西藏宗谱：纪念古格·次仁加布藏学研究文集 Tibetan Genealogies: Studies in Memoriam of Guge Tsering Gyalpo (1961-2015)

主编 〔奥〕恭特朗·哈佐德
沈卫荣

中国藏学出版社

Tibetan Genealogies

Studies in Memoriam of Guge Tsering Gyalpo (1961-2015)

Edited by

Guntram Hazod and Shen Weirong

China Tibetology Publishing House
Beijing • 2018

古格 · 次仁加布 (Guge Tsering Gyalpo, 1961-2015)

图 1　在朗久景区 (In the landscape of Langchu. Photo: Christiane Kalantari, 2007)

图 2　次仁加布和姐姐 (Tsering Gyalpo with his elder sister. Photo: C. Jahoda, 2007)

图 3，4　1997 年次仁加布在雅桑寺，与住持绛巴格勒和恭特朗 · 哈佐德 (Tsering Gyalpo in Yasang 1997, with Abbot Byams pa Dge legs and G. Hazod)

图 5　2010 年在喀孜 (In Khartse 2010. Photo by Huang, Tsering's driver and assistant)

图6　2008年在罗马图齐档案室 (At the Tucci archive, Rome 2008. Photo: Christiane Kalantari)

图7　2015年1月，与恭特朗·哈佐德（左）和沈卫荣（右）在柏林高等研究院 (With Guntram Hazod (left) and Shen Weirong (right) at the Institute for Advanced Study Berlin, January 2015. Photo: Maurice Weiss)

图8　2015年6月26日，在柏林游船上 (On a boat trip in Berlin, June 26 2015)

图9　从擦擦洞俯瞰廓迦寺，次仁加布最后的安息地 (View of the Khorchag monastery from the *tsha tsha* cave and last resting place of Tsering Gyalpo. Photo by a monk from Khorchag, December 2015)

目 录

Table of Contents

前　言

དཀར་ཡོལ་ཆག་ཀྱང་རི་མོ་བློ་ལ་ངེས།།

瓷杯碎了，花纹却印在人们心中。

——西藏民间谚语

今天西藏阿里地区札达县的中心，有一座举世闻名的寺庙托林寺。寺的北边不远处，沿着象泉河支流的上游，人们可以找到一个叫古格的地方。这片小小的区域却对西藏历史有着重要的意义：这里诞生的三位“觉沃主”是形成统治古格王朝的13位核心联盟君主的重要人物；而从古格王朝的兴起到这座佛教王国的全盛时代，重要的宗教场所均坐落在此；更有可能与历史关联的，这片区域就是藏西地区闻名遐迩的矿产区。值得注意的是，古格的西边有座名为“梅乌”（意为“牛祖”）的山，与之相关在当地流传着一个“牛祖神”的故事。这块神奇的岩石传说是曾经冲刷了整个高原的大洪水褪去后出现的。这样的洪水与定居起源的故事在整个喜马拉雅地区均有流传，只是地方的版本有着些许的不同。这一切都是次仁加布告诉我们的。他发现了为什么这片小小的地方会把自己的名字借给一个更大的古格王国来命名，而这样的转变显然发生在古格王国建立之前，因为大古格作为“下象雄”的五区之一在吐蕃王朝时期（公元7—9世纪）就已有记载。

2015年6月，去世前不久，次仁在柏林的一次讲座上首次讲述了这段不为人知的小古格的历史，而在这次公开场合上（同时他私下也说过），他提到了是什么促使自己踏上了这片土地，走上了研究藏西地区历史与民族的：他是在追寻他外公的足迹，而他母亲就是来自这片“小古格”地区。在20世纪20年代，她嫁给了郎楚周边的牧民人家的父亲。所以，“古格·次仁加布”的笔名正是次仁对这段与大小古格相连的准家族血缘关系的情感表达。

次仁出生于朗久村（意为“十牛”），位于今天阿里地区行政总署噶尔县的狮泉河镇以南。郎久这个名字来源于郎久湖，这是牧民夏季放牧安置黑帐篷的点（分有十个“措瓦”小组）；而到了冬季，他们将牧营会搬到山后与湖的西岸交接的地方，这里靠近繁忙的公路。一路上人们可以看到郎楚“梅拉赞”神的象征——牦牛角装饰的地标。这样一种空间与季节的组织结构是印度河上游（即狮泉河）典型的放牧形式。次仁在家中九个孩子里排名老四。他无忧无虑的童年大多是在广袤无边的草原上放牛度过的。他常说放牛是一种理想的人生技能打基础的方式。所以我们发现他在简历“教育”一栏的第一行里写道：“1961—1974 年：放牛、放羊”，第二栏才是“1974—1976 年：噶尔县上小学”。他经常告诉我们他的老师是怎样建议他的父母把他送去拉萨继续学习的，他们愿意这样做因为家里需要懂汉语的人作为家族的生意谈判（诸如卖羊等）代表与新成立的地区政府沟通交流。

实际上，他从来没有得到这份工作。拉萨学校（1976—1981 年）毕业后，他去了北京中央民族大学，然后分到了中国社会科学院民族所工作（1981—1988 年）。而后，他回到了拉萨，娶了自己的江孜籍学生彭宗，在西藏人民政协编辑办找到了一份工作。1994 年，在当时西藏社科院院长平措次仁的推荐下，次仁到了西藏社科院工作，于 2001 年起担任宗教所所长，直至去世。

次仁对宗教所研究工作的影响是巨大的。不仅仅是他与西方学界的紧密学术联络，从 1995 年起他承接了一大批国内和国际的教学与研究项目，使得他作为客座教授常常出现在内地的大学里，作为研究员到访国际知名学术机构。例如，次仁多次到访奥地利维也纳（1996、1998、1999/2000、2010、2011 年），美国弗吉尼亚大学（2001 年）、哈佛大学（2004 年）、普林斯顿大学（2006 年）和最近的柏林高等研究院（2014—2015 年）。他著的书，以合著者和合作人身份写的文章、卫藏民族志（2000，2005，2007 年）和诸多其后研究和合作的作品（2006，2009，2011，2012，2013，2015 年）都与藏西历史紧紧相关。

在这些研究项目和国际访问中，次仁是代表着西藏社科院宗教所，能促成这些国际交流合作是需要极大的个人努力和付出的。理想的情况是，任务各方互帮互助、取长补短。在 20 世纪 90 年代，西藏社科院接到普查登记西藏自治区的文物保护单位的任务，优先方式是驻地调查。在 90 年代末社科院近百所苯教寺庙调查的苯教普查大项目中，次仁作为平措次仁的助理参与其中，并尝试实践自己的民族志研究调查方法。一系列与拉萨雪地区生活的老人关于这片地区的历史或拉萨河谷与雅隆王朝早期相关的信仰崇拜的访谈（部分有录像）体现了这些项目中独特的案例（次仁加布，2005）。而次仁指出，这些研究方法都是受到了自己的西方同事的启发。他与他们分享着一个重大的意识：保护文化遗址区原住民的口述历史传统的迫切性。在这个过程中，他同时学习到了大多通过书本去了解西藏的藏族同胞不知道的事。那些田野生活的每一天都在带来意想不到的对于过去遗迹的发现。即使在西藏自治区的核心区域，也时常能发现一片有过和仍在经历着变革的地方。这些文物遗址的记录，从仅仅有限的技术层面记载开始，因此成为西藏研究者离开办公桌去从另一个不为人知的历史角度探寻藏土的当务之急。

从 2000 年初，次仁开始致力于藏西地区的调查，特别是古格王朝的旧土。他常说他的目标就是在有生之年尽可能地发掘藏西的文化遗产。他相信，这些遗产瑰宝超越了特定的文化、历史和族群的纽带，应该属于全世界。这也是次仁作为一名西藏研究者提出的学术中心思想之一。

在次仁的方法中，有一点很不寻常：他是如此的博学、儒雅，但同时他又如此接地气。当有人咨询他相关信息与历史资料时，他总是温和地为人们打开门。事实上，次仁的研究领域涉及范围十分广阔。不仅从他的出版物可以得知，还有很大部分未经处理的资料等待他的同事和后继者们继承其在民族学、历史学和艺术学上的遗产，有朝一日将之公布于世、发扬光大。同时，还需要后人们能够追随次仁未尽的发现探索，特别是藏西寺庙古籍调查搜集工作。次仁最后的一次发表（2015 年）记述了他于 2014 年常驻西藏东南地区的重大发现：一座高达 4 米的吐蕃晚期的大日如来石刻像。虽然仅仅是对遗址点的首次勘定，但为后来研究者提供了一个可展开长达数年的课题。

在驻留柏林高等研究所期间，次仁手上有好几个任务：一篇有关噶玛噶举支派的文章（主要是基于 18 世纪大司徒确吉穹乃所著《噶举金鬘》里的描述），和计划中一本有关藏西的书的章节写作。这些作品均反映和展现了次仁对古格王朝核心区域民族学与艺术史、历史调查研究的最新成果，其中一章还包括古代象雄的政治地理。而他的研究路径相较于当代中国国内与西方的象雄研究更具有批判眼光。他常说很多研究都是杜撰的无稽之谈，更确切地说："象雄，跟苯一样，就像一个瓶子。大家把这片高原上所有古老却又无法立刻得以解释的东西都扔进去。"他的计划是更精确地定位象雄。根据 15 世纪古格班智达扎巴坚赞所著的《日月族王统记》的一章所述，这正是藏西王国的奠基人吉德·尼玛衮来到的地方。

在次仁的研究中有一个特别的关注点与札达县的石窟寺有关。他首次照相记录了其中很多石窟壁画，包括喀孜河谷的佛教洞窟，并为其勾勒了历史背景。这些田野工作的共通点在于探寻 10—11 世纪阿里地区先驱灵魂人物大译师仁钦桑布的活动足迹。这也让次仁追到了普兰：众所周知，这是藏西王国的雏形"阿里三围"的发源地，也是尼玛衮与其部队 10 世纪初从北边的"然拉卡玛"南下驻扎定居的地方。

在普兰，次仁与奥地利科学院合作的项目工作主要集中在廓迦寺，普兰地区早期皇家（仁钦桑布）遗址和宗教场所。其中发现了一大批珍贵的历史文物和独特的宗教仪式庆典仍被保留了下来。次仁与普兰结下了不解之缘，直到在他生命的最后时期，在柏林，他仍与廓迦寺的前任主持保持着密切联系，请教问学，为了开展中的学术研究，也为了自己的信仰。

廓迦寺会成为他最后的安息之地。在那里，寺院后山的山洞里擦擦像堆积着，守望着廓迦和孔雀河的山水。

*

这部《西藏宗谱：纪念古格·次仁加布藏学研究文集》集合了次仁加布生前一些同事密友的文章。从拉萨的社科院、内地的各大学术机构，到来自西方的同仁，他们有些与次仁一起共事过多年，有些则是学术上有过交流切磋，保持着联系。

“西藏宗谱”也是柏林高等研究院的一个藏学研究小组课题。本书的两位主编在次仁加布过世前与其一同工作学习数月。我们的课题调查围绕西藏历史中不同传承的建构现象：从小范围的特定血亲关系到宗教传承（包括转世）的不同理念，它们已经成为了藏传佛教和苯教在雪域高原喜马拉雅地区创建的特征。我们关心的是，例如在谱系自身的变动性中传承的超验设计与特殊的追溯视角（因为我们发现藏人在传播特定的传承形式时，并不具有地域或者族群的界限），或者到底是怎样的视角主导着不同时期西藏历史中谱系的建立（参见柏林高等研究院 2015 年 5 月期《人物与思想》[Köpfe und Ideen] 中，Michael Oppitz 对柏林高等研究院“西藏视角”小组的评论）。

另一方面，我们要在一个更广的语境当中理解谱系，将之视为历史显现中可触摸和过程性的一部分。这样的话，那些遗迹、政治文化的建构、文物，甚至还有思想与身份认知都具有自己的谱系。

对于“西藏宗谱”这个概念的更广泛用法还可为提炼总结这本大多为历史研究文章的纪念文集找到一把支撑伞。然而更重要的是，贯穿全集的 21 篇研究仍是对杰出的西藏学者、我们的挚友次仁加布的深切悼念之情。

恭特朗·哈佐德　沈卫荣

2017 年 12 月于维也纳和北京

（姚霜　译）

Foreword

དཀར་ཡོལ་ཆག་ཀྱང་རི་མོ་བློ་ལ་ངེས།།
(The cup may have broken yet the
image lingers on in the mind)
Tibetan Proverb

Not far north from Tholing, the famous temple and monastery in the centre of today's Tsamda County (Ngari Prefecture, TAR), on the upper reaches of a tributary of the Langchen River, there is the small district called Guge (Gu ge). The area was obviously of some regional-historical significance: it once saw the seats of three of the 13 Joba ("lords") who formed the core alliance of the rulers of the Guge Kingdom (10th-16th cent.), several significant religious sites from the founder period and heyday of this Buddhist Kingdom were situated here, and – probably historically connected to all these – the area also included one of the productive goldmines for which Western Tibet was widely known. Notable is the story of the local Guge deity Me Bau (Mes Ba'u, "Ancestor Calf"), which is associated with the eponymous mountain situated in the western part of this district. The prominent rock is described as having been the first to emerge after the retreat of the Great Flood that once covered the entire Highlands, a local variant of the flood and settlement origin stories as can be found throughout the Himalayan region. In this prominence, Tsering Gyalpo, to whom we owe this information, saw a key indication why the area had lent its name to the greater Guge area, a transfer that apparently happened long before the founding date of the Guge Kingdom, since a greater Guge is already recorded for the imperial period (7th-9th cent. CE), as the name of one of the five districts of "lower Zhang zhung."

In a lecture which Tsering gave in Berlin shortly before his death in June 2015, he first addressed the history of this otherwise unknown lesser Guge, and on this occasion (as also in private conversations) he also mentioned the personal motives that led him to this place, which formed the starting point for his extensive historical and ethnographic West Tibetan studies: he was following the footsteps of his grandfather on his mother's side, who came from this lesser Guge district and who eventually married into a family from the neighbourhood of the nomadic settlement of Langchu sometime in the 1920s. The fact that Tsering adopted the penname of "Guge Tsering Gyalpo" is the emotional expression that underlines this quasi-genealogical connection of his family with the lesser and greater Guge.

Langchu (Glang bcu, "Ten Bulls"), Tsering's birthplace, is located south of the Ngari's capital Senge Khabab (Chin. Shiquanhe 狮泉河) in present-day Gar County. It is named after Lake Langchu, where the black tents of the summer place of the pastoral community (divided into ten *tsho ba* groups) are located; the houses of the winter place situated on the other side of the mountain ridge bordering the lake area in the west can be reached via the busy route that goes past the central, yak-horn-decorated cairn of the representative Langchu god Me Lhabtsen (Mes Lha btsan) – here reflecting a spatial and seasonal organisation pattern typical for the nomadic communities in this region around the upper reaches of the Indus (Tib. Seng ge kha 'bab). With his siblings – he was the fourth of altogether nine children – Tsering spent an untroubled childhood, often for days cattle herding in the far-flung pastures, as he says, an activity that he also used to describe as an ideal learning ground for life's skills. Thus in his CV under the heading "education" we find as the first entry the words: "1961-1974 – grazing of sheep and goats;" this is followed by the entry "1974-1976: attendance at primary school in Gar." He often told us how his teacher recommended his parents to send him to Lhasa for further education, which they welcomed, because there should be someone from the family who was literate in Chinese when it came to adequately representing the family in business negotiations (e.g. selling goats) with the then newly established district administration.

He actually never got this job. After graduating from school in Lhasa (1976-1981) his education led him to Beijing, with studies at the Minzu University and the Ethnology Department of the Chinese Academy of Social Sciences (1981-1988). Back in Lhasa, he married his fellow student Pendzom, a native of Gyantse, and got a job in the editorial department of the Tibetan People's Political Consultative Conference. In 1994, on the recommendation of Phuntsok Tsering, the then new president of the Tibetan Academy of Social Sciences (TASS), Lhasa, Tsering came to the TASS, where for the last 15 years he served as director of its religious department.

Tsering greatly influenced the research work of this institute, not least through his intensive academic contacts with Western colleagues and institutions. From 1995 he was involved in a number of national and international teaching and research programmes, with guest professorships at universities in China, and as a research associate at several prominent academic institutes abroad – in Vienna (1996, 1998, 1999/2000, 2010, 2011), Virginia (2001), Harvard (2004), Princeton (2006) and most recently in Berlin (Institute for Advanced Study, 2014-15). Widely known are the books – where he essentially participated as co-author or collaborator – text- and ethnography-based studies on medieval Central Tibet (2000, 2005, 2007), and his numerous later studies and co-authored publications (in Tibetan, several also trilingual Tibetan/Chinese/English) related to the history of Western Tibet (2006, 2009, 2011, 2012, 2013, 2015).

It required an enormous personal effort to realise these international sojourns as did the projects that resulted from these activities, since they usually were carried out on the back of his job at the TASS. In an ideal situation the different task areas complemented each other. In the 1990s the TASS programmes were often designed to survey and inventory the historic sites in the TAR, priorities that were associated with longer stays in the field. The "Bon inventory project" of the late 1990s with the visit of more than 90 Bon monastic sites was one of such larger TASS programmes, in which Tsering was involved (in this case as assistant to the TASS president Phuntsok Tsering). In this connection Tsering used to try out the ethnographic methods he adapted for his own purposes. The series of (partly video recorded) interviews with representatives of the older generation on the history of Lhasa Zhol, or on certain cultic traditions related to early Yarlung and the Lhasa Valley (Gyalpo 2005) represent unique examples of such projects, which, as he noted, were methodically inspired by his Western colleagues. With these colleagues he also shared an important awareness: the urgency to follow the remnants of still living oral traditions at historical sites; in this process he at the same time learned something that the majority of Tibetologists – this refers to those who know Tibet primarily from texts – do not know: namely that every day in the field can bring the unexpected discovery of significant relics of the past, even in the core areas of the TAR which had been and still are affected the most in terms of loss and changes. The documentation of sites – initially merely in terms of the available technical means – thus became a priority among the tasks of a Tibet researcher who regularly feel urged to leave his desk to explore his hometown from its lesser-known historical angles.

From the early 2000 Tsering increasingly dedicated himself to his research on Western Tibet, especially the area of the former kingdom of Guge. He often said that his aim was to reveal as much as possible of the cultural heritage of his West Tibetan hometown to the world during his lifetime. He believed that, beyond their specific cultural and historical bonds and national affiliations, these treasures have to be considered as belonging to the whole world. This was in fact one of his central messages as a Tibet researcher.

There was something quite unusual in Tsering's approach, which had to do with his known prudent, gentle and at the same time highly captivating nature. He was a gentle door opener when it came to establishing contacts in order to get access to information and historical material. In fact the range of his findings has been enormous. A number of these are known from his publications, but much more material is still unprocessed, and it remains for his colleagues and successors to make his ethnographic, historic and art-historic heritage accessible to the scientific public, but also to pursue remaining traces leading to discoveries that Tsering was unable to record any longer (this relates, among others, to his discovery of large collections of ancient texts held in West Tibetan monasteries). His last publication (2015) describes the exceptional discoveries in south-east Tibet where Tsering stayed for an extended period in 2014, above all the monumental, four-metre-high stone relief of the Buddha Vairocana with his entourage, a work from the late imperial period. Yet this paper is actually only a first recognition of sites that are expected to occupy the researchers for a fairly long period.

During his stay at the Berlin Institute for Advanced Study, Tsering worked on several projects: a contribution related to the branches of Karma Bka' brgyud (mainly based on Si tu pan chen Chos kyi 'byung gnas' detailed *Bka' brgyud gser phreng*, 18th cent.) and various chapters of his planned book on Western Tibet. This was intended to reflect and highlight the latest results of his ethnographic and (art-)historical surveys to the core areas of the Guge Kingdom, also including a chapter on the political geography of the older Zhang zhung. Tsering's approach was here characterised by a rather critical attitude towards contemporary Zhang zhung studies in Western, Tibetan and Chinese works. Many of them were pure fables, he used to say, or more prosaically: "Zhang zhung (like Bon) is a pot into which everything found in the Highlands that appears to be old and is not instantly explainable is thrown." The plan was to more accurately identify Zhang zhung, which the founding father of the West Tibetan Kingdoms, Skyid lde Nyi ma mgon, came upon on his arrival in the western regions as described in one chapter of Gu ge pandita Grags pa rgyal mtshan's 15th-century *Nyi ma'i rigs kyi rgyal rabs dang zla ba'i rigs kyi rgyal rabs*.

A particular focus in Tsering's Guge surveys was related to the cave temples in Tsamda County, of which he photographically documented many (such as those of Khartse) for the first time, and also outlined their historical contexts. The common element of these and other visits was to follow the historical traces of the Great Translator Rinchen Sangpo (Rin chen bzang po), the pioneering teacher and outstanding founding figure of the 10th-11th-century Ngari region. This also brought Tsering to Purang; as we know, this area was the actual starting point in the formation of the West Tibetan kingdoms (Mnga' ris skor gsum), where Nyi ma mgon and his group settled down in the early 10th century, arriving from their first stop in the north, i.e. the site of Ra la mkhar dmar.

In Purang, Tsering's work (in connection with projects based at the Austrian Academy of Sciences in Vienna) was mainly concentrated on the Khorchag ('Khor chags) monastery, the early royal (Rinchen Sangpo) foundation and religious centrepiece of Purang, where a rich treasure of historical artefacts and also much of the impressive regional festival tradition has survived. Tsering developed a close relationship with this place. Until the last (while in Berlin) he was in constant contact with the former head of Khorchag – in connection with certain questions related to Tsering's ongoing studies, but also in personal matter, regarding questions of faith.

Khorchag was to become his last resting-place, with many of the *tsha tsha* relics placed in the mountain caves behind the convent walls – facing the monastery and the landscape of the Peacock River.

*

This *Tibetan Genealogies* anthology brings together contributions by some of Tsering Gyalpo's closer colleagues – companions from the environment of his home institute in Lhasa and other institutions in China, as well as colleagues from the West who were in regular scientific contact with Tsering or worked with him over a longer period.

"Tibetan Genealogies" was also the title of the Tibet-centred programme at the Berlin Institute for Advanced Study (Wiko) where the editors worked together with Tsering Gyalpo during the months prior to his passing. Our investigations revolved around the phenomenon of different constructions of transmission one encounters in Tibetan history – forms of lineages in the narrower kinship specific sense up to the different concepts of religious lineages (including reincarnation) as they became characteristic in the establishment of Tibetan Buddhism and Bon in the Highlands and Himalayan region. We were interested, for example, in the mobile nature of genealogies (related to the observation that in their distribution certain forms of Tibetan transmission lineages actually had no geographic or national borders), the lineages' transcendental design with its characteristic backward gaze (often beyond the historically accredited bearers of the line), or the question of what exactly visions were linked to genealogical constructions in the different periods of Tibetan history (Cf. here Michael Oppitz's reflections on Wiko's "Tibet focus", in *Köpfe und Ideen*, Wiko, May 2015.)

On the other hand, we can understand genealogy in its much broader context, as an aspect of history that indicates contact-historical and other processual components in historical manifestations. In this sense, sites, political and cultural establishments, objects, and even ideas or identities have a genealogy.

This broader use of "Tibetan Genealogies" may also serve here as an umbrella under which the various, mostly historically oriented contributions can be summarised. But much more, the common thread of the 21 studies in this volume is simply that they are dedicated to Tsering Gyalpo – written as a tribute of an extraordinary person, colleague and friend.

Guntram Hazod and Shen Weirong
Vienna and Beijing, December 2017

古格·次仁加布主要著述目录

一、论文类

1.《试论 1841-1842 年西藏、森巴战争》，中国社会科学院研究生院硕士学位论文，1988 年。

2.《试论清政府对蒙藏地区的宗教政策》，载《中国民族史学会第三次学术讨论会论文集》，北京：改革出版社，1991 年。

3.《西藏阿里托林寺调查报告》，《中国藏学》1992 年第 3 期。

4.《阿里名刹托林寺》，《中国藏学》1992 年第 3 期。

5.《阿里古刹廓迦寺》，《西藏民族宗教》1994 年第 3 期。

6.《浅析藏传佛教长期存在的根源》，《西藏研究》1995 年第 1 期。

7.《阿里噶尔恰钦盛会》，《西藏艺术研究》1995 年第 3 期。

8.《论原始宗教及其产生的历史条件》，《西藏研究》（藏文版）1999 年第 4 期、2000 年第 1、2 期连载。

9.《论我故乡朗久的历史背景及其主供神美拉赞》，《中国藏学》（藏文版）2000 年第 3 期。

10.《以寺养寺是寺庙僧尼自食其力的正确途径》，《西藏研究》2001 年第 3 期。

11.《试析拉喇嘛益西维在噶罗去世真伪》，《西藏研究》（藏文版）2002 年第 2 期。

12.《布达拉宫下面雪村的古迹考略》，《西藏研究》（藏文版）2002 年第 4 期。

13.《阿里三围源流考辨》，《西藏研究》（藏文版）2003 年第 3 期。

14.《拉萨赤宗赞的历史》，《中国藏学》（藏文版）2003 年第 4 期。

15.《阿里羌唐牧民的过年习俗》，《中国藏学》（藏文版）2004 年第 2 期。

16.《日尼寺》，《西藏研究》（藏文版）2005 年第 3 期。

17.《论西藏宗教信仰自由政策的历程》(藏文)，载《西藏自治区成立40周年论文选集》，北京：中国藏学出版社，2005年。

18.《阿里札达县喀泽聂拉康石窟壁画》，《西藏研究》2008年第1期。

19.《江乐金石窟》，《西藏研究》2008年第2期。

20.《阿里札达县喀泽扎宗石窟壁画》，《西藏研究》2009年第2期。

21. The Buddhist Monuments of Khartse Valley, Western Tibet. In *Austrian Academy of Sciences / AAS Working Papers in Social Anthropology 2009*, Volume 9: 1-28. (with Christian Jahoda, Christiane Papa-Kalantari)

22.《阿里扎达夏千佛石窟壁画》，《西藏研究》2010年第2期。

23.《阿里普兰廓迦朗董节考》，《西藏大学学报》(藏文版)2011年第2期。

24.《略论十世纪中叶象雄王国的衰亡》，《中国藏学》2012年第2期。

25. On Ornament, textiles and baldachins depicted on the ceilings of Buddhist cave temples in Khartse Valley, Western Tibet. Form, Function and Meaning. *Kunstgeschichte*. (with Christiane Kalantari) (《美术史》电子刊物，2013年1月28日)。(《西藏西部喀孜河谷佛教洞窟窟顶所绘饰品、织物和华盖之研究》，2018年荣获第四届中国藏学研究珠峰奖英文研究成果类二等奖)

26.《略述西藏昌都芒康县新近发现的吐蕃时期大日如来石刻像》，《西藏大学学报》(藏文版)2014年第3期。

27.《芒康县嘎托镇境内首次发现大型吐蕃摩崖浮雕大日如来像》(第二作者，与巴桑旺堆合著)，《西藏研究》2014年第4期。

28.《西藏阿里古格壁画艺术遗迹》，《西藏日报》2014年9月28日。

29. Gsar du rnyed pa'i bod btsan po'i skabs bzhengs pa'i smar khams rdzong rnam par snang mdzad kyi brag brkos snang brnyan skor la rags tsam brjod pa (A brief report on a rock-carve image of Vairocana, recently traced in Smar khams County and erected during the imperial period). In: Czaja, Olaf and Guntram Hazod (eds.), *The Illuminating Mirror: Festschrift for Per K. Sørensen on the Occasion of His 65th Birthday*. 2015: 181-189.

30. Guge kingdom-period murals in the Zhag grotto in Mnga' ris, Western Tibet. In: Jahoda Christian and Christiane Kalantari (eds.), *Studies and Materials on Historical Western Tibet*. Vol. III. Vienna: Austrian Academy of Sciences. Forthcoming. (with Christiane Kalantari)

二、专著、编译类

1. *Civilization at the Foot of Mount Sham-po. The Royal House of lHa Bug-pa-can and the History of g.Ya'-bzang. Historical Texts from the Monastery of g.Ya'-bzang in Yar-stod (Central Tibet)*. Wien: Verlag der Österreichischen Akademie der Wissenschaften. 2000. (with Guntram Hazod and Per K. Sørensen)（《雅拉香布山下的文明——吐蕃王室拉 · 布巴坚和雅桑之历史》，2006 年荣获第一届中国藏学研究珠峰奖英文研究成果类三等奖）

2.《阿里史话》，拉萨：西藏人民出版社，2003 年。

3. གུ་གེ་ཚེ་རིང་རྒྱལ་པོའི་ཆེད་རྩོམ་ཕྱོགས་བསྒྲིགས། ཀྲུང་གོའི་བོད་རིག་པ་དཔེ་སྐྲུན་ཁང་། ༢༠༠༥. (《古格 · 次仁加布文集》)

4. Thundering Falcon. An Inquiry into the History and Cult of Khra-'brug, Tibet's First Buddhist Temple. Wien: Verlag der Österreichischen Akademie der Wissenschaften. Cooperation with Per K. Sørensen and Guntram Hazod. 2005.（《雷鸣之鹏——西藏第一座佛殿昌珠寺志考》）

5. མངའ་རིས་ཆོས་འབྱུང་གངས་ལྗོངས་མཛེས་རྒྱན་ཞེས་བྱ་བ་བཞུགས་སོ།། བོད་ལྗོངས་མི་དམངས་དཔེ་སྐྲུན་ཁང་། ༢༠༠༦. (《阿里文明史》，2010 年荣获第二届中国藏学研究珠峰奖藏文研究专著类二等奖）

6.《藏传佛教噶举派》，拉萨：西藏人民出版社，2007 年。

7. *Rulers on the Celestial Plain. Ecclesiastic and Secular Hegemony in Medieval Tibet. A Study of Tshal Gung-thang*. 2 Vols. Wien: Verlag der Österreichischen Akademie der Wissenschaften. Cooperation with Per K. Sørensen and Guntram Hazod. 2007.（《天界的统治者：中世纪西藏的政教权力——蔡贡堂研究》）

8. མངའ་རིས་རྩྭ་མདའ་རྫོང་ཁོངས་ཝ་ཆེན་ཕུག་པའི་ལྡེབས་རིས་སྒྱུ་རྩལ། བོད་ལྗོངས་མི་དམངས་དཔེ་སྐྲུན་ཁང་། ༢༠༡༡.（*Mural Paintings of Wa-chen Cave in Rtswa-mda', Mnga'-ris.*《阿里札达额钦石窟壁画艺术》，藏、汉、英对照。2014 年荣获第三届中国藏学研究珠峰奖英文研究成果类二等奖）

9.《西藏宗教实践与理论探索》，拉萨：西藏藏文古籍出版社，2011 年。

10. མངའ་རིས་སྤུ་རངས་ཀྱི་འཇིག་རྟེན་ཆ་འཛུགས་རྟེན་འབྲེལ་གླུ་སྣ་བཞུགས་སོ།། མི་རིགས་དཔེ་སྐྲུན་ཁང་། ༢༠༡༢. (《阿里普兰婚俗婚歌集》)

11. མངའ་རིས་འཁོར་ཆགས་དགོན། བོད་ལྗོངས་བོད་ཡིག་དཔེ་རྙིང་དཔེ་སྐྲུན་ཁང་། ༢༠༡༢. (*Khorchag Monastery: An Overview of Its History and Culture. Studies and Materials on Historical*

Western Tibet. Vol. I. With Christian Jahoda, Christiane Kalantari and Patrick Sutherland)（《廓迦寺文史大观》，藏、汉、英对照）

12. བཀའ་བརྒྱུད་པའི་གྲུབ་མཐའ་ཀྱི་བཤད། བོད་ལྗོངས་མི་དམངས་དཔེ་སྐྲུན་ཁང་། ༢༠༡༣.（《西藏宗教历史文化之噶举派》，2018 年荣获第四届中国藏学研究珠峰奖藏文研究专著类三等奖）

13.《传奇阿里》，北京：中国藏学出版社，2014 年。

三、其他

1.《撤销原藏北总管设立藏北总管及索宗军饷处史略》（藏译汉）、《原西藏地方政府阻止西藏和平解放事件之一》（藏译汉）、《十九世纪一批英国和德国人在西藏山南地区活动情况》（藏译汉）、《为十四世达赖喇嘛制作新宝座的情况纪略》（藏译汉）、《达赖喇嘛及其属下官员经措那逃往印度时的若干见闻》（藏译汉）等，于 1996—1998 年间，分别刊载于《西藏文史资料选辑》，第 18、19 辑等。

2.《神山岗仁布齐峰史话》，《西藏文学》1999 年第 4 期。

3.《藏传佛教如何与西藏的社会相适应问题》，《西藏统一战线》2002 年第 3、4 期。

4. 收集和整理阿里民歌四十多首，均刊载于《邦锦花》，2003 年第 4 集、2004 年第 1 集。

5.《西藏阿里科迦寺一期维修保护工程竣工》，《法音》2009 年第 11 期。

Territory, Kinship and the Grave in Early Tibet

On the identification of the elite tombs in the burial mound landscape of Central Tibet

Guntram Hazod (Austrian Academy of Sciences)

1. Introduction[1]

Burial in larger, chambered mound graves in its various forms and implementations was widely known from the Bronze Age to Early Middle Ages cultures of the Central Euroasian regions, and even beyond.[2] One sees these "tumulus cultures" (OA 471) in connection with the advent of complex socio-political structures and the development of early kingdoms whose political leaders were buried in tombs richly endowed with grave goods and often of enormous proportions. The Scythian princely "kurgans" (ca. 7th-4th cent. BCE) are often exemplary here. The tumulus landscapes on the Tibetan plateau, with the highest density in Central Tibet and the former Tuyuhun area in Qinghai 青海 , are relatively late examples in the history of these forms of burial. In Central Tibet these range from grave fields in the gradation of smaller, round barrows to multi-chambered mound graves with

1 I wish to dedicate this study to my long-time colleague and dear friend Tsering Gyalpo (1961-2015). A number of issues addressed in this study were discussed with him, most recently during our joint stay at the Wissenschaftskolleg zu Berlin (Institute for Advanced Study Berlin; Wiko); in concreto the present contribution forms the extension of a paper held by the author at the workshop "Memories of kings: kingship in the religious imaginings of Asia", organised by the "Kingship and Religion in Tibet" research group, University of Munich, Munich 22-23 May 2015. The research on which this study is based mainly was carried out during the author's stay at the Wiko in the 2014/15 academic year, and it is part of the "The Burial Mounds of Central Tibet", a project financed by the Austrian Science Fund (FWF P 25066-G19, 1/2013-10/2016) and based at the Austrian Academy of Sciences's Institute for Social Anthropology. I am indebted to Reinier Langelaar, Joanna Bialek, Christian Jahoda and Per K. Sørensen for very valuable comments and suggestions related to different contexts addressed in this paper. Any mistakes in what follows remain my responsibility.

2 For the term Central Eurasia as it is used in this paper see Beckwith 2009: XIX, 385-386.

their characteristic rectangular, mostly trapezoidal ground plan. The chronology is rather uncertain with regard to the early stage of the tumulus tradition and archaeologically hardly documented, and our proposed dating to the 4th to 10th century is mainly taken from written sources. This relates to the period of the two consecutive political developments in Central Tibet: the regional principalities or chiefdoms and Tubo (7th-9th century), a time that in the sources is associated precisely with this form of burial.

A special feature in Central Tibetan tumulus research is the issue of a fairly well-documented settlement pattern, especially for the later phase of the tumulus history, with textual sources combined with historical ethnography here forming the basis for a more detailed illustration of the sites' topographical and historical settings. Today more than 400 grave fields in the territories of Central Tibet, the Bod of the imperial period, are known to us, of which about two-thirds contain tombs that can be classified as elite mounds. This is evidently by far not all, but is sufficient to draw further conclusions – in terms of the tombs' specific spatial distribution and their correlation to the reality of early Tibetan society.

The present paper shall focus on the elite burial sites in Central Tibet in the time of the empire. The social category for this type of tumulus entombment mainly included the emperor family and the political and military leadership – in principle the members of the (partly affinally defined) circle of emperor (and his family) and the aristocracy that formed the core of the governmental structure. Similarly to the emperor family, the majority of the aristocratic families traced their origin back to the time of the ancient principalities. The earlier history of these territories and the situation of their later transfer into the administrative system of the imperial period thus form a first reference point in the identification of the elite burial sites. This is linked to the question of who was buried where, which leads us to the issue of kinship, the building of branch territories and other specifics, and not least the concept of paradise is addressed in this study to further specify the elite burial in Central Tibet.

2. Principal classifications of the burial mound landscapes in Central Tibet

2.1 The one tomb and the many

We would like to begin with the view of a well-known painting of the Tibetan plateau lands – the image of the demoness lying on her back. This figure (from the late 17th century) and its specific body arrangement relates to the later Tibetan Buddhist reflection of the extension of Tubo – a narrative that is at the same time composed as a religious memory of a particular king, namely Srong btsan Sgam po, to whom the actual formation of Tubo is ascribed (cf. TF 2005: 171ff.). This narrative seems to ignore any monuments related to the older pre-Buddhist tradition. We only find religious expressions represented by numerous cultural manifestations situated around the 12 "border temples" reportedly founded by Srong btsan Sgam po in the 7th century CE. A particular example of this Buddhist re-writing of history is reflected by way the tomb of this emperor is represented: it is the only reference to an imperial era burial mound in the painting, given in the form of a temple surrounded by a wall, of which some parts still existed when G. Tucci first visited this famous site of the Tibetan kings' tombs in 1948 (Tucci 1950: 32). The temple described as *bang so che* ("great burial mound") refers to the Bang so Dmar po lha khang on top of this impressive tumulus – a foundation from the early 13th century ascribed to a master from the Nyang (Myang) family based in 'Phyong po (the old Phying ba), homeland of the Tibetan kings who were buried there (TF 2005: 209; 263).

On the other hand, several descriptions of this tomb and the *btsan po*'s funeral (651 CE; probably in early winter) have survived in Buddhist chronicles, most notably the lost grave accounts quoted in *Gtam gyi tshogs* (*TT*) and those included in the *Rgyal po bka' thang* (*KT*), both already used in the pioneering studies by Tucci (1950) and Haarh (1969); partly coloured by a Buddhist interpretation, the descriptions give a significant picture of the entombment, which, as already noted elsewhere (van Schaik 2011: 15), are reminiscent of older Central Asian practices widespread since Scythian times. In a way the whole society was present: mentioned by name are the successor emperor (Mang Slon mang btsan) and the "ministers and Tibetan subjects", who in an evidently extensive mourning procession accompanied by music carried countless precious gifts to the tomb, described as quadrangular construction "with the width as far as the stone's throw by Nyang"[3]. Inside the grave, it says, a temple had been built (constructed of materials from the "mountains of 'Breng" (i.e. Grang mo), the actual home of the royal family), in which an image of the

3 Evidently a member of the Nyang (Myang) family and perhaps a distant forefather of the above-mentioned Nyang descendant from 'Phyong po, who founded the Srong btsan Bang so Dmar po lha khang.

emperor, brought there on a "wooden horse" (i.e. waggon), was placed. (After sealing it) they entrusted the tomb to the gods protecting the country and, having offered prayers to them, they returned home (*TT* 287.16-21; 288.18-289.4; 291.9-14). Special grave custodians (*dur bsrung*) guarded the grave (and the grave territory) and every year, on the day of the *btsan po*'s death, the society (*rgyal brgyud rje 'bangs 'khor dang bcas pa*) came together again for celebrations, in the course of which, various gifts were offered and animals (horses, cattle etc.) were sacrificed at the tomb (*KT* 146.12-23).

But what about the burial of the members of (aristocratic) society who were present at the *btsan po*'s funeral and who also served as the addressee in the preceding mourning procedures? In fact there were hundreds of burial-mound fields scattered throughout the Central Tibetan districts; they represent outstanding manifestations of the pre-Buddhist Tibetan cultural lore, but similar to the demoness painting, their existence is hardly mentioned at all in the later written sources. Our current list includes more than 400 tumulus fields (0001-0421, state: 9.2016) in Central Tibet (Dbus and Gtsang regions), many of them of the category of elite burial sites, which we are only gradually capturing in a more documentable form.[4]

The origins of the tumulus tradition can only very roughly be given as the 3rd, or 4th century CE (cf. fn. 36). This is the period to which the beginning of the second, similarly dense burial-mound area within the Highlands should also be dated, those of the Tuyuhun region (in Qinghai) where a branch of the proto-Mongolian Xianbei settled in the 3rd or early 4th century (below chap. 6). The striking parallels with regard to the ritual architecture of the gravesites are evidently due to a common history, to which we will return later (chap. 6). For Central Tibet the chronological control of the pre-imperial phase of the tumulus history is rather poor, and therefore some of our appraisals given in this study are on uncertain terrain. As to the end of the burial-mound tradition, this can be quite clearly dated to the early 10th century (the time of the plundering of the *btsan po* tombs), though

4 For an overview see the website www.oeaw.ac.at/tibetantumulustradition (hereafter TTT), an interactive web page established in the course of the above-mentioned research project (fn. 1). See also Appendix II. This list contains data from earlier archaeological records (in the 1980s and 1990s), the extension of recordings in recent years by the Cultural Relics Bureau (CRB), Lhasa (cf. XWD 2010; Tsewang 2011), and the recordings by the TTT team and the author of this contribution respectively. Actually, most of this list is based on the author's inquiries; these date back to the first (often unexpected) discoveries of grave fields in 2005 and 2007, which were then followed by a number of targeted *in situ* surveys, where later high-resolution satellite imagery formed a significant help in identifying new burial sites. In fact, the identification of about two-thirds of the present list is based on such aerial archaeological information, although the greater part has still not been visited on site.

certain tombs were apparently still used in a Buddhist context over a longer period (Hazod 2013).[5]

2.2 Types of grave fields and mounds

A special feature in the study of the Central Tibetan burial-mound landscape is the fact of relatively good preconditions to reconstruct the settlement patterns related to the time of the empire, but partly even to the earlier period. The basis for this is the relatively high stability of the historical toponyms, about which we are informed by written sources and the complementary data from local oral traditions. For example, the place names mentioned in the sources in connection with the foundation of the 7th-century temple of Khra 'brug (in Lower Yar lung) can mostly be identified on site and cartographically documented (TF 249ff.). Here we find the setting of the burial sites in Lower Yar lung (ca. 16 grave fields, i.e. 0001-0014; 0381, 0382) in a specific settlement situation and the spatial relation of cultivated and non-arable zones, which with some qualification are transferable to the time of the temple foundation. From the data available such reconstructions cannot be carried out in all burial-site areas, but basically we see a pattern where the cemeteries were established in close proximity to the settlements, in whose position in the landscape we can recognise a largely high level of historical continuity.

Within this basic setting several categories of grave fields can be established. The vast majority of cemeteries is located in the nonarable alluvial zones, as mentioned, usually not far from the villages (TTT: field type FT-A). Less frequent are the cemeteries (or groups of tombs) on a mountain or mountain ridge above the valley (FT-B; Fig. 2b), or (still more rarely) even in the midst of the cultivated land, as it were in front of the houses (FT-C). Here, however, one cannot be certain whether the fields already existed when the tombs were constructed. This topographical setting conveys the overall image of a seemingly indiscrete world of the living and the dead (but see below fn. 11); in their occupation of the uncultivated zones the cemeteries appear as a quasi continuation of the settlement history. At the same time, a form of adaptation to the existing topography is characteristic: composed

5 In later sources there is mention of a Buddhist furnishing of the interior of Srong btsan Sgam po's grave, in the form of murals, which, however, include representations that should be dated from the time when the temple on top (chap. 2.1) was founded or even later. This points to a history of opening the tombs in the context of certain ritual care and re-furnishing of the imperial graves' interior (Hazod 2013).

as hills and situated at the edge of the hillside some tombs actually merge with the environs and even larger structures are often almost indiscernible from some distance, although the current situation of the burial sites with mounds in often poor condition is of coursenot comparable with the original one.[6]

According to their external form we find three basic types of grave mound, which after the descriptions in (later) textual sources we can describe as follows: the *zlum po* type (TTT: mound type MT-A; i.e. round or oval mounds of various sizes), the *gru bzhi* type (MT-C; quadrangular tombs, square (rather rare) or trapezoidal; Fig. 3b) and the *mchod rten* type (from late 8th century – MT-D; Fig. 4).[7] The Tibetan terms for tumulus (*bang so, mchad, mchad kha/pa*)[8] do not indicate any specific shape; an exception is the form *se (mo) gru bzhi* mentioned in certain ritual texts (Bialek 2015: 389ff.; Stein 2010: 261f.; 266-67), which indicate a quadrangular grave construction.[9] Among the designations by the locals, apart from *bang so* we find forms such as *sa gru bzhi*, or also *bang so gru bzhi*, but these are rather rare. More dominant are names that do not indicate any grave at all, or deliberately

6 Chinese sources speak of buildings situated next to the mounds, constructed of red earth, and with white tigers (the classical image of the "hero") painted on them (Bushell 1880: 521; Drikung 2011: 487), here it is not clear, however, whether this was a general feature of peripheral cemeteries. Old Tibetan documents also suggest that a wooden pole with the coloured (*mdos* like) "eight-threaded net" (*rgya thag brgyad*) was attached to the (larger) tombs, or placed next to them, at least temporarily, i.e. for the period of the funeral ritual. For the *rgya(l) thag brgyad* see Bialek 2015: 157ff.; see also below fn. 9.

7 In the sources, the MT-D type is ascribed to Buddhist female members of the royal house (see Appendix I), but it had a greater application within the (Buddhist) aristocracy. A special case of evidently "Buddhist mounds" are structures that have countless *tsha tsha* immured in the outer walls, as we recently (2015) discovered at a grave of field no. 0148 (cf. Feiglstorfer, in this volume). (Note that forms of Buddhist funerals reportedly have been practised already in the time of *btsan po* Khri Lde gtsug btsan (namely the Chinese Buddhist *tshe* rites; cf. Kapstein 2000: 38ff.; Uebach 1987: 96-97; Wangdu and Diemberger 2000: 37-39), but we are not informed about any grave architectural adaptions possibly related to this.) Another mound type is MT-B; this refers to smaller round or oval mounds that are covered with grit, perhaps just a variation of MT-A, representing an adaptation of the local conditions of the material available for the tomb construction.

8 Shawo Khacham 2014a suggests a distinction according to which *bang so* was the term for imperial tombs and the tombs of the peripheral aristocracy were designated as *mchad*. This is perhaps true for the imperial period (cf. Appendix I, § 2, no. XIV); yet in post-imperial sources *bang so* is used to describe any tumulus, including those of non-imperial members, and in turn *mchad* is also found for tombs related to members of the royal family, e.g. the *mchad zlum po* of *rgyal po* 'Bro Gnyan lde ru (below chap. 4).

9 *Se gru bzhi*, lit. "a spot of four corners"; see Bialek 2015: 389, *et passim* for *se* (*se mo*), which she explains as a backformation from the diminutive *se'u*, with the latter being a derivation from *so*, originally "spot". In her reading, *se* is "used to avoid in ritual context taboo terms denoting all kinds of places related to funeral, like grave, tomb, etc." (Bialek, ibd.). The preparation of the above-mentioned (fn. 6) **rgya thag brgyad was associated* with the grave construction (cf. e.g. PT 1136: l. 19, 59) and the *se gru bzhi is* described of having a western entrance where the *skyibs lugs* (psychopomp sheep) was positioned (PT 1042: l. 117-118 (*TDD* 43). The same funeral text (1042.136-137) mentions the *bang so* (lit. "spot of a repository") having a *thugs khang* (burial chamber), which apparently

conceal their existence, perhaps to avoid destruction. Even today at many sites the stone material of the graves is being taken by the locals for use in construction projects. On the other hand, in some areas individual mounds or even whole cemeteries have fallen victim to government construction projects. Photographs from previous visits or older satellite images thus often become historical documents of something that has disappeared from one to the next (see TTT, "thematic introduction": "destruction-2").

Several sources which were already used by Haarh in his pioneering attempt to reconstruct the emperor's tombs (Haarh 1969) indicate a cross-shaped inner architecture of the chambered MT-C types – in an order of five (i.e. the *dra mig lnga pa* design), or in the extended form of nine sections (*re'u mig dgu pa*). The inner structure seems to be independent of the external shape, as these two designs are mentioned for (larger) round as well as square mounds. However, excavations and the most recent architectural reconstructions from opened graves (Feiglstorfer, in this volume) suggest that this latticed brickwork, does not indicate any particular chamber arrangement, at least not in the case of peripheral elite graves, but walls above the actual chamber(s), which apparently primarily served stability purposes. In most cases a medium-sized grave of the *dra mig lnga pa* type probably contained only one chamber plus a smaller auxiliary one, both of which were set half below ground and had stone slabs as coverings. A slightly inclined wall, or – for larger and / or hillside graves – two parallel stonewalls filled with earth, formed the outer frame of the tombs. The whole was filled with rammed earth, and usually a final layer of earth covered the structure. In addition to this hill-shaped type, among the larger MT-C graves there is the "coffer-shaped" type of grave, which, so it seems, had either only a partial outer earth covering or none at all (see e.g. Fig. 5).

The vast majority of the *gru bzhi* or MT-C type is trapezoidal, with the longer side facing towards the valley floor. Every grave in a field of several dozen of such trapezoidal graves has its own orientation (cf. TTT: 0112), for which we so far have no other explanation, as

was a separate construction from the *ring se* (PT 1042: l. 48-49), the latter probably a term for the central chamber where the body was placed (Chu Junjie 1991: 106 reads it as "coffin chamber"; cf. PT 1134: l. 56-57 (*TDD* 146) which speaks of a copper vessel (made of iron and copper) placed inside the *se 'brum bzhi* (= *se gru bzhi*); cf. also Appendix I, § 2, no. XIV). From one passage (PT 1042: l. 145; *TDD* 44) we learn that *bang so* and *se* (*se gru bzhi* or *ring se*?) evidently refer to different constructions situated at some distance from one another, when it says that one can go from the *se* (part of the grave complex) to the *bang so* (*se nas bang sor gsheg*). I am grateful to Joanna Bialek for these and other references to terms specific to grave construction in Old Tibetan documents (e-mail from April 2016), whose more detailed analysis of the archaeological situation on site is beyond the scope of this paper.

the individual deviations would be simply due to adaptations to the respective topographical situations. There was obviously no preferred direction in such a compound of tombs, which is particularly visible in the field type FT-A and FT-B, which are often situated on opposite sides of the valley. But this is only an externality, which says nothing about possible concepts of a sky orientation or alignment towards certain constellations related to the actual burial; only knowledge of the position of the corpse, the coffin (to our best of knowledge not evidenced from the Central Tibetan tumulus archaeology) or the (rectangular) grave chamber can provide information in this respect (see chap. 6).

More than half of the fields known to us include groups of graves that, in terms of size or construction features, can be attributed to the social elite, with the significant type of trapezoidal (chambered) mounds that in our opinion should probably not be dated before the 7th century. Other fields have no elite tombs, but consist of only smaller round or oval MT-A mounds; these *zlum po* barrows most likely represent the oldest type of burial mound, which was certainly used even later in parallel to the MT-C tombs. These "non-elite fields" have more graves – up to 500 (0270; Fig. 6). Larger structures of the *zlum po* type are recorded for the royal genealogy both for the imperial as well as pre-imperial period (Appendix I), and it can only be assumed that this tradition was adopted by other families of the chiefdom period, and, as mentioned, is actually not sufficiently attested to by archaeological data.[10] The rather typical situation is a mixture of different types of tomb, with smaller structures alongside larger, round or trapezoidal tombs, the latter being up to 70-80 metres wide at the front. The necropolis of Phying ba represents a similar situation – a mixture of grave types plus the rare type of a square ground plan. Several of the larger trapezoidal tombs situated on a slope have a striking step construction at the front (cf. also Caffarelli 1997: 235), similar to the hillside tombs of the emperors Khri Srong lde btsan and Khri Lde gtsug btsan (0032.M-X, M-XI). Recent archaeological surveys have made it clear that in some cases these "steps" are actually filled up trenches that served for animal sacrifices (below fn. 47), here specifically representing a variant of the sacrificial pits usually situated next to the tombs, sometimes in a salient symmetrical arrangement. Other traces of ritual architecture

10 The earliest example of a (peripheral) tomb that can be classified as elite tomb, is dated to the 5th century CE; information by Shakya Wangdu, Lhasa 2015.

in the graves' environment relate to building remnants, or even wall parts that perhaps were used to mark a kind of grave territory (cf. no. 0015).[11] Finally, several of the (peripheral) elite tombs have grave monuments – steles, stone lions situated at the front, which evidently served to highlight the special status of the deceased. There are only a few of these sites, but it can be assumed that there were originally many more monuments of this sort (Hazod 2015).

2.3 The factor of regional differences in the density of burial mound fields

The highest density of grave fields is clearly in the central areas of the Horn provinces of Dbu ru and G.yo ru, while larger gaps are evident in the western regions (Ru lag and Right Horn) and also in eastern Central Tibet. This imbalance is pronounced. Thus ca. 70 burial-mound fields are to be found just in the area of present-day Lhun grub County (i.e. the old 'Phan po district plus parts of Byang and Klung shod), several with groups of elite tombs, while e.g. in Snye mo, the border district between Dbu ru and G.yas ru, there are only two burial-mound fields, one of them with a smaller, albeit impressive group of (eight) elite tombs (no. 0274). The criteria of population density (and greater density of agriculturally usable zones) or the relations between centre and periphery in terms of regional political concentration seem to provide no adequate explanation for this regional disparity. Rather we must assume that the mound burial was not the only form of funeral practised in Central Tibet, but that there were other forms as well. These may have been forms of cist- or stone-lined pit tombs (as were common in the Highlands from the Neolithic)[12] or forms of exposing the corpse. In fact, the well-known description of the tombs of the early Yar lung kings seems to indicate the practice of "sky burial" or also "water burial", which according

11 A special addition is reported for the grave of emperor Srong btsan Sgam po: a sort of ritually defined (and architecturally marked?) territory around the grave, which the grave guardians apparently also used for the cultivation of crops for their own livelihood or perhaps also for the tomb's ritual aftercare (*KT* 146; 147.4; Haarh 1969: 351-52). This territory is defined as a borderline between the living and the dead, probably related particularly to the protection from grave robbers – an institution for which it remains unclear how far this can also be assumed for peripheral elite fields (cf. in this context the "royal law of not digging up *bang so*" listed in the later chronicls; *Lde'u-2* 271.5; *KG* 192.19). In Khrom chen (0339), one of the most extensive elite fields (4140m^2, with 135 (mostly) elite mounds, 28 sacrificial pits) recent archaeological surveys revealed that the whole cemetery may have been enclosed by stone walls, and some groups of tombs were apparently connected to each other by a wall (Shawo Khacham 2014b).

12 See Aldenderfer 2013 for a survey of the mortuary archaeology in the Neolithic and Bronze Age in the Highlands; cf. also Wei Luyan 2013.

to this account was replaced by mound burial at the time of the Btsan lnga group of kings (Hazod 2007b; Appendix I). In any case we can assume that this old funeral form (with a wide distribution throughout ancient Central Eurasia) was practised in the plateau lands long before it became popular in the milieu of Buddhist mortuary practices.[13]

As already noted, although it is only mentioned in the sources for the Yar lung house, we assume that sometime in the chiefdom period the type of larger mound burial became popular among the social elite outside of Yar lung as well. For the imperial period, apart from the (male and female) members of the emperor family we see the rank-holding nobility and military leadership and probably more generally the battle-tested "heroes" as typical "tumulus candidates". In the portrayal of Chinese observations (noted in the *Xin Tangshu* 新唐书) about Tibetan tombs it says: "[They all represent] tombs of Tibetan nobles who have gained fame in battle" (Bushell 1880: 521). Whether the lower social classes were also buried in barrows we do not know. It should be noted that the social stratification even in the imperial time was not a rigid system, or more precisely it was strongly linked to old patterns of virtue, foremost the behaviour in combat, which indicates a certain flexibility in terms of social status and respect. Often cited is the passage in the *Xin Tangshu*, which notes that for the Tibetans death in war was most honourable, "and if several generations have been killed in battle the family is ennobled" (Bushell 1880: 442-443). Such ennobled ones were apparently customarily buried in tombs. Yet regional differences are likely, and with a view of the Snye mo situation one cannot exclude the possibility that in certain areas traditionally different or older forms of burial were practised even for representatives of the classical tumulus category.

Apart from this imbalance in terms of density, the spatial distribution of the tumuli fields principally seems to reflect the history of the old settlement and territorial situation in

13 This just confirms the observations from archaeology, which says that there are hardly any cultures or societies with only one type of burial, and it also notes that different forms of burial are often correlated with the status of the deceased (Pearson 2009: 31). In 2015, in one cemetery (no. 0148) we identified several round or oval stone marked sites situated in the upper part of this alluvial field, while lower down are mound graves of various sizes. Sacrificial pits, which are sometimes similarly marked are usually situated next to the mounds, so that these structures may actually refer to cist graves or stone-lined burial pits from an older or also parallel historical context. It is also worth mentioning that some mound grave fields are in close vicinity to sky burial sites (0135; 0121; 0182). For early practices of exposing the corpse in the Tibetan plateau lands, cf. the description of Yangtong in Chinese sources (Bushell 1880: 527; Haarh 1969: 345ff.).

the agricultural areas of Central Tibet, where from a certain point in prehistory the major districts were headed by ruling families. Their political domains are referred to in the source (in retrospect and in contrast to the centralised order of the empire) as *rgyal phran* or minor principalities (Dotson 2009a: 37); Yar lung (plus Phying ba), the territory wherefrom the Tibetan emperors came, was originally one of these ancient chiefdoms, which, however, evidently already had the contours of a dominant kingship in the Lho kha area – at least from the time of the Btsan lnga – and is also named as such in the sources.

From the 7th century the old family lines constituted the core of the civil and military elite of the empire, which was entrusted with the task of civil and military administration. Loyalty to the throne – the structural core of the central authority – usually guaranteed the families the maintenance of their ancestral territorial rights. It is thus certainly not wrong to assume that the members of the ruling elite were buried in their respective lands. The concentration of the burial mound fields in Central Tibet within the Highlands underscores this assessment. To the best of our knowledge (with the exception of the 'A zha land) there were no significant cemeteries with elite tombs outside of Central Tibet (including parts of Nag chu, no. 0359-0360) and beyond the classical *rgyal phran* territories.[14] One might think that members of the social tumulus category who have died outside of their country were "brought home" for the funeral – similar to the royal house, whose members (not all but certain categories of members, see below) are described as having been buried in their own country (*rang gi yul*).[15] With regard to location of the elite tombs we are thus first referred to the facts of the territory of the leading families – the latter organised into "lineages".

14 To the best of our knowledge, no comparable grave mounds are recorded for Zhang zhung, which is one of the *rgyal phran*, and interestingly the Central Tibetan regiments stationed there in the imperial period (such as the "western divisions of the heroes" (*stod kyi dpa' sde*), Hazod 2009: 169) apparently left no mound graves. It is also noteworthy that, for example, parts of the 'Bro family (one of the *stod kyi dpa' sde*) very probably settled in Western Tibet as early as the pre-imperial period, but in contrast to the 'Bro branches of Central Tibet they did not practice mound burial there. According to information from Shawo Khacham (Lhasa 2015) there are some tumulus fields in the more immediate surroundings of Dunhuang, which he assigns to Tibetan and other military and their families stationed there.

15 This is namely recorded for Lha Tho tho ri (Lha Tho tho Snya brtsan), and the home actually refers to Grang mo in Upper 'Phyong po (Appendix I; Hazod 2007b).

3. Territory and lineage

3.1 "Chiefdom" and the "early state"

When we speak of the pre-7th-century *rgyal phran* units as chiefdoms, this is a somewhat artificial designation, here following the classic evolutionist concept of pre-state and early state societies. In principle what we see in the old territories is a highly stratified socio-political order, which in some characteristics cannot be differentiated from the early state organisation.[16] Here regionally we can identify the state-like constellation of (hereditary) rulers and ministers (*rje* and *blon*) that commanded land and a labour force, apparently very early controlled the access to the local mines (copper, gold, silver etc.) in their home districts (cf. Hazod 2014a: 55-56), were involved in the control of trade and in this way accumulated wealth and power. But the foundation of the empire constituted a step into another dimension. It initiated a radical change in the direction of an order that transcended regional principles – a centralised organisation of civil and military administration with entirely new developments: the territorial divisions in horn provinces and chiliarchies (the latter with a genealogy that can be traced back to Xiongnu 匈奴),[17] the successive establishment of border garrisons, the gradual conversion of customary law into law books and a comprehensive aristocratic ranking system are only the more prominent new institutions (cf. Dotson 2009a: 37ff.). We are well advised to terminologically differentiate the developments before and after the 7th century where we can rely on the categories of political leadership mentioned in the sources, with the two principal developments of chiefdom (i.e. territorial units headed by a chief (*rje*) or also king (*rgyal po*) and Tubo (headed by the *btsan po*)). One may see a significant structural continuity in the political entourage system, which is mentioned for early Yar lung and apparently represented the Tibetan variant of the "ruler and his comitatus" order that Beckwith has identified as central to the Central Eurasian

16 Cf. here in parallel the observation by Sneath 2013 related to the context of the early Inner Asian (nomadic) societies.

17 This refers to the decimal system and the (three) horn (or wing) division of the military organisation, or also the bodyguard corps (cf. e.g. Kradin 2011; Di Cosmo 1999; cf. also Munkh-Erdene 2016 and his discussion of the post-Xiongnu "continuity of the Inner Asian imperial political traditions"; for the Xiongnu see most recently the contributions in Brosseder and Miller (eds.) 2011.

political cultures (Beckwith 2009: 127).[18] The conquest project of Tubo itself was based on an alliance of leading families, and an adaptation of this system in its specific definition of loyalty and proximity to the throne remained the basic principle of the state order. The assurance of territorial rights to the old families was indeed significant and characteristic of a certain degree of political regionalism, but at the same time the formula of the sworn alliance included a sort of paramount ownership by the throne, as can be seen not least in the case when the oath of loyalty was broken (see below chap. 5.1). In fact, the whole world was nominally "subject" (*'bangs*) to the throne – a significant transformation of the "many worlds order" of the chiefdom period into the summarising system of the early state.[19]

3.2 Structural principles: The territory and the lineage

In our tumulus research we initially assumed a more direct relationship between lineage and mound burial, something that today needs to be revised not just in view of the above-mentioned spatial distribution of elite burial sites, but this relationship seems to be viewed too narrowly also in terms of the social organisation of the individual territories. In the classical historiographical sources the political leadership is referred to as *rus*, *gdung* ("lineage", "clan"), but this situation should not be confused with a tribal or "clan society". For early Central Tibet, the notion of lineage / clan in the sources rather relates to individual families and actually seem to represent family constructs that developed in the context of the settlement history and the establishment of a territory – as an instrument to pass on territorial claims within one family from generation to generation (cf. below chap. 5.1, 5.2).

18 We see the earlier form of the entourage system represented in the institution of the "six subject clans" at the side of the king (i.e. the *yab 'bangs rus drug*, see below 3.3). These are apparently addressed in the well-known statement in Chinese sources about the Tibetan custom of joint entombment, namely the burial of the lord and his ministers – the five or six "common-fated ones"; see Beckwith 2009: 20 for references; cf. also Chu 1991: 146ff. (The mythical counterpart of this institution was arguably represented by the bodyguards (*sku srung*) recorded for the divine house of Phvya; however they are classified as group of seven or seven brothers; *Lde'u-2* 232.9; 234.17). Bialek suggests seeing the *zha 'bring* (entourage) mentioned in the funeral context of PT 1042: l. 125-127 (*TDD* 43) similarly, as a specific group of followers (here specified as *zha 'bring nang pa*) who might have been sacrificed to accompany the deceased in his afterlife (Bialek 2015: 347).

19 In their fundamental comparative study on the "early state" Claessen and Skalnik 1978 have suggested the division into the three types of inchoate, typical, and transitional. In taking up this concept it appears that the Tibetan state organisation of the imperial period beyond its centralising mechanisms largely remained in the inchoate phase, which is characterised *inter alia* by the dominant role of kin and community ties in politics, in contrast to the more typical early state where a gradual disbandment of kinship ties in the governmental structures is specific. Cf. here also Di Cosmo 1999: 8ff., Kradin 2011: 78ff. for more a recent application of the "early state" concept in the discussion concerning the development of early step empires.

The strong and conscious awareness of descent linked to it entered into the corresponding genealogical constructs evident in the historiographical sources, mostly created in the milieu of later (post-imperial) ruling houses.

The actual structuring principle in terms of settlement and community building in the old territories was possibly not that much different from what can be observed from later traditions: the territorial god (*yul lha*) – an entity of enormous charisma which socially and ritually encompassed the house and settlement components of community building and which (as *sku bla*) in earliest records appears to be genealogically linked to the ruling families (cf. Karmay 1998: 432ff.). The *yul*, *lha* (and its demonic counterpart *srin*) are noted as central components in ritual texts (such as ITJ 734 (*TDD* 276ff.); Thomas 1957), which pivot on the complex of healing – of the country and at the same time the safety of the local ruler (*rje*). The name of the country often proves to be the unifying element of these components. For example, the toponym Gnubs (or Snubs), which designated one of the old territories, was the name of a famous lineage, i.e. the lineage of the Gnubs *rje*, and the representative *lha* was called Gnubs lha (ITJ 734: 7r300-303 (*TDD* 287); Hazod 2009: 172; below fn. 51). There was probably never a "tribally" organised Gnubs, but local groups divided into hamlets and villages who were committed to the *lha* and placed under the leadership of a family that adopted this place name as lineage name.[20] We see this interplay of the concepts of *yul*, *lha* and *rje* and the latter's (often multi-branched) lineage constructs as crucial for defining the pre-imperial regional units, which later, with the empire

20 Gnubs forms here one of 100 or more *rus mtshan*, lineage names, that can be identified for Central Tibet for the time of the tumulus tradition and the early post-imperial period. The various lineage classifications as they first appear in respect to the entourage groups of "subject clans" (fn. 18) and the later (and related?) *mi'u rigs* lists (Dotson 2006: 82) refer to certain historical events and cannot be taken as evidence of any original "tribal system" as is often implied in the Western literature, in connection with the picture of "migrated lineages" somewhere in the dark of prehistoric times. Cf. here already Smith 2001: 219, 321, fn. 702, who in his commentary on the representations of "tribal classifications" in the *Bshad mdzod* notes that the classifications of the *nang gi mi'u rigs* into four main groups appear to reflect the situations of past political superimpositions. Thus the "eight servant (clans) of the four Stong ruler" (*stong rje bzhi khol brgyad*) are not to be read as evidence of any original tribal lineage sub-groups, but rather are later records of a historically more or less distant political dominance of Stong people (or Sum pa Stong) over local groups. The Stong as well as the Ldong, two of the classical *rus chen* basic units, are already mentioned in the sources for the pre-imperial period as groups in Central Tibet (Dotson 2006: 124, *et passim*), so that their often asserted eastern Tibetan origin is questionable. The presence of the same lineages in eastern Tibet in several cases certainly goes back to the time of the empire, where lineages (or regiments under the leadership of certain members of a lineage) were sent from Central Tibet to the frontier garrisons (cf. e.g. Hazod 2009: 200). An early example of constructed "tribal classification" seems to be addressed in the fragmentary inscription stone situated by a tomb in the field of Mchad kha (0115; near Zhva'i lha khang of Upper Mal gro, on the border with the Klung shod disctict;

formation, served as the ideal basis for the establishment of the district and regimental divisions (*sde*).

It would be misleading in this sense to assume, for example, that the grave fields we find in Gnubs (largely the present-day Rong district) relate to different lineages situated in this area, but rather reflect the settlement pattern where clusters of villages simply shared the same cemeteries. However, certain fields are outstanding in including an ensemble of larger tombs relating to the resting places of elite families. And in some cases it indeed appears that the field was only provided for one prominent family. The following observations mainly concern the burial situation related to these elite families who served the central government in the period of Tubo and whose graves as it were spatially surrounded those of the imperial family in 'Phying ba. The above statement, according to which the grave of a deceased from the social tumulus category was established in their own country, here represents the first issue that we should examine more closely.

3.3 What does home territory mean?

According to the classical tradition, the grave of Gri gum Btsan po (Dri gum Btsan po) is considered the first Tibetan *bang so*. The descriptions (in PT 1287; Zeisler 2011; Hill 2006) suggest foreign influences – in terms of the mourning tradition, or the origin of the ritual specialists (*gshen, bon po*) entrusted with the funeral – influences from Central Asia, with ancient Persian, proto-Mongolian and other components, an issue that I will not pursue any further here (but see below chap. 6).[21] The somewhat enigmatic figure of Gri gum apparently represents a ruler of the chiefdom period, corresponding to the Btsan lnga of the

for the text see *OTI* 67; Li and Coblin 1987: 299). It speaks of three generations (*tshe gsum*) of respectively "the Cho phyi, the Mda' people (*mda' myi*), the Tse, the Phyug po, the Gyim etc."; they are summarised as the "lineages of exalted peoples of (collateral) brothers" (*spun myi 'phags rigs*) who issued from one Lha ji chen po, son of the gods in heaven (*gnam lha'i sras*). Yet it appears that this classification actually represents the genealogical order of different groups of people who were resident in this area, and to whom the occupant of the tomb in question was evidently related in one way or another. Phyug po probably refers to the Phyug tshams known as one of the leading lineages of the Klung shod district (Hazod 2009: 195, 200); for Gyim po see e.g. the Gyim (or Gyi) spun drug in ITJ 731 (*TDD* 268-270), perhaps related to the Gyi or Kyi people (TF 53), and Cho phyi may refer to a branch (*phyi*) of the Chog(-ro) (Cog ro, Lcog ro), the latter (within Dbu ru) otherwise associated with the areas of Bcom pa (Bcom mdo) or 'Dam gzhung (cf. PT 1287: l. 482, 485; *TDD* 225-226; below chap. 3.3.1).

21 As to the ritualists who are described as having come from outside ('A zha, Bru zha or Gurnavatra), one account noted in Buddhist chronicles has it that the beginning of the spread of the *gshen* (or *bon po*) was in 'On of Central Tibet (also described as Bon mo lung ring of 'On; *KG* 164.8-165.3; *Nyi ma* 93.7.ff.; cf. Ramble 2007; Martin 1999,

Yar lung genealogy, who, as mentioned, are equally associated with the beginning of the *bang so* tradition. One of the problems in the Gri gum account concerns the location of this ruler's tomb, where two sites are mentioned: Kong po and Yar lung (or Phying ba). It seems as if only the later tradition brought the corpse from Kong po back "home" (i.e. to Phying ba), but this is not certain (Hazod 2007b). Kong po was certainly not Gri gum's homeland, and should he be buried in Mi yul Skyid mthing of Kong po (no. 0097) as many assume, the location was evidently based on other criteria than the home.

The much more obvious problem in determining the ancestral home is the factor of mobility of the families and the lineage ramifications linked to it. The classic "lineages" of early Tibetan history were transregional, meaning they were present in different territorial contexts. We can actually find this situation even in the chiefdom period, where people from the same lineage were apparently active in different regions. The specific entourage organisation of Yar lung, the above-mentioned "six lineages, subjects of the father" (*yab 'bangs rus drug*) represent early examples of such transregional situations. With regard to the "subject clans" Lho and Rngegs (alias Lho and Gnyags) Dotson has demonstrated that the paired listing of the six lineages, who among others accompanied the king in the "royal hunt", were not actually individual "clans" but that the *rus* names stand for larger adjacent areas, which also headquartered other family lines. (In this case the Myang / Nyang are registered elsewhere in old Tibetan documents as having lived in Lho Rngegs,

2001). We think the site is related to the place where Gri gum Btsan po's sons reportedly made a longer stop during their flight following the violent death of the father (*Lde'u-2* 245.19-246.6). 'On is considered by pilgrims who visit Bsam yas as the land of the "deaf" (*'on*) people, according to the rumour that the daily wakening call by the white rooster (*bya dkar po*) of Bsam yas is heard everywhere in the (Buddhist) world except in 'On (Tsering Gyalpo and other Tibetan colleagues, personal communication). Perhaps there is a connection with the feature of the first *gshen* priest described in this 'On story, namely the donkey ears that were covered by a headgear resembling a "Phrygian cap", i.e. the one that covers the ears and has a forward-tilted tip as is still worn by members of (the later) Bon communities. The question of whether this account represents a typical "Chos story", as Martin suggests, or whether an older (Inner Asian related) history of the *bon po* origin may lie behind it is something that still needs to be examined. In ritual texts, the funeral priests are often specified as *pha*, father, which refers to a family organisation and the hereditary transmission of priestly qualifications within a family (cf. Stein 2010: 254-258). One should see the spreading (perhaps indeed from 'On) of the priest families involved in the mound burial in some causal relationship with the specific distribution of burial mounds. Cf. also TTT: "thematic introduction" no. 24. In Bon sources (*Mdzod sgra 'grel*, *Bsgrags pa gling grags*, quoted in Bellezza 2002: 85; 2008, chap. 5) on the so-called 37 "assembly places of the *bon po*" (*bon po 'du gnas* – probably an establishment of the 8th century, but with an older history behind) it says that each site was associated with (the ritual care of) burial mounds (*bang so*). The 37 sites refer to the "tumulus land" of the Four Horns. See Uebach 1999; Hazod 2007a: 604-606.

an ethnonymic designation of a large area in Lhokha; Dotson 2007a: 78-83). There are several variants of this *yab 'bangs* list, one of them mentioning the pair Khyung and Snubs (Gnubs). If we assume, for example, that family members who bore the name Gnubs served for generations in this entourage union and thereby arguably lived near the royal residences, meaning in Yar lung, an area with more than 30 cemeteries (Appendix II), then the question of where they were buried is far from clear. Assuming they received their own graves, they may have had their tombs in Yar lung, but also in a more remote Gnubs home such as the Gnubs yul in Rong already mentioned above, which we think was historically associated with this *yab 'bangs* of Gnubs. The toponym Gnubs is also registered for Upper Yar lung (CFS, s.v. index), and apparently had a territorial domain in the neighbouring 'Phyong po for this lineage is registered of having been allocated the *dbang ris* of Phying ba, together with the Mgos; this refers to one of the "18 shares of power" (*dbang ris bco brgyad*), which describes the first major territorial division even before the establishment of the three (later four) horn provinces (Hazod 2009). Here there is a plausible scenario according to which a family originally based in Yar lung and 'Phyong po received some estates in the western region in reward for their services to the king, which then became a separate territory named Gnubs yul. But Gnubs among others was registered very early for Gnyal (south-east of Yar lung), so that members of the family with the name Gnubs were probably buried in different areas. In view of such stories of early branches it seems pointless to speculate about the original home or to propose any family-specific grave assignments. (In the scenario outlined here, we assume that the lineage members were all buried in mounds, for which clear evidence is missing however. As is the case elsewhere, the burial sites in these areas are mostly not dated and, as already mentioned, apart from this one has to consider the situation of joint entombment; above fn. 18).

The factors of mobility and development of branch areas apply still more for the imperial period. In many cases this can be traced back to interventions by the central authority, where officials from high-ranking families were granted lands for their services. But violent relocations of lineages are also recorded, as in the case of Snyags (Gnyags) and 'Bre in the later period of the empire (Vitali 2002; Hazod 2013: 102). Or families emigrated (in connection with the construction of the peripheral temple foundations, such as the Kyi people of 'Phan po; TF 52-53), or were forced to emigrate by certain political circumstances, as with the Thon (Mthon) in the 8th century, where in this context mostly branch territories emerged, often with histories lasting late into the post-imperial period (Vitali 1996: 221ff.). (The term "lineage transfers" as suggested in the sources is misleading; strictly speaking arguably no lineages wandered, but individual families plus groups of common people attached to them. Often the term *mi* is added to the lineage names (e.g. Thon mi (Mthon myi), Sba (Dba') mi, Sha mi, 'Bro mi, Lo mi i.a.), which recalls a situation similar to the above-mentioned context of local groups situated around dominant families).

The Mgos (var. 'Gos) represent one of the better documented examples of territorial multi-presence in the imperial period: the origin of the lineage was reportedly in Skyid rong, from where by order of the emperors several Mgos families came to Dbus in the 7th century. The Mgos are here registered very early for Phying ba (see above), and from the 8th century at latest parts of the lineage served in the region of Lower G.yas ru (or Right Horn), where they provided the Horn commander. At the end of the same century the chief minister Mgos Khri bzang Yab lhag was granted enormous estates in the Nyang/Myang stod area (the famous Mgos yul derived from this), which the family later had to share with other families, in connection with the foundation of the Gnas rnying temple in Nyang stod (Vitali 2002: 82ff.; *CDR* 10a-b; Puchung Tsering 2011: 49). As far as we can see, with the exception of Skyid rong, grave fields are to be found in all of these "Mgos countries", without it being possible to identify any actual "Mgos homeland" or central "Mgos cemetery".

With some qualifications, one may see evidence of early territorial links in the geographical distribution of one and the same place name. The Mgar represent such an example of "wandering toponyms" – a name first recorded in the 6th century as the *blon* lineage of the Ngas po chiefdom (later 'Phan po), and described as the basic lineage for the later establishments of the "three great Mgar homes" (*mgar tshang chen po gsum*) of Central Tibet.[22] There are at least a dozen of Mgar sites (Mgar yul, Mgar grong, Mgar khang, Mgar lung) in the geographically small area around Lhasa alone (in Stod lung, 'Phan po or Mal gro), whose local traditions each claim that they were from the imperial period and related

22 i.e. the "Upper Stod lung Mgar tshang", the "Mal gro Mgar tshang" and the "Bsam yas Mgar tshang"; Hazod 2007a: 584. The Mgar site in upper 'Phan po, locally known as Mgar yul, is not far from the upper Mong valley, where reportedly the *bla mtsho* or "soul lake" of the Mgar is located. Hazod, *op. cit*. p. 582. The Bya pu referred to in the *OTC* (*TDD* 223: 1.462) as home of the Mgar (or the "Mgar bu") remains unknown, unless it means the Mgar seat (locally called Mgar khrungs khang) in Gnyal, not far from the present-day border with Bya yul. (See the map on TTT, site 0070; Richardson (1998: 34) suggested an identification with the Bya tshal of Sgregs.) For the lineage of Mgar Stong btsan see also Garrati 2015; cf. also Thaba Tashi Dondrub 2009.

to the most prominent Mgar member, the celebrated minister Mgar Stong btsan Yul zung. Most of these Mgar places also have burial mounds in closer proximity, such as in Ram pa of Lower Stod lung, which post-imperial sources claim was the actual birthplace of the great minister Mgar Stong btsan yul bzung (RCP 144). But the graves nearby are rather insignificant (see TTT: 0165), while further up in Stod lung (in the side valley of Sgang skyid) there is a significant elite field whose central grave the locals describe as the resting place of the "son of minister Mgar" (no. 0172). There is a similar larger burial ground even further up, in Sdings kha (0182), which is described as the summer residence of the minister Mgar (and also as his birthplace).[23]

Similarly, great family lines such as the 'Bro, Dba's, Tshes pong, Sna nam, Gnyags, Myang, 'Brang, Khuand others clearly had several territorial connections, often with other prominent families in the vicinity, so that in cases where several grave fields are next to each other any family-specific allocation remains speculative.

There are some cases where the assignment of burial site and lineage is relatively clear. The famous Mchims (in present-day Snang County) is one such case (it is actually a local dynasty with the designation of *rgyal* ("royal"); no. 0092, 0093); so is the Lcog ro (or better one group of Lcog ro people, in Bcom mdo; no. 0196; below chap. 3.3.1), the Lo snang (or Lde snang) family in Lho brag (below chap. 6), the Myang (or a branch of the Myang) in Nyang po (no. 0100; Hazod 2009), the Tshes pong (branch) in Rgu rum (below chap. 6), the Sna nam of Brang (0163) (and possible also of Gser khung, 0047; below fn. 40) and the impressive field of Khrom chen (in Lha rtse County; 0339) is assumed to have belonged to the 'Bro (see most recently Tsewang 2011: 83-92; Lobsang Nyima 2011: 208ff.; Shawo Khacham 2014b).[24] A particular example is Ngan lam, as here we find the only peripheral

23 In eastern Mal gro, next to Mgar khang Village, there are the grave fields of 0127 and 0108, the latter situated near the "minister place" of Blon po sgang. In addition, the Ba gor of Snye mo (above chap. 2.3) is mentioned as the home of "five Mgar ministers" of the imperial period (*KT* 436.17), and elsewhere is also given as the seat of a Mgar descendant who occupied the post of a district chief (*yul dpon*) in the 8th century (for references see Hazod 2007a: 582), but interestingly no burial mounds are to be found in this area around Ba gor (in lower Snye mo). In the local traditions around Mgar places there are often allusions to smithery (*mgar*) and nearby sources of iron ore (Hazod, *op. cit.*), and it appears that some of the many Central Tibetan Mgar sites – there are also sites in Byang, Yar lung, Grva phyi, Kha rag, or in Gnyal (fn. 22) – actually relate to sites linked to iron mining or smelting. The spatial distribution of these places itself points to a significant component in the early Central Tibetan settlement history. For recent discoveries of an ancient iron-smelting site in the Mgar grong area of Stod lung see Li Yingfu and Ha Bibu 2014.

24 Hazod 2009 addresses some more links between grave field and lineage (for Dba', 'Bre, Khyung, Ka ba, 'Brang i.a.), which today partly need to be revised or complemented.

elite grave, which is also identifiable. One of the two burial grounds situated next to the place Ngan po in 'Phan yul is arguably to be associated with this line. Yet for some reason this family was allotted a new area in the 7th century. This is the Ngan lam near Lhasa, where a mighty burial mound is to be found. Several indications make it clear that this is the resting place of the famous minister and general Ngan lam Stag ra Klu khong (see below chap. 5.1).

Finally, we have the special case of single (elite) mounds scattered throughout the Central Tibetan regions (Appendix II). It is reasonable to see their location in connection with the country of the respective decedents, but how is country to be defined – as the birthplace of the deceased or the country of his ancestors? And why was the burial site not continued, where were the consort(s) and other relatives buried? We will return to these and other family-specific issues later on (chap. 5).

3.3.1 The organisation of the grave constructions: state regulation and regional autonomy

From a certain point in the empire era the state's responsibility apparently also included the organisation of the (elite) funerals. Some important evidence can be found in the chapters of the "section on law and state" in the early post-imperial chronicles (Dotson 2007a). Mentioned by name are grave buildings of the military leadership (in the gradation *rgod kyi zhang blon* (military minister) and *rgod kyi yang rje* (further (lower ranking) military lords), with the addition that the mound burial (*dur mchad*) should be made together with fields and serfs (*dur mchad bran zhing dang ldan pa la bya'o*; Dotson, *op. cit.*, p. 260). This perhaps refers to the allocation of fields and their maintenance by bondservants in connection with the aftercare of the graves,[25] although such an institution is mentioned or indicated in the sources only in connection with a *btsan po* tomb (above fn. 11).

The labour for the construction of tombs was organised by the government, and a separate paragraph gives the compensation that had to be paid when a worker did not appear at the workplace (for men one goat per day's absence, for women a donkey, Dotson, *op. cit.* 259). The text speaks here of the *bang so* (and not *mchad*) of a lord (i.e. *rje'i bang so*), but this does not necessarily mean a tomb of a member of the imperial house, but more generally may refer to graves of "subject rulers" or chiefs of an administrative unit (above

25 For a different interpretation see Dotson 2006: 266.

fn. 8). Apparently grave goods were also regulated, and in general it seems that with the coming of the age of "law and state" the old regional autonomy in terms of burial tradition was retrenched and subjected to the state administration. In an inscription we learn that the central authority represented by the district administration of the chiliarchy (*stong sde*) was responsible if not for the construction then for the maintenance of the regional elite tomb(s) (below chap. 5.2).

For the present discussion the extent to which government intervention changed the regional tumulus situation is relevant in the sense that the siting of graves perhaps at some time became uncoupled from the families' territorial link and subject to decisions by the state. The situation of the burial ground of Thang stod (no. 0257; Fig. 8) in Lower Skyid shod may serve as an example to speculate on such situations. The field, which I visited in 2009, has a total of ca. 25 burial mounds divided into three groups. Two thirds are trapezoidal elite mounds, the largest (over 50m at the front) has a shrine on top dedicated to the deity called Lug rdzi rgyal po.[26] He is traditionally considered the territorial god (yul lha) of the Dbus sde district, which includes this side valley of Thang stod. This corresponds to the Dbul sde from the list of imperial districts of Dbu ru (Hazod 2009: 209). On the occasion of the annual festival in early spring, the Dbus sde communities traditionally came together in Thang stod, where, it is said that equestrian games among others were held around the central mound. This represents an attractive example of a late "tumulus use", but one may well see here the continuation of older territorial connections that were defined through the *yul lha*. In Buddhism such deities were given a modified radius of protective functions, often associated with new or additional names, but without necessarily changing their socio-political *modus operandi* of protection. The Thang stod grave field could simply be seen as an establishment by the district authority of Dbul sde, which determined that the district officials wherever they came from were to be buried here, in larger or smaller mounds according to rank. Such forms of externally defined tumulus field establishment cannot be excluded, but we rather suspect an originally different context.

The institution of regional administration corresponded with the redistribution system that assured the aristocracy their estates in return for their services to the state and the

26 Possibly there is a relation between this protector god and the classification of the "seven herdsmen" related to the imperial period, where the post of the *lug rdzi* (sheep herders) is registered as having been held by the Mkhar pa lineage (Dotson 2007a: 127).

throne. In other words, the district administration was in the hands of the families who resided there; at least this is the picture that can be drawn from the district catalogues with their mention of regional lineages related to the district leaderships (Hazod 2009). So one should distinguish the element of state control in the tumulus history from the facts of earlier territorial connections of grave field and local families. In this case we do not know which families the administration of the Dbul sde was assigned, but we assume that they were located in this area where they also had their estates. In this sense, we would favour the view that Thang stod served as burial ground of the district administration, and at the same time represented the ancestral home of a local family line (or branch line), whether this territorial link dated from an older (pre-imperial) history, or was the result of a later allocation by the state. (A similar combination of a "district field" and lineage-specific burial site can be assumed for the *stong sde* or military thousand districts. Burial site 0196, the central grave field of Bcom mdo in Byang (northern Dbu ru), here represents one better-documented examples: the area is recorded as *stong sde*, headed by the Lcog ro lineage (Hazod 2009: 200), and elsewhere in a 13th-century text is described as the place where the Lcog ro had their tombs (Roesler 2007: 130). Yet realistically the burial site served as both a burial site for members of the local Lcog ro family and of (higher) representatives of the "Lcog ro regiment" or people who were otherwise associated with this area.)

In addition to Dbul sde, there are 16 more *yul sde* (estab. 8th cent.) registered for the Central Horn, nine of them in the Lhasa area of Skyid stod and - smad, the latter known as the name of two of the altogether ten chiliarchies of Dbu ru. The facts of large number of district units around Lhasa, combined with a likely high population density in this area of the two Skyid *stong sde*, may explain the high density of grave fields and elite graves in the Lhasa valley (see Appendix II).[27] Here and there we can assume a similar territorial relation of grave and family, where in most cases of the local grave fields the elite tombs are situated in the compound of apparently older graves.

What we can deduce from the "grave paragraph" in the "state and law" catalogues is the

27 One may also refer in this context to the group of the "six subject clans of the *btsan (po)*" (*btsan 'bangs rus drug*, i.e. the Lo and Bran ka; Sba and Ngan lam; Gshu rings and Phur pa) – probably an institution from the imperial time parallel to the six *yab 'bangs* of the early Yar lung context; branches of these lineages who are described of having been responsible for the safekeeping of the *btsan po* existed in the Lhasa valley (namely attested for Lo, Bran ka, Sba (Dba') and Ngan lam; RCP s.v. index), where apparently they also had their graves (see chap. 5.1).

situation of an obviously limited autonomy of the aristocracy in the decision on graves and grave size, grave goods etc. Regional varieties can be assumed, and in those chiefdom territories that in the imperial period partly maintained their regional dynastic status (such as the *rgyal* (royal) dynasties of eastern Central Tibet – Dags po, Mchims, Rkong po) the influence by the central authority in terms of funeral issues was probably less than in other areas. On the other hand, state influence was simply a consequence of the *btsan po*'s alliance with his aristocratic allies. Thus *btsan po* Khri Srong btsan (Srong btsan Sgam po) promised his veteran ally Dba's Dbyi tshab to offer the foundation stone for the tomb (*mchad*) after Dbyi tshab's death and to sacrifice 100 horses (PT 1287 (*OTC*, chap. V): l. 264-265, 275-275; *TDD* 211-212; DTH 144-145). The family of Dbyi tshab apparently acted as bride-taker in relation to the *btsan po* house (cf. Dotson 2009a: 31), which explains the rich endowment the *btsan po* promised for this funeral; but apart from that, this passage in the *OTC* more generally suggests that the graves of the loyal nobility were to a certain degree under the aegis of the central authority, which in this case was probably also involved in the organisation of the tomb construction. (The meeting between the *btsan po* and Dbyi tshab (and his paternal relatives (*spad spun*), altogether seven) took place in La mo of Skyid shod. La mo itself has no graves and we assume that the burial mound of Dbyi tshab and his closer relatives was built in one of the other Dba' areas which can be located in the Skyid shod region; see Hazod 2009: 228f.).

Excursus: the organisation of the labour force

Sitting on the grave of Khri Srong lde btsan during our fieldwork in 2014, my colleague Hubert Feiglstorfer made a rough calculation related to its construction, with a size of ca. 120×120m, H: 26m (mound XI of 0032). He comes to the conclusion that approximately 200 people would require two years just for the movement of the rammed earth (ca. 370.000m^3).[28] This does not include the labour-intensive wall constructions – from the construction of the chambers to the outer walls – the (sacrificial) trenches situated in front of the grave or possibly other architectural additions that are no longer visible today. We

28 The parameters for this calculation are: 200 people working seven days a week ten hours a day, where one person moved a maximum of one tonne of earth per hour – with the proviso that the material was brought from the nearby environment (i.e. about 15 minutes walking distance; not counted is the use of working animals). Note that in the case of Srong btsan Sgam po's grave the earth is said to have been brought from some distance (above chap. 2.1). For comparable calculations of a 7th-century princely mound of the Tang dynasty see Eckfeld 2005: 61.

understand why in the case of the *btsan po*-s' tombs the funeral usually took place two years after the death; in the case of Khri Srong lde btsan the construction had reportedly already started while he was still alive (Appendix I, § 2, no. XI).

The organisation of labour force relates to the factor of social stratification, the lowest of which evidently was represented by the category of serfs or *bran*. We can assume that they were an important factor with regard to the procurement of the necessary labour for the grave constructions. *Btsan po* tombs were of a particular dimension, and differ from the usual elite graves not only in terms of size, funeral preparation, the mourning system, the funeral procedure itself, etc., but arguably also in the expenditure of manpower, which here was probably organised on a larger, supra-regional level. Yet commanding *bran* (or *bran khyim*, households of bondservants in a wider sense) was one of the territorial rights that the *btsan po* guaranteed his allies (cf. Dotson 2009a: 50; below chap. 5.1), and regardless of the question of the extent of the state's influence (or the emperors's obligation as in the case of Dbyi tshab's tomb), the necessary workers for the regional graves most likely came from the respective districts, where they were bound to the estates of the local leading families. In relation to the above calculation of the royal 120m-mound, approximately six months to a year of working time can be assumed for the construction of a grave of half this size, such as the M-1 mound of Thang stod, and a correspondingly smaller labour force. Given the enormous number of burial mounds, one can imagine that the organisation of the graves – from the recruitment of labour, architectural planning, ritual care to the subsequent supervision – formed a significant socio-economic factor in the society of the imperial period.

3.4 The situation of lineage specific cemeteries

One of the most important peripheral grave fields is represented by the cemetery of Slebs (or Slebs ri) in Lower Skyems stong, which was surveyed under the direction of the Tibetan archaeologist Sonam Wangdu in the 1980s and early 1990s (Sonam Wangdu 2010; cf. Chayet 1994a: 76ff.). The tombs are probably mostly to be dated to the imperial era. The burial site more precisely consists of two neighbouring cemeteries (known as the eastern and western burial-mound sites, *bang so shar* (0092), *bang so nub* (0093)), with a total of more than 200 graves, largely (trapezoidal) "coffer-shaped" mounds of the *gru bzhi* type, plus several stupa-shaped mounds (MT-D) in the smaller field of *bang so nub* (see Sonam

Wangdu 2010: 47; TTT: 0092; Feiglstorfer in this volume – Fig. 1). Skyems stong was the heartland of the old Mchims yul, whose territorial god, Mchims lha Than tso, is associated with a mountain in the lower section of the valley, not far from Slebs (cf. Lhabdron 2014: 181). This area was the seat of the Mchims rgyal dynasty (Hazod 2009: 175), whose most prominent member, General and Chief Minister Rgyal zigs Shu theng (Zhang Mchims Rgyal zigs Shu theng) is described as the lord over (the unrealistic number of) 90,000 bondservants. It seems obvious to assign the fields of Slebs to the Mchims lineage (see most recently Lhabdron 2014), and the (tortoise-shaped) stone base (situated in *bang so shar*; XWD 118) arguably belonged to the lost inscription stone dedicated to a high representative of Mchims.

One of the most important finds from Slebs, which has been kept for more than a decade in the Cultural Relics Bureau in Lhasa but has not been documented or made public so far, is a seal from the imperial period (Fig. 9).[29] The small artefact (1,8×2 cm), made of (deer?) bone and targeted with an eyelet, bears the inscription "*kha'u* (*khe'u*?) *zhang zig*" over the engraved image of a horse – an indication of a certain rank-holder (*yig tshang*) in the imperial-era aristocracy (cf. Stein 2010: 101ff.). From this name he may have not belonged to the Mchims family.[30] If so, this issue would qualify the assessment of Slebs as being exclusively a Mchims-specific necropolis. Mchims here may rather represent an umbrella name for the specific political domain, including the Mchims regiments, whose ennobled

29 The author wishes to thank Shakya Wangdu from the Cultural Relics Bureau (Lhasa) for approval to visit and photograph the seal. However, the circumstances of this discovery are unclear; some say the item was a surface find from the Slebs burial ground, others that it was found inside of one of the opened graves of Slebs (0092). Writing and drawing are engraved on the bone in a mirror image, where a slightly dash-like recess above the letter *kha* possibly indicates the *'greng bu* or "e" symbol and thus is to be read as Khe'u not Kha'u. Some remains of red pigment are on the seal.

30 The inscription follows the pattern of private seals: image plus name of three syllables related to family name (Kha'u / Khe'u) followed by personal name; cf. Takeuchi 1995: 108ff. Zhang zig is attested as a personal name (e.g. Rlang Zhang zig; Takeuchi 1998: 177, text 538: v1), and theoretically could be short for the Mchims-specific form of *zhang rgyal zigs*, but Kha'u (Khe'u) points to a different family, where Kha'u (Khe'u) was perhaps originally a place name. One Khe'u Bzang gong is recorded (Takeuchi 1995: 191f., text 16:r9, r12), and a Khe'u Gan tshe is known as the name of a temple (Thomas 1935-63, Part I: 127). To the best of my knowledge, a Kha'u family or lineage is not attested in the sources; however, it may well be related to Kha and the Kha myi (Kha people) who are registered as having formed one section of the Nyen kar regiment, headed by Dba': *nyen kar gi sde dba' kha myi* (Thomas 1935-63, Part II: 466; for Nyen kar and the Dba' lineage see Hazod 2009: 224ff.). As place name, a Kha'u (or Kha'u Brag rdzong) is listed as religious site in the area of Grom pa in Lha rtse (TF 212). It is also conceivable that the Kha'u refers here to an area within Mchims or belonged to the wider domain of Mchims and thus the holder of this Kha'u Zhang zig seal was in a wider sense of "Mchims origin". I am grateful to Joanna Bialek for her response concerning the seal photography and for references in this respect (e-mail April 2016).

combatants (above chap. 2.3) were also buried in this Mchims field. (Cf. also the case of the Bcom mdo *stong sde*; chap. 3.3.1.)

But be that as it may, Slebs was in any case also a Mchims burial site in the narrower (lineage-specific) sense, and in this context several questions arise: What happened, for example, to the members of Mchims families who were born and grew up outside of Mchims yul, in a branch territory, as we find in many other families? Were these "Mchims people" buried in a cemetery of their birthplace, or in a cemetery in the vicinity of the house where they lived with wife and family, or as for all the other Mchims name-bearers was the central cemetery of Slebs provided for them? The Tibetan kings and emperors, for example, were not buried in their respective country of birth, but from a certain point in royal history in the necropolis of Phying ba, which in its division into two (0029, 0032) formally corresponds to the situation of the two fields of Slebs in Mchims.[31] We would like to draw attention to the factor of kinship organisation. Kinship means consanguinity and affinal relationship and (within the closer circle of family or household) in the generation of heir and lineage-holder it included his wife (and second wives) and siblings (older and younger brothers and sisters – the latter moving away according to the patrilineal order) – positions which at the same time embodied different social roles and were apparently also criteria in the choice of location of the tomb.

The burials recorded for Phying ba comprise 19 generations, with the first two generations being represented by women (Appendix I). In view of this long period, the 28 graves that today can be made out for the fields 0029 and 0032 (Don mkhar and Mu ra) seems a rather low number, in any case low compared to the Mchims-specific burial ground. A larger number of members of the dynasty were apparently not buried in Phying ba within these generations. Where are their graves? Or were they buried in a joint entombment or was a grave mound intended for them at all? With respect to the imperial necropolis we find textual indications which in fact suggest that the rule of kinship organisation represented an important criterion in the question of who was buried where. Let us take a closer look at this issue and finally ask, how far this specific situation can also be transferred to the regional

31 A similar division of two neighbouring cemeteries is also to be found in several other lineage-specific burial sites – in Khrom chen (0339, 0340), Gser khung (0047, 0048), Bcom mdo (0195, 0196), Sham bu (0278b, c), and also in Ngan lam (below chap. 5.1).

elite burial landscapes and what conclusions can be derived from this comparison.

4. Kinship and tomb I: a view of the necropolis of Phying ba

The relevant sources for this chapter refer to the *Gsang ba yang chung* (*GYC*, known as an appendix to the *Cang lnga* text group, see below) and the Lde'u chronicles (especially *Lde'u-1*), namely the section in the chapter on the royal genealogy, which informs about the members of the royal house who had been discarded as possible candidates for the throne. I will start my brief discussion with this text (*Lde'u-1* 104-05).

The situation of discarded candidates is given by the phrase *thang mtshams su phab ba* – "brought down to the border [of the] plain", i.e. expelled, disqualified for the throne that was transmitted through the agnatic line from father to the son. This *thang mtshams* institution (already addressed by Chayet (1994b: 21-22) and Dotson (2009a: 26ff.), cf. also Karmay 1998: 306-307 (fn. 86); Pezhung 2013: 65; Drikung 2011: 97)is said to have been introduced by the wise ministers (*blon po rig pa can*). It appears in this context as a quasi by-product of the development of the hereditary kingship. It says that at this time (of the *rgyal* or chiefdom period) the ministers decided which of the many potential candidates should be given the throne (*rgyal sa*), and the other (lateral candidates) had to be brought "to the border of the plain". The latter relates to half-brothers (i.e. brothers from an affinal relation of the father different to the one from which the heir to the throne came) as well as to "full brothers" (i.e. brothers who shared the same mother as the king or *btsan po*); in both cases the specification of the maternal origin is indicated by prefixing the name of the mother's paternal lineage or house to the names of the brothers, in the form *tsha* ("nephew") of the mother's lineage/ruling house X (fn. 33).

The description in the *Lde'u* chronicles of the disqualified younger and older (half-) brothers (*gcung po* and *gcen po*) of the heirs to the throne starts by listing the princes related to the periods of the first groups of kings genealogically (i.e. the first groups after the actual founding figure Spu lde gung rgyal): the Eight Lde, Six Legs and Five Btsan (Appendix I). These are usually rendered as mythical kings, however the description nevertheless includes historically reliable material. Thus it states that new lateral lines developed from these groups – lines of younger and elder brothers. These are described as Zhang lnga gcen po and Zhang lnga gcung po, which Dotson (2009a: 29) suggests is identified with the Zha snga lineage mentioned in the *Old Tibetan Annals* and the inscription.[32] As first noted by Chayet (1994b) in this context, this story shows that in the earlier days of the Tibetan kingship it was evidently the middle son who was favoured.

The following *thang mtshams* princes are listed:
(**P** = location of grave in Phying ba (0029 or 0032) as given in *GYC*)

· The *gcen po* of I sho legs (from the Legs drug; grave erected in heaven)
· The *gcen po* of Bse rnol nam (from the Lde brgyad; location of grave not mentioned)
· The *gcung po* of Rgyal to re Longs brtsan (from the Btsan lnga; location in Grang mo, due south of 'Phyong rgyas; above fn. 15)
· The *gcung po* 'Ol god tsha ("nephew of 'Ol god") Blon Ger legs (i.e. the younger brother of Gnam ri Slon mtshan;[33] grave in **P.**, next to his father and mother)
· The *gcung po* Tshes spong *tsha* [Btsan srong] (violently eliminated, in Gnyal; Dotson 2009a: 81; location of grave not mentioned; on Gnyal see TTT: no. 0070)
· The *gcung po* 'A zha tsha Mer ste (i.e. the younger (half-) brother of Mang srong Mang btsan; violently eliminated; location of grave not mentioned)
· The *gcung po* of 'Dus srong (from the father's affinal relation with the Ru yong lineage; location of grave not mentioned)
· Lha Bal po (elder half-brother of Khri Lde gtsug btsan, with *btsan mo* Ga tun as his mother; funeral for the latter in 708-09, in Pying ba?) and his two younger brothers Lod po and Lod chung (tomb (if one was provided at all) outside of Phying ba)

32 Cf. also Uebach 2012: 54. Perhaps this lineage name is related to Zha ma, a prominent lineage in western Gtsang province of the post-imperial period (Hazod 1998). Note that the form Zha lnga (var. Zhal lnga = Zhang lnga, Zha snga?) is also registered for peripheral aristocratic lineages: namely for the "*zhang* lineage" of Sna nam, if we read the place of "'On (var. 'Ol) Sna nam Zha(l) lnga" (RCP 559) as a settlement related to the Sna nam Zha lnga branch in "'On (or 'Ol [kha])"; see Czaja 2013: 97 for a discussion of this place name; cf. also below fn. 40.

33 *Tsha* (*bo*) means nephew (BS (brother-son) as well as SiS (sister-son)) and grandson (*Tshig mdzod* 2246/2), and here in a broader classificatory sense highlight the origin of the mother from the house / lineage of 'Ol god. A similar tagging of maternal origin is also to be found in the name of other (disqualified) brothers, and it has been argued that this form of naming was used to express the disqualified position of these brothers (Dotson 2009a: 28; but note that *tsha* is also to be found in the naming of the heir apparent, albeit only in later sources, namely in the formulation of the origin of Tibet's first king (Gnya' khri Btsan po): *lha'i gdung rmu'i tsha*. "(Offspring) of the divine lineage (of Phvya), nephew (= classificatory SiS) of Rmu (var. Dmu)"; *Lde'u-2* 233.15). Unlike Mer ste and Lha bon, the Blon Ger legs and also Btsan srong were not half-brothers from a second affinal relation, but full brothers – if we assume that Stong btsun 'Bro ga of 'Ol god, who in PT 1286 is mentioned as the mother of Khri Slon btsan, this was also the mother of Blon Ger legs, and the Tshes pong *tsha* Btsan srong and his older brother Srong btsan Sgam po had the same mother (i.e. 'Bring ma Thog dgos). We find also such *tsha* gradations in the branching stories of aristocratic families outside the royal lineage; below chap. 5.

· Khri Lde gtsug btsan's first-born Ljang tsha Lha bon (*alias* Lha[s] bon; grave in **P.**)
· Mu tig btsan po (= Mu rug btsan; grave in **P.**)[34]

The *Gsang ba yang chung* mentions some more disqualified princes:
· 'Bro tsha Rmu btsun and Mon bu Rgyal mtshan (related to 'Bro snyan Lde ru; grave in **P.**)
· Prince(s) (not mentioned by name) related to Sad na legs (grave in **P.**, possibly buried inside the tomb of this *btsan po*)
· Gtsang ma (elder son of Sad na legs); his [body] was left behind in Lho brag.

This certainly incomplete *thang mtshams* listing includes several question marks regarding the location of the graves. What can be stated is that several half-brothers and disqualified throne candidates were evidently buried in one of the two fields of Phying ba. This indicates that the dissociation of the disqualified siblings was not necessary linked with any spatial distancing of their graves. Lcang tsha Lha bon, who received a grave in Mu ra, here represents a special example. But the mention of the *thang mtshams bang so* related to I sho legs whose burial(s) are given in heaven also suggests that the lateral lines were not disqualified socially.

The grave list of the *Gsang ba yang chung* (*GYC*) provides information on the kinship and social implications in the burial tradition of the Yar lung house. This appendix to the *Can lnga* text group (*Lde'u-1* 99) seems to represent the earliest extant description of the burial mounds related to the Tibetan royal house, although the dating of early 10th century suggested for the *Can lnga* (Karmay 1998: 308) appears to be too early for the *GYC* (see foreword of Appendix I). The text lists 28 tombs located in one of the two grave fields, a number that largely corresponds to the situation we find on site. In addition there are tombs listed that relate to various members of the imperial family and which are given as being outside of 'Phyong po; others are without any place information. Appendix I provide a translation of the main part of *GYC* (377.9-380.9), while at this point we single out only some main issues relevant for the present discussion.

The grave list is divided into seven sections:

34 The mention of Mu tig Btsan po (Mu rug btsan; r. ca. 800-02) and also of Lha Bal po (r. 704-05) as *thang mtshams su phab ba* is obviously related to the event of their early dismissal from the throne as stated in later chronicles (Sørensen 1994: 407, 597; Dotson 2007a).

(**P** = tomb in Phying ba (i.e. 0029 or 0032); **O** = location of grave outside of Phying ba)

1. The early burials, from the Khri bdun to the Btsan lnga (the burials of the latter group refer to a place in Upper 'Phyong po)
2. The tombs of the succeeding kings and emperors: from no. I to XVII] **P**
3. The burial mounds of queen-mothers (nine "queens (*jo mo*) endowed with power"[35] are listed, plus 11 grandmothers (*phyi ma*) with only one mentioned by name) **P**
4. Eight junior queens **O**?
5. Six ladies of the imperial house not buried in graves **O**
6. Burials of six junior queens in stupa-shaped tombs **O**, **P**
7. The burial mounds of disqualified [princes] (*thang mtshams kyi bang so*) **P**

As to the first group, as noted above we think the details on the burials of the kings before the Btsan lnga – the burials in *gnam*, *rdza*, *g.ya'*, *spang*, *chu* (Appendix I) – refer to various forms of exposing the corpse, which were practised in some places in pre-historical times. The information may here relate to a specific area in 'Phyong po and Upper Yar lung (Hazod 2007b), but arguably relate a Central Tibetan burial tradition beyond this area, which probably did not disappear either after the practice of building burial mounds for the families of the political and military elite began. The latter form (we assume it was from the very beginning a form of inhumation burial) started with the round (or *zlum po* type) *bang so* of the Btsan lnga in the cultivated zones of the settlement area (*yul*). The geographical position mentioned in this context refers to the area known as Grang mo of Upper 'Phyong po, where later sources locate also the grave of Gri gum Btsan po (0028), the ruler, with whom the beginning of the burial-mound tradition is associated. He represents the paragon of the ruler of the chiefdom period, which with the Btsan lnga may to some degree represent a historically first more localisable dimension.

35 The rendering of the Tibetan terms related to the various kinship specific positions within the imperial family here follows Dotson 2009a: 25f.; however, some renderings, particularly "queen" and "queen-mother", remain imprecise as they do not differentiate between the period of royal families (related to the *rgyal po* period, before the 7th century) and the period of imperial families. The chief wife of an emperor (and heir-bearing mother) was strictly speaking not a "queen" but an "empress". (On the various problems in this context see fn. 37 in Dotson, *ibid.*). In line with the description in post-imperial sources, in *GYC* there is often no distinction between "royal" and "imperial"; thus under this heading of "*jo mo* endowed with power" it indiscriminatingly lists ladies from both periods.

In the *GYC* the actual tumulus tradition starts with Rgyal to re Longs brtsan,[36] the first of the Btsan lnga ("Five [rulers with the name element] *btsan* (mighty)". He was one of the Yar lung rulers who are mentioned in the sources as founder of Phying ba Stag rtse (*KT* 148), the "Tiger Cliff" castle situated opposite the (later) necropolises. His wife and queen mother came from the 'O ma district, which may be the 'O ma not far north of 'Phyong rgyas. (The site has an imperial-era grave field, one of the altogether more than 30 burial-mound fields in the 'Phyong po and Yar lung districts; TTT: "maps".) How far this could be an indication of a still rather regionalised affinal policy at that time is uncertain. His mother was a Nyi btsun, which could be read as princess of the Rnyi ba from Gnyal, the home territory of this family. He was buried in Grang mo, as were the succeeding four kings, including Lha Tho do Snya brtsan. The latter's son and successor, Khri Snya zung brtsan (no. I), was buried in Lower Don mkhar, not far from the place where previously the *bang so* of the wife of Lha Tho do Snya brtsan and the wife of his predecessor Khri thog brtsan were erected. This geographical change from Grang mo to Don mkhar may correlate with an opening/ extension of the Yar lung power and its affinal policy. Lha Tho do Snya brtsan is generally regarded as the ruler who founded the residence (his *sku mkhar*) Yum bu Bla sgang (in the Lower Yar lung, an area also known as Yar mo sna bzhi; TF 228). The history of the heavenly reception of the first Buddhist objects (characterised as *gnyan po gsang ba*) at this location today is generally seen as an indication of a historical first contact with Buddhism. At this time the *nor bu bang so* (tomb with treasures) was allegedly also established in Yum bu Bla sgang, originally for the safekeeping of older royal insignia (TF 101f.).

The graves of the Btsan lnga have not yet been discovered, but we can state that at some point in the history of this Yar lung house there was a change of the location of the family graves. Here it is interesting that the burial mound history of Phying ba started with the *bang*

36 In counting back from Srong btsan Sgam po (d. 649-50), the reign of the first of the Btsan lnga is to be dated to the 4th century or so (30 years per generation) – a chronology which presupposes that the genealogy of this group of five represents historic facts. Otherwise this dating is the only (textual) indication for determining the beginning of the tumulus history. (A similar chronology can be calculated for Zhang zhung, when it says in the "Zhang zhung chapter" of Gu ge pandita Grags pa rgyal mtshan's *Nyi ma* (141.2ff.), that the Snya shur La khva geng rtse, the father of Srong btsan Sgam po's Zhang zhung consort (Li thig sman) lived 11 generations after Snya shur Mu su ring nge who was elected as (first) ruler (*jo bo*) of Zhang zhung (*Nyi ma* 141.4-6). This would lead to a dating of the political origin of Zhang zhung of approx. early 4th century. However, the mortuary archaeology of western Tibet suggests a much earlier presence of centralised power in this area (Aldenderfer 2013; Bellezza 2014), although to label this early archaeological evidence as "Zhang zhung" remains pure speculation.)

so of Stong rgyal Mtsho ma, the grandmother of Khri Snya zung brtsan. The information about the location of this tomb in *GYC* allows us to identify it with one of the smaller (round) tombs situated at the left side of the entrance to the Don mkhar valley, a separate group of *bang so* which can be attributed to queens. It seems that the grave field of Don mkhar was initially reserved for ladies of the Yar lung House, while the kings before Khri Snya zung brtsan were still buried in Upper 'Phyong po. The grave field of Mu ra was established only much later, after the death of Srong btsan Sgam po, with Don mkhar still having been used as burial ground in the imperial period.[37]

The bird's-eye view of the two Phying ba burial sites combined with the grave account gives a good "text" about the history of the tombs related to the royal genealogy (Fig. 1). For example, we can clearly see the development from chiefdom and imperial-era burial mounds (in terms of size and form, starting from the oldest group v.3-4); at the same time a number of differentiations in the grave landscape (in terms of size, shape, distance from each other etc.) can be observed, which in some cases appear consistent, but in others, however, are often not so easy to explain.[38] And we see the basic relationship between kinship and tomb in connection with the question of who was buried where. In summary, this can be graphically shown as follows:

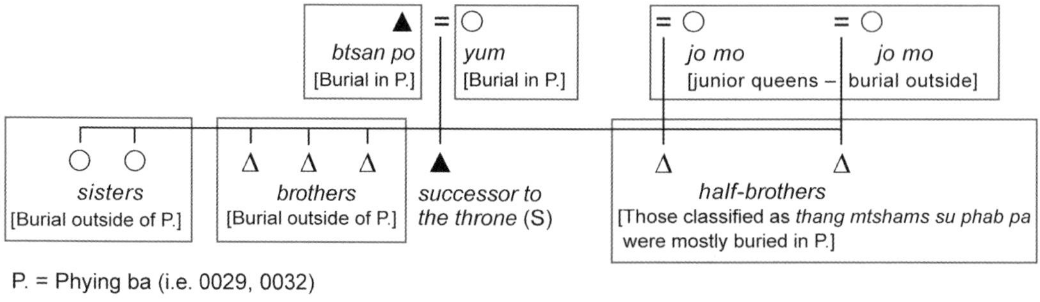

- The *btsan po*-s: All *btsan po-s* (and formerly the kings (*rgyal po*) from the time of no. I, see Appendix I, § 2) were buried in **P.** (in either Don mkhar (0029), or Mu ra (0032)).

37 The two fields are not mentioned in the *OTA*, which only speaks of Phying ba. *Dba' bzhed* 27b (Wangdu and Diemberger 2000: 98-99) gives the form Ra ba thang or Phyi lugs (Phying lung) Ra ba thang.

38 A discussion of the individual tombs and their specific positions, external features or spatial relation to each other goes beyond the scope of the present paper. See here most recently Shawo Khacham 2014a.

- As to the queen-mothers (*yum*) we already have noted that the history of the grave field in Phying ba started with the erection of tombs related to ladies (heir-bearing queens), namely Ru yong Stong rgyal mthso ma (mother of Lha Tho do Snya brtsan), and Mno (Gno/Rno) bza' Mang mo rje Ji dgos (wife of Lha Tho do Snya brtsan), and only from the time of Khri Snya zung brtsan (no. I) were the tombs of the queen-mothers and *btsan po*-s united in the necropolis of **P.**, although usually at some distance from one another (the exception being the "twin grave" of Stag bu and his consort; see Appendix I). Although several queen-mothers are not mentioned in the grave account of the *GYC* (Appendix I) we can state that it was the custom to bury the heir-bearing queens in **P.**, and indeed in separate tombs. If our identification is correct, the largest tomb relates to the *bang so* of Tshes pong 'Bring ma Thog dgos (tomb no. iv.1, in Don mkhar), the mother of Srong btsan Sgam po.
- The *jo mo* (junior queens) – burial outside of **P.**

  The identification of the location of the tombs related to the junior queens (*jo mo*) raises some problems: within the groups 4 to 6 the grave account lists the burials of several junior queens, where the "tombs" noted in group 6 (and partly also in group 5) relate to Buddhist burials, which (perhaps with one exception, i.e. 6.6) are all to be located outside of Yar lung / 'Phyong po. The details of the eight junior queens of group 4 are not clearly readable to me. It says at the end of this list: (...)*'chims bza' dang brgyad bang sor brtsig so //* – "(...) 'Chims bza' [Lha mo btsan] [one of the consorts of Khri Srong lde btsan] – altogether eight [*jo mo*] [whose resting place] was erected in *bang so*"(i.e. inside the tombs of their respective husbands?). Alternatively, and perhaps the better reading would be: " (…) plus 'Chims bza' making eight [for whom graves] were erected as *bang so*". The text gives no details of the locations. If the ladies were buried inside the graves of their husbands, then we have to ask what happened to the body if the grave of the husband had not yet been built, or were they buried together with the king in the form described for 'Brong Gnyan lde ru (no. II) and his chief consort? (see excursus below) In the introductory verse of *GYC* it says that some of the "18 *jo mo* from the marriage with subject (lineages)" (*'bangs la gnyen pa'i jo mo bco brgyad*) were buried in combination with others (*Lde'u-2* 377.3-4).
- The sisters – burial outside of **P.**

  The sisters (and half sisters) are not actually mentioned by name in the *GYC*, but we can assume with some conviction that in line with the patrilineal order they were buried in the land of their husbands.

• half-brothers – they were partly buried in **P.**, namely in "*thang mtshams* graves".

• brothers – burial outside of **P.**

For the imperial period at least, no "full brother" is registered as having been buried in P, unless they became emperors; the phrase *khu chen bang so* apparently relates to the latter situation (Appendix I).

It is striking that in contrast to princes classified as *thang mtshams su phab pa*, other brothers not specified in this way were not included in the funeral of the Phying ba burial grounds, at least they are not mentioned in the grave account. This applies, for example, to Khri Slon khol, known from the *Old Tibetan Chronicle* as the younger brother of Khri Slon btsan (Gnam ri Slon mtshan), who remained in Phying ba, while Khri Slon btsan set out with his army to the north, on the Skyid chu. According to later sources the departure took place from Bug pa can, one of the imperial residences in Yar stod, near grave field no. 0018, one of the possible candidates for the burial of a prince. Rather unlikely but not entirely excludable is that several of the disqualified princes who did not die in exile (as Gtsang ma, no. 8 of group 7), were buried in the graves of their brothers and *btsan po*-s. The not entirely clear passage concerning the Sad na legs *thang mtshams bang so* perhaps relates to such an issue. In any case, what we can summarise in this context are two observations:

1) Several princes were apparently buried in a grave field outside of 'Phyong rgyas. This included the half-brothers of the *thang mtshams* status as well as full brothers of the *btsan po*.

2) We see that from the social category of princes apparently only half-brothers of the *thang mtshams* status were buried in 'Phyong rgyas.

As for those princes who were not buried in **P.**, my explanation is simply that such a funeral was not provided. The princes were rather active in other territorial contexts, or resided in one of the places registered as early residences in the Yar lung area and adjacent districts (Grang mo, Phang thang, Bug pa can, Yuṃ bu bla sgang, Gzan (of Gnyal; possibly the Bzang yul of Gnyal gzhung; no. 0070) are mentioned in this context), or also in areas of the "mobile residence", which gradually became sort of "fixed" sites of the emperor house, such as Bsam yas; and these places outside (i.e. distant from Phying ba) may also have served as the sites for the princes' tombs, not least as these areas indeed mostly have graves of the elite type.[39] The reason why certain brothers were buried in **P**. may have been pragmatic, or it was simply that these princes did not develop separate lines and had no relation to one of the imperial residences either.

· The implications of the *zhang* lineage in the *GYC*

The clear distinction between queen-mothers and junior queens and the classification of the *thang mtshams* princes reflect key elements of the affinal connection of the royal family and the social differentiations related to it. Regulation of the social order caused significant difficulties and was accompanied by internal political power struggles for the throne, which repeated in almost every generation. What was of priority, it seems, was not to follow a specific order of succession to the throne (ultimogenitur, primogeniture or succession by the middle son), but the enforcement by one of the lineages affinally associated with the royal line of their right to become an heir-bearing lineage, which coincided with the convention of declaring other possible candidates to be *thang mtshams*. It has been observed that in the Tibetan royal genealogy we find a certain rhythm in the occurrence of *zhang* lineages, i.e. of those privileged heir-producing mother-brother lineage, whose leading members were addressed as *zhang*, one of the highest ranking titles that was heritable within this line at least for four generations (calculated after the enthronement of a *btsan po*, whose mother (i.e. the *yum* or queen-mother) came from this bride-giver lineage; Dotson 2004).[40] Behind this rhythm of the occurrence of these lineages, Dotson sees a specific variant of "generalised exchange" between the royal line (the bride-taker lineage, *dbon*) and the bride-giver (and mother-brother lineage, *zhang*), which at the same time was linked to the proscription,

39 See the "G.yo ru" map on TTT, for Bsam yas see 0040; Lhasa proper has no mound burial sites as also not the other Buddhist "personal residences" of *btsan po*-s ('On can do, Skar cung).

40 These were the three 'Bro, Mchims, Tshes pong and – after the birth of Khri Srong lde btsan – also the Sna nam was entitled as *zhang* (Dotson, *ibid.*; a note in *Nyang ral* (273.4-11) suggests that the Sna nam pa received the *zhang* status after the prince had reached the age of five). Apart from Mchims, no chief territory with a possible central lineage-specific grave field can be clearly identified for the other lineages. In the case of the 'Bro, as said, the area of Gtsang stod in the Lha rtse district in western Gtsang, around the large elite grave field of Khrom chen (0339) has been proposed as the lineage's main territory within Central Tibet. Among the territories of the Tshes pong was the Rgu rum district in Stod lung, with the significant field 0176 behind present-day Rgu rum village (chap. 6; cf. also fn. 62). The Sna nam in turn were *inter alia* in Lower Stod lung (cf. RCP 430), in 'On (see fn. 32) and in the Grva district (RCP 171), and there are indications that the elite fields of Stod lung Brang (0163) and of Gser khung in Grva (0047) were related to this lineage (see Appendix II: entry 0163 and 0047). *KG* 189.7-9 speaks of the "'Bro in the west", the "Mchims in the east" and the "Sna nam in the middle" (of Central Tibet).

according to which one and the same *zhang* line was not allowed to serve as the heir-producing lineage for two successive generations (Dotson 2004; 2009b). The struggle of the aristocratic elite for the position of an heir-producing lineage and, related to it, the rivalry between the half-brothers (sons of first and secondary wives), formed as it were a phenomenon inherent to the system with respect to the order of succession, with its basic prescription of a "*zhang* rotation" (cf. Dotson 2009b: 236). The grave landscape of Don mkhar and Mu ra here reflects the social system – in the form of a clear distinction between the graves of the *btsan po* and the burials of the (half-)brothers, between queen-mothers and junior queens. And within the group of queens there was again the differentiation, according to which a clearly larger grave was provided for those from a *zhang* lineage. If our grave identification is correct, this is true at least for the graves of Tshes pong 'Bring ma thog dgos (in Don mkhar), Sna nam Mang mo rje Bzhi steng (in Mu ra), and 'Bro Khri ma lod. (The latter, the quasi-empress, is registered as one of the "11 *phyi ma*" (*phyi mo*; grandmothers) in *GYC* and marked as no. IX in our list (Appendix I). The other *phyi ma* or their graves are not mentioned and it remains unclear who they may refer to).

Excursus: The grave in Lower Zhang (0037)

The *zhang* lineage of Khri ma lod, 'Bro, is generally considered one of the most powerful family lines of the empire.[41] The *zhang* system started with this line, at least, the first *zhang* queen-mother of historical time was a 'Bro, namely 'Bro bza' Dung pyang bzher (a.k.a. 'Bro bza' Mo dur yang bzheng), the wife of Khri Sna zung brtsan (no. I), as previously mentioned, the first ruler of the Yar lung house who was buried in 'Phyong rgyas. The lineage name 'Bro was apparently transferred from the mother to the son and successor of no. I, 'Bro Mnyen lde ru (later spelling 'Bro(ng) Gnyan/ Snyan lde ru), and it has been argued that here one can see an indication of matrilineal order that may have been practised in the earlier history of the 'Bro (Yamagucci 1992). According to the classical sources, 'Bro Gnyan lde ru's burial site was erected in Lower Zhang (Zhang mda'), situated outside of 'Phyong rgyas (0037), a toponym that may indeed be related to the history of this Yar lung king, perhaps in the sense of "place of the *zhang*(-line) (of 'Bro)," but this does not

41 See here most recently the study on the 'Bro house by Lobsang Nyima 2011.

indicate "matrilinearity".[42] The *GYC* is the only source that gives the grave of *rgyal po* 'Bro Gnyan lde ru as being in Don mkhar (0029), probably a scribal error. The fact that the local tradition and the on-site survey confirm the existence of a larger single grave in Zhang mda' Village (Fig. 10) is indicative that this is the grave of this king. It is interesting that the tombs of the disqualified brothers of 'Bro Gnyan lde ru, 'Bro tsha Rmu btsun and Mon bu Rgyal mtshan, were built in Don mkhar mda'. (They are situated "below Stag gu", i.e. Stag bu Gnyan gzigs; Appendix I.)

The well-known story of the leper king, therefore (deliberately?) buried outside, has been heavily reshaped by Buddhism when it says that in view of the impending pollution only the worship of the Buddhist objects that had been kept "secret" since Lha Tho tho ri (i.e. the *gnyan po gsang ba*) could secure the lineage. The various versions usually add that in addition a doctor (*sman pa*) from 'A zha should be invited for this purpose. The order came from the father, 'Bro Gnyan lde ru, himself, who expressed it to the young Stag bu as his last will. He declares (in the versions of *KG* 170; *Lde'u-2* 251; *Lde'u-1* 107) that if the son remained blind, he should summon Sum ri ring po in Sum pa yul, his (i.e. 'Bro Gnyan lde ru's) son born to his *chung ma* (second wife) Rgya mo rgya lcam from the (Sum pa) *bon po* (family), and appoint him to the throne (cf. Haarh 1969: 336-337 and Yamaguchi 1992: 70-71 for slightly diff. readings). After this he entered the grave with his two ministers (i.e. the *rje 'bangs gsum*), which was built in Zhang mda', called the "round grave of the living" (*gson mchad zlum po*). The two ministers were Snyags Thang ba yang rje and Snubs Khri Thog rje gzungs (var.: Khri Thog rje gzung btsan; *Lde'u-1*; *Lde'u-2*, *op. cit.*); elsewhere it says the king together with his wife (from Mchims) and one of the two ministers went into the grave, and the account in *Bshad mdzod* has it that "the lord and his attendants, the seven" (*dpon g.yog bdun*) entered the tomb alive (Haarh 1969: 335). These six are very likely an allusion to the *yab 'bangs rus drug* group, which also included Snyags and Snubs.

In this story one may see some evidence concerning the historical links of the Tibetan tumulus tradition: the story of joint entombment represents an example of the "ruler and his comitatus" funeral as mentioned in Chinese sources on Tibet, and, as noted, generally is considered a widespread phenomenon in the ancient political cultures of Central Asia (or even

42 A connection between the Zhang toponym and the much older lateral lineage establishment of the above mentioned Zhang lnga is also feasible, yet its original name – as previously mentioned – is proposed as having been "Zha snga".

Central Eurasia). (The mention in the *Xin Tangshu* (Bushell 1880: 521; above fn. 18) suggests that this form of entombment was still practised in the imperial period, but there is no clear evidence for this in the sources or from archaeology.) The connection to the 'A zha (Tuyuhun) addressed in the story may refer to changes in burial rituals, which were inspired (once more?) by contacts with this important kingdom. The Tuyuhun (and their Xianbei legacy) but also the (affinally related) Sum pa no doubt belong to the closer circle of historical contact links, which we can locate in the early Central Tibetan tumulus history (see also chap. 6).

5. Kinship and tomb II: the situation of the peripheral elite fields

Now the question arises of what in the specific situation that we find for the royal genealogy in *GYC* is transferable to the elite burials outside the imperial necropolis? On this we can state as a principal limit of comparability: the burial ground of Phying ba was exclusively reserved for members of the royal dynasty – and if there was a "joint entombment" of non-relatives as recorded for the grave 0037 this was quasi determined by system. In grave fields of the size similar to Mchims with seven times as many graves it is likely that people outside the closer kinship complex of the regional dynasty were also buried there (members of the Mchims regiments, for example). The fact that there were apparently only these two cemeteries in the core area of ancient Mchims yul (Appendix II) supports this conclusion.

Having said this, similar dynastic order principles can be expected for the dominant elite families. Here we can assume that the similarities are provided by the specifics of the (patrilinear) kinship structure, whose first historical evidence in relation to a regional Tibetan elite family line we find in chapter five of the *OTC* (related to Dba's Dbyi tshab's family, below fn. 44), and, more detailed, in the famous Zhol stele inscription (composed in ca. 764), and also in the (later?) Lho brag inscriptions.

5.1 The Ngan lam

The Zhol inscription is related to the Ngan lam, the family of the well-known general and minister Stag sgra Klu khong (in the following in short: Klu khong). Summarising in the much-quoted North Face inscription it reads (Richardson 1985: 16-25):

— The emperor (Khri Srong lde btsan) ensures by oath that the silver letter (*dngul gyi yi ge*; Dotson 2009a: 61) handed over to Klu khong will forever remain within the lines of Klu gong's descendants (*bu tsha rgyud*), and if the family line (*rabs*) of rank holder is interrupted the silver letter-rank should be passed on to the next (male) relative within the *bu tsha rgyud* of the Klu khong and his father, Zla gong.

— In addition the descendants of Zla gong are likewise ensured an aristocratic position and rank (the rank of *zhang lon*) – connected to the command of 300 soldiers. As long as the loyalty (*glo ba nye*) to the *btsan po* is not broken, the *bu tsha rgyud* of Zla gong should not lose their lives or positions for whatever offence, but be punished with compensation payments. Should a (sub-)line die out, the *khol yul* (land for tax levy), cattle and the general property (of the family line) should not be confiscated, but given to the nearest (male) relatives (*pu nu bo*). Besides loyalty it states that Zla gong's *bu tsha rgyud* "will be honoured by (*btsan po's*) words and praised as capable ones as far as (they are) competent for an official duty (*rje blas*)" (transl. of this line (North Face 17-20) in Bialek 2015: 211).

— Further the *btsan po* declares that the post of the bodyguard district leader (*sku srungs stong dpon*) of 'Phan yul is to be awarded to no one other than members of the *bu tsha rgyud* of Ngan lam Gsas slebs, the grandfather of Klu khong (who first had held this post).

— and he states whatever is in possession of the *bu tsha rgyud* of Zla gong – such as bondservants, fields, pastures, fallow lands, and forests (*bran zhing 'brog sog tshal*) should not be reduced or go to others. And should anyone take action against members of the *bu tsha rgyud*, this will be regulated by orders from above; slanders against the Ngan lam people will not be given any ear, as long as Ngan lam is loyal; if one of the *bu tsha rgyud* would act disloyal, only this one would be punished (i.e. no kin liability).

This agreement may have been concluded at a meeting in Ngan lam near Lhasa, known as one of the residence places of the *btsan po* (see below), where the inscription stele was originally erected (Hazod 2007a; 2010). The old Ngan lam was in 'Phan yul, in the area of the small tributary of Ngan chu, river of Ngan, where it has been argued that Ngan is possibly of Sogdian origin (Richardson 1985: 23, fn. 13). The main river of 'Phan po is also known as 'Phan po Ngan chu, which is indicative of an old Ngan establishment of central regional importance.[43] A family from this Ngan lam area had apparently established some reputation through its service as a bodyguard to the *btsan po*, a position that was evidently

43 Hazod 2007a: 605. On the other hand Ngan lam appears in the list of the "Ma sangs clans", a classification which refers to the period before the emergence of the principalities (*rgyal phran*), in the form *gnyan ma sangs ngan lam rtsang skyes*, the "*gnyan ma sangs* Ngan lam (ancestor) born in Rtsang (Gtsang)"; *Lde'u-2* 225; Hazod 2007a: 602. On *gnyan* and *ma sangs* in this context see Karmay 1998: 444-445.

hereditary and confirmed in this imperial decree. The decree is actually dedicated to the minister Klu khong, who rose to the high rank of a silver-letter holder; but the larger family complex of Ngan lam was simultaneously rewarded on this occasion as well, and provided with certain positions was raised to the rank nobility or reconfirmed in this status. This was accompanied by an entire catalogue of certified rights addressed to the family or family members, with a permanence that actually had no qualification other than the demanded loyalty to the throne.[44]

The family is portrayed in the agnatic succession of three generations (Gen. I: Gsas slebs; Gen. II: Zla gong; Gen. III: Klu khong) plus non-specifically the offspring, who are interestingly divided into the descendants of Gen. I, II, III, or also summarised in Gen. II and III. The term is *bu tsha rgyud*, which describes the section of the (still customarily used today) *pha tsha bu brgyud* family complex (from the point of Ego), literally the "line (*brgyud*) of father (*pha*), sons (*bu*) and grandsons (*tsha* (*bo*))." The (paternal) "nephews" can also be addressed as *tsha bo*, which would mean that the *bu tsha rgyud also* included the collateral side of brothers and brothers-sons. This broader familial context is otherwise indicated by the phrase of relative nearness (*nye ba*) to the office holder, or at one point illustrated by the term *pu nu po* ("older, younger brothers"). This latter formulation usually refers to a larger collateral segment (i.e. including the descendants of the brothers), although the form of an expanding radius of *phu nu* solidarity as for example addressed in the Gesar epic (Karmay 1998: 496f.) is apparently not intended here. Parallel designations of this vertical and horizontal kinship order in relation to the assignment of rank insignia are to be found in old Tibetan documents in the form "from the *bu po spad* down to *pha spun spad*", which, as pointed out by Dotson (*op. cit.*), describe the closer kin group of "son and his descendants" (as viewed from Ego) and the genealogical (collateral) extension of Ego's paternal cousins (father-brother sons) and their descendants (*pha spun spad*).

In its description of the three generations of fathers, the Zhol inscription portrays a patrilineal lineage complex related to an aristocratic family, which was summarised under the name Ngan lam. We do not know the age of these family lines, i.e. how far in prehistory

44 Cf. here in parallel (and in essentially the same terms) the chronologically much earlier example of ennoblement given in *OTC*, chap. V, i.e. the account of the oath between Srong btsan Sgam po and the ally Dba' Dbyi tshab and his paternal relatives (PT 1287: l. 247-298; *TDD* 210-212; DTH 143-147; Drikung 2011: 188-195). See here also Dotson's chapters on ennoblement and nepotism in the time of Tubo, in Dotson 2009a: 60ff.

the peculiarity of a kinship-defined (and usually also ritually expressed) wider "lineage solidarity" had been practised in these Ngan lam of 'Phan po. The North Face inscription rather appears to document the birth of an aristocratic family at the side of the *btsan po*, with the establishment of a larger lineage ramification of *bu tsha rgyud* as the necessary consequence, when it came about in order to anchor the heritage of aristocratic positions conferred by the *btsan po* within the family and to connect it with kinship positions. Inheritance (including the right of access to family-specific resources) and genealogical consciousness were in direct causal relationship: the rights of carriers of the same name, Ngan lam, were defined by descent, a fact which theoretically could have run through endless generations and branchings. Yet this kind of extensive lineage order, so it appears, had its origin not in the family itself but was constructed; at least to a certain extent we see this lineage as the product of the family's close relationship with the authority of the throne.

The old Ngan lam had two cemeteries (0216, 0217), both of the "mixed fields" type, with dozens of small to medium-sized (10m to 30m at the front) trapezoid tombs and numerous traces of (probably older, because heavily eroded) smaller, apparently round graves, a total of nearly 300 tombs or even more. We assume these are mainly the graves of the inhabitants of the ancient Ngan lam districts, including the members of the three *bu tsha rgyud* generations mentioned in the inscription. Outside of 'Phan yul there was, as mentioned, another Ngan lam not far from Lhasa, the area around the side valley of Sri, where next to the original place of the Zhol inscription stone the imposing tomb (65m at the front) is located, which can be assigned to Ngan lam Stag ra Klu khong (0157). The Ngan lam Ts(h)al (g)sar pa ("new garden of Ngan lam"), registered in the *OTA* as a winter residence for 701 CE, most arguably refers to this second Ngan lam, which apparently dated already from the 7th century. This was likely in connection with the establishment of the above-noted six *btsan 'bangs* lineages, which (parallel to the older *yab 'bangs rus drug*) described in the sources as ensuring the physical welfare of the *btsan po* (fn. 27); Ngan lam is included in this list, mentioned in tandem with the Sba (Dba's, Dba'), known as one of the dominant families in the Skyid shod region (above chap. 3.1.1). One later source synonymously calls the area of Ngan lam Btsan 'bangs sa, which evidently relates to the place of this *btsan 'bangs* lineage of Ngan lam (Hazod 2009: 216). This bodyguard position apparently demanded the presence of family members in the vicinity of the *btsan po*, whose mobile residence was predominantly in this section of Skyid shod, where territorial links of other *btsan 'bangs rus* can also be found (above fn. 27).

Our earlier assumption that the Klu khong resting-place was a single tomb now has to be revised, since the Tibetan archaeologist Shawo Khacham has recently discovered other tombs in the Sri valley, which we visited together in 2015. This concerns smaller (trapezoidal) mounds not far from the central mound 0157, and of two smaller cemeteries (by number of tombs) on the other (east) side of the valley (0397, 0398), with the particularity of each including the ruins of a stupa-shaped mound, one of the most significant finds of the Tibetan tumulus archaeology in recent years. We can assume that apart from Klu khong other Ngan lam relatives were also buried in this second Ngan lam; one of the stupa mounds may be the resting place of Ngan lam Rgyal ba mchog dbyangs (fl. late 8th century), known from the list of the first monks of Bsam yas monastery (RCP 605). He was reportedly born in Ngan lam of 'Phan yul (RCP *ibid.*), and was either a direct member of the three Ngan lam *bu tsha rgyud*, or otherwise inherited this noble Ngan lam status.

In all, Ngan lam represents a good example of the various correlations that can be established in the identification of elite burial mounds: the relationship of state authority and the creation of an aristocratic lineage, and, connected to it, the establishment of branch territories as well as the factor of lineage-related burial sites, where both the "home territory" as well as the branchings probably always simultaneously functioned as what one may call a "district grave field".

5.2 The family of *pha* Lo Snang

The Lo brag inscriptions – the "cliff inscription" and the "rock inscription" (cf. Uebach 2013) – are dedicated to a certain Lde sman Lde'u cung, described as the son of one Lo snang (the cliff inscription (l.7) reads: Lde Snang; Uebach 2013). A Lo snang (Lde snang) seems not to be attested in other sources, but the Lde sman Lde'u cung could well be the Lde sman (Lte sman, Lhe sman) inthe list of Buddhist temples founded by ministers in the late 8th and 9th century; the temple ascribed to him isthe *lha khang* of Lho phu Khyer chu (*Lde'u-2* 298.1; Uebach 1987: 114-115) – the district known as the birthplace of Marpa lotsawa (1012-97) in Lho brag. A Lde sman Rgyal mtshan is also recorded for the 8th century – in the context of Padmasambhava activities in Lho brag (Kapstein 2000: 159). It has been argued that the name part Lde sman may relate to a physician (doctor of Lde) or a specialist connected with divination (Richardson 1998: 267). It may originally be a place name, namely short for the area of Lde chung and Sman thang. Lde chung (evidently related to the addressee of the inscription) is the name of the small settlement where the rock inscription (i.e. the better-preserved of the two (largely identical) inscriptions) is located; the other is in the lower Sman thang, a small tributary valley of the central Lho brag river. According to a local account the two inscriptions mark the closer estate of the family mentioned in the inscription (Huo Wei 2010).[45]

Similarly to the Ngan lam example of his (not further detailed) services to emperor and government (*sku* and *chab srid*), the Lde sman Lde'u cung (or more precisely the *bu tsha rgyud* of Lo /Lde snang) is forever guaranteed the family landholdings by the *btsan po*. And should the *phu nu* (*po*) of the *bu tsha rgyud* of the *pha* Lo snang experience any hostility (in connection with the passing on of territorial rights) the families shall be protected from the authority by special decrees. Here it is clear that "older and younger brothers" (*phu nu po*) classification includes some wider collateral segments of the Lo snang family line. In this way the imperial decree ennobled a local family in a lasting form, which was apparently not without hostility from neighbouring families.

A separate paragraph in this sworn edict is dedicated to the tomb of Lde'u cung. It says, that the rituals (*rim gro*; on this term see Walter 2009: 166f.) at this burial mound (*mchad*) shall be conducted by the higher authority (*bla*), and if ever in the future, in the time of the *dbon sras* (descendants of the *btsan po* dynasty), the tomb were to be destroyed then the government authority, or the chiliarchy (*stong sde*) administration, respectively, would take care of its restoration.

It is well conceivable that this Lde'u cung grave relates to the central mound (M-1) of the cemetery of Skyid stod (0065), one of the exemplary elite burial mound fields of Central Tibet, which we so far unfortunately have been unable to visit.[46] The cemetery is located about 6 km. west of the county capital (Lho brag Do ba rdzong), on a slope behind Skyid

45 Geographical position of the Lde chung rock inscription: 28 26 10, 90 48 22; Sman thang inscription: 28 22 15, 90 54 48 (based on SXL 2014: 24). The dating of the inscription is uncertain. Richardson (1998: 268f.) suggests the time of Khri Srong lde btsan's reign (on the basis of certain orthographic parallels with the Zhol inscription); Pasang Wangdu dates it to the time of Khri Lde srong btsan (ref. in SXL 2014). For photographs of the inscriptions see e.g. XWD 120; Uebach 2013 (cliff inscription); TTT: 0065 (Plate 2 with photograph of the Lde chung inscription); SXL 2014: 23; for English translations see Richardson 1998: 266; Li and Coblin 1987: 359.

46 For a description see the archaeological report SXL 2014; Jampel Tsondru 2010: 217-222; Tsewang 2011: 92-94. For illustrations see TTT, site no. 0065; cf. also Shargan Wangdue, in this volume.

stod village. According to SXL 2014 the field includes 68 mounds, for the most part of the (trapezoidal) *gru bzhi* type, as well as 36 sacrificial pits. The central mound may originally have measured ca. 65m (front); there are the remains of a building on top of this typical MT-C type of mound. Such architectural additions are indeed mentioned in the sources (cf. Haarh 1969: 346), but can also come from a later period when locals occasionally used larger mounds as shelters for domestic animals or as pastoralist campsites (*'brog sa*). Extensive steps lead to the front of the grave and also to the two adjacent tombs (ca. 25m), where animal bones were found in one of the two smaller step constructions, and apparently served as sacrificial trenches.[47] What is striking in the field is the location of some individual graves further away (200m, 400m).

The surface archaeology provides no precise evidence of an earlier (pre-imperial) use of the cemetery. The state authority or district administration was certainly involved in the organisation of the tombs – in connection with the ennoblement of the family mentioned in the inscription. It is very likely that representatives of the *bu tsha rgyud* of *pha* Lo snang were buried there, probably already in the period before the inscription. In the archaeological report of SXL 2014 it says that the Lde'u cung family of the inscription "moved to the Lho brag *stong sde*" after its ennoblement (implying that the family was not of Lho brag origin), but it gives no further arguments for this conclusion.

0065 is the largest of six cemeteries we have registered for this central section of Lho brag. The other cemeteries also have some elite graves, otherwise many small, mostly heavily eroded mounds dominate, such as in the field 0369 (due south of Lha lung, the famous village (also registered as "lineage") and *dgon pa*).[48]

The area of Lho brag County is still little documented in terms of tombs. According to the current state, it seems that these six cemeteries were the only ones in the entire Lho brag region. This would indicate the facts already mentioned above: that other forms of burial besides mound burial were practised in the districts of Central Tibet in pre-Buddhist period. For the time being we only can state that mound burial was apparently concentrated in this political heartland on the upper reaches of the Lho brag river, without being able to say how

47 Information by Shawo Khacham, Lhasa 2015; cf. SXL 2014: 18. For similar sacrificial trenches in Dulan 都兰, cf. Heller 2006: 67.

48 On a "Lha lung lineage" specific grave situated in Upper Skyid shod (i.e. no. 0126) see Hazod 2014: 69.

far the fields included the funerals of burial-mound candidates from other parts of the Lho brag area. As a preliminary statement we would conclude that the Skyid stod field was used as a sort of central district cemetery that perhaps originally and primarily was connected with the Lo snang family, but arguably was also used by other leading families of this area.

5.3 Conclusions and further details

The description of lineages in the inscriptions helps us in discussing the issues of kinship and grave in the larger regional context comparatively to Phying ba. A burial ground that can be assigned (though not exclusively) to an aristocratic family may principally have included the burials related to the following kinship positions:

• Leading representatives of the family line and their chief consorts:

There is no reason not to assume that, similar to the burial in Phying ba, the wives were buried in the same field as the husbands, here following the principle of patrilocal residence rule (but see below). In several fields we find the situation of "twin graves" (e.g. 0333; 0112; 0176; 0396; 0329), which, possibly similar to the situation of the Stag bu grave complex (III.1-4), points to the resting place of a married couple. (The tumulus archaeology in the Tuyuhun area reports of a couple (presumably husband and wife) who were found together in one grave (Tong Tao 2008: 95); to our knowledge such finds are not known from Central Tibet, but in any case cannot be excluded.)

We may further assume that most of the hereditary members of the respective territorial domain and heirs of the aristocratic rank insignia were buried in this field. In elite grave fields we often see the situation of a central grave in compound with several smaller mounds, ca. half the size. Grave field 0024 is particularly striking in this respect. It constitutes one of seven grave fields in 'On – the area which is addressed in the cry of the "white rooster of Bsam yas" (above fn. 21). We named this cemetery "bird field": a central MT-C grave mound (50m front, with steps in front), according to the locals the resting place of a "great general", has to its left and right respectively three and four smaller mounds and the "bird's hindquarters" are formed by the arrangement of ten sacrificial pits lying directly in a row at the rear of the central mound (see TTT: 0024). We read this assembly as a kin group, or as the order of graves of two or more generations of related higher officials or holders of a certain military rank (cf. also the similar situation of 0329; below fn. 62). Directly below the "bird design" as well as just north of it there are a number of other medium-sized or smaller graves (no. 0025), which from their condition seem to be older sites and are clearly separated from the ritual ensemble of 0024. A similar kinsman-like situation can be assumed, for example, behind the three prominent grave mounds in field 0076 of G.ye yul (with two of them more than 70m at the front), which locally are described as the residences of "three sons" (or princes; *sras gsum*), who are arguably to be ascribed to the dynasty of G.ye yul (Dbye mo) east of Yar lung (Hazod 2009: 171, 180).

· Some of the *phu nu po* may have founded branch lines in connection with separate territorial domains, where they (and their families) were also buried. Their formation may hark back to similar conditions to the Zhang lnga (Zha snga) sub lineages in the history of the royal genealogy (cf. fn. 32). In the case of the royal (and imperial) family, we saw that for disqualified brothers and half brothers the maternal origin was added to the name (in the form: "nephew (*tsha*) of mother's (paternal) lineage X"). Such *tsha* segments can also be found in genealogies of aristocratic families. One of the better known examples is represented by the late 8th-century history of the 'Khon (known as the family line behind the later Sa skya ruling house), in the form of the 'Bro *tsha spun bdun*: The youngest son born to the 'Khon rje Gung stag (a minister under Khri Srong lde btsan) by a daughter from Rlangs married a daughter from the 'Bro; six of their seven sons, the "seven brothers, nephews/descendants of 'Bro" (*'bro tsha spun bdun*), later scattered from La stod Snyan rtse and founded branch territories in various regions (in Lhoka, Gtsang and the later Lower Mnga' ris),[49] while the youngest brother apparently remained as the principal lineage-holder in this (new) 'Khon territory (*GBY* 308.8-310.6).[50] Similar lateral and territorially anchored *tsha spun* branches can also be found in other regional contexts (cf. TF 314) and more generally can be assumed among the leading families of the empire-era aristocracy. So besides state interference there were internal lineage histories behind territorial branchings

49 Such regional establishments usually followed the old Tibetan policy of "invitation" by local groups.

50 The starting point of this regional spreading, La stod Snyan rtse (var. Gnyan tshe thang, Gnyen Rtse thar), is located in the Gram mtsho area of southern La stod (SCB 33), according to Everding south of the Gram mtsho, in the locality of Mtsho sgo, on the southern shore of the Bong chu (Arun) (Everding and Dzongphugpa 2006: 41). It is noteworthy that this area, considered in the Sa skya tradition as "ancestral home" of 'Khon, was apparently previously the territory of the maternal uncle, i.e. 'Bro Dgra 'dul, who is said to have initiated various competitions in which the seven brothers also were involved, and who later, after fights, had to leave the territory to the youngest, who remained in Snyan rtse. The 'Bro of Snyan rtse were themselves in turn a branch of the multi-branched 'Bro, here described as one of Tibetan athletes' (*gyad pa*) lineages (in the version of the *Sa skya gdung rabs*; Everding 2000: 349). We know the tumulus situation of La stod Lho for the most part only from satellite photographs; several burial grounds are not far north of Mtsho sgo, two apparently with elite mounds (no. 0411, 0413).

comparable with that of the emperor family, and these peripheral places can be principally considered as candidates for burial sites.

• The sisters – as elsewhere, these had to marry outside, where they also had their graves. As we know, some daughters of certain family lines (altogether five) became heir-bearing queens, which means the paternal elite lineage acted as bride-giver (*zhang*) to the imperial house. These ended up in Phying ba. Other sisters became junior queens; as noted above, we do not know exactly where they would customarily have been buried or whether there was any general rule at all in this respect.

• Conversely, some of the aristocratic families received brides from the emperor's family or brides from branches of the imperial family, although we cannot say to what extent this was possibly expressed in the position or size of the graves in question. There is no information about the position of second wives in aristocratic families, and, as in the case of Phying ba, we cannot say anything about possible regulations with regard to the burial of these affinal relatives.

• Deviations:

Patrilocal residence was a fact (lamented as a painful rule by Sad ma mkhar, Srong btsan Sgam po's sister; Uray 1972), but apparently there were deviations from this postnuptial rule, with the married couple moving into the paternal land and household of the wife. The arrival of the 'Khon in the land of 'Bro (fn. 50) seems to be such a case. It is reported that Thumi (Thon mi) Sngang grags, the father of Thon mi Sambhota, came from Lub ra kha (part of Thon, adjacent to Snye mo), later married as second wife a Lady of the Gnubs family in Gnyal (the district south-east of Yar lung) and moved to her home in Gynal, where the famous son was born, in the village of Sa 'bo ra (hence the form Thon mi Sa 'bo ra, Indianised Sambhota). According to his new residence, the father was also called Lho Gnyal ba (Rang sgra 1999). Such forms of uxorilocal rules are repeatedly recorded in the early post-imperial period (RCP 75, 596), and seem to be based on certain pragmatic considerations. In this case one may also consider that the relation between the Thon and the Gnubs of Gnyal followed an older tradition (dating back to pre-historic Yar lung where the two families acted as minister in the time of the early kings);[51] this followed perhaps an affinal circle, something that has not been studied outside the royal house (see above chap. 4). In this place of Sa 'bo ra (now called Thon mi Sambhota), directly behind the ruins of the Sambhota temple (the site of an 11th-cent. religious council; *Rva lo* 290; BA 376-77), there is a larger artificial hill (30m), locally called *lcags ri* (registered in TTT as field no. 0075). The archaeology may one day confirm our presumed identification of this as a burial mound, perhaps the resting place of the famous descendant of Thon.[52] In any case, with regard to the question of who was buried where, deviations from patrilocal principles and generally pragmatic solutions in the rule of residence also have to be considered.

Summarising:
i. In their characteristic geographical limitation to the old districts of Central Tibet the enormous number of burial sites largely reflects the geography of the ancient principalities as well as the (later) historical ramifications of the lineage-based leading families, where the territories linked to these families were also used as place for burial sites, but probably nowhere in the peripheral fields exclusively by only one family or lineage.
ii. For the period of the chiefdoms the graduation of larger and smaller round or oval grave mounds is actually just a supposition, since we have no real chronological control for this time. We see here the territory (*yul*) and its *lha* as the proper structural principles. This also means that the burial grounds that we consider to be of prehistoric origin were simply the cemeteries of the peoples living in the settlement areas – usually situated not far from the houses, somewhere in the non-arable zones of the valley. The outstanding classic (trapezoidal) MT-C type of elite mounds within these grave fields was most likely not common before the 7th century.
iii. In the imperial period the factor of territory received a new dimension through the division into government-controlled (civil and military) districts, which did not make the old territorial family relations obsolete, but apparently reduced regional autonomy in terms of grave-specific

51 i.e. Gnubs Smon to re Sbung brtsan and Mthon myi 'Bring po Rgyal mtshan btsan nu (PT 1287: l. 68-70 (*TDD* 203); on the latter figure and the story of his killing see Bialek 2015: 288-289 (note 5); cf. also Bialek 2016: 117). It should be noted that the original Gnubs yul (Gnubs shul (*yul*) Gling/King drug) apparently extended to the north of Gtsang po, where the Gnubs lha, Gnubs lha Mthon drug, is reportedly also located (Hazod 2009: 172). The latter is perhaps related to the family name (originally a toponym?) and district name of Mthon.

52 Note that there are no grave mounds in Lub ra kha (situated high up in the mountains due east of Thon) and neither are there any in Thon proper.

decisions or were superimposed by governmental order. As a result, one finds the burial situation of "district grave fields" with officials and military personnel and their relatives buried there, not all of whom had direct or ancestral connections to the areas in question.

iv. "Ennoblement and grave" is a central factor, with the large (50m to 70m) mounds being in a league of their own as the resting places of the highest representatives of civil and military society. Generally, the issues of size of the graves, the extent of architectural decorations, the number of sacrificial pits associated with the individual tombs, and the site's architectural combination with steplike trenches etc. were apparently primarily linked to the governmental position and military success of the deceased, but perhaps also to criteria such as respect for the deceased in a more local context. Certain changes or new developments in the process of the imperial period can be assumed in this respect. For example, the "lion decorated" peripheral elite graves were apparently all from the later (Buddhist) phase of the empire (Hazod 2015; Appendix II: 0115, 0242, 0339).

v. There is a crucial identifying feature in elite burial sites: the two grave fields of Phying ba were *not* district grave fields, but reserved only for members of the royal / imperial family (plus the "common fated ones" buried together with the lord; fn. 18). On the other hand, the observation that collateral relatives of the emperor were buried outside of Phying ba followed a pattern that in principle can be assumed for similar dynastically organised peripheral families as well. In other words, in lineage-organised major families the question of who have to be buried where followed rules based on kinship principles similar to those mentioned for the *btsan po* house.

vi. One of the main conclusions from the burial-site distribution is that obviously other forms of burial existed in parallel to mound burial, and perhaps even predominated, with forms of exposing the corpse being one candidate here. The huge gaps in the distribution of elite burial fields were apparently simply due to fact that no aristocratic families of civil or military servants lived in these (traditionally non-mound-burial) areas in question, while otherwise the existence of elite graves concerns persons for whom burial in mound tombs was provided. In the case of single tombs (often truly solitary, with no mound sites far and wide), there were apparently no heirs of the deceased's position to continue this tradition, and in the respective local milieus a different form of burial was traditionally practised. One of the questions that come up in this context is whether the different regional funeral forms also correlated with different conceptions of the afterlife. To narrow down this question, in the concluding chapter we will ask what ideas of afterlife (or paradise) can be identified in association with the tumulus tradition of the imperial period and what in fact was the society for which this concept was intended?

6. The society in paradise

The sealing of a grave represented the conclusion of a ritual procedure that was intended to ensure the deceased's journey to paradise. The latter is usually described as "land of joy" (*dga' yul*, also *skyid yul*), although it is not always clear from the ritual texts whether the respective funerals explicitly refer to mound burials however. There is some information in the sources on how this paradise was conceived, such as in PT 1134 (Orosz 2003: 26), and not least in the meanwhile much-studied painted coffin panels from the tumulus landscape in the Tuyuhun (or 'A zha) area (especially the better-preserved Guolimu M-1, Panel I and II, Heller 2013; Tong Tao 2008: 153-159; Tong Tao and Wertmann 2010). The latter findings from burial sites in the Dulan district[53] are evidently not purely Tibetan but rather point to the situation of a hybrid cultural milieu (significant for this border region), with influences from Tibetan, Chinese, Inner Asian, and local contexts. In this milieu the Tuyuhun, who from the early 4th century CE settled in the areas of the upper Yellow River, represent the legacy of their Xianbei origin, a strong element in the transmission history of proto-Mongol cultures, with genealogies that go back to the steppe empire of the Xiongnu (found. 3rd cent. BCE) and the older Indo-European-influenced Central Asian contact histories (Beckwith 2009), and not least to China, where the multi-branched Xianbei people were

53 For a detailed description of the burial mound sites in the former 'A zha area, mainly in present-day Dulan County, Delingha and Ulan County see Tong Tao 2008: 85ff., who calls the elite burial sites in these dense tumulus landscapes "Tubo-Tuyuhun" cemeteries. The local tradition regards the central and much discussed "Reshui M-1" mound (65m), in the Reshui 热水 tomb cluster of Dulan (Heller 2006: 60-65), as the resting place of *blon chen* Mgar (information Shawo Khacham). In fact, in the course of the Tibetan administration of the 'A zha region contacted by Mgar Stong btsan and the later Mgar presence there (until end of 7th century) the area increasingly became a "Mgar territory", also in the minds of large sections of the 'A zha people (cf. Beckwith 2009: 128-131). From 659-667 Mgar Stong btsan stayed most of the time in 'A zha yul; in 667, when returning to Central Tibet he came to Zrid (most likely the present-day Spra kha 'dam in Dbu ru lung; Appendix II: 0187) to meet the *btsan po*. The following year he died in Ris pu, which we think is the present day Ris bu opposite Spra kha 'dam (Hazod 2014: 55; for an updated map of this area; see TTT: site no. 0187). It is therefore unlikely that Mgar Stong btsan was buried in 'A zha yul, unless we have here the example of "bringing back" the body to a country considered as the chief minister's new (home) territory. After the fall of Mgar (under *btsan po* Khri 'Dus srong) the Tuyuhun region remained a key area of the Central Tibetan administration (and affinal) policies, and, as already noted elsewhere, it is very likely that Tibetan officials were buried in the 'A zha yul grave fields (Heller 2013) – this in addition to leading representatives of Tuyuhun, which as vassal of Tubo continued under the status of *rgyal phran*.

highly formative in the Era of Division (220-589 CE), and also involved in the founding history of the succeeding Sui and Tang dynasties (Holcombe 2013). The pictorial narratives of the coffin panels (unearthed in a mid-size elite tomb of the Guolimu cemetery; Tong Tao 2008: 94f., 153ff., 328) shows scenes of everyday life of the aristocracy and their burial forms that are largely also true for Central Tibet, where the similarities may go back to a shared cultural past in Central Asia transmitted by the Xianbei people. The red-faced people (men and women) in these depictions are today not to be identified with the much quoted red-faced (*gdong dmar can*) Tibetans, but rather with the 'A zha, or groups having lived in the 'A zha area, from whom the Tibetans had adopted this custom (van Schaik 2007); the latter again is thought to have a much older Xianbei origin (Tong Tao and Wertmann 2010; see also Li Yongxian, in this volume).

In my view the images of the Guolimu Panel I and II can be summarised under two main headings: "life" (Panel I) and "afterlife" (Panel II), with the scenes each beginning on the narrower foot sides of the coffin panels (Fig. 12). The scene of the "royal hunt" on the broader head side of Panel I forms a transition to Panel II, which begins with the bringing of the decorated horses (cf. here the *rta rgyan can* in PT 1042: l.130; *TDD* 43) and, following the mourning scenes, scenes of sacrifice, the elimination of a malevolent spirit, it opens the way to the journey to paradise (i.e. the ride on the (*rta*) *do ma*, beloved horse, of the ritual texts). In its description of a banquet around the princely couple, paradise itself appears as a copy of the main scene on Panel I, apparently representing an engagement party (cf. Heller 2013). Both scenes – betrothal and the couple's paradisial sojourn – have a residence tent in the centre, which are quasi superposably positioned on the head side of the panels, and the whole situation is against the background of an identically designed landscape.[54]

Transferred to the context of early Central Tibet, we here propose these images relate to the category of places where the regular assemblies were held and where the "mobile

54 This is, admittedly, a very rough summary of the paintings, and also still somewhat preliminary in its principal interpretation. One uncertainty concerns the scene on the right edge of Panel I, in the reading of Heller 2013: 130 "an archer wearing a tall Tibetan turban (and) aiming at the jugular vein of a large white and black tethered yak" (cf. also Drikung 2011: 379). Whether it should be interpreted as the actual "royal hunt" needs to be further examined. Note that the archer is standing on a small carpet, and the yak is fastened to a stick; this I think points to the sacred act of killing the yak by a royal figure, and the man standing in a waiting position behind is an image of the royal successor (see also next fn. 55). For other interpretations and the issues of the origin of the individual cultural representations of the paintings (Sogdiana (with evidently parallels to Zoroastrian funerary practice; Heller 2013), Chinese, Xianbei/ 'A zha or Tibetan), cf. the literature referred to above.

centre" was customarily located – the park (*tshal*; also *ling tshal*, or other terms that suggest a garden, e.g. *lcang bu*, "willow (park)") from where the elite also set out on the hunt and where the oath-taking and legal and administrative decisions took place.[55] One may speculate whether both regional contexts Tuyuhun / Xianbei and Central Tibet go back to older Persian-coined templates of the garden of the Royal Hunt (i.e. the *paridaida*; Gr. *paradeisos*), which since the Achaemenid time was spread in the assemblage of other cultural elements throughout Central Asia (Allsen 2006: 46-51). In imperial Central Tibet these park sites were located in the lands of the elite families, who probably vied with one another to act as the inviting party for the court. In any case, we can assume that the entry to paradise was also guaranteed for all those who were involved in such park meetings. The pictures on the panels may show a royal or princely couple, but the scenes have a greater social validity; as suggested by Heller, the paintings generally represent "a generic narrative, rather than the actual events of an individual's life" (Heller 2013: 131). In this case, they were probably leading the way for the couple buried together in the M-1 mound of Guolimu (Tong Tao 2008: 95); judging from the size of this mound those buried here were apparently from the lower or middle rank aristocracy.

The panel picture gives us an idea of the nature of paradise: it is simply the social everyday life related to the political culture of the *rgyal po* / *btsan po* and his aristocratic entourage. Interestingly, one finds no religion in these illustrations (there is ritual, but that is not the same thing); what we see is society and its customary laws: laws of hospitality, engagement, socially structured hunting, socially structured mourning – events in which the ritual is inscribed. Presumably this is exactly what the inscriptions of imperial period call (from the view of the emperor) the "tradition" (*lugs*), or the "tradition of the ancestors" (*OTI* 13, l.1-8) – a set of social conventions (*chos*, *gtsug lag*, "customs", (ancient) "principles", cf. Bialek 2015, s.v. index), which also included the religious. In a similar context the anthropologist M. Bloch (2013: 23-40) speaks of the "transcendental social", a concept that helps to overcome the artificial (academic) separation of the religious and the social related

55 Cf. Dotson 2013 for the entries on the hunt (and group hunt) in the *Old Tibetan Annals* (and also in the *Annals of the 'A za Principality*) and the discussion of other hunt-specific (particularly legal) mentions in Old Tibetan documents. Note that these entries mostly relate to huntings organised by high officials and were not royal hunts in the strict sense. The latter (prototypically portrayed in Sad ma kar's song, Uray 1971) was of different quality – namely to demonstrate the king's spiritual power within the political arena of his closer and wider entourage. Cf. Alsen 2006 (esp. 260ff.) for the royal hunt in the ancient Near East and the later steppe empires.

to pre-world-religion cultural contexts. The portrayal of paradise in the Guolimu panels is almost a prime example of a "transcendental social", where the social reality appears as being mirrored in heaven.

Paradise evidently had a specific place in these mirrored worlds. PT 1136 (l. 7; *TDD* 155) and parallel Bon po texts speak of the land of joy as being located in the north (Stein 2010: 263; Bellezza 2008: 460). This is significant when we take into account here B. Zeisler's new interpretation of the origin history of the Tibetan kings (Zeisler 2015). Her reading of the well-known concept and name element *khri* (usually rendered as "throne") in its proposed original meaning as "star" leads her to a reinterpretation of the ancestral group of the Gnam kyi khri bdun ("seven heavenly [kings] [with the name element] *khri*") with whom the genealogy of the Tibetan kings begins (Appendix I), or the (related) "seven *khri* siblings" whose middle one is described as having fathered the ancestor of the Tibetan kings. Behind these terms she sees a constellation, with the seven (brightest) stars of the Great Bear representing the likely candidate (corresponding to this constellation's later naming as Byang gi skar ma spun bdun, "seven brothers, stars of the north").[56] Her suggestion that the name of the eighth king, chronologically the first tumulus-buried Gri gum, should be read as "the star that died" (*khri gum*) sounds only logical. Yet, this new reading is rather questioned by colleagues from the closer linguistic field of old Tibetan studies (Bialek, personal communication). On the other hand, it is also clear that the question of ethno-astronomical components in the rituals of pre-Buddhist Tibet remains largely an unexplored world. One thinks inevitably of those funeral priests (*dur gshen*) who according to the classical chronicles appeared in the period after the Seven khri, and who are described as priests who "observed (and calculated) the star constellation" (Sørensen 1994: 145).[57] Such information are highly relevant for an archaeology that investigates the possible celestial orientation of

56 i.e. the seven stars of the Big Dipper (Ger. Großer Wagen), one of the major constellation in ancient cultural lore – in Mongolia associated with a group of seven gods / divine brothers (or the Seven Buddhas in the (later) Buddhist context; cf. e.g. http://www.constellation-guide.com/big-dipper/). In PT 1038: l. 12-17 the middle one of the *seven khri* (i.e. the Yab lha Bdag drug son Khri Bar la bdun tshig) descended from the 13th level of the sky *to sa gdog drug* (= *sa ga dog drug*), which Zeisler reads as the "six spheres of the Libra constellation"; but see here the critical comment in Bialek 2015: 386.

57 Cf. here e.g. also the mention of star constellation (*skar ma gar*, "dance of the stars") in PT 1042: l. 135-137 (*TDD* 43), in connection with the placing of the *thugs gur* ("soul tent"), or a specific part of it, into the tomb's *thugs khang*. What is still puzzling in this context is the older history of what later, from the 17th century, became known as the Stag phu Nyi thig (observatory of Stag phu), in the Stag phu valley of Mal gro, which is believed to go back 3000 years. (For a brief note on this site see Hazod 2016; cf. also Appendix II: "0110".)

the graves, where – as already noted (chap. 2.2) – with regard to the actual reference point it is less the outer trapezoid position than the architectural components of the grave interiors that have to be considered. Here we are still at the beginning, but there are some indications that the relatively stable Great Bear constellation, visible throughout the year while circling around Polaris, played a significant role not only in the Central Tibetan tumulus history but also comparatively in Central Asian regions (cf. Feiglstorfer in this volume).

In this sense, there was only one paradise (and one direction to paradise), which the circle of *btsan po*, his family and the aristocracy shared. For Central Tibet the conception of paradise indeed appears historically connected to the establishment of the burial-mound practice, presumably inspired by the foreign ritualists who are mentioned in the context of Gri gum's funeral – the *bon po* from the geographically extensive area of influence of the once mighty Tuyuhun kingdom (in the mid-fifth cent. extending as far as Khotan, Beckwith 1987: 18); but this does not necessarily mean that people outside tumulus practice were excluded from such conceptions.

But what about those who were excluded from the "politics of paradise" (Eckfeld 2005) – on the basis of certain social conventions concerning virtue? For example, did those who had proved to be cowards in combat ever get a grave? According the *Xin Tangshu* and old Tibetan Documents (PT 1071) such persons were publicly denounced or banished (Bushell 1880: 443; Dotson 2009a: 48). Generally, what about the non-virtuous – the renegades and the disloyal? Examples from the *Old Tibetan Annals* are Myang Zhang snang or Mgar Btsan nyen Gung rton (the grandson of *blon chen* Mgar); the latter was sentenced to death for disloyalty, and indeed during one of the *tshal* meetings. The decision whether a traditional burial (and participation in the paradise society) was provided in these cases probably followed certain customary laws, of which to my knowledge no information exists. As to the lower classes of commoners, they were not outside the aristocratic world, but bound to it, and also appear in the guise of servants on the Guolimu panels.

The *Old Tibetan Annals* are an authentic witness to the existence of the Central Tibetan "mobile centre", but this is described only very tersely and the entries are primarily concerned with recording decisions that were taken during the assemblies. As to the mobile court (*pho brang*), the entries are mostly only statements of where the court resided in winter / summer of the year X. A somewhat more detailed description of a campsite is given in the

Xin Tangshu, related to the meeting at Sbra stod tshal ("park of the upper tent", in Rgya ma), in connection with the China-Tibet treaty of 821/22 (Hazod 2014). This site was established by the founder Khri Slon btsan (Gnam ri Srong btsan) and in function and layout seems to correspond here to the Fusi, the founding residence of the Tuyuhun (situated due west of the Koko Nor).[58] The descriptions of Sbra stod tshal allow some architectural reconstruction of a Tibetan campsite, and regardless of the specific situation of the treaty ceremony they provide a good picture of the circle of *btsan po* and his ministerial aristocracy, which in its specific composite was always adapted depending on the occasion of the meeting. I would like to conclude this study with a description of a meeting at campsite related to the *OTA* entry of 757-58.

In the winter of this year the court resided in the "willow park of Stod (lung)" (Stod gyi Lcang bu). This most likely refers to the area around present-day Rgu rum, at the entrance to the Tshur phu valley where later the Lcang bu temple was erected in the time of Khri Gtsug lde btsan (Fig. 13). The temple was sponsored by a descendant of the aristocratic Tshes pong family, one of the *zhang* or bride-giver lineages to the emperor house (fn. 40). This park more precisely was in an area called Brag rum, which is recorded in the *dbang ris bco brgyad* catalogue as Tshes pong territory.[59] As already noted by Richardson in the foreword of his translation of the Lcang bu inscription (1985: 92), on this occasion the 15-year-old Khri Srong lde btsan probably visited his (intended) family-in-law, or the meeting of 757-58 refers to the engagement party, namely with Lha rgyal Ldong skar from the house of Tshes pong (Appendix I). We find such meetings with the *btsan po* in his bride's family's camp (*zhang*) prototypically in the affinal connection of the divine houses of Phvya and Dmu as portrayed in the origin history of Gnya' khri Btsan po (in the *Yo ga* (*yi ge*) *lha gyes*

58 Hazod 2015: 192; for a graphical reconstruction see Tong Tao 2008: 277; from the description in Chinese sources (in Tong Tao, *op. cit.*), the geographical position appears to be: 37 01 32, 99 34 52 (Google Earth). For the "centre" in the Xiongnu and the Inner Asian imperial context see Bemmann 2011.

59 See Hazod 2009: 193. This identification of Brag rum was already suspected earlier (Hazod 2014: 71-72) and has recently been supported by statements of the locals from Rgu rum village recorded by Shawo Khacham (personal communication, Lhasa 2015). It says that the two main pillars at the entrance to the Tshur phu monastery were unearthed from a place directly behind Rgu rum village. This refers to the *phyi dar* temple of Brag rum, evidently the successor establishment to the imperial Lcang bu lha khang, from where the Lcang bu inscription stone was brought to Tshur phu *dgon*. On Rgu rum (Gu rum) see also RCP 150 *et passim*.

can of the *Can lnga* text group; Karmay 1998: 295ff.) or also in PT 126.[60] In fact, this form of alliance formed something like the core issue in the discourse of society-building in the early Central Tibetan aristocratic world, which – so it appears – continued in paradise or, better, was transferred there as a "transcendental social". In complementing the brief entry in the *Annals* by the scenes of the Guolimu panel one can imagine a glittering feast of the two parties of bride-giver and bride-taker in the inviting plain of Brag rum, with various ceremonies and not least with a common departure for the hunt by the nobles and their attendants present at this meeting – somewhere in the forests of the upper Mtshur phu. (In this case, it may have been a deer (*sha*) and not a yak hunt as on Guolimu Panel I; note that scenes of deer hunting are already to be found on the prehistoric petroglyphs in the Lhasa valley (near Sbra stod tshal; Hazod 2014), and the closer Lhasa area may have been used as a park for deer hunting, i.e. the Ra sa Sha tshal from the *OTA*,[61] before the site in the wake of the Jo khang foundation gradually was transformed into a new, i.e. Buddhist, paradise.)

Burial ground 0176 (Fig. 13), which I visited in 2008, begins in the alluvial fan some 600 meters behind Rgu rum village – it is a typical "mixed field" of larger and smaller structures. It consists of ca. 17 elite graves, which have mostly been completely destroyed and stripped

60 The narratives in both texts address the invitation of a descendant of the gods of heaven to become lord of men (for this formula see Hill 2013). The *Can lnga* text makes it clear that the respective candidate (Gnya' khri Btsan po) was an offspring of Phyva, who resided (temporarily) in the land of Dmu, the land of the mother brother (and land of the daughter of Dmu, the classificatory matrilateral cross-cousin), from where, provided with the paraphernalia from the house of Dmu (and also of Phvya), he descended to the earth (Karmay *op. cit*; *Lde'u-2* 232-235). Similarly in PT 126 (l. 104-168; *TDD* 22-24) the messengers of Phvya ask the lord of Dmu for a ruler, a request the compliance with which required the worship of the *sku bla* of Dmu (with the divine yak Sham po (l. 146) being mentioned among the (symbolic) offerings in this context – evidence of the text's connection with the Yar lung house; cf. Chu 1990; Ishikawa 2001; but see here the different reading of *lha g.yag sham po* in Drikung 2011: 41). Dmu und Phvya were affinal relatives (*gnyen*), and probably the same narrative "worked" for ruler-specific rituals just as for engagement, and possibly also for funeral ceremonies, if we also understand the Dmu land as the place of return after the kings' death (by means of the *dmu* cord; Appendix I, § 1). This would lead to the conclusion that the land where the preferential bride-giver resided, and from where the lord of men started on his journey to the earth, and the great beyond refer to one and the same heaven.
(Note that in the same text the heavenly Dmu evidently has a geography on earth, when it says that the messengers coming from the sky travelled through the lower part of Rtsang smad (*rtsang smad mdo*, or the lower section of the Gtsang po in Lhoka?) where they first arrived in the land of Srin before they reached Dmu'i yul "situated at the south-east border" (PT 126: l.117-122; *TDD* 22-23; cf. Drikung 2011: 34-40). The Srin land may refer to the Srin mo rong in eastern Lhoka, due west of Kong po (Hazod 2009: 203), i.e. the area associated with the arrival of Gnya' khri Btsan po.)

61 However, geo-ecological studies have observed that there was a considerable process of deforestation in this region from the late Neolithic (4200 BP); see Kaiser et al. 2006; Miehe et al. 2006. For the ecological situation of the Lhasa valley in the 7th century based on textual indications, cf. Sørensen 2007.

of its stone material, so that one hardly can imagine the original layout. The opening of the largest tomb has a diameter of ca. 65m, the next largest about 40m. At the front the graves have the step-like construction, typical of larger (hillside) tombs. 25 or 30 another smaller round-shaped mounds are scattered around, and detailed surveys would certainly bring still more burial traces to light. It seems natural to assign the elite graves to Tshes pong; very likely the sponsor of the Lcang bu lha khang, Zhang Tshes pong Nya sto (Stag bzang Snya sto) and his family are buried there, who – as stated in the Lcang bu inscription – belonged to the *bu tsha* (*rgyud*) of one Zhang Tshes pong Gsas sto (Richardson 1985: 103).[62] Whether this cemetery at the same time functioned as a "district field" in the form as described above we can only guess; in any case the site fits well into the multifaceted framework of elite burial mound fields as we have tried to outline in this study.

* * *

Appendix I

The *Gsang ba yang chung* about the tombs of members of the Tibetan royal family

The following is a translation of the main part of the *Gsang ba yang chung* (*GYC*; in *Mkhas pa Lde'u chos 'byung* (*Lde'u-2* 377.9-380.9), which is specified as appendix to the *Can lnga* (together with Khu ston's (lost) *Lo rgyus chen mo*; cf. *Lde'u-1* 99). The latter text group, which is exclusively dedicated to the history of the Tibetan royal line (Karmay 1998: 282ff.), has been dated to the early 10th century (Karmay 1998: 308), yet for the *GYC* certain entries (such as the mention of the apotheosis of Srong btsan Sgam po and his two consorts; below § 5.1-2) rather a later dating of this "even smaller (account) of the secret (tradition)" (*gsang ba yang chung*) can be assumed. In any case it represents the earliest

62 A similar context of temple foundation and burial ground related to Tshes pong can be assumed for the field 0329 situated in Bo dong of Gtsang. The *nang blon* Zhang Tshe spong Lha bzang Klu dpal (*KG* 412.8-9) reportedly founded the Sbo thong Bya rgod bshongs temple here in the early 9th century (Uebach 1987: 118-119), perhaps the precursor to the early *pyhi dar* temple and monastery of Bo dong E (Diemberger *et al.* 1997: 17; Hazod 1998; for the toponym Bo dong (Bu dong / Bu mo dong) see the popular etymology in *KG* 512.1-5). The significant elite burial mound site (ca. 1km north of Bo dong E) arguably includes the resting places of members of this founder family, although territorial links of Tshes pong to this area in Gtsang are otherwise not attested in the sources. Similar to 0024 (above chap. 5.3) we find here the striking (kin group?) order of groups of three and four mounds, in this case situated below the central tombs of M-1 and M-2.

known and at the same time most extensive written evidence of the burial mounds related to the Tibetan royal house and a significant basis text for the grave accounts in the later chronicles. On the other hand, the quotes from the *GYC* in the same chronicles suggest that the rendering of the *GYC* in *Lde'u-2* is apparently not complete. Other details on the graves in later sources that are not mentioned in the *GYC* show that originally several different records of the royal tombs were in circulation; noteworthy here are the quotes from "older books" (*yig tshang rnying ma*) or the "record of Mgar" (*Mgar gyi dkar chag*) in 'Jigs med gling pa's *Gtam gyi tshogs* (Hazod 2013), or the well-known grave descriptions in the *Rgyal po bka' thang* (Haarh 1969), where information on the graves (and grave interior) from the imperial period appear combined with the situation of a much later period (13th century). Cf. Panglung 1988; Hazod 2013.

The *GYC* starts with a description of the earliest tombs and their respective locations between heaven and the cultivated area, followed by the descriptions of the historical burial mounds, with details on position, names, form of construction and other features (376.15-17). And summarising at the end it says that there is a total of 18 *bang so* of lineage holders, the two *bang so* of the Khu chen (see below, § 2, no. XV), the nine *bang so* of (heir-bearing) queens (*jo mo srid zin gyi bang so*), and the nine *bang so* of junior queens (*srid ma zin pa['i jo mo'i] bang* so). These constitute the middle generations of the spreading of power (*bar gyi mnga' dar*), in all forty generations – from lord Gnya' khri [Btsan po] to Dpal 'khor [btsan], and the generations preceeding Gnya' khri Btsan po are the upper generations of the gods (*stod kyi lha rabs*) (380.7-11) as described in the *Yi ge lha gyes can*, the first of the *Can lnga* (Karmay, *op. cit.*, 282ff.). This rather idealised summary of *bang so* is itemised more precisely in the main text, which lists 28 tombs located in the two grave fields. The number can be largely confirmed by the situation on site, although with roughly half of the cases the precise identification remains uncertain. Other tomb descriptions relate to various members of the royal house, with the positions given as being outside of 'Phyong po, or they are without any place information, and – provided that their location can be assumed as being in 'Phyong rgyas – apparently have not left any trace.

Additions to the translation are given in square and curly brackets. The personal names in bold relate to *btsan po*-s and queen mothers, and are given in the spellings of the older Dunhuang documents (PT 1286 and *OTA* respectively). The numbering I to XVII follows the chronology of the succession to the throne (Dotson 2009a: 143). Cf. Panglung 1988,

Hazod 2013 (with a brief and incomplete summary of *GYC*); Wang Renxiang *et al.* 2005; Tsewang 2011: 120-130; Shawo Khacham 2014a.

Lde'u-2, p. 377.9:

[1] [The early forms of burials: from the Seven Khri to the Btsan lnga]

· Furthermore, the tombs of the seven [kings with the name element] *khri* were erected in heaven. The divine bodies possessed no corpse; they dissolved like a rainbow.

{Elsewhere it is further detailed that the seven *khri* of heaven remained to be connected by the sky rope *dmu thag*, and their departure to heaven coincided to the time when the respective sons were able to control a horse (cf. Haarh 1969: 119; in PT 1286: l.44-48 (*TDD* 198-199) this actually relates to the six *khri* before Dri gum Btsan po, but later it speaks of *gnam la dri bdun*, in the (corrupt) compound "Spu lde Gung rgyal Gnam la Dri bdun"; see Dotson 2009a: 144). It does not say which son (elder, middle, younger), but indicates a rule of succession, which apparently was combined with the regulation of regicide. We find this recalled in the later chronicles' stereotypical formula, which with respect to the historical time claims: "when the son reached the age of 13, the father went to heaven" (cf. Drikung 2011: 261-262; for *gdung du gsheg* ("goes to heaven") see Hill 2008). However, the historical data do not confirm this, and there was apparently no strict rule as to the order of succession to the throne, although there are indications of an ideal type – the preference for the middle son (Chayet 1994b; Dotson 2009a: 27). In a recent paper, Zeisler (2015) proposes reading the term *khri* (*dri*) in this and parallel contexts (such as PT 1038) in its possible older meaning of "star", indicating that we should see a certain constellation behind the group of the seven celestial *khri* (above chap. 6).}

· The grave-sites (*dur*) of the two stengs ("two upper ones") were erected in the rocks and slate zones (*rdza, g.ya'*).

{The Two Upper Ones refer to Gri gum Btsan po (Dri gum Btsan po, occasionally also Khri gum (in the reading of Zeisler 2015: "the star that died") and his son Spu lde Gung rgyal; for the two figures' tombs see Hazod 2007b.}

· The graves (*bang so*) of the six [kings carrying the name element] *legs* ("excellent") were erected between the alpine meadows and the plain.

{The group is also known as the Sa'i Legs drug (Six Legs of the Earth, or Sa la legs drug), with the tombs' position given as being between the slate mountain and the alpine meadows (*g.ya'* and *spang*). The group perhaps similarly to the seven *khri* relates to a certain constellation. It also has been suggested to see behind this and the other (not mound related) burials of the mythical kings an allusion of forms of exposing the corpse (Hazod 2007b; I remember a site full of slate stones erected high up at the Yar lha Sham po circuit route, which the locals only vaguely described as being possibly a sky burial site (*dur khrod*) "that is no longer used" (fieldnotes 1997). It is situated below the G.yag chad la, "the pass where the yak (i.e. Sham po/bu) tired" (see Plate 31 in CFS 2000; cf. also Jampa Tenzin 2010: 116), and indeed at the border of the slate mountain and the *spang* (the latter specified by Tsering Gyalpo as the zone of high-altitude pastures that (among the domestic animals) only can be used by yaks). Note that the birth at this point appears associated with the image of the hero of the earliest period, named as G.ya spang skyes ("Born at the border of *g.ya* and *spang*"), the first in the group of the eight *ma sangs* (nine with G.yang 'brum Si le ma; *Lde'u-2* 224-25; the same figure is known from the Bon po *lde'u 'phrul* divination texts, described as the one who wears "the great helmet of the sun", and on his body "the great armour of the stars" (Smith 2011: 20; Ramble 2015; for a different description, see *PK* 365. 7-15).}

• The place of interment (*dur sa*) of the seven [kings carrying the name element] *lde* were erected in the middle of the river.

{Lde bdun is also the rendering in *Lde'u-2* 248; otherwise this group includes eight members, called the "Eight Lde of the Water". *Ka khol ma* 89.11-12 gives Sham chu (= Yar lha Sham chu, the name of the Yar lung river) as the actual burial site of the Lde brgyad.}

• From the [time of the] Seven [kings with the name element] *btsan* ("mighty") the grave-sites (*dur sa*) were erected in the country (*yul*); the country's name was Yar lung Ngar ma thang. Moreover, they were without *phul*, and resembled raised earthen mounds.

{Yar lung Ngar ma thang refers to a place in the Gzhas phu valley of the Grang mo district in Upper 'Phyong po; Hazod 2007b. This group is usually listed as Five Btsan (as e.g. in PT 1286), or even Three Btsan. With regard to the latter view, Dpa' bo in his *Mkhas pa'i dga' ston* (*KG* 169.8-11) states that this would be nonsense, because it says in the *Gsang ba yang chung* etc.: "The graves (*mchad pa*) of the Five Btsan are piles of earth that resemble tents; they are without *phul*, square tombs were not known [at that time]. This is well known since early times." Dpa' bo evidently used here a version of the *GYC* different to the present one.}

[2] [The tombs of the succeeding kings and emperors: From no. I to XVII]

[**I**] [The grave of] Khri Snyan gzung btsan [**Khri Snya zung brtsan**] was raised in Don mkhar mda'. It is similarly without *phul*, square tombs were unknown at that time, it is said.

[**II**] The *bang so* of 'Bro Gnyan lde ru [**'Bro Mnyen lde ru**] is in Don mkhar mda' (*sic*); ruler and subjects, the three, entered the grave alive.

{For this *rgyal po* see above chap. 4; for his tomb in Zhang mda' (*KT*: Zhang phu'i mda') see the description in the *Rgyal po bka' thang* (*KT* 155.6-156.5).}

[**III**] The tomb of Stag gu snyan gzigs [**Stag bu Snya gzigs**] was erected in Don mkhar mda'. Its position is to the left of Khri snyan [no. I]. It is also without *phul*, and resembles an extended earthen mound.

{A massive wall (L = ca. 80m) is in front of the mounds of no. III and iii.1-4 (Fig. 1); it was made of two separate walls, and the space between was filled with earth and stones (see Shawo Khacham 2014a: 79) – perhaps the remains of a larger enclosure of this part of the Don mkhar mda' tumulus complex.}

[**IV**] Then the [tomb with the] *phul skyed* construction, which has [the form of a] shoulder blade: The name is Gung ri Sog kha. [This tomb of] Gnam ri Srong btsan [**Khri Slon btsan**] was erected in Don mkhar mda'. The position is to the left of Khri Snyan gzung btsan.

{The line *phul skyed rtsig pa sog khar yod* appears to be a somewhat corrupt rendering; elsewhere the tomb is described of having *phul che* (great *phul* – a certain form of architectural addition), and being quadrangular in its form like a shoulder-blade; cf. *Mkhas pa'i dga' ston* (*KG* 172.3): *phul che dbyibs ni gru bzhi sog ka ris*.}

[**V**] [The tomb of] **Srong btsan Sgam po** [r. 618(?)-40 plus ca. 646-49; d. 649-50] was erected in 'Phyong po mda' [*Ka khol ma* 309: Yar lung Don mkhar thang]. Its size (p. 378.1) corresponds to the range of an arrow shot. It has four chapels in the four corners. Name: Smug ri Smug po. Square tombs were constructed from that time onwards.

{The grave account in the *Rgyal po bka' thang* (*KT* 145-47; Haarh 1969: 350f.) speaks of the joint entombment of the father and the mothers, the three (*yab yum gsum gyi pur*), which evidently refers to the classical death story of the btsan po and his two Buddhist consorts (Sørensen 1994: 330ff.) – evidence of the Buddhist influence of this otherwise informative account. On this tomb (and the tomb's inner structure) see Haarh, *op. cit.*; Hazod 2013.}

[**VI**] [The tomb of] **Gung srong Gung btsan** [d. ca. 646] is in Don mkhar mda'. The position is to the left of Gnam ri Srong btsan [no. IV]. Name: Gung ri Gung che, so it is said.

[**VII**] [The tomb of] Mang srong [**Mang slon Mang rtsan**, d. 676-77] is to the left of Srong btsan [no. V.]. Its name is Sngo bzher Hral po. {Funeral in 679-80}

[**VIII**] [The tomb of] 'Dus srong 'phrul rgyal [**'Dus srong Mang po rje**, d. 704-05] is to the left of Ma[ng] srong. Its name is Seng ge brtsegs pa can.

{Elsewhere the name is given as Seng ge brtsig pa, proper name: Lha ri can (Panglung 1988). Later chronicles state that this (trapezoidal) "lion building" was erected by "Hor people" (probably related to the Dru gu, Western Turks); Hazod 2015: 198; Hazod 2013: 94. The funeral of the emperor was in winter 706-07; as calculated by Haarh (on the basis of the *OTA* and PT 1042), the time of the entombment of members of the imperial house appears to have been early winter (Haarh 1969: 358-359; 422; cf. also Chu 1991: 134-137), i.e. ca. the last week of October or first week of November (see here Dotson 2009a: 12-13 for a recent reconstruction of the old Tibetan calendar system and its approx. correspondence with the Western calendar; on the reliability of PT 1042 (composed in a Buddhist milieu) see Walter 2009: 194.}

[**X**] [The tomb of] Ag tshom [**Khri Lde gtsug brtsan**, d. 754] was erected on the Mu ra ri. Its position is to the left of 'Phrul gyi rgyal po [no. VIII], the name is Lha ri Gtsug nam, so it is said.

[For no. **IX** see below, § 3. – No *bang so* is recorded for **Lha Bal po**, the elder [step-]brother of no. X, who ruled from 704-05 (Dotson 2009a: 143), i.e. the Pa tshab *tsha* Lha Bal po in *Lde'u-1* 120.20–21, who together with his two younger brothers Lod po and Lod chung was deposed.]

[**XI**] [The tomb of] **Khri Srong lde brtsan** [d. ca. 800] was erected on the Mu ra ri; its position is behind the father [no. X] to protect [the latter's tomb] against the flood. [The tomb] was built by himself before his death. Its name is 'Phrul ri Gtsug nam [var. 'Phrul ri Gtsug snang].

{In the introductory of the *GYC* (377.1) it more generally says: most were *bang so* (the kings) built themselves before they died. For further details on Khri Srong lde btsan's tomb see Hazod 2015 and the references given there.}

[For no. **XII** and **XIII**, see below.]

[**XIV**] **Khri Lde srong brtsan** [d. 815] is in front of 'Phrul rgyal [no. VIII.] [The ground of the tomb] is inside elevated, due to the queen-mother's vision it could be flooded (*yum gyis chab gang dgongs pas nang gi mtho*). Its name is 'Phrul chen Bzher [var.: Rgyal chen ['Phrul ri]].

{Rgyal chen 'phrul is the name of this burial mound in the famous stele inscription at the tomb of this emperor (*OTI* 27.1.59: .. *rje'i bang so rgyal chen 'phrul zhes mtshan pa 'di lags so*)); as far as we see it, this is the earliest written evidence of the term *bang so* in the meaning of burial mound. In *TT* 293.2-3 it says that the body of the king resided inside the *bang so*, on a pedestal (*gdan*, related to the *gdan /rtan byang* of the *se gru bzhi* burial in PT 1136: l. 19, PT 1134:l. 56?), inside a closed (better: open?) large copper vessel (*zangs chen kha sbyor*) – the latter a form of container / coffin also registered for 'Bro Gnyan lde ru or Gri gum Btsan po (cf. also PT 1134: l. 57; *TDD* 146). See most recently Bialek's analyses of Old Tibetan *kha sprod* and *zangs brgya'* (2015, s.v. index) and her interesting comparative note on the ethnography of the (open) box in the context of Tibetan funeral traditions, both related to mound burial and "sky burial."}

[**XVI**] The position of [the tomb of] Dar ma [**Khri 'U'i Dum brtan**, d. 842] is between 'Phrul and Rgyal chen [i.e. no. VIII and XIV]. Its name is Bang rim 'Khor lo can.

{Some sources mention that the construction remained incomplete; Panglung 1988: 347-349. }

[**XVII**] The position of [the tomb of] 'Od srung [**Khri 'Od srung btsan**] is behind 'Phrul rgyal [no. VIII]. Its name is Skyes bu Lha bsten.

{Other sources call the tomb Skye'u Lha rten; it says that thereafter the tradition of constructing burial mounds ended; cf. Hazod 2013.}

[**XII**] Mu ni btsan po [**Mu ne brtsan**, d. 798] is in front to the right of Ag tshom [no. X]. [The grave's] name is Lha ri Lding bu [var.: Lha ri Ldem bu/ po].

[For no. **XIII** see below § 7.5.]

[**XV**] [The tomb of] Ral pa can [**Khri Gtsug lde brtsan**, d. 841] is situated in Don [mkhar] mda', on the left side. Its name is Khri stag Smang ri.

{In other sources the tomb is called Khri stengs Rmang ri. Mu ne brtsan and Khri Gtsug lde brtsan (XII and XV) are elsewhere described as *khu chen* (cf. Panglung 1988), and the form *khu chen gyi bang so gnyis* in *GYC* (*Lde'u-2* 380.7-8) evidently refers to the graves of these *btsan po*-s. The terms are posthumous classifications, which we think describe the paternal uncle–nephew relations between four *btsan po* of two generations of brothers: Mu ne was *khu* in relation to Khri Gtsug lde brtsan, the other one in relation to Khri 'Od srung btsan. The designation of the two *khu* [*bo*], paternal uncles, as "great" we think simply reflects their status as emperors. In the introduction part of *GYC* it says that the *rgyal po khu chen* who did not hold power were placed in graves or buried somewhere else; *Lde'u-2* 377.1-2.}

[3] The *bang so* of queens endowed with power:

{The group is mistakenly summarised as "queens holding no power" (*srid kyis ma zin jo mo*), but actually relates to (heir-bearing) queens, thus reads: *srid kyis zin jo mo*.}

[3.1] [The *bang so* of] Ong cong [**Khon co Mang mo rje Khri skar**; PT 1288: Mun chang Kong co; funeral in 683-84] is in Don [mkhar] mda', on the left side.

{*Ka khol ma* 309: Phying ba Stag rtse ri. The tomb marked as v.1 on the map (Fig. 1) may relate to the one immediately above no. XV. However, the registration of the Chinese Princess as the mother of Mang slon Mang brtsan (no. VII) in PT 1286 (Royal Genealogy) has been questioned, and based on the entry of 706-07 in the more reliable *Annals* it has been argued that rather Mang pangs (d. 706-07; funeral in 707-708) was the queen-mother. See Uebach 1997: 57; Dotson 2009a: 23.}

[3.2-4] Next to it is Mong bza' Khri mo 'brong [**Mong Khri mo mnyen Ldong steng**? mother of no. VI]; beside that is also Ru yong Btsan mo mthso [**Ru yong Stong rgyal mtsho ma**; wife of Khri Thog brtsan, and mother of Lha Tho do Snya brtsan]; beside that is Mno bza' Mar dkar [Rno bza' Mang Dgar = **Gno bza' Mang mo rje Ji dgos**, wife of Lha Tho do Snya brtsan.]

{The tombs are indicated as v.2, and v.3-4 on the map.}

[3.5] [The tomb of] Tshe spong 'Bri ma Thod dkar [**Tshes pong 'Bring ma Thog dgos**] is located to the right of *yab* [Gnam ri Srong btsan]. It was named Bang so G.yul mo'i thang.

{From Gnam ri Srong btsan onwards the burial mounds of the *btsan po* are specified by individual names, mostly mountain names, indicating that they were also idealised as mountains. There were apparently also names for the tombs of the queen-mothers (or the queen-mothers of the *zhang* status), although this is noted only for the Tshes pong Lady, the mother of Srong btsan Sgam po. Interestingly, this mound has no *ri* name but a *thang* name, where we think *g.yul mo'i thang* is an alternative form of *g.yul kha thang*, "threshing floor".}

[3.6] 'Dos (p. 379.1) bza' Stong btsun 'Bro dkar [**'Ol god Stong btsun 'Bro ga**] is to the left of *yab* [Stag bu Snya gzigs].

{for the other three mounds see § 7.1-3 below.}

[3.7] Tshe spong Dmar rgyal [**Tshes pong bza' Rma rgyal Ldong skar**, the chief consort of

Khri Srong lde btsan; above chap. 6] is in Don mkhar Shu po sna.

{This place still remains to be identified. Satellite photographs indicate the traces of further tombs in Don mkhar (0030 and 0031), with only smaller structures.}

[3.8] Sna nam Dbyibs stang [**Sna nam bza' Mang mo rje Bzhi steng**? d. 742-43] is on the left corner [of the tombs] of *yab* [Khri Lde gtsug brtsan, no. X] and the son [Khri Srong lde btsan, no. XI.].

{The tomb of the queen-mother is marked as x.1 on the map.}

[3.9] 'Bro bza' Stong dkar Phyi mo lod [**Khri ma lod**, d. 712-13; funeral in 713-14] is on the left corner, on the other side of the son ['Dus srong, no. VIII]. There are said to be [respectively separate tombs of altogether] 11 *phyi ma* (= *phyi mo*, grandmothers) of *lde'i sras*. [i.e. heirs with *lde* as element in their names, or *lde' sras* = divine sons / throne-holders?].

{In the *OTA* only two ladies are addressed as *phyi* (*pyi*), Mang pangs (§ 3.1) and Khri ma lod (with *phyi mo* also including the meaning of great-grandmother; Uebach 1997: 57ff.). For this powerful grandmother and "empress", and the 'Bro in general see Lobsang Nyima 2011. The tomb is indicated as no. IX on the map of Fig. 1.}

[Not listed in this group of queen-mothers are **'Bro bza' Dung pyang bzher** (mother of 'Bro Mnyen lde ru), *btsan mo* **Ga tun** (funeral (in Phying ba?) in 708-09; mother of Lha Bal po), **Mchims za Btsan ma thog Thog steng** (d. 721-22; mother of Khri Lde gtsug brtsan), **'Bro bza' Lha rgyal Mang mo rje** (mother of Khri Gtsug lde btsan and 'U'i Dum brtan), and ***p*** [*h*] ***yi*** **Mang pangs** (above §3.1).]

[4] Eight [junior] queens not endowed with power (*srid ma zin pa'i jo mo*):

[4.1] Lcang mo Khri btsun [PT 1288: Jo mo Khri btsun],

{The funeral of this consort of Khri Lde gtsug brtsan was performed in (winter) 745-46. The junior queen (*jo mo*) is identified in later sources as the mother of Lhas bon (below 7.4.), but also the Chinese princess Kim sheng Kong co (d. 739-40) has been discussed as candidate in this context; cf. Dotson 2009a: 124.}

[4.2] Snyen stengs Snyen ma lod (?),

[4.3] 'Bro bza' Ma khang Gsing ma lod (?),

[4.4] Tshe spong bza' Khrim gung rgyal (?),

[4.5] 'Bro btsun Khri mo legs,

{i.e. Jo mo 'Bro bza' Khri mo legs, one of the three (junior) consorts of Khri Lde srong btsan, classified as "sisters"; Sørensen 1994: 409; Dotson 2009a: 30.}
[4.6] Mkhar chen bza' Mtsho rgyal,
{i.e. one of the consorts of Khri Srong lde btsan, from Mkhar chen (due west of Bsam yas); see Gyatso 2006.}
[4.7] Zhang zhung bza' Zngo bzher Lig tig sman, and
{i.e. the consort of Srong btsan Sgam po; for her parent's house see *Nyi ma* 141.4f.}
[4.8] 'Chims bza' [Mchims bza' Lha mo btsan (?), consort of Khri Srong lde btsan] – altogether eight [for whom graves] were erected as *bang so* (*'chims bza' dang brgyad bang sor brtsig so*).
{The last sentence is evidently corrupt, leaving the possible reading that the resting place of the eight *jo mo* were erected inside the tombs [of their respective husbands]. In the introduction of *GYC* it summarises that some of the 18 *jo mo* were buried together with others, while some had burial sites of their own (*Lde'u-2* 377.3-4).}
[Not listed in this group of junior queens is Lhas pangs (Lha span); she is addressed as *lcam* in the *OTA* (d. 730-731; funeral in 732-733), and assumed to have belonged to the consorts of *btsan po* no. VIII or X; Uebach 1997: 63.]

[5] [The ladies] not having entered graves (*dur du ma tshud pa*) were
[5.1-2] Bal mo bza' Khri btsun and Gi shang Ong cong who disolved into [the statue of] the Great Compassionate One.
{This refers to the classical death story in the Buddhist vita of Srong btsan Sgam po (Sørensen 1994: 330ff.), only that the text evidently here conflates the two Chinese princesses, Mun chang Kong co (3.1) and Kim shang/sheng Kong co (7.4).}
[5.3] Tshe spong bza' Mdor rgyal was lodged in Mod (read: Mdo) shod of Mdo stod Khams.
{Unidentified, unless this lady is the Ru yong bza' Mdo rgyal, the chief consort of Mu ne btsan po.}
[5.4] Thag de bza' Bu chung (*sic!*) died after Sman Bag ma (?), and since she was concealed at Zar po, [this site] became known as Se sman of Gra.
{This site in Gr[v]a still needs to be identified.}
[5.5] Pho yong bza' Rgyal mo btsun [– one of the consorts of Khri Srong lde btsan –] was placed in Dbu tshal [i.e. the satellite temple of Bsam yas which she herself had raised; cf.

Sørensen 1994: 389].

[5.6] 'Chims bza' Mu ne lod was strangled in 'Phang thang [in lower Yar stod] and then placed there. These six were left behind.

[6] The building of *mchod rten* replacing *bang so*:

[6.1] 'Bro bza' Khri rgyal Mang po (read: mo) rje, named Jo mo Byang chub rje after she left for liberation – the *mchod rten* was built in G.yi phu; [furthermore the ladies]

{One of the consorts of Khri Srong lde btsan; a founder-figure (cf. Wangdu and Diemberger 2000: 68) and also known as author of an "additional law" (*khrims bu chung*); *Lde'u-2* 268.16-18; *KG* 378.20-23; a G.yi phu (var. Dbyi phu; "upper Lynx") is in the Thang skya district of Mal gro, a religious site centered around a stupa associated with Atisha (cf. Chaka Dawa 2013: 28).}

[6.2] Cog ro bza' Dpal gyi Ngang btsun ma,

{i.e. Khri Gtsug lde btsan's consort Dpal gyi Ngang tshul}

[6.3] 'Chims bza' Rin chen Rgyal ma gtsug (?),

[6.4] Tshe spong bza' Lhun gyi Lha mo, and

{This Tshes pong Lady appears to be the Lhun gyi Bu mo, one of Khri Gtsug lde btsan's consorts; Sørensen 1994: 411.}

[6.5] Lha lung bza' Dpal rab 'Byin rje all had *mchod rten* built for them.

{i.e. Lha lung bza' Me tog ma? – one of Khri Gtsug lde btsan's consorts.}

[6.6] In addition, another [stupa-shaped] *bang so* is [inside?] the son's platform[-constructed] [tomb] (*de las bang so gzhan ma [gru] bzhi stengs sras so*).

{Reading uncertain; otherwise it may refer to the resting place of one of Sad na legs' junior queens.}

[Not listed by name are the ladies summarised as the *jo mo* who acted as generals on the borders (?) and who reportedly were buried in specifically decorated tombs (*Lde'u-2* 377.4-5).]

[7] For the *bang so* of disqualified [princes] (*thang mtshams kyi bang so*, with *thang mtshams* being short for *thang mtshams su phab ba* ("brought to the border of the plain"); *Lde'u-1* 104f.):

[7.1-2] [The burial sites of] the disqualified [princes] [in the time] of 'Bro Snyan lde ru (above 2.II), namely [his brothers] 'Bro tsha Rmu (p. 380.1) btsun and Mon bu Rgyal mtshan [cf. *Lde'u-1* 107] relate to the two piles of earth situated below of Stag gu (no. III);

{The two mounds belong to the group marked as iii.1-4 on the map.}

[7.3] [the tombs of] the disqualified [prince] related to Gnam ri Srong btsan, Blon po Legs nam [i.e. 'Ol god tsha Blon Ger legs; *Lde'u-1* 107], is situated to the left of Stag gu.

[7.4] Lcang tsha Lha dbon [Lhas bon, d. 739/40, funeral in 741-42] is located to the left of the father [Khri Lde gtsug brtsan]. This *bang so* is round-shaped.

{Other sources describe the tomb's position as being in front of the father (Panglung 1988). Following the entry in the *Annals*, according to which the funerals for the son, Lhas bon, and the Chinese Princess (Kim sheng Kong co) were performed in the same year ([winter] 741-42) it has been argued that it possibly relates to only one funeral and the two were buried together. Cf. the discussion in Dotson 2009a: 24; 121-22; 124. This tomb is marked on the map as x.a /x.2, with the second symbol (indicating the Chinese princess) representing a rather uncertain identification.}

[7.5] the tomb of Mu tig btsan po [**Mu rug brtsan**, r. ca. 800-802; d. ca. 804] is in Don mkhar mda'. Skya ldem is the *bang so*'s name.

{The name is alternatively given as Skya ring Ldems pa, or also Gyang ri Rgyang ldam/ ldem; Mu rug brtsan is counted as no. **XIII** in our representation of the royal lineage; on this figure see Dotson 2007b; above fn. 34.}

[7.6] The Sad ne legs [specific *thang mtshams*] grave was added to the square platform [constructed inside the tomb of this emperor].

{Cf. above § 2, no. XIV; § 6.6; perhaps this burial relates to the sons Lha rje and Lhun grub, who died an early age.}

[7.7] The border of the plane grave site[s] of I sho legs were made in heaven.

{These grave(s) relate to the Zhang lnga gcen po lineage; *Lde'u-1* 104; above chap. 4.}

[7.8] Gtsang ma was left in Lho brag. (*Lde'u-2*, p. 380.7)

{In contrast to many Tibetan accounts which say that Gtsang ma was a monk who was assassinated in his exile in Lho brag (or Lho brag Bum thang), in the tradition of eastern Bhutan he arrived as the *lha sras* Gtsang ma who founded the Mi zim pa castle, and is considered the ancestor of the noble families that later dominated this region (see Ardussi 2007). According to *Nyang ral* 437.3-10, Gtsang ma died in Spyal ka, a rock cave where his remains were also buried. For the identification of this site in western Bhutan see Ardussi, *op. cit.*, 9ff.}

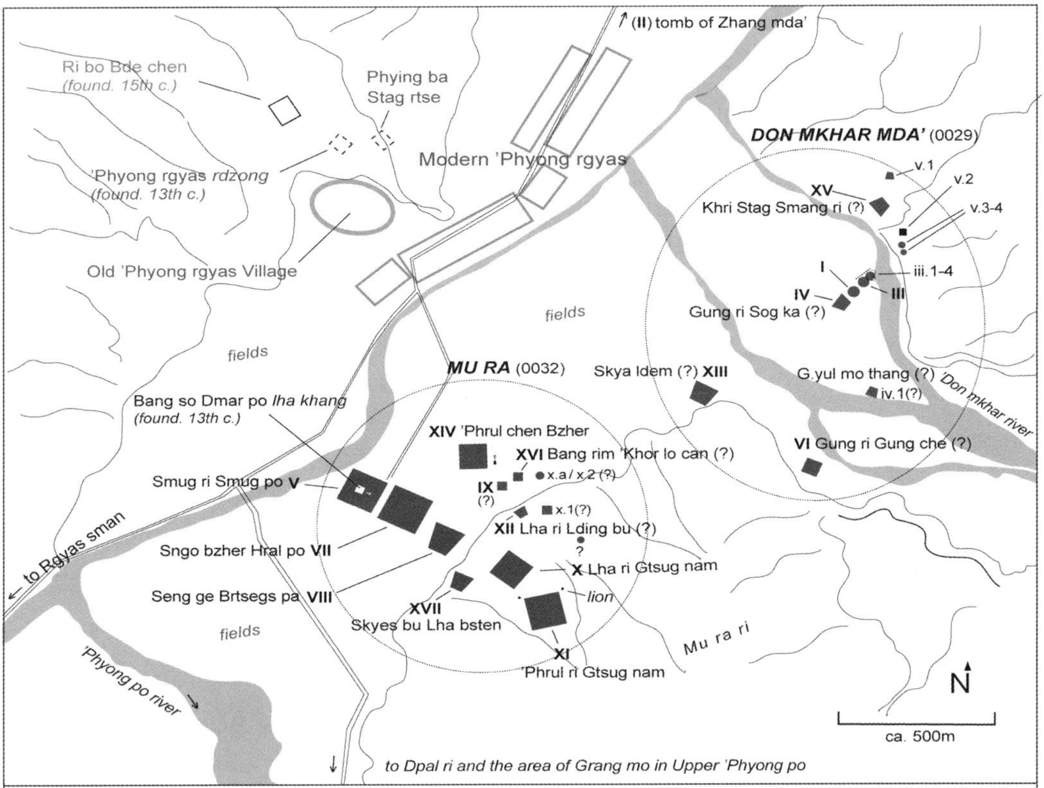

Proposed identification of the tombs (I-XVII):

I	=	Khri Snya zung brtsan
II	=	'Bro Mnyen lde ru
III	=	Stag bu Snya gzigs
IV	=	Khri Slon btsan (grave name (in *GYC*): Gung ri Sog kha)
V	=	Srong btsan Sgam po (grave name Smug ri Smug po)
VI	=	Gung srong Gung btsan (grave name: Gung ri Gung che)
VII	=	Mang slon Man rtsan (grave name: Sngo bzher Hral po)
VIII	=	Khri 'Dus srong (grave name: Seng ge Brtsegs pa)
IX	=	Khri ma lod
X	=	Khri Lde gtsug brtsan (grave name: Lha ri Gtsug nam)
XI	=	Khri Srong lde brtsan (grave name: 'Phrul ri Gtsug nam)
XII	=	Mu ne brtsan (grave name: Lha ri Lding bu)
XIII	=	Mu rug brtsan (grave name: Skya ldem)
XIV	=	Khri Lde srong brtsan (grave name: 'Phrul chen Bzher)
XV	=	Khri Gtsug lde brtsan (grave name: Khri stag Smang ri)
XVI	=	Khri 'U'i Dum brtan (grave name: Bang rim 'Khor lo can)
XVII	=	Khri 'Od srung btsan (grave name: Skyes bu Lha bsten)

(For other entries on the map see Appendix I)

Fig. 1. The royal grave fields of Phying ba (0029, 0032). (Drawing based on Shawo Khacham 2014a: 27)

Appendix II
A list of the major elite burial sites of Central Tibet

This list is based on the burial-site table given on the TTT website (current state (Sept. 2016) 0001-0421) and relates to major fields with tombs from the size of 30m upwards, plus some further sites with notable peculiarities. The details are restricted to some principal information, in the order of: number of site – district (*xiang* 乡) – geographical position / altitude. The counties (*xian* 县) form the outer geographical reference for this listing. A few notes on each cemetery are given in brackets, often not more than the mention of the central mound's (M-1) size (For more details see "site" on TTT). Site numbers highlighted in **bold** refer to fields with the largest tombs. Note that the size specifications (mostly based on satellite imagery) relate to the front of the (trapezoid) mounds, at ground level, where not the actual walls but the earth sloping at the side of the mounds was taken as reference point. Here the factor of erosion allows only approximate conclusions. The height information, usually between 5m and 10m, is not given. For size details of the tombs in Phying ba see Wang Renxiang *et al.* 2005.

SNE GDONG:

0001 – Rtse thang district (*xiang*): 29 12 36, 91 47 32/ 3635m
(Related to a single mound of ca. 40m; TTT: "0001")
0002 – Khra 'brug district: 29 11 32, 91 47 45 / 3800m
(Situated due south of 0001; M-1: ca. 35m; Feiglstorfer 2015.)
0003 – Rtse thang district: 29 10 21, 91 47 22 / 3790m
(Situated behind G.yu gsar Village in Lower Yar lung; M-1: ca. 50m; TTT: "0003")
0012 – Mkhar thog district: 29 10 33, 91 44 19 / 3630m
(In Lower Yar lung; M-1 ca. 30m; TTT: "0012")
0018 – Pho 'brang district: 29 05 31, 91 50 28 / 3740m
(M-1 ca. 40m; situated next to the site of ancient Bug pa can; TTT: "0018")
0024 – Skyer pa district: 29 20 08, 91 49 28 / 3700m (M-1 of ca. 50m)
(The "bird-shaped" group of mounds in the 'On valley; above chap. 5.3; TTT: "0024")

’PHYONG PO:

0028 – ’Phyong po district: 28 53 03, 91 42 40 / 4890m

(Related to the story of “Tibet’s first tomb”; TTT: “0028”; Hazod 2007b)

0029 – ’Phyong-rgyas: 29 01 31, 91 41 50 / 3790m

(The field of Don mkhar mda’ in Phying ba; Appendix 1; Fig. 1.)

0032 – ’Phyong-rgyas: 29 01 10, 91 40 59 / 3785m

(The Mu ra (Mu ra thang) part of the cemetery of Phying ba; Appendix 1; Fig. 1.)

0033 – Spun gsum district: 28 58 59, 91 34 12 / 4050m

(In Rgyas sman of Upper ’Phyong po, not far from Spyan rgyas; M-1: ca. 45m)

0037 – Thang po che district: 29 06 47, 91 42 24 / 3675m

(This relates to the remains of a single (reportedly originally round) burial mound, perhaps originally 60m; above chap. 4; TTT: “0037”.)

0038 – Lha yul district: 29 10 08, 91 40 39 / 3800m (M-1: ca. 45m; TTT: “0038”)

0389 – Lha yul district: 29 10 15, 91 40 59 / 3840m (M-1: ca. 30m)

0396 – Chang khyim district: 29 07 12, 91 35 27 / 3860m

(M-1 ca. 45m; situated in the upper ’Phyos valley)

GRVA NANG:

0040 – Bsam yas district: 29 21 04, 91 31 16 / 3655m

(Situated in the old Brag dmar district, not far from Bsam yas; M-1 of ca. 40m)

0419 – Bsam yas district: 29 20 13, 91 30 50 / 3710 (M-1: ca. 30m)

0042 – Grva phyi district: 29 14 27, 91 24 34 / 3610m (M-1: ca. 30m)

0043 – Smon grub district: 29 08 00, 91 26 07/3855m

(Situated in the upper Grva phyi valley, a field of ca. 50 mounds flanked by two “minister mountains”, M-1: ca. 55m; TTT: “0043”)

0044 – Grva phyi district: 29 11 37, 91 26 58 / 3875m (M-1: ca. 45m; TTT: “0044”)

0047 – Grva thang district: 29 14 02, 91 17 58 / 3660m

(The famous field of Gser khung (M-1 ca. 70m), including a stupa-shaped mound (TTT: “0047”); the Grva district was a territory of the Sna nam (from the late 8th or early 9th century; RCP 171), and this lineage was possibly also behind this field in Lower Grva, namely the branch of Chief Minister Sna nam Zhang Rgyal tshan Lha snang, who is chronicled as having founded the Grva’i lha khang (cf. Uebach 1987: 114-115), probably the precursor to the Grva thang temple (found. 1090), not far from Gser khung. In this sense this chief minister of Sna nam is also a good candidate as the identity of the aristocrat entombed in the impressive M-1.)

0048 – Grva thang district: 29 14 00, 91 17 25 / 3705m

(Situated immediately to the west of 0047, with M-1 of ca. 35m; in the literature usually registered as part of the Gser khung (0047) cemetery.)

0420 – Dkyil ru district: 29 07 08, 91 17 12 / 3875

(Situated in the upper Grva valley, in an area asociated with a branch of the Mchims (BA 95ff.); M-1: ca. 40m)

GONG DKAR:

0053 – Gong dkar district: 29 16 48, 90 53 37 / 3630m (M-1: ca. 35m)

0055 – Rgya ri district: 29 11 46, 90 55 29 / 3810m (M-1: ca. 35m)

0057 – Nya sog district: 29 14 33, 90 31 09 / 3660 (Single tomb; ca. 35m)

SNA DKAR RTSE:

0058 – Kha brag district: 29 14 24, 90 27 49 / 3800m

(Situated behind the village of Sbrang (related to the 'Brang / Sbrang family?), with the special characteristic of exclusively "coffer-shaped" tombs; M-1: ca. 30m; Fig. 5; TTT: "0058".)

0059 – Mkhar lung district: 29 06 18, 90 28 27 / 4615m

(The identification of the field (with M-1: ca. 50) is uncertain)

0063 – Gram mda' district: 28 57 01, 91 04 52 / 4615m (M-1 25-30m).

(The site of ca. 100 mounds is situated next to Dbal sdings, a place possibly related to the old Bal yul (Bal po) district.)

LHO BRAG:

0065 – Skyid stod district: 28 22 57, 90 47 53 / 4140m

(The central burial site of Lho brag, with M-1 of ca. 65m; above chap. 5.2; TTT: "0065".)

0066 – Skyid stod district: 28 23 23, 90 46 05 / 4170m (M-1: ca. 35m; TTT: "0066")

MTSHO SMAD:

0069 – Gtam shul disrict: 28 26 32, 91 26 15 / 4190m (M-1: ca. 30m)

LHUN RTSE:

0070 – Gsum pa district: 28 24 43, 92 20 51 / 3960m

(The central field of Gnyal, largely destroyed by modern constructions, M-1: ca. 40m; TTT: "0070".)

0071 – Gsum pa district: 28 24 34, 92 19 52 / 3976m (M-1: ca. 30-35m)

0072 – Gsum pa district: 28 24 47, 92 19 03 / 3990m (M-1: ca. 30m)

0075 – Zhing ba district: 28 25 03, 92 30 58 / 3870m

(Single hill (ca. 30m) at Thon mi Sambhota; identifcation as grave mound uncertain; above chap. 5.3; TTT: "0075".)

CHU GSUM:

0076 – Shag byang district: 29 05 07, 92 12 08 / 3990m

(The central field of G.ye yul, with three prominent mounds, locally described as the residences of three princes; M-1: ca. 70-80m; TTT: "0076"; Hazod 2009: 180.)

0077 – Shag byang district: 29 04 05, 92 09 39 / 3928m (Single mound of ca. 30m)

ZANGS RI:

0081 – Lcang district: 29 15 56, 91 58 15 / 3590m (M-1: ca. 50m)

0082 – Rong district: 29 13 09, 92 00 34 / 3700m

(The central field in the Rong area; M-1: ca. 40m.)

RGYA TSHVA:

0084 – Ngar rab district: 29 09 10, 92 35 50 / 3450m

(One of the central burial sites of ancient Dvags po, M-1: ca. 50m)

0087 – Rgya tshva district: 29 05 55, 92 44 10 / 3700m (M-1: ca. 30-35m)

0089 – Rgya tshva district: 29 05 14, 92 43 00 / 3226m (M-1: ca. 35-40m)

SNANG:

0092 – Skyems stong district: 28 59 26, 93 20 23 / 3550m

(The eastern burial site (*bang so shar*) of the cemetery in Slebs of ancient Mchims, M-1 of ca. 75m; above chap. 3.4; TTT: "0092".)

0093 – Skyems stong district: 28 58 53, 93 21 02 / 3280m

(The western part (*bang so nub*) of the cemetery in Slebs of ancient Mchims, M-1 of ca. 30m, plus MT-D type of mounds, TTT: "0093".)

SNYING KHRI:

0097 – Stag rtse district: 29 27 26, 94 27 43 / 2956m

(This round grave (ca. 45m) in Mi yul Skyid thing is described as the burial site of Gri gum Btsan·po (Hazod 2007b); with traces of older graves (or pits?) in the immediate surrounding; TTT: "0097".)

0098 – Smad ri district: 29 29 24, 94 33 29 / 3000m

(Identification as tomb uncertain; the site refers to three adjacent hills at the foot of Mt Bon ri (ca. 100m); note that the graves of the ancient Kong dkar po ruler are still not identified; TTT: "0098".)

0099 – Smad ri district: 29 29 38, 94 37 15 / 2985m

(M-1 of ca. 50m; but identification uncertain)

RGYA MDA':

0100 – Nyang po district: 30 13 43, 93 06 02 / 3860m

(Situated in the upper Nyang po valley of eastern Central Tibet; Hazod 2009: 179; TTT: "0100".)

SPO SMAD:

0102 – Dgu shang district: 30 09 27, 95 26 10 / 2930m

(M-1 ca. 25-30m; for this site in Spo bo yul see Hazod 2009: 177; TTT: "0103".)

MAL GRO GONG DKAR:

0104 – Bya ra mdo district: 29 48 02, 91 53 37 / 4235m

(One of the central grave fields of eastern Mal gro, situated next to Chad kha dgon; M-1: ca. 45m; Hazod 2015; TTT: "0104".)

0105 – Bya ra mdo district: 29 47 42, 91 52 30 / 4200m

(The field is situated opposite 0104; M-1 of ca. 40m, originally with two stone lions in front of the grave; TTT: "0105"; Hazod 2015; Feiglstorfer 2015.)

0107 – Bya ra mdo district: 29 48 19, 91 51 41 / 4230m

(In eastern Mal gro, M-1 ca. 35m)

0108 – Dvags pa district: 29 46 08, 91 50 49 / 3970m

(The greatest field of eastern Mal gro in terms of number of elite mounds; M-1: ca. 55m; TTT: "0108")

0110 – Spang mda' district: 29 52 58, 91 49 09 / 4130m

(This group of elite mounds (M-1: ca. 35m) is situated opposite Stag phu dgon in the Stag phu valley of central Mal gro (perhaps the Skyi Stag tsal of the *OTA*). Immediately below Stag phu dgon there is the recently renovated observatory of Stag phu Nyi thig; cf. *Dungkar* 1001-1002.)

0111 – Spang mda' district: 29 54 36, 91 50 02 / 3965m (M-1: ca. 30m)

0112 – Spang mda' district: 29 53 49, 91 51 03 / 4030m

(The largest elite grave field of Mal gro; M-1: ca. 50m; TTT: "0112".)

0113 – Nyi ma lcang rva district: 29 58 05, 91 53 62 / 3990m

(Situated behind Sprin sgang Village; M-1: ca. 30m; TTT: "0113")

0114 – Nyi ma lcang rva district: 29 56 59, 91 58 00 / 4175m

(Single mound in the upper Mang ra valley; ca. 35m)

0115 – Nyi ma lcang rva district: 29 58 50, 91 55 04 / 3950m

(Situated opposite the imperial era temple of Zhva'i lha khang; the burial ground is locally known as Mchad kha ("place of tombs"), M-1 of ca. 35m; behind one of the mounds the fragments of an inscription stone is to be found; for photographs see TTT: "0115"; for transliteration of the text see *OTI* 67; Li and Coblin 1987: 299; above fn. 20.)

0116 – Rtsa zhol district: 30 01 20, 91 47 06 / 4150m (M-1: ca. 30m)

0117 – Gad la hor district: 30 04 37, 91 42 57 / 4005m

(M-1: ca. 35m; situated in Klung shod; TTT, map "Lungshö"; TTT: "0117")

0119 – Gad la hor district: 30 04 58, 91 46 47 / 4025

(M-1 of ca. 30m, but identification uncertain.)

0120 – Klong grol sgang district: 30 02 53, 91 41 10/ 4150m (M-1: ca. 30m)

0127 – Dvags pa district: 29 46 01, 91 50 17 / 4030m (M-1: ca. 30m; TTT: "0127")

0364 – Thang skya district: 29 54 19, 91 45 28 / 3900 (M-1: ca. 30m; TTT: "0364")

<u>STAG RTSE:</u>

0128 – Thang dga' district: 29 51 22, 91 34 27 / 3840m

(M-1 ca. 55m; for a first description of this important burial ground in the Lo valley see Hazod 2009: 228ff.; and TTT site "0128".)

0129 – Thang dga' district: 29 52 41, 91 33 32 / 3865m

(Situated in the Lo valley, M-1 ca. 40m; TTT: "0129".)

0130 – Thang dga' district: 29 52 08, 91 33 36 / 3855m
(M-1 ca. 65m; TTT: Fig. 2 of "0130".)
0376 – Thang dga' district: 29 51 29, 91 32 45 / 3800m
(M-1 of ca. 45; situated in the side valley of Chumbo in Lo; see TTT: "0376", Fig. 2-10; Feiglstorfer, in this volume)
0135 – Chu mda' district: 29 52 07, 91 37 17 / 4050m
(Situated in the Chu mda' valley; M-1: ca. 44m; see TTT: "0135")
0137 – La mo district: 29 47 58, 91 32 34 / 3824m (M-1: ca. 30m)
0138 – Gtsang tog district: 29 47 01, 91 31 48 / 3950m
(Situated behind the ruins of the Bka' gdams pa seat of Dge dgun sgang; M-1: ca. 40m; TTT: "0138")
0141 – Gtsang tog district: 29 45 10, 91 37 37 / 3944m
(On this site in the Cha valley (M-1: ca. 50m), below Ganden monastery see TTT: "0141", and Feiglstorfer 2015.)
0143 – Dar rgyas district: 29 43 54, 91 28 33 / 3859m
(The grave field is situated in the Gru bzhi valley, the ancient Lhas; in its central part there are the ruins of an unidentified monastic complex locally known as Brag gong dgon; M-1: ca. 45m; TTT: "0143"; Feiglstorfer, in this volume)
0402 – Bde chen district: 29 37 55, 91 21 09 / 3880m
(Single mound (ca. 35-40m) in the Shing tshang valley.)
0148 – Bde chen district: 29 39 14, 91 20 58 / 3790m
(For the particularities of this burial ground see TTT: "0148".)
0150 – Bsam grub gling district: 29 38 19, 91 17 01 / 3800m
(Situated in the Chos lung valley; M-1 ca. 45m; TTT: "0150"; Feiglstorfer, in this volume.)

LHASA:

0157 –Tshal Gung thang district: 29 37 00, 91 14 36 / 3820m
(This relates to a single mound (ca. 65m) plus the remains of two smaller mounds situated next to it; on this site in Sri (Ngam lam) see above chap. 5.1; TTT: "0157"; Hazod 2010.)
0397 – Tshal Gung thang district: 29 36 43, 91 15 31 / 3910m
(Situated opposite 0157, including a stupa-shaped mound; TTT: "0397"; Feiglstorfer, in this volume.)

0398 – Tshal Gung thang district: 29 37 29, 91 15 18 / 3800m

(Similarly to 0397, this field includes the ruins of a stupa-mound; Feiglstorfer, in this volume.)

STOD LUNG:

0163 – Gnas chung district: 29 36 15, 90 58 15 / 3785m

(Situated in the Brang district of Lower Stod lung; Hazod 2009: 184; and TTT: "0163" for a new documentation of this site.What is missing in the earlier description is the reference to Brang as old Sna nam land (Hazod 2009: 193), and the story of minister Zhang Ma zhang Grom pa skyes, a member of the Sna nam lineage; the author of the (anti-Buddhist) "small (or additional) law" (*khrims bu chung*) issued during the minority of Khri Srong lde btsan is chronicled as having been buried alive in a tomb in Brang phu of Stod lung (Sørensen 1994: 365; Wangdu and Diemberger 2000: 38). This apparently refers to the elite field of 0163 (with M-1: ca. 50m, M-0: ca. 60m); see Hazod, forthcoming.)

0165 – Sbyar rags district: 29 39 42, 90 51 41 / 3920m (M-1: ca. 30m)

0169 – Rgu rum district: 29 45 25, 90 48 57 / 4010m (M-1: ca. 30m; TTT: "0169")

0171 – Dmar district: 29 48 13, 90 47 27 / 3900m

(Situated behind Gnyan monastery; M-1 of ca. 55m; see TTT: "0171"; Feiglstorfer 2015.)

0172 – Dmar district: 29 49 45, 90 46 07 / 3980m

(Locally related to the Mgar family; above chap. 3.3; M-1: ca. 35-40m; TTT: "0172"; Feiglstorfer 2015.)

0173 – Bde chen district: 29 58 16, 90 44 47 / 4090m

(This relates to a smaller group of mounds (M-1: ca. 30m) situated in the Spang valley.)

0175 – Bde chen district: 29 58 12, 90 46 08 / 4115m

(Single mound (ca. 55m), but identification uncertain.)

0176 – Rgu rum district: 29 45 24, 90 45 41 / 4055m

(This field consists of a group of highly damaged elite mounds (M-1 of ca. 65m) situated behind Rgu rum village at the entrance to the Mtshur phu valley. Rgu rum is most likely the place where the imperial Lcang bu lha khang was situated, sponsored by the Tshes pong family (Hazod 2014: 71-72); TTT: "0176"; above chap. 6.)

0180 – Nam mkha' district: 29 54 26, 90 41 49 / 4070m

(The area of this elite burial site (M-1: ca. 35m) is locally known as Yab chen thang; TTT:

"0180")

'DAM GZHUNG:

0184 – 'Dam chu kha district: 30 29 40, 91 05 21 / 4300m
(M-1 ca. 40m; TTT: "0184" and Fig. 1 with map of the 'Dam gzhung grave fields.)
0186 – Dbu ma thang district: 30 34 05, 91 09 33 / 4340m (M-1: ca. 50m)
0187 – Kong thang district: 30 21 09, 91 03 35 / 4275m
(This highly damaged field is situated at the entrance to Spra kha 'dam Valley, the latter most likely the ancient Zrid (Hazod 2014: 54-55); M-1: ca. 35m; TTT: "0187"; above fn. 53.)

LHUN GRUB:

0191 – Lha khang district: 30 03 15, 91 36 14 / 4130m (M-1: ca. 35m)
0192 – Lha khang district: 30 03 43, 91 33 48 / 4035m (M-1: ca. 35m)
0193 – Lha khang district: 30 04 24, 91 29 40 / 4100m (M-1: ca. 30m)
0194 – Thang mgo district: 30 18 39, 91 29 52 / 4250m (M-1: ca. 30m)
0195 – Bcom mdo district: 30 17 36, 91 24 14 / 4160m (M-1: ca. 30m)
0196 – Bcom mdo district: 30 18 17, 91 24 52 / 4230m
(The central field in this area of Byang (M-1: ca. 40m), west of Rva sgreng; said to be related to the Lcog ro family; TTT: "0196"; above chap. 3.3.1)
0198 – Phu mdo district: 30 08 37, 91 25 53 / 4100m (M-1: ca. 30m)
0199 – Gsum 'phreng district: 30 03 36, 91 17 13 / 4150m
(Single mound (ca. 45m) in the upper Shar valley of 'Phan yul; TTT: "0199".)
0203 – Gsum 'phreng district: 29 59 18, 91 13 14 / 3950m
(The central field of the Shar valley of 'Phan po; M-1: ca. 50m; TTT: "0203".)
0204 – Gsum 'phreng district: 29 58 18, 91 16 16 / 3900m (M-1 ca. 30m; TTT: "0204")
0206 – Gsum 'phreng district: 29 59 01, 91 16 59 / 3930m (M-1: ca. 30m; TTT: "0206")
0207 – Dga' ldan chos skor district: 29 54 55, 91 13 44 / 3810m (A single tomb, ca. 35m)
0213 – Lcang ra shar district: 29 54 25, 91 19 06 / 3825m
(Situated behind the settlement of Brgya grong in central 'Phan po; M-1: ca. 40m; TTT: "0213".)
0368 – Dga' ldan chos skor district: 29 56 40, 91 16 50 / 3900m
(The central field of this part of 'Phan po, situated behind 'Phan po township; M-1 ca. 65m; TTT: "0368".)

0216 – Byang kha district: 29 58 30, 91 10 48 / 3910m

(0216 and 0217 represent the major burial sites of the ancient Ngan lam district of 'Phan yul; M-1: ca. 35m; TTT: "0216"; above chap. 5.1.)

0217 – Byang kha district: 29 58 42, 91 09 48 / 3927m (M-1: ca. 30m; see 0216)

0219 – Byang kha district: 29 57 22, 91 08 04 / 3900m (M-1: ca. 30m, identification uncertain)

0222 – Byang kha district: 29 56 25, 91 07 05 / 3920m (M-1: ca. 35m; identification uncertain)

0225 – Mtsho stod district: 29 57 54, 91 03 54 / 4040m (M-1: ca. 35m)

0227 – Gad po district: 29 53 27, 91 07 54 / 3860m (M-1: ca. 30m)

0230 – Gad po district: 29 53 07, 91 00 06 / 4040m

(Situated in the fields below the Rag ma temple; M-1: ca. 27m; identification unclear; TTT: "0230".)

0235 – Mkhar rtse district: 29 52 28, 91 10 35 / 3940m

(Situated below the Nalendra monastery; M-1 ca. 30m; TTT: "0235".)

0236 – Mkhar rtse district: 29 53 23, 91 10 49 / 3800m

(One of the central elite fields in 'Phan yul; M-1: ca. 45m; TTT: "0236".)

0237 – Grub brgya district: 29 52 52, 91 12 12 / 3810m (M-1: ca. 30m)

0240 – Grub brgya distrct: 29 52 08, 91 13 25 / 3850m

(Situated south of the Glang thang monastery, in terms of number of tombs one of the greatest fields in 'Phan po; see TTT: "0227", "0228" for fields in 'Phan po of similar size.)

0242 – Grub brgya district: 29 51 44, 91 16 39 / 3850m

(Situated next to the ruins of the religious site of 'Bum steng (var. 'Bum sdings) in the small valley due SE of Bon grong, behind Grub brgya Village; two badly damaged stone lions in front of a shrine in 'Bum steng are said to have been found at a tomb of 0242; information by Shawo Khacham, Sept. 2016; see TTT: "0242".)

0244 – Grub brgya district: 29 52 41, 91 15 26 / 3765m

(A single (originally round or oval) mound (ca. 35m), locally described as the resting place of a "lady"; situated in Klu gong village; the latter related to the ritual of Klu gong rgyal po; Hazod 2007a.)

0245 – Lcang ra district: 29 52 01, 91 22 36 / 3820m

(Situated close to Zing ba Village (of ancient Yung ba sna), below the ruins locally related to the seat of one of the pre-historic "Zing po rje" rulers (Stag skya bo and Khri pang sum) who are associated with this area of 'Phan po and the northern part of present-day Stag rtse County (cf. TTT: map "Kyitö"; on the Zing po rje account in PT 1287 see most recently Bialek 2016: 123-126; Dungkar 2011: 157ff.). Next to the graves (MT-1: ca. 25m) are the remains of the village Bänkha (Bran kha), described as the birthplace of the monk minister Bran kha Dpal yon; TTT: "0245"; Hazod 2013.)

0246 – Lcang ra district: 29 51 51, 91 23 28 / 3910m

(Situated behind the village of Ka 'khor (locally spelled as Ka'u), south-east of Zing ba (0245); the ruins of an unknown monastic complex (L: 70m) are in the upper part of the grave field; in Hazod 2009: 184-185 suspected being the remains of a tomb; M-1: ca. 35-40m; TTT: "0246".)

0253 – Dpal 'byor gling district: 29 47 30, 91 24 36 / 3785m (M-1 ca. 30m)

CHU SHUR:

0257 –Tshal sna district: 29 30 11, 90 58 98 / 3665m

(The central elite field of Lower Skyid smad; M-1: ca. 50m; above chap. 3.3.1; TTT: "0257".)

0266 – Gnam district: 29 23 40, 90 53 07/ 3625m (M-1: ca. 35m; TTT: "0266")

0269 – Chu phu district: 29 22 26, 90 44 03 / 6340m (M-1: ca. 30m)

SNYE MO:

0274 – Phu gsum district: 29 30 02, 90 09 43 / 4080m

(The central elite field of this district; M-1: ca. 55m; TTT: "0274".)

0276 – Snye mo district: 29 23 59, 90 06 26 / 3995m (M-1 ca. 35m)

RGYAL RTSE:

0278 – Rtse chen district: 28 55 51, 89 30 26 / 4070m

(The central elite field of ancient Myang ro, the area around present-day Rgyal rtse in Gtsang; M-1 of ca. 55m; TTT: "0278"; Hazod 2009: 187-189; Hazod 2013.)

0280 – Lcang ra district: 28 53 22, 89 33 19 / 4045m (M-1: ca. 30m)

0281 – 'Brong rtse district: 29 00 31, 89 26 54/ 4017m

(Situated in the Ser po valley of central Myang; M-1: ca. 35m; TTT: "0281")

0282 – Ri nang district: 28 55 16, 89 42 36/ 4190m (M-1 ca. 40m)

0283 – (district unknown): 29 02 19, 89 28 26 / 3985m (single mound, ca. 35m)

PA SNAM:

0284 – Khyung rtse district: 29 07 25, 89 17 38/ 4075 (M-1: ca. 30m)

0286 – Dbang ldan district: 28 56 38, 89 10 00 / 4070m (M-1: ca. 35m)

GZHIS KHA RTSE:

0292 – Lhan district: 29 18 13 89 33 54 / 4100m (M-1: ca. 30m)

0295 – Dung dkar district: 29 23 12, 88 59 05 / 3910m (M-1: ca. 30m)

KHANG DMAR:

0298 – Sa ma mda' district: 28 24 35, 89 32 17/ 4470m

(This grave field of smaller (MT-A type?) of mounds is situated next to the imperial Rgyang bu temple; see Fig. 1 of TTT: "0298".)

RIN SPUNG:

0303 – Smon shang district: 29 17 14, 89 45 20/ 3970m (M-1: ca. 30m)

SA SKYA:

0308 – Gzhong ma district: 29 02 48, 88 23 31/ 4110m

(The central grave field in the Shab valley; M-1: ca. 30m; TTT: "0308".)

0313 – (district unclear): Shab dge sdings: 29 11 36, 88 26 53/ 3985m

(Single mound (ca. 35m) not far from the entrance to the Shab valley.)

RNAM GLING:

0315 – Rtse gdong district: 29 23 11, 89 14 39 / 3830m

(This refers to a larger field of mostly smaller (MT-B) mounds not far from the imperial "border temple" of Gtsang 'Bram; Hazod 2009: 191, 221; TTT: "0315".)

0409 – Stag rtse district: 29 36 44, 89 33 36 / 4420m (M-1: ca. 50m)

0410 – Thob rgyal district: 29 27 38, 89 27 03 / 4070m

(Single mound (ca. 35m) in the Thob rgyal valley)

BSHAD MTHONG SMON:

0317 – Mthong smon district: 29 23 04, 88 08 17 / 4078m (M-1: ca. 35m)

0319 – Mthong smon district: 29 24 25, 88 10 20 / 4107m

(One of the central fields of the Left Horn province; at some distance to the east there is a larger single mound, ca. 50m; TTT: "0319".)

NGAM RING:

0323 – Chu 'og district: 29 25 04, 87 34 52 / 4123m (M-1: ca. 40m)

0324 – Chu 'og district: 29 23 02, 87 31 05 / 4150m

(One of the greatest elite fields of imperial Left Horn; M-1 ca. 55m; TTT: "0324".)

0325 – Chu 'og district: 29 23 09, 87 30 13 / 4120m

(Single mound (ca. 65m), situated not far from 0324; TTT: "0325".)

LHA RTSE:

0329 – Bkra shis sgang district: 29 15 40, 88 06 41 / 4040m

(A significant elite burial mound site, not far from the monastery of Bo dong E; above fn. 62; M-1: ca. 65m.)

0330 – Lha rtse district: 29 12 37, 87 26 41 / 4320m

(M-1: ca. 30m; Hazod 2009: 189-190, for a first description of this significant site of ancient Bom ma; TTT: "0330".)

0331 – Lha rtse district: 29 12 31, 87 26 38/ 4315m (Situated next to 0330)

0332 – Lha rtse/ Chu shar district: 29 06 17, 87 35 50/ 4050m

(This represents one of the largest grave fields (in terms of number of tombs), partly destroyed by modern building projects; TTT: "0332".)

0333 – Lha rtse/ Chu shar district: 29 06 16, 87 35 24 / 4050m

(Situated next to 0332; M-1 appears to be a "twin-grave" of ca. 35m; TTT: "0333".)

0335 – Mang phu district: 29 00 17, 87 37 48 / 4290m (M-1: ca. 30m)

0336 – Mang phu district: 28 57 45, 87 38 38 / 4325m (M-1: ca. 35m)

0337 – Gzhis chen district: 29 03 36, 87 41 16 / 4120m (M-1: ca. 45m)

0339 – Lha rtse district: 29 21 33, 87 48 42 / 4120m

(The site of Khrom chen, with more than 130 mounds; M-1 (with two stone lions in front): ca. 75m; TTT: "0339".)

0340 – Lha rtse district: 29 21 31, 87 49 16 / 4110m

(Situated next to 0339, with more than 30 tombs; M-1: ca. 45m.)

GTING SKYES:

0341 – Gting skyes district: 28 18 59, 87 46 18 / 4240m (M-1: ca. 35m)

DING RI:

(An area with 12 grave fields (0343-0349; 0411-0415), including mounds of max. 25m.)

(2a)

(2b)

Fig. 2a-b. The FT-A and -B types of burial mound fields: The examples of Lo (0128, 2a) and Sbrang (0058, 2b). (Hazod 2014, 2010)

Fig. 3a. A round burial mound with square ground-plan: M-1 of 0184. (Hazod 2010)

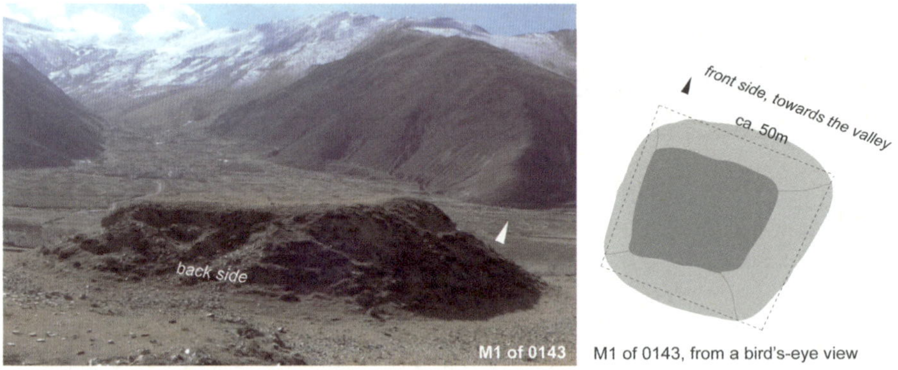

Fig. 3b. The classical trapecoidal MT-C mound: The central tomb of 0143. (Hazod 2015)

Fig. 4. The stupa shaped MT-D mound of Ngan lam Sri (0397). (Hazod 2015)

Fig. 5. The type of "coffer-shaped" mounds: M-1 of 0038. (Hazod 2008)

Fig. 6. The many tombs of 0270 with mostly round tombs of various sizes. (Hazod 2009)

Fig. 7. The grave field of Sgang skyid (0172), central part (Hazod 2013).

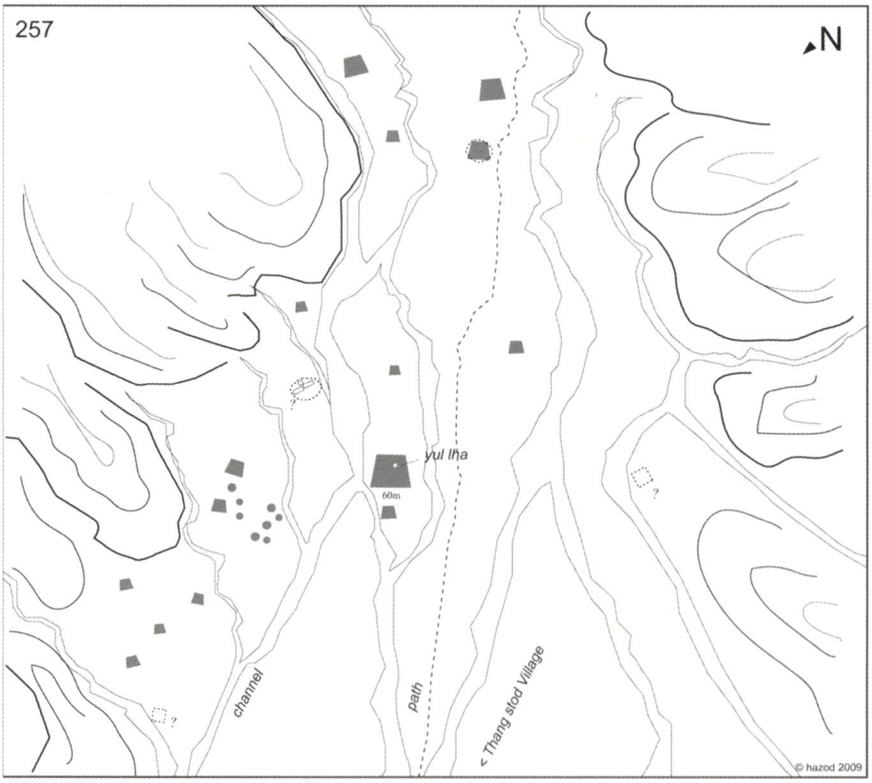

Fig. 8. The grave field of Thang stod (0257). (Hazod 2009)

Fig. 9.
The "Kha'u zhang zig" seal from the burial site of Slebs (0092). (Feiglstorfer, Hazod 2015)

Fig. 10.
The tomb in Zhang mda' (0037).(Hazod 2005)

Fig. 11.
The central burial site of Lho brag (0065).(Phtoto: XWD 119)

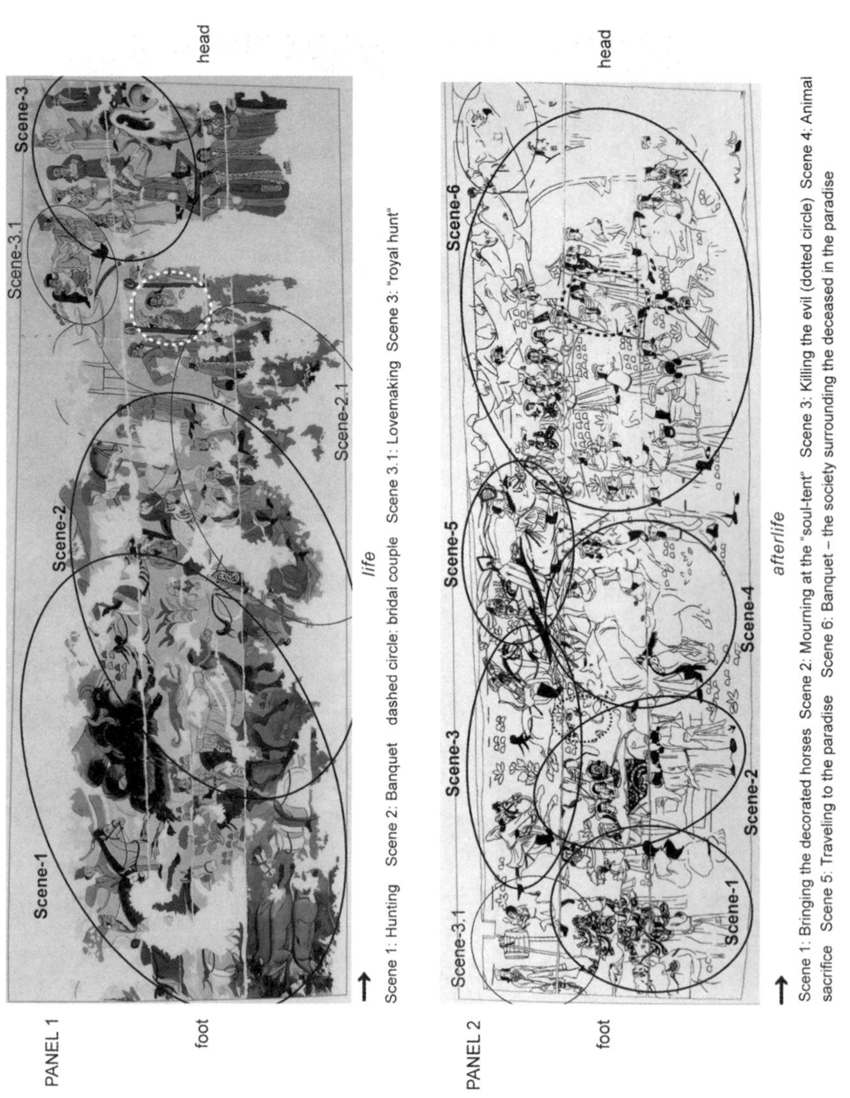

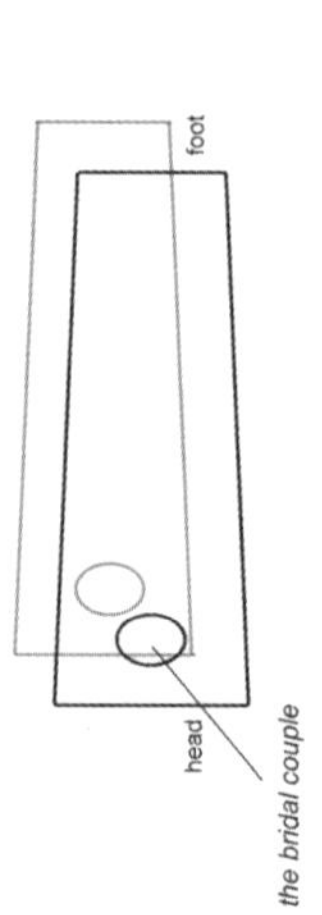

Fig. 12. The Guolimu coffin panels.
(Drawing based on Tong Tao and Wertmann 2010)

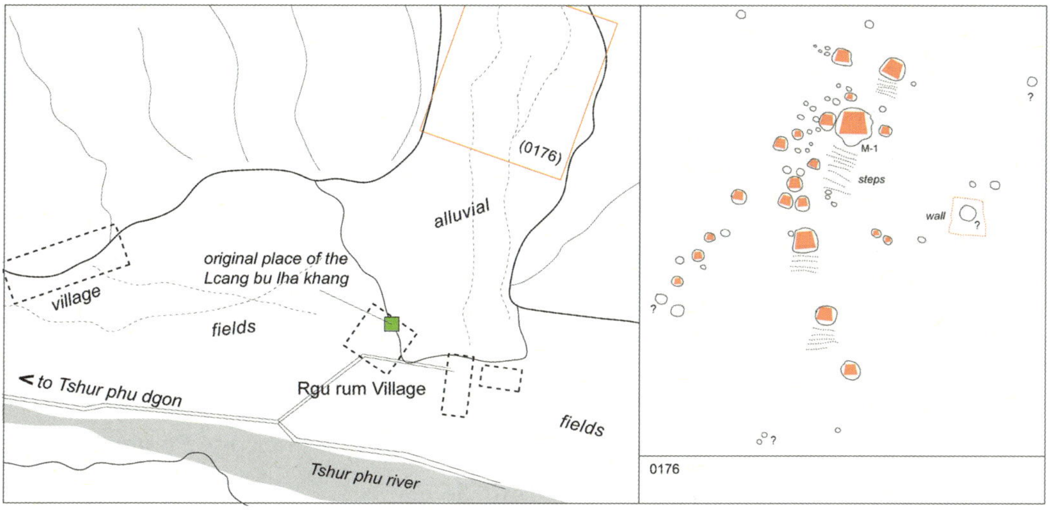

Fig. 13. The area of the "willow park of Stod lung", with the cemetery of 0176 behind Rgu rum Village. (Hazod 2018)

References (Incl. abbreviations)

Aldenderfer, Mark. 2013. Variation in mortuary practice on the early Tibetan plateau and the high Himalayas, *Journal of the International Association for Bon Research*, vol. 1, 293-317.

Allsen, Thomas, T. 2006. *The Royal Hunt in Eurasian History*. Philadelphia: University of Pennsylvania Press.

Annals = *OTA*, see Dotson 2009a.

Ardussi, John. 2007. A preliminary investigation of Bhutanese castle ruins and caves associated with Lha sras Gtsang ma, in: Ardussi, John and Françoise Pommaret (ed.), *Bhutan: Tradition and Changes*. Leiden: Brill, 5-26.

BA = Roerich, George N. 1995. *The Blue Annals*. Delhi: Motilal Banarsidass [Repr. of 1949].

Bacot, Jacques, Frederick W. Thomas, Charles G. Touissaint. 1940-1946. *Documents de Touen-houang relatifs a l'histoire du Tibet*. Paris: Libraire Orientaliste Paul Geuthner.

Beckwith, Christopher I. 1987. *The Tibetan Empire in Central Asia*. Princeton: Princeton University Press.

— 2009. *Empires of the Silk road. A History of Central Eurasia from the Bronze Age to the Present*. Princeton: Pinceton University Press.

Bellezza, Johon V. 2002. *Antiquities of Upper Tibet: Pre-Buddhist Archaeological Sites on the High Plateau*. Delhi: Adroit Publishers.

— 2008. *Zhang Zhung: Foundations of Civilization in Tibet: A Historical and Ethnoarchaeological Study of the Monuments, Rock Art, Texts and Oral Tradition of the Ancient Tibetan Upland*. Wien: Verlag der Österreichischen Akademie der Wissenschaften.

— 2013. *Death and Beyond in Ancient Tibet: Archaic Concepts and Practices in a Thousand-year-old Illuminated Funerary Manuscript and Old Tibetan Funerary Documents of Gathang Bumpa and Dunhuang*. Wien: Verlag der Österreichischen Akademie der Wissenschaften.

— 2014. Tibet Archaeology: Flight of the Khyung, at www.tibetarchaeology.com/december-2014.

Bemmann, Jan. 2011. Was the center of the Xiongnu empire in the Orkhon valley? in: Brosseder, Ulrike and Bryan K. Miller (eds.), *Xiongnu Archaeology*. Bonn Contributions to Asian Archaeology Vol. 5, Bonn: Rheinische Friedrich-Wilhelms-Universität Bonn, 441-461

Bialek, Joanna. 2015. *Studies in the Lexis and Word-Formations of Old Tibetan: Compounds and Compounding*. Dissertation, manuscript submitted in 2015, Marburg University.

— 2016. Side, stench, remnant, plot, oath, and craftiness – the semantic 'capacity' of the OT *dku*, *Revue d'Etudes Tibétaines* 35: 115-167.

Bloch, Maurice. 2013. *In and Out of Each Other's Body: Theory of Mind, Evolution, Truth, and the Nature of the Social*. London: Paradigm Publishers.

Brosseder, Ulrike and Bryan K. Miller (eds.), *Xiongnu Archaeology*. Bonn Contributions to Asian Archaeology Vol. 5, Bonn: Rheinische Friedrich-Wilhelms-Universität Bonn.

Bushell, S.W. 1880. The Early History of Tibet from Chinese sources, *Journal of the Royal Asiatic Society* 12, 435-541.

Caffarelli, Paola M. V. 1997. Architectural style in tombs from the period of the kings, in: Singer J.C. and Phillip Denwood (eds.), *Tibetan Art: Towards a Definition of Style*. London: L. King, 230-261.

CDR = Jo bo lce'i gdung rabs, i.e. Chos grva chen po dpal zhva lu gser khang bdag po jo bo lce'i gdung rabs, TBRC 6087.

CFS = Tsering Gyalbo, Guntram Hazod, Per K. Sørensen. 2000. *Civilization at the Foot of Mount Sham-po. The Royal House of lHa-Bug-pa-can and the History of g.Ya'-bzang. Historical Texts from the Monastery of g.Ya'-bzang in Yar-stod (Central Tibet). Annotated Translation, Transliteration and Facsimile Edition*. Wien: Verlag der Österreichischen Akademie der Wissenschaften.

Chaka Dawa (Lcags kha Zla ba). 2013. *Mal dro gung dkar gyi lo rgyus dvangs gsal chu mo'i rgyun bzang*. Lhasa: Bod ljongs mi dmangs dpe skrun khang.

Chayet, Anne. 1994a. *Art et Archéologie du Tibet*. Paris: Picard.

— 1994b. Les frères écartés: questions sur l'ordre successoral dans la monarchie Tibétaine, in: Kvaerne, Per (ed.), *Tibetan Studies*. Oslo: Institute for Comparative Research in Human Culture, 116-26.

Chu Junjie 褚俊杰 . 1990.Tufan yuangu shizu "qia" "mu" yanjiu 吐蕃远古氏族 "恰"、"穆" 研究 (Study on Phywa and Dmu, two important clans in Ancient Tibet), *Zangxue yanjiu luncong* 藏学研究论丛 2: 1-47.

— 1991. A study of Bon-po funeral ritual in ancient Tibet: Deciphering the Pelliot Tibetan

Mss 1042, in: Hu tan (ed.), *Theses on Tibetology in China.* Beijing: China Tibetology Publishing House, pp. 91-151.

Claessen, Henri and P. Skalnik. 1978. *The Early State: A Structural Approach.* The Hague: Mouton.

Czaja. Olaf. 2013. *Medieval Rule in Tibet. The Rlangs Clan and the Politcal and Religious History of the Ruling House of Phag mo gru pa. With a Study of the Monastic Art of Gdan sa mthil.* Wien: Verlag der Österreichischen Akademie der Wissenschaften.

Di Cosmo, Nicola. 2010 (repr. 2002). *Ancient China and Its Enemies: The Rise of Nomadic Power in East Asian History.* Cambridge: Cambridge University Press.

— 1999. State formation and periodization in Inner Asian history, *Journal of World History* 10(1): 1-40.

Diemberger, Hildegard, Pasang Wangdu, M. Kornfeld, and C. Jahoda. 1997. *Feast of Miracles: The Life and Tradition of Bodong Chole Namgyal (1375/6–1451 A.D.).* Clusone: Porong Pema Choling Editions.

Dotson, Brandon. 2004. A note on zhang: maternal relatives of the Tibetan royal line, *Journal Asiatique* 292.1-2: 75-99.

— 2007a. Administration and law in the Tibetan empire: the section on law and state and its Old Tibetan antecedents. D.Phil. thesis, Oxford University.

— 2007b. "Emperor" Mu rug btsan and the *'Phang thang ma catalogue, Journal of the International Association of Tibetan Studies* 3: 1-25.

— 2009a. *The Old Tibetan Annals. An Annotated Translation of Tibet's First History.* Wien: Verlag der Österreichischen Akademie der Wissenschaften.

— 2009b. The "nephew-uncle" relationship in the international diplomacy of the Tibetan Empire (7th–9th centuries), in: Dotson, Brandon., K. N. Gurung, G. Halkias, and T. Myatt (eds.), *Contemporary Visions in Tibetan Studies. Proceedings of the First International Seminar of Young Tibetologists, London, 9–13 August 2007.* Chicago: Serindia Publications, 223-38.

— 2013. The princess and the yak: the hunt as narrative trope and historical reality, in: Dotson, Brandon, K. Iwao, and T. Takeuchi (eds.), *Scribes, Texts, and Rituals in Early Tibet and Dunhuang: Proceedings of the Third Old Tibetan Studies Panel held at the Seminar of the International Association for Tibetan Studies, Vancouver 2010.* Wiesbaden: Reichert Verlag, 61-85.

Drikung 2011 = H.H. the Drikung Kyabgon Chetsang ('Bri gung Skyabs mgon Che tshang Dkon mchog bstan 'dzin 'phrin las lhun 'grub). 2011. *A History of the Tibetan Empire: Drawn from the Dunhuang Manuscripts*. Translated by Meghan Howard with Tsultrim Nakchu (Orginal published as *Bod btsan po'i rgyal rabs: Tun hong bod kyi yig rnying las byung ba* 2010). Dehra Dun: Songtsen Libary, Center for Tibetan and Himalayan Studies.

DTH = Bacot, Jacques *et al*. 1940-1946.

Dungkar = Lhag pa Phun tshogs *et al*. (eds.). 2002. *Dung dkar tshig mdzod chen mo*. Beijing: Krung go'i bod rigs pa dpe skrun khang.

Eckfeld, Tonia. 2005. *Imperial Tombs in Tang China, 618-907. The Politics of Paradise*. London: Routledge.

Everding, Karl-Heinz. 2000. *Der Gung-thang dkar-chag*. Monumenta Tibetica Historica Abt. 1. Band 5. Bonn: VGH Wissenschaftsverlag GmbH.

Everding, Karl-Heinz und Dzongphugpa, Dawa Dargya. 2006. *Das tibetischen Fürstentum La-stod lHo (um 1265–1642)*. Wiesbaden: Reichert Verlag.

Feiglstorfer, Hubert. 2015. The burial mounds of Central Tibet: Layout, construction, material, unpubl. paper, at http://www.oeaw.ac.at/tibetantumulustradition/de/startseite/.

Garatti, Emanuela. 2015. Shifting memories and changing allegiances: Tracing the descendants of the Tibetan minister mGar through Chinese funerary Inscriptions, *Revue d'Etudes Tibétaines* 33: 155-185.

Gyatso, Janet. 2006. A partial genealogy of the lifestory of Ye shes mtsho rgyal, *Journal of the International Association of Tibetan Studies* 2 (August 2006): 1-27.

GYC = *Gsang ba yang chung* (in *lDe'u-2* 376.15-380.11).

Haarh, Eric. 1969. *The Yar-luṅ dynasty: A Study with Particular Regard to the Contribution by Myths and Legends to the History of Ancient Tibet and the Origin and Nature of Its Kings*. København: Gad.

Hazod, Guntram. 1998. bKra-shis 'od-'bar. On the history of the religious protector of the Bo-dong-pa, in: Blondeau, A.-M. (ed.), *Tibetan Mountain Deities. Their Cults and Representations*. Wien: Verlag der Österreichischen Akademie der Wissenschaften, 57-78.

— 2007a. In the garden of the White Mare – Encounters with history and cult in Tshal Gung-thang, in: Sørensen, P. K. and Guntram Hazod, in cooperation with Tsering

Gyalbo, *Rulers on the Celestial Plain. Ecclesiastic and Secular Hegemony in Medieval Tibet. A Study of Tshal Gung-thang*. 2 Vols. Wien: Verlag der Österreichischen Akademie der Wissenschaften, 571-632.

— 2007b. The grave on the 'cool plane': On the identification of the Tibet's 'first tomb' in Nga-ra-thang of 'Phyong-po, in: Kellner, Birgit *et al.* (ed.), *Pramāṇakīrtiḥ. Papers dedicated to Ernst Steinkellner on the Occasion of his 70th Birthday*. Wien: Arbeitskreis für Tibetische und Buddhistische Studien, 259-283.

— 2009. Imperial Central Tibet – An annotated cartographical survey of its territorial divisions and key political sites, in: Dotson, Brandon, *The Old Tibetan Annals. An Annotated Translation of Tibet's First History*. Wien: Verlag der Österreichischen Akademie der Wissenschaften, 161-232.

— 2010. Wandering Monuments: The Discovery of the Place of Origin of the Shöl Stele of Lhasa, *Orientations* 41(3), April 2010, pp. 31-36.

— 2013. The plundering of the Tibetan royal tombs. An analysis of the event in the context of the uprisings in Central Tibet of the 9th/ 10th century, in: Cüppers, Christopher and Robert Mayer (eds.), *Tibet after Empire: Culture, Society and Religion between 850-1000*. Lumbini: Lumbini International Research Institute, 85-115.

— 2014. The stele in the centre of the Lhasa Mandala: About the position of the 9th-century Sino-Tibetan treaty pillar of Lhasa in its historical-geographical and narrative context, in: Tropper, Kurt (ed.), *Epigraphic Evidence in the Pre-modern Buddhist World*, Wien: Arbeitskreis für tibetische und Buddhistische Studien, 37-81.

— 2015. The lions of 'Chad kha: A note on new findings of stone monuments in Central Tibet from the Tibetan imperial period, in: Hazod, Guntram and Olaf Czaja (eds.), *The Illuminating Mirror: Festschrift for Per K. Sørensen on the Occasion of his 65th Birthday*. Wiesbaden: Reichert Verlag, 189-204.

— 2016. Burial in the Landscape: Remarks on the topographical setting of the grave mounds in early Central Tibet, paper held at the 14th Seminar of the International Association for Tibetan Studies, 19th to 25th June 2016, Bergen, Norway; access of the pdf (incl. illustrations) at www. oeaw.ac.at/tibetantumulustradition.

— Forthcoming. The 'anti-Buddhist law' and its author in eighth-century Tibet: A reconsideration of the story of Zhang Ma zhang Grom pa skyes, in: Eltschinger, Vincent *et al.* (eds.), *Festschrift for Cristina Scherrer-Schaub*.

Heller, Amy. 2006. Preliminary remarks on the archaeological investigations of Dulan: 8th-9th century Tibetan tombs? In: Xie Jisheng 谢继胜, Shen Weirong 沈卫荣, Liao Yang 廖旸 (eds.), *Studies in Sino-Tibetan Buddhist Art* 汉藏佛教艺术研究. Beijing: China Tibetology Publishing House, 57-76.

— 2013. Obeservation on painted coffin panels of the Tibetan Empire, in: Cüppers, Christopher and Robert Mayer (eds.), *Tibet after Empire: Culture, Society and Religion between 850-1000*. Lumbini: Lumbini International Research Institute, 117-168.

Hill, Nathan. 2006. The old Tibetan chronicle – chapter I, *Revue d'Études Tibétaines* 10: 89-101.

—2008. Verba Moriendi in the Old Tibetan Annals, in: Beckwith, Christopher I. (ed.), *Medieval Tibeto-Burman Languages III*, International Institute for Tibetan and Buddhist Studies, Halle (Saale), 71-86.

—2013. 'Come as lord of the black-headed' – an old Tibetan mythic formula, in: Cüppers, Christoph, R. Mayer, and M. Walter (eds.), *Tibet after Empire: Culture, Society and Religion between 850-1000*. Lumbini. LIRI, 169-179.

Holcombe, Charles. 2013. The Xianbei in Chinese history, *Early Medieval China* 19: 1-38.

Huo Wei. 2010. Engraved on the stone: Tubo stone inscription in Lhodrak, *China's Tibet* 117(1): 48-51.

Imaeda, Yoshiro, M. Kapstein and T. Takeuchi (eds.). 2007. *Tibetan Documents from Dunhuang* (Old Tibetan Documents Online Monograph Series Vol. I). Tokyo: Tokyo University of Foreign Studies.

Ishikawa Iwao. 2001. Kodai Chibetto ni okeru reishin saigi no monogatari honyaku hen (Japanese translation of the story about the ancient Tibetan "bla" ritual), *Tōhō* 16: 145-158.

ITJ = IOL Tib J, see *TDD*.

Jampa Tenzin (Byams pa Bstan 'dzin). 2010. *Yar lha sham po'i gnas yig dwangs gsal me long*. Lhasa: Bod ljongs mi dmangs dpe skrun khang.

Jampel Tsondru ('Jam dpal Brtson 'grus). 2010. *Lho brag gnas yig*. Beijing: Mi rigs dpe skrun khang.

Ka khol ma = *Bka' chems Ka khol ma*. Lanzhou: Kan su mi rigs dpe skrun khang 1989.

KG = Dpa' bo Gtsug lag phreng ba, *Chos 'byung mkhas pa'i dga' ston*. 2 Vols. Beijing: Mi rigs dpe skrun khang 1986.

Kaiser, Knut, G. Miehe, W. H. Schoch, A. Zander, A., F. Schluetz. 2006. Relief, soil and lost forests: Late Holocene environmental changes in southern Tibet under human impact. *Zeitschrift für Geomorphologie* (Suppl. 142), 149-173.

Kapstein, Matthew. 2000. *The Tibetan Assimilation of Buddhism. Conversion, Contestation, and Memory*. Oxford: University Press.

Karmay, Samten. 1998. *The Arrow and the Spindle. Studies in History, Myths, Rituals and Beliefs in Tibet*. Kathmandu: Mandala Book Point.

Kradin, Nikolai N. 2011. Stateless empire: The structures of the Xiongnu nomadic super-complex chiefdom, in: Brosseder, Ulrike and Bryan K. Miller (eds.), *Xiongnu Archaeology*. Bonn Contributions to Asian Archaeology Vol. 5, Bonn: Rheinische Friedrich-Wilhelms-Universität Bonn, 77-96.

KT = O rgyan gling pa, *Bka' thang sde lnga*, 5 books. Beijing: Mi rigs dpe skrun khang 1986.

Lde'u-1 = Lde'u jo sras, *Chos 'byung chen mo bstan pa'i rgyal mtshan lde'u jo sras kyis mdzad pa*. Lhasa: Bod ljongs mi dmangs dpe skrun khang 1987.

Lde'u-2 = Mkhas pa Lde'u, *Rgya bod kyi chos 'byung rgyas pa*. Lhasa: Bod ljongs mi rigs dpe skrun khang 1987.

Lhagdron (Lhag sgron). 2014. *Bod kyi gna' rabs mchims kyi rus rgyud skor brdzod pa*, Lhasa: Bod ljongs mi dmangs dpe skrun khang.

Li, Fang Kuei and W. South Coblin. 1987. *A Study of the Old Tibetan Inscriptions*. Taipei Institute of History and Philology, Academica Sinica 91. Nanking, Taipei.

Li Yingfu 李映福 and Ha Bibu 哈比布 . 2014. Xizang Duilongdeqing Gachong cun Yizhi Yelian Yiwu de Faxian yu Chubu Yanjiu 西藏堆龙德庆县噶冲村遗址冶炼遗物的发现与初步研究 (The discovery and preliminary research on smelting remains found in the Gargrong village site, Duilung dechen County, TAR), *Journal of Tibetology* 藏学学刊 10: 1-10.

Lobsang Nyima (Blo bzang Nyi ma). 2011. *'Bro tshang gi lo rgyus dang de las 'phros pa'i 'bro bza' khri ma lod kyi skor rags tsam dpyad pa*. Lhasa: Bod ljongs mi dmangs dpe skrun khang.

Martin, Dan. 1999. 'Ol-mo-lung-ring, the original holy place. In: Huber, Toni (ed.), *Sacred Spaces and Powerful Places in Tibetan Culture*. Dharamsala: LTWA. 258-301.

— 2001. *Unearthing Bon Treasuries. Life and Contested Legacy of a Tibetan Scripture*

Revealer. Leiden: Brill.

Miehe, Georg, Sabine Miehe, Frank Schlütz, Knut Kaiser, La Duo. 2006. Palaeoecological and experimental evidence of former forests and woodlands in the treeless desert pastures of Southern Tibet (Lhasa, A.R. Xizang, China), *Palaeogeography, Palaeoclimatology, Palaeoecology* 242 (2006): 54-67 (Available online at www.sciencedirect.com).

Munkh-Erdene, Lhamsuren. 2016. Political Order in pre-modern Eurasia: Imperial incorporation and the hereditary divisional system, *Journal of the Royal Asiatic Society*: 1-23 (online publication, available on CJO 2016 doi:10.1017/S1356186316000237).

Nyang ral = Nyang-ral Nyi-ma 'od-zer, *Chos 'byung me tog snying po sbrang rtsi'i bcud*. Lhasa: Bod ljongs mi dmangs dpe skrun khang 1988.

Nyi ma = Gu ge Pandita Grags pa rgyal mtshan. *Nyi ma'i rigs kyi rgyal rabs dang zla ba'i rigs kyi rgyal rabs*, in: Gangs can gtsug lag rin chen phreng ba, Vol. 7, Lhasa 2014.

OA = Darvill, Tomothy. 2008. *The Concise Oxford Dictionary of Archaeology*. Oxford: Oxford University Press.

Orosz, Gergely. 2003. Folk religion in the ritual manuscripts of ancient Tibet, in: B. Kelényi, (ed.), *Demons and Protectors: Folk Religion in Tibetan and Mongolian Buddhism*. Budapest: Ferenc Hopp Museum of Eastern Asiatic Art, 19-26.

OTA = *Old Tibetan Annals*, Dotson 2009a.

OTC = Old Tibetan Chronicle (PT 1287; *see TDD*).

OTI = Iwao, Kazushi, N. Hill, and T. Takeuchi (eds.). 2009. *Old Tibetan Inscriptions*. Tokyo: Re-search Institute for Languages and Cultures of Asia and Africa, Tokyo University of Foreign Studies.

PK = O rgyan glingpa, *Padma bka'i thang yig*. Chengdu: Si khron mi rigs dpe skrun khang 1996.

PT= Pelliot tibétain; see *TDD*.

Panglung, Jampa. 1988. Die metrischen Berichte über die Grabmäler der tibetischen Könige. Ihre Überlieferung und ihr Beitrag zur Identifizierung, in: Uebach, Helgaand Jampa Panglung (eds.), *Tibetan Studies*. München, 321-368.

Pearson, Mike P. 2003 (repr. 1999). *The Archaeology of Death and Burial*. Stroud: The History Press.

Pezhung 2013 = Pad gzhung Zla ba chung bdag. 2013. *Btsan po'i rgyal rabs skabs kyi dpon rigs zhib 'jug*. Lhasa: Bod ljongs mi dmangs dpe skrun khang.

Puchung Tsering. 2011. *The History of Zha lu Monastery, Ri sbug Hermitage and rGyan gong Temple*. Dissertation, Oslo: Department of Cultural Studies and Oriental Languages.

Ramble, Charles. 2007. The Aja: Fragments of an unknown Tibetan priesthood, in: Kellner, Birgit, H. Krasser, H. Lasic, M.T. Much, and H. Tauscher (eds.), *Pramanakirtih. Papers Dedicated to Ernst Steinkellner on the Occasion of his 70th Birthday*. Part 1. Wien: WSTB 70.1, 683-720.

— 2015. Fearless dawn, bloodless demon: Literary and iconograpic manifestations of a little-known Bonpo protector, in: Havnevik, H. and C. Ramble (eds.), *From Bhakti to Bon Festschrift for Per Kvaerne*, Oslo: Novus Forlag, 409-430.

Rang sgra. 1999. *Thon mi Sambho ta*. Xining: Mtsho sngon mi rigs dpe skrun khang.

Richardson, Hugh E. 1985. *A Corpus of Early Tibetan Inscriptions*. London: Royal Asiatic Society.

— 1998 *High Peaks, Pure Earth. Collected Writings on Tibetan History and Culture*. Edited with an Introduction by Michael Aris, London: Serindia Publications.

Roesler, Ulrike (2007a). A palace for those who have eyes to see: Preliminary remarks on the symbolic geography of Reting (Rwa-sgreng), *Acta Orientalia Vilnensia* 8(1): 123-144.

Rva lo = Rva Ye shes seng ge, *Rva lo tsā ba rnam thar* [i.e *Mthu stobs dbang phyug rje btsun rva lo tsā ba'i rnam par thar pa Kun khyab snyan pa'i rnga sgra*]. Xining: Mtsho sngon mi rigs dpe skrun khang, 1997.

RCP = Per K. Sørensen and Guntram Hazod, in cooperation with Tsering Gyalbo, *Rulers on the Celestial Plain. Ecclesiastic and Secular Hegemony in Medieval Tibet. A Study of Tshal Gung-thang*. 2 Vols. Wien: Verlag der Österreichischen Akademie der Wissenschaften.

SCB = Pasang Wangdu and Hildegard Diemberger, in Cooperation with Guntram Hazod. 1996. *Shel dkar chos 'byung (History of the "White Crystal") by Ngag dbang skal ldan rgya mtsho: Religion and Politics of Southern La stod*. Wien: Verlag der Österreichischen Akademie der Wissenschaften.

Shawo Khacham (Sha bo Mkha' byams). 2014a. *Tubo wangling de kaogu faxian yu yanjiu* 吐蕃王陵的考古发现与研究 (Archaeological study of Tibetan imperial Tumuli);

Dissertation, Sichuan University.

— 2014b. Chamuqin shibei yu tubo muqun zhuren zhi xinkao 查木钦石碑与吐蕃墓群主人之新考 (A Re-examination of the Khrom chen tombs in Lha rtse, TAR), *Journal of Tibetology* 10, 2014.

Smith, Alexander. 2011. Remarks concerning the methodology and symbolism of Bon pebble divination. *Études mongoles, sibériennes, centrasiatiques et tibétaines* 42. URL: http://emscat.revues.org/1872.

SXL = Shaanxi Province Archaeology Institute and Lho kha Prefecture Cultural Biro. 2014. Report on the Skyid stod bang so of Lho brag, *China Academic Journal Publishing House* 6/2014: 15-26, at http://www.cnki.net (access 3/2015).

Schaik, Sam van. 2007. The red-faced men III: The red-faced women, at http://earlytibet.com/2007/10/05/red-faced-men-iii/

— 2011. *Tibet. A History*. New Haven and London: Yale University Press.

Smith, Alexander. 2011. Remarks concerning the methodology and symbolism of Bon pebble divination, *Études mongoles, sibériennes, centrasiatiques et tibétaines* 42: 2-15.

Smith, Gene E. 2001. *Among Tibetan Texts. History and Literature of the Himalayan Plateau*. Boston: Wisdom Publications.

Sneath, David. 2013. Ayimag, uymaq and bylik: Re-examinng notions of the nomadic tribe and state, in: Paul, Jürgen (ed.), *Nomad Aristocrats in a World of Empires*, Wiesbaden: Reichert Verlag, 161-186.

Sonam Wangdu (Bsod nams dbang 'dus). 2010. A Report of the archeological research done on the Tibetan plateau and conjectures about future developments (English version of the Tibetan original published in *Bod ljong zhib 'jug* vol. 2 (1997), transl. by Yeshi Dhondup), *The Tibet Journal* 35.3 (2010): 41-59.

Stein, Rolf. 2010. *Tibetica Antiqua: With Additional Materials*. Translated and edited. by A. P. McKeown. Leiden: Brill.

Sørensen, Per K. 1994. *Tibetan Buddhist Historiography: The Mirror Illuminating the Royal Genealogies. An Annotated Translation of the XIVth Century Tibetan Chronicle rGyal-rabs gsal-ba'i me-long*. Wiesbaden: Otto Harrassowitz Verlag.

— 2007. Control of the Lhasa mandala zone: Geo-political schemes, national monuments, flood control politics and ideological battlefield, in: Per K. Sørensen and Guntram Hazod, in cooperation with Tsering Gyalbo, *Rulers on the Celestial Plain: Ecclesiastic and Secular Hegemony in Medieval Tibet. A Study of Tshal Gung-thang*. 2 Vols. Wien: Verlag der Österreichischen Akademie der Wissenschaften, 401-550.

Takeuchi, T. 1995. *Old Tibetan Contracts from Central Asia*. Tokyo: Daizo Shuppan.

— 1998. *Old Tibetan Manuscripts from East Turkestan in the Stein Collection of the British Library*, vols. 2; The Centre for East Asian Cultural Studies for Unesco. London: The Toyo Bunko and The British Library.

TDD = *Tibetan Documents from Dunhuang*, see Imaeda *et al*. 2007.

TF = Sørensen, Per K. and G. Hazod, in cooperation with Tsering Gyalbo. 2005. *Thundering Falcon: An Inquiry into the History and Cult of Khra-'brug, Tibet's First Buddhist Temple*. Wien: Verlag der Österreichischen Akademie der Wissenschaften.

Thaba Tashi Dondrub (Mtha' ba Bkra shis Don 'grub). 2009. *Dpa' bo'i bzhud lam: Blon chen po mgar stong btsan yul bzung dang khong gi gdung rgyud la dpyad pa*. Beijing: Krung go'i bod rig pa dpe skrun khang.

Thomas, Frederick William. 1935-1963. *Tibetan Literary Texts and Documents concerning Chinese Turkestan, Part I-IV*. London: The Royal Asiatic Society.

— 1957. *Ancient Folk-literature from North-Eastern Tibet*. Berlin: Akademie-Verlag.

Tong Tao. 2008. The silk roads of the northern Tibetan plateau during the early Middle Ages (from the Han to Tang dynasty) as reconstructed from archaeological and written sources. Dissertation, University of Tübingen.

— 2015. Analyzing the golden masks found in Himalayan area in a Eurasian vision, *Kaogu* 考古 2 (Engl. title of the article in Chinese; English version at: http://bridging-eurasia.org/en/node/344).

Tong Tao and P. Wertmann. 2010. The coffin paintings of the Tubo period from the northern Tibetan Plateau, in: Wagner, M. and Wang Wei (eds.), *Bridging Eurasia*. Mainz: German Archaeological Institute, 187-213.

Tsewang (Tshe dbang). 2011. *Spu rgyal dus kyi bang so'i zhib 'jug las 'phros pa'i gtam*. Lhasa: Bod ljongs mi dmangs dpe skrun khang.

Tshig mdzod = Krang dbyi sun (= Zhang Yisun 张怡荪). 1993. *Bod rgya tshig mdzod chen mo*, 2 vols. Beijing: Mi rigs dpe skrun khang.

Tucci, Guiseppe. 1950. *The Tombs of the Tibetan Kings*. SOR I. Rome.

TT = 'Jigs-med gling-pa, *Gtam gyi tshogs theg pa'i rgya mtsho* (Gangs can rig mdzod 18) Lhasa: Bod ljongs bod yig dpe rnying dpe skrun khang 1991.

TTT = <www.oeaw.ac.at/tibetantumulustradition>

Uebach, Helga. 1987. *Nel-pa Paṇḍitas Chronik Me-tog Phreṅ-ba*, München: Bayrische Akademie der Wissenschaften.

— 1997. Eminent Ladies of the Tibetan Empire according to Old Tibetan Texts, in: S. Karmay and Ph. Sagant eds., *Les habitants du Toit du monde. Hommage à Alexander W. Macdonald*, Paris: Société d'ethnologie, 53-74.

— 1999. On the Thirty-seven Holy Places of the Bon-pos in the Tibetan Empire, in: H. Eimer *et al.* (eds.), *Studia Tibetica et Mongolica (Festschrift M. Taube)*. Indica et Tibetica 34. Swisttal-Odendorf, 261-277.

— 2012. Tibetan official in the 8th-century south-eastern part of the empire, in: Scherrer-Schaub, Cristina (ed.), *Old Tibetan Studies Dedicated to the Memory of R. E. Emmerick*. Leiden: Brill, 53-64.

— 2013. The lHo-brag cliff inscription: an attempt to read it with the help of Katia Buffetrille's photographs of 1988, in: Ehrhard, Franz-Karl and Petra Maurer (eds.), *Nepalica-Tibetica: Festgabe for Christoph Cüppers*. Vol 2. Andiast: International Institute for Tibetan and Buddhist Studies, 261-268.

Vitali, Roberto. 1996. *The Kingdoms of Gu-ge Pu-hrang. According to mNga'-ris rgyal-rabs by Gu-ge mkhan-chen Ngag-dbang grags-pa*. Dharamsala: Tho ling gtsug lag khang lo gcig stong 'khor ba'i rjes dran mdzad sgo'i go sgrig tshogs chung.

— 2002. The History of Gnas rnying, Summarised as its 'Ten Greatnesses,' in: Blezer, H. (ed.), *Tibet, Past and Present. Tibetan Studies I. Proceedings of the 9th Seminar of the IATS. Leiden* 2000. Leiden: Brill, 81-107.

Walter, Michael L. 2009. *Buddhism and Empire: The Political and Religious Culture of Early Tibet*. Leiden: Brill.

Wangdu, Pasang and Hildegard Diemberger. 2000. *dBa' bzhed. The Royal Narrative Concerning the Bringing of the Buddha's Doctrine to Tibet*. Wien: Verlag der Österreichischen Akademie der Wissenschaften.

Wang Renxiang, Zhao Huimin, Liu Jianguo and Guo You'an. 2005. Tibetan royal tombs at 'Phyong-rgyas: Inverstigations and studies, *Chinese Archaeology* 5: 227-233.

Wei Luyan 韦陆艳 . 2013. Shilun Xizang shiqian shiqi shigou muzang 试论西藏史前时期石构墓葬 (A prelimnary study on the stone constructed tombs of pre-historic Tibet). MA thesis, Muzu University of China.

XWD = Editorial Board of the Cultural Relics Bureau, Lhasa. 2010. *Zhongguo wenwu dituji Xizang Zizhiqu fence* 中国文物地图集・西藏自治区分册 *(Atlas of Cultural Relics of the TAR)*. Beijing: Cultural Relics Press.

Yamaguchi, Zuiho. 1992. The establishment and significance of the Zhang Lon system of rule by maternal relatives during the T'u-fan Dynasty. *Memoirs of the Research Department of The Toyo Bunko*. The Oriental Library, no. 50. Tokyo: The Toyao Bungko, 57-80.

Zeisler, Bettina. 2011. For love of the word: A new translation of Pelliot Tibétain 1287, The Old Tibetan Chronicle, Chapter I, in: Imaeda, Yoshiro, M. Kapstein and T. Takeuchi (eds.), N*ew studies of the Old Tibetan Documents: Philology*, History and Religion. Tokyo: Tokyo University of Foreign Studies, 97-213.

— 2015. Gnam gyi khri bdun, the seven stars of heaven: A gift for a reconvalescent, in: Ramble, Charles and Ulrike Roesler (eds.), *Tibetan and Himalayan Healing. An Anthology for Anthony Aris*. Kathmandu: Vajra Books, 747-754.

Notes on the Architecture of Burial Mounds in Central Tibet

Hubert Feiglstorfer (Austrian Academy of Sciences)

1. Introduction[1]

Grave mounds made of clay or a mixture of stone and clay are widespread in the history of burial architecture. In Eurasia the earliest known date back to the 4th millennium BCE (Kipfer 2000: 291, related to sites in the Caucasus area). In China grave mounds first appeared in the Spring and Autumn period (8th to 5th century BCE) (Eregzen 2011b: 279). In the area of Central Tibet the beginning of the practice of burial in mounds is suggested to be related to the development of the regional principalities or chiefdoms some time in the centuries before the founding of the Tibetan empire (7th-9th cent. CE). This appears to mark a change from cist to mound burial, but also the practice of "exposing the corpse" (such as "sky burial") is suspected to have been a predecessor to mound burial, and generally earlier forms of burial were likely still used in the period of the Tibetan tumulus tradition (Hazod, in this volume).

Chronologically largely parallel to Central Tibet, in eastern Tibet there was a second strong tumulus tradition within the Tibetan Highlands, namely in the former Tuyuhun area (around Koko nor and the Upper Yellow River, today part of Qinghai 青海). In both tumulus landscapes we find a similar mixture of small round or oval shaped graves and larger, mostly trapezoidal grave structures of 15m to 70m; as is well known, several of the emperor tombs in the royal necropolis in 'Phyong rgyas of southern Central Tibet are even larger, sometimes almost twice as large. A certain amount of archaeological data

1 This contribution was written in memory of Tsering Gyalbo (1961-2015), with whom I had the honour of working together for some time. Staying with him at Khorchag monastery for several weeks in 2010 was a wonderful experience for me, which I will always remember with pleasure.

is now available for eastern Tibet, mostly related to excavations conducted in Reshui 热水 of present-day Dulan 都兰 County (Qinghai Province), with its dense cluster of tombs described by Chinese observers as "Tubo-Tuyuhun" 吐蕃－吐谷浑 cemeteries (Tong Tao 2008: 85). Towards Central Tibet the number of archaeological surveys related to burial mounds decreases, and relatively few excavations have been carried out in Central Tibet until now (cf. XWD 2010). However, a number of surface archaeological investigations have been conducted in recent years, related to the more than 400 grave fields recorded in Central Tibet today, i.e. largely the provinces of Dbus Gtsang (cf. Hazod, in this volume). Among them were two surveys conducted by the author in 2014 and 2015, which were dedicated specifically to architectural issues, based on selected sites with open graves that allow some significant reconstructions.[2]

From an architectural point of view these grave monuments are mounds of different layout and different forms of (stabilising) construction, which were placed over something below – chamber(s), for example, or simply pits (for the body), an inner working of its own architectural history and orientations. The following observations on the design, construction details and orientation of Central Tibetan burial mounds represent an initial overview of the architecture and development of these monuments. They are based on the data from 2014 and 2015 plus data from previous and also recent surveys on the part of Chinese archaeology (as far as accessible to the author), and they include a look at comparative burial situations in eastern Tibet as well as Mongolia (Xiongnu 匈奴 and Xianbei 鲜卑 context) and also China. These observations primarily relate to monuments of the ruling class or what we may call "elite tombs", which we see as most representative in terms of construction developments.

2. The outer manifestation of Tibetan burial mounds

In contrast to elite burial mounds of the ancient Eurasian regions, such as the Scythian

2 The surveys were conducted together with G. Hazod and Martin Gamon (from the Ludwig Boltzmann Institute for Archaeological Prospection and Virtual Archaeology, Vienna) in the framework of the FWF (Austrian Science Fund) financed project "The Burial Mounds of Central Tibet" (P 25066-G19). For principal documentation of the Central Tibetan burial mound sites, see the interactive project webpage: http://www.oeaw.ac.at/tibetantumulustradition/, in the following in short "TTT". The author wishes to thank G. Hazod and Shawo Khacham (Lhasa) for their observations and suggestions based on earlier drafts of this paper. I also thank Dong Shuyin 董书音 (Vienna) for her help in reading Chinese sources.

kurgans or the Celtic "Hügelgräber", with a mostly spherical design and round ground plan, in Tibet for larger graves the structure with a trapezoidal ground plan was characteristic, either steeply sloping or vertically upright ("coffer shaped"). This form of construction is probably not to be dated before the 7th century or the beginning of Tubo (Hazod, in this volume). Rather rare are mounds with a square ground plan as we find, for example, at the tombs of Srong btsan Sgam po (d. 650 CE) and his successor Mang slon Mang btsan (no. V and VII of 0032).[3] The successor to no. VII, *btsan po* Dus srong, was buried in a trapezoidal grave, and the reason behind such changes in grave form remains an open question. Larger trapezoidal tombs on hillside undoubtedly have a greater stability than round or square structures, but this criterion is not relevant here, as all three graves are situated in the plain on the same level. In post-imperial Tibetan sources both forms are described as *gru bzhi* (square-shaped), in contrast to the *zlum po* or round tumuli and the *mchod rten* or stupa type (Hazod, in this volume). In the eastern Tibetan burial mound sites we also find the trapezoid shape for larger tombs, and as in Central Tibet for smaller structures round or oval barrows are dominant (Tong Tao 2008: 83).

The trapezoidal mounds follow the topography of the slopes, with the centre line being orthogonal to the adjoining contours and in this way defining the outer orientation. This may be related to the situation of a continuous and rhythmical twisting of the mounds along the mountain slope. The layout of the mostly trapezoidal elite tombs at site 0092 (Slebs ri cemetery, dated to the Tibetan imperial period; cf. Sonam Wangdu and Hou Shizhu 2010: 45) shows this effect in a well-organised manner. The individual tombs "dance" along the contour lines of the mountain, with the mound given as M-2 on Fig. 1 (63×42m) being the focus of the surrounding structures.

An idiosyncratic trapezoidal mound is given in the form of a 12-cornered ground plan, namely at M-113 of Slebs ri (Fig. 2), a design which is described as a mandala (*tancheng* 坛城) in Huo Wei 2010: 50. This layout recalls the 12-cornered tower of eastern Tibet and eastern Central Tibet, with the earliest dating given by Darragon (2015: 42) to the 4th century CE (without providing proofs for this dating, however). It is located in the higher reaches of the Nyang chu river of present day Rgya mda' County, not far from the

3 The site numbers follow the grave list as given in the "Tibetan Tumulus" website (fn. 2). For the geographical position of the sites referred to in this paper, see the list at the end of this contribution.

grave field 0100 (cf. Hazod 2009: 179).

In Central Tibet, the tops of the earth mounds are usually flat and the sides either sloping, as can be seen, for example, at mounds M-1 and M-3 of 0141, or vertically straight as "coffer shaped" (cf. Fig. 3).

Several tombs show a kind of ramped access from the rear, which is in a linear elevation, following first the course of the slope downwards and finally rising to the top of the mound. Examples are mound M-1 at site 0157 or mound M-2 at 0172, where the rising part leading to the top of the mound appears to have been made of steps (Fig. 4; cf. also Feiglstorfer 2015).

The clay was in most cases evidently taken from the immediate surroundings and worked up in layers. For larger mounds, Sonam Wangdu and Hou Shizhu (1985: 32) mention the use of rammed earth for the whole mound while for smaller mounds a mixture of clay and stones was rammed. Another method of mound-building was to set the construction into the mountain slope. This method is only possible where there was a rather steep slope, and we observed this type in two neighbouring mounds in the field 0108 (Fig. 5).

The structural stabilisation of burial mounds is in most cases provided by the erection of stone and rammed earth walls. These follow the outline of the mound and define the trapezoidal shape of the mound's ground plan and thus are most relevant for determining the geometry and (outer) orientation of the burial mound.

In coffer-shaped graves, earth walls combined with horizontal rows of flat stone inlays (with a vertical distance of ca. 70cm as found at mound M-2 in Slebs ri (0092) or at mound M-2 at site 0141; Feiglstorfer 2015) are common (Fig. 6). Shuttering on either side of the walls was used in the erection of the walls of mound M-2 in Slebs ri (Wangdu 1985: 34). Wangdu, who conducted the archaeological campaigns in Slebs ri (one of the major Central Tibetan elite fields) in the 1990s, describes the construction of M-2 as vertically organised in the following three phases:

a) The base is made of big stone blocks. In particular, the corner stones show a precise shape for defining the mound's dimension and for levelling and determining its orientation.

b) The middle of the mound is made of ten layers of rammed earth, each ca. 70cm high and separated by ca. 5cm-thick stone layers.

c) The upper part of the mound, ca. 3m high, is a mixture of big stones and rammed earth. (Sonam Wangdu and Hou Shizhu 1985: 33)

The use of different materials in vertically layered constructions is a common feature of Central Tibetan mounds, in the form of rammed earth on a stone base and stabilised by a mixture of clay and stones placed on it. In the case of mounds with a larger span the trapezoidal outer stone structure is divided horizontally in several areas and by that forming a stabilising grid. Tibetan builders evidently had a clear understanding of loads and forces. For example, at mound M-1 at site 0141 parallel stone walls were erected in the edge area of the mound where the pressure from the mass of clay towards outside is greatest (cf. Feiglstorfer 2015). Another example is the erection of a retaining wall downhill of the grave mound. This wall was built in several vertical steps to stabilise the lower part of the hill (0105, Feiglstorfer 2015).

The grid of stone walls was originally covered by clay. Due to weathering the earthen cover on some mounds disappeared and several of the stone walls surfaced at the top of the tomb. Most of the tombs have been partially (some also completely) opened by tomb raiders so that either the stone walls or, after the removal of the stones, the empty ditches of the original walls remained. The dimensions of walls vary, and we found widths of between 50 and 100cm; and their height also varies, for example at mound M-3 of site 0002 (Feiglstorfer 2015) between 80 and 130cm (Fig. 7). At this site, two layers of stone grids were built above one another with a 50cm layer of rammed earth in between. Two layers of walls were built above one another. The external walls are vertically flush-mounted while the internal walls were horizontally shifted against each other to the width of one wall. The gaps between these walls were filled and laterally the walls were also covered with clay.

At one tomb of 0376 it appears that the entire mound was built in several horizontal stone layers (ca. 40cm) situated between rammed earth layers (ca. 40-70cm), to a total height of ca. 5m, similar to the coffer-shaped M-2 mound of Slebs ri (Fig. 8).

The stone walls were used to stabilise the tomb against erosion and collapse and protect it from theft. In Shawo Khacham 2015 and CRC (1992: 369, 370) the example of a tomb in the grave field of Rgya tshva is given, where the layout of the stone grid gives the impression of being related to the structure of the burial chamber below (Fig. 9). The section through tomb M-2 of this field shows the stone grid starting at a height of the hillside terrain and covered with clay. Below the stone grid the mound is a stone construction, and within this massive structure is the burial chamber with a corbelled stone roof. The central area of the 3×3 grid is given as being situated above the main chamber (Fig. 10) and the mid-southern part of this grid is above the antechamber with vertical access to the tomb. Yet actually the structure of the chamber seems to have been erected structurally independently of the stone grid above it, with the latter evidently simply serving a stabilising purpose.

On satellite photograph of mound M-VII of 0032 (exact position: 29 01 75.50, 91 68 06.52) a 3×3 grid (described in Tibetan sources as *re'u mig dgu pa*) is visible, which recalls the often cited 3×3 chamber reconstruction of an emperor tomb given in Haarh (1969). However, there is no archaeological evidence that this grid is directly related to a similar grid structure below, in the area of the chambers. Also at mound M-3, at site 0002, the stone grid followed a 3×3 structure (Fig. 7); (Feiglstorfer 2015), and at mound M-1 at site 0150 we could observe a 8×8 stone grid of 70-80cm / 55cm (width/height), and both were most probably only to stabilise the mound.

A particular variation of burial mounds are stupa-shaped monuments (both with round and square ground-plans) where the chamber construction below is connected to a pagoda-like building. Examples are the stupa tombs found at 0397 and 0398 (in the Sri Valley of Tshal Gung thang; see Hazod, in this volume) (Fig. 11), at Spang mda' (Rgya tshva County; CRC 1992: 367) or at Ser khung (0047). Such developments evidently mark the transition from pre-Buddhist grave mounds to a tradition influenced by Buddhism. Also the findings of *tsa tsa* inside burial mounds as at the site 0143 indicate a burial tradition from the later, i.e. Buddhist period of the empire. At this grave, about a quarter of the mound was opened on one side and the *tsa tsa* were part of the interior mound construction; a later laying of them into the opened mound can be excluded (Fig. 12).

Some of the burial mounds were surrounded by an enclosure wall whose remains are still visible on the surface. One example is at site 0143, next to the ruins of a monastery situated in this grave field. It was erected in a shape close to a square, with a ground plan of ca. 30×26m and there are still some remains of an earlier rammed earth wall along the visible stone foundation (Fig. 13). Another example is given by the remains of stone foundations at site 0402. Artificial terraces were erected in front of this mound, with the stone foundation of a former enclosure wall is still being visible along the lowest terrace. In Khrom chen, besides Slebs ri one of the largest elite grave fields (0339), it appears as if the whole field was enclosed by a wall (cf. Shawo Khacham 2014b).

In Slebs ri (0092), at mound M-27 and at mound M-130, the remains of thick enclosure walls were found (Sonam Wangdu and Hou Shizhu 1985: 35-37). At mound M-130 in this field (Fig. 14) the wall is made in six layers of rammed earth, which are separated from each other by 6cm-thick stone layers. At mound M-27 (Fig. 15), in contrast, the tomb and also the enclosure wall had a circular ground plan. They are constructed with a rather high stone base of ca. 2m with a rammed earth wall on top up to 1.6m high, also made in layers, which are separated by 6cm-thick stone layers.

Not only tombs were surrounded by walls. In Slebs ri (0092) one base for a stele in the form of a turtle with missing head is reported to have been originally surrounded by a wall, as reconstructed from the remains of its foundation (Huo Wei 2010: 54). The burial site of Slebs ri is a good example of the integration into the cemetery of various structures that are not graves. In the south-western area of the same site two structures made of river stones, one with two chambers and the other with one, were used as sacrificial places (Sonam Wangdu and Hou Shizhu 185: 37; marked as J-1 and J-2 at Fig. 1). The smaller structure J-2 partially encloses mounds M-189 and M-190 on this site. Sonam Wangdu and Hou Shizhu (1985: 34, 35) also mention that certain groups of monuments in Slebs ri apparently formed a connected unit, such as mounds M-1, M-8 and the structure F-1 (Fig. 1). The latter is a clay-structure which was not used as grave but rather represented a temple (cf. also Caffarelli 1997: 238). The walls on either side of this structure are ca. 5m apart.

Another characteristic of Tibetan (elite) tombs are staircase constructions in front of the burial mounds, with between five and eleven steps. Some of these steps or terraces relate to trenches used for sacrificial animals.[4] Several examples are to be found in the field of Slebs ri (at M-112, M-113 and M-114; marked as "T" on Fig. 1) and actually almost all larger hillside mounds have this additional architectural feature, most visible on mound no. X of 0032 (tomb of Khri Lde gtsug btsan) (cf. TTT: "thematic introduction", "Around tombs-3"; Shawo Khacham 2014a).

Eastern Tibetan burial-mound constructions include considerably more wood compared to Central Tibet. The trapezoid mound M-1 at Reshui (Tong Tao 2008: 86) was constructed using seven layers of cypress beams. Below this wooden construction there is a trapezoid layer of rammed earth made of loess and pebbles that is 3.5m high and 5m wide. Below the

4 Bones of horses, sheeps, cows, dogs, deer, chicken and doves were found in one of these sites. Apart from the horses, the other (smaller) animals had been cut into pieces, the chicken and doves had been placed in ceramic pots. Cf. Huo Wei 1995: 226, 230, 231. In certain sites in the find, it is thought that the horses were buried alive (Huo Wei, *op. cit.*, p. 226). For an overview of animal sacrifice related to Tibetan elite burials, see Tong Tao 2008: 96-98.

rammed earth wall a circular stone wall made of granite blocks was erected in three steps (each 1m high) 3.3m thick, and 3-6m wide; the upper layer is situated ca. 6.5m below the top of the mound.

We also find smaller earthen mounds whose outline is marked by stones, mostly laid directly on the ground as in the case of a mound at site 0367 (cf. Feiglstorfer 2015). These are of a circular shape with a diameter of up to 12m. They were either built as mounds or the stones were arranged in a circular shape on the terrain. The latter stone structures may relate to sacrificial pits as we found, for example, at 0024 and at 0172 (Fig. 16). At site 0246 and 0148 we found rectangular, stone-lined structures on the ground (Fig. 17) similar to west Tibetan cist tombs (cf. CTRI *et al.* 2001).

2.1 Comparative notes: Mongolia and China

The central terrace of tombs of the Xiongnu context (3rd-1st cent. BCE) have either a rectangular, rhomboid or trapezoidal surface structure (Yeruul-Erdene 2011: 36), with the latter form usually referring to larger structures, smaller tombs are round shaped (Eregzen 2013a: 27). On the south side of several quadrangular tombs, stone structures cover an entrance passage leading northwards into the burial chamber. These tombs were erected as flat earthen mound structures circled by a line of stones giving the impression of a wall. Such a form of stone edging of mounds is in contrast to Central Tibet.

Xiongnu tombs mostly have only flat mounds or even none at all; M-1, the biggest mound in the Gol Mod-II field, rises 3.7m above the surface, with a ground plan of ca. 46×46m (Yeruul-Erdene 2011: 3). Mounds of up to 20m are mostly circular (Eregzen 2011a: 50), similar to what we know from descriptions of eastern Tibetan burial mounds.

In Central China mounds of the Western Han period were primarily square and became round shaped during the Eastern Han period (Eregzen 2011b: 279). The history of earth mounds reportedly started with the Spring and Autumn period and reaches its peak in popularity during the Warring States period (Eregzen 2011b: 279). In the Qin dynasty (221-206 BCE) huge pyramid-shaped tombs were erected (345×350m in ground plan), e.g. Qin Ling of Shi Huangdi 秦始皇 , while during the Tang dynasty a natural hill was often used as a burial mound (cf. here the tomb related to emperor Gaozong 高宗 (r. 650-683 CE); Liu 1989: 219, 222). The layout of the tomb of Li Xian 李 显 (656-710 CE) with the passage way to the chamber (accompanied by three pairs of niches and two further chambers) from the south (Eckfeld 2005: 38) is reminiscent of the layout of the tomb at Shoroon Bumbagar/ Ulaan Kherem in Mongolia dated to the 7th century CE (Erdenebold 2017: Fig. 2) (Fig. 18). This type of tomb with a ramp leading into the chamber is also to be found in Japan (3rd to 7th century CE), but is not attested in the Tibetan burial-mound tradition, either in the Tuyuhun context or in Central Tibet.

3. The grave chamber

Concerning the construction of the burial mounds' inner core we can basically differentiate between earth-walled, stone-walled (example M-121 of Slebs ri (0092); Chayet 1994: 77, see Fig. 19) and wooden-walled chambers, the latter recorded for Dulan, where generally wood, as well as stone and clay, wood and bricks were commonly used (Tong Tao 2008: 86), while wood was not a primary building material in Central Tibetan burial constructions.

The chambers are usually excavated from the earth and the walls are either made of rammed earth, stones, bricks or wood and the roof of stone or wood. We find an exception in M-1 and M-2 in grave field 0330 (Bom ma, Lha rtse County; cf. Hazod 2009: 189-190), where the chambers were built above ground rather than below (Huo Wei 1995: 72, 73; see Fig. 20). At mound M-1 on this site the walls are made of boulders surrounded by a spherical rammed earth mound. The mound was erected in five vertical layers and for each layer the use of stones and logs is mentioned. At mound M-2 the wall construction surrounding the chamber was made of rammed earth and the section above was made of clay mixed with small stones.

3.1 Number of chambers

In several cases in Central Tibet we find chambers with an anteroom, which was built simply as an extension in front of the chamber. It is also found in the form of side niches (Fig. 9) or as a separate chamber laterally adjoining the main chamber, as can be seen at mound M-5 at Ser khung (i.e. M-8 of 0047), the latter dated to the late 8th or early 9th century (Chayet 1994: 75; Caffarelli 1997: 233; Shawo Khacham 2015). Mound M-113 in Slebs ri (Fig. 2) shows the division into two chambers – an entrance chamber (ca. 1.6m×1m) and a directly adjoining main chamber (ca. 2.5×2.2m according to the plan in Huo Wei 2010: 50).

Shawo Khacham (2015) presents larger, multi-chambered elite tombs, in the form we find a reconstruction after Haarh (1969) of the five-chambered tomb of Srong btsan Sgam po (cf.

also Tucci 1973: 62). In eastern Tibet, as well as single-chambered tombs there are double-chambered and multi-chambered tombs, with or without an encircling corridor (Tong Tao 2008: 88, 89).

3.2 Access

The accessibility of the grave through a duct either from the top or the side is characteristic of larger (elite) burial mounds in Central Tibet as well as eastern Tibet. One particular form is access by stairs, as at tomb M-5 of Ser khung (M-8 of 0047) in the form of a double flight of steps with an intermediate landing (Chayet 1994: 75). The upper flight leads downwards south-west to north-east onto an intermediate landing and has nine steps. The second flight turns 90 degrees south-east down from the intermediate landing towards the burial chamber. This flight has seven steps, making 16 steps for the whole construction. Unlike the ramps known from Han or Xiongnu graves, which are straight, these staircases seem to follow a 90° turning pattern. There is another tomb discussed in Shawo Khacham (2015) which likewise has a staircase with a 90° turn; in this case there are only seven steps and they are extremely steep.

3.2.1 Mongolia and Central China

Xiongnu tombs, by comparison, have one-chamber structures, as at the tomb in Noyon Uul with a vertically stepped pit accessible via a ramp (Yeruul-Erdene 2011: 49). Similar structures are also known from the Western Han and the Qin dynasty (Eregzen 2011b: 277). Ramped access is also mentioned for tombs in Mongolia, namely for a burial mound at Ulaan Kherem dated to the 7th century (Fig. 18); this tomb is accessible from the south (Erdenebold 2017). Similar to the Xiongnu tomb of Noyon Uul, which is accessible via a ramp from the cardinal south (in the lower part of the ramp also provided with stairs), the Chinese example from Mawangdui 马王堆 in Hunan 湖南 (Western Han dynasty, 207 BCE to 9 CE) has a cardinal (i.e. absolute) orientation but with the ramp leading to the grave from the north. Much earlier graves in the Xibeigang 西北岗 royal cemetery of the Shang Dynasty (13th-11th cent. BCE) have a similar ramped type but in a cruciform shape. Tombs with a ramp leading from two opposite directions are known from the Qin period (221-206 BCE), at the necropolis of Nanzhihui 南指挥 (Shelach 2015: 207, 285). Ramped and cardinally orientated entrances to the mound are not recorded for Tibet.

3.3 Rock-covered chambers

Graves in western Tibet, found in 1992 and explored in 1999, are generally in the simple form that can be described as stone-lined burial pits or cist tombs (cf. CTRI 2001: 17-20). One of the graves presented in CTRI is a two-chamber type separated by a stone wall, with each chamber measuring ca. 80×180×100 cm (L/W/H).

A stone-built grave in Lhun rtse County of Lhoka dated to 25-125 BCE was made of stone slabs with a mix of sand and clay for the base (Sonam Wangdu 2010: 54). The ceiling consists of ten different layers (materials not mentioned) and spans a space of ca. 180cm in length, 30cm in width and 104cm in depth (*ibid.*). Simple chambers of Central Tibetan grave mounds which are covered with rocks as found at one of the tombs of 0131 (hereafter 0131a) are of a similar or even smaller size. The maximum size of stones for roofing determine the maximum size of these kinds of small chambers. The rock on this 0131 grave is ca. 150×100×40cm (L/W/H) covering a chamber that measures ca. 87×50×50cm (L/W/H) (Fig. 21). The lateral walls are stacked ashlars with no mortar in between. Regarding the use of mortar, the quality of the workmanship is better on more elaborate stone constructions, as noted by Shawo Khacham (personal communication, Lhasa 2015) with regard to larger, excavated tombs at Dulan, where clay mortar was used. At the same field 0131 we found another example of this type of single-chamber burial mound (hereafter 0131b). Two rocks lying on the ground of this opened mound were a similar size to the rock found at the above-mentioned mound in 0131 (Fig. 22). These rocks are obviously remains of the original roofing of the burial chamber.

The rear wall of the burial chamber in 0131a is made of two rocks, which must have been installed first to give stability to the construction. No ashlars or rocks for closing the front were found. The remains of a vertical cylindrical excavation are visible to the left of the chamber (Fig. 23), which may indicate the construction of a vertical access.

The simplicity of this chamber construction below the mound is similar to cist-tomb structures as can be seen at tomb M-1 in Rgyal bzhang, given in Chayet (1994: 74), which was erected with stone walls in a trapezoidal shape and covered with stone slabs. The floor of this type of tomb is clay, as at the tomb 0131a where no particular paving was found. Such a chamber construction may have been common for smaller tombs (20-30m) as well as for pure cist tombs. In fact, from a typological point of view the actual burial place of these tombs of 0131a,b were constructed like cist tombs and later covered with a mound of clay. The much older pure cist tombs were wide-spread and we find them in various places in western Tibet and throughout the Himalayas (cf. Aldenderfer 2013; cf. also Seonbok Yi *et al.* 2008); these are evidently direct predecessors of the simpler (smaller) grave mounds. In the latter case the shaft from the floor of the chamber to the top of the mound represents a characteristic element, and typologically the entire tomb can be described as a "tomb with a shaft leading to a cist like chamber and covered by an earthen mound". In our examples from mounds at 0131 and at 0147 the shaft is between 415 and 320 cm long.[5]

The investigations of the opened graves at these sites revealed a chamber height of 50cm to 90cm. Together with the rectangular ground plan, which is adjusted to the body size, and the size of the roof cover, this may largely represent the basic dimensions of the older cist-tomb constructions. There may be differences with regard to the depth the individual chambers were set below ground level; otherwise the examples indicate that the construction of single-chamber burial mounds were developments from the widespread prehistoric forms of telluric (or earth) burial.

Simple rock-covered chambers also include the type where a big rock is placed in an inclined, overhanging position above the body. We found such a situation at site 0147 (Shing tshang, Stag rtse County) (Fig. 24). A big rock must have been carried into the pit. Its position most probably defines the position of the body. The remains of holes in the wall next to the rock suggest a possible earlier vertical access, or they may have been used to fix the scaffolding in order to lift the stone into the chamber. For north-west China Pan Ling (2011: 464) describes this type as a niche grave (related to tombs at Daodunzi, Ningxia Autonomous Region, China), which is so far not known from contemporary Xiongnu burials.

3.4 Construction of accessible chambers

The span of the chamber defines the choice in building material. For small and in general non-accessible chambers, stone slabs are sufficient for a span of up to 2m. With the

5 Our reconstruction of the shaft's depth is based on the following dimensions: 1) depth from the floor of the chamber to the top of the mound; 2) depth from the floor of the chamber to ground level; 3) height of the actual burial chamber whose roof is below ground level; 4) distance between ground level and the top of the chamber. In details, at mound 0131a the dimensions in cm of 1 = 415; 2 = 190; 3 = 50; 4 = 140 (see Fig. 23); at mound 0131b the dimensions of 1 = 280; 2 = 150; 3 = 90; 4 = 60 (Fig. 22); at 0147 the dimensions of 1 = 320; 2 = 100; 3 = 80; 4 = 20 (Fig. 24).

construction of an access to the chamber(s) the graves reached a new dimension – not least in respect to ritual activities. A corbelled roof of the chamber made of stones was used for a larger spanas found in Ser khung (0047; Chayet 1994: 75). In eastern Tibet wooden planks or trunks joined together were used in bigger chambers, as can be seen at mound M-1 of Reshui where the trunks reach a length of 6m (Fig. 25) (SAM 2005: 60).

For such types of accessible chamber constructions, I would like to follow a classification given by Huo Wei (2010: 52), in 1) vertically arranged constructions made of wooden pillars and beams and 2) a corbelled or dome construction. Both constructions make it possible to span a wider distance than simple roofs with stone slabs.

ad 1) Constructions using wooden pillars: At mounds M-121 and M-130 at Slebs ri (0092) holes for pillars and also some wooden remains 15-20cm in diameter are reported to have been found in the ground (Sonam Wangdu and Hou Shizhu 1985: 36). At mound M-121 (Fig. 19) the holes are set at the corners of the rectangular chamber while at mound M-130 (Fig. 14) they run along two opposite sides of the chamber. According to the plan in Sonam Wangdu and Hou Shizhu (*op. cit.*), the span of the wooden beams must have been ca. 1.75m and the length of the chamber ca. 2m. Such a wooden construction probably followed the technique as used for houses. On several wooden parts at mound M-130 inscriptions were found that probably served to number the individual parts. According to ^{14}C examinations, this mound M-130 dates to 700 CE +/- 70.

ad 2) Corbelled roof: A further development is the corbelled roof technique. Some sources in archaeological reports refer to such vaults, which in Central Tibet were primarily made of stone, not brick. A chamber with a corbelled roof was excavated at mound M-5 in Ser khung (M-8 of 0047), which was plastered with ceramic material (Sonam Wangdu 2010: 52). Further examples of corbelled roof constructions were found at mound M-2 of Spang mda', where mud plaster on the chamber walls is documented (CRC 1992: 370; Huo Wei 1995: 178; see Fig. 9), and at M-27 (0092), which resembles a dome (Sonam Wangdu and Hou Shizhu 1985: 36). A similar dome-like construction is given in Shawo Khacham 2015 (related to M-60 in the field of Dung dkar; see Fig. 26). Huo Wei (1995: 177) points to the close similarity between the corbelled structure found at M-60 and residential buildings.

Several corbelled roofs have a hole on top, which Huo Wei (2010: 52) compares to the hole in the roofs of nomadic tents, i.e. the *gnam sgo* or "sky door" (in parallel, see here the tents on the coffin panels of Guolimu M-2; Tong Tao 2008: 420, 421). Other examples of roofs with a hole are documented for M-2 at Spang mda' (Fig. 9) or M-27 at Slebs ri (Fig. 15) (Huo Wei 2010: 53). At mound M-27 of Slebs ri such a hole was covered with a stone (Sonam Wangdu and Hou Shizhu 1985: 36).

3.4.1. Roof constructions in Chinese tombs

Roof constructions in Central Chinese tombs seem to have developed in a different way compared to roofs in Central Tibetan burial mounds. During the Han dynasty in Xianyang 咸阳, Shaanxi 陕西 Province, a simple pitched roof construction was made of hollow bricks which covered the tomb (the tomb's size is given as 367×186×148cm; IHNS 2000: Fig. II-1). A brick arch was found in a tomb at Shaogou 烧沟 in Luoyang 洛阳, Henan 河南 Province and dated to the Western Han dy-nasty (202 BCE-8 CE), and findings of corbelled roofs at Qinan County / Shang dong Province are dated to the succeeding Eastern Han dynasty (25-220 CE) (*ibid.*, Fig. 7-2-2). In comparison, in Central Tibetan burial mounds' predecessor roof structures in the form of a pitched roof or using a brick arch are so far not known.

3.4.2. Corbelled roofs in western and Upper Tibet

In Tibetan burial mounds, corbelled roof constructions were introduced at a later period compared to western and Upper Tibetan housing structures. Bellezza (2016) gives a hypothesis of corbelled roofs already having been used in the western and Upper Tibetan region in 700 BCE. Based on a radiocarbon dating of a village context in western Tibet by M. Aldenderfer (2003: 8), Bellezza (2015: 7) draws the hypothesis that similarities between the ground plans of structures in this village context and corbelled roof structures point towards their possible dating between 550 and 100 BCE. The earliest actually calibrated radiocarbon date of organic material within a corbelled roof in Upper Tibet is between 200 BCE and 100 CE (Bellezza 2008: 36, 37), similar to the dating given for the early Central Chinese corbelled roof at Qinan County as mentioned before. According to this chronology, the construction of corbelled roofs in Central Tibetan burial chambers at the earliest in the 7th century was at least 600 years after their use for Upper Tibetan housing structures.

3.5 Flooring

Flooring is another feature that indicates technical development in tomb architecture. As we observed at site 0131, the floors of early tombs were bare clay. We find such an architectural approach in the earliest cist tombs recorded for the plateau land (Aldenderfer 2013: 295). A more developed method of flooring is reported from (the imperial era) mounds M-121 (Fig. 19) and M-130 (Fig. 14) at Slebs ri, where the floor is covered with *arga*[6] of a thickness of ca. 10cm (Huo Wei 2010: 53). Here the four stone slabs for the coffin walls must have been laid first and are held in place by ramming the *arga*. This finding of *arga* in Central Tibetan tombs from the imperial period is the first evidence of the use of this flooring method in Tibet (Sonam Wangdu and Hou Shizhu 1985: 38). In its later use, e.g. at monasteries, *arga* appears as a building material of prestige buildings, a relationship which can also be assumed in the material's use in tombs. The deceased were no longer just laid on the earth but on a clean and shining polished floor.

3.6 Plaster

Grass or a mixture of clay and grass, as is known from later house constructions, is mentioned for the decoration of the outside of some coffer-shaped tombs (Sonam Wangdu and Hou Shizhu 1985: 33, related to M-2 at Slebs ri, see Fig. 9); cf. also Huo Wei 1995: 168). Also interior walls were plastered, as in Ser khung (M-8 of 0047), which were plastered with ceramic material (Sonam Wangdu 2010: 52), or at mound M-2 of Spang mda' (Huo Wei 1995: 178).

3.7 Stupa tombs

The stupa tomb at the above-mentioned site 0398 has the stepped base of the stupa and a vanishing shape of its dome (Fig. 27)[7]. Its corbelled roof is made of stones with clay mortar in between (Fig. 28). Most of the stones are angular and some of them have a beginning rounding. On the top of the roof a circular hole is covered with big flat stones, which possibly originally served as the platform for the stupa's base (*bum pa*). On one side of the base, close to the ground, a hole (ca. 10×10cm) leads towards the outside. The photographs

6 Sonam Wangdu and Hou Shizhu (1985: 50) describe the *arga* as made of powder of calcite. Actually it is a method where stones with a high calcite content are crushed and compressed by ramming. The proportion of powder and more coarsely crushed stones plays an important role for the efficacy of this method (cf. Feiglstorfer 2016; Feiglstorfer 2017).

7 Since we were not free to visit this part of the valley during our stay in 2015, Shawo Khacham was so kind as to give detailed information on this object from his earlier visits and to share his photographs.

of the floor show a partial hole surrounded by stones, here recalling the simple pit tombs covered with stone slabs (Fig. 29). Remains of *tsa tsa* lie on the floor, indicating the monument's involvement in the Buddhist environment.

Other sites with stupa tombs are documented in Shawo Khacham (2011) and regionally classified as follows:

a) stupa tomb with a square ground plan (14m / 5.1m; L/H) and the base made of stones of five different layers on top, which are again separated by a layer of stones (examples are found in Khrom chen; 0339).

b) stupa with a trapezoidal ground plan; the building is bordered by a stone wall.

c) the type of M-168 of Slebs ri (0093, i.e. the smaller field of Slebs ri; cf. Hazod in this volume) – a circular stupa situated on a square platform (Fig. 30).

d) the type with a "mandalic" ground plan (related to the stupa tomb of Ser khung, 0047). The base is made of ca. 50cm-high stones and the cross-shaped central part above is made of rammed earth and stone (Fig. 31).

e) the Spang mda' type, with a square base and a dome, and a base made almost completely of rammed earth.

In Slebs ri M-168 represents a circular stupa with a complex vertical construction (Sonam Wangdu and Hou Shizhu 1985: 34): Six circular construction layers were erected on top of the square stone base (height ca. 1m). The lower four layers are each separated with a layer of stones of ca. 13cm. On top of these four layers there are two further layers, and holes of a diameter of ca. 10cm below each of them probably indicate the use of a scaffold for the construction of the monument.

3.8. Bricks

The use of fired bricks in Central Tibet was not common. They were used in eastern Tibet, however, in particular grey bricks as found in the first chamber of mound M-1 in Dulan (Shawo Khacham 2015). Several of the "Tubo-Tuyuhun" tombs presented in Tong Tao (2008: 93, 94) show the use of adobe bricks. At mound M-1 of the cemetery in Ulan (*op. cit.*, p. 93) the upper part of the mound is described as several layers of mud bricks. The adobe brick layer covers a ca. 10cm-thick ash deposit and a layer of rammed earth below. The walls of the chambers at mound M-3 in the same cemetery are built of adobe bricks.

We found the use of adobe walls in Central Tibet only in one wall construction (at site 0376, which we visited in 2015; Fig. 32, 33). The bricks are 48×36×8cm (L, W, H), which corresponds to a weight of ca. 25kg for each brick. To the best of our knowledge, there are no recorded examples of the use of adobe bricks for chambers in Central Tibet.

3.9 Wood constructions

In east Tibetan Dulan excavations show chamber constructions which are partly or wholly made of wood. The main chamber of mound M-1 at Reshui (Tong Tao 2008: 318) is constructed with logs on all six sides. Those used for the roof are up to 40cm in diameter and up to 6m long (SAM 2005: 7, 35). In mound M-3 of the same cemetery, walls in the east and west chambers were made of stone with timber lacing (SAM 2005: 63), a construction form commonly used for structures above ground, in particular to withstand earthquakes and to give the stone wall additional strength.

In general, walls of wooden grave chambers are made either of wooden panels or wooden pegs, which are rammed into the ground side by side. The chamber walls support the roof, which may be made of the same material as the walls (Fig. 25). At mound M-1 at Reshui, cypress roof beams were laid between the rammed earth layers and in medium-sized and small tombs low adobe brick walls were erected to support the load of the clay (Tong Tao 2008: 86). The roof constructions have to withstand the heavy loads of caly and stone above them, which may be roughly calculated at two tonnes/m^3.

3.9.1. Chambers in Mongolia and China

Beside simple cist tombs with stone slabs laterally protecting the coffin, as seen in a cross-section of a Xiongnu tomb (NMK 2003: 63), at the time of the Xiongnu accessible wooden chambers were also built. The shafts above the pit were a tapered form, evidently for structural reasons, with a depth of 7m to 18.3m (Yeruul-Erdene 2011: 45, 49). The use of wood for chamber constructions was widespread among the Xiongnu (Fig. 34). In the Mongolian steppes non-accessible chambers were constructed like wooden coffins as containers for the actual coffin (cf. Miller 2011: 565).

In China, since the Shang period (mid to late 2nd century BCE) wooden-chambered, ramped tombs were built and became widespread during the Spring and Autumn period of late Bronze Age China (8th to 5th century BCE). The form of dividing the main chamber into several sub-chambers by wooden constructions in the Warring States period (5th-3rd cent. CE) differs from Xiongnu-related structures, with no division of the main chamber (Eregzen 2011b: 277, 278).

In Tang China, the northern (rectangular) chamber of the tomb of Li Xian (d. 684 CE), had an "outer coffin" made of stone (ca. 4×3m L/W), in which the wooden coffin with the emperor's corpse was placed (Eckfeld 2005: 42- 43).

4. Placing the body

4.1 Placing of the corpse on the bare clay or in a coffin

In Central and eastern Tibet the main burial form in mound interments was inhumation.[8] The corpse of the deceased was either placed in a coffin made of stone or wood or laid directly on the bare clay. A coffin is theoretically transportable. From a practical point of view, coffins made of heavy wooden pegs or even of stone may have been fixed *in situ*.

Inhumation without a container is very common. For Tibetan burial mounds, this form seems to have been common for smaller structures with simple burial pits where the floor was not further treated in the way it is found in larger mounds with accessible chambers.

In western and Central Tibetan burial pits and cist tombs the corpse seems to have been placed directly into the pit without any separate container. The container was as it were formed by the walls of the pit. In Central Tibetan areas the use of wooden coffins was evidently extremely rare. Examples are known from western Tibet (500 BCE-100 CE) and from Mustang (Aldenderfer 2013: 306). Earlier examples with trapezoidal wooden coffins were found at Neolithic tombs at Chugong (near Lhasa) or at Bronze Age sites in Quiji and Xindian (Aldenderfer 2013: 299; cf. also Chayet 1994: 52-53). In one of these early cist tombs in Lhasa the body was laid on its right side in a bent position in a grave of ca. 80×90cm (He Qiang 1995: 35). In excavated western Tibetan cist tombs, the body was found in different positions, e.g. with scattered parts of the corpse (CTRI *et al.* 2001: 6), with the head separately posed or in flexed position. These forms of placing the body

8 There are some data on cremation and also urn burial in the prehistoric era (CTRI 2001: 20; Chayet 1994: 55), but usually not in combination with mound burial. An impressive exception is the finding in a 7th-century grave mound in Mongolia: a wooden coffin with a wooden box inside, with the ashes of the deceased wrapped in silk (see Erdenebold 2017).

evidently correlated with the small size of these (non-burial-mound) graves (CTRI *et al.* 2001: 5).

A kind of stone coffin found at the (imperial era) mound M-121 at Slebs ri (site 0092) (see Fig. 19) was made of stone slabs on a rectangular ground plan. This suggests the development from stone-lined cist tombs with the stone construction forming the coffin.

The small pit for the body, which we found in the opened grave of 0131a mentioned above, could only have been used for a child or a body in a bent position in the case of an adult. A reconstruction of this tomb constructed for the body in a stretched out position is given below in chapter 5.3. Such kinds of small graves were covered with stone plates or rocks; the smallest examples are of ca. 50×50cm ground plan. In such pits there was not enough space for a coffin.

With the changing concept of accessible chambers the placing of the corpse must arguably have changed accordingly. The greater space also allowed the use of a coffin. The zenith in this development no doubt is represented by the larger elite graves and particularly the *btsan po*-s' tombs, although we have no archaeological data for the latter, but only the descriptions in post-imperial sources. The corpse of Srong btsan Sgam po, for example, is reported to have been placed in a silver coffin in the central chamber of his tomb (Tucci 1973: 62; cf. here also Hazod, in this volume).

4.1.1 Tuyuhun, early Mongolia, and Tang China

As already noted, in contrast to Central Tibet, in the Tuyuhun era of eastern Tibet the use of wooden coffins was common, as is also reported for tombs of the (proto-Mongolian) Xianbei, to whom the Tuyuhun were related. The Xianbei coffins were made by skilled carpenters, as can be seen, for example, in the skilfully worked logs connected with rebate joints (Tong Tao 2008: 153). Some of the coffins were painted with scenes of the everyday life of the aristocracy and their burial culture (Hazod, in this volume). The wooden coffins in eastern Tibet were either rectangular or trapezoid (Tong Tao 2008).

In Tong Tao (2008: 175, 176) the coffin of a Murong Xianbei 慕容鲜卑 descendant (d. 415 CE) from the northern Chinese borderlands is presented. It describes the head end of the coffin as being wider and higher than the foot. Among the coffins found in the Tuyuhun area the depictions of trapezoidal coffins in most cases show the shorter part of the coffin as the head end, however (Tong Tao 2008: 285, 288). Similarly, in the coffin of a 7th-century tomb in Shoroon Bumbagar (Mongolia) the head of the corpse was placed at the smaller leg of the trapezoid container (Erdenebold 2017). In Ochir et al. 2013: 30 this coffin's trapezoid is presented with the longer leg on the south side, which follows the trapezoidal ground plan of the chamber, also with its longer leg on the south side. At a Xiongnu tomb in Uvgant a trapezoidal chamber contains a rectangular coffin with the head placed outside the coffin pointing towards the longer leg of the trapezoid (Eregzen 2013b: 187).

Trapezoid coffins were also used during the Kayue culture (900-600 BCE) of north-west China, e.g. at grave M-39 at Dahua zhongzhuang 大华中庄 (Shelach-Lavi 2015: 240). One reason for placing the head on the longer side of the trapezoid may be the placing of sacrificial goods close to the head, as is described for two trapezoid coffins in a report on the prehistoric site at Kayue (AIQP 1998: 53, 55). At two other tombs at this site (M-7, M-40) the head is at the shorter side of the trapezoid, however; at M-40 the area inside the coffin's longer side was evidently used for placing pots with various different contents (*ibid.*).

In the Xiongnu context the bodies were placed on felt or on birch bark (Eregzen 2011a: 62). Wooden coffins with butterfly joints for the corners are known (Yeruul-Erdene 2011: 45). Depictions of the sun and moon on coffins (Tseveendorj 2013: 170) are reported and textiles with decorations of sun and moon were placed close to the head (*op. cit.* p. 45).

4.2 Position of the corpse

Since archaeological reports on corpse are rare, particularly for Central Tibetan tombs, it is difficult to arrive at a homogenous picture. As already mentioned, the size of the pit may correlate with the position of the body placed in either contracted / bent or stretched position. A supine or lateral and bent position, also with crossed hands or legs, is often mentioned (Chayet 1994: 78). In Dulan (eastern Tibet) it is reported that in many graves the body was placed directly on the stone or timber flooring in a contracted position facing downwards or in a lateral position, while a supine position is rarely found (Tong Tao 2008: 97). In comparison, bodies in Xiongnu tombs are found in both supine and stretched position (NMK 2003).

5. Orientation of burial mounds

Orientation means the relation to a specific point of reference or the following of an absolute cardinal direction, where, as said, in the case of grave mounds we have to differentiate the mound's outer orientation (with the viewing direction defined by the longer side in the case of trapezoid structures) from the orientation of the inner parts. The latter is defined by the shape of architectural elements such as the burial chamber or the coffin, and not least by the position of the body.

As noted, the trapezoid was the most common layout of Tibetan burial mounds in the elite category, with the longer leg of the trapezoid pointing downhill. In the (post-imperial) description of the tomb of emperor Gnam ri Srong btsan (d. early 7th cent.), Hazod has suggested seeing the first evidence for a trapezoidal burial mound (Hazod 2014: 24). Other early evidence of this design is provided in the (reconstructed) form of the enclosure of the residence established by this emperor in Rgya ma, east of Lhasa (*op. cit.*, p. 25). The trapezoidal burial mounds within one grave field are only roughly orientated in the same direction, but in following the topographical situation they are in fact mostly individually oriented. In many cases the mounds are laid out along a slope, which accordingly makes them higher at the front.

As to the symmetrically arranged stupa tombs, the mound M-1 at Spang mda' was constructed in a cruciform "mandala" design with a north-west orientation (CRC 1992: 367). The stupa at site 0397 (Fig. 11), which we visited in 2015, has a square ground plan and its *bum pa* opening faces south-west.

The graves within one burial site usually represent mixed forms partly related to different epochs – stone-lined cist or pit tombs in the immediate vicinity of round or trapezoidal structures, such as the sites of 0246 or 0148, which we visited in 2015 (Fig. 17), and related to this one can also expect different orientation concepts in one and the same grave field.

5.1 Mongolia and China

According to Yeruul-Erdene (2011: 36), the elite Xiongnu tombs usually face north. The tomb M-31 at Noyonuul follows the direction of the chamber and the corpse (*op. cit.*, p. 45). Also the later (7th-century) tomb of the above-mentioned Shoroon Bumbagar burial site at Ulaan Kherem faces north. In China, Tang-period tombs, namely Li Xian's mound, follow exactly the cardinal direction (Eckfeld 2005: 38). Archaeological findings in central China suggest that over the last 9000 years the cardinal orientation was dominant. This is the case, for example, in the field of Peiligang 裴里岗 (7000-5000 BCE), where most of the graves follow a north-south orientation (Shelach-Lavi 2015: 79); so too at the burial mound at Fanshan 反山 (of the Liangzhu 良渚 culture, 3300-2200 BCE; Fagan 1996: 138), or at the cruciform late Shang graves at Xibeigang (13th-11th cent. BCE; *op. cit.*, p. 207), or at the funnel-shaped Western Han tomb at Mawangdui (206 BCE-9 CE; Eregzen 2011b: 277) while graves for the Qin lords at Nanzhihui (221 BCE-206 BCE) are more or less all absolutely E-W orientated (Shelach-Lavi 2015: 285; Allard 2006: 213). The burial mound of the first emperor of the Qin dynasty is part of a large burial complex surrounded by an enclosure wall (Shelach-Lavi 2015: 318). This feature was followed in the Yang-ling burial complex of the Han dynasty (206 BCE-220 CE) where as well as the whole burial complex the single burial mounds also have a surrounding enclosure wall, the latter provided with four cardinally orientated entrance gates (*op. cit.*, p. 327).

5.2 Inner orientation

Containers for corpse were made either as wooden coffins, as stone sarcophagi, or as pits in which the body was placed. At the same time containers were usually used to hold funerary objects, whose number and size correlates with the size of the body. Archaeological documentation of skeletons and their orientation is rather rare and thus a quantifying analysis is difficult. For the most part we only have data on the containers and their orientation, which also allows some conclusions on the body's orientation, based on the assumption that the body and container correlate with each other in terms of orientation (cf. Tong Tao 2008: 288).

The orientation of containers differs in many cases from the orientation of the layout of the mound. Such a deviation can be found, for example, at the cist tomb M-7 at Phu nub (Yar lung) mentioned in Chayet 1994: 73, at the Reshui burial mound M-2 (Tong Tao 2008: 317) (Fig. 35) or also at the above-mentioned burial mound of 0131a.

The *btsan po*-s' tombs at 0032 face downhill and they appear to be orientated in an inter-cardinal – possibly north-west – direction. As already stated the orientation of the outer shape does not necessarily have to correlate with the inner orientations (of chamber, coffin or skeleton), and we have no evidence of the actual alignments of the *btsan po*-s' tombs. In the 7th-century Shoroon Bumbagar tomb at Ulaan Kherem (see above) the wooden coffin (230×85×40cm) (L/W/H) faces ca. 30° north-west (Erdenebold 2017), i.e. divergent from an absolute orientation in contrast to elite tombs of the earlier Xiongnu and also in China of the Tang Dynasty (Eckfeld 2005: 43), where the coffin orientation indeed seems to correlate with the (cardinal) orientation of the outer tombs. In circular graves of the Xiongnu context of the later period, the dominant orientation for the body was towards the north (80%), while for the earlier period ca. 18% of the examples faced east or south-east, and 2% faced south (Turbat 2013: 90).

In western Tibet, one of the more common orientations of the cist tombs was along the NW-SE axis (e.g. tomb M-1 at Dung dkar Pi wang; CTRI et al. 2001: 17). A similar north or north-west orientation is also recorded for some Central Tibetan cist tombs (M-7 or XM-15 of Phu nub, or M-1, M-2 and M-3 at Rgyal bzhang, in Chayet 1994: 73). At Central Tibetan burial mounds such as M-5 in Ser khung (M-8 of 0047) an orientation of the chamber along the NW-SE axis is evident (a coffin was missing, most probably plundered; Sonam Wangdu and Hou Shizhu 2010: 52).

5.2.1 Comparative notes: Tibetan tombs and Han and Jin tombs in Qinghai

Similar to Central Tibet, in eastern Tibet the burial mounds' outer orientation is towards the valley. In Tibet, absolute orientations of burial mounds were apparently not common. Information on their inner orientation is sparse. As one of the few examples, at mound M-2 in Reshui in eastern Tibet, the chamber is orientated towards the north-east and at mound M-1 the chamber faces south-west (Tong Tao 2008: 317, 318; see Fig. 35).

In contrast, at Han and Jin cemeteries in Qinghai (1st cent. BCE to 4th cent. CE) we find a variety of orientations of chambers (north, north-east, north-west, south, south-east and also south-west) and it seems difficult to fix any particular orientation, although the northern (NW or NE) direction appears to predominate. In Shangsunjiazhai 上孙家寨, at mounds M-154 and M-155, the chamber, coffin and the head of the corpse point northwards (Tong Tao 2008: 285, 286); no coffin was found at M-12, but the chamber and the head of the skeleton were facing north. At mound M-37 the chamber, coffin and the head of the skeleton faced north-east (op. cit., p. 288). At mound M-1 in the grave field of Taojiazhai 陶家寨, three skeletons were found facing south and one facing south-east (*op. cit*., p. 289). At mound M-6 in Gucheng, one chamber faces south-east and the head of the skeleton is inclined slightly in the same direction (*op. cit*., p. 289). At the same site, at mound M-7 the chamber and the head of the skeleton faces north-east (*op. cit*., p. 290). At mounds M-1 and M-2 in Gaozhai (Huzhu), the chambers (without skeletons) face north-east (*op. cit*., p. 291).

The examples from Han and Jin tombs in Qinghai given by Tong Tao also show the importance of the orientation of the tomb entrance in determining the position of the coffin and in particular of the head of the skeleton. The head of the skeleton and the grave entrance correlate with each other, a situation which may indicate the custom of carrying the deceased into the burial chamber legs first.

5.3 Reconstruction of the orientation of Central Tibetan burial chambers

Based on the above-mentioned correlation of the orientation of the head of the body with the orientation of the chamber entrance at Han and Jin cemeteries in Qinghai, in a hypothetical comparison the corpse in the chamber of mound M-2 in Spang mda' (Khacham 2015) in Central Tibet would have been facing south-west. On the other hand, in the case of mound M-5 at Ser khung (M-8 of 0047) the skeleton would have been orientated towards the north-west (see plan in Chayet 1994: 75). The *bum pa* opening of the stupa tomb M-1 in Spang mda' presented in CRC (1992: 367) is orientated towards the north-west. The rock at site 0147, which may have been the cover of a niche tomb, is orientated along the east-west axis.

The pit we found at the tomb of site 0131a is aligned at 328° (north-west), based on the orientation of the lateral walls towards the rear wall of the chamber. Compared to the orientation of the neighbouring burial mounds, this opened mound is similarly aligned to the topography and the trapezoid's longer leg faces the valley, at between 345° and 350°. This just underlines our general observation that the orientation of the mound deviates from the orientation of the chamber, in this case an angle of ca. 20°. This means that two different concepts were used to determine the orientation of these two structural components of the burial mound, i.e. the outer shape and the chamber. In tomb 0131a the position of the body was probably along the chamber, parallel to the rear wall of the tomb. Given the size of the chamber, 85×50×50 cm (L/W/H), the position of the corpse (of an adult) was evidently bent with the knees up to the chest, laid on its back or in a lateral position.

At this particular tomb we only found one stone to cover the pit, yet the use of more than one covering rock can be assumed, as we find several cover stones scattered in one of the neighbouring tombs (0131b) and a hypothetical reconstruction of the original form of the grave container for placing the corpses in a stretched out position is given in Fig. 23.

Given the height of the chamber and the chamber's size in general, the deceased was evidently not carried inside from one of the sides as was the case at the larger accessible chambers. In this case the body had to be laid into the chamber from the top; the covering rock here closed a chamber that, as said, was in principle constructed in parallel to the stone-lined pit tomb, only that it was covered by earth to form a burial mound.

6. Concluding remarks

To briefly sum up this contribution in the architecture of the Central Tibetan burial mounds we find the development from simple cist tombs to smaller round or oval mounds and finally to forms where the inner part represents a combination of a pit plus shaft construction, which in a second step was covered by a mound of clay (or caly plus stones), a type which arguably relates to the majority of the smaller trapezoidal mounds. This is followed by variations of larger (trapezoidal) structures with accessible chamber(s), with the chamber floor particularly treated, an architectural feature which together with other elements of the interior such as a staircase (in the (symbolic) number of nine plus seven steps) were characteristic of the walled burial sites of the higher ranking nobility of the imperial period; the latter is also indicated outwardly by the size of the respective monuments or by the step like trench constructions in front of (hillside) elite mounds. The grid construction to stabilise larger mounds (in a 3×3 or even other designs) was probably in most cases not related to a parallel-shaped chamber situation below.

Stupa tombs reveal particular techniques of roof constructions, as are also found in the building history of neighbouring cultures, and possibly represent an adaptation from common house constructions as we also find in some architectural features of larger walled burial mounds. Chronologically we see the stupa tombs as a later development in Central Tibet's tumulus history, related to the Buddhist period of Tubo as also the "*tsa tsa* tombs" or probably also the variety of the 12-cornered trapezoidal burial mound.

Among the larger tombs, round and square structures are rather rare. Notable is the presence of simple stone-marked cist or pit graves together with several forms and sizes of mound graves within one and the same grave field. However, it remains open whether in such mixed fields with different chronologies there were also different forms of (inner) orientation of the burial sites.

The orientation issue is the least explored. What can be stated is that on the one hand there was evidently no consistency in the outer orientation of the trapezoidal structures; they simply adopted the architecture of the topographical situations on site, which resulted in the fact of mixed orientations within one field. On the other hand a deviation in the orientation of the graves' interior (represented by chamber, coffin or body position) compared to the outer direction can be observed, a situation which is remarkable particularly in terms of a burial concept that was possibly celestially oriented in the sense of a relation to certain constellations (see Hazod, in this volume). We see a slight dominance of the northern directions (N, NE, NW), which in contrast to elite burials in inland China is also to be found in elite tombs of eastern Tibet and the early Mongolian context. But this all needs to be further examined on the basis of additional quantitative data on the burial sites' inner construction and information from written sources about the heavens at the time of the Tibetan tumulus tradition.

* * *

List of Central Tibetan burial mound sites mentioned in the article

(Based on the site list given on the Tibet Tumulus website (TTT; fn. 2); the details follow the order of number of site, district, county and GPS value.)

0002: Khra 'brug district, Sne gdong County: 29 11 32, 91 47.
0024: Skyer pa district, Sne gdong: 29 20 08, 91 49 28.
0032: Phyong rgyas (royal necropolis), 'Phyong rgyas: 29 01 10, 91 40 59.
0047: Grva thang (Ser khung field), Grva nang County: 29 14 02, 91 17 58.
0092: Skyems stong (Slebs ri field), Snang County: 28 59 26, 93 20 23.
0093: Skyems stong (second field of Slebs ri), Snang County: 28 58 53, 93 21 02.
0100: Nyang po, Rgya mda' County: 30 13 43, 93 06 02.
0105: Bya ra mdo, Mal gro Gong dkar County: 29 47 42, 91 52 30.
0108: Dvags pa, Mal gro Gong dkar County: 29 46 08, 91 50 49.
0131: Thang dga' (Lo valley), Stag rtse County: 29 51 36, 91 32 59.
0141: Gtsang tog (Cha valley), Stag rtse County: 29 45 10, 91 37 37.
0143: Dar rgyas (Gru bzhi /Lhas valley), Stag rtse County: 29 43 54, 91 28 33.
0147: Bde chen district (Shing tshang), Stag rtse County: 29 36 23, 91 22 01.

0148: Bde chen district, Stag rtse County: 29 39 14, 91 20 58.

0150: Bsam grub gling (Chos lung valley), Stag rtse County: 29 38 19, 91 17 01.

0157: Tshal Gung thang (Sri valley), Lhasa Municipality: 29 37 00, 91 14 36.

0172: Dmar district (field of Sgang skyid), Stod lung County: 29 49 45, 90 46 07.

0246: Lcang ra (Ka'u /Ka 'khor), Lhun grub County: 29 51 59, 91 23 37.

0330: Lha rtse, Lha rtse County: 29 12 37, 87 26 41.

0339: Lha rtse (Khrom chen cemetery), Lha rtse County: 29 21 33, 87 48 42.

0367: Yab, Stod lung County: 29 41 25, 90 57 18.

0376: Thang dga' (Lo valley), Stag rtse County: 29 51 33, 91 32 36.

0397: Tshal Gung thang (Sri valley), Lhasa Municipality: 29 36 43, 91 15 31.

0398: Tshal Gung thang (Sri valley), Lhasa Municipality: 29 37 29, 91 15 18.

0402: Bde chen (Shing tshang), Stag rtse County: 29 37 55, 91 21 09.

Fig. 1. Slebs ri (0092). Drawing by H. Feiglstorfer (after Sonam Wangdu and Hou Shizhu 1985).

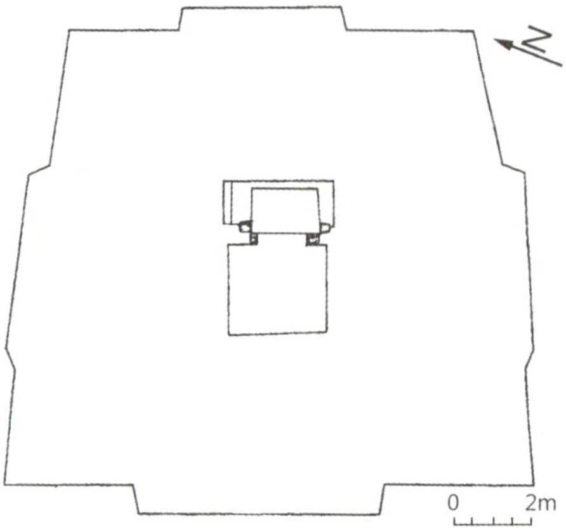

Fig. 2. Slebs ri (0092).
The 12-cornered mound M-113, after Huo Wei 2010: 50.

Fig. 3. The site of 0141 (Cha Valley). Examples of mounds with sloping walls (M-1, M-2) and the "coffer shaped" type (M-3). Based on SfM (Structure from Motion) photography by M. Gamon 2014.

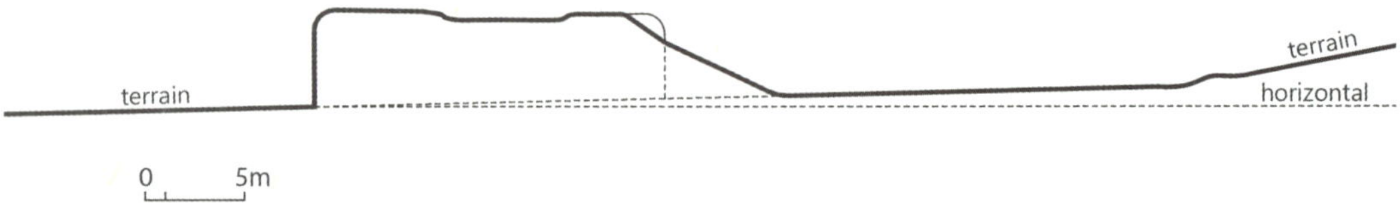

Fig. 4. Site 0172 (Sgang skyid).Section of M-2 with ramp leading from the rear of the mound up to the top. Drawing: H. Feiglstorfer 2015.

Fig. 5. Site 0108 (Blonposgang), an example of a mound (ca. 50m, front) built into the mountainside.
Photograph: H. Feiglstorfer 2015.

Fig. 6. Site 0141 (Cha Valley). The stone inlays separating the rammed earth layers are visible along the walls of this coffer-shaped mound.
Photograph: H. Feiglstorfer 2014.

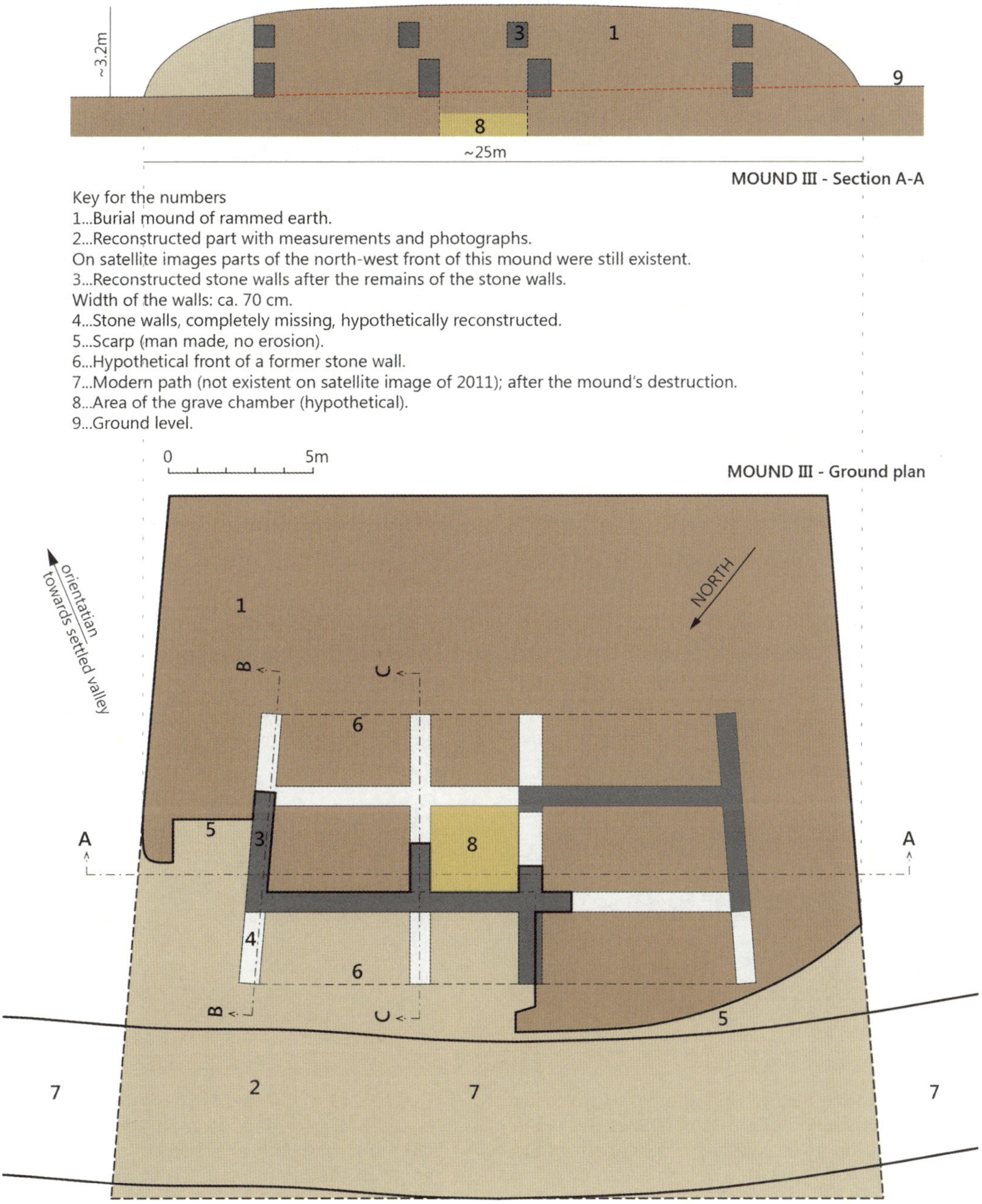

Fig. 7. Site 0002 (Rtse thang, Lower Yar lung). Ground plan and section.
Drawing: H. Feiglstorfer 2015.

Fig. 8. Site 0376 (Lo Valley). Vertically arranged layers of stone and rammed earth (RE = rammed earth, ST, stones; height of the mound: ca. 5m). Photo: H. Feiglstorfer 2015.

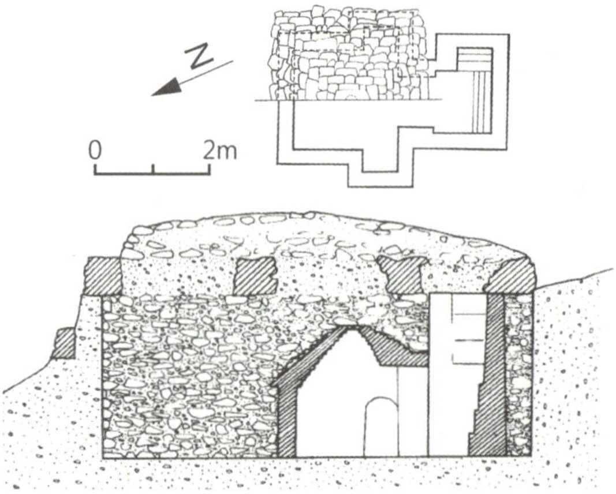

Fig. 9. M-2 in the field of Spang mda' (Rgya tshva County). The section of the tomb shows the stone structure on top as structurally independent of the chamber below.
After Shawo Khacham 2011.

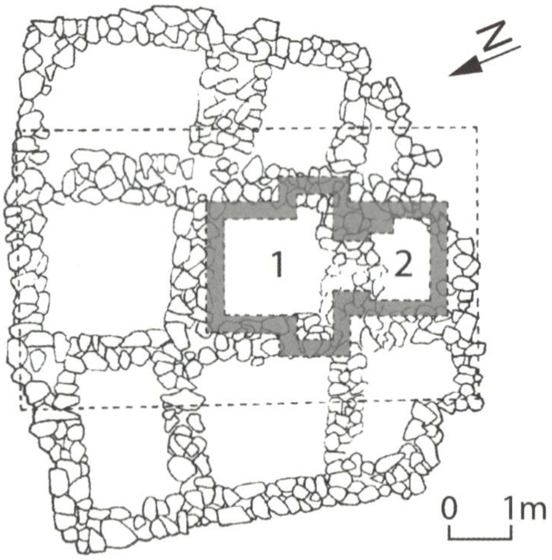

Fig. 10. M-2 in the field of Spang mda'. The core of the 3×3 grid (1) is located above the main chamber, with the antechamber (2) situated south of the central part of the grid. Drawing after CRC 1992: 369.

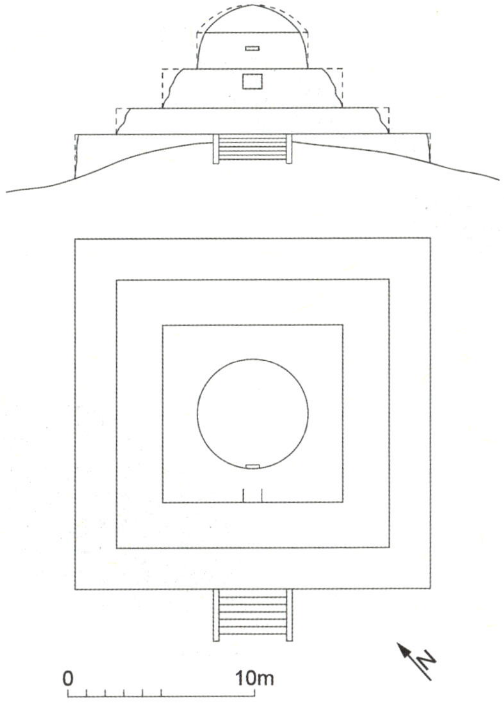

Fig. 11. Site 0397 (Sri Valley). Ground plan and SW elevation of the stupa tomb.
Drawing by H. Feiglstorfer.

Fig. 12a-c. Site 0143 (Gru bzhi). *Tsa tsa* found inside the earth structure of an open mound.
Photograph: H. Feiglstorfer 2015.

Fig. 13. Site 0143 (Grubzhi). Reconstruction of a burial mound enclosure wall, the latter indicated by the remains of the wall's foundations. Drawing: H. Feiglstorfer 2016.

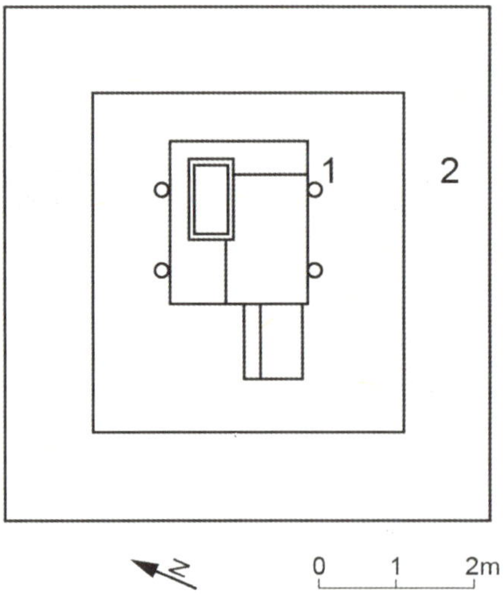

Fig. 14. Site 0092 (Slebs ri). M-130, ground plan (1 = position of wooden pillar; 2 = wall around the grave's central part); after Sonam Wangdu and Hou Shizhu 1985: 36.

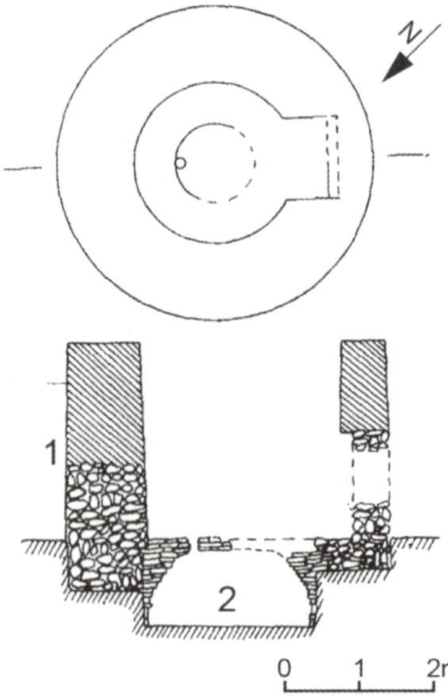

Fig. 15. Site 0092. M-27, section, wall (1) around the burial pit or chamber (2), the latter with a corbelled roof construction; after Wangdu and Shizhu 1985: 36.

Fig. 16. Site 0172 (Sgang skyid). A structure-from-motion (SfM) 3-D visualisation of a sacrificial pit. Feiglstorfer 2015.

Fig. 17. Site 0246 (Ka'u, Lower 'Phanpo).
Example of a stone-marked pit grave.
Photograph by H. Feiglstorfer 2015.

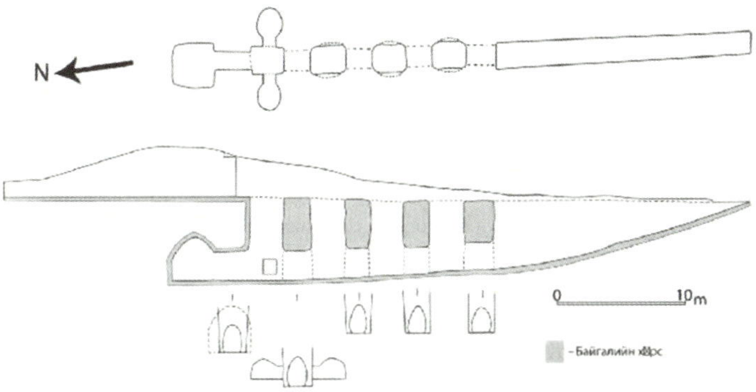

Fig. 18. Ground plan and section of a central (7th-cent.) burial mound in the field of Shoroon Bumbagar, Mongolia; in Erdenebold, forthcoming.

Fig. 19. Site 0092 (Slebs ri), M-121, ground plan and section of the grave with the chamber's floor made of arga; after Sonam Wangdu and Hou Shizhu 1985: 36.

Fig. 21. Site 0131a (Lo Valley). Burial pit or chamber covered by a rock.
Photograph by H. Feiglstorfer 2015.

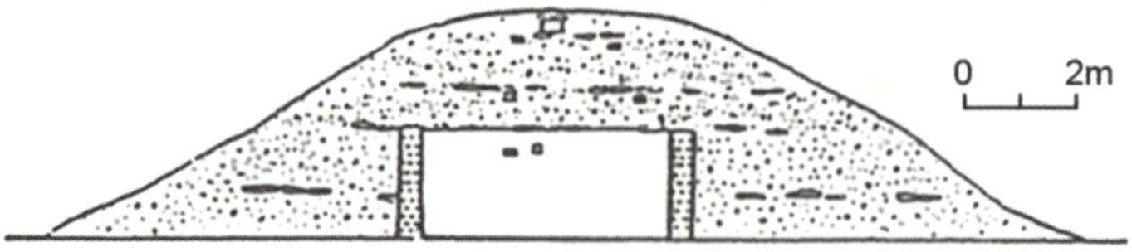

Fig. 20. Site 0330 (Bom ma). Example of a (ca. 20m) round burial mound, with the walled chamber built above ground level; after Huo Wei 1995: 72.

Fig. 22. Site 0131b (Lo Valley). Two rocks, the remains of a chamber's roof construction.
Photograph: H. Feiglstorfer 2015.

Fig. 24. Site 0147 (Shing tshang). View inside the burial chamber of one of the central mounds of this site (A = position of the burial pit; B = Openings (for construction purposes?) in the inner wall.
Photograph: H. Feiglstorfer 2015.

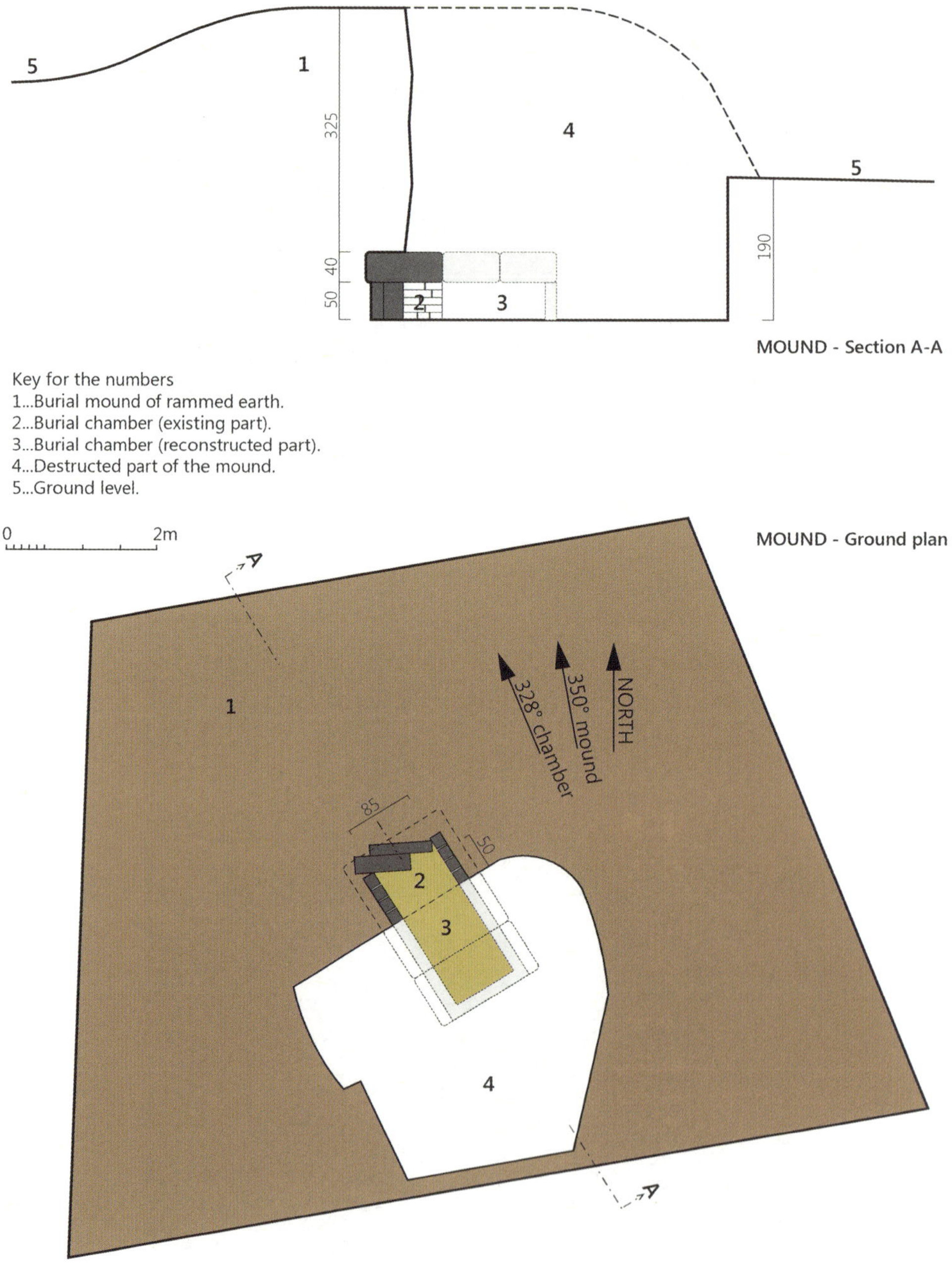

Fig. 23. Site 0131a (Lo Valley), ground plan and section of the reconstructed mound shown in Fig. 21. Drawing by H. Feiglstorfer 2016.

Fig. 25. Dulan, Reshui. M-1, longitudinal section of the tomb.

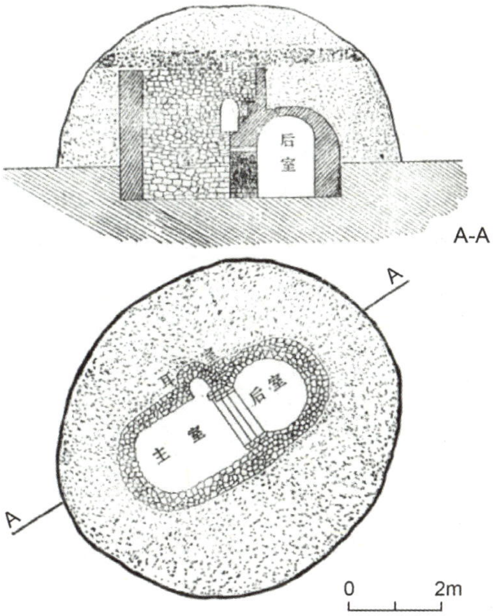

Fig. 26. Dung dkar. M-60, ground plan and section. Shawo Khacham 2015.

Fig. 27. Site 0398 (Sri Valley). Stupa tomb. Shawo Khacham 2011.

Fig. 28. Site 0398 (Sri Valley). Stupa tomb. View of the corbelled roof construction. Shawo Khacham 2011.

Fig. 29. Site 0398 (Sri Valley). Stupa tomb. Some tsa tsa are visible behind the burial pit. Shawo Khacham 2011.

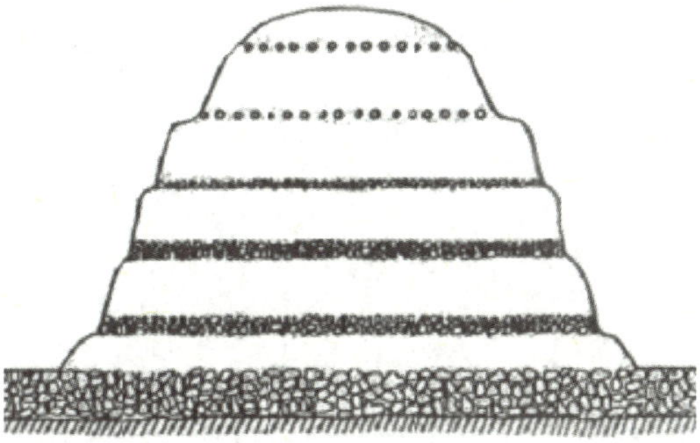

Fig. 30. Site 0093 (Slebs ri). Mound M-168. Stupa tomb with a circular ground plan; in Shawo Khacham 2011.

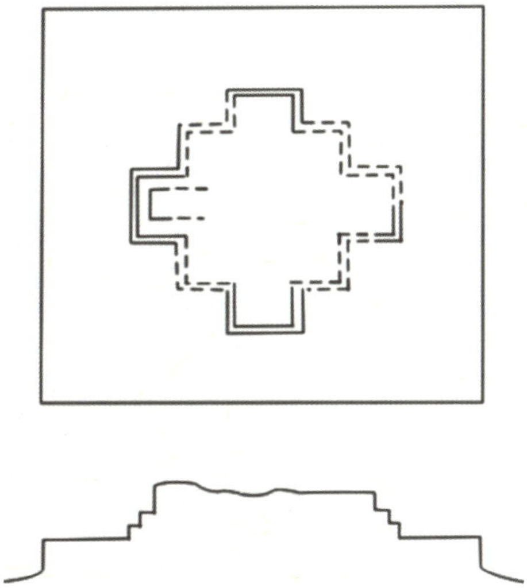

Fig. 31. Site 0047 (Ser khung). Stupa tomb with a cruciform ground plan; in Shawo Khacham 2011.

Fig. 32. Site 0376 (Lo Valley). Adobe brick wall inside the tomb. Photograph: H. Feiglstorfer 2015.

Fig. 33. Site 0376 (Lo Valley). Adobe bricks. Size 48 x 36 x 8cm.
Photograph: H. Feiglstorfer 2015.

Fig. 34. Noyonuul, Mongolia, Xiongnu tomb (M-31) with a wooden coffin inside a wooden chamber; in Yeruul-Erdene 2011: 49.

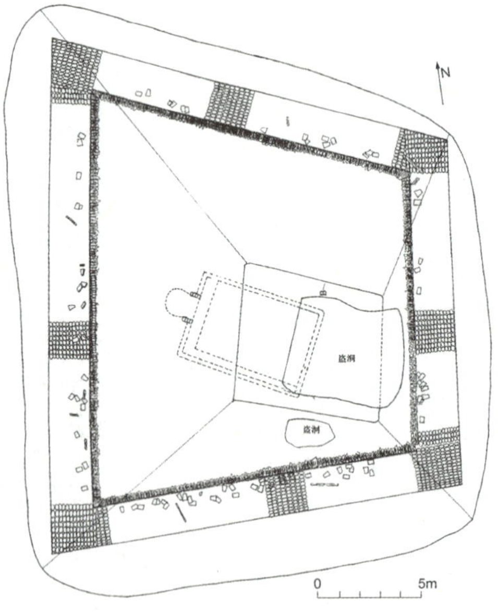

Fig. 35. Dulan, Reshui. Mound M-2. Ground plan with the two orientations of the outer trapezoid and the inner chamber; after Tong Tao 2008: 317.

References (Incl. abbreviations)

AIQP = Archaeological Institute of Qinghai Province (ed.). 1998. Qinghai Hualong xian shangbanzhuwa Kayue wenhua mudi Dierci fajue 青海化隆县上半主洼卡约文化墓地第二次发掘 (The Tomb of the Ka yue culture period in Hualong, Qinghai), *Archaeology* 1: 51-64.

Aldenderfer, Mark. 2003. A New Class of Standing Stone from the Tibetan Plateau, *The Tibetan Journal* 28(12): 3-20.

— 2013. Variation in mortuary practice on the early Tibetan plateau and the high Himalayas, *Journal of the International Association for Bon Research* 1: 293-317.

Allard, Francis. 2006. Frontiers and boundaries: The Han empire from its southern periphery, in: Stark, Miriam T. (ed.), *Archaeology of Asia*. Malden, Oxford: Blackwell Publishing, 233-254.

Bellezza, John Vincent. 2008. *Zhang Zhung: Foundations of Civilization in Tibet:A Historical and Ethnoarchaeological Study of the Monuments, Rock Art, Texts and Oral Tradition of the Ancient Tibetan Upland.* Wien: Verlag der Österreichischen Akademie der Wissenschaften.

— 2015. The Ancient Corbelled Buildings of Upper Tibet. Architectural attribute, environmental factors and religious meaning in a unique type of archaeological monument, in: Feiglstorfer Hubert (ed.), *Architecture and Conservation. Proceedings of the 13th Seminar of the International Association for Tibetan Studies (IATS).Panel 2 – Architecture and Conservation. Ulaanbaatar* 2013.4-18 (Available online http://www.jccs-a.org/issues).

— 2016. *Tibet Archaeology. Flight of the Khyung, newsletter April 2016* (Available online http://www.tibetarchaeology.com/april-2016/).

Caffarelli, Paola M. V. 1997. Architectural style in tombs from the period of the kings, in: Singer J.C. and Phillip Denwood (eds.), *Tibetan Art: Towards a Definition of Style.* London: L. King, 230-261.

Chayet, Anne. 1994. *Art et Archéologie*. Paris: Picard Éditeur.

CRC 1992 = Cultural Relics Committee. 1992. Xizang Yaluzangbujiang zhongyou Qusong, Jiacha liangxian gumuzang de diaocha yu fajue 西藏雅鲁藏布江中游曲松、加查两县古墓葬的调查与发掘 (Ancient tombs in Qusong and Jiacha of Tibet), in: Tong

En'zheng, 童恩正 (ed.), *Southern Ethnology and Archaeology* 5: 359-371.

CTRI = Chinese Tibetan Research Institute of Sichuan, Archaeological Department of Sichuan University, Archaeological Institute of Tibet (eds.). 2001. Xizang zhada xian Piyang-Dongga yizhi gumuqun shijue jianbao 西藏札达县皮央・东嘎遗址古墓群试掘简报 (Archaeological report of ancient tombs in Tibet. Zhada, Piyang-Dongga site), *Archaeology* 6: 14-31.

Darragon, Frederique. 2015. On the ancient cross-shaped towers of Nyangpo and Kongpo in eastern Central Tibet, in: Feiglstorfer Hubert (ed.), *Architecture and Conservation. Proceedings of the 13th Seminar of the International Association for Tibetan Studies (IATS). Panel 2 – Architecture and Conservation. Ulaanbaatar 2013*. 34-50 (Available online http://www.jccs-a.org/issues).

Eckfeld, Tonia. 2005. *Imperial Tombs in Tang China, 618–907. The Politics of Paradise*. London, New York: Routledge.

Erdenebold, Lhagvasuren. 2017. Preliminary excavation findings from Shoroon Bumbagar, Ulaan Kherem, Mongolia, in: Allinger, Eva, Frantz Grenet, Christian Jahoda, Maria-Katharina Lang, and Anne Vergati (eds.). *Interaction in the Himalayas and Central Asia: Processes of Transfer, Translation and Transformation in Art, Archaeology, Religion and Polity*. Wien: Verlag der Österreichischen Akademie der Wissenschaften, 13-28.

Eregzen, Gelegdorj. 2011a. Circular burials of the Xiongnu, in: Eregzen, Gelegdorj (ed.), *Treasures of the Xiongnu. The first Nomadic Empire in Mongolia*, Ulaanbaatar, 50-73.

— 2011b. Comparative Analysis of Xiongnu Noble Tombs and Burials in Adjacent Regions, in: Brosseder, Ursula, Bryan K. Miller (eds.). *Xiongnu Archaeology. Multidisciplinary Perspectives of the First Steppe Empire in Inner Asia*. Bonn: Rheinische Friedrich-Wilhelms-Universität, 275-284.

— 2013a. Belkhiin am tombs, in: Tseveendorj, Dandinsuren (ed.). *Encyclopaedia Xiongnu*, Ulaanbaatar, 27.

— 2013b. Uvgunt tomb, in: Tseveendorj, Dandinsuren (ed.). *Encyclopaedia Xiongnu*, Ulaanbaatar, 187.

Fagan, Brian M. (ed.). 1996. *The Oxford Companion to Archaeology*. New York, Oxford: University Press.

Feiglstorfer, Hubert. 2015. The burial mounds of Central Tibet: Layout, construction, material, unpubl. paper, at http://www.oeaw.ac.at/tibetantumulustradition/de/startseite/.

— 2016. The making of an *arga* roof. Access at: www.youtube.com.

— 2017. *Mineral building traditions in the Himalayas*, Vienna: University of Natural Resources and Life Sciences of Vienna, doctoral thesis.

Haarh, Eric. 1969. *The Yar-luṅ dynasty: A Study with Particular Regard to the Contribution by Myths and Legends to the History of Ancient Tibet and the Origin and Nature of Its Kings*. København: Gad.

Hazod, Guntram. 2009. Imperial Central Tibet – An annotated cartographical survey of its territorial divisions and key political sites, in: Dotson, Brandon, *The Old Tibetan Annals. An Annotated Translation of Tibet's First History*. Wien: Verlag der Österreichischen Akademie der Wissenschaften, 161-232.

— 2014. The stele in the centre of the Lhasa Mandala: About the position of the 9th-century Sino-Tibetan treaty pillar of Lhasa in its historical-geographical and narrative context, in: Tropper, Kurt (ed.), *Epigraphic Evidence in the Pre-modern Buddhist World*, Wien: Arbeitskreis für Tibetische und Buddhistische Studien, 37-81.

He Qiang 何强. 1995. Lhasa Duoren: Tubo jitan yu muzang de diaocha ji fenxi "拉萨朵仁"吐蕃祭坛与墓葬的调查及分析 (Lhasa Duoren. The investigation and analysis of Tubo sacrificial places and tombs), *Cultural Relics* 1: 32-36.

Huo Wei 霍巍. 1995. *Xizang Gudai Muzang Zhidu Shi* 西藏古代墓葬制度史 *(The History of the Ancient Tombs of Tibet)*. Chengdu: Sichuan People Press.

— 2010. Xizang Lieshan mudi xiangguan wenti de zaitantao 西藏列山墓地相关问题的再探讨 (A re-discussion of some issues related to the Sleb ri tombs in Tibet), *Journal of Tibetology* 5: 46-60.

IHNS = Institute for the History of Natural Sciences. 2000. *Zhongguo gudai jianzhu jishu shi* 中国古代建筑技术史 *(A History of Building Technology in Ancient China)*. Beijing: Chinese Academy of Sciences Press.

Kipfer, Barbara Ann. 2000. *Encyclopedic Dictionary of Archaeology*. New York: Springer.

Liu, Laurence G. 1989. *Chinese Architecture*. New York: Rizzoli.

Miller, Bryan K. 2011. Permutations of peripheries in the Xiongnu empire, in: Brosseder, Ursula, Bryan K. Miller (eds.), *Xiongnu Archaeology. Multidisciplinary Perspectives of the First Steppe Empire in Inner Asia*. Bonn: Rheinische Friedrich-Wilhelms-Universität, 559-578.

NMK = The National Museum of Korea, The National Museum of Mongolian history, The Institute of Archaeology / Mongolian Academy of Sciences, Seoul (eds.). 2003. *Hunnu Tombs at Hudgiin Tolgoi in Mongolia. Research Report on Korean-Mongolian Joint Expedition in Mongolia III.*

Ochir, A., L. Erdenebold, S. Kharjaubi, and K. Tantegin. 2013. *Ertnii nüüdelchdin bunkhant bulshny maltlaya sudalgaa (The Excavation and Research of Tomb Graves of the Ancient Nomads)*, Ulaanbaatar.

Pan Ling. 2011. A summary of Xiongnu sites within the northern periphery of China, in: Brosseder, Ursula, Bryan K. Miller (eds.). *Xiongnu Archaeology. Multidisciplinary Perspectives of the First Steppe Empire in Inner Asia.* Bonn: Rheinische Friedrich-Wilhelms-Universität, 463-474.

SAM = School of Archaeology and Museologyof Beijing University, Archaeological Institute of Qinghai Province (eds.). 2005. *Tibetan Tombs at Dulan, Qinghai* 都兰吐蕃墓 . Beijing: Science Press.

Seonbok Yi, *et al.* 2008. *Stone-cist Burials at Erdene, Mongolia.* Ulaanbaatar.

Shawo Khacham. 2011. Tubo taxingmu de qiyuan yu yuanshi tazang 吐蕃塔形墓的起源与原始塔葬 (The origin of the Tubo stupa tomb and the ancient stupa burial), *Journal of Tibet University* 4: 141-145.

— 2014a. *Tubo wangling de kaogu faxian yu yanjiu* (Archaeological study of Tibetan imperial tumuli), doctoral thesis, Sichuan University.

— 2014b. Chamuqin shibei yu Tubo muqunzhuren zhi xinkao 查木钦石碑与吐蕃墓群主人之新考 (A Re-examination of the Khrom chen tombs in Lhatse, TAR), *Journal of Tibetology* 藏学学刊 10.

— 2015. Tubo wangling de mushi fuyuan yanjiu 吐蕃王陵的墓室复原研究 (Tibetan Emperor Tumuli's chamber recovery), *Tibetan Studies* 6: 46-53.

Shelach-Lavi, Gideon. 2015. *The Archaeology of Early China. From Prehistory to the Han Dynasty*, New York: Cambridge University Press.

Sonam Wangdu and Hou Shizhu 侯石柱 . 1985. Xizang Langxian Lieshan mudi de diaocha he shijue 西藏朗县列山墓地的调查和试掘 (The investigation and excavation of the Lie shan tombs in Lang Xian), *Cultural Relics* 9: 32-38.

— 2010. A report of the archaeological research done on the Tibetan plateau and conjectures about future developments, *The Tibet Journal* 35(3): 41-59.

Shin 2000 = Shin Yun min. 2000. *Han de mugguagmyu engu*. Seoul.

Tong Tao. 2008. *The silk roads of the northern Tibetan plateau during the early Middle Ages (from the Han to Tang dynasty) as reconstructed from archaeological and written sources*. Dissertation 2008, University of Tübingen.

Tseveendorj, D. 2013. Sun and moon worship, in: Tseveendorj, Dandinsuren (ed.). *Encyclopaedia Xiongnu*, Ulaanbaatar, 169-170.

Tucci, Giuseppe. 1973. *Tibet*. München: Nagel Verlag.

Turbat, T. 2013. Funeral practices of circular graves of the Xiongnu, in: Tseveendorj, Dandinsuren (ed.). *Encyclopaedia Xiongnu*, Ulaanbaatar, 86-90.

XWD 2010 = Editorial Board of the Cultural Relics Bureau, Lhasa. 2010. *Zhongguo Wenwu Dituji, Xizang Zizhiqu fence* 中国文物地图集・西藏自治区分册 *(Atlas of Cultural Relics of the TAR)*. Beijing: Cultural Relics Press.

Yeruul-Erdene, Ch. 2011. The Xiongnu elite tombs, in: Gelegdorj Eregzen (ed.), *Treasures of the Xiongnu. The First Nomadic Empire in Mongolia*, Ulaanbaatar, 35-49.

Srong btsan sgam po Revisited

Ancestral king, monarchic founder, Buddhist saviour saint and cultural hero

One Body – Multiple Identities

One Identity – Multiple Bodies

Per K. Sørensen (University of Leipzig)

Everything must change in order to stay the same
(*Tutto deve cambiare perché nulla cambi*)
Tomasi di Lampedusa, *The Leopard* (*Il Gattopardo*)

1. Introduction

It is an honour to dedicate this small essay – despite the sad circumstances – to my dear friend, the late Tsering Gyalbo: He was a knowledgable and illustrious scholar, a proud son born in the depth of his beautiful and vast homeland; moreover, a warm and helpful colleague who over many years and across all borders served as a path-breaker by actively promoting academic contacts between Tibet and the West.

Considering the exciting topic of the present volume, there can be little doubt that in the long perspective various strategies and designs were actively deployed by Tibetan historians when it comes to the question of constructing genealogies, here taken in a broad sense, both when recording those who were to hold temporal (most often kinship-related) as much as religious-spiritual power, which in a Tibetan context held a particularly prominent position, indeed the temporal-ecclesiastical inter-relatedness remained an unique, yet viable concept of widespread currency for many centuries as witnessed in well-established phrases like *chos srid zung 'brel.*[1] It is commonly claimed that genealogy deploys history as a series of biographical sketches linked by the principles of hereditary (but as we know now also spiritual) succession, or indeed their fruitful combination. Such attempts to construct a vision and a narrative aimed at supplying legitimacy to present needs, commonly drafted for the sake of upholding secular or clerical claims, legitimising current or erstwhile prerogatives or they had a commemorative motive, being committed to paper in order to ensure the perpetuation of a line's or lineage's memorable past to avoid that their memory disappeared in the haze of historical amnesia. Such reconstructions usually were conceived of as a relatively linear and uninterrupted transmission, in most cases drafted either when knowledge of the individual and successive members of the genealogy in question was still fresh or, as we often meet in numerous (ethnogenetic) tracts of family or ecclesiastical lineage stories, entire narrative constructions were invaded by historical fiction, the more remote the lineage or genealogical origins (not least its often hazy beginnings) went back in time the more fictionalised its reconstruction proved to be. Samples are legion as can be witnessed in countless Tibetan Buddhist and historiographical sources. Nonetheless, genealogical representations and recordings in a Tibetan context usually displayed a weak notion of historical reliability, most often marred by arrant cases of anachronism or, most often, plain mythographical fiction. Not seldom, transcendental aspects and designs too were at play, even mythologies and literary templates as narrative tropes, transgressing the boundaries of time and space, and the formation of such stories of origin involved both allegorical visions and supernatural prodigies vested with transformative powers in the formation of a genealogy. The following modest paper is a case in point of such permutations, but here restricted to a single, albeit prominent figure in Tibetan history that was to stand at the heart of many genealogical and historical beginnings.

2. Ruler with shifting epithets

Rarely do we encounter figures in Tibetan history that were subject to more transformations and permutations in terms of identity than Srong b(r)tsan sgam po (605?-649 AD – with the exception perhaps of the hypertropic role and protean forms assumed by or rather projected upon the omnipresent thaumaturge and yogin Guru Rinpoche by posterity and by his most

1 See Cüppers (ed.) 2005 for this concept.

Fig. 1. Srong btsan sgam po, Central Tibet, 11-12th century. Potala Palace.

ardent followers that at places were to turn into a veritable Guru-mania down through the following centuries).[2] (Fig. 1) We are generally on the safe side when we maintain that the king was the first "historic monarch" in Tibet's history, later a key figure in the construction of genealogies. However, with fair reason, the king should rather be regarded, if not actually as the founding (fx. his grandfather and father were the actual trailblazers in uniting the different local lords and heads of prominent lineages into what became the Yarlung Kingdom), then at least the towering figure in the establishment and expansion of the emergent Tubo, a circumstance not only confirmed by available historical sources but also in tune with the idealised depiction that was ubiquitously transmitted and actively

2 In actual fact, anticipating our discussion here, it would resemble what the Tibetans customarily if only technically, call a case of "superimposition" and attribution (*sgro 'dogs/btags*, Skt. *samāropa, adhyāropa*), here of an "iconic" nature. Our understanding of the phenomenon Padmasambhava, although the questions as to his actual presence, length and not least the nature of his sojourn(s) in Tibet are still largely shrouded in mystery, the better appreciation of his often nebulous role mainly in later historiographical and religious literature has improved greatly following a series of studies by the colleagues Robert Mayer, Lewis Doney, Jake Dalton, and Hirshberg. A similar analysis, arguably a less complex undertaking, concerning the equally bulky "biographic and testamentary" vita literature dedicated to the founding king remains a desideratum.

endorsed in most subsequent Tibetan sources. Above all, this is the most obvious reason why his name pops up in most contexts when Tibet is being mentioned, almost on the verge of becoming an identity marker tagged for the land and hence the actual hero and progenitor in the national master narrative. This depiction of him is now actively propagated and in this role his name appears in countless publications and guidebooks, which foregrounds his role above anything else.

Indeed, his many "larger-than-life" or "trans-or multi-life" roles (indiscriminately designated as "manifestations," "re-incarnations" or "rebirths"; *sprul ba/sku, skye ba*):[3] in brief, the odyssey of his afterlife down through history ensured Srong btsan sgam po (a soubriquet under which he was commonly known, in part a Buddhist-inspired cognomen, original his regal name was Khri Srong brtsan, or Srong lde brtsan)[4] a position and repute that not only remained spectacularly symbolic, highly idealised but also surprisingly stable – one could here add in a *longue durèe* perspective – throughout all stages of Tibet's lengthy and eventful history. Since long he has turned into constituting a rhetoric site for Tibetan national and collective sentiments.

The earliest available (roughly 9th-10th century) sources (prominently those discovered

3 Here it must be stipulated that the initial concept was that Avalokiteśvara manifested or transformed himself in/into this king; however early in the post-dynastic narratives surrounding this king, esp. in the so-called vita corpus, the "testamentary" (*gter ma*) literature, the king by extension was portrayed as the one who effortlessly and proactively manifested himself through magic transformation (*sprul ba*) of sorts into a multitude of identities.

4 The honorific soubriquet or attributive epithet: (*thugs*) *sgam*, "profound" or "deep" (of mind) = "wise or sagacious" was also used for later kings. See Doney 2015: 67, fn. 19; for Khri Srong brtsan, its earliest? use is the late imperial or more feasibly? post-imperial *Old Tibetan Chronicle* (*OTC*; Pelliot Tibétain 1287 line 299: *btsan po srong brtsan sgam po'i ring la*...and the lines 453-55); see also *Myang ral chos 'byung* 175, *Lde'u chos 'byung* 253; *Dba' bzhed* 2b (Pasang Wangdu and Diemberger 2000: 29), followed by the vita corpus (*Ka Khol ma* 72 and *Rgyal rabs*) (Sørensen 1994: 162). We have reason to assume that its origin or first conscious use should be situated in the period of Khri srong lde btsan (756-800) at the earliest (i.e. ca. 800 CE), invented in a court milieu at a point where a "new religious worldview" reigned, an ideological milieu primarily suffused with the newly introduced and massively endorsed Buddhist lore (the "new" state religion in Tibet from 779 CE), an ideology that informed all aspects of the state and society including principal concepts of hegemony, rule and their language, its metaphors and the nomenclatura associated with kings and rulers.

For the application of the epithet *sgam po* to the king, *OTC* offers an brief explanation, arguing that it reflects the unanimous wish on the side of a grateful population to eulogise the rule's sagacity (or mastery of rule), whereas the most later, post-imperial, sources, not surprisingly, argue that his sagacity is due to his wise Buddhist law-making and his righteousness. However, if, more likely, one is looking for a possible Buddhist background or the original inspiration for the concept *sgam po* and its application to the king, one clue may point to the *Gaṇḍavyūha-sūtra* (Vaidhya 1960: 163.10-15) where Avalokiteśvara is characterised by the epithet "wise, profound" (Skt. *dhīra*). The epithetical adjective *sgam po* is rarely seen as a scholastic term to approximately reflect this specific Skt. term, Tib. *zab mo* here commonly is the general term used for "profound."

in Dunhuang but also the earliest edicts, inscriptions and archival documents in Tibetan writing available, such as a number of epigraphic *rdo ring* steles) depict him and his forebears as ancestral beings of celestial origin, endowed with supernatural properties. When and how this exalted status was assigned to the king and his line in pre-historic time still remains unclear. During his lifetime he rose to become a mighty warrior king and dynast with considerable success domestically as well as on the battlefield. His personal contacts with Buddhism must have been dim and brief, yet precisely this aspect in particular should, in the eyes of his descendants and later historians, contribute to perpetuate his role in Tibetan history. Looking at his ritual preoccupation and involvement, little suggests that he was influenced by Buddhism, and he evidently was an illiterate. Still, evidence of his (brief or rudimentary) contact with Buddhism might be gleaned from the Skar cung inscription (l. 4-6) claiming that during his rule Buddhism was practised. It does not indicate neither the nature nor the extent of contact during his era, aside from indicating his role in building a number of temples, foremost the Ra sa gtsug lag khang. The inscription makes a strong point, yet the date of the inscription to the early 9th century, also allows us to assume that it reflects an attempt at posthumous idealisation. Further, the destruction and occupation of Khotan by the Tibetans that occurred, to be true, after the passing of the king in 649/50 CE under the following ruler would suggest that the Tibetans were initially not expressly pro-Buddhist. Buddhist influence from the Kathmandu valley is likely to have been tangibly present during the last years of his reign. Still, it initially remained a religion restricted to the court and a small circle of aristocrats. His (promotional?) identity as a pro-Buddhist ruler, however, obviously was a construction that gained momentum in court circles in the late eighth or early ninth century. This new religion, initially an alien belief-system to the Tibetans challenging the existing "cognitive map" of the Tibetans, later was to turn into a powerful ideological, intellectual and cultural force in Tibet, supplanted and if only – to smooth the passage of this "new religion" from being alien to becoming domestic – absorbed and integrated many local belief systems, to create an unique, if gradually hybrid form of Buddhism, never a coherent and uniform system, that were to change the mindset and the physical universe of the Tibetans for good; in the ninth, perhaps already in the late eighth century, the adoption of Buddhism paved the way for an altered image, theoretical foundation and conceptualisation of the imperial founder figure, gradually replacing the older archaic concepts of a sacral and divine soul into the new role as a Buddhist *cakravartin*-worthy monarch; at that point, like other kings that followed him, he was regarded as an embodiment or manifestation of a *bodhisattva*, gradually being identified as and transfigured into the "Lord of the World" (Lokeśvara) or Avalokiteśvara, commonly known as Mahākāruṇika, the Bodhisattva Lord and Saint of Great Compassion.[5] As has been demonstrated in a number of studies, an image shift in the contemporary sources is to be observed, the Tibetan kings are now grandly eulogised for their accomplishments and perennial service to both religion and state, their feats in terms of proselytism, widespread patronage and promotion of Buddhism, aside from their battlefield accomplishments and expansion of the empire.

Indeed, Srong btsan sgam po's era and rule marked a caesura. His reign during which he was to govern in two turns – the last following the passing of his own son, was characterised by an expansionist policy, and more importantly, by the beginning of international encounters and contacts, opening Tibet to an increasingly cosmopolitan world – in short, his rule heralded the opening of Tibet to the outer world in all directions of the compass. It soon made Tibet a durable and grateful recipient of cultural and intellectual influences from a large number of neighbouring empires, fillips that eventually were to set its indelible mark on Tibet. In hindsight, his regime too signalled the beginning of a phase of transition in the ruler's royal status, not least concerning the very nature of royalty, allowing for an added or revaluated quality of being "a divine being" (*lha*) that gradually assumed new content and forms.[6] It was a process that had taken place and indeed took place during his and that of his father Gnam ri slon mtshan's reign, spanning a period during which the still inchoate regime

5 The idea of "manifestation" and "reincarnation" is documented in dynastic times too, see A.-M. Blondeau 1997; Kapstein 2000.

6 The oldest texts and inscriptions speak about the "kings," mostly in formulaic phrases, being defined as Gods from Heaven descending to become the Kings or Lords (*rgyal po, rje*) of Men/Humans (i.e. mortals), *[g]nam gyI lha las // myi'i rgyal por gshegs*, etc. In the 'Phyongs rgyas inscription (ca. 800 CE), related to the period of Khri srong lde btsan (ca. 742-797/800), it is said / *lha btsan po yab myes lha dang myI'i* (var. *mi'i*) *rjer gshegs te*, thus projecting the imagery and conception of the 'divine or apotheosised chieftain-kings' (*lha btsan po*) as rulers of men/the human world back into the time of (all? former Tibetan) ancestral kings (*yab mes*), no doubt and in the first place including the reign of Srong btsan sgam po. The idea of a heavenly sanctioned or mandated claim to rule is a concept of sacral kingship and sovereign rule that was widespread in East and Central Asia during this period. Nevertheless this phrase obviously signals a retroactive attempt to ancestralise, anachronise and ultimately legitimise a form of sacred monarchy, here perpetuating inheritance. It still does not solve the question as to how and when the term *lha* came into being as an epithet, to indicate a status of royalty (and the Tibetan kings by extension being seen as "Sons of God" or *lha sras*, obviously not just reflecting Skt. *devaputra*). Some references would suggest that the epithet *lha* (seen to reflect a manifestation of or indeed equalising *lha* 'Od lde spu rgyal) as an indigenous term goes back to the era prior to Spu lde gung rgyal (? 4th century of the then Spu rgyal Bod dynasty or later to Lha Tho do/ri snya/gnyan btsan).

succeeded, through conquer and through a network of politically motivated matrimonial alliances in uniting a row of minor lineage-based warring polities in Central Tibet, creating a hegemonic rule that developed from being a minor, rather localised Yarlung Kingdom into what famously should become the powerful Tubo (c. 600-850 CE), roundly feared by most neighbours in Central Asia. At court a complex system of tiered concubinage (the king allegedly championing at least five consorts) proved essential to the integration and coherence of the realm. In fact, royal lineages often derived their prestige, aside from any aura of divinity or numinosity, and survival from alliances with competing people and states that often implied a row of interethnic marriages, so also in Tibet. In this sense, the king was truly a cosmopolitan by contemporary standards.

The crucial question remains: During the *btsan po*'s lifetime what kind of quality did his status of divinity or royalty imply? Unfortunately, we must bite the bullet and confess that we have no sources available or datable to his lifetime. As we know, the first records and written testimonies currently available in Tibetan script emerged at the earliest over one hundred years after his passing. Deplorably, the activities, identity and chronology of the alleged inventor of the Tibetan script, Thon mi (a contemporary of the king, posthumously lauded as the "Good or Noble Tibetan" i.e. Sambhoṭa) still remain nebulous, the first specimen of writing purportedly offered by Thon mi to king Srong btsan sgam po at Byan can/Dzen khog sna rdo in the form known to us dates from earliest the 12th century. This

---

P.T. 1286 anachronistically? chronicles that "the earliest rulers were 'sons of gods' ruling the land of men" (*lha sras myi yul gyI rgyal mdzad*). We obviously have no reason to believe that the concept was fabricated during the reign and lifetime of Khri Srong brtsan. On these terms, see Stein (1980); and latest Doney (2015). Some authors suggest, arguably doubtful, to see the epithet *lha* as a secular term referring to the nobility vis-a-vis *m(y)i*; cf. Walter 2009. So far, we have not come across, below the kings, a minister or nobleman being designated or tagged with the epithet *lha*.

Following this, an essential issue, mainly a semantic and terminological-interpretational one, that would solve many questions behind the study and understanding of Tibet's imperial period is to the crucial question as to when Buddhism were able to assert itself for real against or parallel to the former largely pre-Buddhist, ancient tradition and prevailing belief system(s) (variously described, often commonly represented by the terms *lha'i gtsug lag; yab myes kyi lugs; lugs bzang, chos bzang*; in "Buddhist times" retrospectively *chos rnying*); see Hazod, *forthcoming*. The initial and decisive point as to when Buddhism got the upper hand not least within influential court circles probably followed the mid-750's crisis in Tibet that culminated in the ensuing outmaneuvering and elimination of Ma Zhang Grom pa skyes (punishment: buried alive) during the earlier years of reign of Khri srong lde btsan, probably in the beginning of 760's. This watershed shift, eventually also within the area of semantics, is important for our classification and appreciation of a number of terms and nomenclatura utilised in contemporary sources whether they should be read in a pre-Buddhist or Buddhist sense (as to terms like *lha, chos*, etc.).

piece is not helpful since its language is demonstrably Buddhist, and the diction and metric structure clearly post-dynastic.[7] Yet, written documents or forms of the newly invented script must have been available at the close of his life. One of the most important purposes for the invention of a script, the drafting of law texts, was to be tackled soon after its invention. True, the foray into drafting basic laws in text-form should be initiated after his passing (according to *OTA*, in the year 655-56, *bka' grIms kyi yi gi bris*), yet the decision and the preparation for this important civilising project, likely must have been taken just before 650.

Looking for other clues of "written" or transmitted legacies ascribed to the king and his time, we could take a look at another set or list of ruler or norms, often claimed to stem from the king or originating during his time, among others, the so-called "sixteen pure popular rules of conduct or human norms (*mi chos gtsang ma bcu drug*) as part of the king's legislation.[8] It has been shown that though an almost similar set or list of human norms circulated in 8th-9th century Tibet in various contemporary texts, its ascription to the king remains a later construction.[9]

Looking back on the origin of the Tibetan rulers, we can observe that the king's immediate predecessors and his forebear in the royal line clearly had been barely more than petty ruling chieftains, whose inner organisation consisted of a sort of political alliance or confederation with a towering chieftain as a *primus inter pares* among his peers – recent research now speaks about an Eurasian-derived *comitatus* structure prevailing in early Tibet, an extended form of interdependent war-band associates, and with a ruling court characterised by perpetual mobility with no fixed (or seasonally shifting) centre, and knitted together by political allegiances and plighted loyalty, a sort of sacred contract, sworn between a ruling chief and his most trusted and influential family- or lineage-heads. At some point, with the *btsan po*'s regime expanding and in response to foreign contact and models of rule, the *btsan po* morphed into becoming a royal and divine avatar, but now, as we can see, increasingly with Buddhist markers such as with alternating salvific, tutelary and thaumaturgic properties superimposed or projected upon him – the exact dates for this and these gradual transformations or re-figurations in the royal ideology however still remain to

7 See Sørensen 1994: 175, 540-41 (for the text, i.e. a brief nine-and seven-syllabic piece of poetry in three quatrains, with translation); Hazod in Sørensen and Hazod 2005: 232-35, 247.

8 Sørensen 1994: 183f.

9 Dotson 2006: 323ff.; Roesler 2015.

be clarified, opaque also is whether and to what extent these qualifying epithets and titles reflected forms of self-representation. This is a likely scenario, as in case of Khri srong lde btsan.[10] Interestingly, precisely during the latter's rule, when the pro- and anti-Buddhist controversy reached its ideological climax in around 760 CE, where we can observe the beginning of an altogether reorientation towards Buddhism. It most obvious sign of this reorientation was, as discussed in a number of contemporary sources, that the Tibetan kings were all, from around the 8th century in retrospect now seen as Buddhist saints, *in casu* classified as members of different "families" (*kula, gotra, rigs*) of *bodhisattva-s*.

Nevertheless, his manifestations/embodiments, his "projected identity/-ties" proved permanently context-sensitive. The durable flexibility behind the permutations his figure, and his mythologisation, underwent was due to the overriding role he retrospectively played (or was foreseen to play) in the formation of a national identity and eventually in the formation of an historic and national consciousness among the Tibetans: his birth as a national and cultural hero was also grounded in the circumstance that our knowledge of his real life – as well as the vicissitude of his life in Tibet's remote past – remained fragmentary, from the early post-imperial epoch onwards being caught in a sort of narrative vacuum. His "elusiveness" as a real historical figure, prompted by the chronic state of historic amnesia surrounding him at the dawn of Tibet's recorded history, has only motivated subsequent generations of historians and not least later treasure-finders to fill in the gaps in the fragmented biography. Here in the first place the actual 11th and 12th century "compilers" (lit. "revealers," as the sources were dubbed "treasuries," *gter ma*) behind what we can call the vita corpus of the king, viz. the *Bka' chems Ka khol ma* and *Ma ṇi bka' 'bum* (the latter also called *Rgyal po'i bka' 'bum*) both considered by and large fictional biographies putatively ascribed to the king himself, these writings should radically reinvent his central role in the country's history. Indeed, producing such mythographical narratives turned into a genre in itself. [11]

3. A biography with yawning gaps

To write a brief story, or something remotely resembling a "biography" of this founding

10 See Doney 2015.

11 See Sørensen 1994 *passim*; Sørensen in Sørensen and Hazod 2000 App. II; Dargyay 1988; Neumaier 2007, among others.

king and national hero naturally is not only premature, well-nigh unrealistic, yet anyway from the outset beset with insurmountable obstacles – our knowledge of his life and time is paltry and fragmented at best: Aside from the family name and origin of his mother, Queen Tshes pong za from the Tshes pong clan or family,[12] we know next to nothing about his princely paternal affiliation (or rather when and how the "original paternal lineage or line of his turned royal (in other words, into the Spu rgyal ruling line?)," and hence lost its traditional lineage designation as such),[13] whereas other interesting aspects of his family history remain less opaque and are recorded both in written and oral sources.

The rise of the local dynasty, and their homeland in 'Phyong po / Yar lung, initiated for real during the rule of his grandfather Stag bu snya gzigs and his father Gnam ri slon mtshan, both incidentally should meet a cruel fate by being respectively assassinated and poisoned, leaving it to Srong btsan sgam po to seek revenge and new allies, in the incipient formation of Tubo. The political matrimony of his father and mother had been born from a traditional family or clan alliance that was based upon sworn allegiance and workable coalitions, in which supportive family heads in return for their alliance and loyalty occupied key ministerial posts and either appropriated or were allotted huge landholdings. During the time of his royal parents, the ruling house gradually moved from their heartland and ancestral home in the Yar lung and 'Phyong po valleys, heading northwards to the old (Yar) Snon valley (present-day Rgya ma valley), following, in the wake of continuous conquer, expansion and consolidation, a sort of *via regia* leading from Yar lung to Central Tibet. Here the queen mother eventually gave birth to the prince in *pho brang* Byams pa Mi 'gyur gling – his residential birthplace.[14] Unfortunately, the exact birth year of our protagonist still is an object of continuous speculation.[15] Nevertheless, numerous sites in the nearest vicinity of

12 The Tshe spong (orig. spelling: Tshes pong), one of the bride-giver lineages in the time of the empire, held several land-holdings and territories (*sa ris*) in different areas of Central Tibet, one of them evidently in the Tshe spong valley of Upper Yar lung (see Hazod 2009). Often the 'Phyos valley is mentioned, Dotson 2012: 194-96.

13 Spu rgyal may indeed be the very lineage name itself, yet possibly with the simple and original meaning of "*rgyal* (*po*) of Spu (yul)" i.e. the land wherefrom the ancestor stemmed – according to one tradition. As is well known, this refers to the present-day Spo bo where in the side valley of Yar lung, a local tradition indeed localises the *khrungs yul* of the royal ancestral figure Gnya' khri btsan po. See Hazod 2009.

14 The name of the palace here surely reflects a Buddhist coinage (early 9th century?), a name invented post-humously. For this site's original name – Khri rtsigs 'bum gdugs – and generally for a reappraisal of the local Snon / Rgya ma history in the founding period, see most recently Hazod 2014.

15 Certain seems only that his birth was situated in an ox (*glang*) year. See the long discussion and cultic documentation in Gyalbo, Hazod and Sørensen 2000 and Sørensen and Hazod 2005: 230ff.

Rgya ma valley, many still identifiable, are in numerous historical, cultic and ritual contexts associated with the king.[16]

The transition in the religious and political identity and nature of the Tibetan kings has been the object of considerable research from the time of G. Tucci, Erik Haarh followed in particular by a row of prominent French scholars; recently an increasing flow of studies by Dunhuang and Tubo researchers have made great progress and enriched our understanding of the different stages in the development of royalty during Tubo (see Dotson 2009, Intro.). It will not be reiterated here. What we briefly can say is that Khri Srong brtsan (sgam po) in this process should pass from being an ancestral king (*rgyal po*) and then king of chieftains (i.e. *btsan po*), so his common title during his lifetime, only to be a posthumous recipient of the elevated appellation "Divine Emperor (lit. Mighty One) of Magic Sagacity/ Metamorphosis" (*'phrul gyi lha btsan po*),[17] and of being a manifestation of a *bodhisattva*, and subsequently to be depicted, through further permutations, as a Buddhist saviour-king (*dharmarāja*), and as an universal, Aśoka-style monarch (*cakravartin*) staged with a wholly Buddhist royal scenario and narrative. We have reason to believe that this recast of him largely was the ideological set-up and design orchestrated by the court up to and around 800 CE during the rule of Khri srong lde btsan, who similarly – during his lifetime – and

16 Sørensen and Hazod 2005; Hazod 2014.

17 The terminus *a quo* for the use of these indigenous conceptions, appellations and epithets to refer to and include Srong btsan sgam po (see e.g. the Lhasa Treaty Pillar of 821-22) is difficult to ascertain, but, except for *b(r)tsan po*, clearly the oldest term in use for "king" of sorts, they were not in use during his life time in the early to middle 7th century. *'Phrul gyi lha* as suggested most recently by Doney 2015 appears to constitute an imperial religio-political concept, still its provenience is uncertain. Stein 1981: 241; 1983: 186-87 has feasibly argued that it originally represents a Chinese concept and term reflecting "gloire civile et militaire" (*shengshen*), here used as a qualifying attribute to the more basic concept of *lha*. Another aspect is its association (in post-dynastic sources) to the Chinese Wencheng Gongzhu 文成公主 (d. 683), who was considered a female Master of *'phrul*, "magical transformation" which here alludes to her sagacity in the art of *Yijing* 易经 and geomancy (incl. *fengshui* 风水); see Sørensen 1994: 224, in the same vein is the ascription "King of 'Phrul" to Confucius, here like in the case of Wencheng alluding to the mastery of divination, divinatory competence or of "metamorphosis" – which might be the most appropriate translation for the word. PT 16 adds that the kings possessed or mastered *'phrul* (i.e. *thugs la 'phrul mnga'*), a property of the king, mentally possessing "magical transformative or supernatural power/potence," hence also to be translated as "magical sagacity," or simply the "metamorphotic king." See also Macdonald 1971: 337-39; Karmay (repr.) 2007: 3; Berounsky 2010. Things become no less complicated, however, when we read that the concept *'phrul* was not only reserved for royal members, but also attributable to ministers; see PT 1287... *blon po 'phrul dang ldan*; see Sørensen 1994: 177-178. The term in the sense of illustrating "illusory manifestation/transmutation = miracle" is also qualifying material things, such as temples, see the main temple in Lhasa denoted 'Phrul snang (Sørensen 1994: 285 and *passim*). Finally, the term makes its semantic entry into the Buddhist vocabulary (in later concepts like *'cho 'phrul, rdzu 'phrul*, etc.). Its origin, foreign or indigenous, its coinage and repeated use, it can be assumed, must be situated to the court milieu of the incipient 800's.

obviously in a concerted attempt of self-repre-sentation – was considered a bodhisattva, a Dharma-king and routinely a cakravartin monarch in mimicry of Indian Buddhist model kings, once the ideal of a Dharma king gained momentum and proved a prerequisite for a ruler in a society increasingly founded upon Buddhist ethics, norms and cultural values.

4. New identity by transformation

What is specific – contrary to his royal successors at the Tibetan court – is the conscious fixation of Srong btsan sgam po as a human embodiment of Lokeśvara/Avalokiteśvara. The issue has been addressed several times by fellow scholars, but some crucial questions still vex us. Who initiated this grand tale at the 8th-century court, of interlinking the founding monarch, or even, so it seems, merging him with this universal World Saviour? When did it actually start? Moreover, based upon which textual authorities, indigenous, but far more likely, upon Buddhist canonical scripture? Additional questions can be mooted, nevertheless the first poised questions in part still remain unanswered. A number of clues to this specific emanational nexus between king and deity has been proposed. The most obvious was the paramount importance and popularity of precisely the Lokeśvara cult in neighbouring Nepal/Kathmandu valley in the Licchavi period, wherefrom the artists (bringing along the ideology and the underlying concept, architectural idiom and models) behind the erection of (Ra sa) 'Phrul snang edifice stemmed and surely whereform the initial impetus and influx (aside from Khotan) of Buddhist ideas entered Tibet. As is well known, this edifice and monument in the heart of Lhasa is indisputably linked to the founding monarch and his time. Another interesting clue to the incarnational/emanational deification of the king is the relatively early titulation as Baowang 宝王 ("Precious/Jewelry King") – an imperial title for the King of the West or the Western Paradise, often referring to Amitābha, an honorary title offered to Srong btsan sgam po by the 3rd Tang emperor Gaozong 唐高宗 (reign 649-683) upon the latter's enthronement. It was to be a posthumous title since the Tibetan ruler passed away during the same time. Recorded also, here from *Old Tangshu* 旧唐书 , is the readiness of Srong btsan sgam po, with the arrival of the Chinese princess in 641 CE, to adopt or at least emulate a number of the civilising and cultural achievements and introduce these to Tibet.[18]

18 Bushell 1888: 445; Pelliot 1961: 5; Dotson 2009.

It is naturally impossible to cover the large number of aspects as well as the huge amount of literature dedicated and elaborating on this "later mythographic development" of his person and his role. The following notes therefore only serves as a small precursor to a more comprehensive study of his time and person – for lack of space it will focus on two narrative tropes concerning his "afterlife" as it was fabricated, with an eye to the earliest (?) available (admittedly post-dynastic) narrative components that provided the aetiology behind this ascription as we shall see, associated with stories that "rationally" were used or at least regarded to underpin and logically corroborate his divine and exalted status as an earthy manifestation/emanation of the paramount "Great Compassionate One," the Saviour and Bodhisattva deity *par excellence* of Buddhism. Beyond any doubt it was these iconic and telling histories and ideas which propagated an emanational nexus or ascription of the king's "*trans*-figuration" – we shall conveniently call this phenomenon the acquisition of a "borrowed identity" – that as seminal religious phenomenon were to become the most unique cultural hallmark and a guiding organising principle in Tibetan Buddhism, a feature that exerted an immense impact on Tibetan culture and society. The way of transmitting, indeed upholding "a form of innate or numinous mental-corporeal sanctity" or "spiritual heritage or legitimisation in human form" (in form of *skye ba*, *sprul sku*), was, beginning from the early 12th or 13th century, once introduced and organised, institutionally regulated through a row of trans-life or multi-life "body-strings" (*sku phreng*) lineages,[19] an organising principle unique to Tibet, but later this form of institutionalised reincarnation lineages also disseminated throughout the Himalayas, Mongolia and China, being inspired by the Tibetan innovation of regulating and upholding its religious-spiritual and political heritage.

The uniquely Tibetan innovative concept of religious masters and historical figures,

19 The paradox remains: the person incarnating is in essence diachronically or collectively "identical" or the "same," yet synchronically in each "body" individually or personally "different" or "unique." Indigenous Tibetan literature and discourses on "the (re)incarnation principle" rarely discuss this innate dilemma or "apparent contradiction" as to the nature and *modus operandi* behind the continuum or concatenation of existences. The sources also discuss the difference between 'taking' (re)birth (*skye ba*), usually individual-particular, and magic manifestation/emanation (body) (*sprul ba (/sku)*), that theoretically allows for the proliferation of limitless body forms in time and place – here basically reflecting the *modus operandi* of a *nirmānakāya*. More poignantly, in the former case, some texts occasionally refer to the actual operating conveyance of "rebirth," namely the existence of a 'common mind-continuum' or 'identical mind-stream' (*thugs rgyud gcig pa*) that passes through the successive bodies. Further, it is often argued that the 'incarnation/manifestation substratum' (*sprul gzhi*) – evidently referring to the aforementioned mind-continuum and as such the very agent for the proliferation (simultaneously or successively) of many bodies – remains the operating principle behind the manifestations.

retro-actively being furnished with past lives and bodies of rebirths and proactively living forth in successive bodies according to the Buddhist principle of taking "rebirth" or assuming "new existence/re-embodiment" (*punarbhava, yang srid*) was a refinement and elaboration of a basic Buddhist axiom of the *karman*-driven chain of rebirth in Samsara, that befalls every living being. Basically, the concept's conscious refinement or *novum* in Tibet foresaw a master consciously taking or seeking rebirth in a new body. As said, this development had its root and initial application in 11th-12th century Tibet, usually being seen for the "first" time within the Karmapa school, but the phenomenon and usage might be older. This principle of either identifying a future person as a manifestation of a former person, or in hindsight looking back and identifying a former individual as re-embodied in a present living being thus would seem to be working both ways. Indeed, it might have started by way of an identification that was seen to work regressively, but soon, as in most cases, it was conceived of to operate progressively too. What is particular with the nexus Avalokiteśvara having proactively, so it is described, manifested himself as a Tibetan king, or more precisely, Srong btsan sgam po being staged as a (re)-incarnation of the very deity, would seem to have another accentuation: in its *modus operandi* as conceived of by the Tibetan inventors, it mostly was seen to work regressively. As such it was *ex-post-facto* arrangement. A case in point: It indeed resembles the case of the Indian master Atiśa, who was destined to play a decisive role in promoting this nexus and cult around Avalokiteśvara and who himself was considered a manifestation of the deity, staging his principal pupil 'Brom ston as a manifestation of the very same deity (in the first place by depicting him as such in a number of *jātaka*-style biographical adaptations later contained in the *Bka'*

One example may suffice to highlight this, the case of the prestigious lineage of the Dalai Lamas: The 5th Dalai Lama once was queried as to why there were cases of "body-existence overlappings" in his Dalai Lama lineage (counting up to the present day over sixty manifestations) of former rebirths when referring to the simultaneous presence of more "bodies/lives" at one and the same time. Facing the inherent contradiction in the circumstance that for instance Sa chen (1092-1158), Bla ma Zhang 'Gro ba'i mgon po (1123-1193) and e.g. Myang ral Nyi ma 'od zer (1124/36-1192/1204), three contemporary and recognised pre-existences of the Dalai Lama were alive during the very same century and all recognised as "pre-existences" of him, the apparent simultaneity (or as here at least chronological overlapping) of these lives is argumentatively countered by the 5th Dalai Lama when he maintains – here employing the cherished *udakacandropamā* simile for depicting "illusion" – that it is tantamount to the capability of a moon to be reflected in the waters a multitude of times at one and the same time (*zla ba gcig la chu zla grangs med 'byung ba ltar*). See Sørensen and Hazod 2007: 380. One body – many body reflections – *pratibimba*-like it is, he maintains with the logic of analogy, simply the unfolding of the magic workings of a *bodhisattva's* illusory display (*sgyu 'phrul = sgyu ma, māyā*).

gdams glegs bam anthology) (Fig. 2). The Bka' gdams pa founder and patriarch is depicted in his former embodiments variously as Indian kings and princes among others – indeed, the status of "royalty" or the "royal link" is here essential to keep in mind. Unsurprisingly, 'Brom ston in these narratives or former life-stories was depicted as embodying Srong btsan sgam po, but also in succession of other Tibetan *dharmarāja*-s. The same *modus operandi* of rebirth as principal scheme or as an operational master-plan we find in the entire Dalai Lama lineage succession which is nothing more than an expansion of the 'Brom ston "former rebirth" or "pre-existences" scheme, incorporating the entire list of former rebirths associated with 'Brom ston into the Dalai Lama succession lineage.[20] As we see, the system of inventing lineage construction inflated dramatically.

Fig. 2. The Bka' gdams pa patriarch 'Brom ston. Thangka 17th century. Ethnographic Museum, Univ. of Zürich.

It may not be surprising therefore when we claim that much of the written vita corpus (largely conserved in the *Bka' chems Ka khol ma and Ma ṇi bka' 'bum*), mythographical narratives and "afterlife legends" surrounding Srong btsan sgam po in fact were invented, fabricated or at least strongly promoted exactly in the milieu surrounding Atiśa and his Bka' gdams pa proselytes and students. Still, reference to an earlier fixation of this unique nexus prior to the 11th century "invention" (or rather renewed promotion) of the king being an emanation of Avalokiteśvara, seems to boast older roots, pointing to the late imperial time. Principally, we should be aware that some of the sources (among others, and prominently

20 See Sørensen 2005a, 2005b; 2007; Sørensen and Hazod 2007: 463-68; *Bka' gdams glegs bam* Vol. 2, *Bu chos*.

the Dunhuang dossiers) that point to an imperial-time attribution of this emanation nexus[21] might in fact be situated in the early post-imperial epoch, say roughly late 9th or early 10th century, a period that would approximate the early, initial attempt in the dawning *bstan pa phyi dar* period to disseminate this imagery of the king.

5. A salvific profile and identity with a long history

Post-dynastic mythographics (*gter ma*) conserved in the bulky vita corpus mentioned above ascribed to the founding king as well as well-nigh all national and religious histories (*lo rgyus, deb ther, chos 'byung*), datable from early and later medieval period (in fact continued throughout the entire *bstan pa phyi dar* spell), have disproportionately magnified and embellished the sparse, biographical gaps left behind from the past, and furnished him and the role he was foreseen to play with a blend of supernatural tailorings and trappings that left the depiction of him in a whole new light as an artificial or constructed, indeed imagined figure.

At the centre of our attention stands therefore the cult surrounding him and the ritual and devotional significance related to Lokeśvara/Avalokiteśvara, the pre-eminent Saviour Saint and Bodhisattva of Northern Buddhism. The history of this deity has a long history going back at least to the beginning of the first millennium of our era. In early Mahāyāna scriptures such as the *Lotus Sūtra*, the larger *Sukhāvatīvyūha-sūtra* and not least the *Gaṇḍavyūha-sūtra*, among others, we encounter the importance and worship of the deity in its full glory, often serving as an attendant of Buddha Amitābha. In these key scriptures he is endowed with the qualities and dispositions (most eminently his unselfish *mahākaruṇa*-driven work for the welfare of the sentient beings) that early on laid the foundation for his popularity and paved the way for another key scripture underscoring the immense cult of

21 Recent research now dates a number of these documents such as the *Old Tibetan Chronicle* for example and the celebrated IOL Tib. J 370/6 ll 1-2 "The Scripture/Sutra that Fell from the Sky" (*Gnam babs kyi dar ma*) to the 9th-10th century, where the Tibetan kings were addressed as *myi mgon lha sras rgyal mchog ste // 'phrul gyi rgyal po srong btsan dang*...in other words starting with Srong btsan (sgam po). Despite not being found among the Dunhuang material, another salient example is the letter from the 8th-century Indian Buddhaguhya to Khri srong lde btsan in which the Tibetan kings are considered or addressed as bodhisattvas, starting from Srong btsan sgam po as a manifestation of Avalokiteśvara. Where the letter generally is considered authentic, parts of it might have been interpolated or rewritten at a later point; cf. Dietz 1984: 79-84, 358-400; Dargyay 1988: 102-105. Nevertheless, all in all, it points towards the circumstance that the concept or idea of the king as a manifestation of the compassionate *bodhisattva* deity can be situated to the early 9th century or shortly after.

Avalokiteśvara, namely the 5th-century *Kāraṇḍavyūha-sūtra* dedicated to the sheer endless and inconceivable virtues, magic feats and properties of this *bodhisattva* saint set in scene in a grand cosmogonic/-logical vision. Equally important, it introduces the famous six-syllable formula (*Oṃ maṇi padme hūṃ*), the quintessence (*paramahṛdaya*) of the deity,[22] the most powerful mantric formula of his known to all Tibetans. Later sources suggest that the sūtra along with other cult texts dedicated to the compassionate or tutelary deity were translated into Tibetan in the 7th-century.[23] In these key sources we meet, among others and relevant for our purpose here, the extraordinary and prominent faculty of his to "transfigure himself into various forms," indeed assuming a variety of "protean garbs" (*nānārūpavikurvita*) or manifesting himself according to the disposition of the individual living beings by way of displaying a sheer innumerable number of (emanational) projections tailored to the receptive faculties (*aśaya-anurūpavicitra-aparimāṇa-nirmāṇa-samdarśana*) of the devotee. Significant here is not only the bodhisattva's apparent inborn faculty to appear at will but also in accordance with the relative receptivity among those beholding (or placing faith in) him. This is part, surely, of a soteriological programme designed or tailored to reflect the *modus operandi* of the deity: As a means of the liberating power, he can manifest himself not only in different forms for the sake of living beings, but contextually one and the same corporeal form is seen differently at one and the same time due to the karmic disposition of the beholder in question. This unique gift – skilful in means (*upāya-kauśalya*), being another defining hallmark of Avalokiteśvara's soteriological agenda – ascribed to him was to serve, aside from his active compassionate nature or precisely because of it, as a dynamic and transformative power and as an enduring narrative trope entering much of the post-dynastic literature dedicated to the deity and hence to the founder king. He too was considered to possess precisely the same faculties and magical, illusory power as we find detailed in the vita corpus, primarily the *Bka' chems Ka khol ma* and the bulky *Ma ṇi bka' 'bum* followed by a myriad of later stories and history books drawing extensively on this corpus, notably the Tibetan master narrative *par excellence: Rgyal rabs gsal ba'i me long.*[24]

22 See Studholme 2002; van Schaik 2006; Halkias 2013; Sørensen 1994: 97-108.

23 See Sørensen 1994: 173 – in other words, during the reign of Srong btsan sgam po, moreover by the nebulous Thon mi. If the tradition is to be trusted, its earliest translation happened prior to the version that later entered *Bka' 'gyur*, a translation conducted by Jinamitra and Ye shes sde etc. in the 8th century.

24 See Sørensen 1994: 273, 304 *et passim* and Sørensen in Gyalbo *et al.* 2000: 147-76; Sørensen and Hazod 2007: 463-71; Dargyay 1989.

It was these miraculous transcending faculties (or mastery of magical illusion), his corporeal trans-figurations and projections (*vikurvita, nirmita*)[25] that had the strongest impact on the later socio-religious aspects (incarnations, rebirth-theories) related to the deity cult in Tibet. The references and links to the "fated" relationship between Tibet and the *bodhisattva* deity are endless: It is the vast vita corpus of narratives (also containing non-narrative literature, ritual and meditation-manuals of this deity etc.) that promoted and buttressed this nexus, the key role of the Great Compassionate One is endorsed, when he is described and narratively promoted as the "Father," indeed the very genetrix, of all Tibetans. Popular on that score is the celebrated, but fanciful, legend of the origin of all Tibetans from the union of a rock-demoness and a *bodhisattva*-monkey[26] – a manifestation of Avalokiteśvara – as part of a plighted commitment of his to take upon himself the task of "converting" (i.e. civilising) Tibet or turning Tibet into a vibrant Buddhist stronghold and haven, a country pre-destined to be his future *buddhakṣetra*, his "field of conversion."[27] This national origin myth behind the birth of the Tibetan population was another constitutive legend that later galvanized the deity's towering importance and popularity among the Tibetans. A number of historical episodes in Tibet's remotest past and conserved in innumerable Tibetan histories, most of which with doubtful historicity, were to highlight the central role of the above incarnational nexus. The very beginning (i.e. arrival) of Buddhism onto Tibetan soil was also committed to writing at an early point in what seems to be a deliberately unfolding master-plan. According to this, a Tibetan tradition preserved as an integral part of the above vita corpus, the above *Kāraṇḍavyūha-sūtra* along with other Avalokiteśvara cult texts and items supposedly are said to have arrived in a casket from the sky unto the roof of the palace of the 28th king of Tibet in the pre-historic line, Lha Tho tho ri gnyan btsan. It intended to herald Tibet's first (mythic?) encounter with Buddhism and can be roughly dated to the late 4th / early 5th century if we were to believe the story (Fig. 3). An accompanying prophecy tellingly purports that in the fifth generation from this king, a successor would emerge that shall understand (or decipher, i.e. translate?) these texts: Srong btsan sgam po, during whose

25 Highlighted in various forms in canonical scripture dedicated to the Avalokiteśvara cult, such as the *Lotus Sūtra, Śūraṅgama-sūtra, Gaṇḍavyūha-sūtra*; Dutt 1986; Kern 1963; Watson 1993.

26 Sørensen 1994: 125f. with further references. The legend borrowed a number of narrative topoi and figures from the Hindu epic Rāmāyaṇa.

27 Sørensen 1994: 97f.

Fig. 3. King Lha Tho tho ri gnyen btsan and the texts and relics falling on the rooftop of Yum bu bla sgang Castle. (Details of a mural painting, in: *A Mirror of the Murals in the Potala / Budala gong bihua yuanliu* 2000)

reign allegedly the first (currently non-extant) attempt to translate this key *sūtra* was made.

The vita corpus or set of "biographies" of the king put on display a grand and concerted Buddhist (cosmological) vision, in fact a sort of master-plan from that the very outset that was to gain universal acclaim and approval in all corners of the society, in which Avalokiteśvara was staged to embody the very destiny and the very *raison d'être* of Tibet as reflected, among others, in the phrase that the deity was regarded as "the divine/godly legacy or destiny (lit. "share")" (*lha skal*) of Tibet.[28] In the same vein, the celebrated tutelary statue of Ārya Lokeśvara, later to be regarded as the principal statue in the Potala Palace appositely is denoted the *bod kha pa can gyi lha skal gcig po* or "the uniquely fated or hereditary statue/deity of the Snow-capped Land of Tibet."[29] In other words, the phrase "Divine/Godly Legacy (or Fate) of the Snow-capped Land" together with other similar phrases

28 Myang ral (who played a key role in promoting this nexus in his writings) in his *Chos 'byung me tog snying po* designates Avalokiteśvara as *bod kha ba can kyi rgyal khams spyi mthun gyi lha skal*, the "divine legacy common for the entire Tibetan Realm/Kingdom" and in his Guru Rinpoche hagiography *Zangs gling ma* he is similarly designated as *bod kyi lha skal thugs rje chen po*. The Six-syllable formula is in a similar way designated as *bod kyi lha skal*; Sørensen 1994: 163.

29 Sørensen 1994: 163,195; Sørensen 2007: 863; Ehrhard 2004; Alsop 1990.

simply turned into standard metaphors or kennings for the deity, and by extension for Tibet, purposefully set in a sense of fated interdependence. The visionary scenario originating on a more systematic level from the early 11th century onwards was to last until the present day, losing nothing of its appeal, on the contrary. We therefore are not much amiss when we claim that at the outset of the renaissance period of Buddhism (*bstan pa phyi dar*), in other words, from the beginning of the post-imperial period, the history of Buddhism in Tibet essentially, and in some corners almost exclusively, became a grand and authoritative narrative as to how Avalokiteśvara with his enlightened activities and compassionate agenda as if guided by destiny and divine providence worked for the well-being of people and country and hence singlehandedly orchestrated and shaped the fate of Tibet. Along with the grand thaumaturgic tale of Padmasambhava and his role in "taming = converting" Tibet and its landscape occupied by fiendish spirits during the "Golden (= Imperial) Era," both narratives became standard tropes and references in the nation's religious literature, only to finally turn into becoming what seem to the master narrative or national narrative of the country, known to everyone, high or low, whether among illiterate people or among men of letters. The continuous transmission of these "national narratives" and an expanding interest, doctrinally, liturgically, as well as publicly, of the Avalokiteśvara cult, not least rituals associated among others with meditational practices, but also fasting programmes associated with the deity, forcefully helped promote and widely distributethe cult. The aforementioned Bengali master Atiśa and his incipient Bka' gdams pa milieu (see below) were the selfsame actors that spawned the earliest vita tradition of the deity and the king. In the throes of these post-imperial pioneers, the Rnying ma pa masters soon followed in the trail of the Bka' gdams pa, leading to the compilation of *Ma ṇi bka' 'bum*. Appositely, the motifs transmitted in the above vita corpus have been summarised succinctly: the profound belief that Avalokiteśvara is the fated and unique patron deity of Tibet, the decisive role of the king in establishing Buddhism as an embodiment of the compassionate *bodhisattva* deity and, as detailed above, the ultimate destiny of Tibet being his "field of conversion."[30]

Throughout all milieus, whether monastic or lay, it was mainly the appealing salvific

30 Kapstein 2000: 147.

or soteriological agenda implicating both mundane and otherworldly objectives that contributed to the swift dissemination of the cult and its propitiation. Within the ensuing centuries, leading hierarchs of almost all dominant schools or denominations, not to mention innumerable individual ascetics considered themselves or were regarded as manifestations of the popular patron deity and saviour. The numerous acclaimed manifestations of the patron deity in Tibet surely also had an impact within the political and social field in medieval Tibet. The underlying competition for access to and ultimately control of the central edifice in Lhasa, the Lhasa *Gtsug lag khang*, and of Dmar po ri, the Tibetan Potala, reflecting the mystic abode of Avalokiteśvara was a major ideological and political issue in Tibet.[31]

For the Avalokiteśvara narrative, its national significance was dramatically boosted during the establishment of the Dga' ldan pho brang rule in the 17th century, when the Dalai Lama lineage construction was officially codified, founding its legitimacy on precisely this emanational nexus, at that point, to be true, it was no novelty anymore, the emanation nexus to the compassionate deity had already its forerunners throughout Tibet, finding its way into numerous emanation-based and -legitimised lineages, so among the Karma pa, the 'Bri gung pa, the Sa skya pa, the 'Brug pa, to mention a few prominent lineages.

Among a host of disparate narratives contained in this bulky vita corpus designed to bolster or endorse this grand scheme, we shall briefly highlight a number of disparate stories, or rather tales, that for the Tibetans often are emphasised not only as the first concrete "proof" or indication validating the king as a genuine manifestation of the patron deity. In other words, the episodes were deployed to provide the logical or argumentative rationale (*gtan tshigs*) that bespeaks the emanational concept, toits aetiology so to say.

6. Indigenous arguments for the legitimisation

Let us look at how the indigenous Tibetan literature attempted to present this story. The reasons and arguments are listed in connection with the king's purported "last act," in other words the celebrated story of the ritual departure, i.e. the absorption of the king and his two favourite consorts into the personal Eleven-Headed image[32] of his. The "queens,"

31 Sørensen and Hazod 2007 esp. App. II.

32 For the history of this image or idol, see Sørensen 1994: 266f.

in question were his two celebrated, "foreign" consorts, the Nepalese Khri btsun and the Chinese Kong jo (both queens (*btsun mo*) in the vita master-plan or retelling identified as the king's (i.e. Avalokiteśvara's) "compassionate acolytes", in the *Gestalt* of the Green and White Tara respectively). The scenario is recounted following a farewell-scene where the departing king offers advises to his remaining family members, the key ministers and his court, stating that if they in the future (after his passing) really wanted to meet him, they should request for a meeting with (i.e. see and visit) Avalokita. The reason being, as he assures, that there is no difference between him and his so-called "divine *alter ego*," the Lord of Compassion.

Rgyal rabs gsal ba'i me long, an oft-quoted, popular and influential "national history" in Tibetan religio-historical literature, among others, has summerised the scenario accordingly: Following the absorption of the king and his two queens into his favourite idol, Thon mi Sambhoṭa discloses the reasons mentioned above to a sceptical group of ministers. The incidents, the text informs us, provide the decisive arguments intended to convince those attending of the purported emanational nexus between the deity and king. Thon mi subsumes the reasons under the following three points:

- At the point when the king was born in the palace of Byams pa mi 'gyur gling (see above, fn. 11), he was born with Buddha Amideva (i.e. Amitābha) poised on/above his head.[33]
- At Khra 'brug, the king (as an embodiment of Avalokiteśvara revealed by removing his turban/headgear) the countenance of Amideva (i.e. Amitābha) to an old beggar *bhikṣu*.[34]
- The king (as manifestation of Avalokiteśvara) displayed his Amideva countenance (atop his head) to two novice-monks from Li yul (i.e. Khotan). (Fig. 4)[35]

Noteworthy is the consistent reference to the *dharmakāya*-aspect of Avalokiteśvara, the Buddha Amitābha, that is conspiciously present in all the episodes or narratives – a

33 See Sørensen 1994: 339, 579-80. Some lists are at variance, enumerating another reason, *in lieu* of the first argument, namely: At the time when Lha sa (i.e. Ra sa 'Phrul snang) was inaugurated, the king offered up prayers and in an instant Buddhas and Bodhisattvas made their arrival in space above.

34 Sørensen and Hazod 2005: 93 and fn. 241 for references.

35 Sørensen 1994: 303f.

Fig. 4. The two Khotan monks meeting Srong btsan sgam po. (Scene from a biographical thangka: *Bod kyi thang ga*, Lhasa 1985)

circumstance that is not always the case in similar narratives. It appears that this element represents the defining "proof" in the eyes of the compilers behind these vita stories. In a Tibetan, mainly non-canonical context, Amitābha is commonly considered the "father" of the compassionate deity who is then considered the "son," conceived to represent or reflect the intermediate aspect of *sambhogakāya*, whereas Srong btsan sgam po accordingly is considered to reflect and embody the *nirmānakāya*-aspect (as a human, this-worldly or earthy aspect of the Buddha reality and activity) in the popular *trikāya*-system,[36] the tripartite organisation of a Buddha's entire or total (this-worldly and other-worldly) ontology.

The story of his birth is recorded in numerous sources, the historicity and location, as we have seen, surrounding his birth (except the actual birth year) in Rgya ma valley is well documented.[37] In the revision or legendary overhaul of his "biography" presented in the mythographical literature discussed here, unusual is the legendary addition not only of his magical display of the countenance of Buddha Amitābha already at birth but also that the very moment of his conception in his mother's womb was prompted by rays of light emitted from the heart of the compassionate deity.

More often quoted as a sign or as a reason for validating the emanational nexus are

36 Sørensen and Hazod 2007: 466; Neumaier 2007: 234.

37 Sørensen 1994: 160 *et passim*; Hazod 2002; Hazod in Sørensen and Hazod 2005: 145-46, 155, 243-48.

the two ensuing narratives. Either episodes or scenarios are occasionally found painted or depicted on walls and murals, as well as on thangkas dedicated to the visual representation of the life of the king. Both episodes, fictive as they are, seem to have originated or invented during the reign of Khri srong lde btsan at the earliest.

The story of the king and a begging monk in front of a *caitya* at Khra 'brug recounts the story of an encounter between Srong btsan sgam po and a wandering monk (*bande/ bandhya*) here disguised as beggar in front of the so-called Mchod rten Dbu lnga or (the ensemble of) Five-Pointed Caityas installed next to the temple. The episode in the narrative here evidently serves to indicate the piousness and dedication of the king in his treatment and respect for the emblems and signs of Buddhism and to underpin the depth and extent of the king's devotion. The incident follows in the trail of the king's grand scheme of erecting a row of key temples in Tibet (in the first place the so-called "twelve temples to pin down the demoness"), ultimately leading him to demonstrably revere and pay respect to any upholder of the Buddhist lore, in this case an ascetic in ragged cloth. The king is thereby depicted as a ruler who put on display his status as an universal Buddhist monarch (*cakravartin or dharmarāja*) in his capacity as a manifestation of Avalokiteśvara and Amitābha – thereby embodying in one person as king his faculty of possessing and manifesting "all three bodies," (*trikāya*) at one and the same time.[38] What initiates with a scenario of paying mutual respect between these two, soon developed into an awe-inspiring competition of their pre-eminence and potency in demonstrating magical or spiritual power. The display ends without any clear winner, the ascetic, in one text, finally is elected the king's personal chaplain (*purohita*).

The last narrative is in fact a celebrated story of two Khotanese monks or monk-novices, their wish to meet Avalokiteśvara and the experiences they encountered when meeting Srong btsan sgam po, king of Tibet.[39] The two pious monk candidates from Khotan entertained the wish to propitiate and see the countenance of Avalokiteśvara. In a vision Mañjuśrī appeared and imparted to them that the king of Tibet is Avalokiteśvara in person (other sources: Ava-

38 Sørensen (1994): 280-81 (for further references); Sørensen and Hazod 2005: Text B and D: 145-46, 155, 243-48.

39 See Sørensen 1994: 303f. (with further ref.) as well as a host of other sources such as *Dba' bzhed* 3a (Pasang Wangdu and H. Diemberger 2000: 32-33); see also Mills 2012 who in one of the versions attempts to see a tantric-esoteric reading of the myth; van Schaik (2016) offers a detailed reading of the episode, its historical context and available sources regarding the Tibet-Khotan connection.

lokiteśvara had manifested himself in the king). Arriving in Tibet, they came across a plain strewn with beheaded or slain corpses. Devastated, the monks immediately entertained serious doubts as to how such atrocities were possible in the land of the kingly deity (or divine king). They were told that the corpses were transgressors of the law punished by the king. Appalled, they lost faith in the king and his compassionate nature. They soon resolved to return. Through clairvoyance the king was able to read the thoughts of the Khotanese and ordered them into his presence. Inquiring about their visit, they informed him of the earnest yearning of theirs to behold the face of the compassionate deity. But seeing the many corpses, they had resigned and wanted to return. The king again removed his turban or headdress and uncovered the countenance of Amideva. The compassionate king informed the monks of his benevolent nature and assured them of the illusory nature of the corpses they had seen, these bodies were nothing else but emanations and epiphanies, an illusory display conducted by the king in order to set an example of deterrence and edification for the local population to abstain from committing unwholesome acts. The king in this context offered brief and preliminary instructions to the monk novices. The story ends with the swift return of the Khotanese guests by magical means.

Albeit the moral story is found in a number of versions that display variants readings and display minor deviating details, the story or parable is found uniformly inserted into the vita corpus at the close of the section on the enactment of laws based upon the ten Buddhist virtues initiated by the king. The narrative plot primarily served as a moral antidote in order to display the consequences of conducting heinous actions and crimes, such as killing.

7. A legacy renewed

As indicated above, throughout the entire medieval epoch following the discovery (*cum* compilation) of the bulky vita corpus, the paramount role of Srong btsan sgam po was from the very outset closedly linked to the history of the central temple in Lhasa, the Jo khang.[40] Conducting the *lha sa'i jo skor* or the "Lhasa Circumambulation Tour of the Grand Pilgrim Site of the Jo bo Statue in Jo khang" became increasingly obligatory to all Buddhists from all over Central Asia. In the centre of this ritual and devotional circumambulation stood

40 For details of its significance, see Alexander (2005); Gyurme Dorje *et al*. 2010; Vitali 1990; Larsen and Sinding-Larsen 2001.

the king as the founder of the site. The site soon served as an emblem of national prestige, lineages of spiritual masters and local rulers soon were vying for supremacy in providing patronage and in controlling the site. Remarkable is the unanimously high esteem it held – similar only to the other early national edifices such as Bsam yas *vihāra* – from all denominations and schools down through history. Its key image, the Jo bo statue, counted as the country's most sacred object, the pious object of all devoted pilgrims for over a millennium and a true vortex of Tibetan spirituality. The esteem and prestige of the sanctum as such naturally hailed from the central statue, and its numinous properties that sanctified the site and its surroundings. However, its rise as a national sanctuary was also linked to its central role in the rise and formation of the cult of Avalokiteśvara in Tibet. We now know that the Bengali master Atiśa and his followers among his Bka' gdams pa disciples forcefully promoted the cult of Srong btsan sgam po as a manifestation of Avalokita and not least the meditational precepts of the deity. Behind the detection (-cum compilation) of *Bka' chems Ka khol ma*, the putative testament ascribed to the founding king, we unsurprisingly find the active hand or involvement of Atiśa. It was precisely these legendary vita narratives that became part of the crucial transmission of the Great Compassionate One and its cult in Tibet, as well as of its underlying ideology and its popularisation as a national icon. The seminal *Bka' gdams glegs bam* anthology, an early 14th-century compilation was an anthologisation of teachings, dialogues and biographical materials, most of which with oral roots in the late 11th and early 12th-century Bka' gdams pa circles. It was the portrayal of the Indian patriarch, but not least the depiction of his principal student, the Tibetan-born 'Brom ston who in this anthology was depicted not only as a genuine embodiment of Avalokiteśvara but also as the unique promoter *par excellence* of its cult. More importantly, 'Brom ston is depicted in one of his "former lives" narratives as an embodiment of Srong btsan sgam po as well as a row of former Tibet *dharma* kings, the first case evidently of a Tibetan master being recorded as a manifestation of the king. The Tibetan patriarch is thus purposefully depicted as a cultural hero and as a divine soul – a worthy inheritor and legitimate successor of Atiśa – staged to embody in his person the entire legacy of Buddhism as it was transmitted through the Bengali master from India to Tibet. The anthology's literary corpus therefore must been seen as a specific literary reworked attempt at instantiating an envisaged indigenisation of Buddhism on[to] Tibetan soil. In Tibetan history it seems to be the first overall attempt (or programme) to "invent" and bespeak a largely non-tantric personalised transmission of Buddhism from India to Tibet.

As indicated above, another impetus of equal significance in this early medieval epoch was exerted by another circle of actors for the promotion and ideological fixation on Avalokiteśvara (and, equally important, on Padmasambhava) entered the scene to pave the way for a revival of these traditions. The central role here was held by the mentor and inventor Myang ral Nyi ma 'od zer (1124-1192/ 1136-1204) and his disciples and followers who "detected" (evidently compiled) the *Ma ṇi bka' 'bum*, as we have seen a literary and partly esoteric collection of narratives allegedly related to the king as well as teachings, instructions and precepts of Avalokiteśvara, conceived of as a sort of royal manifesto and testament. The new esoteric actors and treasure-finders obviously were inspired by the strategies that had been successfully implemented by the Bka' gdams pa in disseminating and personalising the Avalokiteśvara cult. It was crowned by the eccentric Fifth Dalai Lama, who equally entertained an obsessive proclivity, spiritually, personally as much as politically for the triad Avalokiteśvara, Srong btsan sgam po and Padmasambhava.[41]

8. The Avalokiteśvara cult and the invention of spiritual genealogies

During the rule of the Fifth Dalai Lama (Fig. 5) and with the establishment of the Dga' ldan pho brang administration and government in mid-17th century, the now deep-seated nexus received renewed attention since it became centrally integrated into the Dalai Lama lineage when a new spiritual genealogy in form of an emanation lineage was invented. The reincarnation-based succession lineage of his, as already indicated above, was largely inspired and founded on the pre-existence list of the Bka' gdams pa patriarch 'Brom ston found in the *jātaka*-style life-stories contained in afore-mentioned *Bka' gdams glegs bam*. When looking for additional candidates that were deemed worthy of being included into the succession list of the Dalai Lama (prior to the posthumously identified "official" 1st Dalai Lama), the personal and physical legacy of Srong btsan sgam po, in particular his edifice, the Jo khang was to play a central role since a number of the "pre-existences" or "former rebirths" in the Dalai Lama lineage following 'Brom ston appeared to have been chosen or sanctified by the Potala court to be included into the official list due precisely

41 For more details, Sørensen and Hazod 2007: 451-71.

Fig. 5. The Fifth Dalai Lama, in royal garb embodying the founding king. (Detail of a 19th-century thangka)

to the service they had rendered to the central edifice in Lhasa.[42] At this point, the king had already assumed the status of being the founder of the nation. A major part of the new government's legitimisation in fact hailed from the achievements ascribed to the "golden days" of Tibet during the imperial period at the constitutive heart of which the king was seen. The significance of the founder king saw still new forms: Any reference to the "golden past" of the country usually started with the role and importance of the king, it manifested itself even in a popular theatrical play or opera (*a lce lha mo*) called "Chinese Bride, Nepalese Bride" (*Rgya bza' bal bza'*) dedicated to his life and staging his marriage to his two senior queens.

9. The king's latest avatar: A national or cultural hero

Aside from the mechanism of religious succession and the transformative nature of emanation/incarnation as briefly discussed above, the force of commemoration naturally were at play throughout the last centuries, a dynamic force – in particular when it concerns any

42 Sørensen 2005a,b; 2007.

retelling of a people's or a nation's past, whether in visual and material art, in oral or written literature, or layered and treasured in people's consciousness. Memories, when shared and transmitted, remain crucial formative constitutents in a people's search for national identity, the process of both generating and formulating such shared identities served, as we see in the case of Srong btsan sgam po, as a telling projection surface. Over the centuries, this ideological foundation served as a stepping stone that enabled the figure ideologically to galvanise his role as an uniting national and cultural hero.

The king's most recent avatar or "incarnation" has taken shape within the last thirty years alone, during a period as Tibet underwent her most dramatic transformation, experiencing waves of turbulent changes under a new regime bent on rapid modernisation and assimilation. The pace with which these changes has taken and still takes place is nothing short of breathtaking. Cultural assimilation is now championed in the name of and perforce of economic development.

In a combination of commercial binge, tourist marketing and promotion strategy emblematic of the development of numerous tourist destinations throughout Tibet, pilgrim sites are now major attractions and tourist stop-overs within the huge tourist industry. Ethno-fascination or exotic romance for Tibet and things Tibetan has embraced an appreciable amount of people in China as elsewhere, driven by a romantic and adventurous mindset that reflects a belated sort of Shangrila idealisation not unlike the fascination that once grabbed Western readers and travellers. Here as elsewhere the founding monarch or Tibet and its nation plays a central role.

When today one arrives at Snon valley (today called Rgya ma valley) *en route* the visitor is most spectacularly welcomed by way of huge modern Tibetan-style *paifang* 牌坊 -shaped archways announcing that the guest or the tourist is about to approach and enter the side valley leading to the "Birth Site of Srong btsan sgam po" (*srong btsan sgam po'i 'khrungs yul*), so grandly proclaimed almost to the point that the ancient valley now has assumed the new name (Fig. 6). At the site of his birth, formerly marked by a small cairn, a new imposing building recently has been raised to welcome tourists – the so-called Srong btsan sgam po Memorial Hall (Fig. 7, 8).[43] In Lhasa, not only at the main attractions associated with the king, the Jo khang or at Potala, under which the erstwhile meditation cave of

43 On this building and the history of Rgya ma, see most recently Hazod 2014.

Fig. 6. Portal entering Rgya ma Valley.

Fig. 7. The shrine marking the birth-place of Srong btsan sgam po in the courtyard of the "Srong btsan sgam po Memorial Hall". (Photo 6, 7: Sørensen 2010)

Fig. 8. The "Srong btsan sgam po Memorial Hall" in Rgya ma. (Photo: G. Hazod 2013)

the king is located,[44] his name and importance remains omnipresent. In the new centralised promotional strategy to rewrite history, the king plays a central role.

The latest development, amid this unprecedented tourist boom mainly targeting Chinese tourists and visitors, now accommodates another state-sponsored mega event, a drama production and a spectacle to be permanently staged in Lhasa. The background for this evidently was the king's erstwhile matrimony that in part had ensured China and Tibet amicable relationships during an otherwise turbulent warring period. For China this *heqin* marriage alliance – granting prospective consorts to rulers of neighbouring states – at the dawn of Tibet's recorded history, was part of the traditional Chinese policy of securing stability and appeasement, a time-tested strategy favoured also by the Tang dynasty especially in times of military distress and threats vis-à-vis mighty neighbours or enemies. According to a Sinocentric worldview, the image of the Chinese emperor as the supreme ruler of the

44 See A. Chayet et F. Meyer 1983.

Fig. 9. Princess Wencheng Opera at the "Potala Hotel" in Grib Valley, opposite Lhasa.

Fig. 10. Srong brtsan sgam po and Wencheng of the opera (Fig. 9).

so-called All-under-Heaven (*Tianxia* 天下 , i.e. the whole world), the neighbouring Tibetan king was seen as a sort of petty or local ruler of the kingdom of Tubo, whose relationship was to be pacified by way of the granting of a princess, as well as bestowing honours and titles (*cefeng* 册封) to chieftains and rulers.[45]

This circumstance, the erstwhile marriage alliance, accounts for her immense role in modern Chinese minority politics. The young Tang princess, merely a minor member of the imperial family, is accorded a centre stage role. At first sight, the new opera seems to represent an elaborate interpretation, yet it is rather an entirely new staging of the popular yet traditional theatrical opera (*a lce lha mo*) as said commonly known as "Chinese Bride, Nepalese Bride" (*rgya bza' bal bza'*), an extremely popular romance between the king and his two favourite queens, depicting the marital alliances between Tibet and her two neighbouring kingdoms, a legend known from the vita copus of the king.[46] This new opera, however, displaying very little resemblance to the operatic play, is called "Princess Wencheng," "the Chinese Princess" (Fig. 9, 10). The main story is now employed to serve

45 It should be recalled that most classical civilisations and regimes throughout history usually conceived of themselves as being cosmically central. For the Sinic world, the literature on the underlying principles behind the age-old Chinese world order and worldview is legion, with its emic, cosmomagic presuppositions and ingrained sinocentric implications of a moral claim to universality and supremacy: see e.g. Fairbank 1968; Piper Rae Gaubatz 1996: 25; further, Wernsdörfer 1998; Slobotník 1998; Blum 2002.

46 See Sørensen 1994: 199-249 for details of these marriages and the basic sources. Josayma 1991.

as a template to describe the overall Sino-Tibetan relationship and galvanise the ethnic brotherhood. In this new drama, the king is exceptionally delegated to a minor role or *Nebenrolle*. The omnipresent king and cultural hero is for the first time eclipsed by someone – by the now iconic Chinese princess and erstwhile queen who here has taken the centre stage; yet on the other hand is it, after all, only theatre.

***

References (incl. abbreviations)

Alexander, André. 2005. *The Temples of Lhasa. Tibetan Buddhist Architecture from the 7th to the 21st Centuries.* Chicago: Serindia Publications.

Alsop, Ian. 1990. Phagpa Lokeśvara of the Potala. *Orientations* 21(4): 51-61.

Benard, E. A. 2000. Transformations of Wencheng Kongjo: The Tang Princess, Tibetan Queen, and Buddhist Tara, in: Benard, E.A. and B. Moon (eds.), *Goddesses Who Rule.* Oxford: Oxford University Press, 149-64.

Bhabh omi K. (ed.). 1990. *Nation and Narration. London*: Routledge.

Blum, Susan D. *et al.* 2002. Reconsidering the Middle Kingdom, in: Blum, Susan D. *et al.* (eds.), *China off Center: Mapping the Margins of the Middle Kingdom.* Honululu: University of Hawaii Press.

Bonnell, Victoria E. and Hunt, Lynn (eds.). 1999. *Beyond the Cultural Turn. New Directions in the Study of Society and Culture.* Berkeley: University of California Press.

Brauen, Martin. 2005. *The Dalai Lamas. A Visual History.* Chicago: Serindia Publication.

Bushell, S.W. 1888. The Early History of Tibet. *JRAS.*

Chayet, Anne and F. Meyer. 1983. La chapelle de Srong-btsan sgam-po au Potala. *Arts Asiatiques* 38: 82-5.

Cüppers, Christoph (ed.). 2005. *Proceedings of the Seminar on the Relationship between Religion and State (chos srid zung 'brel) in Traditional Tibet* (Lumbini 4-7 March 2000). Wiesbaden: Reichert Verlag.

Dargyay Eva K. 1988. Srong-Btsan Sgam-Po of Tibet: Bodhisattva and king, in: Granoff, P. and K. Shinohara (eds.). *Monks and Magicians: Religious Biographies in Asia.*

Oakville: Mosaic Press: 99-116.

— 1989. Srong-btsan sgam-po's "Biography" in the Mani bka' 'bum, *Acta Orientalia Acdemiae Scientiarum Hungaricae* 43(2,3): 247-257.

Doney, Lewis. 2015. Early Bodhisattva Kingship in Tibet: The Case of Tri Songdétsen. *Cahiers d'Extrême Asie* 24: 29-47.

Dotson, Brandon. 2006. *Administration and Law in the Tibetan Empire: The Section on Law and State and its Old Tibetan Antecedents.* D. Phil. Thesis. Oxford.

— 2009. *The Old Tibetan Annals.An Annotated Translation of Tibet's First History*. Wien: Verlag der Österreichischen Akademie der Wissenschaften.

— 2012. At the behest of the mountain: Gods, clans and political topography in post-imperial Tibet, in: Scherrer-Schaub, Cristina (ed.), *Old Tibetan Studies*. Brill Tibetan Studies Library: Leiden. 159-204.

— Forthcoming. A Translation of the *Old Tibetan Chronicle* – Pelliot tibétain 1286 and Pelliot tibétain 1287.

Dreyfus, Georges. 1994. Proto-nationalism in Tibet, in: Kvaerne, Per ed. *Tibetan Studies*. (Proceedings of the 6th Seminar of the International Association of Tibetan Studies Fagernes 1992. Oslo), Vol.I, 205-218.

Dutt, N. (ed.). 1986. *Saddharmapuṇḍarīka-sūtram*. Calcutta: The Asiatic Society.

Ehrhard, Franz Karl. 2004. *Die Statue und der Temple des Arya Va-ti bzang-po. Ein Beitrag zur Geschichte und Geographie des Tibetischen Buddhismus.* Wiesbaden: Dr. Reichert's Verlag.

Fairbank, John. K. 1968. *The Chinese World Order.* Boston: Havard University Press.

Fleming, Zara and Shastri, Lhagvademchig (eds.). 2012. *Mongolian Buddhist Art: Masterpieces from the Museums of Mongolia*. 2 Vols. Chicago: Serindia Publications.

Foucault, Michel (1970). *The Order of Things. An Archaeology of the Human Sciences*. London.

Gaubatz, Piper Rae. 1996. *Beyond the Great Wall. Urban Form and Transformation on the Chinese Frontiers*. Stanford: Stanford University Press.

Geertz, Clifford. 1973. *The Interpretation of Cultures: Selected Essays*. New York: Basis Books.

Gyurme Dorje, Tashi Tsering, Heather Stoddard and André Alexander (eds.). 2010. *Jokhang: Tibet's most sacred Buddhist Temple*. London and Bangkok: Edition Hansjorg Mayer.

Haarh, Erik 1969. *The Yarlung Dynasty: A Study with Particular Regard to the Contributions by Myths and Legends to the History of Ancient Tibet and the Origin and Nature of Its Kings*. København: Gads Forlag.

Halkias, Georgios T. 2013. *Luminous Bliss: A Religious History of Pure Land Literature in Tibet. With an Annotated Translation and Critical Analysis of the Orgyen-ling golden short Sukhāvatīvyūha-sūtra*. University of Hawai'i Press.

Hazod, Guntram. 2002. The royal residence Pho brang Byams pa mi 'gyur gling and the story of Srong btsan sgam po's birth in rGya ma, in: Blezer, Henk (ed.), *Tibet, Past and Present. Tibetan Studies I. Proceedings of the 9th Seminar of the IATS*. Leiden 2000. 27-48.

— 2003. The Kyichu region in the period of the Tibetan empire: A historico-geographical note, in: Mckay, A. (ed.), *Tibet and Her Neighbours. A Study*. 29-42.

— 2009. Imperial Central Tibet – An annotated cartographical survey of its territorial divisions and key political sites in: Dotson, Brandon, *The Old Tibetan Annals. An Annotated Translation of Tibet's First History*. Wien: Verlag der Österreichischen Akademie der Wissenschaften, 161-232.

— 2014. The stele in the centre of the Lhasa Mandala: About the position of the 9th-century Sino-Tibetan treaty pillar of Lhasa in its historical-geographical and narrative context, in: Tropper, Kurt (ed.), *Epigraphic Evidence in the Pre-modern Buddhist World*, Wien: Arbeitskreis für tibetische und Buddhistische Studien, 37-81.

— Forthcoming. The 'anti-Buddhist law' and its author in eighth-century Tibet: A reconsideration of the story of Zhang Ma zhang Grom pa skyes, in: Eltschinger, Vincent et al. (eds.), *Festschrift for Cristina Scherrer-Schaub*.

Hayden White. 1990. *The Content of the Form: Narrative Discourse and Historical Representation*. Baltimore: John Hopkins University Press.

Hill, N. 2105. The sku bla rite in imperial Tibetan Religion, *Cahiers d'Extrême Orient*. 24: 49-58.

Hobsbawn, E. J. and Ranger, T. (eds.). 1983. *The Invention of Tradition*. Cambridge: Cambridge University Press.

Ishihama, Yumiko. 2003 (1993). On the dissemination of the belief of the Dalai Lama as a manifestation of the bodhisattva Avalokiteśvara, in: McKay, A. (ed.), *The History of Tibet 2. The Medieval Period: c. 850-1895*. London 2003: 523-37 (repr.). *Acta Asiatica*

64 (1993): 38-56.

Iwao, Kazushi, Hill, Nathan, Takeuchi, Tsuguhito (eds.). 2009. *Old Tibetan Inscriptions*. Vol. II. Tokyo: Research Institute for Languages and Cultures of Asia and Africa.

Josayma, C.B. 1991 (trans.). *Rgya bza' bal bza'*. LTWA.

Ka khol ma = *Bka' chems Ka khol ma*. Lanzhou: Kan su mi rigs dpe skrun khang 1989.

Kantorowitz, Ernst H. 1957. *The King's Two Bodies. A Study in Medieval Political Theology*. Princeton.

Kapstein, Matthew. 2000. *The Tibetan Assimilation of Buddhism: Conversion, Contestation, and Memory.* Oxford: Oxford University Press.

Kern, H. (tr.). 1963. *Saddharmapuṇḍarīka or the Lotus of the True Law*. New York: Dover.

Lafitte, Gabriel 2013. *Spoiling Tibet. China and Resource Nationalism on the Roof of the World*. Asian Augments. Zed Books.

Lde'u chos 'byung = Mkhas pa Lde'u, *Rgya bod kyi chos 'byung rgyas pa*. Lhasa: Bod ljongs mi rigs dpe skrun khang 1987.

Macdonald, Ariane. 1971. Une lecture des Pelliot Tibétain 1286, 1287, 1038, et 1290: essai sur la formation et l'emploi des mythes politiques dans la religion royale de Srong bcan Sgam po, in: Macdonald, A., (ed.), *Études Tibétaines dédiées à la mémoire de Marcelle Lalou*. Paris: Adrien Maisonneuve, 190-391.

Ma ṇi bka' 'bum = *Chos rgyal srong btsan sgam po'i Ma ni bka' 'bum*. Xining: Mtsho sngon mi rigs dpe skrun khang 1991.

Michael, Franz. 1982. *Rule by Reincarnation: Tibetan Buddhism and Its Role in Society and State*. Boulder: Westview.

Mills, Martin A. 2012. Ritual as History in Tibetan Divine Kingship: Notes on the Myth of the Khotanese Monks. *History of Religions* 51(3): 219-220.

Myang ral chos 'byung = Tārānātha Kun-dga' snying-po, *Myang yul stod smad bar gsum gyi ngo mtshar gtam gyilegs bshad mkhas pa'i 'jugs ngogs*. 1-223. Lhasa: Bod ljongs mi dmangs dpe skrun khang 1988.

Neumaier, Eva K. 2007. Thecult of Amitābha and the apotheosis of the Tibetan ruler, *Pacific World* 3(9): 231-44.

OTC = *Old Tibetan Chronicle* (PT 1287; see *TDD*).

Pasang Wangdu. 2002. King Srong btsan sgam po according to the *Dba' bzhed*: Remarks on the introduction of Buddhism into Tibet and the greatest of the Tibetan royal ancestors, in: Buffe-trille, K. and Diemberger, H. (eds.). *Territory and Identity in Tibet and the Himalayas*. Leiden: Brill, 17-32.

Pasang Wangdu and Diemberger, Hildegard. 2000. *dBa' bzhed. The Royal Narrative Concerning the Bringing of the Buddha's Doctrine to Tibet*. Wien: Österreichische Akademie der Wissenschaften.

Roesler, Ulrike. 2015. "16 Human Norms" (*mi chos bcu drug*) — Indian, Chinese and Tibetan, in: Czaja, Olaf and Guntram Hazod (eds.). *The Illuminating Mirror*. Wiesbaden: Reichert Verlag. 385-405.

Said, Edward 1978. *Orientalism*. New York: Random House.

van Schaik, Sam. 2006. The Tibetan Avalokiteśvara cult in the tenth century: Evidence from the Dunhuang Manuscripts, in: Donaldson, R. M. and C. Wedemeyer (eds.), *Tibetan Buddhist Literature and Praxis* (Proceedings of the Tenth Seminar of the IATS, 2003, Volume 4): Leiden: Brill, 2006: 55-72.

— 2016. Red faced barbarians, benign despots and drunken masters: Khotan as a mirror to Tibet, *RET* 36 (October 2016): 45-68.

von Schroeder, Ulrich. 2001. *Buddhist Sculptures in Tibet*. 2 Vols. Hongkong.

Slobodník. M. 1998. The Chinese Princess Wencheng in Tibet: A cultural intermediary between facts and myth, in: Gálik, M. and T. Štefanovičová (eds.), *Trade, Journeys, Inner- and Intercultural Communication in East and West* (*up to 1250*). 267-76.

Spiegel, Gabrielle M. 1997.*The Past as Text: The Theory and Practice of Medieval Historiography*. Baltimore: Johns Hopkins University Press.

Sørensen, Per K. 1994. *Tibetan Buddhist Historiography. The Mirror Illuminating the Royal Genealogies. An Annotated Translation of the XIVth Century Tibetan Chronicler Gyal-rabs gsal-ba'i me-long*. Asiatische Forschungen 128. Wiesbaden: Otto Harrassowitz Verlag.

— 2005a. A seven thangka lineage set of the 9th Dalai Lama, in: Brauen, M. (ed.), *The Dalai Lamas. A Visual History*. Chicago: Serindia Publications, 242-257.

— 2005b. The Dalai Lama Institution: Its Origin and Genealogical Succession, *Orientations* (Sept. 2005): 53-60.

— 2007. Restless Relic: The Ārya Lokeśvara: Icon symbol of power, legitimacy and pawn for patronage, in: Kellner, B. Krasser, H., Lasic, H., Much, M.T., and Tauscher, H. (eds.), *Pramaṇakīrtiḥ. Papers Dedicated to Ernst Steinkellner on the Occasion of his 70th Birthday.*

Part II. Wien: Wiener Studien zur Tibetologie und Buddhismuskunde Bd. 70.2. 1-29.

— 2008. The sacred junipers of Reting: The arboreal origins behind the Dalai Lama lineage. *Orientations* (Sept. 2008): 74-79.

Sørensen, Per K. and Hazod, Guntram. 2005. *Thundering Falcon. An Inquiry into the History and Cult of Khra-'brug, Tibet's First Buddhist Temple*. Wien: Verlag der Österreichischen Akademie der Wissenschaften.

— 2007. *Rulers on the Celestial Plain. Ecclesiastic and Secular Hegemony in Medieval Tibet*. Wien: Verlag der Österreichischen Akademie der Wissenschaften.

Stein, Rolf. 1981. Saint et divin, un titre tibétain et chinois des rois tibétains, *Journal Asiatique* 269: 231-75.

— 1984. l'Usage de métaphores pour des distinctions honorifiques à l'époque des rois Tibétains, *Bulletin de l'École Française d'Extrême-Orient* 73: 257-77.

— 1985. Tibetica antiqua III: à propos du mot gcug-lag et de la religion indigène, *Bulletin de l'École Française d'Extrême-Orient* 74: 83-133.

— 1986. Tibetica antiqua IV: la tradition relative au début du bouddhism au Tibet, *Bulletin de l'École Française d'Extréme-Orient* 75: 169-96.

— 1988. Tibetica antiqua V: la religion indigène et les Bon-po dans les manuscrits de Touen-Houang, *Bulletin de l'École Française d'Extréme-Orient* 77: 27-56.

TDD = Imaeda, Yoshiro, M. Kapstein and T. Takeuchi (eds.). 2007. *Tibetan Documents from Dunhuang* (Old Tibetan Documents Online Monograph Series Vol. I). Tokyo: Tokyo University of Foreign Studies.

Tucci, G. 1955.The secret characters of the kings of ancient Tibet, *East and West* 6: 197-205.

Vaidhya, P.L. 1960. *Gaṇḍavyūha-sūtra*. (Buddhist Sanskrit Texts 5). Darbhanga: Mithila Institute.

Vitali, Roberto. 1990. *Early Temples of Central Tibet*. London: Serindia Publ.

Watson, Burton (tr.). 1993. *The Lotus Sutra*. New York. Columbia University Press.

Wernsdörfer, Martina. 1998. Chinesischer Himmelsohn – Tibetischer Gottkönig. Die Souverän-Suzerän-Problematik im Lichte der Lama-Schutzherr-Beziehung, *Asiatische Studien* 52(4): 1113-1174.

Yihong Pan. (1992). The Sino-Tibetan treatises in the Tang Dynasty. *T'oung Pao* 78: 116–61.

从《唐书》的“令禁赭面”说起
——再议图文材料中的“赭面”

李永宪[*]

吐蕃王朝时期藏地曾流行“赭面”之俗，《唐书》等历史文献有过记述，在20世纪末期考古出土的图像资料中也得到证实，如青海省都兰县、德令哈市吐蕃时期墓中“棺板画”和“木板画”所绘“赭面”人像等，这为学界讨论吐蕃“赭面”提供了图、文两个方面的依据。本文对吐蕃“赭面”的再议论，是根据有关吐蕃“赭面”现有的文、图资料，将此妆俗在唐蕃两地的表现置于特定的时空背景下，从唐蕃互动的视角试作一些分析，以引求诸家高见。

一、《唐书》等汉文文献中的“赭面”

《唐书》说吐蕃人有“赭面”之俗，是在讲述文成公主由长安抵达逻些（拉萨）之初的一段文字中，如《旧唐书》卷196上·吐蕃（上）所述：

> 贞观八年（634），其赞普弃宗弄赞（即松赞干布——引者注）始遣使朝贡，……太宗遣行人冯德遐往抚慰之。见德遐，大悦。闻突厥及吐谷浑皆尚公主，乃遣使随德遐入朝，多赍金宝，奉表求婚，太宗未许之。使者既返，言于弄赞曰：“初至大国，待我甚厚，许嫁公主。会吐谷浑王入朝，有相离间，由是礼薄，遂不许嫁。”弄赞遂与羊同连，发兵以击吐谷浑。吐谷浑不能支，遁于青海之上，以避其锋，其国人畜并为吐蕃所掠。于是进兵攻破党项及白兰诸羌，率其众二十余万，顿于松州西境。遣使贡金帛，云

* 李永宪：四川大学中国藏学研究所教授。

> 来迎公主，又谓其属曰："若大国不嫁公主与我，即当入寇。"遂进攻松州。都督韩威轻骑觇贼，反为所败，边有大扰。太宗遣……左武卫将军牛进达为阔水道行军总管，右领军将军刘兰为洮河道行军总管，率步骑五万以击之。进达先锋自松州夜袭其营，斩千余级。弄赞大惧，引兵而退，遣使谢罪，因复请婚，太宗许之。弄赞乃遣其相禄东赞致礼，献金五千两，自余宝玩数百事。贞观十五年，太宗以文成公主妻之，令礼部尚书、江夏郡王道宗主婚，持节送公主于吐蕃。弄赞率其部兵次柏海，亲迎于河源。……及与公主归国，谓所亲曰："我父祖未有通婚上国者，今我得尚大唐公主，为幸实多，当为公主筑一城，以夸示后代。"遂筑城邑，立栋宇以居处焉。公主恶其人赭面，弄赞令国中权且罢之，自亦释毡裘，袭纨绮，渐慕华风。仍遣酋豪子弟，请入国学以习诗、书。又请中国识文之人典其表疏。[1]

《唐书》这段文字主要是讲"唐蕃和亲"的起止过程，其中言及吐蕃"赭面"是对藏地习俗的简要记述，但文中所表语意却并不止于此。

先说唐蕃和亲的背景。吐蕃的"请婚"与唐太宗的"许婚"实质上是公元7世纪前期唐蕃政治（政权）层面互动的因果事件。据《唐书》记述，贞观八年（634）吐蕃遣使长安请婚的同时，还有突厥、吐谷浑等多个部族的请婚使者前往。起初，唐太宗对吐蕃使者由待之"甚厚"到"礼薄"而"未许之"，大概因唐太宗当时对唐蕃关系中请婚这件事并无更深远的考虑。而在吐蕃这一方，松赞干布的策略是以联姻为前提，以扩张发展为目的。因此请婚被拒后，吐蕃即联合当时青藏高原的另一个强势部落"羊同"（象雄）举兵征伐"离间"唐蕃关系的吐谷浑等部，尔后甚至不惜在松州（今四川松潘）与唐交战。当然"举战"的目的是为了"求和"，故吐蕃此战虽败于松州，但仍遣大臣禄东赞以"谢罪"之身复使长安请婚，而唐太宗彼时显然对唐蕃关系已有了基于更高层面的认识，于是才有"以文成公主妻之，令礼部尚书、江夏郡王道宗主婚，持节送公主于吐蕃"的主婚和护嫁之举。显然，"唐蕃联姻"对双方来讲都是一项承前启后的重大事件。

其次，《唐书》在记述遣使请婚、公主入藏等历史事件时，其行文修辞是一种"述史叙事"，但在文字的后面，实际上也隐含着修史者从唐王朝的角度意欲阐明的某些主张，例如对唐蕃双方政治角色的"主次定位"。因此《唐书》在言及吐蕃"赭

1 《旧唐书》卷196上·列传146上·吐蕃上，北京：中华书局，1975年，第5221-5222页。

面”的句段中，重点是表述吐蕃赞普对唐王朝的“敬重之心”——公主初入藏地，对当地风俗尚有不适，尤“恶其人赭面”，有鉴于此，松赞干布即“令国中权且罢之”。这种为顾及长安公主观瞻而禁停“国中”之俗的举措，不仅不合“入乡随俗”的常理，而且还为此颁布“禁俗令”，显然是异常之举。为何长安公主就不能“入乡随俗”呢？因为这不符合《唐书》的笔意，如前文先说“……及与公主归国，谓所亲曰：‘我父祖未有通婚上国者，今我得尚大唐公主，为幸实多，当为公主筑一城，以夸示后代。’遂筑城邑，立栋宇以居处焉。”此句意在表述藏王迎娶公主“为幸实多”的敬重之心由来已久，所以对公主的好恶自然应当是言听计从。在“令禁赭面”之后又说：（吐蕃）“自亦释毡裘，袭纨绮，渐慕华风。仍遣酋家子弟，请入国学以习诗、书。又请中国识文之人典其表疏。”

不难看出，《唐书》的笔意是强调吐蕃对唐王朝长存“敬重、崇尚”之心，所以“联姻”必将引导吐蕃“渐慕华风”。说松赞干布已“令禁赭面”，其实是在强调此事与“为公主筑城”“释毡裘而袭纨绮”“习诗书并请典注表疏”等举措一样，意在“塑造”吐蕃对长安王朝应有的治政姿态：在亲族关系上善待汉地公主、在社会习俗上效仿唐风、在文化知识上向汉地学习、在利益关系上确保双方满意，等等。可以说这是对唐蕃“联姻”之后吐蕃政治与文化角色的一种“评估”和“设定”。

《唐书·吐蕃传》的笔意角度，是后世修史者基于其时、其地、其人对吐蕃的认知与理解，不确、不实乃至托想之辞自是在所难免，新旧《唐书》中此种缺陷也明显易见。但这并不影响《唐书》所言“赭面”之俗的真实性，只是若将“令国中权且罢之”理解为“赭面”之俗就此被革除或就此消失，未必是确定的事实；而公主入藏时曾“恶其人赭面”，则是对吐蕃此种习俗的真实记录。

“赭面”之俗可能并非始于吐蕃时期，《隋书》也记述了藏地有“以彩涂面”的习俗。《隋书·西域传》之“女国”条下云：

> 女国，在葱岭之南，……王姓苏毗，字末羯，在位二十年。……男女皆以彩色涂面，一日之中，或数度变改之。……气候多寒，以射猎为业。出鍮石、朱砂、麝香、牦牛、骏马、蜀马。尤多盐，恒将盐向天竺兴贩，……开皇六年，遣使朝贡，其后遂绝。[2]

2 《隋书》卷83·列传48女国，第6册，北京：中华书局，1973年，第1850-1851页。

《隋书》所称“葱岭之南”的“女国”，即指帕米尔高原及昆仑山、喀喇昆仑山等诸山系以南的青藏高原西北部，其“气候多寒，以射猎为业……尤多盐”等等则是对历史上藏北、藏西高海拔区地理与人文特征的描写，故学界多认为《隋书》之“女国”应是吐蕃王朝建立之前统领高原西北大部地区的“羊同”（或“杨童”，亦即象雄）。《隋书》“男女皆以彩色涂面”描述的是公元6世纪“开皇六年”（586）之际的高原习俗，要早于《唐书》“令禁赭面”的7世纪中期“贞观十五年”（641）近一百年。因此从史籍记述的时间顺序上说，西藏“彩面”之俗的形成应在吐蕃王朝建立之前。从地域上看，《隋书》的“以彩涂面”可能主要指高海拔区以猎牧经济为主的部族习俗，而《唐书》的“其人赭面”应是在以农业为主的拉萨河谷流行，及至文成公主入藏时已是“国中”之普遍习俗。所以，在时间和空间上，“赭面”并不限于吐蕃时期的拉萨一带，应有更早的地域传统，并且至吐蕃王朝时期已是高原部族的一种文化标志。如有研究者认为，8世纪后半叶吐蕃占领敦煌等河西陇右地区时，吐蕃统治者（尚乞心儿）曾令沙州一带的汉族居民易服改装、学说蕃语，甚至“赭面纹身”，并举《张淮深碑》“河洛沸腾，……并南蕃之化，……由是行遵辫发，体美织皮，左衽束身，垂肱跪膝”及《阴处士修功德记》“熊罴爱子，拆襁褓以文身；鸳鸯夫妻，解鬟钿而辫发”等语为据，认为其时“赭面”“纹身”出现在河西、陇右地区，是吐蕃对占领区属民实行“蕃化”治政的一种身份表征。[3]

虽然目前未见有考古材料提供的河西陇右“蕃地”汉民被迫“赭面”的证据，但青海多地吐蕃墓出土绘有“赭面人物”的棺（木）板画，则可表明到8世纪中后期时，“赭面”习俗在当时“大蕃”统领的吐谷浑故地已是十分流行，这既是文成公主入藏时“其人赭面”在时间上的延伸，同时也表明吐蕃“赭面”之俗在地域上的扩展。如此看来，《唐书》所言“令禁赭面”并未产生实际的效力，它应是出自修史者意图的“意表之辞”，因为无论是文献材料还是考古材料，并不支持《唐书》中的这种说法。可能的历史的真相则是，被《唐书》否定的吐蕃“赭面”不但没有在7世纪时消失，其后反而流行更远、更长久，随着吐蕃领土的扩张，成为“蕃民”的习俗标志。

3　参见陈国灿：《唐朝吐蕃陷落沙州城的时间问题》，《敦煌学辑刊》1985年第1期。

二、藏文历史文本中“赭面”的分析

然而检阅藏文历史文本[4]则发现，其中的“赭面”一词所指与《唐书》等汉文历史文献并不相同。

简言之，藏文史籍中的“赭面”一词与“赤面”“红面”等词相通，皆是指西藏古代人群的肤色或面色，即所谓“食肉赤面者”。对此黄颢先生认为：“《五部遗教》记载，‘此后由神猴与岩魔女统治，西藏遂称神魔之域（原附藏文略——笔者注），并出现了‘食肉赤面者”（见《王者遗教》18 页上）。其间‘食肉赤面者’一词，在后来的藏籍中即视为是藏人的代称，继而用‘红面域’或‘赤面域’代称西藏……在《唐书·吐蕃传》中所谓吐蕃人喜‘赭面’，当即藏文所指（赤面或赭面），所谓‘赤面域’或‘赤面国’盖源于此。”[5]同类，《汉藏史集》也称：“在吐蕃，有三大处地面。……最初被称为有雪吐蕃之国。中间一段时间期被神魔统治，被称为赭面之区，后来被称为悉补野吐蕃之国，……”[6]

上举两条引文关于“赭面”或“赤面”的表述在藏文文献中具有代表性，其中有三点值得注意：第一，“赤面”“红面”“赭面”皆指高原早期居民的面肤之色，而面肤“赤红”的原因，则是因为最初“直接吞食侵众人类，饮食人畜血肉面变赤”所致。[7]所以，“赤面 / 赭面 / 红面”是因“饮食血肉”的生活方式导致的自然肤色，并不是面部妆式。第二，高原早期居民的“赤红”肤色并非个例，而是整个部族的群体体貌特征，所以才“继而用‘红面域’或‘赤面域’代称西藏”[8]。由此，人群肤色特征便成为“域”“国”等地域区界的指代词，具有与其他人群或其他区域相区别的意义。第三，“食肉赤面者”或“赭面之区”“赤面国”均表述的是“悉补野吐蕃之国”之前的时期，或为“神猴与岩魔女统治”时期的高原人群，是对吐蕃王朝之前高原早期人群特征的一种追忆或追记。

此外，在《拔协》《五部遗教·王者噶塘》等藏文文献中都见有“赤面”“赭面”的同样用法，词意亦均相同。这种以“赭面”来表述藏族、藏地人群面肤之色的词意，晚期的一些汉文著作中也有沿用，如近人陈渠珍《艽野尘梦》中“……沿途所

4 本文所指藏文历史文本主要指汉译藏文读本。
5 参见黄颢译注：《〈贤者喜宴〉摘译》注 [5]，《西藏民族学院学报》1980 年第 4 期，第 40-41 页。
6 见达仓宗巴·班觉桑布：《汉藏史集》，陈庆英汉译本，拉萨：西藏人民出版社，1986 年，第 14 页。
7 此说出自苯教史《法源》，转引自恰白·次旦平措、诺章·吴坚、平措次仁：《西藏通史——松石宝串》，陈庆英、格桑益西、何宗英、许德存汉译本，拉萨：西藏藏文古籍出版社，1996 年，第 11 页。
8 《隋书》卷 83·列传 48 女国，第 6 册，第 1850-1851 页。

见，皆赭面左衽之藏民”之语。[9] 其意亦指肤色或面色。

不过，引文所举黄颢先生将《唐书》所言“赭面”理解为与藏文史籍中的“赭面”“赤面”等词都是同指高原人群的面肤之色，显然是不准确的。在迄今的研究中人们之所以将吐蕃“赭面”视为一种面妆习俗而几无分歧或另解，笔者认为，主要是研究者多依据的是《唐书》等汉文历史文本，而非藏文史籍，且《唐书》言称“赭面”为面妆之俗时，前文后句皆有清楚的语意表达。

汉、藏两种历史文本为何对“赭面”一词所指有着不同的表达或理解？目前隐约可见的线索似乎还不足以回答这个问题。若仅就成书年代和叙事时代而言，《隋书》《唐书》等汉文史籍成书年代比本文所举藏文文献要早，而记述的史事距修史者较近，因此对吐蕃时期民间习俗之类的记述可信度更高。汉译藏文史籍的成书年代不仅晚于前者，而且所言“赭面”是“悉补野吐蕃之国”之前或“神猴与岩魔女统治”的时期。从某种意义上说，包括新旧《唐书》在内的汉文历史文本对“吐蕃赭面”的记述虽仍显字句不多，但终究是一种历史的“记忆”，是对“吐蕃人喜赭面”的一种“他指”。而藏文历史文本中对吐蕃“赭面”的“失忆”，或将其表述为藏地人群面肤之色的“另指”，若视为历史的“自述”显然可信度是不足的。不管如何，这种差异的个中意味都值得深究，此不赘。

三、“吐蕃赭面”在青藏考古材料中的实证

虽然“吐蕃赭面”缺乏藏文史籍的“自述”，但青藏高原的考古出土材料却为我们提供了珍贵的图像实证。

青藏高原考古材料中发现的彩绘“赭面人物”，是了解“吐蕃赭面”的重要具象证据，其重要性主要有三点：第一，考古图像材料显示的“赭面样式”，使我们对“赭面”的讨论可以从“习俗”的无形层面具体到“妆饰”和“样式”的有形层面；第二，考古发现的“赭面”是由绘画中的“赭面人物”所表现的，因此“赭面”人物的身份等固有特征，为分析其“族群背景”提供了可靠依据；第三，有“赭面人物”图像的考古材料都是有可辨识的时间、空间范围和特征，这为观察其流变方向提供了重要参照。而所有这些，在已刊布的考古材料中都是比较清楚的。

1. 青海省都兰热水吐蕃墓

1999 年北京大学考古文博院、青海省文物考古研究所发掘的青海都兰县热水沟

9 陈渠珍：《艽野尘梦》，任乃强校注本，拉萨：西藏人民出版社，1999 年，第 12 页。

三号墓（99DRNM3）[10] 出土“彩绘木箱状木器”的三块侧板上绘有四个面涂红色“可能就是‘赭面’”的人物。[11] 据发掘者分析，99DRNM3 与 99DRNM1 两墓均是等级较高的“中心墓葬”，其墓主为吐蕃外戚，年代“大约在 8 世纪中期”[12]。

热水吐蕃墓箱板画所绘人物的“赭面”妆可分为两式：一是在两颊、鼻头、下巴分别涂以圆点形红色；二是在两颊各涂两三道条形红色。根据报告刊印的照片观察，所绘人物的服装多已褪色而模糊，但面部“赭面”的画痕却十分清晰，说明此种红色与其他颜料的物质成分不同，应为矿物类原料。（图 1）

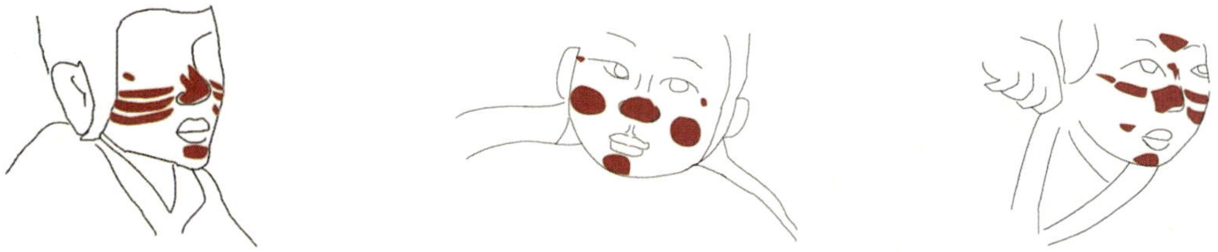

图 1　青海都兰吐蕃三号墓木板彩画中的“赭面”样式
（据《都兰吐蕃墓》图版三四改绘）

2. 青海德令哈果里木吐蕃墓

2002 年青海省文物考古研究所、海西州民族博物馆清理了德令哈市以东果里木[13] 地点的两座吐蕃墓，部分资料最早刊于 2004 年、2006 年[14]。其时代“大体上相当于吐蕃占领敦煌时期。因此我们将这两座墓葬的年代定在八世纪末叶”。[15]

果里木两墓三棺的四面棺板均绘彩画，已刊布的一幅侧板彩画（摹本）中共绘有 42 个人物，其中除背面人物和头部残缺者外，涂饰“赭面”妆的有 34 人（图 2）。与都兰热水墓所见“赭面”样式相同，果里木棺板画的人物“赭面”也是在额、鼻、

10　北京大学考古文博学院、青海省文物考古研究所编著：《都兰吐蕃墓》，北京：科学出版社，2005 年。

11　前引《都兰吐蕃墓》第 100-104 页，图六四、六五，图版三三、三四。

12　前引《都兰吐蕃墓》第 127-128 页。

13　该处墓葬最早曾以“果里木”（乡）为地名，后以墓葬所处该乡的“夏塔图”草场命名。可参见王树芝等：《跨度为 2332 年考古树轮年表的建立与夏塔图墓葬定年》，《考古》2008 年第 2 期。

14　许新国：《唐代绘画新标本——吐蕃棺板画》，《文物天地》2004 年第 3 期，第 17-22 页；青海省文物考古研究所：《棺板上画的是什么人？》，《中国国家地理》2006 年第 3 期，第 84-91 页；另据青海省文物考古研究所所长许新国先生在“第三届西藏考古与艺术国际学术讨论会”（2006 年 10 月，北京）报告中得知，该地点还有部分棺板彩画未予发表。

15　见许新国：《唐代绘画新标本——吐蕃棺板画》，第 21 页。

图 2　青海德令哈果里木吐蕃墓棺板彩画人物摹本（局部）
（采自《中国国家地理》2006 年第 3 期，第 89 页插图）

下颏、两颊等部位涂以点状、条状、块状的红色，依涂抹点数有 13、9、7、5 等单数之分，除额、鼻、下颏外，其余涂点在数量、部位上皆是对称的。（图 3）

3. 西藏自治区定结县恰姆石窟壁画

西藏定结恰姆石窟于 2008 年西藏文物“三普”中发现，2009 年西藏文物保护研究所、首都师范大学、中国藏学研究中心等单位进行了较为系统的调查纪录。该地点各类石窟计有百余孔之多，其中 I 区 1 号窟北壁所绘“供养和礼佛人”中有多位人物饰“赭面”妆。报告中的壁画摹本显示，“赭面”人物皆为右颊或左颊涂抹圆点形红色（图 4、图 5）。调查报告称这种“面颊上涂朱或赭面的习俗，则是吐蕃‘赭面’习俗的遗风”。报告综合了 C14 测年数据及泥塑、壁画等内容推定恰姆石窟的“年代范围介于 10-12 世纪中期。……其开窟的上限时间也不排除早至 9-10 世纪”。[16]

4. “吐蕃赭面”的样式

综观上举考古材料中 40 余位“赭面”人物图像，可知“吐蕃赭面”作为一种面妆习俗，其涂绘样式有着多样变化，尤其青海果里木吐蕃墓棺板画中的“赭面”样式更是丰富多变（参见图 1、图 3），但有两点是共性的：一是“赭面”之色皆为红色。

16　见许新国：《唐代绘画新标本——吐蕃棺板画》，第 21 页。

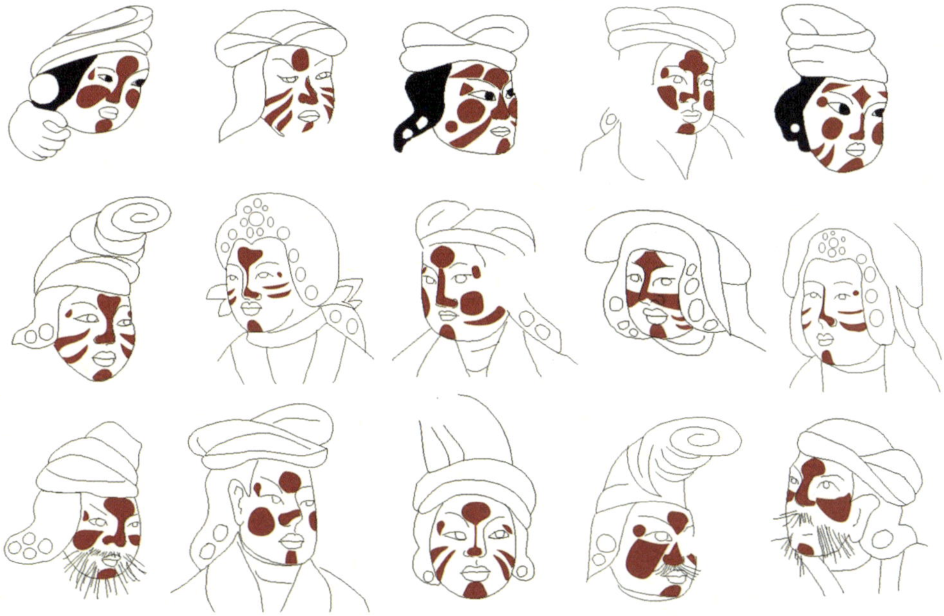

图 3　果里木吐蕃墓棺板画“赭面”的各种样式
（据《中国国家地理》2006 第 3 期第 89 页插图选绘）

图 4　西藏定结县恰姆石窟Ⅰ区 K1 北壁 NI 组壁画“赭面”人物
（采自《考古》2012 年第 7 期图版贰拾：4）

图 5　西藏定结县恰姆石窟Ⅰ区 K1 北壁 N4 组壁画“赭面”人物摹本
（采自《考古》2012 年第 7 期第 74 页：图九）

在考古遗物中有的色相深沉而呈深红或紫红，可能因受出土后光照或氧化作用的影响，原来应是朱砂类矿物颜料的自然色。[17] 二是“赭面”的涂绘样式虽有点数、形状、部位的不同，但都是以面部额（眉心）、鼻、下颏为中轴线，如同面部五官的分布一样完全对称。唯有西藏定结恰姆石窟壁画人物“赭面”是单颊（右颊或左颊）涂红点，有的还在颈部涂有点数不同的红色。在时代上，恰姆石窟的年代要晚于青海的多处吐蕃墓地，稍晚于“吐蕃王朝时期”，所以调查报告认为它们“是吐蕃‘赭面’习俗的遗风”，[18] 或可作为解释二者样式有别的原因之一。

概言之，青藏两省考古材料 40 余例“赭面人物”可代表目前所知吐蕃本土及领地 8-11 世纪“赭面妆”的基本样式。而施行“赭面妆”的人物的身份，根据上述几

17　柳春诚《郭里木棺板彩画临摹手记》中说：“由于棺板彩画出土后接触紫外线和空气，画面颜色会在很短时间内发生改变，……因为棺板画上的颜色在不断地发生变化，要临摹好一幅棺板彩画，至少需要调整 3-5 遍色调，只有这样，才能更加接近它的原始色调。”见《中国国家地理》2006 年第 3 期，第 88 页。关于都兰吐蕃墓中木板画所用朱砂颜料，可参见张晓梅、原思训：《青海都兰吐蕃墓ぅ出土彩绘木构件颜料、金属文物的分析及埋藏环境对文物保存状况的影响》，载北京大学考古文博学院、青海省文物考古研究所编著：《都兰吐蕃墓》，北京：科学出版社，2005 年，第 144-148 页。

18《西藏定结县恰姆石窟》，《考古》2012 年第 7 期，第 75 页。

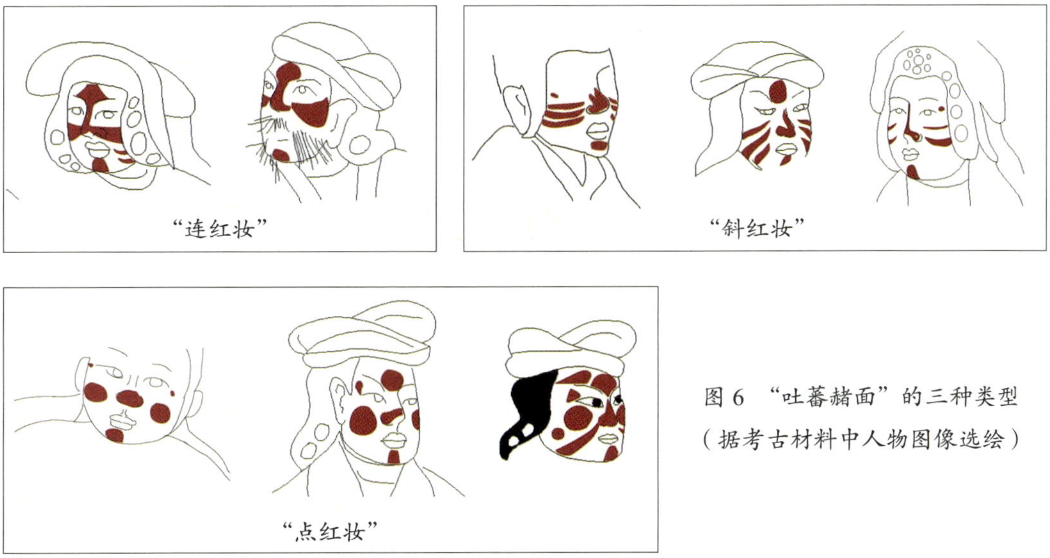

图6 “吐蕃赭面”的三种类型
（据考古材料中人物图像选绘）

处遗存的画面内容分析，包括有王及王后（赞普、赞蒙）、贵族、密宗法师、供养人、商人、武士、乐手、射手、侍者、平民等，几乎代表了吐蕃社会各阶层的人群，但在年龄、性别上似乎并无特定的属性，故可视为吐蕃“国中”之俗，也表明“赭面”具有吐蕃的族群标志意义和地域文化意义。

若将吐蕃“赭面”进行类型划分，可按涂抹样式分为三种：（图6）

其一，将两颊与鼻梁的涂点联为一体通涂红色，如青海果里吐蕃墓棺板画中王后、骑马商人、侍者、射手等人物，此种样式可称为“连红妆”。

其二，在两颊、眼尾、眉稍、腮部等处涂抹向上或向下的条形红色，如青海热水三号墓箱板画中射手、果里木墓棺板画帐篷两侧的男女人物等，这种样式可称为“斜红妆”。

其三，在面部涂抹多处对称（或非对称）的圆形的红色，或间以三角形、条形红色，如青海两处墓地和西藏恰姆石窟的绘画中都有出现，可称之为“点红妆”。

这三种妆式之中还可有更细的区分。从图像人物的数量上看，施行“连红妆”的人物最少，施“斜红妆”的人物较多，而施“点红妆”的人物数量最多。定结恰姆石窟壁画中人物“赭面”为不对称的单颊“点红妆”，可视为稍晚于“吐蕃王朝时期”的“赭面妆”样式的代表。

四、吐蕃“赭面”在唐代汉地的流传

前文已言明，汉文史籍《唐书》“令禁赭面”之说其实并未奏效，“赭面”之俗在吐蕃王朝时期的流行与扩传，已由青藏两省的考古材料提供了实证。有趣的是，被《唐书》“他指”为贞观年间就被禁行的藏地“赭面”，却在元和年间由白居易《时世妆》一诗“自认”流传到了汉地。诗曰：

时世妆，时世妆，出自城中传四方。
时世流行无远近，腮不施朱面无粉。
乌膏注唇唇似泥，双眉画作八字低。
妍媸黑白失本态，妆成尽似含悲啼。
圆鬟无鬓堆髻样，斜红不晕赭面状。
昔闻被发伊川中，辛有见之知有戎。
元和妆梳君记取，髻椎面赭非华风。[19]

作为有治政意识的诗人，白居易在《时世妆》中对当时长安女子“不施朱粉”“乌唇”“八字眉”“啼妆”“无（一作垂）鬓”“堆（一作椎）髻”“赭面”等面妆样式表达了深深的叹惋，批评其为“妍媸不分”“黑白失本”。白居易曾自言：“立采诗之官，开讽刺之道，察其得失之政，通其上下之情。”[20] 所以《时世妆》不仅表达了诗人所言“察政”与“通情”的社会责任感，也包含着诗人源于历史记忆的族别意识。诗末两句，白居易借用《左传》典故[21]将“非华风”的妆俗视为可能导致“礼亡而戎”而须上下“记取”的大事，这才是全诗的主题，也显示了诗人对“蕃俗”的本能排斥。

《时世妆》写于唐宪宗元和年间（806-820），此时距《唐书》之“公主恶其人赭面”已过去了160多年。这一百多年之间远方的吐蕃“赭面”是如何流传到了汉地长安？诗人并未明言。但以“礼亡而戎”的典故来告诫社会，说明诗人是视“吐蕃赭面”为“异族妆俗”，同时诗人对吐蕃的族属及地域也是有所了解的，例如诗人

19 引自范学宗、吴逢箴、王纯洁编：《全唐文全唐诗吐蕃史料》，拉萨：西藏人民出版社，1988年，第454-455页。

20 参见（唐）白居易著，朱金城笺校：《白居易集笺校》（《策林》六十九·采诗），上海：上海古籍出版社，1988年。

21《左传·僖公二十二年》：初，平王之东迁也，辛有适伊川，见被发而祭于野者，曰：“不及百年，此其戎乎！其礼先亡矣。”杜预注：辛有，周大夫。伊川，周地，伊水也。

在《缚戎人》中写道：

……

缚戎人，戎人之中我苦辛。

自古此冤应未有，汉心汉语吐蕃身。[22]

白居易《缚戎人》中所称“戎人”应是泛指西部的非汉族人群，到元和年间长安汉地所认识的“蕃”或“吐蕃”，则包括了8世纪后期（唐代宗李豫，766-779）“大历年中没落蕃。一落蕃中四十载”的河西、陇右等“蕃地”，即吐蕃在安史之乱后占领的西域大部地区。《时世妆》将“髻椎面赭”归为“非华风”的异族或异域妆俗，虽未指明“赭面”来自吐蕃，但《缚戎人》将曾沦为“一落蕃中四十载”的河西陇右汉民称为“汉心汉语吐蕃身”，可见公元8、9世纪之交时，长安等汉地社会对“吐蕃”域界的指认，要比文成公主时代的吐蕃大得多。而彼时唐蕃之间已有一百多年的相互轮动，从未消失的“赭面”之俗从“蕃地”传到长安应不难理解。一方面，从“蕃地”复归汉地的“戎人”与到汉地求法经商的吐蕃僧俗众人或成为民间文化传播的中介，另一方面，如陈寅恪先生所言“贞元元和年间，长安五百里外即为唐蕃边疆，其邻接若斯之近，决无断绝可能。[23]可见当时长安与吐蕃领地的距离已很近，在这样的背景下，“赭面妆”成为长安城中流行的“时世妆”正是文化互动的例证。

吐蕃的“赭面”是否就是《时世妆》中的“斜红不晕赭面状”呢？如果对比本文划分的吐蕃“赭面”的三种样式，可以发现其中的“斜红妆”最有可能就是唐代汉地所仿效的“赭面”妆式。2000年安阳市文物考古所曾发掘了一座“墓主身份应属中层贵族”晚唐砖室壁画墓，建墓年代为唐文宗太和三年（829），在墓室壁画中

22《缚戎人》全诗：“缚戎人，缚戎人，耳穿面破驱入秦。天子矜怜不忍杀，诏徙东南吴与越。黄衣小使录姓名，领出长安乘递行。身被金创面多瘠，扶病徒行日一驿。朝餐饥渴费杯盘，夜卧腥臊污床席。忽逢江水忆交河，垂手齐声呜咽歌。其中一虏语诸虏：‘尔苦非多我苦多！’同伴行人因借问，欲说喉中气愤愤。自云乡贯本凉原，大历年中没落蕃。一落蕃中四十载，遣着皮裘系毛带。唯许正朝服汉仪，敛衣整巾潜泪垂。誓心密定归乡计，不使蕃中妻子知。暗思幸有残筋力，更恐年衰归不得。蕃候严兵鸟不飞，脱身冒死奔逃归。昼伏宵行经大漠，云阴月黑风沙恶。惊藏青冢寒草疏，偷渡黄河夜冰薄。忽闻汉军鼙鼓声，路傍走出再拜迎。游骑不听能汉语，将军遂缚作蕃生。配向东南卑湿地，定无存恤空防备。念此吞声仰诉天，若为辛苦度残年。凉原乡井不得见，胡地妻儿虚弃捐。没蕃被囚思汉土，归汉被劫为蕃虏。早知如此悔归来，两地宁如一处苦！缚戎人，戎人之中我苦辛。自古此冤应未有，汉心汉语吐蕃身。”参见（唐）白居易著，丁如明、聂世美校点：《白居易全集》，上海：上海古籍出版社，1999年。

23 陈寅恪：《元白诗笺证稿》，台北世界书局，1975年，第123页。

图 7　河南安阳北关唐代壁画墓“赭面斜红妆”女像
（采自《考古》2013 年第 1 期第 59-68 页之图 9（左）、图 18（右））

图 8　安阳唐墓“斜红妆”女像（左）与青海吐蕃墓棺板画
“斜红妆”女像（右）比较

的立姿侍女和“更衣女子”的面部都涂抹有斜条形红色（图 7）[24]。这种妆式与青海吐蕃墓棺板彩绘的“赭面斜红妆”极为相似（图 8），或可据为长安《时世妆》之“斜红不晕赭面状”的旁证。唐代的相州（安阳）虽远离长安，但似乎更能说明元和年

24　参见安阳市文物考古研究所：《河南安阳市北关唐代壁画墓发掘简报》，《考古》2013 年第 1 期，第 59-68 页。

间“非华风”的“斜红赭面”同样并未因白居易的告诫而消失，反而在汉地有更广泛的流传。

在时间与空间两个方面，历史文本与考古材料可以勾勒出吐蕃“赭面”流传到唐代汉地的大致脉络。从《唐书》贞观十五年（641）的“公主恶其人赭面”到8世纪中晚期的青海“吐蕃外戚墓”彩绘“赭面人物”，再到《时世妆》元和年间（806-820）的“斜红不晕赭面状”及太和三年（829）的安阳晚唐墓壁画“斜红妆侍女”，在唐蕃两个世纪左右的互动中，“赭面”在本土流行及其东传汉地的过程几乎相伴始终。

五、小结

从史前石器时代的“人体装饰”到历史时期的“妆式”“发式”“物饰”等，世界上很多民族都有自己独特的装扮和妆饰习俗，这些妆饰习俗在该民族古代历史中的意义或功能，或许今天已经很难有准确的了解和质性认定。如吐蕃的“赭面”始于何时、何故似乎已难详考，或许最初只是高原气候环境下用于护肤防晒、美饰面容的一种习俗——在今日西藏牧民中仍流行着这种被称为“兑甲”（*döja*）的女性面妆。[25] 然而到了吐蕃王朝时期“赭面”不仅成为“国中”之俗，还随着吐蕃领地的扩张演化为“蕃化”统治的手段，成为“吐蕃身”中的一项标志，衍生出区别族群文化的特殊意义。

历史上“胡风东渐”与“渐慕华风”一样，都不是单向的文化传播。唐蕃两地双方的文化交流中，“赭面”可称是“胡风东渐”中一个有趣的例子，在记述贞观年间及元和年间史事的《唐书》《时世妆》这样的汉文文本中，“赭面”似乎一直是被否定和排斥的，要么因“公主恶其人赭面”被彼方令禁，要么是“髻椎面赭非华风”的自我告诫。然而不论在蕃地还是汉地，令禁的“国中之俗”仍被吐蕃因领地的扩张所推行，而“非华风”的习俗又总是被开放的唐代社会所吸纳。本文对所引历史文本和考古材料的浅显分析只是提示一种视角，这就是从考古材料与文本之间的差异上有时或可窥见历史的真相。

25 Melvyn C. Goldstein and Cynnthia M. Beall, *Nomads of Western Tibet*, University of California Press, Berkeley Los Angeles, 1990.

洛扎底乌炯刻碑

夏格旺堆 *

底乌炯（ལྡེའུ་ཅུང）[1] 刻碑位于西藏自治区山南地区洛扎县洛扎镇吉堆（རྒྱལ་སྡོད）村委会二组多穷村（འདུས་བྱུང）北约 400 米，[2] 县城西北距离近 8 公里的洛扎雄曲 [3] 左岸（北岸）支流多穷水（འདུས་བྱུང་ཕུ་ཆུ）河谷一处山嘴崖面上（见图 1、图 2）。崖壁地处多穷水东岸，从多穷村向西北行约 400 米后，向北拐过一个山嘴，河谷小路和自北向南流去的多穷水的左侧崖壁上，可以清楚看见面向西南的刻碑文字及其装饰图案雍仲符号（见图 3）。与此处刻碑内容基本相同，但位于洛扎县城东北面的“门塘刻碑”（སྨན་ཐང་བྲག་བཀོས་ཡི་གེ）的形式也与此一样，只是整体尺寸规模要比此处小得多。为了能够更好地保护这两座刻碑，于 2006 年将两处刻碑合并成一个保护单位，公布为第六批全国重点文物保护单位，公布名称为“门塘 · 得乌琼石刻”。但在底乌炯刻碑正前方立的保护石牌上，写的是“洛扎门塘、底乌琼摩崖石刻”。

* 夏格旺堆：西藏自治区文物保护研究所副研究员。

1 关于“底乌炯”地名，在汉文中常有不同的写法。笔者所见的某些地图上标注的是“杜鲁琼”，文物部门公布的文物保护单位名称为“得乌琼”，另外有“底乌琼”等写法，均所指为同一个地点。本文在藏文名称上之所以采纳“ལྡེའུ་ཅུང”的写法，是依据碑文中提到的“底乌炯”这个名称，故为之。

2 1991 年时，多穷村属于吉堆乡一个村庄（参见何强：《西藏吉堆吐蕃墓地的调查与分析》，《文物》1993 年第 2 期，第 13-18 页），但目前撤区并乡后，成为吉堆居委会二组。需要说明的是，为了与已经公布的汉文资料名称上能统一，在此暂用“多穷”二字汉译地名。

3 巴桑旺堆和何强文章中认为，此条河为“洛扎怒曲（ནུབ་ཆུ）”，而巴嘎 · 阿贵的文章中写成了“洛扎夏曲（ལྷོ་བྲག་ཤར་ཆུ）”，但笔者于 2014 年 7 月的实地采访，以及后来与洛扎县文化文物局旺杰等人的再次确认中获知，这条河名为“洛扎雄曲（གཞུང་ཆུ）”。参见巴桑旺堆：《新见吐蕃摩崖石刻》，《西藏研究》1982 年第 2 期，该文同时用藏文发表于《西藏研究》1982 年第 2 期，以及巴桑旺堆：《吐蕃碑文与摩崖石刻考证》（པ་ཚབ་པ་སངས་དབང་འདུས་ཀྱིས། སྤུ་རྒྱལ་བོད་ཀྱི་རྗེ་བཀོས་ཡི་གེ་ཕྱོགས་བསྒྲིགས་ཀྱི་མ་ཡིག་དག་བཤེར་དང་དེའི་ཚིག་འགྲེལ་དྭངས་སང་གངས་ཆུ།），拉萨：西藏人民出版社，2013 年，第 126 页。巴嘎 · 阿贵文章见本文注 10。

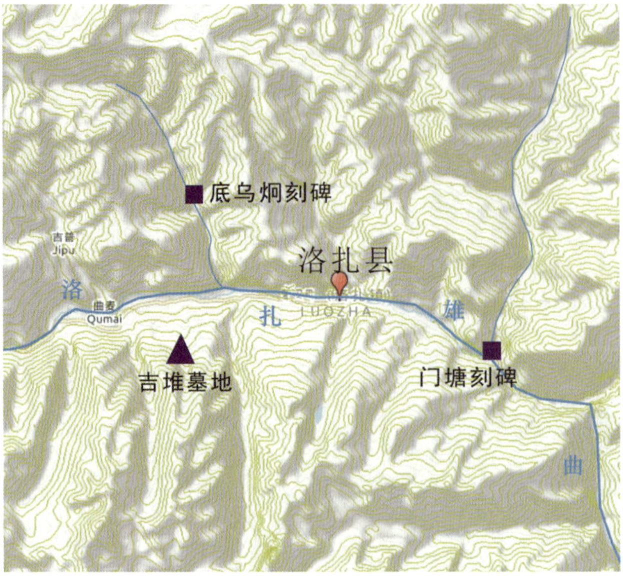

图 1　底乌炯—门塘刻碑位置示意

图 2　底乌炯刻碑外景

图 3　底乌炯刻碑形制情况

一、以往工作与研究情况

1981 年，著名学者巴桑旺堆先生在洛扎境内调查时，首次发现底乌炯及门塘两处刻碑文献，并于 1982 年发表了此碑刻调查研究成果。[4] 在这篇介绍文中，巴桑旺堆先生提出，因这两处刻碑内容相同，建议使用“洛扎摩崖石刻”的名称。但他并没有对这两处刻碑的现状进行介绍。因这两个地点不同，相距近 20 公里，所以笔者建议用不同地点来命名。本文采纳了“底乌炯刻碑”和“门塘刻碑”的命名。

巴桑旺堆先生对这两处刻碑资料的公布，使学界开始关注洛扎境内的石刻文献。李方桂、柯蔚南于 1987 年出版的《古代西藏碑文研究》中，以巴桑旺堆发表的藏、汉文文章中的录文和碑文的藏文威利转写为基础，比较两份文献录文异同，对底乌炯刻碑文献做了相关研究。并且，仍沿用了巴桑旺堆建议的名称“洛扎摩崖石刻”。[5]1991 年西藏文管会文物普查队成员何强等人对洛扎境内的吉堆（རྒྱལ་སྟོད）墓地做调查时，提到过这两座刻碑，并且认为吉堆墓地就是这两座刻碑中提到的“底乌炯”及其家族的墓地。[6] 但对刻碑的研究，引用了巴桑旺堆先生所做的研究，没有进一步对刻碑本身做更深入的记录和研究。2010 年，霍巍和新巴·达娃扎西两位根据实地调查与巴桑旺堆录文，对在这之

图 4　洛扎底乌炯刻碑临摹线条，2012

4　巴桑旺堆：《新见吐蕃摩崖石刻》，第 94-95 页。另，藏文原文辑录于西藏社会科学院民族研究所编：《藏学论文选集》，拉萨：西藏藏文古籍出版社，2005 年，第 197-201 页。

5　〔美〕李方桂、柯蔚南著，王启龙译：《古代西藏碑文研究》，拉萨：西藏人民出版社，2006 年，第 247-250 页。

6　何强：《西藏吉堆吐蕃墓地的调查与分析》。

前学者们对录文进行的研究中存在的问题作了纠正，并提供了一份新的录文转写。[7]但其中仍存在一些小的问题。2011 年，巴桑旺堆先生出版的《吐蕃碑文与摩崖石刻考证》一书中，对他本人 1982 年公布的碑文资料所存在的问题做了较为详尽的纠正，尽管也仍然存在小问题。[8] 2012 年秋季，受山南地区文物局委托，在山南地区文物局、洛扎县文广局的协助下，陕西省考古研究院对吉堆墓地进行考古调查与测绘时，对底乌炯和门塘摩崖刻碑进行了调查、记录（图 4）。并且，制作了两处刻碑的临摹线图，改变了以往没有线图的状况。不过，这次调查工作没有对碑文内容做更深入的核校。[9] 2014 年，巴嘎·阿贵对底乌炯刻碑中出现的德勉底乌炯（ཞེ་སྨན་ཞིའུ་ཙུང）这位历史人物及其家族的历史做了考察，并且进一步强调了地处洛扎雄曲右岸（南岸）、两处刻碑地点中间位置的吉堆墓地，当为德勉底乌炯、其父亲罗囊（ལོ་སྣང）以及他们家族成员们的墓地。[10] 另外，日本学者 Kazushi IWAO（岩尾一史）等人 2009 年编著的《古藏文碑铭》，[11] 以及 2102 年由恰嘎·旦正编著的《藏文碑文研究》[12] 中都收录了洛扎石刻文，但都基本是以巴桑旺堆先生的录文作为基础进行的研究，更不见对刻碑相关信息的进一步介绍。

2014 年 7 月，笔者带队的课题组成员前往底乌炯和门塘刻碑地点，对两处刻碑进行了测量、照相等记录。因风化太严重和崖面条件所限，无法对这两处刻碑进行拓片。幸好，这次因搭了架子，所以获得了较为准确的底乌炯刻碑的相关尺寸。这座刻碑因处于悬崖峭壁，过去许多学者提供的相关尺寸基本为目测或估算的。这次与我们随行协助的有洛扎县文化文物局旺杰及多布杰两位，衷心感谢他们为这次调查工作所做的一切。

7 霍巍、新巴·达娃扎西：《西藏洛扎吐蕃石刻与吐蕃墓地的调查与研究》，《文物》2010 年第 7 期，第 56-62 页。

8 巴桑旺堆：《吐蕃碑文与摩崖石刻考证》，第 126-132 页。

9 陕西省考古研究院、山南地区文物局、洛扎县文广局：《西藏洛扎县吉堆墓地与吐蕃摩崖刻石考古调查简报》，《考古与文物》2014 年第 6 期，第 15-25 页。

10 བར་ཁ་དག་དཀོན། ལྷོ་བྲག་ཞེའུ་ཙུང་བྲག་བརྐོས་ཡི་གེར་གསལ་བའི་བོད་བཙན་པོའི་དུས་ཀྱི་བློན་ཆེན་ཞེ་སྨན་ཞེའུ་ཙུང་དང་འབྲེལ་ཡོད་ཀྱི་ལོ་རྒྱུས་གནད་དོན་སྐོར་མདོ་ཙམ་གླེང་བ། ཀྲུང་གོའི་བོད་རིག་པ། 2014ལོའི་དེབ་གཉིས་པ། ཤོག་གྲངས་39-50.

11 Kazushi IWAO, Nathan HILL, Tsuguhito TAKEUCHI, Izumi HOSHI, Yoshiro IMAEDA, *Old Tibetan Inscriptions*, Old Tibetan Dcuments Online Monograph Series Vol.II, Published by Research Institute Languages and Culturels of Asia and Africa(ILCAA), Tokyo University of Foreign Studies, Tokyo, 2009, 第 66 页（岩尾一史、Nathan HILL、武内绍人、星泉、今枝由郎编著：《古藏文碑铭》，古藏文文献在线丛刊，卷 II，东京外国语大学亚非语言文化研究所，2009 年）。

12 恰嘎·旦正（ཚབ་འགག་རྟ་མགྲིན）：《藏文碑文研究》（བོད་ཡིག་རྡོ་རིང་ཞིབ་འཇུག），拉萨：西藏人民出版社，2012 年，第 91-92 页。

二、刻碑现状

1. 刻碑

刻碑凿刻于一处天然岩厦下面，岩厦上端平面近乎三角，其下端即为平面正方形的刻文碑面。碑面是进行过简单打磨平整加工，但岩性粗糙、平面凹凸不平，崖面上覆盖有许多腐殖物。其顶端、岩厦下三角形空间凿刻一个阴刻雍仲符号，距离碑面顶部边缘 0.65 米。顶部雍仲符号平面长方形，高 0.6 米，宽 0.45 米，阴刻线条宽度 0.06 米、深度 0.015 米。在碑面底部有与碑面顶部凿刻的雍仲符号基本上下对应的一个雍仲符号，方向为右旋或顺时针，其平面正方形，高、宽 0.5 米，符号阴线的宽度、深度基本和顶部雍仲符号相同。凿刻文字的碑面平面基本为正方形，高 3.3 米、宽 3.4 米，含底部雍仲符号到地面的高度为 7 米。

2. 刻碑文字

刻文共有 12 行，第一行 7 个字要比其他行的文字体积略大些，每个字母的高度 0.13—0.35 米、宽度 0.1—0.14 米；第一行、第二行“抬头”空格行距 0.2—0.26 米；其他行的每个字母高、宽约为 0.15—0.16 米，行距 0.15—0.2 米（见图 3、图 5）。

目前发表的录文，都是将底乌炯、门塘两处地点石刻文字合并互补，整理成一份文献的录文版本，并非一个刻碑地点的完整录文。为了能更真实地反映每一个地点刻文内容的现状，本文对录文的整理，不采取合并互补，仅将一处刻碑现存的刻文抄录下来。此处录文是以巴桑旺堆先生惠赠给笔者的电子版录文作为基础，再对照本人拍摄的照片文字进行核对和注解。需要提及的是，霍巍、新巴·达娃扎西两位的录文仅有 11 行，将第一行和第二行合并在一起了，但实际上共有 12 行文字。因巴桑旺堆

图 5　底乌炯刻碑文字现状

先生 1982 年录文不是按照行序抄录，所以李方桂、柯蔚南 1987 年版著本，[13] 以及岩尾一史等人 2009 年编著的《古藏文碑铭》在引用巴桑旺堆先生文本编书时，[14] 未能反映刻碑文字的真实行数。后两本书中，仅列出了 7 行，并且岩尾一史等人是按照李方桂、柯蔚南著本编辑了录文。李方桂和柯蔚南对巴桑旺堆先生于 1982 年发表的藏文原文录文和汉文原文转写中存在的异同进行了梳理，不过，笔者在此不对转写中存在的异同进行整理，因为转写非常容易丧失藏文原文的许多信息。在此需要说明的是，巴桑旺堆先生 2011 年版、2103 年版著本，完全按照刻碑原文行序和行数来做了抄录。

刻碑文字内容，大致讲述了三个部分内容。1. 德勉底乌炯因忠诚于赞普王室，故天神之子赞普下诏，赏赐德勉底乌炯之父亲罗囊及其子孙享有永久性特权，其家族所属的奴隶、封地决不再减少。2. 底乌炯之丧葬应法事优隆，在任何赞普后裔掌政期间，其墓葬若有损毁，当由东岱（སྟོང་སྡེ། 即“千户”）专事修缮。3. 若底乌炯之父罗囊及其子孙后代，以及同宗兄弟闯祸犯事，则（可免去其责任）。[15]

共 12 行，原文如下：

༡ ༄༅། བཙན་པོ་(1)ལྷ་སྲས་ཀྱི་ཞ་སྔར།

༢ (2)ལྡེ་སྨན་ལྡེ་ཙུང་།

༣ སློ་བ་ཉེ་ཉེ། སྐུ་ཏྲ་ཆབ་སྲིད་ལ་དཔེན་པའི། ཇེ་བླས། དཀའ་བ་(3)

༤ བྱེད་བྱེད་ནས་། བཀས་གནང་བ་(4)ལྡེའུ་ཙུང་གི་ཕ་(5)ཕོ་སྣང་གི་བུ་(6)

༥ །(7) ཚ་ཕེལད་རྒྱུད་(8)ནམ་ཞར་སྲིད་གཡུང་དྲུང་ཏྲ་མཚུངས་པ་ཏྲ།(9) ཕོལ།

༦ །།ཡུལ་ལས་(10)སྔོགསྲ་ཀྱི་དབྱི་སྐྱི་སླུང་བ་ཏྲ། ལྡེའུ་ཙུང་གི། མཆད་ཀྱི།

---

13 〔美〕李方桂、柯蔚南著，王启龙译：《古代西藏碑文研究》，第 247-250 页。

14 བར་ཁ་དག་དཀོན། ལྷ་བྲག་ལྡེའུ་ཙུང་བྲག་བརྐོས་ཡི་གེར་གསལ་བའི་བོད་བཙན་པོའི་དུས་ཀྱི་བློན་ཆེན་ལྡེ་སྨན་ལྡེའུ་ཙུང་དང་འབྲེལ་ཡོད་ཀྱི་ལོ་རྒྱུས་གནད་དོན་སྐོར་མདོ་ཙམ་གླེང་བ།.

15 尽管刻碑原文中，因风化等原因，不见“则可免去其责任”，但从上文的转折词“བཀའ་གྲོད་ཅི་ལ་ཆགས་ཀྱང་།”之“ཆགས་ཀྱང་།”中，可以推导出词句含义来。

(1) 原文中为“པྀ་”。

(2) 文前有一个长隔字符，为“།ལྡེ་”。

(3) 文后有两个长隔字符，应为“བ།།”。

(4) 此处文后为一个长隔字符，应为“བ།”。

(5) 此处文后为一个长隔字符，应为“ཕ།”。

(6) 此处文后似是两个长隔字符，应为“བུ།།”。

(7) 此处文前为两个长隔字符，应为“།།ཚ་”。

(8) 此处文后为一个长隔字符，应为“རྒྱུད།”。

(9) 此处有无一个长隔字符“།”，比较模糊不清。

(10) 此处“ལས་”文后是一个长隔字符，应为“ལས།”。

༧ ། །རིམ་གྱི་ལྷ་ནས་མཛད་དེ། ནམ་ཅིག་དབོན་སྲས་ཁྲ་གི་རིང་ལ་རལ་ཡྒྱ།
༨ །ལྷ་ནས་ཕྱོང་ཕྱེས་བསྒྲིག་པར་གནང་། ལྡེའུ་ཅུང་གི་པ་ལོ་སྣང་གི་བུ།
༩ [11]ཚ་ཕེལད་རྒྱུད་དང་ཕུ་ནུ་ཅིག་པ་[12]བཀའ་གྲོད་ □ [13]ཅགས་ཐྲ་ན། །[14]
༡༠ □□□□ བར་[15]གན □□□□□□ [16]འདི་ལྟར་དབུ་སྙུང་བ་ཧྲ། ཀོང་ཀར། །
༡༡ ། །ཕོ་[17]ལྷ་བཙན་[18] □□□□□□□□ ན་[19]ཕོ་ཧྲ།(20) ཏུ་བཞི་[21]ཞང་ལོན་།[22]
༡༢ ། །གིས་[23]ཕྲོ་བོར་བའི་གཙིགས་ཀྱི་སྒྲོམ་[24]བུ་ནི་[25]ཕྱག་སྤྲལ་དུ་བཟུད། །[26]

---

(11) 此处"ཚ་"的文前有两个长隔字符，似为"། །ཚ་"。

(12) 这段"ཕུ་ནུ་ཅིག་པ་"的"ནུ་"和"ཅིག་"之间的崖面石块在刻文之前就已经脱落了，就像巴桑旺堆先生确认出的一样，这两个字之间尽管有一定的空间相隔，似是有什么文字，实际没有刻文。

(13) 此处"བཀའ་གྲོད་□"的"གྲོད་"字之后，似有一个文字被损毁。故用"□"符号来记录此处不清楚的文字。

(14) 此处"ཅགས་ཐྲ་ན། །"是按原文抄录的。巴桑旺堆根据门塘刻碑文字，将这部分文字纠正为"ཅི་ལ་ཆགས་ཀྱང་།"，并指出底乌炯的这处文字是误写文字。从字面上看，确也读不出什么意思来。

(15) 此处"བར་"之前的文字中，与其紧挨之前的文字尽管模糊，但看似为"སྙུང་"字，其余文字基本损毁。

(16) 这段"□□□□བར་གན□□□□□□"文字，在巴桑旺堆录文中，根据门塘刻碑文字，将其复原为"ན་ཅིག་གིས་□□□བར་གནང་སྟེ།"。需要提及的是，即便是门塘刻碑文字，因风化这段"སྟེ། འདི་ལྟར་དབུ་སྙུང་བ་ཧྲ།"已经看不见了。

(17) 此处原文"། །ཕོ་"前面有两个长隔字符，但在巴桑旺堆录文中漏掉了这两个长隔字符。

(18) 原文为"བཙན་"，但在巴桑旺堆录文 2011 年版、2013 年版中皆误录为"བཙན་"。

(19) 这段"□□□□□□□□ན་"文字，在底乌炯刻碑中因风化已经损毁不显。巴桑旺堆根据门塘刻碑文字，将这段复原成了"ལྷ་བཙན་པོ་སྤྱན་མཚན་ཧྲ། སྲིད་ཀྱི་བློན་པོ་"。即便在门塘刻碑，因风化，"སྲིད་ཀྱི་བློན་"等文字已经看不见了。复原的这段文字中，"ལྷ་བཙན་"在底乌炯和门塘刻碑上皆相同；因损毁，在底乌炯刻碑上，不见"སྤྱན་མཚན་ཧྲ།"等文字，但在门塘刻碑中的原文"སྤྱན་མཚན་"二字，在巴桑旺堆录文中写成了"སྤྱན་མཚན་"。

(20) 此处原文的文后仅是一个长隔字符，应为"ཧྲ།"，但在巴桑旺堆录文中，将文后的长隔字符写成了一个短点隔字符"ཧྲ་"。

(21) 在底乌炯刻碑中"ཏུ་བཞི་"的"བཞི་"字元音为反写，但在门塘刻碑中，"བཞི་"字元音字母为顺写。这是一个比较有意思的现象。

(22) 底乌炯原文中，因"ལོན་།"字位于这一行的最右侧，所以其短点隔字符的后面，似是有一个长隔字符。在门塘刻碑中，因"ལོན་"字尚非位于最右侧边、其后仍有文字，故其文后仅是短点隔字符，而不是短点之后再加一个长隔字符。

(23) 此处"གིས་"的"ག"字下半部分因岩体表面脱落，文字结构不是很清楚，这里的录文是根据巴桑旺堆先生的抄录及参考了门塘刻碑原文。另外，即便在门塘刻碑中，"ཕྲོ་བོར་བའི་གཙིགས་ཀྱི་"这段文字因风化，已经不能清楚地辨识。

(24) 在底乌炯刻碑中，"ཀྱི་སྒྲོམ་"这两个词因风化磨损，不能完全识读。但可参考模糊可认的门塘刻碑文字进行判断。此处录文按巴桑旺堆电子版录文。

(25) 在底乌炯刻碑中"ནི་"字很清楚，但目前的门塘刻碑中，"ནི་"字的"ན"的下半部分结构因岩面脱落而不好辨认。若无巴桑旺堆录文和底乌炯刻碑文字可以做参考，有可能将其认读为"ཤི"。

(26) 在底乌炯刻碑中，"ཕྱག་སྤྲལ་དུ་བཟུད། །"这段文字还能清楚地认读，但在门塘刻碑中，这段文字已经因风化，仅认读"སྤྲལ་"字的上加字"ས"，以及这段文字最后的两个长隔字符"། །"，其余文字已经不能认读。另外，在这段文字之后，门塘刻碑中尚有"དུར་ནི་□□ལང་ས། པ □□ན□□"的文字。因底乌炯刻碑上面未见这段文字，故在这里没有抄录。但巴桑旺堆等以往的学者们，将门塘刻碑这段文字合并补充后，抄录成"洛扎摩崖石刻"的文字内容。需要提及的是，以往"洛扎摩崖石刻"文字是将两个地点刻碑的文字比对、互补后编辑而成的，并非一座刻碑的全部文字内容。

三、小结

关于底乌炯和和门塘两处刻碑建造凿刻的时间，学者们几乎一致地认为是赤德松赞时期。1982 年，巴桑旺堆先生公布这两处刻碑的资料时，根据刻碑文中“天神之子（བཙན་པོ་ལྷ་སྲས）”称呼的出现，认为这一称呼在许多吐蕃碑刻中，常被用来称谓赤松德赞（755-797 年在位）之子赤德松赞（ཁྲི་ལྡེ་སྲོང་བཙན）的事实作为依据，推定当在赤德松赞在位期间（798-815 年在位）建造了这两处刻碑。随着有关史籍的不断公开出版，巴嘎·阿贵根据《弟吴贤者宗教源流》《娘氏宗教源流》两部史籍的记载，基本确定了洛扎石刻文献中提到的“德勉底乌炯”为赞普赤松德赞，以及王子牟尼赞普(མུ་ནེ་བཙན་པོ། 797-798 年[16]或 797-799 年[17]在位)和赤德松赞时期的一位大臣。[18]由于他与王妃策崩萨（ཚེ་སྤོངས་བཟའ）联手除掉牟尼赞普，支持赤德松赞即位掌政，且从赞普父王赤松德赞以来，德勉底乌炯一直忠诚于吐蕃王室，所以为他宣誓证盟，下诏颁赏和立碑述德。

笔者认为，洛扎境内的这两处摩崖石刻，从其形制上讲与工布雍仲增刻碑（或第穆萨摩崖刻石）一样，也是一种“刻碑”的形式，还不能归类为简单的摩崖石刻。所以，本文在其名称上，一直使用“刻碑”。尽管门塘刻碑因为严重风化，尚不能更加清楚地看见刻文的崖面是否经过相应的加工处理，但底乌炯刻文崖面是经过加工处理的，其四边轮廓很清楚。而且，两处刻碑上下端的靠近中部，皆有一个雍仲符号作为装饰。这种刻碑上装饰雍仲符号的做法，我们同样可以在工布雍仲增刻碑碑座底部见到。考虑到底乌炯家族地位估计无法与工噶波王相比，所以洛扎两处的刻碑形制略显简单，甚至不排除雍仲符号的数量也与他们各自的社会等级存在某种联系。

尽管底乌炯和门塘刻碑文字内容有许多相同，但也不全同。由于目前我们无法复原门塘刻碑的完整内容，所以不好与底乌炯文字内容作更加深入的比对。从刻碑本身的用途或需要来讲，目前我们尚不确定吐蕃时期的勒石述事传统中是否存在同一内容刻于不同地点的做法，但可以确定的是赤松德赞和赤德松赞父子时期已经有刊立建造两个大致内容碑的做法，一般时间晚的石碑为前一通石碑内容的补充，如夏拉康的

16 参见 འབྲི་གུང་སྐྱབས་མགོན་ཆེ་ཚང་དཀོན་མཆོག་བསྟན་འཛིན་ཀུན་བཟང་འཕྲིན་ལས་ལྷུན་གྲུབ་ཀྱིས་རྩོམ་སྒྲིག་གནང་བའི་ཏུན་ཧོང་བོད་ཀྱི་ཡིག་རྙིང་ལས་བྱུང་བ། བོད་བཙན་པོའི་རྒྱལ་རབས། (《吐蕃王朝史——源自敦煌吐蕃文书》) སྲོང་བཙན་དཔེ་མཛོད་ཁང་གིས་༢༠༡༠ལོར་ཧྲི་ལི་གསར་མར་བསྐྲུན་པའི་ལྷུགས་པར་མ། 第 85 页；王尧：《吐蕃金石录》，载《王尧藏学文集》卷 2，北京：中国藏学出版社，2012 年，第 181 页。

17 〔美〕李方桂、柯蔚南著，王启龙译：《古代西藏碑文研究》，2006 年，第 15 页。

18 陕西省考古研究院、山南地区文物局、洛扎县文广局：《西藏洛扎县吉堆墓地与吐蕃摩崖刻石考古调查简报》。

两通碑，以及工布境内的米林朗嘎碑和雍仲增刻碑大致内容相同，且后一个碑是前一个碑内容补增的做法都反映了这样的情况。但底乌炯和门塘这两座刻碑也是否如此，尚有待今后更多材料的发掘和相关研究的深入。

有关努钦·桑杰益西的人生叙述 *

落桑东知

历史是如何被书写的呢？历史编纂并不仅仅是材料的堆积——文字的抑或图像的，更加重要的是其背后蕴藏着各种张力的存在。这种张力的形成，使得同一个事实，呈现出不同的面向，形成不同的叙述方式（Narrative form）。当某一种叙述方式，获得更多人的共识之后，这就成为了所谓的“真理”。这种“叙述方式”一旦形成，其稳固性是不言而喻的，因为此时它成为了人们认知的主要工具（Cognitive Instrument）。但是，当我们理性地面对此类“叙述方式”时，我们同时也能够发现其脆弱的一面，即虚构的特点。作为历史信息的接受者，我们身边总是充斥着这类叙述方式。它的存在，使得历史本身扑朔迷离，同时也让我们的历史知识陷于混乱。

努钦·桑杰益西（གནུབས་ཆེན་སངས་རྒྱས་ཡེ་ཤེས། 以下将简称“努氏”）作为藏传佛教前后弘期过渡阶段（约 9 世纪中叶至 10 世纪末期）最为重要的佛教上师。他对密乘佛教在藏地的传播，有着伟大而深远的影响。与其同时代的人物相比，努氏的地位是非常显赫的，成就甚是卓越。努氏的生活年代，是个社会混乱、战乱频繁的时期。然而，努氏像是游离于其时代背景的“隐形人”，于他的佛学造诣未能受到多大的冲击。他不仅七次远赴南亚次大陆，依止诸位佛教大德，在藏地传播印度佛教。而且，他也撰写了数部影响深远的佛教经典，包括《禅定目炬》和《密意集经疏·黑暗铠甲》

* 落桑东知：青海民族大学藏学院宗教学教师。

本文为青海民族大学高层次人才（博士）项目阶段性成果，项目名称“宁玛派大圆满法早期状况之研究”，项目编号：2017XJG03。

谨以此文缅怀古格·次仁加布（1961-2015）先生。2015 年 3 月，笔者前去柏林高等研究所拜访沈卫荣教授，他特意安排次仁加布、Guntram Hazod 和 Per K.Sørensen 等学界大腕，与我这个无名小卒共进晚餐。这是笔者与次仁加布先生首次见面，因为语言相近再加上同为藏人，去餐馆的路上我们聊得甚是投机，并赐予我他在拉萨和柏林的联系方式，他提携后辈之心令我感动，此时也是笔者定稿这篇文章之时。我们相约在维也纳大学再次相见，之后也通过邮件联系几次。然而，当我返回北京的第一天，却收到他在柏林仙逝之事，甚是惋惜。这次沈卫荣教授特意召集各路人马整理纪念文集，令我感动不已，也可算是一段学术佳话。

（སངས་རྒྱས་ཐམས་ཅད་ཀྱི་དགོངས་པ་འདུས་པ་མདོའི་དཀའ་འགྲེལ་མུན་པའི་གོ་ཆ་ལྡེ་མིག་གསལ་བྱེད་རྣལ་འབྱོར་ཉི་མ་ཞེས་བྱ་བ་བཞུགས་སོ）等著作。在他的年代佛教几乎在藏地中断，但正是由于他的存在，在很大程度上使佛教之星火燎原，并最终成就了“藏传佛教”这个在佛教世界最辉煌的佛教教派。

对于如此重要的历史人物，后人如何认识他，同他本人是谁的问题一样重要。因为，人们如何认识他，与人们如何建构历史有很大的关系。纵观藏族宗教史，重要历史人物的角色，在后期经过润色、加工是特别明显的，这也许就是所有宗教史的特点吧。倘若我们还相信历史多少还能够重现，那么我们就需要剥离那些虚构的“叙述方式”。所以，笔者在此试图澄清，围绕努氏的那些“叙述方式”，它们是否为历史事实，或者是传统的又一次建构。简言之，这篇文章的主旨与其说是重构努氏其人，倒不如说是在检讨后人如何看待努氏的问题。

一、作为莲花生大士高徒的努氏

莲花生大士在藏地，据传有“二十五位高徒”（རྗེ་འབངས་ཉེར་ལྔ）。这些高徒由于修习密宗，成就甚是高超。19世纪《郭扎佛教史》列出了这些高徒的名氏，并录有简短的生平。根据它的记载，这些高徒的顺序依次为[1]：1. 努钦·桑杰益西、2. 恩兰·嘉瓦乔益西循努（ངན་ལམ་རྒྱལ་བ་མཆོག་དབྱངས）、3. 努·南喀宁布（གནུབས་ནམ་མཁའི་སྙིང་པོ）、4. 娘译师（གཉགས་ལོ་ཡེ་ཤེས་གཞོན་ནུ）、5. 益西措杰（ཡེ་ཤེས་མཚོ་རྒྱལ）、6. 卓弥·贝吉益西（འབྲོག་མི་དཔལ་གྱི་ཡེ་ཤེས）、7. 朗·贝吉僧格（རླངས་དཔལ་གྱི་སེང་གེ）、8. 贝热遮那（བཻ་རོ་ཙ་ན）、9. 玉扎宁布（གཡུ་སྒྲ་སྙིང་པོ）、10. 那囊·多杰杜迥（སྣ་ནམ་རྡོ་རྗེ་བདུད་འཇོམས）、11. 益西央（ཡེ་ཤེས་དབྱངས）、12. 索巴·拉贝（སོག་པོ་ལྷ་དཔལ）、13. 那囊·益西（སྣ་ནམ་ཡེ་ཤེས）、14. 贝吉昂秀（དཔལ་གྱི་དབང་ཕྱུག）、15. 丹玛紫芒（ལྡན་མ་རྩེ་མང）、16. 嘎瓦·贝泽（སྐ་བ་དཔལ་བརྩེགས）、17. 夏布·贝吉僧格（ཤུད་བུ་དཔལ་གྱི་སེང་གེ）、18. 智·嘉瓦洛智（འབྲི་རྒྱལ་བའི་བློ་གྲོས）、19. 曲强译师（ཁྱིའུ་ཆུང་ལོ་ཙཱ）、20. 占巴南喀（དྲན་པ་ནམ་མཁའ）、21. 卧占·昂秀（འོ་བྲན་དབང་ཕྱུག）、22. 玛·仁钦乔（རྨ་རིན་ཆེན་མཆོག）、23. 拉隆贝吉多杰（ལྷ་ལུང་དཔལ་གྱི་རྡོ་རྗེ）、24. 朗卓·官却迥乃（ལང་གྲོ་དཀོན་མཆོག་འབྱུང་གནས）、25. 拉松·嘉瓦香曲（ལ་གསུམ་རྒྱལ་བ་བྱང་ཆུབ）。然而，当我们稍作分析，可知这些序目中的某些人物，显然不会是莲花生大士同时代的人。最突出的一位是“二十五位

1 《གུ་བཀྲའི་ཆོས་འབྱུང》གུ་རུ་བཀྲ་ཤིས་ཀྱིས་བརྩམས། རྡོ་རྗེ་རྒྱལ་པོས་བསྒྲིགས། ཀྲུང་གོའི་བོད་རིག་པ་དཔེ་སྐྲུན་ཁང་། ༡༩༩༠ལོའི་པར་གཞི་དང་པོ། ཤ་༡༥༧ནས་༡༦༥།

高徒”中的第六位，即卓弥·贝吉益西。卓弥译师是后弘期萨迦派“道果法（ས་སྐྱའི་ལམ་འབྲས）”的主要传承者，与宁玛派大宿·释迦迥乃（ཟུར་ཆེན་ཤཱཀྱ་འབྱུང་གནས། 1002—1062）等为同时代。由此可见，卓弥译师为莲花生大士的高徒显然是不妥的，有其时代上的错乱。从这点我们可窥见，所谓的莲花生大士的“二十五位高徒”，有可能为宁玛派人的后期建构。因此，笔者认为所谓莲花生大士“二十五位高徒”中的部分人物，很有可能是后弘期的宁玛派辩护者们将吐蕃历代名人划归为本派祖师莲花生大士的高徒，以此彰显自派的神圣性是有关联的。

根据莲花生大士“二十五位高徒”具有虚构的特点，笔者对努氏作为莲花生高徒的身份产生了怀疑。努氏作为莲花生“二十五位高徒”的记载，最早可见于12世纪的两部文献中，即《娘氏宗教源流》（ཆོས་འབྱུང་མེ་ཏོག་སྙིང་པོ་སྦྲང་རྩིའི་བཅུད། 通常称作“ཉང་རལ་ཆོས་འབྱུང”）和《莲花生传·赤铜洲》（སློབ་དཔོན་པདྨའི་རྣམ་ཐར་ཟངས་གླིང་མ），然而此时莲花生大士俨然是位神化人物，因此这两个材料的相关记述并不可靠。关于努氏的生存年代，郭译师·循努贝（འགོས་ལོ་གཞོན་ནུ་དཔལ། 1392-1481）的概述无疑是最形象的。《青史》在叙述了诸多神通广大的瑜伽大成就者之后，记载：“这些大成就者大部分去世、王法崩坏、纷争之乱事兴起之时，名谓努钦·桑杰益西者依止印度、尼泊尔和勃律之诸先贤。获得113岁时寿，使密乘之教法兴起”（དེ་རྣམས་ཕལ་ཆེར་འདས་ཤིང་རྒྱལ་ཁྲིམས་ཞིག ཕྱོགས་རིས་ཀྱི་འཁྲུག་པ་དར་བའི་དུས་སུ་སྣུབས་སངས་རྒྱས་ཡེ་ཤེས་རིན་པོ་ཆེ་ཞེས་བྱ་བས་རྒྱ་གར་དང་བལ་པོ་དང་བྲུ་ཤའི་ཡུལ་ན་གནས་པ་ལ་སོགས་པའི་མཁས་པའི་སྐྱེ་བོ་མང་པོ་བསྟེན། ལོ་བརྒྱ་དང་བཅུ་གསུམ་དུ་བཞུགས་ནས་གསང་སྔགས་ཀྱི་བསྟན་པ་དར་བར་མཛད།)[2]。从这段叙述中，我们发现努氏的生活年代，与藏族史学传统描述“黑暗时期（མུན་ནག་གི་དུས། 9世纪中叶-10世纪末期）”的景况相一致。在这个特殊的“黑暗时期”，努氏扮演着“密乘之教法”兴起的重任。更加重要的是，透过新近发现的，署名为努氏“自传”的一部文献，

2 《དེབ་ཐེར་སྔོན་པོ》འགོས་ལོ་གཞོན་ནུ་དཔལ་གྱིས་བརྩམས། སི་ཁྲོན་མི་རིགས་དཔེ་སྐྲུན་ཁང་། ༡༩༨༥ ལོའི་པར་གཞི་དང་པོ། ཤ་༡༣༧།

即《努氏之文书·嘉卧切》（གནུབས་ཀྱི་བཀའ་ཤོག་རྒྱ་པོ་ཆེ）[3]，进一步加深了笔者对努氏的生活年代处于“黑暗时期”的看法。《嘉卧切》中，在涉及努氏自己的生存状况时，大篇幅地记述了战乱带给他的灾难，使他颠沛流离、生活窘迫。这种图景，显然不会发生在天下太平、生机盎然的吐蕃时期，而恰好是社会混乱、藩镇割据、民不聊生时期的形象，这正好与后吐蕃王朝的“黑暗时期”相对应。12世纪的《娘氏宗教源流》，在叙述莲花生大士在藏时期的情况时，努氏的名字只被提及一次，且仅仅是在罗列莲花生大士“二十五位高徒”时有所提及。然而，莲花生大士在藏时期所进行的各种活动中，譬如显密经典的翻译、佛事仪轨，皆未有努氏的身影，他完全游离于当时的这些重要的王朝庆典中。努氏在宁玛派后期的文献中，常被视为自派中最为重要的人物之一，他曾七次远赴中亚、印度等地涉猎教授、翻译密续、注疏经典，为密乘教法在藏地弘扬，有其不可磨灭的影响。倘若努氏真为莲花生大士在藏时期的人物，那么他如同当时活跃的其他大德一样，必然会被提及、追溯其个人魅力。值此，笔者认为娘热·尼玛沃色（ཉང་རལ་ཉི་མ་འོད་ཟེར）在撰写教法史时所参考的文献中，皆没有记录

3　学术界对于《嘉卧切》是否为努氏所撰的“自传”尚存质疑。另言之，它更像是一部后人对努氏所写的传记。Jacob Dalton先生认为，虽然《嘉卧切》自始至终都以努氏自己第一人称的口吻在叙述，因此读者可能觉得它是一部自传。然而仔细研读之后发现，虽然它包含努氏自己的某些话语，但整体而言它其实并不是一部自传，而是努氏后弘期继承者们撰写的一部传记。这无非就是说，这部文献的形成当在努氏之后的后弘期时代。那么谁又会是传记的作者呢？后弘期以降，颇章·希瓦沃（ཕོ་བྲང་ཞི་བ་འོད）、郭译师·库巴拉则（འགོས་ཁུག་པ་ལྷས་བཙས）等人对包括努氏在内的，早期宿氏等宁玛派教法传统的真实性问题提出了质疑。宿氏的继承者们为了反驳他们，便有可能托着撰写这部努氏传记，一方面正名自己的传统，另一方面去驳斥这些人的主张。这种猜想，我们可以通过另外几个线索得到进一步的印证。努氏传记中告诫其后辈传承者“教传（བཀའ་མ）”的重要性，而这种“教传”无疑是宿氏传统在宁玛派教法史上最重要的贡献，两者对“教传”重要性的强调有不谋而合之效果。《嘉卧切》用三分之一多的篇幅，详列了各种密续及其仪轨的名称，其中有大瑜伽十八部密续、无比瑜伽四部经、无上瑜伽四部诀窍和七部后续等。在这四部系列下的各个续典的名称，一般而言都与宿氏传统的列举是相一致的。从这些线索，我们有理由相信《嘉卧切》的作者可能出自于宿氏传统。那么这个传记作者又是哪个时代的人物呢？在此Dalton先生提出了两个可能最早（terminus post quem）和最晚（terminus ante quem）的时间点。于最早形成的时间而言，他以《嘉卧切》中所列的“伏藏”之发掘为线索，从实证的角度来说，《嘉卧切》的出现当是“伏藏品”发掘之后的事情。所幸的是这些“伏藏”的“掘藏者”，我们已经能够确定，即来自于嘉氏家族的香春·多吉沃百（རྒྱ་ཞང་ཁྲོམ་རྡོ་རྗེ་འོད་འབར)。多吉沃百是拉杰·努琼（ལྷ་རྗེ་གནུབས་ཆུང）的亲传弟子，而努琼是米拉日巴尊者（1052—1135）的密咒师。通过这样的人物关系，可以推定，多吉沃百的生存年代为11世纪，也就是《嘉卧切》最早的形成年代。于最晚的形成时间，一部14世纪的文献，即《五部伏藏要义之疏释》(གཏད་རྒྱ་ལྔའི་གོ་དོན་གྱི་བརྗོད་བྱང་གི་འགྲེལ་པ)，引用了《嘉卧切》中的某些片段，这便是《嘉卧切》最晚的形成年代。最后，Dalton先生于《嘉卧切》的作者及其形成年代，作出了这样的总结性的断言，“它可能形成于11至14世纪之间（很有可能在14世纪之前），它直接抑或间接地与早期宿氏有关联”。关于《嘉卧切》为后弘期的努氏传记，笔者认为Dalton先生所说的有其合理性，因为从整体叙述形式而言，它更像传记的叙述风格，因此笔者也倾向于他的论断。请参阅Jacob P. Dalton, “Preliminary Remarks on a Newly Discovered Biography of Nupchen Sangye Yeshe,” in *Himalayan Passages: Tibetan and Newar Studies in Honor of Hubert Decleer*, ed. Andrew Quintman, Benjamin Bogin. Boston: Wisdom Publications, 2014, pp.145-161.

莲花生大士时期努氏的情况，这就使他无法叙述此时期努氏的具体作为。因此，我们有理由相信努氏并非是莲花生大士在藏时期的人物。那么，在缺失努氏具体的细节的同时，娘热·尼玛沃色为何又将其归入到莲花生大士的“二十五位高徒”之一呢？笔者认为对这个问题的最有效的解释是，与后弘期以降修习旧译密咒者，遭受新译各派诟病的宗教话语体系是离不开的。旧译密咒修习者们，为了辩护自身传统的有效性，借新译各派也普遍接受莲花生大士的情况下，将本派传统的著名人物，归为莲花生大士高徒的行列中，并形成所谓的“二十五位高徒”。当娘热·尼玛沃色在12世纪撰写自己的教法史时，莲花生大士“二十五位高徒”这种传统的创造业已形成，努氏也被划归为这些所谓高徒的行列当中。娘氏在接受努氏作为莲花生高徒这种传说的同时，又因为相关历史文献的阙如，无法在其教法史中呈现莲花生在藏时期努氏的生平。然而，当《娘氏宗教源流》叙述所谓“黑暗时期”时，我们才第一次接触到了关于努氏的具体的人生细节。它甚至记载了努氏的六个儿子，其中四位死于战乱，其余两位流离失所；孤身一人的努氏，乔装成乞丐模样，在后藏地区活动等的情况[4]。因此，我们有理由认为努氏是后吐蕃王朝时期，即所谓“黑暗时期”的人物，与莲花生大士并没有师徒的关系。

为了使问题得到更进一步的澄清，我们有必要探讨努氏具体的生卒年代。根据宁玛派自己的历史叙述，努氏是位获得“寿自在持明位”（ཚེ་ལ་དབང་བའི་རིག་འཛིན་གྱིས）的大成就者，能够驾驭自己的寿命。一般认为，努氏具有113岁的时寿[5]。按照传统的这种说法，努氏是在公元832年诞生，示寂于944年。传统关于努氏生卒的讨论，在解释努氏为莲花生大士高徒的说法上，也难免产生了矛盾。这就是说努氏降生的832年，莲花生大士是否还在藏地？这里将以两部早期历史文献，说明对此问题的看法，因为两部文献对莲花生大士在藏地弘法时间有不同的叙述。根据《巴协》的记载，莲花生大士在藏只有短暂的停留，他甚至是在桑耶寺未建成前，受到大臣们的弹劾而离开[6]。桑耶寺建成历时五年，即传统所说的“虎年”（公元775年）奠基，“马年”（公元779年）建成。因此，他离开的时间最晚也是在779年之前，因为这一年桑耶寺已经建成。遵照这样的说法，莲花生大士离藏，与努氏的诞生足有半个世纪之差。《娘氏宗教源流》作为莲花生信仰在藏地，逐渐膨胀达到高潮

4 《ཆོས་འབྱུང་མེ་ཏོག་སྙིང་པོ་སྦྲང་རྩིའི་བཅུད》ཉང་ཉི་མ་འོད་ཟེར་གྱིས་བརྩམས། བོད་ལྗོངས་བོད་ཡིག་དཔེ་རྙིང་དཔེ་སྐྲུན་ཁང་། ༢༠༡༢ལོའི་པར་གཞི་གསུམ་པ། ཤ་༨༡༣།

5 《བདུད་འཇོམས་ཆོས་འབྱུང》 བདུད་འཇོམས་ཡེ་ཤེས་རྡོ་རྗེས་བརྩམས། སི་ཁྲོན་མི་རིགས་དཔེ་སྐྲུན་ཁང་། ༡༩༩༦ལོའི་པར་གཞི་དང་པོ། ཤ་༢༨༡།

6 《དབའ་བཞེད་བཞུགས་ས》དབའ་གསལ་སྣང་གིས་བརྩམས། བོད་ལྗོངས་བོད་ཡིག་དཔེ་རྙིང་དཔེ་སྐྲུན་ཁང་། ༢༠༡༢ལོའི་པར་གཞི་གསུམ་པ། ཤ་༢༥་ནས་༢༦།

时期的作品，对莲花生大士在藏的时间，比起《巴协》中的短暂停留，显然是要长很多。《娘氏宗教源流》中记载，莲花生大士应赤松德赞（ཁྲི་སྲོང་ལྡེ་བཙན）之邀而入藏，在赤松德赞之子牟迪赞普（མུ་ཏིག་བཙན་པོ）时期离藏。根据《弟吴宗教源流》（ལྡེའུ་ཆོས་འབྱུང）的说法，赤松德赞有三个儿子，即牟尼赞普（མུ་ནེ་བཙན་པོ）、牟迪赞普和赤德松赞（ཁྲི་ལྡེ་སྲོང་བཙན）。在此我们需要确定，牟迪赞普的执政年代。但是，由于牟迪赞普执政时间极为短暂，我们需要通过他之后的赞普的继位时间，来估算他的执政时间。一般认为赤松德赞 56 岁时离世，即公元 797 年。赤松德赞之后的权利交替，似乎出现了裂缝，纷争不断。赤松德赞的三个儿子依次执政，但牟尼赞普和牟迪赞普的执政，只持续了数月而已，两者都遭到杀害。接着，最小的儿子赤德松赞继位。赤德松赞有五个儿子，其中依次有两个儿子执政王位，分别是赤祖德赞热巴巾（ཁྲི་གཙུག་ལྡེ་བཙན་རལ་པ་ཅན）、达磨乌东赞（དར་མ་འུ་དུམ་བཙན）。根据山口瑞凤的研究，赤祖德赞热巴巾是在公元 815 年继位的[7]。由此我们可以知晓，牟迪赞普的侄子，即赤祖德赞热巴巾执政时为 815 年，那么牟迪赞普自己的执政显然是要早于这个时间点的。另外，大部分藏族史书，一致认为赤德松赞的执政，持续了十几年。从上面的这些线索，我们发现牟迪赞普的执政当在公元 9 世纪之初。如果莲花生大士在牟迪赞普时期离藏，那么这个时间点，距努氏的降生将近有 30 多年的之差。倘若我们确实相信，早期史书对努氏生卒的断定，我们也发现作为莲花生大士高徒的情况，也不过是后世的错误而已。

西方学者 Roberto Vitali 先生关于努氏出生时间的讨论，具有一定的参考价值。Vitali 是根据《嘉卧切》中的记载，鼠年即努氏 61 岁时在卫藏地区发生的“第二次纷争”（ཁེང་ལོག་བར་བ），作为其问题的切入点展开论述。那么，努氏 61 岁时的这个鼠年，即发生“第二次纷争”的年代究竟是哪年呢？吐蕃赞普后裔贝考赞（དཔལ་འཁོར་བཙན། 881—910）时期，总共发生了“三次纷争”。从而，Vitali 断定努氏 61 岁鼠年发生的这次纷争，也可界定于贝考赞统治时期，即公元 881 年至 910 年。通过这样的逻辑，他将这个发生“第二次纷争”的鼠年认定为 904 年。公元 904 年时努氏为 61 岁，那么他的出生时间应该为 844 年[8]。Vitali 将努氏的生存年代界定为 9 世纪中叶至 10 世纪上半叶的观点，笔者认为较为妥贴。这也同时佐证了努氏是所谓“黑暗时期”人物

7 Zuihō Yamaguchi, “The Fiction of King Dar-Ma’s Persecution of Buddhism,” in *Du Dunhuang Au Japon: Études Chinoises et Bouddhiques Offertes À Michel Soymié*, Geneva: Droz, 1996, pp.231-258.

8 Roberto Vitali, *The Kingdoms of Gu.Ge Pu.Hrang: According to Mnga’.Ris Rgyal.Rabs by Gu.Ge Mkhan.Chen Ngag.Dbang Grags.Pa*, 2nd edition, Dharamsala, India: Serindia Publications, 1997, pp.541-551.

的看法。

通过以上的论证，我们发现努氏并不是莲花生大士的高徒，不过是宁玛派学者辩护自派“正统性”的一个策略。这同时说明了，我们所深信不疑的莲花生大士“二十五位高徒”的说法，是需要纠正的。

二、内三密“教传”总持有者

宁玛派的法脉，在其话语结构中通常划为两大体系，即“伏藏”（གཏེར་མ）和“教传”（བཀའ་མ）。其中，“教传”的传承，被宁玛派继承者认为自前弘期以降从未间断。特别是在12世纪“三宿尔”（ཟུར་གསུམ）以来，其重要性尤其得到认可。自公元10世纪后期，藏族的宗教景况（Religious Landscape）相较于吐蕃时期发生了巨大的变化，开始着手翻译印度后期的密乘经典，诸如《胜乐本续》《时轮本续》和《密集本续》等，这被传统藏族史学编纂者标为佛教在藏地的“后弘期”。这些后弘期的新翻译者，在强调他们所翻译经典的印度“正统性”的同时，批判在此之前的某些经典为藏人自己的伪造。面对这些新翻译家的责难，那些认同在此之前佛教传统的辩护者们——他们被冠以“宁玛派”，开始收集、整理自己的经典，这些经典的考订和传承就是我们在此所说的“教传”。这种“教传”的兴起，在很大程度上是用来对抗新的迅速壮大的新译经典，以图在宗教竞争中取得优势。在传统的宁玛派历史编纂文献中，努氏是“教传”这个传统的核心人物，因为他总持有内三密“经、幻、心”（མདོ་སྒྱུ་སེམས་གསུམ）三部的传承。其中“经”指无比瑜伽《集密意经》（དགོངས་པ་འདུས་པའི་མདོ），“幻”指大瑜伽《秘密藏续》（གསང་བ་སྙིང་པོ），“心”指无上瑜伽大圆满《心部十八法》（སེམས་སྡེ་བཅོ་བརྒྱད），从这个意义上说是“内三密教传总持有者”（མདོ་སྒྱུ་སེམས་གསུམ་གྱི་བསྟན་པ་སྤྱིའི་བབས་ཚུལ）。仁增·吉美林巴（རིག་འཛིན་འཇིགས་མེད་གླིང་པ། 1729/1730—1798），在其所撰的《宁玛十万续编纂史·遍满南瞻部洲之庄严》中，说道“经幻心”三部总教法，首始于娘·益西循努，中间承于努氏·桑杰益西，终降于宿氏（ད་ནི་མདོ་སྒྱུ་སེམས་གསུམ་གྱི་བསྟན་པ་སྤྱིའི་བབས་ཚུལ་ལས། གངས་རིའི་ཁྲོད་འདིར་སྔ་འགྱུར་རྙིང་མ་ཞེས་པའི་བསྟན་པ་དང་པོར་གཉགས་ལ་བབས། བར་དུ་གནུབས་ལ་བབས། ཐ་མར་ཟུར་ལ་བབས་ཞེས་འཆད་པར་བྱའོ།）[9]。在此笔者试图探讨，将努氏视为内三密教传总持有者之说法，是否有

9 《དེ་བཞིན་གཤེགས་པས་ལེགས་པར་གསུངས་པའི་གསུང་རབ་རྒྱ་མཚོའི་སྙིང་པོར་གྱུར་པ་རིག་པ་འཛིན་པའི་སྡེ་སྣོད་དམ་སྔ་འགྱུར་རྒྱུད་འབུམ་རིན་པོ་ཆེའི་རྟོགས་པ་བརྗོད་པ་འཛམ་གླིང་མཐའ་གྲུ་ཁྱབ་པའི་རྒྱན་ཅེས་བྱ་བ་བཞུགས་སོ》རིག་འཛིན་འཇིགས་མེད་གླིང་པས་བརྩམས། སི་ཁྲོན་དཔེ་སྐྲུན་ཚོགས་པ། སི་ཁྲོན་མི་རིགས་དཔེ་སྐྲུན་ཁང་། ༢༠༠༨ལོའི་པར་གཞི་དང་པོ། ཤ་༢༠༩།

其一定的历史根据。

（一）努氏与《秘密藏续》

为了随顺宁玛派内三密的次序，我们首先将讨论努氏与“大瑜伽十八部续”（མ་ཧཱ་ཡོ་ག་རྒྱུད་སྡེ་བཅོ་བརྒྱད）之最根本经典《秘密藏续》的传承[10]。毋庸置疑，《秘密藏续》在宁玛派教法史上扮演着很重要的角色，从某种程度上也可视为宁玛派传统的标签，因为它是藏传佛教史上最重要的与新译各派所不共的旧译续典。对此，Dan Martin 这样总结道：“它（《秘密藏续》）的重要性能够被其庞大的注疏著作所证明，从这点而言它至少影响了上一个千年。近来，它在宁玛派‘寺院大学’敏珠林寺（སྨིན་གྲོལ་གླིང）的课程中有其特殊的地位。在很大程度上，它的早期传承史就是宁玛派密续的一般历史。”[11] Martin 先生在此对这部续典的评价，并非是虚夸奉承之辞。这从宁玛派历史上的诸位重要人物，对其作相关注疏之过程，也可见一斑。从最初绒松·曲季桑布[12]（རོང་ཟོམ་ཆོས་ཀྱི་བཟང་པོ，约 11 世纪）的《秘密藏续释·宝疏》（གསང་སྙིང་དཀོན་མཆོག་འགྲེལ），到隆钦巴·智美沃色（ཀློང་ཆེན་པ་དྲི་མེད་འོད་ཟེར། 1308-1363）的《秘密藏

10 传统而言，有“大瑜伽十八部续”之称谓。根据德国汉堡大学（Hamburg University）奥纳女士（Orna Almogi）的研究，于宁玛派传统对大瑜伽这十八部续主要有两大分类方式。第一种为弟吴智者（མཁས་པ་ལྡེའུ）之《弟吴宗教源流》（ལྡེའུ་ཆོས་འབྱུང）所代表的分类方式：（1）根本五部续（གཞིའམ་རྩ་བའི་རྒྱུད་ལྔ），（2）实修五部续（སྒྲུབ་པའི་ལག་ལེན་སྟོན་པའི་རྒྱུད་ལྔ），（3）分支五部续（སྤྱིའི་ཡན་ལག་ཏུ་གྱུར་པའི་རྒྱུད་ལྔ），(4) 两部后续（རྒྱུད་ཕྱི་མ་ལྟ་བུ་གཉིས），(5) 摄总要之一续（བསྡུས་དོན་ལྟ་བུའི་རྒྱུད་གཅིག）。第二种为隆钦巴·无垢光《密续总义·梵音之声》（སྔགས་ཀྱི་སྤྱི་དོན་ཚངས་དབྱངས་འབྲུག་སྒྲ）所代表的分类方式：（1）身三部续（སྐུ་རྒྱུད་གསུམ），（2）语三部续（གསུང་རྒྱུད་གསུམ），（3）意三部续（ཐུགས་རྒྱུད་གསུམ），（4）功德三部续（ཡོན་ཏན་རྒྱུད་གསུམ），（5）事业三部续（འཕྲིན་ལས་རྒྱུད་གསུམ），（6）摄要三部续（སྤྱིའི་རྒྱུད་གསུམ）。奥纳女士认为，传统史料所提及的“大瑜伽十八部续”所列出的每个“指称（List）”并非指单一的或者特定的某部续典，而更应该认为是一系列的续典，包括根本续（རྩ་རྒྱུད）、后续（ཕྱི་མ་རྒྱུད）、后之后续（ཕྱི་མའི་ཕྱི་མ་རྒྱུད）等。奥纳在详细对勘“大瑜伽十八续（按她自己的观点，更应该称为‘大瑜伽十八个系列’）”在藏传佛教各种文献中的不同表述以后，认为这种“大瑜伽十八部续”的说法相对而言比较早，因为“前弘期”所翻译的佛教文献中就初见端倪；但是，在这种说法下的具体的十八部续典却未有固定的指称，随着时空的不同而流于变化，所以“大瑜伽十八续”的说法更像是一种“概念性（mere notion of one）”的提法。详情请参阅 Orna Almogi, “The Eighteen Mahayoga Tantric Cycles: A Real Canon or the Mere Notion One?” *Revue d'Etudes Tibétaines*, no.30, October 2014, pp.47-110.

11 Dan Martin, “Illusion Web-Locating the Guhyagarbha Tantra in Buddhist Intellectual History,” in *Silver on Lapis: Tibetan Literary Culture and History*, ed. Christopher Beckwith, Bloomington: The Tibet Society, 1987, p.178.

12 关于绒松·曲季桑布的生平及著述，请参阅奥纳女士的文章：Orna Almogi, “Sources on the Life and Works of the Eleventh Century Tibetan Scholar Rong Zom Chos Kyi Bzang Po: A Brief Survey,” in *Tibet, Past and Present*, ed. Henk Blezer, vol. 1, PIATS 2000: Proceedings of the Ninth Seminar of the International Association for Tibetan Studies. Leiden: Brill, 2002, pp.67-80. 在这篇文章中，奥纳列出了两部由其弟子叙述绒松生平的著作，对致力于了解这位宁玛派早期人物的学者而言，是个有用的线索。

续释·十方除暗》（གསང་སྙིང་འགྲེལ་པ་ཕྱོགས་བཅུ་མུན་སེལ）[13]，再到当代的居米旁·南杰嘉措（འཇུ་མི་ཕམ་རྣམ་རྒྱལ་རྒྱ་མཚོ། 1846-1912）的《秘密藏续释 · 光明藏》（གསང་འགྲེལ་སྤྱི་དོན་འོད་ཟེར་སྙིང་པོ）[14]，多竹钦 · 吉美丹贝尼玛（རྡོ་གྲུབ་ཆེན་འཇིགས་མེད་བསྟན་པའི་ཉི་མ། 1865—1926）的《秘密藏续总义抉择 · 宝藏之钥》（གསང་སྙིང་སྤྱི་དོན་རྣམ་འབྱེད་རིན་ཆེན་མཛོད་ལྡེ）[15]，可谓绵绵不绝。从这些诠释学家的身份而言，我们可以说几乎宁玛派历史上各时期的代表人物，都对此续典给予很重要的位置。或许是因为它对宁玛派传统的重要，新派某些人物对旧译密续横加指责时，它便首当其冲。对它的责难，主要是围绕其印度来源的“正统性”，认为它是假托印度佛教渊源的藏人之伪造。在这些质疑者中，最严厉者当推 11 世纪的郭译师 · 库巴拉则[16]。郭译师辩驳《秘密藏续》为吐蕃时期翻译家玛 · 仁钦乔（རྨ་རིན་ཆེན་མཆོག）所撰，而非是宁玛派传统所说的印度佛教经典。自郭译师等人以降，《秘密藏续》遭受新译密续某些人物的诟病，直到其梵文原本在藏地被重新发现之后，这种争论才趋于缓和。根据《青史》记载，“克什米尔班智达驻锡于桑耶寺时，发现《秘密藏续》印度原本”[17]。在此所提到的克什米尔班智

13 对隆钦巴的这部注疏的研究，请参阅 Gyurme Dorje, *The Guhyagarbha Tantra and Its Commentary*. Unpublished Ph.D Thesis. SOAS, University of London, 1987. 他的研究是西方研究《秘密藏续》的里程碑，自此以后为相关研究奠定了基础，提供了新的契机。因此这篇未出版的博士论文，成为征引最为频繁的书目之一。这篇论文有 1500 多页，其中包括篇幅较长的对《秘密藏续》的文献史的回顾、对《秘密藏续》藏文本之对勘、《十方除暗》对前者的疏释等。

14 对不败尊者的这部疏释本，近期出版了汉译本，见沈卫荣译、谈锡永释：《幻化网秘密藏续释——光明藏》，北京：华夏出版社，2010 年。英译本参见：Jamgon Mipham, *Luminous Essence: A Guide to the Guhyagarbha Tantra*, Snow Lion Publications, 2009.

15 对多智钦注疏本的研究，以及相关章节的英译，参见 Nathaniel De Witt Garson, *Penetrating the Secret Essence Tantra: Context and Philosophy in the Mahayana System of rNying-Ma Tantra*, Ph.D Thesis, Charlottesville: University of Virginia, 2004.

16 根据宁玛派传统的叙述，郭译师曾打算求拜宁玛派大宿尔，但被后者拒之门外；后又试图随从萨迦派卓弥 · 释迦益西，被后者要求奉送大量黄金作为求学之用，遂又未能成行；对此，他怀恨于心，后来在印度学成返藏后，指责宁玛派的正统性。请参阅：《སྔ་འགྱུར་རྡོ་རྗེ་ཐེག་པ་གཙོ་བོར་གྱུར་པའི་སྒྲུབ་བརྒྱུད་ཤིང་རྟ་བརྒྱད་ཀྱི་བྱུང་བ་བརྗོད་པ》ཞི་ཆེན་པདྨ་རྣམ་རྒྱལ་གྱིས་བརྩམས། བོད་ལྗོངས་བོད་ཡིག་དཔེ་རྙིང་དཔེ་སྐྲུན་ཁང་། ༢༠༠༢ལོའི་པར་གཞི་དང་པོ། ཤ་༧༤། 郭译师对宁玛派传统的反驳文，是否真为其本人所作，宁玛派学者持一定的质疑，主要是因为驳文中出现误解佛学基础知识等的低级错误。郭译师的相关重要论述，在 16 世纪宁玛派传统的辩护者索达巴 · 洛追坚赞（སོག་བཟློག་པ་བློ་གྲོས་རྒྱལ་མཚན། 1552—1624）对其进行反驳的著作，《藏地于旧译密续引起争论之解答 · 了义之龙声》（གསང་སྔགས་སྔ་འགྱུར་ལ་བོད་དུ་རྩོད་པ་སྔ་ཕྱིར་བྱུང་བ་རྣམས་ཀྱི་ལན་དུ་བརྗོད་པ་ངེས་པ་དོན་གྱི་འབྲུག་སྒྲ། སོག་བཟློག་པ་བློ་གྲོས་རྒྱལ་མཚན་གྱིས་བརྩམས། སི་ཁྲོན་མི་རིགས་དཔེ་སྐྲུན་ཁང་། ༡༩༩༧ལོའི་པར་གཞི་དང་པོ། ཤ་༢༡༧ནས་༢༣༠།）中有记载。另外，1979 年在不丹的廷布，将新译密续各派人物对宁玛派传统责难的著作结成一册，名曰《破斥谬咒之辑要》（སྔགས་ལོག་སུན་འབྱིན་གྱི་སྐོར། TBRC No. W23954），郭译师的论述也列于其间。

17 Sam van Schaik 先生在他的文章中提到，释迦师利跋陀罗在桑耶寺发现《秘密藏续》梵文本的记载最早见于 12 或 13 世纪时期萨迦派关于释迦师利跋陀罗的传记中（在此 Sam 未指出是萨迦派哪部文献），后来这个传闻被郭译师接受，并记录在《青史》中。Sam van Schaik, “In search of the Guhyagarbha Tantra,” www.earlytibet.com/2007/08/27/.

达，是噶举派卓普译师（ཁྲོ་ཕུ་ལོ་ཙྪ་བ）迎请的、1204 年赴西藏的释迦师利跋陀罗。他及其随从的到来，又一次将藏人对佛教的兴趣导入印度佛学经院传统[18]。依《秘密藏续》的这个梵文原本，迥丹·日贝热支（བཅོམ་ལྡན་རིག་པའི་རལ་གྲི 1227-1305）作有《秘密藏续之修法·修饰之花》（གསང་སྙིང་སྒྲུབ་པ་རྒྱན་གྱི་མེ་ཏོག）；泰译师·尼玛坚赞（ཐར་ལོ་ཉི་མ་རྒྱལ་མཚན）更是发现了此前未有之《秘密藏后续》，并将其译出。

努氏与摩诃瑜伽类主要续典《秘密藏续》的关系，郭译师·循努贝在其《青史》中认为，努氏很可能有自无垢友（Vimalamitra བྱི་མ་ལ་མི་ཏྲ）以来的传承[19]。郭译师的理由为，努氏的师承关系可以追溯至无垢友本人，因为努氏为无垢友的亲传弟子娘·益西循努的弟子，并且也是娘之弟子索巴·贝吉益西（སོག་པོ་དཔལ་གྱི་ཡེ་ཤེས）的传承人[20]。从这种师承关系，我们或许有理由相信，郭译师的这种断言并非是空穴来风、天花乱坠，有其一定的历史根据。或许是得益于郭译师的论断，当代著名的宁玛派传承人杜迥·吉扎益西多杰（བདུད་འཇོམས་འཇིགས་བྲལ་ཡེ་ཤེས་རྡོ་རྗེ། 1904-1987），在其《杜迥教法史·天鼓之音》中用肯定的口吻说道，努氏具有《秘密藏续》的传承[21]。

倘若努氏具有自无垢友以来的传承，那么努氏的传承从宁玛派传统自身而言，应该算是“最正统”的。因为，根据宁玛派编纂史家的叙述话语，我们可知无垢友不仅是《秘密藏续》在印度本土传承过程中的中枢人物，而且，他曾亲自莅临作为“蛮荒之地”的藏地传授《秘密藏续》，藏人对这部大瑜伽续典的传承首始于他。近代著名的宁玛派传统在卫藏的传承者，多竹钦·吉美丹贝尼玛在其对《秘密藏续》的注疏本，即《秘密藏续总义抉择·宝藏之钥》中概括了续典在印藏的传承。借此我们能够窥探无垢友于此续典在藏地传播的贡献，抑或得益于无垢友的努氏自己的传承。跟其他续典一样，《秘密藏续》的传承主要也有三大传承，即佛密意传（རྒྱལ་བའི་དགོངས་བརྒྱུད）、持明表示传（རིག་འཛིན་བརྡའི་བརྒྱུད）和补特伽罗口耳传（གང་ཟག་སྙན་བརྒྱུད）。多竹钦将续典在人间的传承，主要限定于补特伽罗口耳传。他认为《秘密藏续》的传承首始于国王扎（རྒྱལ་པོ་ཛ）[22]，国王扎由七个梦得到授记，在其殿顶得到密续和持金刚像；他依止此持金刚像修习《秘密藏续》，六个月后圆满证得密续奥义，因而金刚萨

18 Matthew Kapstein, *The Tibetan Assimilation of Buddhism: Conversion, Contestation, and Memory*, New York: Oxford University Press, 2000.xix.

19 关于无垢友的生平，请参照沈卫荣：《无垢友尊者及其所造〈顿入无分别修习义〉研究》，载于《佛学研究中心学报》2005 年第 10 期，第 81-117 页。

20 《དེབ་ཐེར་སྔོན་པོ》འགོས་ལོ་གཞོན་ནུ་དཔལ་གྱིས་བརྩམས། སི་ཁྲོན་མི་རིགས་དཔེ་སྐྲུན་ཁང་། ༡༩༨༥ལོའི་པར་གཞི་དང་པོ། ཤ་༡༦༧།

21 《བདུད་འཇོམས་ཆོས་འབྱུང》བདུད་འཇོམས་ཡེ་ཤེས་རྡོ་རྗེས་བརྩམས། སི་ཁྲོན་མི་རིགས་དཔེ་སྐྲུན་ཁང་། ༡༩༩༦ལོའི་པར་གཞི་དང་པོ། ཤ་༡༦༧།

22 关于这个传奇人物，请参阅 Samten G. Karmay, *The Arrow and the Spindle: Studies in History, Myths, Rituals and Beliefs in Tibet*, Kathmandu, Nepal: Mandala Book Point, 1998, pp.76-93.

垂示现于他；由此《秘密藏续》在人间的传承也已开始，从国王扎传授给古阁热扎（ཀུ་ཀུ་ར་ཛ），其后依次为：因陀罗菩提（ཨིནྡྲ་བྷཱུ་ཏི）、乌巴热扎（ཨུ་པ་ར་ཛ）、郭玛德瓦（གོ་མ་དེ་ཝི）、游戏金刚（Lilavajra སྒེག་པའི་རྡོ་རྗེ）、佛密（Buddhaguhya སངས་རྒྱས་གསང་བ）、莲花生、无垢友，此阶段为《秘密藏续》在印度本土的传承；在藏地，由无垢友传授给玛·仁钦乔和娘·益西循努，后两者的传承分为三个支系，但努氏总摄此三支之传承[23]。从多竹钦对《秘密藏续》传承史的叙述，我们可以想见努氏于《秘密藏续》传承的"正统性"。

挺有趣的是，五世达赖喇嘛（1617—1682）在其《闻法录·恒河之流》中提到，努氏不仅具有莲花生和无垢友两者之《秘密藏续》传承外，还认为具有游戏金刚所作《秘密藏续疏·白凯》（སྤར་བཀབ）传承[24]。此疏释本相传为藏译《秘密藏续》印度两大注疏本之一，另外一部为尼玛沃季僧格（ཉི་མའི་འོད་ཀྱི་སེང་གེ）的《秘密藏续广疏》。

通过梳理以上文献对努氏于《秘密藏续》传承关系的表述，我们可以确信努氏具有自印度以降的《秘密藏续》传承。《秘密藏续》作为"旧译密续"最具特色的一部续典，在努氏的生活年代此续的重要性是不言而喻的，因而努氏对此续的了解应该也是很透彻的。另外，在《禅定目炬》大瑜伽章节中也数次引用了此续典。

（二）努氏与《密意集经》

据宁玛派传统，《密意集经》是内三密无比阿努瑜伽（ཨ་ནུ་ཡོ་ག）的主要续典之一。根据此续典的跋文，与大部分藏译续典不同的是，它是译自勃律文（བྲུ་ཤའི་སྐད），因此扉页上续典的名称也就有了梵文、勃律文和藏文三者的称呼。勃律，古有大、小勃律之划分，今指巴基斯坦北部学者所俗称之"小西藏"的巴尔蒂斯坦地区（Baltistan）[25]。宁玛派传统所言之，此续典译自勃律文的说法在藏传佛教史上颇有争议。11世纪郭译师·库巴拉则认为，此续典并非源自勃律文，而是藏人所杜撰之"谬法"（ལོག་ཆོས）[26]。现代西方学者也对其传统说法提出了质疑，根据 Jacob Dalton

23 《གསང་སྙིང་སྤྱི་དོན་རིན་ཆེན་མཛོད་ལྡེ》རྡོ་གྲུབ་ཆེན་འཇིགས་མེད་བསྟན་པའི་ཉི་མས་བརྩམས། རྡོ་གྲུབ་ཆེན་འཇིགས་མེད་བསྟན་པའི་ཉི་མའི་གསུང་འབུམ་པོད་གསུམ་པ། སི་ཁྲོན་མི་རིགས་དཔེ་སྐྲུན་ཁང་། ༢༠༠༣ལོའི་པར་གཞི་དང་པོ། ཤ་༤༩ནས་༧།

24 《ཟབ་པ་དང་རྒྱ་ཆེ་བའི་དམ་པའི་ཆོས་ཀྱི་ཐོབ་ཡིག་གངྒཱའི་ཆུ་རྒྱུན》རྒྱལ་དབང་ལྔ་བ་ངག་དབང་བློ་བཟང་རྒྱ་མཚོས་བརྩམས། སེར་གཙུག་ནང་བསྟན་དཔེ་རྙིང་འཚོལ་བསྡུ་ཕྱོགས་སྒྲིག་ཁང་གིས་བསྒྲིགས།《རྒྱལ་དབང་ལྔ་པ་ངག་དབང་བློ་བཟང་རྒྱ་མཚོའི་གསུང་འབུམ་བཞུགས་སོ》པོད་གཉིས་པ། ཀྲུང་གོའི་བོད་རིག་པ་དཔེ་སྐྲུན་ཁང་། ༢༠༠༩ལོའི་པར་གཞི་དང་པོ། ཤ་༢༧༡།

25 古勃律，无疑是佛教盛行的一个地区，这点仅仅从吐蕃时期诸多佛教人物从这些地区入藏传法，就能得到佐证。后来，由于伊斯兰教在此地区的盛行，使得佛教传统时至今日已荡然无存，但根据 Dan Martin 先生的研究可知用当地语说唱格萨尔的习俗仍然在传承。苯教中赫赫有名的朱家族（bru）或许也与此处所说勃律者有关。相关讨论请参阅 Dan Martin, "Ol-mo-lung-ring, the original holy place," in *Sacred Space and Powerful Place in Tibetan Culture: A Collection of Essays*, Library of Tibetan Works and Archives, 1999.

26 སྔགས་ལོག་སུན་འབྱིན་གྱི་སྐོར། TBRC No.W23954ཤ་༢༥།

先生的分析指出，此续典从整体而言是贴着“异国标签”（Written for Export）的藏人之创造。他的研究是基于续典中是否出现未进行藏译之勃律文词汇作为判断维度。纵观续典，续典总揽 75 章，所谓勃律文词汇只出现在最为人所熟知的金刚手教化茹达拉（Rudra）恶魔的神话部分，即第 20 章到 31 章中，总共 12 章。“茹达拉神话”部分，作为续典的最初“创作层面”（Textual Stratum）或当是译自勃律文，但这些部分后来又经过佛教哲理的修改、润色和再创造，主要是为其哲理根据提供服务。“茹达拉神话”以外的部分，相对而言哲理较为深奥的余下部分，是在勃律之外的藏地进行创作的，这些部分才是续典在主题上的核心，显然这些部分总体上不是译自勃律文或者梵文[27]。因而，如果 Dalton 先生的研究属实，我们或可断言续典经历了两个创作阶段，这两个阶段分别是在勃律和藏地完成的。

正是基于《密意集经》的这两个创作阶段，11 世纪以降的新翻译家们围绕“正统”抑或“非正统”的话语形式，展开对它的指责。新翻译家们所谓的“正统”，其实质是某种对“地域概念”的考虑，即来自藏地之外异域的文本。新近 Ronald Davidson 先生，基于续典的这种创作模式，提出了“灰色文本（Gray Text）”的概念。这种“灰色文本”是指，像《密意集经》这种翻译作品，它不全然是梵文本的翻译，也不尽然是藏人的伪造，是印藏两者思想融为一体的结果。这种所谓的“灰色文本”，并非仅仅限定于宁玛派续典，在新译续典中也多有出现。新译经典中的这些“灰色文本”，我们可在萨迦班智达（1182-1251）和恰译师却吉贝（ཆག་ལོ་ཆོས་རྗེ་དཔལ། 1197-1264）等学者，于新译经典的这类“灰色文本”的讨论中，能够窥其一二[28]。根据 Davidson 先生的研究，新译翻译家将“正统”之标签，贴在来自异域（尤其是印度）文本上的作为，我们有必要进行质疑。因为，即使在印度本土也无所谓“正统”之话语可言，因为印度佛教文化的一个主要特色就是“经典创作”（Scriptural Composition）。这些印度学者的创作与后期藏人之创造性作品并无二致，两者都在佛教文化的叙述框架内出现，因此也就无所谓“正统”抑或“非正统”的判断。当佛教在藏地吸收之时，印度佛教的这种“经典创作”文化也随之进入藏地，本土学者也积极投入于佛教经典的创作项目中。但为何到 11 世纪初期，在藏地出现了所谓“正统性”的辩论呢？ Davidson 先生指出，这或许可能是受到汉传佛教的影响。因为在汉地最早出现经典编纂的活动，有些经典被标以“疑伪经”而未被视为“正统”佛教，

27 Jacob Dalton, *The Uses of the dGongs Pos 'Dus Pa'i Mdo in the Development of the rNying Ma School of Tibetan Buddhism*. Ph.D Dissertation.University of Michigan, 2002, pp.266-278.

28 《སྡོམ་པ་གསུམ་གྱི་རབ་ཏུ་དབྱེ་བའི་བསྟན་བཅོས་བཞུགས་སོ》 ས་སྐྱ་པཎྜི་ཏ་ཀུན་དགའ་རྒྱལ་མཚན་གྱིས་མཛད། བོད་ལྗོངས་བོད་ཡིག་དཔེ་རྙིང་དཔེ་སྐྲུན་ཁང་། ༢༠༡༢ལོའི་པར་གཞི་གཉིས་པ།

显然在此印度佛教之“经典创作”文化被终止了。从这些维度看“灰色文本”之“正统”与否，更像是一个“社会政治议题”（Socio-Politic Issues），而不仅仅是文本本身的问题那么简单[29]。

根据宁玛派自身传统，努氏与续典的传承，可以追溯到续典本身在印藏最初的传承时期。这点我们通过1681年成书之《密意集经师传承史》所记载的努氏的传承，就能有所了解。《密意集经师传承史》记载：

在尼泊尔，（努氏）向世持寻求经之灌顶，但授记道应向堪布法护求之[30]。（努氏）遂赴印度，在印度中部如何向堪布法护求法之事宜，已在阐述大瑜伽传承史时提及，故不再赘述。如是，堪布法护授予诸灌顶和修法。另外，（努氏）也受益于阿阇梨赛瓦杰。此时（努氏求法之时），堪布法护赴勃律，在勃律堪布曲赞杰的语言沟通协助下，与达纳西塔即释迦之狮莲花生大师和法菩提一道在勃律集市翻译续典[31]，但未获供养遂弃之。尔后，（堪布法护）又折回印度，在此教授给勃律堪布曲赞杰、世持、娘·益西循努、祖拉贝格和努钦·桑杰益西等人。努氏在勃律堪布曲赞杰处也获得续典的教授，此即是说勃律堪布曲赞杰根据达纳西塔的教言重新从勃律文翻译时获得的教授，此处是随顺阿努无比瑜伽的传承。努氏于法菩提处也获得续典的传承[32]。

（བལ་ཡུལ་དུ་སློབ་དཔོན་བ་སུ་དྷ་ར་ལ་མདོ་དབང་ཞུས་པར་མཁན་པོ་ཆོས་རྒྱལ་སྐྱོང་ལ་ཞུས་ཤིག་པར་ལུང་བསྟན་པ་བཞིན་རྒྱ་གར་གྱི་ཡུལ་དུ་བྱོན་ཏེ། མཁན་པོ་ཆོས་རྒྱལ་སྐྱོང་ལ་རྒྱ་གར་དབུས་འགྱུར་ཚལ་དུ་ཞུས་ཚུལ་གོང་དུ་མ་ཧཱ་ཡོ་གའི་བླ་བརྒྱུད་སྐབས་བྲིས་པ་ལྟར་ལ། དེ་ལྟར་མཁན་པོ་ཆོས་རྒྱལ་སྐྱོང་གིས་དབང་བརྒྱུད་སྒྲུབ་ཐབས་མང་དུ་གནང་ངོ༎ གཞན་ཡང་ཨཱ་ཙ་རྱ་གསལ་བའི་རྒྱན་ལ་ཡང་ནོས། དུས་ནམ་ཞིག་གི་ཚེ་མཁན་པོ་ཆོས་རྒྱལ་སྐྱོང་བྲུ་ཤའི་ཡུལ་དུ་བྱོན་ཏེ། དྷ་ན་རཀྵི་ཏའམ་ཤཱཀྱ་སེང་གེ་སྟེ་ཨོ་རྒྱན་ཆེན་པོ། དྷརྨ་བོ་དྷི་གསུམ་ལ་བྲུ་ཤའི་མཁན་པོ་ཆེ་བཙན་སྐྱེས་ཀྱི་ལོ་ཙཱ་མཛད་དེ་བྲུ་ཤའི་ཁྲོམ་དུ་མདོ་འགྱུར་མཛད་པ་མོས་པ་ཆུང་སྟེ་མ་འགྱུར་བར། སླར་ཡང་རྒྱ་གར་དུ་བྱོན་ཏེ་བྲུ་ཤའི་མཁན་པོ་དང་། བ་སུ་དྷ་ར་དང་། ཛྙཱ་ན་ཀུ་མཱ་ར་དང་། གཙུག་ལག་

29 Ronald Davidson, “Gsar ma Apocrypha: the Creation of Orthodoxy, Gray Texts, and the New Revelation,” in *The Many Canons of Tibetan Buddhism*. Edited by Helmut Eimer and David Germano, Brill, 2002, pp. 203-224.

30 洛钦·法贤认为，世持要求努氏去拜见阿阇梨赛瓦杰，而非为堪布法护。参见 ལོ་ཆེན་དྷརྨ་ཤྲཱི་ཡིས་བརྩམས། ལོ་ཆེན་གསུང་འབུམ་པོད་བཅུ་གཉིས་པ། ཤ་༥༧། TBRC No.W22197.

31 洛钦·法贤认为，达纳西塔显然不是莲花生大师，此理由参见 ལོ་ཆེན་གསུང་འབུམ་པོད་བཅུ་གཉིས་པ། ལོ་ཆེན་དྷརྨ་ཤྲཱི་ཡིས་བརྩམས། ཤ་༥༠ནས་༥༧། TBRC No.W22197.

32 བཀའ་མ་མདོ་དབང་གི་བླ་མ་བརྒྱུད་པའི་རྣམ་ཐར། པདྨ་འཕྲིན་ལས་ཀྱིས་བརྩམས། ཤ་༧༥༠ནས་༧༥༢། TBRC No.W21523.

དཔལ་དགེ། སངས་རྒྱས་ཡེ་ཤེས་རྣམས་ལ་གསུངས་ཤིང་། སློབ་དཔོན་སངས་རྒྱས་ཡེ་ཤེས་ཀྱིས་བྲུ་ཤའི་མཁན་པོ་ལ་ཡང་གསན་ཏེ། དེ་ཡང་བྲུ་ཤའི་མཁན་པོས་དྷ་ན་རཀྵི་ཏའི་བཀའ་དང་སྦྱར་ཏེ་སྐད་ཡང་བྲུ་ཤར་བསྒྱུར་བའི་ཚེ་བསྒྱུར་ཏེ་གསན་པས་ཨ་ནུའི་བརྒྱུད་པ་ལྟར་རོ།། དེ་ལྟར་ལོ་ཙྪ་བ་སངས་རྒྱས་ཡེ་ཤེས་ཉིད་ཀྱིས་མདོ་མཁན་དྷརྨ་བོ་དྷི་ལ་ཡང་གསན་པར་བཞེད། ）

下面我们将梳理这些人物关系，从而不仅为我们能提供早期续典传承的轮廓，更加重要的是有助于认识努氏在续典传承过程中的角色。在上述人物中，达纳西塔、法菩提和勃律堪布曲赞杰三人，在《密意集经》跋文中明确记载是藏译者[33]。其中，与努氏关系密切者为法菩提和勃律堪布曲赞杰两人。法菩提此人于努氏而言是其重要的上师之一，因为据称是努氏自己所作的自传《嘉卧切》中，在罗列自己在印藏的主要上师之时，此人就被提及[34]。勃律堪布曲赞杰，被洛钦·法贤认为实为藏地雅隆（ཡར་ལུང）地区人，通三种语言，尔后在勃律地区兴事业，遂称为“勃律堪布”[35]。努氏也得到勃律堪布曲赞杰的传承[36]。最后一个参与续典翻译的人物，达纳西塔在续典传承过程中扮演很重要的角色，因为法菩提、曲赞杰等人的传承都始于它，从而努氏的传承追根溯源也应归于他[37]。通过梳理与努氏相关之《密意集经》的传承，传统宁玛派历史编纂学家，显然是将努氏的传承追根溯源至印度本土的传承，这就为续典在努氏以降藏地的传承树立了所谓的“正统性”。但是，这种“正统性”显然没有赢得新译翻译家们的信任，因而也并非像宁玛派传统所称道的那样的坚固，并且于藏传佛教史造就了一个悬而未决的问题。

不管《密意集经》是全部译自勃律文，抑或是藏人自己的半成品，但显然努氏是《密意集经》在藏地最早传播的中枢人物之一。从现有的资料而言，努氏对这个续典所作的注疏本，《黑暗铠甲》是藏地第一本系统、完整的注疏。自努氏以降，《密意集经》在宁玛派教法史中逐渐显现其作用，为以后的诸位传统自身的诠释学家提供了经典基础。

33 དེ་བཞིན་གཤེགས་པ་ཐམས་ཅད་ཀྱི་ཐུགས་གསང་བའི་ཡེ་ཤེས་དོན་གྱི་སྙིང་པོ་རྡོ་རྗེ་བཀོད་པའི་རྒྱུད་རྣལ་འབྱོར་གྲུབ་པའི་ལུང་ཀུན་འདུས་རིག་པའི་མདོ་ཐེག་པ་ཆེན་པོ་མངོན་པར་རྟོགས་པ་ཆོས་ཀྱི་རྣམ་གྲངས་རྣམ་པར་བཀོད་པ་ཞེས་བྱ་བའི་མདོ། (བཀའ་འགྱུར་དཔེ་བསྡུར་མ) ཀྲུང་གོའི་བོད་རིག་པ་ཞིབ་འཇུག་ལྟེ་གནས་ཀྱི་བཀའ་བསྟན་དཔེ་སྡུར་ཁང་གིས་དཔེ་སྡུར་ཞུས། ཀྲུང་གོའི་བོད་རིག་པ་དཔེ་སྐྲུན་ཁང་། དཔེ་སྐྲུན་དུས་ཚོད་༢༠༠༦ནས་༢༠༠༩ལོའི་བར། པོད་༡༠༣། ཤ་༦༧༢།

34 སངས་རྒྱས་ཡེ་ཤེས་རིན་པོ་ཆེའི་ལོ་རྒྱུས་གནུབས་ཀྱི་བཀའ་ཤོག་ཆེན་མོ་བཞུགས་སོ། (སྔ་འགྱུར་བཀའ་མ་ཤིན་ཏུ་རྒྱས་པ) ཚེ་རིང་རྒྱ་མཚོས་གཙོ་སྒྲིག་བྱས། སི་ཁྲོན་དཔེ་སྐྲུན་ཚོགས་པ། སི་ཁྲོན་མི་རིགས་དཔེ་སྐྲུན་ཁང་། ༢༠༠༩ལོའི་པར་གཞི་དང་པོ། ཤ་༧༥༥། TBRC No.W1PD100944.

35 ལོ་ཆེན་གསུང་འབུམ་པོད་བཅུ་གཉིས་པ། ལོ་ཆེན་དྷརྨ་ཤྲཱི་ཡིས་བརྩམས། ཤ་༥༥། TBRC No. W22197.

36 同上引，p.56.

37 同上引，pp.50-58.

另外，纵观《禅定目炬》全文，其中于大瑜伽和大圆满两章，征引最为频繁的经典，便是《密意集经》。

（三）努氏与心部类文献

心部类文献作为正在形成过程中的大圆满法的最初经典群体，对于其以后的传统有着基础性的意义。努氏作为大圆满法这个传统的最初构建者，在其《禅定目炬》中试图考订这一传统独特的文献，这些文献在后来被称作“心部”类文献。因此而言，大圆满心部类文献，正是通过努氏等人的编纂，才最终形成了像“心部十八法”这样的指称。

从以上的分析我们可知，宁玛派传统所说的，努氏作为内三密教传总持有者的说法，是有其合理性的。正是通过努氏对旧译密咒的传承，在“三宿尔”时期最终形成了“宁玛派”这个教法传统。

三、密法传承的守护者

对许多人而言，对于努氏的最大认知，或许是他施咒迫使赞普朗达玛对其作妥协并承诺从此不再干涉俗家密咒师，任其修持密法之传闻。这种传闻并非仅仅以民间故事之形式在流传。当我们翻阅宁玛派教法史时，确实发现这种传闻之文字叙述。当代影响最广之《杜迥教法史·天鼓之音》中记载：

> 赞普朗达玛迫害佛教之时，赞普对其（努氏）问道：“你有何等功夫？”答道：“请看我仅仅念诵密咒之功夫”，说着将食指（亦即“忿怒手印”）指向天空，在其所指方向显现出大如九个牦牛叠加般之黑色的铁蝎子。赞普见状惧道：“不再责难殊胜之密咒师，任你们修习。”他又言：“再看此功夫。”接着用忿怒手印引出雷电，击中彼方之岩石，将其粉碎。赞普对此恐惧万分，“不再祸害你等群体”，并释放了他。白衣盘发之密咒师们未受到（赞普之）迫害，仰仗于他的功劳。[38]
>
> （རྒྱལ་པོ་གླང་དར་མས་བསྟན་པ་བཤིགས་པའི་དུས་རྒྱལ་པོས་ཁྱོད་ལ་ནུས་པ་ཅི་ཡོད་ཟེར་བས། ངས་སྔགས་ཙམ་བཟླས་པའི་ནུས་པ་འདི་ལ་གཟིགས་ཤིག་ཅེས་སྡིགས་མཛུབ་གནམ་དུ་ཕྱར་བས་སྡིགས་མཛུབ་ཀྱི་སྟེང་ནས་ལྕགས་ཀྱི་སྡིག་པ་ནག་པོ་གཡག་ཙམ་དགུ་བརྩེགས་སུ་འདུག་པ

38 《བདུད་འཇོམས་ཆོས་འབྱུང》 བདུད་འཇོམས་ཡེ་ཤེས་རྡོ་རྗེས་བརྩམས། སི་ཁྲོན་མི་རིགས་དཔེ་སྐྲུན་ཁང་། ༡༩༩༦ལོའི་པར་གཞི་དང་པོ། ཤ་༢༣༤ནས་༢༣༥།

མཐོང་བས་རྒྱལ་པོ་སྐྲག་སྟེ་དཀོན་མཆོག་སྔགས་པའི་སྐུ་ལ་མི་བདོའོ་ཆོས་མཛོད་ཅིག་ཟེར། ད་རུང་ནུས་པ་འདི་ལ་གཟིགས་ཤིག་ཟེར་ནས་སྡིགས་མཛུབ་ཀྱིས་ཐོག་རབ་སྟེ་ཕ་རིའི་བྲག་ལ་བསྣུན་པས་ཚལ་པར་སོང་། དེར་རྒྱལ་པོ་ཤིན་ཏུ་འཇིགས་ཤིང་སྐྲག་ནས་ཁྱེད་འཁོར་དང་བཅས་པ་ལ་གནོད་པ་མི་བྱེད་དོ་ཟེར་ནས་བཏང་། སྔགས་འཆང་གོས་དཀར་ལྕང་ལོ་ཅན་རྣམས་ལ་གནོད་པ་མ་བྱུང་བ་འདིའི་དྲིན་ཡིན། ）

杜迥仁波切关于努氏的这段记载，显然不是他的杜撰。因为从叙述的文字中我们发现，在形容迫害时用了“བདོ”这个词，这个词显然不常用于现代藏文中。从这点我们可以推断，他的这段记述可能引自别处。顺着这样的逻辑，我们发现这个古藏语动词出现在协钦·班玛南杰（1871-1926）所著《协钦教法史》的相关记述中[39]。在《协钦教法史》中，我们虽然见到这个动词，但在叙述赞普朗达玛与努氏的关系时，情节描述比杜迥仁波切的简略很多。从而有理由相信，杜迥仁波切的引文并非来自《协钦教法史》，两者可能来自更早的一部文献。

17 世纪郭若扎西历时 66 年（1807-1873）完成的、卷帙浩大的《郭扎佛教史》中，我们发现与杜迥仁波切的叙述同出一辙[40]。郭若扎西在讲述传奇人物莲花生大士的“二十五位高徒”时，出现了努氏胁迫赞普让步的叙述。在这个叙述中，郭若扎西用“བསྡོ”而非用“བདོ”这个动词表达迫害，显然从现代藏文的角度而言“བསྡོ”更符合表达。因此，我们困惑于杜迥仁波切在整体引用郭若扎西的叙述之时，为何未用“བསྡོ”这个更接近现代藏语的动词呢?

号称宁玛派第一部完整教法史的《娘氏宗教源流》，是由 12 世纪宁玛派早期传统重要人物，娘·尼玛沃色（1124-1192）所著。在这部重要的著作中，我们发现赞普朗达玛时期，拯救密咒师的人物并非是努氏，而是比努氏更早的同处努家族的努·南喀宁布。娘氏如此记载：

彼时迫害密咒师们。此时，具力者为努·南喀宁布。（赞普）曰：“嫁祸于他。”他答道：“请允许禅修本尊。”接着，用食指（亦即“忿怒手印”）引出雷电击中岩石。他言：“对赞普也实施此（忿怒手印）。”赞普答道：“不

39 《སྔ་འགྱུར་རྡོ་རྗེ་ཐེག་པ་གཙོ་བོར་གྱུར་པའི་སྒྲུབ་བརྒྱུད་ཤིང་རྟ་བརྒྱད་ཀྱི་བྱུང་བ་བརྗོད་པ》ཞེ་ཆེན་པདྨ་རྣམ་རྒྱལ་གྱིས་བརྩམས། བོད་ལྗོངས་བོད་ཡིག་དཔེ་རྙིང་དཔེ་སྐྲུན་ཁང་། ༢༠༡༢ ལོའི་པར་གཞི་དང་པོ། ཤ་༡༧༥།

40 《གུ་བཀྲའི་ཆོས་འབྱུང》གུ་རུ་བཀྲ་ཤིས་ཀྱིས་བརྩམས། རྡོ་རྗེ་རྒྱལ་པོས་བསྒྲིགས། ཀྲུང་གོའི་བོད་རིག་པ་དཔེ་སྐྲུན་ཁང་། ༡༩༩༠ ལོའི་པར་གཞི་དང་པོ། ཤ་༡༨༧།

祸害于你，从此不再迫害密咒师。”[41]

（དེ་ནས་སྔགས་པ་རྣམས་ཕབ། དེའི་དུས་སུ་མཐུ་ཆེ་བ་སྣུབས་ནམ་མཁའི་སྙིང་པོ་ཡིན་པས། དེར་ཁོང་ལ་སྐྱོན་འབེབས་ཟེར་བས། ཁོ་ན་རེ། ཡི་དམ་གྱི་ལྷ་སྒོམ་དུ་གསོལ་ཟེར་བས། སྡིགས་མཛུབ་གཅིག་མཛད་པས་ཐོག་ཕབ་ནས་བྲག་ལ་བརྒྱབ་པས། རྒྱལ་པོ་ཉིད་ལ་ཡང་བྱའོ་གསུངས་པས། ཁྱེད་ལ་སྐྱོན་མི་དབབ་བོ། ད་ཕྱིན་ཆད་སྔགས་པ་མི་རྡོ་འོ་ཞེས་ཟེར་རོ།）

在娘氏的这个叙述中，我们终于找到了协钦·班玛南杰和杜迥仁波切所用动词“བརྡོ”的出处，在此用了“རྡོ”这样的动词，但他们为何用前加字“བ”，已无从知晓。“རྡོ”这个动词在现代藏文中有“比拼”之意，但在娘氏的叙述情景中更应指“迫害”。这个不常用古藏语动词的出现，从某种程度上为我们提供了这样的线索，即后期宁玛派编纂史家所言之努氏与赞普朗达玛的叙述，可能最初源自娘氏关于努·南喀宁布的叙述，后来转嫁到努氏身上。

更加重要的是，郭若扎西、杜迥仁波切关于努氏的故事情节，毋庸置疑是复制12世纪娘氏对努·南喀宁布的叙述。不同的两个人物同时都用“忿怒手印”，引出雷电击中岩石，从而让这个“十恶不赦”的赞普恐惧万分，进而妥协于他们，最终成功地挽救了密咒师们。从而我们可断言努氏拯救密咒师的传闻，只不过是后期宁玛派史学编纂者们的臆想，并无多少历史根据。

由于相关资料之缺失，我们无从考证宁玛派史学家们从何时将娘氏关于努·南喀宁布的叙述转嫁到努氏名下，但这可能与努氏在宁玛派传统中影响日趋壮大有必然的联系。如前所述，在后期的宁玛派史学家眼中，努氏是宁玛派传统在雪域藏地传播的“中兴之主”，是内三密教传的总持有者。在这个话语中，整个宁玛派历史中总共也就这么三位重要人物，从这点来说努氏的重要性是不言而喻的。努氏的教传传承随着与新译各派的竞争，对宁玛派来说显得尤为重要，其最重要的传承者宿氏家族将其发扬壮大，并最终形成了藏传佛教史上影响甚广之经典体系——《宁玛派十万续》（རྙིང་མ་རྒྱུད་འབུམ）。相对于努氏在后期宁玛派的重要性，努·南喀宁布显然是较为黯淡的。在后期的历史记忆中，努·南喀宁布是前弘期很活跃的历史人物，但与努氏相比在后来构建宁玛派历史过程中，他的影响可能被打折扣了，或未得到应有的认可。努氏的传承者们，为了维护宁玛派内部自己的传统，宁愿歪曲历史根据也将努氏建构为在教法遭受灭顶之灾时与“暴君”相抗衡，并成为教法的“拯救者”。

41 《ཆོས་འབྱུང་མེ་ཏོག་སྙིང་པོ་སྦྲང་རྩིའི་བཅུད》ཉང་ཉི་མ་འོད་ཟེར་གྱིས་བརྩམས། བོད་ལྗོངས་བོད་ཡིག་དཔེ་རྙིང་དཔེ་སྐྲུན་ཁང་། ༢༠༡༢ལོའི་པར་གཞི་གསུམ་པ། ཤ་༤༠༠།

努氏“拯救者”角色的建构，或可能与另外一则被宁玛派编纂史家所广为叙述之情节有关。在这个叙述形式中，赞普迫害佛教徒的运动正如火如荼地进行，努氏试图运用密宗特殊“诛灭法”（སྒྲོལ་བ），以制止赞普的恶业。14 世纪成书的《龙钦教法史》（《教法源流·如意之宝藏》）中，对其如此记载：

> 其（热巴巾赞普）弟达磨乌东赞，绰号为朗达玛者执政。他是魔力所诱之凡夫，因此祖辈的诸宗教习俗被遗弃、诸法脉之传承被隔断、诸经院被毁坏、诸经典被堕入江河。还强迫出家僧还俗，不听从者被杀害。诸密咒师隐秘于荒野和雪山。见佛法被毁灭之情景，阿阇梨（努氏）感到暴戾之赞普将阻碍正法之兴盛，因此深感需要护法之“忿怒咒”。遂此，立刻赶赴印度。在喇嘛世持和祖拉贝格等处，获得无量护法之忿怒咒后，返回藏地。彼时，获悉赞普已被拉隆贝吉多杰者所弑杀，遂将这些咒语作为伏藏埋入，某些也传授给其弟子们。[42]
>
> （དེའི་གཅུང་པོ་ཁྲི་དར་མ་འུ་དུམ་བཙན་གླང་དར་མར་གྲགས་པ་དེས་རྒྱལ་སྲིད་བཟུང་སྟེ། དེ་བདུད་ཀྱི་བྱིན་གྱིས་བརླབས་པའི་སྐྱེས་བུ་ཞིག་བྱུང་ནས། ཡང་མེས་ཀྱི་ཆོས་ལུགས་ཐམས་ཅད་ནི་བོར། ཆོས་འཁོར་ཐམས་ཅད་ནི་ཉམས་སྨད། གཙུག་ལག་ཁང་ཐམས་ཅད་བཤིག་ཅིང་གླེགས་བམ་ཐམས་ཅད་ཆུ་ལ་འཕོ། རབ་ཏུ་བྱུང་བ་རྣམས་ཀྱང་ཕབ་ཅིང་ཁྲིམ་གྱི་གནས་སུ་བཀོད། མ་ཕབས་པ་དག་ནི་བཀྲོངས། སྔགས་འཆང་ཀུན་ཡང་རི་ཁྲོད་དང་གངས་ཁྲོད་དུ་ཡིབ་ཅིང་། སངས་རྒྱས་ཀྱི་བསྟན་པ་ནུབ་པར་མཐོང་ནས། དེར་སློབ་དཔོན་གྱི་ཐུགས་དགོངས་ལ། སྡིག་སྤྱོད་ཀྱི་རྒྱལ་པོ་འདི་འདྲ་བས། སངས་རྒྱས་ཀྱི་བསྟན་པ་དར་རྒྱས་སུ་མི་སྟེར་བར་འདུག་པས། བསྟན་པ་སྲུང་བའི་དྲག་སྔགས་ཤིག་དགོས་པར་འདུག་སྙིང་དུ་དགོངས་ནས། དེ་མ་ཐག་ཏུ་རྒྱ་གར་ལ་ཕར་ལོག་ཕྱིན་ཏེ། བླ་མ་བ་སུ་དྷ་ར་དང་། གཙུག་ལག་དཔལ་དགེ་ལ་སོགས་པ་རྣམས་ལ་བསྟན་པ་སྲུང་བའི་དྲག་སྔགས་ཀྱི་སྐོར་དཔག་ཏུ་མེད་པ་ཞུས་ནས་བྱོན་ཙ་ན། ལྷ་ལུང་དཔལ་གྱི་རྡོ་རྗེས་རྒྱལ་པོ་བཀྲོངས་ཟིན་ནས་འདུག་པས། བསྟན་སྲུང་དེ་དག་ཕྱིས་གཏེར་དུ་སྦས། ལ་ལ་སློབ་མ་ཀུན་ལ་སྤེལ་བ་ཡིན། ）

我们发现《龙钦教法史》中的这段叙述，被后期的宁玛派史学家们所普遍接受，

42 《ཆོས་འབྱུང་རིན་པོ་ཆེའི་གཏེར་མཛོད་བསྟན་པ་གསལ་བར་བྱེད་པའི་ཉི་འོད》 རྒྱལ་སྲས་ཐུགས་མཆོག་རྩལ་གྱིས་བརྩམས། བོད་ལྗོངས་བོད་ཡིག་དཔེ་རྙིང་དཔེ་སྐྲུན་ཁང་། ༡༩༩༣ལོའི་པར་གཞི་དང་པོ། ཤ་༤༡༡

譬如《宁玛十万续编纂史·遍满世界之庄严》[43]《郭扎佛教史》[44]和《杜迥教法史》[45]都有记述。在这则传统叙述中，所处的时代仍然是赞普毁灭佛法的“黑暗时期”，努氏仍旧被树立为教法的“拯救者”，只是这个形象最终未能建立，因为另外的“拯救者”，即拉隆贝吉多杰先于他。或许得益于这样的叙述，后期的宁玛派才有理由将早期史料中所述之努·南喀宁布的形象，转嫁到努氏的光环之下。

43 《དེ་བཞིན་གཤེགས་པས་ལེགས་པར་གསུངས་པའི་གསུང་རབ་རྒྱ་མཚོའི་སྙིང་པོར་གྱུར་པ་རིག་པ་འཛིན་པའི་སྡེ་སྣོད་དམ་སྔ་འགྱུར་རྒྱུད་འབུམ་རིན་པོ་ཆེའི་རྟོགས་པ་བརྗོད་པ་འཛམ་གླིང་མཐའ་གྲུ་ཁྱབ་པའི་རྒྱན་ཅེས་བྱ་བ་བཞུགས་སོ》 རིག་འཛིན་འཇིགས་མེད་གླིང་པས་བརྩམས། སི་ཁྲོན་དཔེ་སྐྲུན་ཚོགས་པ། སི་ཁྲོན་མི་རིགས་དཔེ་སྐྲུན་ཁང་། ༢༠༠༨ལོའི་པར་གཞི་དང་པོ། ཤ་༡༧༥།

44 《གུ་བཀྲའི་ཆོས་འབྱུང》 གུ་རུ་བཀྲ་ཤིས་ཀྱིས་བརྩམས། རྡོ་རྗེ་རྒྱལ་པོས་བསྒྲིགས། ཀྲུང་གོའི་བོད་རིག་པ་དཔེ་སྐྲུན་ཁང་། ༡༩༩༠ལོའི་པར་གཞི་དང་པོ། ཤ་༢༥༧།

45 《བདུད་འཇོམས་ཆོས་འབྱུང》 བདུད་འཇོམས་ཡེ་ཤེས་རྡོ་རྗེས་བརྩམས། སི་ཁྲོན་མི་རིགས་དཔེ་སྐྲུན་ཁང་། ༡༩༩༦ལོའི་པར་གཞི་དང་པོ། ཤ་༢༣༧།

吉德尼玛衮和他的阿里王朝

陈庆英[*]

谨以此文纪念英年逝世的古格·次仁加布先生

吐蕃王朝崩溃后一百多年的历史，是西藏历史记载最为残缺凌乱的一个时期。842年，赞普朗达玛遇刺后，吐蕃王朝开始崩溃。经过二十多年的云丹（yum brtan）和沃松（vod srungs）两位王子的王位之争，大臣贵族乃至拥兵自重的边将，纷纷卷入到两位王子为争夺赞普王位而进行的战乱中，后来又发生了吐蕃“平民犯上”的起义。到869年造反的平民起义军发掘吐蕃赞普王陵，吐蕃王朝结束。不过，和其他地区的历史发展不同，起义军并没有建立一个新的王朝来取代吐蕃王朝，而赞普的后裔们无力建立一个强大的政权，甚至一位王子的几个儿子也难以合成为一个有能够较长时期统治一片地域的政权，他们分化消解的趋势长期延续不断。因此可以说，吐蕃王朝的崩溃在很大程度上是保持一个君王的赞普王位继承体制的崩溃。在延绵的混战和动荡中，作为赞普后裔的首领们更乐于采取让诸子自立的游牧部落常见的财产和部属分割的办法，以图赞普的名号在自己的家族中能够保持得更加久远一些。虽然他们在心底里有恢复吐蕃王朝的统一的愿望，但是实际行动中却有意无意造成更加分立的局面。当然，与这一大趋势不同，由于吐蕃王朝二百多年中统一青藏高原的文治武功，特别是统一的文字和律法、佛教的推行，社会上也有趋向复兴王朝统一高原的努力的例子，一个是河湟谷地的吐蕃部落，迎请一位赞普的后裔来做首领，在部落联盟的基础上建立起维持了一百多年的唃厮啰王朝。另一个是在高原西部的古格王朝，而拉喇嘛益西沃即是古格王室的一位有深远影响的历史人物。

* 陈庆英：中国藏学研究中心历史研究所研究员。

古格王室是赞普朗达玛的儿子沃松的后裔。据萨迦派三祖扎巴坚赞（grags pa rgyal mtshan）的著作，认为贝考赞为沃松与觉若妃·杰姆之子，于893年（藏历水牛年）生于雅隆旁塘。藏文史籍称沃松是朗达玛的遗腹子，他应该是生于842年，按这一说法，贝考赞出生时沃松已经50岁。沃松占据约茹（今西藏山南），晚年时，在同云丹一系的斗争处于弱势，加上平民犯上起义的打击，使他无法立足于约茹，被迫迁移至后藏叶茹地区。905年，沃松去世，其子贝考赞在后藏的仲巴拉孜（日喀则拉孜县）为他大办丧事后继承王位，在后藏地方建立起贝考赞王系的势力范围，执政18年。贝考赞选择在年楚河上游兴建了嘉喀孜（rgyal mkhar rtse）城堡，作为自己的王宫。由于这一城堡的名称，后来出现了江孜（rgyal rtse）这一地域名称。贝考赞娶有两妃，侧妃琛氏妃·尊尼（mchims bzav btsun ne）为他生有长子赤扎西孜巴贝（khri bkra shis brtsegs pa dpal），长妃那囊氏·勒尊（sna nam bzav legs btsun）生有次子吉德尼玛衮（skyid lde nyi ma mgon）[1]。贝考赞的统治也不稳固，最终激起一场贵族平民大规模反叛，贝考赞也在这场反叛中被杀[2]。贝考赞被杀后，他在约茹的领地大部分丧失，其长子赤扎西孜巴贝在嘉喀孜（今江孜）继承王位；次子吉德尼玛衮被迫移居到更西部的象雄茹（阿里地方）去发展势力[3]。

赤扎西孜巴贝有贝德（dpal lde）、沃德（vod lde）、吉德（skyid lde）等三子，史称下部“三德”。这里说的“下部”是相对于在阿里地区的吉德尼玛衮的后裔来说，阿里地区在上部，年楚河地区的赤扎西孜巴贝的后裔在下部。看来在赤扎西孜巴贝在世时，他的领地还大致维持一种统一的局面，在他去世后又出现了分化，他们的子孙仍然是各据一方，互不统属。其中有一些在后来的历史上也很有名。贝德的后裔向南发展，建立了一个占据今天吉隆地区的贡塘小王朝。沃德的后裔中，有一支去了甘青河湟地区，成为唃厮啰政权的首领，还有一支到了山南雅隆，其中一个子孙玉坚（g·yu spyan）被拉萨河流域的地方首领嘎米·云丹雍仲（gar mi yon tan g·yung drung）迎请至墨竹工卡的恰萨地方（bya sa）[4]掌权后，开始有了雅隆觉卧王系。玉坚的一个儿子出家修法，被称为拉隆·旺秋（lha lung gi dbang phyug），担任恰萨寺法座。其后恰萨寺历任法座都由他们家族的出家僧人担任，形成雅隆觉卧政教结合的地方势

1　岗日瓦·群英多吉：《雪域西部阿里三围历史》，拉萨：西藏人民出版社，1996年，第36-37页。

2　恰白·次旦平措、诺章·吴坚等著，陈庆英等译：《西藏通史——松石宝串》，中国西藏杂志社、西藏藏文古籍出版社，2004年，第226-227页。

3　恰白·次旦平措、诺章·吴坚等著，陈庆英等译：《西藏通史——松石宝串》，第226页。

4　恰萨地方（bya sa）是指噶当派的怯喀寺所在的地方，怯喀寺今译为切嘎寺，在拉萨市墨竹工卡县县城东北。

力[5]。吉德的后裔留在年楚河流域一带，其中的一个孙子介则（lce btsad）兴建了白朗杰喀土城，派兵驻守，统治年楚河下游。在介则的资助下，罗顿·多吉旺秀等人在这里建造了佛教后弘期最早的佛寺娘麦坚贡寺（在夏鲁寺附近，后来属于夏鲁寺）。其再传弟子介尊·西饶森格亦在杰则后裔的资助下建造了夏鲁金殿，其后裔在元代被封为夏鲁万户，其权势和财富均得到很大的发展[6]。

关于吉德尼玛衮前往西部阿里地区的原因和经过，史籍记载也十分简略，学界存在着不同的说法。结合当时的时代和贝考赞父子在后藏地区的境遇看，恰白·次旦平措等先生所著的《西藏通史——松石宝串》的说法应该是最接近实际情形的。该书说："吉德尼玛衮长大之后，云丹派系占据了他的大部分地域，因而被迫移至阿里。据说在临行时，父王说：'（那里）如同张开的南门隅（lho mon）深谷，常受到勃律（vbru sha）、巴尔提（sbal ti）和地上的蚂蚁等人和非人的侵害，故此要按显密宗的仪轨供养本尊及护法神，只要这样做，阿里赞普之政权世系及庶民就会兴旺发达。'他前往阿里时，尚·巴擦·仁庆德（zhang pa tshab rin chen lde）大臣和觉若·列扎拉勒（cog ro legs sgra lha legs）等大臣送行至后藏吉马雍仲（bye ma g·yung drung）地方，临别时巴擦氏敬献了一件狼皮大氅，觉若氏敬献一头骡子，并伤心地痛哭了一场，他们舍不得分离。尼玛衮对二大臣讲：我到阿里后如能成为一名君主，请二位为我各派一名妃子来，说毕就向阿里进发，最后住在玛旁雍湖（ma pham g·yu mtsho，一神湖名）之北边。"[7]又说："《王朝金链》中记载道：'吉德尼玛衮在民变时由白玛苏嘎穷·贝丹珠（vbal ma zug gar khyung dpal ldan grub）和米纳巴·阿嘎拔杂（me nyag pa a ka bdzra）二人为首的成百上千骑士护送前往阿里。途中，因属下用布巾擦拭鱼和蛋，然后敬献与他，故而使用布巾成为上部西藏王族之习俗'[8]。以上记载连贯起来应该是，吉德尼玛衮似乎被某个民变势力逐至阿里，临行时其父不忍心离别，就如何面对今后可能遇到的事情进行劝导，二大臣送至后藏上部，敬献衣服及坐骑骡子。放逐到阿里时以白玛苏嘎穷为首的一队骑兵看护之，食用本不喜欢的鱼和蛋等。总之，可以断定吉德尼玛衮是被逐往阿里的看法是符合历史事实的。"[9]从这些记载看，吉德尼玛衮是其父贝考赞的晚年由于其势力在云丹的子孙和民变势力的打击下而局限于江

5　王森：《西藏佛教发展史略》，北京：中国藏学出版社，2002 年，第 60-61 页。

6　达仓宗巴·班觉桑布著，陈庆英译：《汉藏史集》，拉萨：西藏人民出版社，1986 年，第 228-230 页。

7　恰白·次旦平措、诺章·吴坚等著，陈庆英等译：《西藏通史——松石宝串》，第 230 页。岗日瓦·群英多吉：《雪域西部阿里三围历史》，第 37 页。

8　恰白·次旦平措、诺章·吴坚等著，陈庆英等译：《西藏通史——松石宝串》，第 230 页。

9　恰白·次旦平措、诺章·吴坚等著，陈庆英等译：《西藏通史——松石宝串》，第 231 页。

孜和拉孜，而且形势危急，因此决定以长子赤扎西孜巴贝继承江孜和拉孜地区，而让次子吉德尼玛衮到西部的阿里地区去发展，开辟新的统治地域。因此说吉德尼玛衮被迫前往阿里是符合当时的形势和情理的，不过他前往阿里很可能是贝考赞的一种让他去扩大统治区域的安排，这从他去阿里时有成百上千的骑兵护送就可以看出。

阿里地区古代存在一个象雄王国，古代象雄王国可分为里象雄、中象雄和外象雄三部分（或上、中、下象雄三部分）。[10] 由于位处西藏与克什米尔、印度、中亚、波斯等多个文化圈的楔合部，象雄的西部地区在种族、宗教和文化等方面形成了兼容并蓄的多元化传统，这也是象雄文明的标志性特征之一。著名法国藏学家石泰安很早就注意到这一点："西部地区对西藏文明的形成曾起过重大作用。那里既与犍陀罗和乌仗国（斯瓦特）接壤，又与该地区的小国毗邻，希腊、伊朗和印度诸文明中的古老成分都经由那里传至吐蕃。"[11] 象雄是苯教最早传播的地区，或者说苯教最早是在象雄形成，然后传播到青藏高原的各个地区的。吐蕃王朝从松赞干布时期开始，经过几次战争，征服了象雄，按照吐蕃王朝的军政制度，将象雄编为吐蕃的一个茹，征调象雄的军兵和部落充当前锋参加吐蕃王朝和唐朝的战争以及在中亚和唐朝、大食争夺勃律的战争。由于常年的战争和差役征发，到吐蕃王朝的中后期，许多地区人口减少，民生凋敝。由于地处偏远，交通困难，吐蕃后期的史料中很少提到象雄，那里被认为是一个边远蛮荒之地，所以在吐蕃王朝崩溃之后的初期，各个争霸的地方势力也极少顾及西部的这一片地区。贝考赞和吉德尼玛衮也只是在占据后藏而又地位不稳之时，才被迫决定由吉德尼玛衮前往阿里去谋求发展的。

吉德尼玛衮到阿里以后，经历了一个艰难的开拓过程。据记载，吉德尼玛衮品行高尚、智慧过人，当他抵达热拉（ra la）一带时，受到了当地人的尊敬，权势亦有所增强。于木马年（934 年）兴建了热拉卡玛宫（ra la kha dmar），次年（藏历木羊年、公元 935 年）又修建孜托甲日宫（rtse tho rgya ri）。看来热拉地方当在今天的阿里地区的仲巴县，吉德尼玛衮是以此为根据地，先在这里立足，再向今阿里地区的

10 关于象雄疆域范围，1985 年才让太在《古老的象雄文明》一文中，首次引用了苯教学者扎敦·格桑丹贝坚赞所著《世界地理概说》关于象雄疆域范围的详细记述："里象雄为冈底斯山西面三个月路程之外的波斯（bar zig）、巴达山（bha dag shan）和巴拉（bha lag）一带。中象雄在冈底斯山西面一天的路程之外，东面和蕃（bod）接壤。那里有象雄王国的都城——琼隆银城，这片土地曾经为象雄十八国王统治，亦是著名的苯教四贤竹、许、芭、梅（bru zhu spa rmevu）的诞生地。外象雄以琼波六峰山为中心，也叫孙巴精雪（sum pa gying shod）。包括三十九个部族，嘉德二十五族，即现在的安多上部地区，绝大部分住民信仰苯教。"迄今为止，上述史料为藏文文献中有关古代象雄王国疆域范围的最为详尽的记载，曾在中国藏学界内广为引用。参见才让太：《古老的象雄文明》，《西藏研究》1985 年第 2 期，第 96-97 页。

11 石泰安著，耿昇译：《西藏的文明》，北京：中国藏学出版社，1999 年，第 34 页。

腹地发展。“此后，为了调查阿里三围之实情，吉德尼玛衮派去三位精明大臣，前往三围各地调查，前去布让一带调查的大臣返回后，拜见君王。君王寻问布让一带情况时，大臣回禀曰：其地如同剖开的马腹被雪山所环抱，其地之人像罗刹。前去古格一带调查的大臣回来奏曰：该地如白色鱼肚，由石山所环抱，人似绵羊。从玛尔域调查回来的大臣奏曰：玛尔域如同积满水的洼地，由雪山所环抱，人同蛤蟆一样。君王听了上述情况后下令：我等王臣礼供上师三宝，祈祷发愿，逐步前往那些地方。他们一行先到布让，在那里采取了发展商业、满足人们食品需要等措施，使当地人深受感动，吉德尼玛衮受到人们敬重，于是制定了相应的法规，逐渐把布让收归治下。此后以武力征服了古格（gu ge），复又发兵玛尔城，占据该地区，并制定了适合该地的法规。对那些不服从尼玛衮统治的人员，轻者让其承认罪过，若不如实承认罪过，继续违抗，将给予砍头的处罚，如此软硬兼施，建立了统治整个阿里三围的政权。”[12]从这一记载看，当时西部阿里地区是处在一种部落分散的状态，并没有一个比较强大的势力可以和他对抗，而吉德尼玛衮又采取了一些改善民生、争取人心的措施，减少当地民众的对抗心理。可能还有他的吐蕃赞普后裔的身份，也是一面能够号召民众的旗帜，使得他作为一个外来的势力能够在较短的时期在阿里建立起自己的统治。当然在这个过程中，也免不了有武力征伐甚至有对反抗者的杀戮。

吉德尼玛衮在阿里站住脚以后，在布让（今普兰县）兴建了一座王宫，史称“尼松寝宫”（sku mkhar nyi gzung），其大臣有芒喀（mang dkar）和穷布（khyung po）二人。据说，当举行尼松寝宫完工庆典时，从天上发出了如下预言：“如同灿烂的太阳照耀着众生一样，吐蕃王国出现在布让，才使得佛法兴隆昌盛。”[13]建立城堡实际上即是建立自己领地的首邑，是当时地方势力的首领得到一片领地以后通常都要采取的措施。吉德尼玛衮还给自己的领地起了一个专门的称呼即“阿里”（mngav ris）。这一片地域在吐蕃王朝之前被称为象雄，曾经建立过一个象雄王国，在吐蕃王朝征服象雄以后，在该地区设立了象雄茹，是吐蕃本部的卫藏四茹之外的一个茹。在现今能够见到的吐蕃王朝的文献中，把包括现今阿里地区在内的广大地域统称为象雄，没有见到过“阿里”这一称呼。但是到元代的文献中，“阿里”这一名称就广泛出现，而“象雄”一词就只是作为一种吐蕃王朝及其以前的地理名称才出现。所以有学者推测，“阿里”一词应该是在吉德尼玛衮统治这一片地区之后，才开始出现了“阿里”这一地域名

12 恰白·次旦平措、诺章·吴坚等著，陈庆英等译：《西藏通史——松石宝串》，第230页。
13 岗日瓦·群英多吉：《雪域西部阿里三围历史》，第37-38页。

称[14]。至于吉德尼玛衮这样做的原因，首先可能是为了区分贝考赞的长子赤扎西孜巴贝和次子吉德尼玛衮的领地的不同。赤扎西孜巴贝的领地是在后藏，是吐蕃王朝的本部四茹中的叶茹和茹拉两个茹，而赤扎西孜巴贝作为贝考赞的长子，继承了赞普的名号，被认为是吐蕃王朝的直接的延续，而吉德尼玛衮的领地在吐蕃四茹以外，是他新开辟的一片赞普后裔的领地。这就需要给吉德尼玛衮的身份做出一个新的定义，看来他被臣下称为或者他自己选择了一个“阿达”（mngav-bdag）即“领主”的称号。这一称号表明他和赤扎西孜巴贝的关系，他在初期还未在西部完全站住脚的时候，他作为赤扎西孜巴贝的亲兄弟从赤扎西孜巴贝的势力中分出来而统治这片土地，因而具有一定的从属关系。但是在新开辟的这一批地区中他又是一个有独自行使权力的统治者。到后来他能够完全行使权力的时候，他的“阿达”（mngav-bdag）称号就有了与赤扎西孜巴贝的“赞普”的称号差不多相等的意义。这样，对他的领地就需要有一个新的称呼，这样“阿里”（mngav-ris）即“阿达的领地”就随之出现。对于这一地域名称的来历，《汉藏史集》记载说：“吉德尼玛衮的儿子为贝吉衮与德祖衮、扎西尼玛衮，他们被称为上部的‘三衮’。吉德尼玛衮先到上部，将上部各地收归治下，总称为“阿里”，命长子贝吉衮统治玛域、努热，次子德祖衮统治象雄、吉觉、尼贡、茹托、普兰、玛措等六个地方，幼子扎西尼玛衮统治迦尔夏、桑格尔。由此，产生了‘阿里三围’的名称。”[15]为什么象雄这个地域名称从吉德尼玛衮的时期开始逐渐弃而不用，我们推测可能的原因是：第一，吉德尼玛衮的领地与象雄的地域并不完全重合，他的领地的主要部分是象雄的核心地区，但是这并不是象雄的全部，而且他的领地的西部和南部的一些地域又是在象雄之外。所以象雄并不能准确表示他的领地。第二，象雄是吐蕃的属部，用象雄来表示他的领地，就会使他的身份变成为避居于属地的赞普后裔，比起在卫藏地区的赞普后裔的各个地方势力，那就似乎要低一些。因此需要避免造成自己是逃到象雄去的蛮荒之地的头领的印象。第三，吐蕃王朝早期时就有囊日论赞占领森波杰的岩波后，将岩波更名为澎波的先例，因此吉德尼玛衮选择了将其在卫藏以西占领的地域新起名为“阿里”的办法。由此“阿里”这一地域名称开始出现在西藏的历史中。从这个意义上说，可以认为是吉德尼玛衮建立了一个阿里王朝，这个王朝的君主仍然沿用赞普的名称，但是其领地有了一个明确的称呼即是“阿里”。

14 巴桑旺堆：《11 世纪的上部阿里与下部阿里》，收入中国藏学研究中心和维也纳大学合编《西部西藏的文化历史》，北京：中国藏学出版社，2008 年，第 75-76 页。

15 班觉桑布：《汉藏史集》（藏文版），成都：四川民族出版社，1985 年，第 215-216 页。陈庆英汉译本，西藏人民出版社，1986 年，第 128-129 页。

ལྷ་བླ་མ་ཡེ་ཤེས་འོད་ཀྱི་འདས་ཡུལ་སྐོར་གྱི་དོགས་དཔྱོད།

རྨེ་རུ་ཚེ་རིང་དོན་གྲུབ།*

བཀའ་གདམས་གསར་རྙིང་གིས་གཙོས་པའི་བོད་བརྒྱུད་ནང་བསྟན་གྱི་གྲུབ་མཐའ་སྣ་བ་ཤས་ཆེ་བས། བཙན་པོའི་གདུང་རྒྱུད་ཀྱི་སྐུ་དྲག་དགེ་སློང་ལྷ་བླ་མ་ཡེ་ཤེས་འོད་ཀྱིས་སྐབས་དེར་རྒྱ་གར་དང་ཁ་ཆེའི་ཡུལ་ནས་པཎྜི་ཏ་པཱ་ལ་རྣམ་གསུམ་སོགས་མཁས་གྲུབ་དུ་མ་བོད་ལ་གདན་དྲངས་པ་མ་ཟད། ལོ་ཙཱ་བ་དང་པཎྜི་ཏ་དུ་མ་གསོ་སྐྱོང་གནང་བ་དང་དུས་མཚུངས་བཤད་སྒྲུབ་གཉིས་ལྡན་གྱི་དགོན་པ་གསར་བཞེངས་སོགས་ཀྱི་སྒོ་ནས་སངས་རྒྱས་ཀྱི་བསྟན་པའི་མེ་རོ་སྤོད་ནས་གསོས་པའི་ངོ་མཚར་ཆེ་བའི་མཛད་རྗེས་ལ། དད་སེམས་དང་ཡིད་ཆེས་ཐལ་དྲག་པའི་དབང་གིས་ཁོང་གིས་སངས་རྒྱས་ཆོས་ལུགས་ཀྱི་ཆེད་དུ་རང་གི་སྲོག་ཀྱང་གར་ལོག་གི་བཙོན་དོང་དུ་བློས་བཏང་བའི་དཔའ་བོའི་གཟུགས་བརྙན་ཕྱི་རབས་ཀུན་སྣུ་ལོང་གཡོ་བ་ཞིག་བསྐྲུན་པར་གདའ།

དེ་ཡང་འབྲོམ་སྟོན་རྒྱལ་བའི་འབྱུང་གནས་ཀྱིས་རྭ་སྒྲེང་དགོན་དུ་མཛད་ཞེས་གསུངས་པའི་《ཇོ་བོ་རྗེའི་རྣམ་ཐར་ལམ་ཡིག་ཆོས་ཀྱི་འབྱུང་གནས་》(རྭ་སྒྲེང་དགོན་ཕྱག་འདེབས་པའི་སྤྱི་ལོ་1056ནས་འབྲོམ་སྟོན་གཤེགས་པའི་སྤྱི་ལོ་1064བར་ལ་མཛད་པར་ངེས།) སུ་"རྒྱལ་པོ་ཆེན་པོ་ལྷ་བཙུན་པས་……ངེད་ཁུ་དབོན་གཉིས་ཀྱིས་མི་འདི་གོ་ཆོད་དམ། འདིས་བློ་གཏད་ཐུབ་བམ། འདིས་སངས་རྒྱས་ཀྱི་བསྟན་པ་ལ་སེམས་སྙམ་པ་ལ་བྱ་དགའ་བྱིན་ཅིང་། གསེར་སྲང་བརྒྱ་སྐོར་རེས་མ་མཐའ་བྱས་ནས་དཔོན་གཡོག་རགས་པ་རེ་ཁྲིད་གདན་འདྲེན་དུ་བཏང་བ་ཡིན་ནའང་། ཕལ་ཆེར་ཚད་པ་དང་དུག་སྦྲུལ་གྱིས་ཁྱེར། ནོར་དང་སྲོག་མགོ་གང་ཡང་མ་ཐོན་པར་བྱུང་། ནོར་འཕྲོད་ཁྲིད་རང་དང་མཇལ་ཀྱང་འདི་ལྟར་བསྟན་པའི་བྱ་བ་ཆེས་པས་གདན་མ་འདྲོངས། དེ་ལ་ཡང་བློ་མ་བསད་པར་ལྷ་ཆེན་པོ་དེས། བལ་ཡུལ་གྱི་མཐའ་འཁོབ་ཏུ་ཇོ་བོ་སྤྱན་འདྲེན་པའི་གསེར་འཚོལ་དུ་བྱོན་པས། གར་ལོག་གི་རྒྱལ་པོས་ཆོས་ཀྱི་རྒྱལ་པོ་པཎྜི་ཏ་གསེར་འཚོལ་བར་རིག་ནས། འདིའི་ཕ་མེས་རྣམས་ཀྱིས་སྔོན་ཡང་སངས་རྒྱས་ཀྱི་བསྟན་པ་དར་བར་བྱེད་འོང་བས་བཟུང་ལ་བཙོན་ཁང་དུ་ཆུག་ཅིག་ཟེར་ནས་མནར། དེ་བདག་གིས་ཐོས་ནས་སྡུག་བསྔལ་བའི་སྟོབས་ཀྱིས་རྟ་པ་བརྒྱ་བྱས་ཏེ། ཁུ་བོ་བཀློག་ཏུ་ཕྱིན་པས་གར་ལོག་གི་རྒྱལ་པོ་ཕ་ཚན་ཆེས་ནས་མ་བཀློག་ཡང་དམག་བྱས་ནས་ཁོ་ལ་བརྒྱབ་ན་ལྡོགས་པར་སྣང་སྟེ། དེའི་བར་དུ་མི་དང་འགྲོ་བ་མང་པོའི་སྲོག་ཆད་པར་

* 次仁顿珠，西藏社会科学院宗教研究所助理研究员。

སྣང་བ་དང་། ང་རང་ལ་ཡང་བར་ཆོད་བྱུང་ན་ཇོ་བོ་སྤྱན་མི་འདྲོངས་པར་གདའ་བས་ཁོ་དང་ཐབས་མཁས་པས་བསྟུན་གྱིས་བསླུས་པ་དང་། ལ་ཁོ་ན་རེ། འོ་ན་ཁྱེད་རང་པཎྜི་ཏ་གདན་འདྲེན་པའི་འགྲོ་གསོལ། ཁྱེད་རང་ཡང་ངའི་འོག་ཏུ་ཞུགས། ཡང་ན་གསེར་རྒྱལ་པོ་རང་དང་མཉམ་པ་ཅིག་ཁྱེར་ལ་ཤོག དེ་ནས་རྒྱལ་པོ་བཏང་གི་ཟེར་བ་ལ། གསེར་ལ་འདམས་ནས་གསེར་སྲང་བརྒྱ་ཐམ་པ་ཁྱེར་ཏེ། རྒྱལ་པོ་བསླུས་པས་ཀྱང་ཁོ་མ་ཉན། དེ་ནས་ལུས་དང་མཉམ་པ་ཅིག་ཁྱེར་ནས་བསླུས་པས་ཀྱང་ཐམས་ཅད་ཚང་བ་ཅིག་དགོས་ཟེར་ནས་ཁོ་མ་ཉན། དེར་ཁུ་བོ་ཁྲི་སྨན་ན་བཙུན་དེ་འོ་བརྒྱལ་བར་བཞུགས་པའི་སྒོ་དྲུང་དུ་ཕྱིན་ནས་ཁུ་བོ་ལ་བོས་ཏེ། བཀའ་དྲིན་ཆེན་པོ། སྔོན་གྱི་ལས་ཐོག་ཏུ་བབ་པ་ཡིན་པས། ངས་ཁོ་ལ་དམག་བརྒྱབ་ནས་བཟློག་ན་ནི་སྐྱེ་བོ་ཚན་པོ་ཆེ་ཕུང་ལ་བཏང་ནས་རང་རེ་གཉིས་ཀྱང་ངན་སོང་དུ་འགྲོ་དགོས་པར་སྣང་། པཎྜི་ཏ་གདན་མ་དྲངས་པར་ཁྱེད་རང་ངེད་ཀྱི་འོག་ཏུ་ཞུགས་ཟེར་བ་པ་ནི། ཆོས་བློས་བཏང་ནས་སྡིག་རྒྱལ་གྱི་འོག་དེ་ནས་གསེར་ཁྱོད་རང་ཙམ་ཞིག་དགོས་ཟེར་བ་ལ་གསེར་བཙལ་བས། ཁྱེད་ཀྱི་སྐུ་ལུས་དང་མཉམ་པའི་ཚོད་ཙམ་ཞིག་རྙེད། དེས་ཁོ་མ་ཉན་པས་ད་ངས་དབུ་ཙམ་ཅིག་རྙེད་པ་དང་བསྲུར་འོང་གིས། དེའི་བར་དུ་སྔོན་གྱི་ལས་ལ་སེམས་པ་དང་། དཀོན་མཆོག་གསུམ་ལ་གསོལ་བ་འདེབས་པ་དང་། སྙིང་པོ་ཆེ་བྲང་འོག་ཏུ་བཅུག་པའི་སོ་ནམ་མཛད་དགོས་པ་ཡིན། ཞེས་ཞུས་པ་དང་། ཁུ་བོ་བཞད་ཅིག་མཛད་ནས། ཁྱོད་ལའང་གཅེས་སྤྲུག་སྟུམ་ཟན་མའི་པགས་ཤིག་ཡོད། དཀའ་སྤྱད་དང་སྙིང་རུས་མི་ནུས་སྙམ་པ་ཡིན་ཏེ། ང་ཤི་ཡང་ཁྱོད་ཀྱིས་ཕ་མེས་ཀྱི་རྣམ་སྲོལ་སྐྱོང་བར་སྣང་། ཁྱོད་ཀྱི་དེ་གོ་བ་ཆེ། ང་དེས་ཆོག ངའི་བསམ་པ་ལ་བོད་འདིར་ཆོས་ཁྲིམས་ཤིག་མ་འཚོས་པར་ང་ཤི་ན་མི་ཚུང་བར་འདུག་སྙམ་པ་ཡིན་ཏེ། ད་ང་ན་སོ་ཡང་རྒས་འདིར་ང་ད་ལན་མ་ཤི་ཡང་ཚེ་ལོ་བཅུ་ཡིན། སྔར་ཚེ་འཁོར་བ་ཐོག་མ་མེད་པ་ནས། ཆོས་ཀྱི་ཕྱིར་གཅིག་ཀྱང་ཤི་བ་མེད། ད་ལན་ཆོས་ཕྱིར་ཤི་ན་ལེགས་པ་ཡིན་པས། རྒྱལ་པོ་འདི་ལ་གསེར་སེ་བ་ར་ཏི་ཅིག་ཀྱང་མི་སྟེར། གསེར་ང་རང་ཙམ་རྙེད་པ་ཤིན་ཏུ་ཇམས་ཆེ་ན་ད་མགོ་བོ་ཙམ་པ་ག་ན་རྙེད། གསེར་ཐམས་ཅད་རྒྱ་གར་དུ་ཁྱེར་ལ་ད་ཙུང་དུ་པཎྜི་ཏ་དེ་གདན་ཅི་འདྲོངས་ཀྱིས། པཎྜི་ཏ་ཆེན་པོའི་སྣན་དུ་ཡང་། ང་ན་རེ། ངས་ཁྱེད་དང་སངས་རྒྱས་ཀྱི་བསྟན་པའི་ཕྱིར་ལུས་སྲོག་གར་ལོག་གི་རྒྱལ་པོ་ངན་པ་ལ་བྱིན་ཡོད་པས་ཚེ་རབས་ཐམས་ཅད་དུ་བདག་ལ་ཐུགས་རྗེས་འཛིན་པ་དང་། ངའི་བསམ་པའི་གཙོ་བོ། ཁྱེད་བོད་དུ་བྱོན་ནས་སངས་རྒྱས་ཀྱི་བསྟན་པ་དར་བར་བྱེད་པ་ཡིན་པས། དེ་ཁོ་ན་བཞིན་དུ་མཛད་པ་དང་། སྐྱེ་བ་འདིའི་འོག་རོལ་ཏུ་ཁྱེད་དང་ངེས་པར་མཇལ་བར་བྱིན་གྱིས་བརླབ་ཏུ་གསོལ། ཞེས་ངའི་འཕྲིན་མཛོད་ཅིག་དེ་ལྟར་ལགས་པས་ང་བློས་ཐོངས་ལ་སངས་རྒྱས་བསྟན་པ་ལ་སོམས་ཤིག་གསུངས། དེ་ནས་ཁུ་བོ་གར་ལོག་གི་རྒྱལ་པོས་མེད་པར་བྱས་པའི་གཏམ་དེ་རྣམས་མགོན་པོ་ཨ་ཏི་ཤའི་སྣན་དུ་ཐོངས།"[1]ཞེས་དང་ཐོག་མར་འཁོད་པའི་ལྷ་བླ་མ་ཡེ་ཤེས་འོད་ཀྱིས་ཆོས་ཀྱི་ཕྱིར་རང་སྲོག་གར་ལོག་གི་བཙོན་དོང་དུ་བཏང་བའི་མི་སེམས་འགྱུལ་བའི་སྙིང་གཏམ་དེའི་ཤུགས་རྐྱེན་ལས། ཕྱིས་སུ་བྱུང་བའི་མཁས་པ་ཤས་ཆེས་མངའ་རིས་ཁུལ་གྱི་ཡིག་ཚང་དག་ལ་གཟུ་བོའི་ཞིབ་དཔྱད་ཡེ་ནས་མ་མཛད་པར། སྦུ་མཐུད་གོང་གི་ལྷ་ཚུལ་ལ་གཞི་

1 《བཀའ་གདམས་ཕ་ཆོས》ཤ230ལས་དྲངས། འབྲོམ་སྟོན་རྒྱལ་བའི་འབྱུང་གནས་སོགས་ཀྱིས་མཛད། མཚོ་སྔོན་མི་རིགས་དཔེ་སྐྲུན་ཁང་གིས་1994ལོའི་ཟླ་7པར་པར་དུ་བསྐྲུན།

བཅོལ་ནས་རང་རང་གི་མོས་པ་དང་མཐུན་པའི་ལྷ་བླ་མ་ཡེ་ཤེས་འོད་ཀྱི་གཏམ་སྣ་ཚོགས་གཅིག་མཇུག་གཉིས་མཐུད་དང་སྤེལ་བར་སྣང་།

ཁོ་བོས་ད་ཕན་མཇལ་བའི་དེབ་ཐེར་ལས་ཐོག་མར་ལྷ་ཚུལ་དེའི་རྗེས་འབྲངས་པ་ནི་ཚལ་པ་ཀུན་དགའ་རྡོ་རྗེ་ལགས་ཏེ། དེ་ཡང་ཁོང་གིས་དུས་རབས་བཅུ་བཞི་པའི་དུས་དཀྱིལ་བོད་རབ་བྱུང་དྲུག་པའི་མེ་ཁྱི་ལོར་(སྤྱི་ལོ་1346) མཛད་པའི་《དེབ་ཐེར་དམར་པོ་》ལས་"ཡབ་ནི་ལྷ་བླ་མ་ཡེ་ཤེས་འོད་ཅེས་བྱའོ། ཁོང་རང་ཡང་རྒྱ་གར་དུ་བྱོན་པས། ལམ་དུ་གར་ལོག་གི་དམག་གིས་བཟུང་སྟེ། བོད་ཀྱི་གསེར་བསྡུས་ནས་བླུ་བར་བརྩམས་ནའང་། སྐུ་ལུས་ཙམ་གཅིག་རྙེད་པ་ལ་དབུ་ཙམ་གཅིག་མ་རྙེད་པར་བསྒྲོངས།"[2]ཞེས་པས་མཁྱེན་ནུས། འོན་ཀྱང་དེར་ལྷ་བླ་མ་ཡེ་ཤེས་འོད་གར་ལོག་གིས་བསྒྲོངས་པའི་གནས་ཚུལ་ཙམ་ལས་ཁོང་རྒྱ་གར་དུ་བྱོན་དགོས་པའི་ཀུན་སློང་ངོ་མ་ཅི་ཡིན་གསལ་བཤད་མཛད་མེད། དེའི་རྗེས་ཀྱི་དུས་རབས་བཅུ་བཞིའི་དུས་མཇུག་བོད་རབ་བྱུང་བདུན་པའི་ས་འབྲུག་(སྤྱི་ལོ་1388) ལོར་ས་སྐྱ་བསོད་ནམས་རྒྱལ་མཚན་གྱིས་མཛད་པའི་《རྒྱལ་རབས་གསལ་བའི་མེ་ལོང་》ལས་"འདི་གསུམ་གྱི་དུས་སུ་ལྷ་བླ་མ་ཡེ་ཤེས་འོད་ཀྱིས། སངས་རྒྱས་ཀྱི་བསྟན་པ་ལ་དགོངས་ནས། རྒྱ་གར་དུ་པཎྜི་ཏ་གདན་འདྲེན་བྱོན་པས་ལམ་དུ་མུ་སྟེགས་པའི་དམག་གིས་བཟུང་། དགེ་ཕྱོགས་ཀྱི་ཡོན་ཏན་སྐྱེད་པའི་རྩ་སྒོ་ཐམས་ཅད་མི་བཙས་བསྲིགས་ཏེ་རྫོངས་པར་བྱས་སོ། དེའི་གཏམ་ལྷ་བླ་མ་བྱང་ཆུབ་འོད་ཀྱིས་གསན་ཏེ། གསེར་དཔག་མེད་བསྐུར་ནས་བླུ་རུ་བཏང་བས། གསེར་དང་ལྷིད་མཉམ་པ་དགོས་ཟེར་བ་དང་། ཡང་གསེར་གང་ཡོད་བསྐུར་བས་རྒྱ་མ་ལ་བཏེག་དུས་དབུའི་ཆ་ཙམ་ཅིག་གསེར་གྱིས་མ་ལོང་པར་ཁོང་ན་རེ། ད་ནི་ཁྱེད་རྣམས་ཀྱིས་བདག་བླུས་ཀྱང་ཡོན་ཏན་མེད། ངའི་རྩ་སྒོ་མི་བཙས་བསྲིགས་ནས་དུད་འགྲོ་ལྟ་བུ་ཡོད་པས་བདག་ཤི་ནའང་བླའི། ང་བླུ་བའི་གསེར་རྣམས་ཁྱེར་ལ......ཇོ་བོ་དཱི་པཾ་ཀ་ར་ཞེས་བྱ་བ་བཞུགས་ཡོད་པར་འདུག དེ་ལ་གསེར་ཕུལ་བོད་དུ་གདན་དྲངས་ལ།"[3]ཞེས་པར་ལྷ་བླ་མ་ཡེ་ཤེས་འོད་གར་ལོག་གིས་བཟུང་དོན་ཡང་ཇོ་བོ་གདན་འདྲེན་ཞུ་བའི་གསེར་སྒྲུབ་བྱེད་དུ་ཡིན་པ་གསལ་བར་བསྟན། འོན་ཀྱང་ལྷ་བླ་མ་གར་ལོག་དམག་གིས་བཟུང་བ་དེ་མུ་སྟེགས་དམག་གིས་བཟུང་བས་ཚབ་བྱས་ཁར། བཙོན་རྟུང་དྲག་པོས་རྩ་སྒོ་ཐམས་ཅད་མི་བཙས་བསྲིགས་ཏེ་རྫོངས་པར་བྱས་པའི་ཡ་ང་བའི་གནས་ཚུལ་གསར་པ་ཁ་སྣོན་མཛད་འདུག དེ་བཞིན་སྟག་ཚང་དཔལ་འབྱོར་བཟང་པོས་དུས་རབས་བཅོ་ལྔ་པའི་དུས་དཀྱིལ་བོད་རབ་བྱུང་བདུན་པའི་ཤིང་སྟག་(སྤྱི་ལོ་1434) ལོར་མཛད་པའི་《རྒྱ་བོད་ཡིག་ཚང་ཆེན་མོ་》རུ་《རྒྱལ་རབས་གསལ་བའི་མེ་ལོང་》གི་གསུངས་རྒྱུན་དང་སྤྱིར་མཐུན་པ་ཞིག་སྣར་དྲངས་འདུག

དེའི་རྗེས་ཙམ་བོད་རབ་བྱུང་བརྒྱད་པའི་མེ་སྤྲེལ་(སྤྱི་ལོ་1476) ལོར་འགོས་ལོ་གཞོན་ནུ་དཔལ་གྱིས་མཛད་པའི་《དེབ་ཐེར་སྔོན་པོ་》རུ། "ལྷ་བླ་མ་ཡེ་ཤེས་འོད་ཀྱིས་རང་གི་རྒྱལ་སྲིད་གཏད་ཟིན་ཀྱང་དམག་གི་དཔོན་མཛད་དེ། གར་ལོག་དང་འཐབ་པས་ཕམ་སྟེ་གར་ལོག་གིས་བཙོན་དུ་བཟུང་། གར་ལོག་གིས་ཡེ་

2 《དེབ་ཐེར་དམར་པོ》ཤ43ལས་དྲངས། ཚལ་པ་ཀུན་དགའ་རྡོ་རྗེས་མཛད། དུང་དཀར་བློ་བཟང་འཕྲིན་ལས་ཀྱིས་མཆན་འགྲེལ་བཀོད། མི་རིགས་དཔེ་སྐྲུན་ཁང་གིས་1981ལོའི་ཟླ་10པར་པེ་ཅིན་དུ་པར་ཐེངས་དང་པོ་བརྒྱབ།

3 《རྒྱལ་རབས་གསལ་བའི་མེ་ལོང》ཤ244ལས་དྲངས། ས་སྐྱ་བསོད་ནམས་རྒྱལ་མཚན་གྱིས་མཛད། མི་རིགས་དཔེ་སྐྲུན་ཁང་གིས་1996ལོའི་ཟླ་2པར་པེ་ཅིན་དུ་པར་ཐེངས་བཞི་པ་བརྒྱབ།

ཞིས་འོད་ལ་ཁྲོད་དཀོན་མཆོག་གསུམ་ལ་སྐྱབས་སུ་འཛིན་པ་གཏོང་ན་ངེད་ཀྱིས་བཙོན་ལས་གཏོང་། དེ་ལྟ་མ་ཡིན་ན་ལུས་རིལ་པོ་དང་ལྷིད་མཉམ་པའི་གསེར་བྱུང་ན་གཏོང་ཟེར་”[4]ཞེས་པ་འདིར་ཤཱཀྱའི་དགེ་སློང་ཡེ་ཤེས་འོད་ཀྱིས་དམག་དཔོན་མཛད་པའི་དགོད་བྲོ་བའི་གཏམ་ཐོག་མར་སྨྲོས་ཤིང་། ཕོང་གི་སྲོག་ཡང་བཙོམ་ལྡན་འདས་ཀྱི་རིང་ལུགས་བློས་མ་ཐོང་ཕྱིར་དགྲ་ལག་ཏུ་ཤོར་བ་ཡིན་པ་གསལ་བཤད་གནང་བས། ཤུགས་སུ་སངས་རྒྱས་ཆོས་ལུགས་ལ་ཆེ་བ་བརྗོད་རྒྱུ་དང་ཕྱི་རབས་རྣམས་ཀྱིས་ཆོས་དེ་དང་དུ་བླང་རྒྱུའི་དམིགས་པ་མཐར་ཐུག་དེ་རྟོགས་ནུས།

དེ་བཞིན་ཕྱིས་ཀྱི་པཎ་ཆེན་བསོད་ནམས་གྲགས་པས་སྤྱི་ལོ1538ལོར་མཛད་པའི་《དེབ་ཐེར་དམར་པོ་གསར་མ་》དང་། སྤྱི་ལོ1580ལོར་འབྲུག་པ་པད་མ་དཀར་པོས་མཛད་པའི་《ཆོས་འབྱུང་བསྟན་པའི་པདྨ་རྒྱས་པའི་ཉིན་བྱེད་》དང་། ངག་ཀུན་བསོད་གྲགས་རྒྱལ་མཚན་གྱིས་མཛད་པའི་《བཀའ་གདམས་ཆོས་འབྱུང་》སོགས་སུ་ལྷ་བླ་མའི་གོང་གི་དེབ་ཐེར་བྱིངས་དང་ཉི་ཚེ་བའི་ལྟ་ཚུལ་འགའ་སྣར་དྲངས་འདུག ཨོན་ཀྱང་སྤྱི་ལོ1643ལོར་ལྔ་པ་ཆེན་པོ་མཆོག་གིས་མཛད་པའི་《དེབ་ཐེར་དཔྱིད་ཀྱི་རྒྱལ་མོའི་གླུ་དབྱངས་》སུ་“ལྷ་བླ་མ་ཡེ་ཤེས་འོད་གསེར་འཚོལ་དུ་བྱོན་པ། གར་ལོག་གིས་བཙོན་དུ་བཟུང་བར་བཤད་པ་ནི། སྐྱེ་བོ་ཕལ་པ་ནོར་སློང་བ་ལྟ་བུའི་རྣམ་པར་ཤར་བ་བློ་གྲོས་དམན་པ་སྟེ། འདི་ཉིད་མངའ་རིས་ཀྱི་བཙད་པོ་ཆེན་པོ་ཡིན་པས། རྒྱུ་མཚན་ཞིབ་ཏུ་མ་དཔྱད་པའི་སྐྱོན་ནོ།”[5]ཞེས་པ་ལས་ངེས་ཤེས་འདྲོང་ནུས་པར། རྒྱལ་མཆོག་ལྔ་པ་ཆེན་པོས་སྐབས་དེ་ཤེད་དཔེ་རྙིང་ཕྱོགས་བཏུས་མཛད་པའི་སྐབས། ལྷ་བླ་མའི་འདས་གྲོངས་ཀྱི་གནས་ཚུལ་དངོས་དང་མཐུན་པའི་མངའ་རིས་ཀྱི་ཡིག་ཆ་དག་གཟིགས་རྟོགས་བྱུང་སྟབས་སྔོན་གྱི་ལྟ་བ་གཅིག་གྲགས་ལ་དགག་པ་མཛད་པ་གསལ་པོར་ཤེས། ཨོན་ཀྱང་གནད་དོན་ངོ་མ་ཅི་ཡིན་གསལ་སྤྲོས་མཛད་མེད་པར་སྣང་།

དེ་ནས་བརྩམས་ཏེ་རང་རེ་རྣམས་ཀྱི་ཆོས་ལུགས་ཀྱི་གཙོ་རྒྱུན་དགེ་ལུགས་པས་བསྐྱངས་པ་མ་ཟད། གྲུབ་མཐའ་དེ་འཛིན་གྱི་མཁས་པ་དག་གིས་ཀྱང་བཀའ་གདམས་ལུགས་ཀྱི་ཤིང་རྟ་ཆེན་པོའི་བཀའ་ཡོད་དོ་ཅོག་ལ་སྲོག་དང་བསྡོས་ཀྱང་བློས་མི་ཐོངས་བའི་བརྟུལ་ཞུགས་འཛིན་ཅིང་། ཡང་སྔོས་གོང་མ་ཆན་ལུང་གི་དབུ་བླ་ལྕང་སྐྱ་རོལ་པའི་རྡོ་རྗེ་མཆོག་གི་སློབ་མ། སྐབས་དེ་དུས་བོད་ལ་ཆོས་སྲིད་ཀྱི་དབུ་འཕང་ཤིན་ཏུ་མཐོ་བ་ཐུའུ་བཀྭན་བློ་བཟང་ཉི་མ་མཆོག་གིས་ཉེ་རབས་སྤྱི་ལོ1801ལོར་མཛད་པའི་《ཐུའུ་བཀྭན་གྲུབ་མཐའ་》རུ་“ད་དུང་གསེར་མང་པོ་བཙལ་ནས་སྤྱན་འདྲེན་པར་མངགས་དགོངས་ནས་གསེར་འཚོལ་དུ་ཕེབས་པ་གར་ལོག་གི་རྒྱལ་པོས་བཟུང་ནས་མ་བཏང་། ཡེ་ཤེས་འོད་ཀྱི་དཔོན་པོ་བྱང་ཆུབ་འོད་ཀྱིས་གསེར་མང་པོ་བཙལ་ནས་ཁྲུ་བོ་བླུ་བར་ཕྱིན་ཀྱང་གཏོང་མ་ཉན། དེ་ནས་ཡེ་ཤེས་འོད་གར་ལོག་གིས་བཀྲོངས་སོ།”[6]ཞེས་ལྔ་པ་ཆེན་པོའི་དགོངས་འཆར་ལ་ཁ་ཡ་གནང་ཕོམ་མ་བྱུང་བར་གོང་གི་ལྟ་ཚུལ་དེ་སྔར་སྲ་བརྟན་དུ་བཏང་འདུག

4 《དེབ་ཐེར་སྔོན་པོ》སྟོད་ཆ། ཤ299-300.

5 《དེབ་ཐེར་དཔྱིད་ཀྱི་རྒྱལ་མོའི་གླུ་དབྱངས》ཤ81ལས་དྲངས། རྒྱལ་དབང་ལྔ་པ་བློ་བཟང་རྒྱ་མཚོས་མཛད། པེ་ཅིན་མི་རིགས་དཔེ་སྐྲུན་ཁང་གིས་1980ལོའི་ཟླ་11པར་པར་ཐེངས་གཉིས་པ་བརྒྱབ།

6 《ཐུའུ་བཀྭན་གྲུབ་མཐའ》ཤ85.

ད་ཐེངས་ཁོ་བོས་ལྷ་བླ་མ་ཡེ་ཤེས་འོད་འཚོ་ཞིང་བཞེས་པའི་ཡུལ་མངའ་རིས་ཀྱི་ཡིག་ཚང་དག་ལ་ཞིབ་དཔྱད་མི་དམན་ཙམ་བྱས་པ་ལས་རྙེད་མཐོང་བྱུང་བར། གོང་དུ་ལྷ་བླ་མ་ཡེ་ཤེས་འོད་ཀྱིས་པཎྜི་ཏ་ལྔ་བརྒྱའི་གཙུག་གྱུར་ཇོ་བོ་རྗེ་ཨ་ཏི་ཤ་རྒྱ་གར་ནས་གདན་འདྲེན་པའི་སླད་གསེར་སྒྲུབ་པའི་ལམ་དུ་གར་ལོག་གིས་བཙོན་བཟུང་བྱས་ནས། ཁྲིམས་གཅོད་ཀྱིས་མནར་མཐར་སྲོག་འཚོར་བའི་ལོ་རྒྱུས་དེ་ཅི་ནས་ཀྱང་དུས་རབས་བཅུ་གཅིག་པའི་དུས་དཀྱིལ་དུ་བཀའ་གདམས་བསྟན་པའི་མེས་པོ་འབྲོམ་སྟོན་རྒྱལ་བའི་འབྱུང་གནས་ཀྱི་ཇོ་བོའི་ལམ་ཡིག་ལ་འཕོད་པའི་སྒྲུང་གཏམ་དེའི་རྗེས་སུ་འབྲངས་ནས་ཕྱི་རབས་རྣམས་ཀྱིས་རྗེ་ཚོགས་རྗེ་རྒྱུས་སུ་བཏང་བ་འབབ་ཞིག་ཡིན་པར་སེམས་ཏེ།

དྲན་དབང་དམ་པ་དགེ་འདུན་ཆོས་འཕེལ་མཆོག་གིས"ཕྲུན་པོའི་ངོ་མཚར་བསྐྱེད་པའི་ཧར་གྱི་གཏམ།། ཆེན་པོའི་ངོ་བཟུང་བརྩེགས་པའི་གཅམ་བུའི་ཚིག། དད་པའི་འཕྲུལ་བུ་སློང་བའི་སྒྲུང་གཏམ་དག། རིང་དུ་སྤངས་ཏེ་དྲང་པོའི་ལམ་དུ་ཞུགས།།"[7] ཞེས་གསུངས་པ་ལྟར། ལོ་རྒྱུས་ཀྱི་དོན་གནད་དེའི་དངོས་ཡོད་གནས་ཚུལ་ཇི་ལྟ་བུ་ཞིག་ཡིན་ཞེ་ན། སྐབས་དེ་དུས་གཞན་ཡུལ་དུ་གཤེགས་མཁན་ནི་ལྷ་བླ་མ་ཡེ་ཤེས་འོད་མིན་པར་བཙུན་པ་བྱང་ཆུབ་འོད་ཀྱི་གཅེན་པོ་འོད་ལྡེ་ཡིན་པ《མངའ་རིས་རྒྱལ་རབས་》སུ་གསལ་པོར་འཁོད་ཡོད། དེ་ཡང་དེབ་ཐེར་འདི་ལས"གཅེན་འོད་ལྡེ་བཙན་སྐུ་ཤེད་ཤིན་ཏུ་ཆེ་བས་སྐུ་ན་གཞོན་ནུ་ནས་ཐུགས་རྒྱལ་ཅན་དུ་འཁྲུངས་པ། འཁྲུག་པ་ལ་འཛམ་ཐེངས་གཅིག་མར་ཡུལ་དུ་གཤེགས་པའི་དུས་སུ་དཔེ་ཐུབ་ཀྱི་གཙུག་ལག་ཁང་བཞེངས་མཐུག་ཏུ་བྲུ་ཤའི་ཡུལ་དུ་དམག་མཛད་པས་དེར་དབུ་འཛམ་སོ། གཅུང་གཉིས་ཀྱིས་སྐུ་བླུས་པས། ཁོང་ཉིད་དང་སྐར་བའི་གསེར་དགོས་ཟེར་ནས། མ་ཁྱུགས་ཏེ་རེ་ཤིག་དེ་ཉིད་དུ་བཞུགས་སོ། ......ལྕགས་དྲང་གྲོལ་ནས་བྲོས་པས་སྔོན་ལས་ཀྱི་རྐྱེན་གྱིས་ལྕགས་དུག་བྱུང་ནས། བཤུལ་དཀར་གྲོངས་སོ་ཟེར།"[8] ཞེས་པ་ལས་མཁྱེན་ནུས། ཡང་དེ་མུར་བྱང་ཆུབ་འོད་ཀྱིས་གཅེན་བླུ་བའི་གསེར་མང་པོ་སྒྲུབ་གསོག་མཛད་ནས་ཡུལ་དེར་གཅེན་བསུ་བར་བརྩམས་ཀྱང་གཅེན་ལམ་བར་དུ་ལྕགས་དུག་ཕོག་ནས་གྲོངས་ཟིན་པ་མཁྱེན་ཏེ། མཐུག་ཏུ་གསེར་དེ་དག་ཇོ་བོ་གདན་འདྲེན་ཞུ་བའི་ཡོན་དུ་བཏང་འདུག་པའི་གནས་ཚུལ་ཡང་གསལ་སྟོན་གནང་འདུག་སྟེ།"མཐུག་ཏུ་གཅེན་བླུ་བའི་གསེར་བསྡུད་དུ་དབུས་ཀྱི་ན་སྲ་གསེར་ཁ་ཚུན་དུ་ཕེབས། གསེར་མང་པོ་གཟིགས་སོ། གཅེན་གྲོངས་པ་གསན་ནས། དེར་ཐུགས་དགོངས་རྫངས་པས། གཅེན་ནི་གྲོངས་ཁོང་གི་དོན་དུ་རྒྱ་གར་ནས་པཎྜི་ཏ་མཁས་པ་གཅིག་གདན་དྲངས་ནས་བོད་དུ་སངས་རྒྱས་ཀྱི་བསྟན་པ་སྤར་བས་ཀྱང་དར་བར་མཛད་དགོངས་ནས། ནག་ཚོ་ལོ་ཙཱ་བ་ཚུལ་ཁྲིམས་རྒྱལ་བ་དཔོན་གཡོག་ལྔ། རྒྱ་བརྩོན་སེང་ལ་ཐིག་པོ་ཤིང་སྲང་བཅུ་གཅིག་འཁོར་བ་གཅིག་དང་། གསེར་གྱི་ཕྱེ་མ་མང་པོ་བསྐུར་ནས་རྫངས་པས། ཇོ་བོ་དཱི་པཾ་ཀ་ར་ཤྲཱི་ཛྙཱ་ན་གདན་དྲངས་ནས་ཕེབས་པ་ན།......"[9] ཞེས་པ་འདི་ལས་འོད་ལྡེའི་ལོ་རྒྱུས་དངོས་འདི་གྲུབ་མཐའི་མཁན་པོ་དག

7 《གངས་ཅན་རིག་མཛོད་དེབ་བཅུ་པ། དགེ་འདུན་ཆོས་འཕེལ་གྱི་གསུང་རྩོམ་དེབ་དང་པོ》ཤ6ལས་དྲངས། བོད་ལྗོངས་བོད་ཡིག་དཔེ་རྙིང་དཔེ་སྐྲུན་ཁང་གིས་1990ལོའི་ཟླ་4པར་པར་ཐེངས་དང་པོ་བརྒྱབ།

8 《མངའ་རིས་རྒྱལ་རབས》ཤ61 གུ་གེ་མཁན་ཆེན་ངག་དབང་གྲགས་པས་མཛད། མཐོ་ལྡིང་གཙུག་ལག་ཁང་བཞེངས་ནས་ལོ་1000འཁོར་བའི་དྲན་གསོའི་གྲ་སྒྲིག་ཚོགས་ཆུང་གིས་1996ལོར་པར་དུ་བསྐྲུན།

9 《མངའ་རིས་རྒྱལ་རབས》ཤ63-64.

གིས་ལྷ་བླ་མ་ཡེ་ཤེས་འོད་ལ་ཨུ་ཚུགས་ཀྱིས་སྨྲར་བ་གསལ་བར་རྟོགས་ཐུབ།

གཞན་བརྗོད་གཞིར་གྱུར་བ་ལྷ་བླ་མ་ཡེ་ཤེས་འོད་མཆོག་ཀྱང་མཐའ་མཇུག་མངའ་རིས་གུ་གེའི་མཐོ་ལྡིང་གཙུག་ལག་ཁང་དུ་ཚེའི་འདུ་བྱེད་བཏང་བའི་སྐོར་མངའ་རིས་ཡིག་ཚང་དག་ལ་ཡོངས་གྲགས་སུ་འཁོད་འདུག དེ་ཡང་མངའ་རིས་ས་ཁུལ་ལ་ས་སྐྱེས་རྗེ་སྐྱེས་སུ་གྱུར་བ། ལོ་ཆེན་རིན་བཟང་གི་དངོས་སློབ་ཀ་ཆེན་བཞིའི་ཡ་གྱལ། གུ་གེ་ཁྱི་ཐང་པ་དཔལ་ཡེ་ཤེས་ཀྱིས་མཛད་པའི་《ལོ་ཆེན་རིན་བཟང་གི་རྣམ་ཐར་ཤེལ་ཕྲེང་ལུ་གུ་རྒྱུད་》ལས་ལོ་ཆེན་མཆོག་ལན་གཉིས་པར་རྒྱ་གར་ནས་རང་ཡུལ་གུ་གེར་ཚུར་ཕེབས་པའི་ལམ་བར་དུ་ལྷ་བླ་མ་ཡེ་ཤེས་འོད་སྙུང་གཞི་དྲག་པོས་ཟིན་ཏེ་ཐོན་ལ་འདས་ཀྱིན། ཁོང་དང་ཞལ་མཐའ་མ་མཇལ་ཁོམ་མ་བྱུང་བའི་སྐོར་ལ“ལྷ་བླ་མ་ཡེ་ཤེས་འོད་སྙུང་བར་སན་ནས། མྱུར་དུ་ཞལ་མཇལ་དུ་བྱོན་པས་ལ་སྙུང་གཞི་དྲག་པོ་གཅིག་གིས་ཟིན་ནས་ཞལ་མ་མཇལ་ལོ། གདུང་མཆོད་དན་སོང་བ་ལ་སོགས་པ་ནི་ལོ་ཙྪ་བ་ཁོང་རང་གིས་མཛད་དོ།”[10]ཞེས་པ་འདིས་ཐོག་མར་ལྷ་བླ་མ་ཡེ་ཤེས་འོད་གཞན་ཡུལ་ལ་གྲོངས་མེད་པའི་གནས་ཚུལ་དངོས་དྲངས་ཡོད། ཡང་དེའི་ཕྱིས་ཀྱི་ཡིག་ཚང་《མངའ་རིས་རྒྱལ་རབས་》སུ་“ལྷ་རྒྱལ་ལྷ་མ་ཡེ་ཤེས་འོད་……སྐུ་ན་ཤིན་ཏུ་བགྲེས་པའི་དུས་སུ་ཡང་ཉིད་ཀྱི་ཐུགས་དམ་གླིང་ལ་ཕྱག་མཁར་བསྐྲུམས་ནས་བསྐོར་བ་མང་དུ་མཛད་ཅིང་།……ལོ་གསུམ་བར་དུ་སྐུ་མཚམས་བཅད་ནས་ཐུགས་དམ་མཛད་ཅིང་མཚམས་ལས་ཐོན་པ་དང་རེ་ཞིག་འབབས་ཀྱི་ཚུལ་གྱིས་གདུལ་བྱ་རྣམས་ལ་ཞལ་བསྟན་པ་དང་།……སྐུ་ཚེ་མཐའ་ཕྱིན་པའི་བར་དུ་མཐོ་གླིང་དུ་བཞུགས་ཤིང་བསྟན་པ་དང་སེམས་ཅན་གྱི་དོན་མཛད་པ་ཡིན་ནོ།”[11]ཞེས་པ་དེ་དང་། ལྷག་པར་དུ《ལྷ་བླ་མ་ཡེ་ཤེས་འོད་ཀྱི་རྣམ་ཐར་རྒྱས་པ་》ལས“དེ་ལྟར་རབ་ཏུ་བྱུང་ཞིང་བསྙེན་པར་རྫོགས་ནས་ལོ་སུམ་བཅུ་སོ་གཅིག་གི་བར་དུ་སངས་རྒྱས་ཀྱི་བསྟན་པའི་བདག་པོར་གྱུར་ནས་དར་རྒྱས་མཛད་པ་དང་། སྟོན་པ་ཤཱཀྱ་སེང་གེ་ཉིད་ཁོ་ན་ལྟར་གྱུར་ཏོ། དེ་ནས་ས་མོ་ལུག་གི་ལོ་ལ་མཐོ་གླིང་གཟིམས་ཁང་དུ་ཞི་བར་གཤེགས་པའི་ཚུལ་བསྟན་མོད།”[12]ཞེས་པ་བཅས་དེ་དག་ཀུང་གཅིག་ཏུ་བསྒྲིགས་སྐབས་ལྷ་བླ་མ་ཡེ་ཤེས་འོད་རང་ཡུལ་གུ་གེའི་མཐོ་གླིང་གཙུག་ལག་ཁང་དུ་རབ་བྱུང་གོང་གི་ས་མོ་ལུག(སྤྱི་ལོ་1019)ལོར་དགོངས་པ་རྫོགས་པ་གསལ་བར་རྟོགས་ཐུབ།

མདོར་ན། སྐབས་དེའི་ལོ་རྒྱུས་དངོས་ལ་ཞིབ་དཔྱད་བརྒྱུད་མཐོང་ཐུབ་པར་གཞན་ཡུལ་ལ་གྲོག་འདོར་མཁན་ནི་ལྷ་བླ་མ་ཡེ་ཤེས་འོད་ཀྱི་གཅེན་འཁོར་རེའི་སྲས་ལྷ་ལྡེའི་བུ། འོད་ལྡེ་བྱ་བ་དེ་ཡིན་ཞིང་གསེར་འཚོལ་བར་བསྐྱོད་མཁན་ནི་ལྷ་སྲས་འོད་ལྡེའི་གཅུང་པོ་བཙུན་པ་བྱང་ཆུབ་འོད་ཡིན་ལ། གསེར་འཚོལ་དོན་གྱི་ཐོག་མའི་ཀུན་སློང་ཡང་རང་གི་གཅེན་པོ་འོད་ལྡེ་བླུ་བའི་ཆེད་ཡིན་པ་ར་སྦྲོད་ཐུབ། འོན་ཀྱང་། ཕྱིས་ཀྱི་མཁས་པ་རྣམས་ཀྱིས་ལོ་རྒྱུས་ཀྱི་དོན་རྐྱེན་དེ་ལྷ་བླ་མ་ཡེ་ཤེས་འོད་ཀྱི་སྟེང་དུ་བེད་སྤྱད་ནས་འཁྲུག་པོར་བརྗོད་དོན་ཡང་། ཁོ་བོས་བསམ་ན། གཅིག་ནས་དེའི་དུས་སུ་གངས་ཅན་གྱི་ཡུལ་དབུས་ལ་འདུལ་བ་སྟོད་རྒྱུད་དང་བཀའ་གདམས་པའི་གྲུབ་མཐའི་ཤེན་ཤུགས་ཆེ་བས། བཙོས་མའི་ལོ་རྒྱུས་དེའི་

10 《ལོ་ཆེན་རིན་བཟང་གི་རྣམ་ཐར་ཤེལ་ཕྲེང་ལུ་གུ་རྒྱུད》བྲིས་མ།

11 《མངའ་རིས་རྒྱལ་རབས》ཤ58-59.

12 《ལྷ་བླ་མ་ཡེ་ཤེས་འོད་ཀྱི་རྣམ་ཐར་རྒྱས་པ》བྲིས་མ།

གཞི་འཛིན་ས། བཀའ་གདམས་མེས་པོ་རྒྱལ་བ་འབྲོམ་སྟོན་པའི་《ཇོ་བོ་རྗེའི་རྣམ་ཐར་ལམ་ཡིག་ཆོས་ཀྱི་འབྱུང་གནས་》དུ་འཁོད་པ་དེ་དང་དུ་བླང་བ་དང་། གཉིས་ནས་ལྷ་བླ་མ་ཡེ་ཤེས་འོད་ཀྱིས་འཛིག་རྟེན་ཕུན་ཚོགས་ལ་བློས་བཅད་དེ་སངས་རྒྱས་ཆོས་ལ་ཞུགས་ནས། བོད་ཀྱི་སྟོད་ཁུལ་ནས་བསྟན་པའི་མེ་རོ་གསོ་བ་དང་གསར་མའི་འགྱུར་འགོ་གཏོད་པ། དེ་བཞིན་འདུལ་བ་སྟོད་རྒྱུད་དར་འཕེལ་དང་། ལྷག་པར་དུ་ཕྱི་དར་བོད་ལ་སངས་རྒྱས་ཆོས་ལུགས་འཛིན་སྐྱོང་སྤེལ་གསུམ་ཐད། འཕྲིན་ལས་བླ་མེད་འཛོག་མཁན་ཇོ་བོ་ཨ་ཏི་ཤ་གདན་དྲངས་པ་སོགས་ལ་མཛད་རྗེས་ཆེ་བར་སེམས་ནས་དངོས་དོན་དང་ཡོངས་སུ་འགལ་བའི་བློལ་བསྟོད་བཅོས་མའི་གཏམ་སྨྲ་བ་ཙམ་དུ་སྣམ་མོ།།།།

ཟུར་བལྟའི་དཔྱད་གཞི།

《གུ་གེ་ཚེ་རིང་རྒྱལ་པོའི་ཆེད་རྩོམ་ཕྱོགས་བསྒྲིགས།》ཀྲུང་གོའི་བོད་རིག་པ་དཔེ་སྐྲུན་ཁང་གིས་2005ལོའི་ཟླ་10པར་ཐེངས་དང་པོ་བརྒྱབ།

(དཔྱད་རྩོམ་འདི་2009ལོའི་《བོད་ལྗོངས་སློབ་གྲྭ་ཆེན་མོའི་རིག་དེབ་》འདོན་ཐེངས་བཞི་པར་འཁོད་ཡོད།)

From Death to New Life

An 11th-12th century cycle of existence from southernmost Tibet

Analysis of *Rnel dri 'dul ba*, *Ste'u* and *Sha slungs* rites, with notes on manuscript provenance

Toni Huber (Humboldt University)

every living thing comes from the dead
– Socrates in Plato's *Phaedo*

1. Introduction*

This contribution in memory of our departed friend and colleague Tsering Gyalbo is part of a larger research project documenting contemporary eastern Himalayan rites for revitalisation of the living, promoting fertility and virility, and allowing women to conceive new children. I refer to all the rites and myths, ritual specialists and community festivals related to this phenomenon in my research region as the cult of Srid pa'i lha.[1] The cult is found at some seventy locations within eastern Bhutan and the adjacent Mon yul Corridor of Arunachal Pradesh (India). Many indicators suggest that the immediately neighbouring

* Acknowledgements: Thanks are due to the following persons: Joanna Bialek (Berlin) for constructive exchanges of ideas and feedback on linguistic issues; Mona Schrempf (Saarbrücken) for discussions and literature tips on birth and rebirth in Asia; Reinier Langelaar (Vienna) and Guntram Hazod (Vienna) for proof-reading and useful suggestions; Moke Mokotoff (New York) for his permission to use and publish the *Ste'u* and *Sha slungs* manuscript in his ownership; and Deborah Klimburg-Salter and staff at the Western Himalaya Archive Vienna (Department of Art History, University of Vienna) for access to high resolution images of the manuscript to enable my research.

1 For publications related to the Srid pa'i lha cult, see Huber 2015, 2015a, 2015b, 2015c, 2013 and In Press.

Lho brag district of southernmost Tibet, and adjacent districts including Gtam shul, Gru shul and Mon Mtsho sna, constitute the proximate historical source region for crucial aspects of contemporary revitalisation rites performed in the cult. A little-known population named Shar Dung inhabited these same regions until their displacement and dispersal during the 1350s due to Tibetan military campaigns.[2] The Shar Dung appear to be the most likely southward transmitters of various aspects of the cult into the neighbouring Himalayan valleys where it exists today. Although my informants mainly speak East Bodish languages, their ritual culture of revitalisation rites is recorded in local collections of Tibetan language manuscripts that are hereditarily transmitted and maintained within lineages of community ritual specialists. I thus investigated several collections of old manuscripts that can be sourced back to southernmost Tibet, in order to check for earlier precedents that might inform rites recorded in cult manuscripts and in ethnographic data I collected just south of Lho brag. Results from those investigations are presented herein, and are based upon a chapter in my forthcoming monographic work on the cult, *Source of Life*.

The present study reviews three rites found recorded in old, recently discovered manuscripts. The first rite termed *Rnel dri 'dul ba* occurs in an as yet undated, anonymous text discovered at the Dga' thang shrine in Gtam shul, but which I consider must date from the 11th-12th century period.[3] The two other untitled rites I term *Ste'u* and *Sha slungs* occur in a manuscript currently in private ownership in the United States, and scientifically dated to the 11th-12th century period.[4] All three rites deal with mundane[5] concerns, all are devoid

2 The *Rgya bod yig tshang* 380 describes the eastern Lho brag territory where Shar Dung strongholds (*mkhar btsan sa*) existed within a region defined by Chu skyed lung gsum, Lho brag gya ba bzhi (both possibly a reference to the three river valleys and four ranges – *gya ba*? – which define the actual geography of Lho brag as a region), the highlands of 'A lungs Skyogs mo and lowlands of Tsag sa wa bzhugs. On the Dung and Shar Dung, see Petech 1990; Aris 1979: chapt.5; Aris 1986: 46-55 and especially Ardussi 2004.

3 The *dbu can* transcription and facsimiles can be found in *Dga' thang* 33-59, 131-178. On the whole collection and its discovery, see Pa tshab Pa sangs dbang 'dus and Glang ru Nor bu tshe ring in *Dga' thang* 1-8, and Karmay 2009: 55-65. Most recently, Karmay 2013: 20 stated, "judging by the style of writing, grammatical structure, the type of vocabulary and the notions that are expressed, there is no doubt that the Dga' thang manuscripts are very old, probably pre-11th century." Note that when citing texts in this collection, I always give three references in this order: page no. of *dbu can* transcription; page no. of facsimile; folio/line nos. of the citation.

4 Facsimiles of the manuscript have been published in Klimburg-Salter, Lodja and Ramble 2013: 39-45, and in Bellezza 2013: 30-76. For convenience I adopt the reference system for folios used in these existing publications. Bellezza 2013: 15, n.22 reported an AMS sample dating of the paper to 11th-12th century, which was confirmed to me by Moke Mokotoff (*pers. comm.* March 2016).

5 I intend 'mundane' as a general characterisation for practices and goals related to earthly human existence in the here and now, and the very proximate future, and which lack reference to any soteriological or 'ultimate' horizons.

of any concrete references to either the Tibetan Buddhist or the G.yung drung Bon salvation religions, and all clearly belong to a milieu of autonomous ritual specialists operating within local communities.

The study has four parts. Part I (chap. 2) sets out an analysis *of Rnel dri 'dul ba* rites concerned with the post-mortem status of deceased foetuses or miscarried infants and in some cases their mothers, and how this impacts upon the living. Part II (chap. 3) analyses both the *Ste'u* and *Sha slungs* rites that have the combined goals of posthumously gaining new human lives following deaths, as well as protecting the germinal beings once they have arrived upon the earth.[6] Part III (chap. 4) discusses the results which reveal a cognate cosmological framing and set of reference points across these three rites from the same 11th-12th century milieu and common geographical region. Read together, they indicate what amounts to a local cycle of human existence, at least to the extent that the concepts involved were applied in the rites under study. Moreover, most of the central concepts, identities, technical language and procedures in these three old rites are still evident today in the cult of Srid pa'i lha that I documented in the eastern Himalayas. Part IV (chap. 5) deals with manuscript provenance. I initially demonstrate that manuscripts recording *Rnel dri 'dul ba, Ste'u* and *Sha slungs* rites share certain close similarities with manuscripts recording revitalisation rites used in the cult of Srid pa'i lha. I then set out a wide range of evidence for establishing geographical provenance for the *Ste'u* and *Sha slungs* manuscript. I consider it was most likely composed in southernmost Tibet, within a zone of ca. 100 km diameter encompassing the area of the Dga' thang shrine to the north and the highland valleys of north-eastern Bhutan and adjacent hill regions where the cult of Srid pa'i lha is based upon similar manuscripts to the south. A conclusion proposes how we might best define the status of these three old rites.

Finally, it must be noted that the three old texts being considered herein contain a wide variety of obscure terms and grammatical constructions, and some of my proposed resolutions of them remain tentative.

6 I am aware of the study on the *Ste'u* and *Sha slungs* manuscript and the *Rnel dri 'dul ba'i thabs* by Bellezza 2013. Bellezza's interpretations of these texts and his methodology diverge strongly from my own, while the detailed content in his publication is often flawed to the extent that any reference to it invariably requires a considerable volume of additional corrective commentary. I thus ignore it herein, and simply suggest interested readers compare the results of my study with those offered in Bellezza 2013.

2. *Rnel dri 'dul ba* rites and their cultural background

The Dga' thang manuscript described by its publishers as *Rnel dri 'dul ba'i thabs*, or 'Methods of subduing *rnel dri*', is the longest ritual text discovered at the Gtam shul site, with forty seven surviving folio sides. It records a collection of antecedent crisis tales and models for conducting exorcism and purification rites specifically to combat posthumous possessions appearing in the wake of culturally problematic deaths. Such deaths include those of mothers but especially of their infants occurring during childbirth or in utero due to what we would now medically define as septic abortion or miscarriage, and miscarriages induced by certain violent accidents, for example, being hit by a rock or falling from a precipice or horse are cited in the *rnel dri* tales.[7] Samten Karmay accurately described the *Rnel dri 'dul ba'i thabs* as related to "special purification rites" in cases of unfortunate deaths,[8] while Brandon Dotson correctly understood that these rites are not directly concerned with the dead or their disposal as such, although the antecedent narratives cite deaths and in a few cases briefly refer to death rites as general causal and sequential framing references. Rather, the rites benefit the living by way of purifying surviving kin and spouses, appeasing deities who preside over social communities, averting reprisals by a deceased's family against another party, and so forth.[9] At the end of one *Rnel dri 'dul ba* antecedent narrative, the rite's purpose is explicitly described as being 'In order that the dead do not pursue the living',[10] while in another tale a *bon mo* ritual specialist is described as one who can 'bring a dead person back to life.'[11] Thus, despite death triggering the original problem, life and the living are very much and ultimately in focus here. This is one of various points the *Rnel dri 'dul ba* rites share in common with the rhetoric in the old *Ste'u* text studied in part II (chap. 3), for it, too, explicitly states that when death is concealed with the proper rites this benefits the living, in the form of gaining new, young lives (see below). An identical rhetoric occurs in Srid pa'i lha cult texts based upon the *Yangal* rites in the *Rnel dri*

7 A second Dga' thang manuscript dealing with various exorcisms including *dri* is called *Sha ru shul ston gyi rabs la sogs pa* by its publishers; see *Dga' thang* 60-75, 179-212. Its rites and language share but few similarities with the *Rnel dri 'dul ba'i thabs*, nor does it deal with *rnel dri*, and only features a certain type of *dri bon* rites and thus lacks the elaborate purification of the vertical cosmic axis by the Ya ngal ritual specialist.

8 Karmay 2009: 63-64.

9 Dotson 2008: 61-63.

10 *ShI phyIr gson myi 'brang ngo /; Dga' thang* 52, 167, f.37, l.2.

11 See the *myi shi sos gyi bon mo* named Kod shel lcag (elsewhere God she lcag); *Dga' thang* 55, 172, f.42, l.4-5, cf. 58, 175, f.45, l.7-8.

'dul ba'i thabs.[12]

The ca. 11th-12th century *Rnel dri 'dul ba* rites from Dga' thang occur in the historical context of both older and later rites related to them. Problematic deaths associated with the term *dri* were already a concern expressed in Old Tibetan texts discovered at Dunhuang, although the precise meaning of Old Tibetan *dri* is not yet completely established. Dotson understood *dri* in such formulations as *dri ru bkrongs, drir grongs* or *drir nongs* to mean 'violence', but also noted that "violent death seems to be almost personified by the term *dri*, and is certainly personified by noxious beings such as the *btsan dri*, a particular type of demon."[13] There are *dri bon* ritual specialists mentioned in Old Tibetan ritual texts, just as there are *dri bon* cited in the *Rnel dri 'dul ba'i thabs*. Modified forms of some unknown old rites related to *dri*, or at very least recycling of cultural materials from them, also continued in the later G.yung drung Bon religion, although they became reframed within a formal religious context. These G.yung drung Bon rites include transformation of older vocabulary, and this has frequently confused observers. The orthography of *dri* changed to *gri* in later sources, and hence often became understood literally as 'knife' and 'murder'.[14] Also, *bdur* found in most of the Old Tibetan texts for death rites became written *'dur* by the G.yung drung Bon po, who then specifically assimilated the verb *'dur ba* to the verb *'dul ba*, with *'dur* in its nominal forms often also assigned to 'funeral rites' which obscures the fact that no funerals *per se* need be involved. David Snellgrove – who cautiously preferred to treat these verbs separately – already drew attention to this class of rites, which were explained by his expert Tibetan Bon po informants as "supressing troublesome spirits that return from the dead, especially those who have been murdered; for this purpose there is a ritual known as *gri 'dur byed pa*."[15] Samten Karmay and others describe both *'dur ba* and *gri 'dur* as being used "to perform the posthumous evocation ritual of the killed" and "for exorcising the spirits that cause unnatural death," while the same rites termed *'dur* come to be more

12 For example, in a Ya ngal rite from Kurtö, we read the appeal, 'Today, open the door to the *lha* of the living! Today, close the door to the tomb of the dead!' (*'di ring gson gyi lha sgo phye // 'di ring gshin gyi dur sgo chod //*); *Shawa 1*, Text 3, f.16a, l.1-2.

13 Dotson 2013: 163-165. The *btsan dri* are mentioned in the *Sha ru shul ston gyi rabs la sogs pa* text; *Dga' thang* 67, 194, f.15, l.2.

14 See, for example, *gri* in both the *Gal mdo* and *Gzi brjid* presentations of the *Srid gshen* 'way' respectively in Kapstein 2009: 117, 124 and Snellgrove 1967: 116-117.

15 Snellgrove 1967: 300, cf. 259 n.40.

generally described as some form of "taming" by assimilating *'dul* to *'dur*.[16]

The Old Tibetan and later G.yung drung Bon contexts and terminologies related in certain ways to *Rnel dri 'dul ba* rites are clearly not identical to them, and traces of transformations in vocabulary and concepts across a ca. 11th century watershed era are everywhere to be found. Thus, anachronism is a particular methodological concern in relation to relevant G.yung drung Bon sources written in Classical Tibetan, not least of all because they currently lack any reliable provenance information.[17] I therefore eschew them in my analysis of *Rnel dri 'dul ba.*

Our initial problem is gaining terminological clarity for *rnel* and *dri* and the rite name *Rnel dri 'dul ba.* Earlier, this had been understood by Dotson as "to 'subdue' (*'dul*) [...] various types of impurities (*rnel, dri [ma]*),"[18] presumably reading *rnel* in relation to *mnal/ mnol*, while Karmay understood *dri 'dul ba* as the "taming of knifed deaths"[19] by applying the later G.yung drung Bon meaning for *gri 'dur* to it. Neither explanation is convincing in the context of the *Rnel dri 'dul ba* narratives. I have never seen the word *rnel* attested in any other Tibetan language document, and uncertainties involving the Old Tibetan meaning of *dri* were signalled above.

What is certain in the text under consideration is that a *rnel dri* directly subject to *'dul ba* ('suppressing', 'taming', 'converting', and so forth) must refer to some being endowed with sentience since that is overwhelmingly what the verb *'dul ba* applies to in other contexts. There are occasionally different types of *dri* signalled within the text,[20] but here I

16 Karmay 1972: 349, and Karmay 1994: 419 translating a passage from *Mkhas pa Lde'u* 235, Karmay 2009: 63 for *gri 'dur* has "the taming of the knifed deaths", and for *Mu cho khrom 'dur chen mo* "the Great collection of taming rites performed in public by Mucho". See also *Zhangzhung* 122, *'dur sgo* which is defined as incorporating "taming rituals".

17 A text collection now often cited by others is the *Mu cho khrom 'dur*. Currently, there is no historically and scientifically attested provenance information concerning dates, places of composition or authorship for any of this collection. Concerning internal claims, most of the individual works are anonymous, yet when attributions of origins are given they are often contradictory, some texts being cited as *gter ma*, others very similar not, with different *gter ston* credited, while some commentators state they were never *gter ma*, and so on; see the notes and colophons given in Martin, *et. al.* 2003: entries 31.1-31.54, 39.1-39.64. In my forthcoming monograph, *Source of Life*, I compare a group of texts from the *Mu cho khrom 'dur* with manuscripts containing parallel references in the Srid pa'i lha cult and with the Old Tibetan document PT 1060. Among them, the *Mu cho khrom 'dur* texts exhibit the most deviance, almost all of which involves reframing with discourses and vocabulary from the G.yung drung Bon and Tibetan Buddhist salvational religions.

18 Dotson 2008: 62 n.64.

19 Karmay 2009: 63.

20 See the various *dri* indexed to the sky, earth, intermediate space, stone, fire and later also water in the *Sha ru shul ston gyi rabs la sogs pa* text; *Dga' thang* 60, 180, f.1 and 71, 200, f.21, l. 4.

am only drawing upon those accounts concerning *rnel dri*, which represent the vast majority of cases in the *Rnel dri 'dul ba'i thabs*. Accordingly, *rnel, dri* (or *gri*) and *rnel dri* (or *rnel gri*) are the specific designations given to deceased human victims towards whom *Rnel dri 'dul ba* rites are directed. In the text itself we find them described as 'child *dri'* (*bu dri/gri*), 'female child *dri*' (*bu dri/gri mo*) and 'female *rnel dri*' (*rnel dri/gri mo*). In context, for example, the narratives describe them in scenarios,'In the country Dung yul, at Dung stod, a girl of Dung, a *rnel*, died'[21] or when the infant becomes possessed and is specifically named as such, 'The name of that female *dri* was *rnel dri* Dgab mar ma',[22] and so forth. Here one can note that almost all the score or so of *rnel dri* antecedent tales feature women who are pregnant and their unborn foetuses or babies who die of symptoms matching septic abortion or accident-induced miscarriage. On the one hand, the recurrent parallel phrasing *bu dri/gri* with *rnel dri/gri* and *bu dri/gri mo* with *rnel dri/gri mo* in text passages strongly suggest that *rnel* stands for 'infant' or 'child'. On the other hand, it is conspicuous that within those narrative texts in the collection that place more emphasis upon the pregnant mother as the victim – albeit that her foetus must also die – we only find the term *dri* and not *rnel dri.* [23]

When I discussed the above points with Joanna Bialek, a linguist-lexicographer of Old Tibetan, she suggested[24] that the otherwise unattested *rnel* may be the result of a specific type of as yet little understood developmental pattern evident for Tibetan word formation. Various attested examples of this include *rdo, rde'u, rdel* 'stone/projectile', *ba, be'u, bel* 'cow/calf', or *spra, spre, spre'u, sprel* 'ape/monkey', and so on. Thus, we might consider the development *na, ne'u, rnel,* in which *na* means 'age, stage of life', and diminutive *ne'u* literally 'little age/stage of life', i.e. a 'young one', 'foetus/baby/infant'. The *r* superfix on *rnel* may appear out of place in this development, however lexicons attest the superfix-bearing form *sne'u* in a synonym for *bu tsha* 'child, boy', with an Old Tibetan occurrence of it attested as well.[25] Further evidence comes from the approximately contemporary *Ste'u* and *Sha slungs* manuscript treated in part II (chap. 3), and in which the cognate term *ne'u*

21 Y*ul dung yul dung stod na // dung gyI bo [read: bu] mo rnel te grongs /; Dga' thang* 39, 141, f.11, l.1-2.

22 *Dri mo de'I mying / rnel dri dgab mar ma' /; Dga' thang* 45, 152, f.22, l.6-7. For other *rnel dri* names which share elements with this one, see *Dga' thang* 44, 150, f.20, l.7 *rnel bkrags dgab mar ma*, 50, 162, f.32, l.2-3 *rnel drI thag bshar ma*, and 47, 156, f.26, l.8 *rnel grI thag shal ma'* (cf. *ibid.* 48, 158, f.28, l.4, and 49, 159, f.29, l.4).

23 See the case of Lha lcam Phye ma lam in *Dga' thang* 39-40, 141-142, f.11, l.4-f.12, l.4.

24 *Pers. comm.* 9 May in Berlin, and email of 12 May, 2016.

25 Das 1902: 771, cf. also *sne'u* as 'children' in Thomas 1957: 87 n.4.

zhon 'young ones' derived from *na gzhon*[26] features centrally within a set of cosmological references that are very close in certain respects to those found in *Rnel dri 'dul ba* rites. Based upon the aforementioned evidence, in this study I am provisionally accepting that *rnel* means 'infant' in the text concerned.

In the *Rnel dri 'dul ba'i thabs*, the agency behind a *rnel* victim becoming a *dri* is almost always assigned to members of the *srin* and *sri* classes of spirit. In the narratives, these beings are not some generic or universal agents, but rather very localised figures associated with – and named after – the residence places of their victims in the terrestrial environment, or at sites where the victims perform activities.[27] The same pattern for identifying troublesome *srin* who require 'ransom' (*glud*) rites is already found in the Old Tibetan documents, and I will return to this point in the part III (chap. 4). Unlike any known Old Tibetan sources, the *srin* and *sri* in *Rnel dri 'dul ba* narratives are almost exclusively and intimately related to unborn children and their mothers. *Srin* and *sri* are said to 'infiltrate' (*zhugs*) the bodies – but most specifically the uterus – of women, cause 'death' (*grongs, gum, lcebs*) and 'mishap' (*nongs*) to their foetuses or babies who become *dri*, and also 'drag off' (*drongs*) their victims to become *dri*. One local *srin* even has the name Bu rkun, literally 'Robber of Children'.[28] The *srin* which specifically target child victims in the *Rnel dri 'dul ba* narratives are closely cognate with the *sri*, and likely they are variants of the same older word and class of beings. The more rarely involved *sri* are definitely ancient and dangerous beings from under the earth whose profile is more well-defined in the Old Tibetan sources than the already somewhat generic *srin*. Old Tibetan texts state that '*sri* having risen from the earth appeared', identify them as '*sri* thieves in the earth', while 'up above one offers to *lha*, and down below one suppresses *sri*'.[29] However, the very close connection between *sri/*

26 *Na gzhon BGT* 1495, *lo na gzhon pa*, cf. Jäschke 1881: 298.

27 For examples, in the Rtsang shul tale it is the Rtsang *srin* Zla gar (*Dga' thang* 47, 156, f.26, l.4), in the Dbye mo yul grugs tale it is Dbye *srin* Yug mo (ibid. 50, 161, f.31, l.10), in the [Yar] lungs sogs ka tale it is Yar *sri* Btsan bye Phag po sna rings (*ibid.* 49, 160, f.30, l.6), while in an incident that occurs at the boundary between the alpine slates and the meadows (*g.ya' le spang mtshams su*) it is the G.ya' *srin* Tshubs ma and the Gangs *srin* Phywa ba (*ibid.* 39, 141, f.11, l.9-10). Interestingly, in the tale of the progenitor king from the mid-13th century his first problem on earth is hostile *srin*; *Mkhas pa Lde'u* 236.

28 See the Gnubs yul gling grugs tale; *Dga' thang* 48, 157, f.27, l.7. The name occurs in the later ritual text *Sri gsas bung ba stag chung bzhugs*; see Karmay and Nagano 2002: 186 = f.4a.

29 See, in order of citation, IOL Tib J 0731: r122, *sa las sri lang ste chags* (cf. PT 1134: 74); IOL Tib J 0734: 7r270, *sa la sri rkun ma*; PT 1050: 5, *ya rus ni lha mchod la // mar du ni sri gnon cig //*. Unless otherwise indicated, all citations of Old Tibetan documents are from *OTDO* (see References).

srin and children becomes strongly evident for the first time in *Rnel dri 'dul ba* narratives. Aspects of this cultural complex were preserved in the later Classical Tibetan vocabulary, with *sri'u* and *sri'u phru* positively referring to 'a human child' (*mi'i phru gu*). Yet, *sri'u* is also attested with a negative meaning much closer to the cases we are dealing with in the *Rnel dri 'dul ba'i thabs*, namely for a 'woman whose child dies after birth'.[30] In older Classical Tibetan ritual literature, a somewhat cognate technical term *chung sri*, 'a *sri* of a young one' (*chung ngu'i sri*), occurs although it refers to a child victim and not a mother, and it is a clear synonym of *rnel dri*.[31] A specific class of rites to suppress *sri* for protection of infants do exist within the Srid pa'i lha cult, and are also known from other older '*bon*'-identified manuscripts used by autonomous ritual specialists for mundane rites.[32] There are also cognate terms for rite techniques in earlier and later texts, including *sri khung* for a ritual pit dug in the earth to trap *sri*, which is cited in *Rnel dri 'dul ba* rites and later texts.[33] Moreover, the words *sri'u* and *sri'u phru* are probably the earlier basis for the spoken expression *sifu* or *seefu* used today by speakers of East Bodish languages and the Tibetic language Chochangacha within the Srid pa'i lha cult for rites in which the ancestral sky *lha* descend to the ritual ground to impregnate women who are otherwise unable to conceive a child (see chap. 4). To my present knowledge, this whole cultural complex associating unborn and very young infants with *dri/sri/srin* in a ritual context can be traced back only as far as the *Rnel dri 'dul ba'i thabs* and its cultural-historical milieu. [34]

In summary, one can further note that in the antecedent tales of the *Rnel dri 'dul ba* text,

30 Das 1902: 1288.

31 See *chung sri* in *BGT* 815: *byis pa chung ngu nas 'chi bar byed pa'i gdon nam sri /*, while *chung sri* is used throughout the *Sri gsas bung ba stag chung bzhugs* manuscript (Karmay and Nagano 2002: 185-197). See also the discussion in Blondeau 1997: 208-210, while Rangjung Yeshe Dictionary (consulted at: http://dictionary.thlib.org) cites a text title *sri bzlog 'khor lo 'bar ba* as "ritual work recited after the death of an infant to prevent the malevolent *sri* spirits from harming other children,"; cf. also Karmay 1972: 352, *sri kha (lang ba)* 'to meet one's fate' in G.yung drung Bon religious literature.

32 An example of such rites found in the cult is recorded in the manuscript *Lawa* 2, Text 1, and titled *Bon 'di ni bsbyi bsri 'khor mo bcug gsums bzhug sho* [original orthography], and in which the written forms *sri*, *bsri* and *sri'u* occur. A cognate type of rite is found in the *Sri gsas bung ba stag chung bzhugs* manuscript published in Karmay and Nagano 2002: 185-197.

33 See *Dga' thang* 51, 163, f.33, l.9, and the *Sri gsas bung ba stag chung bzhugs* manuscript in Karmay and Nagano 2002: 188 = f.8a.

34 One can note that the Dri gum tale in the *Old Tibetan Chronicle*, most recently translated and discussed by Dotson 2013, contains the same basic set of words and motifs – *dri, sri*, a death, a child and a ransom – we find in *Rnel dri 'dul ba* rites.

there is an overall pattern for deploying terminology. The initial term used for a deceased infant victim is always *rnel*, while *dri* designates them after death when they become problematic, subject to *'dul ba* and dispatched away from the human world, and *rnel dri* identifies them in relation to more general discussion points, such as when their names are cited, their fates mentioned, and so on. The *dri* status is designated as problematic in various ways, but two verbal markers are most common, *dri yar ba* 'wandering/rambling *dri*', and *dri ma btul* 'unsuppressed *dri*'. If one accepted the suggestions made for *rnel* above, then rites described as *Rnel dri 'dul ba* can be understood to address 'young ones/infants' (*rnel*) who die violently or in culturally problematic ways rendering them susceptible to capture and control by *srin* and *sri*, and who, as resulting *dri*, ramble around posthumously precipitating problems, and thus must be subjected to ritual manipulation. In that case, *rnel dri* occurring as a compound noun is best understandable as 'wandering bad death infant spirit' in the specific context addressed here.

2.1 *Rnel dri 'dul ba* rite sequences

The *Rnel dri 'dul ba'i thabs* describes a whole series of rite techniques performed in part by the ritual specialist *A bo* or *pha* Ya ngal Gyim kong, whose unique identity and purificatory practices were all carried over from the Dga' thang manuscripts into the *Sel rabs* cycle of rites used in the Srid pa'i lha cult.[35] Since my present interest is to compare the overall cosmology expressed in *Rnel dri 'dul ba* rites with that evident in the *Ste'u* and *Sha slungs* texts, and to assess these as possible early precursors for the cosmology of the cult, I will focus upon the first and by far longest and most elaborated rite within the collection, which covers the first eleven folios of the *Rnel dri 'dul ba'i thabs* manuscript. My discussion will also refer to several subsequent and parallel *rnel dri* narratives for clarification. The aim is not to detail every single procedure in the text, but rather to illustrate the basic operations, orientations and agencies a *Rnel dri 'dul ba* rite entails to accurately illuminate the cosmological framing.

The first rite of the *Rnel dri 'dul ba'i thabs* series has no title, narrative or named victim since the initial folios recording its mythical precedent are missing. While we lack the crisis narrative justifying performance of the rite, we know the subject was a female

35 On Ya ngal in the cult of Srid pa'i lha, see Huber 2013.

infant victim,[36] who almost certainly died as an aborted or miscarried foetus following the overwhelming pattern in other *rnel dri* tales within the collection. The overall structure and individual components of all the rite sequences are clearly evident in the surviving materials, yet the language in places is often obscure with my proposed solutions accordingly annotated.

i. First phase: Ya ngal rites

The initial *Rnel dri 'dul ba* rite sequence is divided into two major phases. The first is presided over by *pha* Ya ngal Gyim kong, and the second by a *dri bon* (also *gri bon*) named Ra ljags Skyi rgyal. Between these two phases, a bridging text indicates the main character of each by stating, 'That above was the purification of a *rnel gri mo*, it is completed. [section break] This below is the method for suppressing *rnel dri'*.[37] The first purification phase includes a ransom rite (*blus*) repeated several times, a ritual journey itinerary transiting between eleven zones of cosmic space, within nine of which a series of elaborate procedures summarised as 'purification' (*bsangs*) must be repeated while undertaking the journey, and then a final procedure for closure once the initial goal has been reached. The itinerary of the vertical, upward ritual journey is of prime interest here. Various instructional cues in the text leave no doubt this is a verbal journey that must be chanted aloud at every stage. Initially, a list of ransom items is enumerated for presentation to the offending spirit agent who caused the victim to become a *dri*. In this case, it is a *srin* named Zo zo ring po. Thus, the departure point for the journey in the tale in question is the location of this spirit. While we lack this information due to missing folios, according to the pattern established in all other *rnel dri* tales within the collection these *srin* are always identified within the terrestrial locations of their victims (see below), and in some tales this is very specifically given, for example, at the boundary between alpine slates and meadow. The process commences as follows:

> Offer [ransom items] into the hands of *srin* Zo zo ring po.
> Ransoming [the victim] from the hands of *srin* Zo zo ring po,
> Transit the doors that are upwards, the types of which are
> The doorsill of the pass,

36 At the end of Ya ngal's first phase of rites, the *bu grI mo* is cited, while the completion statement mentions a *rnel grI mo*; see *Dga' thang* 37-38, 139, f.9, l.4, l.7.

37 *De yan chad rnel drI mo'i bsangs lags te / rdzogs sho [= sa + ho] // // // 'di man chad rnel drI gdul ba'i thabs so*; see *Dga' thang* 38, 139, f.9, l.7-8.

The bamboo door of the sheep,

The pine door [of] the horse head, and

The long water reeds[38] [door], and depart. [39]

Following this, a range of helping ritual aids are gained to expedite the journey. One must then 'step upwards over the first doorsill, and depart.'[40] The language of 'door' (*sgo*) architecture here, and how one 'passes' or 'steps over' (*rgal*) the 'doorsills' or 'thresholds' (*ma*[41] *them*) in traditional houses – later also the 'narrow path' (*'phrang*) leading to/from a house door is included – is entirely commonplace terminology and imagery from the domestic sphere. There are nine such 'doorsills' or 'thresholds' to pass over or step across, each numbered, with movement between and through them continually upwards,[42] in order to reach a final point.

Crossing each doorsill, one enters a new spacial level each time in this upward series. These nine levels are generally colour- and substance-coded, have a familiar topography and people (*myi bo*) in them, and sometimes disturbing images are associated with them. The ontological status of these levels is not at all obvious from the text itself. For example, they could be so many 'versions' of the regular world as it appears to a troubled *rnel dri* being. This theme is encountered in another Dga' thang text, the *Byol rabs*, where a man living in the world is troubled by 'bad omens' (*ltas ngan*) which distort reality for him, and we find

38 For the reading *chu rba* > *chu sba* (or *spa*) 'water reed', I follow the pattern in these texts of 'doors' being most often identified with particular types of woods or woody vegetation. A precedent of this type for *rba* and *smyug* together occurs in *Rnel dri 'dul ba* ritual instructions in a list of implements/devices called *shad* ('rake', 'brush'?) made from three types of wood or woody plant stems, *byang gyI rba shad dang / bod gyI shing shad dang / mon gyI smyug shad dang / shad gsum gyis bshad [read: gshad] do //; Dga' thang* 34, 132, f.3, l.3-4.

39 *Srin zo zo ring po'i phag du phul / srIn za za ring po'I phyag nas blus te / la'I them sgo dang / lug gyI smyug sgo dang / rta rgo [read: mgo?] gsom sgo dang / chu rba rang [read: sba ring?] gyI rigs yan chad gyI cig bgrod te gshegs so /; Dga' thang* 33, 131, f.1, l.9-f.2, l.1.

40 *Rma them pa cig yar ru rgal te gshegs pa; Dga' thang* 33-34, 132, f.2, l.7-8.

41 The original *rma* spelling is another example of the *r* superfix added to words which lack it in Classical Tibetan found throughout Dga' thang manuscripts, e.g *brla* for *bla*, while an *r* superfix is written for the *d* prefix of standardised Classical Tibetan, e.g. *rgu* for *dgu*, *rngul* for *dngul*. Moreover, in Srid pa'i lha cult manuscripts from valleys in northeast Bhutan directly adjacent to Lho brag, addition of an *r* superfix which does not occur conventionally is a common scribal practice, e.g. *rdus* for *dus*, *rdang* for *dang*, etc. A *rma* orthography could possibly have other meanings, but I strongly doubt that here due to the cognate and purely conventional vocabulary of house, door and entranceway it occurs with.

42 For example, f.5, l.10 ... *rma them pa gsum yar rgal na*; f.8, l.1 ... *rma them pa bdun yar rgal te*; f.8, l.11 ... *rma them pa rgu ya rol na*', and so on.

Old Tibetan expressions for worldly 'calamities' used in that narrative as well.[43] This *Byol rabs* is a case where a ransom is deployed to free a victim experiencing such perceptions, and thus appears similar to the first *Rnel dri 'dul ba* rite. These nine levels might also be representations of the type of defiled world resulting from the circumstances of death giving rise to a *rnel dri*, and the impure presence of its subsequent uncontrolled wandering. The main defilement concern is explicitly stated to be bodily fluids and matter released into the world during deaths of expectant mothers and their foetuses or new-borns, when conditions such as septic abortions or miscarriages induced by violent accidents occur leading to the advent of a *rnel dri*. This theme is reiterated time and again in parallel antecedent tales throughout the *Rnel dri 'dul ba'i thabs*, for example:

The mother's head was facing upwards.
The child's head was facing downwards.
The pus shot out like a [bolting] horse.
The blood welled up, groaning like an ox.
The placenta was twisted in the covering.[44]
The blood spread out, *tsa ra ra*.
Defilement of the *lha* melted the glaciers.
Defilement of the lakes penetrated to their depths.
Up above, the *lha* were unworshipped.
Down below, the *dri* were unsuppressed.[45]

Thus, the world is 'defiled' (*bnol* > *mnol*) literally from top to bottom, which cuts off vital connections between living persons and their *lha*, and again, we see it is the living who are motivated to perform such rites since they are affected and will be its prime beneficiaries. The main rites for 'purification of defilement' (*mnol bsangs*) up the vertical axis, and leading eventually to the *lha*, are performed by the Ya ngal ritual specialist. However one views the nature of the nine levels of the itinerary, the ritual specialist must perform purification rites

43 For example, *skyin dang babs pa las* and *rma[n] dang sa las*; see the edition of *Byol rabs* sections in Karmay 2009: 79 for l.169-170.

44 In this context, the *dgab* 'covering' (usually in nominal compounds based upon *'gebs*) must be the amniotic sac or membranes which develop together with a placenta, and in which a miscarried foetus is frequently delivered intact.

45 *Ma mgo gyen du bstan / bu mgo thur du bstan / chu ser rta ltar rgyag [/] khrag glangs glang ltar 'khun / sha ma dgab la dkris // gtIng khrag tsa ra ra / lha bnol [read: mnol] gangs bzhu 'o // mtsho bnol [read: mnol] gtIng bkrum mo // yar ste lha ma mchod / mar de [read: te] dri ma btul /*; e.g. *Dga' thang* 48, 157-158, f.27, l.9-f.28, l.1.

each time in preparation for passing to the next level within the ascending ninefold series. These transitions through the levels are expressed using the image of moving out of the door of a village house and closing it behind oneself:

With the occurrence of each included procedure,
Take a step out towards the narrow path, and
Say "Open the door which is like bone-white conch!
Open the door which is like a [black] ink inscription!
Open the door of the copper narrow path and iron narrow path!"
And break each narrow path wooden stave.
In each instance, invite the Ya ngal and his concomitant purification of defilement. [46]

The doors are thus encountered, opened, traversed and a wooden stave is broken to obstruct them once again. This is clearer still in parallel *rnel dri* tales. For instance, in the Skyi ro narrative Ya ngal Gyim kong opens the way to the *lha* and then,

Each of the doors is traversed.
The door of turquoise bamboo.
The door of copper [coloured] wild rose.
The door of fir tree. [47]
Lay down obstructions[48] for the thirteen doors.[49]

Note that the 'doors' are made of various types of wood, sometimes colour-coded, with a total of nine doors for some versions of the rite and thirteen doors in other versions. Furthermore, in a list of procedures at the beginning of the second phase of this first and most elaborate *Rnel dri 'dul ba* rite one of them is termed 'cutting off the narrow path of *dri*' (*dri 'phrang bcad pa*). As we will see shortly, the procedure of breaking wooden staves

46 *Cho ga khongs re lags pa dang / 'phrang mo ngo long cig byas la / rus dkar dung tsam gyI sgo phye cig zer / snag byang tsam gyI sgo phye cig / zangs 'phrang lcags 'phrang sgo phye cig byas la' / 'phrang gdong mong [read: ldong mo] re re gcag go / de re re la yang [read: ya] ngal dang bnol [read: mnol] bsangs khongs re spyan drang ngo /; Dga' thang* 35, 134, f.4, l.2-5.

47 For *'dong mo 'wangs* read: *sdong mo wangs*. The *wang [shing]* refers to fir in my research region, and to my knowledge in southern Tibetan dialects it seems to be a variant of *thang [shing]*, but cf. *wang mo* in *BGT* 2366 *shing mngar gyi rigs shig.*

48 While *'ga 'ga tsam* might conventionally be read as a variation of Classical Tibetan *'ga' tsam* 'a few', I read *'gag 'gag tsam cIg*, parallel to the earlier *sgo sgo cig* preceding the motion verb. On *'gag* 'obstruction', see Jäschke 1881: 92 and 'enge Stelle', see *Wörterbuch*, 12: 362, BGT: 486 *'gag = sgo 'gag.*

49 *Sgo sgo cig bgrod 'tshal lo / smyug ma g.yu'i sgo / se ba zangs gyI sgo / 'dong mo 'wangs gyI sgo / sgo mo bcu gsum la 'ga 'ga [read: 'gag 'gag] tsam cIg bsgyer ro //; Dga' thang* 49, 159, f.29, l.10-11. For *bsgyer* cf. *'gyer* and *sgyer*.

is also used for the final closure of the entire Ya ngal sequence. When the ninth and final doorsill at the end of this first phase of the rite has been crossed, the itinerary then states:

The deceased, an infant (*rnel*), died.

Deliver it. Deliver it to the *sman*.

When it is understood that [crossing] doorsill nine is completed,

The female child *dri* is ready for the *sman*.

Its pus is ready for lustrations. [50]

Concerning ritual requisites for this, excavate a hole for each doorsill, nine of them.

[Use] nine rough stones. [51]

[Use] nine billets of wood.

Place each stone and a billet [in/at each hole?].

Break each wooden stave. [52]

The method of accumulating [the requisites] together with the method of laying down [the obstructions] are one.

That above was the purification of a female infant *dri*; it is complete. [53]

In other *rnel dri* tales within the collection featuring different ritual specialists, the same overall ritual process ensues, but with a clearer account of certain details of purification rites that merely occur in the Ya ngal versions as a single word or phrase. For instance, in several listings of his rite techniques and requisites, a Ya ngal is said to use nine smoke types (*dud*

50 The image here is related to the subdued child *dri* requiring ritual ablution (*bkrus*) and lustration (*tshan*) prior to delivery to the *sman*, for example *bu gri rgod las g.yung du btul / chu sna mang po nas bkrus / tshan sna mang po nas btab / [...] bu gri sman du bskyal /; see Dga' thang* 42, 146, f.16, l.7-9.

51 For *shal ba*, cf. Jäschke 1881: 557 *shal ba* and *shal ma* 'a flint, sharp-edged stone'.

52 For *'dong mo* read: *ldong mo* 'wooden stave' or *sdong po* 'tree branch/trunk', cf. elsewhere *'dong mo 'wangs* for a wooden ritual port or gate (*Dga' thang* 49, 159, f.29, l.11), and further *'dong shas bcu gsum na' / stag pa'I rgam shing dang bcu re gsum /* as ritual materials with other types of wood (*ibid.* 52, 165, f.35, l.8-9), cf. also *shing sna bcu gsum* with *shing bu* and *'gal pa*. (*ibid.* 50, 161, f.31, l.2).

53 *Dga' thang* 37-38, 139, f.9, l.3-8, *grongs yang rnel te grongs / bskyal ba sman du bskyal / rma them pa rgu rdzogs par shes na / bu gri [read: dri] mo sman du rung / de'i chu ser tshan du rung / 'dI'i ya stags nI rma them pa re re la khung bu re re rgu bsko // shal ba rgu / 'gal pa rgu // 'gal pa dang shal ba re re yang gzhag / 'dong mo re re yang gcag / bsag thabs dang gyer thabs bcas gcig go / de yan chad rnel grI [read: dri] mo'i bsangs lags te / rdzogs sho [= sa + ho] //.*

rgu)[54] and 'live birds' (*gson ma*)[55] as part of upward purification of defiled *lha*. In the Glan yul tale we read more fully,

The *lde gshen* Rmun bu and
The *tshe myi* Rmu rgyal
Used thirteen types of wood,
A large surface of woven/plaited material[56] and
Bamboo to make a long wall. [57]
With the nine 'son trees' (*shing bu*) they made wooden billets.
By way of thirteen live birds (*gson ma*),
They purified the *lha* upwards.
They suppressed the *sri* downwards.
They opened the way for the coming of the *lha*.
They shone a bright light for the lord.
Humans and *lha* met up.
Lords and subjects met up. [58]

The nine smoke types mentioned elsewhere are produced by burning wooden staves cut from the nine 'son trees' cited here. This ritual tree classification has been preserved as the 'nine son trees of valleys' (*lung shing bu dgu*) – together with the 'nine father trees of sunny slopes' (*bdag shing pha dgu*), and 'nine mother trees of shady slopes' (*srib shing ma dgu*) already known from Old Tibetan references – in the Srid pa'i lha cult as part of the *Sel rabs*

54 For instance, 'For each included procedure as well, a Ya ngal prepares what is befitting with purification and nine smoke [types].' (*cho ga khongs re re la yang / ya ngal cig gyIs bsangs dang / bdud [read: dud] rgu dang rigs bcas /*); *Dga' thang* 34-35, 133, f.3, l.10-11.

55 For instance, '*Pha* Ya ngal Gyim kong, at the junction of three paths, purified the *lha* upwards again with nine *sri* holes, nine *mjol*, one rough stone, one wooden billet [and] one *gson ma*' (*pha ya ngal gyIm kyong [read: kong] gyis / lam sum mdo shed du / sri gung [read: khung] rgu mdzol [read: mjol] rgu / sha ma [read: shal ba] gIg 'gal pa cIg / gson ma cIg la / yar te lha yang bsang /*); *Dga' thang* 51, 163, f.33, l.8-10, with the readings *khung, mjol* and *shal ba* based upon other precedents in the manuscript, cf. n.50 above.

56 Speculative. For *sle mo ngo cen* read: *sle bo/mo ngos chen*. A *sle* or *sle mo* is 'a coarse blanket' Jäschke 1881: 596, cf. BGT 2996 *sle mo*, while *sle ba/po/bo* refers to 'a flat basket' woven or plaited (*sle ba*) from cane or bamboo; Jäschke 1881: 596, *CDTD* (nouns) entries 8998-8999.

57 For *snyags ma* read: *smyug ma*, for which *snyug(s) ma* is a common variant. For *'dram rings* read: *'gram ring*, apparently a 'long wall/base' as a ritual structure or altar of a sort made from various woods.

58 *Dga' thang* 50, 160-161, ff.31, l.2-6, *lde gshen rmun bu dang / tshe myI rmu rgyal gyIs / shIng sna bcu gsum dang / sle mo ngo cen dang / snyags ma 'dram rings las btang / shing bu rgu dang de las 'gal pa bgyIs / gson ma bcu gsum las / yar te lha bsangs / mar te sri bnan / lha'I gshegs shul phye / rje'i snang gsal sgron / myI dang lha ru mjal / rje dang 'bangs su mjal /.*

cycle whose primordial initiator is Ya ngal Gyim kong.[59] The term *gson ma* here literally means 'a live one' applied to birds,[60] and various species of *gson ma* birds used during rites frequently have something attached to them. This becomes clearer in the Dbye mo yul grugs tale:

> The *lha* were driven off, driven into the sky.
> The wild geese vanished, vanished into the lake.
> The Dbye *gshen* Mkhar bu,
> Attaching a *gshang* of gold [61]
> To a vulture *gson ma*,
> Opened the portal of the sky again.
> Upwards, the *lha* were purified again. [62]

Some of these same lines and motifs occur in *Sel rabs* texts featuring Ya ngal in the Srid pa'i lha cult.[63] Very similar descriptions for using *gson ma* and also bird wings – perhaps still on living birds – occur in Old Tibetan texts recording death rites, apparently to convey the 'bad news' of death and prepare an open path (*lam*) into the sky for a psychopomp animal. [64]

Using all these and still other rite techniques, the Ya ngal's ever upward ritual journey through the levels arrives somewhere beyond the ninth level. It is the second phase of suppression/conversion rites that now commence which crucially inform us where the

59 For instance, in the *Dri zhim dud sel* rite within the *Sel rabs* cycle, the *shing bu dgu* include the species *ba lu, su lu, 'om bu, tsher bu, mkhan bu, srin bu, kham bu, skyer bu* and *star bu*; see *Shawa 1,* Text 3, 37a, 6-39a, 1.

60 *Gson ma* literally 'a live one', cf. Das 1902: 1314 "*gson ma* colloq. for *gson po: phug ron gson ma* a live pigeon". The *gson ma* birds are always prepared – sometimes by having objects attached to them – or at least are present just before a purification, see elsewhere in the *Rnel dri 'dul ba'i thabs* at *Dga' thang* 50, 162, f.32, l.5, *bya rgod gson ma la / gser gyI sha btags pa / gnam gyI mthongs yang phye / yar te lha yang bsangs /; Dga' thang* 51, 163, f.33, l.9-10: *sha ma cIg 'gal pa cIg / gson ma cIg la / yar te lha yang bsang /,* and in the *Byol rabs* at *Dga' thang* 16, 105, f.21, l.6: *bdud bya skyung kha gson ma la / gser gyi dril chen btags /,* and also see PT 1047, l.360: *bya gag gson ma // 'am spyang ki ltong gyis btag ste.*

61 I read the otherwise obscure original *gser gyI sha* or *'sha* of gold' attached to the bird here as an error for *gshang* 'flatbell' since in a *Byol rabs* among the Dga' thang manuscripts we find a *gson ma* rite technique described as 'attach a large bell of gold to a demon bird jackdaw, the *gson ma'* (*bdud bya skyung kha gson ma la / gser gyi dril chen btags /; Dga' thang* 16, 105, f.21, l.6).

62 *Lha 'phangs gnam du 'phangs / ngang yal mtsho ru yal / dbye gshen mkhar bu yIs / bya rgod gson ma la / gser gyI sha [read: gshang] btags pa / gnam gyI mthongs yang phye / yar te lha yang bsangs /; Dga' thang* 50, 162, f.32, l.4-6.

63 For example, in *Shawa 1,* Text 3, f.31a, l.1-2: *des kyang lha yar gnam du yar // des kyang ngang yar mtsho la yar //.*

64 See PT 1194, l.49-50, *gshog la god kad bya rjungs btags na / gnam mthongs [phye? OTDO* reads: *'gyed* here] [---] *sprin gyi go seld to /.* Preceding this line the text successively indicates the *gshog* is a vulture's wings, e.g. l.37 *bya rgod,* l.40 *rgod thang,* l.41 *rgod gshog,* etc., cf. also Stein 2010: 266 on *gshog pa.* Also PT 1047, l.360 *bya gag gson ma // 'am spyang ki ltong gyis btag ste.*

journey ultimately leads to.

ii. Second phase: *Dri bon* rites

At the commencement of the second phase, there follow a series of episodes in the text described as 'explanatory words of *dri* suppression' (*dri gdul ba'i tshig bshad*), which feature the performance of a *dri bon* specialist. He commences his work up at the highest or ninth level – coded 'gold' or 'yellow' (*gser*) in this instance of the rite – and up as far as which Ya ngal has already purified. Then the *dri bon* works his way downwards through the coded levels in the reverse order to that passed through on Ya ngal's upward ritual journey. In these short, formulaic episodes, which are repeated in most of the subsequent antecedent tales throughout the whole text, the location of the victim's *dri* in each case is always first described with the set formula, 'Its *dri* was upwards, rambling in the sky' (*de'i dri yar gnam du yar*). Upwards in the sky is precisely where Ya ngal ended the first phase of the rite. At this point, a fixed, threefold subjugation, purification and dispatch procedure follows, apparently coming to an end in the abode of *sman* and *lha* beings. This was signalled already at the end of the nine level with the words, 'The female child *dri* is ready for the *sman*. Its pus is ready for lustrations.' Here are several descriptions of this procedure from the second phase of suppressing *rnel dri* by the *dri bon*. The first instance concerns Gser yul, reached by Ya ngal at the top of his upward ritual journey after crossing the ninth doorsill:

> In the land Gser yul Gser stod,
> Gser lcam Nyag, an infant (*rnel*), died.
> Her *dri* was upwards, rambling in the sky.
> The *dri bon* Ra ljags Skyi rgyal
> Converted the *dri* from wild to tame.
> It's hide was tanned from thick (i.e. haughty)[65] to fine.
> From the *dri*, [she] was brought down to the *btsun*.
> From the *mtshun*, [she] was delivered to the *sman*. [66]

65 *'Khengs* 'to be full', 'puffed up' (Jäschke 1881: 42, 56) in / *pags 'khengs las zhib du mnyes* / refers to an untanned hide, and has to be read in parallel with the alternate, recurring phrasing / *pags gsar las zhib du mnyes* / (cf. f.10, l.5, l.11, f.11, l.3).

66 *Yul gser yul gser stod na' / gser lcam nyag nI rnel te grongs / de'i dri yar gnam du yar / grI [read: dri] bon ra ljags skyI rgyal gyIs / drI rgod las g.yung du btul / pags 'khengs las zhib du mnyes / drI las btsun du phab / mtshun las sman du bskyal //; Dga' thang* 38, 139-140, f.9, l.11-f.10, l.3.

And again, further down the series,

In the land of Shel, Shel yul stod,
A girl of Shel, an infant (*rnel*), died.
Her *dri* was upwards, rambling in the sky.
The *dri bon* Ra ljags Skyi rgyal
Converted the *dri* from wild to tame.
It's hide was tanned from thick (i.e. haughty) to fine.
From the *dri*, [she] was brought down to the *btsun*.
From the *mtshun*, [she] departed to the *lha*. [67]

Across the range of examples we have, the final dispatch is consistently governed by the verbs *bskyal* 'deliver', *phab* 'bring down' and *gshegs* 'depart/go to'. It represents some kind of spacial descent via *btsun/mtshun*, followed by an exit that ultimately leads to *lha* and *sman* beings.

The ritual step for this phase dealing specifically with defiling bodily fluids and matter associated with a *rnel dri* death is described more explicitly in the later *rnel dri* tale of 'Gos za Phyam 'dar ma:

The child *dri* was converted from wild to tame.
Ablutions were done using many types of waters.
Many types of lustration fluids were cast upon it. [...]
The child *dri* was delivered to the *sman*.[68]

In other *rnel dri* antecedent tales, we find the final dispatch to the abode of *lha* and *sman* characterised by a specific change of identity, and being handled by a particular specialist. In the Lho ga Lang grug tale, the Lord of Lho (an ancient clan) has a daughter Lho za Dril bu Sil sil sman. When pregnant with a female infant, a demon penetrates her womb, illness ensues, and a bad death follows, with 'The deceased, an infant, dragged off for *dri*.'[69] After being ransomed back from her *srin* demon keeper Zo bo ring po,

67 *Yul shel shel yul stod na / shel gyI bo mo rnel te grongs / de'i dri yar gnam du yar / drI bon ra ljags skyI rgyal gyIs / dri rgod las g.yung du btul / pags 'khengs las zhIb du mnyes / grI [read: dri] las btsun du phab / mtshun las lhar [read: lha] ru gshegs //; Dga' thang* 38, 140, f.10, l.16-9.

68 *Bu gri rgod las g.yung du btul / chu sna mang po nas bkrus / tshan sna mang po nas btab / [...] bu gri sman du bskyal /;* see *Dga' thang* 42, 146, f.16, l.7-9.

69 *Grongs pa rnel grIr [read: drIr] drongs /; Dga' thang* 46, 153, f.23, l.5-6. On *[']drongs* in these formulations, cf. also *Dga' thang* 51, 165, f.35, l.2, *drongs yang glan drir drongs /*, Jäschke 1881: 284 *'dren pa* 4. and p. 285 *'drongs, BGT* 1430 *'drong ba.*

[She] was drawn out and departed to the *lha* and *sman*.

[She] was offered into the hands of *sman bon* 'Bring dang.

[She] departed to the *lha* and *sman*.

As for [her] name, it was given as Lha za Dril bu Sil bu sman.

The benefit [of the rite] was like that in times past.[70]

The deceased infant victim, who was first identified only as the 'infant female child' (*bu mo rnel*) or as the 'infant' (*rnel*) gains a new name based upon that of her deceased mother, Lho za Dril bu Sil sil sman, whose name literally means 'Lho Clan Lady, Bell Ringing *Sman*'. The victim now dispatched to the *lha* and *sman* is appropriately renamed Lha za Dril bu Sil bu sman, literally '*Lha* Lady, Bell Tinkling *Sman*', linking her symbolically back to her dead mother but marking her new *lha* category of being. This in no orthographic variant, nor is it incidental. The intentional renaming here is just one instance of a wider pattern evident in *Rnel dri 'dul ba, Ste'u* and *Sha slungs* rites that combines marking of origins or descent together with transitions in modes of existence between *lha* and humans, and one I will explore in more detail in sections below.

It is also apparent here that it was not just *dri bon* who presided over the final dispatch, for *sman bon* also specialised in transfers to the *lha* and *sman* beings. This is based upon older precedents, but represents one of various apparent transformations that I return to again in the part III (chap. 4).

2.2 Cosmological framing

Where exactly *sman, lha* and *mtshun/btsun* are stationed in the cosmos is generally apparent in the *Rnel dri 'dul ba'i thabs*. Unambiguously, the *lha* are repeatedly said to be upwards in the sky. As for *sman*, in one case immediately following the dispatch of a *dri* to such agents, we are told that,

The *dur gshen* Rma da' delivered the infant *dri* to the *sman*.

Sman of the alpine slates (*g.ya*) ground it to fragments.

Today, the infant *dri* is subdued to the core.[71]

70 *Lha dang sman du bsnya [read: bsnyad] ste btang / sman bon 'brIng dang phyag du phul / lha dang sman du gshags [read: gshegs] / mying ni lha za drIl bu sIl bu sman du btags / gna' de ltar phan /; Dga' thang* 46, 145, f.24, l.9-10.

71 *Dur gshen rma da' yIs / rnel drI sman du bskyal / g.ya sman sil mar btags / de ring rnel grI'i [read: dri'i] gzhung du gdul lo /; Dga' thang* 52, 166-167, f.36, l.9-f.37, l.1; cf. also f.21, l.1-2.

Thus, *sman* here are in a terrestrial habitat, albeit a high alpine one. This correlates with many other ecologically-marked *sman* beings in Old Tibetan documents, where they occur in or at the sky, peaks, rivers, lakes, alpine slates, rock cliffs, and so on.[72] It is worth pointing out here that *lha* and ecologically-marked *sman* are already attested among the oldest records of mundane rites surviving in Tibetan language. Wooden slips inscribed with Old Tibetan that were recovered from the Lop Nor region, and dating to the mid-8th to mid-9th century period, record rites addressing *lha, sman, yul sman* and *rtse sman* by specialists termed *lha bon po, sku gshen* and *zhal ta pa.* [73]

As for *mtshun/btsun*, the text only indicates they are somewhere in a stage between the human world and the abode of *lha* and *sman*, nothing more. I have let the original spellings *btsun* and *mtshun* stand in my translations because throughout the *Rnel dri 'dul ba'i thabs* manuscript they continually alternate in formulaic passages without any clear pattern.[74] One can only logically conclude that they refer to the same type of being, with *mtshun* (also *[b]tshun*) the original form of the word, while *btsun* represents a folk etymology.[75] The older attestations of the word apparently can mean 'ancestor', but only within specific contexts. In Old Tibetan sources, the imperial rulers referred specifically to their own 'ancestors' using the term *yab myes/pha myes*, whereas *mtshun* or *btsun* (and variants) almost always occurs in expressions related more directly to *lha* and *phy[w]a*, with *mgon tshun* or *'gon [b]tsun* being a typical example which spanned the ca. 11th-century watershed period as a reference in myths.[76] Classical Tibetan references retained this connection between *mtshun* and *lha*, with a 16th century Tibetan lexicon defining *mtshun*

72 See Stein 2010: 72-73, 267-268 for a summary of references to *sman* in some Old Tibetan and early Classical Tibetan sources, with IOL Tib J 0739 and IOL Tib J 0738 particularly rich in such references, while van Schaik 2013: 242 n.26, 247 cites Old Tibetan references to *rtse sman*.

73 Van Schaik 2013: 241-247.

74 We read alternatively *drI rgod las mtshun du phab / btsun las sman du bskyal (Dga' thang* 38, 140, f.10, l.5-6), *grI las btsun du phab / mtshun las lhar ru gshegs* (f.10, l.8-9), *drI las mtshun du phab / mtshun las sman du bskyal* (40, 143, f.13, l.1), and compare *dri rgod las g.yung du btul / dri las btsun du phab* (44-45, 150-151, f.20, l.10-f.21, l.1) with *rgod las g.yung du btul / drI las mtshun du phab /* (45, 152, f.22, l.4-5).

75 Joanna Bialek *pers. comm.* 9 May, 2016.

76 Variants occur in PT 1134, IOL Tib J 0739, IOL Tib J 0731. A variant of the segment *gnam rim pa dgu steng du mgon tshun* from PT 1134: 11, 19 occurs in the Dga' thang manuscript as *gnam gyI pha mtha' na / 'gon btsun phywa; Dga' thang* 53, 167, f.37, l.10. In *Gsang ba bon lugs* and *Grags pa bon lugs* narratives we find *mgon btsun phya; Mkhas pa Lde'u* 230. The form *mtshun* means 'patrilineal ancestor' in Classical Tibetan. See the discussions of all these early ancestor terms in Stein 1983: 193-194 n.87 and Stein 1985: 104 n.47.

as 'the male's *lha* of patrilineal ancestors',[77] while for *mtshun* (*gyi*) *lha* a mid-20th century lexicon offers 'a *lha* who is of this world, a *'go ba'i lha* which descends from the time of male ancestors'.[78] However, in the *Rnel dri 'dul ba'i thabs* there is no male gender assigned to *mtshun/btsun* and it is often female victims who are delivered to them (see below). In the absence of direct evidence, these categories of being are best left gender unassigned and neutral, and this applies especially to *sman* as well.[79] If one wanted to translate *mtshun/btsun* here as 'ancestor', then *sman* and *lha* must also be accorded ancestor status since they all share the same position in the *Rnel dri 'dul ba'i thabs*. As will be seen in the following analysis of the *Ste'u* and *Sha slungs* texts, this appears to be the case. Concerning the intended location of these beings in *Rnel dri 'dul ba* tales, they are definitely up the vertical cosmic axis. In an Old Tibetan document, the *btsun* appear together with *btsan, bdud, rmu* and the nine *g.yen* (*g.yen dgu*)as a group of spirit 'thieves' (*rkun ma*) who require a ransom rite,[80] or in other cases these beings can all exist arrayed up the vertical cosmic axis as the 'nine *g.yen* in the sky' (*gnam la g.yen dgu*), and 'nine star *g.yen'* (*skar ma g.yen dgu*),[81] while in the document PT 1060 a descending hierarchy indexed to special horses begins with the *lha* land Gung dang (i.e. Gung thang), then the *bdud, dmu, skar, gzha'* (< *gza'*), *sprin, gnyan, klu, sman* and *srin*.

2.3 Summary

The overall sequence of the Ya ngal chanted ritual journey describes an itinerary passing up the vertical cosmic axis through a series of topographically defined levels, via doors that are opened and closed, doorsills that are crossed and paths followed, all indexed to woods and mundane materials and culminating in the sky (Fig. 1). This same pattern is more briefly

77 *Pha mes pho lha*; citation in Stein 2010: 62-63.

78 *Chos grags* 710-711 has *'jig rten pa'i lha zhig ste pha mes kyi dus nas brgyud pa'i 'go ba'i lha*, Another recent lexicon has the same definition, but adds that *mtshun* is a term of 'Bon usage' (*bon lugs*) meaning 'the quintessence of the mobile vitality principle or life force of patrilineal ancestors; see *BGT* 2315, #2, *bon lugs ltar pha mes kyi bla'am srog gi bcud /.*

79 The common idea that the word *sman* refers to female beings is a misconception based upon other readings of that word with the same or very close formal spellings (e.g. *dman*), and any specific gender assigned to generic *lha, sman* and *mtshun/btsun* needs to be justified by evidence in context. In various old myths, the genderless category *sman* is sometimes assigned a gender marker to indicate a female spirit of this type, for example, see *Rlangs* 11 on a *gnam sman ma*, just as *lha* and *mtshun/btsun* can be gender-marked in context.

80 IOL Tib J 0734: 7r267.

81 See IOL Tib J 0731 *passim*, PT 1285, l.v.015, and IOL Tib J 0734, l.7r267.

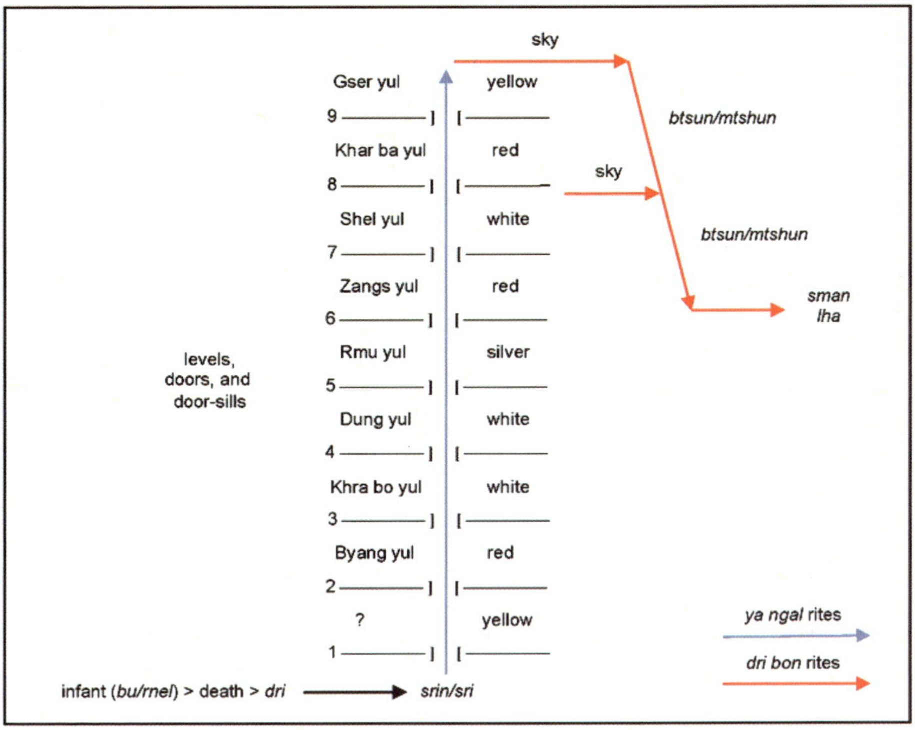

Fig. 1. Sequences and orientations in a *Rnel dri 'dul ba* rite.

reiterated in various of the successive *Rnel dri 'dul ba* tales, and of special significance is the fact that references to both nine level and thirteen level itineraries and rite sequences occur.

3. *Ste'u* and *Sha slungs* rites

3.1 Introduction

Here I analyse the vocabulary, contents and cosmological perspectives in the *Ste'u* and *Sha slungs* texts, respectively. The language in both texts is Classical Tibetan, with a few orthographic and linguistic features indicating their age. The surviving folios on each recto and verso side of the manuscript are comprised of painted illustrations within framed panels, with short passages of text accompanying each of them beneath. Both *Ste'u* and *Sha slungs* texts consist of collections of fourfold folio series (Fig. 2), with first, second, third and fourth folios in each series dedicated to a common theme across all subsequent folios of the same number. Existing complete folios allow nine or ten such series, or surviving sections thereof, to be wholly or partially reconstructed.[82] However, the content of both texts reveals that there were a total of thirteen types of *ste'u* and thirteen types of *sha slungs*, respectively, represented within each complete text. While the individual *sha slungs* are unnumbered, the *ste'u* described on every third folio within each fourfold series are numbered, and *ste'u* numbers four, six, seven, eight, nine, ten and thirteen are present among the surviving folios. This indicates the original manuscript was formed of thirteen fourfold folio series, recto and verso, respectively. The assumption is strongly reinforced by the evidence of the number thirteen being ritually and cosmographically significant in earlier and contemporary sources. We already observed this in Dga' thang manuscripts discussing rites for mundane purposes which are approximately contemporary with the *Ste'u* and *Sha slungs* texts. Moreover, in Dga' thang texts we find recurring reference to the specific motif of the sky or the upward vertical axis composed of thirteen levels (*gnam rim pa bcu gsum*). [83] The same cosmographic motif features in Old Tibetan documents,[84] but also in early Classical Tibetan sources composed in or by authors from and active in southernmost Tibet around Lho brag not long after the three old rites under study in this paper were in circulation.[85] We are thus dealing with an old cosmographic motif which is well-attested as localised in the most likely origin region of the *Ste'u* and *Sha slungs* manuscript (see chap. 5), and, as we will see below, exactly the same motif forms the cosmographic framework for a descent itinerary from sky to earth described across all surviving third folios of the *Ste'u* text.

Along with the text passages, the paintings on each folio of the manuscript are potentially instructive for understanding the rites being described. However, it is not always clear what the various illustrations of human-like figures actually depict since all lack inscriptions directly within their frames, while others do not correlate with the text

82 The second folio in the Na-v/Na-r series in the overview of surviving folios by Klimburg-Salter, Lodja and Ramble 2013: 39, and the Na-2r/Na-2v of Bellezza 2013: 68, 108, offers no evidence for its placement in this position – Bellezza's linking of the text fragments has no philological basis. It might have belonged to any of the missing series except the first one (the initial *yang* on facs. Na-2v, l.1 rules this out), and needs to be provisionally considered as unplaced.

83 See *Dga' thang* 13, 101, f.17, l.2-4, and 59, 177, f.47, 5.

84 See PT 1038, l.12, see Spanien and Imaeda 1978-1979, v.2: pl.312.

85 The most interesting examples occur in the early redaction of the progenitor king narrative by Nyang ral Nyi ma 'od zer (1124-1192) composed in ca. 1170s-1190s (*Nyang ral chos 'byung* 157-158), and in the autobiographical account of Gu ru Chos dbang's (1212-1270/73?) early visionary experience at Gnam skas Brag (*Gu chos rang rnam* 12a, 3-4).

passages beneath them.[86] It is quite possible some groupings of these illustrations represent idealised views of ritual performance of post-mortem rites. For example, ritual actors wearing armour and holding weapons occur very widely in death and post-mortem rites conducted by highland shamans along the extended eastern Himalayas, while they are also represented in Old Tibetan accounts of funerals.[87] Such readings of the paintings deserve further comparative analysis. Neither paintings nor text provide any direct statement concerning the manuscript's geographical provenance, although various internal references and comparisons with other materials allow for well-informed preliminary conclusions about location of origins or composition (see chap. 5). The manuscript leaves the impression of being a rather local production which was not intended to be widely circulated for generic use, although the text passages do contain a range of traces of contact with a greater milieu of older mundane rites and myths, including death rites such as those recorded in Old Tibetan documents. It is noteworthy that both *Ste'u* and *Sha slungs* texts completely lack the word *bon*, and while *gshen* occurs three times within the texts, this is merely as an element within compound names. Thus, as with the *Rnel dri 'dul ba'i thabs*, the only supporting sources we can draw upon with any confidence for an analysis are pre-11th century Old Tibetan ritual texts from Dunhuang, and the approximately contemporary Dga' thang manuscripts recording mundane rites which are of known geographical provenance. Most personal and place names are of the type found in many older Tibetan texts dedicated to mundane rites and the antecedent tales usually accompanying them. They are composed from a pool of meaningful elements that are constantly rearranged into different compound forms. There are, however, a small collection of immediately recognisable, more enduring named identities within the texts, and these, along with other clues and information, also contribute evidence for proposing a location of origin or composition.

86 For example, which – if either – of the two couples mentioned in the text passage on folio Cha-1r translated below is being depicted in the painted panel associated with it (Fig. 12)? Or are these people dressed in lay-persons' garments engaged in a rite or hunt, since a bow-shooting pose and archery equipment are shown in the frame? On folio Na-1r (Fig. 22), only the name 'Od de Gung rgyal is mentioned in the inscription, yet a female figure identical to that upon Cha-1r (Fig. 12) is depicted together with the male figure who looks completely different from the other possible 'Od de Gung rgyal image on Cha-4r (Fig. 15), where an armor-clad figure shoots a bow.

87 For examples, on Gurung see Pignède 1993 [1966]: 370-371, on Tamang see Höfer 1997: 16 n.29, plate 9 following p.122, Höfer 1981: plate 11 following p.99, on Mosuo see Chuan-kang Shih 1998: 116-117, plates, and on Naxi see He Limin and He Shincheng 1998: 157-159, and Rock 1955: 8-9. Note also the presence of those who hold spears and battle-axes in a processional list of ritual actors for a royal funeral recorded in the Old Tibetan document PT 1042: 123-124, *de'i 'og du phyag cha mdung pa / de'i 'og du phyag cha dgra sta / pa.*

Fig. 2. Opposite folio sides of the same section of the continuous, folded manuscript, with intact fourfold folio series from *Ste'u* text (l.), and from *Sha slungs* text (r.).

The *Ste'u* and *Sha slungs* texts represent two separate but complimentary rites dedicated to a common goal. The vocabulary and syntax of both are often closely matched, albeit that the unique term *sha slungs* is never cited in the *Ste'u* text, and *ste'u* never in the *Sha slungs* text. Their most distinctive and significant shared vocabulary are references to 'small *lha'* (*lhe'u* < *lha*) and *sman*, and the designation *ne'u zhon* (< *na gzhon*) or 'young ones' to qualify *lhe'u* and *sman*, as well as the description 'small *lha* offspring who are brother and sister' (*lhe'u sras lcam dral*). These references directly indicate the combined purpose of both texts, which is to safely usher new male and female lives into the world from ancestral realms beyond the domestic sphere of human existence. The diminutive *lhe'u* here is rare, occurring as a proper name element in but a few Old Tibetan myths.[88] However, it is unknown to me from other sources as a stand-alone category designation for a type of being or mode of existence as we find it applied in the *Ste'u* and *Sha slungs* texts. Aside from a partial cognate in an Old Tibetan document,[89] the unique diminutive construct *ne'u zhon* meaning 'young one' is certainly closely cognate with *rnel* 'young one/infant' in the approximately contemporary *Rnel dri 'dul ba'i thabs*.

3.2 The *Ste'u* text and rite

The rites defined in the *Ste'u* text are not "funerals," as previous commentators have claimed, although deceased and burials are briefly alluded to on some of the folios. Rather, these rites define post-mortem procedures with the express goal of bringing new life into the world following a death, and the use of various ritual structures and offerings to enable this. Certain terminology in the *Ste'u* text is somewhat antiquated or rare, and must first be carefully appreciated.

The text features recurring use of *bdur* and *bdur yags* or *bdur yags pa*. The verb *bdur* occurs in Old Tibetan texts for death rites, and has been variously translated as 'funeral rite', 'to bury' (a corpse), and once also as 'to conjure' (the dead).[90] In Classical Tibetan, *dur* (and some compounds containing it) continued to mean 'tomb', 'grave', 'burial ground', 'to bury' (*dur du 'jugs pa*), 'dig a grave' (*dur rko ba*), and so on, while the verbs *'dur ba* and *ldur ba* both mean 'to have gone to pieces' or 'to decay'[91] and are probably semantically related to *bdur* and *dur*. Thus, I understand *bdur* in the *Ste'u* text as meaning 'to bury' (a corpse) and

88 See PT 1068: 6, 9, 20, also PT 1134: 67 *et passim*, also in the divination texts PT 1046B: 37 and IOL Tib J 0740: 2, 104, 155. Cf. the *lhe rje* deities in the *Gsang ba'i bon lugs* narrative, see *Mkhas pa Lde'u* 231.

89 See *sne'u* (written *sne 'u*) in IOL Tib J 0734: 5r198, 'in order to embrace a child...' (*sne 'u khyud pyir [read: phyir]...*), Thomas 1957: 69, 87 n.4, while *sne'u* is a rare synonym for *bu tsha* 'child, boy'; see Das 1902: 771.

90 See Dotson 2013: 132, Stein 1971: 501, n.63 and Stein 2010: 62, 257, 258.

91 See *BGT* 1404, 1455.

referring to 'burial'.

The term *yags pa* is quite rare. We know in Old Tibetan it belonged to the ritual domain of death from a single reference in PT 1042 describing a death rite. In that context, four *yag pa* are ritual actors at the start of a ranked sequence which appears to be a procession to the grave entrance, and who are followed by others holding spears and battle-axes, a *gshen* ritual specialist, and still others presumably holding the different ritual devices listed in the text.[92] In later Classical Tibetan usage, *yags* directly signifies post-mortem procedures related to mourning or memorialising the dead. *Yags* is defined as a rite technique of making offerings with a 'ritual support' for the deceased (*'das mchod 'bul rten*), which Melvyn Goldstein glosses as "utensils for offering prayers for the deceased." [93] Other reported Classical Tibetan usages relate *yags* to consolation for the bereaved and to offerings of gifts intended to effect this.[94] In the context of the *Ste'u* text, I understand *yags [pa]* to mean 'mourning rites'. All indications are that the use of *ste'u* rites that the text is actually describing must occur only after burial and mourning rites have been fully accomplished. The text refers to these rites and ritual devices in some instances explicitly as 'the *ste'u* of completed burial and mourning rites' (*bdur yags grub pa'i ste'u*), leaving no doubt they represent a third and different set of post-mortem procedures later on.

Regarding the terms *ste'u* and *sbre'u* for the series of material objects employed as ritual devices or structures in the text, *ste'u* is very possibly related to Classical Tibetan *ste'u shing* or *te'u shing*. Lexicons define this as "a small wooden frame/seat or sitting bench."[95] As will be seen, various *ste'u* have components of wood (*shing*) fashioned into a lattice-work frame, and are said to function as 'supports' (*rten*). The original concept behind the term is more elusive. Since the term applies to a rite for ushering new life into the world, one proposal

92 See the passage in PT 1042: 123-125, *sor [read: sgor, ? cf. l.41] gshegste [read: gshegs te]* / (123) *gshegs kyi rim pa la / thog mal [read: ma] yag pa bzhi / de'i 'og du phyag cha mdung pa / de'i 'og du phyag cha dgra sta* / (124) *pa / de'i 'og du gshen / de'i 'og du zo rig / de'i 'og du nam ka / de'i 'o du smra zhal / de'i 'og du* / (125) *zhal dang sku rten* /, etc.

93 Goldstein 2001: 989, see *yags* in *BGT*: 2545 *'das mchod 'bul rten* /.

94 See *yags* in Das 1902: 1125 "present sent to a bereaved person as a token of condolence; the present of condolence. *ma yags bya snyam pa la"*, also p. 950 *ma yags bya* "to console, give consolation to one who is in grief: *de'i dus na yab yum gum nas dge bshes la ma yags bya snyam pa la* 'he thought of consoling the Dge-bshes whose parents had died." Das' authority in both cases is the *Jo bo rje A ti sha'i rnam thar.*

95 *Chos grags* 334, *te'u shing – khri'u shing ngam rkub stegs*; cf. Jäschke 1881: 204 *ste'u shing khri* citing Milarepa, and *BGT* 1030, *te'u shing - khri chung ngu zhig.*

is that *ste'u* is related to, or an orthographic variant of, *the'u* and *thi'u*,[96] meaning 'bud', usually for a flower bud, but also applied to the young, fresh shoots of tree saplings. This possibility is strongly supported by representations of the *ste'u* ritual device or structure in the text itself. The painted images in the text (Fig. 3, 4) depict an erect, complex object closely resembling a sapling tree with a growing apical bud and lateral buds, but which also look like elaborate flowers. The accompanying text passages represent them as having 'eight lotus petals spread out' around the base as if the upper part were a flower bud. The meaning 'bud' for *ste'u/the'u* fits completely with the overall symbolism of fecundity and new life applied to these *ste'u* on the same folios as the paintings, which are also said to have ripe fruits and eggs surrounding them (see below). Contextual support for this interpretation of *ste'u* as *the'u* comes in the Old Tibetan document PT 1134 referring to a *gshen* ritual specialist performing death rites whose name is The'u bzhug (l. 61), with the proper name perhaps meaning something like 'stationed (*bzhugs*) [at] the *the'u*'. Since we can trace much otherwise rare terminology in the *sTe'u* and *Sha slungs* texts back to PT 1134 (see chap. 4), including other diminutives like *lhe'u* which also occurs just six lines below the The'u bzhug reference in PT 1134, we should seriously consider some associations here. In a *Klu 'bum* account obviously sharing continuities with Old Tibetan documents, a ritual specialist for death rites named *rgyal gshen* The'u yug is also introduced. This name, whether a variation of Old Tibetan The'u bzhug or not, is also most telling since the syllable *yug* means 'mourning' (mostly as *yug[s] sa*) cognate with *yags*, and is most likely linguistically related to *yags*. A second proposal could be that the local orthography *ste'u* indicates a word complex involving *gte/gte pa/gte ma* and *gta'/gta' ma* (with *gte'u* attested) 'a pawn, a pledge, bail', as well as *gto* 'apotropaic rite' (*gto bcos*) and sometimes 'ransom',[97] in other words something that has to be given – or the process of giving it – in exchange for what is required or wished for. In this case, it would be offerings made for new lives following a death. Finally, there may be a deeper highland Tibeto-Burman ethnolinguistic dimension to *ste'u* in relation to Himalayan shamanic rites of 'welcoming' and fetching the 'mobile

96 *BGT* 1161, *thi'u - gsar du kha 'bus pa'i me tog gi thi'u /*, and entry 1186: *the'u* – 2. *me tog kha ma 'bus pa /*.

97 See Jäschke 1881: 206, 208, and on *gto* Stein 1972: 235, 244 and Karmay 1998: 246. For this suggestion, I thank Joanna Bialek, *pers. comm.* email of 18.6.2016.

vitality principle' or 'soul' in a ritual journey and bringing it to a desired destination.[98] This possibility, as we will see below, is particularly pertinent since the *ste'u* rite involves a vertical itinerary of stations between the place of ritual and the top of the cosmos. Until more data become available, open-minded consideration of various possible derivations for *ste'u* will be required.

The term *sbre'u* in the *Ste'u* text appears to be a diminutive form of *sbra* or *[']brang*, meaning any covered structure, but a canopy, awning or small tent- or hut-like arrangement in this case, and the synonyms *gur* and *khabs* do occur in the text with *sbre'u.* The term is closely related to the verb *'bre ba* meaning 'to draw over', 'to spread', 'to stretch' referring to cloth coverings and wrappings, including awnings and canopies.[99]

The *Ste'u* text is comprised of a series of four folio sequences (Fig. 2)[100] defining four related subjects:

a. First folios give brief descriptions of tree-like ritual structures termed *ste'u* said to support the appearance of *sman* and *btsun.*

b. Second folios give descriptions of beings who are identified as protectors of *lhe'u* and *sman.*

c. Third folios feature trios of male figures and describe a second *ste'u* structure based upon erected awnings or coverings which are said to offer protection and refuge for *lhe'u* offspring who are 'young ones' (*ne'u zhon*).

d. Fourth folios offer a summary of precedents and goals, beginning with reference to ancestral figures, then super-condensed antecedent references to deceased, burials and mourning, and finally state benefits and invoke the goal of a present rite.

a. Tree-like *ste'u*

The *ste'u* of first folios in the series, of which three examples survive, are presented in the same manner as *sha slungs* (see below), with the *ste'u* being numbered, some named, and some described with attributes. These *ste'u* appear to be erect, man-made and decorated

98 For example, the Gurung/Tamu term denoting shamanic rites involving a journey to the spirit world is *tē* (or *tēh*), related to the verb *tēwa* meaning 'to welcome' and 'going to meet'; see Strickland 1982: 234 and references cited therein.

99 See Jäschke 1881: 381 *bre ba*, 402 *'bre ba*, cf. Snellgrove 1967: 284, 304 on *bre* for both cloth canopies and the covering over the dome of a shrine in the G.yung drung Bon religion.

100 See the upper half of the useful overview of surviving folios in Klimburg-Salter, Lodja and Ramble 2013: 39.

tree-like or perhaps flower-like structures. Both text passages and illustrations clearly corroborate this type of *ste'u*, for example on folio Ca-1v (Fig. 3),

> The fifth *ste'u* is given a name: *ste'u* which blazes precious conch light. At its apex, there blazes conch light. In between, small conch birds fly. At its base, eight lotus petals spread out. It supports the appearance of *sman* and *btsun*. [101]

Fig. 3. Folio from the *Ste'u* text (Ca-1v) depicting a tree-like *ste'u* with small birds.

Fig. 4. Folio from the *Ste'u* text (Na-1v) depicting a tree-like *ste'u* with small birds and wild animals.

And for the fragmentary text on folio Na-1v (Fig. 4),

> The twelfth is the *ste'u* which blazes copper light. At its apex, small birds of the *sman* soar. At its middle, lacquered leather[102] eggs [...].[103]

Thus, the function of this *ste'u* is made explicit in that it 'supports the appearance of *sman* and *btsun*' beings. The small birds of the *sman*, and what appears to be a male and female pair of *nyig* or Tibetan gazelle surrounding these *ste'u* are clearly mentioned and depicted in

101 Facs. Ca-1v: *ste'u lnga mtshan gsol ba' / rin chen dung 'od 'bar ba'i ste'u / rtse la dung 'od 'bar / skabs [read: sked] na dung bye'u 'phur / rtsa na phad ma' 'dab brgyad bdal / sman btsun byon ba rten //.*

102 On Old Tibetan *bse'* as a material; see the extensive discussion in Bialek 2015: 115-122.

103 Facs. Na-1v: *bcu gnyis zangs 'od 'bar ba'i ste'u / rtse la sman bye'u lding / sked la bse' sgong [...remaining text illegible].*

the *Sha slungs* text (see below) as markers of the presence of the *sman* and *btsun*. And this supports the idea that the birds and wildlife these beings are said to own, accompany or lead them from the natural wilderness to a ritual site at which *ste'u* have been set up. On another of these folios (Cha-1v), it states that both eggs and ripe fruits occur on or at this tree-like *ste'u* type. Thus, the symbolism is of fecundity and new life.

b. Small *lha* protector lords

Second folios in the series, of which five examples survive, depict beings armed with different weapons, mounted upon various wild animals and birds (Fig.5), and who are designated as *lhe'u mgon rje*, 'small *lha* protector lords'. The text passages mainly describe their attributes. More importantly, each *lhe'u mgon rje* is invoked to either 'appear as the small *lha* and *sman* protector!' or to 'act as the small *lha* and *sman* protector!',[104] while the ritual practitioner is instructed to make offerings to them accordingly.

Fig. 5. Folio from the *Ste'u* text (Ca-2v) depicting a *lhe'u mgon rje* mounted upon a falcon.

c. Tree and trio of male figures *ste'u*

Third folios in the series have survived the best, with seven examples available in the manuscript. These *ste'u* are numbered, with four, six, seven, eight, nine, ten and thirteen, which is the final one in the series, available to us. Each is identified in their text panels with natural phenomena, the sun and moon (four), 'southern' clouds (six), atmosphere (seven), the earth (eight), the cosmic mountain (nine), glacier or snow mountain (ten) and finally the juniper tree (thirteen). Yet, the illustrations on all painted panels each depict a trio of human-like, male figures who display in unison a certain bodily movement or gesture, and these change from folio to folio. If the text actually correlates with the painted images, the

104 Facs. Na-1v: *bcu gnyis zangs 'od 'bar ba'i ste'u / rtse la sman bye'u lding / sked la bse' sgong [...remaining text illegible].*

identities of these trios of male figures are all 'sons' or 'offspring' (*bu, sras*) of *phya, sman, lha, klu* and *yul sa*[105] beings, as well as those of natural elements like earth, stone and green plants, or the Spring, Summer and Autumn seasons of the year.

This group of *ste'u* have diverse descriptions. One instance is actually described as a 'tree'. Other instances are simple 'tent'-like structures comprised of some form of erected awning or covering (*gur, khabs, sbre'u*) above, and a carpet, mat or cushion (*gdan*) below. As with other terminology in both *Ste'u* and *Sha slungs* texts, mention of use of the same range of items also occurs in death rites recorded in Old Tibetan manuscripts, albeit with somewhat different meanings or in contexts we cannot be sure of are the same.[106] A third instance on several folios are descriptions of sublime or 'virtual' awnings and carpets comprised of meteorological phenomena and precipitation, including clouds, mist, rain and snow.[107] This certainly does not occur in any Old Tibetan accounts of death rites. Folios Pa-3v and Pa-4v explicitly mention the purpose of these 'trios of male figures' *ste'u* type:

> Thirteen, the everlasting turquoise juniper *ste'u*. Mgon bu Lha sras, Klu bu Rin cen and Sdings bu G.yu le, the three. The *ste'u* of completed burial and mourning rites. A cloth awning covers it above. A multi-coloured[108] foundation carpets it beneath. [...*illegible text*...] A blooming flower of gold. Its bark is vast and spreading. It exists as the protection and refuge of small *lha* offspring (*lhe'u sras*) who are young ones. [109]

While a tree like the juniper on folio Pa-3v is not mentioned for the other *ste'u* of this

105 Note that *yul sa* is ambivalent. In Old Tibetan documents, it appears to mean both a type of being or deity often cited together with *sman* (e.g. PT 1051: l.30, IOL Tib J 0738: 3v23), and a term for a place or area (e.g. PT 1047: l.37, l.246, IOL Tib J 733: i.1).

106 For a few examples among a whole range, see PT 1042: 42 'tent of the cadaver and tent of the mental principle' (*ring gi gur dang / thugs kyi gur*), and l.118 'spread a striped/multi-coloured felt covering on top of the grave' (*se'i gong du dbyam phying khra bo bting*), in PT 1134: 56 'as for the mental principle tent at/for the *'brang*, pitch a white one. As for the tailored [or: 'rump/seat' *byang* > *byang khog*] cushion/carpet, place the cushion/carpet' (*'brang du thugs sbra / ni / dkar mo pub rtan byang rtan khod*), in PT 1136: 25 'erect a *'brang* for performing death rites' (*shid bgyir 'brang gzugsu*, cf. l.18) which assumes *sbre'u* may be related to *'brang*, and l.28 'spread a covering [on a psychopomp horse]' (*khabs su bkab*), and so on.

107 For examples, see facs. Cha-3v and Ja-3v.

108 I read *mching* as *mching bu*, cf. *BGT* 846, *mdog sna tshogs ldan zhing.*

109 Facs. Pa-3v and 114, Pa-4v, l.1-2 (above painted panel): *bcu dsum [read: gsum] d.yung [read: g.yung] drung g.yu shug ste'u / mgon bu lha sras dang / klu bu rin cen dang / sdings bu g.yu le gsum / bdur yags grub pa'i ste'u / dar bre'u bla'I khabs / mching gram [read: 'gram] 'og kyi gdan / [one line of text with ca. ten syllables illegible here] [Pa-4v] gser yi me thog bkra / shun pa zab dang dar ro / lhe'u sras ne'u zhon yi mgon dang skyabsu [read: skyabs su] yod // /.*

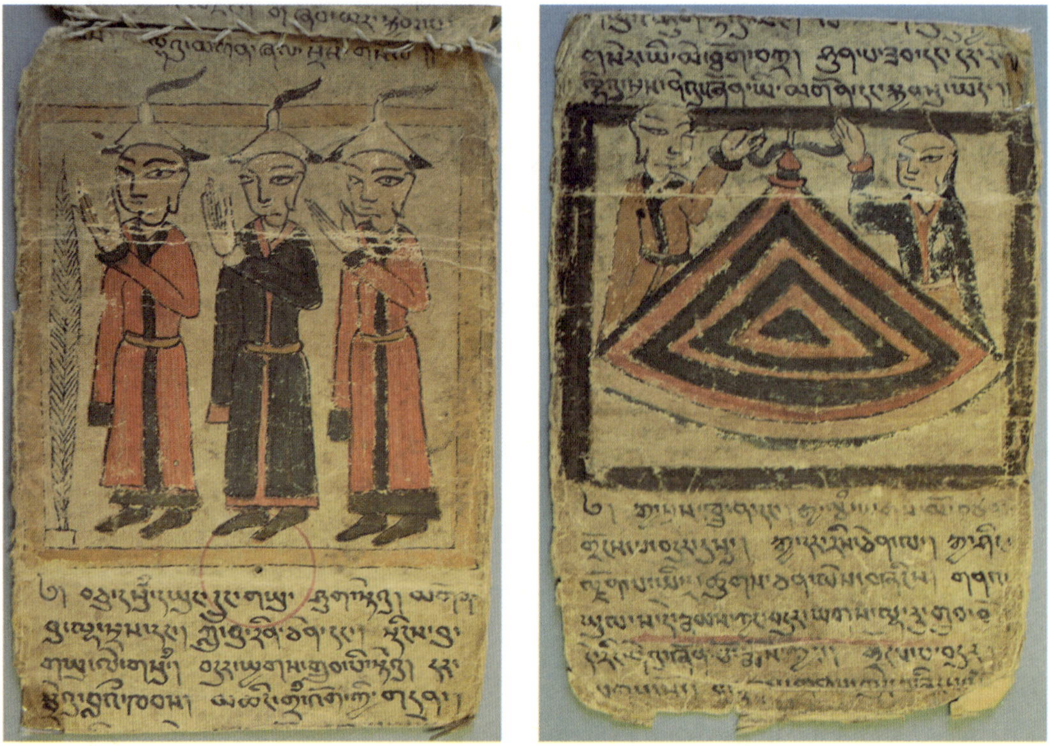

Fig. 6. Folios from the *Ste'u* text depicting the everlasting turquoise juniper *ste'u* (Pa-3v, left frame) with continuous inscription on the top of the following folio (Pa-4v, right frame).

group, on all seven surviving folios we find an erect tree clearly depicted, apparently set into a base as if it were a ritual construction, at the left-hand side of each illustration (Fig. 6, left frame). It is quite possible that what is being depicted here are trees used during any rite performance which represented each of these thirteen *ste'u*. First folio series *ste'u* are also represented by tree-like structures or devices. Moreover, these *ste'u* on third folios are invariably described as being 'of completed burial and mourning rites'[110] clearly defining them as a post-mortem procedure following the main death rites, and employed for 'protection and refuge of small *lha* offspring who are young ones'. The trios of male figures depicted and named upon every folio as 'sons' or 'offspring' of the deities of the natural world and its phenomenal manifestation are those charged with protecting new offspring who come into the world, most likely at the locations of each example of this *ste'u* type.

110 *Bdur yags grub pa,* cf. facs. Cha-3v, l.3-4, Ja-3v, l.5, Nga-3v, l.3, Nya-3v, l.3, Ta-3v, l.2-3.

Crucially, this series of locations together form a descending itinerary (Fig.16), and I will return to this topic in the respective summaries for the *Ste'u* and *Sha slungs* texts below.

d. 'Small awning' *sbre'u*

Fourth and final folios in the series, of which five examples have survived, represent a summary and culmination of each series. They all describe and depict ritual structures termed *sbre'u* or 'small awnings' which are basically the same as those described more simply upon third folios. These consist of components including cloth coverings and awnings, lattice-work frames – some described as wooden – beneath which the cloth covering is set up (Fig. 7, 8), and some with mats inside or under them, yet all of precious or exotic materials because they are being described here as mythical precedents. The text schema on each fourth folio begins with brief reference to possible ancestral beings, a mythical antecedent of burial of a deceased with precedent for a *sbre'u* ritual structure, and finally an invocation for present ritual performers to directly address the main goal of the rite. The text passages on fourth folios are the most explicit concerning the overall purpose of the rite. Folio Nga-4v (cf. Fig. 7) reads,

Fig. 7. Folio Nga-4v from the *Ste'u* text depicting a 'small awning' *sbre'u*.

Fig. 8. Folio Cha-4v from the *Ste'u* text depicting a 'small awning' *sbre'u*.

> In the Bar land Gling drug, the *yul sa* Khri Do re and Khri lcam Gling mo skar. At the time the deceased was buried, a lattice-work which was blue was erected for a white conch small awning.
> Today, [you] give young ones, male and female,[111] for the sake of a positive precedent. [112]

Folio Cha-4v reads (cf. Fig. 8),

> Lha bu 'Brang kar and Lha sman 'Phrul mo. At the time the deceased was buried, a lattice-work which was turquoise was erected for a white conch small awning. By way of burial and mourning rites for the deceased, death is concealed. This benefits the living. [You] give young ones, male and female, for the sake of a positive precedent. [113]

Folio Pa-4v (see Fig. 6, right frame) contains an additional reference to primordial precedents,

> Rgya sras Khru na and Rgya lcam Rgas mo btsun. When the deceased was buried, a lattice-work of Rgya tree wood was erected for a Rgya cloth endowed with motifs. In antiquity, the *yul sa* [beings] completed burial and mourning rites as *lha*. Today, [you give][114] young ones, male and female, and for the deceased there are burial and mourning rites.[115]

3.2.1 Summary

The *Ste'u* text describes a post-mortem rite whose goal is obtaining new life. The rite was performed after burial and mourning rites for a deceased person had been completed. The various ritual devices or structures and beings cited in the text passages of each fourfold

111 I follow Coblin 1991: 320 n.134 who assigned *pho smos* to both genders, while Richardson 1998: 154, 164 n.30 left it unassigned; cf. also *bu pho smos* in PT 1283: 247, and *'di rnams pho smos* in PT 1071: r251-r252, r266.

112 Facs. Nga-4v: *bar yul gling drug du / yul sa khri do re dang / khri lcam gling mo skar / grongs pa bdur dus su / dung bre'u dkar po la mthing yi dra tshugs can les [read: las] bzhingso [read: bzhengs so] // de ring ne'u zhon pho smos la dpe' bzangs don du 'bul lo //.*

113 Facs. Cha-4v: *lha bu 'brang kar dang / lha sman 'phrul mo dag / grongs pa bdur dus su / dung bre'u dkar mo la / g.yu'i dra tsugs [read: tshugs] can les [read: las] bzhings [read: bzhengs] / grongs pa bdur yags pas / shi bgab [read: gab] gson la bzang / ne'u zhon pho smos la dpe' bzangs don du 'bul /.*

114 Cf. the precedents *ne'u zhon pho smos la dpe' bzangs don du 'bul lo* on Nga-4v, l. 4-5 and Cha-4v, l. 5.

115 Facs. Pa-4v: *rgya sras khru na dang / rgya lcam rgas mo btsun / grongs pa bdur dusu [read: dus su] / rgya dar ris cen [read: can] la / rgya shing ljon pa yi dra tshugs can les [read: las] bzhings [read: bzhengs] / gna' yul sa de rnams kyang bdur yags lha ru grub bo / de ring ne'u zhon pho smos kyang / grongs pa bdur yags so / [a final line following here is illegible].*

folio sequence reveal a series of four stages adding up to an overall process.

The first type of *ste'u* are set up to support the arrival of *sman* and *btsun* beings at the site. What the term *btsun* (< *mtshun*) refers to in this context will be discussed below. The wild animals and birds which the *Sha slungs* text states are owned by these beings, are also in attendance at *ste'u*, most probably as symbolic harbingers of, and guides for, the *sman* and *btsun*. The other symbols associated with these *ste'u* are of new life and fecundity. The new lives that arrive with the *sman* and *btsun* are directly identified as 'small *lha'* and 'small *lha* offspring'. This combination of wildlife, its *sman* owners and 'small *lha*' and 'small *lha* offspring' form a very concrete link to the *Sha slungs* text that I will discuss below. The mobile and armed 'small *lha* protector lords' described and depicted on second folios are the guardians of new lives while they travel together with the *sman* and *btsun* to the ritual site.

On third folios of the *Ste'u* text, the numbered series of 'tent'-like structures indexed to natural phenomena and objects proceed from high and rarefied regions down to and ending at a juniper tree, which is the thirteenth and final numbered *ste'u* of this type. Assuming the text was used in order from the first fourfold folio series through to the last, then the series can only mark stratified locations descending the vertical axis, from celestial abodes down to the terrestrial ritual site. The surviving sequence of numbers, locations and the beings indexed to them successively lists the *phya* at the sun and moon (*ste'u* four), the *sman* at the southern clouds (six *ste'u*), the seasons Spring, Summer and Autumn in the atmosphere (*ste'u* seven), the soil, rocks and plants upon the earth[116] (*ste'u* eight), the *yul sa* kings of the cosmic mountain (*ste'u* nine), the high white snows or glaciers (*ste'u* eleven) and the juniper tree (*ste'u* thirteen). Most importantly, it is said that each of these *ste'u* way stations in different, stratified locations offers refuge and protection to small *lha* offspring. This protection is offered not only by the various 'tent'-like structures created of materials appropriate to each stratified location (e.g. awnings of clouds and carpets of mists), but also by the trios of 'sons' or 'offspring' of the deities and natural phenomena associated with each successive way station. Thus, this set of progressive references taken as a whole running through all third folios reveals a thirteen stage descending journey required for new life to come down from ancestral realms above to reach a ritual site marked by a tree.

116 See facs. Nya-3v, i.1: *ma bu khrun snar*, an expression otherwise unknown to me, but perhaps meaning 'mother and child foremost division'?

The fourth and final folios in each series are more complex, and certainly synoptic in function, with three distinct references always appearing in the same order. First, there are beings with named identities, sometimes with a cognate location. Second, the erection of small awnings after burials, sometimes with the rhetoric that after death is ritually concealed, life benefits. Third, there is an appeal for male and female 'young ones' (*ne'u zhon*) who are 'small *lha* off-spring' to be given. The question here is, to whom do these three types of references refer? Whether or not the precedent of burials and erecting awnings applies to the initially named beings is unclear, although it seems rather doubtful. For one, there are no direct grammatical indications of this in any of the passages on surviving fourth folios. Moreover, the idea of synchronous, double burials of one male and one female in each instance appears somewhat unintelligible, and is also without precedent in cognate sources. Whatever the case, the first two references do represent antecedents of a kind.

Since male and female offspring given after death is the *Ste'u* rite's stated purpose, logically these lives and their source must be the precedent being conveyed. The practical, ritual precedent is erecting small awnings after a burial. But who do the two named male and female identities represent? The ultimate source of any human life is an ancestor, while a new life descending from an ancestral realm beyond the human domestic sphere – as is the case in the *Ste'u* rite – will have an identity appropriate to its origins. One or both of these possibilities is what the pairs of named male and female identities in each text passage – and presumably the paired figures on each painting – should represent, viz. ancestors and origin identities of new offspring. Descriptive elements in the named identities indicate this to be so. We find them termed '*klu* off-spring young one' (*klu sras gzhon nu*), '*lha* child/son' (*lha bu*), 'Rtsang offspring' (*rtsang sras*) and 'Rgya offspring' (*rgya sras*) for male figures, with 'sisters' (*lcam*, a synonym of *spun*), *sman* and *btsun* defining the respective female figures. This is precisely the classificatory language used to describe the offspring and young ones found throughout the *Ste'u* text, but also in the *Sha slungs* text, for which we can mention in advance that on the final folio all the *slungs* are explicitly offered to 'small *lha* offspring who are brother and sister' (*lhe'u sras lcam dral*). This same pattern of references exists also for names in the *Rnel dri 'dul ba* tales. [117]

117 For example, Lha lcam Phye ma lam (also Lha lcam Phye leb) (*Dga' thang* 39, 141, f.11, l.7, l.11), and Lha za Dril bu Sil bu sman (*ibid.* 46, 154, f.24, l.10-11).

The above interpretation is further confirmed when locations sometimes associated with the paired, named beings are considered, at least for those we have approximately contemporary and cognate information available. Take, for example, the place named Kha la Rtsang stod on folio Ja-4v (Fig. 9, lower frame). In Old Tibetan documents, Kha la Rtsang stod or Rtsang stod appears as both quasi-mythical realm and principality with geographical location, it is especially associated with *phywa* beings who seem to be both human and divine.[118] The named *lha* in the text must come from the *lha* land Gung thang (also Gung dang), which is explicitly mentioned as being up above the intermediate space of the atmosphere (see below), and cited in the *Sha slungs* text as the *lha* abode. The otherwise unknown Bar land Gling drug most likely refers to the intermediate space (*bar*) of the atmosphere. The initial passage on folio Ja-3v (Fig. 9, upper frame) reads,

> *Ste'u* seven, the ste'u of the floating intermediate space (*bar snang*). Regarding what is upwards, the *lha* land is seen. Regarding what is downwards, the earth is seen. Regarding what is in between, the human land is seen. On account of that, it is the *ste'u* of floating [intermediate space].[119]

Thus, these are all fitting ancestral locations of

Fig. 9. Folio Ja-3v (upper frame) from the *Ste'u* text depicting a trio of 'son' protectors with a tree for the *'ste'u* of the floating intermediate space', and folio Ja-4v (lower frame) depicting Rtsang 'off-spring' Snying khar and Rtsang 'sister' Si le ma.

118 See Hill 2013: 39 citing PT 1060: l.74, IOL Tib J 0734, folio 7, ll. 292, 294, 298, and PT 1286, recto, ll. 186.

119 Facs. Ja-3v, l.1-3: *ste'u bdun bar snang 'phyo ba'i ste'u / yar bltas lha yul snang / mar bltas dog mo snang / bar bltas myi yul snang / de phyir 'phyo ba i [read: ba'i] ste'u /.*

the type we might expect to feature in antecedent references occurring on fourth folios of the fourfold *Ste'u* text series. The *Rnel dri 'dul ba* text also directly confirms that *lha* are like parents who give birth to humans and send their new-born children down to earth. In the [Yar] lungs sogs ka tale, the crisis of a *rnel dri* defilement is described for the living as follows,

The *lha* were driven off, driven into the sky.
The wild geese vanished, vanished into the lake.
Human beings were not begotten by the *lha*.[120]

The verb *btsas* here literally means 'give birth to', while nominal *btsas pa* is used for 'new-born children'. This is one of various explicit correlations between the cosmological framing in the *Rnel dri 'dul ba* and the *Ste'u* and *Sha slungs* texts. This same idea of human origins from *lha* persisted in folk cosmology for some time after the 11th-12th century era of these old texts. In a 14th century source from southern Central Tibet, the progenitor *lha* 'O de Gung rgyal, who features prominantly in the *Sha slungs* text, is explicitly cast as the *lha* ancestor of human beings.[121] The Srid pa'i lha cult in my research region is based upon exactly this idea as well (see below).

3.3 The *Sha slungs* text and rite

Like the *Ste'u* text, the *Sha slungs* text is also arranged into a number of series – apparently originally thirteen – of short, four folio sequences (Fig. 2)[122] defining four related subjects:

a. Two of the surviving trio of first folios – the third represents an exception[123] – have the same text schema with three distinct references as we find on fourth folios on the *Ste'u* text. Initially, pairs of *lha* beings from *lha* abodes are simply named. Second, going to the *sman* beings dwelling in terrestrial mountains and lakes together with *yul sa* beings is described. The strongholds (*mkhar*) and fortresses (*rdzong*) are cited as dwellings of *'small lha'* (*lhe'u*), of 'young ones (*ne'u zhon*) who are small *lha'*, and

120 *Dga' thang* 49, 160-161, ff.30, l.8-31, l.1, *lha 'phangs gnam du 'phangs / ngang yal mtsho ru yal / lha yIs myI ma btsas /.*

121 See *Rlangs* 5, where the passage reads: *srid pa lha rabs mched bzhi zhes kyang bya / mgo gsum tsha [? read: mgon tshun phya] zhes kyang bya / de nas mi rgyud du grol ba ni / sras 'o de gung rgyal /.*

122 See the lower half of the useful overview of surviving folios in Klimburg-Salter, Lodja and Ramble 2013: 39.

123 The exception is facs. Na-1r, with only a very fragmentary text, the first words of which read *'Od de gung rgyal yi thugs kyi sprul pa les / sman rdzong [...]*, and which does not allow us to order the content together with the two other surviving first folios.

of *sman*. Finally, ritual instructions for protection and care of them by other beings are cited.

b. Second folios all depict groups of birds, including 'small birds' indexed to different environments, which are the property of *sman* and 'small *lha*', and larger birds that protect and shepherd them.

c. Third folios all cite *sha slungs* and depict different wild herbivores in male, female and juvenile trios, with mention of their qualities or functions in relation to *sman, btsun* and 'small *lha*'.

d. Fourth folios describe both named *lha* and *myi* beings related to various categories (*yul sa, sgra bla, sa bdag*) who protect and care for *sman*, 'small *lha*' and their property of wild herbivores which live with them.

It is immediately obvious from this overview that 'small *lha'* (*lhe'u*), *sman* and more rarely mentioned *btsun*, all of whom are found in the natural environment together with wildlife and birds, and who are the positive focus of a complex of other types of beings, are the principal object of the *Sha slungs* rite. Before examining examples of each folio type in the fourfold sequence, the meaning of the rare word *slungs* and its unique forms *sha slungs, slungs ma* and *sha mkhar slungs ma* within the text must be considered, since its interpretation is crucial for understanding the rite.

3.3.1 Meanings of *slungs* and *sha slungs*

Slungs is attested in Old Tibetan documents, primarily in relation to administration and law and with only two brief references in relation to descriptions of rites. In the first context, it refers to a 'way station', perhaps 'post station', a halting or dismounting place or fixed spot along a road or route, while in some instances it might be glossed as 'outpost'. F.W. Thomas identified 'government *slungs'* (*mngan slungs*), 'Chinese *slungs*' (*rgya slungs*), 'nomad *slungs*' (*'brog slungs*) and 'soldier *slungs*' (*so slungs*), the latter defined as "messengers responsible for transporting provisions to hill-stations," and he also suggested "military police."[124] In different Old Tibetan documents *slungs* are associated with 'messengers' (*po nya > pho nya*), 'horses' (*rta*), 'horse keepers/grooms' (*rta rdzi*), and 'horse owners' (*rta bdag*).[125] An imperial administrative innovation apparently included regularising distances

124 Thomas 1951: 51-52, 64, 151, 236, 276-277, 296-297, 376, 423, 446.
125 PT 1096: 2r-r5, r16-r19, PT 1290: r10.

between *slungs* 'way stations'.[126] In some Old Tibetan documents the word occurs in *slungs tshugs* and together with *tshugs* in context, and in *slungs sa*,[127] both of which have informed analogous later usages in Classical Tibetan, such as *tshugs sa* 'caravansary', 'way station' and *gru tshugs sa* 'ferry boat station', while *slungs* itself fell out of use.

The common aspects indicated for Old Tibetan *slungs* are fixed and well-defined halting spots, location along a regular route as opposed to any random site, and places occupied by and significant for both persons and animals, especially horses and those who own, ride and care for them. When fully interrogated, 11th-12th century *sha slungs* and its variants are found to preserve most of this older semantic scope.

Beyond administrative and legal contexts, Old Tibetan *slungs* is only known from two references to rite descriptions occurring in antecedent narratives, and both are variants of the same text. *Slungs* occurs in mythical accounts in which the body of a horse is being discussed. The horse is a psychopomp animal termed *do ma snyings dags*, and might also have been sacrificed. In PT 1134, we read of the psychopomp horse, 'as for the mane, it was bound with silk. As for the tail, it was given as/appointed for a *slungs*'.[128] A myth narrative in PT 1136 repeats the same formulation, 'As for the tail, it was given as a *slungs*.'[129] If the horse was sacrificed for the rite, then perhaps the tail was removed and given for use as a flag or standard to mark an actual *slungs* site, for instance, so that such a way station could be seen by travellers from a distance? Or perhaps the ritual arena in which the horse is treated in these texts could have been considered a *slungs*, one subsequently marked by the horse's tail? Such horse tail standards mounted atop poles were widely used in ancient Central Asia and regions of Mongol rule and influence. They were mentioned in the *Marco Polo*, and Henry Yule's notes to his translation report "*Túk* or *Túgk*, is the horse-tail or yak-tail standard which among so many Asiatic nations has marked the supreme military command."[130] An interesting cultural link between *slungs*, horses (*rta*) and standards or flags was carried over into the word *lung rta* (and *klung rta*), a term for a ritual flag depicting a horse, by replacing the obsolete syllable *slungs*.[131]

126 See the *Old Tibetan Chronicle* in Dotson 2013: 297, 388.

127 PT 1096: r2-r4, PT 1290: r12.

128 PT 1134: 123: *pum puM ni dar gis / bchings / rnga ma ni slungs su bchug [read: bcug].*

129 PT 1136: 28-29, *mjug mani [read: ma ni] slungsu [read: slungs su] stsald.*

130 Yule 2010 [1871]: chapt. LIV, 231, n.2.

131 See Bialek 2015a: 33 n.34, Dotson 2011: 92 n.27, Uray 1984: 358–359, n.56.

In the *Sha slungs* text, we find *slungs*, *slungs ma* and more fully *sha mkhar slungs ma* forms. This latter '*sha* stronghold *slungs ma*' appears to be the full form of *sha slungs* as a technical term, since Tibetan systems of abbreviation usually omit every second element in bisyllabic pairs in order to generate a condensed term (*bsdus yig*). This is confirmed by various usages in the text. Certain folios mention a numerical series of *sha slungs* based ideally upon a primordial pattern. After the last *sha slungs* in the text has been described, a summarising etiological reference states, 'The thirteen *sha slungs* also initially came into being like that.'[132] This strongly implies the text is discussing *sha slungs* as being something in the here and now in relation to primordial models. Since *sha slungs* are only mentioned on seven folios, we assume that the other six *sha slungs* of the ideal thirteen must be described upon the missing folios. *Sha slungs* are indexed to wild animals and birds, and the accompanying illustrations attest these correlations. There is a '*sha slungs* of the precious' (*rin chen yi sha slungs*) for species of deer, wild ass and wild goats, a 'small bird *slungs*' (*bye'u slungs*) and a 'final *sha slungs*' (*sha slungs mtha' ma*) assigned to ground dwelling marmot and badger. It is likely that the '*sha slungs* of the precious' type is a general name encompassing them all. When the series are finished with 'the final *sha slungs*', it is stated that 'The *sha slungs* of the precious are completed'.[133] One passage related to the primordial appearance or construction of *sha slungs* states, 'As for the *sha mkhar slungs ma*, being the *sa bdag* queen, Lha mo brten ma adorned it [with] five precious things.'[134] The *sa bdag* queen just cited is identified as a *sgra bla* being. There is also another set of 'three *sha mkhar* men' (*sha mkhar myi gsum*) who are *sgra bla* and who are directly associated with the *sha mkhar [slungs ma]*.

Clearly there is significant semantic overlap between *sha slungs* and Old Tibetan administrative *slungs* 'way stations'. There are a fixed series of *sha slungs*. They are designated as different types depending upon the beings associated with them. They are associated with animals and, as we will see below, these animals are the explicit property of owners, and are further looked after by designated caregivers. This is exactly parallel to the horses of the *slungs* 'way stations' whose owners and carers are cited in Old Tibetan

132 Facs. Pa-3r l.6-Pa-4r, l.1: *sha slungs bcu gsum yang / dang po de ltar bsrid do /.*

133 Facs. Pa-4r, l.3 (above illustration): *rin chen yi sha slungs rdzogs s.ho //.*

134 Facs. Pa-4r, l.1-2 (below illustration): *sha mkhar slungs ma ni / sa bdag rgyal mo ste / lha mo brten ma des / rin cen [read: chen] sna lnga brgyan/.*

documents. Since *sha slungs* are associated with wild animals, they also resemble the administrative *slungs* 'way stations' along a travel route which were necessarily spaced far off from places of intensive human use.

One significant difference between Old Tibetan *slungs* references and *sha [mkhar] slungs [ma]* is the latter term(s) being related to wild animals rather than domestic horses or horses used during rites. The *sha* element marks this distinction. *Sha* appears in the text with *slungs* as a generic term encompassing all wild animals invoked in the rite. Thus, *sha* qualifies the *slungs* which are related to all these animal species regardless, including various deer, wild ass, wild goats, marmot and badger, which are very different types of animals with highly diverse ecologies that do not overlap. Wild avifauna have their own term, 'small bird *slungs*' (*bye'u slungs*), and are not included under *sha slungs*. At the same time, the text also employs the generic category term *ri d[w]ags* to refer to all larger wild animals which are herbivores, while the specific usage *sha* to refer to 'deer' (*sh[w]a ba*) as a sub-set of *ri d[w]ags* only occurs once.[135] Thus, in this text *sha* in *sha slungs* and its compounds is to be understood generally as 'wildlife' exclusive of avifauna.

The *mkhar* element in *sha mkhar slungs ma* means 'stronghold', and is a well-attested term in Old Tibetan for fortified residence places of ruling elites. In Tibetan folk songs, poetic rural depictions of nature, and the culture of hunting we find *mkhar* commonly applied to environments occupied by wild animals of the *ri dwags* category, that is, game species. Moreover, in many such contexts *sha* and *mkhar* are explicitly related to *dgra lha* and *sgra bla* beings as we find in the *Sha slungs* text, since in Tibetan Plateau hunting cultures those beings are appealed to by hunters for success in obtaining game animals.[136] For example, a chanted appeal to *dgra lha* for hunting success I recorded in use among Changthang hunters in Gerze Dzong, far north-western Tibetan Plateau, and one which identifies game with the productive force *g.yang*, includes the lines, 'In the midst of the broad stronghold (*mkhar*) of the meadows, is the multiplying *g.yang* of deer and wild ass

135 Facs. Cha-4r, l.3, while elsewhere we only find *sha yur po* with *yu mo* and *she'u cung* to refer to a specific type of deer on facs. Nya-3r, l.1-2.
136 See Huber 2012: 205-206, 210-211.

females and their offspring. Today, fetch that *g.yang* here.'[137] Thus, the association cited above between *sha mkhar*, the *sa bdag* queen and 'three *sha mkhar* men' who are all *sgra bla* is a wide-spread cultural pattern. Given that the older application of *mkhar* as 'stronghold' is something protective and difficult to access, *mkhar* is perhaps best translated as 'refuge' in *sha mkhar slungs ma* in relation to the known ecology of wild herbivores who can be sought after as game.

The Tibetan language has a very rich vocabulary for designating areas, sites and abodes of all types. From among these extensive possibilities, whoever composed the *Sha slungs* text was very precise in applying a particular Old Tibetan technical term of administration to designate whatever a *sha slungs* was meant to be. Given that use of *slungs* in the *Sha slungs* text is so cognate with Old Tibetan usages, we should precisely understand and translate *sha slungs* as 'wildlife way station', *sha mkhar slungs ma* as 'wildlife refuge way station', and *bye'u slungs* as 'small bird way station'. Analysis of the contents of the *Sha slungs* text supports these meanings.

Aside from what has been cited above, the *sha slungs* as 'wildlife way stations' are given no further locations or attributes within the text. In other passages, only some of which mention *sha slungs*, there are references to wild herbivores abiding in mountain and lake regions, to birds found in both forest and rock areas, and one can also deduce that the *sha slungs* of marmot and badger were on, and partly in, the earth due to their ecology. Thus, all *sha slungs* are located in wilderness areas of the natural world, within the terrestrial realm of the cosmos. Concerning the actions of the wild animal denizens of *sha slungs* in relation to these locations, the text most commonly states that they 'emerge/come out' (*[']byung*) from (*nas/nes*) *sha slungs*, nothing more. Although there are parallel *bye'u slungs* or 'small bird way stations' mentioned, birds in the text 'hatch out' (*rdol*) of 'precious eggs' (*rin cen sgong [nga]*), with one case of a 'lacquered leather egg' (*bse' sgong*) and one of an 'iron egg' (*lcags sgong*), in the rocks, the forest, the realm of the earth, at or within the 'life and death boundary' (*gson gshin 'tshams*) and finally in the 'four directions' (*phyogs bzhi*). While the 'life and death boundary' is obscure, it might just allude to the 'world' within

---

137 *Spang mkhar yangs pa'i dkyil shed na // sha rkyang ma bu'i 'phel g.yang de // de ring 'di ru g.yang du len*; f.51a, l.5-6 of *Gsang ba'i bdag pos gnang ba'i dgra lha dpang[s] bstod ces bya ba bzhugs so //* (block print in 26 folios. paginated 39b-53a within a larger collection, and photographed at Sengkhor, Gertze County, Tibet Autonomous Region, August 2002).

Fig. 10. Folio Ca-1r from the *Sha slungs* text, with continuous inscription on Ca-2r (Fig. 11).

Fig. 11. Folio Ca-2r from the *Sha slungs* text with final lines of inscription for Ca-1r at top.

which everything takes birth and dies, and the other locations all describe the natural world. A third reference parallel to both *sha slungs* and these eggs and their locations which are apparently *bye'u slungs*, but one cited only twice and which is not directly related to wild animals and birds, are agate boulders (*mchong yi pha bong*) from which beings identified as '*sha mkhar* men' (*sha mkhar myi*) who are *sgra bla* 'come into being' (*bsrid*).

An account of each folio type in the fourfold series now follows.

a. Going to the *sman*

First folios are the most instructive in the fourfold series of the *Sha slungs* text, although only two survive with intact text passages. The text schema in these passages is the same as found on fourth folios in the *Ste'u* text. They begin by simply naming a *lha* couple from places that are not on the earth. Then follows the practical precedent of going to the *sman* beings who live in a protected zone of mountains and lakes. Finally, there is the invocation of protective agency addressed to some deity by an actual user of the text during present performance of the rite. The text passage across folios Ca-1r and Ca-2r states:

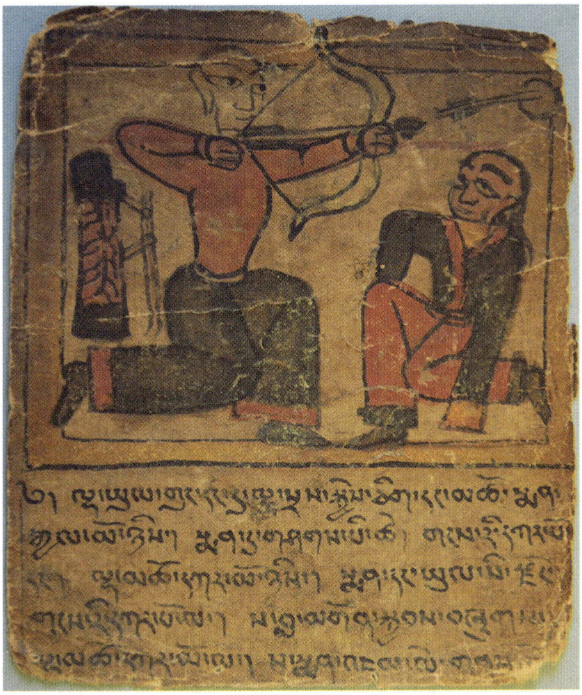

Fig. 12. Folio Cha-1r from the *Sha slungs* text (text passage continued on folio Cha-2r above painting, Fig. 13).

Atop the land Sa le ljon, the stronghold of Smon lam rock [and] the whirling, white Dung lake. In between lake and rock, Lha sras Lha bo che [and] Lha za Gang cig ma. At the time of going to the *sman*, as for the small *lha* stronghold [and] the *sman* fortress, the *dmag dpon* was lord of *sgra bla*, the *sman* fortress was the fortress of *sgra bla*. In his hand, a sharp weapon [*missing text*]. Suppress the *gzed*, *btsan* and *g.yam dri* [or: *g.yam* and *dri*]. Young ones (*ne'u zhon*),[138] male and female, are to be brought together with the fortress of *sgra bla*.[139]

Folio Cha-1r (Fig. 12) states:

138 The initial syllables of this line are unreadable, and I reconstruct *ne'u zhon* here from an identical, recurring phrasing on fourth folios in the *Ste'u* text, see facs. Pa-4v, l.5 *ne'u zhon pho smos kyang*, facs. Nga-4v, l.4-5 and Cha-4v, l.5 *ne'u zhon pho smos la*.

139 Facs. Ca-1r.l.1-Ca-2r, l.2: *yul sa le ljon stingsu [read: steng su] / smon lam brag kyi mkhar / dung mtsho dkar mo 'khyil / mtsho dang brag bar du / lha sras lha bo che / lha za gang cig ma sman du gshags pi [read; gshegs pa'i] tshe' / lhe'u mkhar sman rdzong ni / dmag dpon sgra bli [read: bla'i] rje / sman rdzong sgra bli [read: bla'i] rdzong / phyag na dbal mtsho [= mtshon + missing verb here /]* [Ca-2r] *gzed btsan g.yam dri 'dul / [add: ne'u zhon] pho smos kyang sgra bli [read: bla'i] rdzong dang sprad //.*

> In the *lha* land Gung dang, the two, Lha sras Skyes cig and Mtsho sman Rgyal mo. At the time of going to the *sman*, the two, Gangs ri dkar po and Lha mtsho dkar mo, [were] the fortresses of the *yul sa* beings and *sman*: on Gangs ri dkar po, Sa lha Mgon skyabs dwelt; in Lha mtsho dkar mo, Sa sman 'Jam le abided. [They] were good protectors. Young ones (*ne'u zhon*), who were small *lha* (*lhe'u*) [and] *sman*, and living creatures, who were wild herbivores, resided in the stronghold and fortress of Kha ba 'od mkhar and Lha mtsho dkar mo. This Sa sman 'Jam le is to be cherishing to the *sman*. [140]

The antecedent in both examples here is of descent of 'young ones' who are 'small *lha*' from an ancestral *lha* realm above the earth. The precedent concerns safe dwelling conditions for these new beings upon the earth (*sa*) in specific wild places among certain types of protective and useful co-residents. The final invocations or requests are to ensure young ones reach the appropriate protective abodes, and to designate who will care kindly for them.

The pairs of male and female identities beginning each text passage must either be *lha* ancestor names or origin identities of those who depart their abodes to go to the *sman* in the terrestrial wilderness as 'young ones' who are 'small *lha*'. They are named appropriately in the same manner as on fourth folios of the *Ste'u* text. In one pair, the male is designated as the *'lha* offspring' (*lha sras*) Lha bo che. The male's name in the second pair, Lha sras Skyes cig, can literally mean either '*Lha* offspring a human person' or '*Lha* offspring a gift', signifying the presentation of a human life from the ancestral *lha*. As for the abodes of these ancestors or their offspring, Gung dang (or: Gung thang) is well-known as the ancestral *lha* land above, but the land Sa le ljon is obscure. In fact, it also designates an ancestral *lha* abode high up the vertical cosmic axis, and we learn this from a slightly later manuscript from the same 'neighbourhood' in southernmost Tibet. In the *Bshad mdzod yid bzhin nor bu* redaction of the *Grags pa bon lugs* narrative composed during the 1400s in Gru shul, immediately adjacent to both Gtam shul and Lho brag, we find Dga' Sa le is the name of the

140 Facs. Cha-1r, l.1-5 and Cha-2r, l.1-4 (above painted panel): *lha yul gung dang du lha sras skyes cig dang mtsho sman rgyal mo nyis / sman du gshags pa'i tshe / gangs ri dkar po dang / lha mtsho dkar mo nyis / sman dang yul sa'i rdzong gangs ri dkar po la / sa bla [read: lha] mgon skyabs bzhugs / lha mtsho dkar mo la / sa sman 'jam le gnas* [Cha-2r] *[first two syllables missing/illegible here] sku srungs lags / ne'u zhon lhe'u sman [illegible, add: dang?] chags ri dags rnams / kha ba 'od mkhar dang lha mtsho dkar mo yis mkhar dang rdzong la bzhags / sa sman 'jam le 'di sman la 'o re byams // //.*

fifteenth level of the sky from which *lha* come.[141]

The content of the precedent sections and the final instruction sections in these first folios are somewhat synoptic and prefigure what is described in greater detail upon the subsequent three folios in each fourfold series. That is, they present the range of protective locations that are 'way stations' (*slungs*), the denizens of these places in the form of birds, wild herbivorous animals and different non-human beings, and mechanisms that together ensure safe and caring conditions for the 'small *lha*' who are new 'young ones' sent down to earth.

b. Small bird way stations

Second folios present a series of locations summarised as 'small bird way stations' (*bye'u slungs*), list the avifauna inhabiting them, their characteristics and the relations among these birds and their *sman* owners. For example, folio Cha-2r (Fig. 13) states:

> An iron egg broke open in the forest. The small forest birds *ke ke*, *khu long zer mong* and *bya gshen 'jon mo* continually lead the way in the forest. They are a favoured movable property [of *sman*[142]]. As for the protector of small birds, the long beaked *kang ka* [bird] emerged from the forests of Lho ga. [It] holds sway over the realm of trees. [It] must act as the protector of small birds who stops dispersal of trains of the *sman's* small birds into the trees![143]

I deal with the identification of the birds and locations mentioned in this passage in parts III and IV below. The birds listed and depicted on all five surviving second folios have a range of roles based upon their size and their status as 'property'. Species of small birds (*bye'u*) who are identified both as being existing property of, or which are offered (*'bul*) as property to, *sman*, not only 'lead the way in the forest', but also 'lead the way in the rocks',[144] 'show the way taken by *sman*'[145] and 'do not annoy *sman* with their calls'.[146] Those larger birds mentioned in each group, who are neither classed as property nor offered as property to

141 See the Copenhagen ms. edition by Haarh 1969: 409.

142 For precedents for use of *dkor* in relation to *sman* and birds elsewhere in the *Sha slungs* text, see facs. Ca-2r, 1.4 (beneath painted panel), Na-2r, 1.4-5 (beneath painted panel) and 71, Pa-2r, 1.3-4 (beneath painted panel).

143 Facs. Cha-2r, 1.1-8 (beneath painted panel): *lcags sgong nags la rdol / nags bye'u ke ke dang / khu long zer mong dang / bya gshen 'jon mo des nags la shul yang 'dren / dkor yi dam pa lags / bye'u mgon srungs ma ni / lho ga nags mtshal nes / kang ka mchu rings byung / shing khams dbang du sgyur / sman yi bye'u 'phring rnams / shing la myi byer ba'i [/] bye'u mgon srungs ma mdzod // //.*

144 Facs. Ca-2r. 1.3-4 (beneath painted panel), *gshags shul brag la 'dren /.*

145 Facs. Pa-2r. 1.3-4 (beneath painted panel), *sman lam shul yang[?] mtshon /*, with *lam shul* here understood according to *BGT* 2768, *gzhan dag phyin pa'i rjes kyi lam shul.*

146 Facs. Na-2r. 1.4-5 (beneath painted panel), *sman yi sun ma 'bod /.*

Fig. 13. Folio Cha-2r from the *Sha slungs* text.

Fig. 14. Folio Pa-3r from the *Sha slungs* text.

sman, have a protective, shepherding role over the small birds, one which parallels that of the *lha* and *lha*-descended beings in relation to wild animals on third and fourth folios. Finally, there is no trace of any formal progression from one *bye'u slungs* to the next, no route, nor any obvious development of the arrangement of species and habitats being described on successive second folios. It appears more the case that together they form a network encompassing all of wild nature where birds occur.

c. Wildlife way stations

Third folios describing the 'wildlife way stations' (*sha slungs*), and the range of wild herbivores that dwell in them, are the best represented among the fourfold folio series, with seven surviving examples. Their text schema and content are quite similar to second folios presenting small bird way stations, albeit generally shorter in length. There are six larger sized wild herbivore species mentioned throughout these folios, including wild ass, cervid deer, takin, Indian muntjac or barking deer, alpine musk deer and Tibetan gazelle, and their classificatory identification is discussed fully in chap. 5 below. Most of them are individually listed as property that is being offered to *sman*. Several of the wild herbivores are also designated as messengers (*pho nya*) who run far or fast, and one acts as a mount (*chibs*) of *sman* and *btsun*, much like the messengers and horses of the *slungs* way stations of Tibet discussed in Old Tibetan documents. The idea that *sman* and other beings who dwell in the natural world own and use a range of wildlife in the types of roles and functions just mentioned is entirely commonplace in Tibetan and high Himalayan traditions of myths and rites. By far the most revealing roles any of these animals have are those assigned to the last type of wildlife in the *sha slungs* series, namely the badger and the marmot on folio Pa-3r (Fig. 14):

> As for [what emerges] from the final wildlife way station, marmot and badger, the two. Badger, the colour of turquoise. [They] make the dry mattress[147] of the *sman* by carrying off nectar waters. Marmot, the colour of gold. [They] ready the bed [for] small *lha* [and] *sman*. [These animals] count as movable properties for benefit. [148]

Thus, if the passage is taken literally as an ecological statement, it could mean that small *lha* and *sman* sleep on the ground, or even under the earth, in this type of wildlife way station, since that is where both badger and marmot nest and are active. As with the *bye'u slungs* folios, there is no trace of any formal progression from one *sha slungs* to the next, no route, nor any obvious development of the arrangement of species being described on successive third folios. The final *sha slungs* in the series being the preserve of ground-dwelling animals also appears unsystematic in this regard, since marmots occupy alpine steppes while badgers dwell in forested valleys. Like all the *bye'u slungs*, the *sha slungs* together form a network encompassing all of wild nature where wild animals occur.

d. Wildlife protectors

On the five surviving fourth folios of the series, *lha* and *myi* identified beings, also sometimes related to *yul sa* and *sgra bla* categories, are depicted and described as having a protective and caring role towards wild herbivores that belong to *sman*, but also towards 'small *lha*' and *sman* themselves. Some of these protectors have the high status of progenitor

147 For *gdung sobs* I read *gdung [ba]* as the verb 'to be dried', and *sobs* as *sob* (cf. *gsob*) a 'stuffed' cushion/mattress (*sob stan*, etc.) of some kind. This fits best in relation to the role of the following marmot.

148 Facs. Pa-3r. l.1-6, *sha slungs mtha' ma nes ni / phyi ba' dang grum pa nyis / grum pa' g.yu yi mdog / bdud rtsi chab len bas / sman yi gdung sobs mdzad / phyi ba' gser yi mdog / lhe'u sman gzi' [read: gzim] mal sbyor / longs spyod dkor yi grangs /*. The remaining text of line 6 (*sha slungs bcu gsum*...) begins a three line passage ending on the top of folio Pa-4r which introduces a separate topic following the description of the marmot and badger.

Fig. 15. Folio from the *Sha slungs* text (Cha-4r) depicting a protector of wild herbivores or perhaps the *lha* 'O[d] de Gung rgyal.

lha, and the long enduring identity of 'O[d] de Gung rgyal (Fig. 15), whose cult is already apparent in Old Tibetan documents, is among them, while others are completely unknown beings. For example, folio Cha-4r featuring 'O[d] de Gung rgyal invokes him in relation to other protector beings:

> Protector of wild herbivores, because *lha* 'Od de Gung rgyal, the master of ten thousand *yul sa* [beings], the ultimate source[149] of the *lha*, cherishes the *sman* and is of great assistance to deer, [you] do not send the movable property of *sman*, the wild herbivores, to the enemies which are *bdud, btsan*, and *srin po!*[150]

The most distinctive feature of this and other fourth folio texts is the role of these

149 *Grol phugs*, although *phugs* could also mean 'perpetual' here, see *BGT* 1714, cf. Stein 2010: 152 "men who descend from the gods (*mi rgyud lha las grol ba*)" citing *Rlangs* 5.

150 Facs. Cha-4r, l.1-5: *ri dags srungs ma ni / lha 'od de gung rgyal ni yul sa khri yi dpon / lha yi grol phugs lags / sman la 'o byams la / sha la skyabs che bas / sman dkor ri dags rnams / bdud btsan srin po yi sgra [read: dgra] la ma skur shig /.*

protectors as suppressors (*'dul*) and hunters (*rngon pa*) of a range of negative spirits and forces, including *bdud*, *btsan*, *srin po*, *gzed*,[151] *g.yam dri* (or *g.yam* and *dri*?), who might threaten the useful wildlife property of *sman* and small *lha*. It is noteworthy that some of the vocabulary here on 'hunters of the *bdud*' is shared with texts among the Dga' thang manuscripts,[152] while the notion that these same types of negative spirits act as 'thieves' of other beings' lives is already established in the Old Tibetan ritual texts.[153] Thus, this aspect of the cosmology is fully congruent with older and approximately contemporary ritual texts.

3.3.2 Summary

As a rite, the *Sha slungs* text is concerned with managing a complex of relations among three sets of beings: those representing new life that comes into the natural, terrestrial world; those that aid and protect that first set of beings; and those that potentially threaten the interests of both the first and second sets. Apart from invoking all these beings and their relations by chanting the text, a user must emphatically instruct some beings to act (*mdzod*) as protectors or shepherds in certain ways, while appeasing others by making offerings (*'bul*). There are also a few appeals to bring new life together with (*sprad*) its safest earthly abode. Moreover, on the very final folio in the text, of the thirteen wildlife way stations it explicitly states, 'They are offered to small *lha* offspring who are brother and sister as properties for enjoyment/use. The *sha slungs* of the precious are completed.'[154]

Sha slungs and *bye'u slungs*, and their wild animal and bird inhabitants, formed a network of functional locations throughout the natural wilderness. They served as safe havens for small *lha* who are new lives, together with their *sman* supporters, after descending from ancestral realms. It is reasonable to assume that, like way stations everywhere, *sha slungs* and *bye'u slungs* were temporary halting places on a journey, one that began up in the sky and eventually ended in a mother's womb. Small *lha* offspring who are 'young ones' were destined to be born as human children at some stage, and this brings us back to the *Ste'u* text as a complimentary rite.

151 The rare name *gzed* as a deity identity is found in PT 1060; see Stein 2010: 269.

152 Facs. Ca-4r, l.4 *tsan bdud kyi rngon pa*, cf. *Dga' thang* 60, 181, f.2, l.5, and 63, 185 f.6, l.6 on *bdud kyi rngon pa yin no /* as one of 'the three terrors one encounters there (on a ritual jounrey)' (*'jigs pa gsum dang der phrad do' /*).

153 The idea is old, see IOL Tib J 0734: 7r267-268 on the *btsan, bdud, btsun, rmu, g.yen dgu* and *sri* who are 'thieves' (*rkun ma*) that require a ransom.

154 Facs. Pa-4r, l.1-3 (above painted panel), *lhe'u sras lcam dral la longs spyod dkor du 'bul // // rin chen yi sha slungs rdzogs s.ho //.*

The *Sha slungs* text leaves no doubt that all the beings it presents abide in the wilderness upon the earth's surface, that is, below celestial and atmospheric abodes from where the *Ste'u* text describes descent of small *lha* offspring to a terrestrial end station. It thus stands to reason that the purpose of the *Sha slungs* rite logically followed on from the *Ste'u* rite. When new life was called down from ancestral sky realms using *ste'u*, the *sha slungs* and *bye'u slungs* and their denizens were ritually maintained in wild places to ensure a safe and supportive domain for these potential human lives (Fig. 16).

There is the question of whether or not a rite performed with either or both the *Ste'u* and *Sha slungs* texts could have been conducted using any chosen, individual fourfold series of folios, and thus targeted to the particular content of that series, or if the entire text including all thirteen fourfold series needed to be performed together for a complete rite. I am inclined to think that all thirteen had to be performed following the order of numbered *ste'u* on third folios, since together they define a protected itinerary through the world space from the sky abode of *lha* ancestors, via the *sman, mtshun/btsun* and *yul sa*, to the ritual site and thus the sphere of human activity. It must have been similar with the thirteen numbered *sha slungs*,

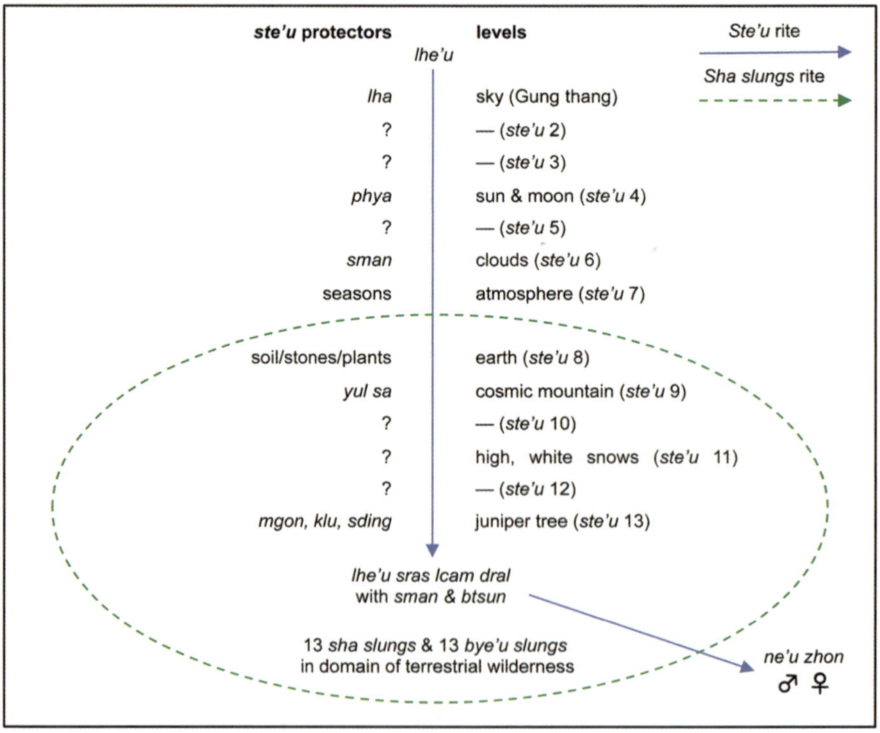

Fig. 16. Combined aspects represented in *Ste'u* and *Sha slungs* rites.

which would have all been performed in order to ensure every part of the wilderness formed a safe and supportive haven for small *lha* waiting to take birth as new human beings. Only information on actual social practice could address this point more definitively, but we are unlikely to gain that.

4.Discussion – An old cycle of existence and its status in relation to regional cultural history and ethnography

Surveying all we know about the *Rnel dri 'dul ba, Ste'u* and *Sha slungs* rites, we have demonstrated they share the same overall cosmological framing and common concepts and reference points. Considered together, they amount to a cycle of human existence, one that circulates or flows up and down the vertical cosmic axis. Its two poles are the social domain of personhood upon the earth below and the ancestral domain of *lha* in the high sky above. When transiting in between these poles, as deceased existences departing back to ancestors, or as vital, new lives given out by ancestors once again, existence must pass through the intermediary custody of *sman* and *mtshun/btsun*. At least, this is obviously so in the two ritual cases we are dealing with, namely, of culturally problematic deaths, and of intentionally bringing new lives into the world in a safe manner. The intermediary transits back and forth between personhood and ancestorhood are obviously critical phases in the circulation of existence. A myriad of other beings located in terrestrial wilderness areas and the proximate atmosphere exist not only to threaten and steal, but also to protect and care for human existence, whether in its deceased or in its vital modes. Hence, these transit phases have such intensive ritual interventions dedicated to them. In general, we should consider the *Rnel dri 'dul ba*, *Ste'u* and *Sha slungs* procedures as merely being particular forms of *rite de passage* within this overall cycle.

Furthermore, these three old rites inform us that the entire cycle of existence operates in the sky, the atmospheric and the terrestrial domains of the cognisable natural world in general. It is purely mundane, and it is a potentially open cycle around which existence can continue to flow. There is no hint here of any 'other-worldly' destination or 'point of no return', but especially no separate 'land of the dead' or 'paradise', nor any 'heaven' and 'hell' types of destinations linked to moral status. We know that a range of such ideas (*gshin yul, dga' yul,* etc.) were already referred to in certain Old Tibetan documents – some possibly influenced already by Buddhism – as well as in early translations of Buddhist doctrines into Tibetan (*sdig yul, dga' dang skyid pa'i yul*, etc.).[155] The *Rnel dri 'dul ba, Ste'u* and *Sha slungs* rites evince no continuity whatsoever with such representations. They express a cosmology completely separate from those promoted by organised salvation religions in the region since the period of Tibetan conversion to Buddhism.

The question arises of how best to identify the status of this old cycle of existence and the sources it occurs within from the perspective of regional cultural history? Materials from the Tibetosphere offer some obvious examples for comparison. One thinks of the Old Tibetan origin mythology of *btsan po* rulers descended from *lha*, or of contemporary Amdo folk notions recognising local mountain deities as community ancestors. Yet, these examples appear as merely superficial, mythological representations alongside the far more specific connections and mechanisms defining relations of existence between *lha* and humans in the *Rnel dri 'dul ba*, *Ste'u* and *Sha slungs* texts, which, as rites, are intended to offer practical procedures to attain specified goals, viz., people acted upon them. Thus, one assumption might be that these three old rites are just elaborated forms of what we already know of from other Tibetan Plateau times and spaces. This is the position taken toward rites in the Dga' thang manuscripts by those who claim them as "Bon ritual traditions" and stress unbroken continuities between Dunhuang documents and later sources,[156] while one commentator claims the "*bon*" he equates with all these old manuscripts is "best defined as a significant part of, if not the sum total, of archaic ritual traditions; those that developed or were redeveloped indigenously in Tibet."[157] Besides the fact that these old texts do not represent themselves in this manner (see below), the ongoing drawback with such sweeping assessments is their repetition of existing generalisations and assumptions, rather than putting these to the test by working with the actual evidence to hand. I consider that these three old rites can be more fruitfully investigated in relation to obvious differences and similarities they exhibit in relation to other known traditions in the region, and their exact relationship with Old Tibetan documents can be more fully established, while comparisons with wider frames of cultural history and ethnographic evidence can be examined. I will

155 See Stein 2010: 58-59, 263-264, van Schaik 2013: 235 and Imaeda 1981.

156 See Karmay 2009: 63. The publishers of the Dga' thang manuscripts identified the collection as *bon gyi gna' dpe*, the rites themselves as *bon gyi cho ga*, and further divided some of them into *bon sde gson bon*, with this latter classification being found in G.yung drung Bon literature; see Pa tshab Pa sangs dbang 'dus and Glang ru Nor bu tshe ring 2007 in *Dga' thang* 1-2.

157 Bellezza 2014: 160.

now offer brief discussions of these three points as a basis for drawing my own conclusions on the status of the *Rnel dri 'dul ba, Ste'u* and *Sha slungs* rites.

4.1 Differences in relation to Tibetan materials

Commenting on the *rnel dri* tales, Samten Karmay observed "I have never come across this particular account in the later Bon tradition,"[158] and such an experienced authority is best placed to offer this assessment, one that accords with my own surveys of rites in Tibetan language sources in which *rnel dri* do appear unique. However, the same ideas and rites are certainly not unique in the adjacent Himalayas. Similar cases of spirit possession of a woman's womb and foetus leading to miscarriage were already a recognised medical diagnosis termed *jātahāriṇī*, or 'seizer of the born', in a ca. 6th-7th century Sanskrit medical compendium titled *Kāśyapasaṃhitā*, old manuscripts of which were first known from Nepal.[159] Exactly the same concept of *rnel dri* as 'wandering bad death spirits', albeit not specifically restricted to – yet frequently applied to – infants born and unborn, represents a wide-spread cultural pattern and concern ethnographically attested along the extended eastern Himalayas. Such rites are focused mainly upon posthumous problems in the wake of in utero, natal and young infant deaths, maternal deaths during childbirth, violent accidents, suicides and less commonly murders. The often elaborate rites involved for dealing with this concern are most frequently the preserve of Himalayan highland shamans.[160]

The identification of ancestors and the concept of a 'soul' – or more precisely 'mobile vitality principle' – as a basis for existence is another interesting point of difference between the *Rnel dri 'dul ba, Ste'u* and *Sha slungs* rites and what we usually find in Tibetan Plateau materials. In the three old rites under study, it is striking that existence is never anonymous or abstract. In each of its four modes – as young life entering the world, in personhood, in being deceased, and in ancestorhood – existence is consistently categorised and named, thus always marked in terms of transformations of state and identity. It is not possible to find

158 Karmay 2009: 64.

159 See Cerulli 2012: chapt. 4 on the miscarriage narrative in the *Kāśyapasaṃhitā*.

160 For examples, see Gaenszle 2007: 37-38 on the Mewahang Rai rites for *hillasi* (accident and murder deaths), *ma: maksi* (maternal deaths in pregnancy or childbirth) and chanu (unborn child deaths), He Limin and He Shicheng 1998 on Naxi *Hâr-lâ-llù'k'ó'* rites for suicide deaths, while together with Gerhard Heller I observed and documented the cognate Idu Mishmi *Brophee* rite in Upper Dibang valley during 2007 staged to benefit the family of a suicide victim experiencing troubles due to the deceased person's wandering spirit.

anything comparable to this in Tibetan Plateau materials beyond these three old rites, yet sophisticated concepts of ancestors and rich vocabularies identifying them are commonplace in eastern Himalayan highland societies. In contrast to, and perhaps because of this feature, it is also striking that the *Ste'u* and *Sha slungs* texts never once refer to existence using any 'soul' terminology. Similarly, the term *brla* (< *bla*)[161] only occurs in two among a score of *Rnel dri 'dul ba* antecedent tales, and then only in a very limited manner to discuss one specific technical operation for establishing support objects (stag's antlers or a stone in these tales) to catch and anchor wandering *dri*, rather than the victim they possess and who is rescued from them.[162]

Moreover, the cultural background provided by Old Tibetan documents and the contemporary context of ethnographic data both inform us of the long-standing and wide-spread notion of a 'soul' or 'mobile vitality principle' among highland speakers of Tibeto-Burman languages, e.g. Tibetan *bla*, Gurung/Tamu *pla/plah*, East Bodish *pra/pla/phla*, Naxi *ó-hâ'*, amongst many others. Yet, there are significant differences in the ways it is understood and represented. The definition of what *bla* means in Tibetan Plateau cultural contexts is repeatedly emphasised by scholars as being singular, with only one *bla* underpinning each human existence. However, this variation of the idea is actually aberrant within the wider region. In contrast, eastern Himalayan highland populations admit multiple souls – nine, seven and three are the more common enumerations – or a soul that is a divisible entity and which can thus exist simultaneously in different locations as 'divisibles'. This is certainly the case immediately south of Lho brag among East Bodish speakers, whose languages also extend northwards to some extent onto the southern fringes of the Plateau very close to the site where Dga' thang manuscripts were discovered. Indeed, the same multiple 'soul' concept is also clearly described in these Dga' thang manuscripts. For example, in the *Gnag rabs* we find an explicit reference to 'the human body with four souls' (*brla bzhi dang myi 'i [read: myi'i] lus po*),[163] and one thus cognate with Himalayan data but not with Tibetan Plateau data.

161 Karmay 2013: 23 n.9-10 convincingly explained the *brla* spelling as *bla* in a *Gnag rabs* from the Dga' thang manuscripts, cf. also *rla* spellings in Old Tibetan documents; Dotson 2008: 44.

162 See *Dga' thang* 39, 141, f.11, l.4-f.12, l.4 for the 'narrative of catching a *rnel dri* [on] stag antlers' and p.40, 142, f.12, l.4-13, l.1 on the 'narrative of a *brla* stone for a *rnel dri mo*'.

163 See the *Gnag rabs* narratives in *Dga' thang* 3, 88, f.4, l.6. See also the transcription in Karmay 2013: 28 but note his citation (p. 26) to p. 97 of the manscript is mistaken for p.87.

Based upon these and other indicators in the content of the three old rites and the manuscript collections they occur in, we cannot unambiguously identify them as 'Tibetan' since they also appear to be 'eastern Himalayan'. As for existing assessments that *Rnel dri 'dul ba, Ste'u* and *Sha slungs* rites belong to a "Bon tradition" which existed across Tibet, this is problematic at best in light of the evidence. The word *bon* does not appear at all in the *Ste'u* and *Sha slungs* manuscript, nor are any rites from the same or an earlier era of the type represented by *Ste'u* and *Sha slungs* known from older manuscripts. In the *Rnel dri 'dul ba* text, the word *bon* is only infrequent, while its meanings there have nothing to do with any formal identity or movement, nor especially with any "tradition," since the application of that word in contemporary English would demand at least internal rhetorical evidence of both time depth and continuity being claimed, and this is definitely not the case here. One *bon* usage in the text merely designates a single type of ritual specialist among a range of such figures appearing in the tales, including the *gshen, tshe myi, ya ngal*, and so forth, and whose roles are often not clearly distinguished from one another. The other *bon* usage – a single occurrence[164] – represents the technical term 'rite' that is attested in both Old Tibetan and other later manuscripts recording rites for mundane purposes.[165] Furthermore, and like

164 'The antecedent narrative of Bkra za Gzig 'brang is wished for. It is the method (*lugs*) of the Phag bon Gsas khri.' (*bkra za gzIg 'brang gyI rabs la 'tshal lo / phag bon gsas khri'i lugs lags so /; Dga' thang* 52, 167, f.37, l.3-4), while the end of the same section reads, 'The rite (*bon*) method of the Phag bon Gsas khri is completed.' (*phag bon gsas khri i [read: khri'i] bon lugs / rdzogs s.ho //; Dga' thang* 54, 170, f.40, l.4).

165 For *bon* as 'rite' in older texts, see Stein 2010: 268 and van Schaik 2013. Examples of *bon* as 'rite' in cognate, post-11th century texts recording mundane rites are common, albeit frequently overlooked and substituted for meanings draw from the G.yung drung Bon vocabulary. For instance, an old manuscript narrating a myth and concomitant rite for overcoming *sri* demons who cause infant deaths, and in which the ritual specialist invokes a deity named Bung ba stag chung, begins with the words 'This rite (*bon*) appoints/invokes the *gsas* [against] the *sri*. Salutations to Bung ba stag chung!' (*bon 'di ni sri gsas bdar ba / bung ba stag chung la phyag 'tshal lo*); Karmay and Nagano 2002: 185 (= f.1b). Also, in the undated *Ming sring dpal bgos dang lha 'dog bcas bzhugs* manuscript, the first section of which relates a myth of origin about the sharing of wealth between siblings in the context of a marriage rite, and in which the ritual specialist in the myth is consistently referred to as the *lha bon thod dkar* or *lha bon* and not as a *bon* or *bon po*, we read a list of materials required for the rite: 'The [father] Rgya rje Ling dkar said, "Such things as a *lha* horse, a *lha* yak, a *lha* sheep, a *lha* goat and a *lha* turban of white silk, those are the materials which are required for the rite (*bon*), and required as the price of a daughter, and having searched for them all, place them in the hands of the seven *gnya'u* men. The seven men who are those *gnya'u*, each mounted upon a speedy stallion and went into space, to the *lha* land."' (*rgya rje ling dkar zhal na re / lha rta dang ni lha g.yag dang / lha lug dang ni lha ra dang / dar dkar lha thod la sogs pa / bon la dgos pa'i rdzas rnams dang / bu mo'i rin du dgos pa rnams / thams cad tshang ma btsal nas ni / gnya'u mi bdun phyag du phul / gnya'u de'i mi bdun gyis / mgyogs pa'i rta pho re re zhon / lha yul de ni dbyings su byon /*); Karmay and Nagano 2002: 218 (= f.425). In Sikkim, Balikci 2008: 338 found "the term *bon* refers to specific oral ritual texts that are chanted and considered to be the core of the *bon* specialists' ritual knowledge," while *bon ban* is the category of ritual specialists who can chant such texts.

the case of *Ste'u* and *Sha slungs*, we know of no rites equivalent to *Rnel dri 'dul ba* dated to the same or an earlier era from Tibet. Since the "Bon" identity now claimed for these little known 11th-12th century rites is often articulated by stressing continuities between Old Tibetan documents and later sources, these, too, can be examined.

4.1.1 Reuse of language from older texts

Leaving aside the major, and to date, unanswered question of how sets of Tibetan Language manuscripts discovered 1500 km apart in the Hexi Corridor of Gansu and in southernmost Tibet might have come to share content, we can examine what continuity actually represents where common words and phrasing occur in both sets of texts. From the earlier work of scholars like Rolf Stein and more recent studies by Joanna Bialek,[166] we are already well aware that shared vocabulary spanning the 11th century period is frequently associated with transformations of meaning and new contexts of application. A term like *slungs* in the *Sha slungs* text cannot be described naively as a 'continuity'or 'survival' from Old Tibetan. It has been subject to an intelligent and subtle creative process, and its later use embodies significant transformations of meaning and application. We can also be quite certain that administrators stationed in East Turkestan during the Tibetan empire, and ritual specialists somewhere in southernmost Tibet several centuries later, represented very diverse types of agents whose intensions for *slungs* served different needs. Other terms such as *bdur, yags, sbre'u* and to some extent *dri* in our sources can more easily be demonstrated as continuities with Old Tibetan usages due to their application in cognate cultural fields over time. Yet, these are not the only two options to explain and define common vocabulary we find in the *Rnel dri 'dul ba, Ste'u* and *Sha slungs* rites and Old Tibetan documents. We have examples of very direct and intentional reuse of words and identities without transformation. We also find reuse with modifications for which we cannot discern transformative intensions, i.e. they may have been incidental or convenient to an extent. There are also forms of creative 'cut and paste' reuse based upon possible misunderstandings or lost context, for instance due to oral transmissions, use of incomplete manuscripts, or as a result of folk etymologisation and language transformation more generally. Here I will give a few examples from my analysis of the *Rnel dri 'dul ba, Ste'u* and *Sha slungs* texts. My intention is limited to revealing the

166 See Stein 1971, Stein 2010 (Tibetica Antiqua III & V), Bialek 2015 and 2015a, but also Blezer 2011 and Gurung 2011 for examples more specific to G.yung drung Bon.

nature and scope of the 'constructedness' of these later texts on the basis of older materials. A full linguistic analysis by a specialist scholar, for example, would yield other results and reveal different aspects.

As an instance of very direct and intentional reuse of words and identities without transformation, we can take the many *srin* names occurring in *Rnel dri 'dul ba* narratives, along with other basic tale settings and additional identities. Consulting the Old Tibetan document IOL Tib J 0734, we can find the following examples – which are not an exhaustive survey – of correspondences (Fig. 17) of identities within respective tale collections:

Source	Land	lord	*srin*	*gshen/bon*
0734	Dbye mo yul drug	Khar ba	Yug mo	Dbye *gshen* Kar bu
Rnel dri	Dbye mo yul grug	Khar ba	Yug mo	Dbye *gshen* Mkhar bu
0734	Mchims yul dgra sul	Ne'u	Pod	*shen* Do rab 'bring rab
Rnel dri	Mchims yul rgu sul	Ne'u sing	Pha	*gshen* Rgu gdo
0734	Skyi ro ljang sngon	Rmang po	Tsa lung zha'i (or: zhal)	*gshen* Rgyan ngar
Rnel dri	Skyi ro ljang sngon	Rmangs po	—	*gshen* Rgyan ngar
0734	Rtsang shul mtho	Phwa'a	Po da, Pod de	*shen* Snyal ngag
Rnel dri	Rtsang shul mthon ba'	Ya bo	Zla gar	*gshen* Snyal ngag
0734	Gnubs shul king drug	Sribs pa	Rkang pran	Rong po lde khar
Rnel dri	Gnubs yul gling grug	Sris pa	Bu rkun	*gshen* Rum po
0734	Yar khyim sogs [yar(/kar)]	'O lde spu rgyal	Pa sna ring po	*lde gshen* Rmun bu
Rnel dri	[Yar] lungs sogs ka	Rmun bu	Pag po sna ring	*lde gshen* Rmun bu

Fig. 17. Examples of narrative identities shared between IOL Tib J 0734 and the *Rnel dri 'dul ba'i thabs*.

These first examples represent quite systematic reuse. Another, more random range of details for building up *rnel dri* tales can also be found occurring in the Old Tibetan documents IOL Tib J 0734 and IOL Tib J 0738. For example, in a *rnel dri* tale set in [Yar] lungs Sogs ka, the beneficiary of the rite is Yar lha Sham po, while in the Old Tibetan Yar khyim Sogs [yar (/ kar)] tale, an effigy (for a ransom?) is set up for Yar lha Sham po by a ritual specialist. [167] Or, a *sman* of the 'alpine slates' (*g.ya sman*) is discussed in a tale with the wording *g.ya sman sil*

167 Cf. *Dga' thang* 50, 161, f.31, l.6 with IOL Tib J 0734: 8r324.

ma[r], while we find closely cognate Old Tibetan wording *g.ya sman ni si li ma* in IOL Tib J 0738.[168] The parts of IOL Tib J 0734 where such correspondences occur contain a series of antecedent tales requiring ransom techniques involving *srin*, and since *Rnel dri 'dul ba* also includes ransoms in relation to *srin*, the reuses here are very rational in terms of common cultural fields with overlapping content. On the other hand, there is also a great deal that differs between these older and later texts in terms of other identities, usages, motifs, rite techniques and most significantly ritual goals. We cannot know which – if any – surviving Old Tibetan documents may have represented potential sources here, and some of the same or similar material just cited also occurs in PT 1285, for example. However, direct access to some written or oral traditions related in ways we do not yet understand to such documents must account for this degree of specific correspondence.

There are examples of reuse with modifications for which it is hard to discern any specific transformative intensions, and which rather appear incidental or convenient. One *Rnel dri 'dul ba* rite features a *sman bon* named 'Bring dang who ensures that the purified existence of a deceased finally 'departs/goes' (*gshegs*) to the *sman*. In the account of death rites in the Old Tibetan document PT 1134, we find a *rgya bon* named Brim tang whose function it is to set up 'nets' (*rgya*) for funeral structures.[169] In another account of death rites in PT 1042, it is said 'the *sman bon po* goes to fetch/leads (*drangs*) the *sman*'.[170] It suggests we might be observing a construction process in the *Rnel dri 'dul ba* text which selects and combines approximately cognate materials to attain a different end result convenient for the author/compiler's specific intentions, albeit that the selections could be fairly arbitrary within certain sub-fields.

For the final type of case, in an above quoted *Rnel dri 'dul ba* description of the doors passed through on the vertical ritual journey, the wording *se ba zangs gyi sgo*, then *sgo cig bgrod* and *sgo mo* occurs in consecutive lines, with *se ba* 'wild rose' logically conforming to the context of a series of doors indexed to woody plant species throughout the text. In the death rites described in PT 1042, one reads *se'i sgor gshegs* (f. 42), and in PT 1134 *se mo bgrod* (f. 9, *et passim*). But in those Old Tibetan contexts, reference to the obscure term *se* relates to the

168 Cf. *Dga' thang* 52, 166, f.36, l.9 with IOL Tib J 0738: 1v26.

169 PT 1134: 119-120, and see especially Bialek 2015: 389-391 on transformations in Old Tibetan vocabulary of death rites.

170 PT 1042: 77, *sman bon pos sman drangs lags*, cf. also the *sman bon* who states a divination result in PT 1043: 72.

'grave' or 'tomb' and its entrance or opening (*se'i sgo*), while we now know that *se* has been the object of a complex series of folk etymologies (e.g. *se gru bzhi, se mo, se mo gru bzhi*, etc.) which began being generated during the era of Old Tibetan use.[171] Such processes most likely informed the development of a ritual vocabulary for *Rnel dri 'dul ba* rites.

The *Ste'u* and *Sha slungs* texts offer the same range of examples demonstrating these types of cases, but two particular variations of them will be the focus here. One remarkable feature of both texts is the number of rare or uncommon diminutive forms they employ to designate crucial aspects of myth references and ritual content. These include *ste'u, ne'u, bye'u, sbre'u* and *lhe'u*, while *rnel* in the *Rnel dri 'dul ba* text is hypothesised to be closely related to *ne'u*. The forms *ste'u, ne'u, bye'u* and *lhe'u* are all found together in a single Old Tibetan document describing death rites, PT 1134, albeit that there we read *the'u*, and while *sbre'u* is absent from the same document two of its likely precursors, *brang* and *sbra*, occur with the same meaning in a closely cognate field. All these diminutives are of interest for different reasons, yet I will focus upon *bye'u* as a concept category because of what it reveals about transformations during contexts of reuse, and possibly also about early ideas of ancestors.

For comparison with usages in the *Sha slungs* and *Ste'u* texts, quite a number of relevant Old Tibetan *bye'u* references are available especially in the document PT 1134, but also in PT 1136 and PT 1285. Here are some examples:

i. *bya gshen 'jon mo* (folio Cha-2r): a 'small forest bird' which 'continually leads the way in the forest', a property of *sman*, found in Lho ga and with a tendency to stay into the trees. In PT 1136, a *bya gshen* 'Jon mo is a human ritual specialist who performs death rites together with *pha* Gshen rab kyi myi bo for the deceased Lho rgyal Byang mo tsun.[172] The only thing in common, apart from their names, in the older and later citations, is the Lho reference occuring in both contexts.

ii. *kang ka* (folio Cha-2r): a long beaked protector of small birds, from Lho ga, holds sway over the realm of trees, and stops dispersal of trains of the *sman's* small birds into the trees. In PT 1134, the *gang ka* performs some undefined role – perhaps by calling *pu ru ru*? – in finding a path for travel (*'gro lam*) in the rocks for the purposes of a ritual journey by a psychopomp sheep during a death rite.

171 See the analysis in Bialek 2015: 389-391, who considers that *se* was possibly employed to avoid use of a taboo term; cf. also Stein 2010: 267.

172 See Dotson 2013: 135-136 for a translation of the narrative.

iii. *rma bya sgag mo* (folio Pa-2r): a peahen, a protector of the *sman's* small birds that must stop them from dispersing, it also shows the way to go, and is offered as property. In PT 1134, the *sgeg sa*, peacock or peahen (cf. Classical Tibetan *sgeg ldan* syn. *rma bya*), together with the *khug sta['}* or swallow (Classical Tibetan *khug rta*), is the direct object of a specific rite technique: 'When the small bird swallow proceeds, tickle the end of its tail. When the small bird peacock proceeds, tickle the top of its tail.'[173]

iv. *brag bye'u*, in context with *brag la* (folios. Ca-2r): they show the way to go in the rocks, which means the way taken by *sman*,[174] whose property they are said to be. In PT 1134, *bye'u* appears in relation to 'seeking a path in the rocks' (l.190, *brag la / lam tshol ba*) as part of an itinerary for a psychopomp sheep accompanying the deceased. In the *Sha slungs* text, 'in the rocks' (*brag la*) is also reused as a generalised setting in which small bird eggs of artificial materials hatch out. In PT 1134, a crane, a very large bird, also hatches out of eggs, but those eggs are without any distinction, nor in the rocks.[175]

v. *gtsos to re* and *lam ba* (Ca-2r): both are unusual and otherwise unattested, untraceable names for birds. They are most likely products of reuse of text where the author/compiler lacked full knowledge of vocabulary meaning. The name *Gtsos to re* can be compared with the PT 1134 wording *gtsos/dgo re* (l.240), and *lam ba* with *lam 'pan* (l.170). Both *gtsos* and *lam* appear multiple times within PT 1134, and while *gtsos* has nothing to do with birds, *lam* is closely related in context to some actions of birds. A strategic and well-informed author/compiler would have had to wilfully and illogically ignore the attested meaning 'Tibetan gazelle' for *dgo*, which is completely incongruous in relation to a bird name. However, since the alternative dialect words *nyi gri* and *nyig* are used elsewhere in the text to define a Tibetan gazelle (see chap. 5), this indicates the word *dgo* with this meaning was unknown to them.

A final comment can be made on a possible source for the name Kha la Rtsang stod

173 PT 1134: 252-254, *bye'u khug sta' / song na / mju [read: mjug] gi mtha [read: mtha'] za reg / bye'u sgeg sa song na / mjugi [read: mjug gi] drung za reg /*, cf. parallel wording at l.213-214 and l.265-266. I derive 'tickle' from Classical Tibetan *za* 'to itch' and *reg pa* 'to touch'.

174 See facs. Ca-2r, l.3-4 (beneath painted panel) *gshags [read: gshegs] shul brag la 'dren /*, with facs. Pa-2r, l.3-4 (beneath painted panel) *sman lam shul yang[?] mtshon /*, where *lam shul* is understood according to *BGT* 2768, *gzhan dag phyin pa'i rjes kyi lam shul*.

175 For example, in PT 1134 we find a crane hatch from an ordinary egg, l.45 *khrung khrung ni sngo rdol na /*, and l.62 *khrung khru[ng] ni sgong rtold /*.

designating an ancestral location from where offspring who will become new humans originate. We only know this particular form of the name in Old Tibetan from the catalogue of principalities section in PT 1060. That document lists Kha la Rtsang stod having a Rtsang *lha* who is *bye'u* and a Rtsang lord who is *phywa*.[176] Rolf Stein considered *bye'u* to be a diminutive of *phya* in this context,[177] in which case it must refer to a type of ancestor who is a *lha*. In the *Ste'u* text, new life comes down from the *lha* abobe via a *phya* abode at the sun and moon where it is protected by *phya* 'sons', and when descending further it is aided by *bye'u* birds. The old associations here are rather telling, and probably also reflect earlier mythical and lexical antecedents of the *Ste'u* text.

4.2 Ethnographic traces

Here I will give summarised cases of contemporary ethnographic data which can be meaningfully compared with content in *Rnel dri 'dul ba, Ste'u* and *Sha slungs* texts. The first two cases are of rites I recorded during field research on the cult of Srid pa'i lha in eastern Bhutan, while the third describes the most common and visible post-mortem practice used throughout Bhutan. The fourth and final case offers reports of a wider, popular belief about the circulation and identity of human existence.

a. Rites for *lha* conceptions

In the Srid pa'i lha cult practiced in eastern Bhutan, directly south of Lho brag, various rites are performed in relation to ancestral deities stationed at the top of the sky, and who are classified variously as *lha* (and *pho lha*), *phya* (plus spoken variants), *pla* and *se*, *zhi* or *[g/b]zhe[s]*. One form of these rites named *sifu* or *seefu* (cf. written *sri'u* and *sri'u phru*) are performed so that barren women or infertile couples conceive new children. The aforementioned ancestors are lead down from the sky via thirteen-level itineraries which can include the *lha* abode, the sun and moon, stars, the intermediate space/atmosphere, clouds, Gtsang stod, the cosmic mountain, the descending slopes of the mountain side and various trees. The ultimate resting point upon earth at the ritual site is a living juniper or other highland tree, and/or a fresh cut tree sapling which has bark and side branches removed up to an apical topknot of leaves, plus some decorations or ritual devices added, and erected

176 See PT 1060: 74.
177 Pointed out in Stein 2010: 150 n.50.

into the earth. The descending ancestral deity is symbolically and linguistically equated with birds, and appearances of white birds before and during the rites are a harbinger of an ancestral deity's arrival. The ritual specialist calls for new children for mothers. Any children conceived following the rites must regularly acknowledge the ancestral deity as their 'parent' by offering rites of thanks and respect to them, and fall under the deity's life-long protection. They are socially categorised as *sifu* or *seefu* meaning 'off-spring' (and more explicitly as *lha sras, lha'i bu, lha'i sras mo, lha'i bu mo*), and named by their human parents after their sky ancestor. If, for example, that is Gurzhe (literally 'Gu[r] Ancestor'), who is regarded as the '*lha* child/son (*lha'i bu*) of progenitor *lha* 'O de Gung rgyal, they receive a name incorporating the element 'Gu-', 'Gur-' or 'Guru-', such that a male child will be named Gurzhe, Gurulha, Guru Tsering or similar, and a female Gurumo, and so on.[178] They may also be named directly after *lha* as their parent/ancestor, with males called Lhadenla, Lhala, and Lhadarla and females Lhamo, Lhadenmo, Lhakey, and so on. Almost all features of these rites and the naming of putative offspring of ancestral deities represent the identical cultural pattern found in *Ste'u* and *Sha slungs* rites.

b. Ya ngal elimination rites

At more northern sites closest to Lho brag, the cult of Srid pa'i lha includes rites termed *sel* 'elimination', for which Ya ngal Gyim kong is the primordial initiator in the *Sel rabs* manuscripts. Different stages purify and thus open the path for transit of the ancestral *lha* up and down the vertical axis, via thirteen and nine levels, between the top of the sky and the door of the domestic house. The rites include fumigation (*bsang*) using combustable materials from ninefold 'father', 'mother' and 'son' types of trees and shrubs, ablution (*khrus*) with an array of waters from different rivers, lustration (*tshan*) employing a variety of waters 'scented' by contact with different plants and environments, as well as downward suppression rites involving sets of *sman* and *bon* auxiliaries. Nearly all the techniques, the cosmographic scheme, the identity of Ya ngal Gyim kong, and a wide variety of other content in the cult also occur in the *Rnel dri 'dul ba* rites from Dga' thang. This applies right down to the fine details of individual rite techniques. To take a single instance from

178 This naming practice represents the genealogical patronymic linkage system widely found among highland speakers of Tibeto-Burman languages, but far less evident or absent among speakers of Tibetic languages; see Lo Ch'ang-p'ei 1945.

Fig. 18. Altar set-up for vertical dispatch of ancestral deities up through the levels of the sky and closure of the path, Tsango, northeast Bhutan.

the Lha mo che festival at Tsango in the Khoma Chu valley, a site a few days foot march from the nearest settlements in Lho brag across a pass formerly used for trade. At the point in the rites when the ancestral *lha* is dispatched back up through the levels of the sky, a series of thirteen small holes are excavated in the earth aligned in a row directly in front of, and facing, the '*lha* tree' (*lha shing*) which is the terminal point of the deity's descending itinerary to the ritual site. Into each hole, a ca. 1.5 m long branch of the woody shrub locally named *sershing* or 'yellow wood' (*Mahonia napaulensis*, Tibetan *skyer ba*), is inserted so that it stands erect. A few flat, plain stones set at the base of each branch form a kind of mini-altar. Upon each of these, three rough, natural white stones are placed in a small pile (Fig. 18). Finally, when the deity has departed again, each stone is hurled up into the sky and each *sershing* stem is broken to seal the path back up to the sky to avoid it becoming defiled.[179] Once the deity departs and reaches the first level of the sky, he is considered to

179 For the same rite sequence employed by Ya ngal in the *Rnel dri 'dul ba* rites, cf. also the wording *gshed khung zur gsum brkos la // de'i khar skyer phur bcu gsum gyls bskor; Dga' thang* 34, 133, f.6, l.5-6.

Fig. 19. Tree-like *ste'u* on folio Cha-1v of the *Ste'u* manuscript (l.), and apical wooden ornaments on pine tree saplings used for post-mortem memorial rites, east Bhutan (r.).

wait there a short time before ascending finally out of range, and thus a last chance to appeal for his favours occurs. For this stage the local expression *them* is used, which in the Khoma dialect of Dzala means both 'tarrying' or 'hesitating' (cf. Tibetan *them bu* 'stopping') upon the 'threshold/doorsill' (*them*, cf. Tibetan *ma them*) going upwards. Apart from very minor variations, every detail I recorded during my field work for this process occurs in the *Rnel dri 'dul ba* rites in the Dga' thang manuscripts.

c. Post-mortem tree rites

It is almost considered compulsory in Buddhist communities throughout Bhutan that the family of a deceased person conduct a post-mortem memorial rite involving the erection of cut pine tree saplings. These are typically set up upon a high hill or remote, open site somewhat distant from habitation. The ideal number nowadays is one hundred and eight, although even erecting a single sapling is considered to fulfil this rite. Each tree stem should have its bark and any branchlets stripped off, with Buddhist prayer flags, ideally printed with the six-syllable mantra, attached to the length of the stem. In some remote rural areas, an apical topknot of foliage can be left atop the sapling's stem, although nowadays this is mostly replaced by a symbolic wooden ornament, in the shape of a sword with a disk around its base (Fig. 19, right frame). Present-day Buddhist representations aside, the form and position of these ornaments strongly resemble the apex of tree-like *ste'u* depicted in the *Ste'u* manuscript (Fig. 19, left frame). The rite has to be performed within a certain period following main death rites, often within twenty-one days, but this varies between practitioners, with forty-nine days being an ideal maximum. The rite can also be repeated annually over several years following a death, and family members can gather with alcohol at any instance of setting up the saplings. The rite is now universally considered Buddhist. However, it lacks a formal doctrinal basis, has no single technical term to describe it, nor any orthodox ritual text, and is performed entirely by lay persons. The number one hundred and eight, which is now taken as a mark of the rite being Buddhist, is also applied to other non-Buddhist mortuary practices of the laity in the region.[180] Opinions about the rite's purpose are generally cognate, including helping to quickly separate the soul of the deceased from the living, or helping the soul find the '*lha*'s white path' (*lha lam dkar po*) to a positive post-mortem destiny, as well as gaining merit for the deceased. I think this rite can most fruitfully be considered a later Buddhist adaptation of the use of tree-like *ste'u* as found in the *Ste'u* text.

d. Aspirations for circulation of lives

In closing these examples, we can cite ethnographically attested conceptions of cycles of existence among Tibetan speaking peoples that closely match the logic of circulation found in the three old texts we are dealing with. Mundane ideas of human life circulating back and forth, via death and birth, across the transitions between realms of ancestorhood and personhood, and in which origins and descent are intimately identified, are not at all uncommon along the extended eastern Himalayas and the eastern Tibetan Plateau margins. The most common form of these ideas I am aware of today are people's express aspirations that their deceased relatives take birth once again within the immediate fold of the family or proximate kin group, and their acceptance that this is what results. Mona Schrempf published documentation of such a case in contemporary Amdo (Qinghai):

> Lhamo's twenty-one year old cousin, who was her dearest female friend, died in a tragic accident. Lhamo's aunt and uncle had expressed their hopes that their deceased daughter would be reborn to Lhamo as her child. The two cousins had been playmates and very close childhood friends, like two sisters. The death of

180 The practice of corpse disposal into a nearby river, which is wide-spread from far northeast Bhutan across to Tawang and down the Mon Yul Corridor, has the number one hundred and eight for the ideal total of dismembered body parts disposed into the water.

> Lhamo's cousin was therefore traumatic for the whole extended family. It was clear that only a rebirth of the deceased young woman within her family would be able to remedy the rupture and pain left behind by her sudden and premature death. [...] Lhamo eventually gave birth to a healthy baby girl. Nobody seemed surprised at the fact that her baby turned out to be a girl. It was obvious to everybody that she was the lost cousin, her former best friend reborn. [181]

The second case of this type, reported by Anne-Marie Blondeau from a Tibetan cleric's oral testimony given during the mid-1980s, is of rites employed for the parents of very young infants who die. As a young cleric, the informant gained his knowledge of apotropaic rites (*gto bcos*) from his uncle, a *sngag pa* practitioner in Khams, and then himself worked as a ritualist for the laity in the Spo bo region of south-eastern Tibet, further along the eastern Himalayas from Bhutan. Following preparation of an infant's corpse with a range of ritual procedures, during which its mother must turn the corpse's head in the direction of the sky *sman* (*gnam sman*), the ritual specialist invoked the deceased multiple times with such appeals:

> Oh, you little baby (*sri'u*) who has passed beyond, by the power of this rite of *Oppressing the Sri* (*sri gnon*), ripen what is not yet ripened. Take the body of a 'black-headed person', and in this intermediate space between sky and earth, come back as a child of your mother and father! [...The informant then reported:] If one pronounces these wishes with execution of the rite in the correct manner, the baby will be reborn within that year as the child of its two parents. [...][182]

In my opinion, these cases demonstrate instances of long-term continuities with the cosmological outlook and rite techniques of the *Rnel dri 'dul ba, Ste'u* and *Sha slungs* texts, and for the first three cases, they do so within a geographical region immediately adjacent to both the known origin location of Dga' thang manuscripts and the highly probable origin location of the *Ste'u* and *Sha slungs* manuscript (see chap. 5).

5. Notes on manuscript provenance

Rnel dri 'dul ba, Sha slungs and *Ste'u* rites not only share features of content in common, a range of evidence indicates that their manuscripts may have the same region of geographical

181 Schrempf 2010: 170-171.
182 Citations translated from the French text in Blondeau 1997: 202 & n.30, 203, with original Tibetan passages on p.219.

provenance. I will first illustrate some close and specific morphological characteristics and orthographic features shared by these two manuscripts and Srid pa'i lha cult manuscripts with very similar content which were produced relatively close to the discovery site of the Dga' thang manuscripts. A second section reviews internal pictorial and textual evidence on *Sha slungs* text folios that can be relevant for establishing geographical provenance, and finally I compare some of this with ethnographic records of *shalung* rites from the Srid pa'i lha cult region.

5.1 Shared morphological and orthographic features

Dga' thang texts, such as the *Rnel dri 'dul ba'i thabs*, were recorded in manuscript booklets, as opposed to loose *dpe cha* folios. They were discovered at Gtam shul, a place that would have been a straightforward premodern journey of 50 km along a major trans-Himalayan river system from the closest extant sites of the Srid pa'i lha cult in Khoma Chu valley and Kurtö. Manuscript folios are made of handmade paper vertically stitched along left/right folio margins to form a simple booklet, with corners on outer folio margins trimmed round (Fig. 20). They have an approximate folio width to height format ratio of 2:1.The texts are penned in black ink with a wooden stylus.[183] All these features of Dga' thang manuscripts are more or less morphologically identical to the older manuscript booklets found at Srid pa'i lha cult sites in the Khoma Chu valley (Fig. 21, 22), that is, in closest proximity to Lho brag.

A second type of manuscript found at Srid pa'i lha cult sites in the Khoma Chu valley are in the form of 'concertina'-like booklets. Their folios are both folded and stitched together to form a long, continuous folding text which is inscribed upon both sides, and which the user can continually turn the pages of to read through one text and then that written upon the reverse folio sides. These folded 'concertina' booklets are morphologically identical to the *Ste'u* and *Sha slungs* manuscript, with the exception that those I have recorded in northeast Bhutan have a more horizontal format while the *Ste'u* and *Sha slungs* manuscript is vertically oriented (Fig. 2).

Parallel to the morphological similarities between the three sets of manuscripts compared here, there also exist unique orthographic characteristics and some older and

183 The handwritten scripts used in Dga' thang manuscripts are all of the 'headed' style, albeit inscribed in what Samten Karmay described as "rapid writing, a style that is very similar to that of the Dunhuang manuscripts," Karmay 2009: 58.

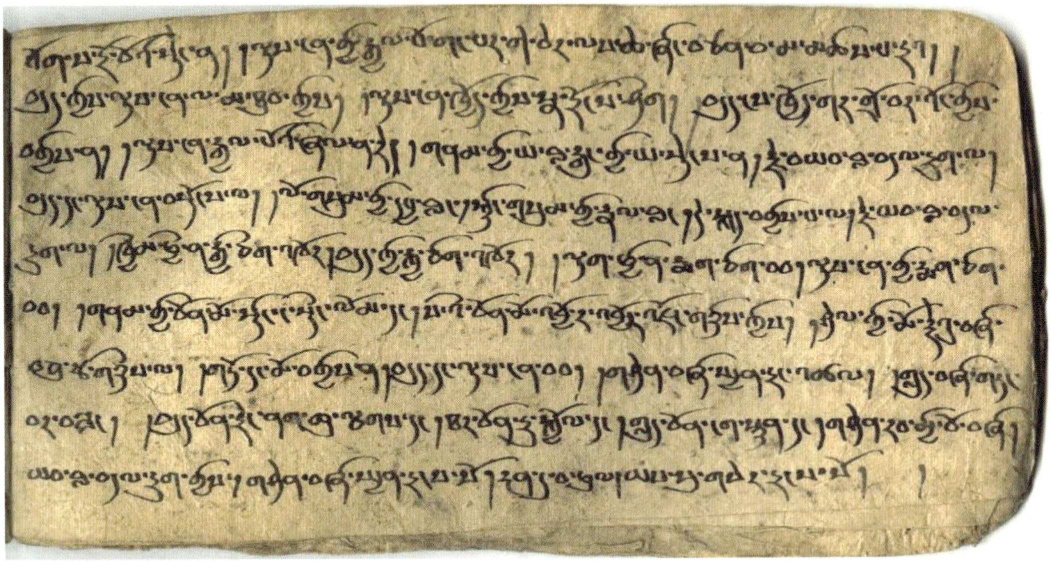

Fig. 20. Manuscript booklet folio with vertical left/right margin stitched spine, from a *Byol rabs* text, Dga' thang 'Bum pa che, Gtam shul.

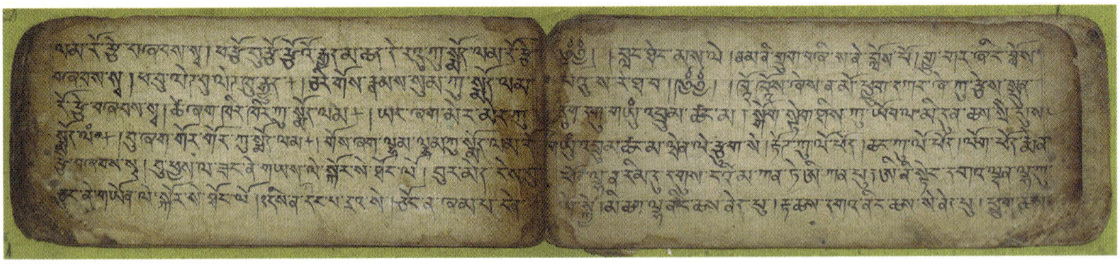

Fig. 21. Srid pa'i lha cult manuscript booklet with vertical, left/right margin stitched binding, lower Khoma Chu valley, northeast Bhutan.

seldom encountered language usages they also all share in common.

One telling example is the orthography of a *sho* terminal particle following final verbs with *sa* as secondary suffixes. It consists of a superfix *sa* above consonant *ha* carrying the vowel *o*, and occurs at title and section endings immediately preceding a double *shad* marker. It is especially found in *rdzogs sho* // and *bzhugs sho* // constructions in the cult's manuscripts (Fig. 23, frames a., b.) and in Dga' thang manuscripts (Fig. 23, frame c.).[184] The identical *rdzogs sho* // feature is also found in the *Ste'u* and *Sha slungs* manuscript (Fig. 23, frame d.).

184 Compare *rdzogs* as final verb with *sa + ha + o* terminals in the *Gnag rabs* (*Dga' thang* 12, 100, f.16, l.1); the *Rnel dri 'dul ba'i thabs* (*Dga' thang* 38, 139, f.9, l.8, and 54, 170, f.40 l.4, and 52, 167, f.37 l.3); and cf. *yegs sho, rdzogs stso* and *stsogs sho* in the *Sman dpyad* (*Dga' thang* 83, 235, f.24 l.6-7).

Fig. 22. Manuscript booklet with horizontal, top/bottom margin stitched binding, recording a *Sel rabs* text narrated by Ya ngal Gyim kong, upper Khoma Chu valley, northeast Bhutan.

A second example of particular orthography common to all three groups of manuscripts are abbreviated forms of representing the ergative, with *'i* or *'is* constructions employed instead of standard *kyis*, *gyis*, *yis* and *final vowel + s* forms. There are also a crop of usages very rarely found in texts from the post-11th century era. One example is the temporal expression *da rung da chung du* in both the *Rnel dri 'dul ba'i thabs* text and Srid pa'i lha cult texts, something which also occurs in Old Tibetan documents.[185] Even more compelling is that both of the features just mentioned and the *rdzogs sho//* orthography are all found occurring

185 For examples, within the *Rnel dri 'dul ba'i thabs* (*Dga' thang* 52, 166 f.36 l.4-5), and *Sha ru shul ston gyi rabs la sogs pa* (*Dga' thang* 69, 197, f.18, l.7). For variations of the *da rung da chung du* string in Old Tibetan documents, see PT 1134: 066 *da rung ni da cung / du*; PT 1285: v52-53 *da rung da chung*; IOL Tib J 0739: 11r 05 *da rung ni da cung du*; cf. IOL Tib J 0731: r012 *da ring da chung du*.

Fig. 23. *Rdzogs sho* orthographies in manuscripts from Srid pa'i lha cult sites in the Khoma Chu valley (a. and b.), a Dga' thang manuscript (c.) and the *Ste'u* and *Sha slungs* manuscript (d.).

together in texts featuring the ritual specialist identity Ya ngal Gyim kong and the type of purification rites he is associated with.[186] Another feature shared between the *Rnel dri 'dul ba'i thabs* text and manuscripts from Srid pa'i lha cult sites in the Khoma Chu valley is that, unlike the vast majority of anonymous older texts for mundane rites preserved in Tibetan language, they contain unique identities of their human composers.[187]

5.2 Localising the *Sha slungs* and *Ste'u* manuscript

5.2.1 Evidence in the *Sha slungs* text

The anonymous manuscript containing both *Ste'u* and *Sha slungs* texts comes down to us bereft of explicit information concerning its provenance, apart from the certainty that its paper is dated to between the 11th and 12th centuries. In light of features discussed in the previous section which are shared with both Dga' thang manuscripts and Srid pa'i lha cult manuscripts found in closest proximity to Lho brag, the *Ste'u* and *Sha slungs* texts contain

186 See especially the *Rnel dri 'dul ba'i thabs* text in *Dga' thang* 52, 166-167, f.36 l.4-5 *da rung da chungs du*, l.7 *ya ngal gyim kyong*, f.37 l.3 *rdzogs sho* // with the *sa* + *ha* + *o* orthography.

187 See the names Gar rgos pa (*Dga' thang* 51, 164, f.34, l.1) and Phag *bon* Gsas khri (54, 170, f.40, l.3-4).

a range of evidence linking them to the same geographical region. This includes the named identities of some beings, settings that are named and described, and classifications and painted images of wildlife species in light of their known distribution and ecologies. We can also compare otherwise unique references in these texts with cognate ethnographic data from Srid pa'i lha cult festivals.

a. Names

In general, one can observe virtually all names for the *lha* and *lha*-related class of beings in the text are very close variations upon the typical 'recombinant' mythical names in nearly all older texts describing mundane rites, myths and cosmology. They are all (re)constructed from a basic pool of syllables and compounds that reoccur and circulate in multiple combinations within this type of literature, and this generation of diversity around common reference points is indeed a characteristic of older antecedent narratives (*rabs*). Some of these syllabic combinations yield so many similar variations there is no way to connect a common identity over time for a single figure.[188] In contrast to this, a few names never vary, and these are of most interest. By far the best known named identity among all the beings listed within the *Sha slungs* text is *lha* 'O[d] de Gung rgyal. This name, with only the most minor orthographic variations, has remained a constant identity in the texts concerning mundane rites from Tibet since sometime during the late imperial era until today. His name is the only identity to occur more than once on the surviving folios of the *Sha slungs* manuscript. This is significant since *lha* 'O de Gung rgyal is the primary and most universal deity featuring in the cult of Srid pa'i lha. In both the *Sha slungs* text and those of the cult, he is accorded the same primordial progenitor status. At the second mention of *lha* 'O[d] de Gung rgyal's name on *Sha slungs* text folio Na-1r (Fig. 24), the phrasing used is the same as that commonly occurring in ritual texts from the Srid pa'i lha cult.[189] In the *Sha slungs* text we also meet the *ne tso smra mkhan*, or 'parrot able to talk', who is a frequent interlocutor and actor in myths about 'O de Gung rgyal within the cult.

Certain individual name elements in both the *Sha slungs* and *Ste'u* texts are of interest for

188 The best example begins with the Old Tibetan name *rje* Bla bo bla sras (IOL Tib J 734, l.3r088, 3r100, 4r165), with Sgam Lha bo lha sras in the Dga' thang manuscripts (Karmay 2009: 71-73, 80-81), Lha 'o lha sras in the *Mu ye pra phud phya'i mthar thug* manuscript (Karmay and Nagano 2002: 35 =f.3a, 42 =16a), Sgam Lha'i lha sras in *Mkhas pa Lde'u* 230, cf. 236, and with Lha bu lha sras in Srid pa'i lha cult manuscripts. For still more variations, see Dotson 2007: 25.

189 Compare facs. Na-1r, l.1, *'od de gung rgyal yi thugs kyi sprul pa les /* with *Lawa* 2, Text 13, *Lha'i nam la dus bzhi'i bzhugs sho*, 1b, 1-2a, 5, *lha 'o de gung rgyal bya ba de // sku gsung thugs kyi sprul ba las //.*

Fig. 24. Folio from the *Sha slungs* text (Na-1r) depicting a figure that could be *lha* 'Od de Gung rgyal.

they also commonly occur in ritual texts from Dga' thang and texts from the Srid pa'i lha cult found closest to Lho brag, while apart from Old Tibetan documents, these same name elements are far less common in other contexts. For example, we find the *-re* final suffix and its *to re* and *do re* forms for the final syllable(s) of names in all the documents in question. In the *Sha slungs* and *Ste'u* texts there are a *yul sa* being Khri do re (*Ste'u* f. Nga-4v, l.1-2), a bird *kon to re* (*Sha slungs* f. Tha-2r, l.3), a bird *gtsos to re* (*Sha slungs* f. Ca-2r, l.3) and a bird *pho re* (*Sha slungs* f. Tha-2r, l.2). In cult texts we find a ritual specialist Rgyal 'byor re and an origin place She re, while in the *Byol rabs* manuscript from Dga' thang there is a protagonist Klu rab Bzang to re.[190] Manuscripts with redactions of *Rgyal rigs* genealogies represent a third 'local' text from the same general geographical zone as the cult and the site of Dga' thang, and they, too, preserve *-re* suffixed proper names.[191] The same *-re, to re* and *do re* forms are very common for proper names in texts such as the *Old Tibetan Chronicle*. Such name forms obviously have a long-term circulation in the region between Lho brag and the Himalayan distribution zone of the Srid pa'i lha cult, yet they are rare in other post-

190 *Dga' thang* 21-22, 113-114, f.29, l.6, f.30, l.1, 4, 5, 8.
191 *Rgyal rigs* f.4b, 6b, Dbas rgyal To re, f.9b Khor re, f.45a Mthong re.

11th century literature written in Tibetan.

Another interesting type of rare name element or epithet has the forms *sman bu* 'son of the *sman*' and *sman sras 'sman* offspring', both forms of which occur in the *Ste'u* text (f. Cha-3v, l.2-3) in the names Sman bu La se, Sman bu Yu ne and Sman sras Skye cig. The name or title Sman sras also occurs in Srid pa'i lha cult texts as the father of a ritual specialist, while Sman bu sheb is the name of a cult site established by Khu clan members who migrated from Lho brag into the upper Kho long Chu river valley.

As for named settings in the *Sha slungs* text, there is only a single identifiable non-mythical place mentioned in the whole text, and this is the forested area of Lho ga on folio Cha-2r (Fig. 13).[192] Lho ga is also called Lho ga lang drug in Old Tibetan documents and Lho ga lang grug in the Dga' thang manuscripts. It was an ancient principality probably related to the Lho clan and adjacent to Ltam (i.e. Gtam shul) where the Dga' thang manuscripts where discovered, and was the basis for the later region of Lho brag.[193] Lho brag is without doubt the proximate origin place for the cult of Srid pa'i lha, and its lowest valleys extending southwards into the immediately adjacent Himalayan watershed are indeed heavily forested places very different from the arid Tibetan Plateau lands close by to the north.

Other settings in the *Sha slungs* text are certainly mythical. Yet, the very occurrence of specific names among them strongly indicates the same zone of geographical origins in southernmost Tibet and Lho brag, while the same names are highly relevant within the Srid pa'i lha cult also. One setting on folio Ca-1r is described as being, 'Atop the land Sa le ljon, the stronghold of Smon lam brag surrounded [by] the Dung mtsho dkar mo [...].' [194] The Dung mtsho dkar mo is the most ubiquitous primordial toponym within the Srid pa'i cult's narratives, and one identified by its participants in local landscapes across the cult's distribution region of eastern Bhutan and the Mon yul Corridor, not to mention in Lho brag itself. Many clues hint that the Dung mtsho dkar mo name is intimately related to the pre-14th century Shar Dung population of Lho brag and surroundings, and I have addressed this topic in detail elsewhere.[195] In addition to the *Sha slungs* text, the Dung mtsho dkar mo name also has its earliest known roots in the Dga' thang manuscripts from Gtam shul,

192 The *Ste'u* text likewise only features a single possibly 'real' place name, Kha la Rtsang stod; see facs. Ja-4v: l.1.

193 See citations to Old Tibetan documents in Hazod 2009: 173 and Map 3, also Dga' *thang* 45, 153, f.23, l.1-2.

194 Facs. Ca-1r: l.1-2: *yul sa le ljon stingsu [read: steng su] / smon lam brag kyi mkhar / dung mtsho dkar mo 'khyil /.*

195 See Chapter Sixteen of my forthcoming monograph *Source of Life.*

that is, ancient Ltam shul adjacent to Lho brag. While the mythical country name Sa le ljon is otherwise unknown, it has noun equivalents in myths within both the Dga' thang manuscripts and the *Bshad mdzod* redaction of the *Grags pa bon lugs* narrative composed in Gru shul immediately adjacent to both Gtam shul and Lho brag.[196] The name Gangs ri dkar po on *Sha slungs* text folio Cha-1r (Fig. 12) is of course generic. However, it too happens to be a prominent mythical toponym in the Srid pa'i lha cult. It names a resort of the progenitor *lha* and 'son' of 'O de Gung rgyal, Gu se Lang ling, while the Gang sri dkar po name and its mythical identity are associated with a high peak in southern Mon Mtsho sna just to the east of Gru shul and the upper Kholong Chu valley,[197] and the name Gangs ri dkar po is invoked in rites of the Srid pa'i lha cult until today.

b. Wildlife Classifications

Confidently assigning zoological classifications to names of any organisms cited in Tibetan texts from most historical periods, or even attempting the same using colloquial conversations with indigenous informants, is a challenging task. This is because ethnographic evidence consistently demonstrates the same indigenous animal name can be locally applied across a number of species of superficially similar appearance, species that nevertheless have quite different zoological classifications, and this occurs to the point of divisions between different family-level classifications of organisms. Experience teaches that correlating indigenous names with physical evidence – live sightings, body parts or scats – of the wild species in question is the only certain methodology. This is unavailable to us in dealing with the *Sha slungs* text. However, that text uniquely provides a series of realistic painted images of most wild species it mentions by name. In a few cases, it also provides habitat information together with the wild species names. While we cannot provide a full and unequivocal zoological classification for all species listed, most are transparent enough to gain an overall impression of the general region those who composed the text – or the earlier traditions they drew upon – must have been familiar with and gained their knowledge and inspirations from. Moreover, around half of the larger wild animal species cited in the text have distributions strictly limited to certain regions and sub-regions of the

196 For example, see Sa le sbram in both a *Byol rabs* and *Gser skyems kyi rabs* in *Dga' thang* 30, 125, f.41, l.4-5, and 31, 128, f.44, l.3. As noted above, in the *Bshad mdzod* (Copenhagen ms. edition Haarh 1969: 409), Dga' Sa le is the fifteenth level of the sky.

197 See Huber 2015b: 228-229.

greater Tibetan Plateau system and Himalayan highlands. This narrows location possibilities down quite considerably.

The large wild animal species listed in the text can be divided into two groups. Those easily identifiable are the *rkyang* 'wild ass', *sha* 'deer species', *phyi ba* (or *'phyi ba*) 'marmot' and *grum pa* 'badger'. Of these, all are found in southern Tibet, while the badger, which must refer to the Asian badger or sand badger (*Meles leucurus*), is strictly limited in distribution along the interface of the eastern Himalayas and south-eastern Tibetan Plateau margins. The more ambiguous names include *skyin, kha, dan* and *nyi gri* or *nyig*, and I will now consider each of them in turn.

Concerning *skyin*, some lexicons indicate it applies to the wild goat species called ibex, although ibex is strictly limited to the extreme northwest of the entire Tibetan Plateau system. However, the name *skyin* and its spoken variants including *kin/kyin/khyin/khying/khyim/kyem/khyem* is applied right along the eastern Himalayan highlands to designate the takin (*Budorcas taxicolor*).[198] That wild caprid is only found in forested mountain tracts eastwards from the Bhutan Himalayan highlands, and across to the very far eastern borderlands of the Tibetan Plateau, although never upon the high plateau itself. The painted images on folio Cha-3r directly above the text passage citing *skyin* (Fig. 25) clearly confirm the intention of the artist to realistically depict a takin rather than an ibex. The horn-bearing male animal on the left has a long-haired shaggy coat which is dark. This long-haired shaggy coat, with Winter hair growing over 20 cm in length, clearly distinguishes the takin from caprids like the ibex which can also be termed *skyin*. Moreover, the darkest of the four subspecies of takin are those inhabiting the eastern Himalayas at the westerly end of takin distribution in Asia, specifically in Bhutan and neighbouring parts of far western Arunachal

198 Words for takin have a complex background in the region. 'Takin' itself may be borrowed from a Mishmi language – probably Digaru – and the 'kin' element is cognate to *kin/kyin/khyin/khying/khyim/khyem* names related to takin in many highland areas along the eastern Himalayas where Tibetic and East Bodish languages are spoken. Various Tibetan and west Bhutanese names for takin incorporate 'yak' references in addition to the *kin/kyin/khyin/khying/khyim/khyem* elements that signal a wild goat species (cf. *skyin* in *BGT* 147 *gzugs dbyibs ra dang 'dra ba'i ri dwags shig*), for example *'brong khyim si* in earlier Bhutanese religious texts (today spoken *jongkhimsi* in western Bhutan), while Frederick Bailey, a keen hunter and wildlife enthusiast who spoke fluent Tibetan, reported east Himalayan names for takin as, "To the Miju Mishmis (i.e. those living near Rima) they are known as "Kyem", while the Mishmis up the Dibang river (Chulik Atta tribe) call them "Akrön." The Abor name is "Siben-ö." Takin is the name used by the Digaru Mishmi" (Bailey 1912: 1069-1070), and "The people of Po Me and Kongbo call them "Kyimyak" [*skyin g.yag*] or "Tsimyak" (Bailey 1915: 74). The 'Brug pa Kun legs hagiography records a myth of the origin of the takin as a hybrid between goat and bovine animals following a sacrifice rite (Kretschmar 1981: 112).

Fig. 25. Folio from the *Sha slungs* text (Cha-3r) depicting *skyin* animals.

Fig. 26. Folio from the *Sha slungs* text (Tha-3r) depicting *kha* animals.

Pradesh. The male's horns in the painting are characteristic of the takin's rather short horns (ibex have very long horns), which first bow forward and then sweep back and up, and which can appear crossed over when viewed from the side. The female depicted to the right in the painting has typical takin coloration, with yellowish hair darkening on the undersides, legs and along the back.

The animal *kha* (*kha po* for male, *kha mo* for female), painted on folio Tha-3r (Fig. 26) is without doubt intended as a realistic depiction of the Indian muntjac or barking deer (*Muntiacus muntjak*). The male animal is a plain reddish brown colour, with short, unbranched horns (or with one small protrusion on the right-hand horn), which matches the morphology of real male muntjac in the wild. As on the painting, female muntjac possess no horns. The name is also found written *kha sha* in Tibetan,[199] and throughout the Srid pa'i lha cult distribution zone this name is pronounced both *kha sha* and *ga sha* depending upon the local mother tongue of the speaker. The muntjac finds its northern limit of distribution along

199 The name and species identity confirmed by the painting on folio Tha-3r are not to be confused with other vague or alternative entries in lexicons for species with longer, branched antlers; cf. Jäschke 1881: 236 *kha sa sha ba* 'snow deer', 'elk', in Sikkim 'the deer', and 'spotted deer', and *kha sha* in *BGT* 213, *ri dwags bye brag cig.*

Fig. 27. Folio from the *Sha slungs* text (Ja-3r) depicting *dan* animals.

the extended Himalayan highlands between Nepal and north Burma.

As for the deer-like animals named *dan* (*dan po* for male, *dan mo* for female) depicted on folio Ja-3r (Fig. 27), one reliable lexicon lists *dan mo* as 'the female of the ibex, and of the musk deer.'[200] Ibex can immediately be ruled out due to the painted image accompanying the text on folio Ja-3r. Rather, the realistic depictions of the painted *dan* animal bodies resemble the alpine musk deer (*Moschus chrysogaster*). Alpine musk deer are found in southern Tibet and along the extended eastern Himalayan highlands between Nepal and northwest Yunnan.

The animal name *nyi gri* (male) or *nyig* (female and juvenile) is unknown to me from all Tibetan reference sources. The name must represent antiquated local usage from the era and area of the text's composition, or a non-Tibetan language. The only realistic candidate for *nyi gri* I have so far come across in terms of location and time period is the Dzala dialect spelling *no'u ge* written in Tibetan script in an old manuscript of the Srid pa'i lha cult from the Khoma Chu valley, directly south of Lho brag. The narrative context is an origin and migration account of the Khu clan who move from southernmost Tibet into north-eastern Bhutan. In that context, *no'u ge*[201] designates a wild animal species being mentioned as an

200 Jäschke 1881: 250.

201 Cf. *CDTD* (nouns) entry 3024 *ʔɲɛn ~ ʔɲin* as the Khams Tibetan Nang chen dialect pronunciation of *gnyan*.

Fig. 28. Folio from the *Sha slungs* text (Ta-3r) depicting *nyi gri* male, female and fawn (l.), and the Tibetan gazelle male, female and fawn (r.).[202]

offering during a rite named *nawan* (or *na ban*) at a site along the Lho brag Shar chu river valley in southernmost Tibet. The other animals mentioned for the same offering include thar or serow, female deer and wild pig. The painted *nyi gri* images on folio Ta-3r (Fig. 28 left frame) very realistically represent the Tibetan gazelle (*Procapra picticaudata*, Fig. 28. right frame). The characteristic dark, thin horns of the male on the right are swept directly back, while the female lacking horns is also accurately depicted. Tibetan gazelle (T. *dgo*) are distributed across the whole of the Tibetan Plateau system.

In summary, half of the larger wild animals depicted in the *Sha slungs* text are geographically limited to southernmost Tibet and the highland ranges of the extended eastern Himalayas as far east as northwest Yunnan and north Burma. The other half all have much wider distributions that all include southernmost Tibet. The badger, whose distribution is restricted to valley systems along the south-eastern Tibetan Plateau margins, is a key indicator. If the provenance of the manuscript is in any way related to the wild animals realistically depicted and named in it, then we can be in no doubt about its regional location in a southernmost Tibetan region bordering the extended eastern Himalayas from Bhutan eastwards.

202 Image source: "The Tibetan Gazelle, *Gazella picticaudata*" in P.L. Sclater and T. Oldfield. 1894-1900. *The Book of Antelopes*, vol.3. London: R.H. Porter, plate LII (Public domain).

There are quite a number of bird species mentioned throughout the *Sha slungs* text. However, for various reasons they are generally more problematic to derive classificatory identifications for as potential aids to geographically locate the text. Due to their mostly small size and somewhat stylised depictions on the manuscript's paintings, most bird images cannot be readily correlated with ornithological data leading to an identification. Unlike the specificity in names for larger animals, some birds are mentioned in the text in purely descriptive terms (e.g. *rlung bya gshog drag* 'wind bird powerful wings'), while other names can refer to so many different species (e.g. *thang kar* or *khyung* for raptors and large carrion-eaters) that they are not reliable indicators. Another group of bird names (e.g. *kon to re, gtsos to re, lam ba*, etc.) are completely unknown from any reference source, and a hypothesis concerning their origins in processes of reusing Old Tibetan textual material was advanced above. Yet another group of birds, including the parrot, cuckoo and peafowl, are all species familiar from the eastern Himalayas and obviously correlate directly in terms of their distributions with those large animal identities limited to the same region discussed above. The most interesting bird names for the present exercise are those of forest birds of Lho ga occurring in the text passage on folio Cha-2r (Fig. 13), which was translated above. Their significance for locating the *Sha slungs* text geographically is best appreciated in relation to the comparison of ethnographic data in the following section.

c. Ethnographic comparisons

During rites for Srid pa'i lha cult festivals in the Dirang region of the Mon yul Corridor, a 'tepee'-like ritual structure termed *shalung* is used. This provides a set of reference point strongly suggestive of continuities with, and later adaptations of, descriptions occurring in the *Sha slungs* text. Here I can provide but an abbreviated summary of *shalung* use and significance, while details are forthcoming in my monograph *Source of Life*.

The *shalung* rite is presided over by a hereditary and autonomous ritual specialist locally termed *bonpo*, but simply written *bon* in local manuscripts. The rite is mainly addressed to the progenitor *lha* 'O de Gung rgyal and some communal and nature deities mythically assimilated to him. There is a local manuscript written in Tibetan script recording chants to these deities. The 2.5 m high 'tepee'-like *shalung* structure (Fig. 29) is fashioned out of freshly cut branches of a specific tree species, and has an inner cavity. The *shalung* structure is said to be 'decorated with/adorned by precious things' (*rinchen gyen*, cf. Tibetan *rin chen [b]rgyan*). This consists of flowering branches of *Rhododendron sp.* (Fig. 29). It is erected

Fig. 29. A hereditary *bonpo* (r.) and his ritual assistant seated in front of a *shalung* structure, upper Sangti Chu valley, Dirang district, 2009.

in a sacred grove, beyond the village precincts. *Lha* are invoked to descend the vertical cosmic axis to the *shalung* during a nocturnal rite in which only the *bonpo* and his assistant participate. The *shalung* is considered a temporary shelter for deities at the ritual site. Its cavity holds the dead bodies or body parts (mainly heads) of certain species of wildlife, including deer, birds and fish, harvested from local hills, forests and rivers. On the following day of rites, which the whole worship community attend, these contents are later taken out of the *shalung* to be used for communal feasting and exchange. Other food items and woollen cords in the *shalung* are used to convey vitality and long-life to participants.

In the festivals I documented, the main wild animal species used in the *shalung* was the Indian muntjac or barking deer, and it was reported that in times past the takin was used. As we saw above in the *Sha slungs* text, the muntjac or barking deer (*kha*) and takin (*skyin*) are both large wild animal species invoked in the old rite. In the local dialect of Tshangla spoken in Dirang, the element *sha* forming part of *shalung* has the meaning of a generic classifier marking 'wild animals'[203] exactly the same generic classifier as written *sha* in the *Sha slungs* text. As for birds used in *shalung*, there are two locally named *jun* and *zhangka* that should be used, although these birds could not be obtained at the times I witnessed the rite. I will discuss these two birds shortly. Finally, there are fish used. The three types of wildlife are representative of all creatures from land, water and air. A *shalung* rite has several goals that coincide. It ensures game and fish for future harvest. It acknowledges and reinforces some older relationship between descent groups in different settlements who participate. It is a meat offering to the ancestral deity, and an opportunity for the worship community to harvest newly arrived vitality from the same deity.

Concerning the two birds *jun* and *zhangka* which must be used in a *shalung*, they appear to be those mentioned on the *Sha slungs* text folio Cha-2r as forest birds of Lho ga. *Jun* and *zhangka* are the colloquial pronunciations used by Tshangla-speaking participants of the *shalung* rite, yet ritual specialist informants say they are actually Dakpa names introduced when the rites where brought southwards from Tawang during the past, and where the names would be spoken *jon* and *changka* or *cangka*. The *jun* pronunciation is typical of the o > u vowel shift made by Tshangla-speakers when using Tibetan vocabulary (e.g. Tibetan *lha mo* is spoken '*lhamu*'). It appears these two local names are equivalent to the two in the text, with Dakpa *jon* matching the 'small forest bird' (*nags bye'u*) named *bya gshen 'jon mo*, and *cangka* the long-beaked *kang ka* bird that holds sway over the realm of trees and acts as guardian of, and shepherds around, the *bya gshen 'jon mo* and its small forest bird fellows. The oral origin narrative of the *shalung* rite reported to me in the Sangti valley included the explicit detail that the *jun/jon* bird is of special significance for the ritual specialist *bon* Shenrab who is locally credited with initiating this rite. This appears to be a cultural memory preserving the old connection cited above between a *bya gshen* 'Jon mo who is associated with *pha* Gshen rab kyi myi bo in PT 1136. The *kang ka* bird appears to be mentioned in PT 1134 as the *rgya bya gang ka*.

Back in the forests of the Mon yul Corridor where the *shalung* rite is performed, both

203 In Dirang Tshangla, *sha* is used as a generic classificatory suffix on the names of larger game animals, such as *gasha* 'muntjac', *basha* 'goral', *rogsha* 'langur monkey' and *omsha* 'bear'. A 'hunter' is thus a *shapa*, and his techniques include that known as *khon sha* (also *sha khon*) for driving large game, and setting leg snares called *shashong* where *shong* is the string or cord used in the snare mechanism. *Sha* also means 'meat', which is a meaning also found in Tibetic and East Bodish languages to the north, while a *sha* classification of wild animals is not.

the *jun* and *zhangka* are real birds. As for local interpretations of these bird names, the *jun* is a small 'russet-coloured' (Tibetan *'jon*) forest bird of not more than 15 cm length, and of good song. Although I have been unable to establish its exact taxonomic status, it is most likely one of the many fine singing thrush or lark species occurring in this part of the eastern Himalayas – note that nightingales are absent in the same region.[204] As a southern forest bird that is 'long-beaked' and holds sway over the realm of trees in this context, the *zhangka* is easily identifiable as the heron or egret. These birds commonly roost in trees, often in large numbers up in trees near water, and some species also nest in trees as colonies. Multiple species of herons and egrets occur across the research region. In Tibetan, *kang ka* is attested as a name for herons and egrets, and is apparently derived from Sanskrit.[205] What *kang ka* in the *Sha slungs* text and *rgya bya gang ka* in PT 1134 once referred to is a more difficult question. In texts that are temporally most proximate to these references, the *kang ka* is a distinct carnivorous, scavenging bird described together in a group with the crow, vulture and owl.[206] But in modern era lexicons, the name is applied to vulture (*bya rgod*), and a bird of burial or funeral sites. Such later definitions would not easily allow for a forest bird, while no species of Tibetan Plateau and high Himalayan vultures can in any way be described as 'long-beaked'. If it is a vulture, then it can only be the slender-billed vulture (*Gyps tenuirostris*) found in Assam and sub-Himalayan environments in India and Nepal. [207] All this brings us back to the region in which *shalung* are used today, or at least the complex ecological frontier between forested Himalayan tracts and the southernmost Tibetan Plateau, as opposed to the arid Tibetan highlands.

Certain of the manuscript illustrations in the *Sha slungs* text might supply further clues linking it to the contemporary performance of *shalung* rites used in the Srid pa'i lha cult. Two of the illustrated panels (Ca-4r, Ja-4r) depict white clad, human-like beings (Fig. 30, 31). Whether or not, and how, the text beneath each painting actually relates to the images

204 According to *CDTD* (nouns) entry 2826, *'jon mo* 'a kind of small bird' synonymous with *'jol mo* (entry 2829, cf. *BGT* 909), for which a number of identities are given in different sources (turkey-hen, peacock, lark, nightingale, etc.), but that seems beside the point in the case being dealt with here.

205 Jäschke 1881: 2.

206 See the *Bstan 'gyur* reference in *Wörterbuch*, 1: 30.

207 The description *rgya bya* may be for an 'Indian/foreign bird', but in relation to burial/funeral sites it could be a bird related to a 'net' (*rgya*) which appears to have been a ritual structure or device (or part thereof) used in earlier Tibetan funeral rites; see Bialek 2015: 157 160.

Fig. 30. Folio from the *Sha slungs* text (Ca-4r) depicting a being who could be a *lha* or idealised ritual specialist, or both.

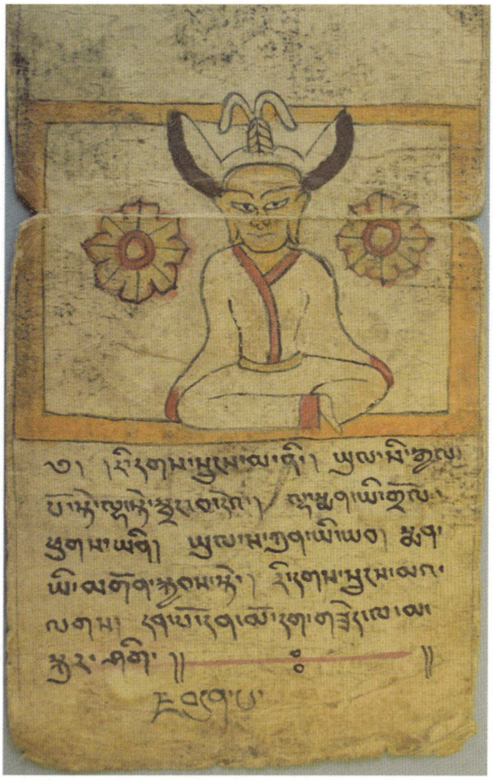

Fig. 31. Folio from the *Sha slungs* text (Ja-4r) depicting a being who could be a *lha* or idealised ritual specialist, or both.

remains uncertain upon various folios throughout the manuscript. These figures may be the *lha* the passages mention, but they may also be ritual specialists, especially of the primordial type who usually represent models and ancestors of living ritual specialists. In any case, one of these beings is flanked by erect trees or branches and a pair of flowers (Fig. 30), while the other sits between two flowers (Fig. 31). Tree branches and flowers are of course the basic material for constructing a *shalung*, while they are among the most common altar components for revitalisation rites performed in the Srid pa'i lha cult. The symbolic value of flowers is intimately related to origins, procreation, mobile vitality and fertility in both older myths from the region[208] and in ritual cultures presided over by shamans along the extended

208 For instance, see *Mkhas pa Lde'u* 228 on a yellow flower of gold and a blue flower of turquoise which are the very first objects in creation, and give rise to the first male and female beings. See also the Naxi *Ts'ò mbêr ssáw* myth informing the *Muân bpò'* festivals of cyclic revitalisation, in which a white flowering tree is the setting for the first union of a human male and a divine female from the sky; Rock 1948: 75.

Fig. 32. Ritual specialist standing before a *shalung* structure decorated with rhododendron flowers; note the central feather plume atop the 'horned' headgear, Rahung, Dirang district, 2011.

eastern Himalayas.[209]

The figure illustrated on folio Ja-4r wears headgear with a distinctive 'horned' appearance topped by a central plume-like device (Fig. 31). This very distinctive headgear of the same construction, with a central plume, and sometimes also white in colour,[210] is worn by some shamans in the central Mon yul Corridor where *shalung* structures are used to deliver offerings to ancestral deities located up the vertical axis (Fig. 32).

To my current knowledge, the *shalung* rites I was able to observe are not described in any other ethnographic accounts from the eastern Himalayas or the Tibetan Plateau. Like the *Sha slungs* text itself, these rites appear to be unique to the region where we find them today. Their character is clearly an amalgam of different cultural patterns which have flowed with

209 On flowers, vitality and fertility during rites among Himalayan shamans, see Gros 2012: 381 n.59, 499 on the Drung, Höfer 1994: 53-55, *et passim* on the western Tamang, Gaenszle 2007: 269-272, *et passim* on Rai groups, and Yang Fuquan 1998: 197-199 on the Naxi.

210 See also Dollfus and Jacquesson 2013: 40 and plates xiv, xvii for a Sherdukpen version of the same headgear termed *keng guthung* 'horned hat'.

migrating peoples down from the north and up from the south, respectively, along the Mon yul Corridor. Although nowadays the Dirang worship communities speak Tshangla, the ritual language for these rites is actually Tibetan influenced by the East Bodish language Dakpa spoken further north up the Mon yul Corridor, and Dirang descent groups involved in the rite often trace their origins either to the Dakpa-speaking Tawang region or further north to Tibet. On the other hand, various features of the rites resemble 'tribal' practices of the foothills and the Assam plains further south, being practices that belong to other populations speaking Tibeto-Burman languages, such as the Bodo-Garo group and the so-called Kho-Bwa cluster of languages, or practices found in areas where such peoples were once the earlier settlers. Structures highly reminiscent of the *shalung*, for example, are used among hill peoples speaking Kho-Bwa languages further south in the Mon yul Corridor during their annual clan revitalisation festivals staged each Winter,[211] as well as on the neighbouring plains of Assam during the well-known post-harvest festival called Bhogali Bihu or Magh Bihu.[212]

Many points of interpretation related to the data presented above remain incomplete with the present state of research. Nevertheless, the combined evidence already indicates a high probability that the origins of the *Ste'u* and S*ha slungs* manuscript can be located somewhere within a zone of ca. 100 km diameter encompassing the area of the Dga' thang shrine to the north and the highland valleys of north-eastern Bhutan and adjacent Himalayan regions to the south, and within which the cult of Srid pa'i lha is still practiced based upon similar manuscripts and where it also preserves a wide range of often closely cognate rites and language references.

211 On the construction of a Sherdukpen equivalent of the *shalung* structure, see Dollfus and Jacquesson 2013: 86 and plate xvii, although the indigenous term used to designate it is unclear from their account. Dollfus and Jacquesson translate *loblang* as 'god residence' (p.146) indicating it specifically as a place name where such structures are erected (p.137), and talk separately of the structure of tree branches resembling a *shalung* as the 'God's home'. They etymologise *loblang* as a Mey/Sherdukpen word meaning 'the Place *blang* of the God (s) *lo*' (p.84) and that *blang* means 'an inhabited place' (p.141). In Mey/Sherdukpen, *toblang* is a 'cattle pen', *langbuche* a 'fence', *langkhung* the 'ground floor' of a house (Rinchen Dondrup 1988: 41, Blench 2011), and apparently *blang* and *lang* refer to structures consisting of a space directly upon the earth surrounded by an enclosure, such as the design of the *shalung* and the 'God's home'. Since *lo* is the Mey/Sherdukpen cognate of T. *lha* used in much ritual terminology, it would appear likely *loblang* is a spoken cognate of T. *lha brang* 'deity's abode/hut' used elsewhere throughout the region to the north to describe the same type of ritual structures, just as *brang* is found in non-Kho-Bwa languages immediately north of the Mey/Sherdukpen area to refer to structures consisting of a space directly upon the earth surrounded by an enclosure and used as livestock pens, sheds and huts, e.g. Tshangla *wa brang* 'cattle-pen', *ta brang* 'stable' (Das Gupta 1968: 75); Brokpaké *ta brang* 'cattle-pen' (Rinchen Dondrup 1993: 36).

212 This is the ritual hut named *bhelaghar*, especially in its older, more conservative 'tent'- or 'tepee'-like forms.

6. Conclusions

Based upon the evidence and analysis in this study, my proposals for assigning a status to the *Rnel dri 'dul ba, Ste'u* and *Sha slungs* rites within a wider perspective of regional cultural history and ethnography are as follows:

i. As ritual literature, these texts are sophisticated later constructions based upon a pool of older linguistic and cultural resources represented in a range of Old Tibetan documents, and not only those dedicated to rites and myths, but also to administration and law. The modes of access later writers had to this older pool of resources remain unknown. The texts evince transformations in which extensive later reuse of Old Tibetan words and phrasing frequently bears only indirect or no meaningful connections back to their original environments of use. Claims of continuity with older ritual literature across a ca. 11th century divide for texts such as the *Rnel dri 'dul ba, Ste'u* and *Sha slungs* should only be advanced in relation to a critical accounting of such transformations.

ii. These texts and the rites they record represent a complex interplay between certain cultural patterns known from the Tibetan Plateau and others recorded from the eastern Himalayas. Their uniqueness appears indicative of localised agency and socio-cultural phenomena present in southernmost Tibet, namely in and around Lho brag, and adjacent Himalayan areas to the south, but so far not known from elsewhere. We cannot simply identify these old texts and rites in any blanket manner as 'Tibetan', but only as being localised within a contiguous interface between southern Tibetan Plateau margins and eastern Himalayan highlands.

iii. Unqualified identifications of *Rnel dri 'dul ba, Ste'u* and *Sha slungs* rites as "*bon*" or "Bon tradition" are unproductive and misleading in scholarly contexts. The most significant problem these sweeping designations represent is masking – by causing us to ignore or be blind to – valuable evidence of diversity and complexity across past times and spaces. Such *bon*/Bon identities can only be analytically useful for discussing old texts containing rites and myths related to mundane concerns when we comparatively justify them using transparent, critical criteria and actual empirical data. Without such support, they are best regarded as nativist claims.

* * *

References and Sigla

1. Works in Tibetan Language

BGT = *Bod rgya tshig mdzod chen mo* (*Zang-Han Dacidian* 藏汉大辞典), 3 vols. Beijing: Mi rigs dpe skrun khang, 1985.

Chos grags = *Dge shes chos kyi grags pas brtsams pa'i brd dag ming tshig gsal ba bzhugs so*. Beijing: Mi rigs dpe skrun khang.

Mkhas pa Lde'u = Mkhas pa Lde'u (ca. mid-13th cent.). 1987. *Mkhas pa lde'us mdzad pa'i rgya bod kyi chos 'byung rgyas pa*. Lhasa: Bod ljongs mi dmangs dpe skrun khang (*Gangs can rigs mdzod* 3).

Gu chos rang rnam = Gu-ru Chos kyi dbang-phyug (1212-1270/73?). 1979. *Ghu ru chos dbang gis sku'i rnam thar skabs brgyad ma' / dharma shwara'i rnam thar, in:The Autobiography and Instructions of Gu ru Chos kyi dbang phyug*, vol.1. Paro: Ugyen Tempai Gyaltsen (*Rin chen gter mdzod chen po'i rgyab chos*, vols. 8).

Dga' thang = Pa tshab Pa sangs dbang 'dus and Glang ru Nor bu tshe ring. 2007. *Gtam shul dga' thang 'bum pa che nas gsar du rnyed pa'i bon gyi gna' dpe bdams bsgrigs*. Lhasa: Bod ljongs bod yig dpe rnying dpe skrun khang.

Rgya bod yig tshang = Dpal 'byor bzang po (15th cent.). 1985. *Rgya bod yig tshang chen mo*. Chengdu: Si khron mi rigs dpe skrun khang.

Rgyal rigs = Tibetan text edition in Aris, M. 1986. *Sources for the History of Bhutan*. Wien (Wiener Studien zur Tibetologie und Buddhismuskunde, Heft 14), 12-77.

Nyang ral chos 'byung = Nyang Nyi ma 'od zer (1124-1192?). 1988. *Chos 'byung me tog snying po sbrang rtsi'i bcud*. Beijing: Bod ljongs mi dmangs dpe skrun khang (*Gangs can rigs mdzod* 5).

Gzi brjid = *Mdo dri med gzi brjid*, 12 vols. Lhasa: Bod ljongs bod yig dpe rnying dpe skrun khang, 2000.

Gsang ba'i bdag pos gnang ba'i dgra lha dpang[s] bstod ces bya ba bzhugs so // (block print in 26 fols. paginated 39b-53a within a larger collection, and photographed at Sengkhor, Gertze County, August 2002).

Lawa 2 = Untitled collection of 15 texts with loose *dpe cha* folios. Private collection, Lawa village, Lhuntse Dzongkhag. Photographed December 2012.

Texts cited in this study:

Text 1: *Bon 'di ni bsbyi bsri 'khor mo bcug gsums bzhug sho*, 14 (r/v) numbered loose *dpe cha* folios, 6 lines per side.

Text 13: *Lha'i nam la dus bzhi'i bzhugs sho*, 7 (r/v), numbered loose *dpe* cha folios, 5 lines per side.

OTDO = *Old Tibetan Documents Online* accessed at: http://otdo.aa.tufs.ac.jp (and http://otdo.aa-ken.jp), and hosted by the Research Institute for Languages and Cultures of Asia and Africa, Tokyo University of Foreign Studies, Tokyo, Japan.

Rlangs = Byang chub rgyal mtshan (1302–1364). 1986. *Rlangs kyi po ti bse ru rgyas pa.* Lhasa: Bod ljongs mi dmangs dpe skrun khang (*Gangs can rig mdzod* 1).

Shawa 1= Title page (= 1a): *Lha rabs rgam chen pha wang bzhugs so*. Handwritten manuscript booklet bound on top margin, 80 unumbered pages (r/v), 6 lines/side. Community property held by the ritual specialist lineage, Shawa village, Lhuntse Dzongkhag. Photographed January 2012.

Text cited in this study:

Text 3: *Lha rab dang bdud rtsi bcas pa bzhugs so*, pages 21a-40b [following page blank].

Zhang zhung = Pasar Tsultrim Tenzin, Changru Tritsuk Namdak Nyima, Gatsa Lodroe Rabsal. 2008. *A Lexicon of Zhangzhung and Bonpo Terms*. Osaka: National Museum of Ethnology (*Bon Studies* 11, *Senri Ethnological Reports*, 76).

2. Works in Other Languages

Ardussi, John. 2004. The Gdung lineages of central and eastern Bhutan – A reappraisal of their origin, based on literary sources, in: Karma Ura and Sonam Kinga (eds.), *The Spider and the Piglet*. Thimphu: Centre for Bhutan Studies, 60-72.

Aris, Michael. 1986. *Sources for the History of Bhutan*. Wien (Wiener Studien zur Tibetologie und Buddhismuskunde, Heft 14).

— 1979. *Bhutan. The Early History of a Himalayan Kingdom*. Warminster: Aris & Phillips.

Bailey, Frederick M. 1915. Notes from Southern Tibet, *Journal of the Bombay Natural History Society*, Sept. 30: 72-78.

— 1912. Miscellaneous Notes no.VIII-Note on Takin (*Budorcas taxicolor*), *Journal of the Bombay Natural History Society*, July 30: 1069-1070.

Balikci, Anna. 2008. *Lamas, Shamans and Ancestors. Village religion in Sikkim*. Leiden:

Brill (*Brill's Tibetan Studies Library*, 17).

Bellezza, John V. 2014. Straddling the millenial divide – A case study of persistence and change in the Tibetan ritual tradition based on the *Gnag rabs* of Gathang Bumpa and Eternal Bon documents, circa 900-1100 CE, *Revue d'Etudes Tibétaines* 29: 155-243.

— 2013. *Death and Beyond in Ancient Tibet: Archaic Concepts and Practices in a Thousand-Year-Old Illuminated Funerary Manuscript and Old Tibetan Funerary Documents of Gathang Bumpa and Dunhuang*. Wien: Verlag der Österreichischen Akademie der Wissenschaften.

Bialek, Joanna. 2015. *Studies in the Lexis and Word-Formation of Old Tibetan. Compounds and Compounding*. Unpublished doctoral dissertation, Fremdsprachliche Philologien, Phillips-Universität Marburg.

— 2015a. Erneuerbare Wörter: Alttibetischer Wortschatz im neuen kulturellen Umfeld. Sprach-wandel durch Übersetzungskultur, in: Schrijver, P. and P.-A. Mumm (eds.), *Dasselbe mit anderen Worten? Sprache, Übersetzung und Sprachwissenschaft, Akten des 2. Symposiums des Zentrums historische Sprachwissenschaften (ZhS) München, 11. und 12. April 2014*. Bremen: Hempen Verlag, 21-42.

Blezer, Henk. 2011. It all happened in Myi yul skyi mthing: A crucial nexus of narratives pointing at the proto-heartland of Bon?, in: McKay, Alex and A. Balicki-Denjongpa (eds.), *Buddhist Himalaya: Studies in Religion, History and Culture. Volume 1: Tibet and the Himalaya*. Gangtok: Namgyal Institute of Tibetology, 157-178.

Blench, Roger. 2011. *Languages of the Mey [Sherdukpen] Cluster*.
http://www.rogerblench.info/Language%20data/South%20Asia/NEI/Kamengic/Mey/General/Linguistics/Comparative%20Mey%20wordlist.pdf. (accessed 20.04.2012).

Blondeau, Anne-Marie. 1997. Que notre enfant revienne! Un rituel méconnu pour les enfants morts en bas-âge, in: Samten Karmay and P. Sagant (eds.), *Les habitants du toit du monde*. Nanterre: Société d'ethnologie, 193-220.

CDTD = Bielmeier, R., F. Haller, K. Häsler, B. Huber and M. Volkart (comps. & eds.). 2008. *Comparative Dictionary of Tibetan Dialects*. Bern (the consulted pdf files for the verb volume in 924 pages and noun volume in 2288 pages represented a 2012 version received from one of the editors, and cited with permission).

Cerulli, Anthony. 2012. *Somatic Lessons: Narrating Patienthood and Illness in Indian Medical Literature*. Albany: State University of New York Press.

Chuan-kang Shih. 1998. Mortuary rituals and symbols among the Moso, in: Oppitz, Michael and E. Hsu (eds.), *Naxi and Moso Ethnography. Kin, Rites, Pictographs*. Zürich: Völkerkundemuseum der Universität Zürich, 103-125.

Coblin, Weldon South. 1991. A study of the old Tibetan Shangshu paraphrase, part I, *Journal of the American Oriental Society* 111: 303-322.

Das, Sarat Chandra. 1902. *Tibetan-English Dictionary*. Calcutta: Bengal Secretariat Book Depot.

Das Gupta, K. 1968. *An Introduction to Central Monpa*. Shillong: North-East Frontier Agency.

Dollfus, Pascal and F. Jacquesson. 2013. *Khiksaba. A Festival in Sherdukpen Country (Arunachal Pradesh, North-East India)*. Guwahati: Spectrum Publications.

Dotson, Brandon. 2013. *The Victory Banquet*. The *Old Tibetan Chronicle* and the Rise of Tibetan Historical Narrative. Unpublished Habilitation script, Ludwig-Maximilians-Universität, München.

— 2011. On the Old Tibetan term *khrin* in the legal and ritual lexicons, in: Turin, M. and B. Zeisler (eds.), *Himalayan Languages and Linguistics: Studies in Phonology, Semantics, Morphology and Syntax*. Leiden: Brill, 77-97.

— 2008. Complementarity and opposition in early Tibetan ritual, *Journal of the American Oriental Society* 128(1): 41-67.

— 2007. Divination and law in the Tibetan empire: The role of dice in the legislation of loans, interest, marital law and troop conscription, in: Kapstein M. and B. Dotson (eds.), *Contributions to the Cultural History of Early Tibet.* Leiden: Brill (*Brill's Tibetan Studies Library*, 14), 3-77.

Gaenszle, Martin. 2007. *Ancestral Voices: Oral Ritual Texts and their Social Contexts among the Mewahang Rai of East Nepal*. Berlin: Lit Verlag.

Goldstein, Melvyn C., *et al.* 2001. *The New Tibetan-English Dictionary of Modern Tibetan.* Berkeley: University of California Press.

Gros, Stéphane. 2012. *La part manquante. Échanges et pouvoirs chez les Drung du Yunnan* (*Chine*). Nanterre: Société d'ethnologie.

Gurung, Kalsang Norbu. 2011. *The Emergence of a Myth. In Search of the Origins of the Life Story of Shenrab Miwo, the Founder of Bon*. Unpublished doctoral dissertation, Universiteit Leiden.

Haarh, Erik. 1969. *The Yar-luṅ Dynasty*. Copenhagen: G. E. C. Gad's Forlag.

Hazod, Guntram. 2009. Imperial central Tibet: an annotated cartographical survey of its territorial divisions and key political sites, in: Dotson, Brandon, *The Old Tibetan Annals: An Annotated Translation of Tibet's First History*. Wien: Verlag der Österreichischen Akademie der Wissenschaften, 161-231.

He Limin and He Shicheng. 1998. The Dto-mba ceremony to propitiate the demons of suicide, in: Oppitz, Michael and E. Hsu (eds.), *Naxi and Moso Ethnography. Kin, Rites, Pictographs*. Zürich: Völkerkundemuseum der Universität Zürich, 138-172.

Hill, Nathan. 2013. The envoys of Phywa to Dmu (PT 0126). Unpublished 56pp. manuscript, cited by permission of the author.

Höfer, Andràs. 1997. *Tamang Ritual Texts II: Ethnographic Studies in the Oral Tradition and Folk-religion of an Ethnic Minority in Nepal*. Wiesbaden: Franz Steiner Verlag (*Beiträge zur Südasienforschung* 66).

— 1994. *A Recitation of the Tamang Shaman in Nepal*. Bonn: VGH Wissenschaftsverlag (*Nepa-lica* 7).

— 1981. *Tamang Ritual Texts I: Preliminary Studies in the Folk-religion of an Ethnic Minority in Nepal*. Wiesbaden: Franz Steiner Verlag (*Beiträge zur Südasienforschung* 65).

Huber, Toni. In Press. Legless and eyeless [and tongueless] in search of incense. Oral and written versions of a Bon *sPos rabs* from northeastern Bhutan, in: Gaenszle, M. (ed.). *Ritual Speech in the Himalayas: Oral Texts and Their Contexts*. Cambridge, MA: Department of South Asian Studies, Harvard University (*Harvard Oriental Series*). 30pp.

— 2015. Hunting for the cure: a Bon healing narrative from eastern Bhutan, in: Ramble. C. and U. Rösler (eds.), *Tibetan and Himalayan Healing: an Anthology for Anthony Aris*. Kathmandu: Vajra Books, 371-382.

— 2015a. Descent, tutelaries and ancestors. Transmission among autonomous, bon ritual specialists in eastern Bhutan and the Mon-yul Corridor, in Havnevik H. and C. Ramble (eds.). *From Bhakti to Bon. Festschrift for Per Kværne*. Oslo: Novus Press (*The Institute for Comparative Research in Human Culture, Serie B*, Skrifter CLV), 271-289.

— 2015b. Naked, mute and well hung: A brief ethnographic comparison of Kengpa and related ritual performers in the eastern Himalayas and beyond, in: Czaja, O. and G.

Hazod (eds.), *The Illuminating Mirror. Tibetan Studies in Honour of Per K. Sørensen on the Occasion of his 65th* Birthday. Wiesbaden: Ludwig Reichert Verlag, 219-242 (text), 592-595 (plates).

— 2015c. An obscure word for 'ancestral deity' in some East Bodish and neighbouring Himalayan languages and Qiang: Ethnographic records towards a hypothesis, in: Post, M.W., S. Morey and S. DeLancey (eds.), *Language and Culture in Northeast India and Beyond: In Honor of Robbins Burling*. Canberra: Asia-Pacific Linguistics (*Asia-Pacific Linguistics*, A-PL 23), 162-181.

— 2013. The iconography of *gshen* priests in the ethnographic context of the extended eastern Himalayas, and reflections on the development of Bon religion, in: Ehrhard F.-K. and P. Maurer (eds.), *Nepalica-Tibetica. Festgabe for Christoph Cüppers*, Band 1. Andiast: International Institute for Tibetan and Buddhist Studies, 263-294.

— 2012. The changing role of hunting and wildlife in pastoral communities of northern Tibet, in: *Pastoral practices in High Asia. Agency of 'development' effected by modernisation, resettlement and transformation*. Dordrecht: Springer, 195-215.

Imaeda Yoshiro. 1981. *Histoire du Cycle De La Naissance et de la Mort*. Geneva-Paris: Librairie Droz.

Jäschke, Hermann August. 1881. *A Tibetan-English Dictionary, with Special Reference to the Prevailing Dialects*. London: Secretary of State for India.

Kapstein, Matthew T. 2009. The *Commentaries of the Four Clever Men*: A doctrinal and philosophical corpus in the Bòn po *rDzogs chen* tradition, in: Karmay, S. and D. Rossi (eds.), *Bon. The Everlasting Religion of Tibet*, special edition of *East and West*, 59: 1-4 (December), 107-130.

Karmay, Samten G. 2013. Queen of the world and her twenty-seven daughters, in: Hill, N. (ed.), *Journal of the International Association for Bon Research* 1(1): 19-35.

— 2009. A new discovery of ancient Bon manuscripts from a Buddhist stupa in southern Tibet, in: Karmay, S.G. and D. Rossi (eds.), *Bon. The Everlasting Religion of Tibet*, special edition of *East and West*, 59(1-4) (December): 55-84.

— 1994. The origin myths of the first king of Tibet as revealed in the *Can-lnga*, in: Kvaerne, P. (ed.), *Tibetan Studies*, vol.1. Oslo: The Institute for Comparative Research in Human Culture, 408-429.

— 1972. *The Treasury of Good Sayings: A Tibetan History of Bon*. London: Oxford

University Press. (*London Oriental Series*, 26).

Karmay, Samten G. and Yasuhiko Nagano. 2002. *The Call of the Blue Cuckoo. An Anthology of Nine Bonpo Texts on Myths and Rituals*. Osaka: National Museum of Ethnology (*Bon Studies* 6, *Senri Ethnological Reports*, 32).

Klimburg-Salter, Deborah, L. Lodja and C. Ramble. 2013. *Bön. Geister aus Butter – Kunst & Ritual des alten Tibet. Katalog zur Ausstellung im Museum für Völkerkunde, Wien* 1.2. *bis 1.3.2013*. Wien: Museum für Völkekunde.

Kretschmar, Andreas. 1981. *'Brug pa kun legs. Das wundersame Leben eines verrückten Heiligen*. Bonn: VGH Wissenschaftsverlag (*Beiträge zur Zentralasienforschung*, 5).

Lo Ch'ang-p'ei. 1945. The genealogical patronymic linkage system of the Tibeto-Burman speaking Tribes, *Harvard Journal of Asiatic Studies* 8(3-4): 349-363.

Martin, Dan, Per Kvaerne and Yasuhiko Nagano (eds.), Tseyang Changngoba *et. al*. (comps.). 2003. *A Catalogue of the Bon Kanjur*. Osaka: National Museum of Ethnology (*Bon Studies* 8, *Senri Ethnological Reports*, 40).

Petech, Luciano. 1990. *Dung-Reng, Acta Orientalia Academiae Scientiarum Hungaricae* 44: 103-111.

Pignède, B. 1993 [1966]. *The Gurungs. A Himalayan Population of Nepal*. Transl. S. Harrison and A. Macfarlane. Kathmandu: Ratna Pustak Bhandar.

Richardson, Hugh E. 1998. Hunting accidents in early Tibet, in: *High Peaks, Pure Earth: Collected Writings on Tibetan History and Culture*. London: Serindia Publications, 149-166.

Rinchen Dondup. 1993. *Brokeh Language Guide*. Itanagar: Directorate of Research, Government of Arunachal Pradesh.

— 1988. *A Hand Book on Sherdukpen Language. Itanagar*, Directorate of Research, Government of Arunachal Pradesh.

Rock, Joseph F. 1955. *The Zhi mä Funeral Ceremony of the Na-khi of Southwest China. Described and Translated from the Na-khi Manuscripts*. Vienna-Mödling: St. Gabriel's Mission Press (*Studia Instituti Anthropos*, 9).

— 1948. The Mùan-bpö ceremony or the sacrifice to heaven as practiced by the Na-khi, *Monumenta Serica* 13: 7-160.

van Schaik, Sam. 2013. The naming of Tibetan religion: *Bon* and *Chos* in the Tibetan imperial period, in: Hill, N. (ed.), *Journal of the International Association for Bon*

Research 1(1): 227-257.

Schrempf, Mona. 2010. Between mantra and syringe: Healing and health-seeking behaviour in contemporary Amdo, in: Adams, V., M. Schrempf and S.R. Craig (eds.), *Medicine Between Science and religion. Explorations on Tibetan Grounds*. New York/Oxford: Berghahn Books, 157-183.

Snellgrove, David L. 1967. *The Nine Ways of Bon. Excerpts from gZi-brjid*. London: Oxford University Press (*London Oriental Series*, 18).

Spanien, Ariane and Yoshiro Imaeda. 1978-1979. *Choix de documents tibétains conservés à la Biblio-thèque nationale: complété par quelques manuscrits de l'India Office et du British Museum*, Tome I & II. Paris: Bibliothèque nationale.

Stein, Rolf.A. 2010. *Rolf Stein's Tibetica Antiqua, with Additional Materials*. Transl. and ed. A.P. McKeown. Leiden: Brill (*Brill's Tibetan Studies Library*, 24).

— 1985. Tibetica Antiqua III: A propos du mot *gcug-lag* et de la religion indigène, *Bulletin de l'École Française d'Extrême-Orient* 74: 83-133.

— 1983. Tibetica Antiqua I: Les deux vocabulaires des traductions indo-tibétaine et sino-tibétaine dans les manuscrits des Touen-Houang, *Bulletin de l'École Française d'Extrême-Orient* 72:149-236.

— 1971. Du récit au rituel dans les manuscrits tibétains de Touen-houang, in: *Études tibétaines dédiées à la mémoire de Marcelle Lalou*. Paris: Librairie d'Amerique et d'Orient, 479-547.

— 1972. *Tibetan Civilization*. Transl. J.E. Stapleton Driver. Stanford: Stanford University Press.

Strickland, S. 1982. *Beliefs, Practices, and Legends: A Study in the Narrative Poetry of the Gurungs of Nepal*. Unpublished doctoral dissertation, Jesus College, University of Cambridge.

Thomas, Frederick W. 1957. *Ancient Folk-Literature from North-Eastern Tibet* (*Introductions, Texts, Translations and Notes*). Berlin: Akademie-Verlag. (*Abhandlungen der Deutschen Akademie der Wissenschaften zu Berlin, Klasse für Sprachen, Literatur und Kunst*, Jahrgang 1952, Nr. 2).

— 1951. *Tibetan Literary Texts and Documents from Chinese Turkestan*, 2. London: Royal Asiatic Society.

Uray, Géza. 1984. The earliest evidence of the use of the Chinese sexagenary cycle in

Tibetan, in: Ligeti, Louis (ed.), *Tibetan and Buddhist Studies Commemorating the 200th Anniversary of the Birth of Alexander Csoma de Korös*, vol. 2. Budapest: Akadémiai Kiadó, 341-360 (*Bibliotheca Orientalis Hungarica*, 19/1-2).

Wörterbuch = Franke, Herbert, J-U. Hartmann and T.O. Höllmann (eds.). 2005-2013. *Wörterbuch der tibetischen Schriftsprache*, vols. 1-22. München: Verlag der Bayerischen Akademie der Wissenschaften.

Yang Fuquan. 1998. The Ssú life gods and their cult, in: Oppitz, M. and E. Hsu (eds.), *Naxi and Moso Ethnography. Kin, Rites, Pictographs*. Zürich: Völkerkundemuseum der Universität Zürich, 189-208.

Yule, Henry. 2010 [1871]. *The Book of Ser Marco Polo, the Venetian. Concerning the Kingdoms and Marvels of the East*, vol. 1. Cambridge: Cambridge University Press.

夏鲁寺般若佛母殿画塑图像研究 *

——以相关仪轨文献为中心

杨鸿蛟

《般若经》（*Prajñāpāramitā Sūtra*）是大乘佛教最为重要的经典之一。由其所化现和衍生出的般若佛母虽不及《般若经》流传广泛，但在佛教神灵体系中亦占有重要地位。10-11 世纪即藏传佛教后弘期初期，以般若佛母与十方佛图像为题材的壁塑在后藏和阿里地区寺院中集中出现，后藏地区的娘曲河沿岸此时即有江浦寺、孜乃萨寺和夏鲁寺三座寺院建有专供此类题材壁塑的般若佛母殿。惜江浦寺、孜乃萨寺业已不存，唯有夏鲁寺般若佛母殿留存至今，虽然殿内塑像为 2004 年新塑，已非原貌，但壁画和土木结构仍为原有遗存，保存状况也相对完整，为进一步的图像研究提供了可能性。本文即是从仪轨文献入手，对夏鲁寺般若佛母殿内图像加以分析和比对，并对般若佛母与十方佛曼荼罗的宗教意涵及其与大日如来和金刚界曼荼罗之间的关系加以阐释。

一、历史与现状

夏鲁寺（zhwa lu dgon）地处西藏年楚河西岸，日喀则东南，古时谓之娘思兑

* 杨鸿蛟：中国藏学研究中心西藏文化博物馆馆员。

本文为 2014 年国家社科基金青年项目“11-14 世纪汉藏印佛教互动背景中的夏鲁寺艺术遗存研究”（项目号：14CZJ004）和 2015 年中国藏学研究中心重点课题“夏鲁寺艺术与汉藏文化交流研究”的阶段性研究成果。奥地利维也纳大学艺术史系的派特拉·穆勒（Petra Müller）曾在已有的拉达克地区那科寺（Nako）译师殿般若佛母图像研究的基础上，对西藏后藏地区夏鲁寺与江浦寺（rkyang phu）般若佛母塑像予以初步研究，撰文“Representing Prajñāpāramitā in Tibet and the Indian Himalayas. The iconographic concept in the Temples of Nako, rKyang bu and Zha lu”, in https://www.asianart.com/articles/mueller/index.html。本文则是从图像文本入手，通过对其仪轨考释，探究其宗教义理与传播原由。此外，对于文中所引部分藏文仪轨文献的解读和汉译文的校正，要特别感谢中国藏学研究中心西藏文化博物馆仁青卓玛和宗教所吉美桑珠两位老师所给予的帮助和指导。

图 1　夏鲁寺般若佛母殿（廖旸摄于 2009 年）

（nyang stod）地区，现为日喀则市甲措雄乡。夏鲁寺由吐蕃后裔杰尊喜饶琼乃（lce btsun shes rab vbyung gnas）始建于 1027 年至 1045 年之间[1]，寺院坐西向东，建筑平面作“回”字型，是由闭合回廊围合四面主体殿堂而形成的建筑布局，沿袭了吐蕃时期桑耶寺的传统。东翼佛殿为三层，其他三面为二层，四面顶层各具琉璃瓦汉式屋顶，是西藏地区典型的汉藏结合建筑样式。

般若佛母殿位于东翼二层，建筑格局分为主殿（内殿）与转经回廊两个部分，分别建于 11 世纪后弘期初期与 14 世纪上半叶，分属夏鲁寺历史上的两次大规模营建工程（图 1、2），本文所要讨论的主要是 11 世纪主殿的图像内容。

1　关于夏鲁寺始建年代的考证亦请参见 Roberto Vitali, *Early Temples of Central Tibet*, London: Serindia Publications, 1990, pp.91-94; 熊文彬：《元代藏汉艺术交流研究》，石家庄：河北教育出版社，2003 年，第 212-213 页。a mogha siddhi, *chos grwa chen po dpal zha lu gser khang gi bdag po jo bo lcevi gdong rab*（《夏鲁金殿世系》），TBRC 扫描本，第 12 页 b 面第 2 行至第 13 页 b 面第 3 行。另参见觉囊达那热他著、佘万治译：《后藏志》，拉萨：西藏人民出版社，2002 年，第 85 页；参见藏文本《夏鲁世系史》（*dpal zha luvi gser khang gi gnas yig dad bskor tshad phan yon bcas*），译文参见 Giuseppe Tucci, *Tibetan Painted Scrolls*, Kyoto: Rinsen Book Co., Ltd. 1980, pp. 656-662。桑珠：《〈夏鲁世系史〉译注》，载《藏学研究》，北京：中央民族学院藏学研究所，1987 年，第 300 页。

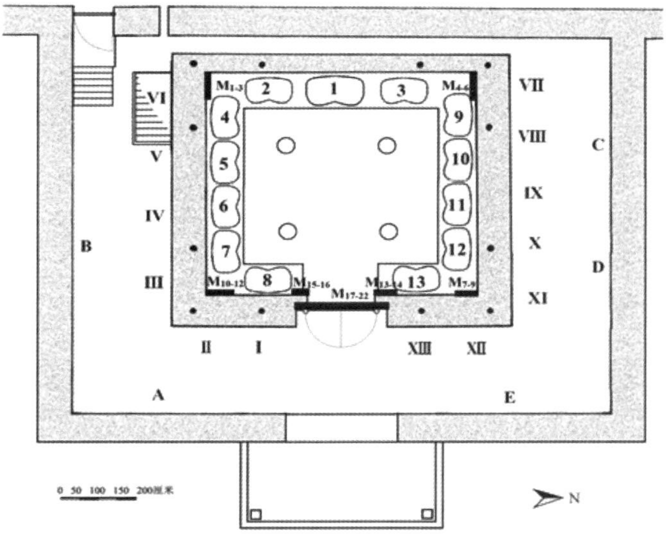

图 2 夏鲁寺般若佛母殿平面示意图（魏文制图）

般若佛母殿的建造时间被认为至晚不超过 1045 年，据《后藏志》《夏鲁金殿世系》《夏鲁寺世系史》等文献记载，杰尊完成夏鲁寺的主体建筑之后，还用极其珍贵的材料制作了一尊观世音菩萨像供于寺中，因此尊观音像的授记，亦因吐蕃戒律不纯正，于是杰尊前往印度菩提伽耶金刚座寺从大阿阇黎无畏笈多（Abhayākaragupta）[2] 学习了许多教旨、法规，带回一尊名为喀萨巴尼（Kasarpāṇi）的观世音菩萨像回到夏鲁寺，并迎请印度大学者阿底峡为夏鲁寺经堂开光，其中提到特别迎神安住于般若佛母的眼睛后部。[3] 另据《佛历精要》，阿底峡于木鸡年（1045）抵达后藏夏鲁寺，并停留了三个月，然后前往前藏。[4] 意大利学者维塔利（Robert Vitali）据此判断，般若佛母殿是在杰尊从印度回到藏地之后，阿底峡至夏鲁寺之前这一阶段建立的。

2 据《究竟瑜伽鬘》(*Niṣpannayogāvalī*)，无畏笈多隶属超戒寺（Vikramaśīla），于罗摩帕拉王（Rāmapāla，1084-1130）当政第三年，也即 1114 年著有《佛觉庄严论》(*Munimatālaṅkāra*）一书，因而此人应是 11 世纪下半叶至 12 世纪上半叶的人，似与杰尊喜饶琼乃前往印度的 11 世纪初期不符。超戒寺建于 8 世纪末叶的达玛帕拉时期（Dharmapāla，775-800)，地处印度比哈尔（Bihar）帕格尔布尔地区的安提查克村，于 1203 年被穆斯林军队焚毁仅存遗址，与金刚座寺辖于同一地域。Benoytosh Bhattacharyya, *Niṣpannayogāvalī of Mahāpaṇḍita Abhayākaragupta*, Baroda: Oriental Institute, 1972, pp. 10-11.

3 前引《夏鲁金殿世系》，第 13 页 b 面第 4 行至第 15 页 b 面第 4 行；前引《后藏志》，第 85-86 页；David Seyfort Ruegg, *The Life of Bu ston Rin po che: with the Tibetan Text of the Bu ston rNam thar*, Roma: Is. M. E. O, 1966, p.90, 附录《布顿传记》藏文本，第 14 页 a 面。

4 chab spel tshe brtan phun tshogs:《佛历精要》(*mang thos klu grub rgya mtsho, bstan rtsis gsal bavi nying byed*）拉萨：西藏人民出版社，1987 年，第 102-104 页。前引 *Early Temples of Central Tibet*, p.92, n.33。

夏鲁寺般若佛母殿内殿现存四臂般若佛母与十二尊佛塑像，以及眷属菩萨和供养天女壁画。据夏鲁寺寺管会主任洛萨加措（blo gsal rgya mtsho）古修拉介绍，殿内现存塑像为 2004 年重塑[5]，现存佛像名号及布局现状参阅图 2 和表 1。

表 1　夏鲁寺般若佛母殿内殿塑像尊像手印、持物及名号

编号	名号[6]	手印 / 持物
1	般若佛母（yum chen mo）	四臂，主臂当胸作转法轮印，其余二臂上举，右手持金刚杵，左手应有持物，已失
2	金寂佛（ston pa gser thub）	双手结禅定印
3	吐蕃赞普赤热巴巾（mngav bdag khri ral pa can）	右手施与愿印，左手作无畏印并持莲托金刚杵
4	下方莲花吉祥佛（vog phyogs kyi sangs rgyas pad mavi dpal）	右手施与愿印，左手作禅定印
5	东北等持象佛（shar byang kyi sangs rgyas ting vdzin glang po）	右手施无畏印，左手作禅定印
6	西南日曼荼罗光明吉祥佛（nub lho kyi sangs rgyas nyi mavi dkyil vkhor snang bavi dpal）	双手施转法轮印
7	北方帝释佛（byang phyogs kyi sangs rgyas rgyal bavi dbang po）	双手施禅定印
8	南方无忧吉祥佛（lho phyogs kyi sangs rgyas mnya ngan med dpal）	右手作触地印，左手作禅定印
9	上方喜吉祥佛（steng phyogs kyi sangs rgyas dgav ba dpal）	双手施转法轮印
10	西北妙盖佛（nub byang kyi sangs rgyas gdugs dam pa）	双手作禅定印
11	东南莲花吉祥佛（shar lho kyi sangs rgyas pad mavi dpal）	右手作触地印，左手作禅定印
12	西方焰炽佛（nub phyogs kyi sangs rgyas rin chen vod vphro）	右手作与愿印，左手作禅定印
13	东方宝生佛（shar phyogs kyi sangs rgyas rin chen vbyung gnas）	右手施无畏印，左手作禅定印

壁面转角空隙有供养天女和四摄菩萨画像，共计 16 尊（$M_{1\text{-}16}$），门内壁上方绘六身菩萨，均有藏文墨书题记，题记多已被污垢遮盖，能辨析者仅有善逝宝自在（bde

5　据其介绍，塑像的复原主要参考了宿白和王毅的文章，以及江孜白居寺吉祥多门塔中般若佛母与十方佛塑像样式。翟跃飞亦于同年考察夏鲁寺时以照片的方式记录了当时工匠于般若佛母殿内塑像的场景。翟跃飞：《深浅看西藏——以经卷艺术为线索》，北京：人民美术出版社，2009 年，第 34 页，图 5-18。

6　笔者根据已有标牌的尊像名称编订，但殿内东北等持象佛、西南日曼荼罗光明吉祥佛、上方喜吉祥佛和东南莲花吉祥佛四尊尊像名称标牌遗失，“西北妙盖佛”汉文译名原为“西北凶妙佛”，有误。

gshegs rin chen dbang）（M_{18}）、善逝金刚手（bde gshegs phyag na rdo rje）（M_{19}）、普贤菩萨（sems pa kun tu bzang po）（M_{20}）（图 5）。除 M_1 为游戏坐姿，其他均作跏趺坐姿。这些壁画均为早期遗存，因殿内粘贴大量彩绘擦擦泥塑，部分门内上方壁画难以辨识（图 3、4，表 2）。

表 2　夏鲁寺般若佛母殿内殿壁画尊像图像志特征

编号	尊格	身色	持物
M_1	金刚钩菩萨	白	右手持钩，左手于右膝作与愿印
M_2	香女	白	左手持香炉，右手当胸作妙供养印
M_3	嬉女	白	双手抵于两侧大腿，右手金刚拳，左手似持金刚杵
M_4	金刚索菩萨	黄	双手持羂索分作期克印，右手上扬，左手当胸
M_5	花女	绿	双手持盆，盆内盛满花状物
M_6	鬘女	绿	双手持鬘 / 念珠
M_7	金刚锁菩萨	红	双手持铁镣，右手当胸，左手置于左膝
M_8	灯女	红	双手持灯
M_9	歌女	红	左手持琴（似琵琶），右手作弹拨状
M_{10}	金刚铃菩萨	绿	双手持金刚铃
M_{11}	舞女	绿	双手于右肋向外交叉，作妙供养印
M_{12}	涂香女	绿	左手持白海螺，右手当胸
M_{13}	菩萨	黄	双手持圆形物体，似轮盘
M_{14}	菩萨	白	双手持摩羯幢
M_{15}	菩萨	黄	双手持宝瓶
M_{16}	菩萨	白	左手持塔状物，又似金刚铃，右手作妙供养印
M_{17}	菩萨	红黄	右手持一茎花，左手作妙供养印
M_{18}	善逝宝自在菩萨	红黄	右手持一茎花，左手当胸
M_{19}	善逝金刚手菩萨	红黄	双手持物，持物不明
M_{20}	普贤菩萨	红黄	右手作无畏印，左手作与愿印
M_{21}	菩萨	红黄	双手当胸，不清
M_{22}	菩萨	红黄	双手持物，不清

图 3-1 夏鲁寺般若佛母殿内殿南壁西端供养天女及菩萨壁画：编号 M_{1-3}（钟子寅摄于 2008 年）

图 3-2 夏鲁寺般若佛母殿内殿北壁西端供养天女及菩萨壁画：编号 M_{4-6}（钟子寅摄于 2008 年）

图 3-3 夏鲁寺般若佛母殿内殿东壁北端供养天女及菩萨壁画：编号 M_{7-9}（钟子寅摄于 2008 年）

图 3-4 夏鲁寺般若佛母殿内殿东壁南端供养天女及菩萨壁画：编号 M_{10-12}（钟子寅摄于 2008 年）

图 4-1 夏鲁寺般若佛母殿内殿门北侧供养天女及菩萨壁画：编号 M_{13-14}（钟子寅摄于 2008 年）

图 4-2 夏鲁寺般若佛母殿内殿门南侧供养天女及菩萨壁画：编号 M_{15-16}（钟子寅摄于 2008 年）

图 5　夏鲁寺般若佛母殿内殿门壁附带题记之菩萨壁画：编号 $M_{17\text{-}22}$（钟子寅摄于 2008 年）

二、般若佛母殿原貌考述

关于般若佛母殿内殿图像内容的具体描述并未见诸《后藏志》《夏鲁金殿世系》《夏鲁寺世系史》《布顿传记》等早期夏鲁寺历史的相关文献中，而是在 20 世纪上半叶至中叶三世噶陀司徒确吉嘉措（kaḥ thog si tu chos kyi rgya mtsho, 1880-1923/25）所撰《雪域卫藏朝圣指南》（*gangs ljongs dbus gtsang gnas bskor lam yig nor bu zla shel gyi se mo do*）和考古学家王毅与宿白两位先生的考古报告中予以较为细致的记录。

《雪域卫藏朝圣指南》成书于 1918-1920 年，记述内殿塑像数量和图像特征，尤其是对般若佛母图像志记录尤详，弥足珍贵：

dbus su yum chen mo phyag dang po gnyis chos vchad/ vog ma gnyi skyabs sbyin dang/ utpala steng du pu ste bsnams pa dang/ phyogs bcuvi sangs rgyas rgya lugs gos vkhyud lhab lhub can/ sngon gyi sman sku gnyis rnying pa thog so re sleb pa/[7]

试译如下：

> 中央般若佛母主二臂作说法印，其次二臂一作无畏印，一持顶置经书的青莲；汉式的十方佛衣缘轻飘摇曳，两尊古旧的香泥佛像均高到屋顶。

意大利藏学家朱塞佩·图齐（Giuseppe Tucci）虽于1937年考察过夏鲁寺，但其著作中对般若佛母殿内殿图像着墨不多。而后于1959年，我国考古学家王毅与宿白两位先生曾率队赴夏鲁寺进行考古调查，发表了《西藏文物见闻记（二）》和《西藏日喀则地区寺庙调查记（上）》二文，文中详细记录了般若佛母殿内殿塑像配置并附照片三幅。[8]《西藏日喀则地区寺庙调查记（上）》一文记：

> 堂内四壁前满列佛像，后壁正中为大佛母，左一释迦，右一着新月冠饰、结定印之坐佛，左右壁前各列四释迦，前壁入口两侧各一释迦。佛像多木雕，衣纹流畅，靠背满雕卷云，座下或雕蹲狮，或饰莲柱，皆与自萨迦以来的藏式佛像有差。壁画为诸像所掩，似皆旧绘。[9]

上述文献和考古资料为我们进一步复原般若佛母殿塑像提供几点线索：（1）主尊四臂般若佛母图像特征；（2）殿内应为十三尊塑像，除十方佛外，主尊左右各为“释迦牟尼”（由宿白先生所述，推知与其他十方佛图像特征一致，具螺发，着袈裟，跏趺坐）和禅定印宝冠佛（大日如来或阿弥陀佛）；（3）根据照片中的塑像及其底座图像（图6、7），风格与图齐和福斯科·马里尼（Fosco Maraini）1937年所拍摄的艾旺寺、江浦寺及扎塘寺中的塑像样式一致[10]（图8），亦是身着装饰中亚大团花的藏式长袍和衣褶堆叠、宽衣帛带的汉式佛装，面呈印度帕拉样式，底座装饰

---

7 chos kyi rgya mtsho, *gangs ljongs dbus gtsang gnas bskor lam yig nor bu zla shel gyi se mo do*, si khron mi rigs dpe skrun khang, 2001, p. 298.

8 王毅：《西藏文物见闻记（二）》，《文物》1960年第9期，第52-65页。宿白：《西藏日喀则地区寺庙调查记（上）》，《文物》1992年第5期，第32-42页。

9 参见宿白：《藏传佛教寺院考古》，北京：文物出版社，1996年，第91页。从照片可知，二先生所述左右应为观者之左右，与笔者所述主尊左右不同。

10 Ulrich von Schroeder, *Buddhist Sculptures in Tibet*, Vol. II, Hong Kong: Visual Dharma Publications Ltd., 2001, pp. 836-850.

图 6　夏鲁寺般若佛母殿西南角隅塑像 1959 年摄，引自《藏传佛教寺院考古》，图 32。

图 7　夏鲁寺般若佛母殿西南角隅塑像（廖旸摄于 2009 年）

图 8　夏鲁寺般若佛母殿塑像底座 1959 年摄 引自《藏传佛教寺院考古》，图 34。

图 9 《诸佛菩萨圣像赞》（1761 年）中四臂般若佛母，引自国家图书馆版本：《诸佛菩萨圣像赞》，北京：中国藏学出版社，2009 年，第 254 页。

繁复的错莲，尤其是承抵莲座的卧羊承托莲柱与卧狮的柱式，如出一辙，同属图齐所命名的“萨玛达”（Samada）风格。

三、四臂般若佛母单尊仪轨文本探析

佛教理论与实践中，般若佛母信仰十分盛行，[11] 般若佛母的观想和修持，不但可增长智慧和见识，另具有禳灾除障，远离病苦、困扰、恶魔附体和危害的功能[12]。般若佛母身色常见有白、黄两色，白色多为一面二臂样式，黄色则主要指一面四臂样式。般若佛母手臂数量常见有二臂、四臂和六臂几种，亦见有多臂者，主要流行于东南亚地区。

现存藏文般若佛母成就法与曼荼罗仪轨多在11世纪藏传佛教后弘期初期之后，诸版《丹珠尔》所收般若佛母成就法即有20余篇[13]，其藏文名称常见有 shes rab kyi pha rol tu phyin ma（般若波罗蜜多母）、rgyal bavi yum（佛母）、yum chen mo（大佛母）等，尤以 yum chen mo 最为常见[14]。

由司徒班钦的记述可知，夏鲁寺般若佛母塑像与13世纪雅砻译师扎巴坚赞（grags pa rgyal mtshan）译《黄色般若波罗蜜多母成就法》图像特征相符，黄色身、主臂双手作说法印、右二施无畏印、左二持莲托《般若经》。为窥其全貌，现将其藏译文录文并试译如下[15]：

vphags ma shes rab kyi pha rol tu phyin ma la phyag vtshal lo// rang gi snying gar aṃ yig las byung bavi zla bavi dkyil vkhor la dhīḥ yig rnam par bkod pa las vod dpag tu med pa/ de las byung bavi vod zer gyis bla ma dang sangs rgyas dang/

11 Benoytosh Bhattacharyya, *The Indian Buddhist Iconography: Mainly Based on the Sādhanamālā and Cognate Tāntric Texts and Rituals*, Firma K. L. Mukhopadhyay, 1958, p.197.

12 Miranda Shaw, *Buddhist Goddesses of India*, Princeton University Press, 2006, p.181.

13 参见杨鸿蛟：《11至14世纪夏鲁寺般若佛母殿绘塑研究》，博士论文，首都师范大学，2012年，指导教授：谢继胜，第53-60页。

14 rgyal bavi yum 出现较晚，见于14世纪《布顿佛教史》中对于《般若十万颂》《般若二万五千颂》的指称，rgyal bavi yum stong phrag brgya pa dang/ nyi khri lnga stong pa dang/

15 藏文：*shes rab kyi pha rol tu phyin ma gser mdog can gyi sgrub thabs*，梵文：*Kanakavarṇaprajñāpāramitāsādhana*，德格版《丹珠尔》，[D. No.]3547，rgyud, mu 183b1-184a4，北京版《丹珠尔》，[P. No.]4369，rgyud vgrel, du, 237a8-238a6 (vol.81, pp.19-20)。本文引用《中华大藏经·丹珠尔（对勘本）》，rgyud, mu，卷40，第868-870页。真言尽可能以Bhattacharyya整理的《成就法鬘》（Sādhanamālā）中第156篇为参照转写。此处要特别感谢四川大学中国藏学研究所罗鸿教授帮助查找梵文版本并进行了版本比对，以及故宫博物院张雅静博士对文中梵文词转译予以校正。

byang chub sems dpav rnams bskul zhing gdan drangs nas mdun du stan sna tshogs pa la bzhugs par bltas nas/ yid kyis phyag dang/ mchod pa dang/ sdig pa bshags pa dang/ bsod nams la rjes su yi rang ba dang/ gsum la skyabs su vgro ba dang/ byang chub tu sems bskyed pa dang/ bsod nams yongs su bsngo ba dang/ bzod par gsol ba rnams byaste/ de nas byams pa dang/ snying rje dang/ dgav ba dang/ btang snyoms rnams bsgoms te/ de nas oṃ shū nya tā dznyā na badzra swa bhā wa ātma konyahaṃ zhes brjod nas stong pa nyid bsgom par byavo//

顶礼圣母般若波罗蜜多母。观想从自心间 aṃ 字生出的月轮上出现 dhīḥ 字放出无量光。自彼生出的光明迎请一切上师、佛和菩萨安坐于面前诸种坐垫之上。用意念去顶礼、供奉、忏悔、福泽欢喜、皈依三宝、发菩提心、福德圆满回向、求宽恕诸种行。然后观想慈、悲、喜、舍诸心。复诵 oṃ śūnyatājñānavajrasvabhāvātmakonyahaṃ 咒并观空。

de nas de bzhin du skad cig gis zla ba la gnas pavi dhīḥ yig bltas la/ de yongs su gyur pa las shes rab kyi pha rol tu phyin ma ral pavi cod pan can/ zhal gcig pa phyag bzhi pa/ phyag gnyis chos vchad kyi phyag rgya mdzad pa/ rin po che sna tshogs pas brgyan pa/ gser mdog vbar ba/ phyag g·yon pas shes rab kyi pha rol tu phyin pa dang ldan pavi utpa la sngon po bsnams pa/ na bzav sna tshogs pavi stod g·yog can/ phyag g·yas pa mi vjigs pa sbyin pa/ padma dmar po dang zla ba la rdo rje skyil krung gis bzhugs pavi bcom ldan vdas ma rnam par bsgoms te/ de nas brtan pavi nga rgyal byavo// gang bcom ldan vdas ma shes rab kyi pha rol tu phyin mavi nga rgyal dang bcas pavi nga rgyal can gang yin pa de bcom ldan vdas ma shes rab kyi pha rol tu phyin mavo//

复次，如是观刹那安住于月轮之上的 dhīḥ 字，由其完全变化为佩戴发冠的般若波罗蜜多佛母，具一面四臂，二臂作说法印，饰诸种珍宝，散发金光，左（二）手持青莲托《般若经》，着诸种衣饰的肩帔，右（二）手施无畏印，结金刚跏趺坐于红莲花和月轮之上的薄伽梵母，如是深入观想。复次，作佛慢坚固。所谓薄伽梵母般若波罗蜜多母即是具有薄伽梵母般若波罗蜜多母佛慢之佛慢者。

de nas sngags dgod par bya ste/ mgrin par oṃ dhīḥ lce la oṃ ghiḥ rna ba dag la dziḥ de nas rang gi snying gar āḥ yig dmar po las byung bavi padma// vdab ma brgyad pa zevu vbru ge sar dang bcas pa bsams la yi ge rnams dgod par byavo// yid kyis padmavi vdab ma dang zevu vbru ser po rnams la shar gyi vdab ma la na mo/ mevi vdab ma la bha ga wa tyai/ lhovi vdab ma la pradznyā pa ra mi tā yai/ bden bral du a mi ta gu ṇā ye/ chu bdag gi vdab ma la bha ga wa ti batstsha lā ye/ rlung gi vdab ma la sarba ta thā ga tā dznyā na pa ri pū rā ye/ lus ngan gyi vdab ma la swa twa batstsha lā ye/ dbang ldan gyi vdab ma la tadya thā oṃ dhīḥkarṇi kā yaṃ/ shar du shru/ me ru ti/ lho ru smrī/ bden bral du te/ chu bdag tuvi/ rlung du dzā/ lus ngan du ye/ dbang ldan du swā hā/ de bzhin du sngags kyi yi ge rnams bkod nas bzlas so/ /yi ge vdi rnams de bzhin du bsam par byavo/ /

复次，安置真言。喉部（安置）oṃ dhīḥ，舌上（安置）oṃ ghiḥ，双耳（安置）dziḥ，然后从自己的心间红色 āḥ 字生出莲花。观其具八片莲瓣、花蕊、果须，种字安置其上。观想所有的莲瓣、黄色花蕊，东方花瓣（安置）nama，东南方花瓣（安置）bha ga wa tyai[16]，南方花瓣（安置）pradznyā pa ra mi tā yai[17]，西南方花瓣（安置）a mi ta gu ṇā ye[18]，西方花瓣（安置）bha ga wa ti batstsha lā ye[19]，西北方花瓣（安置）sarba ta thā ga tā dznyā na pa ri pū rā ye[20]，北方花瓣（安置）swa twa batstsha lā ye[21]，东北方花瓣（安置）tad yathā, oṃ dhīḥkarṇi kā yaṃ[22]，东置 śru，东南置 ti，南置 smrī，西南置 te[23]，西方置 tu'i[24]，西北方置 dzā[25]，北方置 ye，东北方置 swā hā，如此安置和念诵所有咒字。如是观想这些咒字。

thun mtshams gsum du stong phrag brgyad ji srid zla ba drug gi bar ram yang na los de thos pa vdzin par vgyur ro/ / gser mdog can gyi shes rab kyi pha rol tu phyin mavi sgrub thabs rdzogs so//

于六个月中（每日）三座（晚）做八千遍，才能闻持。黄色般若波罗蜜多母成就法圆满！

16 根据 Bhattacharyya 编《成就法鬘》（Sādhanamālā）梵文版本，还原成梵文为 bhagavatī，意为薄伽梵母。
17 根据上引《成就法鬘》，还原成梵文为 prajñāpāramitā，意为般若波罗蜜多母。
18 根据上引《成就法鬘》，还原成梵文为 amṛtaguṇā，意为甘露功德母。
19 根据上引《成就法鬘》，还原成梵文为 bhaktivatsalā，意为虔信母。
20 根据上引《成就法鬘》，还原成梵文为 sarvatathaṅatājñānaparipūritā，意为一切如来依怙智圆满母。
21 根据上引《成就法鬘》，还原成梵文为 sattvavatsalā，意为众生慈爱母。
22 根据上引《成就法鬘》，还原成梵文为 tad yathā, oṃ dhīḥ karṇikāyāṃ，意为“即说：嗡，地，在莲花上”。
23 上引《成就法鬘》为：ti。
24 上引《成就法鬘》为：vi。
25 上引《成就法鬘》为：ja。

此成就法的梵文本名为 *Kanakavarṇaprajñāpāramitāsādhana*，原收录于《成就法鬘》（梵 *Sādhanamālā*）[26] 和《成就法海》（梵 *Sādhanasāgara*，藏 *sgrub thabs rgya mtsho*；又称《成就法集》，梵 *Sādhansamuccaya*，藏 *sgrub thabs kun las btus pa*）中。《成就法鬘》成书时间不晚于 12 世纪下半叶，《成就法海》为其一部分，藏文本由雅砻译师扎巴坚赞（yar klung lo tsā ba grags pa rgyal mtshan，1242-1346）译于 1285 年，被收录于诸版大藏经中。[27] 虽然夏鲁寺般若佛母塑像与扎巴坚赞译《黄色般若波罗蜜多母成就法》相符合，且其施主为与夏鲁寺关系密切的麻吉巴（ma gcig pa），但这些还不能成为判定整体塑像年代的绝对依据，一是由于作为殿内整体壁塑图像组合仍未找到确凿的文本依据，其二是在仪轨文本之外，西藏密法传承中还存在口传形式，并不著述文字。

此一般若佛母主臂作说法印，即转法轮印，源自释迦牟尼最初于鹿野苑宣讲四圣谛，即"初转法轮"，是金刚界五方佛中大日如来的手印，也常见于弥勒菩萨、文殊菩萨和阿底峡、萨迦班智达、宗喀巴等上师图像中 [28]；右二臂持蓝莲花托梵箧，左二手施无畏印。蓝莲花是绿度母和其他金刚乘诸神的持物 [29]，梵箧为其所化现的《般若经》，也是其重要标识，无畏印寓意佛陀令众生脱离轮回的所有恐惧，早期佛像中可见此印，也是金刚界五方佛中不空成就佛的手印 [30]。然而，不同于其他几种常见的四臂般若佛母的是，这一般若佛母手中并未持金刚杵和念珠，金刚杵寓意空性，而念

26 Lokesh Chandra, *Dictionary of Buddhist Iconography*, vol. 9, New Delhi: International Academy of Indian Culture and Aditya Prakashan, 2003, p.2668. Benoytosh Bhattacharyya, *Sādhanamālā*, Baroda: Central Library, 1925, no. 156.

27 据藏文大藏经中的《成就法海》尾跋记载，《成就法海》是经由乔达摩师利（Gautamośri）传至吉祥萨迦大寺。在班智达月称（Kīrticandra）亲请下，依靠大轨范师达玛巴拉（Dharmapālarakṣita）的护持以及大官员贡嘎旬奴（gun dgav gzhon nu）和麻吉巴（ma gcig pa）供养，由外土瑜伽士扎巴坚赞（grags pa rgyal mtshan）于鸡年（1285）在曲米京卡（chu mig rdzing kha）翻译完成，麻吉巴可能为从夏鲁寺嫁到萨迦的麻吉堪卓本（ma gcig mkhav vgro vbum），即夏鲁寺寺主阿梅桑杰益希（a mes sangs rgyas ye shes）女儿。该部成就法集在北京版《丹珠尔》中由 246 个成就法组成（第 4221-4466 号），在德格版中由 245 个成就法组成（第 3400-3644 号），《成就法海》的作者和译成时间判定，参见郝一川：《〈成就法鬘〉中的真实名文殊研究》，收于谢继胜、罗文华、石岩刚主编：《汉藏佛教美术研究——第四届西藏考古与艺术国际学术讨论会论文集》，上海古籍出版社，2014 年，第 223-224 页；Leonard W. J. van der Kuijp, "On the Vicissitudes of Subhūticandra's Kāmadhenu Commentary on the Amarakoṣa in Tibet", in *Journal of the International Association of Tibetan Studies*, no. 5, 1-105, p. 21.

28 〔英〕罗伯特·比尔著、向红笳译：《藏传佛教象征符号与器物图解》，北京：中国藏学出版社，2014 年，第 234 页。

29 前引《藏传佛教象征符号与器物图解》，第 179 页。

30 前引《藏传佛教象征符号与器物图解》，第 233 页。

珠则象征通过背诵咒语、供奉和慈悲觉识体现出的语之纯净[31]。

值得探讨的是，这种样式的般若佛母图像也见于他处。图9清代乾隆时期成书的《诸佛菩萨圣像赞》(1761年)中，同一样式的般若佛母亦被收入，位列第252尊，也即“诸样佛母”之第二十五，以满、汉、蒙古、藏四体朱书尊名，[32]《诸佛菩萨圣像赞》是以乾隆时期清宫所制360尊像擦擦为原本描绘而成，这批擦擦模具系于乾隆十四年(1749)至二十二年(1755)间由清宫造办处所铸，图像来源于乾隆十四年三世章嘉若必多吉(rol pavi rdo rje, 1717-1786)所编藏传佛教图像集[33]。此尊以“四臂般若佛母”命名，以区分“来字二十四”二臂般若佛母。《诸佛菩萨圣像赞》将诸神分为23类，般若佛母位于第18类“诸样佛母”的第25尊，与叶衣佛母、尊胜佛母、大白伞盖佛母等并列。《诸佛菩萨圣像赞》对尊神的分类模式与格鲁派资粮田唐卡中所表现的尊神排列顺序一致，图像集一定程度上反映了清代宫廷藏传佛教神系的基本框架。另据罗凯什·钱德拉(Lokesh Chandra)，在一件晚期的尼泊尔绘本中，也见有此种样式的四臂般若佛母。[34]另有一件尼泊尔《般若经》手写本的鎏金铜夹经板，美国普里茨克(Pritzker)夫妇藏品，纪年约为1207年。夹经板正中雕刻四臂般若佛母，手印和持物与夏鲁寺般若佛母近似，但于左手二臂持物略差，直接持握经书，而非持莲托经书。[35]

四、般若佛母曼荼罗仪轨

1. 三则相关般若佛母曼陀罗仪轨

图齐在对江浦寺马头明王殿般若佛母与十方佛塑像进行分析时，认为由于十方佛较为常见，通常所有的前行仪轨均需迎请其来进行除障，因而很难判定他们的图像确定是

31 前引《藏传佛教象征符号与器物图解》，第197页。

32 前引 *Dictionary of Buddhist Iconography*, vol.9, p. 2668. 国家图书馆版本：《诸佛菩萨圣像赞》，北京：中国藏学出版社，2009年，第254页。像之上方题汉文“四臂般若佛母”，下方题藏文“sher phyin phyag bzhi ma//”，左边题满文（转写）“Duin galangga sure-icargi dalin de akônaha eme fucihi”，右边题蒙古文（转写）“Dörben γartu bilig barmaid eke”，左下页脚朱书千字文编号“来字二十五”；所附汉文像赞为六言四句，墨书，“身似菩提宝树，心存般若波罗。大展我佛宝卷，慧光度世云多。”

33 前引《诸佛菩萨圣像赞》，第18-19页。

34 前引 *Dictionary of Buddhist Iconography*, vol. 9, p.2668.

35 Pratapaditya Pal and Julia Meech-Pekarik, *Buddhist Book Illuminations*, Hong Kong, New York, Paris, New Delhi: Ravi Kumar Publishers, 1988, p. 105, pl. 26.

出自某部经典。[36]然而在夏鲁寺般若佛母殿情况略微不同，殿内四隅壁画中出现有曼荼罗中常见的内外供养天女以及四摄菩萨，即嬉女、鬘女、歌女、舞女、花女、香女、灯女、涂香女、金刚钩、金刚索、金刚锁和金刚铃十二尊，因此推断其壁塑布局很可能为般若佛母曼荼罗的构造。检索仪轨文献，与夏鲁寺般若佛母曼荼罗相关的经典主要有[37]：

（1）9世纪庆喜藏（Ānandagarbha）作《般若波罗蜜多曼荼罗仪轨》（*shes rab kyi pha rol tu phyin pavi dkyil vkhor gyi cho ga*）[38]；

（2）11世纪宝称（Ratnakīrti）作、尼泊尔玛哈帕那（Mahāpāṇa）译《般若波罗蜜多曼荼罗仪轨》（*shes rab kyi pha rol tu phyin pavi dkyil vkhor gyi cho ga zhes bya ba*）[39]；

（3）收录于瑜伽友（Mitrayogi，约12世纪中期）作《密答喇百法》（*mi tra brgya rtsa*）的《般若佛母曼荼罗》[40]，版本有二：一为59尊（图10、11），[41]一为71尊，较前

36 图齐著，魏正中、萨尔吉主编：《梵天佛地》，上海—罗马：上海古籍出版社、意大利亚洲研究院，2009年，第四卷第一册，第84-85页。

37 除此处介绍的三个般若佛母曼荼罗仪轨外，还有其他几种，被收录于其他经续中，但由于主尊图像特征或曼荼罗构造与夏鲁寺一例相去较远，因而未予引用。主要如下：1. 出自13世纪苏吉达室利（Sugataśrī）和萨班衮噶坚赞（kun dgav rgyal mtshan，1182-1251）藏译《一切如来身语意秘密庄严怛特罗王》（*de bzhin gshegs pa thams cad kyi sku dang gsung dang thugs kyi gsang ba rgyan gyi bkod pa zhes bya bavi rgyud kyi rgyal po*）的“般若佛母智慧曼荼罗”和“般若佛母羯磨曼荼罗”，德格版《甘珠尔》，[D. No.] 492, rgyud, tha 83b1-119b5 (vol. 86)，图像分别再现于白居寺吉祥多门塔三层普渡三途殿（ngan song thams cad yongs su sbyong bavi lha khang）的北壁和西壁，主尊般若佛母分别为黄色和红色身的四面四臂忿怒尊；2. 另于白居寺吉祥多门塔五层塔瓶南无量宫东壁上方、西壁上、下出现有三铺般若佛母曼荼罗：般若佛母智慧大曼荼罗、般若佛母大成就法大坛城和般若佛母广大曼荼罗，据题记出自《般若波罗蜜多理趣一百五十颂》（*vphags pa shes rab kyi pha rol tu phyin pavi tshul brgya lnga bcu pa*，德格版《甘珠尔》，[D. No.] 489, rgyud, ta 266a1-272a7(vol. 85)）和《一切如来身语意秘密庄严怛特罗王》，曼荼罗中未见十方佛。参见熊文彬：《中世纪藏传佛教艺术——白居寺壁画艺术研究》，北京：中国藏学出版社，1996年，第82页；前引《梵天佛地》，第四卷第二册，第71、90-91、274-278、359、404页。

38 梵文：*Prajñāpāramitāmaṇḍalavidhi*，德格版《丹珠尔》，[D. No.] 2644, rgyud, ju 247a4-260a7（vol. 170）。

39 梵文：*Prajñāpāramitāmaṇḍalavidhi-nāma*，德格版《丹珠尔》，[D. No.] 2645, rgyud, ju 260a7-270a2（vol. 170）。

40 关于瑜伽友的生活年代，参见贾维维：《榆林窟第三窟顶髻尊胜佛母曼荼罗研究》，《故宫博物院院刊》2014年第2期，第59页。

41 von rgyal sras bskal bzang thub bstan vjigs med rgyal mtshan, *mi tra brgya rtsavi dkyil vkhor gyi mngon rtogs blo gsal mgul rgyan*, Delhi: von chos sdings bla brang gi par khang, 1985, pp.137L4-142L2. 另参见自 Kimiaki Tannka, *Mitrayogin's 108 Maṇḍalas: An Image Database*, Kathmandu: Vajra Publication, 2013, p.67. 但书中将其命名为60尊，待查考，感谢浙江大学文化遗产研究院贾维维博士向笔者提供图片。周绍良、吕铁钢主编：《藏密修法宝典》（卷五），“密答喇百法主尊像”，北京：华夏出版社，2002年，第179-180页。

图 10　瑜伽友作《密答喇百法》的《般若佛母曼荼罗》（59 尊），引自 Kimiaki Tannka, *Mitrayogin's 108 Maṇḍalas: An Image Database*, Kathmandu: Vajra Publication, 2013, p.67.

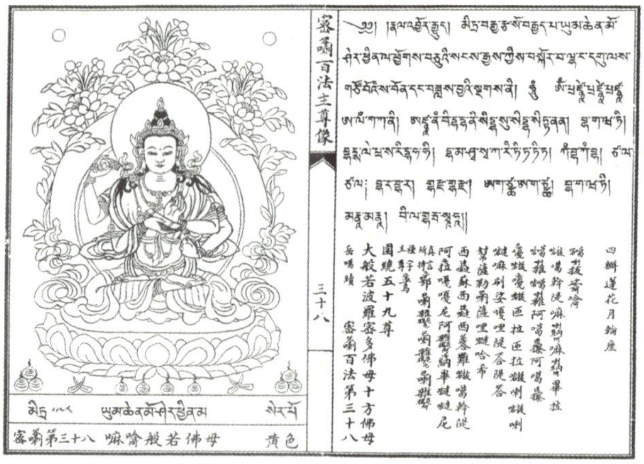

图 11　瑜伽友作《密答喇百法》的《般若佛母曼荼罗》（59 尊），引自周绍良、吕铁钢主编：《藏密修法宝典》（卷五），“密答喇百法主尊像”，北京：华夏出版社，2002 年，第 179-180 页。

者多出内外四供养天女和四摄菩萨[42]。

三则仪轨中的曼荼罗配置均为以般若佛母为中尊，东、南、西、北、东北、东南、西南、西北、上、下十方诸佛及其各自眷属菩萨围绕，四隅和四门置八供养天女和四摄菩萨，与夏鲁寺的般若佛母曼荼罗的主体配置接近。然而，三者之间亦有显著差异，主要体现在十方佛及其眷属、般若佛母眷属尊神。三本中以庆喜藏本时代最早，篇幅最长，以七字偈颂体的方式成文，内容涵盖曼荼罗观想和绘制、手印、咒语以及火供仪式，对于曼荼罗尊神配置、身色、手印记录十分细致，尊神共计 71 尊。瑜伽友本除十方佛名外，另在主尊周围配置四佛母和四波罗蜜菩萨尊神，不同于前者（详见附表）。

42　gnyan vod srung mgon po, *mngon par rtogs pa mu tig phreng ba* (*grub pavi dbang phyug chen po mi tra dzo kivi gsung las byung bavi thugs dam gyi lha mchog brgya rtsa brgyad kyi mngon par rtogs pa mu tig phreng ba rgya gzhung dang khyad med gnyan vod srung mgon povi gsung*), in blo gter dbang po, *rgyud sde kun btus*, Kathmandu: Sachen International, Guru Lama, 2004, TBRC W27883. 23: 345 - 487，pp.389L2-391L5.

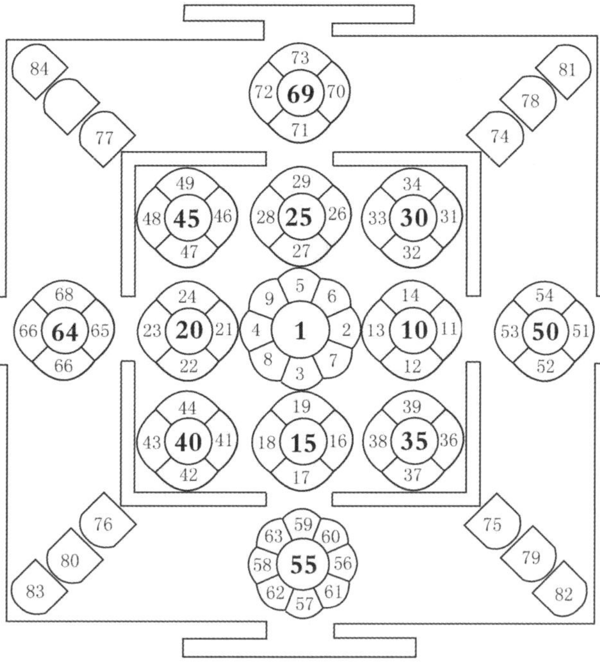

图 12　宝称作《般若佛母曼荼罗仪轨》之曼荼罗布局图示（杨鸿蛟制图）

宝称本为七字偈颂体，含般若佛母曼陀仪轨三则，第一则曼荼罗铺陈最多，亦与般若佛母殿图像构造相近，其中所述尊神共计 84 尊（应为 85 尊，漏灯女一尊），般若佛母 1 尊，佛母眷属 4 尊，诸佛 12 尊，眷属菩萨、天女 67 尊，开篇撰述般若佛母成就法发源及写作缘起："如来佛曾授记龙树（藏文：klu sgrub, 梵文：Nāgārjuna，约 150-250 年）及其弟子月称（藏文：zla grags, 梵文：Candrakīrti，约 7 世纪）、清辨（藏文：bha bya, 梵文：Bhavaviveka, 约 490-570 年）等，亲自向世间宣说无碍般若佛母成就法，然而对于广大曼荼罗，智者们未作演说。因此我等不才，受此上师、本尊恩德，遍览典籍，摄引要义，善说此部曼荼罗仪轨。"[43] 中段述说三则曼荼罗画法及观修仪轨，文末附尾题。从尾题记述可知，在宝称本写作时，参考了庆喜藏本：

43　前引《般若佛母曼荼罗仪轨》，第 520 页第 1 至 3 行。藏文原文：bde gshegs lung stan klu sgrub dang/ de yi slob ma zla grags dang/ mkhas pa yi ni bha bya dang/ de sogs yum gyi sgrubs thabs ni/ legs pa nyi du bstan kyang ni/ sla zhing dkyil vkhor rgyas pa ni/ mkhas pas de dag ma bstan te/ des rgyas bdag gis sla bar bstan/ bdag vdra shin tu blun gyur kyang/ bla ma yi dam drin dang ni/ gzhung rnams kun nas bstus nas ni/ dkyil vkhor cho ga legs par bshad/ 特此感谢中国藏学研究中心西藏文化博物馆副研究馆员仁青卓玛老师对文中藏文本的校正。

以般若佛母摄受善根故，宝称宣说此自性三坛城仪轨，智者们以聪慧对所有般若佛母摄义仪轨稍做接触即已领会，若不是以此等一切为基，即不会有这部仪轨的完满阐说，故在看过并领会庆喜藏本要义之后，宣说这则绝对有别于他本的仪轨。[44]

虽然三本仪轨文本均不能与夏鲁寺般若佛母曼荼罗图像完全契合，主尊与噶陀司徒所记不符，同时也由于未能找到夏鲁寺原存十方诸佛塑像的完整图像资料，细致的图像比对还有待下一步图像资料的获取，门楣上方和门框左右的十尊菩萨也未能全部在三本仪轨中对应出来。但对三本仪轨中的曼荼罗构造予以梳理对于夏鲁寺般若佛母曼荼罗遗存的研究亦有参考之益。

仅就确定的夏鲁寺图像：四臂般若佛母和内外四供养天女、四摄菩萨以及门框上方和左右的菩萨众，均未能与上表所列三个文本严密对应。宝称本记：

（外圈）四方空隙处安置与其他一样的嬉女、鬘女、歌女及舞女，其外安置亦与其他一样的花女、持香熏女、涂香女，复次亦是与其他一样持钩、持索、持铁镣及持铃（者）。分具白黄红绿诸色，内部均具青色，东为大白，南为大黄，西为大红，北为大绿，中为纯青。安置广大供养及朵玛，曼荼罗圆满庄严如是已。[45]

除编号为 M_8 的灯女未出现在仪轨中，其余 11 尊均是有迹可循，位置和身色略微混乱，仅有 M_3、M_8、M_1、M_4、M_7、M_{10} 六尊能够完全契合。门南北两壁上的四尊持宝瓶、塔、伞幢和轮的菩萨以及门壁上方包括金刚手、普贤、宝生自在等在内的六

44 前引《般若佛母曼荼罗仪轨》，第 538 页第 7 行至第 539 页第 2 行。藏文原文：vdi don rin chen grags pa yis/ yum chen dge rtsa bsdu bavi phyir/ dkyil vkhor gsum gyi bdag nyid kyi/ cho ga vdi ni bstan pa yin/ mkhas pa rnams kyis yum kun la/ don bsdus cho ga de tsam zhig/ shes rab gsal bas shes par bya/ de ltar min [pa?] thams cad kyis/ cho ga legs par bstan pa min/ de bas cho ga vdi dang gzhan/ khyad par yod pa kho nar zad/ kun dgavi snying povi don mthong nas/ go ba sla phyir bstan pa yin/。

45 前引《般若佛母曼荼罗仪轨》，第 522 页第 7 行至第 523 页第 2 行。藏文原文：mtshams su sgeg mo phreng ba ma/ glu dang dang gar de gzhan dang mthun/ phyi la me tog bdug ba ma/ dri chab ma ste gzhan dang mthun/ lcags kyu zhags pa lcags sgrog dril/ de yang gzhan dang mthun pavo/ dkar dang ser dang dmar dang ljang/ kun gyi nang rol mthing bavo/ shar du dkar po che ba ste/ lho ru ser po che ba ste/ nub tu dmar po che ba ste/ byang du ljang che ba ste/ dbus su mthing ga yang dag ldan/ mchod dang gtor ma rgyas par bshams/ dkyil vkhor rgyan sogs legs par dgod/ /。

尊菩萨也均未出现在仪轨之中，是为憾事。

而这部宝称本与习见的般若佛母与十方佛的仪轨不同，是在庆喜藏本的基础上，特别地增添了娑婆世界（mi mjed vjig rten khams）之主和清净佛刹土（yongs su dag pavi zhing khams）之主，也即现在佛释迦牟尼佛和过去佛燃灯佛，究其教义，仍是强调释迦牟尼佛演说《般若经》的佛教传承。依据宿白先生的记录和照片可知，夏鲁寺般若佛母塑像左侧一尊应为“释迦”样貌，也即和图片中十方佛图像相似，因此，虽在数量上宝称本与夏鲁寺般若佛母殿内佛尊数量相符，但从宿白先生拍摄的照片来看，般若佛母右侧一尊，也即“着新月冠饰、结定印之坐佛”，显然为报身相大日如来或阿弥陀佛，图像上与常见的燃灯佛特征不符合[46]。

2. 般若佛母曼荼罗与金刚界系曼荼罗关系

从般若佛母曼荼罗图像的尊神配置上来看，Petra 根据拉达克地区的 11 世纪末或 12 世纪的拉隆寺（Lalung）和那科寺（Nako）[47] 等遗迹，将般若佛母图像配置分为两种类型：般若佛母与十方佛组合（类型 I）、般若佛母与五方佛组合（类型 II）以及两者融合的类型[48]。然而综观藏西以及后藏江浦寺、孜乃萨寺、夏鲁寺三寺般若佛母殿遗迹，不难看出其图像配置的另一相似之处，即是般若佛母曼荼罗与大日如来或金刚界曼荼罗图像有着密切关系，后藏三寺的般若佛母殿均是与主供大日如来的佛殿相配，江浦寺为 37 尊金刚界曼荼罗的大日如来殿[49]，孜乃萨寺和夏鲁寺相似，均是大日如来与八大菩萨配置的马头金刚殿，其般若佛母殿内的主尊为并列的般若佛母和四面大日如来像，周围配以十方佛[50]，般若佛母与大日如来的关系十分明确，这与 10-11 世纪的印度尼西亚的一尊般若佛母与大日如来组像具有异曲同工之处[51]。后藏三寺相较而言，夏鲁寺般若佛母殿在整个寺院的地位更为突出。

46 前引 *Dictionary of Buddhist Iconography*, vol. 4, 2002, pp.1001-1005.

47 11 世纪末那科寺译师殿（lo tsā ba lha khang），主壁为金刚界曼荼罗壁塑，悬塑五方佛周围绘制眷属壁画、般若佛母与十方佛；12 世纪初的那科寺上寺（lha khang gong ma）主壁（东壁）悬塑般若佛母和八佛，四周绘诸佛和菩萨及绿度母配八难，北壁为金刚界曼荼罗；主尊均为二臂般若佛母。前引 “Representing Prajñāpāramitā in Tibet and the Indian Himalayas. The iconographic concept in the Temples of Nako, rKyang bu and Zha lu”; Christian Luczanits, *Buddhist Sculpture in Clay: Early Western Himalayan Art, late 10th to early 13th centuries*, Chicago: Serindia Publications, 2004, p.85, 86, Fig. 83.

48 前引 “Representing Prajñāpāramitā in Tibet and the Indian Himalayas. The iconographic concept in the Temples of Nako, rKyang bu and Zha lu”.

49 前引《后藏志》，汉译本，第 35-36 页；前引《梵天佛地》，第四卷第一册，第 84 页。

50 前引《后藏志》，汉译本，第 54 页。前引 *Early Temples of Central Tibet*, pp.50-51.

51 铜合金，高 63 厘米，现藏荷兰国家民族学博物馆，莱顿（RMV 1403-2862, 1883），参见 Susan L. Huntington and John C. Huntington, *Leaves from the Bodhi Tree: The Art of Pāla India (8th-12th centuries) and Its International Legacy*, Dayton Art Institute, University of Washington Press, 1990, pl. 84, p.242.

而这一点与般若佛母与十方佛曼荼罗仪轨的构造和属性相应和，按照布顿仁钦珠（bu ston rin chen grub, 1290—1364）的经典划分方式，宝称本《般若佛母曼荼罗仪轨》被归入瑜伽部密续释论，与《真实摄经》（*Tattvasaṃgraha*）、《恶趣清净怛特罗》（*Sarvadurgatipariśodhanatantra*）等相关仪轨并列[52]。作为重要瑜伽密续上师的庆喜藏，被布顿誉为“瑜伽续部三贤”[53],所造《般若佛母曼荼罗仪轨》在曼荼罗构造上也与其他五部瑜伽续曼荼罗同质[54]。

另从宗教义理来看，般若佛母被视为智慧和空性化现的众佛之母，在部分佛教仪轨文献中，将其与金刚界之主大日如来相对应，例如在《恶趣清净怛特罗》中她被作为金刚界自在母也即大日如来的女性伴偶进行祈求[55]。在13世纪止贡巴吉天颂恭（vjig rten mgon po, 1143-1217）所作《帕木竹巴吉祥多门灵塔目录》（*phag mo gru pavi gdung rten bkra shis sgo mang gi dkar chag*）中将四臂般若佛母称为金刚界女性主宰，即“金刚界自在母”（Vajradhatviśvarī）[56]。在尼瓦尔佛教中，由于其超凡性，等同于金刚界大自在母的般若佛母并未以拟人化的形象表现出来，而是以空龛表示。[57]

四、结论

1. 就夏鲁寺般若佛母曼荼罗壁塑来说，虽未能具体确定其仪轨文本和传规，但从20世纪初噶陀司徒《雪域卫藏朝圣指南》可知其主尊般若佛母原貌，基本可判定

52 布顿·仁钦珠著、蒲文成译：《布顿佛教史》，兰州：甘肃民族出版社，2007年，第200页。另从曼荼罗构造上来看，宝称本（如上图）和瑜伽友本中的主尊般若佛母均为四臂黄色身，周围配置有四佛母（嘛玛基、白衣、佛眼、度母）和四波罗蜜菩萨女尊样式（金刚女、大宝女、法女与业女）。这种布置与金刚界曼荼罗（vajradhātumahāmaṇḍala）、普明大日如来曼荼罗（sarvavidvairocanamaṇḍala）、法界语自在曼荼罗（dharmadhātuvāgīśvaramañjuśrīmaṇḍala）等瑜伽续曼荼罗中心以大日如来或大日如来化身为主尊，周围布四方佛和四佛母或四波罗蜜菩萨的构造相似。

53 转引自王瑞雷：《托林寺红殿壁画研究》，博士论文，首都师范大学，2016年，指导教授：谢继胜，第152页。

54 杉木恒彦：Ānandagarbhaの曼荼羅成就法論，インド哲学仏教学研究，1995-10-31，33-46（L）.

55 Tadeuez Skorupski, *The Sarvadurgatipariśodhana Tantra: Elimination of All Evil Destinies, Sanskrit and Tibet Texts with Introduction, English Translation and Notes*, Delhi: Motilal Banarsidass, 1983, pp.20-21. John C. Huntington and Dina Bangdel, *The Circle of Bliss: Buddhist Meditational Art*, Chicago: Serindia Publications, Inc., 2003, p.122.

56 Christian Luczanits, “Maṇḍalas of Maṇḍalas: The Iconography of a Stūpa of Many Auspicious Doors for Phag mo gru pa.” in *Tibetan Art and Architecture in Context. Proceedings of the Eleventh Seminar of the International Association for Tibetan Studies: Tibetan Studies, Königswinter*, Vol. 2006, 2010, pp. 281-310: 293. “yum chen mo shes rab kyi pha rol tu phyin ma rdo rje dbyings kyi dbang phyug ma zhal gcig phyag bzhi ma”.

57 前引 *The Circle of Bliss: Buddhist Meditational Art*, pp.120-121, fig. 3.

其图像特征与《成就法鬘》一致，与江浦寺等同时期的般若佛母图像不尽相同，为厘清图像原貌提供了基础材料。

2. 般若佛母是金刚乘神灵体系中重要的女性神，其信仰在11-13世纪北传佛教体系中尤其兴盛，地区遍布印度、尼泊尔、印度尼西亚爪哇地区、日本以及藏西拉达克、西藏后藏部分地区、西夏地区，[58]究其根本是由于《般若经》信仰在这一时期持续兴盛，伴随瑜伽密续法的传播和佛教体系中女性尊神崇拜的流行等要素，促成她在这些地区成为特定时期的重要尊神。

3. 后弘期初期以夏鲁寺为代表的后藏三寺般若佛母殿的兴建动因主要有两方面：一是与吐蕃时期《般若经》信仰以及后弘期下路弘法传承有着密切关联[59]，另一方面则是与瑜伽密续经典和图像的传播相应。本文着重于后者，通过仪轨文本和义理的考量和分析，推断出后藏三寺的般若佛母与十方佛图像是伴随后弘期初期以金刚界曼荼罗仪轨为代表的瑜伽密续传入而传入的；由于尚无法确定较为明确的仪轨文本，不排除口传秘诀的可能性。

58 Edward Conze, "The Iconography of the Prajñāparamitā," in *Thirty Years of Buddhist Studies*: *Selected Essays by Edward Conze,* Oxford: Bruno Cassierer, 1967, pp. 243-268.

59 参见前引杨鸿蛟：《11至14世纪夏鲁寺般若佛母殿绘塑研究》，第11-24页。

附表　庆喜藏本 (A)、宝称本 (B)、瑜伽友本 (C、C’)[60] 般若佛母曼荼罗仪轨图像比较

方位		尊名	身色	持物 / 手印				编号
				右手		左手		
				一	二	一	二	
中央/中央	中	般若佛母 shes rab pha rol phyin pavi yum	白	与愿	莲托经箧	A1		
		般若佛母 yum chen	黄	莲托经箧	与愿印	莲托金刚杵	禅定印	B1
		般若佛母 yum chen mo	黄	经箧	金刚杵	说法印	置于侧腰	C1
		般若佛母 yum chen mo	黄	说法印	金刚杵	说法印	持经箧置侧腰	C’1
	东	金刚女菩萨 sems ma rdo rje						B2
		佛眼佛母 sangs rgyas spyan ma	白	持经箧		置于侧腰		C2
	南	大宝母 rin chen ma						B3
		嘛玛基佛母 mā ma kī	青	持经箧		置于侧腰		C3
	西	法女菩萨 chos kyi sems ma						B4
		白衣佛母 gos dkar mo	红	经箧		置于侧腰		C4
	北	业女菩萨 las kyi sems ma						B5
		度母 sgrol ma	绿	经箧		置于侧腰		C5
	东南	嘛玛基佛母 mā ma kī						B6
		金刚女菩萨 rdo rje sems ma	青	金刚杵				C6
	西南	白衣佛母 gos dkar mo						B7
		大宝母 rin chen sems ma	黄	大宝				C7
	西北	佛眼佛母 sangs rgyas spyan ma						B8
		莲花女菩萨 padmavi sems ma	红	莲花				C8
	东北	度母 sgrol ma						B9
		业女菩萨 las kyi sems ma	绿	青莲花				C9

60　C 本为 17 世纪 von rgyal sras bskal bzang thub bstan vjigs med rgyal mtshan 所录 59 尊版本，C’ 为 19 世纪《续部总集》（*rgyud sde kun btus*）所收 gnyan vod srung mgon po 的 71 尊版本，两者基本重合，后者较前者增出内外四供养天女和四摄菩萨十二尊，另两者在主尊般若佛母的四臂手印和持物记录上存在差别。两者相同的部分，笔者仅录 C，不同处另列 C’。

续表 1

方位		尊名	身色	持物 / 手印				编号
				右手		左手		
				一	二	一	二	
东方 / 东方	中	宝生佛 dkon mchog vbyung gnas	淡红 / 粉	施宝印（rin chen mchog sbyin）			置于脐部	A10
		宝生佛 rin chen vbyung gnas	黄	触地印				B10
		无忧佛 mya ngan med pavi dpal	白	予愿印				C10
	东	法幢菩萨 chos kyi rgyal mtshan	白	摩羯幢		莲花		A11
		光明俱生菩萨 sems dpav vod zer kun vbyung		莲花				B11
		法幢菩萨 chos kyi rgyal mtshan	白	摩羯幢				C11
		法幢菩萨 chos kyi rgyal mtshan	白	幢				C’11
	南	自在王菩萨 dbang phyug rgyal po	天青	铁钩		莲花		A12
		大宝焰炽菩萨 rin chen vod vphro		金刚棒				B12
		自在王菩萨 dbang phyug rgyal po	青	铁钩				C12
	西	严饰菩萨 bkod pavi rgyan	白	青莲花		莲花		A13
		宝自在菩萨 rin dbang phyug		宝				B13
		庄严幢菩萨 bkod pavi rgyal mtshan	红	经箧				C13
		庄严王菩萨 bkod pa rgyal po	红	青莲花				C’13
	北	大宝焰炽菩萨 rin chen vod vphro	绿	大宝焰光		莲花		A14
		金刚不动菩萨 rdo rje mi g·yo sems dpav		铁钩				B14
		大宝焰炽菩萨 rin chen vod vphro	绿	宝				C14
第二 / 南方	中	无忧佛 mya ngan med pa	天青	持焰轮		置于脐部		A15
		无忧佛 mya ngan med dpal	青	莲花与愿印				B15
		轮回断续佛 vkhor ba rgyun gcod	青	经箧				C15

续表 2

方位		尊名	身色	持物 / 手印				编号
				右手		左手		
				一	二	一	二	
第二/南方	东	圣光明菩萨 snang mchog	白	日曼荼罗		莲花		A16
		无忧菩萨 sems dpav mya ngan med pa		四莲瓣				B16
		圣光明菩萨 snang ba mchog	白	大宝				C16
		圣光明菩萨 snang ba mchog	白	日曼荼罗				C’16
	南	手印菩萨 phyag rgyavi rgyal po	青	弓箭		莲花		A17
		法幢菩萨 chos kyi rgyal mtshan		宝				B17
		手印王菩萨 phyag rgyavi rgyal po	青	弓箭				C17
	西	香王菩萨 spos kyi rgyal po	红	箧盒 /《宝箧经》		莲花		A18
		庄严王菩萨 bkod pa rgyal		焰火				B18
		香王菩萨 spos kyi rgyal po	红	箧盒 /《宝箧经》				C18
	北	辩积菩萨 spobs pa brtsegs	绿	金玉箧盒		莲花		A19
		自在王菩萨 dbang phyug rgyal		幢				B19
		辩积菩萨 spobs pa brtsegs	绿	伞盖	C19			
第三/西方	中	大宝光明佛 rin chen vod vphro	海螺白	持獠牙		置于脐部		A20
		大宝光明佛 rin chen vod vphro	红	禅定印				B20
		轮回吉祥 vkhor bavi dpal	红	獠牙				C20
	东	莲花王菩萨 padmavi rgyal po	白	莲花花苞		莲花		A21
		行智菩萨 spyod pavi blo gros		莲花				B21
		莲花王菩萨 padmavi rgyal po	白	莲花				C21
		莲花王菩萨 padmavi rgyal po	白	莲花花苞				C’21
	南	莲花善妙菩萨 padma dam pa	青	开敷莲花		莲花		A22
		圣光明菩萨 snang ba mchog		海螺				B22
		莲花瓣菩萨 padmavi vdam ma	青	莲花茎				C22
		莲花善妙菩萨 padma dam pa	青	开敷莲花				C’22

续表 3

方位		尊名	身色	持物 / 手印				编号
				右手		左手		
				一	二	一	二	
第三 / 西方	西	金刚不动菩萨 rdo rje mi g·yo ba	红	经箧		莲花		A23
		手印菩萨 phyag rgya		铁钩				B23
		不动菩萨 mi g·yo ba	红	经箧				C23
		金刚不动菩萨 rdo rje mi g·yo ba	白	经箧				C’23
	北	无著王菩萨 thogs med rgyal po	绿	铁钩		莲花		A24
		辩积菩萨 spobs pa brtsegs		禅定印托梵箧				B24
		无著王菩萨 thogs med rgyal po	绿	铁钩				C24
北方	中	佛王 rgyal bavi dbang po	明绿	持莲花		置于脐部		A25
		佛王 rgyal bavi dbang po	绿	无畏印				B25
		一切控 thams cad dbang sgyur	绿	莲托日				C25
	东	宝自在菩萨 rin chen dbang phyug	海螺白	八角珍宝		莲花		A26
		佛施 rgyal ba byin		莲花				B26
		宝自在菩萨 rin chen dbang phyug	白	大宝				C26
		宝自在菩萨 rin chen dbang phyug	淡黄	八角珍宝				C’26
	南	不动业菩萨 mi g·yovi las	天青	诸种金刚		莲花		A27
		成就天 grub pavi lha		宝				B27
		成就菩萨 sems dpav grub pa	青	十字金刚杵				C27
		成就菩萨 sems dpav grub pa	青	诸种金刚				C’27
	西	言喜菩萨 dgav ba ston pa	红	镜子		莲花		A28
		言喜菩萨 dgav ba ston		钵				B28
		言喜菩萨 dgav ston	红	琵琶				C28
	北	不动菩萨 mi g·yo	纯绿	禅定状		莲花		A29
		不动菩萨 mi g·yo ba		禅定印托十字金刚杵				B29
		不动菩萨 mi g·yo sems dpav	绿	禅定状				C29

续表 4

方位		尊名	身色	持物 / 手印				编号
				右手		左手		
				一	二	一	二	
第五/东北方/北方	中	等持象佛 ting vdzin glang po dam pavi dpal	纯金	说法印		持法衣		A30
		等持象佛 ting vdzin glang po	黄红	转法轮印				B30
		释迦牟尼佛 shākya thub pa	黄	说法印				C30
	东	金刚手菩萨 phyag na rdo rje	海螺白	金刚杵		莲花		A31
		佛降伏 rgyal ba gnon		莲花				B31
		金刚手菩萨 phyag rdor	白	金刚杵				C31
	南	慈悲之主 byams dang snying rjevi bdag nyid can	天青	莲花		莲花		A32
		普贤菩萨 kun du bzang		宝盒				B32
		观音菩萨 spyan ras gzig	青	莲花				C32
	西	虚空藏菩萨 nam mkhavi snying po	绿宝石	法器箧盒		莲花		A33
		文殊菩萨 vjam dpal		金刚杵				B33
		虚空藏菩萨 mkhav snying	绿	法器箧盒				C33
	北	地藏菩萨 sa yi snying po	绿	宝芽（rin chen myug gu）			莲花	A34
		除盖障菩萨 sgrib pa sel ba		花				B34
		地藏菩萨 sa snying	绿	宝芽（rin chen myug gu）				C34
东南方	中	善妙莲花佛 padma dam pavi dpal	白	持莲花		置于脐部		A35
		善妙莲花佛 padmo dam pa	红	说法印				B35
		无贪莲花 ma chags padma	浅蓝	经箧				C35
		无贪莲花 ma chags padma	青	经箧				C’35
	东	普贤菩萨 kun du bzang po	白	宝穗		莲花		A36
		莲花手菩萨 lag na pad mo		莲花				B36
		普贤菩萨 kun bzang	白	宝穗				C36
	南	文殊菩萨 vjam pavi dpal	天青	剑		莲花		A37

续表 5

方位		尊名	身色	持物 / 手印				编号
				右手		左手		
				一	二	一	二	
东南方		大势至菩萨 mthu chen thob		花苞				B37
		文殊菩萨 vjam dpal	青	青莲花				C37
		文殊菩萨 vjam pavi dpal	青	剑				C’37
	西	除盖障菩萨 sgrib sel	红宝石莲花	青莲花		莲花		A38
		药王菩萨 sman gyi rgyal		瓶				B38
		除盖障菩萨 sgrib bsel	红	剑				C38
		除盖障菩萨 sgrib pa rnam sel	红	红色青莲				C’38
	北	弥勒菩萨 byams pa	绿	檀板（？ gundhe）			莲花	A39
		功德藏菩萨 yon tan snying		剑				B39
		弥勒菩萨 byams pa	黄绿	那伽树				C39
		弥勒菩萨 byams pa	绿	那伽树檀板				C’39
第七/西南方	中	日曼荼罗光明吉祥佛 nyi mavi dkyil vkhor snang bavi dpal	绿宝石	持日曼荼罗		置于脐部		A40
		日曼荼罗光明吉祥佛 nyi mavi dkyil vkhor snang bavi dpal	红黄	说法印				B40
		自义解脱 bdag don rnam grol	红	说法印				C40
	东	大势至菩萨 mthu chen thob	莲花根	三股金刚杵		莲花		A41
		日遍照菩萨 nyi ma rab snang		莲花				B41
		大势至菩萨 mthu chen thob	白	金刚杵				C41
	南	药王菩萨 sman pavi rgyal po	天青	甘露瓶		莲花		A42
		金刚手菩萨 rdo rje can		花枝				B42
		药王菩萨 sman pavi rgyal po	青	诃子				C42
		药王菩萨 sman pavi rgyal po	青	甘露瓶				C’42
	西	功德藏菩萨 yon tan snying po	绿宝石	宝穗		莲花		A43
		童饰菩萨 gzhon nu rgyan		金刚杵				B43
		功德藏菩萨 yon tan snying po	青绿	宝穗				C43

续表 6

方位		尊名	身色	持物 / 手印				编号
				右手		左手		
				一	二	一	二	
第七/西南方	北	见喜菩萨 mthong ba dgav ba	蓝宝石	那伽树叶		莲花		A44
		狮子吼菩萨 seng gevi sgra		甘露瓶				B44
		见喜菩萨 mthong na dgav ba	绿	那伽树檀板				C44
		见喜菩萨 mthong na dgav	深蓝	那伽树叶				C’44
第八/西北方	中	妙盖佛 gdugs chen dam pavi dpal	淡绿	持诸种金刚		置于脐部		A45
		妙盖佛 gdugs dam pa	红黄	说法印				B45
		轮回降魔 vkhor bavi bdud vjoms	黄	禅定印				C45
		轮回暗摧 vkhor ba mun vjoms	黄	禅定印				C’45
	东	童饰菩萨 gzhon pavi rgyan chags pa	海螺白	睡莲花		莲花		A46
		宝胜菩萨 rin chen mchog		莲花				B46
		童子菩萨 sems dpav gzhon nu	白	睡莲花				C46
	南	善士菩萨 skyes bu dam pa	天青	剑		莲花		A47
		莲花王菩萨 padmo rgyal		五顶				B47
		善士菩萨 skyes bu dam pa	青	剑				C47
	西	如狮狮子吼菩萨 seng ge vdra bavi seng gevi sgra	红	海螺		莲花		A48
		善妙莲花菩萨 padma dam pa		花				B48
		狮子吼菩萨 seng gevi sgra	红	拂尘				C48
		狮子吼菩萨 seng gevi sgra	红	剑				C’48
	北	金刚目明 rdo rje spyan gsal	绿	自目		莲花		A49
		无著王菩萨 thogs med rgyal		华服				B49
		菩萨 sems dpav	绿	期克印				C49
		金刚目 rdo rje spyan	绿	二目				C’49

续表 7

方位		尊名	身色	持物 / 手印				编号
				右手		左手		
				一	二	一	二	
上方 / 外部东方 / 上方	中	喜吉祥佛 dgav bar bye pav i sems can				莲花		A50
		喜吉祥佛 dgav ba dpal	白	无畏印				B50
		喜吉祥佛 dgav ba sgyur bav i dpal	青	日月				C50
	东	贤护菩萨 bzang skyong	白	瓶		莲花		A51
		乐施菩萨 dgav sbyin		莲花				B51
		贤护菩萨 bzang skyong	白	瓶				C51
	南	宝生菩萨 dkon mchog vbyung gnas	天青	灯芯 / 细枝		莲花		A52
		贤护菩萨 bzang skyong		花				B52
		宝生菩萨 dkon mchog vbyung gnas	青	宝				C52
	西	健行菩萨 dpav bar vgro ba	红	剑		莲花		A53
		宝生菩萨 dkon mchog vbyung gnas		日				B53
		健行菩萨 dpav bar vgro ba	红	剑				C53
	北	童王菩萨 gzhon nu rgyal	绿	月		莲花		A54
		月光处菩萨 zla vod		月				B54
		月光童子菩萨 zla vod gzhon nu	绿	月				C54
外部南方	中	释迦牟尼佛 shākya thub pa	纯金	降魔印				B55
	东	弥勒菩萨 byams pa		莲花				B56
	南	虚空藏菩萨 nam mkhavi snying po		宝				B57
	西	地藏菩萨 sa yi snying		瓶				B58

续表 8

方位		尊名	身色	持物 / 手印				编号
				右手		左手		
				一	二	一	二	
外部南方	北	观音菩萨 spyan ras gzig		黑羚羊皮				B59
		目犍连 maud gal		托钵				B60
		舍利弗 shā rivi bu		托钵				B61
		具喜菩萨 kun dgav po		托钵				B62
		地藏菩萨 sa yi snying		瓶				B58
		护光菩萨 vod srung						B63
外部西方	中	燃灯佛 mar me mdzad	红	禅定印				B64
	东	日光菩萨 nyi vod		宝				B65
	南	月光菩萨 zla vod		宝				B66
	西	弥勒菩萨 byams ba mai tri		宝				B67
	北	善士菩萨 skyes bu dam		宝				B68
第十/外部北方/下方	中	莲花吉祥佛 padma dam pavi dpal	亮金	持莲花		置于脐部		A55
		莲花吉祥佛 padmavi dpal	天蓝	无畏印				B69
		莲花 vdam skyes padma	黄	触地印（sa gnon）				C55
	东	智慧顶菩萨 ye shes tog	海螺白	金饰顶饰		莲花		A56
		莲花善妙菩萨 padma dam/		莲花				B70
		智慧顶菩萨 ye shes tog	白	青莲花				C56
		智慧顶菩萨 ye shes tog	白	金花				C'56
	南	无忧遍摧菩萨 mya ngan kun vjoms	天青	剑		莲花		A57
		智慧顶菩萨 ye shes tog		莲花				B71
		忧苦遍摧菩萨 mya ngan kun vjoms	青	剑				C57
		忧苦暗摧菩萨 mya ngan mun vjoms	青	剑				C'57

续表 9

方位		尊名	身色	持物 / 手印				编号
				右手		左手		
				一	二	一	二	
第十 / 外部北方 / 下方	西	无量智菩萨 blo gros mi zad/	红	经箧		莲花		A58
		忧苦遍摧菩萨 mya ngan kun vjoms		莲花				B72
		无量智菩萨 blo gros mi zad	红	经箧				C58
	北	智光明 ye shes vod zer	绿	具光金刚		莲花		A59
		无量智菩萨 blo mi zad/		莲花				B73
		智光 ye shes vod	绿	三股金刚杵				C59
四隅	内 / 四隅	供养天女 lha mo						A60
		嬉女 sgeg mo						B74
		嬉女 sgeg mo	白					C'60
		供养天女 lha mo						A61
		鬘女 phreng ba ma						B75
		鬘女 phreng ba ma	黄					C'61
		供养天女 lha mo						A62
		歌女 glu mo						B76
		歌女 glu ma	红					C'62
		供养天女 lha mo						A63
		舞女 gar mo						B77
		舞女 gar ma	绿					C'63

续表 10

方位		尊名	身色	持物 / 手印				编号
				右手		左手		
				一	二	一	二	
四隅	中/四隅	供养天女 lha mo						A64
		持香熏女 bdug pa ma bdug pa ma	白					C’64
		供养天女 lha mo						A65
		花女 me tog ma						B78
		花女 me tog ma	黄					C’65
		供养天女 lha mo						A66
		持香熏女 bdug pa ma						B79
		灯女 mar me ma	红					C’66
		供养天女 lha mo						A67
		涂香女 dri chab ma						B80
		涂香女 dri chab ma	绿					C’67
	外/四门	定门 sgo srung						A68
		持铁钩 lcags kyu						B81
		持铁钩 lcags kyu	白					C’68
		定门 sgo srung						A69
		持羂索 zhags pa						B82
		持羂索 zhags pa	黄					C’69
		定门 sgo srung						A70
		持铁镣 lcags sgrog						B83
		持铁镣 lcags sgrog	红					C’70
		定门 sgo srung						A71
		持铃 dril						B84
		持铃 dril bu	绿					C’71

阿里白东波石窟、千佛石窟和译师殿千佛壁画调查记

熊文彬*

笔者自1999年首次前往阿里地区考察，先后考察札达县的皮央、东嘎石窟、托林寺、科迦寺、芒囊寺、热尼拉康、香孜遗址、达巴遗址、琼隆遗址和日土县的丁穹拉康、塔康巴岩画、日姆栋岩画、阿绒沟岩画和宗雄措岩画等众多遗迹，但一直都在学习之中。2015年生于阿里的学长、好友次仁加布先生不幸去世，应清华大学的沈卫荣和奥地利的恭特朗·哈佐德（Guntram Hazod）教授之约，特以阿里文化为题，以纪念次仁加布先生为阿里地区历史和文化研究所作出的重要贡献，并表示崇高敬意。

千佛题材是藏传佛教艺术流行的题材之一，留下了大量的壁画、唐卡和泥塑等作品。自佛教从吐蕃时期传入西藏以来，这一题材的表现一直就未中断。直到18世纪，章嘉活佛还编纂、刊刻了梵文、藏文、满文、蒙古文和汉文的五体《贤劫千佛》。[1]这一题材不仅在西藏和其他藏区流行，同时也传入藏传佛教流传的内地、蒙古族和满族地区。在此，笔者仅就札达县托林镇的白东波石窟、萨让乡日巴村的译师殿和日土县乌江乡的千佛石窟壁画按时代进行简要的记述。

一、白东波石窟壁画

白东波石窟位于札达县托林镇白东波村，距离著名的皮央和东嘎石窟30公里，

* 熊文彬：四川大学中国藏学研究所、历史文化学院考古系教授。

1 Lokesh Chandra, *Iconography of the Thousand Buddhas*, International Academy of Indian Culture and Aditya Prakashan, New Delhi, 1996.

图 1　白东波石窟西壁贤劫千佛壁画

最早被定名为“东嘎第二地点”，[2] 其中唯一一座壁画窟被定名为 1 号窟。[3]1994 年，随着四川大学中国藏学研究所、四川大学历史文化学院考古系与西藏文物局组成的考古队在东嘎、皮央石窟开展工作以来，该石窟逐渐引起了学术界的关注。1997 年，西藏自治区文物局和四川大学首先发表了该石窟调查的简报；2002 年，瑞士独立学者诺依曼首次将该石窟的轮回图和千佛壁画介绍给学术界。[4] 2015 年 8 月 7 日，笔者与浙江大学的谢继胜教授、中国社会科学院的廖旸研究员，以及谢继胜教授和清华大学沈卫荣教授的学生贾维维、王瑞雷、次仁卓玛、孟丽、谢皓玥等一起，在札达县文物

2　西藏自治区文物局、四川联合大学考古专业：《西藏阿里东嘎·皮央石窟遗址考古调查简报》，《文物》1997 年第 9 期，第 8 页。

3　霍巍：《西藏西部石窟壁画中几种艺术风格的分析——兼论西藏西部石窟壁画艺术三个主要的发展阶段》，《藏学学刊》2004 年第 1 辑，第 156 页。

4　Helmut F. Neumann: “The Wheel of Life in the Twelfth Century Western Tibetan Cave Temple of Pedongpo,” *Buddhist Art and Tibetan Patronage: Ninth to Fourteenth Centuries. PIATS 2000: Tibetan Studies: Proceedings of the Ninth Seminar of the International Association for Tibetan Studies, Leiden* 2000, Brill's Tibetan Studies Library vol. 2/7, eds. Deborah E. Klimburg & Eva Allinger, Leiden-Boston-Köln: Brill, 2002, pp. 75-84. 同时参见耿江萍译、廖旸校汉译本：《12 世纪西藏西部白东布石窟寺生死轮图》，张长虹、廖旸主编：《越过喜马拉雅——西藏西部佛教艺术与考古译文集》，成都：四川大学出版社，2007 年，第 79-84 页。

图 2　白东波石窟东壁贤劫千佛及其题记与立佛壁画局部

局洛旦局长的帮助和陪同下，对白东波石窟又进行了考察。

白东波 1 号窟坐北朝南，由甬道和主室组成，为“平面形制也近方形的单室窟，但四角呈抹角圆转角，进深 3.7、面阔 4.2 米，窟门前设狭窄的甬道通向窟室。窟顶底部做成覆斗形，高 5.3 米。在窟内中心设一圆形坛，未开凿龛室塑像。”[5] 甬道藻井为弧形斜坡式，北高南低。主室四壁绘满了整齐排列的千佛壁画（图 1），从上到下绘有 16 行佛像；从左到右每排构图佛像的数量除南壁外，随着从下到上的收分而有不同。其中，底部构图最多，数量介于 15-16 身之间；顶部较少，介于 13-12 身之间。南壁底部中心为甬道入口位置，顶部 3 排佛像的构图与其他三壁相同，只是甬道两侧佛像的构图不同，由甬道一分为二：甬道东侧构图有 5 身佛像，与此相对的西壁只构图有 4 身佛像。这些佛像均为坐像，每身佛像之下，均题写有 2-3 行藏文题记，其中开头为佛像的藏文名字，后部为藏文转写的梵文《缘起偈》：“oṃ

5　西藏自治区文物局、四川联合大学考古专业 :《西藏阿里东嘎 · 皮央石窟遗址考古调查简报》,《文物》1997 年第 9 期，第 10 页。平面图参见图 9。诺伊曼的调查略有出入，他认为该窟坐西朝东，面积略为 3.4 x 4 米（参见 Helmut F. Neumann: “The Wheel of Life in the Twelfth Century Western Tibetan Cave Temple of Pedongpo,” p.75. 同时参见耿江萍译、廖旸校汉译本 :《12 世纪西藏西部白东布石窟寺生死轮图》，第 79 页。）

ye dharmāhetuprabhavā hetuṃ teṣāṃ tathāgato hy avadat teṣāṃ ca yo nirodha evaṃ vādī mahāśramaṇaḥye svāhā”。藏文为邬金体，部分字母的写法仍保持有古藏文的明显特征（图 2）。现存千佛壁画，南壁保存得较为完好，除墙裙上方的 2-3 排佛像变色并有擦痕和顶部个别地方有雨水侵蚀痕迹外，大多得以完整保存；南、西二壁除墙裙一角部分壁画已脱落外，状况与南壁类似；东壁壁画保存状况相对较差，在毗邻墙裙的 1-4 行壁画中，有近二分之一画面已漫漶不清或脱落，中间靠近北壁位置，也有部分壁画脱落。与此同时，除北壁外，其余三壁在各壁相邻位置分别绘有 2-3 身立佛（图 2），周围无题记。经统计，四壁现保存千佛壁画 787 身，其名号与《贤劫经》（*Aryabhadrakalpikasutra*）所载贤劫千佛吻合。[6]

窟顶藻井壁画已经大面积脱落，只有靠近北壁的位置和四周边缘尚存有部分画面。壁画以红色为底色，用白、蓝、绿等色表现的是环状的缠枝花纹。

甬道东西两壁构图有轮回图和供养人壁画，虽然底部画面大多受损，但中部和顶部画面仍完整保存如初。诺伊曼虽然正确识别出西壁的轮回图并对其渊源和图式进行了简要的分析，但未公布涉及该窟名称、施主和壁画内容的重要题记，同时也未提及甬道东壁的叙事性画面和供养人及其题记。

甬道西壁的画面分为上下两个部分，中间由线条相隔。靠近藻井顶部白色底色的长方形区域内构图有 6 位神灵，其中南侧构图的是一位一面二臂的坐式菩萨像，丰乳细腰，天衣飘举，造型具有显著的克什米尔风格特点。其北构图的是 4 位手持弓、箭、剑和盾牌等不同武器兽面人身的神灵，疑为地方神。最北端构图神灵头戴礼帽、身穿三角大翻领长袍，骑在山羊身上。其下区域构图的是西壁表现的主要题材六道轮回图，采用的是流行的基本构图模式，亦即圆轮模式：外圈为圆轮，中心为圆形的轮轴，从轮轴中延伸的六条轮辐将画面分成 6 个区域，分别表现六道。其中，轮轴表现的是象征贪、嗔、痴的蛇、猪和鸡，上三个区域表现的是天道、人道和阿修罗道，下三个区域表现的是畜牲道、饿鬼道和地狱道。六道之外，绘有一圈的十二因缘母题。诺伊曼不仅正确识别出六道，而且还注意到圆轮之外四方的四位女神这一与众不同的特点，她们敞胸露怀，双手张开，分别位居一方，拥抱轮回图。迄今为止，只有托林寺红殿门廊左壁轮回图的构图与此相同，但二者相比，白东波拥抱轮回图的女神绘有头光，显然为神灵，而红殿轮回图则无头光，不具神格。与此同时，红殿轮回图顶部上方正中同时还绘有轮回图常见的拥抱者无常大鬼。诺伊曼借此认为，红殿轮回图的

6 Helmut F. Neumann: “The Wheel of Life in the Twelfth Century Western Tibetan Cave Temple of Pedongpo,” pp. 81-82. 耿江萍译、廖旸校汉译本：《12 世纪西藏西部白东布石窟寺生死轮图》，第 84 页。

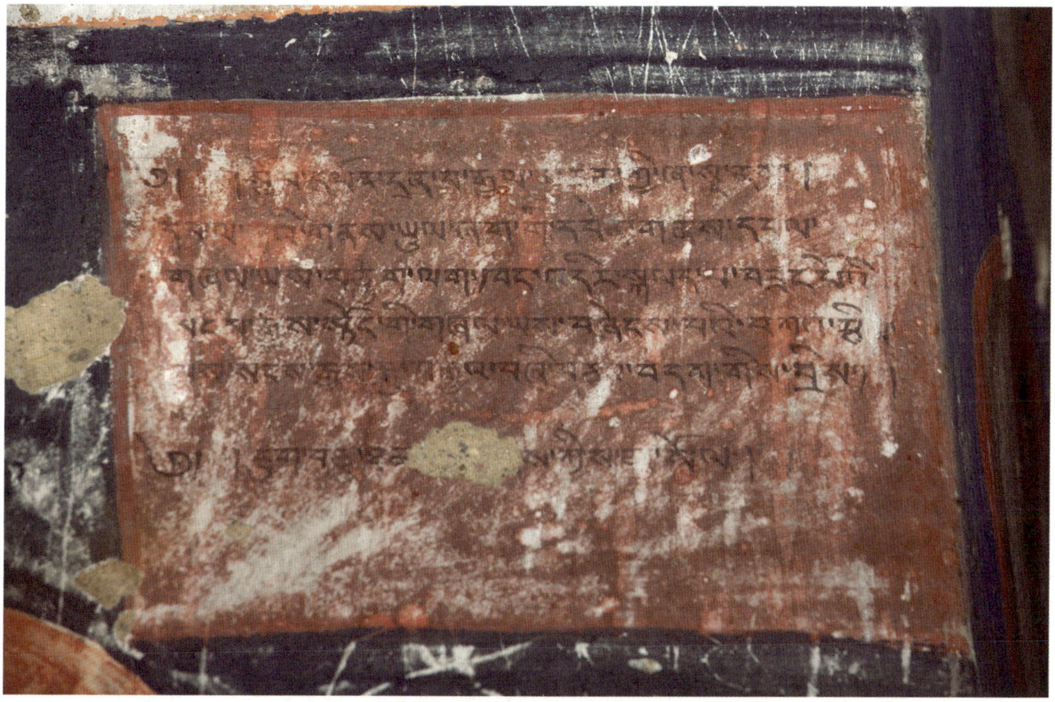

图 3　白东波石窟甬道西壁藏文题记（廖旸拍摄）

构图融合白东波的女神和常见的无常大鬼的构图而成。[7] 经仔细观察，这一结论有待于进一步斟酌，因为白东波甬道西壁轮回图上方正中的同一位置残存了一个类似于头部形状的白色区域，壁面虽然受损，已看不出任何纹样，但其上仍残痕有颜料。由此推测，这一位置原来极有可能描绘的也是无常大鬼的头部。倘若如此，白东波甬道与托林寺红殿门廊轮回图在这一区域的构图并无区别，二者的区别在于白东波轮回图的构图与后世流行的构图模式完全相同，即以轮轴和轮辐来构图六道画面，而托林寺红殿则并非如此。它不仅没有轮辐的分隔，而且中心描绘的是佛教的宇宙世界，以须弥山为中心、大海为背景来构图的。显而易见，二者在圆轮之内的构图来自两个不同传统的粉本。

在轮回图顶部、亦即拥抱轮回图的两位女神和无常大鬼的南侧绘有 2 僧 4 俗 6 位供养人像，同时在北侧题写有一则藏文题记（图 3）。题记书写于方框内，红底墨字，共 6 行，为邬金体。题记虽然不是十分清晰且一处文字脱落，但内容涉及白东波

7　Helmut F. Neumann: "The Wheel of Life in the Twelfth Century Western Tibetan Cave Temple of Pedongpo," pp. 75-84. 耿江萍译、廖旸校：《12 世纪西藏西部白东布石窟寺生死轮图》，第 79-84 页。

石窟所在地及其名称和施主的名字及壁画的内容等重要信息。该则题记的汉译文虽在2007年的《文物》上发表，但未给出藏文原文。其译文是："……陈巴坚赞大师卜算言示，于'白'地方龙行聚处夏卡幽静地方之佛堂内应建千佛之身，鄙人敬绘九百四十尊。六十尊……"[8]

鉴于这则题记的重要性，笔者在此给出藏文的拉丁转写和尝试性的译文：

第一行：// slob dpon dran pa rgyal mtshan gyi zhal snga nas/

第二行：dpal (zhu)vi gnas yul zhag gi dben gnas dpal

第三行：gzhal yas gtsug lag khang vdir skald pa bzang povi

第四行：sangs rgyas stong gi gzhal yas bzhengs pavi bkav rtsi…

第五行：sangs rgyal rgu brgyav bzhi bcuv bdag gis bris //

第六行：// drug bcu tha(m)……s gis (m)a sol //

译文：

遵照上师琛巴坚赞的旨意，在此白（须）之地夏地方吉祥幽静的吉祥无量祖拉康殿中绘制贤劫千佛。本人绘制九百四十身佛像。六十（身）……（未绘）。[9]

上师琛巴坚赞由于缺乏相关记载，迄今虽然无考，但从题记清楚可知，白东波石窟所在地在古代（11-12世纪）被称为"夏（zhag）"，并且属于"白（须）（dpal [zhu]）"这样的一个大地方。石窟原名"无量祖拉康殿（gzhal yas gtsug lag khang）"，其中绘制的千佛为贤劫千佛，而且是"遵照上师琛巴坚赞（slob dpon dran pa rgyal mtshan）的旨意"绘制而成的。同时可知，贤劫千佛壁画都出自一人之手，而且因洞窟面积等原因，只绘制了其中的940身佛像，其余60身未能跃然壁上。对比现存787身佛像，153身佛像已经脱落。

甬道东壁壁画由上、中、下三部分组成，中间由线条分割（图4）。上部区域最小，画由2身神灵和装饰纹样组成，神灵身份有待认定；中部区域为长方形条带，其间构图7身菩萨，其身份也有待进一步辨识。他们都坐于双重仰覆莲座上，造型均为一面二臂，头绘头光，上身裸露，下身着短裙裤，双手所持法器一手相同，均为长条形的叶子；双脚或结跏趺坐，或半跏趺坐，或结舒相坐，姿势舒展，婀娜多姿。下部

8 四川大学中国藏学研究所、四川大学历史文化学院考古系、西藏自治区文物局：《西藏阿里札达县象泉河流域白东波村早期佛教遗存的考古调查》，《文物》2007年第6期，第77页。此译文因题记抄录或其他原因，有漏译之处。

9 感谢中国社会科学院的廖旸研究员提供清晰的题记照片，特别感谢西藏社会科学院的巴桑旺堆研究员在四川大学担任特聘教授期间与笔者识读和讨论这则题记。

图 4　白东波石窟甬道东壁《母虎本生》故事壁画

分区域的构图最大，为东壁壁画表现的主体。除左上方和左下方（亦即北段上下壁）所绘 1 身一面六臂观音和数身一面二臂菩萨外，绝大部分画面构图的都是树木、身着世俗服饰的菩萨（除头上的三叶冠外，均为世俗装束）、俗人、动物和建筑等纹样。他们三三两两为一组，间或题写有墨书藏文题记。其中，在右侧的树林中绘有一只老虎，老虎旁边绘有一人，同时在树上搭有一件衣服。在此场景之下，残存有一处题记框，遗憾的是，题记已无踪迹。此处题写的题记分为两种，一种有题记框，但其内题记均已消失；另一种则无方框，大多数题记虽然漫漶不清，仍有几则题记尚能辨识，它们从上到下依次如下：

顶部头戴白色宽沿帽男子与其右的树上休憩的鸟之间题写有一则题记，为“ngu zhing tshol ba”，意为“边哭边找”。北段顶部六臂菩萨与树冠上嬉戏的猴子下面之间、亦即两位头戴白色宽沿帽男子的头部题写有两行题记：“rim vgro（承事）……//……”；同时在其右侧（南侧）两棵树下绘有一位仰视的妇女，此处题写有三行题记：“rim vgro ba gcig gis // gcig mthong nas // gzhon nu ga re zer ba”，意为“侍者个个面面相觑，问‘童子何处？’”；同时在仰视妇女正下方的一颗树前绘有两位妇女，二人似乎正并肩前行，其右侧题写有两行题记：“……log nas tshol //tu ches pa”，意为

“……返回后前去寻找”；紧接其下位置，绘有一顶蓝色帐篷，其内一位身着红袍的人正躺在床上，一侍女坐在床前，在此场景下方也题写有两行题记：“……rim vgro ba（侍者）// ……”。

在上述题记中，“rim vgro ba”一词反复出现。按《藏汉大词典》，该词主要有两个含义：其一，承事者，即侍者；其二，“诵经祈福的僧侣”，即举行祈福禳灾的人。同时结合老虎及虎前所躺之人和寻找童子等题记内容和场景推测，这组画面表现的内容是一个完整的故事，应为佛本生故事之一《母虎本生》故事。[10] 在这组故事之下，表现的是楼房和大批俗人和供养人，由于画面磨损严重，难以辨认。

弧形斜坡式的甬道藻井北高南低，以蓝色为底色，同时在中心和左右两侧等距地构图了三条红色为底色的装饰条带。其上绘满了各种以树木、团花、联珠等为主的连续植物纹样。其中联珠与枝叶纹组成的纹样与日土县乌江乡丁穹拉康石窟藻井中的枝叶纹如出一辙。[11]

从风格类比来看，白东波石窟千佛坐像和立佛的风格不仅都与毗邻的东嘎 1-3 号窟和皮央 79 号窟壁画表现的佛像非常相似，体现出显著的克什米尔风格（图 1-2），[12] 而且甬道东、西两壁供养人和叙事场景中描绘的人物的服饰（图 4）也与东嘎、皮央石窟、托林寺 55 塔、日土县丁穹拉康石窟、甚至是古代拉达克地区的塔波寺早期壁画中的供养人如出一辙：男人头戴宽沿帽，身着三角大翻领的长袍，腰间系带，足穿靴子；妇女也身着三角大翻领长袍，腰间系带，足蹬靴子，头发或编成数条细长的小辫，悬瀑在身体前后。[13]

其次，从题记保存的文字和书写特征来看，其中保留的部分古藏文书写特征与 11-12 世纪的特征吻合。例如，贤劫之意的藏文“skal dpa”一词中仍保留了古藏文中

---

10 2016 年 11 月，在浙江大学召开的“图像学与风格史：亚洲宗教美术研究方法论”学术会议上，德国莱比锡科学院的孟瑜博士在其发表的论文中认定，此处壁画的题材为《母虎本生》故事，并将其与夏鲁寺同一题材壁画进行了文本与图像之间的比较。

11 分别参见陕西省考古研究院、西藏自治区文物保护研究所、阿里地区文物局、日土县文物局：《西藏日土县丁穹拉康石窟群考古调查简报》，《考古与文物》2014 年第 6 期，第 34 页；四川大学中国藏学研究所、四川大学历史文化学院考古系、西藏自治区文物事业管理局编著：《东嘎·皮央遗迹考古报告》，成都：四川出版集团、四川人民出版社，2008 年，彩图 19-21、图 4-21、图 4-22 等；Deborah E. Klimburg-Salter, *Tabo, A Lamp for the Kingdom, Early Indo-Tibetan Buddhist Art in the Western Himalaya*, Thames and Hudson, New York, 1997, figs.23,123.

12 四川大学中国藏学研究所、四川大学历史文化学院考古系、西藏自治区文物事业管理局编著：《东嘎·皮央遗迹考古报告》，彩图 23 和 25。

13 分别参见四川大学中国藏学研究所、四川大学历史文化学院考古系、西藏自治区文物事业管理局编著：《东嘎·皮央遗迹考古报告》；陕西省考古研究院、西藏自治区文物保护研究所、阿里地区文物局、日土县文物局：《西藏日土县丁穹拉康石窟群考古调查简报》，图八一九、一五、一七和一九。

的再后加字“d”；意为百的藏文“brgyav”和十的藏文“bcuv”保留了早期文字中的后加字“v”；同时，千佛之意的藏文“stong”和“ca”等词语和字母的书写，仍保留了吐蕃时期古藏文的书写特征（图 3）。

再次，千佛名号题记后部分题写的《缘起偈》在 11-12 世纪阿里地区制作的擦擦中十分盛行。[14]《缘起偈》是世尊最初所度的五比丘之一马胜（Aśvajit）为舍利弗所说，仅四句而含摄四谛，示法身不生不灭，是佛法要义的根本体现，因首句而得名缘起（生）偈、缘起法颂等等。最早出自 9 世纪初由天菩提（Surendrabodhi）和智军（Ye shes sde）译入的《缘起大乘经》（梵 *Ārya-Pratītyasamutpāda-nāma-mahāyānasūtra*）[15]，著录于吐蕃时代的译经目录《旁塘目录》（*dkar chag vphang thang ma*）第 225 号、《丹噶目录》（*dkar chag ldan kar ma*）第 234 号。[16] 藏文文献称之为《缘起心要》，强调其精髓、深刻。唐高宗永隆元年（680）中天竺法师地婆诃罗（Divākara“日照”，613-687）与西明寺沙门圆测（613-696）等五人译《造塔功德经》中直接称此偈为《佛法身》。[17] 在稍后唐 · 释义净（635-713）所译的《浴佛功德经》中又被称之为“法颂舍利”。[18] 不仅如此，藏文在此对梵文的转写十分简洁，没有繁复的上下加字的叠缀，这些都属于早期转写的特点。此外，整个题记的字体、字头符号（yig mgo）和表示停顿的音节符号（tshig thung）也与此时期古藏文文献的书写特点完全一致。[19]

综上所述，以千佛为主的白东波石窟壁画应创作于 11 世纪，其下限应在 12 世纪。[20]

14 关于《缘起偈》的内容及其流变和与擦擦等艺术之间关系的详细研究，参见廖旸：《西藏西部擦擦铭文探索》，见熊文彬、李逸之主编：《西藏古格擦擦艺术》，北京：中国藏学出版社，2016 年，第 14-56 页。

15 德格版甘珠尔第 212 号，通帙第六二，tsha125a3-125b7。

16 Adelheid Herrmann-Pfandt, *Die lHan Kar Ma: Ein früher Katalog der ins Tibetische übersetzten buddhistischen Texte, kritische Neuausgabe mit Einleitung und Materialien*, Wien: Verlag der Österreichischen Akademie der Wissenschaften, 2008, S. 123-124.

17《大正藏》卷 16，第 801 页。

18《大正藏》卷 16，第 800 页。

19 详见巴桑旺堆：《关于古藏文写本的研究方法的再探索》，《中国藏学》2009 年第 3 期，第 65-73 页。

20 赫尔穆特 · F. 诺伊曼将该窟壁画的年代定为 12 世纪，见 Helmut F. Neumann, “The Wheel of Life in the Twelfth Century Western Tibetan Cave Temple of Pedongpo,” pp. 82-84. 耿江萍译、廖旸校汉译本：《12 世纪西藏西部白东布石窟寺生死轮图》，第 79-90 页。霍巍教授则将其年代定位于 11-13 世纪，为西藏西部石窟发展第一个阶段的代表。见霍巍：《西藏西部石窟壁画中几种艺术风格的分析——兼论西藏西部石窟壁画艺术三个主要的发展阶段》，《藏学学刊》2014 年第 1 辑，第 156 页。

二、千佛石窟

千佛石窟位于日土县班公湖北面的乌江（dbu byang）村，当地人称为“千佛寺（stong sku lha khang）”。2015 年 8 月 13 日，笔者与西藏文物保护研究所的夏格旺堆和李林辉研究员一起，对该石窟进行了考察。

该石窟入口处的墙体已经全部坍塌，只残存正壁和左右两壁。石窟坐北朝南，高约 2.4-2.6 米。现存平面呈梯形，东西长、南北窄：正（北）壁长 6.8 米，南壁遗迹长 5.85 米；西壁宽 5.5 米，东壁宽 3.6 米，壁画为殿内现存的唯一艺术遗迹，主要由千佛、坛城和佛传故事等组成（图 5）。壁画大多被毁，其中正壁相对完整，左右两壁底部已大部脱落或已漫漶不清，保存状况极差。不过，从图像配置和风格特点来看，该窟壁画仍是西藏西部后弘期佛教艺术发展的重要一环。

左壁壁画由上、中、下三个区域组成。上部为一排上师和大成就者。中部为壁画主体，平行绘有 5 铺坛城；下部绘有一铺坛城和 6 身诸佛菩萨像。各个坛城中心的主尊像或已被毁或已漫漶不清，其题材已无法一一辨认。只有下部唯一的坛城底部因题写有墨书藏文题记，其内容非常清楚，为除盖障坛城，题记原文为“sgrib sel gyi

图 5　日土县千佛石窟及其千佛壁画

dkyil vkhor”。

正壁壁画也由三个区域组成。正壁中心主尊为一佛二菩萨大像，其上为通排千佛小像，宝座下长方形条带内构图有诸菩萨、护法和供养人像。与此同时，主尊像将中部主体壁画分为左右对称的两个部分。其中，两侧顶部分别为 7 排小佛，每排小佛的数量介于 38-37 身不等；中部主尊像两侧同时分别构图有 5 个佛龛，其中最两端的佛龛中分别表现的是一对对坐的上师像，其服饰和造型与左壁中的上师一致；上师像与中心佛像间分别绘有四个佛龛，其内分别绘有四佛。此八佛的构图也与中心佛像相同，为一佛二菩萨组合。每位佛陀组像之间、亦即在二胁侍菩萨的两侧分别绘有 4 排共 8 身的小佛像（图 6）。下部则又在左右两侧分别对称地构图有 6 排千佛小像，每排千佛的数量也在 35 身左右。整个画面虽然受损严重，但主尊像依然可看出身着红色袈裟、袒露右肩，右手下垂，作触地印，左手于胸前结禅定印，双脚结金刚跏趺坐，端坐于双重仰覆莲座上，表现的应是释迦牟尼佛像。须弥座两侧绘有一对白色狮子，中间盖布上绘法轮。背光从下到上仍保存有大象、狮羊、摩羯鱼等纹样。二胁侍菩萨均侧向佛一侧站立，裸露上身，下身着彩色条带裙裤，其身份已难以辨识。由于两侧八佛的造型、尤其是能辨别他们身份的身色、手印、宝座上描绘的乘骑和象征法

图 6　千佛石窟正壁一佛二菩萨及其左右两侧千佛小像

器残损严重，因此难以准确辨认。正壁下部、亦即主尊像的左右两侧是按方框构图的佛传故事，画面严重磨损，只能依稀可辨，部分场景仍残留有墨书邬金体藏文题记，不过已不成句，难以释读。从中心一排 9 身佛陀的数量及其部分手印等来看，中心部分壁画可能表现的是药师佛坛城壁画。

右壁壁画构图也分为三部分：顶部为两排上师和大成就者像；中部主体部分则由一铺巨大的十一面观音像和另外 3 铺坛城组成。坛城题材已难以准确辨识，依稀可看出中心的两铺坛城的主尊分别表现的是两位佛陀。底部为两排菩萨、护法神和供养人像。

从风格上看，千佛寺石窟体现出三个比较明显的特点：其一，上师像大多身披大氅、内着坎肩、袒露右肩，其袈裟的样式和人物的造型与拉萨林周县达隆寺和昌都类乌齐寺保存的 13-14 世纪达隆风格唐卡中的上师像非常类似。其二，9 佛胁侍的造型和装束具有比较明显的波罗风格特征，与札达县卡孜乡的帕尔嘎布石窟胁侍菩萨非常近似。二胁侍菩萨身材修长，高髻、上身裸露、下身着裙裤，造型呈明显的 S 形。佛陀背光的形制和纹样也与帕尔嘎布石窟如出一辙。[21] 其三，背光、头冠等部分纹样带有尼泊尔风格特征。由此推测，千佛寺石窟壁画应绘制于 13-14 世纪左右，其中千佛与众不同的构图样式丰富了这一题材的构图模式。

三、译师殿

译师殿（lo tswa ba lha khang），全称译师白殿（lo tswa ba lha khang dkar po），位于札达县萨让乡日巴（ri pa）村。2014 年 9 月 2-3 日，笔者与陕西省考古研究院的张建林研究员、田有前副研究员和札达县文物局洛旦局长一起对该寺进行了为期两天的考察。殿名来自当地百姓口传，称该殿系阿里地区著名大译师仁钦桑布（958-1055）所建。1933 年对该寺进行过考察的图齐和盖尔西也推测，该寺可能是《仁钦桑布传》记载仁钦桑布曾在 21 个小地方所建的佛寺之一。古格·次仁加布根据仁钦桑布的《中

21 四川大学中国藏学研究所、四川大学历史文化学院考古系、西藏自治区文物局、西藏阿里地区文化广播电视局：《西藏阿里札达县帕尔嘎尔布石窟遗址》，《文物》2003 年第 9 期，第 42-59 页，图一一、一四、一五。关于壁画的年代，该文第 57 页认为："年代的下限当在 13 或 14 世纪前后。"

图 7　札达县译师殿西壁千佛壁画、泥塑背光与供柜

传》认为，该殿为仁钦桑布时期所建，仁钦桑布不仅为寺院开光，并多次造访。[22]

译师殿坐西朝东，平面为正方形，面积不大。殿内现存泥塑背光和壁画，壁画题材主要为千佛、上师、佛传故事、地方护法神和供养人像。泥塑背光和莲座遗迹主要保存在正壁（西壁，图 7）和东壁（殿门所在墙体，图 8），其中正壁底部残存 5 身，均为绘塑结合形式（图 7），亦即背光以壁画形式表现，塑像由雕塑形式表现。中间泥塑背光最大，1933 年图齐和盖尔西考察时，塑像仍较完整，表现的是四面普明大日如来佛[23]，现只存头光顶部巨大的兽面衔摩尼宝珠和双摩羯鱼尾造型壁画。其余 4 身泥塑背光较小，同时背光之间上方的壁面绘有供养菩萨。由此推测，原来此处

22　次仁加布：《阿里教法史·雪域美饰》（*mngav ris chos vbyung gangs ljongs mdzes rgyan*），藏文本，拉萨：西藏人民出版社，2006 年，第 314 页。但次仁加布未给出这本传记的名字，在现有的《中传》中也未发现相同的记载；同时参见谢萧（Christina Scherrer-Schaub）、崔可华（Kurt Tropper）著，杨鸿蛟汉译：《王者、译师、师尊：关于（阿里）日巴译师殿部分壁画和题记的研究》，见艾瑞卡·福特、梁俊艳、黛博拉·克林博格·索特、张云、海尔默特·托舍主编：《8-15 世纪中西部西藏历史、文化与艺术》，北京：中国藏学出版社，2015 年，第 10 页。

23　照片参见谢萧、崔可华著，杨鸿蛟汉译：《王者、译师、师尊：关于（阿里）日巴译师殿部分壁画和题记的研究》，第 11 页图 2。

图 8 译师殿东壁泥塑莲座、背光与千佛壁画

的泥塑表现的是中央的大日如来、东方的阿閦佛、南方的宝生佛、西方的无量光佛和北方的不空成就佛等五方佛像。东壁现存三身泥塑莲座和背光，殿门两侧和上方正中各一身，莲座均高离地面，因此原来的塑像均为悬塑。三身背光均为椭圆形火焰纹，其中殿门上方者在背光内还带有桃形头光。底部两侧背光中原来的塑像表现的疑为护法神像。与此同时，殿门两侧莲座为由莲茎蔓延而成的高大茎状莲座，其中殿门北侧者保存十分完整，其表面绘有缠枝纹，其造型与札达县古格故城、托林寺的红殿、白殿和迦莎殿中保存的形制一致。

壁画主体千佛分布于四壁顶部垂帐纹下方，均为坐像，每身佛像下面都墨书有藏文邬金体的名号。除雨水的侵蚀和部分墙体小面积的脱落外，绝大多数壁画的保存相对比较完好。这些千佛描绘的也是贤劫千佛，其分布如下：

正壁（西壁）顶部为千佛，底部为五方佛泥塑，中部中心壁画为兽面和摩羯鱼等纹样构成的大日如来佛泥塑的背光，背光两侧为两组平行对称的上师像，上师像两侧又为连续构图千佛。其中，两组上师像上方构图有 3 排千佛，每排 26 身；上师像左右两侧又分别构图 2 排千佛，其中第一排 20 身，第二排 10 身（与千佛中的所有佛像相比，这 10 身佛像的形制较大）。由此可知，正壁共绘有 108 身佛像（图 7）。

壁中的两组上师像也分别题写有题记。两组上师像均位于大日如来佛泥塑及其背光上方的左右两侧，均由第一排三身一组的上师和第二排的单身上师组成，亦即每组共绘有 4 身上师像。其中，左侧一组第一排的三位上师像从左到右分别表现的是：佛密大师（头戴黄色尖顶班智达帽、面部右侧，身着袈裟、双手当胸作说法印，结金刚跏趺坐；题记：snangs rgyas bsang ba）、庆喜藏（除面部朝向前方外，其余造型特征都与佛密大师相同；题记为：kun dgav snying po la na mo）和释迦友（除面向左侧外，其余造型与佛密大师相同；题记：don la kas pa sheg kyab shes gnyen la na mo[意为：稽首善了义的释迦友]），其中庆喜藏为主尊；其下构图的单身上师为信作铠（头戴班智达帽、身体右侧，双手作说法印，结金刚跏趺坐；题记：sra ta ka ra la na mo）；右侧上师组像从左到右分别描绘的是：至尊阿底峡大师（阿底峡像大部已被雨水侵蚀的泥渍覆盖；题记：jo bo rje a ti sha la na mo）、天神上师益西沃（身着袈裟、袒露右肩、双手前身持念珠，结金刚跏趺坐；题记：lha bla ma ye shes vod la na mo）和小译师雷必喜饶（面部左侧，身着袈裟、袒露右肩，双手当胸作说法印，结金刚跏趺坐；题记：chun legs she la na mo），其中主尊为益西沃。其下表现的单身上师像为大译师仁钦桑布（身体左侧，其余造型与萨达噶拉像相同；题记：lo chen rin chen bzang po la na mo）。

这两组人物都与仁钦桑布大师密切相关。在布顿大师的著作《入瑜伽续海之舟》（*rnal vbyor rgyud kyi rgya mtshor vjug pavi gru gzing*）中，左侧第一排构图的佛密、庆喜藏和释迦友三人被誉为“瑜伽续之三能者”。其中佛密被冠以“善了义（ton la mkhas pa）”称号，释迦友被誉为“善语词（tshigs la mkhas pa）”，庆喜藏被誉为“精通了义和语词（don tshigs gnyis la mkhas pa）”。在此壁画题记中，“善了义”的桂冠虽然被戴在了释迦友的头上，但这与布顿大师的记载还是吻合，同时“精通了义和语词”的庆喜藏大师位于主尊的位置也在情理之中。他们三人分别与仁钦桑布合作翻译、厘定和撰著了大量的经典，不少著作都被收入藏文大藏经《甘珠尔》。[24] 三人之下的信作铠上师也是仁钦桑布的老师，曾将佛智（Buddhajñāna）的教法传给仁钦桑布。在右侧一组上师像中，中间的古格国王益西沃及其左、右的阿底峡大师和小译师雷必喜饶与仁钦桑布过往甚密。尤其是雷必喜饶，他不仅与仁钦桑布一起前往克什米尔学习、他还是仁钦桑布四大心传弟子之一，也是仁钦桑布的堂弟，经常帮助仁钦桑

24 关于仁钦桑布与该壁画中所表现的上师之间合作翻译、厘定的部分佛经，参见图齐：《仁钦桑波及公元 1000 年左右藏传佛教的复兴》，《梵天佛地》（*Indo-Tibetica*）卷二，魏正中、萨尔吉主编，上海：上海古籍出版社、意大利亚非研究院，2009 年，第 30-46 页。

图 9　译师殿北壁千佛及其题记局部

布主持一些宗教和世俗事务。[25]

此外，在五方佛背光之间还绘有数身供养菩萨，其中左右两端的金刚鬘菩萨（身体左侧，菩萨装，上身着紧身衣，露出乳房和腰部，下身着裙裤；右手当胸作说法印，左手上举，持花鬘；题记：phreng ba ma la na mo）、金刚灯菩萨（身体右侧，左手当胸作说法印，右手上举，持供灯，其余造型特征与金刚鬘菩萨相同；题记：mar me ma la na mo）及其题记尚能清晰可辨。此外，从图齐和盖尔西 1933 年拍摄的四面普明大日如来佛泥塑的照片可知，五方佛下同时还绘有一排诸佛菩萨壁画，现已被供柜全部遮挡。

南、北二壁布局相同，中间靠墙的立柱分别将壁面一分为二，东西两侧壁面面积大体一致。以北壁为例（图 9），其千佛的分布如下：东侧从上到下构图了 14 排佛像，每排 13 身左右，共绘 169 身佛像；西侧壁面千佛的分布与东侧相同，北壁共绘有 338 身佛像。南壁千佛分布与北壁相同，也绘有 338 身佛像。

25　关于这两组上师像及其配置和原因的探讨，参见谢萧、崔可华著，杨鸿蛟汉译：《王者、译师、师尊：关于（阿里）日巴译师殿部分壁画和题记的研究》，第 11-16 页，同时参见图 3 上师分布示意图。

图 10　译师殿东壁礼佛图及其题记

东壁千佛的构图相对复杂，除千佛外，还构图有供养人、地方神灵和个别本尊；与此同时，除壁画外，还构图了 3 尊泥塑。位于中心的殿门将东壁分为南、北两个部分。这些题材的构图从上到下依次是：顶部均对称地构图有 6 排千佛，除第 1 排千佛贯通南北外，其余 5 排每排分别构图千佛 11 身。南、北二侧中心的殿门上方为泥塑，千佛构图在泥塑的四周，同时在泥塑底部和门楣上方千佛的中间构图有数身地方神，并题写有藏文题记。其中牧区夜叉（题记：gnod sbyin vbrog gnas）、正知（题记：yang dag shes）、色邦（题记：sred sbong）和俊钦（题记：rgyun vchan）的题记尚能辨认。殿门两侧南北壁中央，构图的是泥塑及其背光和莲座，千佛则平行对称地构图在它们的周围。经统计，整个东壁总共绘有千佛 226 身。

综合上述，译师殿正壁绘佛像 108 身，南、北二壁各 338 身、东壁 226 身，整个佛殿共绘佛像 1000 身，与《圣贤劫经》等经典所载之千佛之数吻合。

此外，在东壁北侧底部千佛下方，还构图有 30 余位僧人和供养人，他们包括上师、王族、官吏和武士，并分别题写有题记，但保存状况较差，大多斑斑驳驳或模糊不清，部分壁画甚至脱落。画面分别围绕北端和中心表现的三位人物大像展开。北端绘有一位上师坐像，身着袈裟，头左侧，双手当胸作说法印，描绘的是天神喇嘛益西沃（题记：lha bla ma ye shes vod kyi zhal snga nas，意为“天神喇嘛益西沃阁下”），下方为供奉的僧众。与此同时，壁面中心绘有两位人物大像，二者相向而坐（图 10）。左侧人物身着袈裟，描绘的是至尊释迦沃（题记：lha rje btsun shva kya vod kyi zhal snga nas，意为“天神至尊大师释迦沃阁下”）；右侧人物缠头巾、外披大氅，内着长袍，系古格故城和托林寺红殿和白殿壁画表现的古格王朝王族成员的典型装束，表现的是洛桑（饶）丹陛下（题记：lha mi dbang chen po drung blo bzangs（rab）bstan gyi zhal snga nas，意为“神人之主洛桑（饶）丹阁下”）。二人两侧和下方绘有三排僧人、王族、官吏和武士装束的人物，均面向二者，正向他们致礼，整个画面为礼佛场景。礼佛人物周围题写的题记只有个别尚能清晰可辨，如董梅擦（题记：ldong mes tshar）等。

藻井由彩绘木板组成，纹样主要包括几何纹样、缠枝纹、吉祥八宝和相向吹号的金翅鸟等，线条流畅，色彩艳丽，其风格与托林寺和古格故城红殿和白殿现存藻井彩绘十分类似。

从壁画风格来看，译师殿壁画与托林寺和古格故城红、白殿 15-16 世纪的壁画非常一致，在西藏西部流行的克什米尔风格的基础上融合了大量的卫藏绘画的元素。值得注意的是，古格故城的金科殿（dkyil vkhor lha khang，亦即坛城殿）不仅与译师殿一样，也绘有释迦沃和仲洛桑像，而且也题写有相应的题记，[26] 这表明译师殿壁画与古格故城坛城殿壁画都创作于同一时期（待另文考述）。

四、千佛经典在西藏的流布

自佛教传入中国后，千佛在中国的汉传和藏传佛教都十分流行，礼拜千佛的千佛寺或千佛堂繁若星辰。汉传佛教中千佛题材的传入无论文献和图像都早于藏传佛教。据研究，自支谦从公元 223-253 年间译入《梵网经》或《梵网菩萨戒经》（*Brahmajāla sūtra*）以来，与千佛相关的经典《如来不思议秘密大乘经》（*Tathagat-acintya-guhaya-nirdeśa*）、《妙法莲花经》或《法华经》（*Saddharma-puṇḍarīka-sūtra*）、《贤劫经》（*Bhadrakalpika-sūtra*）、《悲华经》（*Karuṇāpuṇḍarīka-sūtra*）、《华严经》（*Avatamska /Gaṇḍavyūha*）、《金刚顶一切如来真实摄大乘现证大教王经》（*Sarva-tathāgata-tattva-saṅgraha*）和《千佛名经》等主要经典也相继译成汉文，成为汉传佛教艺术依据的主要经典。

26 张蕊峡、张建林、夏格旺堆：《阿里壁画线图集》，拉萨：西藏人民出版社，2011 年。

藏传佛教与千佛相关的经典则最早从8-9世纪的吐蕃时期开始译入，译入藏文的千佛内容的经典主要有由作明狮子（Vidyakarasimha）和贝央（dpal dbyangs）于公元755年左右译入的《贤劫经》（Toh 94），胜友（Jinamitra）等人9世纪译入的《悲华经》（Toh 112）、《如来不思议秘密大乘经》（Toh 47），胜友、天菩提（Surendrabodhi/lha dbang byang chub）和智军（ye shes sde）于9世纪合译的《华严经》（Toh 44）和信作铠（Śraddhākaravarman）与仁钦桑布于10世纪译入的《真实义摄经》（*Sarva-tathāgata-tattva-saṅgraha*）等，[27] 也成为藏传佛教艺术千佛表现的主要依据。

藏文《贤劫经》的经名为《贤劫大乘经》（*bskal pa bzang po zhes ba theg pa chen povi mdo*），简称《贤劫经》（*mdo sde bskal bzang*），收录在藏文大藏经《甘珠尔》中，由印度堪布作明狮子、藏族译师贝央翻译，贝孜（dpal brtsegs）校定，全文26品。该经为佛祖释迦牟尼在祇园精舍时应喜王菩萨（mchog tu dgav bavi rgyal po）之请而说，分为三个部分：第一部分论述诸种三昧及其功德；第二部分叙述佛陀的殊胜功德并列举贤劫千佛名称及其出生地、族姓、父母、子嗣、弟子、寿元、神通、涅槃、灵塔等诸事；第三部分讲述持诵本经的各种功德和对千佛的供养等。[28]

《贤劫经》载及的千佛名号鉴于篇幅所限难以一一笔录，其中前十佛分别为拘留孙佛（de bzhin gshegs pa vkhor vjig）、拘那含佛（de bzhin gshegs pa gser thub）、迦叶佛（de bzhin gshegs pa vod srung）、释迦牟尼佛（de bzhin gshegs pa shva kya thub pa）、弥勒佛（de bzhing shegs pa byams pa）、狮子佛（de bzhin gshegs pa seng ge）、明焰佛（de bzhin gshegs pa rab gsal）、大势佛（de bzhin gshegs pa mthus pa）、妙华佛（de bzhin gshegs pa me tog）、华氏佛（de gzhin gshegs pa me tog gnyis pa）。最后十位千佛分别为断势力佛（de bzhin gshegs pa shugs kyis vdor ba）、极势力佛（de bzhin gshegs pa stob can）、智慧华佛（de bzhin gshegs pa shes rab me tog）、坚音佛（de bzhin gshegs pa brtan pavi dbyangs）、众生乐舒心佛（de bzhin gshegs pa sems can snying po bde thang ldan pa）、妙义佛（de bzhin gshegs pa don dag gsal ba）、喜明佛（de bzhin gshegs pa dgyes pa gsal ba）、狮子颜佛（de bzhin gshegs pa seng gevi zhal）、妙髻佛（de bzhin gshegs pa gtsug phud）、光明佛（de bzhin gshegs pa snang ba mdzad pa）。[29] 与汉文本《贤劫经》比较，汉藏译本在千佛排列的顺序上并不完全相同。

本考察记涉及的两座石窟和一座寺院就与贤劫千佛直接有关。其中白东波石窟

27 Lokesh Chandra, *Iconography of the Thousand Buddhas*, pp.1-2.

28 参见拉萨版藏文大藏经《甘珠尔》ka函，165a-588a页。

29 分别参见拉萨版藏文大藏经《甘珠尔》ka函，174b-176b、485b-488a页。

的千佛题记明确说明表现的就是贤劫千佛，[30] 日巴村译师殿中的千佛壁画按图齐描绘的也是这同一题材。日土县千佛石窟中的千佛虽无题记，可能也与贤劫千佛有关。不仅如此，由仁钦桑布创建于 996 年并在 1042 年完成修复的塔波寺主殿的转经道上壁也绘有一圈的贤劫千佛壁画。[31] 由此可见，贤劫千佛这一题材在古代西藏西部比较盛行，它们都来自吐蕃以来译入的《贤劫经》。实际上，《贤劫经》对藏传佛教艺术中千佛题材的影响不仅仅限于西藏西部地区，对整个西藏、甚至全中国藏传佛教流布之地都产生了持续而又广泛的影响。直到清代，拉萨雪印经院仍在根据《贤劫经》刊刻和印刷贤劫千佛版画，如章嘉·乳必多吉编纂的梵文、藏文、蒙古文、满文和汉文五体合璧的贤劫千佛版画。[32] 与此同时，札达县白东波石窟、日土县千佛石窟和札达县译师殿的千佛壁画根据风格类比，大致分别创作于 11-12、13-14 和 15-16 世纪这三个不同的历史阶段，大致勾勒出后弘期以来西藏西部藏传佛教艺术风格演变的大致轨迹和不同历史阶段的风格特点。

30 由于各种因素，笔者尚未将白东波石窟和译师殿题写的千佛名号与藏文本《贤劫经》之载进行一一比对，留待将来进行。

31 Deborah E. Klimburg-Salter, *Tabo, A Lamp for the Kingdom, Early Indo-Tibetan Buddhist Art in the Western Himalaya*, Thames and Hudson, New York, 1998, p.154 and fig.162.

32 关于雪印经院刊印的贤劫千佛版画及其研究，参见 Lokesh Chandra, *Iconography of the Thousand Buddhas*, pp.1-2.

The Bird-faced Monk and the Beginnings of the New Tantric Tradition: Part One*

Leonard W.J. van der Kuijp (Harvard University)

Ter nagedachtenis van Tshe ring rgyal po (ca. 1961-2015), proud son of Gu ge.

rgyal po 'od kyi mtha' can dang //
dge slong bya'i gdong can gyis //
nga'i bstan pa rgyas par byed //

The king with the name ending in *'od* and,
The monk with the face of a bird,
Will increase my Teaching.[1]

1. Preamble

In the late tenth and eleventh centuries, the expected friction of distance separating the Tibetan plateau and the Indian subcontinent was either suspended [a] by the conviction that the spread of Buddhism was a vehicle for good individual and shared karma, irrespective of the potential financial rewards, [b] by the promise of financial advantage and gain – the Buddhist dharma is indeed precious and can easily be made economically advantageous to those who possess it or to those who can convince others that they are in possession of its

* Part Two will be published in the *Zangxue xuekan* 藏学学刊 / *Bod rig pa'i dus deb/ Journal of Tibetology*, vol. 17.

1 The king and monk referred to in this prophecy allegedly by the historical Buddha are, respectively, Lha bla ma Ye shes 'od and Lo tsā ba Rin chen bzang po (958-1055); for this and other prophecies concerning Lha bla ma, see my "A Fifteenth Century Biography of Lha bla ma Ye shes 'od (947-1019/24): Part One: Its Prolegomenon and Prophecies*," *Tibet in Dialogue with its Neighbours: History, Culture and Art of Central and Western Tibet, 8th-15th Century*, ed. E. Forte *et al.*, Wiener Studien zur Tibetologie und Buddhismuskunde, Heft 88 (Wien: Arbeitskreis für Tibetische und Buddhistische Studien/China Tibetology Research Center, 2015), 369-370.

sacred and spiritually efficacious teachings and rituals-, or [c] by an agreeable combination of both. Whatever the suspension, its result was that a veritable avalanche of new, hitherto unknown works, all purporting to represent either the "enlightened word of the Buddha/*buddha*" (*buddhavacana*) or to have issued from the pen of *bona fide* and recognized Indian Buddhist masters, entered and spread over the Tibetan cultural landscape in new translations and/or in revisions of earlier ones. A Tibetan Sanskrit scholar (*lo tsā ba*) who professed Buddhist beliefs – I do not know of any Tibetan Lo tsā ba-translators of Buddhist texts who were not recognized as being Buddhist by religious conviction – and his Indic/Newar/Kashmiri master-informant were usually responsible for crafting these translations that were done either in the northern reaches of the subcontinent, including Kashmir and the Kathmandu Valley, or somewhere in the Tibetan region. The more confident bilingual Tibetans and those Indic/Newar/Kashmiri masters who were *tibétisant* also managed to translate some of these texts by themselves without the assistance of a "native informant" – these translations are usually characterized as *rang 'gyur*. It was thus a time of wide-ranging literary and religious discoveries that were of such a sustained intensity as to have no parallel in the history of the world, let alone in the history of the Tibetan cultural area. It was a time that later Tibetan historians would call the subsequent propagation (*phyi dar*) of Buddhism[2]; the early propagation (*snga dar*), which began in the late eighth century, had come to an abrupt halt in the middle of the ninth century with the collapse of the Tibetan empire.

There is of course nothing wrong with a little religious enthusiasm, but it would be wrong to assume that the outright ebullience with which this flood of new and probably barely understood literature was greeted by a relatively small segment of the population had no serious social and intellectual downsides. The influx of a large number of different Buddhist religious texts of especially the tantric variety, one that proceeded in a rather haphazard way, created a series of problems that some felt needed urgent addressing. And, indeed, the few directives that we possess from the late tenth and eleventh century by the concerned powers – for these, see below – clearly suggest this. For one, this influx must have clouded the better judgment of a few to the extent that it prevented them from

2 For some notes on the *phyi dar*, see H. Stoddard, "'Rekindling the Flame', a Note on Royal Patronage in Tenth Century Tibet," *The Relationship between Religion and State* (*chos srid zung 'brel*) *in Traditional Tibet*, ed. Ch. Cüppers (Lumbini: Lumbini International Research Institute, 2004), 49-104, two plates.

seeing that some of these writings might not be *bona fide* Buddhist texts at all, even if it may not be altogether clear what kind of criteria they might have used to distinguish what was and what was not authentically tantric Buddhist. There is a hint in the literature that at least one individual had simply asked those Indic and Nepalese individuals with whom he had come in contact on his travels whether such and such a work was actually considered Buddhist and that, when they had answered in the negative, he expunged these later from his list of authentic Buddhist writings. This was especially the case with the anonymous (or seemingly anonymous) texts that purported to be the word of the Buddha or *buddha*, and not necessarily those works men in search of a decent (or an indecent) livelihood had composed and propagated. Further, there was no central authority that could vouch for the "canonicity" of these works, let alone one that was able to pass judgment on their authenticity and doctrinal integrity. The vulnerability of this situation was of course further exacerbated by the fact that, in contradistinction to Theravāda Buddhism,[3] even "the very idea" of a canon in Mahayana (and Vajrayana) Buddhism seems to have been absent in the subcontinent. Why this should have been so is certainly worthy of sustained exploration. Further, the itinerancy of some of the South Asian men who had come to Tibet suggests that they were not associated with one or another religious institution such as a monastery. There do not seem to have been many voices that may have objected to the Vajrayana Budddhism or they had been effectively silenced long ago, and the scholarly practice of writing large-scale and intricate commentaries, informed by a sizable "secondary" literature, suggestive of access to a decent library, already enjoyed a long and distinguished history when this form of Buddhist theory and practice was introduced to the Tibetan world. The "authenticity" of these works was not always clear and some were arguably only marginally "Buddhist" in inspiration or were purported to be so by those who carried them into the Tibetan area or by those Tibetans who had acquired copies of these works in the subcontinent. Needless to say, this situation easily lent itself to abuse by unscrupulous individuals, both from the subcontinent as well as native Tibetans, who initiated and led a number of popular cults in the tenth to twelfth centuries after which they either were discredited by the prevailing religious establishment and thus died a natural death, or were stripped from their obvious

3 See here the seminal paper of S. Collins, "On the Very Idea of the Pali Canon," *Journal of the Pali text Society* 15 (1990), 89-126.

problematic parts and silently incorporated into a form of 'orthodox' religious practice.[4] The *lo tsā ba*-translator Rin chen bzang po, this bird-faced son of Mnga' ris, may very well have been the very first individual in Tibetan religious history to essay to bring some form of 'orthodoxy' and structure in Vajrayāna praxis and its textual foundations.

Born in 958 in Zhang zhung, in Mnga' ris, in the far western region of Tibet, Rin chen bzang po was one of the great Tibetan bilingual masters, who was active during this period. His life spanned almost a hundred years and thus coincided with the very inception of this movement, this great on-going experiment in which a large and vibrant portion of one culture was transferred to another, this renaissance that, taking its cues from what had transpired in the Tibetan empire during the late eighth and first half of the ninth century, was to change forever the religious landscape of the Tibetan cultural area and beyond.[5] Rin chen bzang po himself had been among the handful of young West Tibetan men whom King Khri lde srong gtsug btsan (947-1019/24), ruler of the wealthy area of Gu ge in Mnga' ris, had handpicked in *circa* 974 to pursue the study of Sanskrit and Buddhism in general. In order that they accomplish this idea of his, the king had provided them with the necessary financial support and sent them to Kashmir and other areas of the Indian subcontinent. Himself a born-again Buddhist, the depth of the king's religious conviction ultimately motivated him to abandon the secular life and take full monastic vows in 989. At this point, he adopted the name in religion of Ye shes 'od.[6] Owing to the fact that he was a scion of Tibet's royal family and even if perhaps more of an honorary than an actual guru-teacher, his name is prefixed by *lha bla ma*, where *lha* indicates his royal family background and *bla ma*, that is, guru, points to him being regarded as a teacher. While he abdicated his rule over Gu ge in favor

4 The authoritative studies are still D. Martin, "The Star King and the Four Children of Pehar: Popular Religious Movements of 11th- to 12th-Century Tibet," 49 (1996), 171-195, and his "Lay Religious Movements in 11th- and 12th-Century Tibet: A Survey of Sources," *Kailash* 18 (1996), 23-55; but see also C.A. Scherrer-Schaub, "Contre le libertinage. Un opuscule de Tabo adressé aux tantristes hérétiques?," *Le parole e i marmi. Studi in onore di Raniero Gnoli nel suo 70° compleanno*, ed. R. Torella with C. Cicuzza, *Serie Orientale Roma*, vol. 92.2 (Rome: Istituto italiano per l'Africa e l'Oriente, 2001), 703 ff.

5 R.M. Davidson has continued to relate its story in important detail even if his focus on Mnga' ris and Rin chen bzang po *per se* was a bit succinct; see *The Tibetan Renaissance: Tantric Buddhism in the Rebirth of Tibetan Culture* (New York: Columbia University Press, 2005).

6 See my "A Fifteenth Century Biography of Lha bla ma Ye shes 'od (947-1019/24): Part One: Its Prolegomenon and Prophecies*," 341-375, which is based in the first instance on the *Lha bla ma ye shes 'od kyi rnam*[*s*] *thar rgyas pa, Bod kyi lo rgyus rnam thar phyogs bsgrigs*, vol. Pi (= 43), ed. Dpal brtsegs bod yig dpe rnying zhib 'jug khang (Xining: Mtsho sngon mi rigs dpe skrun khang, 2011), 273-355.

of his elder brother Khri dpal 'khor lde, who now added Gu ge to his original domain of Pu hrang, his pursuit of the religious life of a layman and then as a monk did not mean that he had become fully ineffectual where social and political policies were concerned. Indeed, his biography which Gu ge Paṇ chen Grags pa rgyal mtshan (1415-1486) completed in 1480 is replete with quotations of passages from his *bka' shog*-directives and edicts in which he can be seen to promote the rule of secular law with definite underpinnings of Buddhist canon law.[7] We can be sure that these official documents must have carried some weight owing to his continued high social status in addition to having the moral authority of a man of religion. The fact that he embodied in himself a combination of the secular and the religious indeed made him a powerful force for cultural change.

We do not have much information about the development of Buddhism in Mnga' ris before the advent of Lha bla ma, not to mention other forms of religious practices and worship. Indeed, there are still a large number of unclarities about what exactly transpired upon the dissolution of Tubo that must have taken place after the assassination of its last ruler Khri dar ma 'u dum btsan (d. ?842), alias Glang dar ma. Not unproblematically, the tradition asserts that he had two sons, 'Od srung[s] and Yum brtan, whose descendants ruled, respectively, over the vast area that later came to be known as Mnga' ris and Central Tibet. Especially with respect to Yum brtan, a strange name if there ever were one, the veracity of this tradition has come to be questioned in recent years, most notably by G. Hazod.[8] Indeed, he and the lines of his descent are not always as clear as one would like them to be and Nor brang O rgyan has done us a great service by detailing the main differences in the accounts from a variety of historical sources that were available to him.[9] In the interest of economy,

7 Ra se Dkon mchog rgyal mtshan culled these from Gu ge Paṇ chen's Lha bla ma biography and published them in his "Btsan po khri lde srong gtsug btsan gyi bka' gtsigs kyi yi ge thor bu," *Bod ljongs zhib 'jug* 2 (2004), 117-25. Subsequently, S.G. Karmay studied one of these in "A Decree of lHa Bla ma Ye shes 'od," *Cultural Flows across the Western Himalaya*, ed. P. McAllister *et al.* (Wien: Verlag der Österreichischen Akademie der Wissenschaften, 2015), 477-485, as well as in his as yet unpublished "Bon Institutions Referred to in the Newly Discovered Decrees of lHa Bla ma Ye shes 'od." And J.P. Dalton discussed these fragments in his "Power and Compassion: Negotiating Buddhist Kingship in Tenth-century Tibet," *The Illuminating Mirror. Tibetan Studies in Honour of Per K. Sørensen on the Occasion of his 65th Birthday*, ed. O. Czaja and G. Hazod (Wiesbaden: Dr. Ludwig Reichert Verlag, 2015), 101-118.

8 See his "The Yum brtan Lineage," in Tsering Gyalbo *et al.*, *Civilization at the Foot of Mount Sham-po. The Royal House of Lha Bug pa can and the History of the G.ya' bzang* (Wien: Verlag der Österreichischen Akademie der Wissenschaften, 2000), 177-191.

9 See the *Bod sil bu'i byung ba brjod pa shel dkar phreng ba* (Lhasa: Bod ljongs mi dmangs dpe skrun khang, 1991), 261 ff.

I follow the information provided on this line by the *circa* 1200 chronicle of Lde'u Jo sras and the *circa* 1270 chronicle of Mkhas pa Lde'u, for, even when they diverge in many places, they contain extremely detailed genealogies of both branches of the family.[10] We can deduce from the presence of many Uyghur and Tibetan Buddhist names in religion in the genealogical tables of the Mongol imperial families that, during the thirteenth and fourteenth centuries, Buddhism had become quite influential in the uppermost echelons of Mongol society – after all, Qubilai Qaγan's (1215-1294) first son was given the Tibetan name Rdo rje! And we witness the very same changes in the onomasticon of names of indivduals that belong to the various the lines of descent of the royal houses of Mnga' ris. But this may not apply to Lha bla ma, because most sources suggest that he was self-ordained and thus had given himself a name of religion.[11] Referred to as self- or masterless ordination, the *svāmaṃ/ svayambhūtva* or *anācāryakaupasampadā* is rather well known from the Vinaya literature and, for example, Vasubandhu also referred to it in his *Abhidharmakoṣabhāṣya*, as is taking the Bodhisattva vow by oneself, in the *Śrīmālāsiṃhanādasūtra* and the *Bodhisattvabhūmi* on which basis one may become a member of the Mahayana religious community.[12] On the other hand, Gu ge Paṇ chen has a verse that first states, it seems uniquely, that Lha bla ma had received his ordination from a certain Gnas brtan 'Dul 'dzin Gzhon nu 'od concerning whom he writes:[13]

10 See, respectively, the *Lde'u chos 'byung* (Lhasa: Bod ljongs mi dmangs dpe skrun khang, 1987), 152-153, and the *Rgya bod kyi chos 'byung rgyas pa*, ed. Chab spel Tshe brtan phun tshogs, Gangs can rig mdzod 3 (Lhasa: Bod ljongs mi dmangs dpe skrun khang, 1987), 388-390. These have been incompletely dealt with and with some errors in my "Dating the Two Lde'u Chronicles of Buddhism in India and Tibet," Asiatische *Studien/Études asiatiques* XLVI (1992), 468-491. I intend to return to these in the near future. A partial translation of Mkhas pa Lde'u is found in Xu Decun 许德存 , *Diwu zongjiao yuanliu* 弟吴宗教源流 (Lhasa: Xizang renmin chubanshe, 2013), where pp. 195-196 deal with Yum brtan and his descendants.

11 See R. Vitali, *The Kingdoms of Gu.ge Pu.hrang According to the Mnga' ris rgyal rabs by Gu ge Mkhan chen Ngag dbang grags pa* (Dharamsala: Tho ling gtsug lag khang lo gcig stong 'khor ba'i rjes dran mdzad sgo'i go sgrig tshogs chung, 1996), 234-235, n. 333.

12 See, respectively, *L'Abhidharmakośa de Vasubandhu*, Tome III, tr. and ann. L. de La Vallée Poussin (Bruxelles: Institut Belge des Hautes Études Chinoises, 1971), 60, *The Lion's Roar of Queen Śrīmālā*, tr. A. and H. Wayman (Delhi: Motilal Banarsidass, 1990), 64-67, and the *Yuga shidi lun pusa di* 瑜伽师地论菩萨地 [*The Bodhisattvabhūmi of the Yogācārabhūmi: Comparative Edition of Tibetan, Sanskrit and Chinese with the Tibetan Commentaries of Rgya mtsho sprin and Yon tan 'od*], ed. Hadano Hakuyū 羽田野伯 *et al.*, Publications of the Institute of Tibetan Buddhist Textual Studies 2.1 (Kyoto: Hozokan, 1993), 220-222; see also M. Tatz, *Asanga's Chapter on Ethics with the Commentary of Tsong-kha-pa, The Basic Path to Awakening, The Complete Bodhisattva* (Lewiston: The Edwin Mellen Press, 1986), 84, 150-151.

13 *Lha bla ma ye shes 'od kyi rnam[s] thar rgyas pa*, 293.

lhag pa'i tshul khrims ngur mig[a] *gos kyis slubs*[b]*//*
lung rtogs yid bzhin rin chen nor bus brgyan //
thub dbang bstan pa'i rgyal mtshan dpal 'bar ba'i //
gnas brtan 'dul 'dzin gzhon nu 'od de mchod //

[a] Read: *smrig*. [b] Read: *bklubs*.

Bedecked with the saffron[14] attire of superior ethics,
Ornamented with the wishfulfilling gem of scripture and understanding
With the radiant lustre of the victory banner of the powerful sage's teaching,
Homage to the Elder 'Dul 'dzin Gzhon nu 'od!

But he then writes immediately following this verse that Lha bla ma had received his ordination from a Ku ma ra bha ṭa, that is, Kumārabhadra "in the earth-female-ox year [989]." Of course, "Kumārabhadra" reflects Tibetan "Gzhon nu bzang po" and not "Gzhon nu 'od," which would be "*Kumāraprabha." The close homophony of the two Sanskrit names is probably to blame for the confusion and it is not clear whether this Gzhon nu 'od or Kumārabhadra was an ethnic Tibetan. Whatever the case may have been, his presence would indicate that the area was not entirely bereft of Buddhist institutions prior to their resurgence under Lha bla ma's leadership. But there is no question that Lha bla ma was the first scion of the royal family that issued from 'Od srungs to adopt a recognizably name in religion. What also needs to be recognized is that the Gnas brtan was evidently *not* part of the tradition of the Stod 'dul, the Western Vinaya, or what D. Martin has called the "Highland Vinaya," for he does not appear in its line of transmission that was outlined by Zhing mo che ba Byang chub seng ge (12th cent.).[15] In fact, the first person Zhing mo che ba mentioned in this line is

14 Apropos of the term *ngur smrig* that I translated by "saffron," Karma pa VIII Mi bskyod rdo rje (1507-1554) has made an interesting remark in his commentary on the section on the *pratimokṣa* vow of the *Dgongs gcig* precepts of 'Bri gung 'Jig rten mgon po (1143-1217) as arranged by the latter's nephew Shes rab 'byung gnas (1187-1241); see the *Dam pa'i chos dgongs pa gcig las so sor thar pa'i tshoms kyi kar ṭig chen po, Collected Works*, vol. 5 (Lhasa, 2004), 28-29.

15 See his "The Highland Vinaya. A Study of a Twelfth-Century Monastic Historical Source, the 'Transmission Document' of Zhing-mo-che-ba," *Tibet After Empire. Culture, Society and Religion between 850-1000*, ed. Ch. Cüppers *et al*. (Lumbini: Lumbini International Research Institute, 2013), 249-250, 255. Aside from the sources Martin used for his essay, Gu ge Paṇ chen cites Zhing mo che ba's 'document' in the *Lha bla ma ye shes 'od kyi rnam*[*s*] *thar rgyas pa*, 309-311.

a certain Dharmapāla whom Lha bla ma had invited to Mtho gling, the monastery in Gu ge that he had founded in 996. Whether Dharmapāla's arrival coincided more or less with the date of the foundation of this institution is not altogether clear.[16]

Lha bla ma's contemporary, Tsha la na Ye shes rgyal mtshan was a fifth generation descendant of Yum brtan and must be identified as Mnga' bdag Lha Ye shes rgyal mtshan – the prefix Mnga' bdag implies that he was in charge of a domain. In fact, he was a ruler of sorts of Bsam yas monastery and its environs. Mnga' bdag Lha Ye shes rgyal mtshan was an important translator from Sanskrit in his own right and, among other texts, almost single handedly introduced the so-called Ye shes (*Jñāna) traditions of *Guhyasamājatantra* exegesis and practice that ultimately issued from Buddhasrījñāna (ca. 800) and his followers into Tibet's religious history.[17] Lde'u Jo sras [LDE'U 1 A-B] and Mkhas pa Lde'u [LDE'U 2] give the lines of descent of Tsha la na Ye shes rgyal mtshan from Yum brtan as follows:

LDE'U 1 A	LDE'U 1 B	LDE'U 2
Khri Lde mgon smyon	Mgon spyod	Khri Lde mgon snyan
Nyi 'od dpal mgon	Nyi 'od	Nyi 'od dpal mgon
Mgon spyod	Dpal gyi mgon	Mgon spyod
Tsha la [r]na Ye shes rgyal mtshan	Tsha la na…	Tsha la na…
[the eldest of his four sons was:]		
Mnga' bdag Khri pa	Khri pa	Mgon ne

We encounter additional variations in the chronicle of Indo-Tibetan Buddhism the

16 C.A. Scherrer-Schaub, "Was Byaṅ chub sems dpa' a posthumous title of King Ye śes 'od?," *Tabo Studies II. Manuscripts, Texts, Inscriptions and the Arts*, ed. C.A. Scherrer-Schaub and E. Steinkellner, Serie Orientale Roma LXXXVII (Rome: Istituto Italiano per l'Africa e l'Oriente, 1999), 217, n. 36, suggests that he arrived Mtho gling in 1013. For Mtho gling monastery as such, see R. Vitali, *Records of Tho.ling. A Literary and Visual Reconstruction of the 'Mother' Monastery in Gu.ge* (Dharamsala: High Asia, 1999).

17 On this tradition, see now P.–D. Szántó, "Early Works and Persons related to the So-called Jñānapāda School," *Journal of the International Association of Buddhist Studies* 36/37 [(2013/2014)] (2015), 537-561, and its bibliography.

authorship of which is attributed to Nyang ral Nyi ma 'od zer (1124-1192).[18] Whatever the problems with this attribution, Nyang ral states that Yum brtan's descendants settled in the Bsam yas and Lcang rgyab areas, and gives the following line :[19]

Khri lde mgon po [two sons]

Rig pa mgon po	Nyi 'od dpal mgon
Khri lde	Mgon spyod
'Od po	Tsha la na Ye shes rgyal mtshan
[three sons]	[four sons]
A tsa ra Mgon po btsan Mgon brtsegs	

It is clear that the "Ye shes rgyal mtshan" component of his name Tsha la na Ye shes rgyal mtshan is certainly a name in religion, although I have yet to find any information concerning how he may have received it. Tsha la na translated a number of texts with Kamalagupta and I think he must be the same Kamalagupta with whom Rin chen bzang po had worked on some of his translations. Provided that he was not a profligate monk with loose vows, then, if he were a monk, he most probably received his vows after he had fathered his four sons. Alternatively, his name in religion may have its origin in him having taken his layman's vows, the ceremony of which is also accompanied by the recipient being given a name in religion.

It is striking that Rin chen bzang po's parents and siblings all had Buddhist names and he himself was apparently given his novitiate by Legs pa bzang po at the age of twelve, that is, in 970, at which time he received his name in religion. These items also indicate that at a minimum a semblance of Buddhism was very much present in West Tibet prior to Lha bla ma's awakening to the faith, an idea that was also underscored by, to name but a few, Nor

18 See D.A. Hirshberg, *Delivering the Lotus-Born: Historiography in the Tibetan Renaissance*, unpublished Harvard University doctoral dissertation (Cambridge, 2012), 197 ff., and now his *Remembering the Lotus-Born. Padmasambhava in the History of Tibet's Golden Age* (Somerville: Wisdom Publications, 2016), 141 ff. The chronicle is rarely mentioned in the literature. A mes zhabs Ngag dbang kun dga' bsod nams (1597-1659) refers to it – he calls it Nyang ban's *chos 'byung*-chronicle – in his 1644 study of Rje btsun Grags pa rgyal mtshan's (1147-1216) work on consecration, the *Ar ga'i cho ga dang rab tu gnas pa'i don gsal;* see his *Rab gnas don gsal gyi gsal byed dngos grub 'byung ba'i bstan bcos chen po'i dgongs don rnam par bshad pa rab gnas bstan pa rgyas pa'i nyin byed, Collected Works*, vol. 38, ed. Si khron bod yig dpe rnying myur skyob 'tshol sgrig khang (Lhasa: Bod ljongs dpe rnying dpe skrun khang, 2012), 67.

19 For what follows, see the *Chos 'byung me tog snying po sbrang rtsi'i bcud*, ed. Nyan shul Mkhyen rab 'od gsal, Gangs can rig mdzod 5 (Lhasa: Bod ljongs mi dmangs dpe skrun khang, 1988), 446-447, 449.

brang O rgyan, R. Vitali, and the regretted Gu ge Tshe ring rgyal po in their studies,[20] as well as in sources that have only quite recently turned up. Nonetheless, we should be cognizant of the fact that Nyang ral, Lde'u Jo sras, and Mkhas pa Lde'u state in unison that the "flame of the Buddhist teaching" was lit by Lha bla ma, the ruler of Pu hrang, Khri lde mgon btsan of Dbu ru, that is, Central Tibet, and Tsha la na of Bsam yas.[21]

2. Rin chen bzang po: His Biographies and Oeuvre

It is of course unfortunate that Rin chen bzang po's biography by his disciple Khyi thang pa Ye shes dpal (11thc.), alias Jñānaśrī, is so far the most authoritative study of his life that is available. I write "unfortunate," because Khyi thang pa's work in whatever version, and there are several, regrettably falls ever so short on so many fronts that one is almost inclined to question whether it was in fact written by one of Rin chen bzang po's disciples or, to put it somewhat differently and less radically, by one who was a well informed disciple and actually interested in the life of his teacher! While it does contain, to be sure, a number of interesting anecdotes and some valuable information on Rin chen bzang po as well as a number of rather precious lexemes of the local dialect, it is remarkably reticent about the important dates of his subject's life, it is extremely quiet as far as the prodigious output of his translations is concerned, it says nothing about Rin chen bzang po as a physician, and it has nothing to say about the master's own compositions. True, he does refer to a much larger (*rgyas pa*) biography, which apparently contained additional information on Rin chen bzang po's training and education, but it has not come down to us so far. What exacerbates the problems with this biography is that it has been transmitted in several different versions that are of different length.

Zhang Changhong recently edited this surprisingly difficult work on the basis of several recensions and also furnished an integral Chinese rendition that must be judged to be a considerable improvement of the earlier English translation by the pioneers D.L. Snellgrove

20 See, respectively, the relevant passages in the *Bod sil bu'i byung ba brjod pa shel dkar phreng ba, The Kingdoms of Gu.ge Pu.hrang According to the Mnga' ris rgyal rabs by Gu ge Mkhan chen Ngag dbang grags pa* and the *Mnga' ris chos 'byung gangs ljongs mdzes rgyan* (Lhasa: Bod ljongs mi dmangs dpe skrun khang, 2006). See also the *Stod mnga' ris skor gsum gi lo rgyus 'bel gtam rin chen gter gyi phreng ba*, ed. Mnga' ris srid gros rig gnas lo rgyus bsdu rub u yon lhan khang (Lhasa: Bod ljongs mi dmangs dpe skrun khang, 1996).

21 See the *Lde'u chos 'byung*, 154, the *Rgya bod kyi chos 'byung rgyas pa*, 390, and *Chos 'byung me tog snying po sbrang rtsi'i bcud*, 449.

and T. Skorupski.[22] A recent publication included two versions of Khyi thang pa's study plus two other, later, retyped pieces on his life; these are :[23]

1. *Skyes mchog rin chen bzang po'i rnam thar ngo mtshar*[24]
   By Khyi thang pa
2. *Lo tstsha ba rin chen bzang po'i 'khrungs rab[s] rnam thar 'bring po ka dpyad pa rin chen sgron me*
   By Blo gros don yod (?15th cent.)
3. *Lo tstsha ba chen po skyes mchog rin chen bzang po'i rnam thar dka' spyad sgron ma*
   By Khyi thang pa
4. *Lo chen rin chen bzang po rnam par thar pa bsdus pa*
   Unknown

An additional biography is the following:

5. *Lo tstsha ba chen po rin chen bzang po'i rnam thar dad ldan dge 'phel*
   By Blo bzang bzod pa (1922-1995) [25]

A somewhat long piece on Rin chen bzang po's life and disciples is found Nyang ral's chronicle where we are told that Lha bla ma had gathered twenty-one young boys from all over Mnga' ris and, having given them the necessary funding, dispatched them to the subcontinent in order to invite to Gu ge some learned Buddhist intellectuals, including Paṇḍita Dharmapāla from the east and Rin chen sde (*Ratnasena) from Kashmir. Of the twenty-one, nineteen ultimately succumbed to the unfamiliar heat and illness. Not so Rin chen bzang po and Pu hrang Legs pa'i shes rab, who became respectively known as the senior (*lo chen*) and junior translator (*lo chung*). Rin chen bzang po spent a good number

22 See Zhang Changhong 张长虹, "Da yishi Renqinsangbo zhuanji yizhu 大译师仁钦桑波传记译注 (part 1)," *Zhongguo zangxue* 中国藏学 4 (2013), 30-38, and its sequel "Da yishi Renqinsangbo zhuanji yizhu 大译师仁钦桑波传记译注 (part 2)," *Zhongguo zangxue* 中国藏学 1 (2014), 31-41, and the literature cited therein. But see also Kawagoe Eshin 川越英真, "Rin chen bzang po no jinsei to katsudō (Rin chen bzang po の生涯とその活動, The Life and Activities of Rin chen bzang po)," *Bunka* 文化 46 (1983), 79-50, and H.P. Gangnegi, "A Critical Note on the Biographies of Lo chen Rin chen bZang po," *The Tibet Journal* 23(1998), 38-48.

23 These were most recently published in, respectively, *Lo chen rin chen bzang po dang / Chag Lo tsā ba Chos rje dpal dang / Rngog Lo tsā ba Blo ldan shes rab kyi rnam thar*, ed. Ser gtsug nang bstan dpe rnying 'tshol bsdu phyogs sgrig khang (n.p., n.d.), 1-25, 26-73, 74-93, 94-107. Of course, these works were published earlier.

24 This is an artificial title. The actual title given on p. 25 corresponds to the one of no. 3!

25 This recent work was published in *Historical Texts from the Monastery Kyi in Spiti* (Spiti: Lama Rdo rje tshe brtan, 1978), 1-32.

of years in Kashmir and returned to his homeland a very learned man with an excellent knowledge of Sanskrit. The result was that he and his disciples soon stood at the very heart of the aforementioned Buddhist renaissance and the course that Buddhism was to take in Tibet is quite unthinkable without them. Nyang ral also stated that Rin chen bzang po had translated the so-called *Stod 'grel* in the Kathmandu Valley, but he appears to have confused Rin chen bzang po, who never sojourned in the Valley, with Atiśa who did.[26] The *Stod 'grel* or *Commentary on the First Part* is none other than the first part (*stod!*) or the *dum bu dang po*, of Ānandagarbha's (?8th cent.) massive **Tattvālokakāri* commentary on the *Tattvasaṃgrahasūtra/tantra*, the basic *yogatantra* scripture, that was translated by Rin chen bzang po.[27] In a brilliant article, R. Vitali has given a detailed account of the mask of Mahākāla that flew after him from the Indian subcontinent to the Tibetan area; additional material on this mask and Rin chen bzang po's connection can now be found in A mes zhabs' 1624 study of Sa skya Paṇḍita Kun dga' rgyal mtshan's (1182-1251) work on instrumental and vocal music, the *Rol mo'i bstan bcos*.[28] And more than two hundred years after Nyang ral's capsule biography, Chos dbang grags pa (1404-1469), like Rin chen bzang po a native of Zhang zhung, composed a versified biography of his life, which D. Martin recently studied in consummate detail.[29] In addition, Bu ston Rin chen grub's (1290-1364) and A mes zhabs' chronicles on the origins and development of the *yogatantra* literature of respectively

26 *Chos 'byung me tog snying po sbrang rtsi'i bcud*, 463.

27 "Correcting" *Stod 'grel to Bstod 'grel* in his fine study of the biographies of Atiśa (or: *Adhīśa) (982-1054), H. Eimer, in an oversight, suggested long ago that the treatise in question was Buddhaśrīśānti's (10th-11th cent.) Deśanāstavavṛtti, which the author co-translated with Rin chen bzang po; see his *rNam thar rgyas pa. Materialien zu einer Biographie des Atiśa, Teil 1, Asiatische Forschungen*, Band 67 (Wiesbaden: Otto Harrassowitz, 1979), 466-477. We owe to Eimer the reading "Atiśa," but recently Szántó, "Early Works and Persons related to the So-called Jñānapāda School," 539, n. 2, reminded us once again that some seven years H. Isaacson had argued for the possibility of reading his name as *Adhīśa. The Tibetan canon, however, virtually consistently reads his name as "A ti sha".

28 See his "Sa skya and the Mnga' ris skor gsum Legacy: The Case of Rin chen bzang po's Flying Mask," *Lungta* 14 (2001) (= *Aspects of Tibetan History*, ed. R. Vitali), 5-44, and the *Rig pa'i gnas lnga las bzo rig pa'i bye brag rol mo'i bstan bcos kyi rnam par bshad pa 'jam dbyangs bla ma dges pa'i snyan pa'i sgra dbyangs blo gsal yid 'phrog 'phrin las yongs khyab, Collected Works*, vol. 9, ed. Si khron bod yig dpe rnying myur skyob 'tshol sgrig khang (Lhasa: Bod ljongs dpe rnying dpe skrun khang, 2012), 179-183.

29 See the "Veil of Kashmir. Poetry of Travel and Travail in Zhangzhungpa's 15th-Century *Kāvya* reworking of the Biography of the Great Translator Rinchen Zangpo (958-1055 CE)," *Revue d'Etudes Tibétaines* 14 (2008), 1-56.

1342 and 1637 contain fairly substantial narratives of his life.[30] And finally, we should also mention here Rme ru Tshe ring don grub's very recent general survey of Rin chen bzang po and his activities. [31]

The various listings of the large and varied corpus of his translations point to the obvious, namely, that he was among the most versatile and prolific Tibetan scholar-translators who were active in the late tenth and first half of the eleventh century.[32] But we have to be a tad more careful. It now appears that, while he is credited with translating these for the very first time, it turns out that this may not be factual at all. For example, there has hardly been any question that he was the author of the translation of the *Guhyasamājatantra* that is attributed to him and his counterpart Śraddhākaravarman in all the published xylographed and manuscript Kanjur-canons. But as we will see in Part Two of this essay, this may not have been the case. Of course, judging from the listings of his translations, it is clear that he mainly focused his linguistic skills on making tantric literature available in Tibetan translation. However, at the same time, he also made a name for himself in the area of Indian medicine. His *circa* 1015 translations of Vāgbhaṭa's (7th cent.) *Aṣṭaṇgahṛdayasaṃhita* together with the auto-commentary and Candranandana's (9th cent.) large commentary, together with several of his disciples who had studied Indian medicine with him assured him an important place in the history of Indo-Tibetan medicine as one of the founders of a very important tradition of medical knowledge in Tibet. But these translations,[33] too, may have had a partial precedent. In his so far undated history of

30 See, respectively, the passage in the *Rnal 'byor rgyud kyi rgya mtshor 'jug pa'i gru gzings*, Collected Works, repr. L Chandra, Part 11 (New Delhi: International Academy of Indian Culture, 1969), 143-161, which is basically reproduced in the *Rnal 'byor rgyud kyi dam pa'i chos byung ba'i tshul legs par bshad pa yo ga bstan pa'i sgo 'byed, Collected Works*, vol. 15, ed. Si khron bod yig dpe rnying myur skyob 'tshol sgrig khang (Lhasa: Bod ljongs dpe rnying dpe skrun khang, 2012), 225-250, which amount to intellectual histories of the era of Rin chen bzang po and the crucial role he played in the dissemination of these and other tantras.

31 *Lo chen rin chen bzang po'i mdzad 'phrin zhib mo rnam 'byed* (Lhasa: Bod ljongs mi dmangs dpe skrun khang, 2014) as well as his summary in "Lo chen rin chen bzang po'i mdzad 'phrin mdo tsam brjod pa," Bod *ljongs zhib 'jug* 1 (2015), 14-29.

32 For a convenient listing of these, see the *circa* 1270-1280 catalog of Dar ma rgyal mtshan (1227-1305), alias Bcom ldan [rigs pa'i] ral gri, in K.R. Schaeffer and L.W.J. van der Kuijp, *An Early Tibetan Survey of Buddhist Literature: The Bstan pa rgyas pa rgyan gyi nyi 'od of Bcom ldan ral gri, Harvard Oriental Series*, vol. 64 (Cambridge: The Department of Sanskrit and Indian Studies, 2009), 197-208; see also G. Tucci, *Rin chen bzang po and the Renaissance of Buddhism in Tibet around the Millenium* (Indo-Tibetica III), tr. N.K. Smith (New Delhi: Aditya Prakashan, 1988), 40-49.

33 See D. Martin, "An Early Tibetan History of Indian Medicine," *Soundings in Tibetan Medicine. Anthropological and Historical Perspectives*, ed. M. Schrempf (Leiden: Brill, 2007), 311.

the Tibetan medicine, Zur mkhar ba Blo gros rgyal po (1509-?1579) writes that the quartet of Paṇḍita Dharmaśrīvarman, Nye bor Lo tsā ba Dbyig gi rin chen, Mar lo/po Rig pa gzhon nu, and Dbyig gu Dge slong Shākya blo gros had rendered the *Aṣṭaṇgahṛdayasaṃhita* and its autocommentary into Tibetan during the early part of Lha bla ma's life.[34] So far, no other sources known to me have anything to report about these men and Dbyig gi rin chen, for one, is not registered in any of the available listings of Lo tsā ba-translators. This translation appears to be no longer extant, but the recent and ongoing publication of medical texts from inter alia the enormous collection of the Potala libraries may very well prove this to be false. Zur mkhar ba then states that Rin chen bzang po had offered the Kashmirian Paṇḍita Jārandhara the rather princely sum of some one hundred *srang*-measures of gold to aid in the translation of these works plus Candranandana's commentary. These translations then formed the nucleus of a medical tradition that was further developed by the so-called "four physicians from Pu hrang," whereby a certain Mang mo Sman btsun appears to have been the most influential of this quartet. Finally, and not unimportantly, Vitali mentions that Rin chen bzang po had been involved in the translation and dissemination of a work that Pho brang Byang chub 'od (984-1078) had retrieved from Bsam yas monastery.[35] This work was partly written in Zhang zhung, the language of his native birthplace, and was a so-called treasure-text (*gter ma*) that was associated with the Old (*rnying ma*) Tantras! This is not as insignificant as it sounds, because striking in his survey of tantric literature that will be discussed below and in Part Two is the utter absence of any tantras that demonstrably solely belong to the Old Tradition.

In stark contrast to his fame as a Sanskrit scholar and translator, Rin chen bzang po had been up to the present almost unknown as an author in his own right. Indeed, it was only quite recently that manuscripts of several of short studies on tantric subjects that are attributed to him were discovered in one of 'Bras spungs monastery's libraries; these included the following:[36]

34 For what follows, see his *Sman pa rnams kyis mi shes su mi rung ba'i shes bya spyi'i khog dbubs*, eds. Gzhon nu nyi ma and Klu sgrub rgya mtsho (Chengdu: Si khron mi rigs dpe skrun khang, 2001), 262, 300, 302.

35 See *The Kingdoms of Gu.ge Pu.hrang According to the Mnga' ris rgyal rabs by Gu ge Mkhan chen Ngag dbang grags pa*, 226-229.

36 *'Bras spungs dgon du bzhugs su gsol ba'i dpe rnying dkar chag*, Stod cha, ed. Bstan 'dzin phun tshogs (Beijing: Mi rigs dpe skrun khang, 2004), nos. 1927, 4403, 12307, and 12613. I misplaced the catalog number of the fifth manuscript of my listing.

1. *Dpal mngon par rtogs pa'i dka' ba'i gnas bshad pa* with glosses (*mchan bu*) that may have been written by him; fols. 13.
2. *[B]sgrub pa'i thabs mdor byas pa* with glosses; the editors queried: "Were the glosses written by Lo chen Rin chen bzang po?"; fols. 8.
3. *Yo ga'i rab gnas*; fols. 16.
4. *Dam tshig mdor bsdus bstan pa*; fols. 8.
5. *Dpal 'khor lo bde mchog lū yi pa'i bstod pa yid bzhin nor bu*; fols. 2.

Several of these plus two others that are not listed here have now been published in black-and-white facsimile reproductions; these are the following according to their title pages, opening statements, or colophons:

1. *Dpal 'khor lo bde mchog lū yi pa'i bstod pa yid bzhin nor bu*; fols. 2.
2. *Rab tu gnas par byed pa don gsal*; fols. 2. [37]
3. *Dpal mngon par rtogs pa'i dka' ba'i gnas bshad pa lo tsā ba rin chen bzang pos mdzad pa*; fols. 13.
4. *Cho ga bya tshul*; fol. 1.
5. *Bde ba can gyi smon lam*; fols. 3.

To be sure, "Rin chen bzang po" is by no means an uncommon Tibetan name in religion, so that authorial attributions can be a tricky thing. Of these, nos. 1, 3, and 5 are prefixed by Lo tstsha ba or Lo tsā ba and this would perhaps render it more likely that he was in fact their author or that, at a minimum, since these are all copies and not autographs, at least someone in the tradition had ascribed them to him. No. 3 is actually a work he co-authored with Atiśa, and Kano Kazuo 加納和雄 and Kawasaki Kazuhiro 川崎一洋 have recently made a study of it.[38] It must be said that none of these works are especially noteworthy in terms of their content. With the exception of no. 2 (= no. 1), which is a eulogy to according to the transmission of Lūyipāda, they are all expository and tend to discuss their subject in a

37 A mes zhabs cites one line from fol. 1b of this work in his *Rab gnas don gsal gyi gsal byed dngos grub 'byung ba'i bstan bcos chen po'i dgongs don rnam par bshad pa rab gnas bstan pa rgyas pa'i nyin byed*, 295.

38 See their "Hayashi Rin chen bzang po ra 'Cakrasaṃvarābhisamāya chū' –zobun kōtei tekisuto (リンチエンサンポ著『チヤクラサンヴアラ・アビ サマヤ注』— 蔵文校訂テクスト —, A Critical Edition of Rin chen bzang po's *Cakrasaṃvarābhisamāya* Commentary)," Kōyasan Daigaku Ronsō 高野山大学論叢 49 (2014), 1-36. But see also Kawasaki's earlier brief study of this same work in *Indogaku Bukkyōgaku Kenkyū* 印度學佛教學研究 56 (2008), 958-953.

fairly introductory fashion. However, they do allow us a glimpse into his authorship. We do not know the true extent of his oeuvre, but it is for this reason that the recent recovery of his expository survey of tantra is of great importance for our understanding of the inculturation of Buddhist tantra in Tibet. Titled *Rgyud sde spyi'i rnam par bzhag pa 'thad ldan lung gi rgyan gyis spras pa, An Exposition of Tantric Literature Embellished by an Ornament of Correct Scripture*, a manuscript of this work in seventy-eight folios is registered in a recently published catalog of rare [and not so rare] works that are housed in the library of 'Phan po Na lendra monastery, which Rong ston Shākya rgyal mtshan (1367-1449) had founded in 1436.[39] It also made a cameo appearance in a note in Kano's and Kawasaki's excellent study of one of Rin chen bzang po's later works, the *Dpal mngon par rtogs pa'i dka' ba'i gnas bshad pa*.[40] It is too bad that the only text of this work that was available to me for the present essay is a typed, computer-input text [41] and not a facsimile reproduction of the original manuscript. In addition to the usual text-critical issues with which one is confronted when reading a manuscript, it is thus fraught with the possibilities of additional misreadings and mistyped text, not to mention the tacit orthographic sanitation to which the manuscript no doubt has been subjected. Giving it a cursory reading, we notice that its topical outline (*sa bcad*) is quite detailed. In fact, in terms of its complexity, it goes well beyond the ones that we have for the writings of, say, 'Gos Lo tsā ba I Khug pa Lhas btsas, whose name in religion may have been Byang chub rtse mo, Rong zom Chos kyi bzang po (11th cent.), or Rngog Lo tsā ba Blo ldan shes rab (ca.1059-ca.1109). This may not be insignificant when we begin to look more closely into the question of its authorship. Without giving a source for this, W. Verrill recently put forward the idea that an "exposition of tantric literature" (**rgyud sde spyi'i rnam bzhag*) was attributed to 'Gos Lo tsā ba I.[42] The basic title of Rin chen bzang po's work is of course quite reminiscent of the title of the short piece on tantra and the literature associated with it by the early Sa skya pa yogi-scholar Sa

39 *Bod khul gyi chos sde grags can khag gi dpe rnying dkar chag*, ed. Ska ba Shes rab bzang po (Beijing: Mi rigs dpe skrun khang, 2010), 196, no. 4289, under volume 538 Ka.

40 Kano and Kawasaki, "Hayashi Rin chen bzang po ra 'Cakrasaṃvarābhisamāya chū' – zobun kōtei tekisuto (リンチェンサンポ 著『チャクラサンヴァラ・アビ サマヤ注』— 蔵文校訂テクスト —, A Critical Edition of Rin chen bzang po's *Cakrasaṃvarābhisamāya* Commentary)," 1, n. 2.

41 I thank Ms. Kelsang Lhamo of the Tibetan Buddhist Research Center for making a scan of this work available to me.

42 See his *Introduction* in *The Yogini's Eye. Comprehensive Introduction to Buddhist Tantra*, tr. Ngor Thartse Khenpo Sonam Gyatso and W. Verrill, *Classics of the Early Sakya*, vol. 1 (Xlibris Corporation, 2012), 17.

chen Kun dga' snying po (1092-1158),[43] the *Rgyud sde spyi'i rnam gzhag chung ngu*, and the *Rgyud sde spyi'i rnam par bzhag pa* of his eldest son Slob dpon Bsod nams rtse mo (1142-1182), to which I will return severally below.[44] Thus, if this treatise were indeed by Rin chen bzang po, then it is the very first work of its kind in the history of Buddhism and I feel it is a privilege to be able to introduce it to a wider audience.

Its colophon and afterword are a bit perplexing; we read :[45]

...sgra bsgyur gyi lo tsā ba chen po rin chen bzang pos mar yul du sbyar ba'o // dge slong bzang po'i mtha' can gyis sbyar ba'o // // gang mo grub pa dpal bzang gis sbyar ba yin / ***rgyud*** *las /*

rang rig rtogs pa sangs rgyas te //
ma rtogs 'khor ba'i gzhi rtsa can //
de phyir rang rig rtogs byas la //
'khor ba'i gzhi rtsa gcad par bya //

zhes gsungs so // [note: ri brgyad ni / shar du rin po che'i lhun po // byang du maṇya ra ljang khu/ nub tu ke la sha dkar po / lho ru ma la ya ser po / dbang ldan du dbang chen nag po / mer spos ngad ldan ser po / bden bral du gangs can dkar po / rlung du dpal gyi ri sngon po // dge'o // // gcig zhus // //]

…written in Mar yul[46] by the great Lo tsā ba Rin chen bzang po who translates. Written by the monk whose name has the ending of bzang po. Written by Gang mo Grub pa dpal

43 Sa chen's work is now available in translation; see Chr. Wilkinson, tr., *An Overview of Tantra and Related Works, Sakya Gongma Series*, vol. 4 (Concord: Suvarna Bhasa Publishing LLC, 2014), 11-35 - I thank Mr. Chr. Wilkinson for having generously given me a copy of this volume of his translations - and also Yang Jie 杨杰 , "Gongge ningbo suozao *Xubu zong anli* yizhu (公哥宁卜所造《续部总安立》译注 , Annotated Translation of Kun dga' snying po's *Rgyud sde spyi'i rnam bzhag*)," *Xiyu lishi yuyan yanjiu jikan* 西域历史语言研究集刊 / *Historical and Philological Studies of China's Western Regions*, vol. 8, ed. Shen Weirong 沈卫荣 (Beijing: Science Press, 2015), 349-362.

44 The Slob dpon's work is translated in *The Yogini's Eye. Comprehensive Introduction to Buddhist Tantra*, tr. Ngor Thartse Khenpo Sonam Gyatso and W. Verrill. The translation, which must have been completed prior to Ngor Thartse Khenpo's passing in 1988, is an impressive accomplishment, even if it does not show evidence of having engaged in the necessary text-critical work that, for example, we find done in 'Jam dbyangs Kun dga' bstan pa'i rgyal mtshan's (1885-1952) annotated edition of this very text in his *Collected Works*, vol. 2 (Kathmandu: Sa skya rgyal yongs gsung rab slob gnyer khang, 2007), 1-166. With all due respect to the authors, the layout of this work with its intertwining translation of texts and comments is not always as clear as they must have intended.

45 RGYUD, 77/78.

46 For Mar yul, see Vitali, *The Kingdoms of Gu.ge Pu.hrang According to the Mnga' ris rgyal rabs by Gu ge Mkhan chen Ngag dbang grags pa*, 153-161.

bzang [po]. It is stated in the ***tantra***: [47]

Non-referential realization is enlightenment;
Non-realization has the foundational root of samsara.
Thus, when one has created non-referential realization,
One will have cut the foundational root of samsara.

[Note: The eight mountains: the Heap of Jewels in the east, the green Maṇya ra in the north, the white Kelasha [= Kailash] in the west, the yellow Malaya in the south, the black *Mahendra in the north-east (*dbang ldan*), the yellow *Gandhamādana in the Fire [= ?south-east], the White Snowy in the south-west (*bden bral*), the blue *Śrīparvata in the Air [= ?north-west]. Happiness. Corrected once.]

Aside from the problem of the identity of the *tantra*, these lines raise at least two questions, the first of which is: Who is Gang mo Grub pa dpal bzang [po]? The answer is that I have found not one source in which a name with a prefixed toponym or clan name Gang mo occurs. However, the name in religion Grub pa dpal bzang po (?-1237) is famously associated with Zhang Lo tsā ba, who figures not only as a disciple of Nyang ral and the Kashmirian Śākyaśrībhadra (1127-1225) and as a translator, often together with Ratnarakṣita of Patan, Nepal, but also as the exponent of the so-called *Bde mchog snyan rgyud* precepts. His short biographies by Rba'i ban de (= the monk of the Rba/Sba clan) Dha ra shrī and one that is not signed do not make any mention of *gang mo* or that he ever wrote anything remotely resembling a survey of Buddhist tantra.[48] For now, this must therefore be judged a dead end. The second question is: Where do we find the names of these eight mountains? Well, some of these are quite enigmatic and I have found no parallel passages for this enumeration. And this is another dead end! There is much else in the body of this work that is quite interesting if on occasion somewhat puzzling. This has to do with its quotations of many sources that are not found in the collections of canonical literature as well as with its

47 I have been unable to identify this tantra or the origin of the cited verse.

48 See the *Snyan brgyud kyi brgyud pa yid bzhin nor bu'i phreng ba* and the *Brgyud pa yid bzhin nor bu'i lo rgyus, Ras chung snyan brgyud skor*, vol. 2/19, Mes po'i shul bzhag, vol. 257, ed. Dpal brtsegs bod yig dpe rnying zhib 'jug khang (Beijing: Krung go'i bod rig pa dpe skrun khang, 2008), 78-88, 359-370. See also F. Torricelli, "Zhang Lo-tsā-ba's Introduction to the Aural Transmission of Śaṃvara," *Le parole e i marmi. Studi in onore di Raniero Gnoli nel suo 70° compleanno*, ed. R. Torella with C. Cicuzza, *Serie Orientale Roma*, vol. 92.2 (Rome: Istituto italiano per l'Africa e l'Oriente, 2001), 875-896.

quotations of sources that are found in the literature but which have quite different readings than their canonical counterparts. A problem already begins with Rin chen bzang po's very first quotation of a verse that was apparently taken from a work with the title *Dpal brtul shugs* (read: *zhugs*) *grub pa* (**Śrīvratasiddhi*). He cites it in connection with seven factors that would propagandistically indicate the superiority of Buddhist over non-Buddhist precepts; the verse has it that:

lta ba skyabs gnas mchod pa dang //
spyod pa 'bras bu grub pa'i mtha' //
dam chos la sogs bdun gyis ni //
sangs rgyas chos rnams khyad par 'phags //

The view, place of refuge, worship and,
Pratice, result, philosophical system,
The holy religion, etc., due to the seven,
The Buddha's precepts are quite superior.

It is quite reasonable to suppose that this quotation might be found in one of the two fa-mous *Praises* of the Buddha and his teachings written by Udbhaṭasiddhasvāmin (?) or in their commentaries by Prajñāvarman (ca. 790),[49] or even in the discussions of the supe-riority of Buddhist tantra over exoteric Mahayana Buddhism in such tracts as Tripiṭakamālā's (?mid 10th cent.) apparently fairly widely read **Trinayapradīpa*[50] or in Jñānaśrī's (early 11th cent.) **Vajrayānāntadvayanirākaraṇa*,[51] works that are so far only available in Tibetan translations. Unfortunately, it is not. What is more, I have found neither the title of this work nor the wording of the quotation in the other main sources that I have used for this essay. That is to say, the relevant treatises of the Slob dpon, Bu ston, Klong chen Rab 'byams pa

49 For these, see J. Schneider, *Der Lobpreis der Vorzüglichkeit des Buddha. Udbhaṭasiddhasvāmins Viśeṣastava mit Prajñāvarmans Kommentar, Indica et Tibetica* 23 (Bonn: Indica et Tibetica Verlag, 1993), 18, and his "Der Buddha als der wahre Śiva: Udbhaṭasiddhasvāmins *Sarvajñamaheśvarastotra*," *Berliner Indologische Studien* 8 (1995), 153-187. Prajñāvarman's commentary was translated by a Jārandhara and Rin chen bzang po.

50 BSTAN, vol. 41; 19-70.

51 For this work, see Taiken Kyuma, "Superiority of Vajrayāna – Part I: Some remarks on the **Vajrayānāntadvayanirākaraṇa* (*Rdo rje theg pa mtha'i gnyis sel ba*) Ascribed to Jñānaśrī" and Ryugen Tanemura "Superiority of Vajrayāna – Part II: Superiority of the Tantric Practice Taught in the **Vajrayānāntadvayanirākaraṇa* (*Rdo rje theg pa mtha'i gnyis sel ba*)," *Genesis and Development of Tantrism*, ed. Shingo Einoo (Tokyo: Institute of Oriental Culture, University of Tokyo, 2009), 469-485, 487-514.

(1309-1364), and 'Ba' ra ba Rgyal mtshan dpal bzang po (1310-1391),[52] to name but four early expositors of tantra and its literature, do not cite this verse in their discussions of Buddhist tantra, and neither does Klong chen in his other writings nor Kun dga' snying po (1575-1634), alias Tāranātha, in his oeuvre, both of which are now searchable courtesy of tbrc.org. One should perhaps also add the great Sa skya pa commentator Gtsang Byams pa Rdo rje rgyal mtshan's (1424-1498) *Rnam par bshad pa'i chu rgyun log par smra ba'i dri ma 'khrud byed* of 1479 in which is embedded his lengthy defense of the Slob dpon's work against earlier criticism in *inter alia* a work in Paṇ chen Phyogs las rnam rgyal's (1376-1451) massive *De kho na nyid kyi 'dus pa* encyclopedia and Mkhas grub Dge legs dpal bzang po's (1385-1438) *circa* 1425 *Hevajratantra* commentary,[53] as well as Glo bo Mkhan chen Bsod nams lhun grub's (1456-1532) undated partial study of the Slob dpon's treatise.[54]

Commenting on this verse, an unknown glossator of Rin chen bzang po's text – he probably was a member of the Old Tradition persuasion – cites Padmasambhava (8th cent.) to the effect that he had spoken of one hundred and seventy different non-Buddhist points of view and also relates that a Master Snang grags had isolated three hundred and sixty-two of them.[55] In my ignorance, and I stand to be corrected, I believe that the *Man ngag lta ba'i phreng ba* is the only work on different philosophical-cum-religious points of view

52 See, respectively, the Slob dpon in his *Rgyud sde spyi'i rnam par gzhag pa* (Sde dge print), *Sa skya bka' 'bum*, vol. 2, no. 1, ed. Bsod nams rgya mtsho (Tokyo: The Toyo Bunko, 1968), 1-37 – his nephew Sa skya Paṇḍita edited this work much later –, Bu ston in his 1339 *Rgyud sde spyi'i rnam par gzhag pa rgyud sde rin po che'i mdzes rgyan, Collected Works*, repr. L Chandra, Part 15 (New Delhi: International Academy of Indian Culture, 1969), 1-609, Klong chen in his *Grub mtha' rin po che'i mdzod, Mdzod bdun* [Sde dge xylograph], vol. Cha (Gangtok, 1983), 299-335, and 'Ba' ra ba in his undated *Thar par 'jug pa'i gru bo zab don chos kyi gter mdzod las gsang sngags gsar ma'i rnam bshad kyi dka' 'grel, A Tibetan Encyclopdia of Buddhist Scholasticism; The Collected Writings of 'Ba' ra ba Rgyal mtshan dpal bzang,* vol. 3 (Dehradun: Ngawang Gyaltsen and Ngawang Lungtok, 1970), 267-720; pp. 720-727 contain two poetic pieces. For Klong chen's work, see also *The Precious Treasury of Philosophical Systems*, tr. R. Barron (Junction City: Padma Publishing, 2007), 239-288.

53 See, respectively, the *Rgyud sde spyi'i rnam par bzhag pa rgyud ma lus par 'jug pa la rtsod pa spong ba, Sngon byon pa'i sa skya pa'i mkhas pa rnams kyi sngags skor*, vol. Ga [3] (Kathmandu: Sa skya rgyal yongs gsung rab slob gnyer khang, 2007), 81-184, the *Thun mong ma yin pa'i rgyud sde'i rnam bzhag bshad pa, De kho na nyid kyi 'dus pa, Collected Works*, vol. 23 (New Delhi: The Tibet House, 1971), 601-1259 (= Bo dong Paṇ chen gyi gsung 'bum chen mo, vol. 21 (Wa) (Beijing: Mi rigs dpe skrun khang, 2014), 187-435) – in the New Delhi edition, this work is immediately preceded by the *Sngags la 'jug pa'i sgo gsum pa rnal 'byor kyi rnam par bzhag pa* for which the manuscript only has the last two lines (on p. 601) –, and the *Dpal brtag pa gnyis pa'i rnam par bshad pa rdo rje mkha' 'gro ma rnams kyi gsang mdzod, Collected Works* (Lhasa Zhol xylograph), vol. Ja [7] (Dharamsala: Library of Tibetan Works and Archives, 1981), 469-961.

54 See the *Rgyud sde spyi yi rnam par bzhag pa'i gsal byed nyi ma'i 'od zer, Selected Writings*, vol. 4 (Dehra Dun: Pal Evam Chodan Ngorpa Centre, 1985), 1-87.

55 RGYUD, 6.

(*lta ba*) that is generally attributed to Padmasambhava. That said, it does not contain the aforementioned enumeration.[56] Further, I would be inclined to hold that the name "Snang grags" was either miswritten in the manuscript or misread by the typist, and that it should be amended to "Snang bral," that is "*Bhāviveka/*Bhavivikta," one of the many names the Tibetan tradition has used to designate Bhāviveka (6th cent.). This would mean that the number of non-Buddhist positions should be amended to three hundred and sixty-three – numeral 2 may have been misread for 3 –, which is the number that occurs in his *Tarkajvālā* as well as in the *Madhyamakaratnapradīpa* that, by the by, has been (quite wrongly) attributed to him and was written by a much later namesake.[57] Both works are only extant in the Tibetan translations by Atiśa and his disciple Nag tsho Lo tsā ba Tshul khrims rgyal ba (1011/2-ca.1070), although the first was already partly rendered into Tibetan by the beginning of the ninth century.

Now it is generally recognized that the *Man ngag lta ba'i phreng ba* is beholden to the two opening verses of the thirteenth chapter of the famous (or infamous) **Guhyagarbha[tattvaviniścaya]-tantra* [58] – we also find these two used in the tenth chapter of the cognate *Gsang ba snying po nges pa'i bla ma chen po* (**Guhyagarbhaviniścayamahāgurutantra*) [59] – and the same holds quite expressly for Kaḥ thog pa Dam pa bde gshegs' (1122-1192) *Theg pa spyi bcings* in its discussion of different points of view.[60] The Old School writer Rog bande Shes rab 'od (1166-1244) does not cite the *Man ngag lta ba'i*

56 For a study of this work, see S.G. Karmay, *The Great Perfection (rDzogs chen): A Philosophical and Meditative Teaching of Tibetan Buddhism* (Leiden: Brill, 2007), 137-173.

57 For "Snang bral," see He Huanhuan 何欢欢 and my "Further Notes on Bhāviveka's Principal Oeuvre," *Indo-Iranian Journal* 57 (2014), 338, and for the three hundred and sixty-three (!) non-Buddhist points of view that Bhāviveka mentions in his *Tarkajvālā*, see M.D. Eckel, *Bhāviveka and His Buddhist Opponents*, *Harvard Oriental Series*, vol. 70 (Cambridge: Department of Sanskrit and Indian Studies, Harvard University, 2008), 28-36.

58 For this work, see N.D. Garson, *Penetrating the Secret Essence Tantra: Context and Philosophy in the Mahāyoga System of Rnying-ma Tantra*, unpublished University of Virginia doctoral dissertation (Charlotteville, 2004).The first to comment on the Man ngag lta ba'i phreng ba, the Old Tradition scholar Rong zom Chos kyi bzang po, clearly made this point in his undated *Man ngag lta ba'i phreng ba 'grel pa, Collected Works*, vol. 1 (Chengdu: Si khron mi rigs dpe skrun khang, 1999), 303, where the text is reproduced with what appear to be pseudo-archaic spellings. They are absent from his undated *Guhyagarbhatantra* commentary in which he also refers to the *Man ngag lta ba'i phreng ba*; see the *Rgyud rgyal gsang ba snying po dkon cog 'grel, Collected Works*, vol. 1 (Chengdu: Si khron mi rigs dpe skrun khang, 1999), 193-194, 195. On p. 195, Rong zom cites a verse from what he calls "a treatise of grammer" (*byā ka ra ṇa*[*vyākaraṇa*]*'i gzhung*), which turns out to be *Rtags kyi 'jug pa*, 28b-d. To my knowledge, this is so far the earliest quotation of a verse that is part of the *Rtags kyi 'jug pa*.

59 See, respectively, BKA', vol. 102; 317-318, and BKA', vol. 103; 137-138.

60 See the *Theg pa spyi bcings rtsa 'grel*, ed. Bkra shis (Chengdu: Si khron mi rigs dpe skrun khang, 1997), 7, where *Guhyagarbhatantra*, XIII: 1, is cited.

phreng ba in his intellectual history of Buddhism in which lies embedded a defense of Old School thought, but there is hardly any question that he modeled his work after the said passage from the *Guhyagarbhatantra*.[61] The searchable collected oeuvre of Klong chen, again courtesy of tbrc.org, elicits two instances where he cited the *Man ngag lta ba'i phreng ba*, even though neither occur in the context of Klong chen's reflections on the non-Buddhist philosophical systems.

Finally, the figure of three hundred and sixty-two non-Buddhist points of view occurs in the *Anuyoga*-tantra of the *Mdo dgongs 'dus*, LX: 7, where we read the following :[62]

log par rtog 'di ya mtshan can //
brgya phrag gsum dang drug cu gnyis //
nyi shu 'am sde bco lnga gnyis //
tha dad du ma du mar snang //

This misconception, which is amazing,
Appears in many different guises,
Three hundred and sixty-two,
In twenty or fifteen categories.

At one point, Rin chen bzang po discusses the idea of the three types of intelligent compassion and cites *Bodhicittavivaraṇa*, 3, for the one that is focusd on the Buddhist religion (*chos la dmigs pa*) :[63]

snying rjes brlan pa'i sems kyis ni //
'bad pas bsgom pa bya ba yin //
thugs rje'i bdag nyid sangs rgyas kyis //
byang chub sems ni rtag tu bsgom //

61 For Rog bande's work, see now J.I. Cabezón's annotated translation, *The Buddha's Doctrine and the Nine Vehicles. Rog Bande Sherab's Lamp of the Teachings* (New York: Oxford University Press, 2013).

62 BKA', vol.101; 601. See also Gnubs Sangs rgyas ye shes' (early 9th cent.) comments on this verse in his *Sangs rgyas thams cad kyi dgongs pa 'dus pa'i mdo'i dka' 'grel mun pa'i go cha lde mig gsal byed rnal 'byor nyi ma* [Smad cha], *Bka' ma rgyas pa*, vol. 51 (Kalimpong: Dupjung Lama, 1982-1987), 409. The *Mdo dgongs 'dus* is discussed in J.P. Dalton, *Uses of the Dgongs pa 'dus pa'i mdo in the Development of the Rnying ma School*, unpublished University of Michigan doctoral dissertation (Ann Arbor, 2002). See now also Dalton's *The Gathering of Intentions: A History of a Tibetan Tantra* (New York: Columbia University Press, 2016).

63 RGYUD, 55.

One should cultivate with effort,
With an attitude that is moistened by compassion,
The resolve to become *buddha*, which was constantly cultivated,
By the Buḍdha, who embodied enlightened compassion.

The available record shows that this verse quite unambiguously belongs to the translation of the text by the Indian Guṇakara[śrībhadra] and his Tibetan counterpart Lo tsā ba Rab [tu] zhi [ba'i] bshes gnyen of *circa* 1070 or, if not, then to its revised version of *circa* 1100 that was undertaken by the Indian Kaṇakavarman and Lo tsā ba Pa tshab Nyi ma grags.[64] Of course there is the off chance that Rin chen bzang po had translated this work himself, but it does raise some concern in terms of its date and the correctness of its authorial attribution. For now, and unless there is credible evidence that the situation is otherwise, I will provisionally assume that Rin chen bzang po was indeed the author of the *Rgyud sde spyi'i rnam par bzhag pa*. However, if this were indeed the case, then it needs to be pointed out that the only time that I have found a fragment from it cited in the sources used for the present essay is in a late sixteenth century work. In what follows, then, I will briefly discuss the environment in which the *Rgyud sde spyi'i rnam par bzhag pa* may have taken shape. Part Two will discuss in detail the fragment from this work that deals with the meaning of tantra – Sog bzlog pa Blo gros rgyal mtshan (1552-1624) cited it in one of his early works – and will also include an appendix which contains a title-list of the works that he subsumes under each of the four main classes of tantric literature that are so well known and had become standard.

3. Some Classifications of Tantric Literature

In addition to the frantic pace at which Buddhist texts from the subcontinent, including the Kathmandu Valley, were translated into Tibetan, the era of the works and days of Rin chen bzang po and those associated with him was one in which there also seems to have taken place a rediscovery of sorts of the Tibetan translations of Indic esoteric and exoteric Buddhist texts that had been done during the late eighth and ninth centuries, together with re-enactments of the practices associated with these. In particular, the introduction of the

64 See my "Some Text-Historical Issues with the *Bodhicittavivaraṇa* by a Nāgārjuna and the Tibetan Commentarial Literature," *Himalayan Passages. Tibetan and Newar Studies in Honor of Hubert Decleer*, ed. B. Bogin and A. Quintman (Boston: Wisdom Publications, 2014), 135-136.

body of esoteric literature and its associated practices, uncontrolled, immensely varied, and haphazard in the extreme as it was, seems to have caused a great deal of bewilderment among the Tibetan Buddhist intellectual elite of the time, such as this was, and resulted in deep shifts and fissures in the contemporary religious *status quo,* such as that was. The main source for this bewilderment was that each of these very different works identified itself or was identified by one or another authority, recognized or otherwise, as having either emanated from an enlightened source such as the historical Buddha or from one of several exponents of the enlightening experience that is *buddha* such as Vajradhara, Vajrapāṇi, Samantabhadra, etc., or as having been written or inspired by a qualified authority. Earlier translations as well as later ones that had hitherto not been part of the corpus of "acceptable" works or that had not been available in the western regions of the Tibetan cultural area were raising some concern, if not alarm, since their contents, and the practices that devolved from them, seemed to run counter to what had been more or less familiar territory or what had been considered normative.[65] The contents and the practices in question mainly had to do with those that were found in the great-yogatantras (*mahāyogatantra*)[66] and in the more recent corpus of the so-called highest-yogatantras (*niruttarayogatantra*), specifically those of the so-called yogiṇī variety, which, as can be shown, grew out of redefinitions of the tenor of the great-yogatantras and the probably more recent category of the supreme-yogatantras (*yogottaratantra, rnal 'byor bla ma'i rgyud*). These classifications, re-classifications, and the privileging of one practice-system over the other that ensued in the course of the ever-growing body of tantric literature had no doubt as much to do with the politics of religion as with its corollary, namely, with competing interests in the religion market place.

65 See, for example, especially the study of J.P. Dalton, *The Taming of the Demons: Violence and Liberation in Tibetan Buddhism* (New Haven: Yale University Press, 2011), and the literature cited therein as well as the slightly more recent Ch.K. Wedemeyer, *Making Sense of Tantric Buddhism: History, Semiology and Transgression in the Indian Traditions* (New York: Columbia University Press, 2013).

66 For the early literature, see, for example, S. van Schaik, "A Definition of Mahāyoga: Sources from the Dunhuang Manuscripts," *Tantric Studies* 1 (2008), 45-88, "The Sweet Saint and the Four Yogas: A 'Lost' Mahāyoga Treatise from Dunhuang," *Journal of the International Association of Tibetan Studies* 4 (2008 [2009]), 1-67, and "The Limits of Transgression: The Samaya Vows of Mahāyoga," *Esoteric Buddhism at Dunhuang*, ed. M.T. Kapstein and S. van Schaik (Leiden: EJ Brill, 2010), 61-83, J.P. Dalton, "Mahāyoga Ritual Interests at Dunhuang: A Translation and Study of the Codex IOL Tib J 437/Pelliot tibétain 324," *New Studies of the Old Tibetan Documents: Philology, History and Religion*, eds. Y. Imaeda *et al.* (Tokyo: Research Institute for Languages and Cultures of Asia and Africa, 2011), 293-313, and O. Almogi, "The Eighteen Mahāyoga Tantric Cycles: A Real Canon or Merely the Notion of One," *Revue d'Etudes Tibétaines* 30 (2014), 47-110.

Unlike some of his contemporaries, Rin chen bzang po did not countenance the rubric of great-yogatantra, for he recognizes only the four of ritual-(*kriyā-*), conduct-(*caryā-*), yoga- and highest-yogatantra. He thus went counter to the view maintained by Śraddhākaravarman, one of his earliest and main teachers and co-translators, who at one time had maintained four basic categories, namely, ritual-, conduct-, yoga- and great-yogatantras. In a rewarding essay, G. Orofina cites Śraddhākaravarman's somewhat polemical **Niruttarayogatantrārthāvatārasaṃgraha* where he isolated two sub-classes of the great-yogatantras, a natural (*rang bzhin*) and a nominal one (*btags pa*).[67] The first is so identified on the basis of two verses from the *Guhyasamājottaratantra*, 34-35, verses to which we will return in Part Two. The second is divided into the two kinds of the yoga-means-tantra (*rnal 'byor thabs kyi rgyud*, **-upāyatantra*) and the yoga-discriminative insight-tantra (*rnal 'byor shes rab gyi rgyud*, **-prajñātantra*). These are then further subdivided into supreme-yogatantras and highest-yogatantras as well as into a wisdom-tantra (*rig pa'i rgyud*, **vidyātantra*) and fundamental-tantra (*rtsa ba'i rgyud*, **mūlatantra*). Unfortunately, unlike his brief descriptions of the Ritual-, Conduct-, and Yogatantras, Śraddhākaravarman does not align any actual titles of the relevant tantras to his analysis of those works he considered to be great-yogatantras.

Now Rin chen bzang po does not confront any of the other positions on tantra's typology, let alone the ones Śraddhākaravarman had proffered. But he does explain at some length the reasoning behind his fourfold classification under the following five rubrics with the relevant textual sources:[68]

(1) In accord with the time of their origination, the four aeons; citing the [*Dpal 'khor lo sdom pa'i rgyud kyi rgyal po*] *Dur khrod* [*kyi rgyan*] *rmad du byung ba'i rgyud* (**Adbhutaśamaśānālaṃkāratantra*):

bskal pa rdzogs ldan gsum gnyis dang //
rtsod ldan dus bzhi rim pa yis //

67 See her "Notes on the Early Phases of Indo-Tibetan Buddhism," *Le Parole e I Marmi. Studi ni Onore di Raniero Gnoli nel suo 70 Compleanno*, ed. R. Torella *et al.*, Serie Orientakle Roma XCII, 2 (Rome: Istituto Italiano per l'Africa e l'Oriente, 2001), 546-547, this passage is also cited in part in J.P. Dalton, "A Crisis of Doxography: How Tibetans Organized Tantra during the 8th-12th Centuries," *Journal of the International Association of Buddhist Studies* 28 (2005), 155-156. For Śraddhākaravarman's work, see BSTAN, vol. 41; 284-285. He seems to have worked with Rin chen bzang po rather early on, perhaps as early as the 980s and 990s. At the outset of his work, he cites two verses from Tripiṭakamālā's **Trinayapradīpa* (BSTAN, vol. 41; 35, 43) in BSTAN, vol. 41; 280-281.

68 RGYUD, 57-61.

rgyud kyang rnam pa bzhir gsungs te //
bya spyod rnal 'byor bla med do //[69]

The *Satya-, the Treta-, the Dvapara-, and,
The Kali-aeon, due to the four successive tempora,
Tantra, too, was pronounced four-fold,
Ritual, practice, yoga, highest.

Part of the so-called *Ra li* corpus of thirty-two tantras that are connected with the *Cakrasamvaratantra*, this work is available in the translation of Gayādhara and 'Brog mi Lo tsā ba Shākya ye shes (ca.995-1075).[70] In the early 1320s, Bu ston expressed a very positive opinion about this corpus, stating in the catalog portion of his famous chronicle that it was wrong to hold that these were written by Tibetans, since Gayādhara had explained their Sanskrit texts to 'Brog mi Lo tsā ba and Gnyos Lo tsā ba Yon tan grags.[71] However, he later began to harbor serious doubts about its overall authenticity, and the final word in his general survey was that while these had earlier been controversial, some were authentic tantras. And he writes that the authenticity of the others appears to be quite open to doubt and that this should be further looked into.[72] Rin chen dpal bzang po (1403-1479), who is better known by the name of Ratna gling pa, cites a similar passage from the *Dpal phreng dam pa'i rgyud* in his important chronicle of Buddhism-cum-defense of the Old School, which he wrote over a period of eight years, from 1458 to 1466.[73]

69 BKA', vol. 79; 779.

70 For these men, their contributions, and the problem of 'Brog mi Lo tsā ba's dates, see Davidson, *The Tibetan Renaissance: Tantric Buddhism in the Rebirth of Tibetan Culture*, 161-183.

71 See his *Bde bar gshegs pa'i bstan pa'i gsal byed chos kyi 'byung gnas gsung rab rin po che'i mdzod, Collected Works*, repr. L. Chandra, Part 24 (New Delhi: International Academy of Indian Culture, 1971), 988.

72 *Rgyud sde spyi'i rnam par gzhag pa rgyud sde rin po che'i mdzes rgyan*, 438. Si tu Paṇ chen Chos kyi 'byung gnas (1700-1774) cites both statements in his 1733 catalog of the Sde dge Kanjur; see his *Sde dge'i bka' 'gyur dkar chag* (Chengdu: Si khron mi rigs dpe skrun khang, 1988), 396. See further H. Eimer, *Der Tantra-Katalog des Bu ston im Vergleich mit der Abteilung Tantra des tibetischen Kanjur, Indica et Tibetica* 17 (Bonn: Indica et Tibetica Verlag, 1989), 67, n. 049.

73 See *The Nyingma Apology of Rin chen dpal bzang po* (= *Chos 'byung bstan pa'i sgron me rtsod zlog seng ge'i nga ro*) (Tashijong: The Sungrab Nyamso Gyunphel Parkhang Tibetan Craft Community, 1972), 107. For problems surrounding the authenticity of the *Dpal phreng dam pa'i rgyud*, see the long note in Almogi, "The Eighteen Mahāyoga Tantric Cycles: A Real Canon or Merely the Notion of One," 49-50, n. 8, where she also notes that Rog Bande cites this very same verse from the same tantra; see Cabezón, *The Buddha's Doctrine and the Nine Vehicles. Rog Bande Sherab's Lamp of the Teachings*, 126. Ratna gling pa nods severally in the direction of Rog Bande and his cognate work and it is possible, perhaps even likely, that he simply adopted its quotation.

(2) In accord with those who are to be disciplined, the four caste-types (*rigs*, **varṇa*) of individuals; citing the *Dpal bde mchog sbyangs pa rol pa*:

bya ba bram ze gtsang dang bstun //
spyod pa rje [*rje'u*] *rigs bde* [*de*] *bas* [*nas*] *lhag //*
rnal 'byor rgyal po 'khor tshogs mang //
gzhi [*bzhi*] *dmangs gdod nas grol ba ste //*
gzhan du su la'ang ma bstan par //
mdzes pa [*ma*] *khyod la bstan pa yin //*[74]

Ritual, the brahmin [caste], accords with purification,
Conduct, the mercantile caste, is better than that,
Yoga, the king (*rgyal po*) and the many hosts of the entourage (= *rgyal rigs*, **kṣatriyavarṇa*).
The fourth, the people at large (*dmangs, śudra* [*varṇa*]), is being free from the beginning.
Not at all taught to anyone else,
Oh, beautiful lady, it was taught to you.

Bu ston quotes these lines from what he describes as the alleged (*zer*) *Dpal bde mchog sbyangs pa rol pa*, albeit with the much better readings that I have provided in brackets and which I follow in my translation. Verrill also translated this passage from Bu ston's text.[75] Aside from the fact that he renders the title *Dpal bde mchog sbyangs pa rol pa* by "the short *Cakrasamvara…Tantra*," which is incorrect, not to mention that these lines are not found in that tantra, he also omitted to signal that Bu ston closes this quotation by writing "…one should investigate whether the aforesaid explanation [or text] is or is not false" (*…bshad zer rdzun ma yin min brtag go //*). Klong chen cites this very same verse, albeit from what he calls the *Bde mchog rol pa'i rgyud* and with one variant, *gzhi rmongs* for *gzhi dmangs*, in his work on the philosophical systems (*grub mtha'*).[76] And he cites the very same passage from the very same work in his *Ngal gso skor gsum gyi spyi don legs bshad rgya mtsho* and

74 See also *Rgyud sde spyi'i rnam par gzhag pa rgyud sde rin po che'i mdzes rgyan*, 39.

75 *The Yogini's Eye. Comprehensive Introduction to Buddhist Tantra*, tr. Ngor Thartse Khenpo Sonam Gyatso and W. Verrill, 230-231.

76 *Grub mtha' rin po che'i mdzod*, 322. Hence, *The Precious Treasury of Philosophical Systems*, tr. R. Barron, 270, has for this line: "Primordial freedom is for those who are fundamentally deluded."

Sngags kyi spyi don/bcings tshangs dbyangs 'brug sgra.[77] But there the reading in both is *gzhi dmangs*! And this goes to show once again that when reading Tibetan texts we must consult every possible witness!

(3) In accord with the four types of individuals who engage in them; he cites these lines from a work he does not identify but which turns out to be the *Rdo rje gur* [*Vajrapañjara*, XIII: 6]:

dman pa rnams la bya ba'i rgyud //
bya med spyod pa de bas lhag //
sems can mchog la rnal 'byor rgyud //
rnal 'byor bla med de lhag pa'o //[78]

Ritual-tantra for the inferiors,
Conduct without ritual is superior to that,
Supreme yoga is for supreme sentient beings,
Highest yoga is beyond that.

(4) In accord with the four kinds of cupidity-attachment as the sites that need to be purified; he citesthe *Brtag gnyis* (= *Hevajratantra*):

lta dang dgod dang lag bcangs dang //
'khyud dang gnyis spyad la sogs pa //
rgyud kyang rnam pa bzhi rnams su //

Gazing, smiling, embracing, and,
Enjoying intercourse, etc.,
Tantra, too, [is stated] to be four-fold…

77 See his *Collected Works*, ed. Dpal brtsegs bod yig dpe rnying zhib 'jug khang (Beijing: Krung go'i bod rig pa dpe skrun khang, 2009), vol. 22, 313, and vol. 25, 37.

78 This verse is cited in, for example, Slob dpon, *Rgyud sde spyi'i rnam par gzhag pa*, 16/4 (= *The Yogini's Eye. Comprehensive Introduction to Buddhist Tantra*, tr. Ngor Thartse Khenpo Sonam Gyatso and W. Verrill, 205), and Bu ston, *Rgyud sde spyi'i rnam par gzhag pa rgyud sde rin po che'i mdzes rgyan*, 39. Ratna gling pa, *The Nyingma Apology of Rin chen dpal bzang po* [= *Chos 'byung bstan pa'i sgron me rtsod zlog seng ge'i nga ro*], 107, cites the *Rdo rje sa 'og gi rgyud* (**Vajrapātālatantra*) for a very similar idea. Translated by Sugataśrī and Sa skya Paṇḍita, the text by this title in BKA', vol. 94; 667-739, does not include such an idea, let alone have this passage.

Rin chen bzang po's quotation from the *Hevajratantra* only runs parallel to but is by no means equivalent to either *Hevajratantra*, II, iii: 11, or II, iii: 54.[79] The first reads in connection with the four types of empowerment:

dgod pa dag pa slob dpon nyid //
lta ba gsang ba de bzhin no //
lag bcangs las ni shes rab nyid //
gnyis gnyis 'khyud la de yang nyid //

And the second reads correlatively with the number of tantra-types:

hasitaṃ cekṣaṇābhyān tu āliṅgaṃ dvandakais tathā /
tantreṇāpi caturṇāṃ ca saṃdhyābhāṣaṃ na śabditaṃ //
dgod dang lta ba dag gis dang //
'khyud dang de bzhin gnyis gnyis kyi //
rgyud kyang rnam pa bzhi rnams kyis //
dgongs pa'i skad ni ma bsgrags pa //

One of the last verses of *Laghucakrasaṃvaratantra*, III, expresses a similar sentiment, albeit perhaps somewhat problematically.[80] Something like it is also cited in the *'Phags pa 'jam dpal gyi mtshan yang dag par brjod pa'i phan yon gyi 'grel pa*, a commentary on the *Mañjuśrīnāmasaṃgīti* that was allegedly written by a *Kālacakrapada, but which was widely held in Tibet as being of Tibetan (*bod ma*) rather than of Indic origin; the citation runs as follows:[81]

rgod dang lta dang lag bcangs //
gnyis gnyis khyud rnam pa bzhi //
srin bu'i tshul gyis rgyud bzhi gnas //

79 BKA', vol. 80; 42 and 46; see also *The Hevajratantra, A Critical Study*, Part II, ed. D.L. Snellgrove (London: Oxford University Press, 1959), 55, 61. The full and authentic verse is cited in Slob dpon, *Rgyud sde spyi'i rnam par gzhag pa*, 17/2-3 (= *The Yogini's Eye. Comprehensive Introduction to Buddhist Tantra*, tr. Ngor Thartse Khenpo Sonam Gyatso and W. Verrill, 220, 258-259), and Bu ston, *Rgyud sde spyi'i rnam par gzhag pa rgyud sde rin po che'i mdzes rgyan*, 32-33.

80 BKA', vol. 77; 611 (= D.B. Gray, The *Cakrasamvara Tantra* (*The Discourse of Śrī Heruka*, New York: The American Institute of Buddhist Studies at Columbia University, 2007), 176, and n. 16).

81 BSTAN, vol. 8; 645.

According to Bu ston and Tsong kha pa, these lines are found in the *Saṃpuṭatanta* and Bo dong Paṇ chen cites these as being taken from the *Kha sbyor*, where the latter is of course a synonym of *Saṃpuṭa*.[82] Of some interest is that the otherwise little known commentator Dhaṅkadāśa, that is, Taṅkadāśa, cites the component parts of *Hevajratantra*, II, iii: 54, as follows in his Hevajratantra commentary in favor of a five-fold classification of tantric literature:[83]

> *...bya ba spyod pa'i rgyud ni dgod pa zhes brjod do // rnal 'byor gyi rgyud ni lta ba zhes pa'o // rnal 'byor bla ma'i rgyud ni lag bcangs zhes pa'o // rnal 'byor bla na med pa'i rgyud ni gnyis gnyis 'khyud ces pa ste / rgyud ni bzhi po rnams kyis kyang // dgongs pa'i skad ni ma bsgrags pa zhes bshad do //*
>
> The action- and conduct-tantras are "smiling"; the yogatantra is "gazing"; the supreme-yogatantra is "embracing"; the highest-yogatantra is "intercourse"; it is stated:
> The four tantras, too,
> Do not proclaim the intentional language.

According to its colophon, the Kashmiri scholar Vimalaśrībhadra and Shong Lo tsā ba Blo gros brtan pa had translated Taṅkadāśa's work in Sa skya monastery. The team had done so by order of Bla ma dam pa Chos kyi rgyal po, that is, 'Phags pa Blo gros rgyal mtshan (1235-1280), and with the financial support of the official (*dpon*) Zhang btsun.[84] And this five-fold characterization is also found in the *Bla ma'i bsnyen bkur gyi dka' 'grel*,[85] the undated commentary on the *Gurupañcāsikā* by Vāpilladatta (?9th-10th cent.), which is

82 Bu ston, *Rgyud sde spyi'i rnam par gzhag pa rgyud sde rin po che'i mdzes rgyan*, 32, *Tantra in Tibet. The Great Exposition of Secret Mantra by Tsong kha pa*, tr. J. Hopkins, *The Wisdom of Tibet Series*-3 (London: George, Allen & Unwin, 1977), 156-157, and Bo dong Paṇ chen, *Thun mong ma yin pa'i rgyud sde'i rnam bzhag bshad pa*, 613 [= Beijing ed., 199].

83 BSTAN, vol. 2; 540-541.

84 He was the grand-nephew of the more famous Kashmirian Śākyaśrībhadra (1127-1225) and some notes on him may be gleaned from my "On the Vicissitudes of Subhūticandra's *Kāmadhenu* Commentary on the *Amarakoṣa* in Tibet," *Journal of the International Association of Tibetan Studies* 5 (2009), 26, n. 82, 28, n. 92, and my "Studies in Btsun pa Ston gzhon's *Pramāṇavārttika* Commentary of ?1297, Part One: Preliminary Observations and the Import of its Title," *Revue d'Etudes Tibétaines* 30 (2014), 36, 53-54. He is also known for his role in a change in the Tibetan calendar and this will be studied on another occasion.

85 BSTAN, vol. 41; 602.

extant in a translation 'Gos Lo tsā ba II had prepared in Lha khang steng.[86]

In connection with his citation of *Hevajratantra*, II, iii: 54, the Slob dpon makes the interesting statement – but see below for an important text-critical remark – that some earlier scholar-yogis such as Virūpa, the founder of the Path-and-Result (*lam 'bras*) system in which the *Hevajratantra* occupies a center-stage position, felt that this verse indirectly indicated a five-fold classification of tantric literature and practice where the so-called supreme-yogatantra (*rnal 'byor bla ma'i rgyud, yogottaratantra*) was inserted between the yogatantra and the highest-yogatantra. He does not provide a source where Virūpa and company may have asserted this, but he does suggest that this indicated that some had privileged the *Hevajratantra* as *the* highest-yogatantra. Himself an exponent of what arguably was to become the most important transmission of the Path-and-Result system, the Slob dpon states that since both the supreme-yogatantra and the highest-yogatantra include the unsurpassed secret gnosis (*gsang ba'i ye shes bla na med pa*) as a key category, there are actually only four tantra classes. He thus collapses these two into one category. The expression *rnal 'byor bla ma* (**yogottara*) appears only in such yoginītantras as the **Ratnamālātantra* and the**Jñānatilakatantra*.[87] The *Guhyasamājatantra* is possibly the best-known tantra in the academy where it is au courant as a highest-yogatantra. But it was not always thusly classified in the Indian subcontinent. Possibly a disciple of a certain Rin chen rdo rje (Ratnavajra), the otherwise unkown Indian Longs spyod rdo rje (*Saṃbhogavajra) refers to it as a supreme-yogatantra in his *Dpal gsang chen padma* (**Śrīmāhaguhyapadma*) commentary,[88] which he translated by himself, and this trend persisted as late as the early twelfth century when Abhayākaragupta (ca.1050-ca.1125) still classified the *Guhyasamājatantra* as a supreme-

86 In the colophon, 'Gos Lo tsā ba II pays homage to his teacher Vanaratna (1384-1468) for the blessings he had received from him and who may even have given him the Sanskrit manuscript of this work; see BSTAN, vol. 41; 659. Zhwa dmar IV Chos grags ye shes (1453-1524) acknowledges, in his 1517 biography of 'Gos Lo tsā ba II, that the manuscript had no author's colophon (*mdzad byang med pa*); see the *'Gos lo gzhon nu dpal gyi rnam thar*, ed. Ngag dbang nor bu (Beijing: Mi rigs dpe skrun khang, 2004), 107; see also my forthcoming "Notes on the Spiritual Teacher in Tibet and a Case of Upward Social Mobility in the Fourteenth Century."

87 IBKA', vol. 79; 609, and vol. 80; 313.

88 BSTAN, vol. 10; 666. Beginning with Bu ston, this work is listed in the *Cakrasaṃvara* corpus; see his *Bstan 'gyur gyi dkar chag yid bzhin nor bu dbang gi rgyal po'i phreng ba, Collected Works*, Part 26, ed. L. Chandra (New Delhi: International Academy of Indian Culture, 1971), 425. Bu ston notes there that some had claimed it to be a commentary on the *Cakrasaṃvaratantra* as well as on the *Buddhasamāyogatantra*, but he is of the opinion that it mainly focused on the former.

yogatantra and not as a highest-yogatantra.[89]

Based on Bu ston's work on the classification of tantric literature, the said tract in Bo dong Paṇ chen's encyclopedic *De kho na nyid kyi 'dus pa* provides the same sources for a pentad typology of tantric literature in connection with the ideas that are expressed in the *Hevajratantra* and the *Saṃpuṭatantra*.[90] But he on occasion disagrees with Bu ston. In the series of quotations concerning the five different classes, they both cite the *Rab tu sgron gsal*, which would be Candrakīrti II's (ca. 900) highly influential *Pradīpoddyotana* exegesis of the seventh century *Guhyasamājatantra* in the seventeen-chapter recension, and have it that the five of action-, conduct-, yoga-, supreme-yoga-, and yoginī-tantra are found therein. Be this as it may, the *Pradīpoddyotana* does not contain such a classification. And, indeed, it turns out that the quotation is from Bhavyakīrti's lengthy study of the *Pradīpoddyotana*, which is only extant in the Tibetan translation by a certain Kumāra, who may be the same as Kumārakalaśa![91] Bo dong Paṇ chen then cites *Hevajratantra*, II, iii: 54, and partly quotes the passage where the Slob dpon addressed Virūpa's alleged classification of action-, conduct-, yoga-, supreme-, and highest-yoga-tantra. At this point, he first rhetorically queries whether this does not contradict the passage of the *Hevajratantra* and then cites Bu ston who, without having referenced the *Hevajratantra*, held that there was no problem with such a classification.[92] Bo dong Paṇ chen disagrees with this for reasons that will not concern us here. A little later he turns his attention to the distinction between the supreme- and the highest-yogatantra. In so doing, he cites a statement in which such a distinction is made – *rnal 'byor bla ma dang / rnal 'byor bla na med pa'i rgyud kyis dbye bas so // zhes*

89 BSTAN,vol. 4; 255.

90 For what follows, see Bu ston, *Rgyud sde spyi'i rnam par gzhag pa rgyud sde rin po che'i mdzes rgyan*, 91-92, and Bo dong Paṇ chen, *Thun mong ma yin pa'i rgyud sde'i rnam bzhag bshad pa*, 635-636 (= Beijing ed., 222-223). At least at its outset, the latter work is highly polemical. The author makes a series of references to the views of those anonymous individuals - he signals these with such expressions as *kha cig na re…*, "some allege…" and *gzhan dag na re…*, "others allege…," etc., with whom he disagrees. Fortunately, an unknown glossator has identified these by barely (or wholly) undecipherable glosses that are placed above these expressions in the manuscript. The Beijing edition of Bo dong's work is here of some help.

91 See BSTAN, vol. 16; 565. For a study of Bhavyakīrti and aspects of his interesting work, see Tomabechi Toru, "Bhavyakīrti's Sub-commentary on the *Pradīpoddyotana* as a Doxography: Some Preliminary Remarks and a Synopsis," *Toyo Bunka* 東洋文化 (*Oriental Culture*) 96 (2016), 81-94, and my "Tantric Buddhist Scholasticism: Bhavyakīrti and his Summary of Sāṃkhya Philosophy," which is under preparation.

92 *Thun mong ma yin pa'i rgyud sde'i rnam bzhag bshad pa*, 636 (= Beijing ed., 223). The gloss above the not clearly legible kha cig na rereads bu, and, indeed, we find the passage in Bu ston, *Rgyud sde spyi'i rnam par gzhag pa rgyud sde rin po che'i mdzes rgyan*, 92.

pa – and then, no doubt with an eye on the Slob dpon's remark, critiques it on five counts.[93] Sometime later, he in turn is taken to task point by point by Gtsang Byams pa, who quotes this very same passage, states in his turn that these critiques are not reasonable (*de ni rig*[*s*] *pa ma yin te*], and then offers his reasons for having said so.[94] Of interest is that he held that there was a wording problem (*nor tshig*) with the statement *bla ma* and *bla na med pa*, and that the Slob dpon did not speak of Virūpa but rather of ?Bha ba pa. The latter points suggest of course that Gtsang Byams pa was working with a manuscript of the Slob dpon's text that was differently filiated from the ones that are currently available.

(5) In accord with the four foundations of spiritual practice where he cites from each of the four types of tantras:

a. Ritual-tantra: *Rtag pa bsdus pa'i rgyud*
b. Conduct-tantra: *Blo gros rgya mtshos zhus pa'i rgyud*
c. Yogatantra: *Dam tshig mngon par 'byung ba'i rgyud*[95]
d. Highest-yogatantra: *Dpal dam tshig chen po'i rgyud* (**Mahāsamayatantra*)[96]

bde ba chen po'i sku gsung thugs //
ye shes gcig sbyor sdom pa'o //
dpal ldan chos kyi sku gsung thugs //
ye shes gcig sbyor sdom pa'o //
longs spyod rdzogs pa'i sku gsung thugs //
ye shes gcig sbyor sdom pa'o //
sprul pa yi yang sku gsung thugs //
ye shes gcig sbyor sdom pa'o //

In vain do we look for the first three titles in the title-list of tantras of the four classes that are mentioned towards the end of the text – this list is reproduced in the appendix of Part

93 *Thun mong ma yin pa'i rgyud sde'i rnam bzhag bshad pa*, 637-638 (= Beijing ed., 224-225).

94 *Rgyud sde spyi'i rnam par bzhag pa rgyud ma lus par 'jug pa la rtsod pa spong ba*, 129-130.

95 Cabezón, *The Buddha's Doctrine and the Nine Vehicles. Rog Bande Sherab's Lamp of the Teachings*, 120, n. 18. This work is also mentioned in Buddhaguhya's (ca. 800) *Piṇḍārtha* commentary on the *Mahāvairocana-abhisaṃbodhitantra*; see S. Hodge, *TheMahāvairocana-abhisaṃbodhitantra with Buddhaguhya's Commentary* (London: Routledge Curzon, 2003), 561, n. 6. As Hodge remarks, "No tantra of this name is known to have survived."

96 BKA', vol. 79; 619.

Two of this paper.

Profound reservations were voiced by some in the Indian subcontinent as well as in Tibet concerning the monastic, that is, the celibate integrity of the ordained clergy, especially in connection with the secret- (*guhya-*, *gsang-*) and insight-gnosis- (*prajñājñāna-*) empowerments (*abhiṣekha, dbang*) in which coital sacraments play a fundamental role, and the unambiguously antinomian and thus *prima facie* ethically counterintuitive nature of some of the pronouncements found in these tantric writings. We find these reservations well articulated in, for example, the first chapter of the **Vajrācāryakriyasamuccaya* as well as, more famously, in Atiśa's **Bodhipathapradīpa*, a work that he wrote at the request of Byang chub 'od while he was staying in the Gu ge-Pu hrang region, and its *pañjikā*-commentary that is notentirely unproblematically attributed to him.[97] Rin chen bzang po defines the idea of empowerment and the two kinds of empowerments just mentioned as follows:[98]

The Secret Empowerment

> [29] *gsang dbang gi ngo bo ni / phyogs bcu dus gsum gyi de bzhin gshegs pa thams cad khu ba'i rang bzhin nyi zla rgyun gyis dbang bskur ba'o // de'ang* ***rin chen 'khor lo*** *nas /*
>
> *ji srid sangs rgyas thams cad kun //*
> *rdo rje'i lam nas padmar 'khyil //*
> *shu tra rakta 'dres pa las //*
> *yab yum bde'i ba'i ngang du gsal // zhes so //*
>
> *nges tshig ni / ghu ya du a bhi ṣe kha ta / zhes pa* [30] *dbang rdzas te / gsang chen gyi dam tshig yin pas na'o // de yang* ***bla ma brgyud rim*** *nas /*
>
> *thabs dang shes rab gnyis sbyar ba'i //*

97 For the first, see *Adarśa's (?-?) **Ācāryalakṣaṇavidhi*. *Adarśa is styled *Mahāpaṇḍita Maṇḍalācārya and his little work forms part of the *Vajrācāryakriyasamuccaya*, for which see BSTAN, vol. 39; 986-994. It was translated by Mañjuśrī, a scholar of Vikramaśīla, and Lo tsā ba Blo gros rgyal mtshan dpal bzang po (= Sa bzang Ma ti Paṇ chen (1294-1367) in accordance with the last wishes of Chos grags dpal bzang po (1283-?1363). Built by *Atiśa in 1040-1041, Vikramaśīla is another name for Tham Bahīl in Patan, Kathmandu Valley, for which see J. K. Locke SJ, *Buddhist Monasteries of Nepal. A Survey of the Bāhās and Bahīs of the Kathmandu* Valley (Kathmandu: Sahayogi Press, 1985), 404-413, as well as H. Decleer, "Master Atiśa in Nepal: The Tham bahīl and Five Stupas' Foundations According to the 'Brom ston Itinary," *Journal of the Nepal Research Center* 10 (1996), 27-54. A certain Vajraśrī, that is, Rdo rje dpal, who had apparently studied Sanskrit with Lo tsā ba Byang chub rtse mo (1315-1379/80), subsequently revised their earlier translation. For the other two, see R. Sherburne, SJ, tr., *The Complete Works of Atīśa, Śrī Dīpaṁkara śrījñāna* (Delhi: Aditya Prakashan, 2000), 19, verses 64-66, 293-301.

98 For what follows, see RGYUD, 25, 29-30, and 31.

gsang ba las byung gsang ba'i dbang / zhes so //

The essence of the secret empowerment is an empowerment by means of the stream of the sun (= menses) and moon (= seminal fluid), the essence of the sexual fluids of all the tathāgatas of the ten directions and the three times. That, too, is stated in the *Rin chen 'khor lo* (= **Ratnacakrābhiśekhopadeśakrama*) :[99]

> As long as all Buddhas,
> From the path of the *vajra (penis), are gathered in the *padma* (vagina),
> From the admixture of white (**śukla*) and red (*rakta*), they are obviously in the state of the father-mother bliss.

The "origin" (*nges tshig*, **nirukta*): it is called *guhyābhiśekha*, because the empowerment (*dbang*) being the "substance," it involves the spiritual commitment for what is a great secret (*gsang chen*). Moreover, the *Bla ma brgyud rim* (**Guruparaṃparakrama*) states:[100]

> What has taken place on the basis of the secret of joining the means (= male) with discriminative insight (= female), is the secret empowerment.

The Discriminative insight-gnosis Empowerment

[31] *shes rab ye shes kyi dbang gi ngo bo ni / las rgya byin gyis brlabs nas / snyom par 'jug pa'i dbyings dang ye shes dpe don ci rigs par ngo 'phrod do // de yang* ***sku gsung thugs kyi rgyud*** *nas /*

> *chos dbyings shes rab ces bya ste //*
> *ye shes bzhi ni ye shes yin/*

zhes pa dang / rin chen 'khor lo nas /

> *bud med sgyu ma la brten nas //*

99 BSTAN, vol. 27; 595; there the entire passage reads: *ji srid sangs rgyas thams cad kun // gtso gzungs zhal du thim pa las // sku yi dbus su thim pa dang // bde ba'i 'bru tshogs gsal ba'i rgyan // rdo rje'i lam nas padmor 'khyil // shu kra rakta 'dres pa ni // yab yum bde'i ba'i [pa yi]ngang du gsal //*. According to the colophon, this work was written by Master Avadhūtipa who, in his introductory remarks, calls himself Indrabhūti. The last line is found verbatim in the Rnying ma tantra of the *Bcom ldan 'das gnyis med kyi rgyal po*, for which see BKA', vol. 103; 582. The title is absent from the title listing of tantric treatises in the appendix of Part Two of this paper.

100 BSTAN, 41; 469, which is in prose!

dga' ba dang po sems kyis myong //

zhes so / nges tshig ni / pradznyā dznyā na a bhi śe ka ta/ zhes shes rab ma la brten nas lhan cig skyes pa'i ye shes rgyud la gnas pa'o // ***sku gsung thugs kyi rgyud*** *nas /*

shes rab la ni brten nas ni //
bde ba'i ye shes skye bas na //
shes rab ye shes dbang du gsungs //

zhes so //

The essence of the discriminative insight-gnosis empowerment involves the instruction in all the variety of meanings and similes of the sphere of being absorbed by the blessing-bestowing actress-seal (**karmamudrā*) [woman] and gnosis. Now the *Sku gsung thugs kyi rgyud* (**Kāyavākcittatantra*) states:

The range of meaning (**dharmadhātu*) is called discriminative awareness;
The four types of gnosis involve gnosis.

And the **Ratnacakrābhiśekhopadeśakrama* states:[101]

Depending on an illusory woman,
One mentally experiences the first bliss. [102]

The "origin": *prajñājñānābhiśekha*. Relying on a *prajñā*-consort, the innate gnosis remains in one's life-stream. The **Kāyavākcittatantra* states :[103]

In as much as the gnosis of bliss arises,
On the basis of discriminative insight,
It is stated to be the discriminative insight-gnosis empowerment.

4. Rejecting Allegedly Spurious Tantras and Allegedely Unorthodox Practices

The first recorded Tibetan reaction to the ethical and social problems that seem to have arisen from the misinterpretation of the religious texts, willful or otherwise, or from texts

101 BSTAN, vol. 27; 598; there the lines read: *bud med sgyu ma la brten te // bde de dang po sems kyis myong //*.
102 This is the first of the four kinds of bliss that are mentioned in the higher tantric literature.
103 BKA', vol. 79; 596.

that were considered non-Buddhist was the famous open *bka' shog*-letter/directive of Lha bla ma that S.G. Karmay studied some time ago.[104] In this document, Lha bla ma did not mention any personal names or book-titles, but he did take issue with what he said village "tantric practitioners" were doing in the name of Buddhism, with those who, practicing the religion of the non-Buddhist 'Ba' ji pa,[105] had said that whatever they were doing was a form of Buddhism, with those who practiced what they called Rdzogs chen – this is of course different from saying those who practiced Rdzogs chen! –, and with what he considered to be false, that is, inauthentic tantric texts (*sngags log*), the titles of which he did not name. The following two lines from his open letter are especially pertinent as their sentiment continued to resonate in the Tibetan cultural area in various forms throughout the subsequent centuries:[106]

sgrol ba dar bas ra lug nyal thag bcad //
sbyor ba dar bas mi rigs 'chol bar 'dres //

Due to the proliferation of *sgrol ba*, "effecting liberation,"
goats and sheep are sacrificed.[107]
Due to the proliferation of sbyor ba, "effecting intercourse,"
the social groupings of people are confusingly mixed.

There is a good reason for using this order, namely, *sgrol* and *sbyor*, instead of *sbyor sgrol*, as later authors beginning with his great-nephew Lha btsun/Pho brang Zhi ba 'od (1016-1111), alias Lha btsun Zhi ba 'od, commonly used – Zhi ba 'od was Byang chub 'od's younger brother. The tantras of the so-called Old School (Rnying ma pa) such as the *Guhyagarbhatantra*, the *De bzhin gshegs pa thams cad kyi gsang ba'i ye shes don gyi snying po rnal 'byor grub pa'i rgyud*, and the *Dpal he ru ka snying rje rol pa'i rgyud gsang zab mo'i mchog*, to name but three, use this binome or *dvandva* compound. The intent

104 See "The Ordinance of Lha bla ma ye shes 'od," *The Arrow and the Spindle. Studies in History, Myths, Rituals and Beliefs in Tibet* (Kathmandu: Mandala Book Point, 2009), 3-16.

105 For a searching but still inconclusive discussion of this puzzling expression, see D. Martin, *Unearthing Bon Treasures. Life and Contested Legacy of a Tibetan Scripture Revealer with a General Bibliography of Bon* (Leiden: Brill, 2001), 109, n. 8; see also C.A. Scherrer-Schaub, "Contre le libertinage. Un opuscule de Tabo adressé aux tantristes hérétiques?," 698, n. 16, and 709, n. 62.

106 "The Ordinance of Lha bla ma ye shes 'od," 14-15, ll. 49-50.

107 I am not sure about the exact meaning of *nyal thag bcad*, and only very tentatively follow Karmay's translation.

of the latter is not always as clear as one might think. Indeed, in his commentary on the *Guhyagarbhatantra*, the possibly ninth century *Sūryasiṃhaprabha isolated as many as six different senses for the expression *sbyor sgrol*.[108]

Gu ge Paṇ chen notes in his biography of Lha bla ma that the latter had written a *Sngags log sun 'byin gyi bstan bcos, Treatise that Confutes False Mantras/Tantras*, which, right or wrong, I take to be this very same open letter, and he adds with some enthusiasm that:[109]

> *'di ni mdo dbus khams rnams kyi mkhas shing grub pa brnyes pa mtha' dag gi yid kyi shing rta gang bar byed pa bcom ldan 'das kyi bka' ltar tshad mar gyur to //*
>
> This work, which fulfills "the vehicle of the mind" (= the desires) of all the scholars and spiritually realized ones of [A]mdo, Dbus and Khams, became authoritative like the enlightened speech of the one who, having overcome the embodiments of evil, passed beyond (*bcom ldan 'das*) (= the Buddha).[110]

It is of course quite doubtful that Lha bla ma in distant Mnga' ris was able to exert any influence over whatever was being done or practiced in distant Amdo and Khams. It is also relevant to note that in this particular directive, Lha bla ma made no use of the words "Bon" or "Bon po," let alone that he used these to refer to the adherents of the area's indigenous beliefs that were not alleged to be Buddhist. It is therefore *prima facie* difficult to interpret Gu ge Paṇ chen's explicit and repeated remarks that he had taken great pains at eradicating anything that had to do with the Bon religion, even to the point of throwing its texts into the rivers.[111] Perhaps the latter statement is a bit over the top, because Gu ge Paṇ chen's quotations of pieces from his other directives do unambiguously support the notion that Lha bla ma did subject what he called Bon and its adherents to a persecution of sorts.[112] Gu ge Paṇ chen wrote his work at Mtho ling monastery, which Lha bla ma had caused to be

108 See the text in BSTAN, vol. 43; 654 ff.

109 *Lha bla ma ye shes 'od kyi rnam[s] thar rgyas pa*, 315.

110 This is of course but one of several Tibetan interpretations of the meaning of Sanskrit *bhagavān*, that is, the Buddha, see Mie Ishikawa, *A Critical Edition of the Sgra sbyor bam po gnyis pa. An Old and Basic Commentary on the Mahāvyutpatti, Studia Tibetica No.* 18, *Materials for Tibetan-Mongolian Dictionaries*, vol. 2 (Tokyo: The Toyo Bunko, 1990), 6, no. 2.

111 *Lha bla ma ye shes 'od kyi rnam*[*s*] *thar rgyas pa*, 284-289, etc.

112 See here S.G. Karmay's as yet unpublished "Bon Institutions Referred to in the Newly Discovered Decrees of lHa Bla ma Ye shes 'od."

built in 996, and no doubt had access to her archives. Thus, if this were a historical fact and not a mere trope – there is an echo here of what is said to have happened during the large-scale introduction of Buddhism in the reign of Khri srong lde btsan (d. 800) –, then we can at least at a minimum assume that there was a Buddhist surpression, if not persecution, of those who held competing beliefs, whatever they and their literary foundations, if any, may have been. C. Scherrer-Schaub has drawn attention to yet another work *contra* questionable tantric practices. This is the brief text that was recovered from the manuscript holdings of Tabo monastery.[113]

Of course, the notion of killing and sacrifice as religious sacrements and sundry antinomial practices were not foreign to the more "orthodox" tantric literature. Thus, for example, *Hevajratantra*, I, vii: 21c-d, states :[114]

> *'bad pas snying rje bskyed pa yis* (var.: *bskyed nas ni*) //
> *bsad* (var.: *gsad*) *par bya ba brjod pa nyid* //
>
> By having (or: Having) effected enlightened compassion with effort,
> It is simply said that one should kill.

These lines are also found at the end of the fifth chapter of the *Saṃpuṭatantra* [I: 5], albeit with a variant reading in the second line:[115]

> *'bad pas snying rje bskyed nas ni* //
> *mkhas pas gsad* (var.: *bsad*) *par bya ba nyid* //

113 See especialy "Contre le libertinage. Un opuscule de Tabo adressé aux tantristes hérétiques?," 693-733. For Tabo in general, see D. Klimburg-Salter, *Tabo, A Lamp for the Kingdom. Early Indo-Tibetan Buddhist Art in the Western Himalaya* (New York: Thames and Hudson Inc., 1997).

114 *The Hevajratantra, A Critical Study*, Part II, ed. D.L. Snellgrove, 24-25. The Sanskrit text reads: *kṛpām utpādya yatnena māraṇaṃ krīyate viduḥ* //. Note that *viduḥ* is also rendered by *brjod pa nyid* in the fourth chapter of the *Śrīvajramahākāla...tantra*, in BKA', vol. 79; 808, where we have *'bad pas snying rje bskyed pa nyid // gsad par bya ba brjod pa nyid* //. But *viduḥ* derives from the verb *vetti*, which can be used in the sense of "to call" as well as "to consider" and "to know."

115 BKA', vol. 79; 285. The **Suviśadasaṃputaṭīkā* [*Rab tu gsal ba'i kha sbyor gyi rgya cher 'grel pa*], a *Hevajratantra* commentary, also has this reading and interprets *mkhas pa* as "the five kinds of gnosis" (*ye shes lnga*); see BSTAN, vol. 3; 189. The colophon does not indicate its author or translator, but Zhu chen Tshul khrims rin chen (1697-1774) states in his 1744 catalog of the Sde dge Tanjur that it was written by Master Old Kāyastha (= scribe) and that it was translated by Glan [Lo tsā ba] Dar ma blo gros (11th cent.); see *Bstan 'gyur dkar chag*, ed. Blo bzang bstan 'dzin *et al*. (Lhasa: Bod ljongs mi dmangs dpe skrun khang, 1985), 612.

Having effected enlightened compassion with effort,
Expertise should simply kill.

And elsewhere, for example, in Sa skya Paṇḍita's translation of the **Vajrakīlayamūlatantrakhaṇḍa*, we read the following:[116]

snying rjes bsgral ba'i dam tshig ni //
bsad cing mnan[a] *pa nyid min*[b] *te //*
phung po rdo rje'i bdag[c] *nyid de //*
rnam par shes pa rdo rjer bsgom //

[a] Yongle, Li thang, Beijing, and Co ne Kanjurs: *gsad cing gnan*; Snar thang and Zhol Kanjurs: *bsad cing mnan*.
[b] Snar thang and Zhol Kanjurs: yin.
[c] Yongle, Li thang, Beijing, and Co ne Kanjurs: phung *po rdo rje'i bdag*; Snar thang and Zhol Kanjurs: *phur pa'i rdo rje de*.

The sacred oath of 'delivering' with enlightened compassion,
Is not simply to kill or suppress, that is,
It is to meditate on the very essence of the adamantine
psycho-physical constituents,
On consciousness as admantine.

Another deity in this tantra is Rdo rje gzhon nu, that is, Vajrakumāra. Kumāra is the son of Śiva and he is also known as Skandha. Of course, Tibetan *phung po* reflects Sanskrit *skandha*, so that *phung po rdo rje* could also reflect or at least point to the personal name Skandhavajra.

The great Tāranātha, cites both passages in his 1600 commentary on his very own versified homage to the deity Cakrasaṃvara. Signaling that the first derives from the

116 BKA', vol. 81; 145. For a slightly different translation, see C. Cantwell, "To meditate upon consciousness as Vajra: Ritual 'killing and liberation' in the rNying-ma-pa tradition," *Tibetan Studies. Proceedings of the 7th Seminar of the International Association for Tibetan Studies*, *Graz* 1995, vol. 1, ed. H. Krasser *et al.* (Vienna: Österreichische Akademie der Wissenschaften, 1997), 107-118, and especially p. 115, and the same in C. Cantwell and R. Mayer, "Why did the Phur pa tradition become so prominent in Tibet?," *Tibetan Studies: Proceedings of the 11th Seminar of the International Association for Tibetan Studies, Königswinter 2006*, ed. O. Almogi, *Beiträge zur Zentralasienforschung* 14 (Halle: International Institute for Tibetan and Buddhist Studies, 2008), 254, n. 12.

Hevajratantra, his quotation of *Hevajratantra*, I: vii: 21c-d, is entirely unproblematic. On the other hand, he does not source the origin of the second one as taken from the *Vajrakīlayamūlatantrakhaṇḍa*. His reading of the verse is:[117]

snying rjes bsgral ba'i dam tshig ni //
bcad cing mnan pa ma yin te //
phung po rdo rjer gtams byas nas //
rnam par shes pa rdo rjer spar //[118]

It turns out that similar variations of this verse are found in a good number of Vajrakīlaya texts. For example, Boord records the reading of the last two lines of this verse in the *Dpal rdo rje phur ba spu gri nag po rab tu gsang ba'i rgyud*, an Old School tantra, which comes close to Tāranātha's readings; there we have:

phung po rdo rjer gtams byas nas //
rnam par shes pa rdo rjer sgom //[119]

Having "filled" the psycho-physical constituents as adamantine (?),
One meditates on consciousness as adamantine.

Note: Kong sprul Blo gros mtha' yas (1813-1899) commented on both readings, the one by Sa skya Paṇḍita and from what he refers to as an "early translation" (*snga' gyur*), in his study of this tantra, which he had written in 1899 at the age of eighty-six and thus shortly before his passing![120]

117 See his *Bde mchog bstod chen gyi rang 'grel phan bde'i rgya mtsho zhes bya ba'i stod cha, Jo nang rje btsun tā ra nā tha'i gsung 'bum dpe bsdur ma*, vol. 17/45, Mes po'i shul bzhag, vol. 59, ed. Dpal brtsegs bod yig dpe rnying zhib 'jug khang (Beijing: Krung go'i bod rig pa dpe skrun khang, 2008), 106; the same readings are also found in this work in in his *Collected Works* ('Dzam thang xylograph), vol. 9, 129 (see tbrc.org, W22276), and in his *Collected Works* (Rtag brtan phun tshogs gling xylograph), vol. 8; Leh: C. Namgyal and Tsewang Taru, 1982-1987), 117 (tbrc. org,W22277).

118 M.J. Boord, *The Cult of the Deity Vajrakīla, According to the Texts of the Northern Treasures Tradition of Tibet (byang-gter phur-ba)* (Tring: The Institute of Buddhist Studies, 1993), 138, 242-243. His translation is as follows: "... the sacred oaths of killing by compassion and never to harm or oppress are gathered together in the form of a *vajra* and one should meditate upon it as the *vajra* of the mind."

119 The same reading is also given in Ratna gling pa's quotation of the *Phur pa rtsa thung gi rgyud*; see *The Nyingma Apology of Rin chen dpal bzang po* (= *Chos 'byung bstan pa'i sgron me rtsod zlog seng ge'i nga ro*), 159.

120 See his *Dpal rdo rje phur pa rtsa ba'i rgyud kyi dum bu'i 'grel pa snying po bsdus pa dpal chen dgyes pa'i zhal lung, Bka' ma shin tu rgyas pa*, vol. 12 (Chengdu: Kaḥ tog Mhan po 'Jam dbyangs, 1999; tbrc.org, W25983), 37b-40a [88-93], but he does not countenance the reading of *spar*.

Tāranātha states immediately following these two citations:[121]

> *yang lo tsā ba rin chen bzang po'i zhal snga nas / bsad chog byas pas sems can de rnams grol bar 'gyur na / de bzhin gshegs pas kyang bsad chog kho na mdzad cing ston rigs par 'gyur gsung ba ni thugs brtse ba chenpos gsang sngags log par spyod pa 'gog pa'i dgos pa yod par mkhyen zhing gzigs nas gsungs par snang bas lan brgyar phyag bya'o //*
>
> Further, since the statement by Lo tsā ba Rin chen bzang po "If sentient beings become liberated through ritual killing, it is reasonable that the Tathāgata, too, can simply do and teach ritual killing." appear to have been stated on the basis of having understood and intuited with great compassion that there was a need for confuting wrong tantric practices, I should bow a hundred times.

At the outset, the moving force behind the reinvestment in Buddhism that took place in Mnga' ris in the late tenth century had a semblance of having acentral authority. The royal patronage that it received at least initially made the influx of purported Buddhist works from the subcontinent possible and no doubt, later on, added clout to one of the first tasks the royal family had set for itself, namely, to bring order into this literary chaos and the apparent free-for-all practices. At the same time, this reinvestment also had an unintended consequence in that it led to the introduction of competings forms of authority by the different forms of texts all claiming to be sacred scripture, together with their exponents. This influx of a very large body of purportedly sacred literature soon necessitated a sifting out of works of questionable origin, provenance, and what was perceived to be of questionable theoretical and practical orthodoxy, even if the exact criteria for such sifting were usually left unarticulated and lacked any tangible degrees of detail. Lo tsā ba Rin chen bzang po was, if not the first, then among the very first intellectuals who were Sanskritists and translators (*lo tsā ba*) in their own right to make an attempt to sort out and distinguish among this large variety of different works those that were Buddhist, those that were non-Buddhist, and those that were contaminated with non-Buddhist notions and practices. His *Sngags log sun 'byin* or *Confutation of False Tantras* may thus have been the very first

121 *Bde mchog bstod chen gyi rang 'grel phan bde'i rgya mtsho zhes bya ba'i stod cha*, 106-107.

Tibetan attempt at separating the orthodox from the heterodox and at setting things straight as far as "false" and counterproductive practices were concerned.

Evidently a rather substantial tract,[122] it has not [yet] been recovered, let alone published, so that we cannot make any pronouncement on the kind of criteria he may have used in making his determinations. But we do have fragments from it. For example, Nya dbon Kun dga' dpal (?1285-?1379) cites several passages from this work in his post-1371 defense of the Jo nang pa tradition and criticism of the Old School and 'Gos Lo tsā ba II Gzhon nu dpal (1382-1481) observed in his *pañjikā*-commentary on the Kālacakra corpus' *Vimalaprabhā* of 1467 that it contained citations of some passages from the "Kālacakra."[123] As yet unpublished, 'Gos Lo tsā ba II's work is available to me in a xylograph with one hundred and ninety-nine folios with a marginal notation Ca. The scribe of the original text was his very own disciple and biographer Smon lam grags pa, and the printing blocks were carved in 1472 with the financial support of Ngag gi dbang po (1439-1495), the Phag mo gru Spyan snga hierarch of Gdan sa mthil. Rin chen bzang po does mention the Kālacakra corpus in the *Rgyud sde spyi'i rnam bzhag* in his exposition of the so-called non-dual tantras of which there are two.[124]

Glo bo Mkhan chen was yet another author who cites this work, but he refers to it as the *Chos log sun 'byin*,[125] which I take to be a variant of *Sngags log sun 'byin*. Also called *'byam[s] yig* or "document for public circulation" – Dorji Wangchuk has suggested "propaganda pamphlet"[126] – other key-figures in the composition of works belonging to this genre of literature were Pho brang Zhi ba 'od and the late eleventh century Sanskritist 'Gos

122 Klong rdol Bla ma Ngag dbang blo bzang's (1719-1794) *Bka' gdams pa dang dge lugs pa bla ma rag rim gyi gsung 'bum mtshan tho* registers a manuscript in forty-eight folios; see *Materials for a History of Tibetan Literature*, Part 3, ed. L. Chandra (New Delhi: International Academy of Indian Culture, 1963), 673, no. 15801.

123 See, respectively, the *Gzhi lam 'bras gsum las brtsams pa'i dris lan yid kyi mun sel*, ed. 'Bras Rab 'byams pa Dkon mchog chos kho *et al.* (Beijing: Mi rigs dpe skrun khang, 2006), 102 ff., and the *Dpal dus kyi 'khor lo'i rgyud kyi dka' 'grel snying po'i don rab tu gsal ba'i rgyan*, 2b.

124 See RGYUD, 72, for which see the appendix of Part Two of this paper. The *Kālacakratantra* is also mentioned in a note in RGYUD, 70.

125 *Sdom pa gsum gyi rab tu dbye ba'i dris lan lung gi tshad ma 'khrul spong dgongs rgyan, Rgyud sde spyi rnam gsal byed sogs* (Dehra Dun, 1985), 253-254.

126 See his "An Eleventh Century Defense of the Authenticity of the *Guhyagarbhatantra,*" *The Many Canons of Tibetan Buddhism*, eds. H. Eimer and D. Germano (Leiden: Brill, 2002), 275. Some sources have the homophonous *'jam yig* instead of *'byam[s] yig*.

Lo tsā ba I.[127] They were followed[128] by Tsa mi Lo tsā ba Sangs rgyas grags (ca. 1150) and his *Spring yig chen mo*, Rngog Lho brag pa (or: Lha btsun Rngog) and his *Gsangs sngags kyi byung tshul rnam par bshad pa'i gtam chen mo*, Chag Lo tsā ba II Chos rje dpal (1197-1264) and his **Sngags log sun 'byin*,[129] Dar ma rgyal mtshan and his contribution,[130] and Zhang Bsod nams grags pa's (1292-1370) disciple 'Bri gung (or: Thang skya) Dpal 'dzin (ca. 1400) and his *Chos dang chos ma yin rnam par dbye ba'i bstan bcos*.[131] A treatise that shares considerable similarities with the last named, and I do not mean merely in terms of its title, is the one written by the great Bka' brgyud pa hierarch Karma pa VIII.[132] One word of caution: While most of these writers had reservations about the authenticity of certain specimen of tantric literature that we now associate with the Old and the New Schools (Gsar ma pa), most would no doubt side with Dar ma rgyal mtshan when he wrote the following passage – we find this cited time and again in the literature – in his yet to be fully studied

127 For the first, apparently written in 1092, see S.G. Karmay, "An Open Letter by Pho brang Zhi ba 'od," *The Arrow and the Spindle. Studies in History, Myths, Rituals and Beliefs in Tibet* (Kathmandu: Mandala Book Point, 2009), 17-41, and also, briefly, Martin, *Unearthing Bon Treasures*, 110 ff. The Tibetan text of this work is also found in A mes zhabs' undated *Jo gdan bla ma mang thos bshes gnyen pas dris lan yid kyi mun sel, Collected Works*, vol. 40, ed. Si khron bod yig dpe rnying myur skyob 'tshol sgrig khang (Lhasa: Bod ljongs dpe rnying dpe skrun khang, 2012), 28-32. For the second, see the *Sngags log sun 'byin gyi skor* (Thimphu: Kunsang Topgyel and Mani Dorji, 1979), 18-25, and A mes zhabs, *Jo gdan bla ma mang thos bshes gnyen pas dris lan yid kyi mun sel*, 32-35.

128 These are enumerated in Gser mdog Paṇ chen Shākya mchog ldan's (1428-1507) *Le'u gsum pa rig 'dzin sdom pa'i skabs kyi 'bel gtam rnam par nges pa, Collected Works*, vol. 7 (Beijing: Krung go'i bod rig pa dpe skrun khang, 2013), 146.

129 See the untitled work in the *Sngags log sun 'byin gyi skor*, 1-18, and the analysis in K. Raudsepp, "The Dating and Authorship Problems in the *Sngags log sun 'byin* Attributed to Chag Lo tsā ba Chos rje dpal," *Contemporary Visions in Tibetan Studies. The First International Seminar of Young Tibetologists, London, September 2007*, ed. B. Dotson et al. (Chicago: Serindia Publications, 2009), 281-297. Gser mdog Paṇ chen refers to Chag Lo tsā ba II's work as a "letter" (*spring yig*).

130 He alluded to this tract in his catalog of translated scripture (and a few other works besides), for which see Schaeffer and van der Kuijp, *An Early Tibetan Survey of Buddhist Literature: The Bstan pa rgyas pa rgyan gyi nyi 'od of Bcom ldan ral gri*, 257, 262.

131 A manuscript of this work with glosses in different hands is available from tbrc.org, W1CZ885. The *Sngags log sun 'byin gyi skor*, 17, also mentions Śākyaśrībhadra's *Zhu lan* and the *Gzer ma mgo* by a certain Lho brag.

132 See his *Chos dang chos ma yin par rnam par 'byed pa'i gtam chen po zab mo nang don 'khrul par ngo sprod par byed pa grub mtha'i spyi ching, Collected Works*, ed. Karma Bde legs, vol. 4 (Lhasa: 2004), 21-68. Undated, this work was written under the inspiration of his revered teacher Sangs rgyas mnyan pa (1457-1525).

Bslab pa gsum rgyan gyi me tog:[133]

> *gter ma rnying pa snyan rgyud sogs //*
> *sde snod gsum* [3] *dang rgyud sde bzhi'i //*
> *don dang mthun na skyon med yin //*
> *mi mthun rang bzor shes par bya //*
>
> If the old treasure-texts, the aural transmission, etc.
> Comport with the intent of the Tripiṭaka,
> And the four tantric classes, there is no fault.
> One should know what was does not comport to be self-fabricated.

Gu ge Paṇ chen cites the concluding verses of Mantrakalaśa's and Pho brang Zhi ba 'od's revision of the earlier translation of Ānandagarbha's (?8th cent.) *Śrīparamādhyaṭīkā* by Śraddhākaravarman, Kamalagupta, and Rin chen bzang po to the effect that Lha bla ma had dispatched Rin chen bzang po to Kashmir precisely because he felt that so much had gone awry with what he considered to be the orthopraxy associated with Buddhist tantric literature, that is to say:[134]

> *gsang sngags spyod pa'i lugs kun nyams pa dang //*
> *dkyil 'khor sbyin sreg cho ga nyams pa dang //*
> [*cho ga*] *dkyil 'khor cho ga padma stong ldan de //*
> *de bzhin sbyin sreg shan ti shug ti byed //*
> *gzhan yang gsang sngags sbas don kun nub cing //*
> *sbyor sgrol dang ni tshogs la sogs pas slad //*
> *'di yi don rnams btsal phyir bka' gnyer te //*

133 See his *Collected Works*, vol. 1, ed. Khams sprul Bsod nams don grub (Lhasa: Khams sprul Bsod nams don grub, 2006), 334-335. Undated, the *Bslab pa gsum rgyan gyi me tog* must have been one of his later works, since in it he refers to his very own *Rgyud sde rgyan gyi me tog* [306-307, 425], *Dgyes pa rdo rje rgyan gyi me tog* [321], *Kun gzhi rgyan gyi me tog* [324], *Bsngo ba rgyan gyi me tog* [325], *'Jig rten rgyan gyi me tog* [370], *Bstan pa rgyan gyi me tog* [393], *Grub mtha' rgyan gyi me tog* [395], *Dbu ma rgyan gyi me tog* [399], *Ngag gi dbang phyug grub pa* [417], and *Mngon par rtogs pa'i rgyan gyi me tog* [433]. He wrote this work in the monastery of Me tog mdangs can in Gtsang. A manuscript of the *Bslab pa gsum rgyan gyi me tog* was published in the *Bka' gdams gsung 'bum phyogs bsgrigs*, vol. 51, ed. Dpal brtsegs bod yig dpe rnying zhib 'jug khang (Chengdu: Si khron dpe skrun tshogs pa/Si khron mi rigs dpe skrun khang, 2007), 161-317; the cited passage is found on p. 226. The second passage is also cited in Cabezón, *The Buddha's Doctrine and the Nine Vehicles. Rog Bande Sherab's Lamp of the Teachings*, 30.

134 *Lha bla ma ye shes 'od kyi rnam*[*s*] *thar rgyas pa*, 307-308.

lo chen rin chen bzang po kha cher brdzangs //

All the methods of practicing the tantras were corrupted and,
The mandalas, burnt offerings, and rituals were corrupted and,
The Padma stong ldan mandala-ritual and,
Likewise performing ???? burnt offerings.[135]
Furthermore, all of the secret intent of the tantras had disappeared and
Were contaminated by such notions as *sbyor, sgrol*, and *tshogs*.
Because he searched for their intent, he made an effort and,
Dispatched Lo chen Rin chen bzang po to Kashmir.

The text in the Tanjurs is somewhat different:[136]

gsang sngags spyod pa'i chos lugs kun nyams dang //
dkyil 'khor sbyin sreg cho ga nub gyur pas //
dkyil 'khor cho ga padma stong ldan te //
de bzhin sbyin sreg shag ti shug tis byed //
gzhan yang gsang sngags sbas don nub gyur cing //
sbyor sgrol dang ni tshogs la sogs pas slad //
'di rnams don nges btsal phyir bkas gnyer te //
lo tsā rin chen bzang po kha cher brdzangs //

Finally, Bu ston and A mes zhabs cite these verses as follows in their chronicles of the Yogatantra literature:[137]

gsang sngags spyod pa'i lugs kun nyams pa dang //
dkyil 'khor sbyin sreg cho ga nub gyur pas //
dkyil 'khor cho ga padma stong ldan te[a] *//*

135 I have not found *shan ti shug ti* or the variant *shag ti shug ti* as given below in the dictionaries that are available to me, including Sumatiratna's marvelous 1877 two-volume *Bod hor gyi brda yig ming tshig don gsum gsal bar byed pa mun sel sgron me, Corpus Scriptorum Mongolorum*, T. 6-7 (Ulaan Baataar: Ulsyn Khèvlèl, 1959) (tbrc.org, W1PD95802) and Dpa' ris Sangs rgyas, *Dpe chos rna ba'i bdud rtsi* (Xining: Mtsho sngon mi rigs dpe skrun khang, 1985), nor in the work on the Mnga' ris dialects in Qu Aitang 瞿霭堂 and Tan Kerang 谭克让, *Ali zangyu* 阿里藏语 (Beijing: Zhongguo shehui kexue chubanshe, 1983).

136 BSTAN, vol. 31; 465-466.

137 See, respectively, the *Rnal 'byor rgyud kyi rgya mtshor 'jug pa'i gru gzings*, 143, and the *Rnal 'byor rgyud kyi dam pa'i chos byung ba'i tshul legs par bshad pa yo ga bstan pa'i sgo 'byed*, 224-225.

de bzhin sbyin sreg shag ti shug ti[b] *byed //*

[a] A mes zhabs: *de.*

[b] A mes zhabs: *cho ga shag ris.*

gzhan yang gsang sngags sbas don[a] *nub gyur cing //*
sbyor sgrol dang ni tshogs la sogs pas slad[b] *//*
'di rnams don gnyer btsal phyir bka' gnyer te //
lo tstsha[c] *rin chen* bzang po kha cher brdzangs //
[a] A mes zhabs: *don rnams.* [b] A mes zhabs: *bslad*
[c] Bu ston: *lo tstsha.*

Rin chen bzang po's *Rgyud sde spyi'i rnam bzhag*, as does his *Sngags log sun 'byin*, not only reflects the deeply felt concerns of the time, but also sheds light on the beginnings of a body of Tibetan intellectual practices that no doubt had an Indic background in which certain individuals were trying to make sense of and classify the baffling corpus of Buddhist tantric texts, large and small. The *Rgyud sde spyi'i rnam bzhag* has of course to do with a rational classification of the varieties of "authenticated" Buddhist tantric literature and the second, the *Sngags log sun 'byin*, with an inquiry into this literature and a dismissal of what he considered to be spurious and inauthentic writings. In the first, he does not once hint at what he might have considered objectionable either in terms of the authenticity of some of its literary sources or spiritual practices. But he does discuss the difference between non-Buddhist (*phyi*), and Buddhist (*nang*) tantras towards the end of his *Rgyud sde spyi'i rnam bzhag.*[138] Truth be told, the *Rgyud sde spyi'i rnam bzhag* is a "modernist" (*gsar ma pa*) treatise per excellence, since it makes no mention whatsoever of the tantric literature that is specific to the "old" (*rnying ma pa*) tradition. Although we cannot be absolutely certain of this, it would appear that the *gsar ma pa versus rnying ma pa* distinction may have been made towards the end of his life, but certainly not long after his passing.[139]

138 RGYUD, 72-74.

139 For a recent survey of history of this dictinction, see K. Raudsepp, "*Rnying ma* and *Gsar ma*: First Appearances of the Terms During the Early *Phyi dar* (Later Spread of the Doctrine," *Revue d'Etudes Tibétaines* 22 (2011), 25-45.

Abbreviations:

BKA' *Bka' 'gyur* [*dpe sdur ma*], ed. Krung go'i bod rig pa zhib 'jug lte gnas kyi bka' bstan dpe sdur khang (Beijing: Krung go'i bod rig pa dpe skrun khang, 2006-2009), 108 vols.

BSTAN *Bstan 'gyur* [*dpe sdur ma*], ed. Krung go'i bod rig pa zhib 'jug lte gnas kyi bka' bstan dpe sdur khang (Beijing: Krung go'i bod rig pa dpe skrun khang, 1994-2008), 120 vols.

RGYUD Lo tsā ba Rin chen bzang po, *Rgyud sde spyi'i rnam par bzhag pa 'thad ldan lung gi rgyan gyis spras pa, Sngon byon sa skya pa'i mkhas pa rnams kyi rgyud 'grel skor*, vol. 1 (Kathmandu: Sa skya rgyal yongs gsung rab slob gnyer khang, 2007), 1-77/78.

Postscript: Rin chen bzang po's *Sngags log sun 'byin* has recently been recovered by way of a fifty-two-folio *dbu med* manuscript, which Dr. Sha bo Mkha' byams of Tibet University ever so kindly made available to me. The main thrust of this work involves a detailed explication of the way in which the expression *sgrol sbyor* ought not be taken literally (*sgra ji bzhin pa*). I hope to return to it in the near future.

《秘密藏续》与旧译无上密法于西藏的传播 *

沈卫荣 杨杰

《秘密藏续》是藏传佛教旧译密咒的根本经典，也是所有佛法之心要、诸乘之绝顶、密法中最为殊胜秘密之金刚乘究竟见地自生大圆满法的根本所依。近年来于东西方日渐流传开来的中有法门，即以供养与观想一百寂忿本尊坛城为主要内容的《寂忿密意自解脱甚深法》（*zab chos zhi khro dgongs pa rang grol*），追本溯源也必以《秘密藏续》为其最直接的根源。自 8 世纪开始，《秘密藏续》就已经在雪域蕃地流传，虽毁誉不一，但其传承仍不绝如缕，日见广泛。

一、《秘密藏续》之名称

《秘密藏续》于藏文典籍中以各种繁略不同的名称出现，最常见的名称是：*dpal gsang bavi snying po de kho na nyid rnam par nges pavi rgyud chen po*，汉译作《吉祥秘密藏真实决定大续》，相应的梵文名称是：*Śrīguhyagarbhatattvaviniścaya-mahātantranāma*。其他的名称则有：《秘密藏续》（*rgyud gsang ba snying po*）、《幻化根本续》（*sgyu vphrul rtsa rgyud*）、《幻化秘密藏》（*sgyu vphrul gsang ba snying po*）、《秘密藏》（*gsang ba snying po*）、《根本续秘密藏》（*rtsa rgyud gsang ba snying po*）及《秘密幻化》（*gsang ba sgyu phrul*）等。甚至只需略称为《藏》（*snying po*）或《藏续》（*snying povi rgyud*）[1]，亦已代表此续，由是可见其重要性与代表性。

---

* 沈卫荣：清华大学人文与社科高等研究所教授；杨杰：中国人民大学国学院讲师。

本文于旧稿基础上扩充了部分正文内容，增加了注释，依据藏文原文重新订正了文中所涉翻译，纠正了部分欠妥表述，并依据国际学术届最新研究成果补写了第十八部分。

1 Dudjom Rinpoche, *The Nyingma School of Tibetan Buddhism, Its Fundamentals and History*, translated and edited by Gyurme Dorje with the collaboration of Matthew Kapstein, Boston: Wisdom Publications, 1991, Vol. II, pp. 262, 275.

二、《秘密藏续》于藏传佛教中的位置

简言之，《秘密藏续》乃藏传佛教宁玛派（rnying ma ba）或称旧译密咒（gsang sngags snga vgyur）幻化部的一部根本经典，是该派摩诃瑜伽（Mahāyoga，大瑜伽）修习之根本所依。该续说生圆无二，心智自显现坛城，于智自显现本性中成佛。包括《秘密藏续》在内的幻化部续典绝大部分都收录于《宁玛十万续》（*rnying ma rgyud vbum*），而《秘密藏续》的释论则主要收录于《宁玛教传广集》（*rnying ma bkav ma rgyas pa*），[2] 有些也见于藏文大藏经之《丹珠尔》（*bstan vgyur*）部。[3]

《秘密藏续》对于宁玛派之重要，或可于该派著名大德龙青巴上师（klong chen rab vbyams pa, 1308-1363）与米庞蒋扬尊者（mi pham vjam dbyangs rnam rgyal rgya mtsho，意译“文殊胜海不败尊者”，1846-1912）对它的评价中知其梗概。龙青巴上师于其名著《幻化网秘密藏续释论·十方除暗》（*phyogs bcu mun sel*）中说：

> 此殊胜吉祥秘密藏续真实决定，乃诸乘之绝顶，一切经教传承之根源，三世诸佛法乘之捷径，一切秘密之秘密。

而米庞尊者则于《秘密藏续》之另一部重要释论《秘密藏续释·十方除暗总义·光明藏》（*gsang vgrel phyogs bcuvi mun sel gyi spyi don vod gsal snying po*）[4] 中说：

> 此大续无隐藏显示无上密咒见与修之末摩（marman），如理抉择一切金刚乘密意，是故乃三界唯一如意宝、一切续之王、一切乘之绝顶、一切法之源头、一切圣言之总释、一切觉者之大捷道、一切佛密意之究竟。此续具微妙稀有大功德。故若无此（《秘密藏续》）所说末摩，仅各各凭自心（分别）力，将密咒乘金刚语引入推理（分别）境，如是随意所造诸论，乃如离命之尸身，当知其为无精要者也。

---

2 Dudjom Rinpoche, *rNying ma bka' ma rgyas pa: A Collection of Teachings and Initiations of the rNing-ma-pa Tradition Passed Through Continuous and Unbroken Oral Lineages from the Ancient Masters*, Kalimpong: Dudjung Lama, 1982-1987, Vol. 23-36, 48, 49.

3 见于《丹珠尔》的释论有：《大续王吉祥秘密藏疏》（*rgyud kyi rgyal po chen po dpal gsang bavi snying povi vgrel*）、《吉祥秘密藏唯一真实大疏》（*dpal gsang bavi snying po de kho na nyid nges pavi rgya cher bshad pavi vgrel pa*）、《吉祥秘密藏略义疏》（*dpal gsang bavi snying povi don bsdus vgrel pindartha*）、《吉祥秘密藏二次第义》（*dpal gsang bavi rim pa gnyis kyi don*）。

4 该释论汉译见沈卫荣译，谈锡永释：《幻化网秘密藏续释·光明藏》，台北：全佛文化，2010 年。

于金刚乘具增上信念之诸有缘众，当为授受如是之续，不惜身命而精进。

藏传佛教密乘部按译经时间的先后分成新、旧两派，一般说来以弥底尊者（Smṛtijñānakīrti）入藏以前所译续部经典为旧译密咒，是即宁玛派，而以大译师仁钦桑布（rin chen bzang po, 958-1055）以后所译续部经典为新译密咒。[5]

宁玛派教法传统有“九乘次第”（theg pa rim pa dgu）之说，简言之，声闻、缘觉、菩萨为共通三乘，乃化身佛释迦牟尼所说；事部、行部、瑜伽部为密咒外三乘，乃报身佛金刚萨埵所说；生起摩诃瑜伽、圆满阿努瑜伽、大圆满阿底瑜伽为无上内三乘，乃法身佛普贤王如来所说。共通三乘即通常所说之显宗三乘，而后六乘则是所谓甚深密咒（gsang sngags zab mo），亦即是密乘，也称金刚乘。

密乘经典，或称“续”（rgyud）、“怛特罗”（tantra），指分别表示本性、方便及身、智的基续（gzhivi rgyud）、道续（lam gyi rgyud）及果续（vbras buvi rgyud），以及说明这三续的事部、行部、瑜伽部及无上瑜伽部等四部之密典。事部、行部和瑜伽部三部为外续，由见（lta ba）而成为“外”者，因彼等不能通达诸法自性无别，更不能宣说自然智；由修（sgrom pa）而成为“外”者，因彼等不能观修誓句尊与智慧尊无贤劣差别；其灌顶（dbang）而成为“外”者，因彼等不能教示甚深三灌顶，所以被称为外续。无上瑜伽部又分成摩诃瑜伽（Mahāyoga，大瑜伽）、阿努瑜伽（Anuyoga，无比瑜伽）和阿底瑜伽（Atiyoga，无上瑜伽）三部，因为见地、果位都胜于外续，故被称为内续。说其见地殊胜，是因为外续不能通达二谛无别，许胜义谛为清净空性之一边，或离八边戏论，世俗谛被分成三种、四种或五种；而内续许胜义为离戏论边之本觉，世俗为身与智之显现，二者于心间无差别，亦即所谓之胜义谛与世俗谛无别。说其果位殊胜，是因为外续认为人当经过七世或五世修持，得三部、四

5　详见循努班（gzhon nu dpal）:《青史》（*deb ther sngon po*）；土观洛桑曲吉尼玛（thuvu bkwan blo bzang chos kyi nyi ma）:《土观宗派源流》（*thuvu bkwan grub mthav*）藏文版，兰州：甘肃民族出版社，1984 年，第 55-56 页。对新、旧密法的区分有种种不同的说法，或以在金刚座译出的为新密法，在邬仗那译出的为旧密法；或以空行母所译为新密，持明所译为旧密；还有人力主以四无量或七无量来区分，译因位金刚持至果位金刚持之间内容者为新密法，译果位金刚持之圆满修行法者为旧密法；金刚持所说为新密法，普贤王如来所说乃旧密法。而 15 世纪藏族杰出史家班觉桑布（dpal vbyor bzang po）则以为上述种种说法均不可靠，划分新、旧密法的标准只能是译经时间的先后。他以拉喇嘛益西沃（lha bla ma ye shes vod）之前所译密典为旧译密咒，以大译师仁钦桑布以后所译密典为新译密咒。详见班觉桑布：《汉藏史集》（*rgya bod yig tshang*），成都：四川民族出版社，1985 年，第 447-449 页。近年来，学界对新旧两译密咒划分问题的讨论，见 Kadri Raudsepp, “rNying ma and gSar ma: First Appearances of the Terms during the Early Phyi dar (Later Spread of the Doctrine),” *Revue d'Etudes Tibétaines*, 22, 2011, pp. 25-46。

部或五部的金刚持悉地。内续认为经灌顶、开示教诫即可登初地，由修习生起次第，可登第八地，由修习圆满次第可登第九地，由修习光明可登第十地，由修习双运可登第十三悉地，亦即金刚持地，最终生起身、语、意、功德、事业共二十五种，从而利益无边有情。[6]

摩诃瑜伽、阿努瑜伽及阿底瑜伽合称内续三瑜伽，也称方便瑜伽。摩诃瑜伽如诸法之基，重金刚乘地或本性，属生起次第，以“三等持”（ting vdzin gsum）渐次生起本尊，证知一切法乃心性“现空无二”之幻化；阿努瑜伽乃诸法之道，属圆满次第，证知一切法乃心性“界智无二”之力用；阿底瑜伽是诸法之果，是大圆满，为无生，因已超越生起及圆满二次第故，证知一切法乃心性自显现，即无始以来无生无灭之自生本智。龙青巴尊者于其名著《大圆满心性休息》（*rdzogs pa chen po sems nyid ngal gso*）中对此三方便内续总结如下：

> 大瑜伽续修生起次第
> 修风为主是即方便道
> 无比瑜伽修圆满次第
> 修乐为主且空乐双运
> 无上瑜伽主修无二智
> 三者皆知诸法本一如
> 如是了知而修习行持[7]

藏文大藏经《甘珠尔》之旧译续部（rnying rgyud）及藏传佛教宁玛派之内续经典总集《宁玛十万续》收录了摩诃瑜伽、阿努瑜伽及阿底瑜伽三内续的主要经典。虽然《秘密藏续》归类于摩诃瑜伽部，但其内容涉及所有三部方便内续。

三、摩诃瑜伽续部与修部之经典

摩诃瑜伽的经典被分成“续部”（rgyud sde）和“修部”（sgrub sde），前者是经典的外示主体，后者出于前者，主密修。而所有摩诃瑜伽密续之根本续乃《幻化网秘密藏续》。与五大本尊相应，摩诃瑜伽之“修部”经典分成五大部：

6 《汉藏史集》，第438-439页。
7 龙青巴造论、谈锡永译释：《大圆满心性休息导引》，台北：全佛文化，2010年，第158-159页。

1.《文殊阎摩敌续部》（*vjam dpal gshin rje gshad pavi rgyud skor*，文殊阎摩敌身，如来部）

2.《吉祥马头明王莲花语自在胜马游戏续部》（*dpal rta mgrin padma dbang chen rta mchog rol pavi rgyud sde rnams*，莲花马头语，莲花部）

3.《吉祥真实意续部》（*dpal yang dag thugs kyi rgyud sde rnams*，吉祥嘿噜嘎，不动部）

4.《无死甘露功德续部》（*vchi med bdud rtsi yon tan gyi rgyud sde rnams*，殊胜甘露功德，宝生部）

5.《出有坏吉祥金刚橛续部》（*bcom ldan vdas dpal rdo rje phur pavi rgyud sde rnams*，金刚橛事业，不空成就部）

这五部被称为出世间五部，此外还有世间三部：

1.《非人世间持母成就大续部和非人十万根本续》（*ma mo srid pavi dzong lung chen mo yum bzung mavi dngos grub chen movi rgyud rnams dang ma mo rtsa rgyud vbum tiggi skor*，差遣非人）

2.《供赞世间神》（*vjig rten mchod bstod*）

3.《猛咒诅詈》（*dmod pa drag sngags*）

旧译密法之法要有三种传承，即远传佛语（ring brgyud bkav ma）、近传伏藏（nye brgyud gter ma），以及甚深净相（zab mo dag snang）。远传佛语复分为幻（sgyu vphrul）、经（vdus pa mdo）、心（sems phyogs）三部。《秘密藏续》即是幻化部最重要的一部经典，故被称该部的根本续（rtsa bavi rgyud）。

摩诃瑜伽部“续部”经典有所谓十八部大续（tantra chen po bcu brgyad），[8] 传统上被认为是从《十万品幻化网续》（*sgyu vphrul drwa ba levu stong phrag brgya pavi rgyud*）中划分出来的。其中属身续者有三：

1.《诸佛平等和合续》（*sangs rgyas mnyam sbyor*）

2.《大象渡涉续》（*glang po che rab vbog*）

3.《大象入水续》（*glang po che chur zhugs*）

属语续者有三：

1.《月密明点续》（*zla gsang thig le*）

2.《从一放射续》（*gcig las vphros pa*）

8　关于这十八部大续名目的研究见 Orna Almogi, “The Eighteen Mahāyoga Tantric Cycles: A Real Canon or the Mere Notion of One?” *Revue d’Etudes Tibétaines*, No. 30, 2014, pp. 47-110.

3.《从多放射续》(*du ma las vphros pa*)

属意续者有三：

1.《密集续》(*gsang ba vdus pa*)

2.《山王连绵续》(*ri bo brtsegs pa*)

3.《聚于一顶续》(*rtse gcig vdus pa*)

属功德续者有三：

1.《最胜吉祥续》(*dpal mchog dang po*)

2.《最胜甘露续》(*bdud rtsivi mchog dang po*)

3.《如意宝续》(*yid bzhin nor buvi rgyud*)

属事业续者有三：

1.《羯磨磨勒续》(*skar ma ma le*)

2.《燃灯续》(*sgron me vbar ba*)

3.《金刚橛十二字续》(*ki la ya yig vbru bcu gnyis kyi rgyud*)

属总续者有三：

1.《幻化网续》(*sgyu vphrul drwa bavi rgyud*)

2.《三昧耶十万部庄严续》(*dam tshig sa ma ya vbum sde bkod pavi rgyud*)

3.《金刚方便羂索续》(*rdo rje thabs kyi zhags pavi rgyud*)[9]

另按《汉藏史集》的说法，旧译经典幻化部共有八部经典，称为幻变八部（*sgyu vphrul sde brgyad*），它们是：

1.《幻化根本续秘密藏续》(*sgyu vphrul rtsa bavi rgyud gsang bavi snying po*)，说心智自显现；[10]

2.《天女幻化续》(*lha mo sgyu vphrul*)，明说庄严；

3.《八幻化续》(*sgyu phrul brgyad pa*)，示现圆满坛城；

4.《四十幻化续》(*sgyu vphrul bzhi bcu pa*)，示现圆满事业；

5.《无上幻化续》(*sgyu vphrul bla ma*)，主示灌顶；

6.《八十幻化续》(*sgyu vphrul brgyad bcu pa*)，说究竟功德；

7.《文殊大幻网续》(*vjam dpal sgyu phrul drwa ba chen mo*)，说遍布一切根器；

8.《支分幻化续》(*sgyu vphrul le lag*)，说殊胜三昧耶。

9 《汉藏史集》，第443页。关于十八部大续的划分，历史上众说纷纭，莫衷一是。

10 于桑杰林巴（sangs rgyas gling pa, 1340-1396）之《遗教金鬘》(*bkav thang gser phreng*)中，此续被称为《幻化秘密金刚续》(*sgyu vphrul rdo rje gsang ba*)。

复有解释《幻化根本续秘密藏续》之所谓《四部释续》(*bshad rgyud sde bzhi*), 它们是：

1.《智慧藏续》(*ye shes snying po*)

2.《金刚镜续》(*rdo rje me long*)

3.《幻化尘续》(*sgyu vphrul thal ba*)

4.《幻化海续》(*sgyu vphrul rgya mtsho*)

前两部总说解脱道次第，后两部总说方便道次第。[11]

四、《秘密藏续》之科判

《秘密藏续》共分二十二品。依宁玛派的教传（bkav ma）传统，此二十二品分别与基、道、果三续相应：

甲　寂静坛城

基续

第一：缘起品

第二：发胜义及世俗菩提心本智品

第三：抉择一切法品

道续

第四：字鬘轮庄严品

第五：幻网成就三昧品

第六：坛城之幻化品

第七：坛城摄入及密咒品

第八：一切支分坛城加持幻化手印品

第九：金刚庄严秘密三昧耶品

第十：施灌顶品

第十一：会供坛城品

第十二：会供修持品

第十三：甚密诀窍藏品

11《汉藏史集》，第 449-450 页。关于宁玛派九乘次第的解说参见 S. G. Karmay, *The Great Perfection (rdzogs chen): A Philosophical and Meditative Teaching of Tibetan Buddhism*, Leiden: E. J. Brill, 2007。另见杨杰：《论藏传佛教四续部分类之形成及其印度源流》，《中国哲学史》2015 年第 4 期，第 56-61 页。

果续

第十四：大乐赞品

乙　忿怒坛城

基续

第十五：忿怒尊自性坛城如云化现品

道续

第十六：大忿怒尊众语坛城化现品

第十七：示现忿怒尊坛城品

第十八：示现净妙供施品

第十九：三昧耶品

第二十：任运成就加持品

果续

第二十一：忿怒尊赞品

结续

第二十二：欢喜与护持品

五、关于《秘密藏续》之真伪的争论

佛教密法于公元8世纪经莲花生大师传入雪域，其主要典籍即由莲花生（Padmasambhava）、无垢友（Vimalamitra）等印度上师和毗卢遮那（Vairocana）、娘班·定增桑布（nyang ban ting vdzin bzang po）等西藏译师翻译传承下来。由于他们传译的密法典籍都是秘密传授，禁止公开宣扬，再加上密法的传承遭到了热巴巾等吐蕃赞普的限制，密法的经典只有在得到王室的许可后才准许翻译，故而不像显乘经论那样流行广泛，以至于后世对诸如《秘密藏续》这样的密法经典是否真的源于圣地印度也产生怀疑。但当末代吐蕃赞普朗达玛灭法、王权衰败以后，显乘损失惨重，一时难以为继，而密法则反而大行于世，引起了残存之吐蕃宗室子弟的反对。其中，最早对《秘密藏续》等密法经典提出质疑，并对当时流行的密宗修法提出尖锐批评的是被人尊称为上师菩萨的天喇嘛益西沃（lha bla ma ye shes vod）。智光是10世纪末、11世纪初积极倡导佛教复兴的吐蕃宗室子弟中的杰出代表，为振兴佛法而不惜舍弃生命。他对佛法于雪域弘传的贡献主要在于派大译师仁钦桑布（rin chen bzang po, 958-1055）等人往迦湿弥罗（Kashmir）寻求正法之宗，开启了新译密咒的新时代。而其动机则在于他对旧译密法之真伪的怀疑，以及对交合、诛杀（sbyor sgrol）等密宗修法的反感。由于《秘密藏续》之十一品专门解释交合、诛杀，故特别为智光垢病，被其视为伪经。在保存至今的一份文诰中，天喇嘛益西沃用极端刻薄的语言对《秘密藏续》所描述的交合、诛杀等法严加谴责，说宁玛派教徒是借修法之名，行杀生、淫欲之实，并断言谁若将《秘密藏续》当作经典来奉行，则来世定将转生为罗刹。[12]

天喇嘛益西沃对宁玛派大圆满法——特别是对交合、药修、尸修、诛杀等修法的批评，在当时影响巨大，这一时期其他藏传佛教教派之僧人很少有人相信《秘密藏续》的真实性。根据土观洛桑曲吉尼玛尊者（thuvu bkwan blo bzang chos kyi nyi ma）所著《土观宗派源流》的记载，在大译师仁钦桑布所造《辨法与非法》（*chos dang chos min rnam vbyed*）一书和天喇嘛益西沃、希瓦沃（zhi ba vod）、咱米译师（tsa mi lotsāba）、恰译师（chag lotsāba）等人的书简，以及俄译师（rngog lotsāba）之《蒺藜论》（*gze ma ra mgo*）、萨迦班智达之《三律仪判别》（*sdom gsum rab dbye*）等著作中虽未明说宁玛派之过失，但在对藏地所传宗派凡有不纯正者均加驳斥，隐约中也有一二语暗刺宁玛派之处。此外，如噶当派的廓库巴拉孜（vgos khug pa lhas btsas）、止贡噶举派的止贡巴增（vbri gang dpal vdzin）也提出许多论点，证明宁玛派之教法之不纯正；附和其说的还有萨迦派的释迦乔丹（śākya mchog ldan）、噶玛噶举派的米觉多杰（mi bskyod rdo rje）等。然而支持宁玛派的各派大德也还不少，例如五世达赖喇嘛、衮邦图杰尊追（kun spungs thugs rje brtsun vgrus）、三世噶玛巴让琼多杰（rang byung rdo rje）、邬金珠乔（o rgyan grub mchog）、迥丹日贝热支（bcom ldan rig pavi ral gri）、塔译师尼玛坚赞（thar lo nyi ma rgyal mtshan）、竹巴噶举派上师白玛噶波（padma dkar po, 1527-1592）及藏族大史学家巴卧·祖拉成瓦（dpav bo gtsug lag vphreng ba, 1504-1566）等，以及宁玛派本派大师如昆敦·班觉伦珠（vkhon ston dpal vbyor lhun grub）及绒宋·曲吉桑布（rong zom chos bzang）等，皆曰宁玛派教法乃纯正之法。[13]

事实上，到13世纪噶当派上师迥丹日贝热支在桑耶发现了《秘密藏续》的梵文原本，这场争论已基本上告一段落。按照《青史》的说法，最早迦湿弥罗班智达释迦师利（Śākyaśrī, 1127-1225）来到桑耶时，发现了《秘密藏续》之梵本，后落入达敦·斯吉（rta ston gzi brjid）之手，后者复将此原本献给侠格译师（sha ge lotsāba），

12 Samten G. Karmay, “The Ordinance of Lha Bla-ma Ye-shes-’od,” *Tibetan Studies in Honour of Hugh Richardson, Proceedings of the International Seminar on Tibetan Studies Oxford* 1979, edited by M. Aris, and San Suu Kyi Aung, Warminster 1979, pp.150-162. 该文汉译见卡尔迈：《天喇嘛意西沃〔智光〕的文告》，严审村（谢继胜）译：《国外藏学译文集》第三辑，拉萨：西藏人民出版社，1985年，第106-118页。

13 土观洛桑曲吉尼玛：《土观宗派源流》藏文版，第73-74页。

侠格译师将其转给迥丹日贝热支上师，后者据此梵本造《秘密藏修习庄严花》（*gsang snying sgrub pa rgyan gyi me tog*）。最终，这个珍贵的梵本落到了《青史》的作者廓译师·循努班吉祥（vgos lotsāwa gzhon nu dpal, 1392-1481）手中，于是，这场争论终于烟尘落定。廓译师本人深信《秘密藏续》之真实性，作为例证，他还引述了布顿大师所编藏论目录中收录的许多引用《秘密藏续》之论著。[14] 像《秘密藏续》这样真实性受到他派上师怀疑的宁玛派典籍还有许多，例如宁玛派行人所坚信的由莲花生大士所传之《普巴根本品续》（*phur pa rtsa bavi dum bu*）也一直被疑为伪经，最后萨迦班智达贡嘎坚赞（sa paṇ kun dgav rgyal mtshan, 1182-1251）于香曲河谷塞兴地方古寺中发现了此续之梵文原本，别人才不得不信其真实。[15]

廓库巴拉孜也是11世纪时人，是噶当派祖师阿底峡的弟子，因向宁玛派上师大宿氏（zur chen po）求法不果而心生怨恨，当其自参拜圣地归回雪域后即宣称宁玛派所传经典不见于印度，故是伪经。对宁玛派之根本大续《秘密藏续》则更提出有所谓四大缺点（邪误）（skyon bzhi），并缺乏导师、眷属、处、法及时共五种圆满。他指责《秘密藏续》与其他续不同，没有出现菩萨为眷属，故犯界之错误；它不像其他经续通常说三时，而独说有四时，故犯时之错误；《秘密藏续》之坛城不以毗卢遮那佛为主尊，却以金刚萨埵为主尊，故犯坛城之错误；在表明修行之良辰吉日时，《秘密藏续》援引其他续部经文，故犯续文之错误。[16]

对于这些对宁玛派、特别是对《秘密藏续》的批评，宁玛巴给予了有力的回击。

---

14 廓译师循努班：《青史》（*The Blue Annals*）, New Delhi: Motilal Banarsidass, 1979。

15 19世纪不分派运动（ris med）著名上师康楚·罗珠塔耶（kong sprul blo gros mthav yas）曾为该续造释论《吉祥普巴金刚根本续品摄要释·大吉祥欢喜言教》（*dpal rdo rje phur pa rtsa bavi rgyud kyi dum buvi vgrel pa snying po bsdus pa dpal chen dgyes pavi zhal lung*），其开篇偈颂中即提及萨班据梵本重译该续从而令争论得以平息一事。有关包括该续在内的一系列普巴续典真实性问题的探讨，见 Robert Mayer, *A Scripture of the Ancient Tantra Collection: The Phur-pa-bcu-gnyis*, Oxford: Kiscadale Publications, 1996。

16 值得注意的是，以廓库巴拉孜为代表的这一批新译密咒上师往往被学界视为反感宁玛派交合、诛杀修习的宗教改革家，然而从廓库巴拉孜针对宁玛派教法所写的《破除邪密咒》（*sngags log sum vbyin*）一文来看，其中根本只字未提交合与诛杀修习，只是质疑宁玛派教法来源的可靠性与真实性。事实上，与交合与诛杀有关的修法也广见于新译密咒，因此，这些修法并不足以成为新译密咒攻击旧译密咒的把柄，有关这方面的论述，见 Christian K. Wedemeyer, "Sex, Death, and 'Reform' in Eleventh-century Tibetan Buddhist Esoterism: 'Gos Khug pa Lhas btsas, spyod pa (caryā), and mngon par spyod pa (abhicāra)'," in Todd Lewis and Bruce McCoy Owens (eds.), *Sucāruvādadeśika: A Festschrift Honoring Professor Theodore Riccardi*, Kathmandu: Himal Books, 2014, pp. 240-260.

龙青巴尊者在其《秘密藏续释 · 十方除暗》及《龙青教法源流》[17] 中都为此花了不少笔墨。此外，像前面提到的迥丹日贝热支，以及西藏著名史家、《贤者喜宴》（*mkhas pavi dgav ston*）的作者巴卧 · 祖拉成瓦以及索多巴 · 罗珠坚赞（sog bzlog pa blo gros rgyal mtshan, 1552-1664）等，也都对此作出过激烈的反应。索多巴在其《问答 · 教理雷音》（*dris lan lung dang rig pavi vbrug sgra*）中对天喇嘛益西沃的说法逐条予以批驳，特别是对受到批评的一些特殊的密宗修法作出了说明和辨正。例如，他申辩说，宁玛派之双修与世俗的男女交媾不是一回事，药修、尸修并不是宁玛派的独有之法、新密咒中也有救度法，救度和供修之法有差别，因救度和尸供而杀生，不是直接的杀生等等。[18] 从今天的眼光来看，索多巴的辩解实在不够有力，相反在很大程度上，他实际上接受了天喇嘛益西沃的非难，承认在天喇嘛时代确有人借修法之名，行种种恶行。

与此相比，迥丹日贝热支对廓库巴拉孜关于《秘密藏续》有四大缺点的反驳则有力得多。他对《秘密藏续》的注疏题为《秘密藏修习庄严花》（*gsang snying sgrub pa rgyan gyi me tog*），全书已不再单独存世，但从嘉色图确匝（rgyal sras thugs mchog rtsal）之《教法源流大宝藏论》（*chos vbyung rin po chevi gter mdzod*）、五世达赖喇嘛之《恒河水流》（*gang gavi chu rgyun*）、《索多巴全集》、龙青扎西南杰（klong chen bkra shis rnam rgyal）之《善说无垢恒河之水流》（*legs bshad dri med gang gavi chu rgyun*）以及巴卧 · 祖拉成瓦之《贤者喜宴》对其的大段引述中，尚可基本见其全貌。

迥丹日贝热支尊者先以众友上师所著《吉祥密集大疏》（*dpal gsang ba vdus pa vgrel chen*）等名著中曾引述《秘密藏续》为由，证明其非伪经。因为像《密集》部的这些著名的印度续部经典是不可能直接在西藏写成的，因而若在这些续部文献中援引了《秘密藏续》中的段落，则无疑再没有理由将《秘密藏续》归结到直接在西藏写成的伪经行列中去了。

迥丹日贝热支尊者写道：

> 解说此续（《秘密藏续》）为真经之理由如下：
> 阿阇梨众友（Viśvamitra）于其《吉祥密集大疏》（*dpal gsang ba vdus*

17 此书原名为《教法源流大宝藏论 · 阐明圣教之日光》（*chos vbyung rin po chevi gter mdzod bstan pa gsal bar byed pavi nyi ma vod*），习称《龙青教法源流》。此书之藏文原版由西藏藏文古籍出版社于 1991 年重新刊印。此书中有一章专论旧译密咒是否存在于印度（gsang sngags rnying ma rgya gar yul du bzhugs min sogs kyi skor），参见该书第 430-451 页。

18 对于尸修，新译密咒有《空行修尸法》（*ro langs mkhav spyod sgrub pa*）和《修尸金法》（*bam sgrub ro langs gser sgrub*）等。关于供修（mchod sgrub）有伯希和敦煌藏文写卷 840 号专述其修法。

pavi vgrel chen）中疏解《密集续》（*Guhyasamāja*）中“智慧勇识触何处”一句时，引证《秘密藏续》所云：“于离边离中之密严刹土，无量根本智周遍光明坛城，有智宝炽燃之越量宫，十方虚空遍满无间缺。”以及“于一切不可思议之（有情世界），普现种种身、语、意”。

又，当他在疏解《密集续》中“当知此塔乃诸佛之天宫”句时，引证《秘密藏续》所云：“无上本智居一切之中央，其间所有一切十方四时正觉坛城各各不可分别，都成一味。”

他在疏解“无自性之因”一句时，同样又引证《秘密藏续》所云如下：

如是稀有奇妙法
一切圆觉之秘密
由无生而生一切
生者本来是无生

随后，当众友上师解释“秘密”之含义时，他又提到《秘密藏续》所说自性、隐、密、不显示之秘密，以及《秘密藏续》所说五灌顶。复援引其（第一品）如下：

“所有行相颜色各异，或深蓝、或白、或黄、或赤、或绿，皆光辉灿烂。有最上王后，或为幻界、或为坚硬界、或为柔软界、或为温界、或为动界，如是王后聚悉皆无二，无边无际，周遍法界。如是，若芝麻剖荚盈满。”

他又说：“据《秘密藏续》有三种真实。”在所有这些和其他同类的例子中，众友上师都提到了《秘密藏续》。

紧接着，迥丹日贝热支又对廓库巴拉孜所提出的《秘密藏续》之所谓四大缺点一一反驳。

第一，若经文以“如是我闻”为开场白，通常则表明这些经、续乃由诸佛编纂而成，因为即使是已登十地之菩萨也不可能编集所有佛陀之教法。就如阿阇梨萨如儒诃（Saroruha）在其所著《密集续》之释论《吉祥秘密悉地》（*Śrīguhyasiddhi*）中所说：“大多数阿阇梨皆言，具德大光明《密集续》之结集者乃名为世间自在之勇者。大恩上师云：‘具德《密集续》之结集者非是他人，而是宣说此续者。”按照这种解释，宣说者本人即是结集者乃属传统。

第二，至于越量基者，阿毗达磨亦说色究竟天广大无量。

第三，至于所谓四时，众友于《吉祥密集大疏》中云：“如是，当知四时平等。”另外，“一切十方四时之怙主”这样的说法也见于新译密咒中。佛密上师解释说，此四时乃指四劫。

第四，至于何以金刚萨埵居于坛城之中央，新译密咒也说坛城之主尊可改变位置。

至于“尾点（tig）说为智慧名”句，在《秘密藏续》》之梵文原本中读作：sūtrī prajñātiṣyati。窣都利（sūtrī），梵文原意为线条，与藏文字 thig 正好相对等。日光狮子上师在《幻网秘密藏续真实疏》（*Guhyagarbhatattvanirṇayavyākhyānatākā*）中解释说：tig 实际上等同于 thig，tig 是一种古代的写法。

至于说在《秘密藏续》中提到了其他一些秘密续，则是因为所有后来传播的续典，都会提到比其先问世的其他续典；如《喜金刚续》等就提到过比其先传出的《摄真实续》（*Tattvasaṃgraha*）。

通过以上这些论据，迥丹日贝热支为宁玛派之根本大续《秘密藏续》重新树立起了真经的权威。如前所述，这场关于《秘密藏续》是真是伪的讨论，以 14 世纪廓译师亲自得到该续之梵文原本而告终。接着，索多巴在其所著《第二佛阿阇梨莲花生传 · 除意之暗》（*slob dpon sangs rgyas gnyis pa padma vbyung gnas kyi rnam par thar pa yid kyi mun sel*）中宣称，幻化网八部之梵文原本由莲花生大士亲自从印度那烂陀（Nālandā）寺带到桑耶寺，并在桑耶南边一个叫做伽噶札举岭（rgya dkar sgra bsgyur gling）的地方，以其神变将其译成藏文。所以，这些梵文原本即收藏于桑耶寺之葛藏（ke tshang），而不存于印度。

经过这一关于《秘密藏续》等宁玛派所传教法之真伪的讨论，宁玛派作为藏传佛教之一派的合法地位得到了肯定。以后，宁玛派当不再需要为证明其所持经续之真实性而大费笔墨。后来的宁玛派上师如吉美林巴（vjigs med gling pa，1729-1798）等人即拒绝再对像廓库巴那样的人提出的批评逐一予以批驳，认为迥丹日贝热支和索多巴等上师所作的响应已无法再予置喙。对此，就连新密咒派的译师如萨迦派大班智达释迦乔丹（śākya mchog ldan, 1428-1507）也出来主持公道，支持宁玛派，他提出没有必要劳神费力地去证明宁玛派的教法确是译自印度之梵文原本，若能证明它们是莲花生大士的教法，便足已证明其真经的地位了。尽管他们或与后来译自印度原本的密咒和表义语不完全一致，但他们的共与不共成就无可置喙地证明了其真实性。他们或可与那些并没有在印度被单卷单卷地译解，而由一些高僧大德自不同的地区获取的教法相比较。据云，经金刚萨埵同意，那些编集流传教法者本身也获准在不同的地方、用不同的语言来传播这些教法。宁玛派的教法传统传译自印度，这当然不需要作任何证明。若深文周纳，处心积虑地构想证据，人们或可证明一种不确定的经书是真经，而从前来到西藏的大师们发现这是一条人为假设的道路，为避免在这条道路上行走，他们便自己开始说法。

敦珠仁波切也说：

> 一般说来，一种教法并不是仅仅因为它源自印度就异常重要。以其出自哪个地区来作为分辨经书好坏之标准，此为学界所不齿。若一个作者乃得地之大德，那么，他所著作的经书就应当是真实可靠的。所以事实证明它们是来自印度或者西藏并不说明任何区别。西藏本土的经书有时甚至好过印度的经书。人们应当相信那些由藏地显现本智的成道者所编集的经书较之印度那些由只懂语法、因明的平庸学者所写的经书要可靠得多。[19]

六、《秘密藏续》在印度的历史传承

关于无上密咒乘摩诃瑜伽在人间瞻部洲传播的历史，佛经曾作过种种授记。《佛说教诫传授王经》有云：释迦牟尼佛行年八十，心知己身行将涅槃，遂于三月上旬告众弟子曰："吾将入于涅槃，汝等当召三界众天人至此，听吾为其析疑解惑，转最后一次法轮。"目犍连遂召集众弟子来会。释迦曰："吾之利他事业至此已告圆满，旋将入于涅槃。汝等几有疑惑，吾今当为汝等解之。"众弟子当即请求世尊不要入寂，有弟子持明王贡罗阇者，自座位起立，趋赴释迦牟尼佛身前曰："世尊！汝功德虽或圆满，惜尚未开示正法精要、甚深道大乘无上密法。"释迦答曰："吾离人世一百一十二年后，有教法心要之圣人，自色究竟天及须弥山顶四方城楼等天界三处降世，于瞻部洲之东方向人间之具福者、名字中有札（tsa）字之国王开示此法。"《幻化授记》亦云："释迦牟尼佛入灭后百十二载，内传之乘以咒语出现，传布于邬金等地，有名札者，及文殊、阎罗等无数持明师出现。此后，在印度传播，有无数获成就者出现。"根据这些授记，大乘无上密法，即所谓摩诃瑜伽在瞻部洲的传播，首先当从名子中有札字的那位国王算起。

这位带有传奇色彩的国王到底是谁？对此，众说纷纭，莫衷一是。或云即因大陀罗菩提（Indrabhūti），亦云乃大陀罗菩提之子，抑或为较晚的一位与古古罗阇（Kukkurāja, 犬王）、钦婆罗波陀（Kambalapāda）、萨如儒诃（Saroruha）、阇烂达罗巴

19 Dudjom Rinpoche, 1991, Vol.I, p.917.

（Jālandharipā）等人同时代的因陀罗菩提。[20]关于他的事迹，在藏文史籍中记载甚详，其云：

释迦牟尼入灭后百十二载，玛拉雅山东南有止香阿输罗（Triśam-asura）岩洞，乃诸种珍宝所成。有具福国王名札者，在洞中修外续密法，七次梦见秘密部主降临玛拉雅山顶，转动内续密法之法轮，并为他加持赐福。于最后一次梦中，空中有无身形之本尊发声授记曰："汝乃具善缘与大福德之人，即是化身佛所作授记之人，佛陀授记所言集正法精要之圣者，即具福之汝。"国王自梦中醒来，即刻爬上山顶，见一尊紫色珍宝所成之秘密主金刚手身像，高约一肘。他即向此像顶礼三次，绕行三匝，并作赞颂曰：

呜呼汝身甚希有
殊胜导师具善德
往昔我以敬信意
修汝殊胜之本尊
遂得结成此业缘
愿于百劫长时中
终不弃舍汝胜尊

尔后，他即以此佛像为观想本尊，修行达七月之久，乃有种种经典于其梦中显现，并现前降临。藉此加持，一切境相皆显现为经书。国王札虽能通达此等经典之真义，然为了调伏愚鲁凶暴之所化，故而佯装不解，而后遂四处打听，当今世间，谁最博学？人云于萨霍尔国之邬巴罗阇（Uparāja）最为博学。国王札遂遣人迎请，不料邬巴罗阇担心不能消除国王札心中的疑问，所以没有应允，于是将经典归还，顺便捎话说："若依阿阇梨昔日之授记，是等经典该当由大王自己解读。"国王札复遣佛宝等诸多菩萨化身，前往有大学识之比丘古古罗阇（Kukkurāja）处求教，请其解读这些经典。古古罗阇曰："此乃《十万品幻化网续》之金刚萨埵意成就品，或面见金刚萨埵品。若照此修习七月，于禅定中，可见金刚萨埵迅即降临。善男子，尔可随愿而得悉地。"国王札再请赐予领会正法及诸乘之悉地，比丘古古罗

20 Samten G. Karmay 有专文讨论有关国王札的传说，King Tsa/Dza and Vajrayāna（国王札和金刚乘），*The Arrow and the Spindle: Studies in History, Myths, Rituals and Beliefs in Tibet*, Kathmandu: Mandala Book Point, 1998, pp. 76-93.

阇答曰："此等悉地均在金刚手之授记中。"言毕即隐没不见。国王札照此修习七月，金刚手果然亲临，三次点燃金刚杵，说道："今以善德赐汝断取禁戒行灌顶，愿汝远离诸罪。"又说："汝当舍弃具勤作之性相乘，实修无勤作之密咒乘，吾已圆满授汝义之教法及诸乘之灌顶，至于言词开示，当求诸善知识离车子维摩诘。"古古罗阇依秘密主之吩咐而行，将十万品幻化网续分为十八大续部，而后为具缘国王札宣讲。[21]

古古罗阇乃著名的"犬王"，因其时常于白天扮作犬相向成千菩萨与瑜伽士传法，而于晚间带他们去墓地行会供及其他一些仪轨。他曾往邬金详细讲述摩诃瑜伽之五内续续典，包括《诸佛平等和合续》（*Buddhasamāyoga*），并为该续造《密义六庄严》（*Ṣaḍguhyārthadharavyūha*）、《一切坛城之五重仪轨》（*Sarvamaṇḍalānuvartipañcavidhi*）等释论。他将摩诃瑜伽十八续传给了沙克罗普特罗（Śakraputra）或国王札之子小因陀罗菩提，后者传给僧哥罗阇（Siṃharāja），僧哥罗阇传给沙克刺菩提（Śakrabhūti），沙克刺菩提传给邬帕罗阇，最后传给公主果玛德妃（Gomadevī）。

《幻化网道次第》（*Māyājālapathakrama*）云："在瞻部洲之东，依靠金刚座，有一众宝所成之宫，宫内有一吉祥殊胜之室，古古罗阇、因陀罗菩提与僧哥罗阇、邬帕罗阇及公主果玛德妃等人，同受幻化网之灌顶。他们以会众形式受幻化网坛城，并荣登金刚持地。"

按照藏文史书《汉藏史集》的记载，印度共有五百名班智达得到摩诃瑜伽部教法，通达密咒之内、外二续，并获成就。《法藏日光疏》（*chos mdzod rnam bshad nyi mavi vod zer*）云：释迦能仁入寂后百十二年，有具福国王札出，五百年时，有妙吉祥友（Mañjuśrīmitra）出，一千年时，有后妙吉祥友出，千五百年时，有阿阇梨莲花生出，两千年时，有吉祥狮子（Śrīsiṃha）出；在这段时间内，密咒内外续寺院中有学者五百名，最善巧之学者二十一名，得成就者十八名。[22]其中有不同的传承系统，自具缘国王札与古古罗阇而下，最著名的一支传承由游戏金刚（Līlāvajra）及佛密（Buddhaguhya）二位上师继承。

游戏金刚乃桑萨刺国（Ṣaṃṣara）人，幼时于邬金剃度出家，并于此学习三藏及大小五明，学有所成，尤擅无著上师（Asaṇga）所造大乘论典及幻化网部续典。后于邬金一名为玛底玛之岛上，修习《妙吉祥真实名经》（*Mañjuśrīnāmasaṃgīti*），并获成

21 节译自《龙钦教史》，拉萨：西藏藏文古籍出版社，1991 年，第 183-185 页。
22《汉藏史集》，第 443-444 页。

就。复住那烂陀寺十年，造论无数，其中关于幻化网续者有：据无上瑜伽续之解释所作《妙吉祥真实名经释》（*vjam dpal mtshan brjod kyi vgrel pa*）、《吉祥秘密藏续巴甲疏》（*Śrīguhyagarbhaṭika*）、《心明点》（*Cittabindu*）、《六次第》（*Kramaṣaṭka*）、《誓句明释》（*Samayacitraprakāṣa*）和《誓句随眠》（*Samayānuśayanirdeśa*）等。于其众多弟子中，以佛密及佛智足（Buddhajñānapāda）习《幻化网续》最精、最著名。

佛密上师乃中天竺人，于那烂陀寺出家，与佛寂（Buddhaśānti）上师一起同为佛智足上师之弟子。因修文殊菩萨而得道，后往邬仗那，遇游戏金刚上师，随其学瑜伽续与五部无上内续，特别是幻化网续。其著作甚丰，著名者有：《秘密藏续判别疏》（*gsang bavi snying po lavgrel ba rnam bshad / rnam bye kyi vgrel*）、《幻化网金刚业次第》（*Māyājālavajrakarmakrama*）、《法坛城经》（*Dharmamaṇḍalasūtra*）、《圣庄严经》（*Tattvālokaparamālaṃkāra*）、《幻化网续简疏》（*Sūkṣmajāla*）、《幻化网续详疏》（*drwa chen*）、《幻化网道次第》（*Māyājālapathakrama*）和《幻化网道小疏》（*sgyu vphrul lam gyi rnam bshad chung ba*）。

摩诃瑜伽的另一脉传承也传自国王札和古古罗阇，他们的传人先是俱生喜金刚（Sukhasidhi, dgav rab rdo rje），俱生喜金刚先传金刚笑（Vajrahāsya），再传萨霍尔之光象尊者（Prabhāhasti），后者复从佛密上师获幻化网续部之口传。光象尊者即是莲花生大士之主要师尊。莲花生大士著有《秘密藏续广释》（*rnam bshad chen mo*），于西藏时曾给吐蕃赞普及其具福弟子讲述其名作《口诀见鬘》（*man ngag lta phreng*），[23] 专门解释《秘密藏续》之第十三品。

《秘密藏续》于印度传承中的另一位重要祖师无垢友（Vimalamitra），[24] 乃西天竺之哈思提瓦那（Hastivana）人，幼随佛密等上师学法：通大小五明与显密二乘之经典，尤擅幻化网续。他于解释、弘扬摩诃瑜伽密法——特别是幻化网续有特殊贡献，曾将以《秘密藏续》为根本、与金刚萨埵幻化网有关的经典归结为幻化网八部而总说之。无垢友上师造论甚多，其中有关幻化网续者有：《幻化口诀明灯》（*sgyu vphrul man ngag gsal bavi sgron me*）、《无上幻化网续注疏·除暗》（*sgyu vphrul bla mavi vgrel ba mun sel*）、《金刚萨埵幻化网吉祥秘密藏续开眼疏》（*Vajrasattvamāyājālatantra-śrīguhyagarbhanāma-cakṣuṣṭikā*）、《第八十品略释》

23 该论汉译见谈锡永、沈卫荣、邵颂雄、许锡恩译著：《宁玛派四部宗义释》，北京：中国藏学出版社，2012年，第140-170页。

24 有关无垢友生平的考证，见沈卫荣：《无垢友尊者及其所造〈顿入无分别修习义〉研究》，《佛学研究中心学报》第10期，2005年，第81-117页。

（*brgyad bcu pavi bsdus grel*）、《入摩诃瑜伽慧眼口诀》（*Mahāyogaprajñāpraveśa-cakṣurupadeśanāma*）、《幻化网口诀三次第》（*Māyājālopadeśakramatraya*）、《幻化火供次第摄略》（*Māyājālahomasaṃkṣiptakrama*）、《幻化手印禅定》（*Māyājālamudrādhyāna*）、《幻化火烧仪轨》（*Māyājālaghudṛṣṭāntasvāśrayakrama*）、《明点次第》（*thig rim*）和《秘密藏续简疏》（*Guhyagarbhapiṇḍārtha*）等。

现存印度上师所造关于幻化网续部经典之注疏，包括以上所列诸论在内，均收集于北京版藏文大藏经丹珠尔部卷八十二至卷八十三中。据法吉祥译师之《秘密主言教》（*gsang bdag zhal lung*），这些注疏大致可分为总义释（spyivi don bshad pa）与普通释论（vgrel pa）两类。前者以游戏金刚的《心明点》（*thugs thig*）和无垢友之《内典明灯》（*khog gzhung gsal sgron*）为代表。后者包括本注（rtsa vgrel）与释注（bshad vgrel）两类，本注包括印度上师所造解释《秘密藏续》本续之大论，如游戏金刚所造《巴甲疏》、日光狮子所造《广注》（*rgyal chen vgrel pa*）、佛密所造之《判别疏》、莲花生所造《广疏》（*rnam bshad chen mo*）、无垢友所造《秘密藏续简疏》等；释注则是对幻化网续部其他经典的注疏，如无垢友所造《无上幻化网续注疏·除暗》《支分眼疏》（*le lag gi spyanvgrel*）和《第八十略释》等。

此外，组成续部经典主题之所谓密咒十事（mantradaśatattva）的每一部，各有其自身的注释传统。

1. 见部（lta ba）

俱生喜金刚（dgav rab rdo rje）之《判别见之灯》（*la shan lta bavi sgron ma*）、莲花生（Padmasambhava）之《口诀见鬘》（*man ngag lta phreng*）、龙树（Nāgārjuna）之《碧玉散布九平原》（*g·yu thang ma kras dgu*）、噶瓦译师班则（ska ba dpal brtsegs）之《见次第十七明相》（*lta rim snang ba bcu bdun pa*）。[25]

2. 行部（spyod pa）

《摄行明灯论》（*spyod bsdus sgron ma*）与《金刚文殊怙主》（*rdo rje vjam mgon*）。

3. 坛城部（dkyil vkhor）

佛密（Buddhaguhya）造《二金刚业次第上部》（*rdo rje las rim gnyis kyi stod*）及无垢友（Vimalamitra）造《三明点胜》（*thig sum par rgyal*）。

4. 灌顶部（dbang）

25 噶瓦·班则（吉祥积）为吐蕃王朝赤松德赞时著名的噶、焦、祥三大译师（ska cog zhang gsum）之一。该论汉译参见许明银：《吉祥积的〈见次第说示〉藏文本试译》，《圆光佛学学报》创刊号，1983 年，第 165-180 页。另见《宁玛派四部宗义释》，第 255-279 页。

佛密造《二金刚业次第下部》（*rdo rje las rim kyi smad*）、《要论》（*gal po*）、《大小抉择》（*nges vbyed che chung*）、《三滴》（*thig pa gsum*）。

5. 誓句部（dam tshig）

游戏金刚造《誓句明示》（*dam tshig gsal bkra*）、《誓句随眠增》（*dam tshig phra rgyas*）。

6. 事业部（phrin las）

无垢友造《火供》（*sbyin sreg*）、《烧尸》（*ro sreg*）、《舍利业鬘》（*sku gdung las phreng*）、《喜乐寒林之小喻本位》（*dur khrod bde bavi dpe chung rang gnas*）。

7. 修证部（sgrub pa）

因陀罗菩提造《道庄严》（*lam rnam bkod*）、《二次第》（*rim pa gnyis pa*），佛密造《大小道次第》（*lam rim che chung*），游戏金刚造《六次第》（*rim drug*），无垢友造《三次第》（*rim gsum*）、《光次第》（*vod rim*）、《大疏》（*drwa chen*），及佛密造《小疏》（*drwa chung*）、《妙庄严》（*dam pa rgyan*）等。

8. 等持部（ting nge vdzin）

无垢友造《手印禅定》（*phyag rgya bsam gtan*）、《忿怒一手印》（*khro bo phyag rgya gcig pa*）、《专一四手印禅定》（*rtse gcig bsdus pa phyag rgya bzhi pavi bsam gtan*）。

9. 供养部（mchod pa）

莲花生造《食会供》（*za tshogs*）、《寒林》（*dur khrod*）、《喜乐小食子》（*bde ba gto chung*）、《大火供》（*ho chen*）、《小火供》（*ho chung*）、《大小食谱》（*g·yos yig che chung*），以及无垢友上师造《无量妙法》（*thabs mchog dpag gis mi lang ba*）、《宝灯》（*dbyig gi sgron ma*）。

10. 密咒与手印部（sngags dang phyag rgya）

《八掌事业》（*phrin las sbar ba brgyad*）。

七、以幻化网续部为中心之摩诃瑜伽教法于西藏的传译

对于无上密咒乘摩诃瑜伽部的教法于何时、怎样传入西藏，藏文史书中有种种不同的说法。最普通的一种说法是，无上密主要分三次传入西藏，第一次是莲花生之弘传，第二次是毗卢遮那（Vairocana）之弘传，第三次是努·桑杰益西（gnubs sangs rgyas ye shes）之弘传。若细述之，则更分八次传入。

早在吐蕃赞普赤松德赞在位时，为修建吉祥桑耶任运神殿而首先要降伏地魔，故特从西方邬金国请来莲花生，莲花生在桑耶寺说圆满八教（bkav brgyad yongs rdzogs）

等，是为密咒在雪域传播之始。随后，于桑耶寺开光时，有名辛底噶巴（Śāntigarbha）者来临，讲说事续部经典，是为密法第二次传入；此后，有译师藏提烂陀（gtsang thig lenta）、波烂伽目底（Brankamukti）、绛白敦恰（vjam dpal go cha）三人赴岗底斯山，从师阿阇梨佛密学法，得《毗卢遮那现证菩提续》，弘传讲论，是为密法在西藏的第三次传入。此后，则有俄译师（rngog lotsāba）及所谓六试人出，他们去印度随阿阇梨吽迦罗（Hūṃkara）学《真实意》部，并大作弘扬，是为密法在西藏的第四次传入。此后，有学者毗卢遮那出，翻译无数《文殊身》部经典，是为密法之第五次传入；于赞普赤德松赞在位时，迎请迦湿弥罗译师咱那迷得剌（Jinamitra）、答剌摩伽剌（Dharmakara）、室烂答剌（Śīlendra）等，由噶、焦、祥三译师任厘订，丹玛泽芒（ldan ma rtse mangs）等为传译，翻译了密咒身、语、意续之大部分经典，是为密法之第六次传入；于法王赤祖德赞在位时，迎请无垢友上师，由称为六学者译师的玉扎宁波古达（g·yu sgra snying po ku mdar）、占巴南喀仁钦乔（dran pa nam mkha' rin chen mchog）、占巴益西嘉绛（dran pa ye shes rgyal byang）等，将以前所译的所有经典按梵文原本重译，以前所译不完整者则予补足，并厘订新译语，凡属心部、界部、幻化部、经部教授等众多大小续典均被译出，是为密法第七次传入西藏；最后，继末代赞普朗达玛灭法，正法后弘时，有玛（rma）、聂（snyegs）二位译师之再传弟子努·桑杰益西上师出，值年五十又四，因不满雪域先前所有密咒，遂往尼婆罗，见国王跋苏达罗（Bhasudhara），又赴印度，遇阿罗牙瑟坚（Ārya gsal rgyan）、戎博咱牙昝特罗（rom po jayacantra）等，译出内、外、密三部密咒护法，是为密咒在西藏的第八次传入。据说，努·桑杰益西上师还自印度往勃律，与当地译师班智达答剌那乞悉答（Dhanarakṣita）、梅赞结（me btsan skyes）、康巴达喀（vkhams pa dar mkhar）等一起，将《诸佛密意总集经》译成勃律语，再从梵语译成藏文。他前后七次往尼婆罗、印度等地求法，获内外密咒之一切续典，并作弘扬，故其于密咒在西藏传播之功德尤其巨大。

八、《秘密藏续》的藏文翻译

以上是无上密咒在西藏传播的一般情况，具体到摩诃瑜伽部之根本大续《秘密藏续》何时何地由何人译成藏文，也有种种不同的说法。无畏洲上师在其《宁玛派续部典籍目录》中谓《秘密藏续》无疑是由无垢友上师及聂·阇那古摩罗（gnyags Jñānakumāra）、玛译师仁钦乔（rma rin chen mchog）等一起翻译成藏文的。不过在此以前，佛密与毗卢遮那二位上师也已曾将此续译成藏文，而且莲花生及聂·阇那古摩罗译师于这两个译本之间的某个时期也曾翻译过这部续典。故通常以为，佛密曾在冈底斯山（Kailash）向贝·绛班（sbas vjam dpal）及瞻伽目提（bran ka mukti）讲述属于《秘密藏续》部之其他法要，包括《口诀妙庄严》（*man ngag rnam par bkod pa*），他在毗卢遮那的协助下翻译了《秘密藏续》，是为《秘密藏续》的第一个藏文译本。其后，莲花生将《秘密藏续》及其本人所造的《口诀见鬘》传授给聂·阇那古摩罗译师，他们二人合作翻译了《秘密藏续》，是为《秘密藏续》的第二个藏文译本。聂·阇那古摩罗将此传授给索波·贝杰益西（sog po dpal gyi ye shes）；贝吉益西与尚·嘉维云丹（zhang rgyal bavi yon tan）一起将此教法传予努钦·桑杰益西（gnubs chen sangs rgyas ye shes）。

随后，无垢友在桑耶寺讲授《金刚萨埵幻化八部》（*sgyu vphrul sde brgyad*），其中即包括作为十八部续部经典之根本的《秘密藏续》。无垢友乃由吐蕃赞普赤热巴巾派堪布鲁依旺波（mkhan po kluvi dbang po）、属卢·鲁依坚赞（cog ro kluvi rgyal mtshan）、娘索·鲁依旺秋（nyang so kluvi dbang phyug）等人专程从印度迎亲至桑耶寺，于此住一年之久，在玛胜宝译师及聂·阇那古摩罗协助下，也将《秘密藏续》等幻化部续典翻译成藏文，此为《秘密藏续》的第三个藏文译本。聂译师翻译了经部和心部，玛译师翻译了性相部和幻化部。以上这三种译本被称为本译。

此后，塔译师尼玛坚赞（thar lo nyi ma rgyal mtshan）及廓译师循努班合作，根据新发现的梵文原本又重新翻译，由于他们没有大班智达为其翻译作监督，故其译本被人称为技译（rtsal vgyur）。此外，于该译本中，塔译师根据其新发现的梵文原本，补译了该续之二十三及二十四品。

龙青巴曾对现存《秘密藏续》之各种藏文译本作了详细的比较、研究，此后得出结论，认为《秘密藏续》于印度本身就存在不同的版本，故这三种不同的藏译本不只是简单重复劳动，而是根据三种不同的原本所作的三种不同的翻译。对此他在其名著《十方除暗》中特别就《秘密藏续》各种译本中或有附加偈语或无附加偈语一事作出如下评论，他说：

> 或以为此类附加偈语于根本续中本不存在，乃玛译师仁钦乔自幻网部其他续典中抽出，分别添加于根本续各品之中。以后，又有祖茹仁钦循努（gtsug rum rin chen gzhon nu）将这些不同的译本分成有附加偈语本及无附加偈语本两种。复次，或以为没有附加偈语之译本乃聂·阇那古摩罗译师所译，有附加偈语之译本乃玛仁钦乔译师所译。甚至，或以为玛译师出于对

> 喇宋嘉瓦绛秋（la gsum rgyal ba byang chub）[26]的嫉妒而故意将这些译本隐藏了起来。事实是，这些附加的偈语既不见于佛密及毗卢遮那合译的第一个译本，也不见于莲花生与聂·阇那古摩罗完成的第二个译本，它们只见于由无垢友上师与聂·阇那古摩罗、玛仁钦乔译师等合作完成的第三个译本。因而，显然梵文原本即有许多不同的版本。此或可于其他续典中见到同样的例子，如《般若八千颂》本身有许多梵文原本，其中就有般利伐罗句迦（Parivrajikā gzo sbyangs）、具鬘（vphreng can）和具众（sde can）三种不同的版本存世。同样，像《白伞盖经》（*Sitātapatrā*）这样的经典，也已发现有许多不同的版本。因此，我们无法肯定这些不一致的段落是否为藏人所添加。当知此续各种译本之间的不一致之处即已出现于其各种梵文原本。因于这些译本中有达意及不达意之别，故出现有各种不同的梵文原本版本。[27]

以上所述《秘密藏续》之三种不同的译本，及其幻网部其他续典的藏译本，即组成所谓旧译密咒的主要内容。

九、教传经典传承

旧译密咒于西藏的传承系统极为复杂，说法不一。或说有诸佛密意传承（rgyal bavi dgongs pavi brgyud pa）、持明表示传承（rig vdzin brdavi brgyud pa）、补特伽罗口耳传承（gang zag snyan khung gi brgyud pa）三种，又有奉教授记传承（bkav babs lung bstan gyi brgyud pa）、祈愿灌顶传承（smon lam dbang bskur bavi brgyud pa）、空行付印传承（mkhav vgro gtad rgyavi brgyud pa）三种，此即名为“具六传承”（brgyud pa drug ldan）。或曰旧译密咒之法要，总分三类，远传佛语传承（bkav ma ring brgyud）、近传伏藏传承（gter ma nyer brgyud）以及甚深净相传承（dag snang zab brgyud）。教传佛语以《幻化网秘密藏续》《遍集明经》和《菩提心遍作王续》三大本续为基，分为幻、经、心三部（mdo sgyu sems gsum）。其中《幻化网秘密藏续》由无垢友传玛译师仁钦乔，玛译师复传予祖茹仁钦循努及吉热乔迥（gye re mchog

26 喇宋嘉瓦绛秋乃著名的吐蕃最早受剃度的“预试七人”之一，与玛译师同为当时著名的八大译师之一，曾在昌珠受莲花生大士灌顶，故能在空中打坐修禅。

27 《十方除暗》，收《宁玛教传广集》（*bkav ma rgyas pa*），Kalimpong: Dupjung Lama, 1982-198, Vol. 26, ff. 247-248。

skyongs），此二师再传予达吉 · 贝吉扎巴（dar rje dpal gyi grags pa）及尚 · 嘉维云丹二师，其中达吉 · 贝吉扎巴学识过人，提出“即便吾师亦乃有漏众生，故对其所传教法也当加以观察”。但其所传以普传教典传承著称，对众生利益不大。达吉在康、卫、藏各地弘传，其传人后分为卫派和康派二支。尚 · 嘉维云丹则仅按上师所传授徒，世称“青浦教传”（bkav vchims phu ba），对众生利益甚大。

也有人说，旧译密咒依止三大传承，第一传承由聂 · 阇那古摩罗所传教传生起、圆满、大圆满三部之四河；第二传承由努 · 桑杰益西传出；第三传承由大宿 · 释迦迥乃（zur po che śākya vbyung gnas）所传教传四大河（bkavi chu bo chen po bzhi）。所谓教传四大河指的是莲花生、无垢友、毗卢遮那和玉扎宁波四位上师之教法，分别是：一、具注疏及大纲之共通经典河；二、具要点与直指导引之耳传教授河；三、具赐授（灌顶）方便之加持灌顶河；四、具护法忿怒密咒之实修与事业成就河。[28]

在西藏被称为“远传佛语”（ring brgyud bkav ma）的传承系统包括所有自印度传入西藏，并渐次以口耳或文字相传下来的属于摩诃瑜伽、阿努瑜伽及阿底瑜伽之续典和经教，它与所谓的“近传伏藏”（nye brgyud gter ma）形成鲜明对比，后者指后世渐次新发现的密法部类。远传系统通常以其综合摩诃、阿努及阿底三瑜伽著称，它以幻、经、心三部为名，即取旧派密咒生起、圆满、大圆满三部之主要续典——幻化部《秘密藏续》、经部《遍集明经》和心部《菩提心遍作王续》之首字。这一西藏宁玛派传统的共同遗产首先传至聂 · 阇那古摩罗，再传至努 · 桑杰益西，最后传至宿氏家族。

聂 · 阇那古摩罗由寂护（Śāntarakṣita）剃度出家，精通甘露功德及普巴金刚之修习。他追随印度诸位最博学、最有成就的大师学法，得通大小五明，尤擅内外密续，汇聚教传四大教河。阇那古摩罗专精经、幻、心三部，通过他的阐幽发微，将《幻化网续》传予许多弟子，特别是通达普巴的“八大吉祥行者”。这八大吉祥行者指的是他的前期弟子索波 · 贝吉益西（sog po dpal gyi ye shes）、俄瞻 · 贝吉循努（vo bran dpal gyi gzhon nu）、念庆 · 贝央（gnyan chen dpal dbyangs）及塔桑 · 贝吉多杰（thag bzang dpal gyi rdo rje）四人，和其后期弟子朗乔 · 贝吉多杰（lam mchog dpal gyi rdo rje）、达吉 · 贝吉扎巴（dar rje dpal gyi grags pa）、扎 · 贝吉宁波（gra dpal gyi snying po）及拉隆 · 贝吉多杰（lha lung dpal gyi rdo rje）四人。

努 · 桑杰益西于妙吉祥坛城中得灌顶并获成就。他曾随莲花生、无垢友、吉祥狮子、伐苏答剌（Vasudhara）及莲花戒（Kamalaśīla）等印度上师，以及聂 · 阇那古摩

28《敦珠教法史》，成都：四川民族出版社，1996 年，第 226 页。

罗、索波·贝吉益西及尚·嘉维云丹等藏土大德学习包括《秘密藏续》在内的内外密咒及其口诀。他留下了很多著作，主要有：

1.《密意总集经广注·除暗铠甲》（*mdovi grel chen mun pavi go cha*）

2.《幻化网八十品现证疏》（*sgyu vphrul brgyad bcu pavi mngon rtogsvgrel*）

3.《大圆满口诀·禅定目炬》（*rdzogs chen gyi man ngag bsam gtan mig sgron*）

4.《断难·语剑》（*dkav bcod smra bavi mtshon cha*）

努上师最嫡传的弟子是库隆·云丹嘉措（khu lung yon tan rgya mtsho），他将所有灌顶、密续及口诀悉数传予这位高足，后者复将其所得传授给了益西加措（ye shes rgya mtsho）、班玛旺嘉（padma dbang rgyal）、拉杰吽穹（lha rje hūṃ chung）、娘·喜饶却（nyang shes rab mchog）、娘·益西迥乃（nyang ye shes vbyung gnas）、拉杰宿波切（lha rje zur po che）等弟子。这一传承系统根据其传承者之部族名通常被称为绒派（rong）传承，或者娘派（nyang）传承。

绒宋班智达·曲吉桑布（rong zom paṇḍita chos kyi bzang po）[29] 是 11 世纪宁玛派著名的大班智达，后藏茹拉（ru lag）那隆戎（snar lung rong）人。因获得了莲花生的口诀传承而名闻一时。这系传承自莲花生经那囊·多吉堆迥（sna nam rdo rje bdud vjoms）、喀庆·贝吉旺秋（mkhar chen dpal gyi dbang phyug）、扎·多杰循努（sgra rdo rje gzhon nu）、尚尚·云丹扎（zhang zhang yon tan grags）、绒班·云丹（rong ban yon tan）、绒班·崔臣仁波切（rong ban tshul khrims rin po che）等上师一脉相传。而名列此系传承之末的绒班·崔臣仁波切即是绒宋·曲吉桑布之父。据说，曲吉桑布从十三岁起，即以通达经典、学识优异著名。他通因明、吠陀及非宗教典籍；会梵文，善译经，除译有密教典籍以外，还有若干关于密教典籍的注疏及论著。他亦曾为念称智所著《语门利器》（*smra sgo mtshon cha*）作过注释，自己也写过几部藏文文法书，因此得享班智达之雅号。曲吉桑布年轻时曾随一法师朵敦僧格（mdo ston seng ge）学习旧译密咒，一天他梦见自己正在吃他自己用《秘密藏续》熬成的稀粥，喝用《秘密藏续》烧成的菜汤。惊异之余，他将此梦中之情景告诉了上师。不料上师当即连呼：“善哉！善哉！此乃汝已圆满领会此等教法之征兆。尔当为《秘密藏续》与《诸佛平等和合续》各撰一疏。”于是，绒宋班智达留下了西藏历史上第一部重要的《秘密藏续》的藏文注疏。因三宝之自性乃菩提心故，他特将此书命名为《宝疏》（*dkon cog*

29 针对绒宋班智达生平与著作相关材料的研究，见 Orna Almogi, “Sources on the Life and Works of the Eleventh-Century Tibetan Scholar Rong zom Chos kyi bzang po: A Brief Survey,” in Henk Blezer (ed.), *Tibet, Past and Present*, Leiden: Brill, 2002, pp. 67-80.

vgrel）。

绒宋班智达的这部注疏与后来龙青巴尊者所造《十方除暗》被认为是从阿底瑜伽的观点出发解释《秘密藏续》的两部最重要的藏文注疏，与教传派所强调的《秘密藏续》属摩诃瑜伽的观点形成对比。[30] 对此敦珠法王曾说：

> 大遍知者龙青巴所著释论《十方除暗》乃依诸乘之王（阿底瑜伽）阐发（《秘密藏续》）；而遍知绒宋巴之释论则为法界之广注，显现如密封之大匣。若知此二释论乃《秘密藏续》乃最主要至藏文释论，即可令智慧具大力。[31]

绒宋班智达作为第一位评注《秘密藏续》的藏土学者，遭到了众多其他教派的上师，包括宁玛派的著名批判者廓库巴等人的尖锐批评。绒宋班智达所传宁玛派密法以“心品”（sems phyogs）为主，在那些甚至不承认宁玛派为佛教之一派的他派上师们看来，尤其不像是来自印度的传统佛教，故不惜用相当激烈的语言对其作猛烈的批判。事实上，绒宋班智达的贡献在于他复兴了在西藏佛教后弘期以前由噶瓦·班则（ska ba pal brtsegs）、娘·贝央（gnyan dpal dbyangs）及努·桑杰益西等人创立的注疏传统。尽管在11世纪时，西藏本土上师造论者尚属凤毛麟角，故易遭非议，但即使是他的批评者也都承认，绒宋班智达所作忠实于原续经文之权威，经得起量理考察，既不违因明三式，又不背离上师之教法。绒宋班智达一系所传内容以心品为主，与其同时的宿氏家族传承则以集经及幻化网为主。自绒宋班智达至14世纪宁玛派大师龙青巴之间的传承系统史载不详。

大圆满教法分为心部（sems sde）、界部（klong sde）和口诀部（man ngag sde，或称要门部）三个系统。这三个系统各有师承，又彼此相互影响。心部说随现何境，皆为心性自然智，除此自然智之外，更无余法。界部说法性不出普贤界，遮破从法性界外之别处有他法出现，此部着重于光明。凭借离所缘之甚深关要，安住于离勤作之境界，藉甚深光明之双运智成就虹体金刚身。口诀部说藉离取舍之双运无二智，将轮回涅槃一切法归入离空执之法性境界，由此要点，令轮涅无别之本觉现前显现法性境，遂于本觉金刚链身中成熟解脱。至于大圆满之名，则说轮涅万有所摄一切法于觉

---

30 宁玛派教法分外、内、密三层意趣来解释一切经、续、论，是故可以视为《宝疏》及《十方除暗》所说者为《秘密藏续》之密义。

31《敦珠教法史》，第372页。另见Dudjom Rinpoche上揭书，第707页。

空中圆满，故曰“圆满”，再无较此更为超胜之解脱轮回法，故曰“大”。[32] 继绒宋班智达之后真正承前启后、建立起大圆满法之见地、实修传统的是 14 世纪西藏佛学大师、被人称为宁玛派掌教学者之巅峰（mkhas pavi rtse mo）的龙青巴尊者。[33]

龙青巴尊者通常被人称为遍智龙青饶绛巴智美沃色（kun mkhyen rab vbyams pa dri med vod zer），乃宁玛派之大阿阇梨，大圆满法在雪域传播的中流砥柱。尊者于藏历第五胜生周之土猴年（1308 年）生于乌思藏四茹之一夭茹（yo ru）西部名札恰堆仲（grvavi cha stod grong）的地方。父名阿美拉松（a mes lha srung，又称阿阇梨教护，slob dpon bstan pa srung），乃莲花生大师亲炙弟子吉祥胜马游戏之证果者确央（dpal rta mchog rol pavi grub thob mchog dbyangs）之第二十五代孙，其母仲氏女索南坚（vbrom bzav bsod nams rgyan）乃噶当派祖师仲敦巴嘉维迥乃（vbrom ston pa rgyal bavi vbyung gnas）之后裔。

尊者自幼聪颖，五岁即能读、写无碍，七岁失怙，九岁能背诵《般若二万颂》及《般若八千颂》。以闻、思、修博通经律论三藏，融会内外五明，除障增益。年十二，于桑耶寺随亲教师桑珠仁钦（bsam grub rin chen）、屏教师衮噶沃色（dun dgav vod zer）出家，取法名崔臣罗珠（tshul khrims blos gros）。因擅习正法毗奈耶，年甫十四即能说法。年十六，随阿阇梨扎西仁钦（bdra shis rin chen）学《道果》（*lam vbras*）、《两系六法》（*chos drug gnyis*）、《亥母六法》（*phag movi chos drug*）、《铃派胜乐》（*bde mchog dril bu lugs*）、《大轮金刚手》（*phyag rdor vkhor chen*）等许多灌顶、口传和导引。复随阿阇梨旺益西（dbang ye shes）与上师楚普巴（ston khro phu pa）等学《金刚帐》（*rdo rje gur*）、《时轮》（*dus vkhor*）等密法，随萨龙巴上师（za lung pa）等听闻蔡巴噶举派始祖尚贡塘上师尊追扎巴（zhang gung thang bla ma brtson vgrus grags pa, 1122-1193）之教授、竹巴噶举派上师郭仓巴贡波多吉（rgod tshang pa mgon po rdo rje, 1189-1528）之导引及前、后、中三部希解教法（*zhi byed snga phyi bar gsum*）等。年十九，居前藏噶当派名刹桑普乃乌托寺（gsang phu nevu thog gi chos grwa），先后

32 参见土官洛桑却吉尼玛：《宗教源流史》，兰州：甘肃民族出版社，1984 年，第 70-71 页。对应汉译见刘立千译：《土观宗派源流》，北京：民族出版社，2000 年，第 40 页。

33 1996 年四川人民出版社出版了藏文版《遍智龙青饶绛传（*kun mkhyen klong chen rab vbyams kyi rnam thar*）一书，将索南曲珠确（bsod nams chos vgrub mchog）所著《遍智龙青饶绛传·三种信之津梁》（*dad pa gsum gyi vjug ngogs*）与曲扎桑布之子当巴（chos grags bzang po pha yi bu mchog dam pa）所著《遍智无垢光传·见即具利》（*kun mkhyen dri med vod zer gyi rnam thar mthong ba don ldan*）两种传记合成一书出版。这是目前所能见到的最详细的龙青巴尊者传。截至目前《三信津梁》已有汉译本，见李学愚译：《发现雪山的全知法王：贡钦·龙钦饶绛巴全传》，台北：大千出版社，2008 年。另可参见 Dudjom Rinpoche 上揭书，第 238-277 页。

随该寺上院第十五代住持阿阇梨赞贡巴（btsan dgon pa）和第十六代住持曲班坚赞（chos dpal rgyal mtshan），以及著名的邦译师罗珠丹巴（dpang lo blo gros brtan pa）学法。

此外，龙青巴尊者曾遍礼雪域无数名刹大寺，一时名贤若噶玛噶举派黑帽系第三世活佛让琼多杰（rang byung rdo rje, 1284-1339）、萨迦派座主圣上师索南坚赞（bla ma dam pa bsod nams rgyal mtshan, 1312-1375）、萨迦派大德雅德大班智达（g·yag sde paṇ chen）等都曾与他结下师生之缘，故尊者对量学、般若、中观、《慈氏五论》等性相乘教法，以及声明、修辞、声律、戏剧等所有大小明处皆有听闻，并达究竟，获无碍辩才。尊者通雪域各大教派之殊胜教法，对各路密法不存门户之见。对智者三事——讲、辩、著生无碍之心。于是，尊者于雪域巡回辩经，无往而不胜。人称其为“桑耶龙芒瓦”（bsam yas lung mang ba，意为桑耶通众经教者），或称“龙青饶绛巴”，意为“大界无央”。[34]

作为宁玛派上师，龙青巴尊者对旧译密咒自然用心最多，成就最大。他曾随胆八巴（dan bag pa）、阿阇梨循努顿珠（gzhon nu don grub）、纽巴亭玛瓦·桑杰扎巴（myos pavi mthing ma ba sangs rgyas grags pa）等上师听闻经、幻、心三部及《宁玛十万续》等教授，其用心之专一若幼蜂沉醉于蜂蜜醍醐之中。年二十九，得遇宁玛巴大圆满法祖师仁增古摩罗阇（rigs vdzin Kumārāja, 1266-1343），于其座前学法两年，受赐《大圆满秘密心髓》（*rdzogs pa chen po gsang ba snying thig*）之灌顶、口传及导引，以及大圆满三部密续（rdzogs chen sde gsum gyi rgyud）之教授，成为其当之无愧的衣钵传人。年三十一，龙青巴往涅普休瑟（snye phuvi shug gseb）广转法轮，说秘密心髓法。年三十二，复往白顶雪山乌仗那宗之光云乐园（gang ri thod dkar o rgyan rdzong vod zer sprin gyi skyed mos tshal）建阿兰若。随后，又往门苯塘（mon bum tang）建立僧伽，造寺院解脱洲（thar pa gling）。一时为高僧大德、王公贵族所重，故佛事隆盛、供养无算。是为宁玛派教法在今不丹境内弘传之始。

龙青巴尊者在达到闻、思之极顶后，常遁迹山林、幽禁独修，最后得证光明身，达到大圆满心髓见地之究竟。据称尊者于三十二岁时，修大圆满入甚深止观，定中面见莲花生与智慧海，获授灌顶及口诀传承，即《空行心要》（*mkhav vgro yang tig*）之教授，遂尽得宁玛派大圆满两部心髓之传承。尊者修行处遍布雪域，无远弗届，著

34 按照土观上师的说法，饶降巴作为一个称号是萨迦派上师大慈饶绛巴桑杰培（byams chen rab vbyams pa sangs rgyas vphel）在世时创立并立为制度的。《土观宗派源流》，第 187 页。饶绛巴后为格鲁派寺院所赠格西学位之第一等者的称号。

名的有：桑耶青浦、乌仗那宗、神山岩（lha ri brag）、扎普（gra phu）、休瑟、白顶雪山、雪堆提珠（gzhu stod tis gro）、耶尔巴（yer pa）、雅拉香波、苯塘、绛布班吉格定（skyam bu dpal gyi dge sdings）、贡布山之拉瓦陇（gong po rivi gla ba lung）、工布扎贡噶普（kong po rtsa gong gi phu）等等。此外，像洛卓（lho vbrog）、乌夭（dbu g·yor）、门域等边荒之地也成了他修行、布道之场所。

尽管尊者淡泊功名，但其令誉若“圣识一切法主”“语自在”“无垢光”等仍不胫而走，传遍雪域。

龙青巴尊者一生著述宏富，[35]造显密二乘之共与不共论著达九十八部之多，另有专门的内论百二十八部，秘密了义论二百六十三部。其中最著名的有《龙青七宝藏》（*klong chen mdzod bdun*）、《四部心要》（*snying thig ya bzhi*）、《三休息》（*ngal gso skor gsum*）、《三自解脱》（*rang grol skor gsum*）等。其中《龙青七宝藏》指的是：《宗轮藏》（*grub mthav mdzod*）、《妙乘藏》（*theg mchog mdzod*）、《如意藏》（*yid bzhin mdzod*）、《口诀藏》（*man ngag mdzod*）、《法界藏》（*chos dbyings mdzod*）、《实相藏》（*gnas lugs mdzod*）及《句义藏》（*tshig don mdzod*）；[36]《四部心要》指的是《空行心髓》（*mkhav vgro snying thig*）、《无垢心髓》（*vima snying thig*）、《上师心要》（*bla ma yang tig*）、《空行心要》（*mkhav vgro yang tig*）及《甚深心要》（*zab mo yang tig*）；《三

35 Dorji Wangchuk 曾依据龙青巴的传记、其各部著作的跋尾以及这些著作之间互相提及的线索，按时间先后整理出了龙青巴著作的一个列表，见 Dorji Wangchuk, “Cross-Referential Clues for a Relative Chronology of Klong chen pa’s Works,” in Orna Almogi(ed.), *Contributions to Tibetan Buddhist Literature* (PIATS 2006: Tibetan Studies: Proceedings of the Eleventh Seminar of the International Association for Tibetan Studies, Königswinter 2006), Beiträge zur Zentralasienforschung 14, ed. Peter Schwieger, Halle: IITBS, 2008, pp. 195-244.

36《七宝藏》中的一部分近年来已有 Richard Barron 陆续英译出版，《宗轮藏》英译见 Richard Barron (trans.), *The Precious Treasury of Philosophical Systems: A Treatise Elucidating the Meaning of the Entire Range of Spiritual Approaches*, Junction City: Padma Publishing, 2007；《口诀藏》英译见 The Precious Treasury of Pith Instructions（同上，2006）；《法界藏》根本颂英译见 *The Precious Treasury of the Basic Space of Phenomena*（同上，2001），其自释英译见论 *A Treasure Trove of Scriptural Transmission: A Commentary on the Precious Treasure of the Basic Space of Phenomena*（同上，2001）；《实相藏》英译见 *The Precious Treasury of the Way of Abiding and the Exposition of the Quintessential Meaning of Three Categories*（同上，1998）；有关《宗轮藏》的英译及研究可见 Albion Moonlight Butters, *The Doxographical Genius of Kun mkhyen Klong chen rab ’byams pa*, PhD thesis, Columbia University, 2006。《句义藏》的英译及研究可见 David Germano, *Poetic Thought, the Intelligent Universe, and the Mystery of Self: The Tantric Synthesis of rDzogs Chen in Fourteenth Century Tibet*, PhD thesis, The University of Wisconsin, 1992。《七宝藏》中有两部已由刘立千翻译完成，见刘立千译：《实相宝藏论详释》，北京：民族出版社，2007 年；同译者：《句意宝藏论广讲》，2009 年。

休息》是《心性休息》（*sems nyid ngal gso*）[37]、《禅定休息》（*bsam gtan ngal gso*）、《虚幻休息》（*sgyu ma ngal gso*）[38] 及其自释论；《三自解脱》指《心性自解脱》（*sems nyid rang grol*）、《法性自解脱》（*chos nyid rang grol*）、《平等性自解脱》（*mnyam nyid rang grol*）。[39]

龙青巴是从阿底瑜伽之观点出发来解释《秘密藏续》的，他一共留下了三部专门解释《秘密藏续》的注疏，命名为《除暗三部》（*mun sel skor gsum*），分别是：

1.《略义无明除暗》（*bsdus don ma rig mun sel ba*），长 14 页，分析《秘密藏续》之科判；

2.《总义意语除暗》（*spyi don yid bkav mun pa sel ba*），长 89 页，分析佛教与非佛教教义的范围及结构；

3.《文义十方除暗》（*gzhung don phyogs bcu mun pa sel ba*），长 313 页，先介绍《秘密藏续》各品内容，然后对其金刚偈作详细的笺注。通常所言龙青巴所造的《秘密藏续》释论即是指他的这部《文义十方除暗》。

此外，龙青巴尊者尚有《教法源流大宝藏论·阐明圣教之日光》（*chos vbyung rin po chevi gter mdzod bstan pa gsal bar byed pavi nyi vod*）、《法行道次第》（*chos spyod lam gyi rim pa*）、《回向宝鬘》（*bsngo ba rin po chevi phreng ba*）等名著传世。《教法源流宝藏》是继夏鲁派大师布顿仁钦竹（bu ston rin chen grub, 1290-1364）之名著《善逝教法源流大宝藏论》之后又一部著名的教法源流类史著，通常被译名为《龙青教法源流》。书中的主要内容是印度佛教史及佛教于西藏传播、特别是前弘期佛教各种显、密教法于西藏传播的历史。对吐蕃王国时期，西藏佛经翻译的历史记载尤详。书中有一章专门讨论旧派密咒是否存在于印度，对有人提出《秘密藏续》有四条邪误故为伪经的说法逐条予以驳斥。

37 《心性休息》的英译由 Guenther 完成并分三卷出版，见 Herbert V. Gurnther, *Kindly Bent to Ease Us (Part One: Mind)*, Emeryville: Dharma Publishing, 1975; Kindly Bent to Ease Us (Part Two: Meditation), 同上, 1976; *Kindly Bent to Ease Us (Part Three: Wonderment)*, 同上, 1976。该论汉文节译见谈锡永译释：《大圆满心性休息导引》，台北：全佛文化，2010 年。

38 《禅定休息》英译见 Herbert V. Gurnther, *Mind in Comfort and Ease: The Vision of Enlightenment in the Great Perfection*, Boston: Wisdom Publications, 2007；《虚幻休息》英译见 Keith Dowman, *Maya Yoga: Longchenpa's Finding Comfort and Ease in Enchantment*, Kathmandu: Vajra Publications, 2010。《禅定休息》与《虚幻休息》二论汉译合编本见刘立千译：《大圆满虚幻休息妙车释 / 大圆满禅定休息清净车释 / 深法寂静忿怒尊密意自解之直指觉性赤见自解（合编）》，北京：民族出版社，2000 年。

39 汉译见法护译：《大圆满三自解脱论》，台北：大藏文化，2002 年。

十、宿氏派传承与宁玛派僧伽的建立

宁玛派旧译密咒最初的传播乃父子相承、口耳相传，虽有若干法门分散的传承，但不仅没有寺院僧伽组织，也没有形成为一套高度体系化的密教教义。直到 11 世纪有所谓三宿氏出，宁玛派才建立寺庙，并有较大规模的活动。这三宿氏乃指三位来自宿氏（zur）家族的宁玛派上师。第一位宿氏被人称为宿波切（zur po che，意为大宿氏），本名释迦迥乃（śākya vbyung gnas, 1002-1062），又称邬巴龙巴（vu pa lung pa），来自康区之亚宗（yar rdzong）或萨摩（gsar mo）。幼时从朗达玛灭佛后于西藏东南部维系戒律传承的大上师贡巴绕赛（bla chen dgong pa rab gsal）出家。后随其祖父仁钦嘉措（rin chen rgya mtsho）学习显密经续，包括幻化网部诸续。随后，复从曲龙（chos lung）之娘·益西迥乃（nyang ye shes vbyung gnas）上师处获幻化网及心部之要门，从南喀德（nam mkhav sde）上师处获《遍集明经》（*mdo dgongs pa vdus pa*）、《巴甲疏》（*vgrel pa par khab*）及大圆满口诀；又从娘·哲卓琼（vbre khro chung）上师处得《幻化网道次第》之口诀。宿波切善于融合本续与释续、根本文及其注疏、续典及其成就法仪，且施之于行。从他开始，宁玛派始有教派规模。他曾多年住于香地之邬巴龙（vug pa lung）地方，于此亲见四十二寂静本尊与五十八饮血忿怒本尊，并于此建庙。他曾说："邬巴龙之土、石、山、岩于我皆是寂忿本尊之居处；而于温瑟摩（dben ser mo）之南峰，我常见五部佛。是故，我欲于此建寂静尊庙。"并许以按密宗传统造五部佛像，像之右画以幻网之寂相本尊像，像之左画以幻化网之忿怒尊像。

宿波切建邬巴龙寺时已有很多弟子，常随左右者有一百零八位大修行人，其中以所谓"四顶峰"（rtse mo bzhi）为最胜，他们是：见地与密意之顶峰小宿氏喜饶扎（zur chung shes rab grags）、解释《幻化网续》之顶峰梅聂·琼扎（me nyags khyungs grags）、博学之顶峰尚·廓琼（zhang vgos chung）及修行之顶峰桑贡喜饶嘉波（bzang sgom shes rab rgyal po）。此四顶峰中又以宿波切的养子宿琼巴（小宿氏，1014-1074）最有名。

宿琼巴又称嘉沃巴（rgyal bo pa），本是行乞僧塔巴贡钦（thags pa sgom chen）之子，父子二人行乞至宿波切处，遂为后者收养。宿琼巴随其养父学法多年，得益甚厚，但终因贫困而不能得到密法传授。宿波切遂令其与一富家寡母之女婚配，用他们的钱来学密法，学成之后，母女二人资粮圆满，宿琼巴也遵师教敕而舍离二人。宿波切又令其讲经，曾有弟子三百人听其讲《遍集明经》。此后，他继其养父之后住持邬龙巴寺，广传包括《秘密藏续》在内的宁玛派远传佛语传承诸法。此后，他将邬龙巴寺托付于他人管理，自己到有九峰、九泉及九草坪之嘉沃地方静修十三年，故人称其为嘉沃巴。他于此地证得一切法皆金刚萨埵本性，达大圆满境界。他亦曾谒见廓库巴拉孜上师，听他讲喜金刚法。后复于娘茹（nyang ru）地方与四名显教上师辩论，四人同时向他问难，依然辩他不倒，结果四人都成了他的弟子。宿琼巴之名声随之响亮起来。随其学密法者日众，他也因此而变得十分富有，据称为当时一般佛教徒中最富有之人。

宿琼巴之弟子有四柱（ka ba bzhi）、八梁（gdung ma brgyad）、十六椽（phyam bcu drug）、三十二桷（dral ma sum cu rtsa gnyis）等，其中最著名的是四柱，他们是：心部之柱贡布之鸠敦释迦叶（gung bu skyo ston śākya ye）、《密意总集经》之柱迥隆之阳铿喇嘛（skyong lung yang kheng bla ma）、《幻化网》之柱曲巴之朗·释迦桑布（chu bar gyi glang śākya bzang po）上师以及仪轨、事业修习之柱纳摩若之丹底觉释（nag mo revi mdav tig jośāk）。

宿琼巴有子三人，女数人，均修宁玛派密法，且有成就。其中最著名且继承其衣钵者为宿卓浦巴（zur sgro phug pa, 1074-1134）。卓浦巴，名释迦僧格，是宿琼巴尊者之幼子。出生之年，其父示寂，故由母舅抚养成人。年十五开始师从朗·释迦桑布上师学《秘密藏续》；年十九，因需管理众多的家财而无暇外出求学，遂将其父之号称四柱的四大弟子请回家中，请授宁玛派之经、幻、心三部密法之灌顶、口传、导引等，获宿氏家族传承的《秘密藏续》之完整的注疏传统。此后，卓浦巴又师从其他上师，获大圆满教法，遂成为名重一时之宁玛派上师。他于《秘密藏续》之成就从以下例子可见一斑：一次，当他于卓浦说法时，坐于一四周无靠背之法座上，众弟子从四方将其团团围住，而他恰似面向所有方向之听众。人们遂信其为金刚萨埵幻化网坛城主尊之化身。从此他便成了一位著名的化身佛。

尽管卓浦巴住世时，宁玛派的教法正受到天喇嘛益西沃、廓库巴拉孜等人的激烈批评，但卓浦巴尊者依然能传法收徒，招收弟子达千余人之多。他在卓浦地方建新寺，据传冬、夏随其学法的弟子有五百余众，春、秋随其学法者也有三百余众。因卓浦巴精熟《秘密藏续》，从他又衍传出两支主流，一支在卫藏流传，另一支则在康区流传。

十一、宿氏派于卫藏的传承

在卫藏地区，卓浦巴的主要弟子有所谓四黑（nag po bzhi）、四师（ston pa bzhi）及四祖（mes bzhi）等十二人。四黑中最胜者是节敦伽那（lce ston rgya nag），他精中观、量学等显宗经典，曾来卓浦与卓浦巴辩经获胜，卓浦巴遂将其所有教授悉数授之，成为上部宿氏传承系统之主要掌门。伽那自三十岁起随卓浦巴学法十一年，因其根器不凡，卓浦巴即赐其以摩诃瑜伽、阿努瑜伽及阿底瑜伽之根本续与修行要门。伽那的弟子中著名的有来自前藏的敦夏（ston śāk）及锡波（zhig po），以及伽那的侄儿云丹松（yon tan gzungs）等。

该支传承之次第为：

节敦伽那（lce ston rgya nag）→云丹松（yon tan gzungs）及卫巴人锡波（dbus pa zhig po）→锡波堆孜（zhi po bdud rtsi）→达敦觉耶（rta ston jo ye）→达敦斯吉（rta ston gzi brjid）。

达敦斯吉曾造《秘密藏续广注》，并编撰了此派传承上师的传记。

此外，云敦·多杰班（g·yung ston pa rdo rje dpal, 1284-1365）于其所造《秘密藏续云师疏》（*gyung vgrel*）中，基于《秘密藏续巴甲疏》，提出了一条不同的传承系统，其传承之上师先后为：[40]

卓浦巴（sgro phug pa）→后藏人金敦（bying ston）及贡真人涅敦·曲吉僧格（sgong drings nye ston chos kyi seng ge）→藏那沃巴（gtsang nag vod vbar）→梅敦贡波（mes ston mgon po）→喇嘛宋（bla ma srong）→巴希·释迦沃（pakshi śākya vod）→达那敦都（rta nag bdul vdul）→达释迦培（mdav śākya vphel）→宿·强巴僧格（zur byams pa seng ge）→云敦巴·多杰班（g·yung ston pa rdo rje dpal）。

云敦巴乃学、修皆优之大德，其行传为新、旧两派所共许。其师尊宿·强巴僧格（zur byams pa seng ge）乃宿·尼玛僧格（zur nyi ma seng ge）之子、巴希·释迦沃法师之曾孙。宿·强巴僧格十五岁时，在邬巴龙寺随达释迦培学《秘密藏续》，两年后即自造《密续建立》（*rgyud kyi rnam bzhag*）。他先后从节敦竹巴蚌（grub pa vbum）领受大圆满法及幻化网续部密法，复从拉堆（la stod）之达敦斯吉获宿氏派传承之幻化网利益、能力及甚深三种灌顶及其他教法。强巴僧格自己也有众多弟子，其中有十六人精通《幻化网道次第》（*Māyājālapathakrama*）、《秘密藏续》及《秘密藏续巴甲疏》；他最著名的弟子是云敦·多杰班及达那卓玛瓦·桑珠多吉（rta na sgrol ma ba bsam grub rdo rje, 1295-1376）。

云敦·多杰班乃朗族（glan）人，通显、密经教，为第三世噶玛巴让琼多杰之亲

40 这支传承系统也记载于《土观宗派源流》（藏文版），第63-64页。

传弟子。但他亦习宁玛派教法，自宿·强巴僧格处获其远传经、幻、心三部教法，造释论《吉祥秘密藏续义能显明镜》（*dpal gsang ba snying povi rgyud don gsal byed me long*）。此论于藏土甚受欢迎，其流行程度盖过早于它问世的其他各种《秘密藏续》释论。他于其所造释论中重新排列了《秘密藏续》第五品之次序，这成为后出大师如宿·秋英让卓（zur chos dbyings rang grol）等人参究的焦点。以后造《秘密藏续》释论的大师如南喀仁钦（nam mkhav rin chen）、噶陀·格泽班智达（kaḥ thog dge brtse paṇḍita）及久美潘德沃色（vgyur med phan bde vod zer）等皆深受其影响。

值得一提的是，这支宿氏传承的掌门中有多人曾往中原传法，并与元朝王室发生了关系。例如，释迦沃曾托元朝的使者将他掘藏所得之关于长寿水仪轨的经书献给元世祖忽必烈。作为回报，忽必烈赐给他一个“八哈失”（Baγši，意为法师）的称号。这个称号虽比不上萨迦派大师八思巴所获的帝师称号，但在当时也只有少数几位来自西藏的高僧得享此殊荣。另一位著名的八哈失是第二世噶玛巴噶玛八哈失。[41] 以后，云敦·多杰班上师又因其善咒术、精《时轮》而受元成宗之邀进京，在元廷献金刚舞，受赐丰厚。随后，又奉成宗命赴内地求雨。另外，还有一位名桑吉扎（sangs rgyas grags）的宁玛派上师也曾进京谒见元帝，获赐大量土地。[42]

达那卓玛瓦·桑珠多吉来自达那新寺（rta nag gnas gsar），师从宿·强巴僧格学法，专擅幻化网。亦曾于朗聂蔡巴·索南贡波（glang nya tshal pa bsod nams mgon po）处获灌顶。在其弟子中以宿宏·释迦迥乃（zur ham śākya vbyung gnas）、桑吉仁钦（sangs rgyas rin chen）父子为最胜，所谓“宿氏传规”（zur brgyud）和“子传规”（sras brgyud）即分别出自此父子二人。

宿宏·释迦迥乃前面提到过的宿·桑布扎西之子。五岁时，即不可思议地写出了一部解释《秘密藏续》的论典。他师从著名的梵文专家大班智达萨桑玛底班钦（sa bzang mati paṇ chen）、云敦巴、蒋扬桑珠多吉（vjam dbyangs bsam grub rdo rje）等学显、密教法，包括《幻化网道次第》《吉祥秘密藏续》《秘密藏续巴甲疏》等。他有得其所传宁玛派经、幻、心三部教法之徒众甚多，其中有名者有桑吉仁钦及涅巴格勒巴（gnyel pa bde legs pa）。

桑吉仁钦，全名桑吉仁钦·坚赞班桑布（sangs rgyas rin chen rgyal mtshan dpal

41 参见 Leonard W. J. van der Kuijp, "'Baγši'and Baγši-s in Tibetan Historical, Biographical and Lexicographical Texts"（《在藏文历史、传记、字书类文献中的八哈失》）, *CAJ* 39/2, 1995, pp. 275-299.

42 参见格西班玛次仁（Pema Tsering），"rNying ma pa Lamas am Yüan Kaiserhof"（《在元廷的宁玛派上师》）, in L. Ligeti (ed.), *Proceedings of the Csoma de körös Memerial Sympösium*, Budapest, 1978, pp. 511-517.

bzang po, 1350-1431），乃卓玛瓦·桑珠多吉之子，师从乃父及宿宏·释迦迥乃学法，专精包括《秘密藏续》在内的幻化网部续典。年仅十四即能为他人灌顶。年四十，造《秘密藏续大疏》（*gsang snying vgrel chen*）及《幻化网道庄严》（*lam bkod la rnam bzhag*）。此外，他还著有《忿怒尊现证广论》（*khro bo la mngon par rtogs pa rgyas pa*）、《超度仪轨广释》（*gnas lung lavang cho ga rgyas pa*）。年七十，收藏土著名史家、《青史》作者廓译师循努班为徒，授其以《幻化网寂忿尊灌顶》（*sgyu vphrul zhi khrovi dbang*）、《幻化网长寿灌顶》（*sgyu vphrul gyi tshe dbang*），并为其讲解《秘密藏续》及各种释论，根据其自造释论而对《幻化网道庄严》作详细疏解。他还赐循努班以《内典明灯》（*khog gzhung gsal sgron*）、《四十品幻化网》（*sgyu vphrul bzhi bcu pa*）、《八十品幻化网》（*sgyu vphrul brgyad cu pa*）和《无上幻化网》（*sgyu vphrul bla ma*）之传规。

廓译师循努班（vgos lotsāba gzhon nu dpal, 1392-1481）是五世噶玛巴、明封大宝法王德兴协巴（de bzhin gshegs pa）、俄·绛曲班（rngog byang chub dpal）及大班智达伐那若答那（Vanaratna）的弟子，他订正、重译了《妙吉祥真实名经》（*Mañjuśrīnāmasaṃgīti*）及《秘密藏续》等其他续典。他于桑吉仁钦大师处获得远传佛语之传规，成为宁玛派远传系之传人。他自称对旧译密咒宁玛派的传统有特殊的热忱，尚未为拒受正法之毒沾染。他的主要弟子是噶玛噶举黑帽系的第七世活佛曲扎嘉措（chos grags rgya mtsho）及噶玛噶举红帽系第四世活佛曲吉扎巴（zhwa dmar bzhi pa chos kyi grags pa），后者是此派传承之掌门。

曲吉扎巴（chos kyi grags pa, 1453-1525），乃哲雪康玛（tre shod khang dmar）人，随廓译师循努班学新、旧密咒，然后将学得之教法悉数传予止贡派的宿巴·仁钦彭措（zur pa rin chen phun tshogs）。宝圆满不仅精通以经、幻、心三部续典为主的远传佛语经典，而且也博闻与《八大修部》（*bkav brgyad*）[43]、《四部心要》（*snying thig ya*

43 宁玛派摩诃瑜伽修部主要以八位忿怒尊为观修所依，此八者分别为文殊身（vjam dpal sku）、莲花语（padma gsung）、真实意（yang dag thugs）、甘露功德（bdud rtsi yon tan）、普巴事业（phur pa phrin las）、差遣非人（ma mo rbod gtong）、世间供赞（vjigs rten mchod bstod）、猛咒诅詈（dmod pa drag sngags），是即名为八大修部，有关这一教法体系的历史源流及其宗教内涵的全面论述，见杨杰：《宁玛派八大修部研究》，博士论文，中国人民大学，2015年。

bzhi）[44]、《上下伏藏》（*gter kha gong vog*）[45] 等相关的伏藏。他依止阿里班钦班玛旺嘉王（padma dbang rgyal, 1487-1543）[46] 之传规，以教传法布局，复以伏藏口诀加以庄严。自止贡仁钦彭措以下之传承为：

让卓 · 尼达桑杰（rang grol nyi zla sangs rgyas）→ 泽旺诺杰（tshe dbang nor rgyas，萨迦款氏家族之上师）→ 款敦班觉伦珠（vkhon ston dpal vbyor lhun grub，1561-1637，前者之子）。

款敦班觉伦珠早年随其父学习《秘密藏续》、幻化网部其他各种续典及其释论，特别是云敦巴的著作及龙青巴尊者的《十方除暗》等。因其专擅幻化网续故，被人视为卓浦巴之化身。在其弟子中以扎那 · 邬金旦增（brag na o rgyan bstan vdzin）及大宿 · 秋英让卓（zur chen chos dbyings rang grol, 1604-1669）为主。前者曾根据云敦所著《秘密藏续》释论为该续前五品作注。款敦晚年，曾给在帕邦喀（pha wang kha）闭关的第五世达赖喇嘛授法。

大宿 · 秋英让卓乃大宿 · 循努顿珠成（zur chen gzhon nu don grub）之子，宿氏家族的直系传人。于款敦班觉伦珠上师处，获得了结合《秘密藏续》《秘密藏续巴甲注》及云敦所作藏文释论之要门。他曾将班觉伦珠所讲《秘密藏续》前五品教法记录成文。1622 年，他专学龙青巴上师之《十方除暗》。1624 年，他在泽塘寺（rtses thang）为金刚岩持明三世阿格旺波（rdor brag rig vdzin III ngag gi dbang po）及其他弟子讲述《秘密藏续》，建立起他自己的解释体系。其后，他又在噶陀寺给达拉·班玛玛底（stag bla padmamati）讲述龙青巴上师的《十方除暗》。班玛玛底复将此口传经教传给了洛扎松珠（lho brag gsungs sprul），以保证此系传承宏传不绝。秋英让卓尊者晚年住贡塘（gung thang），授桑达 · 呈列伦珠（gsang bdag phrin las lhun grub）以《秘密藏续》之口传经教。第五世达赖喇嘛也曾授事业任运以与《秘密藏续》之《巴甲疏》及与云敦巴之释论一致之口传。因此，远传佛语系这支传承之次第如下：

大宿 · 秋英让卓及第五世达赖喇嘛 → 桑达 · 呈列伦珠 → 大译师曲嘉丹增（lo chen chos rgyal bstan vdzin）。

---

44 《四部心要》共十三卷，属大圆满口诀部（man ngag sde）修习法要，由龙青巴上师编纂而成，包括他领受的伏藏教法《空行心髓》（*mkhav vgro snying thig*）和《无垢心髓》（*vima snying thig*），以及他本人的伏藏《上师心要》（*bla ma yang tig*）和《空行心要》（*mkhav vgro yang tig*）及《甚深心要》（*zab mo yang tig*）。

45 上下伏藏指分别由著名掘藏师娘热 · 尼玛沃色（nyang ral nyi ma vod zer, 1136-1204）和古茹曲旺（gu ru chos dbang, 1212-1270）所发现的伏藏。

46 阿里班钦是教传传承的重要传人，也是一位著名的伏藏师，相传伏藏《后部佛语集持明总集祈请法部七品成就法》（*bkav vdus phyi ma rig vdzin yongs vdus kyi chos skor gsol vdebs levu bdun mavi sgrub thabs*）即为其所发现，他自造之大论《三律仪决定论》（*sdom gsum rnam par nges pavi bstan bcos*），在宁玛派传统中影响甚巨。

从这个时期开始，此远传佛语系注释传统得以毫无减缺地在卫藏流传下来，此当首先归功于秘密主事业任运的两位儿子持明德达林巴（rig vdzin gter bdag gling pa, 即久美多杰 [vgyur med rdo rje], 1646-1714）和大译师达摩师利（lo chen dharmaśrī, 1654-1717）。自达摩师利译师又传出几大支，强调经、幻、心三部。

十二、噶陀康区传承

宿氏远传佛语传承于康区的传播或可推毗卢遮那大师于奥尔朵（vo rdu）之大慈寺（byams chen）翻译、宣讲尼玛僧格所造《吉祥秘密藏续广释》（*Śrīguhyagarbhatattvaviniścayavyākhyānaṭīkā*）为其开端。但真正使旧译密咒之教法在康区得到广泛传播的是噶陀巴当巴德协（kaḥ thog pa dam pa bde gshegs, 1122-1192）。

噶陀巴本名喜饶僧格（shes rab seng ge），又名博巴塔耶（spobs pa mtha vyas），乃噶举派帕木竹巴（phag mo gru pa）大师的姨表兄弟，来自朵甘思六岗之一的博波岗（bu vbur sgang）。早年随宿·卓浦巴之弟子赞敦·卓维贡波（vdzam ston vgro bavi mgon po）学《秘密藏续》及心部诸续等，故当为卓浦巴之再传弟子。但五世达赖喇嘛在其《闻法录·恒河水流》（*gsan yig gang gāvi chu rgyun*）中说，噶陀巴曾亲遇卓浦巴大师，是其亲炙弟子。噶陀巴也曾随贝吉旺秋（dpal gyi dbang phyug）学《内典明灯》（*khog gzhung gsal sgron*）之释义。1159 年，噶陀巴在其家乡位于金沙江畔的博波岗，今甘孜州德格南部地区和云南西部一带，一地形酷似梵文“噶”字的地方，建噶陀寺。此后便于此说法授受，向来自朵甘思、朵思麻各个地区的弟子按宿氏派传统讲授大圆满法、《秘密藏续》及其大小各种注疏，以及《文殊幻化网》（*vjam dpal sgyu vphrul drwa ba*）等，为密咒教法在康区的传播打下了坚实的基础。此寺受历代德格土司支持，寺主以转世相承。

宿氏派远传佛语传承在康区的授受次第为：

噶陀巴当巴德协→藏敦巴（gtsang ston pa）→强巴蚌（byams pa vbum）→金厄芒普瓦·索南蚌巴（spyan snga mang phu ba bsod nams vbum pa）→邬沃益西蚌（dbu vod ye shes vbum）→绛曲班瓦（byang chub dpal ba）→索南桑布贤（bsod nams bzang po）→衮噶蚌巴（kun dgav vbum pa）→旺秋班瓦（dbang phyug dpal ba）→罗珠蚌巴（blo gros vbum pa）→罗珠僧格（blo gros seng ge）→绛曲罗珠（byang chub blo gros）→绛曲僧格（byang chub seng ge）→绛曲坚赞（byang chub rgyal mtshan）→克珠·益西坚赞（mkhas grub ye shes rgyal mtshan）。

经、幻、心三部之远传系统在噶陀的传播发生于 14-16 世纪之间，即介乎邬巴龙寺昌盛与卫藏地区寺院中心兴起之间。在上述传人中特别值得一提的是德证兼具的益西坚赞（ye shes rgyal mtshan）。他是博波岗之土著，为绛曲坚赞（byang chub rgyal mtshan）与扎沃曲蚌（bravo chos vbum）之弟子。他对无上密法于康区传播之主要贡献在于他重新整理了《秘密藏续》根本续及其诸种注疏。他有多种著述存世，著名的有：

《寂忿本尊释》（*zhi khrovi vgrel pa*）、《秘密藏续之注疏、科判及略义》（*gsang bavi spying pa la vgrel pa/ sa bcad/ bsdus don*）、《幻化网道庄严之释论及笺注》（*lam rnam bkoḍ la ṭīkā dang mchan bu*）、《巴甲疏与心明点笺注》（*spar khab dang thugs thig la mchan bu*）、《誓句明释疏 · 明镜》（*dam tshig gsal bkra la vgrel pa gsal bavi me long*）、《持寂忿本尊手印方便文》（*zhi khrovi phyag rgya bcings thabs kyi yi ge*）、《正士仁波切之〈诸乘总义〉疏》（*dam pa rin po chevi theg pa spyi bcing gi vgrel pa*）、《会供轮释》（*tshogs kyi vkhor lovi rnam bshad*）。

在克珠 · 益西坚赞的弟子中有名喀瓦噶波瓦 · 南喀嘉措（kha ba dkar po ba nam mkhav rgya mtsho）者，也曾造《秘密藏续》与《幻化网道庄严》之释论。

十三、宿氏派远传佛语传承于卫藏的复兴

17、18 世纪，正当宁玛派远传佛语传承于康区得到迅速发展时，它于卫藏地区的传播却渐趋式微。此时，有德达林巴及其兄弟大译师达摩师利出，挑起了在卫藏地区重振远传佛语传承之重任。

持明德达林巴（rig vdzin gter bdag gling pa, 1646-1713），本名班玛噶旺久美多杰（padma gar dbang vgyur med rdo rje），乃桑达·呈列伦珠之子，生于今西藏扎囊县（gra nang）达结曲林（dar rgyas chos gling）。他所习教法涵盖包括幻化网续部在内的所有现存的旧译密咒所传经典。据传，他十三岁时，即能背诵《秘密藏续》，并从其父亲那儿获得口传。其后，他不仅精通宿氏派传规，而且也通努、绒等派传规，对迥丹日贝热支所著《续部总建立》（*bcom ldan ral grivi spyi rnam*）也有独到的研究。尤因对龙青巴尊者所造诸论有独到的解悟，故获得了无碍辩智。

德达林巴于 1676 年于扎囊建敏珠林寺（smin grol gling），在此弘传三宿氏以来所传承之经典，重建起以经、幻、心三部为主的远传佛语派传承。敏珠林寺与金刚岩寺齐名，是宁玛派在卫藏的两所主寺；金刚岩寺以弘传北伏藏（byang gter）为主，兼弘三宿氏以来所传经典，寺主以转世相承；敏珠林寺则以弘传南藏（lho gter）为

主，也兼传三宿氏以来所传经典，寺主以父子或翁婿相承。[47]

远传佛语派得以作为一个活的传统继续存在下去，与德达林巴及其传人的努力密不可分。他曾传《宁玛十万续》之教授予第五世达赖喇嘛、其摄政桑吉嘉措（sangs rgyas rgya mtsho）及金刚岩寺第四世持明活佛班玛呈列（padma phrin las）、佐钦班玛仁增久美特确丹增（rdzogs chen padma rig vdzin vgyur med theg mchog bstan vdzin）、噶陀嘉色索南德赞（kaḥ thog rgyal sras bsod nams ldevu btsan）及其他众多来自康区与卫藏的弟子。他最亲近的弟子是他的弟弟大译师达摩师利及他的儿子班玛久美嘉措（padma vgyur med rgya mtsho）、沙布隆益新勒珠（zhabs drung yid bzhin legs grub）、珍钦仁钦南杰（drin chen rin chen rnam rgyal），以及他的女儿杰尊米久班准（rje btsun mi vgyur dpal sgron）。

大译师达摩师利（Dharmaśrī, 1654-1718）由五世达赖喇嘛剃度出家。随其兄长德达林巴学习龙青巴尊者、绒宋班智达及其他宿氏派传承上师的著作，获经、幻、心三部及《宁玛十万续》之完整教授。随后，他于敏珠林寺为该寺僧伽之六十名学僧讲说《秘密藏续》，先后八次授《幻化网续寂忿尊》之灌顶。为了使远传佛语久为流传，达摩师利译师勤于造论，其全集达十八卷之多，其中有对《密意总集经》及《幻化网》的多部注疏。特别是当他听其兄长结合《巴甲疏》及云敦上师所作之释论，口述其自己对《秘密藏续》之解释时，对《秘密藏续》之甚深精义有了透彻的理解，遂造论多卷，通称《幻化部文书》（*sgyu phrul skor gyi yig cha*）。其中有两部即是根据远传佛语派传承所造的对《秘密藏续》之权威注疏，二者分别是：《由总义抉择吉祥秘密藏真实决定续王之善说·秘密主言教》（*dpal gsang bavi snying po de kho na nyid nges pavi rgyud kyi rgyal po sgyu vphrul drwa ba spyi don gyi sgo nas gtan la vbabs par byed pavi legs bshad gsang bdag zhal lung*）与《吉祥秘密藏续真实决定续释·秘密主密意庄严》（*dpal gsang bavi snying po de kho na nyid nges pavi rgyud kyi vgrel pa gsang bdag*

47 关于敏珠林寺的历史，晚近有藏族学者丹贝仲美（bstan pavi sgron me）著《敏珠林寺志》（*o rgyan smin grol gling gi dkar chag*）可供参考，北京：中国藏学出版社，1992 年，第 1-387 页。有关敏珠林寺在宁玛派传承的重振上发挥的重要作用，参 Jacob Dalton, "Recreating the rNying ma School: the mDo dbang Tradition of sMin grol gling," in Bryan J. Cuevas & Kurtis R. Schaeffer (eds.), *Power, Politics, and the Reinvention of Tradition: Tibet in the Seventeenth and Eighteenth Centuries*, Leiden: Brill, 2006, pp. 91-101。15、16 世纪时，有伏藏师热那林巴（Ratna gling pa）把前述"上部伏藏"和"下部伏藏"，加上他自己所掘伏藏汇刻在一起，是即所谓"南伏藏"；16 世纪初，另有一位伏藏师名仁增郭之登浦津（rig vdzin rgod kyi ldem vphrul can），乃后藏北部拉堆绛王室子弟，他曾将其所掘伏藏汇刻在一起，被称为"北伏藏"，参见 Peter Schwieger, "Collecting and Arranging the gTer ma Tradition: Kong sprul's Great Treasury of the Hidden Teachings," in Anne Chayet, Cristina Scherrer-Schaub, Françoise Robin and Jean-Luc Achard (eds.), *Edition, Éditions: l'écrit au Tibet, évolution et devenir*, München: Indus Verlag, 2010, pp. 321-335.

dgongs rgyan），前者称颂《秘密藏续》于整个宁玛派传统中的地位，后者则提供了对该续原偈文之解读。对其后一部著作现有其弟子邬金曲培（o rgyan chos vphel）所造两部注疏存世，它们是：《吉祥秘密主密意庄严总义零散讲授笔录 · 上师口诀宝鬘》（*dpal gsang bdag dgongs rgyan gyi spyi don yan gyi bshad pavi zin bris bla mavi man ngag rin chen phreng ba*）和《吉祥秘密藏真实决定续王秘密主密意庄严之略义及科判 · 摩尼鬘》（*dpal gsang bavi snying po de kho na nyid nges pavi rgyud kyi rgyal po gsang bdag dgongs rgyan gyi bsdus don sa bcad nor buvi phreng ba*）。

敏珠林寺远传佛语派传承之次第如下：

大译师达摩师利 → 嘉色 · 仁钦南杰（rgyal sras rin chen rnam rgyal）→ 堪钦 · 邬金丹增多杰（mkhan chen o rgyan bstan vdzin rdo rje）→ 赤钦 · 呈列南杰（khri chen phrin las rnam rgyal）→ 赤钦 · 班玛旺嘉（khri chen padma dbang rgyal）→ 赤钦 · 桑吉贡嘎（khri chen sangs rgyas kun dgav）→ 多昂丹增诺布（mdo sngags bstan vdzin nor bu）→ 久美潘德沃色（vgyur med phan bdevi vod zer）→ 敦珠吉扎益西多杰（bdud joms vjigs bral ye shes rdo rje）。

其中，久美潘德沃色曾造《秘密藏续》释论，题为《开启百门甚深义之钥匙》（*zab don sgo brgya vbyed pavi ldevu mig*）。久美潘德沃色是 20 世纪著名宁玛派上师敦珠法王吉扎益西多杰尊者之上师，也是该传承系列中晚近之重要人物。

十四、远传佛语传承于康区的广泛传播

自五世达赖喇嘛时代起，远传佛语派传承之教法于整个康区得到了广泛的传播。于平定准噶尔（jun gar pa）入侵之后，及于吉美林巴（vjigs med gling pa）时代，宁玛派之主要活动中心事实上已东移至康区，源出于嘉色 · 仁钦南杰及堪钦邬金丹增的敏珠林系传承不仅于康区的噶陀寺（kaḥ thog）、白玉寺（dpal yul）、协庆寺（zhe chen）、竹庆寺（rdzogs chen）等地，而且也于康区东部之嘉莫绒（rgyal mo rong）及安多（amdo）的果洛（mgo log）等地得到广泛传播。于上述地区，经、幻、心三部之远传一直持续不衰，及至晚近。

噶陀金刚座寺自 12 世纪开始就是宁玛派教法于康区的大本营，至 16 世纪又为持明敦都多杰（rig vdzin bdud vdul rdo rje）及龙萨宁波（klong gsal snying po）两位大师开展。龙萨宁波的弟子索南德赞（bsod nams ldevu btsan）于敏珠林寺的德达林巴尊者处得卫藏之传承，遂于噶陀寺重振注疏传统。经由直美信雄贡布（dri med zhing skyong mgon po）等索南德赞之历辈转世，以及仁增泽旺诺布（rig vdzin tshe dbang nor bu, 1698-1755）及格泽班智达久美泽旺确珠（dge brtse paṇḍita vgyur med tshe dbang mchog grub）等上师的努力，这一传承系统一直流传到晚近之二世噶陀司徒活佛衮斯曲尼嘉措（kun gzigs chos kyi rgya mtsho, 1880-1925）、大堪布仁增阿旺贝桑（rig vdzin ngag dbang dpal bzang, 1879-1941）、堪布努丹（mkhan po nus ldan）、堪布觉丹（mkhan po vbyor ldan）及夏扎桑吉多杰（bya bral sangs rgyas rdo rje）等上师。于这些传人中，格泽班智达曾为宁玛派续部经典编目，并于1764年为《秘密藏续》作疏，题为《内密咒之道次第广释·第二佛陀之密意庄严》（*gsang sngags nang gi lam rim rgya cher vgrel pa sangs rgyas gnyis pavi dgongs rgyan*）。

竹庆寺，全称竹庆邬金禅定法洲（rdzogs chen dgon pa o rgyan bsam gtan chos gling），是宁玛派在四川甘孜藏族自治州德格县境内的著名寺庙之一。1685年，高僧班玛仁增（padma rig vdzin, 1625-1697）经五世达赖喇嘛授意来到康区一个名为茹丹吉昌（ru dam skyid khram）的地方，在德格土司阿旺扎西（ngag dbang bkra shis）支持下，建造了一个禅修中心，后世称竹庆寺。班玛仁增在该寺首创依据梵本释论教学十三部大论之例，讲修显宗密乘以及其他学问之风，极一时之盛。各地宁玛派僧人纷纷来此求学，许多通人证士如著名的米庞尊者等均由此出身，其声望甚至超过了前藏的金刚岩寺及敏珠林寺。

该寺之住持位先由班玛仁增上师之弟子大伏藏师尼玛扎巴（gter chen nyi ma grags pa）、本乐南喀沃色（dpon slob nam mkhav vod gsal）及协庆饶降丹贝坚赞（zhe chen rab vbyams bstan pavi rgyal mtshan）继承，此后则由尼玛扎巴之历辈转世，即二世竹庆活佛久美特确丹增（vgyur med theg mchog bstan vdzin, 1699-1785）、三世竹庆活佛俄顿丹增桑布（nges don bstan vdzin bzang po, 1759-1792）、四世竹庆活佛米久南喀多杰（mi vgyur nam mkhav rdo rje, 1793-1870）、五世竹庆活佛丹曲多杰（thub bstan chos kyi rdo rje, 1872-1935）及六世竹庆活佛吉扎绛曲多杰（vjigs bral byang chub rdo rje, 1935-1959）继承。在南印度新建的竹庆寺由七世竹庆活佛吉美罗萨旺波（vjigs med blo gsal dbang po, 1964- ）住持。

于四世竹庆活佛在世时，有高僧名嘉色仙藩塔耶（rgyal sras gzhan phan mthav yas），或称格芒尊者（sku zhabs dge mang）于竹庆寺建吉祥狮子（Śrīsiṃha）佛学院，并因敏林赤钦·桑吉贡嘎（smin gling khri chen sangs rgyas kun dgav）及巴珠·班玛旺嘉（dpal sprul padma dbang rgyal）的请求，造包括幻网部在内的远传佛语传承之纲要，长达十卷。其转世甲贡堪布仙藩曲尼囊瓦（rgya kong mkhan po gzhan phan chos kyi snang ba），即堪布贤嘎（mkhan po gzhan dgav, 1871-1927），曾为印度的十三部显乘

大论作疏，[48] 他为《秘密藏续》所造释论题为《幻化网续之笺注 · 日月藏》（*sgyu phrul drwa bavi rgyud kyi mchan vgrel nyi zla snying po*），虽通常被认为是龙青巴上师所造《十方除暗》之夹注部分的重述，但于竹庆寺仍深受重视。

协庆寺，全称协庆二教兴盛洲（zhe chen bstan gnyis dar rgyas gling），为竹庆寺僧、二世协庆饶绛活佛久美衮桑南杰（vgyur med kun bzang rnam rgyal）于 1735 年所建，位于竹庆寺东不远处。此寺规模远比不上竹庆寺，至 20 世纪 50 年代有寺僧约百人，而竹庆寺有五六百人。寺主以转世相承，有三世协庆饶绛活佛仁增班觉嘉措（rig vdzin dpal vbyor rgya mtsho, 1771-1809）、四世协庆饶绛活佛久美图朵南杰（vgyur med mthu stobs rnam rgyal）、五世协庆饶绛活佛桑昂丹增（gsang sngags bstan vdzin）及嘉察久美班玛南杰（rgyal tshab vgyur med padma rnam rgyal, 1871-1927）等。[49]

白玉寺，全称白玉尊胜菩提洲（dpal yul rnam rgyal byang chub gling），位于今四川省白玉县，创始人是仁增衮桑喜饶（rig vdzin kun bzang shes rab），建于公元 1665 年。该寺所传教法由宁玛派及帕竹噶举派之玛仓支派（smar tshang bkav brgyud）合流而成，[50] 在显密教法传习方面与宁玛派其他寺院不同，以热那林巴尊者（ratna gling pa）之伏藏法为重。寺主也以转世相承，称噶玛再世（karma yang srid），历代噶玛再世活佛均去德格噶玛噶举派司徒活佛之根本道场八邦寺受戒。值得一提的是，著名的蒋扬钦哲旺波（vjam dbyangs mkhyen brtsevi dbang po, 1820-1892）及秋吉林巴（mchog vgyur gling pa）曾在白玉寺鼓励甲珠活佛班玛多昂丹增（rgya sprul padma mdo sngags bstan vdzin）举办与远传佛语派传承之现存二十七坛城有关的年度大修法会（sgrub chen），后者于 1857 年在今青海省久治县白玉乡建白玉寺子寺达塘显密讲修院（dar thang mdo sngags bshad sgrub gling）。该寺在当地也以白玉寺著称，百年来发展迅速，乃川甘青边界地区一座规模宏大、影响很广的宁玛派寺院。

白玉寺的传承系统现于印度南部由白玉贝玛诺布 · 绛班竹贝罗珠（dpal yul padma nor bu vjam dpal grub pavi blo gros）之转世维持。现存远传佛语派所传承之经论先由邬金显密法多昂曲吉尼玛（o rgyan mdo sngags chos kyi nyi ma）结集，由白玉寺以影印方式重印，约二十卷；后又由敦珠法王在印度重印。敦珠法王刊本共有五十八卷，

48 有关堪布贤嘎“十三部大论注疏”的写作背景及其在藏土的影响，见 George Dreyfus, “Where Do Commentarial Schools Come From? Reflections on the History of Tibetan Scholasticism,” in *Journal of the International Association of Buddhist Studies* 28, no. 2, 2005, p. 293.

49 参见蒲文成主编 :《甘青藏传佛教寺院》，西宁 : 青海人民出版社，1990 年，第 294-295 页。

50 E. Gene Smith, *Among Tibetan Texts: History and Literature of the Himalayan Plateau*, Boston: Wisdom Publications, 2001, p.45.

题为《宁玛教传广集》（*rnying ma bkav ma rgyas pa*），其中前二十卷乃保持白玉寺影印版之内容和结构，后面部分则为新编排进原典的注疏类文献，最新的版本乃是历时九年搜集整理并于2010年于成都发行的《古译文献宝典》，其藏文标题为《旧译宁玛教传极广集》（*snga vgyur snying ma bkav ma shin tu rgyas pa*），该版本补充了众多重要的注疏论典，共计一百三十三卷，规模较敦珠法王版扩增了一倍多，这是迄今为止最为全面的宁玛派教传文献汇编集。

蒋扬钦哲旺波，本名班玛沃色多昂林巴（padma vod gsal mdo sngags gling pa），因出生于德格之德隆顶果（gter lung dil mgo），故又以宗萨钦哲或顶果钦哲知称。平生修学不断，所有教传、地伏藏、再伏藏、意伏藏、随念、净相、耳传七种应机，皆得具备；著有阐述宁玛、噶当、萨迦道果、噶举之四大八小、香巴噶举、希解、时轮六支瑜伽、三金刚近修等八派修习教法，以及声明、诗韵、医方之书甚多。与蒋贡康楚活佛（vjam mgon kong sprul）及秋吉林巴（mchog vgyur gling pa）一道，蒋扬钦哲旺波上师是远传佛语派传承于康区再次兴盛的主要推动者。他于二十一岁时，受敏珠林寺上师仁增桑布（rig vdzin bzang po）上师剃度，正式出家为僧，并在萨迦派上师多吉仁钦（rdo rje rin chen）处受菩萨戒。其后三十余年间修学包括《秘密藏续》在内的一切显密经论及其注疏，得《甘珠尔》《丹珠尔》及《宁玛十万续》之传承。特别是，他从协庆寺久美图朵南杰（vgyur med mthu stobs rnam rgyal）处获得有关《幻化网寂忿尊》之教授。

蒋扬钦哲旺波上师最主要的弟子是局·米庞南杰（vju mi pham rnam rgyal）上师、二世噶陀司徒活佛曲吉嘉措（kaḥ thog si tu II chos kyi rgya mtsho, 1880-1925）、阿宗珠巴（a vdzom vbrug pa, 1842-1924）、三世多竹千活佛吉美丹贝尼玛（rdo grub vjigs med bstan pavi nyi ma, 1865-1926）、伏藏师索甲（gter ston bsod rgyal, 1856-1926）、堪布衮桑班丹（kun bzang dpal ldan）、白玉寺贝玛诺布绛班竹贝多吉（padma nor bu vjam dpal grub pavi rdo rje）、五世竹庆活佛土丹曲尼多吉（thub bstan chos kyi rdo rje）等。其中三世多竹千活佛曾为《秘密藏续》作疏，题为《吉祥秘密藏续总义略释·宝藏钥匙》（*dpal gsang bavi snying povi rgyud kyi spyi don nyung nguvi ngag gis rnam par vbyed pa rin chen mdzod kyi lde mig*）。此书乃由多竹千活佛口授、伏藏师索甲笔录而成，侧重讨论《秘密藏续》之观修要诀。于多竹千寺之秘密藏殿中，每逢冬季法会即有上师按远传佛语系传承之注疏传统开讲《秘密藏续》。

米庞尊者（1846-1912）是继龙青巴尊者之后，宁玛派远传佛语派中的另一位极富盛名的大德。米庞尊者全名蒋扬南杰嘉措（vjam dbyangs rnam rgyal rgya mtsho），他出生于德格土司所辖雅砻江畔之定琼（ya chuvi ding chung），幼时随其父学习书写诵读，十二岁入宁玛派寺院密咒法洲（gsang sngags chos gling）为僧，后赴拉萨入甘丹寺游学，一年后回德格，皈依蒋扬钦哲旺波上师为根本上师，随该师及旺钦杰绕多吉（dbang chen dgyes rab rdo rje）、巴珠活佛吉美曲旺（vjigs med chos dbang）等大德学法，遂通大小五明及显密教法，特别是对工巧、医方与历算尤有慧解。随后，即以讲经、辩论和著述三途利益正法、有情。其常修处有噶摩达仓寺（dkar mo stag tshang dgon）、局地之山居（vju ri khrod）、邓柯顶果山居（ldan khog ding mgo ri khrod）等。年六十七，于局地山居圆寂，故后世习称其为局·米庞大师。他留下著述共三十二卷，由其弟子噶陀司徒曲吉嘉措及巴珠活佛等整理、编排，于德格印经院木刻印行。其著作中有一部《十方除暗总义·光明藏》（*spyi don vod gsal snying po*），是对龙青巴上师之名著《十方除暗》的注疏，该论依绒宋班智达与龙青巴二位尊者之无上密意，从见地、等持、行为、坛城、灌顶、誓句、修证、供养、事业及手印等"密续十事"（rgyud kyi dngos po bcu）来解释《秘密藏续》之甚深义。据传，当米庞尊者造此论圆满时，密主护法阿松玛（sngags srung ma，即一髻佛母 Ekajaṭī）于光明梦境中示现，以身供养，发誓怙佑。次日，米庞尊者造内外祈供密主护法仪轨时，复有格萨尔王亲现，发誓与不败尊者如影随身，不相分离。

十五、《秘密藏续》之近传伏藏传承

除了远传佛语传承外，旧译密咒法要之传承还有近传伏藏传承。按宁玛派的传统，莲花生大士及其他少数具德大师，为了教化未来众生，将很多修证共与不共两种悉地的教授作为伏藏埋藏，大力加持，令不失坏，付于守藏护法掌管，并发净愿，愿此法得遇有宿缘之化机。若到取藏之时，则先示现取藏之预兆，由谁得此藏，则应将掘藏者的名号氏族、容貌等记在取藏的简札上。若时、地与掘藏师一切因缘具备，则可将此藏取出，以之普传有缘，称为伏藏法（gter ma）。伏藏之法，印度自古有之，[51] 藏地其他宗派中也屡见不鲜。伏藏法存在之理论根据可见诸许多正法经典中，其主要理由在于远传佛语传承之活力必然会随时间的流逝而衰退，因此，旧译经典之纯洁性只有在近传之伏藏中重新获得。每一代人只有在其重新发现的伏藏中得到更直接的影

51 关于伏藏传统在印度的先例，见 Robert Mayer, "Scriptural Revelation in India and Tibet: Indian Precursors of the gTer-ma Tradtion," in Per Kvaerne (ed.), *Tibetan Studies: Proceedings of the 6th Seminar of the International Association for Tibetan Studies*, vol. I, Oslo: Institute for Comparative Research in Human Culture, 1994, pp. 533-544.

响。因为伏藏是在近传中获得，其发现者比任何旧密大师更接近教法之源头，所以由他们传播的伏藏法比师徒相承的远传教法更为殊胜。

伏藏法按其被发现的不同方式分成地伏藏（sa gter）、密意藏（dgongs gter）、净相藏（dag snang）及随念藏（rje dran gyi gter），或称再伏藏（yang gter）。[52] 地伏藏通常指的是由后世掘藏师在地下、佛像内或院墙中发现的文献，而密意藏则指被隐埋在某人心识相续中被发现之伏藏。由于宿愿，菩萨或可在野兽之声音中，或在五大中听到法音。佛与菩萨也常常在得道者之梦境及净相中示现，并授之以特殊的教法。所谓净相藏与随念藏，亦被称为甚深净相传承，即是指已得道者在入定时面见本尊或上师，由本尊或上师亲口宣说教授，无间相承之伏藏法。这类传承虽也见于他派，但以旧密传承中最为普遍。它甚至被藏族宗教史家单列为区别于远传之经典传承、近传之伏藏传承之外的第三种传承。[53]

西藏之伏藏法的根源通常主要归结于莲花生。虽然除了莲花生外，还有赤松德赞、无垢友、毗卢遮那、努·桑杰益西、南喀宁波、聂·阇那古摩罗、纳囊·多吉堆迥、娘班·定增桑波等上师也都被认为是伏藏的掩埋者，后世的掘藏师也分别是他们的转世，但到著名的掘藏师娘热·尼玛沃色（nyang ral nyi ma vod zer, 1124-1192）时，莲花生与他的藏土明妃益西嘉措佛母（ye shes mtsho rgyal）则已被认为是西藏伏藏法之主要来源。据传莲花生将众多摩诃瑜伽、阿努瑜伽及阿底瑜伽的教法传给了益西措嘉佛母，后者将它们重新编排成象征五部佛的五种黄卷，隐藏在不同的伏藏库中，留待被后世发现。当然严格说来，莲花生在此扮演的也不过是一个中间人角色，因为伏藏本身最初是诸佛密意传承（rgyal bavi dgongs brgyud），是由本初佛于本初刹土中传承的；其次是所谓持明表示传承（rig vdzin brda brgyud），是持明——即宁玛派之印度先师们以表义相传的。旧密所有不共之特殊口诀的传承只由上师以象征性符号、标帜进行直指教授。再其次才是由莲花生大师于 8 世纪的吐蕃宫廷用语言传授，此即被称为补特伽罗口耳传承（gang zag snyan khung du brgyud）。

具体说来，诸佛密意传承又经三传，即由法身佛普贤王如来父母于色究竟天之法界宫中将所有密意传于第六大金刚持，加持佛法大净瓶；第六大金刚持又亲将密意授予金刚萨埵，并赐加持；金刚萨埵将密意加持后传授给大持明嘎绕多吉（dgav rab

52 关于伏藏类文献的历史、内容、种类及其教法意义参见 Janat B. Gyatso, “Drawn from the Tibetan Treasury: The gTer ma Literature”, *Tibetan Literature, Studies in Genre*, Edited by Jose Ignacio Cabezon and Roger R. Jackson, Ithaca: Snow Lion, 1996, pp. 147-169. 另见 Andreas Doctor, *Tibetan Treasure Literature: Revelation, Tradition, and Accomplishment in Visionary Buddhism*, Ithaca: Snow Lion Publications, 2005.

53 参见《土观宗派源流》，第 62、69 页。

rdo rje）。大持明嘎绕多吉乃印度金刚座西一邦国国王邬波罗阇（Uparāja）与王妃显明具光（Ālokabhāsvatī）之女妙法（Sudharmā）公主之子，传说公主于一茅篷修法时夜梦一白人将五轮种子字（oṃāḥ hūṃ svāhā）所饰宝瓶安其顶，于是受孕从左肋间生下一子。此小儿七岁时，即能难倒邬波罗阇国王及国内著名的五百学者，故受众敬仰，得名嘎绕多吉。后去日光遍照山修禅三十二年，显种种神通，挫败外道无算。其后，复赴金刚座东北大寒林中修行，向诸空行母说法，并于此将佛说所有法藏、要诀传予弟子妙吉祥友（Mañjuśrīmitra）。妙吉祥友随嘎绕多吉修习七十五载，获证菩提，并将大圆满六百四十万颂分为心部、界部、口诀部。妙吉祥友复将密乘所有修持，及清净解脱之灌顶，尤其是所有自性大圆满阿底瑜伽等之修持法要作为具相宝瓶，赐予弟子无垢友、佛智足及莲花生三位大师，是为持明表示传承。所谓补特伽罗口耳传承者，乃指吐蕃赞普赤松德赞父子与大译师属卢·鲁依坚赞等于莲花生座前听得普贤王如来密意之六百四十部大圆满续。因如是之法，小乘种姓无福享受，非但不悟，反遭毁谤，是故莲花生只能将其藏之名山，以利益未来浊世之众。[54] 为准备隐埋伏藏又在一祈愿灌顶仪轨中传授伏藏法，在此期间特别委任某位弟子由其将来的转世在某个特定的时间重新发现这些伏藏。为此他特作所谓奉教授记（bkav vbabs lung bstan），以确保这些伏藏由合适的人在合适的时间、地点被重新发现。然后，他任命护法去隐藏这些伏藏文书，保证在合适的时间、人物出现以前不为人发现。

宁玛派发现之伏藏不仅数量惊人，而且内容广泛、形式多样，包罗万象。19 世纪时，康楚罗珠塔耶尊者（kong sprul blo gros mthav yas）曾将其所见之佛教伏藏法汇编成集，名之为《大宝伏藏》（*rin chen gter mdzod chen mo*），共一百一十一卷。其中尚不包括像《玛尼全集》《五部遗教》等伏藏法中属于历史类的著作，以及那些已经收录进《宁玛十万续》中的伏藏及被归入口诀部之阿底瑜伽类续典，可见伏藏数量之多。[55]

若对伏藏作粗略的分类的话，则主要可分两大类：一是历史类，主要内容是雅隆王朝时佛教传入西藏的历史；二是宗教类，包括教法和实修。第一类作品出现于

54 详见《深法寂忿密意自解脱传承简史·摩尼宝鬘》（*zab chos zhi khri dgongs pa rang grol gyi brgyud pavi lo rgyus mdor bsdus pa nor buvi phreng ba*），收《寂忿密意自解脱法汇》（*zhi khro dgongs pa rang grol gyi chos skor*），Delhi: Sherab Lama, 1975-1976, Vol.1, ff. 27.

55 德国波恩大学中亚语言文化研究所 Peter Schwieger 博士多年来从事对德国柏林国家图书馆所藏楚卜寺版《大宝伏藏》之编目、整理工作，至今已出版目录 3 册：Tibetische Handschriften und Blockdrucke, Teil 10, 11, 12, Die mTshur-phu-Ausgabe der Sammlung Rin-chen gter-mdzod chen-mo, nach dem Exemplar der Orientabteilung, Staatsbibliothek zu Berlin-Preussischer Kulturbesitz. Beschrieben von Peter Schwieger, Franz Steiner Verlag Stuttgart, 1990, 1995, 1999.

12-14世纪，以前面提到的《玛尼全集》和《五部遗教》为典型代表。虽然书中保留有许多今已失传的古代文献中的一些段落，但主体部分则为神话、幻想的成分所充斥，以致无法将它们当作第一手的历史材料使用。这些伏藏的主要内容就是粉饰、神化雅隆王朝的历史，特别是对松赞干布等吐蕃赞普如何将佛法引入，并加以大力扶植的历史浪慢化、教条化。《玛尼全集》实际上就是记载松赞干布之种种弘化的传记，它用大量笔墨来证明松赞干布是观音菩萨的转世。[56]

第二类宗教类作品之主题包括教义、修法和仪轨。这类作品占所有伏藏之大部。除了莲花生及一些伏藏师的传记以外，卷轶浩繁的《大宝伏藏》汇集的主要就是成就法（grub thabs, sadhana）。与远传佛语之经、幻、心三部相应，伏藏法则主要是关于莲花生上师、大圆满及大悲观音（bla rdzogs thugs gsum）三类的修习，其中最核心的部分是《修部八教》《密意总集经》及《金刚橛》部（bkav dgongs phur gsum）之文本。《大宝伏藏》之主要组织原则是旧译法藏之内续三部，即摩诃瑜伽、阿努瑜伽及阿底瑜伽。其中摩诃瑜伽在三部中占绝对主导地位，包括《大宝伏藏》之第三至第八十五卷；阿努瑜伽仅占八十五卷和八十六卷中的部分，阿底瑜伽则占第八十六至第九十一卷。摩诃瑜伽部诸尊被划分为上师、本尊和空行三组，合称为三根本（rtsa gsum）。上师修法在《大宝伏藏》中占去十四卷，本尊修法占三十二卷，主要即是摩诃瑜伽之修部八教，空行修法占五卷，其中包括一些母尊之修法。阿底瑜伽在实修时也用一些同样的本尊，但更重那些直指心性一类的修行方法。

在众多的掘藏师中，有事业洲尊者等掘藏大师发现了与寂忿百尊（即四十二寂静尊和五十八忿怒尊）之坛城有关的伏藏法。而寂忿百尊坛城即《秘密藏续》及幻化网部续典之坛城，所以《秘密藏续》乃《深法寂忿密意自解脱》之主要源头。于是，修供寂忿本尊坛城法的传承也就与《秘密藏续》之传承息息相关。[57]

十六、伏藏师略传

为说明伏藏传承的历史，兹据康楚仁波切《大宝伏藏》中所收《百名掘藏师传·大宝琉璃美鬘》（*gter ston brgya rtsavi rnam thar rin chen baidurya vphreng mdzes*）

56 参 Matthew Kapstein, "Remarks on the Maṇi Bka'' bum and the Cult of Avalokiteśvara in Tibet," in Ronald M. Davidson and Steven D. Goodman (eds.), *Tibetan Buddhism: Reason and Revelation*, Albany: State University of New York Press, 1991, pp. 79-94.

57 参 Henk Blezer, *Kar gling Zhi khro: A Tantric Buddhist Concept*, Leiden: Research School CNWS, School of Asian, African, and Amerindian Studies, 1997, pp. 39-93.

一书的记载，对与《秘密藏续》有关的几位最著名的掘藏师之生平及其所掘伏藏作简单介绍。

1. 雅尔结邬金林巴（yar rje o rgyal gling pa, 1329-1367）

邬金林巴传说为天子确珠杰波（lha sras mchog grub rgyal po）之第七辈转世，藏历第五胜生周阴水猪年（1323 年）生于今西藏自治区扎囊县名雅尔结的地方。家中素有密续渊源，故尤擅咒术、医方、历算等。年二十三，于桑耶寺之红塔发现伏藏法之标牌授记（kha byang），并于雅隆协扎（shel brag）背后一个由莲花岩堆砌而成的稀有水晶洞中发现了大量伏藏。此岩洞本为莲花生大士作甘露药修仪轨之处，洞中有众寂忿本尊之天然石像，一尊大遍入护法[58]像为其守卫。[59]邬金林巴从这尊护法像的头部及身体的其他部位中，抽出了许多伏藏经典。其中自其头顶获属上师、大圆满、大悲观音三部的《寂忿上师生起次第二教三部》（*bskyed rim bla ma bstan gnyis skor gsum zhi drag*）、《大悲莲花心髓》（*thugs rje chen po padma snying thig*）、《大圆满长寿修习》（*rdzogs chen tshe sgrub*）、《阿底、吉底、仰底》（*a ti spyi ti yang ti*）等。复于此像下部三首中，获《本尊教集大法海》（*yi dam bkav vdus chos kyi rgya mtsho chen po*），百三十二节；自其喉部，获《寂忿教集》（*zhi khro bkav vdus*）、《黑忿怒空行母》（*mkhav vgro khros nag*）、《黄门怙主部》（*mgon pa ma ning gi skor*）；自其心间获《大莲花遗教》（*padma bkav yig thang yig chen mo*）；自其下部蛇尾中，获《本智怙主暨众本尊》（*ye shes mgon pa lha mang*）之密续、修法及事业集、医术、甚深护法教授；自手部与蛇尾余部，获《损益事业方便》（*phan gnod kyi las thabs*）及《工巧花饰》（*bzo rig pa tra*）。[60]

此外，邬金林巴还在扎玉工札（gravi g·yu gong brag）获《密咒道次第广论》

58 即宁玛派三大护法之一喇呼拉（Rāhula）。

59 据蒋扬钦哲旺波上师《卫藏胜迹志》记载："（于雅隆）北部山岭上有最驰名的雅隆协吉扎浦（yar lung shel gyi brag phug, 水晶岩洞）等大修道圣地的中心岩洞内，有莲花生的真身替代像，是开口显过圣的神像，还有为数不少的其他天然生成的佛像。协扎山的下面不远的地方有村吉拉康（mtshan brgyad lha khang, 八相神殿）、乃提拉章宫（gnas mthil bla brang 中央宫）等，内中有莲师的替身像、日光法衣，还有禅仗等内供佛宝甚多。在巧策拉喀山口（phyag vtshal la kha, 礼拜山口）有特别殊胜的弃尸场和大宝塔，离尸场不远处有耶协措杰（智慧胜海）的秘密修道岩窟（mtsho rgyal gsang phug）。山左边的背后有邬坚林巴（邬金洲）取伏藏的地方，名白马协浦（padma shel phug, 莲花水晶洞），但距离比较远。"见钦则旺布著，刘立千译注：《卫藏道场胜迹志》，北京：民族出版社，2000 年，第 15-16 页。另参 Alfonsa Ferrari, *mkvyen Brtse's Guide to the Holy Places of Central Tibet*, Roma, IsMEO, 1958, pp. 271-277.

60 此经已佚，但在蒋扬钦哲旺波在之《教集总摄部》（*bkav vdus snying po mdor bsdud skor*）中仍可见其全貌。见《大宝伏藏》，卷 23，第 209-429 页。

（*gsang sngags lam rim chen mo*）[61]、《莲花生略传》（*padmavi rnam thar chung ba*）、《希解遗教明义》（*zhi byed bkav chem don gsal*）、《缘起精粹集》（*rten vbrel yang snying vdus pa*）等伏藏法；又在桑耶寺之另一伏藏库获《五部遗教》，于宿喀（zur mkhar）[62]石塔中获《大悲本智殊胜光》（*thugs rje chen po ye shes vod mchog*）、《吉祥骑虎怙主》（*dpal mgon stag zhon*），于温普达仓（von phug stag tshang）获《忿怒上师与护法类》（*guru drag po dang bstan srung skor*），于扎其之扎波且（gra phyi brag po che）获《阎罗寿主类》（*gshin rje tshe bdag gi skor*）等伏藏法逾百卷，其中仅《教集》部就约有三十卷。但因邬金林巴无法将它们定于黄卷之上，故不得不将其再次作为伏藏重新封藏，遂成再伏藏（yang gter）。在他发现的伏藏中与《秘密藏续》有最直接关联的是《寂忿教集》。

2. 嘎玛林巴（意译"事业洲"，karma gling pa, 1376/7-1394/5）[63]

嘎玛林巴乃吐蕃王国时三大著名译师之一属卢·鲁依坚赞（cog ro kluvi rgyal mtshan）之化身。约于藏历第六胜生周（1327-1387）中降生于达波[64]上部名克珠（dwags povi stod khyer grub）的地方，父名尼达桑杰（nyi zla sangs rgyas），享百二十五之高寿。嘎玛林巴善密咒，具无量功德，乃事业、神通无碍之大圣者。年十五，因授记与缘起圆满和合，遂于达波之形若山神起舞的岗波达山[65]中获《寂忿密意自解脱》（*zhi khro dgongs pa rang grol*）与《大悲莲花寂忿》（*thugs rje chen po padma zhi khro*）及其他岩藏法宝。他将《大悲莲花寂忿》传给了他的所有十四位弟子，使其成为此法之传承上师。但仅将《寂忿密意自解脱》单传给他唯一的儿子尼达曲杰（nyi zla chos rje），并要求在三代以内必须是秘密单传。三代之后，才准由其第三代传人广为传播。由于与授记之妙印母缘起不合，嘎玛林巴于掘藏后不久即示寂。

61　此论乃莲花生所造。

62　宿喀位于桑耶寺附近，自桑耶逆雅鲁藏布江往上游走便到宿喀。此地最稀有的圣迹是象征五部如来的大佛塔。见刘立千译《卫藏道场胜迹志》，第 10 页；另见 Ferrari 上揭书，p. n. 161。

63　迄今为止，未有嘎玛林巴之传记面世，仅在《深法寂忿密意自解脱题记》（*zab chos zhi khro dgongs pa rang grol gyi them byang*）中有关于嘎玛林巴之出处、授记、所掘伏藏及其传承的简略记载。嘎玛林巴之简传另见 Dudjom Rinpoche 上揭书，第 800-801 页。关于嘎玛林巴的生平，特别是生卒年代的考证见谈锡永为《寂静忿怒密意自解脱·六中有圆满次第导引》所撰导论，收莲花生大士岩藏，事业洲尊者岩传，谈锡永译注：《事业洲岩传法——六中有自解脱导引》，北京：华夏出版社，2011 年，第 3-24 页；沈卫荣：《幻想与现实：〈西藏死亡书〉在西方世界》，同上，第 173-239 页。

64　关于达波之地参见《卫藏道场胜迹志》，第 12 页；据译注者言，达波指今西藏自治区桑日县以东的雅鲁藏布江流经的沿岸一带地区，包括今加查、古如朗加、朗、金东等县。

65　此 sgam po gdar gyi ri 疑即为位于沃卡达孜与达波之间的圣山达拉岗波山（dwags la sgam po）。达拉山在今加查县境内，岗波又为寺庙名，乃噶举派达布系的最大道场，由冈波巴上师建成于 1121 年。

嘎玛林巴的第三代传人南喀曲吉嘉措（nam mkhav chos kyi rgya mtsho）即按其授记所言，将《寂忿密意自解脱》之法在卫、藏、康三区，特别是在南北康区，广为传播，其灌顶、口授及导引系统一直延续至今。《寂忿密意自解脱》中的一部分，即《中有大闻解脱》（*bar do thos grol chen po*）被译成英文，以所谓《西藏死亡书》（*The Tibetan Book of the Dead*）闻名于西方。[66]

3. 喜饶沃色（shes rab vod zer, 1518-1584）

喜饶沃色习称为掘藏师称波（vphreng po gter ston），乃大译师毗卢遮那之转世。他发现了《莲花教诫》（*padmavi zhal gdams*）及《解脱滴密意自解脱》（*grol tig dgongs pa rang grol*）。后一伏藏与《秘密藏续》相关，其修法在般若光之本寺琼结白日寺（vphyong rgyas dpal ri, 吉祥山寺）尤为流行。该寺位于琼结藏王墓后方，日窝德庆（ri bo bde chen，大乐山）寺之河东，全名吉祥山大乘洲，古名金刚成熟吉祥山（rdor smin dpal ri），原是宁玛派大寺，乃当地土司索南多嘉（bsod nams stobs rgyal）所建。但至蒋扬钦哲旺波上师于 19 世纪中后期造访此庙时，它已成为一座小庙。庙内尚有莲花生大士的替身像和其他佛宝。[67]

4. 持明嘉村宁波（vjav tshon snying po, 1585-1656）

持明嘉村宁波又名掘藏师勒绰林巴（las vphrog gling pa），或持咒尊者吽那美巴（hūṃ nag me vbar），被誉为一身兼三名之大金刚持比丘。传说他是得莲花生大士嫡传、并得证无漏光明身的一百零八位弟子中之娘班 · 定增桑波（nyang ban ting vdzin bzang po）的化身。他出生于藏历第十胜生周之阴木鸡年（1585 年），出生地是工布的瓦茹南泽（lba ru gnam tshal），父名曲迥贡布（chos skyong mgon po），母名南朗普赤（nam langs bu khrid）。自幼为教法熏习，三岁即能识字念咒，自十二至二十岁，习一般之科目，尤擅医方明，达贤者之顶。是时常在日常、净相与梦境中遇莲花生，遂决意脱离火宅，潜心佛法，在曲杰米庞扎西罗珠（chos rje mi pham bkra shis blo gros）座前出家，受赐法名阿旺曲嘉旺波（ngag dbang chos rgyal dbang po）。随上师听闻一切密咒灌顶、口传、导引等无数教授，且时时潜修。后又随沙布隆诺布坚巴（zhabs drung nor bu rgyan pa）、竹巴汤杰钦巴（vbrug pa thams cad mkhyen pa）和娘美拉泽瓦（mnyam med lha rtse ba）等上师学法，通显密新旧一切教法。并随无比天顶

66 关于《西藏死亡书》及其在西方的流布和影响见 Donald S. Lopez, Jr., *Prisoners of Shangri-La*, Chicago: The University of Chicago Press, 1998, pp. 46-87; David Germano, “Dying, Death, and Other Opportunities,” in *Religions of Tibet in Practice*, Donald S. Lopez, Jr.(ed.), Princeton: Princeton University Press, 1997, pp. 458-493.

67《卫藏道场胜迹志》，第 17-18 页。

上师受近圆戒。

嘉村宁波尊者曾在一泥封之隐舍修行十七年，虽获许多有关伏藏之授记，但他不曾理会。当他念诵金刚手仪轨达一亿遍时，再次出现令其掘藏之授记，遂在扎西罗珠上师鼓励下，于阳铁猴年（1620年）正月初十开始掘藏，最初于一座铁合金所铸金翅鸟像内掘出佛母益西措嘉亲手写下的伏藏标牌授记。按此授记所示，他在扎陇虹帐（brag lung hom vphrang）之铁门内，掘出《极深至宝总集》（*yang zab dkon mchog spyi vdus*）等秘密伏藏，他的伏藏修行及秘密手印与之完全相合。随后，他渐次在工布布楚（kong po bu chu）、称作绛真泽（byang vphreng mdzes）的大林地的入口、聂木神山（snye mo lha ri）、工帐根敦乃（kong vphrang dge vdun gnas）和乌茹夏拉康（dbu ru zhwavi lha khang）等地，掘出《大悲观音》（*thugs rje chen mo*）、《马头金刚与亥母·如意宝》（*rta phag yid bzhin nor bu*）、《寂忿了义藏》（*zhi khro nges don snying po*）、《长寿修习·霹雳金刚》（*tshe sgrub gnam lcags rdo rje*）、《金刚卓洛》（*rdo rje gro lod*）、《吉祥怙主黄门法类》（*dpal mgon ma ning skor*）、《莲花岗圣地指南》（*padma dkod kyi gnas kyi lam yig*）许多甚深伏藏法。其中有些如《至宝总集》等为秘密伏藏法，而大部分则是当众发掘的伏藏。

嘉村宁波尊者享世寿七十又二，后人将其所掘伏藏汇编成集，名《六卷彩虹》（*vjav tshon pod drug*）。其中《寂忿了义藏》与《秘密藏续》之传统最有关联。

5. 敦都多杰（bdud vdul rdo rje, 1615-1672）

持明敦都多杰尊者据传乃大译师卓班车琼（vbrog ban khyevu chung）之化身，于藏历第十胜生周之阴木兔年（1615年）出生于康区德格名额普囊（dngul phu nang）谷之山阴，父亲属岭氏家族（gling gi rigs），名龙树（klu sgrub），行医为业；母亲名柏绿玛（Boluma）。自幼随父从学，识文断字，兼习医道。六岁时，即显现许多净相，居吉祥任运顶法苑（dpal lhun grub steng gi chos grwa），顶礼仁增果登之化身、德格成道者贡嘎嘉措（kun dgav rgya mtsho），得法号贡嘎索南曲帕（kun dgav bsod nams chos vphags）。先闻思修萨迦派教法，后随导师贡却坚赞（dkon mchog rgyal mtshan）习大圆满法，得开证悟之门。复赴前藏学法，于娘布（nyang po）遇大德扎西才旦（bkra shis tshe brtan），听闻许多解脱之教授。后于扎噶拉曲（brag dkar lha chu）行禁食，仅以辟谷术为生，于甚深道之脉、气、明点瑜伽得究竟。其后，往后藏萨迦鄂尔派（ngor）寺院学道果法，回程过邦日（bang ri）顶礼嘉村宁波藏尊者，圆满听闻以尊者自家甚深伏藏法为主之灌顶、导引及口诀。后往波密，于玉海宫（pho brang g·yu mtsho）精进于修习《宝洲极密无上金刚橛》（*rat gling phur pa yang gsang bla med*）时，梦中被诸空行母引往莲花生大士的净土铜色吉祥山，居此二十八日。莲师赐其圆满成熟灌顶及有关伏藏之授记。后往晋见吉祥邬金持教上师，请其释梦。后者大喜，献其以丰盛之供养，并封其为金刚阿阇梨。

敦都多杰尊者最初发掘之甚深伏藏，与所得之伏藏标牌授记相合。年二十九，他以具种姓之班马吉（padma skyid）为其业印，在玉海宝岩（g·yu mtsho rin chen brag）取出标牌授记，于波密东河大乐秘密洞中，取出《正法密意遍总集法类》（*dam chos dgongs pa yongs vdus kyi skor*）。按尊者自己的说法，此藏是他所有掘藏中最为重要的一部，以后所掘伏藏不过是它的支分而已。随后，他渐次在擦瓦卓扎（tsha ba sgro brag）掘出《正法化身心髓》（*dam chos sprul skuvi snying thig*）及其护法刹土神之仪轨，于普日达宗（spu ri dwags rdzong）取出《甚深义秘密心髓》（*zab don gsang ba snying thig*）、《吉祥胜乐四臂护法类》（*dpal bde mchog dka vsrung phyag bzhi pavi skor*）等，于普日协结央仲（spu ri shel gyi yang sgrom）掘出《心髓——无量寿、真实忿怒尊、普巴金刚三部及护法一髻佛母自生佛母类》（*snying thig tshe yang phur gsum dang srung ma ekajaṭī rang byung rgyal movi skor*），复于彼密东河北岸岩石中掘出《莲花岗秘境胜迹志》（*sbas yul pad mo bkod pavi gnas yig*），复于康区德格境内掘得《红、黑阎摩敌与大威德三本尊类》（*yi dam dmar nag vjigs gsum gyi skor*）；但除了《寂静文殊修习类》（*vjam dpal zhi sgrub kyi skor*）外，他似乎并未建立其他伏藏法。

此外，经敦都多杰尊者之手在西藏各地掘出的伏藏还有《吉祥四面怙主及大天修习类》（*dpal mgon gdong bzhi pa dang lha chen sgrub skor*）、《上师持明总集》（*bla ma rig vdzin vdus pa*）、《长寿修习·炙热红霞》（*tshe sgrub tsha ba dmar thag*）、《娘舅护法与庞若类》（*bdav srung zhang blon dang spom ravi skor*）、《耳传顶严·如意宝类》（*snyan brgyud gtsug rgyan yid bzhin nor buvi skor*），对这些伏藏法他同样未作安立。

特别值得一提的是，有行者名冬呈坚（dung phreng can）在波密之南迦巴瓦山（gnam lcags vbar ba，天铁炽燃）中取出《幻化网寂忿尊》《修部八教》及其护法类，于若扎（ra tsag）的石塔中取出《吉祥骑虎怙主类》（*dpal mgon stag zhon skor*）等伏藏，并将它们交到了敦都多杰尊者的手中。这部名为《幻化网寂忿尊》的伏藏于藏地《秘密藏续》之传承意义重大。

敦都多杰尊者晚年以位于波密西部之德庆塘（bde chen thang）及玉日岗果（g·yu ri sgang vgo）二寺为根本道场，并在康区各宁玛派丛林巡游示教，广弘密法。藏历阳水鼠年（1672 年）往生莲花光明大宫，享世寿五十八。

6. 南确米久多杰（gnam chos mi vgyur rdo rje, 1645-1667）

他发现的伏藏达二十三卷之多，多为净相传承。据说自十二岁至其二十四岁时圆寂为止，他于净相中共得到十五卷伏藏法，被称为《天法》（*gnam chos*），该法已成为白玉寺之主修传统之一，其中著名的有《寂忿天法》（*gnam chos zhi khro*）。

7. 秋吉林巴（mchog gyur gling pa, 1829-1870）

秋吉林巴尊者全名秋吉德钦希波林巴（mchog gyur bde chen zhig po gling pa），传说为吉祥天子木迪赞普、亦名益西若巴匝（ye shes rol pa rtsal）之化身。藏历第十四胜生周阴土牛年（1829 年）出生于西康南部与叶尔堆（yer stod）相连的一个名宫德扎囊（sgom sde grwa nang）的地方。其父名班玛旺秋（padma dbang phyug），其母名泽仁央措（tshe ring g·yang mtsho）。自幼灵异，显现稀有正行，识文作颂，了无碍难，人称罗布丹增（nor bu bstan vdzin）。后随八世巴俄祖拉曲吉嘉布（dpav bo gtsug lag chos kyi rgyal po）、止贡派诸殊胜化身、八邦寺堪布司徒班玛宁杰旺波（si tu padma nyin byed dbang po）等著名大师学习各派教法。自蒋贡康楚仁波切处获得了宁玛派之大部分教法传统，包括幻化网之寂忿本尊修法。他与蒋扬钦哲旺波二人都兼具关于经、幻、心三部之教传和伏藏、净相传承之七种传承（bkav babs bdun）。他所发现的众多伏藏如《殊胜洲伏藏法》（*mchog gling gter chos*）等，共达三十卷之多。其中，《甚深七幻化》（*zab bcun sgyu vphrul*）以及在十万空行宗（*mkhav vgro vbum rdzong*）发现的《大悲莲花幻化网》（*thugs rje chen po padma sgyu vphrul drwa ba*），皆依远传佛语传承之名相及义理结构。

8. 蒋扬钦哲旺波（vjam dbyangs mkhyen brtsevi dbang po, 1820-1892）

又名班玛沃色多昂林巴，为大班智达无垢友与法王赤松德赞之双运幻变、嘉色拉杰伏藏师降巴（rgyal sras lha rje gter ston rkyang pa，即赤松德赞）的第十三辈转世。藏历十四胜生周之铁龙年（1820 年）出生于西康德格，父为内氏仲钦仁钦旺嘉（drung chen rin chen dbang rgyal），母是索萨索南措（sog bzav bsod nams mtsho）。幼年时，其大乘种姓已然觉醒，时以出家为念。年二十一，由邬金敏珠林寺堪布仁增桑布（rig vdzin bzang po）上师授近圆戒，随后十三年间，他师从萨迦派上师多吉仁钦（rdo rje rin chen）等一百五十位上师修习大、小乘及显、密教法，遂通大小五明，精各派教法要义。对《幻化秘密藏》和《时轮》《胜乐》《密集》等续典及其释论，如《甘珠尔》《宁玛十万续》《丹珠尔》等都毫无偏见地通习无余。

蒋扬钦哲旺波具经、幻、心三部之佛语远传及伏藏、净相传承之七种传承，曾掘出众多伏藏法，其中与《秘密藏续》直接相关的有在司峨韵措湖（si ngu g·yu mtsho）发现的《三根本幻化网类》（*rtsa gsum sgyu vphrul drwa bavi skor*）。此外，当他在宗雪德协度巴（rdzong shod bde gshegs vdus pa）时，曾在净相中游商羯罗矩陀（Śaṇkarakūṭa）塔，受到莲师及其八位化身的灌顶及关于《修部八教》《幻化寂忿尊》等成熟解脱之心要。

十七、对《秘密藏续》之摩诃瑜伽和阿底瑜伽的诠释

粗略言之，与《秘密藏续》相关的藏文释论可分成两类：一类将在远传佛语系传承中的《秘密藏续》解释为摩诃瑜伽的典型代表；而另一类则将它当作果乘、阿底瑜伽、大圆满法来解释。如米庞尊者在《光明藏》中所言，用于疏解此本续大义之法有两大传规，即共通广大说与不共甚深说。共通广大说即是持明之王、具德宿氏家族之稀有传承，此派将《秘密藏续》按照摩诃瑜伽自宗之传统来解释；而不共甚深说即指绒宋班智达与龙青巴二位尊者之无上意趣，他们将《秘密藏续》解释为“摩诃瑜伽中的阿底部”，即最高部；从其根本言之，它与大圆满法三个分支中“阿底瑜伽的摩诃部”的密意相同。秘密大圆满中有三类教法：一说生圆无二，心智自现坛城；二说不依生圆，心性即本初佛自性；三说于智自显现本性中成佛。米庞尊者认为《秘密藏续》所取为其中第一种说法。虽然这两种传规之究竟密意并无二致，但米庞尊者在其自己的著作中取第二种传规，因为它具有甚深口诀之精要。

虽然这两种传规相互间并不对立、矛盾，但依然明确表明二者各自之侧重有细微的差别。用大译师达摩师利在《秘密主事业善说教授》中的话说，摩诃瑜伽证知一切法乃心性之幻化，阿努瑜伽证知一切法乃心性之力用，而心性中之法界与本智无二无别，而阿底瑜伽则证知一切法乃心性自显现，此心性即无始以来法尔具存之本觉智，无生无灭。尽管标准的摩诃瑜伽修习强调基之自性以及生起次第之渐修，但《秘密藏续》已然平等地显示了生起、圆满次第，以及为阿底瑜伽所重之心智自显现。事实上，《秘密藏续》的修习包罗了生圆二次第，以及大圆满之种子，这就表明了在这些不同的解释传规之间并不存在根本性的矛盾。

在《秘密藏续》诸释论中，属共通广大传规者，以出自远传佛语系之论典为代表，其名目如下：

1. 游戏金刚（Līlāvajra）造，《大续王吉祥秘密藏疏》（*Mahārājatantraśrīguhyagarbhanāmaṭīkā*），简称《巴甲疏》

2. 佛密（Buddhaguhya）造，《秘密藏续判别疏》（*rnam dbye vgrel*）

3. 云敦·多吉班（g·yung ston rdo rje dpal）造，《吉祥秘密藏续义能显明镜》（*dpal*

gsang ba snying povi rgyud don gsal byed me long）

4. 达那·卓玛桑珠多吉（rta nag sgrol ma ba bsam grub rdo rje）造，《秘密藏续纲要》（*khog dbub*）

5. 南喀仁钦（nam mkhavi rin chen）造，《秘密藏真实决定续疏·能显续义之如意宝灯》（*gsang bavi snying po de kho na nyid nges pavi rgyud kyi vgrel bshad rgyud don gsal bar byed pavi sgron ma yid bzhin gyi nor bu*）

6. 曼陇巴·米觉多杰（sman lung pa mi bskyod rdo rje）造，《秘密藏疏及总义》（*gsang snying vgrel pa dang spyi don*）

7. 大译师达摩师利（lo chen Dharmaśrī）造，《由总义抉择吉祥秘密藏真实决定续王之善说·秘密主言教》（*dpal gsang bavi snying po de kho na nyid nges pavi rgyud kyi rgyal po sgyu vphrul drwa ba spyi don gyi sgo nas gtan la vbabs par byed pavi legs bshad gsang bdag zhal lung*）

8. 大译师达摩师利造，《秘密主密意庄严》（*gsang bdag dongs rgyan*）

9. 班玛久美嘉措（padma vgyur med rgya mtsho）造，《总义·见即证义》（*spyi don mthong bas don rtogs*）

10. 噶陀久美泽旺确珠（kaḥ thog vgyur med tshe dbang mchog grub）造，《内密咒之道次第广释·第二佛陀之密意庄严》（*gsang sngags nang gi lam rim rgya cher vgrel pa sangs rgyas gnyis pavi dgongs rgyan*）

11. 三世多竹千·吉美丹贝尼玛（rdo grub III vjigs med bstan pavi nyi ma）造，《吉祥秘密藏续总义略释·宝藏钥匙》（*dpal gsang bavi snying povi rgyud kyi spyi don nyung nguvi ngag gis rnam par vbyed pa rin chen mdzod kyi lde mig*）

12. 久美潘德沃色（vgyur med phan bdevi vod zer）造，《开启百门甚深义之钥匙》（*zab don sgo brgya vbyed pavi ldevu mig*）

属第二类不共甚深传规之释论有：

1. 日光狮子（Sūryaprabhasiṃha）造，《吉祥秘密藏广释》（*dpal gsang bavi snying po rgya cher vgrel pa*）

2. 莲花生（Padmasambhava）造，《口诀见鬘》（*man ngag lta phreng*）

3. 莲花生造，《广疏》（*rnam bshad chen mo*）

4. 绒宋班智达（rong zom paṇḍita chos kyi bzang po）造，《续王秘密藏宝疏》（*rgyud rgyal gsang bavi snying povi vgrel pa dkon mchog vgrel*）

5. 龙青巴（klong chen pa）造，《除暗三部》（*mun sel skor gsum*）

6. 米庞南杰（vju mi pham rnam rgyal）造，《光明藏》（*spyi don vod gsal snying*

po）

7. 仙藩曲吉囊瓦（gzhan phan chos kyi snang ba）造，《幻化网续笺注 · 日月藏》（*sgyu vphrul drwa bavi rgyud kyi mchan vgrel nyi zlavi snying po*）

不管是将《秘密藏续》依主流解释为摩诃瑜伽之教法，还是依阿底瑜伽对其加以诠释，在宁玛派传统中，《秘密藏续》均被视为其最根本之大续。

十八、有关《秘密藏续》的翻译与研究

随着国际藏学研究的迅猛发展，对于藏传佛教宁玛派的历史与教法的研究层出不穷，作为宁玛派教法的根本性文本，《秘密藏续》及其相关的释论、传承史录等自然备受学术界的关注与重视。以下分别就围绕《秘密藏续》所展开的翻译与研究作一简要的回顾与评述。

《秘密藏续》根本续的藏译本本身就有广、中、略三个版本，广本共八十二品，中本共四十六品，略本共二十二品，而迄今为止所有的英译与汉译本都是依据无垢友、聂 · 阇那古摩罗、玛 · 仁钦乔合译之略本而译。最早的英译当见于 Hubert Guenther 于 1984 年出版的 *Matrix of Mystery: Scientific and Humanistic Aspectcs of rDzogs-chen Thought*（Boulder & London: Shambhala），此书严格说来只是《秘密藏续》的节译本，作者的写作意图在于借助《秘密藏续》的文本阐发其中蕴含的大圆满法义，[68] 其针对的受众却非一般读者，因为书中大量借助了传统西方哲学以及现代物理学乃至人工智能等专业性极强的理论工具，并以作者独有的一套创造性的英文翻译体系来表达相关的藏文名相，故而对于书中所涉专业领域及 Guenther 本人的理论与写作风格不熟悉的读者而言，此书确显晦涩，阅读实非易事。尽管如此，全书仍然体现了作者对《秘密藏续》相当深刻而独到的见解，它将这一古老的东方宗教文本置于西方哲学与自然科学的语境中加以释读，为我们展示了迥异于藏土注疏传统的另一种阐释窗口。

此后，《秘密藏续》的完整英译首见于 Gyurme Dorje 至今仍未正式发表的博士论文 *The Guhyagarbhatantra and its XIVth Century Tibetan Commentary phyogs-bcu mun-sel*（Uniersity of London, 1987），作者在导论中详细介绍了《秘密藏续》在印度与西藏的

68 有学者指出，《秘密藏续》从根本上而言仍属于摩诃瑜伽部，然而 Guenther 并未对该续在摩诃瑜伽层面的法义作出应有的解读。参 A. W. Hanson-Barber, "Review of *Matrix and Mystery: Scientific and Humanistic Aspectcs of rDzogs-chen Thought,*" in *The Journal of the International Association of Buddhist Studies*, 1985, Volume 8, No. 2, pp. 138-140.

弘传史，继而整理了该续的精校本，最后作者对根本续及龙青巴的释论《十方除暗》作了完整翻译，然而作者对于《秘密藏续》的法义及其于修习上的重要，并未作出深入探讨。

2011 年，《秘密藏续》的第二个完整英译本由毗卢遮那光明翻译组（The Light of Berotsana Translation Group）的 Lama Chönam 和 Sangye Khandro 合作完成，二人将根本续的翻译及其所译龙青巴之《十方除暗》合并出版，书名为 *The Guhyagarha Tantra: Secret Essence Definitive Nature Just as It is with Commentary by Longchen Rabjam*（Ithaca: Snow Lion Publications），书中为重要的名相提供了较为详细的注释。二位译者在翻译过程中得到了印度南卓林寺（rnam grol gling）的总堪布、当代宁玛派内以教授《秘密藏续》闻名的南卓次仁（rnam grol tshe ring, 1953- ）的亲力指导，二人致力于与《秘密藏续》相关的文本的整理与翻译，已有数部译著出版（余者详见下文）。

《秘密藏续》最为晚近的英译当属德雄仁波切（sde gzhung rin po che, 1906-1987）的弟子 Christopher Wilkinson 的译本，Wilkinson 将《秘密藏续》与阿底瑜伽心部的续典《乐无央》（*bde ba rab vbyams*）的翻译合为一书，于 2015 年出版，题名为 *The Tantra of Great Bliss: The Guhyagarbha Transmission of Vajrasattva's Magnificent Sky*（North Charleston: Create Space Independent Publishing Platform），译者认为这两部续分别代表了摩诃瑜伽的阿底瑜伽、阿底瑜伽的摩诃瑜伽，在法义上可彼此融通、交相辉映，故而译之以供读者合参，与此同时，作者基于此二续讨论了早期大手印与大圆满之间的关系。

《秘密藏续》根本续的汉译本仅有一种，乃沈卫荣依据敦珠仁波切所编《宁玛教传广集》中所收的版本而译，于 2001 年由香港密乘佛学会出版，本文之初版即以导论形式附于书中，该书还收录了莲花生所造《口诀见鬘》的汉译以助读者理解本续，[69] 此论乃由沈卫荣依据 Samten G. Karmay 于其名著 *The Great Perfection: A Philosophical and Meditative Teaching in Tibetan Buddhism*（Leiden: E. J. Brill, 1988）中提供的转写校勘本而译。全书于 2010 年由台北全佛文化出版社再版发行。

就《秘密藏续》的释论而言，最早正式出版的英译本乃 Dharmachakra Translation Committee 所翻译的米庞尊者所造之《光明藏》，题名为 *Luminous Essence: A Guide to the Guhyagarbha Tantra*（Ithaca: Snow Lion Publications, 2009），该译本并未在必要的

69《口诀见鬘》从根本上源出《秘密藏续》，依绒宋班智达的观点，它是为《秘密藏续》第十三品《开示诸法无始以来于大圆满中任运成就相之口诀品》所作之补充。参 Karmay 上揭书，第 139 页。

地方提供相应的注释，也未对原文征引的文献的出处加以说明。

其后，于 2010 年，*Lama Chönam* 和 *Sangye Khandro* 连续出版了两部《秘密藏续》释论的英译，亦即不败尊者之《光明藏》以及第三世多竹千之《吉祥秘密藏续总义略释 · 宝藏钥匙》，分别题为 *Essence of Clear Light: An Overview of the Secret Commentary through Dispelling Darkness throughout the Ten Directions*（Ithaca: Snow Lion Publications）和 *Key to the Precious Treasury: A Concise Commentary on the General Meaning of the Glorious Secret Esence Tantra*（同前），二者皆为藏英双语对照版。迄今为止，实际上仅有龙青巴、米庞尊者、第三世多竹千三人所造《秘密藏续》释论有完整英译，而绒宋班智达的《宝疏》目前仅有一篇幅不长的节译。[70] 至于《秘密藏续》释论之汉译，目前仅有一种，乃沈卫荣所译米庞尊者之《光明藏》，题名为《幻化网秘密藏续释 · 光明藏》，书中对重要名相均加以注释，同时对所有引文都作了考订，谈锡永先生对译文作了逐段疏解，以显明不败尊者之甚深密意，该书 2001 年由香港密乘佛学会出版，2010 年由台北全佛文化出版社再版发行。

与《秘密藏续》相关的研究最早可见于 Kenneth Eastman 于 1983 年在 *Bulletin of the Institute of Cultural Studies* 第 22 期上发表的文章 "Mahāyoga Texts at Tun-huang"（Ryukoku University, pp. 42-60），[71] 作者注意到了敦煌所出的摩诃瑜伽文本中，一些成就法（sādhana）征引了《秘密藏续》的内容，例如 IOL Tib J 540 即罗列了《秘密藏续》所说四十二寂静尊之密咒与名号，Pelliot tibétain 849 则提到了该续的标题，这些细节或可视为《秘密藏续》在 10 世纪末以前于藏土弘传的见证。此后，Dan Martin 于 1987 年发表了题名为 "Illusion Web: Locating the Guhyagarbha Tantra in Buddhist Intellectual History"（in Christopher I. Beckwith (ed.), *Silver on Lapis: Tibetan Literary Culture and History*, Bloomington: The Tibet Society, pp. 175-220），该文以整个印度佛教传统为依托，结合小乘《巴利三藏 · 长部》所收之《梵网经》以及大乘《华严经》等，梳理了"网""法界""越量宫"等名相的演变历程，从而追溯了"幻化网"这

70 见 Orna Almogi, *Rong-zom-pa's Discourses on Buddhology: A Study of Various Conceptions of Buddhahood in Indian Sources with Special Reference to the Controversy Surrounding the Existence of Gnosis (jñāna: ye shes) as Presented by the Eleventh-Century Tibetan Scholar Rong-zom Chos-kyi-bzang-po*, Tokyo: The International Institute for Buddhist Studies, 2009, pp. 277-297.

71 最早注意到《秘密藏续》的欧洲学者当属 Alexander Csoma de Kőrös（参下文所提 Dan Martin 文，第 200 页，注 11），在 20 世纪 80 年代以前，几乎没有单独对《秘密藏续》所作的研究，仅有散见的零星论述，例见 David S. Ruegg, *The Life of Bu-ston Rin-po-che*, Roma: Istituto Italiano per il Medio ed Estremo Oriente, 1996, p. 68; Samten G. Karmay, "A Discussion of the Doctrinal Position of Rdzogs-chen from the 10th to the 13th Centuries," in *Journal Asiatique*, 1975, p. 148.

一理念的历史渊源，并考量了《秘密藏续》在佛教思想史的地位。2002 年，汉堡大学教授 Dorji Wangchuk 发表了题为 "An Eleventh-Century Defence of the Authenticity of the Guhyagarbha Tantra"（in Helmut Eimer & David Germano (eds.), *The Many Canons of Tibetan Buddhism*, Leiden: Brill, pp. 265-291）的文章，[72] 作者首先介绍了《秘密藏续》在宁玛派传统中的地位及其于新译密咒初期在真实性问题上遭受的批评，继而以 11 世纪绒宋法贤的《秘密藏续宝疏》为考察依据，着重分析了绒宋巴在当时梵本尚未找到的情况下，如何以教证与理证对批评者所指出的种种过失逐一回应。此后，Nathaniel De Witt Garson 于 2004 年发表了博士论文 *Penetrating the Secret Essence Tantra: Context and Philosophy in the Mahāyoga Systemof rNying-ma Tantra*（PhD Thesis, Department of Religious Studies, University of Virginia），这是继 Gyurme Dorje 博士论文之后又一部较为全面的关于《秘密藏续》的研究，本文在结构安排上与后者近似，然而不同的是，本文选择了以宿氏为代表的教传佛语（bkav ma）传统的诠释为研究对象，重点考察了《秘密藏续》的教传传承史，并依据达摩师利译师的《秘密主言教》分析了摩诃瑜伽在宁玛派九乘次第中扮演的角色，最后通过翻译第三世多竹千所造《宝藏钥匙》的前半部分，比较了宿氏教传传规与绒宋巴、龙青巴一系传规在《秘密藏续》的诠释上的不同，并尝试性地探讨了该续在印度的源流，本文相对于 Gyurme Dorje 论文而言，对法义上的挖掘更为深入。在此之后的很长一段时期内，学界未见有关《秘密藏续》的集中研究，仅有零星的短篇讨论见于部分学术博客，其中比较有代表性的是 2007 年 Sam van Schaik 于 Early Tibet 博客上发布的博文 "In Search of the Guhyagarbha Tantra"（2007 年 8 月 27 日），[73] 其中基于 Eastman 此前关于敦煌摩诃瑜伽文本的研究和作者本人近年来对敦煌文本的分析，发现这些文本对同属摩诃瑜伽部的《密集续》的征引，从频率和内容的完整性上都超过《秘密藏续》，由此指出 11 世纪以前《密集续》在藏土的影响可能胜于《秘密藏续》。针对此文，Robert Mayer 的补充回复也提供了重要的信息，亦即萨迦派之所以在历史上对《秘密藏续》的真实性鲜有批评，其原因除了传统上认为的迦湿弥罗班智达释迦师利跋陀罗（Śākyaśrībhadra，萨迦班智达的上师之一）在桑耶寺发现了《秘密藏续》梵本外，

72 该文汉译见李梦妍译：《11 世纪关于〈秘密藏续〉真实性的一个辩护》，收沈卫荣主编《大喜乐与大圆满：庆祝谈锡永先生八十华诞汉藏佛学研究论集》，北京：中国藏学出版社，2014 年，第 580-599 页。

73 https://earlytibet.com/2007/08/27/in-search-of-the-guhyagarbha-tantra/ 此外，有关以《秘密藏续》为根本的摩诃瑜伽部誓句（samaya）的研究，见 Sam van Schaik, "The Limits of Transgression: The Samaya Vows of Mahāyoga," in Matthew T. Kapstein and Sam van Schaik (eds.), *Esoteric Buddhism at Dunhuang: Rites and Teachings for This Life and Beyond*, Leiden: Brill, 2010, pp. 61-83.

甚至可以追溯至萨迦三祖扎巴坚赞（grags pa rgyal mtshan, 1147-1216）在其所编《续部目录》中收录了《秘密藏续》，而后来的八思巴（vphags pa blo gros rgyal mtshan, 1235-1280）在为续部编目时也同样收录了《秘密藏续》。最为晚近的有关《秘密藏续》的研究应属 2014 年汉堡大学 Orna Almogi 发表的文章“The Eighteen Mahāyoga Tantric Cycles: A Real Canon or the Mere Notion of One?”（*Revue d'Etudes Tibétaines*, no. 30, pp. 47-110），文中集中讨论了以《秘密藏续》为根本的摩诃瑜伽十八主续，通过比较藏文文献中有关这十八主续名目列表的不同版本，作者认为“十八大续”（tantra chen po bco brgyad）这一概念起源甚早，然而具体的续典名目则为后世的填充，这些续典标题绝大部分可见于敦煌文献，其流通年代早至 10 世纪，不少续典甚至早至 9 世纪。

十九、结语

《秘密藏续》作为宁玛派的根本大续，其弘传史实际上就是旧译密咒在西藏传播的核心主干，由其辐射出的文本、人物、教法几乎涵盖了宁玛派传统的方方面面。通过上文的讨论，笔者初步厘清了《秘密藏续》的续名、文本源流、内容架构及基本法义，呈现了该续典及附属文献之间的相互关系，并梳理出该续及其代表的摩诃瑜伽教法在印度与西藏的传承脉络，从而明确了该续在藏传佛教史上的地位，也为读者大致勾勒出了旧译密咒教法在西藏传播的宏观图景。最后，笔者简要介绍了国际学界有关《秘密藏续》的翻译与研究概况，通过比较不难发现，国内迄今为止对该续典相关的历史与教法研究、文本的整理翻译均明显匮乏，这无疑阻碍了我们深入了解宁玛派密教传统、澄清对“交合”“诛杀”等密教修习的误解，此外，鉴于敦煌密教文献中与摩诃瑜伽部仪轨、义理相关者占有相当大的比重，如果不能对作为摩诃瑜伽之根本所依的《秘密藏续》作出全面而深入的研究，我们实难对这些敦煌文献作出正确的释读。在此，笔者谨以本文作抛砖引玉之用，期望能有更多的学界同仁致力于该续释论的翻译、相关文献的整理，以及对其甚深法义的挖掘与比较研究工作。

装藏用五部大陀罗尼的组合过程

——以西藏西部擦擦铭文为基础的考察 *

廖 旸

关于装藏、尤其是藏传佛教塔像装藏仪轨的文本，以清蒙古族学者工布查布（mgon po skyabs, 1690-1750?）节取二世章嘉阿旺洛桑却丹（lcang skya ngag dbang blo bzang chos ldan, 1642-1716）语录并译述的《造像量度经续补·装藏略安像总持附》[1]最为权威、广为人知，不再赘引。其中指出，装藏用法舍利为第一，身舍利次之；[2]法舍利之中，则以五部大陀罗尼（藏 gzungs chen sde lnga）为上首，即：佛顶尊胜（梵 uṣṇīṣavijaya, 藏 gtsug tor rnam rgyal）、佛顶无垢（梵 vimaloṣṇīṣa 或 uṣṇīṣavimala, 藏 gtsug tor dri med, 原文作“佛顶放无垢光明”）、宝箧印（梵 guhyadhātu, 藏 gsang bavi ring bsrel za ma tog“正法秘密箧印”）、菩提场庄严陀罗尼（梵 bodhimaṇḍālaṃkāra, 藏 byang chub snying po rgyan vbum）以及缘起偈（梵 pratīyasamutpādagāthā, 藏 rten vbrel snying po. 又名十二因缘咒、因缘法颂、法身舍利偈、法舍利真言等等）。以最为常见的缘起偈为例，它们出现的形式与位置是多种多样的：既可能以泥“印”（梵 mudrā,

---

* 廖旸：中国社会科学院民族学与人类学研究所研究员。

本文得到中国社会科学院基础研究学者资助，为国家社科基金重大项目“文物遗存、图像、文本与西藏艺术史构建”（15ZDB120）子课题“从噶当塔到吉祥多门塔——11 至 14 世纪西藏佛塔研究”的阶段性研究成果。深切感念古格·次仁加布老师的学术建树与热忱，谨以小文献给这位阿里赤子。

1 《大正藏》卷 21，第 951 页。

2 原文措辞分别为“法身舍利”与“生身舍利”。西藏存在将舍利划分为五种的分类体系，其中“法舍利”（chos kyi ring bsrel）为经咒，“法身舍利”（chos kyi skuvi ring bsrel）则是塔与塔形擦擦。本文遵循这种分类体系使用相关术语；引文则保留原措辞，请读者体察。详细讨论可参见 Yael Bentor, “Tibetan Relic Classification,” in P. Kvaerne (ed.): *Tibetan Studies: Proceedings of the 6th Seminar of the International Association for Tibetan Studies, Fagernes, 1992* vol. 1, Oslo: The Institute for Comparative Research in Human Culture, 1994, pp. 16-30. 另可参见 Idem, “ The Content of Stūpas and Images and the Indo-Tibetan Concept of Relics,” *The Tibet Journal* vol. XXVIII, no. 1 & 2 (2003), pp. 24-26; Dan Martin, “Pearls from Bones: Relics, Chortens, Tertons and the Signs of Saintly Death in Tibet,” *Numen* vol. 41, fasc. 3 (Sept. 1994), pp. 297-305.

藏 phyag rgya，图 1-2）[3] 或者纸卷的形式装入塔像内部；也可能以铭刻（图 3）、捺印（图 4）、浮雕（图 5）、书写等形式出现在表面。

擦擦曾广泛流行于佛教世界。从宗教学角度观察，它既可以作为神像的载体，也可以充当真言的载体。装藏或铭刻以为加持的真言被视同“法舍利”（dharmadhātu），内装这种真言的塔形擦擦（香泥小窣堵波）则称“法舍利窣堵波”。[4] 在西藏，它发展成为重要的艺术门类，从目前的标本采集与图像发表情况看，西藏西部的擦擦相对谱系完整、资料丰富。[5] 装藏虽然是营造塔像必不可少的步骤，学者们对古代若干重要的装藏实例的文本记载也已开始展开研究，[6] 但目前尚缺乏科学严谨的考古记录、尤其是层位学记录以资对照。鉴于此，作为装藏本身的擦擦的表面铭文，以及擦擦内的装藏就成为目前阶段应予充分利用的材料。本文将主要以西藏西部擦擦铭文为主线，尝试探察装藏中陀罗尼的组合过程。

一、从考古发现看各种陀罗尼的出现

可以想见，五大陀罗尼次第形成并译传，逐渐形成一组文本，最终在装藏中具有独特地位。在早期阶段，于五部大陀罗尼中独崇一种是最常见的现象。下文将会讨论，缘起偈可能是其中最早用于装藏者，其资料浩繁，兹不赘举。[7]

---

3 内置的具铭文小泥块。擦擦收藏与研究者范久辉赐教，从宗教学意义上讲应称作“母擦擦”。参见 Kunsang Namgyal Lama, “Tsha Tsha Inscriptions: A Preliminary Survey,” in *Tibetan Inscriptions: Proceedings of a Panel Held at the Twelfth Seminar of the International Association for Tibetan Studies, Vancouver 2010*, Brill, 2013, p. 19, fn. 70. 莱比锡大学博士研究生侯浩然惠赐材料，谨申谢忱。

4 （唐）释玄奘、释辩机原著，季羡林等校注：《大唐西域记校注》卷第九“摩伽陀国下”，北京：中华书局，1985 年，第 712 页。

5 资料刊布较为集中的有张建林主编：《中国美术分类全集·藏传佛教雕塑全集 4·擦擦》，北京美术摄影出版社，2002 年；熊文彬、李逸之主编：《西藏古格擦擦艺术》，北京：中国藏学出版社，2016 年。
本文利用的擦擦主要为李逸之藏品，感谢藏家惠示图片并慨允发表。

6 可参见安海燕：《元大都大圣寿万安寺白塔之装藏、装饰——释注〈圣旨特建释迦舍利灵通之塔碑文〉相关段落》，载沈卫荣主编《西域历史语言研究集刊》第六辑，北京：科学出版社，2013 年，第 17-52 页；魏文：《五世达赖喇嘛灵塔装藏仪轨系列研究之一：法身舍利装藏目录的初步整理与研究》（初稿）。除以上两个案而外，Losang Paldhen Gyalzur 和 Antony H. N. Verwey 利用二世章嘉造《向所依奉献真言之法·水晶镜及加持奉献与装藏真言》（rten la gzungs gzhug vbul tshul shel dkar me long sogs gzungs vbul skor dang gzungs gzhug rab gnas bcas）展开研究并对照 1968 年的一次佛像装藏与开光，见 “Spells on the life-wood: An Introduction to the Tibetan Buddhist Ceremony of Consecration,” in Dirk Jan Hoens and Rita Kloppenborg (eds.), *Selected Studies on Ritual in the Indian Religions: Essays to D. J. Hoens*, Leiden: E. J. Brill, 1983, pp. 169-196.

7 相关重要发现见 Maurizio Taddei, “Inscribed Clay Tablets and Miniature Stûpas from Ĝasnî,” *East and West* vol. 20 (1970), pp. 70-86; Daniel Boucher, “The Pratītyasamutpādagāthā and Its Role in the Medieval Cult of the Relics,” *The Journal of the International Association of Buddhist Studies* vol. 14, no. 1 (1991), pp. 1-27.

图 1　塔形擦擦（内置梵文真言母印）。青海乌兰县大南湾吐蕃遗址出土。8-9 世纪。李逸之藏。

图 2　塔形擦擦（内置梵文真言母印）。赤陶。东印度比哈尔邦那烂陀（Nālandā, Bihar）遗址出土，11-12 世纪。大英博物馆藏，Mrs. A. Churchill 捐赠，OA 1932, 11-2.1. 廖旸摄。

阿富汗昆都士（Qunduz）发现过铭刻有 5-6 世纪婆罗谜字（Brāhmī）的印章，印文为菩提场庄严陀罗尼的根本咒、心咒与心中心咒；与该陀罗尼相关的其他遗物可见于 7/8 世纪的克什米尔（例见图 6）、8-10 世纪的舍卫城（Śrāvastī），那烂陀等其他著名佛教圣地[8]，以及中印度恰蒂斯加尔邦锡尔布尔（Sirpur, Chattisgarh）遗址的考古

8　对相关考古发现的综合介绍以及对梵藏文本的对勘详见 Gregory Schopen, "The *Bodhigarbhālaṅkāralakṣa* and *Vimaloṣṇīṣa Dhāraṇīs* in Indian Inscriptions: Two Sources for the Practice of Buddhism in Medieval India, "in idem: *Figments and Fragments of Mahāyāna Buddhism in India: More Collected Papers*, Honolulu: University of Hawaii Press, 2005, pp. 314-332, 338-340 "Addenda".

图 3　三十三天降下（局部。伞盖上从左至右刻梵文缘起偈）。玄武岩，全大 78×43.6×18.5 厘米。比哈尔邦库基哈尔（Kurkihar），约 10 世纪。加尔各答印度博物馆（Indian Museum, Kolkata）藏。廖旸摄。

图 4　观音菩萨像（主尊右肩侧上方捺印梵文）。赤陶，30.4×20.4×10.8 厘米。比哈尔邦佛陀迦耶（Bodhgayā），波罗时期，约 10 世纪。加尔各答印度博物馆藏。廖旸摄。

图 5　金刚法菩萨像擦擦（边缘右绕藏文转写梵文的缘起偈）。泥，高 6 厘米。采集于西藏阿里地区札达县托林寺遗址，11-12 世纪。李逸之藏。《西藏古格擦擦艺术》，图版 81。

图 6　菩提场庄严陀罗尼（根本、心、心中心陀罗尼）与缘起偈原始夏拉达体（proto Śāradā）梵文印章（印文作水平翻转处理）。滑石，3×6.3×4.9 厘米。克什米尔，7-8 世纪。大英博物馆藏，1880.168. © The Trustees of the British Museum.

发现中。[9] 东印度奥迪萨邦（Odisha，旧名奥里萨 Orissa）勒德纳吉里（Ratnagiri“宝山”）的情形尤其引人瞩目，因为有四块该陀罗尼的模制陶像发现在第 55 号奉献塔（votive stūpa）内。[10]

尊胜陀罗尼经先后数译，在内地它以幢为载体的形式流行不衰，学界多有关注。[11] 佛顶无垢陀罗尼早期的例子在勒德纳吉里这个繁荣于 6 世纪上半叶至 12 世纪的佛教遗址也有发现。元至正五年（1345）北京居庸关云台过街塔券洞内两侧壁梵、藏、八思巴、西夏、回鹘、汉六体文字石刻分别以尊胜陀罗尼与佛顶无垢陀罗尼为主题，[12] 可见这两种陀罗尼的重要地位。此外，我们还关心另一种名称字面与佛顶无垢陀罗尼容易混淆的咒——无垢净光陀罗尼（另见下文）。唐武周长安元年（701），睹货逻国僧弥陀山（Mitraśānti“寂友”）共法藏译《无垢净光大陀罗尼经》[13]，并很快传入日本。奈良时代女帝称德天皇（764-770 年在位）为纪念平定惠美押勝（一名藤原仲麻吕，706-764）之乱、祈愿护国灭罪，从天平宝字八年（764）起造三重小木塔

9　那須真裕美：「縁起法頌から見る中インド・シルプル遺跡——テラコッタ製銘文を手がかりに」，『印度學佛教學研究』第 57 卷第 1 号（2008 年），第 405-399 页。

10　Debala Mitra, *Ratnagiri* (1958-61) vol. I, New Delhi: Archaeological Survey of India, Memoirs of the Archaeological Survey of India No. 80, 1981, pp. 30-31, 43.

11　刘淑芬：《灭罪与度亡——佛顶尊胜陀罗尼经幢之研究》，上海：上海古籍出版社，2008 年。

12　村田治郎編著：『居庸関』第一卷，[京都]：京都大學工學部，1957 年，第 123-223 页。

13　《大正藏》卷 19，第 1024 号经。此系第二出，于阗实叉难陀初译本名“离垢净光陀罗尼”，早阙。见《开元释教录》卷第九“总括群经录上之九大唐传译之余”，《大正藏》卷 55，第 566 页。此经亦迅速流入朝鲜半岛和日本。参见潘吉星：《〈无垢经〉：中、韩学术论争的焦点》，《印刷科学》2000 年第 4 期，第 33-41 页。

图 7a　百万塔。木雕。日本，约 764 年。大英博物馆藏。廖旸摄。

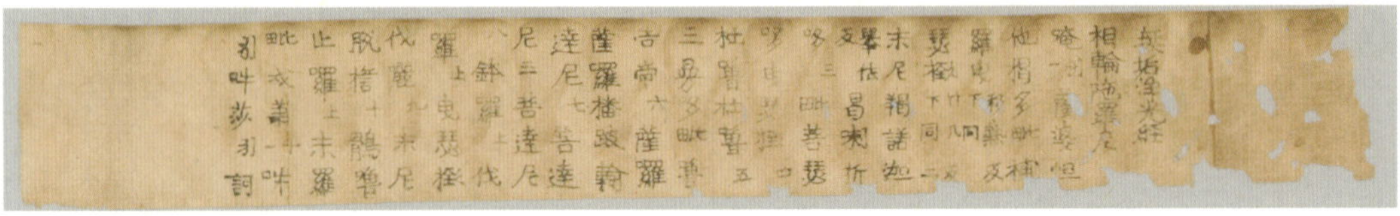

图 7b　百万塔内藏《无垢净光经·相轮陀罗尼》。约 764 年。法隆寺旧藏，愛知学院大学図書館情報センター藏。http://kicho.lib.agu.ac.jp/photo_l/agu_0799.html.

百万件，内藏《无垢净光大陀罗尼经》中所说的根本、相轮、自心印与六度共计四种陀罗尼，分奉于法隆寺等十大官寺（图 7）。[14] 百万塔也是大规模应用雕版印刷术的早期珍贵实物遗存，曾被视为存世最早的雕版印刷品，早已成为世界印刷史上的佳话。辽崇佛重塔，实物遗存相当丰富。如北京辽圣宗开泰二年（1013）净光舍利塔经幢刻无垢净光大陀罗尼与法舍利真言，辽宁朝阳东塔塔基内发现开泰六年该大陀罗尼经幢。特别地，内蒙古巴林右旗辽重熙十六至十八年（1047-1049）章圣皇太后特建庆州白塔天宫相轮樘五室内按照《无垢净光大陀罗尼经》所云安置陀罗尼，碑文记载和考古记录吻合，是目前探讨作为法舍利的陀罗尼用于装藏的珍贵实例。[15]

除了百万塔，宝箧印经制作数量巨大，传世品亦为数不少。从后周显德三年

14　称德天皇即女帝孝谦天皇（749-758 年在位）重登宝祚后的称号。『続日本紀』宝亀元年四月二十六日（770 年 5 月 25 日）条记载，将造完的百万塔分置官寺，其中元興寺、東大寺和西大寺还专设小塔院进行供奉。

关于百万塔及其所纳经咒的讨论参见中根勝：『百万塔陀羅尼の研究』，東京：八木書店，1987 年；蓮池利隆：「観貨邏僧弥陀山と百万塔」，『仏教学研究』64 号（2008 年 3 月），第 1-20 页；湯浅吉美：「百万塔の思想的背景—南都仏教史における位置付けを考える—」，『埼玉学園大学紀要』（人間学部篇）第 5 号，第 219-232 页。

15　参见德新、张汉君、韩仁信：《内蒙古巴林右旗庆州白塔发现辽代佛教文物》，《文物》1994 年第 12 期，第 4-33 页；邱瑞中：《辽庆州白塔佛教文物安置规矩与建塔缘起考》，《内蒙古社会科学》1996 年第 4 期，第 35-40 页。

（956）起，吴越国王钱弘俶（948-978 年在位）曾先后三次印宝箧印经八万四千卷，供养于宝塔内，亦愿心闳阔之举。[16]

二、缘起偈——最早用于塔装藏的真言

据唐三藏玄奘法师（602-664）西行印度的见闻，香泥小塔（即塔形擦擦）内藏[17]经文。经文内容未见详述，而有的仪轨则明确指出，应内置缘起偈：

又欲求成就殊胜果者，于神通日月白分[18]，就趣海河侧印沙、印泥为塔，[19]中置缘起偈（即法身舍利偈）。置像于塔前念诵，行者以水和麨[20]食之。取遏迦（梵 arka）木搵酥投火，护摩十万遍已，地动转，身飞腾，为忉利天主。[21]

若欲除业障，应当印佛塔。
或沙及香泥，皆安缘起偈。
积数如经说，终毕现奇特。[22]

从以上拈出的两种引文看，至少在其译者不空（Amoghavajra，705-774）的时代，塔擦中仅安缘起偈仍是流行的做法，尽管他本人就曾译出五部大陀罗尼及其仪轨中的佛顶尊胜、宝箧印和菩提场庄严三种（T. 972, 1022, 1008）。

唐德宗贞元二十年（804）译出的《造塔延命功德经》专门讲述如何制作塔形擦擦，详解从加持妙华供养如来直至安伞盖等十二个步骤，其中：[23]

第五，次以泥团入模时，用陀罗尼加持一遍，然后入模。陀罗尼曰：

唵 嚩日罗（二合、引）驮都蘖陛 娑嚩（二合、引）贺（引）（oṃ vajradhātugarbhe svāhā）。

第六，次入法身真言时，用此陀罗尼加持一遍，然后入印子中。陀罗尼曰：

唵 达摩驮都蘖陛 娑嚩贺（引）（oṃ dharmmadhātugarbhe svāhā）。

---

16 钱弘俶印经等中国佛教相关文物遗存具见黎毓馨主编：《远离尘垢——唐宋时期的〈宝箧印经〉》，北京：中国书店，2014 年。

17《大唐西域记校注》卷第九“摩伽陀国下”，第 712 页。

18 “日”字衍。此指正月、五月、九月的一日至十五日，一年之中最善。

19 关于这种修行传统、尤其是其在敦煌的实践，见谭蝉雪：《印沙·脱佛·脱塔》，《敦煌研究》1989 年第 1 期，第 19-29 页。

20 麨（chǎo），炒的米粉或面粉。

21（唐）不空译：《圣迦柅忿怒金刚童子菩萨成就仪轨经》卷上，《大正藏》卷 21，第 122 页。

22（唐）不空译：《阿閦如来念诵供养法》，《大正藏》卷 19，第 20 页。

23 罽宾国三藏沙门般若译场译（牟尼室利说梵语，释圆照笔受，释鉴虚润文），《大正藏》卷 19，第 727 页。

图 8　塔像擦擦。泥，高 8.5 厘米。采集于札达县麦龙沟遗址，11—12 世纪。李逸之藏。《西藏古格擦擦艺术》，图版 236。

图 9　塔擦。泥，高 5.5 厘米。采集于托林寺遗址，11—12 世纪。李逸之藏。《西藏古格擦擦艺术》，图版 240。

第六步在泥团入模后、椎打压紧之前需要加入法身真言，至于这个法身真言的媒介形式以及具体内容没有清楚揭示，但从相应真言提到 dharmmadhātu“法舍利”、以加持内藏此法舍利的泥团来看，推论为缘起偈是合理的。[24] 在分十步介绍如何模制擦擦的梵藏文仪轨中，这句真言也被提及，它用在印模（mudrākṣepaṇa）这一阶段，正与上引文中第五、第六步相当。[25] 在藏西塔擦中可以看到铭刻有缘起偈以及加持它的陀罗尼的例子（图 8-9），为我们思考擦擦铭文与擦擦制作过程的关系提供了生动的材料。[26]

直至印度大师无畏藏护（Abhayākaragupta，1064-1125）撰《金刚鬘》（*Vajrāvalī*）之时，根据其中《尊像开光仪轨》（*Pratimādipratiṣṭhāvidhi*）一文所述，加持塔像的真言已增加，包括神祇真言[27]、缘起偈，以及在置入陀罗尼和封藏时分别要用到的两

24　此外，还有以“阿鍐览唅欠”（a vaṃ raṃ haṃ khaṃ）五字为法身真言者（唐·善无畏译：《三种悉地破地狱转业障出三界秘密陀罗尼法》，《大正藏》卷 18，第 910 页），此为大日如来自体，特指大日法身之真言，与本文讨论的“法身真言”不同。

25　包括梵文《初业者灯》（*Ādikarmikapradīpa*）、《除灭恶见》（*Kudṛṣṭinirghātana*）及其藏文译本《摹制擦擦仪轨》（*tsha tsha gdab pavi cho ga*），见〔意〕图齐：《梵天佛地》第一卷“西北印度和西藏西部的塔和擦擦——试论藏族宗教艺术及其意义”，魏正中、萨尔吉主编，上海古籍出版社 / 罗马：意大利亚非研究院，2009 年，第 35-37 页。

26　详见拙文《西藏西部擦擦铭文探索》，载熊文彬、李逸之主编：《西藏古格擦擦艺术》，第 23-25 页。

27　引文中用释迦牟尼真言，这是因为功德主发心崇礼的是“如来舍利”，这在制作其他尊神造像时应可引申。

种真言，但仍未明确提及五部大陀罗尼中的其他四种：[28]

若欲加意崇敬如来舍利，应在造作时将像头或像背、支提的中央留空。完成时应在桦树皮（梵 bhūrja, 藏 gro ga）上用藏红花（梵 kuṃkuma, 藏 gur gum）或牛黄（梵 gorocanā, 藏 gi wang）书写：namo bhagavate śākyamunaye tathāgatāya arhate samyaksaṃbuddhāya oṃ munc mune mahāmuneye svāhā; ye dharmā hetuprabhavā hetun teṣān tathāgato hy avadat teṣāñ ca yo nirodha evaṃ vādī mahāśramaṇaḥ; 以及特定的陀罗尼。将灌沐净化后的舍利用它们缠裹起来。念诵 oṃ mantradhātugarbhāya svāhā, 将它们置于空腔内。然后念诵 oṃ vajra-dhātugarbhāya svāhā [29] 并用金刚泥将空腔的口子封上。应如是开光。

札达县托林镇白东波石窟（pad mavi sdong po phug pa，一称夏温乃 zhag dben gnas）内周壁所绘贤劫千佛是西藏西部最早的佛教艺术遗存之一。[30] 千佛图以佛像匹

图 10　贤劫千佛图局部（右图为左图右下角局部。第一行大部为 de bzhin gshegs pa ye shes mthu brtsal ｜“智慧力如来”字样，后三字连下为缘起偈）[31]。壁画。白东波石窟左侧壁，约 11 世纪。廖旸摄。

28 yadā tu tathāgatadhātoḥ satkāraviśeṣo 'bhimatas tadā ghaṭanakāla eva pratimāyāḥ śirasi pīṭhe vā caityasya garbhe kuharaṃ kārayet niṣpattau bhūrje kuṃkumagorocanābhyāṃ | *namo bhagavate śākyamunaye tathāgatāyārhate samyaksambuddhāya* | *oṃ mune mune mahāmunaye svāhā* | *ye dharmā hetuprabhavā hetuṃ teṣāṃ tathāgato hy avadat teṣāṃ ca yo nirodha evaṃ vādī mahāśramaṇaḥ* | iti dhāraṇīviśeṣaṃ ca likhitvā tena snāpitadhātuṃ veṣṭayitvā *oṃ mantradhātugarbhāya svāhā* | iti paṭhan kuhare prakṣipet | tadanu *oṃ vajradhātugarbhāya svāhā* | iti japan vajralepena kuharadvāraṃ lepayitvā pūrvavat tatpratiṣṭhāṃ kuryād iti | (Masahide Mori 森雅秀, *The Vajrāvalī of Abhayākaragupta: A Critical Study, Sanskrit Edition of Selected Chapters and Complete Tibetan Version*, Ph.D. diss., University of London, 1997, pp. 148-149)

相应藏文本见无畏藏护共 vkhor lo grags 译：*dkyil vkhor gyi cho ga rdo rje phreng ba zhes bya ba*, 德格版丹珠尔通帙第一七七，folio phu 64. 英译文见 Yael Bentor, “On the Indian Origins of the Tibetan Practice of Depositing Relics and Dhâraṇîs in Stûpas and Images,” *Journal of the American Oriental Society* vol. 115, no. 2 (1995), p. 255.

29《金刚鬘·尊像开光仪轨》着眼于大塔像开光仪式，与描述泥塔模制过程的《造塔延命功德经》自不相同，而此句真言字面与后者在入模时加持泥团的第五步真言类似。

30 详见熊文彬：《阿里白东波石窟、千佛石窟和译师殿千佛壁画调查记》，载本文集，第 383-402 页。

配名号的情形固然司空见惯，但此石窟壁画（图 10）题记在佛名之后再缀以缘起偈的做法则绝无仅有。虽与《尊像开光仪轨》所言在尊神真言后续书缘起偈的做法小有区别，但藏西当时奉行以缘起偈为尊像加持的做法则一望可知。

与西藏转写缘起偈的做法不同，汉传佛教中意译的做法更为普遍，在多种文献中反复引用，文字亦甚多译法，[32] 以唐译《浴佛功德经》和《造塔功德经》较通行。前者宣扬“或写法颂安置其中，如上珍奇而为供养，随己力能，至诚殷重，如我现身，等无有异”[33]；后者明确要求“如是偈义名佛法身，汝当书写置彼塔内”[34]。8 世纪初唐长安地区发现的擦擦造像、今称作“苏常侍造像”者，存三种表面有缘起偈文字。[35] 不过，内地也有据梵文音写缘起偈的做法，辽人将二者从文体上区分为“法舍利真言”与“法舍利颂”，见于道宗大安八年（1092）建辽宁兴城白塔峪塔地宫内东北立板石碑铭文：[36]

> ……法舍利真言：唵达囊摩吠覩钵啰婆嚩吠冻帝爽」怛他誐党唵鑁缚捺多瑟者育你噜驮唵鑁嚩你摩贺瑟啰嚩拏野娑嚩」贺。法舍利颂曰：诸法因缘生，缘射（谢）法还灭。吾师大沙门，常作如是说。」

此处真言与颂所据文本尚未比定。与音写（或直接用梵字写刻）相伴而来的是缘起偈的真言化，即按照真言的格式在偈文前加 oṃ、后加 -ye svāhā；[37] 而白塔峪塔地宫仅加后者，这种做法也见于因奉藏佛牙舍利而闻名的北京西山灵光寺辽咸雍七年（1071）招仙塔（西藏的例子见后文图 19b）。招仙塔一名画像千佛塔，1900 年毁，残存塔基上镶嵌的砖所铸缘起偈有两种，一同于白塔峪塔译文，一则取《造塔功德经》

---

31 占堆记录东嘎 2 窟南壁东段第 32 号千佛像题记为 byang chub sems dpav ye shes mthu tsal（四川大学中国藏学研究所、四川大学历史文化学院考古学系、西藏自治区文物事业管理局编著：《皮央·东嘎遗址考古报告》，成都：四川人民出版社，2008 年，第 298 页），两处末字拼写均与厘定后的正字 rtsal 不同，见 *vphags pa bskal pa bzang po zhes bya ba theg pa chen povi mdo*, 德格版甘珠尔通帙第四五，folio ka 210v2.

32 巴利文、梵文、藏译文的介绍见湯山明:「《十二因緣呪》覚え書き」,『印度學佛教學研究』20 卷 1 号（1971 年），第 448-444 页。专注于汉译文的篦梳见風間敏夫：「緣起法頌の一考察」,『印度學佛教學研究』34 卷 1 号“花園大学における第三十六回学術大会紀要（一）”（1985 年），第 177-186 页。

33 （唐）释义净译：《浴佛功德经》,《大正藏》卷 16，第 800 页。

34 唐高宗永隆元年（680）地婆诃罗译：《造塔功德经》,《大正藏》卷 16，第 801 页。特别针对此版译本的探讨见三友量順：「緣起法頌と『造塔功德経』」, 载平川彰博士古稀記念会『仏教思想の諸問題：平川彰博士古稀記念論集』, 東京：春秋社，1985 年，第 125-138 页。

35 李翎：《擦擦与善业泥续考——关于汉地擦擦图像类型的研究》,《故宫学刊》2013 年第 2 期，第 216-218 页。

36 陈术石、佟强：《兴城白塔峪塔地宫铭刻与辽代晚期佛教信仰》，载《辽金历史与考古》第四辑，2013 年，第 237 页。

37 参见拙文《西藏西部擦擦铭文探索》，第 26-30 页。汉传佛教中俱全的真言化可见于西夏天庆七年（1200）释智广、释慧真编集、金刚幢译定的《密咒圆因往生集》(《大正藏》卷 46，第 1012 页），或许体现出时代性的变化。

图 11 “法舍利塔”图案砖。辽。北京房山云居寺北塔内出土。魏文摄。

图 12 “追为头陀释智玄”造塔砖（拓片）。40.5×20.5 厘米。原砖出自云南祥云水目山塔林，后大理国神宗段智祥天开十六年（1220）。祥云县文化馆藏。《大理丛书·金石篇 8》，第 64 页图。

译本，而其汉白玉露盘底部[38]所刻梵字缘起偈则为后加 -ye svāhā 的真言化形式。朝阳北塔地宫宫室内置辽重熙十三年（1044）石经幢顶所刻方形单重檐塔身刻《浴佛功德经》本的“法舍利颂”[39]及梵字 oṃ。北京房山云居寺北塔（上部为元明重修补葺）附

38 拓片见栗加有：《招仙塔与郑氏》，载政协北京市石景山区委员会编：《石景山文史》第 9 辑，2001 年，第 176 页。

39 录文见辽宁省文物考古研究所、朝阳市北塔博物馆编：《朝阳北塔——考古发掘与维修工程报告》，北京：文物出版社，2007 年，第 85 页；拓片见同书图三六上图。

近有不少浮雕单层小塔图案的砖，所雕小塔在塔身部分刻《造塔功德经》译本缘起偈（图 11），塔刹两侧分布“法舍利塔”字样及梵字净法界真言 oṃ raṃ。意译的偈颂与梵字真言的共同出现也暗示出真言化的倾向。目前这些浮雕砖多镶嵌在北塔的塔基上，辽塔研究者认为过去应该大量藏在塔宫之中，情形类似的还有天津蓟县福山塔。[40] 从铭文可确知浮雕的小塔以“法舍利”亦即缘起偈为藏（garbha），由此小塔即法舍利塔，藏于北塔内充当法身舍利。若然，这些“法舍利塔”砖与铭刻缘起偈的塔擦作用相同，其与藏西早期擦擦的年代接近，亦足证塔内装藏法舍利的早期形态。另一个例证出现在云南祥云水目山塔林[41]，从拓片（图 12）看出砖横断为两截，中心刻一塔幢，顶部莲花宝珠，整体结构与云居寺北塔砖上“法舍利塔”类似，但缺乏相轮等细节，形制更倾向于幢。虽然目前墓碑尽毁，不过从砖下部铭文可知当出自皎渊智玄禅师（1149-1214）墓塔。[42] 此砖中塔幢身亦刻《造塔功德经》译本缘起偈，提供了僧人墓塔用法身舍利的例子。就两地的情形而言，从译文版本和塔所处环境来判断，可考虑《造塔功德经》对于这种做法的推动力，这与辽热衷起塔的风尚一致，并波及西南之大理。

三、佛顶无垢大、小陀罗尼——藏西擦擦铭文中另一种高频出现的陀罗尼

五部大陀罗尼的出现频率并不平均。就藏西古代擦擦而言，除最常见的缘起偈而外，四咒中仅佛顶无垢陀罗尼大量出现。该经中释迦牟尼说两种陀罗尼，分别是“佛顶放无垢光明入普门观察一切如来心三摩耶陀罗尼”（samantamukhapraveśaraśmi-vimaloṣṇīṣaprabhāsasarva-tathāgatahṛdayasamaya-dhāraṇī）与“佛顶无垢普门三世如来心陀罗尼”（buddhoṣṇīṣavimala-samantamukhatrailokyatathāgatahṛdaya-dhāraṇī），前者较

40 参见 http://blog.sina.com.cn/s/blog_5f9ebe700102ee73.html. 福山塔与云居寺北塔浮雕砖非常接近，包括塔形、四句偈乃至塔形上方两侧的“法舍利塔”和悉昙体梵字净法界真言。1976 年唐山大地震时福山塔受到严重破坏，维修时在塔身内部发现大量法舍利塔砖，后回填。福山塔简况见政协天津市蓟县委员会编：《古蓟州》，天津古籍出版社，2006 年，第 157-159 页。

41 对水目山塔林的综述见张崇礼：《祥云县水目山塔林的调查及浅议》，载胡人虎主编，大理白族自治州规划建设局、大理白族自治州土木建筑学会编：《大理建筑文化论》，昆明：云南民族出版社，2006 年，第 202-204 页。

42 智玄为号，俗名高成宗，法名本月，字皎渊。父高量成为大理相国，母段氏为昭庆公主。事迹可见于天开十六年（1220）赵佑撰《大理国渊公塔之碑铭并序》，录文见《金石萃编》；现仅存两残片，其拓片见张树芳主编：《大理丛书·金石篇 1》，北京：中国社会科学出版社，1993 年，第 36-37 页。

长，以下分别简称为佛顶无垢大、小陀罗尼。[43] 根据 Kunsang Namgyal Lama 对藏传佛教擦擦铭文的综合研究，五大陀罗尼中也仅提及缘起偈和佛顶无垢，可见这种不平衡性在藏族地区是普遍现象。她将这两种真言以及三字总持咒归为一类，称作“加持性铭文”（consecratory inscriptions）。[44]

西夏时期也出现该陀罗尼经的多件西夏文写本或刻本，包括发现于内蒙古额济纳旗黑水城遗址、译自汉文的残写本（俄罗斯科学院东方文献研究所藏。Танг 389, инв. № 2830。10 面，面 18.5×9 厘米、5 行 17-18 字。题署 [illegible]“兰山觉慧法师德慧校”）和刻本《无垢净光总持》（[illegible]。инв. № 811。麻纸，经摺装，面 26.5×11 厘米、6 行 16 字）[45]，以及额济纳旗绿城子出土的西夏文写本《佛顶无垢光明入普门观察一切如来心陀罗尼经》两卷（[illegible]。封面题 [illegible]“顶尊无垢总持”。内蒙古博物馆藏，M11 · 015-016）[46]。俄藏西夏文本后序中称“威力难量，神功叵测。施宝周邦，未若抄书一句；舍身千万，不如片刻受持”，[47] 极力渲染听闻可离恶趣灭罪业，受持则消业障得安康。在元居庸关云台券洞西壁六体陀罗尼石刻、约铸于明永乐十六至十八年（1418-1420）[48] 的永乐大钟梵字铭文 [49]、清乾隆（1743-1752）建裕陵地宫梵字铭文 [50] 中，均可见到此咒的身影。

无垢净光陀罗尼名中同样有“无垢”字样，易于混淆，致藏传佛教中有“二无垢”（dri med rnam gnyis）的说法。它也同样与造塔有密切关系，唐代以“无垢净光”命名塔的例子已很普遍，足见此经的传播及其与塔的联系。大致来说，佛顶无垢〔净光〕与无垢净光陀罗尼可据有无“佛顶 / 顶髻”字样区分开来。如根据咒文不难判断，《密咒圆因往生集》中的“佛顶无垢净光咒”[51]、大理崇圣寺三塔之中塔（千寻塔）所出塔砖上的“佛顶无垢净光陀罗尼”（图 13）即指佛顶无垢〔小〕陀罗尼，显然“净

---

43 『居庸関』等论著中分别简称为如来心大、小陀罗尼。小陀罗尼亦称心咒。

44 Lama: *op. cit*., p. 15.

45 以上两件著录信息见 *Каталог Тангутских Буддийских Памятников*, Составитель Е.И.Кычанов, Киото: Университет Киото, 1999, с. 428-42, № 232, 233.

46 史金波、陈育宁主编 :《中国藏西夏文献》第 17 册“内蒙古编 · 内蒙古自治区博物馆藏卷”，兰州 : 敦煌文艺出版社，2006 年，卷上（M11 · 015）见第 84-115 页，卷下（M11 · 016）见第 116-122 页。

47 此据聂鸿音译文，见《西夏文〈无垢净光总持后序〉考释》，《兰州学刊》2009 年第 7 期，第 2 页。

48 关于永乐大钟的铸造年代尚存不同看法，此据高凯军 :《关于永乐大钟若干问题的探讨》，《中国历史文物》2004 年第 2 期，第 66 页。

49 张保胜 :《永乐大钟梵字铭文考》，北京 : 北京大学出版社，2006 年，第 51-54、117-120 页。

50 Françoise Wang-Toutain, “Les cercueils du tombeau de l’empereur Qianlong,” *Arts asiatiques* t. 60 (2005), p. 72.

51 《大正藏》卷 46，第 1010 页。

图 13 “佛顶无垢净光陀罗尼”砖印拓片。梵字陀罗尼部分顺序与汉文类似，竖书、左行。18×36 厘米。原砖于 1978 年维修云南大理千寻塔时自塔内拆出。姜怀英、邱宣充编著：《大理崇圣寺三塔》，北京：文物出版社，1998 年，图版一八九。

光”字样并不具备决定性。[52] 不过，二者偶见混淆，在一些语境中实需具体辨析。如前所述，存在名为“无垢净光总持”的西夏文本内容却是佛顶无垢。西夏时期流行的“无垢净光〔总持〕”是番羌（党项与西藏）僧人应会诵的十一种经颂之一，[53] 从用语习惯、流传实物来看或指佛顶无垢陀罗尼。藏传《日诵要道全函》中亦有佛顶无垢达哈喇尼（dhāraṇī 陀罗尼）[54]，侧面可证番僧应诵之“无垢净光”总持之所指。因此，在对待西夏、大理乃至同时代汉文文献中出现的“无垢净光”时，必须考虑其指实为佛顶无垢经咒的可能性。[55]

关心佛顶无垢陀罗尼的多名西夏学学者追溯过西夏文译本的来源，认为分两个系

52 千寻塔塔顶鎏金铜函内出《无垢净光大陀罗尼经》，参见邱宣充：《大理三塔塔藏写经》，载《云南民族文物调查》(修订本)，北京：民族出版社，2009 年，第 110-111 页。梵咒砖往往与之并举，其实二者归属不同的体系，恐不察致误。

53 史金波、聂鸿音、白滨译注：《天盛改旧新定律令》第十一“为僧道修寺庙门”，北京：法律出版社，2000 年，第 404 页。

54 吕铁钢主编：《藏密修法秘典》卷 1，北京：华夏出版社，1995 年，第 469-470 页。

55 如关于北京白塔寺塔址原为辽道宗寿昌二年（1096）建永安寺释迦舍利之塔，据元·释祥迈撰碑文其内发现有“无垢净光等陀罗尼经五部”，但三世章嘉若贝多杰（rol pavi rdo rje, 1717-1786）则写作“顶髻无垢、白伞盖等五部法身舍利”(gtsug tor dri med gdugs dkar sogs chos skuvi ring bsrel sde lnga，转引自扎洛、敖见：《章嘉·若贝多杰〈京城西城白塔志——增信之具〉译注》，载郝时远、罗贤佑主编：《蒙元史暨民族史论集——纪念翁独健先生诞辰一百周年》，北京：社会科学文献出版社，2006 年，第 667 页)，字面上显存分歧，未知其所据。见安海燕：《元大都大圣寿万安寺白塔之装藏、装饰》，第 26-29 页。

统，分别从汉文本和藏文本译出。[56] 由于小陀罗尼（俄藏西夏文本称为“真心咒”）的相关研究成果较丰富，这里仅就小陀罗尼略作讨论。孙伯君对照了北宋施护（?-1017）汉译本、西夏时期的俄藏与绿城子西夏文本、《密咒圆因往生集》所录汉文本以及元居庸关梵汉西夏文本，指出“俄藏黑水城出土西夏文本和居庸关西夏文本更接近〔居庸关〕梵文本，而绿城出土西夏文本与施护汉文本、密咒本颇为一致。如梵文本 namas 和 hūṃ hūṃ hūṃ hūṃ aṃ vaṃ saṃ jaḥ，见于前三种西夏文本，唯不见于绿城西夏文本与施护汉文本和密咒本”。[57] 这个观察非常准确。在此基础上进一步扩大这种对比工作的范围，对判断藏西擦擦铭文所处的时空位置颇有帮助（见表 1）：

表 1 佛顶无垢小陀罗尼诸版本对照

<table>
<tr><th colspan="3">第一组</th><th colspan="3">第二组</th></tr>
<tr><td>施护汉译本 [58]</td><td>一切智究竟成就支提陀罗尼藏文本 [59]</td><td>PT 350 藏文本 [60]</td><td>居庸关西壁梵字本 [61]</td><td>永乐大钟梵字本 [62]</td><td>德格版藏文本 [63]</td></tr>
<tr><td colspan="2"></td><td>tad yathā</td><td colspan="3"></td></tr>
<tr><td colspan="4">唵引、一 oṃ</td><td></td><td>oṃ</td></tr>
<tr><td></td><td colspan="2">s- [64]</td><td colspan="3">namas</td></tr>
<tr><td colspan="5">怛赖二合、引地吠二合、三 traiyadhve [65]</td><td>traiyadhvikānāṃ|</td></tr>
<tr><td colspan="6">萨哩嚩二合、三 怛他引誐哆四 纥哩二合那野五 誐啰鼻二合、引 sarvatathāgata hṛdaya garbhe |</td></tr>
</table>

56 参考聂鸿音：《西夏文〈无垢净光总持后序〉考释》；段玉泉、惠宏：《西夏文〈佛顶无垢经〉考论》，《西夏研究》2010 年第 2 期，第 49-57 页；孙伯君：《〈无垢净光总持〉的西夏文译本》，《宁夏社会科学》2012 年第 6 期，第 77-87 页。

57 孙伯君：《〈无垢净光总持〉的西夏文译本》，第 78-80 页。

58《佛顶放无垢光明入普门观察一切如来心陀罗尼经》卷下，《大正藏》卷 19，第 724 页。梵文还原可参考 É. Chavannes, “Le sūtra de la paroi occidentale de l’inscription de Kiu-yong koan,” in *Mélanges Charles de Harlez. Recueil de travaux d’érudition offert à Mgr. Charles de Harlez à l’occasion du vingt-cinquième anniversaire de son professorat à l’Université de Louvain* 1871-1896, Leiden: E. J. Brill, 1896, p. 71.

59 *shes pas thams cad mthar phyin par grub pavi mchod rten zhes bya bavi gzungs*，德格版甘珠尔通帙第九〇，folio pha 260r3-266v4.

60 转写见 Scherrer-Schaub, *op. cit.*, p. 711; 综合参考藏汉大藏经等材料还原为梵文见 p. 712.

61 村田治郎编著：『居庸関』第一卷，第 210 页。其中藏文版本的转写见同书，第 147 页。

62 拓片见张保胜：《永乐大钟梵字铭文考》，图版 XXIII、XXXII；转写及考述见第 51-54 页、117-120 页。

63 德格版甘珠尔通帙第九〇，folio pa 253v7-254r.

64 Schopen 指出，吉尔吉特本与一切智究竟成就支提陀罗尼起首处突兀的 s- 是 namas“归命”一词中 nama 脱落所致。

65 居庸关和永乐大钟作 vi.

续表

<table>
<tr><td colspan="3">第一组</td><td colspan="3">第二组</td></tr>
<tr><td>施护汉译本[58]</td><td>一切智究竟成就支提陀罗尼藏文本[59]</td><td>PT 350 藏文本[60]</td><td>居庸关西壁梵字本[61]</td><td>永乐大钟梵字本[62]</td><td>德格版藏文本[63]</td></tr>
<tr><td colspan="6">入嚩二合罗六jvala</td></tr>
<tr><td colspan="3"></td><td colspan="3">jvala |</td></tr>
<tr><td colspan="6">达哩摩二合驮引睹七 誐啰鼻二合、引、八 dharmadhātugarbhe |</td></tr>
<tr><td>僧贺啰九</td><td>saṃharaṇa</td><td colspan="2">saṃhara</td><td></td><td>saṃ bha ra</td></tr>
<tr><td colspan="3">阿引喻十 āyuḥ</td><td>mamâyus</td><td>mamāyuḥ[66]</td><td>ma ma ā yuḥ |</td></tr>
<tr><td colspan="3"></td><td>sandhara,</td><td>sambhara</td><td></td></tr>
<tr><td colspan="6">僧输引驮野十一 saṃśodhaya |</td></tr>
<tr><td colspan="5"></td><td>saṃśodhaya |</td></tr>
<tr><td colspan="3"></td><td>. mama sarva-</td><td>sarva-</td><td>ma ma sarba</td></tr>
<tr><td colspan="6">播引波十二 pāpaṃ |</td></tr>
<tr><td colspan="6">萨哩嚩二合、十三 怛他引誐哆十四 三满睹引、十五 坞瑟抳二合洒十六 尾摩罗十七 尾秫第引、十八
sarvatathāgata samantoṣṇīṣa[67]vimalaviśuddhe |</td></tr>
<tr><td colspan="3"></td><td colspan="3">hūṃ hūṃ hūṃ | hūṃ aṃ vaṃ saṃ jaḥ</td></tr>
<tr><td colspan="6">娑嚩二合、引贺引、十九 svāhā|</td></tr>
</table>

比对上述材料，不难看出前三者可划为一组，反映的是 10-11 世纪的普遍情形；后三者为另一组，年代稍晚。从目前采集并发表的藏西擦擦观察，小陀罗尼铭文大部分[68]（例见图 14 和下文图 17）更接近早期版本、尤其是施护译本，并不同于藏文大藏经所录。但是除了不少例子在咒起首处脱落 namas 之外，还有数例在这个位置以 sarvatathāgatatraiyadhvi“三世一切如来”当之（例见图 14）。[69] 只有少数个案（例见图 15）[70] 才更接近元明以来藏文本的面貌；这个时期的梵文本与藏文本高度一致，尚

66 一作 mama āyuḥ.

67 永乐大钟其一、一切智究竟成就支提陀罗尼、PT. 350 等作 samanta-uṣṇīṣa.

68 参见《西藏古格擦擦艺术》，图版 184、185、197、238（本文图 17）、245、246、250、256、264、269、附录 2 图 63。

69 参见《西藏古格擦擦艺术》，图版 250、256。

70 参见《西藏古格擦擦艺术》，图版 214（本文图 18）。

图 14　佛顶无垢大小陀罗尼铭文擦擦。泥，高 10 厘米。采集于托林寺遗址，11-12 世纪。李逸之藏。《西藏古格擦擦艺术》，图版 263。

图 15　佛顶无垢大小陀罗尼铭文擦擦。泥，高 10 厘米。采集于托林寺遗址，11-12 世纪。李逸之藏。《西藏古格擦擦艺术》，图版 252。

没有证据表明梵文本反映的是其在印度的形态，换言之不能排除系根据厘定通行的藏文本还原为梵字的可能性。不过，根据研究者为藏西擦擦的断代，两组情形均在 11-12 世纪的擦擦铭文上得到反映，尽管出现的概率不均，但看起来它们在当时的藏西并行不悖，这显然值得继续考察和探讨。

四、五部大陀罗尼的组合过程

在勒德纳吉里的考古工作发现了三种本文关心的陀罗尼文本，但它们分别在不同的情形下单独出现：缘起偈出现在几块 6 世纪的孔兹岩（khondalite）石板上；菩提场庄严陀罗尼出现在四件模制泥塑上；而在一件发髻冠观音像（Jaṭā-mukuṭa Lokeśvara，从图像志角度看亦可称为大悲 Mahākaruṇa）像背则铭刻有佛顶无垢小陀罗尼。[71] 三者虽同地出现，但显然彼此无涉、尚未成组。临近的另一处遗址乌德耶吉里（Udayagiri）则揭示另一种景象：这里发掘出至少六件铭刻材料连写缘起偈、宝箧印和菩提场庄严陀罗尼；断代在 8-10 世纪间的另一件陀罗尼石刻（Reg. No. 70）更

71　Mitra, *op. cit.*, p. 104; Thomas E. Donaldson, *Iconography of the Buddhist Sculpture of Orissa: Text*, New Delhi: Indira Gandhi National Centre for the Arts, 2001, p. 59.

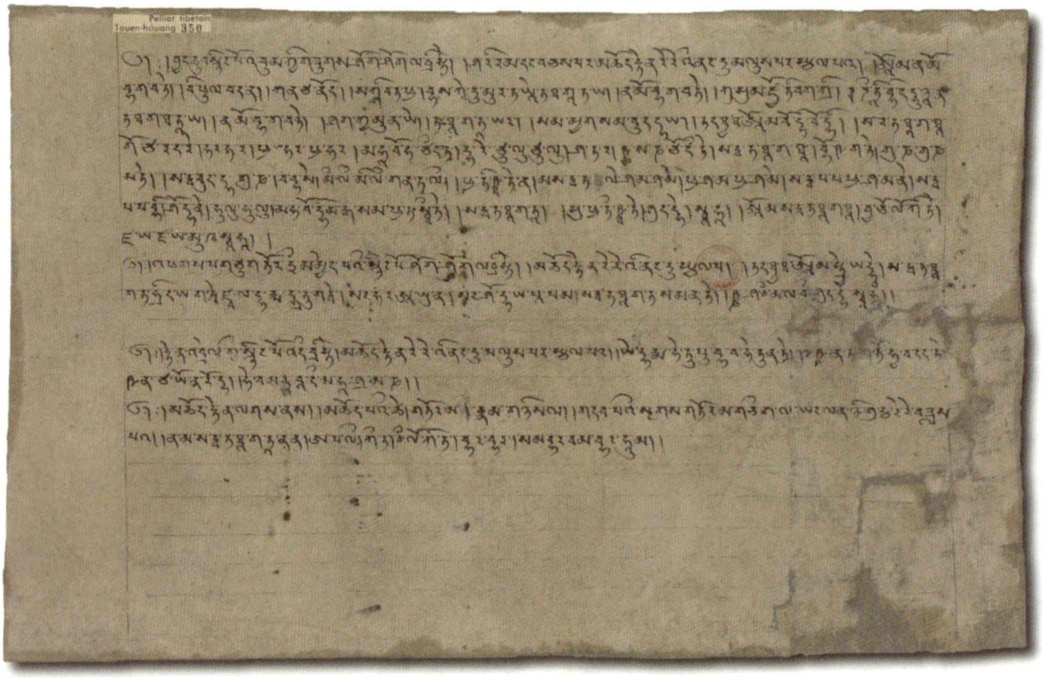

图 16　三种塔装藏用陀罗尼藏文文书。纸本、墨书，31×48 厘米。发现于敦煌藏经洞。Bibliothèque nationale de France, Pelliot tibétain 350. 图片来自 IDP 网站。

在末尾增加佛顶无垢陀罗尼。[72] 这件石刻在宗教实践中的具体用法尚不明确，其铭文与五部大陀罗尼相比仅阙佛顶尊胜，已近定型。它在时代和传播路线方面堪称坐标，有待详加研究。

将目光转向中国，约 10 世纪的敦煌藏文文献 PT. 350（图 16。法国国家图书馆藏）依次录写菩提场十万陀罗尼（byang chub snying po vbum kyi gzungs，包括根本咒、心咒和心中心咒）、圣佛顶无垢心要（vphags pa gtsug tor drI ma myed pavI snying po）与缘起心要（rten vbrel gyI snying po）三种，并反复强调三种真言完整写出后置于塔中（mchod rten re revi nang du ma lus par stsal pava）。[73] 该文献反映出装藏所用的核心陀罗尼发展至一个特定的阶段。

72　Bimal Bandyopadhyay, *Excavations at Udayagiri-2 (1997-2000)*, New Delhi: Archaeological Survey of India, 2007, pp. 128-137; 田中公明 :「オリッサ州ウダヤギリⅡ出土の石刻陀羅尼について」,『東洋文化研究所紀要』第 166 册（2014 年），第 134-124 页。

73　对该文本的研究详见 Cristina Anna Scherrer-Schaub, "Some Dhāraṇī Written on Paper Functioning as Dharmakāya Relics: A Tentative Approach to PT 350", in Per Kvaerne (ed.), *op. cit.* vol. 2, pp. 711-727.

图 17　塔擦（铭文为第一组佛顶无垢小陀罗尼与缘起偈）。泥，高 4.5 厘米。采集于札达县玛囊寺遗址，11-12 世纪。李逸之收藏。《西藏古格擦擦艺术》，图版 238。

图 18　塔擦（铭文为第二组佛顶无垢小陀罗尼与缘起偈，后附不空羂索真言）。泥，高 9 厘米。采集于札达县麦龙沟遗址，11-12 世纪。李逸之藏。《西藏古格擦擦艺术》，图版 214。

天竺胜诸冤敌节怛哩巴（Jetāripa，活动于 10 世纪）上师述，明初持咒沙门莎南屹啰（bsod nams grags）译汉《圣像内置总持略轨》开篇即申明：[74]

夫欲造大菩提塔或尊胜塔等八塔之时，其内所安总持神咒应如是书，即应从上至下次第书之也。谓法轮之内，应当书写顶髻转轮及佛顶髻白伞盖咒；谓八山之内，书诸相传上师之名、尊佛心咒、上师真容、身语意咒、萨哩八二合毕底牙二合等咒也；谓瓶上分中，应当书置悟室尼二合沙毕麻辣咒（按即佛顶无垢陀罗尼）、宝楼阁咒、白毫宝珠咒、如意宝珠咒；谓瓶下分中，书置尊胜陀罗尼咒、无垢净光咒，及应安置舍利咒宝函咒（前一“咒”字衍，此即宝箧印陀罗尼）、菩提亿庄严咒、长因缘咒……

其中已经提到五种陀罗尼，它们分置两处，与其他真言等并用。同书随后还讲解如何装藏骨塔（即身舍利塔）和佛像，与八塔之法相通。

目前所知最早提及装藏用五部大陀罗尼的藏文文献当是萨迦第三祖札巴坚赞（grags pa rgyal mtshan，1147-1216）造《经堂佛塔地基仪轨和开光法明义》，其中明确提及“法身舍利是按所教置于塔内的五种陀罗尼”（chos kyi skuvi ring bsrel la

74　收入《大乘要道密集》第四册，北京大学出版社，2012 年影印版。据沈卫荣研究，其藏文原本尚未勘定，见《八思巴帝师造〈略胜住法仪〉研究》，载达力扎布主编：《中国边疆民族研究》第二辑，北京：中央民族大学出版社，2009 年，第 163 页。

mchod rten gyi nang du bzhugs par bshad pavi gzungs lnga yin te）[75]，索其名目即五部大陀罗尼。从文意来看，装藏五部大陀罗尼的做法渊源有自，必定可以追溯到更早的仪轨文本；希望将来还能够从实物的角度予以印证。

目前藏西擦擦铭文提供的五部大陀罗尼出现的情况，可分为三种：

1. 单独出现缘起偈（或其与尊神真言的组合）或者佛顶无垢陀罗尼。

2. 其中两者的组合，主要表现为缘起偈与佛顶无垢陀罗尼共同出现（图 17-18）。在其他地区的例子中存有不同组合，如发现于克什米尔的梵文印章（图 6）铭文为菩提场庄严陀罗尼及缘起偈。总的来看，通常会采用缘起偈、并置于另一种陀罗尼之后。

3. 五部大陀罗尼〔以及其他真言〕的组合。

第三种情况的例子相对稀见，尚可觅得。在一件大约 15 世纪的塔形擦擦内塞有真言纸卷作为装藏（图 19），上印藏文转写的 10 种真言。分三行横书，无音节点，用垂符分隔各真言，依次为（还原为梵文）：

1. 佛顶尊胜佛母心中心真言与心真言：oṃ bhrūṃ svāhā| oṃ amṛta ayur dade svāhā|

2. 顶髻、项喉、心间、脐孔、密藏五处种字：oṃ aḥ hūṃ trāṃ hrīḥ [76]

3. 白伞盖陀罗尼（略本）：oṃ aḥ rakṣa rakṣa maṃ sarvasatvāṃṣ(ś)ca svāhā| [77]

4. 佛顶无垢小陀罗尼：oṃ namas traiyadh[v]ikānāṃ sarvatathāgatahṛdayagarbhe jvala jvala dharmadha(ā)tugarbhe saṃbhara mama āyuḥ saṃśodhaya mama sarvapāpaṃ sarvatathāgatasamantoṣṇiṣavimale viśudb(d)he hūṃ hūṃ hūṃ hūṃ aṃ vaṃ saṃ jaḥ svāhā|

5. 宝箧印陀罗尼（略本）：oṃ sarvatathāgatoṣṇiṣa dhātumudraṇi sarvatathāgata

---

75 grags pa rgyal mtshan, "argavi cho ga dang rab tu gnas pa don gsal ba," dpal brtsegs bod yig dpe rnying zhib vjug khang (bsgrigs): *sa skya bkav vbum dpe bsdur ma las grags pa rgyal mtshan gyi gsung vbum pod bzhi pa,* pe cin: krung govi bod rig pa dpe skrun khang, 2007, p. 530. 相关英文节译见 Bentor, "On the Indian Origins of the Tibetan Practice of Depositing Relics and Dhâraṇîs in Stûpas and Images," pp. 256-257; 汉文节译见安海燕：《元大都大圣寿万安寺白塔之装藏、装饰》，第 50-51 页。

76 此五字亦五方佛种字。另，《装藏略》中脐孔种字作 traṃ saṃ（saṃ 实则为六根种字之一）；密处作 hri（《大正藏》卷 21，第 951 页），应无实质的不同。

77 *vphags pa de bzhin gshegs pa thams cad kyi gtsug tor nas byung ba gdugs dkar mo can zhes bya ba gzhan gyis mi thub ma phyir zlog pavi rig sngags kyi rgyal mo chen mo,* 德格版甘珠尔通帙第九〇，folio pha 207r5（阙前后的 oṃ aḥ 与 svāhā），209v6 及 211v1（阙首二字）；不见于楞严咒。仅从字面看，也与不空羂索（德格版甘珠尔通帙第九一，folio ba 282r）、随求大护明王大心陀罗尼部分字样（不空译：《普遍光明清净炽盛如意宝印心无能胜大明王大随求陀罗尼经》，《大正藏》卷 20，第 626 页）近似。从装藏仪轨选择的真言种类入手，此处定名为白伞盖真言。

图 19a　塔形擦擦与内部装藏。泥，底部直径 11.5 厘米、高 8.5 厘米。采集于札达县东嘎乡扎西曲林寺，约 15 世纪。李逸之藏。《西藏古格擦擦艺术》，图版 180-1、2。

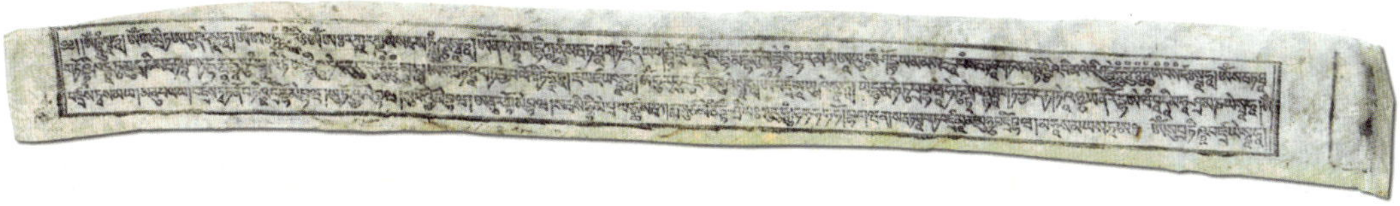

图 19b　展开的装藏真言纸卷。纸本、墨印，4×42 厘米。《西藏古格擦擦艺术》，图版 180-3。

dharmādhātu vaṃ bhūṣite adhiṣṭhi(a)te huru huru hūṃ hūṃ svāhā|

6. 菩提场庄严心真言与心中心真言：oṃ sarvatathāgata vya(ā)valokite svāhā| jaya jaya svāhā| oṃ huru huru jaya muṣ(khy)e svāhā| [78]

7. 金刚寿命真言：oṃ vajra āyuṣe svāhā|

8. 真言化的缘起偈：ye dharma(ā) hetuprabhavā hetun teṣa(ā)n tathāgato hy avadat| teṣāñ ca yo nirodha evaṃ vādī mahāśramana[ḥ]ye svāhā|

9. 百字明：oṃ vajrasatva samaya| manupa(ā)laya| vajrasatva teno patiṣṭha dṛḍho me bhava| sutoṣyo me bhava| supoṣyo me bhava| anurakto me bhava| sarvasidhī me prayaccha sarvakarmasu ca me citti śriyaḥ kuru hūṃ| ha ha ha ha ho[ḥ]| bhagavan| sarvatathāgata vajra mā me muñca vrajri(ī) bhava| mahāsamayasatva aḥ

10. 巩固（坚巩）善住真言（梵 sthirāsana）：oṃ supratiṣṭhavajraye svāhā|

1、4-6、8 即属五部大陀罗尼，就这件藏西中期的塔形擦擦装藏真言的选择与书

78　以上两种见 *byang chub snying povi rgyan vbum zhes bya bavi gzungs*，德格版甘珠尔帙第八十八，folio na 23r；另见 Tôh. 920, folio e 264r.

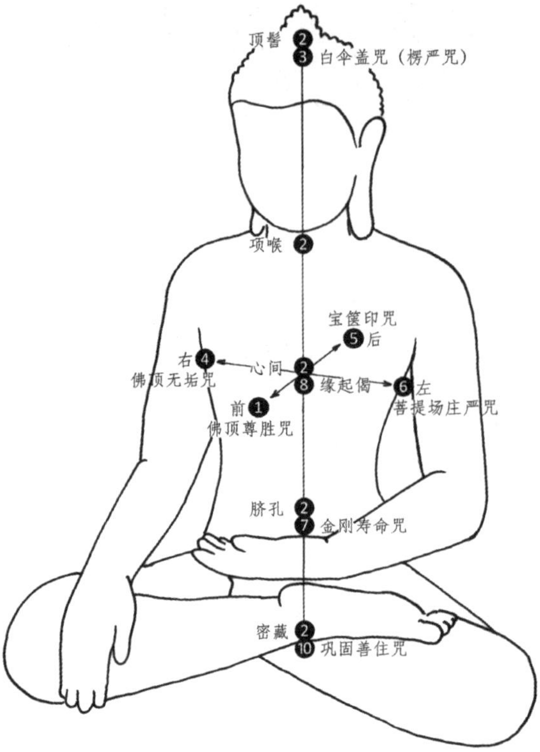

图 20　按《装藏略》复原图 19b 真言位置示意图。

图 21　显密圆通法师道殿建舍利塔记拓片。辽寿昌二年（1096）。梁启超旧藏，现藏国家图书馆，轴 333。

写顺序，可对照《造像量度经续补·装藏略安像总持附》：[79]

> 藏有五方之分。其中纖之藏，则顶上种字下，安楞严总持（按与白伞盖陀罗尼相当）；项喉种字下或傍，安音声字母；心间种字下或傍，安一切智咒；脐间二种字上下及其周围，安金刚寿命心咒；密藏种字下，安巩固善住咒。其四方之藏，则前面佛顶尊胜，右边无垢光明，后面秘密箧印，左边菩提场庄严。此四咒之尾续及中纖之下，俱安十二因缘总持。

印本选用的真言与上引文所述大体吻合，尤其是次序亦能逐一对应，井然有序（图 20）。可见体量较小的擦擦虽难与塔像等量齐观，但对装藏真言却也谨事之，一丝不苟。不过，二者亦有数处不同，可视为当时装藏真言的独特之处：一、所取白伞

79《大正藏》卷 21，第 951 页。

盖真言，《装藏略》中列示为白伞盖陀罗尼之摄受咒与坚甲咒，[80] 与印本不同；二、佛顶无垢陀罗尼取代了《装藏略》指定的无垢光明，不过正如前文所述，存在标称“无垢光明”却实指佛顶无垢陀罗尼的例子；三、选用百字明是此装藏真言印本的特色，不见于《装藏略》。

五、11 世纪末所见另一种五陀罗尼装藏体系

需要注意的是，除西藏西部擦擦铭文所反映的装藏情形而外，在其他地区的佛教传统中，用作装藏的五部大陀罗尼组合可能微有调整，不可一概而论。宗教实践中的实例还在寻觅之中，若从金石文字材料出发，则已得明证（图 21）：[81]

> 今依宝箧陀罗尼经、无垢净光陀罗尼经、菩提场庄严陀罗尼经、最胜摠持陀罗尼经、无垢法，特建舍利塔。
>
> 时大辽寿昌二年三月望日
>
> 显密圆通法师道殿建，弟子性悟施。

此石由周肇祥（养庵，1880-1954）访得于奉天（今辽宁沈阳），未知该舍利塔是否就位于沈阳附近。而根据（元）如意祥迈撰《圣旨特建释迦舍利灵通之塔碑文》记载：[82]

> ……永安寺殿堂废尽，惟塔存焉。观其名额，释迦舍利之塔，考其石刻，大辽寿昌二年三月十五日显密圆通法师道殿之所造也。内有舍利戒珠二十粒、香泥小塔二千、无垢净光等陀罗尼经五部[83]，水晶为轴。

显然北京永安寺释迦舍利塔（今白塔寺塔前身）的石刻内容较为丰富，描述有塔内装藏圣物。但二者所涉及的人物（道殿）、时间（寿昌二年三月十五日）以及装藏陀罗尼种数（五种）如此密合，联想二者的关系令人振奋。显然，“无垢法”应指佛顶无垢陀罗尼。11 世纪末在宗教实践当中已出现完整的装藏用真言体系，辽无垢

---

80 白伞盖陀罗尼之摄受咒为 tad yathā oṃ anale anale khasame khasame vaire vaire saume saume sarvabuddhādhiṣṭānādhiṣṭhite sarvatathāgatoṣṇīṣasitātapatre hūṃ phaṭ [svāhā]；坚甲咒为 hūṃ mama hūṃ ni svāhā. 参见林光明编著：《兰札体梵字入门》，台北：嘉丰出版社，2004 年，第 265-266 页。

81 北京图书馆金石组编：《北京图书馆藏中国历代石刻拓本汇编》第 45 册，郑州：中州古籍出版社，1989 年，第 95 页。

82 引自宿白：《元大都〈圣旨特建释迦舍利灵通之塔碑文〉校注》，收入同氏：《藏传佛教寺院考古》，北京：文物出版社，1996 年，第 325-326 页。

83 安海燕正确指出“此处《碑文》所谓的‘陀罗尼经五部’当是包括《无垢净光陀罗尼经》在内的另一种组合”，见《元大都大圣寿万安寺白塔之装藏、装饰》，第 27-29 页。

净光陀罗尼仍然不可或缺，如前所述庆州白塔还是以其法装藏的实例，对无垢净光的重视使得当时的五部大陀罗尼体系中它取代缘起偈而出现，成为不同于藏式五部大陀罗尼的关键。当然，这并不意味着当时轻视缘起偈的地位，云居寺北塔法舍利塔砖等实物足以为证。道殿堪称一代宗教领袖人物，他对于准提法的观修贡献最巨，[84]在其《显密圆通成佛心要集》影响下辽金时期经幢的陀罗尼在辽末乾统年间（1101-1110）发生突变[85]……鉴于此师在信众中具有如此广大的影响力，则两种金石材料反映的装藏用无垢净光等五种陀罗尼的做法应非孤例，当可断言。

六、小结

对照不空译经和《造塔功德经》《浴佛功德经》的说法，推测 7-8 世纪中不但存在单独以缘起偈作为法舍利的情况，而且有可能在一定的时空范围内径以该偈等同于法舍利。至于五部大陀罗尼乃至更繁复的装藏，则是在佛学发展过程中、伴随象征主义体系的复杂化、精密化而发展起来的。后宏期初以来，逐渐出现缘起偈与其他真言的固定组合，基于西藏西部擦擦铭文的考察表明，以佛顶无垢陀罗尼最为突出。根据 10 世纪节怛哩巴所造仪轨文本，当时已经形成繁密严谨的塔像装藏做法，以真言为主，并及上师名、上师真容、伏藏宝、偈颂、宝藏神父母轮等项内容，不过五部大陀罗尼杂厕其中，并未突出强调，亦未视作一个整体。11 世纪末辽起塔亦用五种陀罗尼，只是用无垢净光而非缘起偈。最后，至迟在 13 世纪初西藏形成五部大陀罗尼为主的装藏真言组合，该组合可能隐含方位等象征意义，具体的宗教内涵尚有待逐一详考。相信随着有关考古报告的发表、公私收藏佛教塔像装藏的公布，以及对当代装藏实践的观察与调查，这个课题将拥有更广阔的研究视野。

五部大陀罗尼组合在藏区不同地域和宗派之间的奉持情况亦有待考察。从空间角度来审度，依据缘起偈和佛顶无垢陀罗尼的流行以及字面演变，在 11-15 世纪的国际化时代，时代共性不容忽视。在佛顶无垢小陀罗尼一例中，从东印度到藏西擦擦、大理梵咒砖、施护汉译本高度相似，呈现出 11 世纪以来佛教世界的文化交流事业之繁荣。

84 详见蓝吉富：《〈显密圆通成佛心要集〉与准提信仰》，载杨曾文、方广锠编：《佛教与历史文化》，北京：宗教文化出版社，2001 年，第 476-480 页；唐希鹏：《〈显密圆通成佛心要集〉与元明准提信仰的流行》，《宗教学研究》2003 年第 3 期，第 123-126 页；郭祐孟：《印度佛教密宗的汉化——以唐、宋时期准提法为中心的探索》，载吕建福主编：《密教的思想与密法》，北京：中国社会科学出版社，2012 年，第 282-287 页。

85 张明悟：《辽金经幢研究》，北京：中国科学技术出版社，2013 年，第 99-125 页。

Tibetan Inscriptions at Alchi, Part I
Towards a reassessment of the chronology

Amy Heller (CNRS Paris) and Shawo Khacham (CNRS Paris)

1. Introduction

This article is dedicated with profound respect and esteem to the memory of our departed colleague and friend Guge Tsering Gyalpo, who has been a key source of new discoveries and inspiration to study in depth the kingdoms of his beloved Mnga' ris Skor gsum, to seek new insights to contribute to the establishment of a clearer chronology of these regions and better understanding of the dynamics within early artistic schools in Western Tibet. His publications document his outstanding achievements in art, history and religion. In the present modest contribution, we focus on elements of inscriptions from Alchi which, in our understanding, help to clarify some aspects of the chronology of the foundation of Alchi and phases of construction of specific sanctuaries.[1]

The data collated here relates crucially to the vexed problem of the chronology of Alchi Sumtsek (Al lci Gsum brtsegs) temple, which has been attributed a 13th century foundation date due to a small section of murals on the second floor which, according to their name inscriptions, portray a series of Drigung ('Bri gung) monks and hierarchs, the last member of which died in 1217 (Goepper 1990, 1993, 1996, 2003). However the iconography and

1 This research stems in part from a lecture by Amy Heller at the Collège de France, Paris, 3 June 2014 "Why re-assess the chronology of Alchi Sumtsek: historical, art-historical and philological considerations." I thank the Centre de Recherche sur les Civilisations de l'Asie Orientale (CRCAO) for the kind invitation to the seminar "Archéologie, arts et culture matérielle du monde tibétain" and for astute criticism from the scholars present. A subsequent article, Tibetan Inscriptions at Alchi, Part II (Heller, A. and R. Vitali, forthcoming), will study the historical and biographical inscriptions of the Dukhang and Sumtsek.

aesthetic milieu of the clay sculptures and mural paintings on the ground floor and all surrounding murals on the second floor, tend to suggest a date roughly a century earlier, slightly later than the Alchi Dukhang (Al lci 'Du khang) temple. Although the precise date of the Dukhang's foundation remains unknown, this temple was initially attributed by Snellgrove and Skorupski to the second half of the 11th century (Snellgrove and Skorupski 1977: 42) and subsequently by Denwood to the mid-11th century (Denwood 1980: 152 and Denwood 2014: 159) while Goepper proposed late 12th to early 13th century (Goepper and Poncar 1996: 18) for the foundation of the Sumtsek.[2] In contrast, Snellgrove and Skorupski date the ground floor of the Sumtsek to late 11th-early 12th c. (Snellgrove and Skorupski 1977: 79) while Denwood dates the Sumtsek to the last third of the 11th century (Denwood 2014: 159). Taking Goepper's findings of the historic lineage into account,[3] one may formulate the following hypothesis: rather than a foundation in the early 13th century, the Alchi Sumtsek was founded shortly after the Alchi Dukhang (in the late 11th to early 12th century) and re-consecrated as a Drigung sanctuary ca. 1220 in the wake of Drigung expansion from the Kailash region throughout western Tibet, including Ladakh.[4] This follows the model of the phenomenon of a phase of Drigung re-consecration ca. 1220 of late 11th to early 12th century temples in Khojarnath (Vitali 1996b: 23) and in northwestern Nepal in both Dolpo and Limi (Heller 2009). Goepper formulated his hypothesis of early 13th century foundation 25 years ago, thus it behooves us to review subsequent research, as well as consult Tucci's 1935 photographs of the inscriptions, and subsequent photographs.[5] This will allow, in our opinion, a far more nuanced understanding of the chronology of Alchi.

2 Goepper 1990: 165 "most likely even after the turn of the century, probably between 1200 and 1220 A.D."

3 Goepper's discovery of the dated segment of mural provided the basis for a chronological framework attributing the Alchi temple complex to ca. 1200 in all successive research by Luczanits (2005: 77) and Linrothe (1999, 2015).

4 Vitali 1996a: 382 discusses the ca. 1220 restoration of earlier temples in Ladakh due to the patronage by the Ladakhi king Dngos grub mgon of the 'Bri gung monk Shes rab byung gnas who left Kailash to teach in Ladakh. Petech 1977: 20 discusses Dngos grub mgon's patronage of the 'Bri gung pa in Kailash ca. 1215, following which Shes rab byung gnas travelled to Ladakh. The phenomenon of a phase of Drigung re-consecration ca. 1220 has also been documented in northwestern Nepal, where two late 11th to early 12th century temples in Dolpo and Limi were re-consecrated by Grub thob Seng ge Ye shes (Heller 2009: 36; 2009: 198).

5 Oscar Nalesini has kindly helped consultation of the Tucci photographic collection in Museo Nazionale Rome; Helga Uebach and Ven. Panglung Rinpoche kindly allowed study of their photographs of 1980 and 1982, for which we are most grateful. In addition, Amy Heller hand copied inscriptions during her 2008 visit, as photography was forbidden.

2. Historical considerations

While Snellgrove and Skorupski first published their tentative chronology in 1977, this date was based on the ancient appearance of the architecture, and also the understanding that murals and clay sculptures of the original construction related to the iconological cycles of the Vajradhatu which prevailed in Guge during the early *phyi 'dar* and throughout thc 11th century. It was in 1980 that Denwood first formulated his hypothesis of an 11th century date due to a phrase he interpreted as crucial for chronology in one Dukhang inscription:

dus la ... 'brom ston

Due to his reading, Denwood was convinced that he was looking at an inscription which was to be dated to the lifetime of 'Brom ston Rgyal ba'i byung gnas (1005-1064), the principal Tibetan disciple of Atisha (982-1054), thus he attributed the inscriptions of the Dukhang to mid-11th century. Understandably!

In succeeding years, the photographs which Denwood used for his readings have unfortunately been lost.[6] However, consultation of the Tucci collection of photographs was fruitful. There are no less than 11 photographs which are all attributed to 1935-10-11 in the archive and all to Sumtsek.[7] However, in fact, several of these photos are inscriptions in the Dukhang. One must recall that these photographs were taken under extreme conditions of light, humidity and stress, as the photographs had to be developed each night, in the dark, beside the candlelight of the tent! In 2016, we can hardly imagine the great difficulties and protocol of photography and development which must have been the routine of Eugenio Ghersi, Tucci's compagnon, who was both physician and photographer. The photographs were taken under duress in terms of light – they are not contiguous, far from it, despite the sequential numbering. It was a fascinating task, as if a puzzle, to attempt to bring together the different photos and make a single continuous line of whichever inscription appear. The results are worthwhile.

In the photograph of the Tucci archive number N. 6008_32 (below Fig. 1), the Dukhang inscription no. 2 read by Denwood is visible. Where Denwood read:

dus la mtshan mtshan gsol slob dpon 'brom ston te (?) ...[8]

6 Only temple Inscription no. 6 of the Sumtsek was published (Snellgrove and Skorupski 1980, fig. 79).

7 Klimburg-Salter, Nalesini and Talamo 1994, films 148-149.

8 Denwood 1980: 127, inscription 2 of Dukhang Alchi. One must recall that Denwood's readings were made in difficult circumstances.

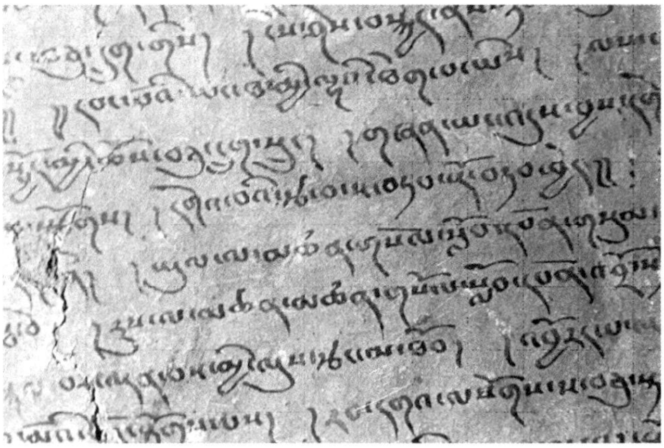

Fig. 1.
Dukhang Inscription no. 2 (detail).
(MNAO photographic archive, G. Tucci's collection, N. 6008_32; photo by Eugenio Ghersi, 1935; courtesy National Museum of Oriental Art, Rome)

At the time Ghersi and Tucci observed the inscription, the letters are clearly legible. We read:

rus la mtshan mtshan gsol slob dpon 'bro ston ...

This reading of the letters gives a completely different connotation to the reading by Denwood. The confusion of *ra* and *da* are well known, thus to read *dus* instead of *rus*, it is quite understandable.[9] But the element *'bro ston*, the teacher of the 'Bro clan, instead of 'Brom ston, this is indeed a very significant distinction in consideration of the major role of the 'Bro clan in western Tibet.[10] Let us recall that the 'Bro clan provided brides for Skyid lde Nyi ma mgon;[11] and Snellgrove, followed by Petech, supported the idea that "the creation of the West Tibetan kingdom was due to the initiative of the 'Bro clan which invited Skyid lde Nyi ma mgon to their country in order to give a cover of legitimacy to their local power."[12] The 'Bro clan was previously documented among rock inscriptions near Alchi[13] and as the clan of Skal ldan Shes rab, founder of the Dukhang, according to Dukhang inscription no. 3[14], as well as Tshul khrims 'od, founder of the Sumtsek[15], according to the Sumtsek

9 Amy Heller first presented this data in June 2012, at the Munich conference "Merkmals and Mirages: A Conference on Dating (Old) Tibetan Writing" (25th to 26th of June, 2012, IBZ; Ludwig-Maximilians-Universität), which discussions lead Uebach to generously share her slides of Alchi.

10 Vitali 2003: 54.

11 Dotson 2012: 185.

12 Dotson, ibid. 185.

13 Takeuchi 2012: 53.

14 Denwood 1980: 146 Inscription 2 of Dukhang Alchi. The accuracy of this reading is confirmed by Heller's hand-copy of this inscription and has recently been reviewed thanks to the 1982 photographs by Helga Uebach and Ven. Panglung Rinpoche.

15 Denwood 1980: 148, Inscription 7 of Sumtsek Alchi.

inscription no. 7. Thus this passage is a further confirmation of the importance of the 'Bro clan at the time of the construction of the Dukhang. Further documentation is necessary to understand more about their patronage in Alchi, and their authority as an extension of royal favour from the ruling house of Guge-Pu hrang. One may recall that the foundation of Nyar ma (996 A.D.) is associated with Rin chen bzang po, in his capacity as royal chaplain (*mchod gnas*) of Lha Bla ma Ye shes 'od and Nyar ma, which we will discuss more below, was documented as the place where Skal ldan Shes rab studied prior to his foundation of the Dukhang. In 1024, the foundation of the monastery of Spithuk (Spe thub) was another example of royal patronage not far from Nyar ma and Alchi.[16]

For the present, in the context of the Dukhang inscription no. 2, while Denwood's chronological framework of the time of 'Brom ston thus becomes moot, we may consider that in other respects, his chronological assessment of the inscription remains valid in consideration of the frequent archaic spellings (reverse *gi gu*, superabundant *'a chung, da drag*, et al.). In the intervening years, there has been considerable progress in understanding the development of Tibetan palaeography in particular thanks to studies of *rdo ring* stele and Dunhuang manuscripts notably by Helga Uebach, Sam van Schaik, Brandon Dotson, which allow better appreciation of the actual shapes and distinguishing characteristics of the letters and the features of handwriting in *dbu can* and *dbu med*. Their research has crucially influenced our understanding of the text of the inscriptions and their chronology in both the Dukhang and Sumtsek at Alchi.

3. Remarks on the historical inscription of the Sumtsek ("Temple Inscription 7")

The detailed study of this inscription is now in progress.[17] Already, at this time, a few salient clarifications may be given in relation to the reading of the inscriptions by Denwood and subsequent research by Vitali. The 1980 photograph of this inscription by Uebach and Ven. Panglung Rinpoche has provided the basis for our remarks, as well as discussion with Roberto Vitali. This inscription discusses the history of the 'Bro clan, notably the ancestor

16 See Vitali 1996a: 301, n. 466 for phases of temple foundations in Ladakh during the 11th century.

17 See detailed readings of several inscriptions in Tibetan Inscriptions in Alchi, Part II (Heller and Vitali, forthcoming). See also Martin, forthcoming, for discussion of infrared photography of several murals which allow better reading of the ancient inscriptions.

Stag bzang of the 'Bro, the migration from Guge Pu rangs to Mar yul, the subjugation of enemies and political appointment during residence in Nyar ma as minister. Denwood had translated "resided in Nyar ma in ... acted as governor of Pho brang dbang lnga."[18](*nyar mar bstad// pho brang dbang lnga'i blon po byas*). Denwood's reading and interpretation of *pho brang dbang lnga* may be subject to question. Clarification of this reading is provided by Nils Martin's study of infrared photographs of inscriptions at nearby Mangyu which record this name as Pho brang Dbang lde, which is also the name of the successor of Mnga' bdag Rtse lde, ruler of Guge Pu rangs at the time of the 1076 Council of Buddhism.[19] The reading of the 1980 photograph of the Alchi inscription clearly reads *pho brang dbang lde'i blon po byas* which must refer to an ancestor of Tshul khrims 'od who served as minister to Pho brang dbang lde. Although his precise dates are not known, he was certainly alive during the second half of the 11th century.[20]As to the translation of "governor" for blon po, it may now be clarified by a subsequent passage in the inscription: (*b*)*lon po slob dpon chen po ni / bstand pa'i sgron me 'bro dngos gyi dpal*, which refers to a minister who is simultaneously a teacher, Bstand pa'i sgron me, the true glory of the 'Bro clan. There is also discussion of Skal ldan 'od as deceased at the time of writing of this inscription in the Sumtsek.

4. The inscriptions of the Great Chorten

Roger Goepper was able to see inscriptions on four walls inside the stupa, which were deciphered and transcribed by Konchok Panday, his Ladakhi friend.[21] Two inscriptions, on the north and west wall, he considered to be prayers without any historical information. The south wall Goepper did not discuss.

a) East wall

Roger Goepper published Klaus Sagaster's translation of the inscription of the east wall of the Great Chorten in 1993. Unfortunately all photographs of this inscription were long lost and the inscription is no longer legible.[22] It is fragmentary in many sections. It is in

18 Denwood 1980: 148.

19 I thank Nils Martin for discussion of this reading at Mangyu; see Martin, forthcoming.

20 According to *Mnga'ris rgyal rabs*, he was enthroned at age 13 and died in his youth (Vitali 1996a: 126). Vitali (2003: 66) situated the enthronement ca. 1088.

21 Goepper 1993: 112.

22 Personal correspondence from Prof. Sagaster. As this article goes to press, thanks to Jaro Poncar we learned that some photographs of this inscription were recently recovered.

heptasyllabic meter, which facilitates understanding of the gaps in the text as presently transliterated.[23] Goepper interpreted the opening phrase as if "*bdag*", reading "I (Tshul khrims 'od) make praise"; but the inscription in fact reads *dus gsum bde(r) gshegs rnams la bstod*. This leads to consider that the chorten inscription which Goepper insisted was written by Tshul khrims 'od is probably written by someone who knew him, but it is descriptive, instead of 1st person singular (I built this, ... I make praise), one may consider the possible interpretation as 1st person plural imperative (let us praise, may we praise…), while *dngos rang* "I myself" may also translate "he himself" (*dngos rang 'bro ban tshul 'khrims 'od*). In terms of grammar, there are several sections which are quotations, describing his work (*snyams*) which would be inconsistent with speech in the first person.

b) West wall

Goepper stated that the inscriptions on the west wall were prayers without any historical information. It was deciphered and transcribed by Konchok Panday, his Ladakhi friend, however today no trace of his research remained as it was not published. As photographed in 2008, the west wall has a fragmentary inscription in seven lines (see appendix) in *dbu can* script. The archaisms of the spelling (*da drag, ya btags*) and letter shapes are retained in this inscription. Although fragmentary, the inscription which is known as the "Words of the Rosary of Pearls" describes the Sumtsek with its three large clay sculptures and successive phases of statues therein, and subsequent construction of the Great Chorten as part of funerary dedication, offerings and rituals. On one hand, this inscription clarifies that the Great Chorten was made after the Sumtsek. On the other hand, the discussion of *bar mdo* (sic: *bardo*) and rebirth in the realm of Akṣobhya tend to imply that this chorten was constructed in homage after the decease of an esteemed teacher, possibly indeed Tshul khrims 'od.

5. Observations on the lineage of teacher portraits of the Sumtsek

When Goepper first published this lineage inscription in 1990, the historic identification of the names of the teachers was clearly established, concluding with 'Jig rten mgon po who died in 1217, thus the *terminus post quem* of 1220 for the painting was made. The identification of the lineage masters portrayed was analysed as a 'Bri gung Bka' brgyud

23 We gratefully acknowledge Abel Zadoks for correspondence on specific linguistic aspects of this inscription (March 2014), as well as Dan Martin.

Fig. 2a. Lineage portraits and inscriptions in the Sumtsek.
(Photograph by Jaro Poncar, 1984)

Fig. 2b. Section of Fig. 2a.

pa lineage stemming from the Buddha Vajradhara to Naropa, Tilopa, Marpa, Milarepa, Milarepa's disciples leading to culmination with the foundation of the 'Bri gung by 'Jig rten mgon po. Subsequently, research on lineage portraits particularly in paintings of the diverse schools of the Bka' brgyud pa tradition has burgeoned. The identification of specific iconographic features for certain portraits has been particularly refined thanks to research by Jane Casey, David Jackson and Christian Luczanits. In 2003, Luczanits discussed the unusual depictions of the lineage in Alchi in comparison with other lineage depictions.[24] Among the anomalies he mentioned, "the portrait of Marpa in white robes with a red cape holding vajra and bell as well as Milarepa as a naked white siddha holding a scarf are unique." He further remarked that the subsequent portraits of the lineage cannot be considered as individualised, and that the portrait of 'Jig rten mgon po differs considerably from comparable portraits within the Alchi complex of sanctuaries. He concluded that the lineage reflected "painter's problems in rendering a new subject."

This analysis of the lineage portraits and their inscription is subject to question in the light of subsequent research. Denwood recently has drawn attention to the very clumsy *dbu can* handwriting of the dedication and name inscriptions of the lineage, leading him to conclude that it is a "later forgery, designed to claim a 'Bri gung pa inspiration behind the foundation of the Sumtsek."[25] In our opinion, Denwood's observations on the handwriting are salient – the inscriptions may be added later to complement the portraits of the masters, which appear to be earlier. Denwood's insights lead us to further observations, notably, that the inscription reads from *left to right*, while the lineage depiction in historical order portrays the masters from *right to left* (Fig. 2).[26]

At far right, there are two seated mahasiddhas with the Buddha Vajradhara. According to the names inscribed, these would be Tilopa at far left, then Naropa.

Immediately beside the two mahasiddhas, there is the man with black hair, wearing a long sleeve v-neck white robe with sash and boots, he is holding a vajra over his heart and a bell in his hand. The inscription above this person reads "*bla ma mar pa lo tsa ba la na mo*," and in terms of well known Tibetan hagiography, Marpa was a disciple of Naropa. Thus the

24 Luczanits 2003: 27.
25 Denwood 2014: 364.
26 We thank Jaro Poncar for kindly authorising reproduction of his photograph.

lineage makes sense, historically. The representation of mahasiddhas is not surprising as grub thob are mentioned in the inscriptions as are the *Phyag rgya chen po* studies of Skal ldan Shes rab during his youth.[27] However, we question the identification of this person as Marpa due to the representation of royal *bla ma* as recognised in 11th century murals from Tholing and Tabo.[28]

In particular, at Tholing a stupa has been identified as the funerary chorten of Ye shes ’od, ca. 1025, with his successor, Lha lde, portrayed as both *sbyin bdag* (donor) and *dge bsnyen* (lay practioner).[29] He is represented in long sleeve v-neck collar white robes cinched at the waist, wearing boots; he holds the conch shell and a ritual implement, he is seated beside offering bowls, conch shells, butter lamp and bells, all ritual implements. Although his coiffure cannot be clearly seen, it appears there are wisps of black hair on his shoulders. There is striking resemblance in the iconography of the two portraits of these lay practitioners in Alchi and in Tholing. In light of the new insights in the historic inscriptions of the Alchi Sumtsek, it is tentatively suggested that this portrait may represents the ancestor of Tshul khrims ’od and Skal ldan Shes rab, who served as minister of Pho brang Dbang lde, as part of the lineage of Alchi. Further research and hopefully infrared photography of the actual inscriptions of the lineage of the Sumtsek may bring refutation or confirmation of this hypothesis.

27 Denwood 1980: Dukhang inscription 3.

28 See Tshe ring rgyal po, Christiane Papa-Kalantari and Christian Jahoda 2009 on the appearance of lay practitioners and Jahoda and Kalantari 2015 for discussion on *pho brang* and on the characteristic features of royal portraits as lay practitioners.

29 Tholing stupa excavation photograph courtesy of the archaeologist Zhang Jianlin 张建林, first studied in Heller 2010. Although Heller first identified this man as Byang chub 'od in 2010, subsequent research by Tsering Gyalbo and Christian Jahoda tend to indicate that this portrait represents Lha lde, not Byang chub ’od. See Jahoda and Kalantari 2016: 95 and below Fig. 3.

Appendix

Translation and transliteration, west wall of Great Stupa, Alchi[30]

(1) First line: totally effaced

(2) xxxxxx may there be birth (in the realm of) the Buddha(s) possessing the five wisdoms. Because of constructing the images of the Bodhisattva and all the Buddha of the ten directions, may there be birth in the first entourage of all the Buddha of the ten directions. By making manifest the body of Bhagavat sugata Akṣobhya, may there be birth at the feet of Akṣobhya in his eastern paradise of Abhirati. By having made manifest the body of the Buddha Amitābha, may there be birth in the Sukhāvatī paradise.

(3) By having made the bodies of the Thousand Buddha of the Bhadrakāla and the Three Great Protectors, may there be birth in the close entourage of Mañjuśrī and Maitreya and so on. By making all the bodies of the Sugata (Bhagavat) xxx Tārā xxx and Prajñāpāramitā, may all the noble ones guide to the celestial realms. By having meditated on developing and completion stages of co-emergence, as for the great joy which is the union of wisdom and compassion, may ordinary and extraordinary *siddhi-s* be obtained.

(4) And, by the meditation on the wrathful ones of the Gsum brtsegs temple, may all inner and outer (esoteric and exoteric) obstacles be appeased. By the assembly of the *mahāsiddha-s* (*ku su lu*) and the initiation of complete meditation, may there be protection from all potential damages and may bad karma be perfectly purified. By making offerings of *gtor ma* and ritual assemblies devoted to the *dharmapāla* and the *ḍākinī* at all six times of the day and full and new moon, may there appear genuine signs of spiritual accomplishment. May there be benedictions thanks to constantly taking refuge in the assembly of all the gods and *yi dam* and the lamas and the Triple Jewels as the place of refuge.

(5) By obeying whatever the lama and abbot and teachers say, and respecting the word of the parents, may the obstacle creating deities become favourable. For all sentient beings of the six realms of existence, because of firmly generating the loving mind and compassion, may become xxxxx love. May all humans and animals who have experienced the difficulties

30 We thank Lionel Fournier, Gérard Joudet, Yvon Heller, Gerald Kozicz, and Nils Martin for their pho tos, Kurt Tropper for his video, Sreekumar Menon for infrared photographs of 2016, and Samten Karmay, Helga Uebach and Ven Panglung Rinpoche for suggestions on the translation.

of suffering in order to making the stupa and (images of) gods, may all their impurities be purified. May there be liberation from the suffering of all bad rebirths, and may one obtain the liberation of the higher realms!

(6) As for having obtained the rank of human or gods, may there be the meeting with the holy Dharma. As for me, at the time of death, at the moment of cessation of the inner and outer breath, may the Buddha Akṣobhya appear in front of me in the sky. After the Buddha's personal appearance xxx may he kindly accept me as pupil xxxxxx, without passing the *bar do* ... at the feet of Bhagavat Akṣobhya, may I be born (there) instantaneously! Even having been born at the feet of the Bhagavat, may I meet the holy Dharma and understand the meaning of no-rebirth.

(7) Having thus accumulated the root of virtue and the two accumulations (of merit and wisdom,) I thus make this prayer and may it be truly accomplished. Having constructed the support of the body, the support of the word and the support of the mind of the Buddha, and ... accumulated merits, ... by the writing of this holy .... by oneself .... having written this prayer as a support, if there are errors in my words, I ask the sages to forgive.

(8) The so-called "Words of the Rosary of Pearls" is now complete!

(1) First line completely effaced

(2) rgyal ...sku xxxxxxxxxx..rigs...ye shes lnga ldan pa.xxxxxxxxx..skye par shog // phyogs (bcu'i) sangs rgyas thams cad dang // byang chub sems pa'i sku bzhengs pas // phyogs bcu'i sangs rgyas thams cad kyi// mkhor gyi dang por skye par shog // bcom ldan bder gshegs myi 'khrugs pa'I // sku'i bkod pa bzhengs pa yis // shar phyogs mngon dga'i zhing khams su// myi 'khrugs zhabs dang skyes par shog // bcom ldan 'od dpag myed ba'i // sku'i bkod pa bzhengs pa yis //

(3) Bde' (ba can gyi zhings khams su) xxxxxxxxxxx skye bar shog // bskal ba stong gi sangs rgyas dang// rigs gsum mgon po'i sku bzhengs pas // 'jam dbyang byams pa la stogs kyi // nye ba'i 'khor du skye bar shog // bder gshegs sku gzugs thams cad dang// sgrol ma xxxxxxxxxx. yum sku // bzhengs bas rje btsun la sogs kyis // mkha' spyod gnas su khrid par shog // skyed rdzogs zung 'jug bsgoms pa yis // thabs dang shes rab gnyis myed pa'i // bde' ba chen po'i ngang las ni // mchog mthun gyi dngos

(4) sgrub thob par shog // xxxxxxxxxx gtum po gsum rtsegs bsgoms pa yis // phyi nang bar chod (> bar cad) zhi bar shog / ting nge 'dzind gyi dbang bskur dang // ku su lu'i

tshogs sog (> gsog) gis // nyams chag thams cad skongs pa (> skung pa) dang // las ngan sgrub pa dag par shog/ nya shi dus drug thams cad du // mkha' 'gro chos skyong thams cad la // tshogs dang gtor mas mchod pa yis // grub rtags dngos su 'byung bar shog // skyabs gnas dkon mchog gsum po dang // bla ma yi dam lha tshogs la // skyabs 'gro rgyund tu byas pa yis // byin rlabs
(5) rgyun chad myed par shog // bla ma mkhan po slob dpon gyis // ci gsung bka' la mnyan pa dang // pha ma'i ngag 'di ma bcag pas // sgra sgegs (> dgra bgegs) rnaṃs kyis byaṃs par shog / 'gro drug sems can thams cad la / byams sems brten cu btang pa dang // rtseg gdung rdung (> gdung) sems xxxxxxx yis // xxxxxxxxx dang byams par shog // lha dang mchod rten thams cad kyi // mched du myi phyugs thams cad kyis // sdug bsngal dka' ba spyad pa yis // las ngan sgrib pa dag par shog // ngan song sdug bsngal las thar nas // mtho ris thard pa thob par

Fig. 3. Donor depiction, presumably king Lha lde; mural painting inside the Northwest stupa, Tholing monastery, ca. 1025; h: 70 cm. (Photograph courtesy of Zhang Jianlin)

(6) shog // myi lha'i go phang thob nas ni // dam ba'i chos dang 'phrad par shog // bdag ni mchi ba'i dus kyi tshe / phyi nang dbugs ni chad ka ru // mdund kyi bar snang nam mkha' la / myi khrugs pa ni dngos su gshegs par shog // bder gshegs dngos su gshegs nas kyang // bdag la thugs ...... sa 'dzind par shog // gshegs // xxx shog / bar mdo'i (> bar do'i) snang ba ma nyod 'di // bcom ldan myi khrugs zhabs drung du // skad cig tsam la skye par shog // bcom ldan zhabs drung skyes nas kyang // dam pa'i chos dang prad par shog // dam ba'i chos dang prad nas kyang //
(7) skye ba myed ba'i don rtogs shog // bdag gi dge ba'i rtsa ba dang // tshogs gnyis ji ltar bsags pa yis// smon lam ji ltar btab pa bzhin // de bzhin nyid du grub par shog // sku yi rten dang gsung gi rten // thugs kyi brten (> rten) rnams bzhengs pa dang // bsod nams xxxx bsags pa'i // kar xxx dam pa bris pa 'di // rang gis xxx lags te // smon lam rten du bris pas lags // tshig sbyor ngag sdes 'khrul 'gyur // mkhas pa rnams (kyis) bzod
(8) par gsol // tshig sbyor mu tig gi 'phreng ba zhes bya pa / rdzogs s.ho //

Editorial signs:

(1), (2), etc.	beginning of a line
xxx	indicates lacuna, with approximate count of letters which are illegible.
>	proposed reading
/	*shad*
ṃ	*bindu*

Fig. 4. Inscription on West Wall, Great Chorten; infrared photography by Sreekumar Menon, 2016.

* * *

References

Casey Singer, Jane. 1995. Early Portrait Painting in Tibet, in: van Kooij, K.R. and H. van der Veere (eds.), *Function and Meaning in Buddhist Art.* Gonda Indological Series; Groningen: E. Forsten Verlag, 81-99.

Denwood, Philip. 1980. Temple and rock inscriptions of Alchi, in: Snellgrove, David and Tadeusz Skorupski (eds.), *The Cultural History of Ladakh*, vol. II. Warminster: Aris and Philips, 119-163.

— 2014. The dating of the Sumtsek temple at Alchi, in: Lo Bue, Erberto and John Bray (eds.), *Art and Architecture of Ladakh.* Leiden: Brill, 159-166.

Dotson, Brandon. 2012. At the Behest of the Mountain, in: Scherrer-Schaub, Cristina (ed.). *Old Tibetan Studies Dedicated to the Memory of R. E. Emmerick.* Leiden, Boston: Brill, 159-204.

Dotson, Brandon and Agnieszka Helman-Ważny. Forthcoming. *Codicology, Paleography, and Orthography of Early Tibetan Documents Methods and a Case Study.* Vienna: Wiener Studien zur Tibetologie und Buddhismuskunde.

Goepper, Roger. 1990. Clues for a dating of the three-storey temple (Sumtsek) in Alchi, Ladakh, *Asiatische Studien* 44(2): 159-75.

— 1993. The Great Stupa at Alchi, *Artibus Asiae* 53(1-2): 111-143.

— 1996. Murals in the early temples of Alchi, in: Pal, Pratapaditya (ed.), *On The Path to Void: Buddhist Art of the Tibetan Realm.* Bombay: Marg Publications, 226-243.

— 2003. More evidence for dating the Sumtsek in Alchi and its relations with Kashmir, in: Kreide-Damani, Ingrid (ed.), *Dating Tibetan Art.* Wiesbaden: Ludwig Reichert Verlag, 15-24.

Goepper, Roger and Jaro Poncar. 1996. *Alchi Ladakh's Hidden Buddhist Sanctuary: The Sumtsek.* London: Serindia Publications.

Heller, Amy. 2009. *Hidden Treasures of the Himalayas Tibetan Manuscripts, Paintings and Sculptures of Dolpo.* Chicago: Serindia Publications.

— 2010. Preliminary Remarks on the Donor Inscriptions and Iconography of an 11th-century *Mchod rten* at Tholing, in: Lo Bue, Erberto and Luczanits, Christian (eds.) *Tibetan Art and Architecture in Context.* Andiast: International Institute for Tibetan and

Buddhist Studies GmbH, 43-74.

Heller, Amy and Vitali, Roberto. Forthcoming. Tibetan inscriptions at Alchi, Part II: The historical and biographical inscriptions.

Jahoda, Christian and Christiane Kalantari. 2016. Kingship in Western Tibet in the 10th and 11th Centuries. *Cahiers d'Extrême-Asie* 24: 81-107.

Jackson, David, with contributions by Christian Luczanits and Kristen Muldowny. 2014. *Painting Traditions of the Drigung Kagyu School.* New York: Rubin Museum of Art.

Kalantari, Christiane and Tsering Gyalpo. 2011. On ornament, textiles and baldachins depicted on the ceilings of Buddhist cave temples in Khartse Valley, Western Tibet. Form, Function and Meaning; at www.kunstgeschichte-ejournal.net; urn:nbn:de:0009-23-27670.

Klimburg-Salter, Deborah, Oscar Nalesini and Guilia Talamo. 1994. *Inventory of the Tucci Photographic Archives, 1926-1935* (*Western Himalayas, Nepal, Tibet*). Roma: Istituto Italiano per il Medio ed Estremo Oriente.

Linrothe, Robert. 1999. Talisman, reliquary and instrument of enlightenment: The Alchi Sumtsek as a mandalic site, *Orientations* 30(1): 22-29.

— 2015. Site unseen: Approaching a royal Buddhist monument of Zangskar (Western Himalayas), in: Bray, John, Petra Maurer and Andrea Butcher (eds.), *Ladakh: Historical Perspectives and Social Change; The Tibet Journal* 40(2), *special issue*, 29-88.

Luczanits, Christian. 2003. Art historical aspects of dating Tibetan art, in: Kreide-Damani, Ingrid (ed.). *Dating Tibetan Art.* Wiesbaden: Ludwig Reichert Verlag, 25-58.

— 2005. The early Buddhist heritage of Ladakh reconsidered, in: Bray, John (ed.), *Ladakhi Histories: Local and Regional Perspectives.* Leiden: Brill, 65-96.

Martin, Nils. Forthcoming. The lDe, the 'Bro, and the sMer. Inscriptional Evidence from the Thugs rje chen po lha khang at Mangyu, in Heller, Amy (ed.), *Towards a Study of the Visual Culture of Tibet and the Himalayas, Proceedings of a Panel Held at the International Association for Tibetan Studies, Bergen 2016* (www.asianart.com).

Petech, Luciano. 1997. Western Tibet: historical introduction, in: Klimburg-Salter, Deborah (ed.). *Tabo: A Lamp for the Kingdom.* Milan: Skira, 229-56.

Snellgrove, David L. and Tadeuz Skorupski. 1977. *The Cultural Heritage of Ladakh, vol. I.* Warminster: Aris and Philips Ltd.

Snellgrove, David L. and Tadeuz Skorupski. 1980. *The Cultural Heritage of Ladakh, vol. II.*

Warminster: Aris and Philips Ltd.

Takeuchi, Tsuguhito. 2012. Old Tibetan rock inscriptions near Alchi, in: Takeuchi, Tsuguhito and Noihiko Hayashi (eds.), *Historical Development of the Tibetan Languages (Journal of Research Institute* 49). Kobe City University of Foreign Studies, 29-70.

Tropper, Kurt. 2013. The Buddha-vita in the White Temple of Tsaparang, in: Tropper, Kurt and Cristina Scherrer-Schaub (eds.). *Tibetan Inscriptions: Proceedings of a Panel Held at the Twelfth Seminar of the International Association for Tibetan Studies, Vancouver 2010.* Leiden: Brill, 43-106.

Tshe ring rgyal po, Christiane Papa-Kalantari and Christian Jahoda. 2009. *The Buddhist Monuments of Khartse Valley, Western Tibet.* Austrian Academy of Sciences / AAS Working Papers in Social Anthropology 2009, Volume 9: 1-28 (http://epub.oeaw.ac.at/wpsa9).

Uebach, Helga. 2011. Notes on the paleography of the Old Tibetan inscriptions: Zhol and bSam yas, in: Chayet, Anne, Cristina Scherrer-Schaub, Françoise Robin, and Jean-Luc Achard (eds.), *Edition, éditions: l'écrit au Tibet, évolution et devenir.* (Collectanea Himalayica 3) München: Indus Verlag, 411-28.

van Schaik, Sam. 2014. Towards a Tibetan palaeography: Developing a typology of writing styles in early Tibet, in: Quenzer, Jörg, Dmitry Bondarev, and Jan-Ulrich Sobisch (eds.), *Manuscript Cultures: Mapping the Field.* Berlin and Boston: De Gruyter, 299-340.

Roberto Vitali. 1996a. *The Kingdoms of Gu ge Pu hrang according to mNga' ris rgyal rabs by Gu ge mKhan chen Ngag dbang grags pa.* Dharamsala: Tho gling gtsug lag khang lo gcig stong 'khor ba'i rjes dran mdzad sgo'i go sgrig tshogs chung.

— 1996b. Jo bo dngul sku mched gsum dkar chag by Wa gindra karma, Introduction, in: *Jo bo Rin po che dngul sku mched gsum rten dang brten par bcas pa'i dkar chage rab dga'i glu dbyangs.* Dharamsala: Organizing Committee for the Commemoration of 1000 Years of Tholing Temple, VII-XIX.

— 2003. A chronology (*bstan rtsis*) of events in the history of mNga' ris skor gsum (tenth-fifteenth centuries), in: McKay, Alex (ed.), *The History of Tibet*, vol. II. London and New York: Routledge Curzon, 53-89.

西藏阿里帕尔嘎尔布石窟的图像程序 *

张长虹

帕尔嘎尔布（par dkar po）石窟位于西藏自治区阿里地区札达县境内，是西藏西部地区象泉河流域佛教后弘期留存的重要遗址之一，早在20世纪90年代，考古学家们已经进行过调查,并公布了调查简报[1]。这座石窟的发现对于西藏西部地区乃至整个西藏地区佛教发展史、艺术史的研究具有重要价值，已经有学者指出了该窟考古发现的重要意义[2],笔者也曾对该窟的题记和两幅曼荼罗图像进行过公布[3],但是该窟的整体图像内容一直未有详细全面的公布，本文拟对该窟的图像程序包括图像细节、题记等进行一个全面的介绍与分析。

该窟除顶部壁画已毁外，四壁皆满绘壁画，并且大部分尊像下面均有题记，系对尊像的偈颂体赞辞，一般为四句，每句九字或七字。为了叙述方便，我们分别对四壁的图像进行了编号，用字母N表示北壁（主壁），W表示西壁（左壁），E表示东壁（右壁），S表示南壁（后壁），下面依次进行叙述。

一、北壁

北壁为该窟的主壁，中央原塑有一尊泥塑像，现已不存，仅有塑像两侧的壁画

* 张长虹：故宫博物院副研究馆员，四川大学中国藏学研究所客座研究员。
本项研究得到四川大学中国藏学研究所教育部人文社科重点研究基地项目“西藏西部佛教史迹综合研究”资助。

1 霍巍：《西藏阿里札达县帕尔嘎尔布石窟遗址》，《文物》2003年第9期，第42-59页。外国学者David Pritzker亦进行过简要介绍，见“The Treasures of Par and Kha-tse,” *Orientations,* September 2000, pp. 131-133.

2 霍巍：《变迁与转折——试论西藏西部帕尔嘎尔布石窟壁画考古发现的意义》，《文物》2003年第9期，第36-41页。

3 张长虹：《西藏阿里帕尔嘎尔布石窟壁画题记释读与相关问题》，《文物》2016年第7期，第63-84页。张长虹：《西藏阿里帕尔嘎尔布石窟的两幅曼荼罗图像及相关问题研究》，《西藏大学学报》（社科版）2013年第4期，第95-106页。

图 1　北壁壁画

图 2　北壁壁画

留存（图 1）。塑像背后绘制有大象、狮羊、骑兽童子、摩羯鱼、金翅鸟等作为塑像的背屏装饰；狮羊两侧绘制有两位胁侍菩萨，左侧的一位身色为粉色，头戴三花冠，冠后束高髻，胸部呈正面，面部呈四分之三侧面看向主尊，身体呈 S 形，上身袒露，下身着裙，双脚均朝向主尊，左肩的植物上方放置有一个宝瓶，因此该菩萨为弥勒；右侧的菩萨身体呈红褐色，装束、姿态同右侧的菩萨相似，两肩侧的白花上方分别横置经书、竖置宝剑，这是文殊菩萨的典型标志物。

两位菩萨的外侧各绘有两位上师，分别编号为 N1—N4。N1 的身色为红色，头戴尖顶班智达帽，身穿袒右僧袍，应为一名印度上师，其余三位上师身色均为白色。四位上师均双手于胸前结印，结跏趺坐，面部呈四分之三看向中央主尊。其中 N1 上师像的下方有藏文题记，共八句，前四句是对 N1 的赞颂辞，后四句应该是对 N1 下方的 N2 的赞颂辞，因为 N2 的下方没有题记；右侧两位上师像的藏文题记书写在 N4 的下方，仅有四句，N3 的下方没有题记。此外，N2、N4 的下方还分别绘制有一排小像，分别编号为 N5 和 N6，其中 N5 的六位小像下方没有题记，从图像特征推测，左侧的四位为四大天王，左起第五位蓝色身体、右手执颅骨碗、左手执猫鼬的为黑瞻巴拉，第六位白色尊神有待进一步辨识。N6 的七尊小像下方各有一则题记，系佛教七政宝（图 2）。

N1 下方的藏文题记（图 3）：

skuvi mdzad pa phyogs bcur sna tshogs bston [ston] //
gsung gi mdzad pa ma tshogs dbang du vdud //
thugs kyi mdzad pas vgro bavi re vdod skongs //
pad mavi rgyal po khyed la phyag vtshal bstod //
sku gsung dbyer med lhun kyis grub //
thugs dam mthar phyin vgro don mdzad //
rgyu ma nor [sgyu mavi nor] [4] gyis vgro bavi re vdod skongs //
bla ma gsal ba vod zer gyi sku la phyag vtshal bstod // [5]

4　对于题记拼写有误的，本文以 [ ] 注出正确的拼写；对于题记有遗漏的，本文在（ ）内补充完整。

5　该句 gsal 与 ba 之间有空格，但原先有字迹被抹去的痕迹，推测为写错之后涂去，重又书写的结果，而非 gsal 与 ba 之间还有字母遗漏。类似的情况也出现于 S4 大黑天像下面的题记的最后一句中 vtshal 和 bstod 之间，两者中间有空隙，有涂抹痕迹，显然系写错之后的涂抹。

译文：身之行教化十方众生，语之行降伏种种女妖 (?)[6]，
意之行满足众生意愿，白玛嘉波（意译：莲花王）我赞礼！
身语无别、任运成就，修行圆满、利益众生，
幻化货财、满足众生之愿，喇嘛色哇沃塞之像我赞礼！

N4 下方的藏文题记（图 4）：

rtag tu ri khrod mgon [dgon] pa vgrim //
thugs dam chos nyid ngang la bzhugs //
vphrin las rnam bzhivi dngos grub brnyes //
drin can rtsa bavi bla mavi sku la phyag vtshal bstod //

译文：恒常游学于山间小庙，修持法性而自性存焉，
证得四种事业之成就，恩人根本喇嘛之像我赞礼！

图 3　N1 下方的藏文题记

图 4　N4 及 N6 下方的藏文题记

从题记可知，主壁左侧的两位上师，N1 上师为白玛嘉波（pad mavi rgyal po），N2 上师为喇嘛色哇沃塞（bla ma gsal ba vod zer）。右侧的 N3 上师下方没有题记，无从知道其身份，N4 上师下方的题记中最后一句为“恩人根本喇嘛之像我赞礼”（drin can rtsa bavi bla mavi sku la phyag vtshal bstod），这位喇嘛应该是建造该窟的功德主的上师，但其具体身份目前也尚不可知。

6　此处 ma tshogs 不知何意，ma 指女性，tshogs 有“集合体”的意思，推测可能指女妖。本文对题记或翻译有存疑的地方用（？）注出。

图 5　西壁壁画

N6 下方的藏文题记（图 4，从左至右）：glang po rin po che、vkhor lo rin po che、dmag mi rin po che、blon po rin po che、btsun mo rin po che、nor bu rin po che、rta mchog rin po che，即：象宝、轮宝、兵宝、臣宝、女宝、摩尼宝、马宝，与壁画的描绘一致。

二、西壁

西壁的北半部绘制一幅曼荼罗，南半部分上下两排共绘有六尊像（图 5）。

该幅曼荼罗，在简报中已正确辨识为金刚界曼荼罗。这是一幅标准的 53 尊配置的金刚界曼荼罗，为叙述方便，本文对图像进行了编号，并与记录西藏早期曼荼罗图像的一部重要文献——《究竟瑜伽鬘》第 19 章中对于该曼荼罗各尊图像的记述进行

图6　西壁北半部金刚界曼荼罗的图像配置和编号

图7　西壁曼荼罗中央主尊大日如来

图 8　阿閦佛及其四大菩萨

比较[7]，编号的顺序与文献中描述的顺序一致（图 6），主要图像特征见表一。

曼荼罗的中央是白色的大日如来（1），但是其形象不是常见的四面八臂或一面二臂，而是四面二臂（图 7）；通常与其一起处于内圆的四波罗蜜女神（2-5）也是罕见地绘制在位置稍远的处于两种色块交界的对角线上。

大日如来的下方绘制的是阿閦佛及其四大菩萨（6-10），按照图像学上的规定，阿閦佛一般为蓝色，其所在的方位为东方，属金刚部。但是这里的阿閦佛为白色，不符合造像学的规定，其身色也看不出有重绘补色的痕迹，不过其所在的三角形区域的

7　《究竟瑜伽鬘》(*rdzogs pavi rnal vbyor gyi phreng ba*, *Nispannayogāvalī*，以下叙述该书时简称 NPY）是关于西藏早期曼荼罗图像的一部重要文献，由大班智达无畏护 (Mahāpandita Abhayākaragupta，约 11 世纪下半叶至 1125? 年）编辑而成，该书的藏译本现存于藏文大藏经丹珠尔中（德格版 No. 3141，北京版 No.3962，中国藏学出版社《中华大藏经〈丹珠尔〉(对勘本)》第 39 册）。《究竟瑜伽鬘》为一部密续文献，全书分为 26 章，每一章分别描述一种不同的曼荼罗。其中第 19 章描述的就是金刚界曼荼罗，第 22 章描述的是净除恶趣清净曼荼罗。巴达恰里雅据梵本对该部著作进行了翻译，见 *Niṣpannayogāvalī of Mahāpaṇḍita Abhayākaragupta*, ed. B. Bhattacharyya, Baroda: Oriental Institute, 1972。本文引用藏文本《究竟瑜伽鬘》中对各尊图像的描述与本窟的壁画进行列表比对，所用版本为《中华大藏经〈丹珠尔〉(对勘本)》(藏文)，第 39 册，北京：中国藏学出版社，1998 年，其中第 19 章对于金刚界曼荼罗的记载（简称 NPY19）见于该书第 324-329 页；第 22 章对于净除恶趣清净曼荼罗的记载（简称 NPY22）见于该书第 357-364 页。

颜色是蓝色，但是在城门及其两侧则各有一小块区域能够辨出是在蓝色上又涂绘了白色（图 8）。关于这种差异出现的原因有待进一步探讨。除了阿閦佛的身色和金刚喜的执物与文献记载有明显不同外，其余图像特征均同于文献记载。

大日如来的右侧绘制的是宝生佛及其四大菩萨（11-15）（图 9），宝生佛所在的方位为南方，属于宝部。除金刚宝的执物和金刚幢的身色与文献记载略有不同外，其余诸尊的图像特征均与文献记载相同。

大日如来的上部绘制的是阿弥陀佛及其四大菩萨（16-20）（图 10），阿弥陀佛所在的方位为西方，属于莲花部。除金刚利的身色、金刚因的契印与文献记载不同外，其余诸尊的图像特征均与文献记载相同。

大日如来的左侧绘制的是不空成就佛及其四大菩萨（21-25）（图 11），不空成就

图 9　宝生佛及其四大菩萨

图 10　阿弥陀佛及其四大菩萨

图 11　不空成就佛及其四大菩萨

图 12　金刚界曼荼罗的左下角

图 13　金刚界曼荼罗左上角

图 14　金刚界曼荼罗的右上角

图 15　金刚界曼荼罗的右下角

图 16　金刚链

佛所在的方位为北方，属于羯磨部。其中除金刚业、金刚拳的身色和执物与文献记载不同外，其余诸尊的图像特征均与文献记载相同。

在第一重方城的四角绘制内四供养女神（26-29），造型特征同四波罗蜜女神相同，只是身色和手中执物有区别（图 12-15），图像学的表现与文献记载几乎完全吻合。

第一重方城外侧，与四佛相对应的位置绘制有十六贤劫菩萨（30-45），造型相似，均头戴三花冠，佩戴各种装饰，上身袒露，下身系带，半跏趺坐（图 12-15）。由于这些贤劫菩萨造型几乎完全相同，文献记载也仅提到其图像类似于其对应的四佛，没有一一详细描述其图像特征，因此难以对其身份一一进行辨识，姑且按顺时针顺序对他们进行编号。

第二重方城的四角绘制外四供养女神（46-49），造型特征同内四供养女神类似，只是身色和手中执物有区别（图 12-15），图像学的表现与文献记载几乎完全吻合。

在外城墙中央的四方城门处，各有一位摄护菩萨（50-53），均呈忿怒相，一面三目二臂二足，头戴三花冠，冠后橙色焰发高束，上身袒露，佩有各种装饰，下身穿虎皮短裙，呈右展姿站立，右手均上举执各自的法器，左手均外伸结期克印（图 16）。

表 1　西壁金刚界曼荼罗诸尊图像与《究竟瑜伽鬘》第 19 章中的描述对照一览表

编号	名称	壁画描绘	NPY19 记载
1	大日如来	四面二臂，身色为白色，双手结最胜菩提印，头戴宝冠，佩有装饰，有坐骑狮子	①四面八臂，四面：白、黄、红、绿；八臂：主双手最胜菩提印，另一双手禅定印，二右手：念珠、箭，二左手：法轮、弓 ②一面二臂：白色，双手最胜菩提印
2	心金刚女	白色，右手持金刚杵，左手期克印置腿上	蓝色，右手红色五股金刚杵，左手期克印执羂索
3	宝金刚女	黄色，右手执宝，左手期克印置腿上	黄色，右手执宝，左手期克印
4	法金刚女	红色，右手执莲茎，白莲开在右肩侧，左手期克印置腿上	红色，右手执红白八瓣莲，左手执莲花
5	业金刚女	绿色，右手羯磨金刚杵，左手期克印置腿上	绿色，右手羯磨金刚杵，左手期克印
6	阿閦佛	白色，大象坐骑，右手结触地印，左手结禅定印	蓝色，大象坐骑，右手执蓝色五股金刚杵指地，左手手掌向上置于腹前
7	金刚萨埵	白色，右手持金刚杵，左手结印置腿上	白色，右手旋绕金刚杵，左手执金刚铃
8	金刚王	黄色，右手持金刚钩，左手结印置于腿上	黄色，右手执金刚钩，右手执金刚索，有时双手执金刚钩
9	金刚爱	红色，双手执弓箭	红色，双手执弓和箭

续表 1

编号	名称	壁画描绘	NPY19 记载
10	金刚喜	绿色，双手上举于头侧作弹指状	宝石绿，双手持金刚杵于胸前结印
11	宝生佛	黄色，右手施与愿印，左手禅定印，坐骑为马	黄色，右手持宝施与愿印，左手禅定印，坐骑为马
12	金刚宝	黄色，右手上举指向额上，左手结印置腿上	黄色，右手执宝鬘，左手执金刚铃
13	金刚光	红色，右手持日轮，左手结印置腿上	红色，双手执日轮
14	金刚幢	白色，右手执宝幢，左手结印置腿上	绿色，双手执如意宝幢
15	金刚笑	白色，双手执金刚牙鬘	白色，右手牙鬘金刚杵，左手同右手
16	阿弥陀佛	红色，双手结禅定印，坐骑为孔雀	红色，双手定印，右手执莲花，坐骑为孔雀
17	金刚法	红色，左手执莲花，右手催开状	红色，左手执莲茎，右手催开状
18	金刚利	白色，右手执剑，左手执经书	天蓝色，右手持剑，左手执般若经
19	金刚因	黄色，右手持辐轮，左手置于腿外	黄色，右手结法轮印，左手持八辐轮
20	金刚语	红色，双手于胸前执一物，已残	红色，右手执金刚舌，左手执法螺
21	不空成就佛	深绿色，右手施无畏印，左手结禅定印，坐骑为格鲁达	绿色，右手执羯磨金刚杵结无畏印，左手手掌向上置腹前，坐骑为鹏鸟
22	金刚业	面部为黄色，肩部、腰部及二臂、二腿上部为红色，手、足为黄色	绿色，右手执羯磨十二股金刚杵，左手金刚铃；有时双手执羯磨金刚杵
23	金刚护	黄色，双手持铠甲	黄色，双手持金刚铠甲
24	金刚牙	黑色，双手各执一金刚牙	黑色，双手持金刚犬牙
25	金刚拳	红色，右手于胸前手掌向内，左手置于左腿上	黄色，结金刚拳，执金刚杵
26	金刚嬉	白色，双手金刚拳按于胯上	白色，双手执金刚杵按于胯上
27	金刚鬘	黄色，双手上举执宝鬘	黄色，双手执宝鬘
28	金刚歌	红色，双手执乐器（弦琴？）	红色，双手执琵琶
29	金刚舞	绿色，身体作舞蹈状	绿色，双手舞蹈状
30	弥勒菩萨	白色，右手持金刚杵，左手结印按于胯上	类似阿閦佛
31	不空见菩萨		
32	灭恶趣菩萨		
33	除忧暗菩萨		

续表 2

<table>
<tr><th>编号</th><th>名称</th><th>壁画描绘</th><th>NPY19 记载</th></tr>
<tr><td>34</td><td>香象菩萨</td><td rowspan="4">黄色，右手均执宝珠，左手结印按于胯上</td><td rowspan="4">类似宝生佛</td></tr>
<tr><td>35</td><td>大精进菩萨</td></tr>
<tr><td>36</td><td>虚空藏菩萨</td></tr>
<tr><td>37</td><td>智幢菩萨</td></tr>
<tr><td>38</td><td>无量光菩萨</td><td rowspan="4">红色，右手执莲茎，一朵白莲位于右肩侧，左手结印按于胯上</td><td rowspan="4">类似阿弥陀佛</td></tr>
<tr><td>39</td><td>月光菩萨</td></tr>
<tr><td>40</td><td>贤护菩萨</td></tr>
<tr><td>41</td><td>光网菩萨</td></tr>
<tr><td>42</td><td>金刚藏菩萨</td><td rowspan="4">褐色，右手持交杵金刚，左手结印按于胯上</td><td rowspan="4">类似不空成就佛</td></tr>
<tr><td>43</td><td>无尽意菩萨</td></tr>
<tr><td>44</td><td>辩积菩萨</td></tr>
<tr><td>45</td><td>普贤菩萨</td></tr>
<tr><td>46</td><td>金刚香</td><td>白色，右手执香炉，左手于胸前结印</td><td>白色，执物如其名</td></tr>
<tr><td>47</td><td>金刚华</td><td>黄色，右手持供物，左手结印按于胯上</td><td>黄色，执物如其名</td></tr>
<tr><td>48</td><td>金刚灯</td><td>红色，右手持灯烛，左手于胸前结印</td><td>红白色，执物如其名</td></tr>
<tr><td>49</td><td>金刚涂香</td><td>绿色，右手上举结印，左手执白色海螺</td><td>绿色，执物如其名</td></tr>
<tr><td>50</td><td>金刚钩</td><td>白色，右手执金刚钩</td><td>白色，执物如其名</td></tr>
<tr><td>51</td><td>金刚索</td><td>黄色，右手执绳索</td><td>黄色，执物如其名</td></tr>
<tr><td>52</td><td>金刚链</td><td>红色，右手执链?</td><td>红色，执物如其名</td></tr>
<tr><td>53</td><td>金刚铃</td><td>绿色，右手执金刚铃</td><td>绿色，执物如其名</td></tr>
</table>

西壁南半部分两排绘制六尊像，分别编号为 W1-W6（图 17），其中除了 W6 图像下方没有题记外，其余五尊像均在图像下方写有一排藏文题记。此外，在这六尊像的下方还绘有一排共 9 尊小像，编号为 W7，每尊小像下面均有一则题记，从右至左依次编号为 W7-1 至 W7-9。

这六尊像均结跏趺坐于马蹄形红色大背光内（图 5），背后有靠垫和六拏具装饰的背屏，莲座均为彩色仰覆莲座，莲座下面的基座中央搭有一块 U 形花布，基座两

图 17　西壁南半部壁画

端各有一位狮子。其中 W1-W4 均为佛像造型，身色印契各异，但均着袒右袈裟，两侧各有一位胁侍菩萨（图 43）。W1 身色为白色，右手于胸前施无畏印，左手于腹前结禅定印，根据题记可知该尊像为药师七如来中的第一位：善名称吉祥王如来；W2 身色为深红色，右手下伸施与愿印，左手于腹前结禅定印，根据题记可知该尊像为药师七如来中的威音王如来；W3 身色为黄色，双手于胸前结说法印，根据题记可知该尊像为药师七如来中的金色无垢如来；W4 身色为浅红色，双手结禅定印，根据题记可知为无忧最胜如来。

W5 身色为深红色，一面四臂，头戴三花冠，上身袒露，胸部突出，下身着条纹长裙，主双手于腹前持宝瓶，里面插有三叶植物，另两手分别执金刚杵和经书，根据其图像学特征和题记，可知该尊像为般若佛母。W6 为佛像造型，面部为白色，身体为蓝色，着袒右袈裟，双手于胸前结印，头顶有七蛇围绕，两侧站立有红色、白色两位胁侍菩萨，基座两侧有龙族升起，尽管没有题记，但是根据其鲜明的图像特征可知该尊像为龙尊王佛。

图 18 W1 下方的藏文题记

图 19 W2 下方的藏文题记

各尊像下方的题记转录、翻译如下：

W1 下方的藏文题记（图 18）：

de bzhin g(she)gs[8] pa bdun la phyag vtshal lo //
mtshan gyis [gyi] me tog rgyas pas dag pa la //
dpe byad bzang pos vbru chags mdzes pavi sku //
gang gis mthong thos dran na dpal gyur pavi //
mtshan gyi rgyal po de la phyag vtshal bstod //

译文：礼敬七如来！

妙相华开而清净，随好果严端正身，
见闻忆念获吉祥，名称王佛我赞礼！[9]

W2 下方的藏文题记（图 19）：

rin cen za [rin chen zla] dang pad mas rab brgyan cing //
shes bya kun la mkhas pas mkhyen pas vphags //
rgya mtsho lta bur zab pavi sku mngav ba //
sgra dbyangs rgyal po de la phyag vtshal bstod //

译文：宝月莲华妙庄严，遍知一切所知法，
犹如大海身广博，威音王佛我赞礼！

8 壁面上 she 字已被毁。

9 本文 W1-W4，E1-E4 藏文题记的汉译参考了元代法师沙啰巴译的《药师琉璃光王七佛本愿功德经念诵仪轨供养法》和清代工布查布译的《药师七佛供养仪轨如意王经》中的译文，这两部经均收录于《新修大正大藏经》（以下在叙述该经时均简称《大正藏》）第 19 册，No.926 和 No.927，第 43-45 页和第 61 页。

图 20　W3 下方的藏文题记

图 21　W4 下方的藏文题记

W3 下方的藏文题记（图 20）：

vdzam buvi [vdzam bu chu bovi] [10] gser ltar lham me pa //
nyi ma stong bas lhag pavi vod mngav ba //
dri med gser gyi mchod sdong lta buvi sku //
gser bzangs dri med snang la phyag vtshal bsto [bstod] //

译文：瞻部河金胜光明，威光炽盛超千日，
犹如无垢金塔身，无垢金光我赞礼！

W4 下方的藏文题记（图 21）：

mya ngan vdas zhi bde bavi mchog brnyes nas //
vgro bavi bsdug [sdug] bsngal gdung ba sel mdzad pa //
vgro drug vgon [mgon] dang dpal du gyur pa po //
mya ngan me [med] mchog dpal la phyag vtshal bstod //

译文：永得涅槃胜安乐，消除有情苦恼热，
救护六道具吉祥，无忧最胜我赞礼！

10　此处藏文的偈颂均为每句九字，该句仅有七字，推测为题记书写时的失误，这里根据吐蕃时期大师喜瓦措（zhi ba vtshos，亦即寂护大师）的赞文进行恢复，见 *de bzhin gshegs pa brgyad la bstod pa*（《八如来赞》），收入《中华大藏经〈丹珠尔〉（对勘本）》（藏文）（在下文叙述中均简称为《丹珠尔》），第 1 卷，北京：中国藏学出版社，2006 年，第 709 页。

图 22　W5 下方的藏文题记

图 23　西壁左侧下方的十二天

W5 下方的藏文题记（图 22）：

smra bsams brjod med shes rab pha rold phyind //

ma skyes mi vgag nam khavi [mkhavi] ngo bo nyid //

bcom ldan so so rang rig ye shes spyod yul bavi //

dus gsum rgyal bavi yum la phyag vtshal bstod //

译文：离言思之般若波罗密，无生无遮虚空般自性，

各各自证智慧所缘处，三世诸佛之母我赞礼。

W6 下方无题记。

在上述六尊像的下方有一排九尊小像，每尊小像下方均有一则题记，从右至左分别为：

W7-1：zla ba　月天

W7-2：savi lha mo bstan ma　地天母丹玛

W7-3：dbang ldan　自在天

W7-4：gnod sbyin　药叉天

W7-5：rlung lha　风天

W7-6：chu lha　水天

W7-7：srin pho [po]　罗叉天

W7-8：gshin rje　阎摩天

W7-9：me lha　火天

从题记可知，这一排小像为十二天的前九位（图 23），另有三位绘在与之相邻的南壁右侧下方。各位天神均为一面二臂，骑坐在各自的标志性坐骑身上，他们的图像特征如下表所示。元朝沙啰巴译《药师琉璃光王七佛本愿功德经念诵仪轨供养法》和清朝阿旺扎什补译的《修药师仪轨布坛法》中有对于十二天的描绘，大体可以与壁画绘制的图像进行对比。不过，元朝沙啰巴译本中仅描述了八方天的图像特征，此外还提到了日天月天，为守护十方的天神，但是未提及地天和梵天。清朝译本则提及了十二天。两译本中诸天的方位布置也有所不同，元朝沙啰巴译本从东方天神帝释开始描述，清朝译本也是从帝释天开始，但其方位为东南。本窟的壁画因主要画在南壁和东壁的下方，似乎是按顺时针顺序从南壁下方左侧开始，从日天、梵天、帝释天、火天至月天结束，表 2 编号的 12 号至 1 号。

表 2 西壁、南壁下侧十二天图像特征

编号	名称	壁画描绘的图像特征	《大正藏》No.926 中的记载[11]	《大正藏》No.928 中的记载[12]
1	月天	白色，双手胸前结印，两肩侧各有一轮白色弯月，坐骑为一对红鹅	仅提到名号	鹅座，白色手持月轮
2	地天母丹玛	黄色，双手于胸前捧瓶，坐骑为一头白色的猪？	缺	猪座，黄色二手持瓶
3	自在天	白色，右手执叉，坐骑为一头红色的牛	东北，白色执宝叉，乘坐青色牛王座	牛座，白色持叉
4	药叉天	黄色，右手持棒，左手握吐宝鼠，乘坐黄色宝马	北方，黄色执鼠囊，乘坐青色马王座	西方，马座，黄色持棒
5	风天	绿色，右手执拂尘，乘坐一头白鹿	西北，烟色执彩旗，乘坐绿色大鹿座	西南，鹿座，浅蓝色持风幡
6	水天	白色，双手执蛇索，乘坐摩羯鱼状的水兽	西方，白色执蛇索，乘坐那伽水兽座	水兽座，白色二手持蛇索
7	罗叉天	红色，右手举剑，左手执盾牌，坐骑为一俯跪人体	西南，黑色执宝剑，乘坐大力起尸鬼	起尸座，青色持剑
8	阎摩天	白色，持棒，乘坐一头灰色的水牛	南方，青色执宝杖，乘坐青色水牛座	水牛座，蓝色持棒
9	火天	红色，右手执三叉戟，左手执瓶，乘坐一头红色的公羊	东南，红色执军持，乘坐红色羖羊座	南方山羊座，红色手持火炉
10	帝释天	黄色，右手执金刚杵，乘坐一头白象	东方，黄色执宝杵，乘坐白色大象座	东南象座，白色持杵

11 《大正藏》No.926，沙啰巴译：《药师琉璃光王七佛本愿功德经念诵仪轨供养法》，第 48 页。

12 《大正藏》No.928，阿旺扎什补译：《修药师仪轨布坛法》第 65-66 页。

续表 1

编号	名称	壁画描绘的图像特征	《大正藏》No.926 中的记载	《大正藏》No.928 中的记载
11	梵天	黄色，三面，右手执物不详，乘坐一对白鹅	缺	黄色，右手持宝施与愿印，左手禅定印，坐骑为马
12	日天	已残，仅见身下有一对马，应该为拉车的马	仅提到名号	车座，红色二手擎日轮

三、东壁

东壁的布局同西壁一样，也是北半部绘制一幅曼荼罗，南半部分上下两排共绘有六尊像（图 24）。

东壁南半部的这幅曼荼罗，简报在正文中未进行定名，但是在图片说明中将之命名为“金刚界曼荼罗”[13]，后有学者提出不同意见，认为是“胎藏界曼荼罗”[14]。霍巍教授在对西藏西部新发现的两幅密教曼荼罗进行对比研究时，又将该曼荼罗比定为《恶趣清净怛特罗》中的普明曼荼罗，主尊为普明大日如来[15]。笔者通过将壁画图像与《究竟瑜伽鬘》中记载的图像特征进行比较，将该幅曼荼罗命名为净除恶趣清净曼荼罗[16]，王瑞雷博士经过认真分析，又认为该曼荼罗为恶趣清净系的九佛顶曼荼罗[17]。下面就这两幅曼荼罗中描绘的诸尊图像的身份进行一一辨识并与文献记载相比对（图 25）。

该曼荼罗是一幅标准的圆形宫殿式曼荼罗，共绘制有 37 尊像。画面正中央绘制释迦如来（1），文献中称为“释迦狮子大日如来”（Shākya seng ge rnam par snang mdzad）[18]，身色为金色，高肉髻顶上有宝珠庄严，比较引人注目的是佛像的肉髻前面还戴有花冠，这也许正是文献中命名为“释迦狮子大日如来”的原因所在，将释迦牟尼佛像和大日如来像的特点结合在了一起，双手于胸前作转法轮印，身着袒右袈裟，袈裟的领口、袖口和裤边饰有一道白边，结跏趺坐，身有白色的头光和褐色卷草纹的靠背，靠背后还有金翅鸟、摩羯鱼、狮羊和大象装饰的背龛，宝座为狮子莲花座。围绕着中央的释迦如来像有两重八朵莲瓣，内重的八朵莲瓣中各绘有一个三昧耶宝，东南西北四个方位分别为：金刚杵、宝珠、莲花和交杵金刚，分别象征着心、宝、法、

13 前引霍巍：《西藏阿里札达县帕尔嘎尔布石窟遗址》。
14 罗炤：《关于西藏帕尔嘎尔布石窟的一幅壁画》，《文物》2004 年第 11 期，第 86 页。
15 霍巍：《对西藏西部新发现的两幅密教曼荼罗壁画的初步考释》，《文物》2007 年第 6 期，第 43-48 页。
16 前引张长虹：《西藏阿里帕尔嘎尔布石窟的两幅曼荼罗图像及相关问题研究》。
17 王瑞雷：《敦煌、西藏西部早期恶趣清净曼荼罗图像探析》，《故宫博物院院刊》2014 年第 5 期，第 81-98 页。
18 NPY22：357。

图 24　东壁壁画

图 25　东壁北半部净除恶趣清净曼荼罗的图像配置和编号

图 26　净除恶趣清净曼荼罗的中央部分

图 27　净除恶趣清净曼荼罗的左下角

图 28　净除恶趣清净曼荼罗的左上角

图 29　净除恶趣清净曼荼罗的右上角

图 30　净除恶趣清净曼荼罗的右下角

业四金刚波罗蜜女；四维绘制四个不同形制的宝珠。外重的八朵莲瓣中绘制八大佛顶（2-9），从下方的东方开始，按顺时针方向先是东、南、西、北四方，然后是四维的顺序进行排列。八大佛顶的造型类似，均头戴花冠，上身袒露，下身着短裙或腰间系带，佩戴耳环、项链、胸链、臂钏、手镯、脚镯等装饰，半跏趺坐于龛形的大背光内（图 26）。中央主尊和八大佛顶的图像描绘，除宝佛顶的身色与文献记载不同外，其余诸尊的身色和执物均与文献记载一致（表 2）。

在第一重方城的四角绘制的是内四供养女神（10-13），造型相似，均呈四分之三侧面朝向中央主尊，均头戴花冠，冠后黑发挽髻并披散在两肩，上身袒露，胸部女性特征突出，下身穿短裙或腰间系带，佩戴耳环、项链、胸链、臂钏、手镯、脚镯等装饰，呈半跏趺坐，身后也均有头光、靠背和大身光，但是四女神的身色和手势各不相同（图 27-30）。

图 31　净除恶趣清净曼荼罗的外城南门

在第一、第二重方城之间，城门的两侧各绘有两尊菩萨，共计有十六尊，为十六贤劫菩萨（14-29）。这十六尊贤劫菩萨的造型相似，也是均呈四分之三侧面朝向中央主尊，均头戴花冠，冠后黑发束成高髻，上身袒露，下身穿短裙或腰间系带，佩戴耳环、项链、胸链、臂钏、手镯、脚镯等装饰，身后有头光和靠背，半跏趺坐于龛形大身光内

图 32　净除恶趣清净曼荼罗的外城西门

（图 27-32）。幸运的是，文献中对这十六尊菩萨的身色和手中执物均有详细描述，并且定名除甘露光菩萨外（在金刚界曼荼罗中为无量光菩萨），其余诸尊均与金刚界曼荼罗中十六菩萨的名字一致，因此我们能够对照文献对这十六尊菩萨的身份进行一一辨识，并且能够为我们辨识前述金刚界曼荼罗中十六尊菩萨的身份和排列顺序提供参考。这十六尊菩萨中，除智幢菩萨、贤护菩萨和普贤菩萨的身色与文献记载不一致外，其余诸尊菩萨的图像描绘基本与文献记载相吻合（参见表 2）。

第二重方城的四角绘制外四供养女神（30-33），造型特征同内四供养女神类似，只是身色和手中执物有区别（图 27-30），图像学的表现与文献记载相吻合，只是文献描述中，华女和香女的顺序进行了互换。

在外城墙中央的四方城门处，各站立有一位摄护菩萨（34-37），均呈忿怒相，一面三目二臂二足，头戴三花冠，冠后橙色焰发高束，上身袒露，佩有各种装饰，下身穿虎皮短裙（图 31-32）。除金刚索的身色与文献描述不符外，其余诸尊的图像描绘均与文献记载相符。

表 3 东壁净除恶趣清净曼荼罗诸尊图像与《究竟瑜伽鬘》第 22 章中的描述对照一览表

编号	名称	壁画	NPY22 记载
1	释迦狮子大日如来	一面二臂，金色，说法印	金色，转法轮印
2	金刚佛顶	白色，右手不详 ，左手禅定印	白色，触地印
3	宝佛顶	白色，右手施愿印，左手禅定印	蓝色，施愿印
4	莲花佛顶	红色，双手禅定印	红色，禅定印
5	羯磨佛顶	绿色，右手无畏印，左手禅定印	绿色，无畏印
6	光明佛顶	白中略泛红，右手持红日，左手置髋部	红白色，右手执日轮，左手按于胯上
7	宝幢佛顶	红色，右手执宝幢，左手于胸前结印	红黑色，双手执宝幢
8	利佛顶	蓝色，右手执剑，左手于胸前结印	蓝色，右手执剑，左手执经书
9	白伞盖佛顶	白色，右手执伞，左手置髋部	白色，双手执伞
10	金刚嬉	白色，双手按于胯上，手中执物不详	白色
11	金刚鬘	黄色，双手执宝鬘	黄色
12	金刚歌	红色，双手执弦琴?	红色
13	金刚舞	绿色，身体作舞蹈状	双手作各种姿势
14	弥勒菩萨	黄色，右手执花茎，一朵龙树花开在右肩外侧，左手持净瓶	黄色，右手执龙树花，左手持净瓶
15	不空见菩萨	黄色，右手执花茎，一朵带把儿球状花开在右肩外侧，左手金刚拳按于胯上	黄色，右手执莲，莲上有目，左手金刚拳按于胯上
16	灭恶趣菩萨	白色，双手执金刚钩	白色，双手执金刚钩
17	除忧暗菩萨	白色，右手执棒，左手金刚拳按于胯上	白色，右手执棒，左手金刚拳按于胯上
18	香象菩萨	白色，右手执物不详，左手金刚拳按于胯上	白绿色，右手执芳香海螺碗，左手金刚拳按于胯上
19	大精进菩萨	白色，右手执剑，左手金刚拳按于胯上	白色，右手执剑，左手金刚拳按于胯上
20	虚空藏菩萨	白色，右手执花茎，一朵白莲开在右肩外侧，上面置经书，左手金刚拳按于胯上	白黄色，右手执莲花法藏，左手金刚拳按于胯上
21	智幢菩萨	白色，右手执宝幢，左手结金刚拳按于胯上	蓝色，右手执如意宝幢，左手金刚拳按于胯上
22	甘露光菩萨	白色，双手捧净瓶	白色，右手持甘露瓶，左手金刚拳按于胯上

续表 1

编号	名称	壁画	NPY22 记载
23	月光菩萨	白色，右手拈花茎，一朵白莲开在右肩外侧，上面置弯月，左手金刚拳按于胯上	白色，右手执莲花月，左手金刚拳按于胯上
24	贤护菩萨	粉红色，右手执火焰宝珠，左手金刚拳按于胯上	白色，右手执焰宝，左手金刚拳按于胯上
25	光网菩萨	红色，右手执花茎，一朵白莲开在右肩外侧，上置宝珠，左手金刚拳按于胯上	红色，右手金刚拳，左手金刚拳按于胯上
26	金刚藏菩萨	白色略泛灰，右手于胸前拈花茎，一朵白优钵罗花开在右肩外侧，上面横置金刚杵，左手金刚拳按于胯上	蓝灰色，右手执蓝色优钵罗花，花上有金刚杵，左手金刚拳按于胯上
27	无尽意菩萨	白色，双手捧净瓶	白色，双手执甘露瓶
28	辩积菩萨	粉红色，右手执白球状物，上置宝珠，左手金刚拳按于胯上	红色，右手执水生宝积，左手金刚拳按于胯上
29	普贤菩萨	灰黑色，右手于胸前结印，左手金刚拳按于胯上	金色，右手执穗，左手金刚拳按于胯上
30	金刚香	白色，右手于胸前结印，左手执香炉	黑色
31	金刚华	黄色，右手于胸前结印，左手持供物	白色
32	金刚灯	粉红色，右手执灯烛，左手于胸前结印	红色
33	金刚涂香	深绿色，右手上举，左手执白海螺	绿色
34	金刚钩	白色，右手执金刚钩，左手于胸前结印	白色，双手执金刚钩
35	金刚索	深褐色，右手执羂索，左手于胸前结期克印	蓝色，又手执羂索
36	金刚链	红色，双手执锁链	红色，双手执锁链
37	金刚铃	绿色，右手执金刚铃，左手于胸前结期克印	绿色，双手执金刚铃

通过对壁画的描绘和文献的记载进行对比，我们可以发现，除极少数图像在身色、印契上略有差异，绝大部分壁画图像的描绘符合文献的记载。

东壁南半部同西壁南半部两两相对，也绘制两排六尊像，分别编号为 E1-E6，每尊像的下方均有一行藏文题记。此外，在这六尊像的左侧有一竖排小像，共七尊，编号为 E7-1 至 E7-7，仅上面两尊有题记；在这六尊像的下方也有一排小像，共十二尊，编号为 E8-1 至 E8-12，像下无题记（图 33）。

E1-E4 均结跏趺坐于马蹄形红色大背光内，着袒右袈裟，两侧各有一位胁侍菩萨，背后有靠垫和六拏具装饰的背屏，莲座均为彩色仰覆莲座，莲座下面的基座中央搭有一块 U 形花布，基座两端各有一位狮子，同 W1-W4 的造型相同，只是身色印契各异，是药师七如来中的后面三位和释迦牟尼如来。E1 身色为白色，双手于胸前结说法印，根据题记可知该尊像为药师七如来中的第五位：法海雷音如来。E2 身色为深红色，右手于胸前施无畏印，左手于腹前结禅定印，为药师七如来中的第六位：神通王如来；E3 身色为蓝色，右手于膝前施与愿印，手捏药诃子，左手结禅定印持钵，为药王如来；E4 身色为黄色，右手施触地印，左手结禅定印，是释迦牟尼如来。这四位如来和西壁的四位如来一起共同构成药师八如来（图 43）。

E5 身色为白色，一面四臂，头戴三花冠，上身袒露，下身着花布短裙，主双手于胸前合什，另两手分别执念珠和莲花，背后有红色的头光和背光，再后有三叶拱形的蓝色背景，象征岩窟，周边有几何形的山、树环绕，两侧各有一位跪坐的胁侍。根据其图像学特征和题记，可知该尊像为四臂观音（图 34）。E6 身色为绿色，头戴花

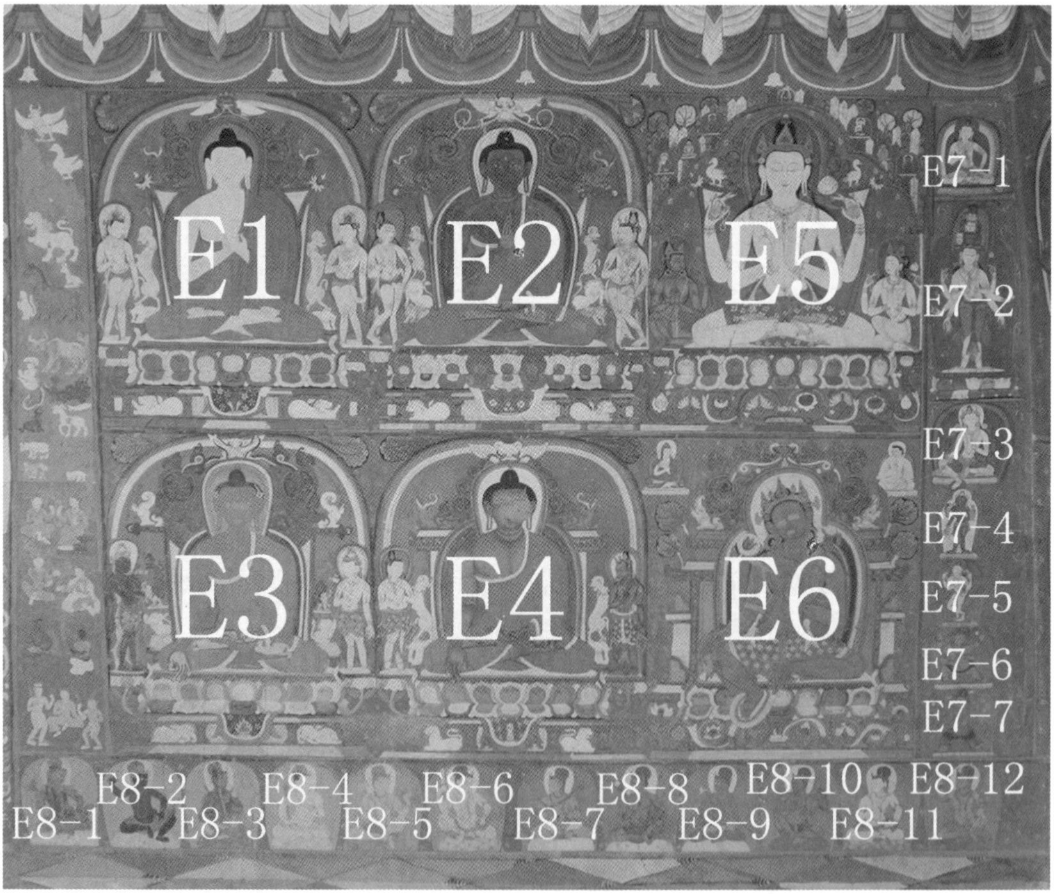

图 33　东壁南半部壁画

图 34　四臂观音

图 35　绿度母

冠，上身袒露，胸部突出，右手外伸，自然地搭在右膝上，执花茎，左手于胸前结印执花茎，根据其鲜明的图像特征和题记可知该尊像为绿度母（图 35）。

各尊像下面的题记转录、翻译如下：

E1 下方的藏文题记（图 36）：

chos sgra chen pos pha rol rgol ba vjoms //

rgya mtsho lta bur zab pavi sku mngav zhing //

vgro bavi dug gsum ma lus sel mdzad pavi //

chos grags rgya mtshovi dbyangs la phyag vtshal bstod //

译文：广大法音破彼难，如海甚深威德身，

悉除众生三种毒，法扬海音我赞礼！

E2 下方的藏文题记（图 37）：

chos kyi blo gros gting pag [dpag] dkav bavi tshul //

图 36　E1 下方的藏文题记

图 37　E2 下方的藏文题记

图 38　E3 下方的藏文题记

rnam dag chos kyi dbyings la rol mdzad cing //
shes bya ma lus mngon gsum [sum] gzigs pa po //
mkhyen pavi rgyal po de la phyag vtshal bstod //
译文：不可测量法之慧，清净法界而游戏，
　　　能观一切所知法，神通王佛我赞礼。

E3 下方的藏文题记（图 38）：
vgro bavi (nad)[19] gso mdzad bavi sman pavi mchog //
be tu rya [bai ḍūr ya] ltar dang bavi sku mngav zhing //
skuvi [sku yi] vod kyis vgro ba sgrol mdzad pa //
sman pavi rgyal po de la phyag vtshal bstod //
译文：能除众疾最胜药，如同琉璃纯净身，
　　　身光照耀度众生，药王如来我赞礼。

19　壁画题记中的 nad 因为涂抹已模糊不可辨，这里根据吐蕃时期喜瓦措大师的赞文进行了恢复，见 *de bzhin gshegs pa brgyad la bstod pa*（《八如来赞》），《丹珠尔》第 1 卷，第 710 页。

图 39　E4 下方的藏文题记

图 40　E5 下方的藏文题记

图 41　E6 下方的藏文题记

E4 下方的藏文题记（图 39）：

nyi mavi mnyen [gnyen] gyur bde gshegs vgro bavi mgon //
srid pa gsum gyi mchog vgyur [gyur] lhavi lha //
shag [shā] kyavi rgyal po bcom ldan mivi [mi yi] mgon //
thub pa rab mdzes khyed la phyag vtshal bstod //

译文：日友善逝众生主，殊胜三有天中天，
　　　人主释迦王世尊，端严牟尼我赞礼。

E5 下方的藏文题记（图 40）：

vphags pa spyan ras gzigs dbang phyug vjig rten gsum gyi mgon //
gzhan la phan phyir brtson bavi go cha rnams [bsnams] //
thugs rjevi rang bzhin dri med dkyil vkhor zhal //
vgro bavi bsdug [sdug] bsngal sel la phyag vtshal bstod //

译文：圣观自在三世主，为利他持精进甲，
　　　慈悲自性无垢相，除众生苦我赞礼！

图 42-1　东壁下方的十二药叉大将（E8-1 至 8-6）

图 42-2　东壁下方的十二药叉大将（E8-7 至 8-12）

E6 下方的藏文题记（图 41）：

lha dang lha min cod pan gyis //
zhabs gnyis pad ma la btud de //
vphongs po kun las sgrol mdzad pavi //
sgrol ma yum la phyag vtshal lo //

译文：天及非天以顶冠，礼敬至尊二足莲，
　　　一切困厄尽救度，救度之母我赞礼！

在 E5 和 E6 的右侧，还绘有一竖排小像，共有七尊，将这部分内容编号为 E7-1 至 E7-7，其中只有最上方的两尊像下面写有藏文题记，分别为：

E7-1：rdo rje sems dpav　金刚菩萨

E7-2：zhal bcu gcig ba la phyag vtshal lo //　礼敬十一面（观音）。

从题记可知，第一位和第二位分别为金刚萨埵菩萨和十一面观音，从图像特征可知第六位为马头金刚，一面四臂，身红色，头顶升起一颗马头。

在 E1-E6 这六尊像的下方，如同 W1-W6 的下方一样，也绘有一排小像，但共有 12 尊，且没有题记，将这部分内容从左至右依次编号 E8-1 至 E8-12（图 33）。根据文献记载，结合壁画描绘的图像特征，可知这十二尊为十二药叉大将，系守护药师佛所立十二誓愿的十二神将（图 42）。在元朝沙啰巴译本和清朝译本中均对这十二药叉大将进行了图像描述，不过关于这十二药叉的名字，元朝沙啰巴译本用的是音译，清朝工布查布和阿旺扎什译本用的意译[20]。这十二药叉大将“右手各结自印当胸，左手皆持宝鼠，口吐宝珠，众宝庄严，身著天衣，腹大体胖，形相可畏，皆犹帝王游戏而坐”[21]。结合文献记载，笔者对这十二位药叉大将的身份进行了一一辨认，其识读顺序应该为从左至右，与编号顺序一致。

表 4　东壁下方十二药叉大将图像特征

编号	名称	壁画描绘的图像特征	《大正藏》No.926 中的记载[22]	《大正藏》No.928 中的记载[23]
1	宫毗罗（极畏药叉大将）Khumbīra	已褪色，右手执宝珠？左手握吐宝鼠	黄色执宝杵	黄色持杵
2	跋折罗（金刚药叉大将）Vajra	红色，右手执宝剑，左手握吐宝鼠	白色执宝剑	青色持剑
3	迷企罗（执严药叉大将）Mihira	黄色，右手执棒，左手握吐宝鼠	黄色执宝棒	黄色持棒
4	安底罗（执星药叉大将）Andīra	白色，右手执棒，左手握吐宝鼠	绿色执宝槌	浅蓝色持棒
5	额你罗（执风药叉大将）Anila	红色，右手执三股叉，左手握吐宝鼠	红色执宝叉	红色持三股叉
6	珊底罗（居处药叉大将）Śāṇḍilya	白色，右手执剑，左手握吐宝鼠	烟色执宝剑	烟色持剑
7	因陀罗（执力药叉大将）Indra	红色，右手执棒，左手握吐宝鼠	红色执宝棍	红色持棒
8	波夷罗（执饮药叉大将）Pajra	黄色，右手执槌，左手握吐宝鼠	红色执宝槌	黄色持棒
9	摩虎罗（执言药叉大将）Mahoraga	蓝色，右手执斧，左手握吐宝鼠	白色执宝斧	黄色持斧
10	真达罗（执想药叉大将）Sindūra	黄色，右手执羂索，左手握吐宝鼠	黄色执羂索	黄色持索
11	招住罗（执动药叉大将）Catura	白色，右手执槌，左手握吐宝鼠	青色执宝槌	蓝色持棒
12	毗羯罗（圆作药叉大将）Vikarala	红色，右手指环扣一小圆轮，左手握吐宝鼠	红色执宝轮	红色持轮

20（元）沙啰巴译《药师琉璃光王七佛本愿功德经念诵仪轨供养法》中将十二药叉大将译为：宫毗罗、跋折罗、迷企罗、安底罗、额你罗、珊底罗、因陀罗、波夷罗、摩虎罗、真达罗、招住罗、毗羯罗，见《大正藏》No.926，第 47 页。（清）工布查布译《药师七佛供养仪轨如意王经》中将十二药叉大将译为：极畏药叉大将、金刚药叉大将、执严药叉大将、执星药叉大将、执风药叉大将、居处药叉大将、执力药叉大将、执饮药叉大将、执言药叉大将、执想药叉大将、执动药叉大将、圆作药叉大将，见《大正藏》No.927，第 51 页。（清）阿旺扎什补译《修药师仪轨布坛法》中沿用了工布查布的译名，见《大正藏》No.928，第 65 页。

21（清）阿旺扎什补译：《修药师仪轨布坛法》，《大正藏》No.928，第 65 页。

22（元）沙啰巴译：《药师琉璃光王七佛本愿功德经念诵仪轨供养法》，《大正藏》No.926，第 47 页。

23 阿旺扎什补译：《修药师仪轨布坛法》，《大正藏》No.928，第 65 页。

图 43　八药师佛

在元朝沙啰巴译《药师琉璃光王七佛本愿功德经念诵仪轨供养法》和清朝阿旺扎什补译的《修药师仪轨布坛法》中，对药师八如来的图像特征也有记载，与壁画描绘的图像相比较后可以发现，尽管藏传佛教的图像学相对比较保守，少有变化，但是这八位如来中有四位的身色发生了变化，壁画为我们保存了流行于西藏西部地区的一个早期版本（图 43）。

表 5　药师八如来的图像特征

编号	名称	壁画描绘的图像特征	《大正藏》No.926 中的记载[24]	《大正藏》No.928 中的记载[25]
W1	善名称吉祥王如来	白色，右手施无畏印，左手结禅定印	黄色无威印	北方，黄色，右手施无畏印，左手正定印

24　元朝沙啰巴译《药师琉璃光王七佛本愿功德经念诵仪轨》中八如来的名字译为：善名称吉祥王佛、宝月智严光音自在王佛、金色宝光妙行成就佛、无忧最胜吉祥王佛、法海雷音佛、法海胜慧游戏神通佛、药师琉璃光王佛、本师释迦牟尼佛。《大正藏》No.925，第 34 页。清朝工布查布译《药师七佛供养仪轨如意王经》中八如来的名号为：善名称吉祥王如来、宝月莲花智严威音王如来、金色无垢宝光妙行成就如来、无忧最胜吉祥如来、法海雷音如来、法海胜慧游戏神通如来、药师琉璃光王如来、释迦牟尼如来。《大正藏》No.927，第 50 页。

25《大正藏》No.928，阿旺扎什补译：《修药师仪轨布坛法》，第 65 页。

续表 1

编号	名称	壁画描绘的图像特征	《大正藏》No.926 中的记载	《大正藏》No.928 中的记载
W2	威音王如来	红色，右手施与愿印，左手结禅定印	黄色施妙印	南方，黄色，右手施愿印，左手正定印
W3	金色无垢如来	黄色，双方结说法印	黄色说法印	东南，黄色，二手说法印
W4	无忧最胜如来	浅红色，双手结禅定印	红色三昧印	西方，浅红色，二手等持印
E1	法海雷音如来	白色，双手结说法印	白色说法印	西南，浅红色，二手说法印
E2	神通王如来	红色，右手施无畏印，左手禅定印	青色说法印	西北，红色，右手施愿印，左手正定印
E3	药师璃璃光如来	蓝色，右手施与愿印捏诃子，左手禅定印持钵	青色施妙印	东北，蓝色，右手施愿印,持阿噜喇果（即诃子），手左正定印，上安钵盂
E4	释迦牟尼佛	黄色，右手触地印，左手禅定印	黄色说法印	东方，黄色，右手镇地印，左手正定印

四、南壁

南壁中央开有窟门，窟门两侧及上方均绘有壁画（图 44），其中窟门左侧共绘有两排四尊像，下方有一排供物和供养人；窟门右侧共绘有上下两尊像，下方绘有一排三尊小像，是十二天中的三位；门楣上方也绘有一排壁画，但残毁严重，仅存少许。本文该壁的壁画按分布的不同单元分别编号为 S1 至 S9（图 45）。

S1 身色为红色，一面四臂，头戴双层花冠，上身袒露，佩有各种装饰，主右手上举执剑，主左手于胸前执乌波罗花茎，白色的乌波罗花开在肩左侧，花蕊中央有宝剑，上面横置经书，另两只手分别执箭和弓。下身穿有碎花短裤，结跏趺坐于仰覆莲座上，莲座下在基座底端有一排藏文题记（图 46），题记中称其执持剑、弓、箭，与壁画描绘吻合。该尊为真实名文殊。

S1 下方的藏文题记（图 47）：

shes rab ral gri mdav gzhuv thogs //

nyon mongs mi shes g·yul ngo sel //

dpav bo bdud sgra [dgra] bdud vdul ba //

图 44　南壁壁画

图 45　南壁壁画

图 46　南壁的真实名文殊 S1

图 47　S1 下方的藏文题记

bdud bzhivi vjigs pa sel par byed //
ye shes dpav che la phyag vtshal bstod //
译文：执持智慧剑弓箭，破除烦恼贼和军，
英雄能降魔和敌，四魔苦难尽除去，
智慧大勇我赞礼！

S2 身色为蓝色，一面二臂，头戴三花冠，桔色头发用小蛇束系，面相忿怒威猛，额上有第三只眼，眼睛和嘴巴均被毁。上身袒露，佩有耳环、项链、臂钏、腕饰等各种装饰，右手上举执金刚杵，左手于胸前执铃，腰系虎皮围裙，双腿粗短，左展姿站立于覆莲座上，莲座下的基座底端有一排藏文题记（图 48），题记中称其“力大无比极忿怒”“执金刚”，与壁画描绘吻合，为金刚手。

S2 下方的藏文题记（图 49）：
stobs po che la drag shul che //
rigs [rig] sngags rgyal po dge ba po //
vdul dkav mthav dag vdul mdzad pavi //
rdo rje snams la phyag vtshal bstod //
译文：力大无比极忿怒，真正妙善明咒王，
调伏一切难调者，执金刚者我赞礼！

文殊菩萨的下方为一尊印度成就者的形象（S3），身色为深褐色，黑色的头发呈波浪状盘于头顶，双手于胸前结印，双腿交叉，全身赤裸，仅在交叉的双腿处缠绕以白布（图 50）。题记中称其为“米帕衮波”（mi pham mgon po），这是希解派创始人、印度大成就者帕当巴桑结（pha dam pa sangs rgyas, ?-1117 年）的别名之一[26]。他的典型形象特征是肤色呈黑色（文字描述为黑色，绘画一般为深褐色），除下半身缠绕以布帛外，全身赤裸[27]，题记中亦描述为“大黑”（nag po chen po），因此从题记及形象两方面均可判定该尊形象即为帕当巴桑结。

26 chos kyi seng ge，*pha dam pa dang ma cig lab sgron gyi rnam thar*，西宁：青海民族出版社，1994 年，第 14 页。
27 关于帕当巴图像特征的分析，见 Dan Martin, “Padampa Sangye: A History of Representation of a South Indian Siddha in Tibet”，收录于 *Holy Madness: Portrait of Tantric Siddhas*, ed. Rob Linrothe. New York, Rubin Museum of Art, 2006, pp.108-123。

图 48　南壁的金刚手 S2

图 49　S2 下方的藏文题记

图 50　南壁的帕当巴桑结 S3

图 51　S3 下方的藏文题记

图 52　南壁的大黑天 S4

图 53　S4 下方的藏文题记

S3 下方的藏文题记（图 51）：
nag po chen po gzi mdangs can //
smra bavi seng ge grags pa che //
vdzam bu gling gi rgyan cig po //
mi pham mgon po khyed la phyag vtshal bstod //
译文：大黑风采光华具，言如狮子声名传，
赡部洲之一庄严，米帕衮波我赞礼！

金刚手的下方为一尊蓝色身、一面四臂的怒相护法神的形象（S4），头戴骷髅花冠，桔色头发上有小蛇，面相忿怒，眼睛和嘴巴被毁；上身袒露佩有各种装饰和断头大花环，主双手于胸前执颅骨碗和剥皮刀，另两手上举执剑和三叉戟，腰系虎皮裙，游戏坐于人魔身上，是典型的四臂大黑天的形象（图 52）。仰覆莲座下的基座底端有题记，题记中称其为"善逝慈悲化身之众生怙主"（bder gshegs thugs rjes sprul pavi // sems can rnams la mgon skyabs mdzad //）（图 53）。

S4 下方的藏文题记：（图 53）
hūṃ bder gshegs thugs rjes spruld pavi //
sems can rnams la vgon [mgon] skyabs mdzad //
vog min gnas na bzhugs pa la //
rab tu btud de phyag vtshal bstod // [28]
译文：善逝慈悲幻化身，有情众生依怙业，
居于色究竟天处，极其恭敬赞礼您！

窟门右侧仅绘有一排上下两位主尊神，编号为 S5、S6，由于雨水的冲刷，已经部分残毁，题记也所剩不多，且模糊不易识读。S5 身色为蓝色，三面六臂四足，六只手中主双手于胸前执颅骨碗和金刚杵，最上两手扯白色人皮，另一只左手外伸执金刚橛，另一只右手执物已残，佩戴有断头花环和骷髅冠，身后有翅膀，腰系虎皮裙，四只脚下踩踏蓝色男魔和白色女魔，该像为金刚橛，亦称为普巴金刚。S6 位于 S5 下方，身色为红色，一面二臂，左手上举执长棒，右手外伸作期克印，桔色的焰发中升出有绿色马头，因此该尊为马头金刚（图 54）。

28　该句 vtshal 和 bstod 之间有较长空隙，系写错之后的涂抹，与 N1 的情况一样。

图 54 南壁左侧的金刚橛和马头金刚

S5 下方的藏文题记仅存后半句：

……[rdo rje] zhon [gzhon] nuvi sku la phyag vtshal bstod

……金刚童子身我赞礼。

S6 下方的题记已经大多已不可识读（图 55）：

……klu gya……dbang che……brdzod[?] pavi //

khro da ……vgrin[?] khyed la phyag vtshal bstod //

在 S6 的下方还绘有三尊神，从右至左依次编号为 S7-1 至 S7-3，其中 S7-3 因雨水的冲刷，已残毁殆尽，如前文所述，根据图像组合，该尊应为十二天中的日天，另两尊分别为帝释天和梵天，像下有题记（图 55），图像特征和辨识参见前文关于西壁下方十二天的图像描述。

图 55　S6 和 S7 下方的藏文题记

图 56　门楣上方 S8 左起前二尊像

图 57　南壁左侧下方 S9 的供养人像

S7-1：brgya byin　　帝释天

S7-2：tshangs pa [？]　　梵天

在门楣的上方可辨残存有六尊形象，均骑乘不同的动物，将该部分编号为 S8。其中左起第一尊和右起第一尊的题记尚存，右起第二尊的题记仅存部分，分别为：re ma ti（热玛蒂）、dgra bla dmag（札拉玛）、……chen mo（大……女），应为地方保护神（图 56）。从早期的东嘎 1、2 号窟开始，西藏阿里地区即有在门楣上方绘制此类地方保护神的传统。

南壁在窟门左侧大黑天像的下方有一排五位供养人的形象，均有题记，从左至右分别为：grub gsal shes rab、grub mdzes shes rab、dge tshul slob bu、dpal ldan vgon、chos nyid mdzes，可译为珠色喜饶、珠则喜饶、格楚洛布、贝丹衮、却尼则（图 57）。

五、小结

通过以上对各壁图像的辨识和题记的转录、翻译，我们大致可以了解整个石窟的图像程序（图 58）。该窟主壁原先主供主尊是一尊泥塑像，尽管现在已经佚失，但是从其两胁侍菩萨——弥勒、文殊或许可以推断原选的主尊是释迦牟尼佛。主尊两侧绘制有四位上师像，四位上师的两侧及头顶两侧还各绘有一列小像，系祖师传承系列，应该是该窟功德主的上师的师承序列。

东西壁两两相对各绘制了一幅曼荼罗和八药师佛以及般若佛母、龙尊王佛、四臂观音和绿度母。这一对曼荼罗为金刚界曼荼罗和净除恶趣清净曼荼罗，这一对曼荼罗在西藏西部 11-12 世纪的石窟和寺院中非常常见，金刚界曼荼罗出现最早，在聂拉康、塔波寺主殿、东嘎 1 号窟均有发现，净除恶趣清净曼荼罗发现于东嘎 3 号窟、卡俄普石窟等。可以说，曼荼罗是西藏西部早期石窟壁画的主要题材[29]。如阿里札达县的东嘎 1 号窟，整窟绘制了七幅曼荼罗[30]；卡俄普石窟的三个壁面均各绘制一大幅曼荼罗[31]；阿契寺杜康殿各壁共绘制了六幅不同的曼荼罗[32]，等等。在这座石窟东西两壁各绘制一幅曼荼罗的做法显然是该地区前期传统的延续，不过曼荼罗题材的地位有所

29 关于西藏西部石窟壁画的几个主要发展阶段，参见霍巍：《西藏西部石窟壁画中几种艺术风格的分析——兼论西藏西部石窟壁画艺术三个主要的发展阶段》，霍巍、李永宪主编：《西藏考古与艺术国际学术讨论会论文集》，成都：四川人民出版社，2004 年，第 245-273 页。

30 霍巍、李永宪：《西藏阿里东嘎、皮央石窟考古调查简报》，《文物》1997 年第 9 期。

31 霍巍：《西藏阿里札达县象泉河流域卡俄普与西林衮石窟地点的初步调查》，《文物》2007 年第 6 期。

32 Pratapaditya Pal & Lionel Fournier, *A Buddhist Paradise, The Murals of Alchi Western Himalayas*, Basel, 1982.

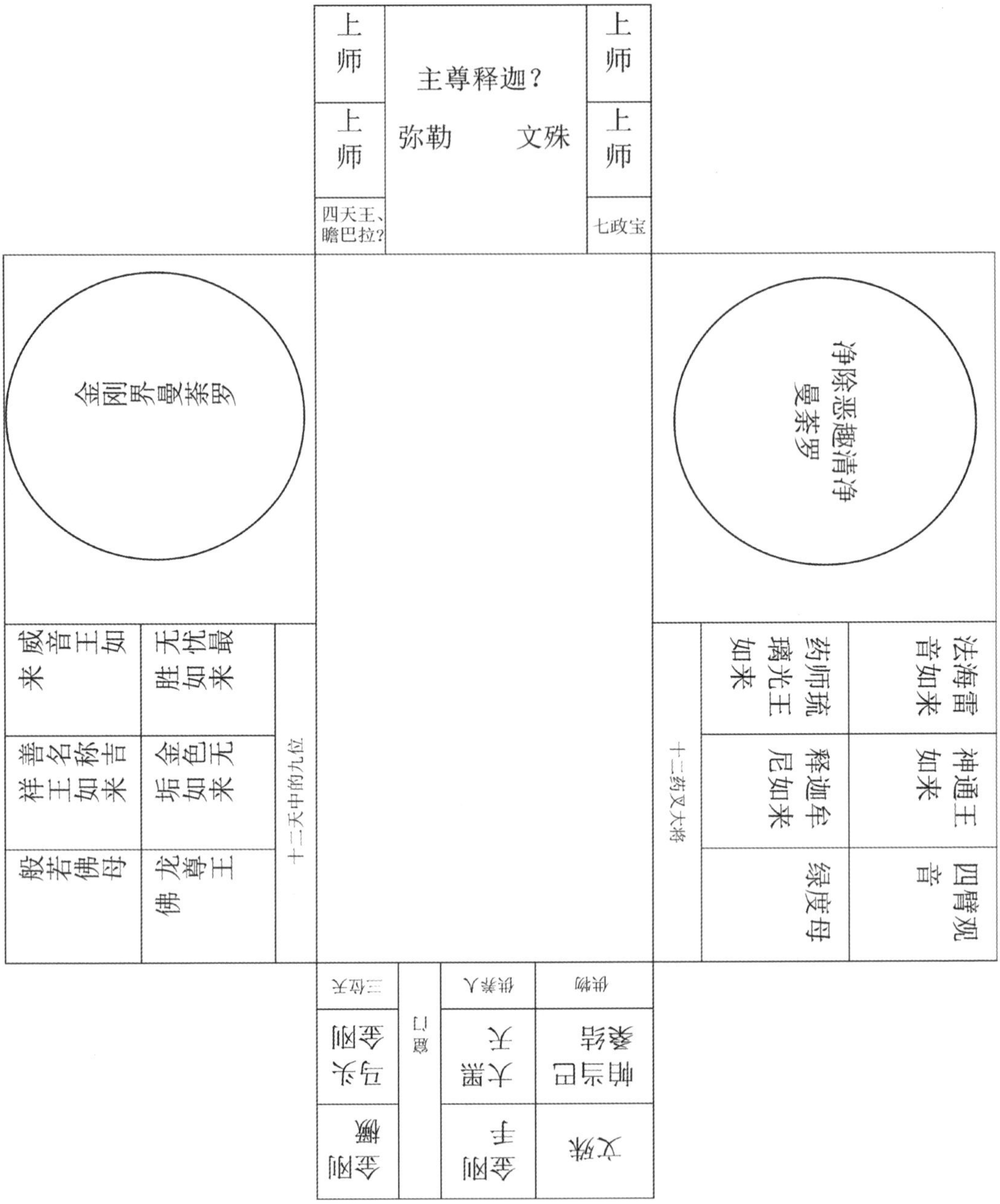

图 58　石窟图像配置示意图

弱化，不再成为主导石窟的主要题材。

东西壁绘制的八位药师佛是西藏西部地区这一时期出现的新题材，彰显了石窟壁画题材和风格的转变。八位药师佛的图像特征鲜明，每一位均配有两位胁侍菩萨，有偈颂体赞颂题记，并且组合完备，十二诸天、十二药叉大将均有清楚完整的描绘。

从这一时期开始，药师佛成为整个藏文化区比较流行的一种题材，在拉达克地区、西夏故城、河西地区等都发现有药师佛的题材，其肇始可能与古格王室的信仰有关[33]。但是八药师佛与般若佛母、龙尊王佛、四臂观音和绿度母的组合配置显得十分独特而新颖，似乎是这一地区比较典型的一种图像组合，其出现的原因还需要进一步的深入探讨。不过，这种组合似乎并未持续多久，在与该窟题材、风格非常类似的邦察石窟以及晚期的科迦寺、查宗贡巴中[34]，龙尊王佛则消失不见，被佛顶尊胜佛母所替代，显然这种组合持续的时间更长，成为藏西比较常见的题材之一。

南壁除了文殊菩萨和帕当巴桑结，其他四位均为忿怒相的护法神，金刚手、大黑天、金刚橛和马头金刚，这四位尊神均是藏传佛教中非常著名的护法神。值得注意的是希解派创始人帕当巴桑结形象的出现，反映出西藏西部地区 13 至 14 世纪宗教派别流传的复杂情况，还需要更多更深入的研究。

关于这些题材出现的原因还可以从其功能来探讨。净除恶趣清净曼荼罗具有超度亡者、净除恶趣、往生善趣天界等功能；供养药师佛能够断绝苦恼病患、远离恶道地狱，解脱轮回苦难。 考虑到本窟中出现的上师题记和供养人题记，推测该窟可能是供养人珠色喜饶、珠则喜饶、格楚洛布、贝丹衮、却尼则等为纪念其亡逝的根本上师而建，这位根本上师即为正壁壁画右侧下方的那位（N4），他的上师又为喇嘛色哇沃塞。

综上所述，本窟所绘制的壁画及其题记，为研究这一时期西藏西部的宗教史、艺术史提供了丰富的历史信息。本窟清晰的图像程序也是一部难得的图像学文献；壁画的图像细节与组合、题材内容和艺术风格，更是对于研究西藏西部地区乃至整个藏传佛教艺术流行地区 13-14 世纪的佛教艺术和宗教信仰有着非常重要的价值和意义，是现存为数不多的、有题记的、有确切地点的、时间相对较为清楚的遗址之一，对于它的研究可起到一种标尺性的作用，能够为其他类似绘画的研究提供可靠的参照。

33 具体分析见前引张长虹：《西藏阿里帕尔嘎尔布石窟壁画题记释读与相关问题》。

34 关于科迦寺的药师佛曼荼罗，参见杨竹：《科迦寺药师佛曼荼罗解析》（指导老师：罗文华），中国社会科学院研究生院硕士论文，2015 年。关于查宗贡巴的药师佛题材，参见霍巍、张长虹、吕红亮：《西藏阿里象泉河流域卡孜河谷佛教遗存的考古调查与研究》，《考古学报》2009 年第 4 期，第 556-562 页。

附表 1　本窟题记与各种文献记载中的药师八佛名称对照表

编号	据题记本文使用的名称及藏文	藏文本《八如来赞》中的名称	藏文本《读诵仪轨》中的名称	汉文本《念诵仪轨》中的名称[35]	汉文本《如意王经》中的名称	梵文名称[36]
W1	善名称吉祥王如来 mtshan gyi rgyal po	mtshan gyi rgyal po	mtshan legs par yongs bsgrags dpal gyi rgyal po	善名称吉祥王如来	善名称吉祥王如来	Suparikīrtitanāmaśrīrāja
W2	威音王如来 sgra dbyangs rgyal po	sgra dbyangs rgyal po	rin po che dang zla ba dang padmas rab tu brgyan pa mkhas pa gzi brjid sgra dbyangs kyi rgyal po	宝月智严光音自在王如来	宝月莲花智严威音王如来	Ratnacandrapadmapratimaṇḍita paṇḍita？ tejaḥsvara ghoṣarāja
W3	金色无垢如来 gser bzangs dri med snang	gser bzang dri med snang	gser bzangs dri med rin chen snang brtul zhugs grub pa	金色宝光妙行成就如来	金色无垢宝光妙行成就如来	Suvarṇabhadravimalaratnaprabhāsavrata
W4	无忧最胜如来 mya ngan med mchog dpal	mya ngan med mchog dpal	mya ngan med mchog dpal	无忧最胜吉祥王如来	无忧最胜吉祥如来	Aśokottamaśrī
E1	法海雷音如来 chos grags rgya mtshovi dbyangs	chos bsgrags rgya mtshovi dbyangs	chos bsgrags rgya mtshovi dbyangs	法海雷音如来	法海雷音如来	Dharmakīrtisāgaraghoṣa
E2	神通王如来 mkhyen pavi rgyal po	chos blo mngon par mkhyen	chos rgya mtshovi mchog gi blos rnam par rol pas mngon par mkhyen pa	法海胜慧游戏神通如来	法海胜慧游戏神通如来	Dharmakīrtisāgaragra？ mativikrīḍitābhijñārāja
E3	药王如来 sman pavi rgyal po	sman pavi rgyal po	sman gyi blo Baiḍūyavi vod kyi rgyal po	药师琉璃光王如来	药师琉璃光王如来	Bhaiṣajyaguruvaiḍūryaprabharāja
E4	释迦牟尼如来 thub pa rab mdzes	shakyavi rgyal po	dpal shākya thub pa	释迦牟尼如来	释迦牟尼如来	Śākyamuni

35　因《供养法》的经文为偈颂体，各佛的名称未能显示完整，因此此处使用同样由沙啰巴翻译的《药师琉璃光王七佛本愿功德经念诵仪轨》中各佛的完整名称，见《新修大正大藏经·密教部》第 19 卷，No.925，第 34 页。

36　此外所用梵名来自《诸佛菩萨圣像赞》，北京：中国藏学出版社，2009 年，第 415-416 页。

附表 2　金刚界曼荼罗诸尊汉藏梵名对照表

序号	汉名	藏名	梵名
1	大日如来	rnam par snang mdzad	Vairocana
2	心金刚女	sems pa rdo rje ma	Sattvavajrī
3	宝金刚女	rin chen rdo rje ma	Ratnavajrī
4	法金刚女	chos kyi rdo rje ma	Dharmavajrī
5	业金刚女	las kyi rdo rje ma	Karmavajrī
6	阿閦佛	mi bskyod pa	Akṣobhya
7	金刚萨埵	rdo rje sems dpav	Vajrasattva
8	金刚王	rdo rje rgyal po	Vajrarāja
9	金刚爱	rdo rje chags pa	Vajrarāga
10	金刚喜	rdo rje legs pa	Vajrasādhu
11	宝生佛	rin chen vbyung ldan	Ratnasambhava
12	金刚宝	rdo rje rin chen	vajraratna
13	金刚光	rdo rje gzi brjid	Vajratejas
14	金刚幢	rdo rje tog	Vajraketu
15	金刚笑	rdo rje bzhad pa	Vajrahāsā
16	阿弥陀佛	snang ba mthav yas	Amitābha
17	金刚法	rdo rje chos	Vajradharma
18	金刚利	rdo rje gnon po	Vajratīkṣṇa
19	金刚因	rdo rje rgyu	Vajrahetu
20	金刚语	rdo rje smra ba	Vajrabhāṣa
21	不空成就佛	don yod grub pa	Amoghasiddhi
22	金刚业	rdo rje las	Vajrakarma
23	金刚护	rdo rje bsrung ba	Vajrarakṣa
24	金刚牙	rdo rje gnod sbyin	Vajrayakṣa
25	金刚拳	rdo rje khu tshur	Vajrasandhi
26	金刚嬉	rdo rje sgeg mo	Vajralāsyā

续表 1

序号	汉名	藏名	梵名
27	金刚鬘	rdo rje phreng ba ma	Vajramālā
28	金刚歌	rdo rje glu ma	Vajragītā
29	金刚舞	rdo rje gar ma	Vajranṛtyā
30	弥勒菩萨	byams pa	Maitreya
31	不空见菩萨	mthong ba don yod	Amoghadarśī
32	灭恶趣菩萨	ngan song kun vdren	Sarvapāyāñjaha
33	除忧暗菩萨	mya ngan dang mun pa thams cad vjoms pavi blo gros	Sarvaśokatamonirghātamati
34	香象菩萨	spos kyi glang po	Gandhahasti
35	大精进菩萨	dpav bar vgrob	Śūraṅgama
36	虚空藏菩萨	nam mkhav mdzod	Gaganagañja
37	智幢菩萨	ye shes tog	Jñānaketu
38	无量光菩萨	vod dpag med	Amitaprabha
39	月光菩萨	zla pavi vod	Candraprabha
40	贤护菩萨	bzang skyong	Bhadrapāla
41	光网菩萨	dra ba can gyi vod	Jālinīprabha
42	金刚藏菩萨	rdo rje snying po	Vajragarbha
43	无尽意菩萨	blo gros mi zad pa	Akṣayamati
44	辩积菩萨	spobs pa brtsegs pa	Pratibhānakūṭa
45	普贤菩萨	kun du bzang po	Samantabhadra
46	金刚香	rdo rje me spos ma	Vajradhūpā
47	金刚华	rdo rje bdug tog ma	Vajrapuṣpā
48	金刚灯	rdo rje mar me ma	Vajradīpā
49	金刚涂香	rdo rje dri chab ma	Vajragandhā
50	金刚钩	rdo rje lcags kyu	Vajrāṅkuśa
51	金刚索	rdo rje zhags pa	Vajrapāśa
52	金刚锁	rdo rje lcags sgrog	Vajrasphoṭa
53	金刚铃	rdo rje vbebs pa	Vajrāveśa

附表 3　净除恶趣清净曼荼罗诸尊汉藏梵名对照表

序号	汉名	藏名	梵名
1	释迦狮子大日如来	rnam par snang mdzad	Vairocana
2	金刚佛顶	sems pa rdo rje ma	Sattvavajrī
3	宝佛顶	rin chen rdo rje ma	Ratnavajrī
4	莲花佛顶	chos kyi rdo rje ma	Dharmavajrī
5	羯磨佛顶	las kyi rdo rje ma	Karmavajrī
6	光明佛顶	mi bskyod pa	Akṣobhya
7	宝幢佛顶	rdo rje sems dpav	Vajrasattva
8	利佛顶	rdo rje rgyal po	Vajrarāja
9	白伞盖佛顶	rdo rje chags pa	Vajrarāga
10	金刚嬉	rdo rje sgeg mo	Vajralāsyā
11	金刚鬘	rdo rje phreng ba ma	Vajramālā
12	金刚歌	rdo rje glu ma	Vajragītā
13	金刚舞	rdo rje gar ma	Vajranṛtyā
14	弥勒菩萨	byams pa	Maitreya
15	不空见菩萨	mthong ba don yod	Amoghadarśī
16	灭恶趣菩萨	ngan song kun vdren	Sarvapāyāñjaha
17	除忧暗菩萨	mya ngan dang mun pa thams cad vjoms pavi blo gros	Sarvaśokatamonirghātamati
18	香象菩萨	spos kyi glang po	Gandhahasti
19	大精进菩萨	dpav bar vgrob	Śūraṅgama
20	虚空藏菩萨	nam mkhav mdzod	Gaganagañja
21	智幢菩萨	ye shes tog	Jñānaketu
22	甘露光菩萨	vod dpag med	Amitaprabha
23	月光菩萨	zla pavi vod	Candraprabha
24	贤护菩萨	bzang skyong	Bhadrapāla
25	光网菩萨	dra ba can gyi vod	Jālinīprabha
26	金刚藏菩萨	rdo rje snying po	Vajragarbha

续表 1

序号	汉名	藏名	梵名
27	无尽意菩萨	blo gros mi zad pa	Akṣayamati
28	辩积菩萨	spobs pa brtsegs pa	Pratibhānakūṭa
29	普贤菩萨	kun du bzang po	Samantabhadra
30	金刚香	rdo rje me spos ma	Vajradhūpā
31	金刚华	rdo rje bdug tog ma	Vajrapuṣpā
32	金刚灯	rdo rje mar me ma	Vajradīpā
33	金刚涂香	rdo rje dri chab ma	Vajragandhā
34	金刚钩	rdo rje lcags kyu	Vajrāṅkuśa
35	金刚索	rdo rje zhags pa	Vajrapāśa
36	金刚锁	rdo rje lcags sgrog	Vajrasphoṭa
37	金刚铃	rdo rje vbebs pa	Vajrāveśa

后记

谨以此文纪念著名藏学家、古格之子古格·次仁加布先生！

次仁加布先生于2008年受聘于四川大学中国藏学研究所，任客座研究员，主持教育部人文社科重点研究基地重大项目《西藏西部佛教史迹综合研究》，笔者有幸得以参与该项目，近距离接触先生，同先生一道于2011年9月前往阿里进行石窟考察。尽管早已经知道出生于西藏阿里地区噶尔县的次仁加布先生是阿里名人，但是跟着他一块儿在阿里考察，才知道古格·次仁加布这个名字几乎已经成为了阿里的一张名片，无论多么边远的窟寺，提到他的名号都能得到额外关照，他的藏文著作《阿里文明史》也在僧人的手中被翻得皱巴巴的。由于加布老师科研任务繁重，因此此次考察时间并不算长，仅有二十多天，只考察了东嘎、香孜、达巴等地的几座石窟，但是可以感受到加布老师一踏上阿里的土地，就浑身地放松、自在、踏实。的确，那里是生他养他的故土，他对那里的一草一木是那么熟悉，他单人匹马走遍了阿里的山山水水，踏察了无数的窟寺塔城，可以说对于阿里的佛教遗迹，没有比他再熟悉的人了，对于阿里的历史，没有比他再熟悉的人了。2012年，先生又应邀至四川大学中国藏学研

图 59　加布老师三件宝：相机、梯子和水壶
(2011 年 9 月作者摄于阿里皮央石窟前)

究所进行四场阿里历史文化系列讲座，令人吃惊的是，他的讲座，居然没有稿子、没有 PPT，就那么两手空空台前一座，各种文献、各处史迹，如竹筒倒豆般倾泻而出，回头整理笔记和录音，发现光是要消化这大量的历史文献信息就得好几天，他是如何做到如数家珍、信手拈来的呢？

记得那是 2015 年一个明媚春天的午后，我正在川大藏学所的大门口无聊地张望，忽然看见一个熟悉的身影走过来，“小张，我给你带了本书”，“啊！原来是加布老师”，他说他要出国了，路过成都，顺便来看看我，讨论一下下一步的阿里考察计划，他知道我最近在做大译师仁钦桑布的研究，因此拉萨新出版了仁钦桑布的传记，他就特地买来赠我。简短的聊天中我们拟定了下一步的考察计划，约定等他这次出国回来就着手进行下一次的阿里考察，上次考察之后，帐篷、梯子、煤气罐等野外考察用具都还存放在他家里呢，就等着他访学归来呢……谁知道6月29号竟等来了噩耗……天妒英才，他才只有54岁！造化弄人，他竟逝世于遥远的别国他乡，永别于他挚爱的故土阿里！

不知不觉，加布老师已经离开我们近两年了，他敦厚善良的音容笑貌仍然宛若眼前，但是再也听不到他亲口讲述阿里的前世今生了，听不到他在石窟前就着月光讲他小时候和羊一起冬日互暖共眠的日子了，呜呼哀哉！惟愿他能够早日魂归阿里，往生上界！

帕尔嘎尔布石窟不是2011年与加布老师一同考察的石窟，但是加布老师生前仍然允准我使用他拍摄的质量更好的照片对题记进行拼接，使得该窟的题记能够全部呈现，善莫大焉！

致谢：笔者有幸于2007年参加四川大学考古队对该窟的复查，期间得到领队霍巍教授和同事吕红亮教授以及札达县文物局的同事们给予的帮助！该年度的考察得到了托马斯·普瑞茨克先生（Thomas J. Pritzker）的资助，谨致谢意！

Drinking for Enlightenment

Remarks on a beer song (*chang gzhas*) from Western Tibet and its comparative historical context

Christiane Kalantari (Austrian Academy of Sciences)

1. Introduction[1]

Tibetan poetry and music not only focus on the Buddhist contemplative life and spiritual realisation, but they also address more mundane concerns and aspects of sensual and sensory experience, having an important role to play in feasting, drinking and making offerings of beer during ceremonies and social events. These aspects of life include all sections of society: monks, ritual specialists such as trance media, performers of Buddhist plays, physicians, craftsmen and the lay community. Women in particular play a special, visible role in this (Fig. 1-4).

This preliminary contribution presents a short song praising beer (*chang*) and its qualities, which was drunk in specific ceremonies, as documented by the late Tsering Gyalpo and the author during our research trip to Western Tibet in 2007 in the context of a research project conducted at the Austrian Academy of Sciences, Vienna (Fig. 5).[2] Three remarkable songs from the 11th-13th century advocating beer drinking will be added (largely relying on the translations and analyses by Schaeffer 2013 and Ardussi 1977). Two of them elucidate

1 Saying farewell to a friend: the study was undertaken within the framework of several research projects on the cultural history of Western Tibet in cooperation with late Prof. Tsering Gyalpo, and under the direction of Christian Jahoda, at the Austrian Academy of Sciences, Vienna.

2 This relates to the research project "Oral and Festival Traditions in Western Tibet" financed by the Austrian Science Fund (FWF P20637). The question of material culture and festival traditions in Western Tibet will be a task of future trans-disciplinary research by the author. In general, the research topic of the culinary culture of Tibet is of course an important source for studies of economy, trade and cross-cultural interaction as well as the Tibetan worldview.

Fig. 1. Bowl (*phor ba*) made of porcelain with silver cover on stand featuring animals, plants and religious symbols (photo: Christiane Kalantari 2007).

Fig. 2. Donor depiction, the "royal drinking scene", Alchi, Dukhang, entrance wall (photo: Christiane Kalantari 2009).

Fig. 3, 3a. Ritual offerings of beer in the Jokhang of Khorchag: a wooden beer flask is offered by a woman in front of the Jowo; another placed in the centre among other ritual offering objects of wealthy families during the annual Namthong festival (photos: Christiane Kalantari 2010).

Fig. 4. Drummers are served barley beer outside the temple during the Namthong festival at Khorchag monastery (photo: Patrick Sutherland 2010).

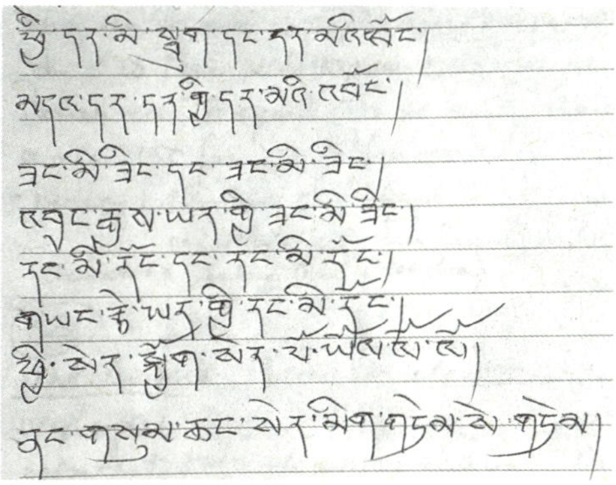

Fig. 5. Song, documented and hand-written by Tsering Gyalpo in Western Tibet, 2007.

the wider social context of barley and beer and their position in Tibetan cosmogony, while the third song focuses on the role of the intoxicating drink in meditation, in rituals and as analogies to spiritual endeavours by famous religious masters such as Milarepa (Mi la ras pa, 11th cent.).

An important but little studied source illustrating the wider historical context of such songs are the drinking ceremonies shown in early Western Tibetan Buddhist paintings. The prominent representations of cup-holders in donor depictions in Buddhist temples, and in Alchi (Fig. 2) and Kanji (Kan'ji; also Rkan/Gangs bzhi) [cf. Tropper 2015] both Ladakh, India) in particular, triggered my interest in the drinking traditions of Tibet. They appear not only to reflect the aspect of alcohol in Buddhist cults but they also mirror cosmopolitan drinking and status culture, connecting Tibet with the Persianate world and Central Asia.

2. Drinking ceremonies in Western Tibet

Visiting Tsering Gyalpo's family on several occasions in Lhasa and in his place of origin in Ngari (Mnga' ris), we had the privilege to experience the exquisite hospitality and in particular the unique and refined Western Tibetan drinking culture. It includes the use of fine traditional Tibetan- and Chinese-style drinking bowls (*phor ba*) of different materials such as porcelain, jade with silver and wood, placed on elaborate silver stands (*khra lcag*) and gracefully offered to the guests who put them on low lacquered tables (Fig. 6). The elegant movements and gestures of women in Western Tibet in serving beer as well as the consciousness for etiquette with regard to the sitting order and hierarchy of guests involve a

Fig. 6. Jade bowls (*phor ba*) in the house of Tsering Gyalpo, Western Tibet (photo: Christian Jahoda 2007).

Fig. 6a. Bowls (*phor ba*) and metal stands in which beer and dried yak meat (in the centre) were offered to us; farmhouse in Tayab village, near Khorchag (photo: Christiane Kalantari 2007).

high degree of refinement and beauty.

Drinking songs, often performed by women, resonate this beauty, and they have probably been composed to further uplift those who enjoy the good qualities of a well-brewed beer.[3] They are presented on both formal and informal private occasions, revealing the sophistication and the discrete charm of the host. Tsering's sister told us that beer songs performed at private gatherings help to further contacts between people, and that toasting songs can even be designed in the form of a dialogue as a prelude to a possible relationship or marriage. Usually women are the ones making a toast to everyone at the table, starting with the oldest person. The person being toasted must dip one finger into the beer and tap the finger three times to the points of the compass before drinking. The guest has to drink from the cup three times, and every other time the host refills the cup. Tsering's sister told us that drinking without this etiquette and toasting songs – as is becoming common nowadays according to her – is regarded as barbaric and uncultivated by the older generation.

The important role of beer (*chang*) in Tibet and Nepal as a drink as well as a substance with medical qualities is due to the distinctive geographic and climatic features of these high mountain regions. Barley also grows in the harsh climate. When the boiled barley has cooled, some yeast or dried barm (*phab*) is added and then the liquid is left to stand for two

3 Songs in traditional Tibet were composed by religious leaders for all concerns of life: for religious and moral instruction, and ritual devotion, they were used for grieving as well as entertainment and critique – e.g. performed by Buddhist bards, the Buchen (*bu chen*) as documented by the author in Pin-valley and Tabo, Himachal Pradesh/India.

Fig. 7. Raised wooden cup (*lba phor*; lathed wood from a protuberance of the tree) covered with silver-sheet and silver spoon (Western Tibet, family of Tsering Gyalpo; photo: Christian Jahoda 2007).

Fig. 8. Factory-produced "Lhasa Beer" served to our team during our research trip in Western Tibet in 2007. (The brewery was established on the northern outskirts of Lhasa, south of Sera Monastery, in the 1980s. However, it is a fact that our skilled Chinese driver Chuan-Sir exclusively drank a specific "energy drink" (Red Bull) created in Austria during the trip and when we started from Lhasa he even stated he would not drive us to the mountains without a sufficient reserve in the car.)

or three days when fermentation begins. After the fermentation process, water is added and the brew is ready for consumption. Chang is drunk at room temperature in summer and it is often served hot in winter, producing an intense feeling of warmth and well-being.[4] Today factory-brewed beer "from the roof of the world" produced near Sera Monastery, north of Lhasa, is also served in Western Tibet (Fig. 8).

The frequent production of *chang* in monasteries – despite the general prohibitive beliefs towards alcohol in Tibetan Buddhism – reflects its important role as commodity in trade, ritual and social life. As far as drinking songs in Buddhism is concerned, prominent thinkers from all sects usually condemned the use of alcohol. Hagiographies inform us that in spite of their vows of abstention, "the monk's fondness of beer was a frequent cause of disciplinary unease in Tibetan monasteries" (Ardussi 1977: 121). However, alcohol was sometimes advocated even among certain religious traditions. Nyingmapa (Rnying ma pa) followers of the older religious schools were allowed to drink alcohol. It was legitimised given the fact that the school's founding figure, Padmasambhava, occasionally drank alcohol (Fig. 9).

4 It is said to be the best remedy against the severe cold of the mountains, and reputedly it has many healing properties for adverse conditions like the common cold, fever and allergic reactions. Beer was used against colds in Austria as well (i.e. heated beer with honey, information by Heiko Heinisch).

Fig. 9. Padmasambhava and his two wives drinking from a vat of beer, *thangka* (image after Müller 1982: 174).

Toasting songs during social gatherings are about congratulation, humour and expression of feelings. They can also praise the setting of a ceremony and the qualities of the objects served. A good example is the following song in prose, documented in 2007 (Fig. 5):

phyi dar mi sbug dang dar ma'i 'bong |
mda' dar gyi dar ma'i 'bong |
zang mi zing dang zang mi zing |
'brang rgyas yar gyi zang mi zing |
rang mi rong dang rang mi rong |
g.yang rtse yar gyi rang mi rong |
phyi ser skyogs ser po yos [*yol*] *lo lo* |
nang gsum chang ser mig gtem se gtem | [5]

5 The song specified as *yangtse* (*g.yang rtse*, "good fortune song") was noted down by Tsering Gyalpo in Seng ge kha 'bab (2007). It is an oral version sung by a female singer who descends from a Western Tibetan nomadic family. I am grateful to Tsering Utruk, Vienna, for editing and paraphrasing the text, Per Sørensen for some further editorial remarks and to C. Jahoda for information on the context.

Fig. 10. Ewer decorated richly with butter offerings. This beer offering is made in front of the house of the groom in Ladakh (image after Brauen 1980: Fig. 22).

This type of beer song (*chang glu, chang gzhas*) is usually performed during weddings and composed as an antiphon, i.e. alternating songs between men and women. Thereby the task is to show the skill in reproducing as many songs as possible. Anyone who cannot respond with a song has to drink. An important aspect of this sung dialogue is the demonstration and confirmation of cultural knowledge, as remarked by Christian Jahoda (verbal communication). The song is full of onomatopoetic expressions, exclamations and local terms typical of folk literature. Here it describes the altar as being fully decorated with ritual offerings such as the *mda' dar* (arrow with five different coloured silk ribbons) and the *'brang rgyas*, the heart-shaped *gtor ma* or offering cakes topped with many butter flakes. These butter flakes (*dkar rgyan*, 'white ornament') are offered by the invited guests as they say their good wishes for the new couple. The bride and the groom are seated below the altar and very elegantly dressed. The house is over full with guests. Somewhere at the side one can find a very large buffet, presented in the best of utensils. One cannot oversee the magnificent beer vessels with elaborate brass ladles in them. The beer itself looks golden and tasty. *Dkar rgyan* are on all the utensils and beer bowls everywhere, since they are considered to be very auspicious.

The song performance is typical of the role of beer plays in festivities and for making offerings during ceremonies. The genre is part of a long tradition of description of offerings, rich of imagery and allegories, designed to confirm, praise and enhance the merit-granting act. Brauen (1980) described a series of beer gatherings during wedding ceremonies in Ladakh (Fig. 10). All sections of society in such festivities take part and each social group had specific duties. He emphasises the "comunitas aspect" of feasting: "Festivals are designed to preserve world order through the practice of certain symbols" (*ibid.* 78 ff.). Ceremonies for the benefit of the deceased and the commemoration and feeding of the ancestor (in the hope of their favourable rebirths) involving the offering and drinking of beer, as described by Brauen (*ibid.*), are an important aspect of affirmation of this social cohesion.

During the festivals the drinking vessels, shallow Chinese-style low cups or drinking bowls (*phor ba*; traditionally every male Tibetan carried a bowl in his robe, *chu pa*), beer pitchers, ewers and flasks are often most exquisite. Ewers can be made of clay (*rdza bum*; earthen jar), metal, or wood; frequently they are adorned with butter offerings and *kataks* on the bottleneck during offering ceremonies (Fig. 10). In the wedding ceremony (*bag ston*) in a farming area a large ceramic vat with full highland barley beer is put in the centre or on the altar of the festival place (with large ceramic spoons or ladles (*dra zu*) hanging on the vessel's rim; Fig. 11, 11a). The neck and body of the flasks are usually decorated with finely worked silver mounts (Fig. 12). Wooden or jade bowls (Fig. 14, 14a) often have silver rims or are lined with pure silver and gold. In addition, valuable stones such turquoise may be placed on the bottom of the vessel, as the author observed together with C. Jahoda when we were guests in Tsering Gyalpo's household (Fig. 7). We were told that it is commonly believed that gold neutralises possible poison. Of course only wealthier people can afford jade bowls resting on stands, richly decorated with metalwork in repoussé technique.

Remarkable are the sumptuous ensembles of cups (*phor ba*) with covers (*kha khebs*) – which recall the shape of a stupa – resting on decorated stands (*kha lcags*), frequently made of silver. One example presented here is in the shape of an eight-petal lotus flower with the sides of cover and stand richly decorated with auspicious symbols (Fig. 15). This

Fig. 11. Clay beer vessels: the bigger one for storage and the small pot for serving beer (image after Müller 1982: 138).

Fig. 11a. Clay ewer, Gyantse (Rgyal rtse) monastery (photo: Christiane Kalantari 2007).

Fig. 12. Tsering Gyalpo and Christian Jahoda served beer in a wooden flask by local village people during the documentation of oral traditions in Western Tibet (photo: Christiane Kalantari 2007).

Fig. 13. Metal flask for spirits such as arak in the shape of a toad (*a rag sbal bum* – perhaps from China); frequently arak is drunk together with *chang* during festivities (former collection H. Harrer, sold at the Dorotheum, 2015 Vienna; photo: Christiane Kalantari 2015).

Fig. 14, 14a. Wooden cup with silver cover, served to Tsering Gyalpo during his documentation of texts for songs in a private house at Khorchag (photos: Christiane Kalantari 2007).

refinement of drinking objects is of course related to the long tradition of metal ritual paraphernalia created for the Buddhist temple and the private altar as well as the important role of traditional jewellery (Fig. 15a).[6] In addition, Tibet became acquainted with a long and lasting tradition of toreutics created as luxury objects and the status culture of the ruling elites in Central Asia (Fig. 16). From this transfer during the period of Tubo, a purely Tibetan tradition of elaborately crafted metal objects emerged (see below; cf. also Heller 2002; Grenet 2016; Pritzker 2016). From the 12th century onwards we find lavish banquets full of luxury vessels represented in Buddhist temples in Western Tibet. The form and

6 In contrast to smiths, who belong to the lowest group, skilled metalworkers, makers of fine metal objects, and woodcarvers occupy a middle position in society, due to the fact that they are charged with religious and ceremonial themes (Müller 1982: 184).

Fig. 15 (l.). Porcelain bowl (*phor ba*) with a silver lid on an elaborate lotus-shaped stand (photo: Christiane Kalantari 2007).
Fig. 15a (r.). Bowl for offerings, Gyantse monastery (photo: Christiane Kalantari 2007).

Fig. 16. Cup with a gold and silver handle, period of Tubo, featuring grapes and vines (after Heller 2002).

meaning of such ritual and offering drinking ceremonies in donor representations will be discussed below.

However, beer not only has an important role to play in various rituals and ceremonies. In Tibet barley and its product beer is part of a universal, cosmogonic relationship and order that can be traced back to Indic myths of creation.

During the festival of the "first ears of grain" in She (She (l), Ladakh, Brauen (1980: 166) documented a marriage song with its main themes as the description of world order, the origin of the crop (*ibid.*, 125 ff.), how the gods brought it down to earth, and the production of beer:

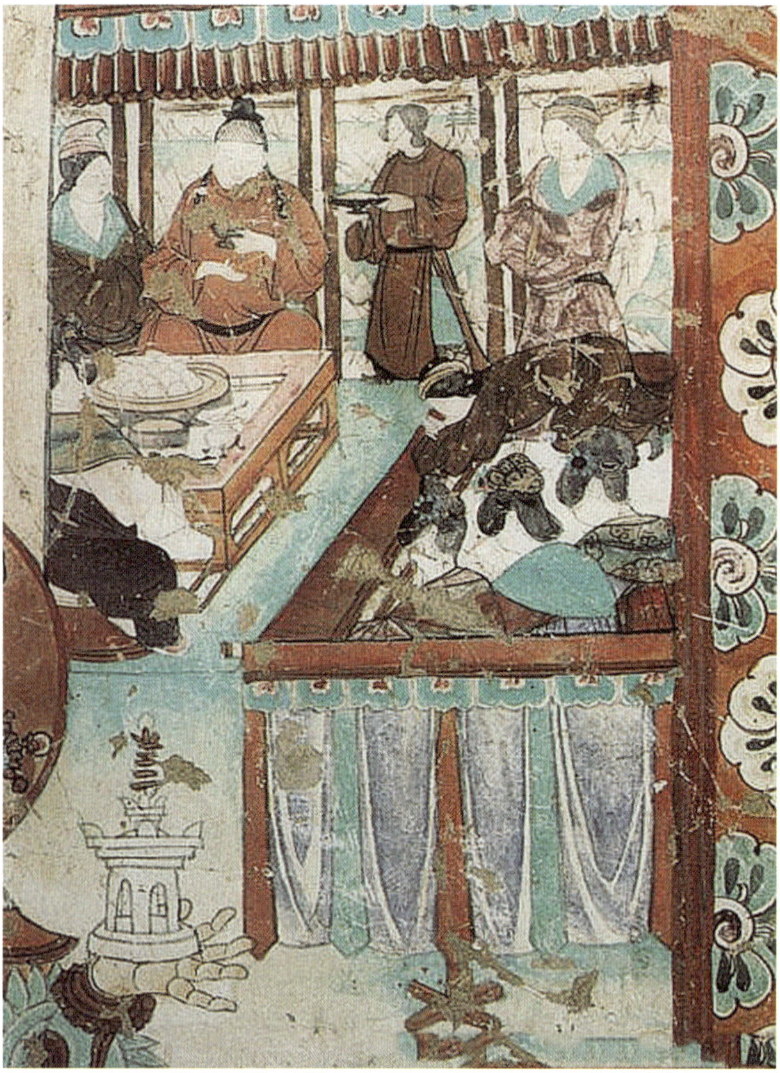

Fig. 17. Yulin cave (near Dunhuang, Gansu province), cave 25, north wall, 8-9th century, featuring a Tibetan drinking ceremony perhaps representing a marriage (photo: www.china-tours-online.com/2012/11/the-yulin-caves-is-most-beautiful.html).

Ja, es wurden drei den drei Bergbrüdern gleiche Herdsteine aufgestellt.
Darauf wurde ein der rötlichen Erde gleicher Kupferkessel gesetzt.
In diesen wurde eine dem Manasarowarsee gleiche Flut geschüttet.
Dann wurde ein den Korallenfunken gleiches Feuer angeblasen
Und ein einem Sandelholzblock ähnliches Holz aufgelegt.
Körner von weißer und grüner Gerste wurden eingeschüttet,
Und den Plejadensternen gleiche Hefe dazugefügt.
Darauf wurde alles in ein buntes Säckchen gefüllt,

Und bis zum nächsten Tag durfte das gärende Getreide schlafen.
Dann wurde es in einen roten, kleinen Tonkrug gefüllt
Und Wasser, so kalt wie Gletscherwasser daraufgegossen.
Nun wurde es in den Bierkrug mit dem Schlangekopfausguss gefüllt
(Brauen 1980: 127-128).
[Yes, three hearth stones similar to the three mountain brothers were arranged.
A copper vat of reddish earthen appearance was put on it.
A flood like Lake Manasarowar was poured into it
[i.e. water similar to the original water of the flood that created the Manasarowar],
then a fire like sparkling coral was blown onto it.
And wood like sandalwood was put on it.
Grains of white and green barley were shaken into it.
And barm like the Pleiades was added.
Then everything was poured into a coloured bag,
and the fermenting grain was allowed to rest until the next day.
Then this was filled into a small, red clay pot
and water as cold as glacier water poured on it.
Finally it was filled into a clay beer ewer with a snakehead spout.]
(English translation by the author)

A remarkable song composed by the great Dzogchen master and philosopher Longchenpa (Klong chen Rab 'byams pa Dri med 'od zer, 1308-63; cf. Schaeffer 2013) says a lot about the social history of beer in Tibet and its role as a commodity in Tibetan economy. The song below is composed to address the benefits of drinking beer, praising the perfect qualities of a carefully crafted beer and its positive effects on health. It also describes the psychological impact of intoxication, " … how esteem and attraction increase and perception loses solidity" (Schaeffer 2013: 474). The author of the song praises its positive effect for all sections of society: "Men use beer for anything at all. Women use it to master wool. Distinguished people use it in place of work" (*ibid.*). The song also addresses the different positions and conflicts between various types of religious communities, namely monastic Buddhism and non-celibate Buddhism. The climax of the song is an indictment of hypocrisy: "It is better to partake of the world and be honest about it than to claim to be pure and lie" (*ibid.*).

In order to explain the qualities of beer and the reason everyone drinks Longchenpa recited the Diamond Song entitled: "Sweet nectar describing the origins and qualities of beer" striking for its poetic richness of images and allegories (Schaeffer 2013: 475 ff.):

> Homage to the Master. In praise of the good qualities of beer.
> Homage to Vajravārāhã
> Ancestors of beer, Vajradhāra, and
> The masters, deities, and muses – homage to you.
> I relate the good qualities of beer.
> Nectar supreme, drunk by the fortunate. Listen ...
>
> From the city of beautiful heavenly gods,
> A single supreme nectar drop falls,
> From the merit of every being in the world,
> Nutritious barley becomes the grist for beer.
>
> With taste and color like honey, and
> Perfect fragrance like the nectar of the gods,
> Just the sight of it raises the spirits; one cannot be without it.
> Sweet beer – its qualities are simply perfect.
>
> Drinking it is bliss, tasting it is delicious.
> When it goes down, body and mind are totally blissed out.
> Appearances are blissful, loose, as for one who understands what's real.
> Sweet beer – its qualities are simply perfect.
>
> After dinking, in carefree repose,
> In an unconscious state, one falls asleep easily,
> Like one who has mastered stabilization, luminosity, and concentration.
> Sweet beer – its qualities are simply perfect.
>
> No sooner drunk than happy tales and
> Lovely melodious songs come aplenty.
> Courage and fearlessness toward others know no depths.
> Sweet beer – its qualities are simply perfect.

At first sweet, taste somewhat bitter,
Because it smells soft, it lingers, and one can't do without,
Consider it, its supreme wonderful flavour is unfathomable.
Sweet beer – its qualities are simply perfect.
…
From the powerful king on high,
To the supreme guru, the monk, the scholar,
All the influential upper classes rely upon it.
Sweet beer – its qualities are simply perfect.

Rule-Following Kadampa so proud of their cleverness,
Philosophers and monks alike,
Drink it on the sly, who is more covetous?
Sweet beer – its qualities are simply perfect.

Another song advocating the consumption of beer is by Phagpa ('Gro mgon Chos rgyal 'Phags pa, 1235-1280), "Flask of Ambrosia: Verses of Praise to Beer" (Dan Martin 2014):[7]

Homage to the Wrath King Swirling Nectar Amṛtakuṇḍali

The essence of earth that sustains the lives of beings,
likewise the collection of flowers and fruits,
with the yeast starter prepared with varied tinctures and herbs
and the very stuff that serves as cleanser of beings, the pure water

The vessels, required condition, and varied recipes work together to
bring it to the complete maturity over a good length of time,
bringing out the pure essence of the pure essence.
These are its perfect causes and conditions.

It seems as if ornamented by strings of pearls,
But these strings are of bubbles shining like the sheerest crystal.

7 Dan Martin, Web Log, 7.2014: "*In praise of beer*", Tibeto-logic.blogspot.co.at/2014/07/in-praise-of-beer.html. See also in this context Shen Weirong 2004.

Seeing it is a glory for the eyes,
hearing its bubbly chil-chil sound

a glory for the ears, with its fragrance
satisfying the organ that has the sense of smell,
its every taste both glory and pleasure for the tongue.
Depending if the weather is cold or hot, it brings on warmth

or coolness to our sense of touch, so we feel comfortable.
It is a sun for exorcising the dark tinges of suffering,
a moon that generates the coolness of happiness and contentment.
It is a wind that fans the flames of insight,

is the most glorious prod to eloquence for would-be speakers.
It generates vowed behaviour on those entering into battle,
and increases the pleasures of those possessed by desire.
Yet this same drink, for minds desirous of peace,
Endows its drinkers with holy meditative absorptions.

For these reasons this is offered as a drink.
It forms the very heart of wealth and leisure.
So it is a thing worthy to be offered,
And ought to be given to those worthy of the gift.

There are also spiritual songs using the preparation and drinking of beer as an analogy of yogic endeavour. They represent a unique Tibetan elaboration of the Indian yogic *dohā*, a tradition of lyrics which emerged from rituals and contemplative techniques of Indian Tantric Buddhism. Some of them are related to the symbolism of the Diamond Song (*rdo rje glu*), performed during tantric rituals. Ardussi (1977: 116) analysed these songs composed by highly accomplished tantric yogins, mostly of the Kagyupa (Bka' brgyud pa) sect in contemplative practice. The earliest example is from the "collected songs" (*mgur 'bum*) of Milarepa (1010-1123), the famous Tibetan yogin (Ardussi 1977: 118). The author posits that they can mainly be understood as analogies between brewing and drinking of beer to the cultivation of certain meditative experiences. But they do not seem to understand drinking as a means of comprehending the "intoxication" of enlightenment (*ibid.* 124). The function of spiritual song appears thus as a means of contemplation and religious instruction, "guiding the listener through analogy and paradoxical juxtaposition of symbols to more subtle levels of meditative realization," comparable to the function of painted icons, as proposed by Ardussi.[8] As far as any real connection between alcohol and Buddhist practice is conceivable, Ardussi (*ibid.* 123) elaborates on the contemplative act of conceiving oneself as the mandala of the deity and its retinue during specific rituals. The rite is regularly performed as a mental event, however, he noted that during the performance sacra-mental beer was consumed by the monk participants, though in small quantities and only if assured that it was ritually purified.[9]

3. Transregional intoxications: drinking cultures in imperial Tibet and in the Western Himalayas

Isabelle Henrion-Dourcy (2005: 202) described the beautiful and expressive performing art of drinking songs with the role of female ceremonial beer servers (*trungshuma*, *khrung zhu ma*). Trungshuma having an important position at the Dalai Lama's family mansion or during the New Year celebration in Lhasa, or marriage ceremonies providing a joyful atmosphere full of wit and refinement and singing drinking songs to the guest.[10]

This sophisticated drinking culture, which can perhaps be traced back to the status culture during Tubo period, is also reflected in donor depictions in early Buddhist temples as well as in luxury articles such as cups and vessels represented in wall-paintings. Some of them are presented in this context for the first time (see below).

The first historical record of beer in Tibet is found in a peace agreement between Tang and Tubo under Songtsen Gampo (Srong btsan Sgam po, d. 649 CE) from 638 CE (Twitchett and Fairbank 1979: 228-230), which included the transfer of the knowledge of

8 They may have been influenced by popular peasant folk themes and related songs and dances.

9 As described by the author, in it the *yogin* strives to fuse his now divine being with the clear light and great bliss of emptiness, in this experience the analogy of intoxication from beer is commonly used. In this particular tantric practice of the circle of hosts (*tshogs 'khor*), *yogins* and their ritually purified consort assemble to perform the physical and contemplative process of generation and perfection, which is celebrated by symbolic consumption of alcohol, with the diamond song being performed (*ibid.*). Beer or alcoholic drink as a symbol for nectarous essence, *amçta*, Tib. *bdud rtsi*, the refined essential of teachings or contemplative experiences, is common in Tibetan Buddhist writing, and initially derives from Indian usage.

10 The best *trungshuma* sing a different drinking song to each guest. They should be renowned as gifted singers for their pleasant manners, for being lively and having an elegant way of expression and language in everyday life (Henrion-Dourcy 2005: 202 ff.).

silk, paper, watermills and beer production. There are ample accounts that Songtsen Gampo enjoyed beer drinking and that it constituted an important aspect of the royal status culture. Vessels of various kinds to obtain beer as well as perhaps also wine,[11] which may have been imported, constitute central objects of self-representation of the Tibetan king. Among the most sumptuous silver and gold Tibetan royal drinking vessels is the famous imperial beer jug (*chang snod rta 'go can*; see Heller 2002: Fig. 4) reputedly used by the king. The jug features a horse-, or rather a camel- headed, round-bellied silver jar with a long neck, 80 cm high. This ewer from the Tibetan king house, which is clearly an item of Eurasian luxury trade, was used to dispense mildly intoxicating beverages to the king and his most honoured guests. The sides have repousée work depicting Sogdian-style dancers, drunken men, and musicians.[12]

Hugh Richardson (1998: 254, cited after Dan Martin 2014[13]) presents sources describing how the *chang snod rta 'go can* was discovered by Tsongkhapa (Tsong kha pa, 1357-1410, founder of the Gelug school) in a hidden treasure and how this jug was brought back to the Lhasa Jokhang, Tibet's most sacred Buddhist temple. It appears to have been used once a year during the *Dpal lha ri khrod* ceremonies, during which it was filled. Heller (2002) reports: "It weighs some 35 kg when full of liquid, and monks fill it daily with *chang*, Tibetan barley beer." In his "Ceremonies of the Lhasa Year" Richardson (1993: 96, cited after Dan Martin 2014) further describes an earthen mug, also a reputed relic of Songtsen Gampo: "… annually in the sixth month, the mug is ceremonially taken to the Dalai Lama's morning reception for officials and offered to those present, who ritually flick a drop of its contents into the air."

Etiquettes in Tibetan drinking ceremonies, such as during wedding ceremonies and festivities in front of the monastery during religious festivals – as documented at Khorchag

11 Cf. also a flask and rhyton from Tibet, 7th-8th century, recently discussed by David Pritzker on the occasion of the IATS 2016, Bergen, Norway. The decorations feature various animals among vines, clearly reflecting also the function of the object. I wish to thank David Pritzker for discussions on this topic (for images, see Heller 2002: Fig. 46).

12 An important Chinese funerary couch made of marble in the Miho Museum from the 6th century, perhaps created by Sogdian artists, shows various detailed scenes of banqueting and drinking scenes (Papa-Kalantari 2008); a remarkable evidence of Tibeto – Sogdian exchange is a related Tibetan painted wooden coffin from Dulan: various different drinking rites are depicted – among them is perhaps a marriage ceremony and a confirmation of a treaty or expression of loyalty. For further interpretations of the scene and images see the study by Amy Heller 2013.

13 Dan Martin, Blog Tibeto Logic: "*The Emperor's Beer Jug*", tibeto-logic.blogspot.co.at/2014_11_01_archive.html).

('Khor chags) monastery together with Tsering Gyalpo in a multi-disciplinary team with C. Jahoda (director) and P. Sutherland – are perhaps late echoes of this ancient status culture, transmitted by aristocratic families in Lhasa, the centre of the "haute monde" of Tibet. It served as a kind of role model, involving a strict hierarchy expressed in seating arrangements, the right to wear certain clothes, and a refined tradition of cuisine (with 108 dishes which have to be served), drinking ceremonies and, of course, polite speech, as Tsering Gyalpo often explained to us from his personal experiences. In particular the social gatherings in front of the temple during the Namthong (Nam mthong) festival commemorate the foundation of the temple and its conse cration. During this occasion inside the Khorchag Jokhang, wealthy families also put offerings of beer in front of the offering tables (Fig. 3, 3a).

3.1. Drinking in a Buddhist temple – the pictorial evidence

Wall paintings have hitherto been little studied sources in the context of drinking cultures in Tibet; they give insight into questions of rituals, social relations – roles of women in particular – as well as material culture. A donor depiction from the Tubo era in a Buddhist cave at Yulin 榆林 (100 km east of Dunhuang 敦煌) gives an insight into the life of the Tibetan nobility of that time; besides wine-making it features a couple engaged in a ceremony, perhaps a marriage, with the groom holding a stemmed cup surrounded in attendants in typical Tibetan long-sleeved robes with lapels and turbans (Fig. 17).

Drinking ceremonies in images of aristocratic donors at Alchi (Fig. 18) around 1200 (and Kanji, from a later period; Fig. 20, 20a, 20b), and the elite's self-representations of various kinds are particularly informative in this respect.

In general, the depiction of principal donors (among the most prominent is the royal lama Yeshe Ö (Lha Bla ma Ye shes 'od (947-1019) [biodata according to Jahoda and Kalantari 2016: 83, Fn. 4; Vitali 2003 gives the date: 947-1024]) and the dharma king and lord monk Jangchup Ö (*chos rgyal rje btsun* Byang chub 'od (984-1078) [biodata according Vitali 2003]) together with high clan members of different regions of their political domain) is a constant theme in the temples such as at Khorchag, Tabo (Rta bo) and Tholing (Tho ling), which they founded or supported from the end of the 10th century onwards, in their aim of establishing a Buddhist kingdom. They are often portrayed in the art they commissioned in sense of reverence, or making gestures of salutation or offering. Often they are depicted close to the sacred performing a gesture of offering with a lotus in the hand. One of the various examples which can be found in early Western Tibetan art, as yet little known, features donors engaged in a consecration ritual and standing in reverence next to the image of Avalokiteshvara at Zhag cave in Be ('Bye) valley, Tsamda (Rtsa mda') County (Fig. 21; Kalantari and Tsering Gyalpo, forthcoming).

In the Alchi donor frieze the noble family is depicted in various seemingly secular ceremonies (including banqueting, feasting scenes as acts of demonstrating loyalty and hunters on horseback performing the famous Parthian shot), as well as in explicitly religious rituals (Fig. 18). It shows high dignitaries of aristocratic lineages in a completely new mode of self-representation, contrasting to related images in earlier periods. In this process of adaptation of images of supremacy typical of this phase not only religious-political conditions but also religious and social life of the time become visible.

The meaning of individual images in the frieze has been a subject of various different speculations (see Flood 2016: 227-254, for a summary; cf. also seminal studies by Esin 1980) but the overall context as a programmatic whole has not been looked at as yet. The focus is on lively and detailed scenes full of objects of material culture, featuring vivid interactions between the protagonists, in particular engaged in drinking rituals of various kinds.[14] Remarkable is also the high visibility of female donors in such scenes and fine robes – including the use of *tirāz*-strips with pseudo-Arabic script – reflecting Iranicate status culture and cross-cultural self-fashioning in that region around 1200 (cf. Flood 2016: 227-254).

A scene hitherto overlooked in scholarly debate features a couple positioned either side of a large round-bellied vessel and a bowl resting on its opening; all this is subordinated to a religious scene showing a seated high religious dignitary, perhaps Kalden Sherab (Skal ldan Shes rab), as mentioned in inscriptions. They are holding bowls and making some collective gesture of reverence appropriate to a religious setting. The vessel is perhaps filled with wine or beer, which is still a common feature in Tibet during religious festivals today.

In contrast to toasting images in purely religious contexts is the famous "royal drinking scene", which clearly translates a mode ultimately derived from Persianate images of

14 This image-friendly mode can also be found in images of the Buddha-vita which regularly occupy a prominent position inside the temples, with many more scenes narrating an event than is usual in India. This can be explained by the fact tha – while in India the scenes were familiar to the devotees – Tibetan practitioners had to be introduced to the content and details of the life of the Buddha.

Fig. 18. Aristocratic couple in the donor frieze with flask and cup in their midst. Detail below a religious ritual, probably featuring the consecration of the temple (photo: Jaroslav Poncar).

Fig. 19. Ceramic plate featuring a cup-holding loving couple, Kashan, 11-12th century, Museum of Islamic Art, Teheran (photo: Christiane Kalantari 2016).

loving couples holding cups of wine with their bases raised (Fig. 19) – an ancient topos in the Iranicate cultural sphere. In the Alchi donor frieze the royal drinking scene featuring a noble lady holding aloft and offering a stemmed cup; opposite her is a male dignitary, most likely her husband, who is shown in a gesture of reverence, perhaps holding a jewel in his right hand; below are attending figures perhaps servants. The scene clearly echoes the imagery of Persianate status culture and sartorial trends which may have been adopted in greater Kashmir to project authority and perhaps transmitted by representations of status culture of small Turkic kingdoms in the region. However, one also has to bear in mind that lower parts of Ladakh are part of the Hindukush cultural sphere; thus Iranicate drinking customs and ideas are familiar in this region – in particular among the Dards – including ritual wine – offerings and large banquets and prestige feasts in which wine consumption plays a central role. The cup rite has not been simply copied at Alchi but consciously adapted to articulatepurely Western Tibetan ideas of drinking culture. In this case, apart from their essential function in rituals of offerings, they appear to exhibit and confirm cultural knowledge and social cohesion, in analogy to the function of elaborate drinking songs composed as antiphones. In a wider sense the various cup-offering scenes can be understood as celebration and commemoration of the pious donors who offer their wealth for the well-being of the community, as is also described in inscriptions (Papa-Kalantari 2008). A toasting couple depicted to the right, holding a cup and with standing infants in their midst, further corroborates this assumption, with the emphasis being on the couple of noble descent as givers of birth and perhaps also reflecting the sponsor's desire for health and prosperity of their offspring.[15] One can conclude that the various scenes in the frieze have to be understood in the context of a consecration ceremony; the drinking mode reflects the interest of the donor in showing off both representation and devotion. Drinking and offerings of alcohol are important elements in such rituals up to the present day in Western Tibet in religious- and non-religious contexts (Fig. 3, 3a).

15 See also several festivities with beer offerings on the occasion of childbirth as described by Brauen in Ladakh 1980: 39.

Fig. 20, 20a, 20b. Kanji temple, donor depiction with donors in the centre engaged in a drinking ritual and dancing, ca. 15th century (photos: Heinrich Poell).

Fig. 21. Donor standing next to Avalokiteshvara and receiving his blessing; painting in a narrative featuring the Tigress Jātaka, Zhag cave temple (photo: Tsering Gyalpo 2007).

Images of cup rites in the Persianate cultural sphere[16] reflect long and lasting wine traditions in Iran and Afghanistan.[17] The eastern limits of this wine-producing tradition appears to be in northwest Pakistan and in the Dardic regions in Ladakh, on the lower riches of the Indus in the western Trans-Himalayas. Up to the present day a mildly intoxicating grape wine called *rgun chang* is produced and drunk, in the Dahanu region of Ladakh, which is the easternmost part of the Hindukush cultural sphere connecting NE Afghanistan, NW Pakistan and lower regions of Ladakh.[18] Grape-wine and grapes were commodities which Sogdian merchants appear to have transported not only to inland China until the 10th century, but

16 The consumption of wine long dominated the Iranian world: Herodotus, who described the Achaemenids as great wine drinkers, transmitted his observation as follows: if there was a decision to be made on an important question they discussed the topic twice, once sober, once drunk; then they would compare the results (I wish to thank Patrick Reza Burger for this information). Famous wine producers and perhaps the oldest wine cultivation cultures are in the southern Hindukush, near the border between Afghanistan and Pakistan (see Klimburg 2014). Wine is considered haram (forbidden) for most of Iranian society today; its official production has been continued mostly by the Armenian minority up to the present day.

17 Accordingly, the visual models for Kubera as a northern wine-drinker, to be found at Ajanta, are depicted as cup-holders attired in dresses from those regions, as observed by Monika Zin. See also recently Klimburg 2014.

18 In Ladakh grapes are grown in the lower valleys, in the Dahanu region where the Brogpa or Dards live (oral information by John Bellezza and Stefan Kloos, 2016, IATS Bergen/ Norway). There the fermented, mildly alcoholic *rgun chang* ("grape beer") is produced. The Kalash of the Hindukush call wine "dah" and traditionally women were in particular fond of drinking wine (Alberto Cacopardo, verbal information 7.2016).

most probably also to Lhasa.[19] The tradition of wine drinking and its relation to images of love-making, pair-ship and images of social cohesion in general is strongly reflected in Iranian literature from very early on.[20] This "symbolic capital" was appropriated in order to visualise rituals of ceremonial drinking in a Buddhist context, underlining the generosity of offerings and thus their wealth and power in the service of Buddhism. Their donations to found and support monasteries is in line with the task of the West Tibetan royal lama Yeshe Ö aiming at transforming the region into a Buddhist sacred land.

3.2 Beer and/ or wine rites in a Buddhist temple

Later reflections of cup rites in Western Tibet can be found at Kanji (Fig. 20-20b). In particular fine images from Tsaparang (Rtsa brang; Fig. 22), datable to the late 16th, early 17th century, further elucidate the roles of such rituals in religious ceremonies and their longevity.

The image features a related representation of the merit-granting act, depicting the royal donors attired in sumptuous costumes (adopting the turban and boots of Yar lung kings), with a lacquered offering table in front on which are placed offering cakes and various white cups, perhaps of porcelain, on stands while a servant on the right border holding aloft an elaborate copper pitcher, perhaps filled with beer or wine. As observed by Linrothe (2014: 202), golden rays shining on their heads indicate that they are receiving the blessing of Amitayus, depicted seated directly above them. The deity, the Buddha of limitless life, is shown with a golden vase in his lap from which golden threads connect the heads of the royal figures; the cup rites and drinking ceremonies thus clearly connect humans and deities in their desire for well-being promoted by those who sponsored these images.

In a detailed chapter in his 2014 book on Kashmiri art and its legacy in Western Tibet, dealing with donor tableau on *thangka*, Linrothe presented several images of drinking scenes. One of these panels is found in the bottom zone of a painting featuring the Supreme

19 Wood (2002) posited that from the second century BC until the end of the Tang dynasty (9th cent.), Sogdian merchants dominated much of the trade of the Silk Roads and they also traded grape and grape-wine.

20 Cf. the poet Nizami (1141-1209; composer of the well-known love epics 'Khosrou and Shirin' – describing the love of the Persian king for Shirin – as well as 'Leila and Majnun') and earlier authors from the 11th century. The popularity of the imagery of wine drinking and love-making had its peak in the courtly art of the Safavid era (17th cent.) in Iran, despite the strong Shiite Islamic orientation of the rulers of that time. However, the Safavid ruler Hussein (1694-1722), who was a devout Muslim, criticised these sensual pictorial traditions and prohibited the consumption of alcohol and opium.

Physician/ Bhaisajyaguru and stems from Western Tibet, ca.15th century. In this, non-celibate monks and high religious dignitaries, and lay persons, including women with children on their laps, are all holding drinking bowls and showing reverence to a deity (Fig. 23; see also Linrothe 2014: 168). They are depicted in a shared spatial context with the wealth deity Jambhala seated on the right; in addition all persons are directed to him, reflecting the desire for long-life and perhaps that for her new-born child in particular. The mode of cup-holders alludes to the image of royalty and cuprites in the context of consecration ceremonies established in Alchi. The author further concludes that the scene on the 15th century Western Tibetan *thangka* reinforces that the idea of *laukika*, mundane, worldly concerns were included in rituals of spiritual value and the role of offerings and drinking of alcohol had an important role in them (*ibid.* 202).

In summary, the famous Alchi donor images (and the paintings in Kanji and Tsaparang, 15th century taking up this theme) clearly demonstrate the role of alcohol, whether beer or wine, not only in donor scenes with toasting couples, and scenes expressing reverence and loyalty. They also reflect the introduction of the image of the Persianate cup rite into an unquestionably Buddhist ritual, which features some collective gesture of reverence appropriate to a religious setting. Thus drinking ceremonies from the Persianate world connoted with love, celebration, royalty and sumptuousness were adopted to create images of purely Tibetan Buddhist devotion.[21]

4. Conclusion

The paper is a preliminary attempt to contextualise aspects of the Western Tibetan beer-drinking culture in view also of the material culture, songs and imagery. As an important factor in the economy of monasteries – centring on trade and technology – in the ritual and social life beer became a frequent subject of folk songs (for ceremonies of different kinds) as well as the focus of many songs composed by eminent religious figures. These songs feature an image-rich language full of allusions to the qualities of a well-crafted beer, its creation by the gods and intoxication as a metaphor or real instrument for spiritual endeavours. This image-friendly culture of poetry is also found in Tibetan visual art. It is well-known

21 During our various stays in Western Tibet we could recognise the development of a wine drinking culture appropriate for official banquets; including a tasty Chinese sort of mulled wine, made of wine, Coca Cola and ginger.

Fig. 22. Tsaparang, royal couple, with cups on their lacquered tables and servants offering *chang* (photo: Christiane Kalantari 2007).

Fig. 23. Donor cartouche, featuring a ceremony with lay persons, among them women toasting with cups and with their infants on their laps, receiving the blessings of Jambhala, bestower and protector of wealth and well-being (after Linrothe 2012: Fig. 4.9).

that drinking traditions were aspects of the status culture of the Tibetan rulers from very early on; but visual sources in Western Tibetan Buddhist temples have as yet hardly been looked at from this perspective. Significant are the donor depictions at Alchi, contrasting to rather formulaic donor images at Tabo. They best reflect the process of appropriation, i.e. the integration of the rich treasure of the Western Tibetan imagination and world-view into local visual culture around 1200.[22] They feature an 'Iranicate' drinking mode and other social interactions which meet the needs of the ruling elites for the expressionof both social cohesion and representation as well as the notion of donation, veneration of the sacred as well as rituals of consecration. Remarkable is the new, visible role of women in a hitherto unknown form.

22 This characteristic has also been mentioned by David Pritzker discussing Tibetan imperial toreutics, IATS 2016, Bergen, Norway.

In particular the Kashmir-style and Persianate elements indicate the important position of these monasteries and socio-political elites on the transcontinental trade routes. Through this historical and trans-regional palimpsest of Indic, Tibetan and Persianate visual and beer-related poetry and drinking traditions, highly complex and refined mutually enhancing cultural practices emerged. The study of material and culinary cultures in Western Tibet as important sources for the study of trans-regional flows is a task for future research.

Acknowledgements: I wish to thank the family of Tsering Gyalpo, in particular his wife and his sisters, for their support and kind hospitality.

***

References

Ardussi, John A. 1977. Brewing and drinking the beer of enlightenment in Tibetan Buddhism: The Doha tradition in Tibet, *Journal of the American Oriental Society* 97(2): 115-124.

Brauen, Martin. 1980. *Feste in Ladakh*, Graz: Akademische Druck- u. Verlagsanstalt.

Esin, Emels. 1980. *A History of Pre-Islamic and Early-Islamic Turkish Culture*. Istanbul: Ünal Matbaasi.

Flood, Finbarr B. 2016. A Turk in the Dukhang? Comparative perspectives on elite dress in medieval Ladakh and the Caucasus,in: Allinger, Eva, F. Grenet, C. Jahoda, M.-K. Lang, and A. Vergati (eds.), *Interaction in the Himalayas and Central Asia: Processes of Transfer, Translation and Transformation in Art, Archaeology, Religion and Polity*. Vienna: Austrian Academy of Sciences Press, 227-254.

Grenet, Frantz. 2016. The Deydier vase and its Tibetan connections: a preliminary note,in: Allinger, Eva, F. Grenet, C. Jahoda, M.-K. Lang, and A. Vergati (eds.), *Interaction in the Himalayas and Central Asia: Processes of Transfer, Translation and Transformation in Art, Archaeology, Religion and Polity.* Vienna: Austrian Academy of Sciences Press, 91-104.

Gyalpo, Tsering, C. Jahoda, C. Kalantari, and P. Sutherland. 2015.*Khorchag Monastery.* Vienna: Austrian Academy of Sciences Press.

Heller, Amy. 2002. The silver jug of the Lhasa Jokhang. Some observations on silver objects and costumes from the Tibetan Empire (7th-9th century), online–publication: http://www.asianart.com/articles/heller/

— 2013. Observations on painted coffin panels of the Tibetan Empire, in: Cüppers, Chistopher, Robert Mayer, and Michael Walter, *Tibet after Empire. Culture, Society and Religion between 850-1000.* Kathmandu: Lumbini International Research Institute, 117-168.

Henrion-Dourcy, Isabelle. 2005. Women in performing art, in: Gyatso, Janet and H. Havnevik (eds.), *Women in Tibet: Past and Present.* New York: Columbia University Press, 195-258.

Jahoda, Christian and C. Kalantari. 2016. Kingship in Western Tibet in the 10th and 11th centuries, in: *Cahiers d'Extrême Asie* (*Special issue "Kingship, Ritual, and Narrative in Tibet and the Surrounding Cultural Area",* ed. Brandon Dotson), 24 (2015), 81-107.

Kalantari, Christiane and Tsering Gyalpo. Forthcoming. The Zhag cave sanctuary, in: Jahoda Christian and C. Kalantari (eds.), *Studies on Western Tibet II.* Vienna: Austrian Academy of Sciences.

Klimburg, Max. 2014. Viticulture in Kafiristan, in: Fragner, Bert *et. al.* (eds.), *Wine Culture in Iran and Neighbouring Countries* (*Conference Proceedings* 2001), Vienna: Austrian Academy of Sciences, 53-70.

Linrothe, Rob. 2014. *Collecting Paradise. Buddhist Art of Kashmir and its Legacy*, New York: Rubin Museum of Art.

Martin, Dan. 2014. In praise of beer; web log, 7.2014: Tibeto-logic.blogspot.co.at/2014/07/in-praise-of-beer.

Müller, Claudius C. (ed.) 1982. *Der Weg zum Dach der Welt.* Innsbruck: Pinguin-Verlag.

Papa-Kalantari, Christiane. 2008. Celestial architecture, Dissertation, Universität Wien. Historisch-Kulturwissenschaftliche Fakultät (2 vols.).

Pritzker, David. 2016. Allegories of kingship: a preliminary study of a Western Asian gold ewer in the royal court of Tibet, in: Allinger, Eva, F. Grenet, C. Jahoda, M.-K. Lang, and A. Vergati (eds.), *Interaction in the Himalayas and Central Asia: Processes of Transfer, Translation and Transformation in Art, Archaeology, Religion and Polity.* Vienna: Austrian Academy of Sciences Press.

Richardson, Hugh. 1998. *High Peaks, Pure Earth: Collected Writing on Tibetan History and Culture.* London: Serindia.

Richardson, Hugh. 1993. *Ceremonies of the Lhasa Year.* London: Serindia.

Shen Weirong. 2004. Magic power, sorcery and evil spirit. The image of Tibetan monks in Chinese literature during the Yuan Dynasty (1260-1366), in: Cüppers, Christoph (ed.), *The Relation between Religion and State (chos srid zung 'brel) in Traditional Tibet. Proceedings of a Seminar Held in Lumbini, Nepal, March 2000*, Lumbini. Lumbini International Research Institute, 151-168.

Schaeffer, Kurtis R. 2013. A drinking song, in: Schaeffer, Kurtis R. *et al.* (eds.), *Sources of Tibetan Tradition.* New York: Columbia University Press, 474-478.

Tropper, Kurt. 2015. The Inscription in the Lo tsa ba lha khang of Kanji, Ladakh, *Wiener Zeitschrift für die Kunde Südasiens* 55: 145-180.

Twitchett, Denis C. and J. K. Fairbank (eds.). 1979. *The Cambridge History of China: Sui and T'ang China, 589-906*, vol. 3. Cambridge: Cambridge University Press.

Vitali, Roberto. 2003. A chronology (*bstan rtsis*) of events in the history of mNga' ris skor gsum (tenth-fifteenth centuries), in: McKay, Alex (ed.), *The History of Tibet. Vol. II. The Medieval Period: c.850-1895. The Development of Buddhist Paramountcy.* London: Routledge Curzon.

Wood, Frances. 2002. *The Silk Road: Two thousand Years in the Heart of Asia*, Berkely: University of California Press.

古格时期西藏阿里地区的重要城堡与村镇略考

黄博 *

阿里地处西藏高原的高海拔地区，平均海拔在 4500 米以上，其北部又是不宜于农耕的羌塘高原，且整个阿里地区都不易于农业生产，只有南部的河谷地带能够从事少量的农业生产。在以游牧活动为主的经济形态下，形成西部西藏区域人口密度小，区域人口流动频繁等牧区居住特点，严重制约了这一地区古代早期城镇的产生。古代阿里境内的城镇发展水平，一般而言至少要到清代才显现出某些城镇的形态。因此本文的主旨不是就阿里地区的古代城市（城镇）发展情况和水平进行描述和评估，仅仅是就历史上阿里地区曾经出现过的一些重要城堡和村镇的情况加以梳理。因此这些所谓的城堡和村镇并不具备现代意义上的城镇的含义，它更多的是一种地名上的意义。当然这些有名的地点之所以出现在历史上，与它们曾经是一些相对繁荣的居民点和拥有巨大实力的军事要塞有关，它们在古代阿里地区发挥过重要的军事和政治意义，其中一些居民点因为佛寺的兴建也成为十分重要的宗教中心，在体现军政意义的同时也就具有了弘扬和发展宗教文化的功能。

9 世纪中期吐蕃王朝的崩溃导致整个青藏高原陷入割据和混战之中，到 10 世纪时，赞普后裔进入西部，在象雄故地建立古格王国，西藏西部地区出现相对稳定的割据局面。直到 17 世纪初古格王国的覆灭，西部西藏的政治地理格局才发生新的变化，因此在整个古格王国时期，阿里境内的重要城堡和村镇在区域历史时间上尚能具有一定的连续性，在城镇发展的特点上自然也有某种程度的一致性。这些城堡和村镇基本上都分布在今天阿里地区境内的札达和普兰两县之内，而阿里地区其他几县则没有找到相关的资料。虽然就地理环境而言，阿里大部分地方都是荒凉的草原或沙漠，但是它的南部地区由于朗钦藏布、森格藏布、马甲藏布等大小河流的影响而形成了不少河

* 黄博：四川大学中国藏学研究所副教授。

谷平原和台地，有些区域在古代可能其植被还相当茂密，在河流两岸也有一些可供农耕的田地，故而札达和普兰两地的半农半牧型经济也具备了早期城镇产生的一些基本的物质条件。所以札达与普兰正好是阿里地区的少数几个能够从事农业生产的地区，现有历史资料的表现并不是偶然的，而是历史事实的一种合理的沉淀。因此本文尝试结合现有的历史资料和国内外学者的研究成果，综合考述西藏历史上割据时期阿里境内的重要城堡和村镇的历史面貌及其相关事件，并梳理出它们同现今阿里地名的比较粗略的对应关系。

一、古格地区

东嘎（དུང་དཀར），这里近二十年来早已成为阿里考古成就中最著名和最重要的发现之一。不过关于它的文献记录情况，各期考古调查报告则大多语焉不详。考古研究估计东嘎遗址中的晚期石窟群的年代当不早于公元 13 世纪，大致在公元 13-15 世纪前后，因为现有遗存发现中尚未出现关于格鲁派和宗喀巴及其弟子信息的内容。[1] 东嘎在《阿里王统记》中早期拼写为 དུན་བཀར，文献记载 11 世纪末，古格王旺德上台后将首都从托林迁到东嘎，他在东嘎修筑城堡，作为自己的依止之地[2]。东嘎作为古格的政治中心一直保持到 14 世纪末南杰德迁都芒囊时为止。东嘎位于朗钦藏布以北，是古格北部地区的重镇，一度与南部地区的托林一起成为古格最重要的两个政教中心。割据时期习惯上将古格地区以朗钦藏布为标界进行区域划分，朗钦藏布以北为北部地区，称为“羌”，包括东嘎、皮央等地；朗钦藏布以南的地区则为南部地区，称为“洛”，包括扎布让、托林、芒囊等地。南北两部拥有不同的贵族势力集团，经常争权夺利。古格在 12 世纪中期分裂成南北两个王国，东嘎成为北朝的都城所在地。这期间东嘎的贵族发挥过重要作用，也是造成国家分裂的一支破坏性力量，古格王泽巴赞死后，“象泉河北边东嘎皮央的一些僧人与杂布让卡的某些人不怀好意，挑拨离间，两位王妃间产生矛盾，互不相服，对峙的裂痕渐增。最终南北分裂，势不两立”。[3]

1　西藏自治区文物局、四川联合大学考古学业：《西藏阿里东嘎、皮央石窟考古调查简报》，《文物》1997 年第 9 期，第 21 页。

2　ཟངས་ཁ་ཚ་ཁྲི་བཀྲ་ཤིས་འབར་ལྡེ་བཙན་ཏེ། དཔལ་ལྡེ་ཡང་ཟེར། ཕོད་སྐུ་བསོད་མི་ལྷུར་འབར་ནས། གུ་གེ་ཞང་ཞུང་ལྡོ་བྱང་ལ་མངའ་གསོལ་ཏེ། གུ་གེ་མཁན་ཆེན་ངག་དབང་གྲགས་པས་བརྩམས། 《མངའ་རིས་རྒྱལ་རབས》1996ལོར་ཐོ་ལིང་གཙུག་ལག་ཁང་ལོ་གཅིག་སྟོང་འཁོར་བའི་རྗེས་དྲན་མཛད་སྒོའི་གོ་སྒྲིག་ཚོགས་ཆུང་གིས་པར་དུ་བསྐྲུན། ཤ74།

3　古格·次仁加布：《阿里史话》，拉萨：西藏人民出版社，2003 年，第 23 页。

东嘎作为古格的政教中心大约有三百年的时间，古格历代统治者对东嘎的经营使得这里在古代曾经相当繁荣。20 世纪 90 年代以来，阿里地区考古工作中最为著名的东嘎遗址的发现也证实东嘎曾经的繁荣。东嘎遗址位于今阿里地区札达县城以北约 40 公里的河谷地带，其西面有一条小河流入朗钦藏布，河谷两地有农田，可以耕种小麦、青稞等农作物，这在阿里也算是自然条件比较好的地方了。据考古调查，在现在的东嘎村北面的断崖上分布着庞大的石窟群，在南面的台地上还有一些残存的佛塔群和寺庙遗址群。另外在东嘎村东面 30 公里处的山沟中还有一处石窟群，这些石窟中包括进行佛教宗教仪式的礼佛窟、用于僧侣们居住和生活的禅窟和僧房窟，此外还有仓库窟和厨房窟，石窟中的精美壁画经考古发现后早已为世人所惊叹。[4] 这不但表明东嘎城堡之外聚有大量居民，而且因佛寺的兴建而更为繁荣。15 世纪前半期古格王南喀旺波彭措德在扎布让山峰上修筑王宫 [5]，从此将都城迁到扎布让王城（即后来举世闻名的古格故城），到这时东嘎才失去了首都地位，随后逐渐衰落。这很可能就是为什么现在未能在东嘎遗址中发现关于格鲁派和宗喀巴及其弟子的画像或题名之类信息的主要原因。不过早期格鲁派在阿里的弘法活动肯定是到过东嘎的，因为在《黄琉璃》的记载中，这里曾是宗喀巴的阿里弟子阿旺扎巴从卫藏地区学法回到古格后最早的落脚之处。[6]

皮央（ཕྱི་ཡང 或 པི་ཡང），按卫藏语音应当读作齐旺或毕旺，阿里地区一般读作皮央。在割据时代这里是古格北部的一个重要村镇，位于东嘎以南，在朗钦藏布北岸，古格前期这里是一个重要的佛教中心，益西沃弘法时代曾在这里建有皮瓦寺，[7] 到古格中期这里已经成为政治和宗教上的重要村镇之一。1424 年古格王南喀旺波彭措德（ནམ་མཁའི་དབང་པོ་ཕུན་ཚོགས་ལྡེ）曾在此举行过登基大典，阿旺扎巴也参加了这次盛典并在《阿里王统记》中记下了这一盛大的场面：南喀旺波彭措德在他 16 岁时在皮央由他的父王南杰德主持迎娶了拉达克公主为妃，同时南杰德将王位传给了他，古格的大臣和僧侣们都聚集到皮央来参加这一大典，阿旺扎巴也亲自率领僧众到皮央参加了

4 西藏自治区文物局、四川联合大学考古学业：《西藏阿里东嘎、皮央石窟考古调查简报》，第 6-22 页。

5 Roberto Vitali, *The Kingdoms of Gu.ge Pu.hrang*, New Delhi: Indraprastha Press, 1996, p.503.

6 སྡེ་སྲིད་སངས་རྒྱས་རྒྱ་མཚོས་བརྩམས།《དགའ་ལྡན་ཆོས་འབྱུང་བཻཌཱུརྱ་སེར་པོ》1989ལོར་ཀྲུང་གོའི་བོད་ཀྱི་ཤེས་རིག་དཔེ་སྐྲུན་ཁང་གིས་པར་དུ་བསྐྲུན། ཤ272།

7 Roberto Vitali, *The Kingdoms of Gu.ge Pu.hrang*, p.269.

南喀旺波彭措德的登基大典[8]。

古格两代国王将传位大典和与拉达克王室联姻的重大典礼都选在皮央举行，从中可见在 15 世纪前半期时，皮央所具有的政治地位和繁荣局面。关于皮央的历史记载在最近 20 多年来为考古发现所证明，1992 年以来经过西藏自治区文物局和四川大学的考古工作者的调查和发掘，皮央已经成为举世闻名之地。皮央现在是阿里地区札达县下属的一个村庄，地处朗钦藏布北侧支流的一条山谷中，距著名的托林寺约 40 公里，海拔 4050 米。考古队在紧靠皮央村西侧的山崖上发现了有近千孔石窟及部分佛寺遗迹，包括所谓的格林塘佛寺遗址和皮央村西侧佛寺遗迹，残存有集会大殿和僧房等遗迹；此外还有礼佛窟和生活窟以及一些佛塔残存建筑等，整个遗址的规模十分庞大。[9]

噶林（ཀ་ཞིང 或 ཀ་སྡིང），此地纯粹是一个古老的村镇。因为在该地既无城堡建筑，也没有什么著名的寺院，仅仅是因为他是古格高僧阿旺扎巴的出生地而被史册所记录，可见当地可能是一个拥有一定数量的定居人口的普通村庄。《黄琉璃》在记载阿旺扎巴的出生时提到此地位于恒河南岸附近一带，是著名的格鲁派高僧、宗喀巴的弟子古格 · 阿旺扎巴的出生地。[10] 此处所指的恒河就是发源于冈底斯山的朗钦藏布（象泉河），象泉河被认为是著名的恒河的上源。此地在地域上属于古格的洛堆（南部的上部）地区。它除了诞生出阿旺扎巴这样的高僧之外，此前还诞生过一位英明神武的国王。据史料记载，在阿旺扎巴之前，拉达克国王的弟弟热吉喇嘛桑波（རས་ཀྱི་བླ་མ་བཟང་པོ）曾经在古格王扎巴德（1230-1277）统治时来到噶林，在这里他预言古格将来会诞生一个德才兼备、崇敬佛法的王子。这位王子就是后来著名的古格王南杰德（1372-1439），阿旺扎巴在《阿里王统记》中生动地记下了在他的家乡发生的这一政

8 དཀྱུང་ལོ་བཅུ་དྲུག་པ་ལ་བྱུང་ངོས་ཀྱི་ཕྱི་ལྷང་དུ་སྤྱན་དྲངས། ས་སྐྱོང་རྣམ་རྒྱལ་ལྡེ་གཙོ་བོ་ཡོད། གུ་གེ་ཏི་དགེ་སྐུ་བཀའ་གྲོས་ལ་དབང་བ་རྣམས་ཚོགས་ནས་མར་ཡུལ་གྱི་རྒྱལ་མོ་ཁྲི་ལྕམ་རྒྱལ་མོར་བཞེས། མཁས་པའི་དབང་པོ་ངག་དབང་གྲགས་པ་ལ་སོགས་པ་དྲུང་མིག་འཛིན་པའི་འདུས་པ་རྒྱ་མཚོ་ལྟ་བུ་དང་། ཁྲི་རྣམ་རྒྱལ་ལྡེ་དཔལ་བཟང་པོའི་ཞབས་དྲུང་ནས་གདན་ཆགས། སློན་པོ་འདུན་ན་འདོན། དྲུང་འཁོར་སྐྱ་བོའི་ཚོགས་ཀྱི་ཀུན་ནས་གང་བའི་དབུས་སུ་མེས་ལྷ་བླ་མ་ཡེ་ཤེས་འོད་ནས་གཙོས་ཏེ་ཉི་མའི་རིགས་ཀྱི་རྒྱལ་ཚབ་མཐའ་དག་གི་ཞབས་ཀྱི་རྟུལ་དང་། འགྲོགས་པར་འོས་པའི་གཉིས་འཕྲུང་དབང་པོའི་ཁྲི་སྟེང་དུ་ཡངས་པའི་རྒྱལ་ཁམས་ལེགས་པར་སྐྱོང་བའི་རྒྱལ་སྲིད་ཀྱི་དབང་ཕྱུག་ལ་མངོན་པར་དབང་བསྐུར། གུ་གེ་མཁན་ཆེན་ངག་དབང་གྲགས་པས་བརྩམས།《མངའ་རིས་རྒྱལ་རབས》ཤ84།

9 参见四川大学历史文化学院考古学系等：《西藏札达县皮央—东嘎遗址 1997 年调查与发掘》，《考古学报》2001 年第 3 期，第 397-422 页。

10 སྡེ་སྲིད་སངས་རྒྱས་རྒྱ་མཚོས་བརྩམས།《དགའ་ལྡན་ཆོས་འབྱུང་བཻཌཱུརྻ་སེར་པོ》ཤ272།

治预言故事[11]。这个故事不但表明噶林位于古格的南部，而且还说明它的地位颇为重要。噶林作为阿旺扎巴的故乡和南杰德预言故事的发生地，尽管我们无法考订其具体位置和人口规模，它在14世纪前后很可能只是古格境内的一个普通村镇，但是两个重大事件的发生都与它有关，他的普通或许更能够加深我们对于古格王国中期的一般村庄的了解。罗伯特 · 维他利猜测其具体地点可能位于著名的托林寺附近的朗钦藏布左岸的某个地方。[12]

芒囊（མང་ནང），又称玛朗（མ་ནམ），也是割据时期古格的一个重要村镇。此地位于古格和普兰的交通要道上，芒囊河流过域内，地理环境比较优越。河流两岸是古格人民定居生活的重要选择地，因为河流附近一般都有适宜于耕种的土地存在。后弘期初期，拉喇嘛绛曲沃（984-1078）曾在此兴建了绛曲根埃林寺（བྱང་ཆུབ་དགེ་ངས་གླིང་གཙུག་ལག་ཁང）[13]，俗称芒囊寺。现在在札达县的古格故城东南17公里处的芒囊村的山道中仍有芒囊寺遗址，寺庙建在山道中平坦的地面上，其中著名的强巴佛殿仍然保存得比较完整。[14] 阿底峡入藏之初，也曾在芒囊与绛曲沃相见，讨论过一些佛教问题。[15] 古格王南杰德时曾在芒囊修建过王宫，并长期居住于此[16]。看来芒囊在15世纪前期一度成为古格的首都。芒囊是典型的因佛寺的兴建，成为宗教重镇而兴盛的古代村镇之一。

桑达尔（སང་དར），是古格的一个重要村镇，而且还是后弘期初期的一个佛教圣地，著名的拉喇嘛悉瓦沃曾在这里供养僧人，大兴佛法[17]。桑达尔位于一个河谷地带，面向托林的东北，处于朗钦藏布的右岸，此地景色壮丽，连结着托林、齐旺和东噶尔等古格要地，是重要的交通要道。图齐曾在这里发现过废弃的佛塔。[18]

木让卡尔波切城堡（མུ་རང་མཁར་པོ་ཆེ），此为古格早期城堡之一，修建者为著名

11 དེ་ཡང་མངའ་བདག་གྲགས་པ་ལྡེའི་རྒྱལ་སྲིད་ལ། ལྷ་སྟོད་ཀྱི་ཀ་གླིང་ན། མར་ཡུལ་གྱི་མངའ་བདག་རས་ཆེན་གྱི་གཙུང་པོ་རས་ཀྱི་བླ་མ་བཟང་པོ་གཅིག་བཞུགས་པའི་རྗེ་ལམ་ལ། བདག་མོ་ལ་སྲས་མཚན་དང་། བསོད་ནམས་དང་ལྡན་པ། སངས་རྒྱས་ཀྱི་བསྟན་པ་ལ་ཕན་པ། མངའ་རིས་ཐམས་ཅད་ཀྱི་མགོན་སྐྱབས་སུ་གྱུར་པ། རྒྱལ་སྲིད་མངའ་ཐང་ཕུན་སུམ་ཚོགས་པ་ལ་མངའ་མཛད་པ་ཅིག་འབྱུངས་པར་ལུང་བསྟན། གུ་གེ་མཁན་ཆེན་ངག་དབང་གྲགས་པས་བརྩམས། 《མངའ་རིས་རྒྱལ་རབས》ཤ80།

12 Roberto Vitali, *The Kingdoms of Gu.ge Pu.hrang*, p.93.

13 གུ་གེ་མཁན་ཆེན་ངག་དབང་གྲགས་པས་བརྩམས།《མངའ་རིས་རྒྱལ་རབས》ཤ63།

14 参见索朗旺堆主编 :《阿里地区文物志》，拉萨 : 西藏人民出版社，1993年，第97-102页。

15 གུ་གེ་མཁན་ཆེན་ངག་དབང་གྲགས་པས་བརྩམས།《མངའ་རིས་རྒྱལ་རབས》ཤ64།

16 གཙོ་ཆེར་མ་ནམ་དུ་རྒྱལ་པོའི་ཕོ་བྲང་མཛད་ནས་དེར་གདན་ཆགས། གུ་གེ་མཁན་ཆེན་ངག་དབང་གྲགས་པས་བརྩམས།《མངའ་རིས་རྒྱལ་རབས》ཤ 84།

17 སང་དར་དུ་དབུ་སྡེ། བཙུན་པ་བཞི་བཅུའི་ཆ་རྐྱེན་དང་བཅས་པ་བཙུགས། གུ་གེ་མཁན་ཆེན་ངག་དབང་གྲགས་པས་བརྩམས།《མངའ་རིས་རྒྱལ་རབས》ཤ 67།

18 Roberto Vitali, *The Kingdoms of Gu.ge Pu.hrang*, pp.315-316.

的古格王泽德（活动时间在 11 世纪后半期）。藏文传记《丹巴却列参坚喇嘛传》（1524 年成书）记载了泽德王曾在托林寺西南五天路程的叫做木让的地方建造了这座城堡[19]。罗伯特·维他利据此推断木让卡尔波切城堡可能就在多香（དོ་ཤང）。[20] 多香现为札达县的一个村名，在古格王城遗址西南约 20 公里处，现在多香村尚有一座叫做木卡尔的寺庙。据上世纪考古调查发现在多香村北 1 公里的多香河东岸台地上的一个独立土山上坐落着一个已经荒废已久的古城堡遗址，城堡中有佛殿、碉堡、塔、防卫墙等，同时在当地还发现有大量的铠甲、头盔等武器装备，调查认为这里应当是古格王国下属的一个治所。[21] 综合藏史记载和考古发现，基本可以确定这里应当就是古格前期木让卡尔波切城堡的所在地，并且在后来发展成为一个较为庞大的军事重镇。

二、普兰地区

尼松堡[22]，也许是割据时期普兰地区最著名的城堡，现存大多数的藏族史书中都记载着阿里王朝的开创者吉德尼玛衮进入阿里地区之后建造尼松堡的事实，尼松堡即是吉德尼玛衮政权的政治中心，也是该政权的军事总部，因此该城堡所在地则相当于吉德尼玛衮的首都。《佛教史大宝藏论》（1321 年）记载，“利玛贡（尼玛衮）被放逐到后藏阿里地区，因此他也就在布让（普兰）那里建筑了古喀利绒城堡（སྐུ་མཁར་ཉི་གཟུངས），遂掌握了那里的政权。”[23] 其中古喀利绒城堡即尼松堡，古喀为藏语城堡之意，利绒的准确译音应是尼松。《雅隆尊者教法史》（1376 年）关于此事记述是参考了布顿大师的，书中说“尼玛衮抵阿里，于普兰建尼松宫堡（སྐུ་མཁར་ཉི་བཟུངས）。即位执政。”[24]《新红史》（1538 年）记载：“贝阔赞之次子尼玛衮前往阿里，在布让地方建造尼松堡（སྐུ་མཁར་ཉི་བཟུང）。”[25]《贤者喜宴》（1564 年）记载吉德尼玛衮到阿里后，由于他行为高尚、智慧广博而得到阿里三围臣民之欢心，遂即请其为王。尼玛衮在普

19 ཐོ་ལིང་ནས་མི་རྒྱང་གི་དགོངས་ལྔ་ཙམ་ལྷོ་ནུབ་ཏུ་ཕྱིན་པ་ན་མུ་རང་ཞེས་བྱ་བའི་ཡུལ་ཅིག་ཡོད། དེ་དང་པོ་གུ་གེ་པའི་འོག་ཡིན་པས་དེ་ན་མངའ་བདག་རྩེ་ལྡེས་བཏབ་པའི་མུ་རང་མཁར་པོ་ཆེ་ཞེས་བྱ་བ་ཡོད། དབང་ཕྱུག་དཔལ་ལྡན་གྱིས་བརྩམས། 《དཔལ་ལྡན་བླ་མ་དམ་པ་ཆོས་ལེགས་མཚན་ཅན་གྱི་རྣམ་ཐར》 ཤིང་པར་མ། ཤ7།

20 Roberto Vitali, *The Kingdoms of Gu.ge Pu.hrang*, p.318.

21 索朗旺堆主编：《阿里地区文物志》，第 94-97 页。

22 尼松堡的藏文写法各书不尽相同，但其藏语发音却一致，可见只是拼写的不同而所指不异。至于不同的写法行文时再给出相应的藏文对应词，在此不一一列出。

23 布顿大师著，郭和卿译：《佛教史大宝藏论》，北京：民族出版社，1986 年，第 181 页。

24 释迦仁钦德著，汤池安译：《雅隆尊者教法史》，拉萨：西藏人民出版社，2002 年，第 40 页。

25 班钦索南查巴著，黄颢译：《新红史》，拉萨：西藏人民出版社，2002 年，第 26 页。

兰建造了著名的尼松堡（སྐུ་མཁར་ཉི་བཟུངས）。[26]《拉达克王统记》则明确写下了尼松堡就是阿里王朝的首都，书中说吉德尼玛衮是在格西赞的支持下来到普兰，娶妻生子，然后修建尼松堡作为首都[27]。综上所述，从古到今所有的藏史著作中，吉德尼玛衮修建尼松堡的举动都是与他在阿里的建政立国的标志性事件有关，可见城堡寨在军政上具有的重要意义。

吉德尼玛衮死后，尼松堡为其子扎西衮所继承。《汉藏史集》称“扎西尼玛衮住在尼桑城堡（སྐུ་མཁར་ཉི་བཟུངས）”[28]。《阿里王统记》也将尼松堡（སྐུ་མཁར་ཉི་ཟུང）作为扎西衮的封地之一，并且将尼松堡与穆、珠牧区三湖（འབྲོག་མཚོ་མུ་རྒྱུད་གསུམ）、巴噶（བར་སྣ）、颇朗（བོ་ལངས）、嘉和尼玛（གྱ་དང་ཉི་མ）等地并列，同属于所谓的右翼地区（གཡས་སྐོར་བ）[29]。所谓的牧区三湖，据苯教的《西藏朝圣指南书》（བོད་ཡུལ་གནས་ལམ་ཡིག）所说，“穆”是对著名的圣湖玛旁雍错和鬼湖拉昂错的简称，此二湖又名穆列苦错（མུ་ལེ་ཁྱུད་མཚོ）和吐错穆列多林（དུག་མཚོ་མུ་ལེའི་རྡོ་གླིང）。[30]而“珠”则是对现在普兰县霍尔乡东南的公珠错（གུང་རྒྱུད་མཚོ）的简称。[31]巴噶这一地名现在仍然在用，[32]该地地处冈仁波齐峰下，玛旁雍错和拉昂错湖边，是朝拜神山圣湖的集散地，笔者2009年夏在阿里考察时曾经过此地，这里是转山和观湖人群的中转站，因此店铺林立，商业繁荣。至于颇朗的确切位置现在则不清楚，罗伯特·维他利认为二者为一地，藏文史著《邬坚巴传》记载，邬坚巴曾经过巴噶颇朗，从该书行文来看，巴噶颇朗是一个地名，此处土地易于农耕，而且有些土地还相当肥沃[33]。邬坚巴（1230-1309）是13世纪后半期西藏著名的高僧，也是一位大旅行家。他是竹巴噶举派上竹巴支派的创始人郭仓巴（1189-1258）的弟子，大约在13世纪中期奉郭仓巴之命经阿里进入

26 ཅེས་གྲགས་པ་ལྟར་སྤྱོད་པ་ཞིགས་ཤིང་བློ་གྲོས་ཆེ་བས་མངའ་རིས་བསྐོར་གསུམ་གྱི་མི་རྣམས་མགུ་སྟེ་རྗེ་ཞུས། སྤུ་རངས་སུ་སྐུ་མཁར་ཉི་བཟུངས་བརྩིགས། དཔའ་བོ་གཙུག་ལག་ཕྲེང་བས་བརྩམས། 《ཆོས་འབྱུང་མཁས་པའི་དགའ་སྟོན》2006ལོར་མི་རིགས་དཔེ་སྐྲུན་ཁང་གིས་པར་དུ་བསྐྲུན། ཤ228།

27 དེའི་ཚེ་དགེ་བཤེས་བཙན་གྱིས་པུ་ཧྲངས་སུ་ཞུ་སྟེ། འགྲོ་ཟ་འཁོར་སྐྱོང་བཙུན་མོར་ཕུལ་བ་ཁབ་ཏུ་བཞེས་པ་ལ། སྲས་གསུམ་བྱུང་ཞིང་། སྐུ་མཁར་ཉི་ཟུངས་རྩིག་སྟེ། རྒྱལ་ས་བཏབ་ནས།《ལ་དྭགས་རྒྱལ་རབས》1987ལོར་བོད་ལྗོངས་མི་དམངས་དཔེ་སྐྲུན་ཁང་གིས་པར་དུ་བསྐྲུན། ཤ42།

28 达仓宗巴·班觉桑波著，陈庆英译：《汉藏史集》，拉萨：西藏人民出版社，1986年，第114页。

29 སྤུ་ཧྲང་སྐུ་མཁར་ཉི་ཟུང་། འབྲོག་མཚོ་མུ་རྒྱུད་གསུམ། བར་སྣ་དང་། བོ་ལངས། གྱ་དང་ཉི་མ། བྱང་པུ་སྤྲུལ་ནག་ཕྱུར་ལ་རྒྱུགས་པ་འདྲ་ཡན་ཆད་གཡས་སྐོར་བ། གུ་གེ་མཁན་ཆེན་ངག་དབང་གྲགས་པས་བརྩམས།《མངའ་རིས་རྒྱལ་རབས》ཤ51།

30 Roberto Vitali, *The Kingdoms of Gu.ge Pu.hrang*, pp.153-154.

31 公珠错意为中流湖，海拔4768米，面积61平方公里，为咸水湖。参见武振华主编：《西藏地名》，第175页。

32 武振华主编：《西藏地名》，第18页。

33 ཏི་སེའི་ས་ཆ་བར་ཀ་བོང་ལ་བྱ་བའི་ཐང་གཅིག་ཡོད་པ་ཐམས་ཅད་ཞིང་དུ་འདུག་པས་ལ་ལ་བཟང་པོ་འདུག ཁ་གཅིག་ངན་པར་འདུག ལ་ལ་ཐ་བ་རེངས་པར་འདུག ཞིང་དེ་རྣམས་སློམ་ཆེན་པ་རྣམས་ཀྱི་དགེ་སྦྱོར་གྱི་རྐྱ་རུ་འདུག་གསུང་། རྟོགས་ལྡན་བློ་བ་སེང་གེས་བརྩམས། 《ཨོ་རྒྱན་པའི་རྣམ་ཐར་རྒྱས་པ》ཤ41།

克什米尔然后到印度的邬坚（今巴基斯坦斯瓦特河谷地区）地方游学，所以人称邬坚巴，他从邬坚地方回到西藏时，郭仓巴刚圆寂不久。[34]最后，嘉和尼玛，后世一般合写在一起，是为姜叶马（རྒྱ་ཉི་མ）。姜叶马现在是札达县的一个牧点，[35]它在近代是十分著名的地区性夏季市场，20世纪初英印当局曾试图迫使西藏地方政府将此开放为通商口岸，[36]从现有地图上看，此地有公路相通，大约在巴噶西南60公里处。现代考古学者还在这里发现过两块石碑，当地牧民称之为达热石碑和仁钦曲顶石碑，属于古代象雄文化遗迹之一。[37]综上所述，尼松堡的大致位置当在普兰东部（右翼地区）的神山圣湖一带的某个地点。

泽杰城堡（རྩེ་རྒྱལ），曾经是普兰王国前期的首都之一，位于普兰的杰蒂（རྒྱལ་ཏི）地方。《阿里王统记》记载，大约于13世纪初在位的普兰王南德衮就曾居住在泽杰宫中[38]，泽杰的藏文含义乃是"胜利峰"，正是王者应居之所。其后古格王扎巴德（1230-1277）征服普兰，也曾驻锡杰蒂，并在此地接见了第三任止贡多津衮噶坚赞，《止贡冈底斯山志》记载，衮噶坚赞到冈底斯山担任止贡多津之后，得到古格王扎巴德和王后拉坚珊珠的邀请前往普兰的杰蒂城堡传法[39]。止贡多津是止贡派在冈底斯山一带的教团主持，由止贡寺寺主委任，是整个止贡派在西部西藏的最高领袖，驻锡在冈仁波齐峰以南山谷中的远声寺，可见在13世纪中期古格征服普兰之后，杰蒂仍然具有十分重要的政教地位。这种地位甚至一个世纪以后仍然没有衰落，15世纪时，普兰人与洛巴人还在这里发生过激烈的战斗，表明杰蒂仍然是普兰重要的军政中心之一。

1436年萨迦派高僧俄尔钦·衮噶桑波（ངོར་ཆེན་ཀུན་དགའ་བཟང་པོ）得到古格王南喀旺波彭措德的邀请前往传法，二人会见之地即在杰蒂[40]。俄尔钦·衮噶桑波（1382-1456），出生于萨迦，并在萨迦学法，9岁出家，曾经担任过萨迦寺的堪布，后来在俄

34 关于邬坚巴的事迹参见廓诺·迅·伯著、郭和卿译：《青史》，拉萨：西藏人民出版社，2003年，第412-416页。

35 武振华主编：《西藏地名》，第221页。

36 H.K. 格雷西：《关于在西藏西部适宜建立一个开放性商埠的地点的备忘录》（1904年5月2日），英国外交部档案第四卷第6号文件附17，1906年编印。

37 顿珠拉杰：《西藏西北部地区象雄文化遗迹考察报告》，《西藏研究》2003年第3期，第107页。

38 དེའི་སྐབས་གཉིས་པ་རྣམ་ལྡེ་མགོན་རྒྱལ་ས་རྩེ་རྒྱལ་དུ་བཞུགས་ནས། གུ་གེ་མཁན་ཆེན་ངག་དབང་གྲགས་པས་བརྩམས།《མངའ་རིས་རྒྱལ་རབས》ཤ 69།

39 དེའི་རྗེས་སུ་རྗེ་འཛིན་པ་ཀུན་དགའ་རྒྱལ་མཚན་པ་བྱོན། རྗེ་འདི་གུ་གེ་རྒྱལ་པོ་གྲི་གྲགས་པ་ལྡེ་དང་། ལྷ་ལྕམ་བསམ་གྲུབ་རྒྱལ་མོ་ཡབ་ཡུམ་གྱིས་སྤུ་རང་རྒྱལ་ཏི་མཁར་དུ་གདན་དྲངས་ནས་ཆོས་ཞུས་པའི་ཡོན་དུ་སྤུ་རང་ཐང་ཡབ་སྟོད་སྨད་ལ་སོགས་པ་ཕུལ་ལོ། དཀོན་མཆོག་བསྟན་འཛིན་གྱིས་བརྩམས།《གངས་རིའི་གནས་བཤད་ཤེལ་དཀར་མེ་ལོང་ཞེས་པ་བཞུགས་སོ》1992ལོར་བོད་ལྗོངས་མི་དམངས་དཔེ་སྐྲུན་ཁང་གིས་པར་དུ་བསྐྲུན། ཤ59།

40 Roberto Vitali, *The Kingdoms of Gu.ge Pu.hrang*, p391.

尔地方创建艾旺却丹寺，简称俄尔寺，他本人因此被称为“俄尔钦”。他以精通萨迦派密法闻名，是萨迦派密教三支派中俄尔支派（ངོར་པ）的创始人[41]。15世纪时普兰长期处在珞俄政权[42]的统治之下，15世纪末，普兰为摆脱珞俄的统治，首先要收复的就是珞俄人控制下的杰蒂。据《后藏疯子亥如伽传》记载，传主本人经过普兰时，正好遇上普兰与珞俄交战。后藏疯子亥如伽（གཙང་སྨྱོན་ཧེ་རུ་ཀ）是乳毕坚金（1452-1507）的绰号，他是后藏娘堆地方人，为噶举派僧人，出家后取法名为桑结坚赞，学法期间遍游各地，他崇尚山中苦修，行为怪异，衣衫褴褛，故被称为后藏疯子，又因为他得到圆满四灌顶，在密教中被誉为“胜乐金刚饮血王”，亥如伽在藏文中即意为“胜乐金刚”（འཁོར་ལོ་བདེ་མཆོག）或饮血王[43]。他是著名的《米拉日巴传》和《玛尔巴传》等噶举派祖师传记的作者，是15世纪西藏最有成就的传记文学大师[44]。他的传记中记载了普兰和珞俄人在杰蒂发生过激烈的战斗，打得日月无光，血流成河，之后普兰攻下了杰蒂，而珞俄人则驻兵城外，准备再战[45]。可见杰蒂在整个15世纪，不但是普兰的军政中心，也是外来势力控制普兰的重要据点，成为兵家必争之地。

噶尔东（དཀར་དུམ）城堡，该城堡位于普兰的圣湖南岸，历史相当悠久，据《科迦寺志》记载它是由10世纪晚期著名的古格王柯热所建。不过该城堡真正发挥军政作用则是在13世纪晚期，这一时期贡塘王朝统治者成为萨迦派在西部地区的代理人，监管古格和普兰等政权，为加强对西部地区尤其是对古格和普兰的控制，贡塘王朝

41 关于俄尔钦的生平详情，参见王森：《西藏佛教发展史略》，北京：中国藏学出版社，2010年，第86-87页。

42 珞俄，又称洛门塘，全区信奉萨迦派，位于西藏与尼泊尔交界处，其首府即今尼泊尔的木斯塘县，距西藏边境仅18公里，海拔3700米左右，居民主要是从西藏各地迁居而来形成的洛巴人。7世纪时起处于吐蕃王朝的统治之下，吐蕃王朝崩溃后这里先后被阿里地区的古格王国、亚泽王国和贡塘王国统治。1440年贡塘王朝任命的珞俄宗本阿玛贝脱离贡塘王朝的统治宣布自主建国，阿玛贝成为第一任国王。珞俄建国后趁着亚泽和贡塘的衰落而迅速强大起来，直到1580年以前在这一地区的竞争中都居于优势地位。参见 Remesh Kumar Dhunkel, *Political History of the Kingdom of Lo/Mustang*, Submitted in partial fulfillment of the requirements for the degree of Doctor of Philosophy in the Graduate School of Arts and Sciences, Columbia University, 1999.

43 张怡荪主编：《藏汉大辞典》，北京：民族出版社，1993年，第3069页。

44 攘卓著，克珠群佩译：《〈米拉日巴传〉的作者——乳毕坚金》，《西藏民族学院学报》1986年第1期，第34-43页。

45 དེ་ནས་ཕྱིར་སྤུ་རངས་ལུང་པ་ཐམས་ཅད་ཉི་མས་ནུབ་དུ་ཁྲིགས། མིག་མཐོང་མས་ལུང་པ་ཁྲག་ཆེར་མཐོང་། མོ་རྒྱིས་ཐམས་ཅད་ངན་པ་ལུང་པ་མི་ཆགས་པར་ཐག་ཆོད། མི་ཐམས་ཅད་སེམས་ལས་དང་མྱ་ངན་གྱི་ནོན། རྒྱལ་ཁྲིའི་རྫོང་སྤུ་རངས་པ་ཕྱིས་བཟུང་། བློ་བོ་སྔོན་ཐང་པས་དམག་རྣམས་ཞིབ་རྒྱིས་བྱས་ཏེ། རྫོང་གི་མཐའི་མ་ལ་སྐར་སྒྲོངས་བྱས། རྟོད་ཚང་རས་པ་སྣ་ཚོགས་རང་གྲོལ་གྱིས་བརྩམས།《གཙང་སྨྱོན་ཧེ་རུ་ཀའི་རྣམ་ཐར》ཤ184།

重建了噶尔东城堡，该城堡遂成为贡塘王朝控制西部的一个重要的军事据点[46]。因此噶尔东城堡是外来者的军事堡垒，经常威胁西部王国的安全，此后在 14-15 世纪期间贡塘王国和珞巴人（ཀློ་པ）经常侵犯普兰地区，此城也往往成为他们在普兰的军事中心[47]。1427 年前后，珞俄门塘王朝（ཀློ་བོ་སྨོས་ཐང）的开国之君阿玛贝（ཨ་མ་དཔལ）委任绕丹衮波（རབ་བརྟན་མགོན་པོ）为普兰宗本，其驻地就在噶尔东[48]，可见该地对于普兰的重要意义。此外，普兰地区还有一个较为著名的外来者据点，即细德（ཞི་སྡེ）城堡，该城堡位于普兰下部，即普兰南部地区，当地现在为细德村[49]，20 世纪 90 年代曾在附近发现过著名的普兰观音碑，可见这里历史相当悠久。13 世纪后半期（约 1250-1275）该地为蔡巴噶举派在西部的据点之一。15 世纪中期锡德的控制权又转移到了萨迦派密教系统俄尔支派的手中。[50]

上面所提到的城堡和村镇仅仅是古格时期阿里境内众多城堡和村镇中的少数几个较为著名的居民点，尤其是村镇，由于村镇的存在十分普遍，事实上数量是很大的，而这里所提到的只是在历史上发挥过一定的政教作用或是跟某个重要的宗教、政治人物的事迹有关联的为数极少的几个村镇。当然，这一时期古格王国后期的王城扎布让宫堡和托林寺所在地托林这两个最重要的城堡和村镇本文并没涉及，主要是因为该城堡的早期情形和建筑遗址在经过几十年的考古发掘和调查研究之后，学术界对其面貌已经相当清晰。另外还有一些城堡没有涉及则是因为资料描述不清晰，无法识别其基本情况，比如《红史》曾提到普兰王驻地“太索”[51]，但关于此地除这条材料外，再也找不到相关资料印证，也无法说明“太索”所指究竟为何，故而在上述城堡的清理过程中也只好从略了。与村镇材料的寥寥无几相比，阿里地区的城堡史料则相对丰富得多。城堡或堡寨一类的居民点由于其军事和政治上的重要功能和对政权的特别意义在藏族历史资料中颇为引人注目，也就更容易被记录在册，可以为今天的研究提供较为丰富的材料。综合这些史料，本节也只能在很低的程度上再现了阿里地区的这些

46 གུ་གེ་ཕུ་རོང་ཁ་ཆེན་དུ། དཀར་དུམ་གནམ་གྱི་ཁྲུང་རྫོང་བཙིགས། ཀ་ཐོག་རིག་འཛིན་ཚེ་དབང་ནོར་བུས་བརྩམས།《བོད་རྗེ་ལྷ་བཙད་པོའི་གདུང་རབས་མངའ་རིས་སྨད་གུང་ཐང་དུ་ཇི་ལྟར་བྱུང་བའི་ཚུལ་དེབ་ཐེར་དྭངས་ཤེལ་འཕྲུལ་གྱི་མེ་ལོང་》《བོད་ཀྱི་ལོ་རྒྱུས་དེབ་ཐེར་ཁག་ལྔ》1990ལོར་བོད་ལྗོངས་བོད་ཡིག་དཔེ་རྙིང་དཔེ་སྐྲུན་ཁང་གིས་པར་དུ་བསྐྲུན། ཤ108།

47 Roberto Vitali, *The Kingdoms of Gu.ge Pu.hrang*, p.392.

48 Roberto Vitali, *The Kingdoms of Gu.ge Pu.hrang*, p.488.

49 武振华 :《西藏地名》，第 498 页。

50 Roberto Vitali, *The Kingdoms of Gu.ge Pu.hrang*, p.392.

51 蔡巴·贡噶多吉著，陈庆英、周润年译，东嘎洛桑赤列校注 :《红史》，拉萨：西藏人民出版社，2002 年，第 119 页。

古代居民点或则说是早期城镇的简单情况。

古格和普兰的城堡建筑都很发达，而且这种城堡还并不仅仅只具有军事功能，它往往在建筑之初可能是为了军事防御，比如吉德尼玛衮最初修建尼松堡，是为巩固刚刚取得西部地区的战果，但据后来史书所言尼松堡基本上发挥着阿里王朝前期实际上的首都的作用。因此这些军事型的城堡后来大多又被赋予了政治总部的功能，成为区域内的政治指挥中心。当然，城堡的军事功能并不全部都是为了防御，有些也是为了实施进一步的军事扩张，比如普兰地区的噶尔东和细德等城堡，最初是外来征服者为了巩固对新征服地区的统治而修筑的，但最后噶尔东等城堡也变成外来者在这一地区的政治治理的中枢，甚至普兰宗本也驻扎于此。可见这一时期，阿里地区这些城堡的纯军事的功能向军政合一型的总指挥部转化对这些早期居民点来说有一定的必然趋势。另外，城堡作为军政指挥部其本来的地域空间是很狭窄的，但是为了维持城堡中的统治者的生活，城堡周围逐渐也聚集起了一定规模的人口，城堡及其附近逐渐成为相当繁荣的居民点，甚至一些重要的寺院也在城堡附近兴建起来，从而更加促进了该区域的繁荣，像东嘎、皮央就是这种多种因素互相作用而形成的一个政教中心，现在留下了庞大的遗址群也证明了这一点。而西部地区城堡的这一发展趋势与卫藏地区是大致相同的。西藏古代特有的行政单位“宗”（རྫོང），就是由早期的城堡演变而来的，而“宗”的本意就是堡垒、山寨、要塞的意思[52]。事实上，卫藏地区最初的十三大宗其实就是由十三个重要的城堡及其附近的属民组成的一个有机的居民聚居区，最后在大司徒绛曲坚赞的法令下才成为行政单位的建置。

当然，这一时期的阿里地区也正是西藏佛教后弘期最活跃的年代，宗教生活在贵族和民众的日常生活中占据着越来越重要的位置，这一因素自然也会注入到阿里的早期城镇形成过程中。上面提到的一些村镇，因为后弘期寺院的兴建而成为兴旺的宗教活动的聚集地，增加了村镇的繁荣，比如芒囊、皮央等地最初都是因为佛寺的兴建而发展起来的。而城堡型的居民点附近也一定会有寺院的兴建。比如东嘎附近就先后修建了不少的寺院，现存东嘎遗址中有一些僧人窟和居民生活窟，可见东嘎的繁荣局面与这一因素的紧密关系。而这一特点与卫藏地区同期大兴佛寺之下的早期城镇发展的基本特点大致契合。

52 张怡荪主编：《藏汉大辞典》，第 2361 页。

The Buddha-vita in Cave 1 of Dung dkar (Mnga' ris)[1]

Kurt Tropper (Austrian Academy of Sciences)

1. Introduction

The present article provides an edition and translation of an epigraphic cycle on the life of the Buddha that is found in cave 1[2] of Dung dkar[3] (Mnga' ris). It forms one of a series of articles on similar epigraphs found in the *skor lam chen mo* of Zha lu Monastery, the cave temple of Pang gra phug, the White Temple in Rtsa pa rang, the Red Temple in Mtho lding, the 'Brom ston lha khang chen mo in Rta bo, and the Sgrol ma lha khang in Rtsa pa rang.[4] In all of these places the inscriptions are combined with paintings and thus constitute important evidence for the latters' identification and art-historical treatment.

In Dung dkar, the inscriptions are integrated into a band of painted scenes that runs across the western section of the south (or entrance) wall and the entire west and north walls (Fig. 1). The lower edge of this band is situated directly above the small stepped platforms extending over all four walls, while the space above it is mostly filled with several large *maṇḍala* paintings (Figs. 2-4).

1 The fieldwork and research for this study were financed by the Austrian Science Fund (project nos. S 9811-G21 and P 25479-G19). I would also like to express my thanks to Cynthia Peck-Kubaczek for correcting my English and to Jürgen Schörflinger for his help with processing the images and sketch plans. The photos reproduced as figs. 2-4 and 11-15 were kindly made available to me by Tshe ring rgyal po and Christiane Kalantari.

2 Here I follow the numbering of the caves by Pritzker (1996), which was later also adopted by other authors (see, e.g., Rhie 1999: 48, Klimburg-Salter 2001 and Luczanits 2004: 113-123).

3 In this article, the spelling of Tibetan toponyms largely follows Tshe ring rgyal po 2006. For the various attested spellings of Dung dkar, see Luczanits 2004: 313, n. 329.

4 Tropper 2007, 2012, 2013, in preparation a, b, c.

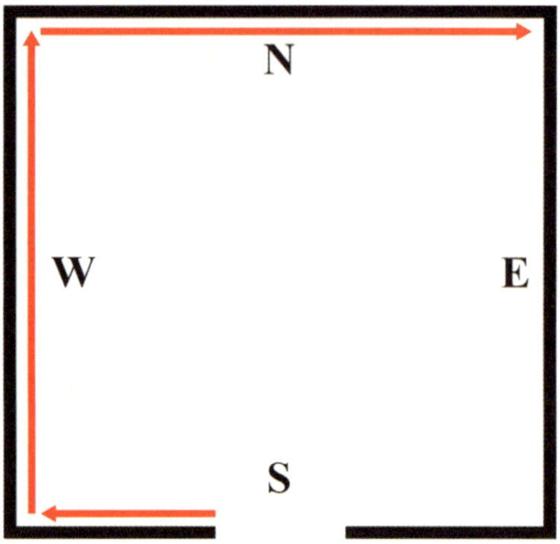

Fig. 1. Sketch plan of cave 1 with the location and progression of the Buddha-vita marked in red.

Fig. 2. Start of the band of painted scenes with integrated inscriptions on the western section of the south wall and the southern section of the west wall. (Photo courtesy of Tshe ring rgyal po; markings in red added by author)

Fig. 3. Band of painted scenes with integrated inscriptions on the western section of the south wall, the west wall, and the western section of the north wall. (Photo courtesy of Tshe ring rgyal po; markings in red added by author)

Fig. 4. Band of painted scenes with integrated inscriptions on the northern section of the west wall and the north wall. (Photo courtesy of Tshe ring rgyal po; markings in red added by author)

The entire composition of paintings and inscriptions is in a poor state of preservation, with many sections almost entirely lost. According to Tshe ring rgyal po (2006: 232), some of the paintings in Dung dkar were destroyed by unnamed researchers, who applied a thin plastic foil to the walls, whereby the paint of the murals was detached. In the process, quite a number of the inscriptional panels also appear to have been ruined, and in some places it is even unclear if the extant outlines of a rectangle constitute the frame of an erstwhile inscription. It is thus difficult to establish how many inscriptional panels the original composition contained.

Figures 5-7 show the location of the 13 panels in which more than just the occasional letter or vowel sign can be made out and which I have edited and translated below. My numbering is based on the progression of the narrative as found in the *Lalitavistara*, which largely correlates with the general arrangement of the paintings and inscriptions from left to right. The only exception is panel no. 8, which is found to the left of panels no. 5, 6 and 7. The reason for this deviance is probably lack of enough space to the right of the large painted scene (the archery contest) to which the inscriptional text refers, and thus the panel was placed to the left above it.

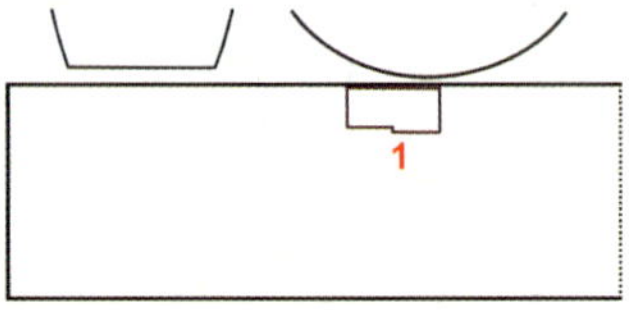

Fig. 5. Location of panel 1 on the western section of the south wall.

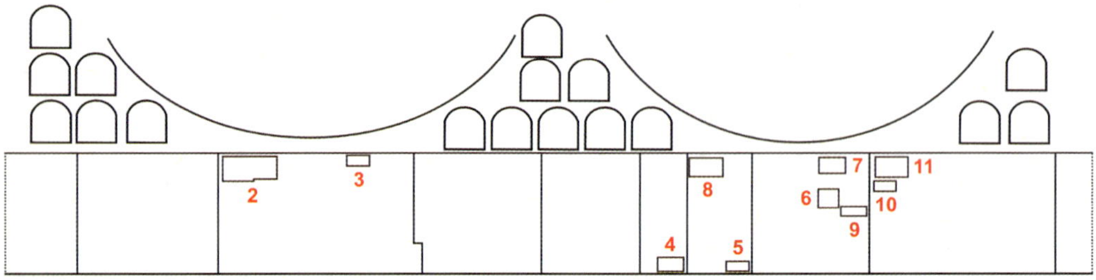

Fig. 6. Location of panels 2-11 on the west wall.

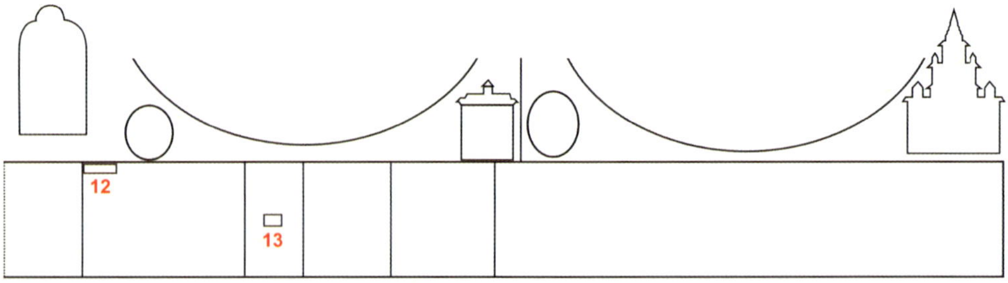

Fig. 7. Location of panels 12-13 on the north wall.

The inscriptions exhibit some of the typical orthographical and palaeographical hallmarks of early Tibetan sources, such as *da drag, ya btags* with *m* before *e* and *i*, and semi-horizontal ligatures of superscript and root letter (Figs. 8-10). As is well known, dating early witnesses merely on the basis of their palaeography and orthography is somewhat problematic, but by and large these characteristics tally well with the attribution to approximately the late 11th or 12th century that has been proposed for the artwork of the cave (see Rhie 1999: 48, Klimburg-Salter 2001: 324, Luczanits 2004: 118). Thus the inscriptions of Dung dkar may well be the oldest epigraphic sources on the life of the Buddha that are still extant in the Tibetan cultural realm.

Figs. 8-10. Examples of old orthography and palaeography: (8) *phyind* (for the editorial signs, see below), (9) *gyurd*, (10) *myi, spobs* (with semi-horizontal *sp* ligature), *myed*. (Video stills, by author)

Unlike most of the inscriptions in the above-mentioned cycles in Zha lu and Rtsa pa rang, the inscriptions in Dung dkar do not seem to be made up of clearly definable literal quotations from (an)other text(s) – at least I could not identify any such quotations. In general, however, the Dung dkar epigraphs concur with the way in which the events are described in the familiar works on the life of the Buddha, most notably the *Lalitavistara* (Tib. *Rgya cher rol pa*), and many phrases in the latter text and in the inscriptions are similar or even identical. In fact, in quite a few places the inscriptions appear to summarize or paraphrase the corresponding passages in the *Lalitavistara*. But there are also some notable differences.[5] Moreover, the episode to which panel 13 refers is not found in the *Lalitavistara* but in the *Vinayavastu* (Tib. *'Dul ba gzhi*) and thus it is clear that the drafter(s) of the inscriptions drew on more than just one source. Oral traditions may have also played a major role, but this is of course difficult to prove.

2. General remarks on the edition and the translation

The edition of the inscriptions is based on stills extracted from large-scale video recordings which I prepared in 2010. In addition, I was given access to a number of high-resolution photos that were taken by Tshe ring rgyal po and Christiane Kalantari in 2007. Because the entire documentation is too extensive to be included in the present article, it has been made available at: www.univie.ac.at/Tibetan-inscriptions.[6]

As in my previous publications, the text of the inscriptions is provided in the form of a diplomatic edition, with all conjectures and emendations relegated to the footnotes. There,

5 See, in particular, n. 58, 159, 160, 189.

6 Links: Ngari → Dungkar → Cave 1.

the reading of the inscription is first repeated and the respective conjecture or emendation is given after a colon;[7] slightly doubful cases are followed by a question mark in brackets[8] and in more speculative instances the brackets are omitted.

In the translation, conjectures are given in square brackets within the running text. As in the edition, the text of slightly doubtful cases is followed by a question mark in (round) brackets.[9] In more speculative cases (i.e., conjectures that are followed by a question mark without brackets in the edition) the translation of the suggested text is provided in a footnote (with question mark)[10] and the running text shows an ellipsis (...).

For ease of understanding and to provide the reader with the wider context of the sometimes extremely fragmentary inscriptions, the edition and translation of each panel is preceded by a short summary of the corresponding passage in the *Lalitavistara* (panels 1-12) and the *Vinayavastu* (panel 13), including references to page and line numbers of the respective editions and/or translations of these two texts.

2.1 Editorial signs

{1}, {2}, {3}, etc.	beginning of a line
*	*dbu*
/	*shad*
d	uncertain reading (underlined)[11]
=	illegible 'letter'[12]
-	illegible letter(s) that formed part of a partly legible 'letter', with one hyphen representing up to three letters (e.g., *-o*, *-rub*, and *-od*; respectively for partly damaged *lo*, *sgrub*, and *spyod*)
$xxx_{pa}\,xxx$	insertion below the line

7 E.g., "*=ngs* : *gangs*" and "*gzho* : *gzhon*".

8 E.g., "= : *so*(?)".

9 E.g., "[a goddess(?)]".

10 E.g., "Read: 'without number'?".

11 Following Tauscher 1999: 50, a letter is marked in this way even in those cases where it is "'partly damaged', but the reading is obvious and quite certain from the context."

12 Cf. Steinkellner and Luczanits 1999: 15 (n. 12), where '*letter*' is defined as "any combination of letters in the Tibetan alphabet that occupy in vertical arrangement of the letter sequence the space of a single grapheme", while *letter* "refers to the single signs for consonants or vowel modification only." Thus a '*letter*' can be composed of up to four *letters*. E.g., *=ng chub sems dpa'* (partly damaged *byang chub sems dpa'*) or *bsod na=s* (partly damaged *bsod nams*).

In the annotations to the translations the following signs are used for quotations from the inscription:

{ } emendations

<> conjectures

3. Panel 1-13

3.1 Panel 1

The remaining fragments in lines 3-5 correspond to the following passage in *Lv*: The Bodhisattva, while still abiding in the Tuṣita realm, manifests eight prognostic signs[13] in the residence of his father-to-be, King Śuddhodana. Thereupon, his future mother Māyādevī calls on her husband and speaks to him in verses about her wish to retreat for some time in order to fast and practice moral conduct. (Hokazono 1994: 348.9-354.8; D: 24v4-26r4; Bays 1983: 72-76)

{1} =====rgy-=================================

{2} ======================= b- la -ogs[14]========ng[15]/

{3} ====================-r-[16]=== pa[17] -as[18]==== -tas[19]

{4} b=d[20] byung[21] bar gyur=t-[22] / / =[23] mo -gyu=phrul[24] yang / rgyal po=s=tsang[25] gi drung tu

13 Described in detail in *Lv* (D: 24v4-25r7).

14 la -ogs : *la sogs*(?).

15 =ng : *dang*?

16 The 'letter' had a *ra btags*, with its root letter and the space above the line being almost completely damaged. The space below the *ra btags* is not damaged and does not contain a *zhabs kyu*. The 'letter' thus only may have contained a *gi gu*, a *'greng bu*, a *na ro*, or no vowel sign at all.

17 The syllable could also be read as *pha*.

18 The syllable probably read *las* or *mas*.

19 *-tas* : *ltas*. The preceding syllable may have read *snga*. Cf. *Lv* (D: 24v4): *snga ltas brgyad ston to*.

20 *b=d* : *brgyad*.

21 The syllable could also be read as *phyung*.

22 *gyur=t-* : *gyurd to*.

23 = : *lha*. Cf. n. 26.

24 *-gyu=phrul* : *sgyu 'phrul*. Cf. n. 26.

25 *po=s=tsang* : *po zas gtsang*. Cf. n. 26.

Fig. 11. Scene showing the birth of the Bodhisattva from the right side of his mother, who is holding on to the branch of a tree with her right hand. A number of other beings that were born at the same time can be made out to the left and above the central composition (note in particular the elephant baby with its mother); for a similar depiction in Pang gra phug, see Tropper, in press. The right side of panel 2 and the entire panel 3 can be seen in the top left and top right corners. (Photo courtesy of Christiane Kalantari)

{5} phyind te -i==$_{s}$su[26] bcad pa zhu ba ====[27]

... [etc.(?)] ... ...[28]... ...[29]... [it came about] that [eight (prognostic) signs] manifested[.][30] [Māyādevī], for her part, went to the presence of king [Śuddhodana] and ... uttering [verses] ...[31]

26 -i==$_{s}$su : *tshigs su*. The remaining traces are somewhat difficult to align with this conjecture, and the s below the line is probably the result of some makeshift correction. However, *tshigs su* (*bcad pa*) is confirmed by *Lv* (D: 25v1-3): *lha mo sgyu 'phrul yang ... rgyal po zas gtsang ma ... bde bar gnas pa'i drung du phyin te ... tshigs su bcad pa 'di dag smras so.*

27 ==== : *lags* (/) or similar? The rest of the line does not seem to have been inscribed. Likewise, the space below line 5 provides enough room for another two or three lines but probably did not contain any text.

28 Read: "and"?

29 Read: "after" ((*pa*) *las*) or "by (his) parents" (*pha mas*)?

30 Or: "... [it came about] that [eight (prognostic) signs] were caused to manifest (by the Buddha *in spe*)[.]"?

31 Read: "(and) was uttering [verses]."?

3.2 Panel 2

The fragments in lines 4-5 strongly suggest that the end of the inscriptional text referred to the numerous other beings that were born at the same time as the Bodhisattva (*Lv*: Hokazono 1994: 462.13-464.19; D: 51r4-51v4; Bays 1983: 142-144). The beginning of the panel may have contained a description of the Bodhisattva's birth, during which his mother was holding on to the branch of a *plakṣa*-tree (*Lv*: Hokazono 1994: 438.21-440.17; D: 45r1-45v1; Bays 1983: 129-130). All this is corroborated by the painted scenes below and to the right of the panel (Fig. 11).

{1} * ====================================

{2} == pl-==[32]========-e===-o=====s ==-o==========

{3} ======================= la so==[33]============

{4} =========== na ======ng[34] / br-=='dun =[35] d-=[36] / -t-========[37]

{5} =====[38] pa sems can ==s===r[39] btsa=[40]=[41] / /

... [*plakṣa*(-tree)(?)] ... [etc.(?)] ... in/at/after ... [and(?)] [the servant Chandaka and] ... [horse(s)/foal(s)] ...[42]... ...[43] sentient beings [were(?)] [born] ...[44].

32 *pl-==* : *plag sha*(?). Cf. *Lv* (Hokazono 1994: 438.23, 440.7, 440.9, 440.11; D: 45r3,5,6) and Tropper 2012 (inscription A, lines 15-16).

33 *la so==* : *la sogs*(?).

34 *=ng* : *dang*(?).

35 *br-=='dun=* : *bran po 'dun pa.* Cf. *Lv* (D: 51v3) and *Chos 'byung* (ed. Rdo rje rgyal po 1988: 85.24-25): *'dun pa la sogs pa bran lnga brgya.*

36 *d-=* : *dang.*

37 The first 'letter' most likely read *rta* or *rte*. For the next one it is difficult to come up with a conjecture that tallies with the remaining traces, and the rest of the line is almost completely lost. Assuming that the semicircular sign above the second 'letter' is a blotch rather than a *gi gu*, *rta sngags ldan* (i.e., irregular for *rta bsngags ldan*) and *rta lnga brgya* are perhaps the closest fits for the first three syllables after the (just slightly uncertain) *shad*. The former is supported by *Lv* (D: 51v3: *bsngags ldan la sogs pa rte'u pho khri*) and *Chos 'byung* (ed. Rdo rje rgyal po 1988: 85.25: *bsngags ldan la sogs rte'u khri*), the latter by caption 5 in the cave temple of Pang gra phug (ed. Tropper 2012): *<de'i(?)> dus su blon mo lnga brgya' {r}god ma lnga brgya' lo<ḍ> pa* (i.e., *bskungs yig* of *la sogs pa*) *thaṃd* (i.e., *bskungs yig* of *thams cad*) *la yang phrug gu lnga {b}rgya lnga brgya' ya<ng* (?)>*btsas so*, "At [that(?)] time, five hundred children respectively were [also(?)] born to five hundred wives of ministers, to five hundred mares, and also to all [the others]."

38 The remaining traces allow for the rather speculative conjectures *las sogs* and *la sogs*.

39 *==s===r* : *grangs med par*?

40 *btsa=* : *btsas*.

41 = : *so*(?).

42 Read: "the horse/foal Kaṇṭhaka (i.e., the Bodhisattva's horse)," or "five hundred horses/foals,"?

43 Read: "etc.,"?

44 Read: "without number"?

3.3 Panel 3

Lv: After the Bodhisattva's birth, his father is sought out by a seer, who asks to see the child and subsequently predicts that he will become a Buddha. (Hokazono 1994: 476.4-496.23; D: 54r7-60v1; Bays 1983: 150-163)

{1} ===[45] de nas =ngs[46] ri'i ngos nas drang srong
{2} ===zhe==ba[47] mngon bar[48] shes pa l-[49]
{3} ====ba[50]=-o[51] nu bltam[52] pa ltar ===
{4} ==[53] gzho[54] nu ltar gsol zhes zhus pa dang
{5} =-o[55] nu g=d[56] log gïs re shig sod ces s-==[57]

Then, from the slope of the [snowy] mountain, a seer [called Asita, who was provided with(?)] the [five] higher perceptions [came/went] to see the (newly) born [youth.] He said: "(I) request to see the youth", and because [the youth had fallen asleep], [he said]: "wake (him) up for a while!"[58]

3.4 Panel 4

Lv: The adolescent Bodhisattva meditates under a *jambu*-tree in a grove, and while doing so impedes five seers on their journey through the sky. Being told by the goddess of the grove

45 === : * / /(?). Cf. panels 4, 9, 10 and 12.
46 =*ngs* : *gangs*. Cf. *Lv* (D: 54r7).
47 ===*zhe*==*ba* : *nag po zhes bya ba*(?). Cf. *Lv* (D: 54r7-v1) and *Chos 'byung* (ed. Rdo rje rgyal po 1988: 86.21).
48 *bar* : *par.*
49 *l*- : *lnga*. Cf. *Lv* (D: 54v1) and *Chos 'byung* (ed. Rdo rje rgyal po 1988: 86.21).
50 ====*ba* : *dang ldan ba* (i.e., with *ba* for *pa*)(?). Cf. *Lv* (D: 54v1) and *Chos 'byung* (ed. Rdo rje rgyal po 1988: 86.21-22).
51 = -*o* : *gzho* (i.e., with *gzho* as irregular spelling of *gzhon*; cf. n. 54, 55, 111, 129, 133, 177, 198, 221).
52 *bltam* : *bltams.*
53 The end of line 3 and the beginning of line 4 most likely read *yong, phyin*(*d*), *gshegs* or similar, followed by a single *shad*, a double *shad* or a particle like *ngo, nas, te* etc.
54 *gzho*: *gzhon* (cf. n. 51, 55, 111, 129, 133, 177, 198, 221).
55 = -*o* : *gzho* (i.e., irregular spelling of *gzhon*; cf. n. 51, 54, 111, 129, 133, 177, 198, 221).
56 *g*=*d* : *gnyid.*
57 *s*-== : *smras* /, *smras* //, *smras so* or similar.
58 In *Lv* (Hokazono 1994: 480.5-6; D: 55v3), the seer does not ask for the Bodhisattva to be woken up but simply points out to the king that such eminent beings do not sleep much and have a disposition to stay awake: *na mahārāja tādṛśā mahāpuruṣāś ciraṃ svapanti jāgaraṇaśīlās tādṛśāḥ satpuruṣā bhavanti; rgyal po chen po skyes bu chen po de lta bu ni ring por mi nyal te / skyes bu dam pa de lta bu dag ni sad par gnas pa'i ngang tshul can no //.*

that they have been held back due to the power of the Bodhisattva, the seers look down and are amazed by his radiant appearance. They praise and circumambulate the Bodhisattva and continue on their path through the sky. (Hokazono 1994: 534.1-540.8, 544.17-546.8; D: 68r5-69v3, 70v1-4; Bays 1983: 199-203, 206-207)

{1} * / / drang sr-ng[59] -u[60] 'phrul dang ldan =====[61]

{2} mkha' la -o=[62] ba las shing 'dzam bu'i ===[63]phy-n[64]

{3} pa na / ph-ir[65] phul ===[66]dong ma nus pa la====[67]

{4} gis ==-u=sem==='i[68] bsa==tan[69] gyi===[70]

{5} rdzu 'phrul nyams pa =n[71] zhes smras========[72]

{6} =l-s[73] na bsam g==[74]==d[75] pa=thong[76] na=[77] bst-==[78]

59 *sr-ng* : *srong*.

60 *-u* : *rdzu*.

61 ===== : *pa lnga nam* or similar. Cf. *Lv* (D: 68v3-4): *de'i tshe phyi rol gyi drang srong ... rdzu 'phrul dang ldan pa nam mkha' las dong ba lnga zhig ...* . The conjecture is also corroborated by the painting above the inscription, which shows five(!) figures soaring in the sky (cf. Fig. 12).

62 *-o=* : *dong*. Cf. n. 61 and line 3.

63 === : *steng du*(?). Cf. *Lv* (D: 68v4): *de dag tshal stug po de'i steng du phyin pa dang ...* .

64 *phy-n* : *phyin*. Cf. n. 63.

65 *ph-ir* : *phyir.*

66 === : *ba ltar*(?). Cf. *Lv* (D: 68v4): *phyir phul ba ltar 'dong ma nus nas ...* .

67 *la====* : *la lha mo zhig*(?). Cf. *Lv* (D: 68v6): *de nas tshal stug po de na lha mo zhig gnas pa des drang srong de dag la tshigs su bcad de smras pa ...* .

68 *==-u=sem==='i* : *byang chub sems dpa'i*.

69 *bsa==tan* : *bsam gtan*. Cf. *Lv* (D: 68v6-7): *shākya'i rgyal sras ... bsam gtan dgongs shing tshal stug 'di na bzhugs // ... de yi mthu yis rdzu 'phrul stobs bzlog go /*.

70 *gyi===* : *gyi mthus*. Cf. n. 69.

71 *=n* : *yin*.

72 *smras========* : *smras so / 'og logs su*(?). Cf. *Lv* (D: 68v7-69r1): *de nas de dag gis 'og logs su bltas pa dang ...* .

73 *=l-s* : *bltas*. Cf. n. 72.

74 *g==* : *gtan*. Cf. *Lv* (D: 69r6): *byang chub sems dpa mi g.yo ba'i lus kyis bsam gtan byed cing / me'i phung po ltar 'bar ba mthong nas ...* .

75 The remaining traces allow for the conjecture *mdzad*. Cf. n. 74.

76 *pa=thong* : *pa mthong*. Cf. n. 74.

77 *na=* : *nas*. Cf. n. 74.

78 *bst-==* : *bstod de* (/). Cf. *Lv* (D: 69r6 and 69v2-3): *de dag byang chub sems dpa' la sems shing tshigs su bcad pas bstod de /*, and *drang srong de dag gis byang chub sems dpa' la tshigs su bcad pa de dag gis bstod de /*.

Fig. 12. Five seers soaring in the sky (cf. n. 61). (Photo courtesy of Christiane Kalantari)

{7} ====m =s-o==byas[79] =nam k- =[80] dong ng-==[81]

[Five seers], provided with [magical power, proceeded] through the sky and [reached] [(the space) above(?)] the *jambu*-tree; [when][, as if(?)] driven [back,] they could not proceed, [a goddess(?)] said (to them): "(your) magical power [is] impaired [by the force of the Bodhisattva's meditative absorption.]" When [(they) looked] [down(?)], [(they) saw (the Bodhisattva) practicing meditative absorption, praisingly circumambulated (him) three times] [and(?)] proceeded [through the sky(?)][.]

3.5 Panel 5

The remaining fragments in lines 1-2 strongly suggest that the inscriptional text referred

79 *====m =s-o==byas* : *lan gsum bskor ba byas*. Cf. *Lv* (D: 69v3): *lan gsum bskor ba byas nas nam mkha' las dong ngo //*.

80 The remaining traces allow for the somewhat uncertain conjecture *ste nam ka la*. Cf. n. 79. For the spelling *nam ka*, see Zhang *et al.* 1993, s.v.

81 *ng-==* : *ngo /(/)*. Cf. n. 79.

Fig. 13. The Bodhisattva (centre right) offering a ring(?) to Gopā (centre left). (Photo courtesy of Christiane Kalantari)

to the following episode in *Lv*: After Śuddhodana has sent out a brahmin priest (Skt. *purohita*) to look for a suitable wife for his son, the priest encounters Gopā, the daughter of Daṇḍapāṇi, and tells Śuddhodana about her. To let the prince make his own choice, the king arranges for a meeting of all the young women of Kapilavastu during which his son distributes jewelry to them. Gopā arrives last, and because all the jewelry has been given away already, the Bodhisattva offers her a ring that he is wearing on his finger. Gopā does not accept the gift and leaves. (Hokazono 1994: 556.5-562.3; D: 72v2-73v7; Bays 1983: 214-217) This is corroborated by the painting above and to the left of the inscriptional panel, which seems to show the Bodhisattva offering his ring to Gopā (Fig. 13).

{1} * ===[82] d-[83] nas sa 'tsho=[84]====dus=[85]
{2} c-=[86]=======[87] chud =======
{3} ======== p-=======
{4} ================
{5} ================

[Then, Gopā] ...[88] entered ...[89] ...

3.6 Panel 6

Lv: As demanded by Daṇḍapāṇi, a contest in various skills is organized to determine who is the most suitable husband for his daughter Gopā. On his way to the place where the contest will take place, the Bodhisattva's rival Devadatta sees a white elephant that is brought along for the Bodhisattva and kills it. Sundarānanda, another competitor, drags the corpse outside the city gate, but the Bodhisattva is still afraid that the decomposing animal will fill the city with a foul smell and hurls it over the seven ramparts and seven ditches that surround the

82 === : / /(?). Cf. panels 4, 9, 10 and 12.
83 *d-* : *de.*
84 *sa 'tsho=* : *sa 'tsho ma.*
85 ====*dus=* : *'khor 'dus pa*? Cf. n. 86 and *Lv* (D: 73v3-4): *de nas ... sa 'tsho ma ... bran mo'i tshogs kyis bskor cing mdun du bdar te / 'dun khang ga la ba dang / byang chub sems dpa' ga la ba der song ste.*
86 *c-* : *can?*
87 ====== : *'dun khang der* or similar? Cf. n. 85.
88 Read: "with her assembled retinue"?
89 Read: "that assemby hall" or similar?

city. The impact of the elephant creates a hole in the ground that is now called *hastigartā* ('elephant hole'). (Hokazono 1994: 564.11-566.10; D: 74v2-75r2; Bays 1983: 219-220)

{1} =[90] / / gla===l-=byin[91] gyis thal cag[92]
{2} gis bsa== /[93] mdzes d='[94] bos glang
{3} =khyer[95] te grong =r[96] gyi gud du bor ro / /
{4} ==chub-e=s[97] dpa' shing -ta[98] la 'dug
{5} =zhin -u[99] zhabs=-i=[100] gi mthe bos glang
{6} po d-[101] blangs te rgyang gra=s=cig[102] tu 'phangs
{7} pa las glang po===[103] zhes bya ba'i mcho=
{8} -te=[104] b-engs -o /=/[105]

[An elephant was killed] by [Devadatta] with a slap of his hand ...[106] [Sundarānanda] took [the elephant(?)[107] and got rid of it outside [the city]. [The Bodhisattva,] sit[ting] on [a chariot,] took up [that] elephant with the toe of [one] foot, hurled it for [(a distance of) one *krośa*] and [the site for worship(?)] called elephant [hole(?)] ...[108].

90 = : *.
91 The remaining traces allow for the conjecture *glang chen lhas byin.*
92 *cag* : *lcag.*
93 The remaining traces allow for the conjectures *bsad de /, bsad na /, bsad do /* and *bsad do //*. Cf. Tropper 2013: 64.
94 *d='* : *dga'.*
95 The beginning of line 3 could have read *de khyer* or *po khyer*, the latter perhaps being somewhat more likely. Cf. the end of line 5 and the beginning of line 6.
96 *grong =r* : *grong khyer.*
97 *==chub-e=s* : *byang chub sems.*
98 *-ta* : *rta.*
99 *=zhin -u* : *bzhin du.*
100 The remaining traces allow for the conjectures *zhabs gcig* and *zhabs ya cig*, the latter perhaps being somewhat more likely. Cf. *Lv* (D: 75r1: *rkang pa ya gcig*; for the spelling *ya cig*, see Orofino 2007: 116).
101 *d-* : *de.*
102 *gra=s=cig* : *grags gcig.*
103 *glang po===* : *glang po gshong* or *glang po'i shong*(?). Cf. *Lv* (D: 75r2: *glang po'i shong*) and *Chos 'byung* (ed. Rdo rje rgyal po 1988: 89.13: *glang po'i gshong*).
104 *mcho= -te=* : *mchod rten*(?).
105 The conjecture "*bzhengs so / /*" would make good sense, but it is difficult to align it with the remaining traces.
106 Read: "and then" or "."?
107 Or: "that elephant"?
108 Read: "was created"?

3.7 Panel 7

Lv: After being victorious in several other disciplines, the Bodhisattva engages in a wrestling contest with his competitors, including the boastful Devadatta, and also wins it. (Hokazono 1994: 584.2-20; D: 78v1-6; Bays 1983: 229-230)

{1} ===[109] de nas======== ba ==========
{2} ==== -ob[110]===================
{3} ===== g=-us[111] nga rgyal bcag ========[112]
{4} g.yas pas ======-kor[113] t-[114] / ========[115]
{5} gyad rna==-yang[116] reg pa tsam gyis sa la '=l[117] bar
{6} =r=[118] te / -ya=-u=sems=='[119] stobs kyis ==[120]
{7} =======================[121]

Then, ...[122] ... ...[123] [in order to] break (Devadatta's) pride[, whirled (him) around in space] with (his) right [hand].[124] ...[125] wrestler[s, too,(?)] [fell] to the ground due to a mere touch (by the youth/Bodhisattva), and thus [the Bodhisattva] ...[126] in[127] strength.

109 === : * / /(?). Cf. panels 4, 9, 10 and 12.
110 The remaining traces may have been part of the syllable *stobs*, which occurs quite frequently in the corresponding narrative of *Lv*.
111 The remaining traces allow for the rather speculative conjecture *gzho nus* (i.e., irregular for *gzhon nus*; cf. n. 51, 54, 55, 129, 133, 177, 198, 221).
112 The end of the line is completely damaged, but *pa'i phyir* (*de*) *lag pa* is a likely conjecture. Cf. *Lv* (D: 78v4-5): *byang chub sems dpas ... gzhon nu lha sbyin lag pa g.yas pas bteg ste ... nga rgyal bcag pa'i phyir ... nam mkha' las bskor bskor te.*
113 ======-kor : *nam mkhar bskor* or similar. Cf. *Chos 'byung* (*nam mkha' la bskor*; ed. Rdo rje rgyal po 1988: 89.19-20) and *Lv* (*nam mkha' las bskor bskor*; D: 78v5).
114 *t-* : *to* or *te*.
115 ======== : (/) *de nas gzhan gyi* or similar?
116 *gyad rna==-yang* : *gyad rnams kyang*(?).
117 *'=l*: *'gyel*. Cf. *Lv* (*byang chub sems dpas reg pa tsam gyis sa la 'gyel bar gyur to* //; D 78v6)
118 *=r=* : *gyurd*. Cf. n. 117.
119 *-ya=-u=sems=='* : *byang chub sems dpa'*.
120 It is unclear if the damaged space following *kyis* contained more text.
121 At the beginning of the line there are faint traces of about six 'letters', but it is unclear if the space that follows contained text. The end of the panel may have read (*byang chub sems dpa' stobs kyis*) *rgyal bar gyur*(*d*) *to* /(/) or similar.
122 Read: "strength"?
123 Read: "the youth,"?
124 Or: ";".
125 Read: "Then/then, the other"?
126 Read: "turned out victorious"?
127 Cf. Hahn 1996: 62.

3.8 Panel 8

Lv: The wrestling is followed by a contest in archery with Ānanda, Devadatta, Sundarānanda and Daṇḍapāṇi.[128] The Bodhisattva's competitors respectively hit one drum they have set up as a target at various distances. The Bodhisattva, using a special bow (cf. panel 9), shoots an arrow that pierces the four drums of his competitors, the iron drum he has set up for himself, seven *tāla* trees, the iron image of a boar, and finally penetrates the ground. At this spot a spring appears, which now is still called *śarakūpa* ('arrow spring'). (Hokazono 1994: 586.12-590.8; D: 79r3-80r3; Bays 1983: 231-233)

{1} ==========ky-================gzh-[129] nu=[130]

{2} ======== / / ===[131]shag kya -nams[132] dang g= -u[133] 'ph-ng[134] 'gran ba =[135]

{3} =========[136] -cags[137] kyi=cig[138] phug=[139]-has by-=gyis[140] g-is[141] phu=[142]

128 The latter is obviously not Gopā's father but a younger namesake.

129 *gzh-* : *gzho* (i.e., irregular for *gzhon*; cf. n. 51, 54, 55, 111, 133, 177, 198, 221).

130 It is unclear if *nu* was followed by another 'letter'.

131 === : *de nas*(?).

132 *-nams* : *rnams*.

133 *g= -u* : *gzho nu* (i.e., irregular for *gzhon nu*; cf. n. 51, 54, 55, 111, 129, 177, 198, 221).

134 *'ph-ng* : *'phong*.

135 It is unclear if "*ba_*" (i.e., with irregular sandhi for *pa*) was followed by another 'letter' (e.g. *la*).

136 The three syllables preceding *-cags* most likely read *kun dga' bos*, which may have been preceded by another short syllable (e.g., *la*; cf. n. 135). For the conjecture *kun dga' bo* and those provided in the following footnotes, cf. *Lv* (D: 79r3-v1): *de'i tshe kun dga' bos rgyang grags gnyis kyi pha rol tu lcags kyi rnga gcig 'ben du btsugs so // de'i 'og tu lha sbyin gyis rgyang grags bzhi'i pha rol tu lcags kyi rnga gcig 'ben du btsugs so // de'i 'og tu mdzes dga' bos rgyang grags drug gi pha rol tu lcags kyi rnga gcig 'ben du btsugs so // de'i 'og tu shākya lag na be con can gyis rgyang grags brgyad kyi pha rol tu lcags kyi rnga gcig 'ben du btsugs so // de nas byang chub sems dpas rgyang grags bcu'i pha rol tu lcags kyi rnga gcig 'ben du btsugs te / de'i drung du shing ta la bdun dngar nas de'i pha rol tu lcags kyi phag rgod kyi gzugs 'khrul 'khor du byas pa gcig btsugs so // de nas kun dga' bos rgyang grags gnyis kyi pha rol na rnga'i 'ben 'dug pa la 'phangs na phog par gyur te / de phan chod kyi la phog par ma nus so // lha sbyin gyis rgyang grags bzhi'i pha rol na rnga'i 'ben 'dug pa la 'phangs na phog par gyur te / de phan chad kyi la phog par ma nus so // mdzes dga' bos rgyang grags drug gi pha rol na rnga'i 'ben 'dug pa la 'phangs na phog par gyur te / de phan chad kyi la phog par ma nus so // lag na be con can gyis rgyang grags brgyad kyi pha rol na rnga'i 'ben 'dug pa la 'phangs na phog par gyur te / thal byung du phyin nas de phan chad kyi la phog par ma nus so //.*

137 *-cags* : *lcags*. Cf. n. 136.

138 *kyi=cig* : *kyi rnga cig* (with *cig* for the more regular *gcig*). Cf. n. 136.

139 The remaining traces allow for the conjectures *phug de* and *phug /*.

140 *-has by-=gyis* : *lhas byin gyis*. Cf. n. 136.

141 *g-is* : *gnyis*.

142 *phu=* : *phug*. The *g* was probably partly written on the red line framing the panel.

{4} ============[143]-ug=[144] las=-on =s[145] bzhi phu===[146] nus s-[147]

{5} ==[148]lcags===dun[149] dang / shing ta la ===[150]=====-cags ===== da=

{6} ==da===s la=[151]byas pa'i phag -nams[152] =phung[153]==========

{7} ===ph-====[154]chu -yung[155] -e=[156] da ltar yang=da'i===========[157]

{8} ================================

{9} ================================

{10} ================================[158]

... [the youth(s)] ... . [Then,(?)] the Shākya[s] and [the youth] competed [in archery] (and) [Ānanda] pierced [one iron drum; Devadatta pierced two, Sundarānanda pierced three, and Daṇḍa(pāṇi)] could [pierce] four[.(?)][159] [Seven] iron [drums][160] and [seven] *tāla* trees ...[161] ...

143 The four syllables preceding *-ug=* most likely read *mdzes dga' bos gsum*, which may have been preceded by another short syllable (e.g. *nas*). Cf. n. 136.

144 *-ug=* : *phug pa*.

145 *las=-on =s* : *las be con gyis* (i.e., with *be con* for the usual [*lag na*] *be con can*). Cf. n. 136.

146 *phu===* : *phug par.*

147 *s-* : *so*(?).The *s* is written on the red line framing the panel.

148 It is unclear if *lcags* was preceded by one or more 'letters'. The conjecture *gzho nus* (i.e., irregular for *gzhon nus*; cf. n. 51, 54, 55, 111, 129, 133, 177, 198, 221) would make good sense, but the available space is definitely too small for it. Perhaps the passage could have read *de nas*, but the letters would have to have been very compact.

149 *===dun : kyi rnga bdun.*

150 === : *bdun.* Cf. n. 136.

151 The erstwhile text at the end of line 5 and the beginning of line 6 is rather uncertain. A very speculative conjecture that more or less tallies with the remaining traces is (*shing ta la bdun*) *dngar / lcags kyi rnga bdun dang shing dang lcags las.* Cf. n. 136.

152 *-nams* : *rnams.*

153 *=phung* : *kyi phung?*

154 The end of line 6 and the beginning of line 7 are almost completely destroyed. A very speculative conjecture that fits the general context is (*phag rnams kyi phung*) *po de las mda' thal te sa phug nas /*. Cf. n. 136 and *Lv* (D: 80r3): *phag rgod kyi gzugs 'khrul 'khor du byas pa las kyang thal te mda' de sa la zug nas mi snang bar nub par gyur to // sa phyogs gang du mda' de zug ste nub pa'i sa phyogs der khron pa lta bu'i khung zhig byung nas da ltar yang mda'i khron pa zhes bya ba yin no //.*

155 *-yung* : *byung.*

156 *-e=* : *ste* /(?).

157 *yang=da'i===========* : *yang mda'i khron pa zhes bya ba yin no / /* or similar(?). Cf. n. 154.

158 Lines 8-10 are almost completely destroyed. It is unclear how much (if any) text they contained.

159 Here, the inscription differs notably from the account in *Lv* (cf. the short summary above and n. 136).

160 Again, the inscription and *Lv* differ substantially. Cf., however, caption 8 of the epigraphic Buddhavita in Pang gra phug (Tropper 2012), which also has "seven [iron] drums" (*lcag<s> ky<i >rnga bdun*). In both Dung dkar and Pang gra phug, the paintings also show seven drums.

161 Read: "were (then) arranged (i.e., by the Bodhisattva)."?

boar made ...[162] water [came out][;(?)] even today [it is called arrow's spring.(?)] (...)

3.9 Panel 9

The text of the inscription corresponds to the following short episode, which forms part of the contest in archery (cf. panel 8): After Ānanda, Devadatta, Sundarānanda and Daṇḍapāṇi have hit their respective targets, each bow that is given to the Bodhisattva, breaks when he draws it. The exceptionally strong bow of his grandfather is brought from the temple where it is kept. While none of the other young men can bend it, the Bodhisattva manages to do so easily and shoots his arrow with it. (Hokazono 1994: 586.24-590.2; D: 79v1-80r1; Bays 1983: 232-233)

{1} =[163] / / de nas mes seng ge 'gram gyi zhu[164] l-=ng[165] nas
{2} =ngs[166] te khyad m-d p-=[167] br-ungs[168] nas===-o=[169]
{3} c-s[170] zhabs mthe bos mnan nas ====cu=
{4} ====-ungs -o==== //[171]

Then, the bow of (the Bodhisattva's) grandfather Siṃhahanu [was brought] from [the temple]; after (the Bodhisattva) [– with nothing special about it –(?)][172] [had bent (it)], ...[173]

162 Read: "Having passed through that accumulation of seven iron drums, the trees and a boar made of iron, the arrow pierced the ground and then"?

163 = : *.

164 *zhu* : *gzhu.*

165 *l-=ng* : *lha khang*. Cf. *Lv* (D: 79v2).

166 The remaining traces allow for the conjectures *drangs* and *blangs* (with similar meanings), the latter perhaps being somewhat more likely. Cf. *Lv* (D: 79v3).

167 *m-d p-=* : *med par*(?).

168 The syllable probably read *brdungs* (i.e., irregular for *bdungs*; cf. *Lv* [D: 79v5]).

169 *===-o=* : *rgyal* (*ba*) *thob, rgyal shog* or similar?

170 *c-s* : *ces*?

171 For the end of the panel it is difficult to come up with a convincing conjecture that is in line with the remaining traces. The last three 'letters' of line 3 may have read *bcu la* or *bcu'i*, but the preceding space seems too narrow for *rgyang grags* (cf. *Lv*: rgyang grags *bcu'i pha rol tu* ... [D: 80r2]) unless it was spelled in an 'irregular' way. Line 4 may have read "'*ben brdungs so // //*", but again this is very speculative.

172 Provided that the conjecture *khyad med par* is correct, this probably refers to the fact that the bow was unusually difficult to bend and none of the Bodhisattva's competitors could do so.

173 Read: "(he) said 'may (I) be victorious!' (and)" or similar?

Fig. 14. The Bodhisattva bends the bow of his grandfather Siṃhahanu, pressing it down with his big toe (cf. n. 174). (Photo courtesy of Christiane Kalantari)

pressed (it) down with his big toe;[174] then, ...[175].

3.10 Panel 10

The beginning of the panel[176] corresponds to *Lv*'s description of how Daṇḍapāṇi gives his daughter Gopā to the Bodhisattva after the latter has excelled in sixty-four skills (Hokazono 1994: 590.19-592.18; D: 80r7-81r1; Bays 1983: 234-235). The rest of the text refers to the Bodhisattva's conjugal life, but not all of it seems to have a clear correspondence in *Lv*.

{1} * / / de nas gzho[177] nu s-bs[178] dang rtsis laso==[179]
{2} pa las khyad bar[180] du gyurd nas / sa=tsho=[181] ==
{3} =r[182] phul nas mkhar ngang skya ldan gna====[183]
{4} ==-yod -i -ogs[184] =ng[185]=-i=======[186]

174 See the painted scene above the inscription (Fig. 14). For a similar representation, cf. http:// www.sumana-dissanayake.com/wp-content/uploads/2011/05/The-Archery-ContestIMG_0303.jpg.

175 Read: "(he) hit the target at (a distance of) ten *krośas*" or similar?

176 I.e., up to *phul nas* in line 3.

177 *gzho* : *gzhon* (cf. n. 51, 54, 55, 111, 129, 133, 198, 221).

178 *s-bs*: *stobs*. Cf. inscription C in Pang gra phug (*stobs dang sgyu rtsal y<i>g rtsis* ...; ed. Tropper 2012) and *Lv* (*'gyed stobs, bāhuvyāyāma*; D: 80v1; Hokazono 1994: 592.1).

179 *laso==* : *lasogs.*

180 *bar* : *par.*

181 *sa=tsho=* : *sa 'tsho ma.* Cf. *Lv* (D: 80v7-81r1; Hokazono 1994: 592.15-17): *thams cad la'ang byang chub sems dpa' 'ba' zhig khyad par du 'phags par gyur to // de'i tshe shākya lag na be con can gyis rang gi bu mo sa 'tsho ma / byang chub sems dpa' la phul lo //, sarvatra bodhisattva eva viśiṣyate sma. atha khalu punas tena samayena daṇḍapāṇiḥ śākyaḥ svāṃ duhitaraṃ gopāṃ śākyakanyāṃ bodhisattvāya prādāt.*

182 Above the damaged section at the beginning of the line there are indistinct traces of what could have been a *na ro*. Possible conjectures for the end of line 2 and the beginning of line 3 include *bag mor* (with *bag mo* as a variant of *bag ma*), *bag mar* and *bag por.* Cf. *Lv* (D: 81r1, Hokazono 1994: 17-18): *rgyal po zas gtsang mas kyang / de rim gyis bag mar blangs te byang chub sems dpa' la phul lo, sā ca rājñā śuddhodanenānupūrveṇa bodhisattvasya vṛtābhūt.*

183 *gna====* : *gnang ngo* (/)/?

184 While the remaining traces of the syllable preceding *-ogs* only allow for the conjecture of one of the three forms of the genitive particle (i.e., *kyi, gyi* or *gi*), the erstwhile wording of *==-yod* and *-ogs* is more doubtful. There are faint traces of a small hook above the upper right corner of the (damaged) root letter in *-ogs* and thus the syllable may have read *tshogs* or *rdzogs*, but these conjectures cannot so easily be brought in line with the other remains of the letter(s) below the *na ro*. Similarly, the vowel sign of the syllable preceding the genitive particle could, perhaps, also have been a *'greng bu* instead of a *na ro* (although the latter seems more likely). Thus there are various possible conjectures for the beginning of line 4, including *long spyod kyi tshogs* (with a horizontal *sp* ligature?), *long spyod kyi rdzogs* and *bud med kyi tshogs*. For the latter, cf. *Lv* (D: 84r2).

185 *=ng* : *dang*(?).

186 *=-i=======* : "*/ khyim dam pa yo byad*"(?). See n. 187.

{5} ==-u=tshogs[187] ==ng /[188] rgyal srid chen po=[189]

{6} ==s pa=== /====[190]

Then, after the youth had turned out superior in [strength], calculation[, etc.], [Gopā] was given ...[191]; subsequently, ...[192] the grey teal castle[193]...[194]...[195] [, an excellent residence that was perfectly furnished,(?)] a great dominion ...[196]

3.11 Panel 11

Lv: After he has taken the decision to become a renunciate, the Bodhisattva goes to see his father and asks for his permission. In the ensuing dialogue, the king tries to change his son's mind, but eventually realizes that he has to let him go. (Lefmann 1902: 198.1-200.11; D: 99r4-100r1; Bays 1983: 301-303)

{1} ==============================

{2} =sku============================

{3} ====================gts-====du b-on ==[197]

{4} ==-u============= / de nas gzho[198] nus 'o na =====[199]d-m =[200]

187 *==-u=tshogs* : *phun sum tshogs*(?). Cf. *Lv* (D: 83v1-6): (*byang chub sems dpa'*) *khyim dam pa mchog yo byad phun sum tshogs pa (thams cad dang ldan pa ... de na 'dug ste*).

188 *==ng /* : *pa dang*(?).

189 It is unclear if the damaged space following *po* contained a (*tsheg* and a) 'letter'.

190 It is unclear if the damaged space following "/" contained more text; (the end of line 5 and) line 6 could have read "*la ( )sogs pa mnga'(o)* / (/)", "*la( )sogs par ldan* (*no*) / (/)" or similar.

191 Read: "as a bride (to him)" or "to the groom (i.e., the young Bodhisattva?)"?

192 Read: "(he/they) was/were given"?

193 *Lv* does not mention the place in connection with the Bodhisattva's and Gopā's marriage and their subsequent life together, but much earlier, in its description of the situation before Māyādevī's conception. There, the Sanskrit equivalent of *ngang skya* (*ldan*) (D: 25v7, 26r6, 28v4) is *dhārtarāṣṭra*/*dhṛtarāṣṭra* (Hokazono 1994: 352.18, 354.19, 368.7). Also cf. *Mvy* (ed. Ishihama and Fukuda 1989: no. 4881; ed. Sakaki 1981: no. 4882), Lefmann 1874: 36, 37, 41, 190, 192, 203, and Edgerton 1953: 286, s.v. *dhṛtarājya* and *dhṛtarāṣṭra*.

194 Read: "He had", "He was provided with" or similar?

195 Read: "a multitude of enjoyment", "complete enjoyment" or "hosts of women"?

196 Read: "etc."?

197 The remaining traces at the end of the line allow for the rather speculative conjecture *zas gtsang gi drung du byon nas*.

198 *gzho* : *gzhon* (cf. n. 51, 54, 55, 111, 129, 133, 177, 221).

199 *=====* : *bdag gis*?

200 *d-m =* : *dam pa*.

{5} =sum[201] =g[202] slo=[203] / ’di =d[204] na bdag rab tu myi ’byung / =sum[205] gang zhe na /
{6} ======[206] da=[207] ’chi ba ’di gsum -ed[208] pa rgyal ==[209] spyod dam zhes -mra=[210]
{7} ’====[211] sby-n =’-[212] nus pa myed do / +[213] / yang g-o nus[214] smras pa / yab rgyal
{8} po====dag[215] dam pa cig cig slong / ’di spyod na bdag ra= -u -yi==ng=/[216]
{9} =====ng[217] zhe na ’di nas ’chi ’phos nas nying mtshams myi sbyor b-=[218]
{10} rgyal ==-od[219] dam zhes smras pas / rgyal po spobs pa myed par gyur[220]
{11} de / gzho[221] nu la rjes su yi rang ngo zhes smras so / /
({12}) + zhes s-s so[222]

… …[223] …[224]

Then, the youth [said]:

201 *=sum* : *gsum.*
202 *=g* : *dag.*
203 *slo=* : *slong.*
204 *=d* : *spyod.*
205 *=sum* : *gsum.*
206 ====== : *rga ba dang na ba* (or similar)(?).
207 *da=* : *dang.*
208 *-ed* : *myed* (cf. lines 7 and 10) or *med.*
209 == : *pos.*
210 *-mra=* : smras.
211 ’==== : *’di gsum*(?).
212 *sby-n =’-* : *sbyin pa’i.* Cf. *Chos ’byung* (ed. Rdo rje rgyal po 1988: 93.21): *de sbyin pa’i mthu med do.*
213 The cross-shaped sign indicates that the short phrase *zhes s-s so*, added at the bottom of the panel and preceded by an identical marker, has to be inserted here. Cf. n. 222.
214 *g-o nus* : *gzho(n) nus* (cf. n. 51, 54, 55, 111, 129, 133, 177, 198, 221).
215 *po====dag* : *po mnga’ bdag*? At any rate, the syllable before *dam* most likely read *bdag*. As subject of (the transitive) *slong*, however, one would rather expect it to be followed by the instrumental particle *gis* (i.e., *bdag gis dam pa cig cig slong*).
216 *ra= -u -yi==ng=* / : *rab tu myi ’byung ngo* / or *rab tu myi ’byung* / /.
217 The syllable preceding *zhe na* must have read *gang* (i.e., yielding the common phrase *gang zhe na*), while the conjecture *rgyal pos* for the beginning of the line is more speculative.
218 The remaining traces allow for the conjectures *sbyor ba* and *sbyor bar.*
219 The beginning of the line probably read *rgyal pos spyod*, with a horizontal *sp* ligature in *spyod* (as in lines 6 and 8).
220 The space following *gyur* is completely bleached out; it may have contained a *da drag.*
221 *gzho* : *gzhon* (cf. n. 51, 54, 55, 111, 129, 133, 177, 198).
222 + *zhes s-s so* : + *zhes smras so.*
223 Read: “After (the Bodhisattva) went to (his father) Śuddhodana”?
224 If the conjecture for the end of line 3 is correct, the almost completely destroyed passage at the beginning of line 4 most likely contained a condensed account of Śuddhodana’s promise to grant his son everything he asked for (if only he did not become a renunciate).

"Well, ...[225] [ask for three boons];[226] if (you) [accomplish] this, I will not become a renunciate. If (you) ask 'which [three]?': Will [the king] accomplish it that (for me) [there is no] [old age, illness(?)] [and] death, these three?"[227]

(")(I) do not have the power [to grant] [these three (boons)(?)].(")[+]

Again, [the youth] said:

"(Oh) father, king ...[228] (I) ask for just one boon.[229] If this is accomplished, I [will not become a renunciate]. If [the king(?)] ask[s(?] '[which (boon)]?': Will [the king accomplish it that] (I) will not be reborn after I have passed away from this (life)?"

As a result, the king became discouraged (with arguing) and said to the youth: "(I) feel happy (i.e., for you to become a renunciate)."[230]

+ Thus (the king) said.

3.12 Panel 12

The remaining fragments of the first line suggest that the entire text of the short panel corresponded to the following episode in *Lv*: On his way to Bodhimaṇḍa, the Bodhisattva emits a radiant light illuminating the home of the *nāga* king Kālika. Joyfully, Kālika, his wife Suvarṇa-prabhāsā and a host of *nāga* girls praise the Bodhisattva with manifold verses and predict his enlightenment. (Lefmann 1902: 281.9-285.16; D: 139r1-140v4; Bays 1983:

225 Read: "I"?

226 Here, *d<a>m <pa>* equates to Skt. *vara*. Cf. n. 227.

227 In *Chos 'byung* (ed. Rdo rje rgyal po 1988: 93.21) the Bodhisattva asks for being spared four things, namely old age, illness, death and decay: *rga na 'chi rgud bzhi med pa stsol cig* (also cf. *ibid*.: 93.23: *mchog bzhi 'di dag*). This tallies with *Lv* (D: 99v4-6; Lefmann 1902: 199.12-200.5): *lha cig dam pa bzhi 'tshal de ni bdag la stsol // ... // rga na 'chi ba'i 'jigs dang rgud par mi 'gyur ba //, icchāmi deva caturo vara tān mi dehi / ... jaravyādhimṛtyubhayataś ca vipattitaś ca /*.

228 Read: "(and) master,"?

229 Cf. n. 226 and *Lv* (Lefmann 1902: 200.6): *varaika(ṃ)* (here, D [99v6] has *mchog* instead of *dam pa*).

230 The intended meaning of *de* and *rjes su yi rang ngo* is not entirely clear. In *Chos 'byung* (ed. Rdo rje rgyal po 1988: 93.24-25), the king says "may your intentions be accomplished" (*khyed kyis bsam pa rdzogs par gyur cig*), which rather seems to relate to the Bodhisattva's desire to become a renunciate than his wish not to be reborn. Similarly, in *Lv* the dialogue between the Bodhisattva and his father ends with the following words of the latter (D: 99v7-100r1; Lefmann 1902: 200.10-11): *phan byed 'gro ba thar byed rjes su yi rang ngo // khyod kyi bsam pa rnams ni yongs su rdzogs gyur cig /, anumodanī hitakarā jagati pramokṣam, abhiprāyu tubhya paripūryatu yan mataṃ te //* – with *rjes su yi rang ngo* clearly corresponding to *anumodanī* (which Edgerton 1953: 32 gives as an equivalent of *anumodanā* "(expression of) *thanks, gratification* or *approval*"). In the inscription the phrase thus should probably rather be understood as the king's approval of his son's wish to become a renunciate, even though the connotation of approval is not explicitly mentioned for *rjes su yi rang* in the various Tibetan dictionaries. Alternatively, *rgyal po spobs pa myed par gyur(d) de / gzho{n} nu la rjes su yi rang ngo zhes smras so* could have been intended to have the slightly different meaning "the king became discouraged but (not wanting to disclose his feelings) said to the youth: '(I) feel happy.'"

427-433)[231]

{1} * / / de nas klu nag po'i gnas snang bas khyab ==nu========

{2} =cas[232] pas ===m(-)=====s(-)===================

{3} ===========================

{4} ===========================

Then, the abode of the *nāga* Kālika was pervaded with light ... [along with] ...

3.13 Panel 13

The panel as a whole is too damaged to allow for a reasonably certain reconstruction, but the extant fragments in combination with the painting below the panel (cf. Fig. 15) make it clear that the text referred to the story of the monkey who gave honey to the Buddha and subsequently fell into a well. This story is not found in *Lv* but in *Vv* (D: *nga* 143r2-v5). Variations of it are also included in the epigraphic cycles on the life of the Buddha in Pang gra phug and Rtsa pa rang.[233]

{1} ===[234] d- na=[235]=========

{2} ===du phy-n[236]=========

{3} =ch- ba'-[237] -u==========

{4} == sbrang rtsi===n======

{5} =============

[Then,] ... [went] to ... [great(?)] ... honey ...

231 Also cf. the extremely shortened version of the Kālika episode in *Chos 'byung* (ed. Rdo rje rgyal po 1988: 97.14-15): *byang chub sems dpas 'od bkye ste nyon mongs dang sdug bsngal zhi zhing snod dag par sbyangs te klu nag pos bstod do //*, "The Bodhisattva radiated light, pacified afflictions and suffering, immaculately purified the vessels – and the *nāga* Kālika uttered praise."

232 =*cas* : *bcas*.

233 Edited and translated in Tropper 2012 (caption 17) and 2013: 99.

234 === : * / /(?). Cf. panels 4, 9, 10 and 12.

235 d- na= : *de nas*.

236 phy-n : *phyin*.

237 ch- ba'- : *che ba'i*(?).

Fig. 15. A monkey gives honey to the Buddha and then falls into a well. Panel 13 (top centre) is framed by a thin red line. (Photo courtesy of Christiane Kalantari)

References (incl. abbreviations)

Bays, Gwendolyn (transl.). 1983. *The Lalitavistara Sūtra. The Voice of the Buddha: The Beauty of Compassion.* 2 Vols. Berkeley: Dharma Publishing.

Chos 'byung, see Rdo rje rgyal po 1988.

D = Derge Kanjur: *The Tibetan Tripitaka.* Taipei Edition. Taiwan 1991: SMC Publishing.

Edgerton, Franklin. 1953. *Buddhist Hybrid Sanskrit Grammar and Dictionary. Vol. II: Dictionary.* New Haven: Yale University Press.

Hahn, Michael. 1996. *Lehrbuch der klassischen tibetischen Schriftsprache.* 5. verbesserte Auflage. Bonn: Indica et Tibetica Verlag.

Hokazono, Kōichi. 1994. *Lalitavistara no kenkyū, jōkan.* Tokyo: Daitō-shuppan-sya.

Ishihama, Yumiko and Yoichi Fukuda. 1989. *A New Critical Edition of the Mahāvyutpatti. Sanskrit-Tibetan-Mongolian Dictionary of Buddhist Terminology.* Tokyo: The Toyo Bunko.

Klimburg-Salter, Deborah. 2001. Dung dkar / Phyi dbang, West Tibet, and the Influence of Tangut Buddhist Art. Tucci Archive Report, 4. *East and West* 51/2, 323-348.

Lefmann, Salomon. 1874. *Lalita Vistara. Erzälung von dem Leben und der Lere des Çâkya Siṁha. Aus dem Original des Sanskrit und des Gâthâdialects zuerst ins Deutsche uebersetzt und mit sachlichen Erklaerungen versehen.* Berlin: Ferd. Dümmler's Verlagsbuchhandlung, Harrwitz and Gossmann.

Lefmann, Salomon. 1902. *Lalita Vistara. Leben und Lehre des Çâkya-Buddha: Textausgabe mit Varianten-, Metren- und Wörterverzeichnis. Erster Teil: Text.* Halle a.S.: Verlag der Buchhandlung des Waisenhauses.

Lefmann, Salomon. 1908. *Lalita Vistara. Leben und Lehre des Çâkya-Buddha: Textausgabe mit Varianten-, Metren- und Wörterverzeichnis. Zweiter Teil: Varianten-, Metren- und Wörterverzeichnis.* Halle a.S.: Verlag der Buchhandlung des Waisenhauses.

Luczanits, Christian. 2004. *Buddhist Sculpture in Clay. Early Western Himalayan Art, Late 10th to Early 13th Centuries.* Chicago: Serindia.

Lv = Lalitavistara: D: *mdo sde, kha*, 1v1-216v7 (The Tibetan Tripitaka. Taipei Edition. Taiwan 1991, vol. 10). For the Sanskrit text see Hokazono 1994 and Lefmann 1902, 1908.

Mvy = Mahāvyutpatti: See Ishihama and Fukuda 1989 and Sakaki 1981.

Orofino, Giacomella. 2007. From Archaeological Discovery to Text Analysis: The Khor chags Monastery Findings and the *Mañjuśrīnāmasaṃgīti* Fragment, in: Heller, Amy and Giacomella Orofino (eds.), *Discoveries in Western Tibet and the Western Himalayas. Essays on History, Literature, Archaeology and Art. PIATS 2003: Tibetan Studies: Proceedings of the Tenth Seminar of the International Association for Tibetan Studies, Oxford, 2003.* Leiden, Boston: Brill, 85-127.

Pritzker, Thomas J. 1996. A Preliminary Report on Early Cave Paintings of Western Tibet. *Orientations* 27/6, 26-47.

Rdo rje rgyal po (ed.). 1988. Bu ston: *Chos 'byung gsung rab rin po che'i mdzod.* Xining: Krung go'i bod kyi shes rig dpe skrun khang.

Rhie, Marylin 1999. Tibetan Painting. Styles, Sources and Schools, in: Rhie, Marylin and Robert Thurman (eds.), *Worlds of Transformation. Tibetan Art of Wisdom and Compassion.* New York: Tibet House, 45-79.

Sakaki, Ryōzaburō 1981. *Honyaku myōgi taishū* (*Mahāvyutpatti*). 2 vols. Tokyo: Kokusho Kannkōkai. (First edition published in Kyoto, 1916-1925)

Steinkellner, Ernst and Luczanits, Christian. 1999. The Renovation Inscription in the Tabo gTsug lag khaṅ. New Edition and Translation, in: Petech, Luciano and Christian Luczanits (eds.), *Inscriptions from the Tabo Main Temple. Texts and Translations.* Roma: Istituto Italiana per l'Africa e l'Oriente, 9-28.

Tauscher, Helmut. 1999. The «Admonitory Inscription» in the Tabo 'Du khang, in: Petech, Luciano and Christian Luczanits (eds.), *Inscriptions from the Tabo Main Temple. Texts and Translations.* Roma: Istituto Italiana per l'Africa e l'Oriente, 29-94.

Tropper, Kurt. 2007. The Buddha-vita in the *skor lam chen mo* at Zha lu Monastery, in: Kellner, Birgit *et al.* (eds.): *Pramāṇakīrtiḥ. Papers Dedicated to Ernst Steinkellner on the Occasion of his 70th Birthday.* Vienna: Arbeitskreis für Tibetische und Buddhistische Studien, 941-973.

— 2012. Inscriptions and Captions of the Buddha-vita in Pang gra phug, in: Heller, Amy (ed.), *The Arts of Tibetan Painting: Recent Research on Manuscripts, Murals and Thangkas of Tibet, the Himalayas and Mongolia (11th to 19th century). Proceedings of the Twelfth Seminar of the International Association of Tibetan Studies, Vancouver 2010.* (http://www.asianart.com/articles/tropper/index.html)

— 2013. The Buddha-vita in the White Temple of Tsaparang, in: Tropper, Kurt and Cristina

Scherrer-Schaub (eds.), *Tibetan Inscriptions. Proceedings of a Panel Held at the Twelfth Seminar of the International Association for Tibetan Studies, Vancouver 2010.* Leiden, Boston: Brill, 43-106.

— In press: Inscriptions, Captions and Murals of the Buddha-vita in Pang gra phug (Mnga' ris, Western Tibet), in: Munier-Gaillard, Cristophe (ed.), *Mural Art.*

— In preparation a: The Buddha-vita in the Red Temple of Tholing.

— In preparation b: The Buddha-vita in the 'Brom ston lha khang chen mo of Tabo.

— In preparation c: The Buddha-vita in the Sgrol ma lha khang of Tsaparang.

Tshe ring rgyal po. 2006. *Mnga' ris chos 'byung gangs ljongs mdzes rgyan.* Lhasa: Bod ljongs mi dmangs dpe skrun khang.

Vv = *Vinayavastu*: D: *'dul ba, ka* 1v1-nga 302r5 (The Tibetan Tripitaka. Taipei Edition. Taiwan 1991, vol. 1).

Zhang, Yisun 张怡荪 *et al.* 1993. *Bod rgya tshig mdzod chen mo / Zang-Han da cidian* 藏汉大辞典 . 2 vols. Beijing: Mi rigs dpe skrun khang (Reprint of the 1985 edition in 3 volumes).

Notes on the Performance and Meaning of the Sherken and Namtong Festivals in Areas of Historical Western Tibet [1]

Christian Jahoda (Austrian Academy of Sciences)

This article is dedicated in honour of the memory of my friend and colleague Tsering Gyalpo (b. 1961 Glang chu, Western Tibet, China; d. 2015 Berlin, Germany).

Buddhist festivals count among the cultural heritage of areas belonging to historical Western Tibet (Mnga' ris skor gsum). They constitute in particular one of their unbroken traditions. In the course of joint field research and during research guest stays in Vienna, the late Guge Tsering Gyalpo often expressed the view which is shared by many people all over historical Western Tibet that this particular heritage and many others for which these areas are well-known should be documented in order to make them known also outside Western Tibet and at the same time to preserve them as well as related knowledge and performance traditions for future generations.

1 The research for this article was conducted within the framework of two research projects funded by the Austrian Science Fund (FWF): "Oral and Festival Traditions of Western Tibet: Processes of Cultural Memory and Renewal" (P20637-G15) and "Society, Power and Religion in Pre-modern Western Tibet: Interaction, Conflict and Integration" (P21806-G19). These projects were carried out under the direction of the author at the Institute for Social Anthropology, Austrian Academy of Sciences, Vienna. These research projects focused on the one hand on the Tibetan-speaking areas of Spiti and Upper Kinnaur in the Indian state of Himachal Pradesh and on the other also included comparative research in Ngari (in Tibetan transliteration [henceforth T.] Mnga' ris) Prefecture in the west of the Tibet Autonomous Region, PR China. The basis for the latter was a research agreement between the Tibetan Academy of Social Sciences in Lhasa and the Austrian Academy of Sciences in Vienna which afforded me (and other researchers working in these projects, such as Christiane Kalantari, Hubert Feiglstorfer and Patrick Sutherland) the privilege of close scholarly collaboration with the late Tsering Gyalpo. Above all I am immensely grateful for his companionship and friendship.

I wish to thank Guntram Hazod and Ernst Steinkellner (Austrian Academy of Sciences, Institute for Social Anthropology and Institute for the Cultural and Intellectual History of Asia, respectively) for helpful and inspiring comments on earlier versions of this contribution. This paper appeared in a slightly different form in Slovak language in *Slovenský národopis* (*Slovak Ethnology*), vol. 59 (2011), no. 4, pp. 385-400.

1. Introduction

The scholarly interest in communal ritual performances or festivals as well as in ritual behaviour has increased over the last decades. Questions dealing with ritual in a variety of aspects, such as conflict and consensus, performance, etc. constitute the topic of many recent and ongoing studies which is also demonstrated by a growing number of related publications in social and cultural anthropology. Increased scholarly interest in ritual, communal ritual performances or festivals can also be observed in various other disciplines (see Kiliánová 2012).

This paper has as its starting point simple everyday-language questions about the meaning of festivals or the main purpose for the celebration of certain festivals or the performance of certain communal rituals. Such questions that researchers will usually also ask their informants in the field and that colleagues, relatives and other interested parties often request them to answer after returning from the field, not seldom result in a variety of more or less unsatisfying answers. This experience is common to most researchers. I would like to cite here examples of such answers by Brahmins concerning the meaning of Agnicayana, a 3,000-year-old Vedic ritual, recorded in 1975 in a village in southwest India by Frits Staal, a great authority in the field of ritual studies: "[W]e do it because our ancestors did it; because we are eligible to do it; because it is good for society; because it is good; because it is our duty; because it is said to lead to immortality; because it leads to immortality. A visitor will furthermore observe that a person who has performed a Vedic ritual acquires social and religious status, which involves other benefits, some of them economic." (Staal 1979: 3). Staal's answer to the question in this case and his more general view, that "[r]itual is pure activity, without meaning or goal." (*ibid.*: 9) and that "ritual consists in the precise execution of rules" (*ibid.*: 15), are well known.[2] What he expressed as a vision or hope was that an "*adequate* theory of ritual will not only elucidate ritual; it will throw light on the origins of language, religion, and perhaps man." (*ibid.*: 21; my emphasis). Conforming to Staal's credo, in my view, the goal of an adequate theory or at least a better understanding of festivals cannot be reached without a reflective re-evaluation

2 "Why has it proved so difficult to define the meaning, goals and aims of ritual? Why are there so many different answers and theories, not only often contradictory between themselves, but of such disparate character that it is difficult to even compare them with each other? There is one simple hypothesis which would account for all these puzzling facts: the hypothesis that ritual has no meaning, goal or aim" (Staal 1979: 8).

or re-assessment of research methodology and of the condition(s), frame(s) and goal(s) of respective research on communal ritual performances.

The question about the meaning of communal ritual performances or festivals implies a holistic approach or perspective. Its focus is therefore not on certain parts or aspects of festivals but towards the very general concept informing them: What are these festivals about? What is their meaning? What is the reason to celebrate a certain festival? It is in this sense that the present article aims to contribute some thoughts on the meaning of Buddhist village festivals in Upper Kinnaur (T. *Khu nu*) and Purang (T. *Spu rang*, etc.) constituting areas of Historical Western Tibet and thereby also throw some light on neglected aspects in the debate of such communal ritual performances. For this purpose, two case studies will be discussed. The first is the Sherken (T. *Shar rgan*?) festival in Pooh (T. *Spu*) in Upper Kinnaur, which I managed to document in October 2009 together with Christiane Kalantari and with the assistance of Thinley Dorje from Tabo village (Spiti).[3] The other one is the Namtong (T. *Nam mthong*) festival in Khorchag (T. *'Khor chags*, etc.) village in Purang County in the Ngari Prefecture of the Tibet Autonomous Region. This festival was documented in the course of a joint field research of the above-mentioned research group with the late Tsering Gyalpo in February/March 2010 (see Tsering Gyalpo 2012; Jahoda 2012a).

2. Preliminary notes on theoretical issues and questions

It was already clear to Frits Staal that, in order to clarify the question of meaning or theory of ritual, one should not confine this task to asking practising ritualists or people taking part in one way or another in the ritual. In fact, it was long before Staal's investigations took place that what became known as participant observation was established by Bronisław Malinowski as characteristic field research method of social anthropologists.[4] This method which was later also adopted by other disciplines seeks to comprise emic views as well as etic (or observers') perspectives and concepts. In keeping with this method, the topic of the meaning of communal ritual performances or Buddhist village festivals in Upper Kinnaur and Western Tibet discussed here will also pay attention to relevant emic and etic concepts.

3 See Jahoda 2011 for an ethnographic account of the Sherken festival, as it was celebrated in October 2009.

4 The final goal of the ethnographer in his view was "to grasp the native's point of view, his relation to life, to realize his vision of his world" (Malinowski 1961: 25).

The societies of Upper Kinnaur and Western Tibet are characterised historically by strong religious traditions, mainly but not exclusively those belonging to Tibetan Buddhism. The oral and ritual traditions performed on the occasion of these festivals, in particular the songs but also performances by trance mediums, are largely determined by concepts from the world of Tibetan Buddhism, although elements of folk religion and other religious traditions (for example, Bon religion) were/are also sometimes present. With this in mind, the analysis and evaluation of these communal ritual performances and festivals needs to take into account in particular also this religious aspect. In the case of Tibetan Buddhism, elaborate philosophical systems and highly complex religious practices have developed which are of great importance for an adequate understanding of religious performances. Moreover, also the political context and historical framework of festivals and various aspects of formalised language (oratories, formalised speeches, intoned prayers and formulae, songs, etc.) and body movements (or dance), symbolic or material aspects of village festivals (such as seating order and dress) are of relevance in this context (see also Bloch 1989).

3. The Sherken festival in Pooh (Upper Kinnaur)

This festival can be characterised essentially as follows: various divination and sacrificial rituals are held at sacred sites and places within the village area which are specifically designated for cultic practices (Fig. 1). These rituals are directed towards local and protective deities, some of whom appear and speak to the villagers through a trance medium. They are accompanied by communal dancing, singing, feasting and ritual processions. For all ritual performances of this festival the participation of representatives from all the village houses is deemed necessary or obligatory. All major rituals as well as related songs and dances are performed mainly by and under the guidance of a lay Buddhist priest, a function that is inherited within his family (Fig. 2). He is also at the top of the internal social village hierarchy and sits at the highest place of the seating order in assemblies, for example, in the community hall of the village when meals are served there for the performers and participants in this event during festival time. The person next to him in status is the village headman, who is elected from a group of ca. 60 houses in Pooh with full rights according to

Fig. 1. Performance of dances and songs, Sherken place, Sherken festival, Pooh, Upper Kinnaur (photo: Christiane Kalantari, 2009).

Fig. 2. Lay village priest (with village headman and musicians) performing ritual dance and speech songs, Sherken festival, Pooh, Upper Kinnaur (photo: Christiane Kalantari, 2009).

customary law.[5]

For all ritual practices of any importance during this festival that are related to the cult of local and/or protective deities musical performance (playing drums and other instruments) is essential. This requires in particular the participation of musicians, who are considered low caste (and referred to as "Chipa" [T. *phyi pa*, literally "outsider"]). The members of the higher families see this as the musicians' duty and as part of an inherited system of intra-village cooperation and exchange. In recent years, revolts by musicians occurred in this and other villages in the area who refused to perform and thereby protested against their social discrimination.

In the case of one of the most important sacrificial rituals of this festival a great change seems to have occurred in the past ca. 100 years. Evidence of this is contained in an unpublished early-20th-century account of the festival by Sir Herbert William Emerson who largely draws on information and eye-witness reports provided by the Moravian missionary Hermann Marx (see Emerson, n.d.). According to this account, on the fourth day of the festival "women carry baskets filled with offerings for the shades of the dead, while each man drives before him a sheep or goat, the ransom of a male child born during the year. The 'life ransom' is known as the 'blessed sheep,' and is dedicated to the goddess [Dabla, T. *Dgra lha*, also *Sgra bla*] at the festival and previously. Before it is driven from the house of the sacrificer, it is placed in the centre of the family. A little wool is picked from the tail and from the back of the head and is waved towards the child first and then towards each member of the family in turn. 'We now lay all harm on you,' say the people, as the tufts of wool are replaced on the victim. Red earth is sprinkled over the back of the animal to keep away all evil influences, and prayers are said for the long life, health and prosperity of the boy. The sheep is then handed over to a 'soft, good-natured man' who leads it to the place of sacrifice." (Emerson, n.d., Chapter XVII: 59-60). As soon as there were signs that the Dabla deity had accepted a sheep as ransom for the boy, Marx observed that the trance medium of

5 The members of these houses describe themselves as "Chayang" in Pooh and adjacent areas in Upper Kinnaur, a word which seems to correspond to "Chazang" in Spiti (in phonetic transcription *tɕʰāzāŋ*, T. *cha bzang / tshang*?). They can be compared to the category of households known as "Khangchen" (T. *khang chen*, lit. "great house") in Spiti, who are identifiable with the former "Threlpa" (T. *khral pa*, lit. "taxpayer") households whose agricultural holdings until the mid-20th century constituted "the fundamental, indivisible [...] units of taxation [...] as well as fundamental units of residence, production and consumption" (Jahoda 2008: 11) not only in Spiti and Upper Kinnaur but also in Ladakh as well as in adjacent areas of Western Tibet, such as Purang (see Levine 1992; Jahoda 2015: 170, *passim*).

Fig. 3. Dabla (*Dgra lha*) deity speaking through trance medium, ritual ground, Sherken festival, Pooh, Upper Kinnaur (photo: Christiane Kalantari, 2009).

the "eagle spirit [Dabla] seized it with both hands, throwing it over his head on to the ground where men were waiting ready to kill it." (*ibid.*: 61). According to the village people's statements collected in 2009, the sacrifice of goats and sheep as described by Marx in the early 20th century was not performed anymore for some decades but ritual offerings to the deity who "enters" the body of a trance medium still constitute one of the key moments of the ritual performances (Fig. 3). Not only the Dabla deity (who is conceived as a female) but also other deities usually "appear" on the occasion of the festival and speak through different trance mediums. Partly they appear also in the form of a material manifestation – called "phobrang" (T. *pho brang*, usually meaning palace or court, king's residence; see also Bielmeier *et al.*, forthcoming) in the case of Dabla, or represented by a sacred vase [T. *bum pa*] in the case of others.

Another fundamental element of the festival that seems to have remained unchanged, however, is the repeated performance of certain ritual songs, which are sung only on the occasion of this festival by the before-mentioned lay village priest. In these songs which contain various references to Buddhism (*lha chos*), also to Bon religion (*bon chos*) and ethical codes of conduct (*mi chos*), Dabla and other deities are directly addressed and praised (Fig. 4). Moreover, the area of Pooh village is portrayed as a sacred landscape embedded within a wider framework of Buddhist cosmology, and the local social order, as it also becomes manifest during the time of the festival, is presented within the framework

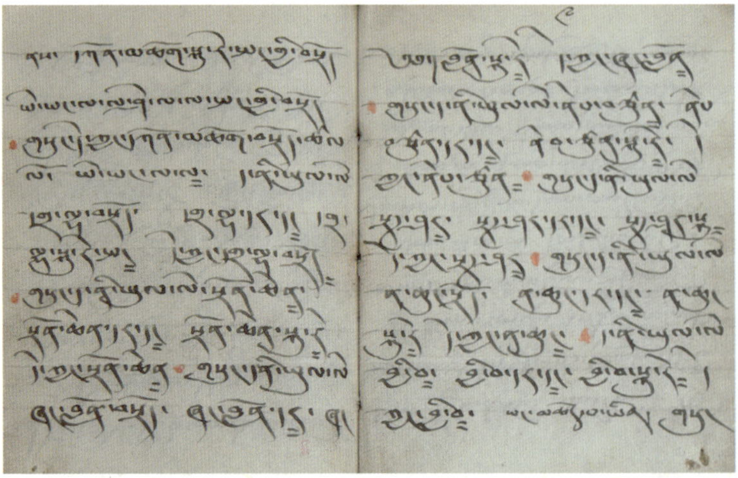

Fig. 4. Manuscript of ritual speech songs performed at Sherken festival, Pooh, Upper Kinnaur (photo: Christiane Kalantari, 2009).

of an older, pre-modern order. This is expressed by the use of archaic concepts, symbols and language that are otherwise only known from wedding songs (see also Tucci 1966: 69).[6]

4. The Namtong festival in Khorchag (Purang)

The Namtong festival in Khorchag village in Purang County is a monastic festival in the sense that it takes place within the walled compound of the monastery and that, except for folk dances and songs, the ritual performances which are carried out by monks of the local monastic community are of a religious nature (and as such require a more or less thorough religious knowledge and training) (Fig. 5). Nevertheless, due to the considerable degree of secular performances and on account of the extent of active involvement by lay village people throughout the festival (Fig. 6), it is legitimate to class it as a communal ritual performance or village festival that is comparable in this regard to the Sherken festival in Pooh. As this, the Namtong festival can be defined as a rather fixed and coherent set of an annual sequence of ritual practices and performances of central importance for the local village community. This includes the participation and presence of members from all social

6 In *Tibetan Folk Songs* (1966) Tucci considered these ritual songs to be part of ceremonies and rituals the main purpose of which was "to produce a renovation" (*ibid.*: 61). He interpreted the local deity, *Dgra lha*, which is represented in the manuscript of the songs, as *Dog lha* or *Dog mo*, the god of the *dog* or soil. The place where this god appears was the *dog ra*, which should be conceived as a sacred area "which by a magical transference represents the universe" (*ibid.*: 65). In his view, in certain passages of these songs, this female deity, *Dog mo*, is referred to as accomplishing a journey through this universe up to heaven and he understood this journey which he found portrayed in the songs by a hierarchy of religious, social and cosmic strata or levels as a superimposition of themes of ancient Indian or Tibetan origin, and related with Bon religion, Buddhism and the Gesar legend, respectively.

Fig. 5. Ritual for the renewing of religious offerings, Namtong festival, Khorchag (photo: Patrick Sutherland, 2010).

Fig. 6. Villagers performing dances, Namtong festival, Khorchag (photo: Christiane Kalantari, 2009).

groups – lay villagers, including musicians, as well as monks, who are to a large degree also of local origin – acting in interrelated roles as performers, audience, sponsors/donors and donees (cf. Ruegg 1991, 1995 and 2008 for a discussion of these terms and related concepts in Tibetan-speaking areas).

In the centre of this festival are sacrificial rituals dedicated to the main protective deities of Khorchag monastery which was founded in the late 10th century. Since the 15th century it belonged to the Ngor subschool of the Sakya (T. *Sa skya*) order of Tibetan Buddhism. The deities who are worshiped and who are personated by monks and occasionally also by lay people in the mask dances during this festival also include an important female deity (Dorje Chenmo, T. *Rdo rje chen mo*) (Fig. 7). She is seen as the original spiritual owner and protectress of the monastery and is historically linked with the medieval royal lineages of Western Tibet and also with one of the key religious figures of the 10th/11th century, the Great Translator Rinchen Zangpo (T. *lo chen Rin chen bzang po*) (958-1055), who was active throughout this region.

The ritual performances of the monks and lay people during the Namtong festival

Fig. 7. Female protective deity of Khorchag monastery and her retinue during Namtong festival, Khorchag, Western Tibet (photo: Patrick Sutherland, 2010).

serve to recall the founding of the monastery and the original establishment of a religious, namely Buddhist order of the local society. Part of this historical Buddhist transformation was the establishment of a particular socio-economic organisation of the local community and a certain social order, which accorded the highest status within the framework of the lay village community to the group of cultivators/taxpayers/religious sponsors. The performance of these rituals can therefore be seen as an act of memory to this old religious and social (also socio-economic) order and to some degree also as a public expression of the perseverance or confirmation of the inherited belief system as far as this is compatible with the present political system.

At the Namtong festival in Khorchag a similar social order comes to light as that in Pooh, with the exception that instead of a lay village priest the monks of the Buddhist monastery occupy the position with the highest ritual status. The dominant social group in the village, as it becomes evident during this festival and also on other occasions, are peasants who live in so-called "great houses" (T. *khang chen*) and who were previously known as "Threlpa" (T. *khral pa*, literally "taxpayers"), because of the land they cultivated for which they had to pay taxes and in return render obligatory services to the owners, mainly a religious estate (see Levine 1992). Of particular importance is the fact that a close relationship between this social group of peasants and the monastery continues to exist in the form of cooperation and exchange (in economic and religious fields), which seems to be of considerable antiquity. A number of these houses also constitute the so-called sponsoring families (*sbyin bdag* in Tibetan) of the monastery. Their donations are the main regular economic support for the monastery and in particular they also sponsor the monks during certain festivals and religious ceremonies. In between the mask dances of the monks villagers from these houses not only perform particular folk dances and songs but also dances where they personate historical figures and local village deities (T. *yul lha*) (Fig. 8).

5. Meaningful or meaningless?

This brief general account of both festivals is based on participant observation and in addition on a preliminary analysis of relevant historical reports and sources. The characterisation of these festivals included some general references to the question concerning their meaning or some aspects which are considered as most important by local informants and some observers (including the author). A more detailed look at available

Fig. 8. Masked dance performance by villagers impersonating local village deities (photo: Patrick Sutherland, 2010).

written, oral and visual source materials, also in terms of relevant emic concepts, is attempted below.

5.1 Assessing evidence from oral and written sources

Sometimes the meaning of a certain ritual or festival becomes clear by way of an investigation of the name under which it is generally known or referred to. In the case of rituals, the semantic denotation of their names most often does not seem to be apt for an adequate clarification of their meaning. An example for this is the Agnicayana ritual studied by Staal, the meaning of which can be rendered as "piling of the Fire Altar" (Kramrisch 2002: 24). The same difficulty yields a closer investigation of the name of the two festivals studied here.

In my enquiries made in Pooh in 2002 and 2009, all local informants, including the officiating lay village priest, referred to this festival by the name of "Sherken". With the exception of Tucci (see below), all reliable written sources mentioning this festival refer to it as Shergen (Emerson, n.d., *passim*), Shirgin (Mamgain 1971: 333), Sherkan (Hein 2007:

238) or Sher rgen (Nyima Senge, n.d.). The meaning of Sherken – pronounced *ɕērkān* in the local dialect (Hein 2007: 238) – is unclear. It is not even clear if it is really a Tibetan name that might be spelt as Shar rgan as suggested by Francke (1914: 20f.).[7] It was perhaps a manuscript containing the written versions of the ritual songs sung during this festival (referred to by him as "The Songs of the Shar rgan festival"; cf. *ibid.*: 118) that led him to use this spelling. The common meaning of *shar* and *rgan* in Tibetan – east and old, respectively – does not provide an expedient enlightening clue.

With reference to the central cult of a female deity [Dabla] and a manuscript with ritual songs in her honour (another version of the manuscript collected by Francke), Tucci (1966) called this festival *Dgra lha* [Dabla] festival. He based his analysis of this festival more or less exclusively on textual materials, in particular a manuscript of these ritual songs. He did not ascribe much value to the actual performance of the festival which "was said by old people to have become *only* a dance, and the occasion for rejoicings; it is quite possible that these songs have altogether disappeared. The dance has a great part in the ritual; I did not see the dance as it is performed in this festival, but I was told that two rows of young men and young women participate in it, advancing and drawing back as it is *usual* in Tibetan dancing." (*ibid.*: 70; my emphases). His approach clearly reflects the view that the meaning of the festival is contained in the text and that for an adequate understanding of the festival aspects of the performance, such as dance, are not enough meaningful (anymore). The result of his analysis is that "[t]he festival is a gathering (..) of those who participate in it, but *also of the gods* protecting the territory […]. The ritual is considered as a cause; the ceremonies which are accomplished, the blessing, the worship, etc. are meant to produce *skyid* [T. *skyid skyid*], happiness and to renew it. The main purpose of the ceremony is therefore that of conducting a ritual intended to produce a renovation; it is a new-year festival which should assure all sorts of prosperity for the coming year [..]." (*ibid.*: 61; my emphasis).

From Emerson's account and from my own recent observations, it is quite clear that

7 Francke's remarks on the festival in *Antiquities of Indian Tibet*, vol. 1 (1914), were based on oral accounts and legends and a preliminary study of written versions of the ritual songs sung during this festival he had collected during a short 4-day-stay in Pooh in July 1909, when also a limited photographic documentation of selected dancing grounds was made by a photographer who accompanied him during this mission financed by the Archaeological Survey of India (ASI). Neither he nor Giuseppe Tucci (who briefly stayed in Pooh in 1933) were able to directly observe this festival. Francke stressed the pre-Buddhist and Bon traditions discernible in the songs and ritual traditions related to this festival, a view which was also followed by Giuseppe Tucci in the travel account which was published in Italian twenty years after Francke's *Antiquities* (Tucci and Ghersi 1934).

the Sherken festival is not a new-year festival (T. *lo gsar*), at least not in the sense that such festivals are commonly understood. Nevertheless, Tucci's statement that the festival is a gathering of village people and also a gathering of gods who protect the village territory deserves attention for two reasons. Firstly, because it characterises this festival as a communal village affair and secondly, because it includes an important emic perspective in the explicitly mentioned gathering or presence of deities.

The Sherken festival can be conceived as an event related to and carried out by the village community of Pooh as the crucial social reference unit. In Upper Kinnaur as well as in Spiti and adjacent areas of Western Tibet, festivals of this kind are considered a collective communal activity with obligatory participation by all social groups and households belonging to the local community. This accords with the insight that the village organisation in these areas as well as in Ladakh historically was and still is characterised by a strong notion of community and local legal autonomy (see, for example, Pirie 2006, Jahoda 2015: 68, *passim*) and that communal ritual performances constitute a fundamental category of festival traditions for which a common designation in Tibetan is demo (T. *ltad mo*).[8] In a more general sense, festivals are referred to as *dus ston* and for any specific rites or rituals *cho ga* is the usual word in written Tibetan (see, for example, Tsering Gyalpo 2012: 214).

5.2 A Brief look at emic and etic concepts

The issue of the gathering or presence of deities is closely related to the question of the meaning of the Sherken festival. In a similar way, this is also true for the Namtong festival where the presence or rather public appearance of deities protecting the monastery and in extension also the village is one of the key aspects – together with the gathering of village people and other visitors. I would like to discuss this issue on the basis of concepts and models used by Joanna Pfaff-Czarnecka and Andre Gingrich in recent contributions to the topic of ritual (see Pfaff-Czarnecka 2012 and Gingrich 2012). Central to their approach is the analytical differentiation between "script" (texts, myths, rules, local and global ideologies, doctrines), "ritual stage" or "arena" and the (re-) production of meaning(s) by

8 The category of "village festivals and rituals" was also identified by Mark Trewin as one of three fundamental categories of festival traditions in the pre-modern kingdom of Ladakh; the other two being "public monastic ritual-dramas" (that is, monastic offering rituals performed at the climax of the annual ritual cycle, T. *dus mchod*) and "state ceremonial" or "royal festivals" (see Trewin 1995: 8, 84, *passim*).

actors or performers. Taking the Durgā Pūjā ritual complex in Nepal as example, Pfaff-Czarnecka holds that ritual performance does not follow simply predetermined rules or a "script", and that consequently the action by performers is "embodied and transformative" and characterised by a dynamic ritual production of meanings. Gingrich attempts to define the ideological part in the production of ritual reality and demonstrates, on the basis of ritual sites (or "stages") in the mountain regions of south-western Arabia, how the "scripts" tend to constrain the production of meanings and rather lead to a reproduction of meaning.

The notion of "script" suggests that the underlying concept is strongly focussed on a text (or texts) or at least on a "scenario" that is predominantly based on written textual sources. In my view, script or scenario should be conceptualised in a wider sense that also includes visual and material aspects as well as music and dance, in the case of Buddhist village festivals in particular all manifestations which (pre-)define, symbolise or express forms of "presence" of deities. These aspects are usually not part of the scripts in a limited textual sense. Still, they exist and in the case of the Sherken and Namtong festivals, from emic perspectives, they are highly impressing and powerful.

When we look at "script" (in the wider sense) and ask about the meaning of rituals, texts, ritual paraphernalia or music and dance in terms of Buddhist concepts, the answer is still not easy. The reason for this is that the notion of meaning itself is explained and understood in various different ways in the societies practising one or the other form of Tibetan Buddhism. The differences depend only marginally on the respective school traditions but primarily on social categories like literate (T. *dpe cha ba*) versus illiterate (T. *thos chung ba*). In agreement with a suggestion made by Bryan Cuevas, it is proposed that the distinction between the sacred and the profane should not be too inflexible and that a rather flexible one should be made between "'formal' religious doctrine and 'informal' religious understanding" (see Cuevas 2008: 6f.).

In formal religious Buddhist doctrine, as it is contained in Buddhist scriptures, such as early Indian Mahāyāna *sūtra*s, the concepts of truth and meaning were object of debates that were continued also in the later Buddhist traditions of Tibet. In order to reconcile the inconsistencies the diverging and expanding conceptual development brought with it and still adhere to the authenticity and pragmatic truth of the Buddhist texts, scriptures were differentiated in terms of meaning (Skt. *artha*) in those of direct or definitive as against those of indirect meaning (Skt. *nītārtha*, T. *nges don*; Skt. *neyārtha*, T. *drang don*) (cf.

Cabezón 1981). Texts like the *Laṅkāvatārasūtra* even hold that meaning "must be *realized* in secluded meditation, *not through verbal understanding*" and that "[i]nfernal rebirth and uninterrupted saṃsāric experience await those who indulge in such mistake [..]." (Lugli 2010: 145; my emphases). Popular views of festivals or rituals in the sense of the above-mentioned informal religious understanding are commonly not or not directly concerned with the question of direct or indirect meaning of scriptures (and their visual or material equivalents). They are rather informed by soteriological value or pragmatic points of view, that is, gathering religious merit in order to come closer to the goal of liberation from the cycle of rebirth.

In fact, both concepts – the radical realisation of meaning *and* pragmatic worldly performance – are often present at Buddhist festivals. In the case of the Namtong festival, for example, meditation, spiritual realisation and initiation are a precondition for the performance of mask dances on the side of the monks who impersonate Buddhist deities. Moreover, the monks spend many long sessions in meditative recitation, more or less in spatial segregation from lay people. On the other hand, if not the physical appearance at least the presence of these deities impersonated by monks is considered as real by most believers which gives them a precious opportunity to perform a "religiously significant action" (Skt. *kuśalakarman*; T. *dge ba'i las*) and acquire merit (cf. Wilson 1996: 381).

In the case of the Sherken festival, at least from a doctrinal Buddhist view, the "spiritual level" is not as high as in the case of the Namtong festival. The reason is that in the former no high-ranking Buddhist deities are personated by monks. The deities who appear – Dabla and others – belong to the class of personal protective deities or village deities and are of a lower, "worldly" or "mundane" order (Skt. *laukikadevatā*, T. *jig rten pa'i lha*) as compared to Mahākāla and other deities appearing at the Namtong festival who are considered as transmundane (Skt. *lokottara*, T. *'jig rten las 'das pa*) (cf. Ruegg 2008: 42). Nevertheless, in terms of presence and agency, there is not much difference. From the viewpoint of informal religious understanding, the deity's presence by way of speaking through a trance medium or through a dance performed by its material manifestation is maybe even considered more "real". One reason for this can be seen in the mingling of lay devotees and deities on the same level of reality and the close direct interaction which takes place between them on the ritual and dancing grounds. Besides the trance medium who is actually "chosen" by the deity (and not considered of any additional importance beyond this; the literal meaning of trance medium – T. *lus g.yar* – is "the one who borrows his/her body to the deity"), the only mediator and person of superior importance for the ritual interaction with the deities is the lay priest "who rejoices in the title of 'the lord of the dancing ground of the lha' [deity]" [T. *dog ra mgon po*] (Emerson, n.d., p. 54; underlined in the original).

5.3 Forms of presence of deities

In the context of communal Buddhist ritual performances or festivals, such as the Sherken and Namtong festivals, the presence of deities – understood in the above-mentioned sense – is certainly one of the most important if not the most important aspect in terms of meaning. Their presence materialises or becomes manifest in various forms. Based on the example of the two festivals, it is possible to differentiate roughly five different forms of manifestation: 1) trance medium (voice), 2) personification (mask), 3) material manifestation ("phobrang", etc.), 4) music and 5) dance.

In the case of the Sherken festival, Dabla as well as other deities are present by speaking through a trance medium (see Fig. 3). The explanation for this is that protective deities of this kind are bodyless beings (T. *gzugs med*) and need to enter a human being's body in order to express herself/himself.[9] In Spiti and Upper Kinnaur the speeches of these deities when they "borrow" the bodies of trance mediums are known as Molla (T. *mol ba*). In other parts of Kinnaur, they are known as "Chironing" oder "Chirāning" (see Mamgain 1971: 332f., Singh 1989: 49). In Khorchag, too, there used to be a trance medium for the female protective deity of the monastery (again Dorje Chenmo – or Dorje Yudön [T. *Rdo rje G.yu sgron*] in the Ngor school tradition to which Khorchag belongs) but this practice was stopped following a ban on trance-mediumship in Tibet by political authorities some decades ago.[10]

9 Dorje Chenmo, a female protective deity (T. *srung ma*) in Tabo, when speaking through her (male) trance medium in 2000 on the occasion of a village festival, stated this many times: "I am a bodyless being. [..] Whether I go inside the *lus g.yar po* [trance medium] or not, it makes no difference [to me]. If I enter into his body, it is of no benefit and if I do not enter, it is no loss either" (translation by the author, based on a transliteration of the speech made by Dechen Lhundup, Tabo).

10 It is remarkable that, according to legendary accounts and local oral tradition, also the famous Jobo (Mañjuśrī) silver statue of Khorchag spoke, altogether seven times in the course of history. Even the name of this place is said to go back to a statement made by this statue (see Jahoda 2012b: 49). Speaking deities are also reported for Central Tibet, for example, the Rje btsun Sgrol ma at Khra 'brug was also known as a "Speaking One" (*gsung byon ma*); see Sørensen and Hazod, in cooperation with Tsering Gyalbo 2005: 68-69.

Nevertheless, the presence of Dorje Chenmo during the Namtong festival, personated by a monk who wears a mask and rides on a wooden horse, is actually the climax of this festival (Fig. 7). Her performance (together with her retinue of four minor deities) is explained as auspicious horse-racing that is meant to suppress demonic beings living below the ground where the monastery was to be built. It is accompanied by a particular musical performance of kettledrums (T. *brda rnga*, according to Trewin 1995: 18 also *brda man*) and the sound of oboes (T. *sur na*). Her appearance, which serves to recall the foundation of the monastery, can certainly be seen in a way – not only in terms of an informal religious understanding – as a re-staging of and ritualised memory to one of the key moments of the historic foundation process. But more importantly, at least from an emic perspective, her appearance during the annual celebration demonstrates her uninterrupted vital presence and (protective) power over this place and signifies rather an act of confirmation than one of a memory. In commercial advertisements and official statements, the presence of this deity, which constitutes one of the most meaningful ritual highlights of this festival, is not even mentioned. There the meaning of the festival is reduced to the mere celebration of the anniversary of the foundation of the monastery.[11]

Nearly all deities as well as secular figures appearing during the Namtong festival are personated by masks (and with an appropriate outfit of garments, ritual items, etc.) (Figs. 9 and 10). Highranking Buddhist deities are personated by monks, low-ranking deities (according to formal religious understanding), such as local deities, as well as secular figures are personated by lay people. In particular the masks but also others ritual items belonging to these deities are not considered as mere artefacts or props but function themselves as manifestations of the related deities. As such they are endowed with agency, sometimes including the capability to fly. One of the most famous masks in this respect – a leather mask of Mahākāla (T. *Gur* [*gyi*] *mgon* [*po*]) that according to certain accounts was given to the Great Translator Rinchen Zangpo by one of his teachers – is referred to as *'cham/s sku* in Tibetan sources. This term carries the double meaning of "a mask used in *'cham*" (in the

11 "Every year on January 12 [actually on the 12th day of the first month] in the Tibetan calendar, the anniversary of the day on which the construction of the monastery was completed, a big ceremony is held. Considered as the most important religious festival by the locals, the ceremony attracts people from all over Purang County to enjoy the carnival of Tibetan dances and chants." (http://www.tibettrip.com/ngari/khojarnath-monastery.htm; last accessed April 14, 2016).

Fig. 9. Demonic being, Namtong festival, Khorchag, Western Tibet (photo: Patrick Sutherland, 2010).

Fig. 10. Raven and Garuḍa deities, Namtong festival, Khorchag, Western Tibet (photo: Patrick Sutherland, 2010).

sense of an artefact) *and* "dancing mask" (in the sense of mask/deity dancing on its own) (cf. Vitali 2001: 7f., 22). This double meaning is also found in the case of other forms of material manifestation as well as in music and dance (see below). Such personated mask dances are typical of monastic Buddhist festival traditions and seem to have developed in this context. In non-monastic Buddhist festival traditions and in particular also in local, non-Buddhist festival traditions, for example, in central and lower Kinnaur – both characterised by a predominant presence of deities speaking through trance mediums – masks do not appear at all (as, for example, in the case of the Sherken festival) or they appear attached to another form of material manifestation of the deity.

Among the forms of material manifestation of deities we find in the case of the Sherken festival the "phobrang"[12] (see Fig. 11), usually explained by local informants "as seat or place of residence" of Dabla, or a sacred vase (T. *bum pa*) in the case of others. We have seen that in the case of Dorje Chenmo's appearance at the Namtong festival, she is nowadays present not only by way of a mask but also through a corporeal structure covered with a ritual cloth made in accordance with the iconography of the image or statue of the

12 According to Tsering Gyalpo (personal communication, Vienna, April 22, 2011), this word, which is consistently pronounced as "phobrang" in Spiti, Upper Kinnaur and adjacent areas of Western Tibet (where dialects belonging to the group of 'Western Innovative Tibetan' are spoken; cf. Hein 2001: 35), stands for T. *pho brang* (see above).

Fig. 11. Material manifestation ("phobrang") of Dabla (*Dgra lha*) deity with lay village priest, trance medium, musicians and villagers, Sherken festival, Pooh, Upper Kinnaur (photo: Christiane Kalantari, 2009).

deity (T. *sku rten*)[13] (Tsering Gyalpo 2012: 239).[14]

In the case of Dabla, this deity who is conceived as a bird – as an eagle (or lammergeyer according to another account) – is even equated with the village area of Pooh. According to this concept of a sacred, bird-like landscape (consisting of natural features where a divine bird is present or materialises), "[t]he goddess keeps the village under the shadow of her wings, resting over the village 'as an eagle sits on her eggs'. The *head* of the eagle *is* at a spot above the village marked by two ancient pencil cedars; the *left wing is* to the west above a group of cedars, while *the right wing* touches a single cedar to the east. The *tail is* at the bottom of the village [..] and *the body rests* on Poo-mad [T. *sPu smad*, Lower Pooh] [..].

13 In the word *sku rten*, literally "body support", which also carries the meaning "man possessed of deity", the same double meaning as before is implied.

14 A comparable example of such a material manifestation of a deity (here, too, appearing fully attired and riding on a horse made of wood) can be found in the case of the protective and territorial deity Dzongtsen (T. *Rdzong btsan*) in Central Tibet (see Hazod 2007: 573ff.).

The four places first mentioned are particularly sacred to the lha [T. *lha*, god, also spirit], and are always visited at the various festivals held in her honour, and especially at the Shergen, the greatest of them all" (Emerson, n.d., Chapter XVII, pp. 53-54; underlined in the original; italics my emphases).

Finally, also certain forms of music and dance are to be seen as forms of the presence of deities. The music played by low-caste musicians on occasions like the Sherken festival and to some degree also in the case of the Namtong festival constitutes a form of "Lharnga" music (T. *lha rnga*, literally "drum of the gods"). In a West Tibetan context (as described by Trewin 1993 with regard to Ladakh), "Lharnga" denotes the music that is played at village festivals and rituals, in particular that which is offered to local deities on these occasions. This kind of music is considered as auspicious, in a religious as well as in a mundane sense (T. *bkra shis* and *rten 'brel*, respectively). Analysing the range of uses of different "Lharnga", Trewin reached to the conclusion that "the form operates at two levels: the social *and* the supernatural" (Trewin 1993: 378; my emphasis) and that it "(re-)presents and (re-)enacts the encounter between human practitioner and supernatural being" (Trewin 1995: 101).[15] In this sense, "Lharnga" can be understood as "drumming *of* the gods" as well as "drumming *for* the gods". In the same way, "Lha-rtse" (T. *lha rtses*, literally "god-dance" / "god-dancing"), that is, the dances which are accompanied by drums, can be understood to carry the meaning of dances *for* as well as dances *of* deities (see also Trewin 1995: 93, 101f.) (Fig. 11).

6. Concluding remarks

The analysis of manifestations which from an emic perspective (pre-)define, symbolise, express or represent forms of "presence" of deities and of their relationship with the meaning of festivals reveals that what is termed "script" should be conceptualised in a wider sense as it is commonly the case. Moreover, a brief look at concepts found in informal and formal Buddhist understanding showed that we are confronted with a variety of scripts – also in the sense of textual materials – which appear quite multifaceted, sometimes perhaps

15 "Musically, the transcendental and the worldly are juxtaposed: *lha-rnga* is identified as the music of the gods, having a level of meaning and beauty beyond the grasp of humans, but at the same time it is no more than an emulation of this ideal, and is merely an immanent ritual tool with familiar (humanly-derived) properties." (Trewin 1995: 101)
An inscription on a votive bell in the temple of the Thundering Falcon (T. *Khra 'brug*), according to Tibetan tradition the earliest foundation of a Buddhist temple in Tibet, represents perhaps the oldest reference to the concept of divine drum (T. *lha'i rnga*) (see Sørensen and Hazod, in cooperation with Tsering Gyalbo 2005: 159).

even inconsistent.

In terms of the question of ritual production of meanings or reproduction of meaning and the dynamics of this process, it becomes clear that this process is of a dialectic nature. This means that "script" and performance are linked and influence each other over time. The assessment if the "scripts" in the sense defined above tend to constrain the production of meanings and rather lead to a reproduction of meaning or if a dynamic ritual production of meanings takes place, needs to be investigated and answered separately in each case. From a methodological point of view, it is certainly helpful if not necessary to include a diachronic perspective and a greater variety of sources and aspects, including emic concepts, such as those related to the presence of deities, as was commonly done so far. Staal's provocative statement concerning the meaninglessness of rituals not only served to demonstrate the deficits of inadequate ritual theories. In a positive sense, it can and still should also be understood as a plea to search for an "adequate theory of ritual", that is, also for more encompassing approaches which is also supported by the evidence discussed in the present article.

On the basis of initial ethnographic, comparative and historical case studies of the two festivals, a few general preliminary results and conclusions can be delineated. In the case of the Sherken festival, a considerable amount of reliable historical accounts and sources is available, which allows to reconstruct quite well the actual dynamics of this process for a wide range of aspects and over a prolonged timespan. In the course of a period of over 130 years (since the 1870ies), the "script" appears to have been amended, revised and renewed to some degree. This is evidenced, for example, by the introduction of a new deity (Little Kālī, Hindi: Choṭī Kālī) and the termination of animal sacrifice, mainly the effect of the influence of reformist Buddhist and Bon lamas, and their substitution by symbolic offerings (see Jahoda 2011 and 2012a). In addition to what was said above, "[s]cript, performance and arena in such a perspective on religious and other ideological rituals" – such as communal ritual performances and village festivals discussed here – are "of course intrinsically permeated by relations of power" (Gingrich 2012: 66). This is evident in particular in the case of the Namtong festival the script(s) and performance(s) of which were subject to severe constraints (ban of trance mediums) and re-writing (as a type of culture festival).

* * *

References

Bielmeier, Roland *et al.* Forthcoming. *Comparative Dictionary of Tibetan Dialects (CDTD): Nouns*. University of Berne.

Bloch, Maurice. 1989. Symbols, song, dance and features of articulation: Is religion an extreme form of traditional authority? in: Bloch, Maurice, *Rituals, History and Power: Selected Papers in Anthropology*. London: The Athlone Press, 19-45.

Cabezón, José I. 1981. The concepts of truth and meaning in the Buddhist scriptures, *The Journal of the International Association of Buddhist Studies* 4(1): 7-23.

Cuevas, Bryan. 2008. *Travels in the Netherworld. Buddhist Popular Narratives of Death and the Afterlife in Tibet*. New York: Oxford University Press.

Emerson, Sir Herbert William (n.d.) *Treatise*. Unpublished manuscript, British Library, Oriental and India Office Collection, shelfmark MssEur.E321.

Francke, August Hermann. 1914. *Antiquities of Indian Tibet*. Part I. Personal narrative, with map, 45 plates and 4 text-illustrations. Archaeological Survey of India. New Imperial Series, Vol. 38. Calcutta: Superintendent Government Printing, India (reprint New Delhi: Asian Educational Services, 1992).

Gingrich, Andre. 2012. Paradise lost, or paradise regained? Conceptions and ideologies of *Himah* as a ritual site in the highlands of South-Western Arabia, in: Kiliánová, Gabriela, Christian Jahoda and Michaela Ferencová (eds.), *Ritual, Conflict and Consensus: Comparing Case Studies in Asia and Europe.* Vienna: Austrian Academy of Sciences Press, 65-73.

Hazod, Guntram. 2007. Appendix IV: In the Garden of the White Mare. Encounters with history and cult in Tshal Gung-thang, in: Sørensen, Per K. and Guntram Hazod, in cooperation with Tsering Gyalbo, *Rulers on the Celestial Plain. Ecclesiastic and Secular Hegemony in Medieval Tibet: A Study of Tshal Gung-thang*, Volume II. Vienna: Austrian Academy of Sciences Press, 571-632.

Hein, Veronika. 2001. The role of the speaker in the verbal system of the Tibetan dialect of Tabo/Spiti, *Linguistics of the Tibeto-Burman Area* 24(1): 35-48.

—— 2007. A preliminary analysis of some songs in Tibetan language recorded in Spiti and Upper Kinnaur, in: Klimburg-Salter, Deborah E., Kurt Tropper and Christian Jahoda (eds.), *Text, Image and Song in Transdisciplinary Dialogue* (Proceedings of the Tenth

Seminar of the IATS, 2003). Leiden: Brill, 235-47.

Jahoda, Christian. 2008. Political space and socio-economic organisation in the Lower Spiti Valley (early nineteenth to late twentieth century), *Journal of the International Association of Tibetan Studies* 4 (December 2008) (*In the Shadow of the Leaping Dragon: Demography, Development, and the Environment in Tibetan Areas.* Proceedings of the Eleventh Seminar of the International Association for Tibetan Studies, Bonn / Königswinter, 2006): 1-34. (http://www.thlib.org?tid=T5559; http://www.jiats.org/)

—— 2011. Das Scherken Fest in Pooh im oberen Kinnaur, Himachal Pradesh, Indien, 2009, in: Lechleitner, Gerda and Christian Liebl (eds.), *Jahrbuch des Phonogrammarchivs der Österreichischen Akademie der Wissenschaften* 2. Göttingen: Cuvillier, 9-41.

—— 2012a. Rituals between conflict and consensus: case studies of village festivals in Upper Kinnaur and Western Tibet, in: Kiliánová, Gabriela, Christian Jahoda and Michaela Ferencová (eds.), *Ritual, Conflict and Consensus: Comparing Case Studies in Asia and Europe.* Vienna: Austrian Academy of Sciences Press, 31-49.

—— 2012b. History, in: Tsering Gyalpo, Jahoda, Christian, Kalantari, Christiane and Sutherland, Patrick (with contributions by Eva Allinger, Hubert Feiglstorfer and Kurt Tropper) *'Khor chags / Khorchag / Kuojia si wenshi daguan* [Kuojia Monastery: An Overview of Its History and Culture]. (Studies and Materials on Historical Western Tibet, Volume I). Lhasa: Bod ljongs bod yig dpe rnying dpe skrun khang, 46-66 (second, revised edition 2015, Vienna: Austrian Academy of Sciences Press, 48-68).

—— 2015. *Socio-economic Organisation in a Border Area of Tibetan Culture: Tabo, Spiti Valley (Himachal Pradesh, India).* Vienna: Austrian Academy of Sciences Press.

Kiliánová, Gabriela. 2012. Introduction: ritual, conflict and consensus, in: Kiliánová, Gabriela, Christian Jahoda and Michaela Ferencová (eds.), *Ritual, Conflict and Consensus: Comparing Case Studies in Asia and Europe.* Vienna: Austrian Academy of Sciences Press, 1-11.

Kramrisch, Stella. 2002. *The Hindu Temple,* Volume I. Delhi: Motilal Banarsidass (first published Calcutta: University of Calcutta, 1946).

Levine, Nancy E.1992. Traditional taxation systems in Western Tibet: a comparative perspective, *China Tibetology* (Special Issue 1992): 322-45.

Lugli, Ligeia. 2010. Meaning without words: the contrast between *artha* and *ruta* in

Mahāyāna *sūtras, Buddhist Studies Review* 27(2): 139-176.

Malinowski, Bronislaw. 1961 [1922]. *Argonauts of the Western Pacific: An Account of Native Enterprise and Adventure in the Archipelagoes of Melanesian New Guinea.* New York: Dutton.

Mamgain, M.D. (ed.). 1971. *Himachal Pradesh District Gazetteers: Kinnaur.* Ambala Cantt.: Quick Printers.

Nyima Senge (Nyi ma seng ge) (n.d.): *sPu rgyal sa'i chags rab mdor 'dus bshad pa / A short story of how this Pooh village came into existence* (unpublished account in Tibetan and draft English translation by Thinley Dorje, Pooh, ca. February-March, 2010).

Pfaff-Czarnecka, Joanna. 2012. Frictions, frames and fragments: belonging and ethnic boundary-making in Nepal's contested ritual communication, in: Kiliánová, Gabriela, Christian Jahoda and Michaela Ferencová (eds.), *Ritual, Conflict and Consensus: Comparing Case Studies in Asia and Europe.* Vienna: Austrian Academy of Sciences Press, 15-30.

Pirie, Fernanda. 2006. Legal autonomy as political engagement: the Ladakhi village in the wider world, *Law and Society Review* 40(1): 77-103.

Ruegg, David Seyfort. 1991. *Mchod yon, yon mchod and mchod gnas/yon gnas*: on the historiography and semantics of a Tibetan religio-social and religio-political concept, in: Steinkellner, Ernst (ed.), *Tibetan History and Language. Studies Dedicated to Uray Géza on His Seventieth Birthday* (Wiener Studien zur Tibetologie und Buddhismuskunde 26). Wien: Arbeitskreis für tibetische und buddhistische Studien Universität Wien, 441-53.

—— 1995. *Ordre spirituel et ordre temporel dans la pensée bouddhique de l'Inde et du Tibet.* Paris: de Boccard.

—— 2008. *The Symbiosis of Buddhism with Brahmanism / Hinduism in South Asia and of Buddhism with 'Local Cults' in Tibet and the Himalayan Region.* Vienna: Austrian Academy of Sciences Press.

Singh, Jogishwar. 1989. *Banks, Gods and Government: Institutional and Informal Credit Structure in a Remote and Tribal Indian District (Kinnaur, Himachal Pradesh)* 1960–1985. Wiesbaden: Steiner.

Sørensen, Per K. and Guntram Hazod, in cooperation with Tsering Gyalbo. 2005. *Thundering Falcon. An Inquiry into the History and Cult of Khra-'brug: Tibet's First*

Buddhist Temple. Vienna: Austrian Academy of Sciences Press.

Staal, Frits. 1979. The meaninglessness of ritual, *Numen*, 26(1), 2-22.

Trewin, Arthur Mark. 1993. Lha-rnga: A form of Ladakhi « folk » music and its relationship to the Great Tradition of Tibetan Buddhism, in: Ramble, Charles and Martin Brauen (eds.), *Anthropology of Tibet and the Himalaya.* Zurich: Völkerkundemuseum der Universität Zürich.

—— 1995. *Rhythms of the Gods: The Musical Symbolics of Power and Authority in the Tibetan Buddhist Kingdom of Ladakh.* PhD City University, London.

Tsering Gyalpo. 2012. Nam mthong dus ston gyi skor, in: Tsering Gyalpo, Jahoda, Christian, Kalantari, Christiane and Sutherland, Patrick (with contributions by Eva Allinger, Hubert Feiglstorfer and Kurt Tropper) *'Khor chags / Khorchag / Kuojia si wenshi daguan* [Kuojia Monastery: An Overview of Its History and Culture]. (Studies and Materials on Historical Western Tibet, Volume I). Lhasa: Bod ljongs bod yig dpe rnying dpe skrun khang, 212-253 (second, revised edition 2015, Vienna: Austrian Academy of Sciences Press, 214-255).

Tucci, Giuseppe. 1966. *Tibetan Folk Songs from Gyantse and Western Tibet* (2nd edition). Ascona: Artibus Asiae.

Tucci, Giuseppe and Ghersi, Eugenio. 1934. *Cronaca della missione scientifica Tucci nel Tibet occidentale, 1933.* Roma: Reale Accademia d'Italia.

Vitali, Roberto. 2001. Sa skya and the mNga' ris skor gsum legacy: the case of Rin chen bzang po's flying mask, *Lungta* 14: 5-44.

Wilson, Joe Bransford. 1996. The monk as bodhisattva: a Tibetan integration of Buddhist moral points of view, *The Journal of Religious Ethics* 24(2): 377-402.

The Yogini and the Hidden Valley

Did Kun tu bzang mo open the gate of Mkhan pa lung?

Hildegard Diemberger (University of Cambridge)

1. Introduction

As I was reading the biography of Kun tu bzang mo, the consort of Gtsang smyon Heruka, I came across a passage (folio 44r-46v) in which she is described as opening the gate of the holy site of Sbas lung Khams pa lung in the region of Pha drug (southern La stod). Although the spelling is slightly different, it is plausible that this was identical with the Sbas yul Mkhan pa lung I studied a few years ago, which is linked to Rig 'dzin Rgod ldem can (1337-1408) and is located in the same region (east of Mt Qomolangma). In this paper I examine this identification and investigate the context in which the famous yogini explored this remote Himalayan area in the early 16th century and the significance hidden valleys had at that time.

Kun tu bzang mo's biography, written by one of her disciples in 1551 on the basis of her own notes and pre-existing biographical accounts, is a valuable testimony written close to the events that shaped the life of one of the most influential spiritual masters of the time. According to its narrative, after the death of Gtsang smyon Heruka in 1507, Kun tu bzang mo spent several years producing print editions of his works, reviving printing houses and travelling around the region of La stod and Mang yul Gung thang. At one point while she was dwelling in Bla 'khor in southern La stod, great anxiety spread because of possible attacks by Mongolian armies (Hor *dmag*). The biography (folio 44r) states that because of the widespread fear of potential disruption and invasion, she felt compassion for the hardship that the living beings would endure and for the misery that would affect lay and monastic communities. She thus thought that it would be useful to go and open the door of the holy site in the Hidden Valley of Khams pa lung (*sbas lung khams pa lung gi gnas sgo phyed*), i.e. ritually open the access to the relevant Himalayan area. This plan was also supported by a request that she received from a local spiritual master called Sngags chang Rdo rje bzang po who stated that it was necessary to open the gate of the holy site and offered the relevant guide texts (*gnas kyi lde mig dkar chag lam yig nams*). Bla ma Rgya le ba and other members of her retinue were sent to scout out the place and performed various assessments described as *sa spyad* (geomancy), *sa rtags* (the interpretation of signs in the landscape), *sa cha gnas tshul* (the description of the holy site). Eventually they went to open the gate taking along male and female yaks and a lot of equipment crossing the Pha drug area on the way.

After this episode she took residence in Brag stod where she met the nun Ani Chos kyi dpal mo who dedicated a song to her. She then went to Mkhar stod, in the winter she dwelled in Zangs mkhar phug, a site linked to Rgod tshang pa, and then spent the spring in Gangs la phug. She was then invited to go to central Tibet but before leaving with her disciples she went to a place described as being a southern hidden place in the upper area of Mkhar rta (*mkhar rta'i lung stod sbas pa blo* [*lho*] *mon gyi yul*) which was full of miraculous signs including hot springs of Rig gsum mgon po; earth, rocks and crags displaying hand and footprints of local male and female deities (*lha dang lha mo*) as well as sacred letters; springs of different colours, white, yellow and dark-blue and birds of all sorts. In this holy site she gave a lot of profound teachings to whoever was there. Eventually she left for central Tibet (Biography of Kun tu bzang mo, folio 47r) and after a visit to Ras chung phug she travelled to Tsari. Not long after leaving Gtsang she met Brug pa Kun las (1455-1529) (Biography of Kun tu bzang mo, folio 51r) and eventually established herself in the Kong po and Dag po region where she spent the second part of her life and passed away aged 85 in 1549.

2. Are Sbas lung Khams pa lung and Sbas yul Mkhan pa lung the same place?

The events described above as reported in Kun tu bzang mo's biography clearly took place in the region of Pha drug, an area in southern La stod that has a history of historical references going back to the imperial period. This was also a well-known place for a number of spiritual masters of the early *phyi dar*, including Ma chig Zha ma (1062-1149) who was born there and remains a locally celebrated heroine (see Roerich 1988: 219; Diemberger and Hazod 1999: 34-51) and Rgod thangs pa Dgon po Rdo rje (1189-1258) and his disciples (see Roerich 1988: 686-687). The area of Mkhar rta was its southernmost part and was often considered to be part of or connected to it. For example Mkhar rta Pha drug are often mentioned together in the autobiography of Rdza rong phu bla ma Ngag dbang Bstan 'dzin nor bu (1867-1940), who was born in this area and became famous for having established Rdza rong phu monastery north of Mt. Qomolangma South of Mkhar rta three high passes (Langma La, Shao La and Chao La) lead into different parts of the Mkhar ma chu (also known as Kama Valley), the densely forested valley of the river that collects the waters from the east face of Mt. Qomolangma and the north face of Mt. Makalu. In the upper reaches of the Mkhar ma chu valley there are two important holy sites, Tshe chu and Gangs la, where hermitages were built in and around meditation caves and where Kun tu bzang mo reportedly spent some time. This is the northern part of Sbas yul Mhhan pa lung (see Diemberger 1996: 219-232), a *sbas yul* considered to have been revealed by Rig 'dzin Rgod ldem (1337-1408) and 'opened' again and again by several masters in subsequent centuries (most notably Snyid zla klong gsal, see Diemberger 1997: 287-334). It is one of the Himalayan "hidden valleys", which are typically located in secluded areas on the ecological boundary between the dry plateau to the north and the vegetation rich valleys to the south.

The most important protector of Mkhan pa lung is Chos skyong Zur ra ra skyes, a wrathful mountain deity, located in the Mkhar ma chu valley and regularly worshipped by the people of Mkhar rta. At the foot of the northern slope of this holy mountain there is a set of ruins of settlement that is currently dilapidated but until the early 20th century was an important centre for trans-Himalayan trade to which people converged from all directions. It was also a sacred site both in terms of the specific worship of Chos skyong Zur ra ra skyes and local Buddhist traditions that were expanding into these places. Kha rta Sa skya gdeng appears in a list of branch monasteries assigned by the Tibetan government to Shel dkar in the period 1710-1718, at the time of abbot Grags pa Rgya mtsho (see *Shel dkar chos 'byung* folio 90r; cf. also Diemberger 1996: 226-227). Mkhar rta chos sde located in the Mkhar rta chu valley was also a branch monastery of Shel dkar chos sde and was located in the vicinity of a village called Mkhar rta Khams pa and Ma gchig Zha ma's monastery Thar pa gling.

Geographically speaking the only areas that can be plausibly identified as a hidden valley or hidden land (*sbas yul*) to the south of Pha drug are Sbas yul Mkhan pa lung and Sbas yul Stag so (immediately to the south-east of Mkhar rta beyond the Bong chu river), as both are Himalayan sites that are remote but accessible through passes. Whilst both are currently considered by the local population as a place of pilgrimage as well as a precious source of wood, bamboo and many other forest products, it is Mkhan pa lung that is closely associated with the protector deities and the ancestral mythology of the people of Mkhar rta, which are also referred to in the guide-texts (see Diemberger 1996: 219-232)[1]. It is therefore probable that Khams pa lung and Mkhan pa lung are just variants of the same name. If this is the case, the guide texts that Kun tu bzang mo and her disciples used to identify the place were presumably texts by Rig 'dzin Rgod ldem can who had a close connection to the Mang yul Gung thang royal court (see *Gung thang rgyal rabs*; Everding 2000) and whose teachings spread across the Himalaya including Mkhar rta and Pha drug. These texts were popular in the area where Kun tu bzang mo and Gtsang smyon Heruka had been active and had inspired the opening of other hidden valleys before her quest for Khams pa lung/Mkhan pa lung. The very heterogeneous nature of the guide text (*gnas yig*) to Sbas yul Mkhan pa lung (which is currently to be found among the people who inhabit the region) is certainly consistent with repeated efforts to explore the sacred site of Mkhan pa lung and with different people inserting passages into the base text reflecting specific geographical features and routes that are not necessarily consistent with each other.[2]

3. *Sbas yul* and the Tibetan expansion in the southern Himalayan valleys

These guide texts to the Hidden Valley of Mkhan pa lung explicitly refer to threats by the Mongolian army (Hor *dmag*) and a range of disasters afflicting Tibet as the signs that indicate the appropriate time for opening the door of the holy site (*gnas sgo phyed pa*). There is also specific reference to unrest and lawlessness in the Gtsang area, the destruction of monasteries in Ru lag and killings within the royal lineage of Mang yul Gung thang. This type of narrative was not exclusive for the hidden valley of Mkhan pa lung. The trope of the

1 More unlikely but not impossible is the next hidden land to the west, Khum bu in the current homeland of the Sherpa but the route leading from Tibet into Khum bu over the Nang pa la does not pass via Pha drug. It is also possible that the exploration included both Mkhan pa lung and Khum bu as these areas are connected.

2 Some parts clearly refer to southern La stod geography whereas others describe places that seem to be located in Bhutan (see Diemberger 1997: 287-334).

sbas yul as a hidden place to take refuge in at a time of crisis was present in many prophetic texts that indicated the way to other remote areas in the Himalaya such as Skyid mo lung, the *sbas yul* most closely connected to Mang yul Gung thang kingdom (see Solmsodorf 2013: 113-136).

In the case of Kun tu bzang mo's decision to open the gate of the holy site of Khams pa lung/Mkhan pa lung this type of narrative was clearly inspirational and particularly appropriate at a time of turmoil and anxiety due to a concrete Mongolian threat. This was most likely the echo of the Mongolian incursion into Mang yul Gung thang around 1523 reported by Mnga' ris pan chen Padma dbang rgyal (see Schuh 1981: 354; Everding 2000: 563; Solmsdorf 2013: 120). Mongolian armies coming in from the west had appeared repeatedly on the scene and their incursions in the 1520s had prompted the invitation of Gter ston Mchog ldan mgon po (1497-1531) to the court of Mang yul Gung thang, when he arrived he observed the heavy damage Mongols had caused to the Byams sprin Lha khang, one of the dynastic temples taming the border regions. As a *gter ston*, Mchog ldan mgon po was involved in re-opening the hidden valley of Skyid mo lung and had the mandate from the Gung thang court to protect the kingdom ritually against the Mongolian army. The Gter ston Bstan gnyis gling pa was also invited to provide the kingdom of Mang yul Gung thang with ritual protection from the Mongols around the same period (Everding 2000: 253). Ritual measures had already been deployed earlier in addressing similar foreign threats. Towards the end of the fifteenth century Mongols arriving from the west (Stod Hor) had terrorised the region, so much so that the short biographical sketch of Kun dga' bzang mo (1459-1502) reported in 'Gyur med bde chen's biography of Thang stong rgyal po (*Thang rgyal rnam thar* 311) mentions a miraculous rain of mice which, by destroying the Mongols' supplies, averted their invasion of Tibet (see also Stearns 2007).

Kun tu bzang mo's decision to open the hidden valley as a refuge is remarkable for other reasons as well. It seems that on that occasion she expressed a remarkable level of leadership, responding to a perceived collective threat by suggesting a wise, if adventurous, solution to avert danger. Leadership enacted by a woman was rare but not unheard of and Kun tu bzang mo may have drawn on powerful exemplars from the past. The Mongolian threat causing the need for a place of refuge was certainly a strong motivating factor driving the opening of hidden valley but was not the only one. Kun tu bzang mo was possibly following the example of previous female sources of inspiration such as Ma chig

Zha ma (1062-1149). Born in southern Pha drug, this female disciple of Pha dam pa Sang rgyas is still celebrated in the Mkhar rta area for her ability to tame the landscape (see Diemberger and Hazod 1999: 34-51). A renowned master of the Lam 'bras tradition, she is also considered the founder of one of Mkhar rta monasteries, Thar pa gling, located in the Mkhar rta chu valley. Coming to Pha drug from Glang 'khor, the dwelling place of Pa dam pa Sangs rgyas, Kun tu bzang mo was certainly aware of her as she was in many ways following in her footsteps.

Another potential source of inspiration was the Gung thang princess Chos kyi sgron ma (1422-1455), who according to the biography of Thang stong rgyal po by 'Gyur med bde chen (*Thang rgyal rnam thar* 284), had expressed a desire to open such a secluded land. This aspiration had led her to leave for the east towards Tsari in a journey that Kun tu bzang mo would reenact in a very similar way, with the difference that she survived much longer: Chos kyi sgron ma died aged 33, Kun tu bzang mo aged 84.

4. Drivers and (unintended?) consequences of the quest for the *sbas yul*

Mystical aspirations and the immediate need for refuge at time of turmoil were certainly the stated drivers for the process of opening *sbas yul*. However it is worth noticing that hidden valleys were located in areas rich in wood and plants that could be used to make paper and medicines as well as dyes. It is not clear whether the sourcing of such materials was a driver for the opening of these places or access to them was originally an unintended positive outcome. Certainly the opening of *sbas yul* provided an increased availability of materials that were good for book production and a range of other activities. Whilst trans-Himalayan trading routes were important in connecting centres located south and north of the Himalaya, *sbas yul* tended to be *cul de sac*, criss-crossed by a web of minor often arduous routes. As sites that provided access to a wide range of materials, they are likely to have played a significant part in the economic and cultural development of the Himalayan region and the Tibetan plateau. Perhaps it is not a coincidence that Kun bzang Nyi zla grags pa, the Gung thang king who invited Mchog ldan mgon po and promoted his re-opening of the hidden valley of Skyid mo lung, was also an extremely prolific patron of printing. At this time an increasing number of print editions started to be actually produced in hidden valleys such as Skyid mo lung and Yol mo (Helambu).

Kun tu bzang mo did not spend a long time in Khams pa lung/Mkhan pa lung and there is no mention of book production in the context of her exploration of the hidden valley. However, other parts of her biography clearly highlight her commitment to producing print editions and her exploration of regions with ecological features that made them relevant to the sourcing of wood and paper such as La phyi (see Diemberger 2016: 267, 308). The specific mystical and political drivers behind her journey to Khams pa lung/Mkhan pa lung are clear. Her explorations, however, can also be seen as reflecting a wider process of opening up the southern Himalayan slopes in ways that transformed the socio-economic and cultural landscape of Tibet and was tightly connected to the evolution of Tibetan book culture and the rapid spread of printing in the 15th and 16th centuries. Mkhar rta and Pha drug were important sourcing places for materials needed in print editions produced at Shel dkar, which had become an important printing centre since the beginning of the 15th century and was the place where the blocks for the Nar thang bka' 'gyur were carved in the 18th century. Rdza rong phu monastery established in 1902 by Ngag dbang bstan 'dzin nor bu in the highest part of Pha drug became an important printing centre, catering for the entire region north and south of the Himalaya.

5. Conclusion

Kun tu bzang mo's opening of the hidden valley of Khams pa lung is likely to represent a so far unknown step in the history of the revelation of the hidden valley of Mkhan ba lung. A complex process of miraculous disclosure and detailed mapping shaped the way in which this and other similar places became increasingly accessible and inhabited over the centuries. At the time of Kun tu bzang mo opening hidden valleys was clearly a wide-spread narrative trope and an inspiration for actual deeds that combined mystical pursuits with practical ones: not only refuge in time of hostility but also the sourcing of forest products and access to new pastures. From this point of view Kun tu bzang mo's exploration precedes and might even be linked to wider Tibetan migration into the Himalayan areas south of Mt. Qomolangma as recorded in Sher pa histories. [3]

* * *

3 See Sangs rgyas Bstan 'dzin and Macdonal 1971; Oppiz 1982.

Fig. 1. Gangs la in the upper reaches of the Mkhar ma chu valley.

Fig. 2. Gangs la, ruins of monastery built around cave.

Fig. 3. Chos skyong Zur ra ra skyes (see also Fig. 5).

Fig. 4. Qomolangma and Makalu towering above the hills of Pha drug.

Fig. 5. Khar rta, painting of Chos skyong Zur ra ra skyes.

Fig. 6. Kun tu bzang mo as depicted in her biography.

Fig. 7. Shel dkar, people from Mkhar rta trading wood and bamboo.

Fig. 8. The valley of the Mkhar rta chu river from Thar pa gling.

Fig. 9. Woman carrying wood in the Mkhar ma chu valley.

References

Tibetan sources

Gung thang rgyal rabs = Rig 'dzin Tshe dbang nor bu. *Gung thang rgyal rabs*, in: *Bod kyi lo rgyus deb ther khag lnga*. Lhasa: Bod ljongs bod yig dpe rnying dpe skrun khang, 1990. [For a German translation, see Everding 2000.]

Ngag dbang bstan 'dzin nor bu rang rnam = Ngag dbang bstan 'dzin nor bu, *Dus mthar mchos smra ba'i btsun pa ngag dbang bstan 'dzin nor bu'i rnam thar 'chi med bdud rtsi rol mtsho'i glegs pa ma gnyis pa zhes bya ba*. Blockprint of 496 folios printed at the Rdza rong phu monastery.

Kun tu bzang mo rnam thar = *Dus gsum rgyal ba ma lus pa bskyed pa'i yum chen kun tu bzang mo'i rnam par thar pa zab don gter mdzod mthong ba don ldan*, by Mkhyen rab dbang phyug, manuscript of 73 folios, 1551.

Lcags spon sangs rgyas dpal'byor rus yig, in: Oppiz, M. 1982. *Die Sherpa und ihre Nachbarn*. Innsbruck-München: Verlag Wagner, 285-295.

Sbas yul mkhan pa lung gi gnas yig = Rig 'dzin Rgod ldem can, *Sbas yul mkhan pa lung gi lam yig sa spyad bcas pa*, manuscript of 20 folios (orginally 14th century, presumably with later additions).

Sangs rgyas Bstan 'dzin and A. W. Macdonal. 1971. *Shar pa'i chos'byung sngon med tshang pa'i dbyu gu*. Junbesi-Paris Nanterre.

Shel dkar chos'byung = Pasang Wangdu and H. Diemberger, in cooperation with Guntram Hazod. 1996. *The History of the White Crystal: Religion and Politics of Southern La stod*. Wien: Verlag der Österreichischen Akademie der Wissenschaften.

Thang rgyal rnam thar = 'Gyur med bde chen, *Thang rgyal rnam thar.* Chengdu: Si khron mi rigs dpe skrun khang 1982.

Sources in other languages

Diemberger, Hildegard. 2016. Tibetan women as patrons of printing and innovation, in: Diemberger, Hildegard, Franz-Karl Ehrhard, and Peter Kornicki (eds.) *Tibetan Printing: Comparisons, Continuities and Change*. Leiden: Brill, 267-308.

— 1996. Political and religious aspects of mountain cults in the hidden valley of Khenbalung-tradition, decline and revitalization, in: Blondeau, Anne-Marie and Ernst

Steinkellner (eds.), *Reflections of the Mountain.* Wien: Verlag der Österreichischen Akadmie der Wissenschaften, 219-231.

Diemberger, Hildegard, Franz-Karl Ehrhard, and Peter Kornicki (eds.). 2016. *Tibetan Printing: Comparisons, Continuities and Change.* Leiden: Brill.

Diemberger, Hildegard and Guntram Hazod. 1999. Machig Zhama's Recovery: Traces of Ancient History and Myth in the South Tibetan Landscape of Kharta and Phadrug, in: Huber, Toni (ed.), *Sacred Spaces and Powerful Places in Tibetan Culture.* Dharamsala: Library of Tibetan Works and Archives, 34-51.

Everding, Karl-Heinz. 2000. *Das Königreich Mang yul Gung Thang.* Bonn: Wissenschafts-verlag.

—2006. *Das tibetische Fürstentum La stod lHo* (um 1265-1642). Wiesbaden: Reichert Verlag.

Oppiz, Michael. 1982. *Die Sherpa und ihre Nachbarn.* Innsbruck-München: Verlag Wagner.

Roerich, George N. 1988. *The Blue Annals.* Delhi: Motilal Banarsidass.

Schuh, Dieter. 1981. *Grundlagen der tibetischer Siegelkunde.* St.Augustin: Monumenta Tibetica Historica.

Solmsdorf, N. 2013. Sojourning in the 'Valley of Happiness': Shedding New Light on the *sbas yul* sKyid mo lung, *Bulletin of Tibetology* 49(1): 113-136.

Stearns, Cyrus. 2007. *Tangtong Gyalpo: The King of the Empty Plain.* Ithaca: Snow lion Publications.

且听本土发声

马丽华

题记：次仁加布先生离开我们两年多了，感谢沈卫荣教授有情有义也有心，主持编辑这本纪念文集，让我们得以借助文字形式表达思念感念之情。回想当初噩耗传来，一时的震惊之后竟是长久的痛惜；再回想与次仁加布先生相识多年，但每一次交谈居然都是带了问题请教，不乏“功利”目的，而每一次都不由得生发“胜读十年书”之慨。其中有两次受益最丰，一为2010年，即将踏上印度河之旅，由于访问巴尔蒂斯坦“小西藏”也在行程安排内，特意向这位来自阿里的专家专题求教。能够想到的是可以从他那里得知此地历史的框架脉络，没想到的是居然描述得如此具细，阿里—拉达克—巴尔蒂斯坦的古往今来，尤其古代交通，牦牛（驮羊绒）的路，绵羊（驮盐）的路，过往行人的路……那么多书本上查不到的知识啊！另一次在2013年夏季，我们同去阿里狮泉河镇参加“象雄文化论坛”，会议期间交流之外，返程航班上又恰巧邻座，一路上就听他讲阿里古史民风，对于个人认知有充实有颠覆，何其丰富的内容！最终结果是，飞机落地前达成一协议：次仁加布同意书写这本有关阿里的大众读物，让更多人分享。

于是就有了这本《传奇阿里》，他生前出版的最后一本书。现在想来唯一感到欣慰的是，他看到了这本书，听说很满意。这一刻我不在现场，只记得出书前不久的另一场合，在拉萨，当我将特意带来的封面小样打开征求意见时，见他目光中流露出欣喜。

仅以这篇为《传奇阿里》所写导读文章表达长久的怀念。

2017岁末于北京

迄今为止，当代人写阿里的图书，我所见者不下一二十本，从旁涉猎的更多，体裁也不限于文字，画册和纪录片都有，尤其摄影作品每见发表，从山水的奇异美到服饰的古典美，无不耀眼且养眼。须知这都是1980年代结束了新疆代管时期，这一地区被重新“发现”以及“阿里热”延续二三十年的部分成果，之密集推出，甚至可用“爆发式”来形容了。至于作者，来自不同行业领域，考古学家、藏学家有之，记者、援藏干部等公职人员有之，职业写手反倒不太多，共同特点是对阿里一见倾心并满怀惊奇的外来人。

介绍这一背景，就为接下来强调《传奇阿里》何以与众不同。不同处首先体现在作者身份——古格·次仁加布，从名字看得出古格故地出身，意味着代表本土参与发言；显然又不属于民间“草根”一派，是走出家乡后的再回首，目光有遥视，有俯瞰，有仰望，理性与情感尽在其中。不同处之二，体现在身为精通藏文的史学研究者，其独具的优势无人可比，在遍阅相关阿里地区古书、潜入历史长河钩沉索隐之后的发言，权威性自不待言。所以说，是文本典籍＋人生经验，在很大程度上成就了这本书。

所以当书稿提交中国藏学出版社的时候，我的心情和表现用“迫不及待”形容没错：迫不及待作为第一读者看稿，迫不及待写下一篇小文忝为代序，意在检示自己也知会朋友，从前在哪些方面有过误读误解，本书作者怎样为之匡正纠偏，从而使我们对于阿里的认知深入一些，或者进一步接近真实。

这就说到初识阿里时，因为陌生而生发的诸多之“谜”，其中首推延续了六七百年的古格王国何以突然消亡。于是种种猜测纷起，不过很快得知这一疑问实属孤陋寡闻——先是格勒博士提醒说，“古格灭国”在西方藏学界并非神秘事件，来龙去脉都在17世纪二三十年代传教士信件里写着哪！继之中译本《魂牵雪域》（伍昆明译，中国藏学出版社，1998）问世，一众关注阿里的人通过此书得出印象：由于葡萄牙传教士的到来，末代古格王意欲改宗信仰，内部矛盾激化，终致灭亡。一时间，“导火索”论占了上风。

次仁加布先生不认同此说，是有依据的。他曾遍查典籍文档，未见该时期传教士活动记载，认为这首先说明其影响甚微，不足以掀起改变历史进程的巨浪。那么古格何以终结，藏史或早有定论，是“狮虎结合导致了古格的灭亡”。这其中的前因后果说来话长，简言之大致这样子：藏传佛教后弘期几百年间，噶举派率先开辟了神山冈仁波齐作为修行圣地，在古格和拉达克等西部西藏长期保持了一派独大局面。然而情况有了变化，在古格王室支持下，以托林寺为首的多座寺庙由噶举派转向格鲁派，及至百余年后的1618年，即传教士到来的前几年，末代古格王扎巴扎西德盛情邀来后藏扎什伦布寺四世班禅大师，弘法授徒，一住三年，所到之处，莫不顶礼。由于新兴格鲁派的传播意味着前后藏政教势力的渗透，拉达克王森格朗杰深感威胁——这期间拉达克地区仍为竹巴噶举传统领地，该派大师达仓不仅贵为国王上师，同时身兼辅政之责。“森格”是“狮子”，“达”是“虎”，被时人视之为一对不可战胜的“狮、虎”组合。当这二人与古格内部反叛势力联起手来，正如历史的完成时：古格在劫难逃。

当然，一个政权的垮台往往是多种因素共同作用的结果，如果说导致古格覆灭之因尚可继续讨论的话，那么，对另一段历史人事的考证，似可一锤定音了。

古格立国早期的拉喇嘛益西沃（或作益西维、意希沃，947—1019）是藏传佛教“上路弘法”的一面旗帜，经由后世多部藏文史书传扬，其舍身护法的故事深入人心：古格王益西沃不仅自己舍弃王位出了家，还影响到两个儿子、一个女儿做了僧尼。当他与“黑衣大食”作战被俘后，面临或改宗信仰或以等身黄金赎身的选择，尽皆坚拒，他还嘱托家人用赎金作聘金，前往印度超岩寺迎请佛教大师阿底峡，自己则从容赴义。

这个故事于后世被写进史书，不是一两本，是两位数的多种版本，以至于借助口碑，在西藏几乎尽人皆知。可是次仁加布注意到阿里人撰写的、成书年代更早的事主生平中，拉喇嘛益西沃既从未参战，何来被俘？而是终其一生虔心事佛，寿终正寝于托林寺。于是以学者的严谨予以深究，查阅史籍不下二十部，厘清了故事原委，最终还原的史实是：主人公实为益西沃侄孙维德，在与“竹夏”人作战时被俘，其弟江久维施救，等身赎金已筹集大部、仅差头部时，可惜功亏一篑，维德客死异乡。之后，阿底峡大师确由江久维迎请而来。

继续追问后世史家移花接木的动机，结论是，由于新兴格鲁派完成了政教一统，已将阿底峡尊为先哲祖师，借由拉喇嘛益西沃名人效应，安排了大师轰轰烈烈的出场——一个壮烈，一个辉煌，相得益彰。翔实考证一似抽丝剥茧，把几百年里如何添枝加叶的“重构”演绎过程逐层揭示，看故事怎样渐渐丰满完整，终成传奇。

通过这一事件，还让我们得知所谓“黑衣大食”原是“竹夏”，藏语习称的“竹夏”实为巴尔蒂斯坦，巴尔蒂斯坦古今别号“小西藏”，曾经归于吐蕃又游离开去，现属巴基斯坦北部地区。竹夏人本与西藏人同文同种同信仰，16 世纪时全面伊斯兰化。

对于古格之后两场战事的记述很有必要，也很到位，缘起，过程，结局，前因后果。至少在我，原先只知其大概，现在得以明晰，并且加深了对其意义的认识和对阿里人的感佩之情。一次在 1680 年代，从拉达克治下收复阿里；一次在 1841 年，系抗击外敌入侵。皆属保家卫国性质，全都取得了胜利。不同处在于，前者以拉达克为敌，后者与拉达克结盟；前者是在古格灭亡半个世纪后，拉达克联合不丹等地的竹巴噶举派，欲以阿里为跳板，向西藏腹地的格鲁派发难。貌似宗派之争，然则争夺属地属民，实与领土和世俗利益交关。以现代眼光看取，17 世纪的这场收复之战还算是内战，可是联系到诸地后来的命运，意义就非同一般了。

由此我们还“顺便”得知为时三百余年的阿里“噶尔本”机构，因何得到“帐篷政府”雅号，何以各有冬、夏驻地的噶尔雅莎和噶尔昆莎，实为个人风格所致——收复阿里的将军并做了阿里第一任行政长官的甘丹才旺本是蒙古族，他把游牧人生活方式引进了官府。与此相关，据说遍布阿里的千年城堡就是在甘丹才旺当政时被弃用的，从此荒芜。对于这一点，作者次仁加布难免遗憾惋惜。

待阿里收复，历经康乾盛世，拉达克作为大清藩属之地，与近邻阿里相安无事。却不料鸦片战争前后，共同经历了一场生死存亡考验：印度境内具有帝国主义背景的查谟地区信奉锡克教的道格拉人——藏语称其为“森巴人”，先是攻占了拉达克和巴尔蒂斯坦，继而入侵阿里。三地揭竿而起，不分佛教、伊斯兰教，噶举派还是格鲁派，救亡时刻结成统一战线，历经浴血奋战，结局却是大不同：阿里保住了，拉达克和巴尔蒂斯坦沦陷了。保住阿里的不光是英勇的阿里人，更是动员了整个西藏的力量，来自驻藏大臣、噶厦政府的意志和全体军民万众一心的信念。这在当时清政府抵御列强连遭败绩、无暇西顾之际，为维护国家统一，确保西南边陲无虞，得建如此奇功，实在了不起。西藏人民由此做出的历史贡献，值得全中国铭记。

次仁加布先生复述了“森巴战争”始末，将这一史迹彪炳史册，告知今人，同样成就了大功一件。这得益于他对所存档案原件不辞辛劳的查阅整理。关于同一场战争在拉达克和巴尔蒂斯坦两个战场上的表现，近年间中国藏学出版社接连推出译著《巴尔蒂斯坦（小西藏）的历史和文化》《巴基斯坦北部地区史》，均有涉及，可以参看比较。总之，当我从中了解到这段历史，后怕之余是庆幸，尤其感念：我们之所以能够在此欣赏阿里，畅言阿里，凭什么？若无当年的流血牺牲，恐怕不排除某种可能：阿里一如拉达克，迄今仍深陷克什米尔争端中——在国力衰弱的百多年前，类似的失地并非一例两例。

被历史选中，为阿里代言。这位出生于阿里的学者在《传奇阿里》中再现了一部古格兴衰梗概，包括介绍名人名刹及王统的篇什，同时也记述有民间生活。在此我想特别提到必读的两篇，一为对狩猎文化那一逝去风景的追记，二为源远流长的乡土神崇拜。二文忠实记录并本质反映了与高原人类生活史同样绵长、以山水崇拜为表征的自然观——永远守望于此的山川大地、自然万象，才是人类家园的真正主人。人生在世，无非过客，“借宿”期间，难免多有打扰，必得心存敬畏歉意；对天赐之物若有取用之需，必得经过准许，以感恩之心分享，而无权糟践，遑论占有。

感动之余，不禁想道，没错，我们都是“借宿者”。在发展进步已成主题的今天，现代文明的种种好处伴随着问题和危机纷至沓来，不由人不左顾右盼。在这种时候，重温古训，学会谦卑，从古已有之的思想资源里汲取，是否可以增益现代人的观念体系，在更高层面上，实现人与自然的和谐相处？

2014 年 8 月 12 日于北京

《传奇阿里》，古格·次仁加布著，中国藏学出版社 2014 年 12 月版

阿里王子，你真的就走了吗？

沈卫荣

阿里王子，你真的走了吗？这几天我走到哪里，见到的依然都是你灿烂的笑容，听到的都是你爽朗的笑声，研究院四周这片绿森林（Grunewald），曾经是我们的最爱，林中方圆好几公里到处都留下我们共同的足迹和欢快的笑声，你那么多开心、愉悦的瞬间都深深地刻印在我的脑海之中，可你怎么就走了呢？你让我怎么还能忍心再走进这一年间几乎每天都让我们流连忘返的绿森林呢？

我们在柏林高等研究院为期一学年的 fellow 生涯很快就要结束了，周五（6 月 26 日）院里组织了一年一度的新旧 fellow 聚会，早上我们一起去了柏林郊外的 Wannsee 湖上泛舟，一边领略湖边旖旎的风景，一边笑谈这一年来的收获和趣事，我们说好了十年后还要一起再来柏林参加高研院的重聚的。下午，我们一起接待了一位在英国求学的有志于研究藏传佛教艺术的博士生，你对这位聪明、美丽的成都姑娘的指点为她的学术研究打开了一片灿烂、吉祥的新天地，你们约好两周以后要在拉萨再见的。晚上，我们一起参加了院里的烤肉晚会，虽然肉烤得不是你喜欢的那么熟，也不是你最爱吃的羊肉，但酒还是你平日很爱喝的那种红酒，同桌都是你喜欢、也是喜欢你的朋友，一个晚上好吃好喝、说说笑笑，可以说是热气腾腾、其乐融融啊！大概快到九点的时候，我与你在食堂门口道别，你直接从楼下另一侧上楼去了你的房间，我还要走出研究院的大门回我临近的住所，这一切都与平日没有什么两样，我们无数次地这样别过，可今天这一别竟然就是天人永隔了！这怎么可能？这怎么可能？阿里王子，你真的就走了吗？

我记不清我是在哪里、在什么时间第一次见到阿里王子的，我俩都研究藏学，也都已经在这个国际性的学术领域内游牧了近三十年，应该有过很多机会见面的，但是，从前的见面只不过是点头之交，我俩真正相识、成为朋友是从去年 10 月才开始的，缘分就是我们有幸一起被选为柏林高等研究院 2014/2015 年度的 fellow。原本我是前一年的 fellow，因故推迟了一年，令我喜出望外的是今年的 fellow 中竟然还另有两位藏学家，其中一位是来自奥地利科学院的 Guntram Hazod 研究员，另一位就是阿里王子。我知道他们两人早已是多年的学术伙伴，合作研究中世纪西藏地方贵族、寺院的历史，一起出版过好几本厚重的英文专著，这次他们二位一起来到柏林高等研究院，结成了一个焦点小组（focus group），专门研究西藏宗谱。能与他们结伴这是何等幸运的事情，出发来柏林前，我写信给高研院申请参加这个焦点小组，被欣然接纳。想不到的是，这一年间，我们三人成了今年柏林高等研究院内最令人瞩目的“焦点小组”，院内四十名同事来自世界各地，各有专攻，平常除了每日一餐必须集聚在一起外，很少见到有人像我们这样如此紧密地联系在一起的。我们三人不但学术上有共同的专注，而且日常生活中也常常形影相随。衷心感谢柏林高研院让我们聚集到了一起，这近十个月的朝夕相处，让我们成了不是兄弟而胜似兄弟的好朋友。

记得阿里王子比我们大家晚到了两三周，但好像他比我和 Guntram 更快地和大家融成了一片，经常看到他和同事们在一起谈笑风生，大家显然都很喜欢这位来自拉萨的朋友。阿里王子在西方藏学界有很好的口碑和很广的人脉，在欧洲各地，包括柏林都有不少曾经和他有过学术合作的朋友们，所以，除了 Guntram 显然待他亲如兄弟以外，很快就有不少朋友陆续从汉堡、莱比锡、维也纳等地专程来柏林和他团聚、向他请教，其中来得最勤的无疑是阿里王子的老朋友、莱比锡大学的藏学教授 Per K. Sørensen 先生。有一次，Per 问我阿里王子在高研院过得如何？我脱口而出：“他可是我们这里的明星！”口无遮拦的 Per 大笑起来，说那一定是因为他是“高研院的稀有物种”。话虽是玩笑，却也道出了真情。阿里王子大概真的就是柏林高研院的“稀有物种”，但这绝不是因为他是柏林高研院有史以来获选为 fellow 的第一位藏族学者，而是因为常挂在他脸上的那份发自肺腑的憨厚、友善、真诚、坦荡和热情，这样清澈，甚至带着几分孩子气的神态不只是在高研院，在世界任何地方也都已经非常稀有了，但它实在非常迷人，没法不让人耳目一新、如沐春风！我相信正是阿里王子脸上时刻洋溢着的微笑和散发出的极为亲和的人格魅力，让他深受同事和研究院工作人员的喜爱，成了我们中间的一位稀有的明星。

在高研院与我们共处的四十位同事可以说个个优秀，各有各的卓越。但这一年间来的来去的去，让我同样感受到阿里王子这种迷人的亲和力的，唯有天才的钢琴家 Andras Schiff 先生一人。Schiff 先生仅仅和我们共处了三个月，可每当他和他的小提琴家太太走进我们的食堂或者会议室时，我都会有春风扑面、满堂生辉的感觉。而若要说 Schiff 先生最喜欢的同事，那一定就是我们的阿里王子。记得 Schiff 先生即将要离院的那天早晨，我们三位藏学家结伴去他寓所和他道别，先生欣然在他的音乐 CD 上为我们签名留念，随后拿出没喝完的大半瓶威士忌送给了阿里王子，说他希望很快能去西藏访问、演出，到时一定要阿里王子亲自陪他去各地参观西藏的文化和宗教名胜，先生对阿里王子的厚爱溢于言表，而阿里王子脸上也写着满满的幸福。分别前，先生提议和我们三位打一个小时的乒乓球，Guntram和我在今年的fellow中乒乓球球艺数一数二，Schiff先生打球和他弹琴一样优雅，而平日不敢与我们对阵的阿里王子，那天破例披挂上阵，和我们结对双打，动作虽然显得有点笨拙，却令这场送别成了我们一年高研院生活中最温馨和最值得记忆的场景之一。可是，阿里王子，你真的走了吗？下次我们若再见到Schiff先生，可怎么向他交待呢？

我和阿里王子的友谊与我们身边的这片绿森林紧密相连。我们最先发现的一个共同特点是对肉食的饕餮般的嗜好。对阿里王子来说，喜欢肉食大概是游牧民与生俱来的天性，对我来说则更多是少年时渴求不得而遗留下的病态的情结，总之高研院食堂每天为我们提供的健康美食绝对无法满足我们对肉食的渴望，于是高研院四周的德国饭店中常常能见到我俩的身影，德国的烤猪蹄成了我们最常吃的佳肴。可是，肉虽好吃，吃多了总也觉得有些不妥。有一天饭桌上，我对阿里王子说："你太胖了，以后每天跟我去绿森林散步吧！"在座包括Guntram在内的几位同事对我如此"出言不逊"小吃了一惊，可阿里王子却兴高采烈地说："好啊，以后你去散步时请一定带上我吧。"从此，我俩的身影就时常出现在这片连绵数十里的绿森林中。我们一次又一次地走进这片自然、宽阔的树林中，一起从秋天走过了冬天和春天，刚刚走进夏天，尽情地呼吸着清爽的空气，常常嘲笑Guntram的懒惰，竟然不来和我们一起享受这人生难得的美妙。记得是11月初的一个周六的下午，我俩决定远足去Krumme Lanke湖边散步，由于不熟悉道路，从研究院出发走到目的地就花了近两个小时，而在湖边散步时享受到的那份宁静和美妙让我们流连忘返，觉得意犹未尽，决定在林中另找一条新路走回研究院。意想不到的是，秋天的柏林下午四点半天就黑了，我们很快就迷了路，在林中不知方向地转悠着，看到有灯光处就一路前行，直到近七点才终于转出了这片林子。当我们走回到绿森林火车站时，虽然已是精疲力竭，但心中的喜乐却难以言表，于是，又坐在车站旁一家德国餐馆的露天啤酒园中冒着寒风大吃了一顿烤肉。

这次的经历让我俩久久难忘，兴奋不已，一直计划着再来一次。大概快到圣诞节前夕了，有两位中国人民大学国学院的同学来高研院参观，我建议她们和我们一起去绿森林散步，原计划再去Krummer Lanke湖边散步，然而当我向一位德国老太太问路时她说那实在太远了，建议我们不如就近去Teufelsee（鬼湖）散步。当我们到达鬼湖时见天色还早，意犹未尽，于是决定继续往前远足，这回当然不能说是没料想到天色一下就暗了下来，而是有点有意要铤而走险的意思，待我们一路摸黑朝着有光亮的方向前行，最终走出森林时，发现我们已经走到了城市西北的大湖Havel的边上了，路上一共走了五个多小时。阿里王子一路十分开心，也非常喜欢这两位活泼可爱的、与他自己女儿一般大的女学生，坚持要请她们去我们常去的一家在酷党大街上的名叫"百家啤酒"的德国餐馆吃烤猪蹄，尽兴而归。我相信这是这两位人大学生于柏林短期访学中最难忘的一段经历，阿里王子请她们吃的烤猪蹄也是她们在柏林吃过的一顿最美味的佳肴，开心、慈爱的阿里王子给她们留下了难以忘怀的深刻印象。当她们得知阿里王子的不幸消息，含泪问我："老师，阿里王子老师真的走了吗？"

我俩一起在绿森林中散步的难忘经历还有很多，一开始我们只是隔三岔五地进入森林中散步，后来慢慢变成了经常性的必修功课，有时甚至一天要去林中散两次步。每周一、二、三、五，高研院同事们集中午餐，餐后我们常常要一起围绕研究院周边的小湖 Halensee 走上一圈。每周四晚上，同事们集中晚餐，德国式的晚餐讲究仪式，一坐下开吃就至少要三个小时，每次我俩都经受不住好酒、好菜的诱惑，待到警觉自己又吃得太多、喝得太多时多半已经太晚了。好几次酒足饭饱时，阿里王子会起身提议说："沈教授，我们出去走走吧？"于是，我俩经常在别的同事们还酒兴正隆时起身摸黑去绿森林中散步，环绕绿森林湖（Grunewaldsee）转上一圈通常需要一个半小时。每次走完这段路程回到住处时常常快十一点了，可我们总是感觉良好，不再为自己今天又吃多、喝多了而发愁、愧疚。

随着我俩日接一日地结伴在绿森林中散步，我们的兄弟情谊也越来越深厚。我们不停地走着，也不停地说着、聊着，谈天说地，谈学问、谈人生，常常是越谈越投机，越谈越有味，每次都觉得意犹未尽。当然，我们在一起说得最多的还是我们共同从事的藏学研究，我们聊我们已经读过的、正在读的和还没有读过的书，谈我们互相熟识的朋友和他们的学问，讨论我们各自感兴趣的学术话题。我和阿里王子有不少共同认识的西方藏学家朋友，他们告诉我每当他们读不懂藏文文献、认不准藏传佛教图像时，他们常常会说："让我们去问阿里王子吧！"阿里王子是研究他家乡文明史的最杰出的权威，他对阿里的文献、社会、历史、宗教和艺术的研究都是这个领域的权威作品，特别是通过他亲自勘查而发现的大量吐蕃及其前弘期早期的佛教石窟、图像，为西部藏区佛教史的研究打开了一个崭新的天地。迄今为止，他已经和西方藏学家们合作，写作、出版了五大部英文专著，对中世纪西藏历史和宗教研究的进步做出了极为卓越的贡献，于国际藏学界享有极其崇高的学术声望。中国之大、藏学家之多，可有阿里王子这样的学术成就者却是绝无仅有的。

可是，阿里王子偏偏又是一位天生温良恭俭让的谦谦君子，虚怀若谷是他最突出的品牌，明明是别人从他那里学到了很多、很多东西，得到了很多、很多的帮助和新资料，可他在我面前却总是赞扬他的学术合作伙伴们科学的学术方法和百折不挠、精益求精的专业精神。他多次给我讲述 Guntram 如何在昌珠寺一下扎营好几个月，把本来觉得无从下手的寺院历史资料一点一滴地积聚起来，把文献研究和实地考查的结果完美地结合起来，最终凝成一部皇皇巨著的故事。恕我直言，藏族学者中很少有像阿里王子这样的学者，对本民族十分宗教化的学术传统具有深刻的批判精神，推崇理性的、科学的现代学术研究方法，并努力把现代学术研究方法用于自己对民族古文化研究的实践之中。他多次对我说，他最钦佩的藏族学者是桑木丹噶尔迈先生，因为他不但对藏族的历史和文化做了最好、最深入的研究，而且也超越了藏传佛教传统学术方法的束缚，是一位有世界学术意义的藏学大家。中国的藏学研究若要真能领先于世界，则必须首先出现几位像噶尔迈先生这样的优秀藏族学者。可见，谦虚的本质并不影响阿里王子内心远大的学术抱负，虽然他已经取得的学术成就早就令世人瞩目，但他的学术志向显然更加高远，他对他自己今后的学术研究有一整套的计划和设想，他内心一定有志于要成为像噶尔迈先生这样的国际藏学巨子，让中国的藏学真正领先于世界。每次谈到这些，我都忍不住要为阿里王子喝彩，为有他这么一位杰出的学术朋友而感到自豪。可苍天何忍，怎么竟然让我们的阿里王子就这么走了呢？

我们在一起当然也常常谈论我们目前置身其间的柏林高等研究院，我们都深为自己能被选为高研院的年度 fellow、并组成为本年度仅有的两个“焦点小组”之一而感到万分荣幸，与此同时，我们也常常对自己的语言能力和学术训练的不足而感到不安。同年的这些 fellow 实在都太优秀，而我俩都是在“文化大革命”的年代中长成的，先天营养不良，在这样一个完全西方主流的学术环境中，与这些优秀的同事相比我们在很多方面都有难以弥补的不足。特别是，尽管我们是一个“焦点小组”，但在学术上我们的研究离主流实在太远，我们身边的这些同事多半是杰出的科学家，或者是西方哲学、文学、艺术和历史研究的大家，对他们研究的课题我们多半缺乏最基础的知识，要很好地理解和吸收他们的学术成果并不是一件非常容易的事情，我们常常因为听报告听得一知半解而觉得非常的惭愧。为此，我俩常常互相安慰、互相鼓励，尽我俩最大的努力去吸收同事们的优秀学术成果，体会他们的学术方法。

柏林高研院为 fellow 们提供的学术和生活条件之好简直是无以复加，而对 fellow 们最主要的一项要求则仅仅是一年内做一场全院性的学术报告。而也正因为如此，这次报告的重要性就变得异乎寻常了，它是对每位 fellow 一次严峻的考验。为了做好这次报告，同事们都各具匠心、各显神通，每次报告基本上都是一场十分精彩的学术汇报演出。为了演好这场大戏，我们这些本来已经在学术界混油了的人物，却一个个都像是初出茅庐的菜鸟。作为“焦点小组”的组长，Guntram 不但对自己的报告做了远远超出必需的准备，而且也对阿里王子的报告予以了十二分的关注，阿里王子本人自然也体会到了不小的压力，对这场报告做了十分精心的准备。报告那天，Guntram 亲自为他主持，把这位国际藏学界的“真龙”的学术贡献向大家做了详细介绍，而专程从莱比锡赶来的 Per K.

Sørensen 教授和我则坐在前排最显要位置为阿里王子助阵，却见阿里王子镇定自若，娓娓道来，一场报告比平常多讲了半个多小时，他从自家的帐篷开始，谈论阿里的风土人情，然后引入他自己于家乡发现的吐蕃时期的岩洞壁画，进而学术地重构出古格王国的历史，整场报告扣人心弦、引人入胜。事后有位来自斯坦福大学的同事对我说，她觉得阿里王子的报告是今年度所有报告中最好、最有趣的报告之一。然而在我看来，阿里王子的报告是今年度所有报告中最吸引人、最给人以新知、并最能把学术和学人的个人认同完美地结合在一起的报告，没有之一。记得阿里王子作完报告时，我立即起身拥抱了他，眼睛甚至有点湿润，我衷心为我的朋友的成功感到高兴、感到自豪！

写到这里，我强忍了多日的泪水终于滚滚而下，阿里王子，你怎么就走了呢？你是次仁加布啊，你是长寿王啊，你怎么这么快就走了呢？正如 Elton John 曾经唱过的那样：人生多么美妙，就因为有你在这世界上（How wonderful life is while you are in the world），可你怎么就走了呢？难道仁者果真不寿吗？你可知道：你的好兄弟、外表比高仓健还酷的奥地利硬汉 Guntram 现在天天以泪洗面，舌头打着结，说不成一句完整的句子，整天想着各种各样的可能性，设想要是他早点如何如何的话，你现在一定还在我们中间。阿里王子，我们的好兄弟，我们三人到底是什么样的缘分啊？我应该是你走前看到的最后一人，而 Guntram 是你走后第一个看到你的人，他至今还没从巨大的震惊中缓过神来，没法理解你为何真的就这样走了。而我依然没法相信你是真的已经走了，因为我现在不管走到哪里见到的依然都是你灿烂的笑容，听到的依然都是你爽朗的笑声。阿里王子，你真的没有走，你将永远留在我的心中！

（原载《上海书评·东方早报》，2015 年 7 月 12 日）

图书在版编目(CIP)数据

西藏宗谱：纪念古格·次仁加布藏学研究文集 /（奥）恭特朗·哈佐德（Guntram Hazod），沈卫荣主编 .—北京：中国藏学出版社，2018. 11
ISBN 978-7-5211-0062-4

Ⅰ . ①西… Ⅱ . ①恭… ②沈… Ⅲ . ①藏学 - 文集 Ⅳ . ① K281.4-53

中国版本图书馆 CIP 数据核字（2018）第 125780 号

西藏宗谱：纪念古格·次仁加布藏学研究文集
Tibetan Genealogies: Studies in Memoriam of Guge Tsering Gyalpo (1961-2015)

责任编辑　徐华兰
藏文编辑　南加才让
特邀英文编辑　张宁
封面设计　翟跃飞
出版发行　中国藏学出版社
印　　刷　中国电影出版社印刷厂
版　　次　2018 年 11 月第 1 版第 1 次印刷
开　　本　787 毫米 ×1092 毫米　1/16
字　　数　883 千字
印　　张　46.75
印　　数　1000 册
定　　价　198.00 元
书　　号　ISBN 978-7-5211-0062-4 / K · 530

图书如有印装质量问题　请与本社发行部联系
E-mail: dfhw64892902@126.com　电话：010-64892902